Lecture Notes in Computer Science 12252

More information about this series at http://www.springer.com/series/7407

Osvaldo Gervasi · Beniamino Murgante ·
Sanjay Misra · Chiara Garau ·
Ivan Blečić · David Taniar ·
Bernady O. Apduhan · Ana Maria A. C. Rocha ·
Eufemia Tarantino · Carmelo Maria Torre ·
Yeliz Karaca (Eds.)

Computational Science and Its Applications – ICCSA 2020

20th International Conference
Cagliari, Italy, July 1–4, 2020
Proceedings, Part IV

Springer

Editors
Osvaldo Gervasi ⓘ
University of Perugia
Perugia, Italy

Sanjay Misra ⓘ
Chair- Center of ICT/ICE
Covenant University
Ota, Nigeria

Ivan Blečić ⓘ
University of Cagliari
Cagliari, Italy

Bernady O. Apduhan
Department of Information Science
Kyushu Sangyo University
Fukuoka, Japan

Eufemia Tarantino ⓘ
Polytechnic University of Bari
Bari, Italy

Yeliz Karaca ⓘ
Department of Neurology
University of Massachusetts
Medical School
Worcester, MA, USA

Beniamino Murgante ⓘ
University of Basilicata
Potenza, Potenza, Italy

Chiara Garau ⓘ
University of Cagliari
Cagliari, Italy

David Taniar ⓘ
Clayton School of Information Technology
Monash University
Clayton, VIC, Australia

Ana Maria A. C. Rocha ⓘ
University of Minho
Braga, Portugal

Carmelo Maria Torre ⓘ
Polytechnic University of Bari
Bari, Italy

ISSN 0302-9743   ISSN 1611-3349   (electronic)
Lecture Notes in Computer Science
ISBN 978-3-030-58810-6   ISBN 978-3-030-58811-3   (eBook)
https://doi.org/10.1007/978-3-030-58811-3

LNCS Sublibrary: SL1 – Theoretical Computer Science and General Issues

This Springer imprint is published by the registered company Springer Nature Switzerland AG
The registered company address is: Gewerbestrasse 11, 6330 Cham, Switzerland

Preface

These seven volumes (LNCS volumes 12249–12255) consist of the peer-reviewed papers from the International Conference on Computational Science and Its Applications (ICCSA 2020) which took place from July 1–4, 2020. Initially the conference was planned to be held in Cagliari, Italy, in collaboration with the University of Cagliari, but due to the COVID-19 pandemic it was organized as an online event.

ICCSA 2020 was a successful event in the conference series, previously held in Saint Petersburg, Russia (2019), Melbourne, Australia (2018), Trieste, Italy (2017), Beijing, China (2016), Banff, Canada (2015), Guimaraes, Portugal (2014), Ho Chi Minh City, Vietnam (2013), Salvador, Brazil (2012), Santander, Spain (2011), Fukuoka, Japan (2010), Suwon, South Korea (2009), Perugia, Italy (2008), Kuala Lumpur, Malaysia (2007), Glasgow, UK (2006), Singapore (2005), Assisi, Italy (2004), Montreal, Canada (2003), and (as ICCS) Amsterdam, The Netherlands (2002) and San Francisco, USA (2001).

Computational science is the main pillar of most of the present research, industrial and commercial applications, and plays a unique role in exploiting ICT innovative technologies. The ICCSA conference series has provided a venue for researchers and industry practitioners to discuss new ideas, to share complex problems and their solutions, and to shape new trends in computational science.

Apart from the general track, ICCSA 2020 also included 52 workshops in various areas of computational science, ranging from computational science technologies to specific areas of computational science, such as software engineering, security, machine learning and artificial intelligence, blockchain technologies, and of applications in many fields. We accepted 498 papers, distributed among 6 conference main tracks, which included 52 in workshops and 32 short papers. We would like to express our appreciation to the workshops chairs and co-chairs for their hard work and dedication.

The success of the ICCSA conference series in general, and of ICCSA 2020 in particular, vitaly depends on the support from many people: authors, presenters, participants, keynote speakers, workshop chairs, session chairs, Organizing Committee members, student volunteers, Program Committee members, Advisory Committee members, international liaison chairs, reviewers, and others in various roles. We take this opportunity to wholeheartedly thank them all.

We also wish to thank our publisher, Springer, for their acceptance to publish the proceedings, for sponsoring part of the Best Papers Awards, and for their kind assistance and cooperation during the editing process.

We cordially invite you to visit the ICCSA website http://www.iccsa.org where you can find all the relevant information about this interesting and exciting event.

July 2020

Osvaldo Gervasi
Beniamino Murgante
Sanjay Misra

Welcome to the Online Conference

The COVID-19 pandemic disrupted our plans for ICCSA 2020, as was the case for the scientific community around the world. Hence, we had to promptly regroup and rush to set in place the organization and the underlying infrastructure of the online event.

We chose to build the technological infrastructure using only open source software. In particular, we used Jitsi (jitsi.org) for the videoconferencing, Riot (riot.im) together with Matrix (matrix.org) for chat and asynchronous communication, and Jibri (github.com/jitsi/jibri) for live streaming sessions on YouTube.

Six Jitsi servers were set up, one for each parallel session. The participants of the sessions were helped and assisted by eight volunteer students (from the Universities of Cagliari, Florence, Perugia, and Bari), who assured technical support and smooth running of the conference proceedings.

The implementation of the software infrastructure and the technical coordination of the volunteers was carried out by Damiano Perri and Marco Simonetti.

Our warmest thanks go to all the volunteering students, to the technical coordinators, and to the development communities of Jitsi, Jibri, Riot, and Matrix, who made their terrific platforms available as open source software.

Our heartfelt thanks go to the keynote speakers: Yaneer Bar-Yam, Cecilia Ceccarelli, and Vincenzo Piuri and to the guests of the closing keynote panel: Mike Batty, Denise Pumain, and Alexis Tsoukiàs.

A big thank you goes to all the 454 speakers, many of whom showed an enormous collaborative spirit, sometimes participating and presenting in almost prohibitive times of the day, given that the participants of this year's conference come from 52 countries scattered over many time zones of the globe.

Finally, we would like to thank Google for letting us livestream all the events via YouTube. In addition to lightening the load of our Jitsi servers, that will allow us to keep memory and to be able to review the most exciting moments of the conference.

We all hope to meet in our beautiful Cagliari next year, safe from COVID-19, and finally free to meet in person and enjoy the beauty of the ICCSA community in the enchanting Sardinia.

July 2020

Ivan Blečić
Chiara Garau

Organization

ICCSA 2020 was organized by the University of Cagliari (Italy), University of Perugia (Italy), University of Basilicata (Italy), Monash University (Australia), Kyushu Sangyo University (Japan), and University of Minho (Portugal).

Honorary General Chairs

Antonio Laganà	Master-UP, Italy
Norio Shiratori	Chuo University, Japan
Kenneth C. J. Tan	Sardina Systems, UK
Corrado Zoppi	University of Cagliari, Italy

General Chairs

Osvaldo Gervasi	University of Perugia, Italy
Ivan Blečić	University of Cagliari, Italy
David Taniar	Monash University, Australia

Program Committee Chairs

Beniamino Murgante	University of Basilicata, Italy
Bernady O. Apduhan	Kyushu Sangyo University, Japan
Chiara Garau	University of Cagliari, Italy
Ana Maria A. C. Rocha	University of Minho, Portugal

International Advisory Committee

Jemal Abawajy	Deakin University, Australia
Dharma P. Agarwal	University of Cincinnati, USA
Rajkumar Buyya	The University of Melbourne, Australia
Claudia Bauzer Medeiros	University of Campinas, Brazil
Manfred M. Fisher	Vienna University of Economics and Business, Austria
Marina L. Gavrilova	University of Calgary, Canada
Yee Leung	Chinese University of Hong Kong, China

International Liaison Chairs

Giuseppe Borruso	University of Trieste, Italy
Elise De Donker	Western Michigan University, USA
Maria Irene Falcão	University of Minho, Portugal
Robert C. H. Hsu	Chung Hua University, Taiwan

Tai-Hoon Kim   Beijing Jaotong University, China
Vladimir Korkhov   Saint Petersburg University, Russia
Sanjay Misra   Covenant University, Nigeria
Takashi Naka   Kyushu Sangyo University, Japan
Rafael D. C. Santos   National Institute for Space Research, Brazil
Maribel Yasmina Santos   University of Minho, Portugal
Elena Stankova   Saint Petersburg University, Russia

Workshop and Session Organizing Chairs

Beniamino Murgante   University of Basilicata, Italy
Sanjay Misra   Covenant University, Nigeria
Jorge Gustavo Rocha   University of Minho, Portugal

Award Chair

Wenny Rahayu   La Trobe University, Australia

Publicity Committee Chairs

Elmer Dadios   De La Salle University, Philippines
Nataliia Kulabukhova   Saint Petersburg University, Russia
Daisuke Takahashi   Tsukuba University, Japan
Shangwang Wang   Beijing University of Posts and Telecommunications,
                              China

Technology Chairs

Damiano Perri   University of Florence, Italy
Marco Simonetti   University of Florence, Italy

Local Arrangement Chairs

Ivan Blečić   University of Cagliari, Italy
Chiara Garau   University of Cagliari, Italy
Ginevra Balletto   University of Cagliari, Italy
Giuseppe Borruso   University of Trieste, Italy
Michele Campagna   University of Cagliari, Italy
Mauro Coni   University of Cagliari, Italy
Anna Maria Colavitti   University of Cagliari, Italy
Giulia Desogus   University of Cagliari, Italy
Sabrina Lai   University of Cagliari, Italy
Francesca Maltinti   University of Cagliari, Italy
Pasquale Mistretta   University of Cagliari, Italy
Augusto Montisci   University of Cagliari, Italy
Francesco Pinna   University of Cagliari, Italy

Davide Spano   University of Cagliari, Italy
Roberto Tonelli   University of Cagliari, Italy
Giuseppe A. Trunfio   University of Sassari, Italy
Corrado Zoppi   University of Cagliari, Italy

Program Committee

Vera Afreixo   University of Aveiro, Portugal
Filipe Alvelos   University of Minho, Portugal
Hartmut Asche   University of Potsdam, Germany
Ginevra Balletto   University of Cagliari, Italy
Michela Bertolotto   University College Dublin, Ireland
Sandro Bimonte   CEMAGREF, TSCF, France
Rod Blais   University of Calgary, Canada
Ivan Blečić   University of Sassari, Italy
Giuseppe Borruso   University of Trieste, Italy
Ana Cristina Braga   University of Minho, Portugal
Massimo Cafaro   University of Salento, Italy
Yves Caniou   Lyon University, France
José A. Cardoso e Cunha Universidade Nova de Lisboa, Portugal
Rui Cardoso   University of Beira Interior, Portugal
Leocadio G. Casado   University of Almeria, Spain
Carlo Cattani   University of Salerno, Italy
Mete Celik   Erciyes University, Turkey
Hyunseung Choo   Sungkyunkwan University, South Korea
Min Young Chung   Sungkyunkwan University, South Korea
Florbela Maria da Cruz Polytechnic Institute of Viana do Castelo, Portugal
    Domingues Correia
Gilberto Corso Pereira Federal University of Bahia, Brazil
Alessandro Costantini   INFN, Italy
Carla Dal Sasso Freitas Universidade Federal do Rio Grande do Sul, Brazil
Pradesh Debba   The Council for Scientific and Industrial Research
                          (CSIR), South Africa
Hendrik Decker   Instituto Tecnológico de Informática, Spain
Frank Devai   London South Bank University, UK
Rodolphe Devillers   Memorial University of Newfoundland, Canada
Joana Matos Dias   University of Coimbra, Portugal
Paolino Di Felice   University of L'Aquila, Italy
Prabu Dorairaj   NetApp, India/USA
M. Irene Falcao   University of Minho, Portugal
Cherry Liu Fang   U.S. DOE Ames Laboratory, USA
Florbela P. Fernandes   Polytechnic Institute of Bragança, Portugal
Jose-Jesus Fernandez   National Centre for Biotechnology, CSIS, Spain
Paula Odete Fernandes   Polytechnic Institute of Bragança, Portugal
Adelaide de Fátima Baptista University of Aveiro, Portugal
    Valente Freitas

Noelia Faginas Lago	University of Perugia, Italy
Giuseppe Modica	University of Reggio Calabria, Italy
Josè Luis Montaña	University of Cantabria, Spain
Maria Filipa Mourão	IP from Viana do Castelo, Portugal
Louiza de Macedo Mourelle	State University of Rio de Janeiro, Brazil
Nadia Nedjah	State University of Rio de Janeiro, Brazil
Laszlo Neumann	University of Girona, Spain
Kok-Leong Ong	Deakin University, Australia
Belen Palop	Universidad de Valladolid, Spain
Marcin Paprzycki	Polish Academy of Sciences, Poland
Eric Pardede	La Trobe University, Australia
Kwangjin Park	Wonkwang University, South Korea
Ana Isabel Pereira	Polytechnic Institute of Bragança, Portugal
Massimiliano Petri	University of Pisa, Italy
Maurizio Pollino	Italian National Agency for New Technologies, Energy and Sustainable Economic Development, Italy
Alenka Poplin	University of Hamburg, Germany
Vidyasagar Potdar	Curtin University of Technology, Australia
David C. Prosperi	Florida Atlantic University, USA
Wenny Rahayu	La Trobe University, Australia
Jerzy Respondek	Silesian University of Technology, Poland
Humberto Rocha	INESC-Coimbra, Portugal
Jon Rokne	University of Calgary, Canada
Octavio Roncero	CSIC, Spain
Maytham Safar	Kuwait University, Kuwait
Francesco Santini	University of Perugia, Italy
Chiara Saracino	A.O. Ospedale Niguarda Ca' Granda, Italy
Haiduke Sarafian	Penn State University, USA
Marco Paulo Seabra dos Reis	University of Coimbra, Portugal
Jie Shen	University of Michigan, USA
Qi Shi	Liverpool John Moores University, UK
Dale Shires	U.S. Army Research Laboratory, USA
Inês Soares	University of Coimbra, Portugal
Elena Stankova	Saint Petersburg University, Russia
Takuo Suganuma	Tohoku University, Japan
Eufemia Tarantino	Polytechnic University of Bari, Italy
Sergio Tasso	University of Perugia, Italy
Ana Paula Teixeira	University of Trás-os-Montes and Alto Douro, Portugal
Senhorinha Teixeira	University of Minho, Portugal
M. Filomena Teodoro	Portuguese Naval Academy, University of Lisbon, Portugal
Parimala Thulasiraman	University of Manitoba, Canada
Carmelo Torre	Polytechnic University of Bari, Italy
Javier Martinez Torres	Centro Universitario de la Defensa Zaragoza, Spain
Giuseppe A. Trunfio	University of Sassari, Italy

Pablo Vanegas	University of Cuenca, Ecuador
Marco Vizzari	University of Perugia, Italy
Varun Vohra	Merck Inc., USA
Koichi Wada	University of Tsukuba, Japan
Krzysztof Walkowiak	Wroclaw University of Technology, Poland
Zequn Wang	Intelligent Automation Inc., USA
Robert Weibel	University of Zurich, Switzerland
Frank Westad	Norwegian University of Science and Technology, Norway
Roland Wismüller	Universität Siegen, Germany
Mudasser Wyne	SOET National University, USA
Chung-Huang Yang	National Kaohsiung Normal University, Taiwan
Xin-She Yang	National Physical Laboratory, UK
Salim Zabir	France Telecom Japan Co., Japan
Haifeng Zhao	University of California, Davis, USA
Fabiana Zollo	University of Venice, Italy
Albert Y. Zomaya	The University of Sydney, Australia

Workshop Organizers

Advanced Transport Tools and Methods (A2TM 2020)

Massimiliano Petri	University of Pisa, Italy
Antonio Pratelli	University of Pisa, Italy

Advances in Artificial Intelligence Learning Technologies: Blended Learning, STEM, Computational Thinking and Coding (AAILT 2020)

Valentina Franzoni	University of Perugia, Italy
Alfredo Milani	University of Perugia, Italy
Sergio Tasso	University of Perugia, Italy

Workshop on Advancements in Applied Machine Learning and Data Analytics (AAMDA 2020)

Alessandro Costantini	INFN, Italy
Daniele Cesini	INFN, Italy
Davide Salomoni	INFN, Italy
Doina Cristina Duma	INFN, Italy

Advanced Computational Approaches in Artificial Intelligence and Complex Systems Applications (ACAC 2020)

Yeliz Karaca	University of Massachusetts Medical School, USA
Dumitru Baleanu	Çankaya University, Turkey, and Institute of Space Sciences, Romania
Majaz Moonis	University of Massachusetts Medical School, USA
Yu-Dong Zhang	University of Leicester, UK

Affective Computing and Emotion Recognition (ACER-EMORE 2020)

Valentina Franzoni	University of Perugia, Italy
Alfredo Milani	University of Perugia, Italy
Giulio Biondi	University of Florence, Italy

AI Factory and Smart Manufacturing (AIFACTORY 2020)

Jongpil Jeong	Sungkyunkwan University, South Korea

Air Quality Monitoring and Citizen Science for Smart Urban Management. State of the Art And Perspectives (AirQ&CScience 2020)

Grazie Fattoruso	ENEA CR Portici, Italy
Maurizio Pollino	ENEA CR Casaccia, Italy
Saverio De Vito	ENEA CR Portici, Italy

Automatic Landform Classification: Spatial Methods and Applications (ALCSMA 2020)

Maria Danese	CNR-ISPC, Italy
Dario Gioia	CNR-ISPC, Italy

Advances of Modelling Micromobility in Urban Spaces (AMMUS 2020)

Tiziana Campisi	University of Enna KORE, Italy
Giovanni Tesoriere	University of Enna KORE, Italy
Ioannis Politis	Aristotle University of Thessaloniki, Greece
Socrates Basbas	Aristotle University of Thessaloniki, Greece
Sanja Surdonja	University of Rijeka, Croatia
Marko Rencelj	University of Maribor, Slovenia

Advances in Information Systems and Technologies for Emergency Management, Risk Assessment and Mitigation Based on the Resilience Concepts (ASTER 2020)

Maurizio Pollino	ENEA, Italy
Marco Vona	University of Basilicata, Italy
Amedeo Flora	University of Basilicata, Italy
Chiara Iacovino	University of Basilicata, Italy
Beniamino Murgante	University of Basilicata, Italy

Advances in Web Based Learning (AWBL 2020)

Birol Ciloglugil	Ege University, Turkey
Mustafa Murat Inceoglu	Ege University, Turkey

**Blockchain and Distributed Ledgers: Technologies
and Applications (BDLTA 2020)**

Vladimir Korkhov	Saint Petersburg University, Russia
Elena Stankova	Saint Petersburg University, Russia
Nataliia Kulabukhova	Saint Petersburg University, Russia

Bio and Neuro Inspired Computing and Applications (BIONCA 2020)

Nadia Nedjah	State University of Rio de Janeiro, Brazil
Luiza De Macedo Mourelle	State University of Rio de Janeiro, Brazil

Computer Aided Modeling, Simulation and Analysis (CAMSA 2020)

Jie Shen	University of Michigan, USA

Computational and Applied Statistics (CAS 2020)

Ana Cristina Braga	University of Minho, Portugal

Computerized Evidence Based Decision Making (CEBDEM 2020)

Clarice Bleil de Souza	Cardiff University, UK
Valerio Cuttini	University of Pisa, Italy
Federico Cerutti	Cardiff University, UK
Camilla Pezzica	Cardiff University, UK

Computational Geometry and Applications (CGA 2020)

Marina Gavrilova	University of Calgary, Canada

**Computational Mathematics, Statistics and Information Management
(CMSIM 2020)**

Maria Filomena Teodoro	Portuguese Naval Academy, University of Lisbon, Portugal

Computational Optimization and Applications (COA 2020)

Ana Rocha	University of Minho, Portugal
Humberto Rocha	University of Coimbra, Portugal

Computational Astrochemistry (CompAstro 2020)

Marzio Rosi	University of Perugia, Italy
Cecilia Ceccarelli	University of Grenoble, France
Stefano Falcinelli	University of Perugia, Italy
Dimitrios Skouteris	Master-UP, Italy

Cities, Technologies and Planning (CTP 2020)

Beniamino Murgante	University of Basilicata, Italy
Ljiljana Zivkovic	Ministry of Construction, Transport and Infrastructure and Institute of Architecture and Urban & Spatial Planning of Serbia, Serbia
Giuseppe Borruso	University of Trieste, Italy
Malgorzata Hanzl	University of Łódź, Poland

Data Stream Processing and Applications (DASPA 2020)

Raja Chiky	ISEP, France
Rosanna VERDE	University of Campania, Italy
Marcilio De Souto	Orleans University, France

Data Science for Cyber Security (DS4Cyber 2020)

Hongmei Chi	Florida A&M University, USA

Econometric and Multidimensional Evaluation in Urban Environment (EMEUE 2020)

Carmelo Maria Torre	Polytechnic University of Bari, Italy
Pierluigi Morano	Polytechnic University of Bari, Italy
Maria Cerreta	University of Naples, Italy
Paola Perchinunno	University of Bari, Italy
Francesco Tajani	University of Rome, Italy
Simona Panaro	University of Portsmouth, UK
Francesco Scorza	University of Basilicata, Italy

Frontiers in Machine Learning (FIML 2020)

Massimo Bilancia	University of Bari, Italy
Paola Perchinunno	University of Bari, Italy
Pasquale Lops	University of Bari, Italy
Danilo Di Bona	University of Bari, Italy

Future Computing System Technologies and Applications (FiSTA 2020)

Bernady Apduhan	Kyushu Sangyo University, Japan
Rafael Santos	Brazilian National Institute for Space Research, Brazil

Geodesign in Decision Making: Meta Planning and Collaborative Design for Sustainable and Inclusive Development (GDM 2020)

Francesco Scorza	University of Basilicata, Italy
Michele Campagna	University of Cagliari, Italy
Ana Clara Mourao Moura	Federal University of Minas Gerais, Brazil

Geomatics in Forestry and Agriculture: New Advances and Perspectives (GeoForAgr 2020)

Maurizio Pollino	ENEA, Italy
Giuseppe Modica	University of Reggio Calabria, Italy
Marco Vizzari	University of Perugia, Italy

Geographical Analysis, Urban Modeling, Spatial Statistics (GEOG-AND-MOD 2020)

Beniamino Murgante	University of Basilicata, Italy
Giuseppe Borruso	University of Trieste, Italy
Hartmut Asche	University of Potsdam, Germany

Geomatics for Resource Monitoring and Management (GRMM 2020)

Eufemia Tarantino	Polytechnic University of Bari, Italy
Enrico Borgogno Mondino	University of Torino, Italy
Marco Scaioni	Polytechnic University of Milan, Italy
Alessandra Capolupo	Polytechnic University of Bari, Italy

Software Quality (ISSQ 2020)

Sanjay Misra	Covenant University, Nigeria

Collective, Massive and Evolutionary Systems (IWCES 2020)

Alfredo Milani	University of Perugia, Italy
Rajdeep Niyogi	Indian Institute of Technology, Roorkee, India
Alina Elena Baia	University of Florence, Italy

Large Scale Computational Science (LSCS 2020)

Elise De Doncker	Western Michigan University, USA
Fukuko Yuasa	High Energy Accelerator Research Organization (KEK), Japan
Hideo Matsufuru	High Energy Accelerator Research Organization (KEK), Japan

Land Use Monitoring for Sustainability (LUMS 2020)

Carmelo Maria Torre	Polytechnic University of Bari, Italy
Alessandro Bonifazi	Polytechnic University of Bari, Italy
Pasquale Balena	Polytechnic University of Bari, Italy
Massimiliano Bencardino	University of Salerno, Italy
Francesco Tajani	University of Rome, Italy
Pierluigi Morano	Polytechnic University of Bari, Italy
Maria Cerreta	University of Naples, Italy
Giuliano Poli	University of Naples, Italy

Machine Learning for Space and Earth Observation Data (MALSEOD 2020)

Rafael Santos	INPE, Brazil
Karine Ferreira	INPE, Brazil

Building Multi-dimensional Models for Assessing Complex Environmental Systems (MES 2020)

Marta Dell'Ovo	Polytechnic University of Milan, Italy
Vanessa Assumma	Polytechnic University of Torino, Italy
Caterina Caprioli	Polytechnic University of Torino, Italy
Giulia Datola	Polytechnic University of Torino, Italy
Federico dell'Anna	Polytechnic University of Torino, Italy

Ecosystem Services: Nature's Contribution to People in Practice. Assessment Frameworks, Models, Mapping, and Implications (NC2P 2020)

Francesco Scorza	University of Basilicata, Italy
David Cabana	International Marine Center, Italy
Sabrina Lai	University of Cagliari, Italy
Ana Clara Mourao Moura	Federal University of Minas Gerais, Brazil
Corrado Zoppi	University of Cagliari, Italy

Open Knowledge for Socio-economic Development (OKSED 2020)

Luigi Mundula	University of Cagliari, Italy
Flavia Marzano	Link Campus University, Italy
Maria Paradiso	University of Milan, Italy

Scientific Computing Infrastructure (SCI 2020)

Elena Stankova	Saint Petersburg State University, Russia
Vladimir Korkhov	Saint Petersburg State University, Russia
Natalia Kulabukhova	Saint Petersburg State University, Russia

Computational Studies for Energy and Comfort in Buildings (SECoB 2020)

Senhorinha Teixeira	University of Minho, Portugal
Luís Martins	University of Minho, Portugal
Ana Maria Rocha	University of Minho, Portugal

Software Engineering Processes and Applications (SEPA 2020)

Sanjay Misra	Covenant University, Nigeria

Smart Ports - Technologies and Challenges (SmartPorts 2020)

Gianfranco Fancello	University of Cagliari, Italy
Patrizia Serra	University of Cagliari, Italy
Marco Mazzarino	University of Venice, Italy
Luigi Mundula	University of Cagliari, Italy

| Ginevra Balletto | University of Cagliari, Italy |
| Giuseppe Borruso | University of Trieste, Italy |

Sustainability Performance Assessment: Models, Approaches and Applications Toward Interdisciplinary and Integrated Solutions (SPA 2020)

Francesco Scorza	University of Basilicata, Italy
Valentin Grecu	Lucian Blaga University, Romania
Jolanta Dvarioniene	Kaunas University of Technology, Lithuania
Sabrina Lai	University of Cagliari, Italy
Iole Cerminara	University of Basilicata, Italy
Corrado Zoppi	University of Cagliari, Italy

Smart and Sustainable Island Communities (SSIC 2020)

Chiara Garau	University of Cagliari, Italy
Anastasia Stratigea	National Technical University of Athens, Greece
Paola Zamperlin	University of Pisa, Italy
Francesco Scorza	University of Basilicata, Italy

Science, Technologies and Policies to Innovate Spatial Planning (STP4P 2020)

Chiara Garau	University of Cagliari, Italy
Daniele La Rosa	University of Catania, Italy
Francesco Scorza	University of Basilicata, Italy
Anna Maria Colavitti	University of Cagliari, Italy
Beniamino Murgante	University of Basilicata, Italy
Paolo La Greca	University of Catania, Italy

New Frontiers for Strategic Urban Planning (StrategicUP 2020)

Luigi Mundula	University of Cagliari, Italy
Ginevra Balletto	University of Cagliari, Italy
Giuseppe Borruso	University of Trieste, Italy
Michele Campagna	University of Cagliari, Italy
Beniamino Murgante	University of Basilicata, Italy

Theoretical and Computational Chemistry and its Applications (TCCMA 2020)

| Noelia Faginas-Lago | University of Perugia, Italy |
| Andrea Lombardi | University of Perugia, Italy |

Tools and Techniques in Software Development Process (TTSDP 2020)

| Sanjay Misra | Covenant University, Nigeria |

Urban Form Studies (UForm 2020)

| Malgorzata Hanzl | Łódź University of Technology, Poland |

Urban Space Extended Accessibility (USEaccessibility 2020)

Chiara Garau	University of Cagliari, Italy
Francesco Pinna	University of Cagliari, Italy
Beniamino Murgante	University of Basilicata, Italy
Mauro Coni	University of Cagliari, Italy
Francesca Maltinti	University of Cagliari, Italy
Vincenza Torrisi	University of Catania, Italy
Matteo Ignaccolo	University of Catania, Italy

Virtual and Augmented Reality and Applications (VRA 2020)

Osvaldo Gervasi	University of Perugia, Italy
Damiano Perri	University of Perugia, Italy
Marco Simonetti	University of Perugia, Italy
Sergio Tasso	University of Perugia, Italy

Workshop on Advanced and Computational Methods for Earth Science Applications (WACM4ES 2020)

Luca Piroddi	University of Cagliari, Italy
Laura Foddis	University of Cagliari, Italy
Gian Piero Deidda	University of Cagliari, Italy
Augusto Montisci	University of Cagliari, Italy
Gabriele Uras	University of Cagliari, Italy
Giulio Vignoli	University of Cagliari, Italy

Sponsoring Organizations

ICCSA 2020 would not have been possible without tremendous support of many organizations and institutions, for which all organizers and participants of ICCSA 2020 express their sincere gratitude:

Springer International Publishing AG, Germany
(https://www.springer.com)

Computers Open Access Journal
(https://www.mdpi.com/journal/computers)

IEEE Italy Section, Italy
(https://italy.ieeer8.org/)

Centre-North Italy Chapter IEEE GRSS, Italy
(https://cispio.diet.uniroma1.it/marzano/ieee-grs/
index.html)

Italy Section of the Computer Society, Italy
(https://site.ieee.org/italy-cs/)

University of Cagliari, Italy
(https://unica.it/)

University of Perugia, Italy
(https://www.unipg.it)

University of Basilicata, Italy
(http://www.unibas.it)

Monash University, Australia
(https://www.monash.edu/)

Kyushu Sangyo University, Japan
(https://www.kyusan-u.ac.jp/)

University of Minho, Portugal
(https://www.uminho.pt/)

Scientific Association Transport Infrastructures, Italy
(https://www.stradeeautostrade.it/associazioni-e-organizzazioni/asit-associazione-scientifica-infrastrutture-trasporto/)

Regione Sardegna, Italy
(https://regione.sardegna.it/)

Comune di Cagliari, Italy
(https://www.comune.cagliari.it/)

Referees

A. P. Andrade Marina	ISCTE, Instituto Universitário de Lisboa, Portugal
Addesso Paolo	University of Salerno, Italy
Adewumi Adewole	Algonquin College, Canada
Afolabi Adedeji	Covenant University, Nigeria
Afreixo Vera	University of Aveiro, Portugal
Agrawal Smirti	Freelancer, USA
Agrawal Akshat	Amity University Haryana, India
Ahmad Waseem	Federal University of Technology Minna, Nigeria
Akgun Nurten	Bursa Technical University, Turkey
Alam Tauhidul	Louisiana State University Shreveport, USA
Aleixo Sandra M.	CEAUL, Portugal
Alfa Abraham	Federal University of Technology Minna, Nigeria
Alvelos Filipe	University of Minho, Portugal
Alves Alexandra	University of Minho, Portugal
Amato Federico	University of Lausanne, Switzerland
Andrade Marina Alexandra Pedro	ISCTE-IUL, Portugal
Andrianov Sergey	Saint Petersburg State University, Russia
Anelli Angelo	CNR-IGAG, Italy
Anelli Debora	University of Rome, Italy
Annunziata Alfonso	University of Cagliari, Italy
Antognelli Sara	Agricolus, Italy
Aoyama Tatsumi	High Energy Accelerator Research Organization, Japan
Apduhan Bernady	Kyushu Sangyo University, Japan
Ascenzi Daniela	University of Trento, Italy
Asche Harmut	Hasso-Plattner-Institut für Digital Engineering GmbH, Germany
Aslan Burak Galip	Izmir Insitute of Technology, Turkey
Assumma Vanessa	Polytechnic University of Torino, Italy
Astoga Gino	UV, Chile
Atman Uslu Nilüfer	Manisa Celal Bayar University, Turkey
Behera Ranjan Kumar	National Institute of Technology, Rourkela, India
Badsha Shahriar	University of Nevada, USA
Bai Peng	University of Cagliari, Italy
Baia Alina-Elena	University of Perugia, Italy
Balacco Gabriella	Polytechnic University of Bari, Italy
Balci Birim	Celal Bayar University, Turkey
Balena Pasquale	Polytechnic University of Bari, Italy
Balletto Ginevra	University of Cagliari, Italy
Balucani Nadia	University of Perugia, Italy
Bansal Megha	Delhi University, India
Barazzetti Luigi	Polytechnic University of Milan, Italy
Barreto Jeniffer	Istituto Superior Técnico, Portugal
Basbas Socrates	Aristotle University of Thessaloniki, Greece

Berger Katja	Ludwig-Maximilians-Universität München, Germany
Beyene Asrat Mulatu	Addis Ababa Science and Technology University, Ethiopia
Bilancia Massimo	University of Bari Aldo Moro, Italy
Biondi Giulio	University of Firenze, Italy
Blanquer Ignacio	Universitat Politècnica de València, Spain
Bleil de Souza Clarice	Cardiff University, UK
Blečić Ivan	University of Cagliari, Italy
Bogdanov Alexander	Saint Petersburg State University, Russia
Bonifazi Alessandro	Polytechnic University of Bari, Italy
Bontchev Boyan	Sofia University, Bulgaria
Borgogno Mondino Enrico	University of Torino, Italy
Borruso Giuseppe	University of Trieste, Italy
Bouaziz Rahma	Taibah University, Saudi Arabia
Bowles Juliana	University of Saint Andrews, UK
Braga Ana Cristina	University of Minho, Portugal
Brambilla Andrea	Polytechnic University of Milan, Italy
Brito Francisco	University of Minho, Portugal
Buele Jorge	Universidad Tecnológica Indoamérica, Ecuador
Buffoni Andrea	TAGES sc, Italy
Cabana David	International Marine Centre, Italy
Calazan Rogerio	IEAPM, Brazil
Calcina Sergio Vincenzo	University of Cagliari, Italy
Camalan Seda	Atilim University, Turkey
Camarero Alberto	Universidad Politécnica de Madrid, Spain
Campisi Tiziana	University of Enna KORE, Italy
Cannatella Daniele	Delft University of Technology, The Netherlands
Capolupo Alessandra	Polytechnic University of Bari, Italy
Cappucci Sergio	ENEA, Italy
Caprioli Caterina	Polytechnic University of Torino, Italy
Carapau Fermando	Universidade de Evora, Portugal
Carcangiu Sara	University of Cagliari, Italy
Carrasqueira Pedro	INESC Coimbra, Portugal
Caselli Nicolás	PUCV Chile, Chile
Castro de Macedo Jose Nuno	Universidade do Minho, Portugal
Cavallo Carla	University of Naples, Italy
Cerminara Iole	University of Basilicata, Italy
Cerreta Maria	University of Naples, Italy
Cesini Daniele	INFN-CNAF, Italy
Chang Shi-Kuo	University of Pittsburgh, USA
Chetty Girija	University of Canberra, Australia
Chiky Raja	ISEP, France
Chowdhury Dhiman	University of South Carolina, USA
Ciloglugil Birol	Ege University, Turkey
Coletti Cecilia	Università di Chieti-Pescara, Italy

Coni Mauro	University of Cagliari, Italy
Corcoran Padraig	Cardiff University, UK
Cornelio Antonella	Università degli Studi di Brescia, Italy
Correia Aldina	ESTG-PPorto, Portugal
Correia Elisete	University of Trás-os-Montes and Alto Douro, Portugal
Correia Florbela	Polytechnic Institute of Viana do Castelo, Portugal
Costa Lino	Universidade do Minho, Portugal
Costa e Silva Eliana	ESTG-P Porto, Portugal
Costantini Alessandro	INFN, Italy
Crespi Mattia	University of Roma, Italy
Cuca Branka	Polytechnic University of Milano, Italy
De Doncker Elise	Western Michigan University, USA
De Macedo Mourelle Luiza	State University of Rio de Janeiro, Brazil
Daisaka Hiroshi	Hitotsubashi University, Japan
Daldanise Gaia	CNR, Italy
Danese Maria	CNR-ISPC, Italy
Daniele Bartoli	University of Perugia, Italy
Datola Giulia	Polytechnic University of Torino, Italy
De Luca Giandomenico	University of Reggio Calabria, Italy
De Lucia Caterina	University of Foggia, Italy
De Morais Barroca Filho Itamir	Federal University of Rio Grande do Norte, Brazil
De Petris Samuele	University of Torino, Italy
De Sá Alan	Marinha do Brasil, Brazil
De Souto Marcilio	LIFO, University of Orléans, France
De Vito Saverio	ENEA, Italy
De Wilde Pieter	University of Plymouth, UK
Degtyarev Alexander	Saint Petersburg State University, Russia
Dell'Anna Federico	Polytechnic University of Torino, Italy
Dell'Ovo Marta	Polytechnic University of Milano, Italy
Della Mura Fernanda	University of Naples, Italy
Deluka T. Aleksandra	University of Rijeka, Croatia
Demartino Cristoforo	Zhejiang University, China
Dereli Dursun Ahu	Istanbul Commerce University, Turkey
Desogus Giulia	University of Cagliari, Italy
Dettori Marco	University of Sassari, Italy
Devai Frank	London South Bank University, UK
Di Francesco Massimo	University of Cagliari, Italy
Di Liddo Felicia	Polytechnic University of Bari, Italy
Di Paola Gianluigi	University of Molise, Italy
Di Pietro Antonio	ENEA, Italy
Di Pinto Valerio	University of Naples, Italy
Dias Joana	University of Coimbra, Portugal
Dimas Isabel	University of Coimbra, Portugal
Dirvanauskas Darius	Kaunas University of Technology, Lithuania
Djordjevic Aleksandra	University of Belgrade, Serbia

Duma Doina Cristina	INFN-CNAF, Italy
Dumlu Demircioğlu Emine	Yıldız Technical University, Turkey
Dursun Aziz	Virginia Tech University, USA
Dvarioniene Jolanta	Kaunas University of Technology, Lithuania
Errico Maurizio Francesco	University of Enna KORE, Italy
Ezugwu Absalom	University of KwaZulu-Natal, South Africa
Fattoruso Grazia	ENEA, Italy
Faginas-Lago Noelia	University of Perugia, Italy
Falanga Bolognesi Salvatore	ARIESPACE, Italy
Falcinelli Stefano	University of Perugia, Italy
Farias Marcos	National Nuclear Energy Commission, Brazil
Farina Alessandro	University of Pisa, Italy
Feltynowski Marcin	Lodz University of Technology, Poland
Fernandes Florbela	Instituto Politecnico de Bragança, Portugal
Fernandes Paula Odete	Instituto Politécnico de Bragança, Portugal
Fernandez-Sanz Luis	University of Alcala, Spain
Ferreira Ana Cristina	University of Minho, Portugal
Ferreira Fernanda	Porto, Portugal
Fiorini Lorena	University of L'Aquila, Italy
Flora Amedeo	University of Basilicata, Italy
Florez Hector	Universidad Distrital Francisco Jose de Caldas, Colombia
Foddis Maria Laura	University of Cagliari, Italy
Fogli Daniela	University of Brescia, Italy
Fortunelli Martina	Pragma Engineering, Italy
Fragiacomo Massimo	University of L'Aquila, Italy
Franzoni Valentina	Perugia University, Italy
Fusco Giovanni	University of Cote d'Azur, France
Fyrogenis Ioannis	Aristotle University of Thessaloniki, Greece
Gorbachev Yuriy	Coddan Technologies LLC, Russia
Gabrielli Laura	Università Iuav di Venezia, Italy
Gallanos Theodore	Austrian Institute of Technology, Austria
Gamallo Belmonte Pablo	Universitat de Barcelona, Spain
Gankevich Ivan	Saint Petersburg State University, Russia
Garau Chiara	University of Cagliari, Italy
Garcia Para Ernesto	Universidad del Pais Vasco, EHU, Spain
Gargano Riccardo	Universidade de Brasilia, Brazil
Gavrilova Marina	University of Calgary, Canada
Georgiadis Georgios	Aristotle University of Thessaloniki, Greece
Gervasi Osvaldo	University of Perugia, Italy
Giano Salvatore Ivo	University of Basilicata, Italy
Gil Jorge	Chalmers University, Sweden
Gioia Andrea	Polytechnic University of Bari, Italy
Gioia Dario	ISPC-CNT, Italy

Giordano Ludovica	ENEA, Italy
Giorgi Giacomo	University of Perugia, Italy
Giovene di Girasole Eleonora	CNR-IRISS, Italy
Giovinazzi Sonia	ENEA, Italy
Giresini Linda	University of Pisa, Italy
Giuffrida Salvatore	University of Catania, Italy
Golubchikov Oleg	Cardiff University, UK
Gonçalves A. Manuela	University of Minho, Portugal
Gorgoglione Angela	Universidad de la República, Uruguay
Goyal Rinkaj	IPU, Delhi, India
Grishkin Valery	Saint Petersburg State University, Russia
Guerra Eduardo	Free University of Bozen-Bolzano, Italy
Guerrero Abel	University of Guanajuato, Mexico
Gulseven Osman	American University of The Middle East, Kuwait
Gupta Brij	National Institute of Technology, Kurukshetra, India
Guveyi Elcin	Yildiz Teknik University, Turkey
Gülen Kemal Güven	Namk Kemal University, Turkey
Haddad Sandra	Arab Academy for Science, Technology and Maritime Transport, Egypt
Hanzl Malgorzata	Lodz University of Technology, Poland
Hegedus Peter	University of Szeged, Hungary
Hendrix Eligius M. T.	Universidad de Málaga, Spain
Higaki Hiroaki	Tokyo Denki University, Japan
Hossain Syeda Sumbul	Daffodil International University, Bangladesh
Iacovino Chiara	University of Basilicata, Italy
Iakushkin Oleg	Saint Petersburg State University, Russia
Iannuzzo Antonino	ETH Zurich, Switzerland
Idri Ali	University Mohammed V, Morocco
Ignaccolo Matteo	University of Catania, Italy
Ilovan Oana-Ramona	Babeş-Bolyai University, Romania
Isola Federica	University of Cagliari, Italy
Jankovic Marija	CERTH, Greece
Jorge Ana Maria	Instituto Politécnico de Lisboa, Portugal
Kanamori Issaku	RIKEN Center for Computational Science, Japan
Kapenga John	Western Michigan University, USA
Karabulut Korhan	Yasar University, Turkey
Karaca Yeliz	University of Massachusetts Medical School, USA
Karami Ali	University of Guilan, Iran
Kienhofer Frank	WITS, South Africa
Kim Tai-hoon	Beijing Jiaotong University, China
Kimura Shuhei	Tottori University, Japan
Kirillov Denis	Saint Petersburg State University, Russia
Korkhov Vladimir	Saint Petersburg University, Russia
Koszewski Krzysztof	Warsaw University of Technology, Poland
Krzysztofik Sylwia	Lodz University of Technology, Poland

Kulabukhova Nataliia	Saint Petersburg State University, Russia
Kulkarni Shrinivas B.	SDM College of Engineering and Technology, Dharwad, India
Kwiecinski Krystian	Warsaw University of Technology, Poland
Kyvelou Stella	Panteion University of Social and Political Sciences, Greece
Körting Thales	INPE, Brazil
Lal Niranjan	Mody University of Science and Technology, India
Lazzari Maurizio	CNR-ISPC, Italy
Leon Marcelo	Asociacion de Becarios del Ecuador, Ecuador
La Rocca Ludovica	University of Naples, Italy
La Rosa Daniele	University of Catania, Italy
Lai Sabrina	University of Cagliari, Italy
Lalenis Konstantinos	University of Thessaly, Greece
Lannon Simon	Cardiff University, UK
Lasaponara Rosa	CNR, Italy
Lee Chien-Sing	Sunway University, Malaysia
Lemus-Romani José	Pontificia Universidad Católica de Valparaiso, Chile
Leone Federica	University of Cagliari, Italy
Li Yuanxi	Hong Kong Baptist University, China
Locurcio Marco	Polytechnic University of Bari, Italy
Lombardi Andrea	University of Perugia, Italy
Lopez Gayarre Fernando	University of Oviedo, Spain
Lops Pasquale	University of Bari, Italy
Lourenço Vanda	Universidade Nova de Lisboa, Portugal
Luviano José Luís	University of Guanajuato, Mexico
Maltese Antonino	University of Palermo, Italy
Magni Riccardo	Pragma Engineering, Italy
Maheshwari Anil	Carleton University, Canada
Maja Roberto	Polytechnic University of Milano, Italy
Malik Shaveta	Terna Engineering College, India
Maltinti Francesca	University of Cagliari, Italy
Mandado Marcos	University of Vigo, Spain
Manganelli Benedetto	University of Basilicata, Italy
Mangiameli Michele	University of Catania, Italy
Maraschin Clarice	Universidade Federal do Rio Grande do Sul, Brazil
Marigorta Ana Maria	Universidad de Las Palmas de Gran Canaria, Spain
Markov Krassimir	Institute of Electrical Engineering and Informatics, Bulgaria
Martellozzo Federico	University of Firenze, Italy
Marucci Alessandro	University of L'Aquila, Italy
Masini Nicola	IBAM-CNR, Italy
Matsufuru Hideo	High Energy Accelerator Research Organization (KEK), Japan
Matteucci Ilaria	CNR, Italy
Mauro D'Apuzzo	University of Cassino and Southern Lazio, Italy

Mazzarella Chiara	University of Naples, Italy
Mazzarino Marco	University of Venice, Italy
Mazzoni Augusto	University of Roma, Italy
Mele Roberta	University of Naples, Italy
Menezes Raquel	University of Minho, Portugal
Menghini Antonio	Aarhus Geofisica, Italy
Mengoni Paolo	University of Florence, Italy
Merlino Angelo	Università degli Studi Mediterranea, Italy
Milani Alfredo	University of Perugia, Italy
Milic Vladimir	University of Zagreb, Croatia
Millham Richard	Durban University of Technology, South Africa
Mishra B.	University of Szeged, Hungary
Misra Sanjay	Covenant University, Nigeria
Modica Giuseppe	University of Reggio Calabria, Italy
Mohagheghi Mohammadsadegh	Vali-e-Asr University of Rafsanjan, Iran
Molaei Qelichi Mohamad	University of Tehran, Iran
Molinara Mario	University of Cassino and Southern Lazio, Italy
Momo Evelyn Joan	University of Torino, Italy
Monteiro Vitor	University of Minho, Portugal
Montisci Augusto	University of Cagliari, Italy
Morano Pierluigi	Polytechnic University of Bari, Italy
Morganti Alessandro	Polytechnic University of Milano, Italy
Mosca Erica Isa	Polytechnic University of Milan, Italy
Moura Ricardo	CMA-FCT, New University of Lisbon, Portugal
Mourao Maria	Polytechnic Institute of Viana do Castelo, Portugal
Mourão Moura Ana Clara	Federal University of Minas Gerais, Brazil
Mrak Iva	University of Rijeka, Croatia
Murgante Beniamino	University of Basilicata, Italy
Muñoz Mirna	Centro de Investigacion en Matematicas, Mexico
Nedjah Nadia	State University of Rio de Janeiro, Brazil
Nakasato Naohito	University of Aizu, Japan
Natário Isabel Cristina	Universidade Nova de Lisboa, Portugal
Nesticò Antonio	Università degli Studi di Salerno, Italy
Neto Ana Maria	Universidade Federal do ABC, Brazil
Nicolosi Vittorio	University of Rome, Italy
Nikiforiadis Andreas	Aristotle University of Thessaloniki, Greece
Nocera Fabrizio	University of Illinois at Urbana-Champaign, USA
Nocera Silvio	IUAV, Italy
Nogueira Marcelo	Paulista University, Brazil
Nolè Gabriele	CNR, Italy
Nuno Beirao Jose	University of Lisbon, Portugal
Okewu Emma	University of Alcala, Spain
Oluwasefunmi Arogundade	Academy of Mathematics and System Science, China
Oppio Alessandra	Polytechnic University of Milan, Italy
P. Costa M. Fernanda	University of Minho, Portugal

Parisot Olivier	Luxembourg Institute of Science and Technology, Luxembourg
Paddeu Daniela	UWE, UK
Paio Alexandra	ISCTE-Instituto Universitário de Lisboa, Portugal
Palme Massimo	Catholic University of the North, Chile
Panaro Simona	University of Portsmouth, UK
Pancham Jay	Durban University of Technology, South Africa
Pantazis Dimos	University of West Attica, Greece
Papa Enrica	University of Westminster, UK
Pardede Eric	La Trobe University, Australia
Perchinunno Paola	Uniersity of Cagliari, Italy
Perdicoulis Teresa	UTAD, Portugal
Pereira Ana	Polytechnic Institute of Bragança, Portugal
Perri Damiano	University of Perugia, Italy
Petrelli Marco	University of Rome, Italy
Pierri Francesca	University of Perugia, Italy
Piersanti Antonio	ENEA, Italy
Pilogallo Angela	University of Basilicata, Italy
Pinna Francesco	University of Cagliari, Italy
Pinto Telmo	University of Coimbra, Portugal
Piroddi Luca	University of Cagliari, Italy
Poli Giuliano	University of Naples, Italy
Polidoro Maria João	Polytecnic Institute of Porto, Portugal
Polignano Marco	University of Bari, Italy
Politis Ioannis	Aristotle University of Thessaloniki, Greece
Pollino Maurizio	ENEA, Italy
Popoola Segun	Covenant University, Nigeria
Pratelli Antonio	University of Pisa, Italy
Praticò Salvatore	University of Reggio Calabria, Italy
Previtali Mattia	Polytechnic University of Milan, Italy
Puppio Mario Lucio	University of Pisa, Italy
Puttini Ricardo	Universidade de Brasilia, Brazil
Que Zeli	Nanjing Forestry University, China
Queiroz Gilberto	INPE, Brazil
Regalbuto Stefania	University of Naples, Italy
Ravanelli Roberta	University of Roma, Italy
Recanatesi Fabio	University of Tuscia, Italy
Reis Ferreira Gomes Karine	INPE, Brazil
Reis Marco	University of Coimbra, Portugal
Reitano Maria	University of Naples, Italy
Rencelj Marko	University of Maribor, Slovenia
Respondek Jerzy	Silesian University of Technology, Poland
Rimola Albert	Universitat Autònoma de Barcelona, Spain
Rocha Ana	University of Minho, Portugal
Rocha Humberto	University of Coimbra, Portugal
Rocha Maria Celia	UFBA Bahia, Brazil

Rocha Maria Clara	ESTES Coimbra, Portugal
Rocha Miguel	University of Minho, Portugal
Rodriguez Guillermo	UNICEN, Argentina
Rodríguez González Alejandro	Universidad Carlos III de Madrid, Spain
Ronchieri Elisabetta	INFN, Italy
Rosi Marzio	University of Perugia, Italy
Rotondo Francesco	Università Politecnica delle Marche, Italy
Rusci Simone	University of Pisa, Italy
Saganeiti Lucia	University of Basilicata, Italy
Saiu Valeria	University of Cagliari, Italy
Salas Agustin	UPCV, Chile
Salvo Giuseppe	University of Palermo, Italy
Sarvia Filippo	University of Torino, Italy
Santaga Francesco	University of Perugia, Italy
Santangelo Michele	CNR-IRPI, Italy
Santini Francesco	University of Perugia, Italy
Santos Rafael	INPE, Brazil
Santucci Valentino	Università per Stranieri di Perugia, Italy
Saponaro Mirko	Polytechnic University of Bari, Italy
Sarker Iqbal	CUET, Bangladesh
Scaioni Marco	Politecnico Milano, Italy
Scorza Francesco	University of Basilicata, Italy
Scotto di Perta Ester	University of Naples, Italy
Sebillo Monica	University of Salerno, Italy
Sharma Meera	Swami Shraddhanand College, India
Shen Jie	University of Michigan, USA
Shou Huahao	Zhejiang University of Technology, China
Siavvas Miltiadis	Centre of Research and Technology Hellas (CERTH), Greece
Silva Carina	ESTeSL-IPL, Portugal
Silva Joao Carlos	Polytechnic Institute of Cavado and Ave, Portugal
Silva Junior Luneque	Universidade Federal do ABC, Brazil
Silva Ângela	Instituto Politécnico de Viana do Castelo, Portugal
Simonetti Marco	University of Florence, Italy
Situm Zeljko	University of Zagreb, Croatia
Skouteris Dimitrios	Master-Up, Italy
Solano Francesco	Università degli Studi della Tuscia, Italy
Somma Maria	University of Naples, Italy
Sonnessa Alberico	Polytechnic University of Bari, Italy
Sousa Lisete	University of Lisbon, Portugal
Sousa Nelson	University of Algarve, Portugal
Spaeth Benjamin	Cardiff University, UK
Srinivsan M.	Navodaya Institute of Technology, India
Stankova Elena	Saint Petersburg State University, Russia
Stratigea Anastasia	National Technical University of Athens, Greece

Šurdonja Sanja	University of Rijeka, Croatia
Sviatov Kirill	Ulyanovsk State Technical University, Russia
Sánchez de Merás Alfredo	Universitat de Valencia, Spain
Takahashi Daisuke	University of Tsukuba, Japan
Tanaka Kazuaki	Kyushu Institute of Technology, Japan
Taniar David	Monash University, Australia
Tapia McClung Rodrigo	Centro de Investigación en Ciencias de Información Geoespacial, Mexico
Tarantino Eufemia	Polytechnic University of Bari, Italy
Tasso Sergio	University of Perugia, Italy
Teixeira Ana Paula	University of Trás-os-Montes and Alto Douro, Portugal
Teixeira Senhorinha	University of Minho, Portugal
Tengku Izhar Tengku Adil	Universiti Teknologi MARA, Malaysia
Teodoro Maria Filomena	University of Lisbon, Portuguese Naval Academy, Portugal
Tesoriere Giovanni	University of Enna KORE, Italy
Thangeda Amarendar Rao	Botho University, Botswana
Tonbul Gokchan	Atilim University, Turkey
Toraldo Emanuele	Polytechnic University of Milan, Italy
Torre Carmelo Maria	Polytechnic University of Bari, Italy
Torrieri Francesca	University of Naples, Italy
Torrisi Vincenza	University of Catania, Italy
Toscano Domenico	University of Naples, Italy
Totaro Vincenzo	Polytechnic University of Bari, Italy
Trigo Antonio	Instituto Politécnico de Coimbra, Portugal
Trunfio Giuseppe A.	University of Sassari, Italy
Trung Pham	HCMUT, Vietnam
Tsoukalas Dimitrios	Centre of Research and Technology Hellas (CERTH), Greece
Tucci Biagio	CNR, Italy
Tucker Simon	Liverpool John Moores University, UK
Tuñon Iñaki	Universidad de Valencia, Spain
Tyagi Amit Kumar	Vellore Institute of Technology, India
Uchibayashi Toshihiro	Kyushu University, Japan
Ueda Takahiro	Seikei University, Japan
Ugliengo Piero	University of Torino, Italy
Valente Ettore	University of Naples, Italy
Vallverdu Jordi	University Autonoma Barcelona, Spain
Vanelslander Thierry	University of Antwerp, Belgium
Vasyunin Dmitry	T-Systems RUS, Russia
Vazart Fanny	University of Grenoble Alpes, France
Vecchiocattivi Franco	University of Perugia, Italy
Vekeman Jelle	Vrije Universiteit Brussel (VUB), Belgium
Verde Rosanna	Università degli Studi della Campania, Italy
Vermaseren Jos	Nikhef, The Netherlands

Contents – Part IV

International Workshop on Future Computing System Technologies and Applications (FiSTA 2020)

International Workshop on Geodesign in Decision Making: Meta Planning and Collaborative Design for Sustainable and Inclusive Development (GDM 2020)

International Workshop on Geographical Analysis, Urban Modeling, Spatial Statistics (GEOG-AND-MOD 2020)

**International Workshop on Geomatics for Resource Monitoring
and Management (GRMM 2020)**

International Workshop on Data Stream Processing and Applications (DASPA 2020)

Dealing with Data Streams: Complex Event Processing vs. Data Stream Mining

Moritz Lange[1], Arne Koschel[1], and Irina Astrova[2(✉)]

[1] Faculty IV, Department of Computer Science, University of Applied Sciences and Arts Hannover, Ricklinger Stadtweg 120, 30459 Hannover, Germany
moritz-lange@outlook.de, akoschel@acm.org
[2] Department of Software Science, School of IT, Tallinn University of Technology, Akadeemia tee 21, 12618 Tallinn, Estonia
irina@cs.ioc.ee

Abstract. Recently, data generation rates are getting higher than ever before. Plenty of different sources like smartphones, social networking services and the Internet of Things (IoT) are continuously producing massive amounts of data. Due to limited resources, it is no longer feasible to persistently store all that data which leads to massive data streams. In order to meet the requirements of modern businesses, techniques have been developed to deal with these massive data streams. These include complex event processing (CEP) and data stream mining, which are covered in this article. Along with the development of these techniques, many terms and semantic overloads have occurred, making it difficult to clearly distinguish techniques for processing massive data streams. In this article, CEP and data stream mining are distinguished and compared to clarify terms and semantic overloads.

Keywords: Data streams · Complex event processing · Data stream mining · Data mining

1 Introduction

Nowadays, massive amount of data is generated by plenty of different sources. Smartphones, social networking services and the Internet of Things (IoT) are just a few examples of these data-generating sources. This trend is often referred to the term *Big Data*. Data is valuable. In some cases, even a company's value is measured by the amount of data it keeps and collects. Therefore, processing and analyzing data is a key challenge of modern businesses [7, 16].

Over time, data generation rates have increased rapidly. Nowadays there are almost continuous flows of information - data streams. Due to limited resources, it is no longer feasible to persistently store all the incoming data. Computer systems, and in particular data analysis techniques, must adapt to these new conditions to meet the needs of today's businesses. For example, streams of transactions need to be analyzed in real time to be able to respond to credit card frauds [1, 10, 16].

© Springer Nature Switzerland AG 2020
O. Gervasi et al. (Eds.): ICCSA 2020, LNCS 12252, pp. 3–14, 2020.
https://doi.org/10.1007/978-3-030-58811-3_1

In the last 20 years various techniques have been developed to deal with massive data streams [10]. These include complex event processing (CEP) and data stream mining, which are examined in this article. Along with the development of these techniques, many terms and semantic overloads have occurred, making it difficult to clearly distinguish techniques for processing massive data streams. In this article, CEP and data stream mining are distinguished and compared to clarify terms and semantic overloads.

The remainder of this article is organized as follows: Sect. 2 focuses on the basics of data streams. Section 3 shows the central concepts and characteristics of CEP. Furthermore, Sect. 4 introduces the general techniques of data mining and shows how they can be applied to data streams. This is commonly referred to as data stream mining. In Sect. 5, both techniques CEP and data stream mining are compared. Section 6 summarizes the results and gives a recommendation as to when each technique should be used.

2 Data Streams

As mentioned in the introduction, CEP and data stream mining are both techniques for dealing with massive data streams. Since data streams are the central concept of both approaches, this section defines the characteristics of data streams and shows the differences to traditional data.

According to Henzinger et al. [15] a data stream is defined as a sequence of data items $x_1 \ldots x_i \ldots x_n$ such that the items are read once in increasing order of the indices i. In combination with the work of Gama et al. [13], the following characteristics of a data stream can be defined:

1. The data items in the stream arrive online.
2. The system has no control over the order in which the data items arrive.
3. Data streams are potentially unbounded in size.
4. Once an item from a data stream has been processed, it is discarded or archived.

The first fundamental difference to traditional data is that there is no random access. Data items arrive in an online fashion. A second characteristic is that the system has no control over the order or timing of their arrival. Especially with several distributed data stream sources it is not possible to predict when which source will send how many data items. As the definition of Henzinger et al. has shown, another difference to traditional data is that there is a potentially infinite sequence of data items and not a finite set. Since it is not feasible to store data items of the stream persistently, there is a one-pass constraint. Once a data item has been read and processed, no further (fast) access is possible. This is because memory and computation time are restricted when processing data streams. The one-pass constraint is the key challenge that needs to be overcome by an algorithm to guarantee real time processing [1,3,13].

Due to the potentially infinite length of data streams, besides the four characteristic differences to traditional data, there are also potential differences in the content of data:

Concept Drift

Concepts in data streams may evolve over time. Unlike traditional data, there is no finite number of static concepts. Statistical properties and relations between data items can change during the runtime. An illustrative example showing a concept drift is the analysis of e-mail traffic. Especially the detection of spam mails shows that concepts in data streams are not always static. For example, if the author of a spam mail notices that his mails do not pass through the mail filter anymore, he will change some words in his mail to trick the filter. Therefore, the concept has drifted. Because concept drifts can occur anywhere in data streams, handling them is a key challenge for many algorithms and systems [1,12].

Massive Domain

Another aspect is that the potentially infinite size of the data stream implies a potentially very large domain. Especially in data streams, discrete attribute values can have a large number of distinct values. This phenomenon can also be seen well in the example of the analysis of e-mail traffic. For example, if the goal is to determine communication routes, a record must be kept for every pair of e-mail addresses. Considering the amount of possible e-mail addresses, the task is not trivial. Such discrete attribute values with huge ranges are very common in streams, because data items usually have individual identifiers [1,12].

In summary, data streams differ in many ways from traditional data. In particular, algorithms computing on data streams must be able to handle the special characteristics. Stream processors like Apache Spark (Streams) or Apache Flink are implementations that deal with exactly these requirements, which is why CEP and data stream mining systems often rely on such a stream processor.

3   Complex Event Processing

After introducing the basics of data streams in the previous section, this section will introduce a technique for processing massive data streams, evolved from active databases in the 1990's and early 2000's - CEP [9].

3.1   Events

The central concept of CEP, as the name suggests, is the Event. According to David Luckham [18] an event is an object that is a record of an activity in a system that has three characteristic aspects:

1. **Form:** The form of an event is an object, which may have attributes or data components. For example, if a system writes to a logfile, it could generate a log event containing the content of the log message as an attribute.

2. **Significance:** An event signifies an activity. The form of an event usually contains data describing the activity it signifies. In the above example, the log event signifies the activity of the system log. Events can signify any activity, which is why events in literature are also defined as records of anything that happens.
3. **Relativity:** An event can be related to other events by time (an event may have prior to before another event), causality (an event may have been occurred in consequence to another event) or aggregation (an event can consist of several other events). The form of an event usually encodes its relativities.

A complex event is an aggregation of other events. Complex events become visible with CEP. They are usually not explicit. A complex event could be, e.g., a series of suspicious transactions which are individually uncritical but together constitute a credit card fraud.

3.2   Event Streams

As mentioned above, CEP is a technique to deal with massive data streams. In the context of CEP, data streams are considered as event streams. From the definition of a data stream (see Sect. 2) it is easy to derive the definition of an event stream by replacing the concept data item with the concept event defined above. The goal of CEP is to understand and interpret the relativity of events in event streams. In other words, to find and respond to complex events near real-time [9].

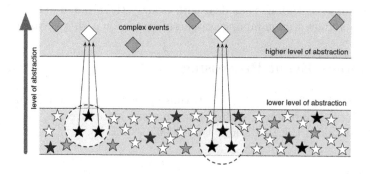

Fig. 1. Event streams and complex events [5]

Figure 1 shows the relation of event streams and complex events (streams). CEP systems analyze the stream of events of a lower abstraction level to find events on a higher abstraction level. CEP systems follow the sense-process-respond cycle (see [4]), which means that they respond to complex events. This response can be a new event representing the complex event or any activity (e.g., a service call).

3.3   Processing Event Streams

Having introduced the central concepts and objectives of CEP in the sections above, this section discusses how implementations of CEP systems can process massive event streams.

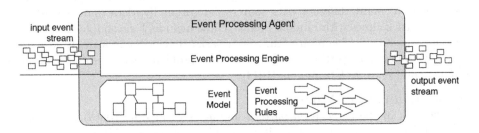

Fig. 2. Architecture of CEP systems [5]

Figure 2 shows the basic architecture of CEP systems. It can be seen that CEP systems belong to the rule-based systems. Rules can be defined declarative in event processing languages (EPL). Rules that are placed in the CEP system are always structured as follows: $\boldsymbol{CONDITION}\ P(e_1 e_2 \ldots e_n) \rightarrow \boldsymbol{ACTION}$ $action(e_1 e_2 \ldots e_n)$. If the event pattern P occurs, the CEP engine will execute the action. All events that may occur are known a priori by the event model.

As mentioned in Sect. 2 the length of data streams is potentially infinite and the resources are limited. This requires a method to allow the data stream to fit into the memory for processing. A sliding window is used for this purpose. The idea is to restrict the considered events to the last recently occurred ones. In general, a distinction is made between a length window, which takes into account the last N events, and a time window, which considers the last events in a fixed time interval [5, 9, 18].

In summary, CEP is about matching predefined structures in data streams. The concept of the event abstracts from the raw data. Rules are defined in an EPL and executed by the CEP engine on a sliding window. When a rule fires, it will result in a new event or activity. Typical applications for CEP include Business Process Management or Algorithmic Trading. In these cases, the patterns are known a priori. However, CEP (alone) does not cover the case if the patterns are unknown.

4   Data Stream Mining

After CEP was introduced in the previous section as an established rule-based approach with a priori known patterns, this section presents data stream mining as a technique for extracting previously unknown patterns and knowledge from data streams. Compared to CEP, data stream mining is a relatively new technique that has only become useful for practical applications by the advances in hardware and software over the past decade [10, 12].

4.1   Mining Data

As the term data stream mining suggests, there is a connection to data mining. Therefore, the following is an introduction to the basics of data mining.

According to Han et al. [14], data mining is the process of discovering interesting patterns and knowledge from large amounts of data. This process can be applied to many different data sources. Traditionally, data mining is operated on data sources with random access. These include, for example, databases or data warehouses. There are four major tasks that occur repeatedly in data mining applications, so that the following four problems are considered as the fundamental ones in data mining [1][14]:

Association Pattern Mining
The task of the association pattern mining is to identify (data) items that imply the appearance of other items within a transaction. If a certain item often occurs together with others, association rules can be deduced. An illustrative example of the use of association pattern mining is the mining of transactions in an online shop. The transaction data can be used to determine which products were often bought together. This knowledge can be used to recommend additional products to customers when they buy a product. In literature, this specific problem is also referred to as frequent itemset mining [1,14].

Clustering
Clustering is the task of grouping (data) items into homogeneous classes. These classes of items that are similar in some ways are called clusters. For the process of clustering, certain properties of the items are taken into account. An example of the application of clustering is customer segmentation. The goal of customer segmentation is to divide a company's customers into groups of individuals that are similar in specific ways relevant to marketing. The properties taken into account could be, for example, age and sex of the customer [1,14].

Classification
Classification is about assigning (data) items to groups. Unlike clustering, the groups are predefined and are not found during the process. That is the reason classification is considered as an instance of supervised learning. This means that a training set of correctly identified observations is available. A sample application domain is pattern matching. With the appropriate knowledge, for example, it is possible to classify e-mails as spam [1,14].

Outlier Detection
An outlier is a (data) element that is significantly different from the rest of the data. The task of outlier detection is to find such anomalies in data. For example, outlier detection is used in the detection of credit card frauds, since the transaction data in a fraud is significantly different from that in normal behavior. Outlier detection can be unsupervised or supervised [1,14].

For each of the above problems, there are a variety of algorithms, such as e.g. the famous k-means algorithm for clustering or the k-nearest neighbor algorithm for classification. However, this article does not aim to elaborate on specific algorithms.

4.2 Mining Data Streams

As mentioned in the previous section, the process of data mining can be applied to many different data sources. These include data streams. Data mining on streams is considered as data stream mining.

The problem is that many conventional data mining algorithms can not handle the constraints of streams. This is because these algorithms have been designed for traditional data and therefore assume random access to the data and potentially infinite processing time. Data streams do not offer these conditions. Because of this, various techniques exist for adapting algorithms to data streams. According to Gaber et al. [10], these techniques can be divided into data-based and task-based techniques:

Data-based techniques
One way to deal with massive data streams is to reduce the incoming data to an amount that the algorithm can handle. This is the goal of the data-based techniques [10].
Sampling
An old established statistical method is sampling. The idea is to select probabilistically whether a data item is processed or not. A well-known instance is the reservoir sampling, where each element has a certain probability that it will be included in the sample. One of the challenges of sampling on streams is that due to the potentially infinite length, the calculation of error bounds for certain sampling rates is not trivial [1,3,10].
Load Shedding
Load shedding refers to the process of dropping sequences of data items from a stream. The problems of load shedding are very similar to those of sampling. It is hard to decide which and how much data can be disregarded. Dropping the wrong data can be quite critical if, for example, during the outlier detection an outlier is ignored [3,10].
Sketching
Another approach is to randomly project a subset of features, which corresponds to vertically sampling the incoming stream. This method works well to compare data streams but is less relevant in the context of data stream mining [3,10].
Synopsis Data Structures
The creation of synopsis data structures refers to the process of applying summary techniques to the incoming data stream. The resulting structures can be used for further analysis. An example for the creation of synopsis data structures is wavelet analysis, where the incoming data

stream is converted into a wavelet by a Fourier transformation. It is possible that in the creation of the synopsis data structures characteristics of the data are lost, which is why in these cases approximate results must be expected. Aggarwal et al. [1] present synopsis data structures as the basis of almost every data stream mining application [1, 10].

Aggregation

Another technique that has evolved with the advent of data streams is aggregation. Aggregation refers to the process of calculating statistical measures (e.g., mean or variance) that summarize the incoming data stream. Furthermore, these measurements can be used by the mining algorithms. A concrete example of aggregation are cluster features which is a method to enable clustering on streams. The idea is to keep statistical variables for each cluster which are updated iteratively. Algorithms using an extension of this technique (micro-clusters) are, e.g. CluStream (see Aggarwal et al. [2]) and DenStream (see Cao et al. [6]) [1, 10, 22].

Task-based techniques

Another way to adapt algorithms to data streams is to change not the data but the algorithms themselves. These approaches are referred as task-based techniques [10].

Approximation algorithms

One approach is to use approximation algorithms, as is done in other areas when hard problems need to be solved. In this approach, mining algorithms are seen as hard computational problems and an inaccurate result is accepted, which can be calculated faster [3, 10].

Sliding Window

One technique that has been briefly presented in the context of CEP is the use of sliding windows. The idea is to restrict the considered data elements to the last recently occurred ones. Algorithms using sliding time windows are e.g.. the STREAM algorithm (see [20]) for clustering on data streams or the Online Information Network (see [17]) for classification on streams [10, 11].

Algorithm Output Granularity

Algorithm Output Granularity (AOG) is an approach that can respond to limited resources and fluctuating data rates. The idea is that the mining algorithm is designed so that its output can be throttled when it runs out of memory. Then the results are merged until enough memory is available again. An algorithm based on this technique is the LWClass Algorithm (see Gaber et al. [11]) [10, 11].

The above list shows that there are many different techniques to enable computing on streams. However, there is not the one technique that enables mining on data streams. Depending on which data mining problem has to be solved and what the concrete application case looks like, variations of the above techniques have to be combined. In addition, the concrete algorithmic techniques have not yet been discussed. For example, the list above does not show how an algorithm can react to a concept drift or the massive domain constraint. More details can be found in the survey papers by Gaber et al. [11] and Silva et al. [22]. The listed examples for algorithms were also taken from mentioned papers.

In summary, data stream mining is an open research field that has emerged through the advances in hardware and software and is still evolving [8].

5   Comparison

After the previous sections have introduced CEP and data stream mining separately, the following section will explicitly compare the two techniques.

Table 1. Comparison of CEP and data stream mining

Complex event processing	Data stream mining
For processing massive event streams	For processing massive data streams
Rule-based	Data analysis/Data Mining
Pattern matching (matching predefined structures)	Pattern and knowledge discovery (discovering unknown structures)
Follows the sense-process-respond cycle	Results need further processing to react
...	...

Table 1 shows some of the major characteristics of CEP and data stream mining discussed in this article. First of all, we can say that both techniques are used to process massive data streams. In the context of CEP, the concept event abstracts from the raw data elements, but under the hood event streams are the same as data streams. This is also the reason why both techniques are using the methods for processing streams presented in Sect. 4.2. In literature, however, the techniques used in CEP are limited to sliding windows.

Although both techniques deal with data streams, they have their origins in quite different fields of computer science. While CEP has evolved from rule-based systems, data stream mining has evolved from classical data analysis through advances in hard and software. Due to the rapidly growing RAM sizes, the operations that can be performed in-memory are also increasing. As a consequence, CEP and in particular data stream mining become more and more practicable.

The main difference between CEP and data stream mining is that the former is about simple matching of predefined structures on sliding windows and the latter is about finding new patterns and knowledge on data streams. In some cases, however, the tasks of the two techniques are very similar. For example, if spam mails had to be detected, both CEP and data stream mining (classification or an outlier detection) can be used. Specifically, the supervised learning methods come very close to CEP and its applications, since there are also predefined structures used as a knowledge base. The difference is how this knowledge base is used. For CEP, a pattern can match or not, whereas for pattern matching by classification it is fuzzier. Incoming data does not have to match exactly. Data can be similar to a pattern in a certain way. The outlier analysis can also enable the detection of spam mails. But again, it's not about whether a pattern matches or not, but whether the incoming data elements are significantly different from the rest of the data. In CEP, the pattern that is found must be expressed explicitly by rules and event models, while data stream mining can also find structures that have not been explicitly modeled. As the clustering shows, the areas of data stream mining and CEP can also be very different. Clustering is about finding new structures, which is not possible with CEP. An interesting comparison would be CEP and the association pattern mining on streams. With CEP it is quite possible to carry out an association analysis by explicitly modeling the possible combinations and then counting the triggered events. With a larger number of combinations, however, this becomes impractical very quickly.

Another important difference between CEP and data stream mining is that CEP follows the sense-process-respond circle. Therefore, when a complex event occurs, there is always an action (response). This is because complex event processing was originally intended to control event-driven architectures (EDA) (see Luckham [18]). Data stream mining applications are natively non-reactive. Results of the data mining need further processing to react to situations. As the last row of the table shows, there are other similarities and differences that can not be considered further in the context of this article. Another interesting aspect, e.g., is the fact that there are only a few scientific papers on handling concept drifts with CEP, although this characteristic of streams occurs there. Because the rules in a CEP system are very static, CEP systems can be combined with other techniques to change the rules at run-time (see e.g. [19] or [21]). This could also be a possible approach to dealing with a concept drift. For example, the combination of CEP and data stream mining is possible. In this case, data stream mining finds new patterns and knowledge, which is fed into the CEP system in the form of rules and event models.

In summary, CEP and data stream mining differ in many ways. Surprisingly, there are many overlaps in the fields of application. For CEP, patterns can either match or not, while the matching for data stream mining is fuzzy. Therefore, comparing data stream mining to CEP, knowledge does not always have to be explicitly modeled.

6   Conclusion and Future Work

In this article, we first looked at the special characteristics of data streams and compared them to traditional data. Therefore, CEP was presented as a rule-based method for processing massive data streams. It has been determined that CEP can only be applied if the complex events to be found are defined a priori in the form of rules and event models. However, CEP (alone) does not cover the case if the patterns are unknown. As a solution, the technique of data stream mining was introduced. It has been shown that it is data mining on streams, which is why the fundamentals of data mining have been introduced. In the following sections it was discussed that data mining techniques were originally designed for traditional data and can not handle the special characteristics of streams without adjustments. For this purpose, some techniques for the processing of data streams were presented and enriched with example algorithms from survey papers. In the end there was a comparison of CEP and data stream mining, which, in addition to many differences, also revealed overlaps in the areas of application.

To summarize the results of this article as a recommendation, CEP should be used when it is necessary to react directly to complex events that can be explicitly modeled before. Data stream mining should be used to discover previously unknown patterns and knowledge from data streams.

While this paper gives an overview of the two techniques and aims to show the origins and differences of both, further papers will deal with more recent findings from the two research fields. One part of our future work will be the development of a decision framework that allows a user to determine the right technique (or the right combination of these techniques) for a specific application.

Acknowledgements. Irina Astrova's work was supported by the Estonian Ministry of Education and Research institutional research grant IUT33-13.

References

1. Aggarwal, C.C.: Data Mining. Springer, Cham (2015). https://doi.org/10.1007/978-3-319-14142-8
2. Aggarwal, C.C., Han, J., Wang, J., Yu, P.S.: A framework for clustering evolving data streams. In: Proceedings of the 29th International Conference on Very Large Data Bases-Volume 29, pp. 81–92. VLDB Endowment (2003)
3. Babcock, B., Babu, S., Datar, M., Motwani, R., Widom, J.: Models and issues in data stream systems. In: Proceedings of the Twenty-First ACM SIGMOD-SIGACT-SIGART Symposium on Principles of Database Systems, pp. 1–16. ACM (2002)
4. Bruns, R., Dunkel, J.: Event-Driven Architecture: Softwarearchitektur fürereignisgesteuerte Geschäftsprozesse. Springer, Heidelberg (2010). https://doi.org/10.1007/978-3-642-02439-9
5. Bruns, R., Dunkel, J.: Complex Event Processing. Springer, Wiesbaden (2015). https://doi.org/10.1007/978-3-658-09899-5
6. Cao, F., Estert, M., Qian, W., Zhou, A.: Density-based clustering over an evolving data stream with noise. In: Proceedings of the 2006 SIAM International Conference on Data Mining, pp. 328–339. SIAM (2006)
7. Chen, M., Mao, S., Liu, Y.: Big data: a survey. Mobile Netw. Appl. **19**(2), 171–209 (2014)
8. Domingos, P.M., Hulten, G.: Catching up with the data: research issues in mining data streams. In: DMKD (2001)
9. Etzion, O., Niblett, P., Luckham, D.C.: Event Processing in Action. Manning, Greenwich (2011)

10. Gaber, M.M., Zaslavsky, A., Krishnaswamy, S.: Mining data streams: a review. ACM Sigmod Rec. **34**(2), 18–26 (2005)
11. Gaber, M.M., Zaslavsky, A., Krishnaswamy, S.: A survey of classification methods in data streams. In: Aggarwal, C.C. (ed.) Data Streams. Advances in Database Systems, vol. 31, pp. 39–59. Springer, Boston (2007). https://doi.org/10.1007/978-0-387-47534-9_3
12. Gama, J.: Knowledge Discovery from Data Streams. Chapman and Hall/CRC (2010)
13. Gama, J., Gaber, M.M.: Learning from Data Streams: Processing Techniques in Sensor Networks. Springer, Heidelberg (2007). https://doi.org/10.1007/3-540-73679-4
14. Han, J., Pei, J., Kamber, M.: Data Mining: Concepts and Techniques. Elsevier, Amsterdam (2011)
15. Henzinger, M.R., Raghavan, P., Rajagopalan, S.: Computing on data streams. External Memory Algorithms **50**, 107–118 (1998)
16. Hilbert, M., López, P.: The world's technological capacity to store, communicate, and compute information. Science **332**(6025), 60–65 (2011)
17. Last, M.: Online classification of nonstationary data streams. Intell. Data Anal. **6**(2), 129–147 (2002)
18. Luckham, D.: The Power of Events, vol. 204. Addison-Wesley, Reading (2002)
19. Mehdiyev, N., Krumeich, J., Enke, D., Werth, D., Loos, P.: Determination of rule patterns in complex event processing using machine learning techniques. Procedia Comput. Sci. **61**, 395–401 (2015)
20. O'callaghan, L., Mishra, N., Meyerson, A., Guha, S., Motwani, R.: Streaming-data algorithms for high-quality clustering. In: Proceedings 18th International Conference on Data Engineering, pp. 685–694. IEEE (2002)
21. Pielmeier, J., Braunreuther, S., Reinhart, G.: Approach for defining rules in the context of complex event processing. Procedia CIRP **67**, 8–12 (2018)
22. Silva, J.A., Faria, E.R., Barros, R.C., Hruschka, E.R., De Carvalho, A.C., Gama, J.: Data stream clustering: a survey. ACM Compu. Surv. (CSUR) **46**(1), 13 (2013)

Anomaly Detection for Data Streams Based on Isolation Forest Using Scikit-Multiflow

Maurras Ulbricht Togbe[1][(⊠)], Mariam Barry[2,3], Aliou Boly[4],
Yousra Chabchoub[1], Raja Chiky[1], Jacob Montiel[5], and Vinh-Thuy Tran[2]

[1] ISEP, LISITE, Paris, France
{maurras.togbe,yousra.chabchoub,raja.chiky}@isep.fr
[2] BNP Paribas, IT Group, Division Data, Montreuil, France
{mariam.barry,vinh-thuy.tran}@bnpparibas.com
[3] Télécom Paris, LTCI, Institut Polytechnique de Paris, Palaiseau, France
[4] Université Cheikh Anta Diop de Dakar, Dakar, Senegal
aliou.boly@ucad.edu.sn
[5] Department of Computer Science, University of Waikato, Hamilton, New Zealand
jacob.montiel@waikato.ac.nz

Abstract. Detecting anomalies in streaming data is an important issue in a variety of real-word applications as it provides some critical information, e.g., Cyber security attacks, Fraud detection or others real-time applications. Different approaches have been designed in order to detect anomalies: statistics-based, isolation-based, clustering-based. In this paper, we present a quick survey of the existing anomaly detection methods for data streams. We focus on Isolation Forest (iForest), a state-of-the-art method for anomaly detection. We provide the implementation of IForestASD, a variant of iForest for data streams.

This implementation is built on top of scikit-multiflow, an open source machine learning framework for data streams. In fact, few anomalies detection methods are provided in the well-known data streams mining frameworks such as MOA or StreamDM. Hence, we extend scikit-multiflow providing an additional tool. We performed experiments on 3 real-world data sets to evaluate predictive performance and resource consumption (memory and time) of IForestASD and compare it with a well known and state-of-the-art anomaly detection algorithm for data streams called Half-Space Trees.

Keywords: Anomaly detection · Streaming · Scikit-multiflow · Survey

1 Introduction

Data streams mining is the era that deals with extracting relevant and meaningful patterns from data arriving in a continuous way. It is a challenging problem especially when applied to evolving data streams or is subject to big data

© Springer Nature Switzerland AG 2020
O. Gervasi et al. (Eds.): ICCSA 2020, LNCS 12252, pp. 15–30, 2020.
https://doi.org/10.1007/978-3-030-58811-3_2

constraints where optimized storage and fast processing are required. When it comes to some streaming applications, such as network attacks, frauds, or failures warning from vital maintenance predictive tools, abnormal patterns (aka outliers) need to be detected as fast as possible to get insights for decision-making. Therefore, anomaly detection in data streams is a major task for some business applications which activities depend on continuous streams from real time events. Anomaly detection algorithms for data streams refer to methods able to handle a continuous and possibly infinite streams and at the same time, extract enough knowledge from the streams to compute anomaly score.

Many frameworks for Data stream mining have been proposed in the literature. Scikit-Multiflow [20] is the main open source machine learning framework for multi-output, multi-label and data streaming. Implemented in Python language, it includes various algorithms and methods for streams mining and in particular the popular Half-space Trees algorithm [24], a fast Anomaly Detection for Streaming Data. One of its motivations is to encourage researchers and industrials on data streams mining field to easily integrate and share their methods inside the framework and make their work easily accessible by the growing Python community.

Our contributions is two-fold: first, we provide a structured overview and categorization of anomaly detection methods for data streams along with a discussion about the main advantages and disadvantages of the approaches. Second, we implement in Scikit-MultiFlow framework an algorithm proposed by [11] (Ding & Fei, 2013), an isolation based anomaly detection (IForestASD) and highlight the simplicity of the framework to accelerate contributions. We performed experiments with 3 real data sets to evaluate predictive performance and resource consumption (memory and time) of IForestASD and compare it with a well known and state of art anomaly detection algorithm for data streams called Half-Space Trees. To our best knowledge there is no open source implementation of IForestASD, neither in Github neither in a streaming framework.

1.1 MOA: Massive Online Analysis

MOA [8] is the most popular open source framework for data stream mining in Java. It includes a collection of machine learning algorithms (classification, regression, clustering, outlier detection, concept drift detection and recommender systems) including data generators, tools for evaluation and an interface to visualize experiments results. MOA is related to Waikato Environment for Knowledge Analysis (WEKA) [28]. In the recent book [7], the authors covered the field of Online Learning from Sketches and Drift detection approaches to supervised and non supervised algorithms for Data Streams. Some practical examples with MOA are also provided. More information can be found in the MOA Manual[1].

The authors of [5] provided a comparative study of distributed tools for analyzing streaming Data, with a qualitative comparison between Apache Spark, Storm, Samza and Apache S4.

---

[1] https://moa.cms.waikato.ac.nz/documentation/.

Others Software Libraries and Frameworks. Multiple open-source software libraries use MOA to perform data stream analytics in their systems [7], including ADAMS, MEKA, and OpenML.

Others big data streams frameworks are SAMOA [6] and StreamDM. Apache SAMOA is an open source platform for mining big data streams. It is a framework that contains a programming abstraction for distributed streaming ML algorithms. StreamDM [9] is an open source data mining and machine learning library, designed on top of Spark Streaming, an extension of the core Spark API that enables scalable data streams processing.

1.2 Scikit-Multiflow: A Machine Learning Framework for Multi-output/Multi-label and Streaming Data

Scikit-multiflow [20] is an open-source framework in Python to implement algorithms and perform experiments in the field of machine learning on evolving data streams. Scikit-multiflow is inspired by the popular frameworks Scikit-learn[2], MOA and MEKA. One advantage of scikit-multiflow compared to the other frameworks is that it serves as a bridge between research communities that have flourished around the aforementioned popular frameworks, providing a common ground for researchers and practitioners.

Scikit-multiflow includes a collection of various algorithms and learning methods: From Rule and Trees based methods such as Hoeffding Anytime Tree or Extremely Fast Decision Tree [19] to ensemble methods such as Adaptive Random Forest classifier [13]. The list of existing algorithms can be found in the package map on the official webpage https://scikit-multiflow.github.io/scikit-multiflow/package_map.html.

Half-Space Trees is the only method for anomaly detection in the current scikit-multiflow release.

Half-Space Trees - Fast Anomaly Detection for Data Streams
Half-Spaces-Trees [24] - Fast Anomaly Detection for Data Streams - is the only anomaly detection algorithm currently implemented in scikit-multiflow. The authors of the algorithm shown that the training phase has constant amortized time complexity and constant memory requirement. When compared with a state-of-the-art method (Hoeffding Trees) its performs favorably in terms of detection accuracy and run-time performance. Thus, we expect HS-Trees to perform better than Isolation Forest ASD as well in term of speed, we will discuss the experiments results in Sect. 4. Compared to Isolation Tree, Half-Space Tree has a fixed depth for each tree in the ensemble and update policy consists of updating the mass profile using the nodes of trees.

1.3 Motivation of the Work

From the review of Big Data Streams Mining Frameworks, scikit-multiflow seems to be the most promising one as it implements the majority of well known stream

---

[2] https://scikit-learn.org/stable/scikit-learn.

learning methods using the very well known programming language Python with a growing community. And since it contains only one anomaly detection method, which is Half-Spaces-Trees [24], we thus decided to extend the framework by implementing an anomaly detection approach based on Isolation Forest algorithm proposed by Ding & Fei [11].

Hence, the motivations behind our implementation providing an isolation-based algorithm in Scikit-multiflow are the follow:

- **Isolation Forest** is a state-of-the-art algorithm for anomaly detection and the only ensemble method in scikit-learn's and widely used by the community. Also, it is a tree-based model easily suitable for online and incremental learning.
- **Scikit-multiflow** is the main streaming framework in Python which includes a variety of learning algorithms and streaming methods.

The paper is organized as follows: Sect. 1 introduces our work and its motivations. In Sect. 2, we provide a survey and classification of anomaly detection adapted to data streams. In Sect. 3, we focus on algorithms description: first batch Isolation Forest and its variant implemented for streaming setting (IForestASD). In Sect. 4 we present experimental evaluations, comparing IForestASD to Half-Space Trees and discuss the results. Finally, Sect. 5 concludes the work by providing future research directions.

2 Anomaly Detection in Data Streams: Survey

2.1 Survey

Anomaly Detection in Data Stream (ADiDS) presents many challenges due to the characteristics of this type of data. One important challenge is that data stream treatment has to be performed in a single pass to deal with memory limits and methods have to be applied in an online way. Thus, the several existing offline anomaly detection approaches such as statistical approach, clustering approach, etc. [1,10,16] are not adapted for data stream because they require many passes over dataset. They also need to have the entire dataset to be able to detect anomalies. We find in the literature some approaches that have been adapted or new designed methods for ADiDS. In [14], authors give a survey on outlier detection methods that can be applied to temporal data with a focus on data streams. They presented evolving prediction models, distance based approach and outlier detection in high dimensional data streams. [25,26] and [22] are all surveys about outlier detection in data stream context. In [26] authors present the issues of outlier detection in data stream like concept drift, uncertainty and arrival rate. A detailed study on time series and multidimensional streaming outlier detection methods is proposed in the book [1, Chap. 9]. It presents different approaches such as probabilistic-based, prediction-based and distance-based methods.

2.2   Approaches and Methods Classification

Generally, anomaly detection methods are based on the facts that anomalies are rare and have a different behavior compared to normal data. These characteristics are true for static datasets and also data streams. The most used anomalies detection approaches are statistics, clustering, nearest-neighbors that we will present below. We will focus on an approach based on isolation: Isolation Forest, proposed in 2008 by Liu *et al.* in [17].

Statistics-Based: Statistics-based approaches generally establish a model that characterizes the normal behavior based on the dataset. The new incoming data which don't fit the model or have very low probability to fit the model are considered as abnormal. Some methods give a score for the data based on the deviation degree from the model [29]. Statistics-based methods can be parametric in which case they need to have a prior knowledge about the dataset distribution. They can be non parametric where they learn from the given dataset to deduce the underlying distribution. In the context of data stream, such prior knowledge is not always available.

Clustering-Based and Nearest-Neighbors-Based: Clustering and nearest neighbors approaches are based on the proximity between observations. The methods in this category are based either on the distance (distance-based) or the density (density-based). Clustering methods divide the dataset in different clusters according to the similarity between the observations. The most distant cluster or the cluster which has the smallest density can be considered as an anomaly cluster [2,4]. Nearest-neighbors methods determine the neighbors of one observation by computing the distance between all the observations in the dataset. The observation which is far from its k nearest-neighbors can be considered as an anomaly [3]. It is also characterized as the observation which has the most less neighbors in a radius r (a fixed parameter) [21]. These approaches need to compute the distance or the density between all the observations in the dataset or they need to have some prior knowledge about the dataset. So they can suffer of a high CPU, time and memory consumption or a lack of information.

Isolation-Based: Introduced by [17], the principle of the isolation-based approach is to isolate abnormal observations from the dataset. Anomalies data are supposed to be very different from normal ones. They are also supposed to represent a very small proportion of the whole dataset. Thus, they are likely to be quickly isolated. Some isolation-based methods are presented in Sect. 3. Isolation based methods are different from others statistics, clustering or nearest-neighbors approaches because they don't compute a distance or a density from the dataset. Therefore, they have a lower complexity and are more scalable. They don't suffer from the problem of CPU, memory or time consumption. Thus, isolation based methods are adapted to the data stream context.

The Table 1 summarizes advantages and disadvantages of the existing approaches for ADiDS.

There are many methods adapted or designed for ADiDS in the literature. They usually use the data stream concept of window to compute anomaly [22].

Table 1. Comparison of ADiDS approaches.

Approaches	Advantages	Disadvantages
Statistics-based	Non-parametric methods are adapted to data stream context	– Parametric methods are difficult to apply to data stream – Non-parametric methods can only be used for low dimensional data stream
Nearest-neighbors	Distance-based methods – Adapted for global anomalies detection	Distance-based methods – Are not adapted for non-homogeneous densities – Have high computational cost for high dimensional data stream
	Density-based methods – Adapted for local anomalies detection – More efficient than distance-based methods	Density-based methods – Have high complexity – Are not effective for high dimensional data stream
Clustering-based	Adapted for clusters identification	Not optimized for individual anomaly identification
Isolation-based	– Have less CPU, time and memory consumption – Are efficient for anomaly detection	– Performance depend a lot on the window and model update policy choices – Hard to adapt for categorical data

The Fig. 1 presents a classification of some anomaly detection methods for each category that exist in the literature and applicable to data stream.

A recent work [27] on anomaly detection approaches has shown that isolation forest algorithm has good performance compared to other methods. Thus we decided to implement an adaptation of isolation forest in a data streams mining framework that will be detailed in the next sections.

3   Isolation Forest and IForestASD for Streaming

The first method proposed in isolation-based category is Isolation forest (IForest) [17,18]. One of IForest's limits is that it was designed for static dataset and not for data stream. In [11], authors propose an improvement of IForest to adapt it to data stream context using sliding windows. The proposed method is named Isolation Forest Algorithm for Stream Data (IForestASD).

There exists other improvements and adaptations of Isolation Forest such as Extended Isolation Forest [15] or Functional Isolation Forest [23] but they are designed for batch settings and not adapted for data streaming.

In this section we will present the IForest algorithm then we will explained the implemented algorithm IForestASD.

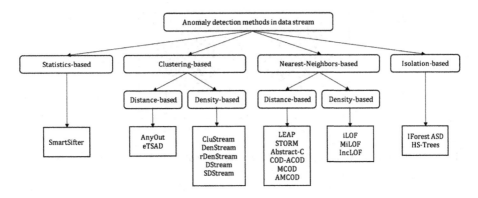

Fig. 1. Classification of data stream anomaly detection methods

3.1 Isolation Forest Method

Isolation forest (IForest) is an isolation-based method which isolates observations by splitting dataset. Anomaly data have two properties which have been exploited by isolation-based methods: They have a behavior which is different from normal data and they are rare in the dataset. With those properties, a relatively small number of partitions is needed to isolate anomalies as shown in Fig. 2. IForest is based on a forest of random distinct itrees. Every tree has to decide if a considered observation is an anomaly or not. If a random forest of itrees globally consider an observation as an anomaly, then it is very likely to represent an anomaly. IForest is composed of two phases: the first one is the training phase which is the construction of the forest of random itrees and the second one is the scoring phase where IForest gives an anomaly score for every observation in the dataset.

In the training phase, all the t random and independents itrees of the forest are built. Using the sample of ψ randomly selected data, every internal node of the binary itree is split in two other nodes (left and right). To split one node, IForest randomly chooses one attribute: d from the m data attributes. Then it randomly chooses a split value v between the min and the max value of d in the considered node. IForest splits internal nodes until a complete data isolation or reaching a maximal tree depth called max_depth which is equal to $ceilling(log_2(\psi))$. After the forest training phase, the scoring phase can begin. In this phase, every new observation x has to pass through all the t itrees to get its path length $h(x)$ [17]. The anomaly score of x is computed with this formula: $s(x, n) = 2^{-\frac{E(h(x))}{c(n)}}$ where $E(h(x)) = \frac{\sum_{i=1}^{t} h_i(x)}{t}$ is the average path length of x over t itrees and $c(n)$ is the average path length of unsuccessful search in Binary Search Tree (BST). $c(n) = 2H(n-1) - (2(n-1)/n)$ with $H(i) = ln(i) + \gamma$ (γ is Euler's constant). Finally, if $s(x, n)$ is close to 1, x is considered as an anomaly. If $s(x, n)$ is less than 0.5, x is considered as a normal data.

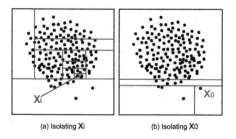

Fig. 2. Normal data X_i needs 11 split steps to be isolated. X_0 has been isolated very quickly in 3 steps.

3.2   IForestASD: Isolation Forest Algorithm for Stream Data Method

Isolation Forest is an efficient method for anomaly detection with relatively low complexity, CPU and time consumption. It requires all the data in the beginning to build t random samples. It also needs many passes over the dataset to build all the random forest. So, it is not adapted to data stream context. In [11], authors have proposed the so called IForestASD method which is an improvement of IForest for ADiDS. IForestASD uses sliding window to deal with streaming data. On the current complete window, IForestASD executes the standard IForest method to get the random forest. This is the IForest detector model for IForestASD. IForestASD method can also deal with concept drift in the data stream by maintaining one input desired anomaly rate (u). If the anomaly rate in the considered window is upper than u, then a concept drift occurred so IForestASD deletes its current IForest detector and builts another one using all the data in the considered window. Figure 3 represents the workflow used in IForestASD to update the model. In Sect. 4 we present our experiments results of this algorithm in scikit-multiflow framework using incremental fit and prediction methods.

4   Experimental Evaluation

In this section, we present the methodology followed in our tests and discuss the results. We compare and discuss the impact of the data window size and the number of estimators in the performance of both Half-Space Tree and IForestASD in terms of F_1 score, training and testing time, and model size.

Performance is measured following the prequential (test-then-train method) evaluation strategy designed specifically for stream settings, in the sense that each sample serves two purposes (test then train), and that samples are analyzed sequentially, in the order of arrival, and become immediately inaccessible. This approach assures that the model is tested on new samples that have not been used in the training yet. All the results and performance metrics reported in this paper correspond to the output of scikit-multiflow from prequential evaluator[3].

---

[3] https://scikit-multiflow.github.io/scikit-multiflow/documentation.html.

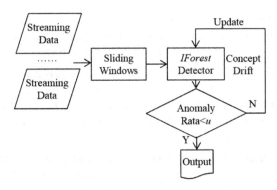

Fig. 3. Isolation Forest ASD algorithm workflow for Drift Detection implemented in Scikit-multiflow. Image extracted from the original paper by [Ding & Fei, 2013] [11]

4.1 Search Space, Data Sets and Metrics

Data Sets Description
To prove the effectiveness of our implementation of IForestASD, we benchmark it against the Half-Space Trees method on a variety of configurations (12 for each dataset). We used some well known public datasets [12] which have been used in the IForestASD paper. Their characteristics are resumed in Table 2.

Experimental Setup
The hyper-parameters setting we used to perform various experiments to compare the two models HSTrees and IForestASD is the following:

Table 2. Datasets and hyper-parameters set up

	Shuttle	Forest-cover	SMTP
Attributes, number of features	9	10	3
u - Drift rate = anomaly rate	7.15%	0.96%	0.03%
Number of samples	49,097	286,048	95,156
W - Window size range tested	[50, 100, 500, 1000]		
T - Number of trees in ensemble	[30, 50, 100]		

The anomaly threshold was set to 0.5 and number of observations (samples) was limited to 10 000 for both Datasets for each experiment. For the parameter u, we set the value to the anomalies rate in the datasets as did the authors of IForestASD algorithm [11]. This value is used to detect drift and reset the anomaly detection model as described in Fig. 3.

The source code to replicate experiments can be found in the Github at https://github.com/MariamBARRY/skmultiflow_IForestASD.

Evaluation Metrics

In the results table, we reported 3 metrics: F1, Running Time (training + testing) ratio (IForestASD/HSTrees) and Model Size ratio (HSTrees/IForestASD).

F1 Metric. It corresponds to the harmonic mean of precision and recall and is computed as follows: $f_1 = 2 \times (precision \times recall)/(precision + recall)$. F1 is a popular metric if there is an imbalanced class distribution and we search for a balance between precision and recall. This is the case of abnormal data which is less represented than normal data.

Running Time Ratio (IForestASD Coefficient Ratio) - IRa. Since Half-Space Trees (HST) is always faster than IForestASD (IFA), for both training and testing time, by an order of 400 for the worst case, we reported the ratio between running time (training and testing) of the two models: IFA over HST. For example for the Forest-Cover data, IFA is 3 times slower than HST for $W = 50, T \in \{30, 50, 100\}$, and for $W = 1000, T = 100$ the running time ratio is 391 in the Table 3 meaning that IFA is 391 slower than HST. Absolute values of running time (in seconds) and their evolution over hyper-parameters variation in reported in Fig. 5.

Model Size Ratio (HSTrees Coefficient Ratio) - HRa. In the opposite of the running time, when we consider the model size, we observe that IFA always used less memory then HST. So, to compare these two methods, we compute the ratio of the higher value (HST) over the smaller value (IFA) to get the HST coefficient. Figure 4 reports the impact of parameters choice on resources used (model size absolute value in Kilo-bytes) for both HSTrees and the evolution of resources used for the 3 datasets when window size and number of trees varies. Interpretation are provided below.

4.2   Results Discussion

Table 3 reports the results obtained for each hyper-parameter combination (window size and number of trees) for both datasets.

We observed that, based on the F1 score, IForestASD performs better than HS-Trees for both Shuttle and SMTP datasets, no matter the windows size or the number of trees. Three further points are observed:

First, we noticed that the number of trees has not a significant impact on the prediction performance for all the datasets. However, when the window size increases (varying from 50, 100, 500 to 1000), the score is better as F1 score increases for all data sets. Second, while for HS-Trees, F1 improves for window size >= 500, it decreases for IForestASD. This can be explained by the fact that unlike HS-Trees, IForestASD deletes its current anomaly detector model (isolation forest) and builds another one using all the data in the current window when the anomaly rate in the window is upper than u. Thirdly, there is a large difference between the performance of the two models depending on the dataset, especially for Shuttle which has a larger anomaly rate of 7%, IForestASD outperforms HSTrees with 80% F1. Therefore we assume that IForestASD performs better on data set with relatively high anomaly rate.

Table 3. Comparison between HS-Trees (HST) and IForestASD (IFA) - We fixed the window size w (50, 100, 50, 1000) and varied the number of trees T for each dataset Forest Cover, Shuttle and SMTP (36 configurations) - HRa and IRa represent HSTRees ratio and IFA ratio described in Sect. 4.1

		Forest cover				Shuttle				SMTP			
		F1		Time	Size	F1		Time	Size	F1		Time	Size
W	T	HST	IFA	IRa	HRa	HST	IFA	IRa	HRa	HST	IFA	IRa	HRa
50	30	**0.36**	0.22	**3**	702	0.13	**0.64**	**3**	817	0	**0.34**	**3**	926
50	50	**0.36**	0.23	**3**	694	0.13	**0.64**	**3**	854	0	**0.34**	**3**	940
50	100	**0.36**	0.22	**3**	737	0.13	**0.64**	**3**	950	0	**0.34**	**3**	986
100	30	**0.39**	0.30	12	367	0.14	**0.71**	12	461	0	**0.36**	9	596
100	50	**0.39**	0.29	12	404	0.13	**0.72**	14	505	0	**0.36**	9	734
100	100	**0.39**	0.30	12	416	0.13	**0.71**	16	551	0	**0.36**	9	808
500	30	0.39	**0.49**	158	108	0.14	**0.80**	519	28	0	**0.39**	106	288
500	50	0.39	**0.47**	152	129	0.13	**0.80**	393	36	0	**0.40**	111	372
500	100	0.39	**0.47**	156	140	0.15	**0.80**	363	92	0	**0.40**	111	434
1000	30	**0.54**	0.40	372	**63**	0.17	**0.78**	1757	21	0	**0.39**	264	**127**
1000	50	**0.54**	0.40	387	**74**	0.14	**0.78**	1175	28	0	**0.39**	272	**155**
1000	100	**0.55**	0.40	391	**86**	0.14	**0.77**	1678	23	0	**0.39**	272	**176**

In complement with predictive performance, two important notions in data streaming applications are time and memory usage of models. Here we analyze the impact of hyper-parameters (windows size W and number of trees T) on the amount of resources used by each model and compare them.

Models Memory Consumption Comparison

Regarding the model size evolution from Fig. 4, where model size of both models are represented in 2 Y axis (IForestASD in right), we can highlight 3 points:

- IForestASD used less memory than HSTrees ($\approx$20 times less), this is explained by the fact that with IForestASD, update policy consists on discarding completely old model when drift anomaly rate in sliding window $> u$ (updates by replacement) while HSTrees continuously updates the model at each observations
- For HSTrees, Window size W has no impact on the model size, only the number of trees T increases the memory used (barplots). This is consistent with the HSTrees update policy which consists on updating statistics in Tree nodes with a fixed ensemble size.
- For IForestASD, both window size w and number of trees T have a positive impact on model size, for both 3 datasets (in 3 linesplot). This is due to the fact that IForestASD uses all the instances in the window (W) to build the ensemble with T trees.

When it comes to some critical streaming applications, such as a predictive model for Network security intrusion, a fast model but less accurate is often

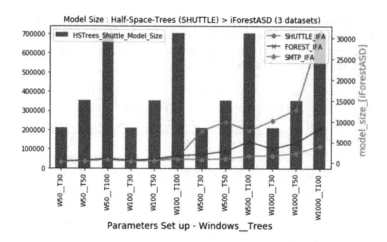

Fig. 4. Model-size metric (kilo-bytes): we fixed the window size (50, 100, 500, 100) and varied the number of Trees (30, 50, 100). For each setting we run HSTrees (barplot - Left Y axis) with Shuttle and IForestASD (lines - Right Y axis) for each dataset - 36 measures - and plot lines (right Y axis). HST is 20x bigger than IFA

preferred over a slow and more accurate model. Indeed, having a high rate of false positive anomalies to investigate is preferred than missing critical true positive anomalies (attack). Therefore, we aim to analyze below the behavior of the models in terms of training and testing time.

We can observe from Fig. 5 that IForestASD is faster with a small window size while Half-Space Trees is faster with bigger window size. The number of estimators increases the running time of both of them. This is consistent with the time complexity of the two base estimators: isolation Tree and Half-Space Tree. Indeed, the worse-case time complexity for training an iForest is $O(t\psi_1^2)$ [18] while for the streaming HS-Trees, the (average-case) amortized time complexity for n streaming points is $O(t(h + \psi_2))$ in the worst-case [11], where t is the number of trees in the ensemble, ψ_1 is the subsampling size of the iForest, ψ_2 the window size in HS-Trees and h the maximum depth (level) of a tree.

Furthermore, the testing time of IForestASD – in the right axis in red line – can be 100x longer than HSTrees testing time (40, 000 vs 400) which is a constraint for critical applications that need anomalies scoring quickly. The difference is significant between the two models because in IForestASD, each instance in the window is tested across each of the isolation trees to compute the anomaly score, thus the exponential increase regarding hyper-parameters.

Our results highlight that a trade-off must be made between resources consumption, processing time and predictive performance (F1 for anomalies) to get acceptable results. In the context of anomaly detection (predictive performance), we can conclude that in terms of F1 score, IForestASD is better than HS-Trees. However, in the context of data streaming applications running time is an important factor and faster models are preferred. In this sense, Half-Space Trees is a

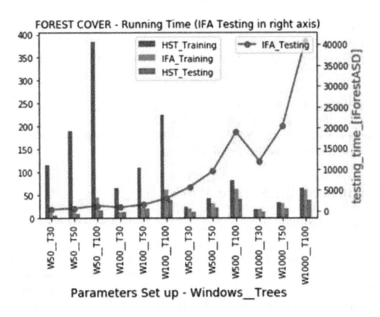

Fig. 5. Running time metric (secondes): forest-cover dataset - we fixed the window size (50, 100, 500, 100) and vary the number of Trees (30, 50, 100) to compare HST and IForestASD running time. IForestASD testing time is represented in another scale on the right Y axis and plot in red line. (Color figure online)

good option due to its lower processing time in the opposite to IForestASD which is exponential with respect to the windows size.

4.3 Guidelines for Setup Depending on Application Requirements

The number of experiments (36 configurations - 3 nb-estimators × 4 window-size × 3 datasets) used to obtain previous findings and discussions provides some insights about good grids of parameters and which model to use in which context.

Since models performance can vary a lot from one choice to another, depending on the characteristics of the data and hyper-parameters setting, we provide some guidelines for deciding between these anomaly detection methods. Thus, based on our experiments, depending on specific application requirements and resources constraints (running time and model size), one can note:

- **Window w for F1**: If the priority is F1 performance for anomaly detection, then setting W close to 500 gives better results with IForestASD.
- **Time & Memory**: If a fast model and especially a fast scoring time is needed, HSTrees should be the privileged option as it is still the state-of-the-art among fast streaming models.
- **IForestASD set up**: When fast model is not a prioritized requirement, IFA gives better results with low running time when using a smaller windows

(lower than 100) and low model size with number of estimators T between 30 and 50.

- **HSTrees set up**: When a fast model is required, HSTress with $w = 1000$ and number of $T = 30$ lead to the best results with optimal resources cost.

We have seen that the best model can be either HSTrees or IForestASD depending on the dataset and application requirements, thus we recommend testing models with dataset sample using scikit-multiflow framework to identify the best parameters for a each application.

5   Conclusion and Future Work

We presented a structured and comprehensive overview of anomaly detection algorithms for streaming data and categorized them by anomaly based approaches: statistical, nearest-neighbors, clustering and isolation based. For each category, we highlighted the advantages and disadvantages of the different approaches. From this study, Isolation forest seems to be an accurate method but not adapted to data streams [27]. We thus proposed an implementation of an anomaly detection approach based on isolation forest for streaming data using sliding window (IForestASD algorithm) in Scikit-multiflow, a machine learning framework for multi-output/multi-label and stream data. The motivation behind this work is that there exist very few anomalies detection methods in streaming frameworks reviewed, and the contribution on scikit-multiflow can help companies, researchers and the growing python community exploit methods and collaborate for the challenging area of Anomaly Detection in Streaming context.

Future Research Direction
This work is the first step of research project about streaming methods in scikit-multiflow which involves multiple stakeholders (co-authors).

The IForestASD approach requires a parameter for drift detection that is manually fixed. As a perspective, one can focus on optimizing the approach to be more efficient for drift detection in streaming data or use existing methods in scikit-multiflow such as ADWIN to automatically adapt the sliding window size. One major improvement of this work would be to update properly the anomaly detection model by taking into account previous anomaly detectors and observations instead of discarding them completely. This can be done using adaptive learning approaches.

Another future work is to implement in scikit-multiflow a novel anomaly or isolation based methods to reduce the running time complexity of original Isolation Forest approach. Implementing a method to justify and interpret anomalies for data streams using trees based algorithms is a promising work as well as in many industries models recommendations need to be justified or understood by the final users to be implemented in production environments. These improvements could then be implemented on top of scikit-multiflow framework in order to provide new open source methods for anomaly detection in streaming data.

Acknowledgements. We would like to thank Albert BIFET from the University of Waikato and Télécom Paris for his insightful discussions about Big Data Streams mining, Adrien CHESNAUD and Zhansaya SAILAUBEKOVA for their contributions on the code, and Fabrice LE DEIT from BNP Paribas IT Group for supporting the project.

References

1. Aggarwal, C.C.: Outlier Analysis, 2nd edn. Springer, Cham (2017). https://doi.org/10.1007/978-3-319-47578-3
2. Aggarwal, C.C., Han, J., Wang, J., Yu, P.S.: A framework for clustering evolving data streams. In: Proceedings of the 29th International Conference on Very Large Data Bases-Volume 29, pp. 81–92. VLDB Endowment (2003)
3. Angiulli, F., Fassetti, F.: Detecting distance-based outliers in streams of data. In: Proceedings of the Sixteenth ACM Conference on Information and Knowledge Management, pp. 811–820. ACM (2007)
4. Assent, I., Kranen, P., Baldauf, C., Seidl, T.: AnyOut: anytime outlier detection on streaming data. In: Lee, S., Peng, Z., Zhou, X., Moon, Y.-S., Unland, R., Yoo, J. (eds.) DASFAA 2012. LNCS, vol. 7238, pp. 228–242. Springer, Heidelberg (2012). https://doi.org/10.1007/978-3-642-29038-1_18
5. Behera, R.K., Das, S., Jena, M., Rath, S.K., Sahoo, B.: A comparative study of distributed tools for analyzing streaming data. In: 2017 International Conference on Information Technology (ICIT), pp. 79–84 (2017)
6. Bifet, A., Morales, G.D.F.: Big data stream learning with SAMOA. In: 2014 IEEE International Conference on Data Mining Workshop, pp. 1199–1202, December 2014. https://doi.org/10.1109/ICDMW.2014.24
7. Bifet, A., Gavaldà, R., Holmes, G., Pfahringer, B.: Machine Learning for Data Streams with Practical Examples in MOA. MIT Press (2018). https://moa.cms.waikato.ac.nz/book/
8. Bifet, A., Holmes, G., Kirkby, R., Pfahringer, B.: MOA: massive online analysis. J. Mach. Learn. Res. **11**, 1601–1604 (2010). http://portal.acm.org/citation.cfm?id=1859903
9. Bifet, A., Maniu, S., Qian, J., Tian, G., He, C., Fan, W.: StreamDM: advanced data mining in spark streaming. In: International Conference on Data Mining Workshops (ICDMW). IEEE, November 2015. https://doi.org/10.1109/ICDMW.2015.140. https://hal.inria.fr/hal-01270606
10. Chandola, V., Banerjee, A., Kumar, V.: Anomaly detection: a survey. ACM Comput. Surv. (CSUR) **41**(3), 15 (2009)
11. Ding, Z., Fei, M.: An anomaly detection approach based on isolation forest algorithm for streaming data using sliding window. IFAC Proc. Vol. **46**(20), 12–17 (2013). https://doi.org/10.3182/20130902-3-CN-3020.00044
12. Dua, D., Graff, C.: UCI machine learning repository (2017). http://archive.ics.uci.edu/ml
13. Gomes, H.M., et al.: Adaptive random forests for evolving data stream classification. Mach. Learn. **106**(9), 1469–1495 (2017). https://doi.org/10.1007/s10994-017-5642-8
14. Gupta, M., Gao, J., Aggarwal, C.C., Han, J.: Outlier detection for temporal data: a survey. IEEE Trans. Knowl. Data Eng. **26**(9), 2250–2267 (2014)
15. Hariri, S., Kind, M.C., Brunner, R.J.: Extended isolation forest. arXiv preprint arXiv:1811.02141 (2018)

16. Hodge, V., Austin, J.: A survey of outlier detection methodologies. Artif. Intell. Rev. **22**(2), 85–126 (2004)
17. Liu, F.T., Ting, K.M., Zhou, Z.H.: Isolation forest. In: 2008 Eighth IEEE International Conference on Data Mining, pp. 413–422. IEEE (2008)
18. Liu, F.T., Ting, K.M., Zhou, Z.H.: Isolation-based anomaly detection. ACM Trans. Knowl. Discov. Data (TKDD) **6**(1), 3 (2012)
19. Manapragada, C., Webb, G.I., Salehi, M.: Extremely fast decision tree. In: Proceedings of the 24th ACM SIGKDD International Conference on Knowledge Discovery & Data Mining, KDD 2018. Association for Computing Machinery (2018). https:// doi.org/10.1145/3219819.3220005
20. Montiel, J., Read, J., Bifet, A., Abdessalem, T.: Scikit-Multiflow: a multi-output streaming framework. J. Mach. Learn. Res. **19**(72), 1–5 (2018). http://jmlr.org/papers/v19/18-251.html
21. Pokrajac, D., Lazarevic, A., Latecki, L.J.: Incremental local outlier detection for data streams. In: 2007 IEEE Symposium on Computational Intelligence and Data Mining, pp. 504–515. IEEE (2007)
22. Salehi, M., Rashidi, L.: A survey on anomaly detection in evolving data: [with application to forest fire risk prediction]. ACM SIGKDD Explor. Newslett. **20**(1), 13–23 (2018)
23. Staerman, G., Mozharovskyi, P., Clémençon, S., d'Alché Buc, F.: Functional isolation forest (2019)
24. Tan, S.C., Ting, K.M., Liu, F.T.: Fast anomaly detection for streaming data. In: IJCAI (2011)
25. Tellis, V.M., D'Souza, D.J.: Detecting anomalies in data stream using efficient techniques: a review. In: 2018 International Conference ICCPCCT. IEEE (2018)
26. Thakkar, P., Vala, J., Prajapati, V.: Survey on outlier detection in data stream. Int. J. Comput. Appl. **136**, 13–16 (2016)
27. Togbe, M.U., Chabchoub, Y., Boly, A., Chiky, R.: Etude comparative des méthodes de détection d'anomalies. Revue des Nouvelles Technologies de l'Information Extraction et Gestion des Connaissances, RNTI-E-36, pp. 109–120 (2020)
28. Witten, I.H., Frank, E., Hall, M.A., Pal, C.J.: Data Mining: Practical Machine Learning Tools and Techniques, 4th edn. Morgan Kaufmann, Amsterdam (2017)
29. Yamanishi, K., Takeuchi, J.I., Williams, G., Milne, P.: On-line unsupervised outlier detection using finite mixtures with discounting learning algorithms. Data Min. Knowl. Disc. **8**(3), 275–300 (2004)

Automatic Classification of Road Traffic with Fiber Based Sensors in Smart Cities Applications

Antonio Balzanella, Salvatore D'Angelo[✉], Mauro Iacono, Stefania Nacchia, and Rosanna Verde

Dipartimento di Matematica e Fisica, Università Degli Studi Della Campania "L. Vanvitelli", Viale Lincoln 5, 81100 Caserta, Italy
{antonio.balzanella,salvatore.dangelo,mauro.iacono,stefania.nacchia, rosanna.verde}@unicampania.it

Abstract. Low cost monitoring of road traffic can bring a significant contribution to use the smart cities perspective for safety. The possibility of sensing and classifying vehicles and march conditions by means of simple physical sensors may support both real time applications and studies on traffic dynamics, e.g. support and assistance for car crashes and prevention of accidents, and maintenance planning or support to trials in case of litigation.

Optical fibers technology is well known for its wide adoption in data transmissions as a commodity component of computer networks: its popularity led to large availability on the market of high quality fiber at affordable price. As a purely physical application, its optical properties may be exploited to monitor in real time mechanical solicitations the fiber undergoes. In this paper we present a novel approach to using optical fibers as road sensors. As quite popular in literature, fiber is used to sense the vibrations caused by vehicles on the road: in our case, signals are processed by functional classification techniques to obtain a higher quality and a larger flexibility for the reuse of results. Classification aims at enabling profiling of road traffic. Moreover in our approach we would like to optimise the analysis and classification computations by splitting the process among edge nodes and cloud nodes according to the available computation capacity.

Our solution has been tested by an experimental campaign to show the suitability of the approach.

Keywords: Optical fiber · Sensing · Automatic classification · Smart cities

1 Introduction

The smart cities paradigm promises the provisioning of a vast basket of advanced services for citizens, society and managers. Achieving this goal requires a number

O. Gervasi et al. (Eds.): ICCSA 2020, LNCS 12252, pp. 31–46, 2020.
https://doi.org/10.1007/978-3-030-58811-3_3

of factors to enable success: as first, a proper vision over all the city framework and needs; planning capacity and skills; a holistic maintenance policy both for preventive and corrective interventions; an ubiquitous communication infrastructure; the availability of affordable, dependable, available, reliable and secure computing resources to run supervision, management, monitoring, control and service applications; proper scalable and reconfigurable software solutions; and, finally, heterogeneous sensing hardware capable of covering all the needs of the applications all over the city. Out of these factors, the ones related to software and computing capabilities may be easily allocated in one or more datacenters, while the communication infrastructures are in general already available or easily deployable in terms of a (usually existing) wired backbone and a last mile based on wireless technologies: installation or integration of this infrastructure may be done at affordable costs that may be shared with other uses, and rarely, in the urban tissue, pose significant challenges. The deployment of sensors may instead be problematic, because of the needed capillarity of coverage to guarantee sufficient information, of the installation costs, of the needed protection apparels against vandalism or environmental weariness, and connected costs are non negligible both for the possible recurrence and the number of installation needed.

Alternative solutions to the same sensing need may be available, and fit for different scenarios: this is the case of interest of this paper, in which the aim of sensing activities is road traffic monitoring. Two possible solutions are the use of cameras, with subsequent image processing, and the use of optical fiber as vibration sensors, with subsequent signal processing. Cameras may cover large spaces and are a traditional solution, allowing both automatic detection and human surveillance: image processing is a well established approach, but it is easily affected by errors when monitoring is not related to small areas and does not provide direct knowledge on dynamics and details of traffic, vehicles and road. Cameras have the significant advantage of being installed easily if there is room, but optics and in general the whole device may be easily damaged or stolen, or disturbed by dirt or other obstructions, and may pose problems in terms of privacy, or may be hacked. Fiber has a very modest acquisition cost but a high installation cost, as it is generally deployed inside the top level of the road structure to catch vibrations when vehicles pass by, and, additionally, to statically diagnose road deformations or problems, as every alteration of its condition influences light transmission and is measurable: fiber is only affordable when building or rebuilding road infrastructures, or for highways, but also provides remote diagnostic capabilities and detailed position and movement information independently in each point of their length, pose no privacy issue and are protected against weariness or vandalism by the road itself.

In this paper we focus on the use of optical fiber as a road sensor. The system we propose follows the most shared choices of solutions existing in literature, with some variations in the setup, in the clustering approach and in the testing campaign: the original contribution of this paper is the introduction of a pre-processing step for extracting appropriate features from DAS signals and an online clustering algorithm which discriminates the type of vehicles. The proposed algorithm is also able to evaluate the evolution of the clustering model itself over time through a continuous stream analysis of the data coming from the fiber road sensors. The use of on-line algorithms allows to analyze real time data and to cope with devices pervasively deployed in a smart city scenario which might not be performing enough to carry put the entire execution.

The need to analyze the data collected from the distributed sensors to make real-time intelligent decisions to control the system is nothing new. In fact, these decisions are often performed on data that is continuously streaming from the edge devices at high input rates [19]. Since not every analysis can be performed directly by or nearby the sensors, as they may be too computing-intensive, some of the computation, according to the problem that must be solved, can be executed in a more performing data center. Splitting the computation among edge devices and datacenter infrastructure is more and more common in data-stream analysis [8].

For this reason, our approach aims at following the evolution of the model over time by splitting the overall analysis and classification computation among the edge nodes, thus nearby the optical fiber sensors and the datacenter, according to the needs. This may also be of fundamental importance if we consider the extensive use that can be done of optical fiber for road sensing and control, that requires the system to correctly scale and distribute the computation, in order to grant a certain level of performance and results quality.

The paper is organized as follows: in Sect. 2 related works from literature are presented and examined; in Sect. 3 the approach followed in this paper for the definition of the system and the analysis of data is presented; in Sect. 4 the feasibility and the applicability of the approach are demonstrated; finally, conclusions close the paper.

2   Related Works

Considering the physical and financial growing of modern smart cities, researchers must look out for new strategies and technologies to improve traffic congestion, as it is known as the main cause of air pollution in urbanized areas. In recent years, technological developments have enabled collection and transition of real-time traffic information, and this, coupled with the increase of traffic trips and congestion, has increased the interest in traffic modeling, not only to improve traffic conditions but also to monitor traffic flows and detect potentially dangerous situations.

Advanced traffic management systems (ATMSs) [20], such as adaptive traffic control (ATC), are enabling a higher efficiency of the traffic management ecosystem and can help integrate the expected growth in vehicle numerousness without overwhelming existing infrastructures.

One specific area, which is also the focus of this work, is the *automatic vehicle identification (AVI)*, that refers to the technology used to identify a particular vehicle when it passes a particular point. Early development of AVI occurred in the United States, beginning with an optical scanning system in the 1960s to identify railroad boxcars [12]. AVI systems can be of various types, such as automatic toll collection systems [4], vehicle-mounted transponders of different types and roadside beacons [18], video cameras and license plate matching techniques [15,28], and the more recent Bluetooth and WIFI based detection systems [1,3]. However, these systems are partly subjected to some inefficiencies:

- video based solutions and technologies have high costs of installation and maintenance;
- the detection effect is also highly sensitive to environmental and weather conditions;
- wireless sensor network technologies are affected by the communication environment and nodes performances.

In contrast, the distributed acoustic sensing technology, that is the use of distributed optical fiber acoustic sensing (DAS), is being used more and more for traffic detection, discrimination and counting [16]. The solutions based on the DAS technology are more sensitive and offer lower costs and higher resistance to temperature, corrosion and interference phenomena. The first experiments involving the DAS technology revolved around the vertical seismic profiling [14] and surface seismic surveys with active sources [5,24]. However, due to their low cost and low power consumption, a large number of these sensors can be deployed in a certain area for purpose of detection, classification, identification and tracking of approaching targets; thus they have been lately used, also quite extensively, to detect and classify vehicles in order to improve traffic flow management.

In [17] the authors studied traffic-related seismic vibrations measured by an urban geophone network with a spacing slightly shorter than a typical city block dimension, a vibration source with a speed of $25 \pm 3 \, \text{m/s}$ was detected on the expressway. However, since there were no traffic flow data available, it was ultimately impossible to verify whether the vibration source was the vibration caused by the vehicle.

On the other hand [13] describe the deployment of a shallow gully (DAS) array on a highway where cars on the road parallel to the array direction were the main source of noise. Analysis of the source of the beam-form confirmed that most of the noise came from cars driving on adjacent roads.

Important results have also been reported in [11]; here the authors use a wavelet-denoising algorithm and a dual-threshold algorithm to reconstruct the signal for feature extraction, and the vehicle count and speed are obtained. When all features have been extracted, the classification of vehicle types is implemented by a support vector machine (SVM) classifier.

As explained in the previous section, another focal point to ensure a performing streaming analysis as well as a scalable solution. We would like to distribute the computation among computational nodes and sensors close to the fiber and the datacenter. In the current state of the art, this strategies are referred to as "cloud/edge analytics" and there are many research activities that withness the successful aspects of deploying the analysis on both cloud and edge according to the computational needs of the tasks to be performed on the data.

Authors of [22] analyze performance trade-offs of hybrid cloud/edge-based in the data analysis scenarios using multiple workloads, reporting how hybrid cloud/edge processing speeds-up stateless and simple stateful operations: specifically, edge computing helps reduce the amount of data being uploaded to the cloud and, consequently, improves the overall performance, in terms of end-to-end throughput, and better supports real-time requirements. In [23] the authors propose a novel distributed deep neural network architecture (DDNN) that is distributed across computing hierarchies, consisting of the cloud, the edge and end devices to improve object recognition accuracy. In [25] the authors present a new computing framework, namely Firework, that facilitates distributed data processing and sharing for IoE applications via a virtual shared data view and service composition, specifically crafted for real-time video analytics. Vigil [26] is a distributed wireless surveillance system that partitions video processing (e.g., object/face recognition or trajectory synthesis) between edge nodes and the cloud with a fixed configuration.

Focusing on the challenge of data clustering, the algorithms which can be run on the edge of the overall system architecture have to fulfill some stringent restrictions: data arrive continuously; single instances have to be processed as soon as they arrive; the size of a stream is potentially unbounded; data objects are discarded after they have been processed; the monitored phenomenon evolves over time.

A recent survey [21], reviews the methods addressing the data stream clustering issue posing the accent on the data structure used for summarizing data, on the capability to discover outliers and to deal with data evolution, on the required input parameters, on the shape of the discovered clusters. Some of the most effective methods, also emerging from such review, are [2,7,27].

3 Architecture and Processing Strategy for DAS Data

Since the traffic monitoring and management has become more and more important and challenging in the current smart cities environment, as stated in the previous section, our main objective is to recognise and classify the signals coming from the deployed optical fiber used as road sensor. In order to achieve this we propose a scalable and distributed architecture and a specific process for sensing and processing the signals coming and for performing the online classifications of the vehicles.

3.1 Overall System Architecture

The general structure of the proposed system is composed of 3 main functional blocks (see Fig. 1) that satisfy the two main duties of the system, sensing and processing, in the most flexible way, to reduce costs and facilitate management, expansion, upgrading and maintenance while lowering the costs. The blocks are: the sensing infrastructure, the interconnection network and the processing facility.

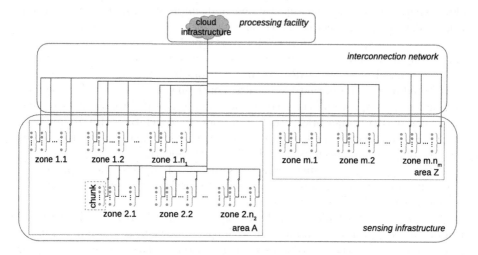

Fig. 1. Logical organization of the system

The *sensing infrastructure* consists in a number of fibers, distributed along the road network that has to be monitored and hierarchically organized into areas, zones and chunks. A chunk is a linear section of a road covered by a number of fibers, that is considered as the elementary component of the sensing infrastructure; a zone is a contiguous portion of the road system (e.g. the roads that embrace a number of blocks or a portion of a highway) the chunks of which are managed as a unit by the interconnection network[1]; an area is a logical portion of the road network, including many zones, that is considered a management unit, e.g. a district, a town, a highway.

The *interconnection network* is the communication infrastructure that collects data from the sensing infrastructure and vehicles it towards the processing facility. Standard networking technologies, possibly exploiting an existing network, are used, and a sensing hub exists per zone, with the task of collecting data from fibers and send them to the computing facility by standard TCP/IP based messaging.

The *processing facility* is implemented in the cloud[2], to minimize costs and exploit advantages such as elasticity and centralized management and

---

[1] This is similar to what happens in the organization of sensing and control in other transportation networks, e.g. the high speed trains standard ERTMS/ETCS [6].

[2] An alternative solution, that offers the possibility of having zone services enabled and enacted locally, is to design, at a higher cost, the software infrastructure as a edge computing infrastructure, e.g.. to implement real time services computed zone by zone locally in the sensing hub.

maintenance, and to integrate data processing with other functionalities provided by other software services in the smart city solution.

In the rest of the paper, we focus on the end-to-end computing process for data from a single fiber, for the sake of simplicity.

3.2   Workflow

The general workflow applied by the system is divided into 4 phases: sensing, processing, de-noising, classification (see Fig. 2).

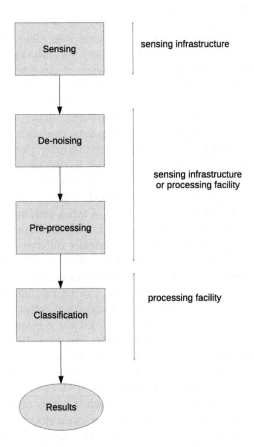

Fig. 2. The workflow and its mapping on the organizational blocks of the system

Sensing - In the *sensing* phase, that is performed by a fiber, the rough signal is measured in space, along the length of the fiber, and time, in terms of variation of the sensed vibration in each point of the fiber in each instant, actually organizing the fiber in sections to compensate the non-ideal conditions in which signal is generated and propagated. The sensing phase is divided into two sub-phases:

- The pose of the fiber
- Events detection

The laying of the fiber can be external or internal, the latter is in general the best configuration to avoid noise as it is blocked by immersing it in a material or fixing it on supports. Another challenging aspect of the sensing phase is the right sampling phase and acquisition rate that must be chosen correctly to not lose valuable information.

Pre-processing and De-noising - In the *pre-processing phase*, the physical signal is measured and converted to be manipulated as a sequence of images that represent the state of the fiber and its evolution over time. However to better apply the clustering algorithm or, more generally, to perform data analysis algorithms on the signal, we have defined a sequence of steps to clean up or better to *de-noise* the signal as it can be highly subjected to noise in the sensing phase but also because the final signal can have a high dimensionality that can badly affect the final clustering results. In the *de-noising* phase, standard de-noising numerical techniques are applied to enhance data readability and improve the effectiveness of the classification and to better identify the sections where we can clearly see the transit of the vehicle. Specifically, in the de-noising phase we have opted for the wavelet transform, [10], a powerful tool for the analysis and processing of signals which is extremely efficient in various fields such as compression and de-noising, and in general when dealing with not stationary signals. The discrete wavelet transform (DWT) is a linear signal processing technique, it transforms a vector into a numerically different vector (D to D') of wavelet coefficients. The two vectors are of the same length, however it is useful for compression in the sense that wavelet-transformed data can be truncated; a small compressed approximation of the data can be retained by storing only a small fraction of the strongest wavelet coefficient e.g., retain all wavelet coefficients larger than some particular threshold and the remaining coefficients are set to zero. One interesting aspect is that the resulting data representation is sparse, thus the computations that can take advantage of sparsity are very fit if performed in wavelet space. Given a set of coefficients, an approximation of the original data con be got by applying the inverse DWT.

Once we have obtained a better signal, both in terms of nodes and in terms of dimensionality reduction, we use the Hough's transform, [9], which is a feature extraction technique used in image analysis, computer vision, and digital image processing. This technique aims at isolating the features that characterize a specific shape in an image, and proved to be specially useful in obtaining an overall description of one or more features from noisy local measures when there is no previous knowledge about the number of solution classes. Each point, expressing a measure, contributes to a globally consistent solution, e.g. a line we want to recognize as such. The classical Hough's transform is concerned with the identification of lines in the image, and use it to find sheaf of parallel lines that identify the vehicle transit and, ideally, the inclination of such lines should suggest the vehicle speed.

In *clustering* phase, that is described and discussed in details in the rest of the Section, images are used to extract knowledge from the available signals and to recognize the type of Tracy Lorraine the vehicles that transit along the fiber.

3.3   Data Definition and Clustering Approach

Hough's transform provides one or more lines for each image. Among the lines, we select one or more sets of parallel ones, which provide information about behaviors of vehicles in transit, anomalies, new emerging trends.

Considering the parametric equation of a straight line $x \cdot cos(\theta) + x \cdot sin(\theta) = r$, the set of J parallel lines ℓ_j $(j = 1 \ldots J)$ is described by the orientation θ and by r_j with respect to the X-Axis. Thus, for each image we get a set of tuples $\{(\theta, r_j); j = 1 \ldots J\}$, with constant θ.

We consider as input of the clustering procedure a set of on-line arriving events E_i which represent the set of tuples of each image, as: $E_i = (\theta_i, a_i)_{i=1,\ldots,\infty}$, where $a_i = [max(r_{i,j}) - min(r_{i,j})]$ $(j = 1 \ldots J_i, i = 1 \ldots M)$. That is, we focus on the orientation and on the distance between the external parallel lines of the sheaf to capture information about vehicle transit.

The clustering process aims at discovering groups of similar vehicles according the two mentioned features. It is made by three main phases: 1) Initial typologies construction; 2) On-line clustering; 3) Typologies updating and outlier detection. These steps are based on micro-cluster algorithm.

In our implementation of the micro-cluster, we assume that a set of similar events can be summarized by the following set of statistics:

- $\overline{G}$: Micro-cluster centroid;
- MD: Micro-cluster boundary;
- n: Number of allocated items;
- ST: Sum of times;
- SST: Sum of squared times.

The centroid G is the representative of the events summarized by the micro-cluster. Since we assume that each sheaf of parallel lines can be described by two quantities (θ_i, a_i), G is the tuple $[\overline{\theta}, \overline{a}]$ such that a set of events is summarized by the average $\overline{\theta}$ of the θ_i's and by the average $\overline{a}$ of the a_i's.

The field MD records the maximum of the distances between the allocated events and the micro-cluster centroid. This allows to get a measure of the micro-cluster radius.

The parameter n stores the number of allocated events E_i.

The parameters ST and SST record the sum ST and the sum of squares SST of the time instants of each allocation to the micro-cluster. Indeed, by means of ST, SST and n we can get the average and variance of the allocation times which give, for instance, a measure of the obsolescence of a typology or information about if a typology is very recurrent only in recent or old time instants.

To define the initial set of event typologies, we cluster, off-line, an initial set $\mathcal{E}$ of M training events $E_i = (\theta_i, a_i)$ by using a standard k-means clustering algorithm. The algorithm provides a set of k clusters $C_1, \ldots, C_k, \ldots, C_K$ and the corresponding set of centroids.

For each cluster C_k (with $k = 1, \ldots, K$) we compute the sum of distances to the centroid and the number of allocated items in order to record them in a micro-cluster. The parameters ST and SST are set to 0 since the micro-cluster initialization is performed on the training set.

The second phase analyzes the on-line arriving events. The first step on each event E_i is to evaluate if it can be allocated to an existing micro-cluster or a new micro-cluster has to be added. In the first case, the event E_i can be traced back to one of the existing typologies; in the second case, it can be an outlier or the first one of a new emerging typology.

The choice is performed by evaluating the Euclidean distance between the event and the nearest micro-cluster. If the distance is lower than the boundary MD of the micro-cluster, E_i can be allocated to it by increasing the number n of allocated events and updating the parameters ST and SST summing to their value the time stamp and the square of the time stamp of the event.

Alternatively, the E_i is used as seed of a new micro-cluster having the event as centroid, $n = 1$, ST and SST set to the value the time stamp and the square of the time stamp of the event. Finally, the parameter MD is set in heuristic way to the MD value of the nearest micro-cluster.

The third phase updates the set of typologies in order to reflect the current behavior of the monitored environment and provides a set of outliers.

With the flowing of data it is possible that too many micro-clusters have been generated due to emerging typologies or outliers. We select initially the outliers by bringing out the micro-clusters for which the parameter n is set to 1. Then we run a new k-means algorithm on the micro-cluster centroids to get a new reduced set of typologies.

Different typologies can provide a detection of several directions, number and speed of vehicles.

4   A Case Study

In this section we present the results obtained by applying the workflow steps in a real environment. In our case the fiber has been placed outside the road surface blocked to the ground, as the environment chosen for the experiments has posed a series of technical limitations. Four sections of fiber have been laid down from about 75 m for a total of about 300 m. The four sections are parallel to each other and the light travels in both directions twice. In this way the data has been detected 4 times in order to have a double validation of the detected vibration.

During the detection of test events, the data has been collected. Three different sets of data, depending on the acquisition signal frequency (152 Hz, 19 Hz and 9 Hz), have been collected. The measurement unit returns frames containing the measured values of the 512 "distributed microphones" in 128 s, which at 152 Hz corresponds to a total of 832 ms, at a frequency of 19 Hz the acquisition interval is about 7 s and the last test at a frequency of 9 Hz the acquisition interval is about 12 s. We have carried out from 5 to 9 car passages for each frequency with two different car models, a B-segment car (approx. 1.105 kg in running order) and a minivan (approx. 1460 kg in running order).

The collected data has been processed in MATLAB by another team that provided us with the raw data. Each file consists of a three-dimensional matrix $sd = z \times tfast\_ms \times time$ where:

- z are the "microphone" along the fiber;
- $tfast\_ms$ the instants of time in which the intensity of the vibration from the "microphones" is measured;
- $time$ the number of measurement windows elapsed during the experiments.

Every matrix is a frame that represent the acquisition interval (832 ms, 7 s, 12 s). The section of fiber laid in a straight line was about 75 m, so two lines close to each other, in addition to having opposite slope, must be between 0 and 150 m apart (depending on the point where the car was at the time that frame was acquired). In the classic approach, on each frame we look for oblique uniform color bands that indicate a moving object, using Hough's transform to identify the external parallel lines and the inclination of the bundle in order to deduce the speed of the moving object Fig. 3.

For data analysis and cleaning we use python scripts and the numpy, scipy, pandas and pywt (for wavelet decomposition and reconstruction) libraries. These libraries allow us to import matlab data and to define the necessary steps to obtain a clean signal without loss of information.

We first rearrange the matrix by combining the measurement windows into one window. It should be noted that the windows have a delay of approximately 100 ms between them due to the processing time of the windows by the signal acquisition control unit.

We then clean up the matrix of the peaks present at the ends of the fiber. Before proceeding with the signal cleaning steps, it is good to remember that after the unification of the windows the matrix is a two-dimensional matrix. On the row there are 512 "microphones" distributed along the fiber, on the columns the instants of time of the unified windows. Each single line represents the signal measured by a single "microphone", and it is precisely on each of these that we are going to carry out the cleaning of the signal.

The steps we perform for de-noising are the following:

- each of the 512 signals is decomposed with a wavelet transform up to the fifth level using the "db1" wavelet;
- the coefficients of the five levels are then selected using customized thresholds for each level;
- the signal is then reconstructed with the filtered levels.

Once the signal has been cleaned up, we can proceed with the functional analysis and with Hough's transform for the identification of the test steps.

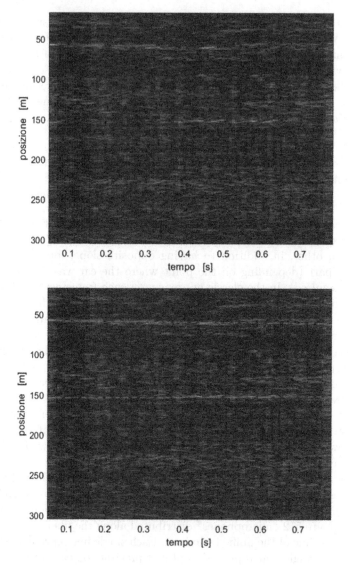

Fig. 3. A frame at 152 Hz with a car passage (top) and the same frame processed with Hough's trasform (bottom)

To apply Hough's transform, the windows relating to the test steps carried out and the windows in which we are sure of the absence of steps are selected. We only translate the windows into space (therefore along the microphones), translated only in time or translated both in time and in space. The first case allows us to verify the presence or absence of a vehicle in space, in the second case we can verify the mobility of the vehicle (if the vehicle moves it is no longer detected by the selected "microphones"), in the last case we are able to follow the vehicle along its movement.

Below are some images of events allocated to micro-clusters describing vehicle behaviors lines identified with Hough's transform. The data analyzed were those relating to the frequency of 152 Hz, in which the test steps were carried out on the windows:

- 130–151 passage at a speed of 10 km/h (Fig. 4)
- 170–195 passage at a speed of 10 km/h
- 205–216 passage at a speed of 20 km/h (Fig. 5)
- 236–249 passage at a speed of 20 km/h
- 265–272 passage at a speed of 30 km/h (Fig. 6)

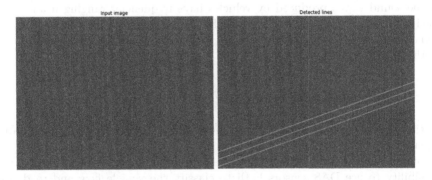

Fig. 4. The fiber section from 130 to 151 at 152 Hz processed with Hough's transform)

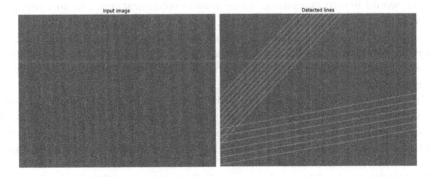

Fig. 5. The fiber section from 205 to216 at 152 Hz processed with Hough's transform)

Following the analysis of the results obtained and studies on the frequencies produced by moving vehicles, we had confirmation of the results obtained,

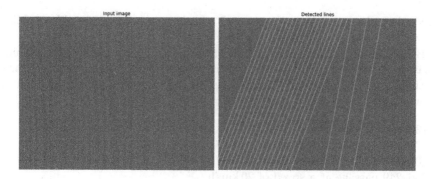

Fig. 6. The fiber section from 265 to 272 at 152 Hz processed with Hough's transform)

as the sound waves produced by vehicles have frequencies ranging from about 150 Hz to rise. For this reason we are already proceeding with further tests at higher frequencies and different setups to get better results and validate the methodology.

5   Conclusions and Future Works

In this article we have shown a new method for traffic monitoring using distributed fiber optic sensors. Some tests have been carried out to validate the presented method, even though they are quite preliminary the results show the possibility to use DAS sensors both to classify the vehicle flow and to detect heavy traffic situations and take actions based on the flow velocity.

Jointly with another team we are working on improving the measuring instruments to get cleaner and better results, specifically in the next experiments we are going to use a better fiber to improve the signal noise ratio of almost 15dB and we would like to experiment more vehicle configurations: not to track just one vehicle movements, but to also track more vehicles driving simultaneously that go for example in opposite direction, or forming queues, in order to have more data about real environmental situations and to improve the classification system to recognize more specific and articulate vehicles configurations without losing accuracy.

In the future, we will continue to work on the possibility to classify not only the vehicle flow but also to be able to classify types of vehicles or groups of vehicles. In addition, experiments may be conducted on road sections using the existing fibre-optic infrastructure provided by telecommunication companies.

Acknowledgements. This work is partially funded by the POR FESR 2014/20 - Project "Quick&Smart" of Università degli Studi della Campania "Luigi Vanvitelli". We are grateful to professor Aldo Minardo for his precious collaboration during the experiments and useful suggestions about the treatment of data.

References

1. Abbott-Jard, M., Shah, H., Bhaskar, A.: Empirical evaluation of Bluetooth and Wifi scanning for road transport (2013)
2. Aggarwal, C., Han, J., Wang, J., Yu, P.: A framework for clustering evolving data streams, June 2003
3. Barcelö, J., Montero, L., Marqués, L., Carmona, C.: Travel time forecasting and dynamic origin-destination estimation for freeways based on Bluetooth traffic monitoring. Transp. Res. Rec. **2175**(1), 19–27 (2010)
4. Bhavke, A., Pai, S.: Advance automatic toll collection & vehicle detection during collision using RFID. In: 2017 International Conference on Nascent Technologies in Engineering (ICNTE), pp. 1–5. IEEE (2017)
5. Daley, T.M., et al.: Field testing of fiber-optic distributed acoustic sensing (DAS) for subsurface seismic monitoring. Lead. Edge **32**(6), 699–706 (2013)
6. Flammini, F., Marrone, S., Iacono, M., Mazzocca, N., Vittorini, V.: A multiformalism modular approach to ERTMS/ETCS failure modeling. Int. J. Reliab. Qual. Saf. Eng. **21**(1), 1450001 (2014)
7. Gama, J., Rodrigues, P., Lopes, L.: Clustering distributed sensor data streams using local processing and reduced communication. Intell. Data Anal. **15**, 3–28 (2011). https://doi.org/10.3233/IDA-2010-0453
8. Gonzalez, N.M., et al.: Fog computing: data analytics and cloud distributed processing on the network edges. In: 2016 35th International Conference of the Chilean Computer Science Society (SCCC), pp. 1–9. IEEE (2016)
9. Illingworth, J., Kittler, J.: A survey of the Hough transform. Comput. Vis. Graph. Image Process. **44**(1), 87–116 (1988)
10. Lang, M., Guo, H., Odegard, J.E., Burrus, C.S., Wells, R.O.: Noise reduction using an undecimated discrete wavelet transform. IEEE Signal Process. Lett. **3**(1), 10–12 (1996)
11. Liu, H., Ma, J., Xu, T., Yan, W., Ma, L., Zhang, X.: Vehicle detection and classification using distributed fiber optic acoustic sensing. IEEE Trans. Veh. Technol. **69**, 1363–1374 (2019)
12. Martin, B., Scott, P.: Automatic vehicle identification: a test of theories of technology. Sci. Technol. Hum. Values **17**(4), 485–505 (1992)
13. Martin, E., et al.: Interferometry of a roadside DAS array in Fairbanks, AK. In: SEG Technical Program Expanded Abstracts 2016, pp. 2725–2729. Society of Exploration Geophysicists (2016)
14. Mateeva, A., et al.: Distributed acoustic sensing for reservoir monitoring with vertical seismic profiling. Geophys. Prospect. **62**(4), 679–692 (2014)
15. Oliveira-Neto, F.M., Han, L.D., Jeong, M.K.: An online self-learning algorithm for license plate matching. IEEE Trans. Intell. Transp. Syst. **14**(4), 1806–1816 (2013)
16. Parker, T., Shatalin, S., Farhadiroushan, M.: Distributed acoustic sensing-a new tool for seismic applications. First Break **32**(2), 61–69 (2014)
17. Riahi, N., Gerstoft, P.: The seismic traffic footprint: tracking trains, aircraft, and cars seismically. Geophys. Res. Lett. **42**(8), 2674–2681 (2015)
18. Rillings, J.H., Betsold, R.J.: Advanced driver information systems. IEEE Trans. Veh. Technol. **40**(1), 31–40 (1991)
19. Satyanarayanan, M.: The emergence of edge computing. Computer **50**(1), 30–39 (2017)
20. Shahgholian, M., Gharavian, D.: Advanced traffic management systems: an overview and a development strategy. arXiv preprint arXiv:1810.02530 (2018)

21. Silva, J., Faria, E., Barros, R., Hruschka, E., de Carvalho, A., Gama, J.: Data stream clustering: a survey. ACM Comput. Surv. **46** (2014). https://doi.org/10.1145/2522968.2522981
22. Silva, P., Costan, A., Antoniu, G.: Investigating edge vs. cloud computing trade-offs for stream processing. In: IEEE International Conference on Big Data in 2019 (2019)
23. Teerapittayanon, S., McDanel, B., Kung, H.T.: Distributed deep neural networks over the cloud, the edge and end devices. In: 2017 IEEE 37th International Conference on Distributed Computing Systems (ICDCS), pp. 328–339. IEEE (2017)
24. Wang, H., et al.: Field trial of distributed acoustic sensing using active sources at Garner Valley, California. In: AGU Fall Meeting Abstracts (2014)
25. Zhang, Q., Zhang, Q., Shi, W., Zhong, H.: Firework: data processing and sharing for hybrid cloud-edge analytics. IEEE Trans. Parallel Distrib. Syst. **29**(9), 2004–2017 (2018)
26. Zhang, T., Chowdhery, A., Bahl, P., Jamieson, K., Banerjee, S.: The design and implementation of a wireless video surveillance system. In: Proceedings of the 21st Annual International Conference on Mobile Computing and Networking, pp. 426–438 (2015)
27. Zhang, T., Ramakrishnan, R., Livny, M.: BIRCH: a new data clustering algorithm and its applications. Data Min. Knowl. Disc. **1**(2), 141–182 (1997). https://doi.org/10.1023/A:1009783824328
28. Zhou, J., Gao, D., Zhang, D.: Moving vehicle detection for automatic traffic monitoring. IEEE Trans. Veh. Technol. **56**(1), 51–59 (2007)

A Dynamic Latent Variable Model for Monitoring the Santa Maria del Fiore Dome Behavior

Bruno Bertaccini$^{(\boxtimes)}$ (iD), Silvia Bacci (iD), and Federico Crescenzi (iD)

Department of Statistics, Computer Science, Applications "G.Parenti",
University of Florence, Florence, Italy
{bruno.bertaccini,silvia.bacci,federico.crescenzi}@unifi.it

Abstract. A dynamic principal component analysis is proposed to monitor the stability, and detect any atypical behavior, of the Brunelleschi's Dome of Santa Maria del Fiore, in Florence. First cracks in the Dome appeared at the end of the 15th century and nowadays they are present in all the Dome's webs, although with an heterogenous distribution. A monitoring system has been installed in the Dome since 1955 to monitor the behavior of the cracks; today, it counts more than 160 instruments, such as mechanical and electronic deformometers, thermometers, piezometers. The analyses carried out to date show slight increases in the size of the main cracks and, at the same time, a clear relationship with some environmental variables. However, due to the extension of the monitoring system and the complexity of collected data, to our knowledge an analysis involving all the detected variables has not yet conducted. In this contribution, we aim at finding simplified structures (i.e., latent common factors or principal components) that summarize the measurements coming from the different instruments and explain the overall behavior of the Dome across the time. We found that the overall behavior of the Dome tracked by multiple sensors may be satisfactorily summarized with a single principal component, which shows a sinusoidal time trend characterized, in a one-year period, by an expansive phase followed by a contractive phase. We also found that some webs contribute more than others to the Dome's movements.

Keywords: Monument monitoring system · Missing-data imputation models · Dynamic factor analysis · Forecasting · Architectural heritage preservation

1 Introduction

Santa Maria del Fiore is the cathedral of Florence, begun in 1296 it was completed in 1436. The Dome, engineered by Filippo Brunelleschi, was built in 18 years. With more than 4 millions bricks, Brunelleschi's Dome was the greatest architectural feat in the Western world (because the Brunelleschi's idea was to

© Springer Nature Switzerland AG 2020
O. Gervasi et al. (Eds.): ICCSA 2020, LNCS 12252, pp. 47–58, 2020.
https://doi.org/10.1007/978-3-030-58811-3_4

build an octagonal dome higher and wider than any that had ever been built). It is characterized by eight webs resting on an octagonal supporting tambour and converging to the lantern that crown its top. First cracks in some webs appeared at the end of the 15th century. The evolving of the issue gave rise of concern and already in 1695 the Grand Duke of Tuscany established a first commission with the task to investigate the stability of the Dome. Nowadays, cracks are present in all webs, although particularly numerous in the even ones, mainly in webs 4 and 6 that are located on the opposite sides of the nave (Fig. 1).

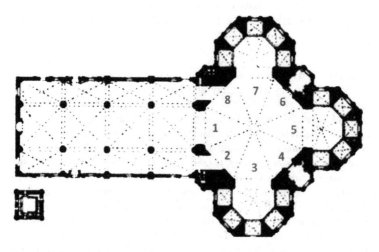

Fig. 1. Planimetry of the Santa Maria del Fiore church and dome, with numbered webs (source: Opera di Santa Maria del Fiore Foundation)

The monitoring system, installed in the Dome since 1955, today counts more than 160 sensors (mechanical and electronic deformometers, thermometers, piezometers, . . .). Due to the variety and number of instruments involved, this monitoring system is one of the most accurate static control systems around the world installed on an historical building. The extension of the monitoring system and the amount of data collected by each sensor make it very difficult to obtain an overall evaluation of the static evolution of the Dome. However, the analysis carried out on data collected by single sensors applied upon the main cracks have allowed to highlight a constant pejorative increase in width over time, and a clear relationship with the main (exogenous) environmental (meteorological and seismic related) variables involved [5].

We are confident that the static "behavior" of the Dome and its ability to answer to the environmental action can be correctly interpreted jointly analyzing all the information gathered by the monitoring system in all these years. To our knowledge, such an analysis has never been presented in any of the studies conducted in the past. A first tentative in this direction was made by Bertaccini [2] who estimated a structural equation model to explain the behavior of the fourth web (in which 13 deformometers and 3 thermometers are installed) in response to the external events (of exceptional and non-exceptional nature).

In this paper, we exploit the use of Generalized Dynamic Principal Components (GDPC) [7] to summarize the "breathing mechanism" of the entire Dome. Similarly to other methods of factor/principal component analysis, the GDPC carries out a dimensionality reduction of the vector of observations coming from different sources (in our case, the deformometers installed upon cracks), taking explicitly into account the correlation between consecutive observations. Thus, the amount of information characterizing the time series of the cracks width is synthesized in a small number of factors (principal components), which should simplify the understanding of the static evolution of the Dome as a whole.

The rest of the paper is organized as follows. After a brief presentation of the functioning of electronic sensors that constitute the monitoring system installed on the Dome, particular attention will be paid to the statistical techniques employed to impute missing data in case of sensors fault (Sect. 2). In general, a complete data matrix is needed when statistical models have to be estimated on the basis of a multivariate time series structure. The imputation process will be propedeutic to the estimation of a dynamic principal components model whose results will be presented and discussed in Sect. 3. Some final remarks and further perspective of analysis will be discussed in the conclusive section (Sect. 4).

2 Data from the Monitoring System

The electronic instruments taken into account in the analyses presented in this work are the 66 deformometers and 56 air and masonry thermometers installed by ISMES (Istituto Sperimentale Modelli e Strutture[1]) in 1987. These sensors record data every six hours (4 measures per day) since January 8, 1988. This means just less than 47.000 measures per sensor, for a total of about 6 million measurements. Data used in this work were limited to about the last 20 years of monitoring activity, from January 1, 1997 to February 28, 2017. Information (metadata) on the location of instruments are available and will be of primary importance in building the statistical model (for the sake of brevity, Fig. 2 shows only the location of the instruments installed on web 4).

The whole dataset (measurements and metadata) was provided by the Opera di Santa Maria del Fiore, in the context of a scientific collaboration with the Department of Statistics, Computer Science, Applications "G. Parenti" of the University of Florence under the responsibility of Prof. Bruno Bertaccini.

Given the extent of the monitoring system in terms of installed instruments, it was decided to reduce the dataset dimension using the daily average of the valid measures acquired by each sensor. The variations of temperature between night and day within the 24 h are considered irrelevant because the masonry is not able to react instantly to changes in air temperature, especially those within

---

[1] http://www.asim.it/ismes/IsmesUk/default.htm.

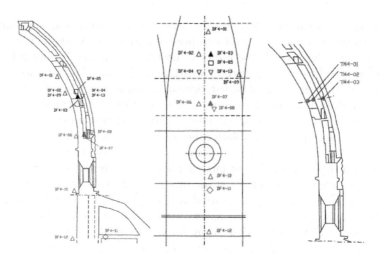

Fig. 2. Location of deformometers and thermometers on web 4 (source: Opera di Santa Maria del Fiore Foundation)

a day; thus, a very slight variation range is expected for the daily detections produced by each deformometer. Under these assumptions, arithmetic mean does not present drawbacks and has the advantage to solve any cases in which daily measurements, for temporary faults, are less than 4.

Figure 3 shows data from the deformometers installed in the even webs. The figure clarifies what is commonly referred as the "breathing" mechanism of the Dome in time: the cracks tend to expand and shrink cyclically according to seasons. This behavior is due to the structure of the Dome that may be assimilated to a physic "closed system", where the structural constraints define the relationship of forces between the various cracks, which in turn are subjected to the action of meteorological and other environmental variables [3].

The preliminary analysis of the measures acquired by the monitoring system highlighted the presence of missing data and outliers in almost all the series of data acquired by the deformometers as well as by the air and masonry thermometers. This phenomenon is generally due to storms and blackouts; it is probable that certain sensors (see, for instance, those represented in Fig. 4) have gone out of calibration due to the action of lightning, producing anomalous oscillations for a shorter or longer period. Due to their lack of (correct) information [1], outliers have been assimilated to missing data and preliminary deleted.

Unfortunately, statistical models for time series generally require a complete data matrix; otherwise, it would not be possible to take full advantage from time related information. Hence, 9 deformometers having more than 10% of missing observations have not been taken into account. With the detections acquired by the remaining 57 deformometers, we designed a statistical algorithm for the imputation of missing values.

Cracks width in web 4

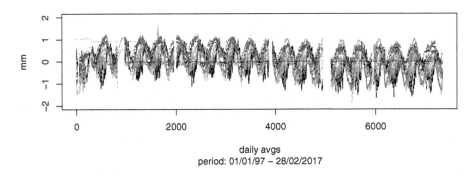

daily avgs
period: 01/01/97 – 28/02/2017

Cracks width in web 6

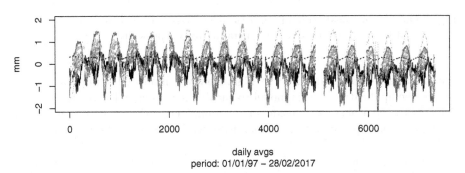

daily avgs
period: 01/01/97 – 28/02/2017

Fig. 3. Deformometers installed in the 4th and 6th webs: cracking pattern over time (width in *mm*)

On clean data, a five-parameters quadratic-sinusoidal regression model was fitted for each type of sensor (air thermometers, masonry thermometers, and deformometers) imposing a sine of period equal to the length of one year, to take into account both the seasonal fluctuation of the measurements or the possible variations produced by systematic changes in the structural framework. The regression model estimated for each sensor is thus formalized as:

$$y = \alpha + \beta t + \gamma t^2 + \delta \sin(\eta + t\frac{2\pi}{365}) + \epsilon, \tag{1}$$

where y is the measure detected by each sensor (i.e., air or masonry temperature and crack width), t is the number of days elapsed from the activation of the monitoring system, and ϵ is an error component that accounts for the stochastic nature of the relationship between y and t.

In the missing data imputation process, the quadratic-sinusoidal regression model allows us to impute an average value consistent with the information that each sensor has detected in the period (one or more days of the year) to which missing data refers to. The fitting indicators produced by each quadratic-

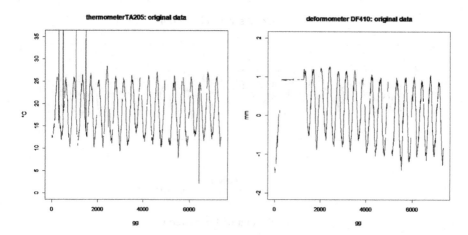

Fig. 4. Outliers and missing data in the cracking pattern over time measured by sensors TA2-05 and DEF4-10 (respectively, temperature in °C and width in mm)

sinusoidal regression model are very high. However, limiting the imputation process to the application of this model to each sensor independently of the values detected by the others was considered not completely satisfactory, because of the strong relationships among air temperature, web walls temperature, and cracks width.

For this reason, we adopted a cascade procedure that provided, through the use of linear regression models, the preliminary imputation of missing values present in the air thermometers time series. In turn, the complete series of air thermometers was used to impute missing data in the time series of the masonry thermometers. Finally, the complete series of masonry thermometers of each web were used to predict missing values of the deformometers installed in that web. In particular, for each air thermometer, the week of the year to which data refers to, the minimum, average and maximum daily temperature recorded in the city and the values estimated by the respective quadratic-sinusoidal regression model were provided as covariates (explicative variables) of the model used to impute missing values present in the corresponding series. For each masonry thermometer series, missing values have been imputed using the following covariates: the week of the year to which data refers to, the complete series of the air thermometers installed in the relative web and the estimations produced by the quadratic-sinusoidal regression model applied on the masonry thermometer series that has to be imputed. Similarly, missing values in the deformometer series have been imputed using a regression model with covariates: the week of the year to which data refers to, the complete series of the masonry thermometers installed in the relative web and the estimations produced by the quadratic-sinusoidal regression model applied on the deformometer series that has to be imputed. For the sake of brevity, the results of the imputation process are presented only for some sensors.

Figure 5 shows the result of the imputation process for the air thermometers TA7-03 installed on web 7: the imputation model shows an outstanding R-squared goodness of fit index ($R^2 = 98.15\%$).

Figure 6 shows the result of the imputation process for the masonry thermometers TM4-03 installed on web 4: the R-squared fitting index is excellent also in this case ($R^2 = 98.48\%$).

Figure 7 shows the result of the imputation process for the first three deformometers (DF2-01, DF2-02, DF2-03) installed on web 2. The fitting indices for those models were, respectively, 92,12%, 87,30% and 96,60%.

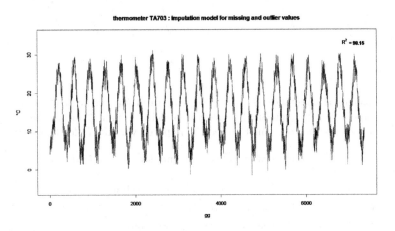

Fig. 5. Air-thermometer TA7-03: result of the imputation process (respectively, in green the seasonal fluctuation from the quadratic-sinusoidal regression model, in red the imputed values)

The R-squared goodness of fit indices computed for all the deformometers that compose the ISMES monitoring system are reported in Table 1. Almost all the indices show a very good performance of the relative model used to impute missing data. In very few cases, the fitting is unsatisfactory: these cases happen when the pattern of detections is quite inconsistent with the typical fluctuation of temperatures (i.e. when the sinusoidal regression model does not fit properly).

3   Modeling the Dome's Breathing Behavior

In this section, we present a suitable statistical approach to reduce the dimensionality of sensors measurements in order to facilitate the comprehension of the overall static evolution of the Dome. The adopted approach is based on Generalized Dynamic Principal Components (GDPC) which should be able to discover some synthesised (latent) trends of the Dome from the time series of the 57 deformometers installed on the eight webs. The suitability of the approach was verified by limiting the analysis to the measurements acquired in the last year.

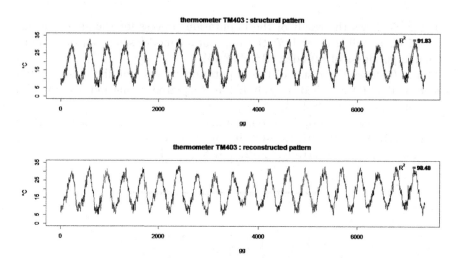

Fig. 6. Masonry thermometer TM4-03: the structural pattern of temperatures over time from the quadratic-sinusoidal regression model (top panel) and the result of the imputation process (bottom panel, in red the imputed values) (Color figure online)

Table 1. R-squared goodness of fit indices computed for all the ISMES deformometers

web 1		web 2		web3		web 4		web 5		web 6		web 7		web 8	
DF	R^2	DF	R^2	DF	R^2	DF	R^2	DF	R^2	DF	R^2	DF	R^2	DF	R^2
101	.945	201	.921	301	.938	401	.818	502	.861	601	.643	701	.961	801	.807
102	.920	202	.873	302	.934	402	.722	503	.877	604	.718	702	.929	802	.941
103	.891	203	.966	303	.606	404	.741	504	.933	605	.872	703	.320	803	.923
104	.773	204	.849			405	.861			606	.790			804	.878
105	.957	205	.847			406	.787			607	.878			805	.941
106	.789	206	.948			407	.881			608	.911			806	.947
		207	.943			408	.861			609	.928			807	.902
		208	.943			409	.923			610	.906			808	.941
		209	.961			410	.798			611	.956			809	.688
		210	.937			411	.935			612	.920			810	.923
						412	.931								
						413	.672								

Several methods have been proposed in the literature to deal with dimensionality reduction in time series analysis building on Dynamic Factor Analysis (DFA; examples are provided by [4,10] and references therein). DFA models are closely related to GDPC models because they assume that one important part of the original series can be explained in a dynamic way by a relatively small number of common factors. However, while DFA relies on a series of assumptions

deformometer DF201 : reconstructed pattern

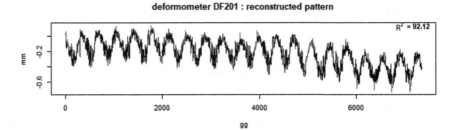

99

deformometer DF202 : reconstructed pattern

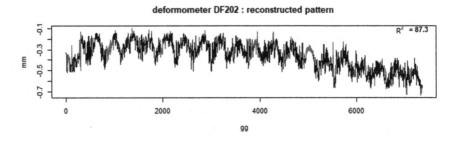

99

deformometer DF203 : reconstructed pattern

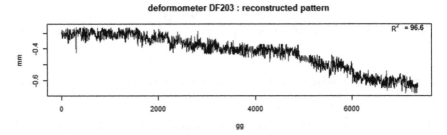

99

Fig. 7. Deformometers DF2-01 to DF2-03: result of the imputation process (in red the imputed values) (Color figure online)

regarding the distribution of error terms and on the variance-covariance matrices of the state-space equations, GDPC is more flexible because it only assumes that the time series share a common latent factor.

Let $z_t = (z_{1t}, ..., z_{mt})'$ denote a time series vector, where m is the number of series and $1 \leq t \leq T$. The first dynamic principal component with k lags is defined as the vector $\boldsymbol{f}_t = (f_t)_{-k+1 \leq t \leq T} = (f_{t-k}, ..., f_{t-1}, f_t)'$ such that the reconstruction of the series z_{jt} $(1 \leq j \leq m)$, defined as a linear combination of $f_{t-k}, \ldots, f_{t-1}, f_t$, is optimal with respect to the mean squared error (MSE) criterion. More precisely, given a factor $\boldsymbol{f}_t$ of length $(T+k)$, an $m \times (k+1)$ matrix of coefficients or loadings $\boldsymbol{\beta} = (\beta_{jh})_{1 \leq j \leq m, 1 \leq h \leq k+1}$ and $\boldsymbol{\alpha} = (\alpha_1, ..., \alpha_m)'$, the reconstruction $\tilde{z}_{jt}$ of original series z_{jt} is defined as $(1 \leq j \leq m; 1 \leq t \leq T)$

$$\tilde{z}_{jt}(\boldsymbol{f}_t, \boldsymbol{\beta}, \alpha_j) = \alpha_j + \sum_{h=0}^{k} \beta_{j,h+1} f_{t-h}. \qquad (2)$$

Note from Eq. 2 that f is not depending on the specific series j. The MSE to minimize is

$$MSE(\boldsymbol{f}_t, \boldsymbol{\beta}, \alpha_j) = \frac{1}{mT} \sum_{j=1}^{m} \sum_{t=1}^{T} [z_{jt} - \tilde{z}_{jt}(\boldsymbol{f}_t, \boldsymbol{\beta}, \alpha_j)]^2. \tag{3}$$

The minimization routine is efficiently implemented in the gdpc R package [6]. The original and reconstructed time series for deformometers DF101-104 are displayed in Fig. 8.

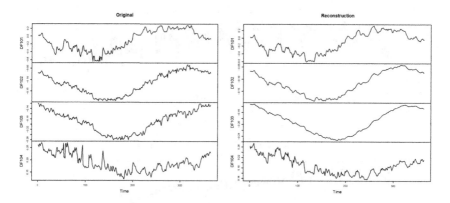

Fig. 8. Original and reconstructed time series for deformometers DF1-01 to DF1-04.

For the last year data the procedure took approximately 3 days on a 16 vCPU virtual machine with a RAM of 64 GB. The goodness of the reconstruction is evident, being the MSE of the reconstruction equal to 0.066. Indeed, the fitted model with one dynamic principal component with four lags, which represents the common factor underlying the time series of the 57 deformometers, explains the 93.4% of the whole variance in the dataset. The estimated time series of the common factor as well as the loadings for the 57 deformometers are displayed in Fig. 9.

We interpret the smooth behavior of the factor as the breathing mechanism of the Dome. Figure 9, top left panel, shows the values of the first principal component along the time, suggesting that, during a one year period, the Dome has a sort of sinusoidal trend with a period of expansion, followed by a period of contraction. This is corroborated by the estimates of loading parameters β_{jh} ($j = 1, \ldots, m$; $h = 1, \ldots, k + 1$) that move together, alternating positive and negative values (Fig. 9). More in detail, measures of deformometers detected at 0, 2, and 4 lags (Fig. 9, panels "0 loading", "2 loading", and "4 loading") contribute, with a few exceptions, to the expansive phase, whereas measures detected at 1 and 3 lags (Fig. 9, panels "1 loading" and "3 loading") contribute to the contractive phase. Also, we notice that the highest loadings are due to cracks recorded by the deformometers in webs 4 (blue lines in Fig. 9) and 6 (pink

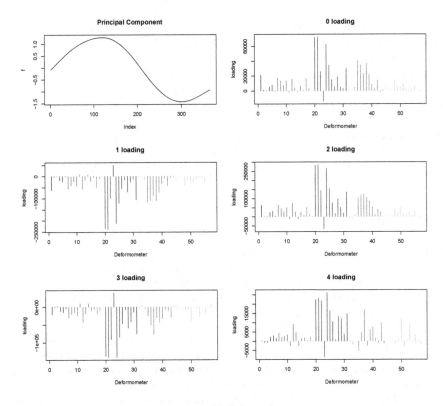

Fig. 9. GDPC results

lines in Fig. 9). In other words, webs 4 and 6 provide the maximum contribution to the movements of the Dome.

4   Conclusions

In this contribution, we performed an analysis of the web cracks reported by the sensors installed on the Brunelleschi's Dome of Santa Maria del Fiore. The complex data structure, resulting by the 57 deformometers over a period of 20 years with some random blackouts, suggested to adopt an approach based on two steps. First, we imputed the missing observations adopting a quadratic-sinusoidal regression model in order to build the complete time series for each deformometer. Second, a dynamic principal component model has been estimated to identify the overall breathing mechanism of the Dome and the contribution of each web crack to the overall movement. This model showed an excellent goodness of fit, clearly revealing the underlying breathing mechanism of the Dome. Compared to the dynamic factor analysis performed in [2], where the algorithm did not converged but stopped after reaching the maximum number of iterations, the GDPC provided much better convergence properties (results not shown here). The proposed analysis represents a useful instrument for the professionals (architects and structural engineers) to globally evaluate the behavior of the Brunelleschi's Dome. In fact, this approach gave satisfactory results in financial applications (see [9]) and its consistency has been investigated in [8]. For the future developments of the work, we intend to relate the movements of the webs each other as well as to assess the impact of external observable (exogenous) variables on the evolution of the cracks.

Acknowledgements. Authors thank the Opera di Santa Maria del Fiore Foundation for providing the data acquired by the monitoring system installed on the Dome. Authors also acknowledge the financial support provided by the "Dipartimenti Eccellenti 2018–2022" Italian ministerial funds.

References

1. Barnett, V.: Outliers in statistical data. Technical report (1978)
2. Bertaccini, B.: Santa Maria del Fiore dome behavior: statistical models for monitoring stability. Int. J. Architectural Heritage **9**(1), 25–37 (2015)
3. Chiarugi, A., Bartoli, G., Bavetta, F.: La meccanica della cupola. In: Cupola di Santa Maria del Fiore, il Cantiere di Restauro 1980–1995, pp. 47–62. Istituto Poligraco e Zecca Dello Stato (1995)
4. Forni, M., Hallin, M., Lippi, M., Reichlin, L.: The generalized dynamic-factor model: identification and estimation. Rev. Econ. Stat. **82**(4), 540–554 (2000)
5. Ottoni, F., Blasi, C.: Results of a 60-year monitoring system for Santa Maria del Fiore dome in Florence. Int. J. Architectural Heritage **9**(1), 7–24 (2015)
6. Peña, D., Smucler, E., Yohai, V.J.: gdpc: an R package for generalized dynamic principal components. J. Stat. Softw. **92**(1), 1–23 (2020)
7. Peña, D., Yohai, V.J.: Generalized dynamic principal components. J. Am. Stat. Assoc. **111**(515), 1121–1131 (2016)
8. Smucler, E.: Consistency of generalized dynamic principal components in dynamic factor models. Stat. Probab. Lett. **154**, 108536 (2019)
9. Trucíos, C., Hotta, L.K., Pereira, P.L.V.: On the robustness of the principal volatility components. J. Empir. Finance **52**, 201–219 (2019)
10. Zurr, A.F., Fryer, R.J., Jolliffe, I.T., Dekker, R., Beukema, J.J.: Estimating common trends in multivariate time series using dynamic factor analysis. Environmetrics **14**, 665–685 (2003)

International Workshop on Frontiers in Machine Learning (FIML 2020)

Comparing Statistical and Machine Learning Imputation Techniques in Breast Cancer Classification

Imane Chlioui[1], Ibtissam Abnane[1], and Ali Idri[1,2(✉)]

[1] Software Project Management Research Team, ENSIAS,
Mohammed V University in Rabat, Rabat, Morocco
imanechlioui@gmail.com, ibtissam_abnane@um5s.net.ma,
ali.idri@um5.ac.ma

[2] CSEHS-MSDA, Mohammed VI Polytechnic University, Ben Guerir, Morocco

Abstract. Missing data imputation is an important task when dealing with crucial data that cannot be discarded such as medical data. This study evaluates and compares the impacts of two statistical and two machine learning imputation techniques when classifying breast cancer patients, using several evaluation metrics. Mean, Expectation-Maximization (EM), Support Vector Regression (SVR) and K-Nearest Neighbor (KNN) were applied to impute 18% of missing data missed completely at random in the two Wisconsin datasets. Thereafter, we empirically evaluated these four imputation techniques when using five classifiers: decision tree (C4.5), Case Based Reasoning (CBR), Random Forest (RF), Support Vector Machine (SVM) and Multi-Layer Perceptron (MLP). In total, 1380 experiments were conducted and the findings confirmed that classification using imputation based machine learning outperformed classification using statistical imputation. Moreover, our experiment showed that SVR was the best imputation method for breast cancer classification.

Keywords: Missing data imputation · Data mining · Breast cancer

1 Introduction

Breast cancer have been considered as the most dangerous type of cancer, and the second leading cause of death especially among women [1]. It is a tumor that can be malignant or benign, mortal if it is not early diagnosed [2]. The main cause of this disease is not well known, although several factors were identified such as: late age at first child, not breastfeeding, early menarche and late menopause, longer term use of hormone replacement therapy in post-menopausal women and current or recent use of the combined oral contraceptive pill, increased alcohol intake, post-menopausal obesity and reduced physical activity [3, 4]. An early diagnosis can prevent the tumor from spreading to other body parts, thus several clinical methods have been used by practitioners such as: Positron Emission Tomography (PET), Magnetic Resonance Imaging (MRI), mammography, and Biopsy [1].

© Springer Nature Switzerland AG 2020
O. Gervasi et al. (Eds.): ICCSA 2020, LNCS 12252, pp. 61–76, 2020.
https://doi.org/10.1007/978-3-030-58811-3_5

Missing data (MD) is an ubiquitous problem in real data, and it can occur due to defective equipment [5], missed entries when filling in data [6], loss of information, human errors [7], patient data safety and policies [8], and information not provided by patients [9]. Several MD techniques were proposed in the literature, and in general imputation proved to be the most efficient solution compared to toleration and deletion [10, 11]. Imputation techniques can be grouped into two groups [12]: i) Statistical imputation techniques common in the literature, many techniques have been proposed including mean [13], hot deck [14] and expectation-maximization [15], ii) since 2000's a new approach has emerged where missing values has been treated as an output of machine learning models [16]. In this framework, the observed data are considered as a training set for the learning model, which is then applied to the data with missing values to impute. K-Nearest Neighbor (KNN) [17], Decision Tree (DT) [18] and Support Vector Regression (SVR) [19] are the most used ML techniques for imputation and achieved great success [20].

With the introduction of ML imputation techniques, several researchers tend to compare the impacts of both statistical and ML techniques on the performance prediction and classification systems. In breast cancer, few papers were published tackling this issue: (1) Acuña and Rodriguez [21] carried out experiments with twelve medical datasets including BC databases, to evaluate the impacts of four MD techniques: deletion, mean imputation, median imputation, and KNN imputation on the misclassification measured in terms of error rate; Their findings suggested that KNN imputation may be the best approach to impute missing values. And (2) Jerez et al. [12] conducted an experiment to evaluate the impacts of several statistical imputation techniques (e.g., mean, hot-deck and multiple imputation), and machine learning imputation techniques (e.g., multi-layer perceptron (MLP), self-organisation maps (SOM) and k-nearest neighbour (KNN)) on an Artificial Neural Network based BC prognosis system. The results showed that according to the Area Under Cover (AUC), the ML imputation techniques outperformed the statistical ones, and Friedman test revealed a significant difference in the observed AUC.

To the best of our knowledge a minority of papers discussed the comparison of imputation techniques for breast cancer classification [22]; moreover none of them used several evaluation metrics to support their findings. This paper investigates whether ML imputation techniques may lead to better results compared to statistical techniques based on different evaluation metrics. Two statistical techniques including mean imputation which is the simplest reference [12] and Expectation Maximization (EM) which assumed to generate unbiased parameter estimates [23]. Two machine learning (ML) imputation techniques, including K-Nearest Neighbor (KNN) which is the most used ML imputation technique [17] and Support Vector Regression (SVR) which have proven to achieve good results for MD imputation [19, 24]. For classification five classifiers were applied over two Wisconsin datasets: Case-based reasoning (CBR), Decision Tree (C4.5), Support Vector Machines (SVM), Random Forest (RF) and Multilayer Perceptron (MLP). And for comparison three evaluation metrics were used: balanced accuracy, Area Under Cover and Kappa value along with Scot-Knott algorithm and Borda count method. In order to draw conclusion on which technique is the best, two research questions were addressed:

RQ1: Does ML imputation techniques significantly outperform statistical imputation ones?

RQ2: Among the ML imputation techniques used, which one achieve the highest performance?

The paper is structured as follows: MD techniques and classification algorithms as well as the datasets used are described in Sect. 2, the experimental design followed is detailed in Sect. 3. The results are presented and discussed in Sect. 4. Finally, Sect. 5 presents conclusion and future work.

2   Materials and Methods

This section describes the techniques used for either handling missing data or classification. As well as the datasets used for the experiments.

2.1   Missing Data Techniques

Thereafter, we briefly present the four imputation techniques used.

- Mean imputation (MI): considered as the simplest method to deal with missing data, widely used as an alternative of Deletion [12]. It consists of replacing the missing data with the mean of all observed cases [25].
- Expectation Maximization (EM): considered as a sophisticated method to deal with missing data. It consists of two steps: the expectation step which uses an initial estimate parameter and conditions it upon the observed variables, the maximization step which provides a new estimation of the parameter using Maximum Likelihood. This process is iterated until convergence [26].
- K-nearest neighbor (KNN): Considered as the most ML technique used for MD imputation [21], based on KNN algorithm. It consists of imputing the missing value considering the K closest instances according to a given distance metric [27].
- Support Vector Regression (SVR): Considered as the regression model of Support Vector Machines (SVM) developed by Vapnik [28]. The SVM is a non-linear algorithm implementing the structural risk minimization inductive principle [29]. They are most known for classification but With the introduction of Vapnik's ε-insensitivity loss function [19], the regression model (SVR) achieved excellent performances [30–32]. However, to the best of our knowledge there is no study investigating the use of SVR imputation for MD in breast cancer datasets.

2.2   Classification Techniques

This study uses five classifiers:

2.2.1   C4.5

C4.5 is a decision tree algorithm developed by Quinlan in 1993 [33]. C4.5 generates classifiers expressed as decision trees; the nodes contain test that will divide-up the training cases, and the results of which permits to decide which bough to follow from the node. The leaf nodes are the class labels instead of nodes [33]. C4.5 mainly has two parameters [33, 34]:

- CF (confidence factor): affects the confidence with which error rate at the tree nodes is estimated, lower CF values incur heavier pruning.
- MS (minimum numbers of split-off cases): affects the size of the grown tree by disallowing the formation of tree nodes whose number of cases is smaller than the chosen MS parameter; thus, higher MS parameter values lead to grown trees that are of smaller size.

2.2.2 SVM

SVM is a group of supervised learning methods developed by Vapnik in the 90's [34]. It is used to model data not linearly separable. To classify data, the algorithm generates an optimal hyper plane which separates different classes and assigns every input of test set data to one of the defined classes [35, 36]. SVM has three parameters [37]:

- C: is the regularization parameter.
- Kernel: specifies the kernel type to be used in the algorithm. It can be 'linear', 'polynomial', 'Gaussian radial basis function', 'sigmoid', 'precomputed', or a callable.
- Kernel parameter: depends on the chosen kernel. For example: Gamma is the kernel coefficient for 'The Gaussian radial basis function', 'polynomial', and 'sigmoid'.

2.2.3 CBR

Case-based reasoning (CBR) is a method of lazy learning known as a nonparametric method. It consists of aggregating the outputs of the most similar cases in order to predict the output of a new case. It uses as a measure of cases similarity the distance between their data to determine the most similar cases to a given new case. Several distance metrics can be used, such as Hamming distance, Manhattan distance and Euclidean distance [38, 39]. Thereafter, the adaptation step of CBR aggregates the outputs of the k most similar cases in order to predict the output of the new case: the median and the mode are the most used aggregation methods for continuous and categorical outputs respectively [40]. CBR mainly has two parameters some of them are [39]:

- Number of neighbors (K).
- Distance metric to use.

2.2.4 RF

Random forest (RF) algorithm is defined as a generic principle of randomized ensembles of decision trees [41]. It is one of the most powerful techniques in the pattern recognition and machine learning for high-dimensional classification and skewed problems [42]. The accuracy of a forest classifier depends on the strength of each individual tree in the generalized forest and the correlation between them. Indeed, increasing the strength of the individual trees increases the forest accuracy rate while increasing the correlation reduces the forest accuracy rate [42]. RF has several parameters, important ones are [43]:

- Number of iterations (I).
- Number of features (K).
- Number of execution slots: default = 1
- Seed = 1

2.2.5 MLP

Multi-Layer Perceptron (MLP) is a type of artificial neural network (ANN) that can represent complex input-output relationships [44]. MLP consists of neurons organized in three layers: input, hidden, and output layers which each one performs simple task of information processing by converting received inputs into processed outputs. Although each neuron implements its function slowly and imperfectly, collectively a neural network is able to perform a variety of tasks efficiently and achieve remarkable results [45]. MLP has several parameters, important ones are:

- L: Learning Rate of its back-propagation learning algorithm. (In general within the interval [0, 1], Default = 0.3).
- M: Momentum Rate of its back-propagation algorithm. (In general within the interval [0, 1], Default = 0.2).

2.3 Datasets Description

The experiments were conducted using two datasets collected at the University of Wisconsin–Madison Hospitals [46]. The first one is the Wisconsin breast cancer original dataset, which contains 699 instances periodically collected within the period 1989–1992 [47]; each patient is described by 10 numerical attributes. The second one is the Wisconsin breast cancer prognosis dataset; it contains 198 records and each one represents follow-up data for one breast cancer case, and only includes those cases exhibiting invasive breast cancer and no evidence of distant metastases at the time of diagnosis. Each record is described by 35 attributes and 30 among them were computed from a digitized image of a fine needle aspirate (FNA) of a breast mass.

All cases containing missing data were deleted, which reduced the size of each dataset: 683 instances remain in Wisconsin original and 194 instances in Wisconsin prognosis. Moreover, we normalized the attributes of Wisconsin breast cancer prognosis dataset within the interval [1, 2] in order to avoid bias of attributes' ranges. Note that the attribute values of the Wisconsin breast cancer original dataset were already normalized within the interval [1–10]. Table 1 presents datasets information, including the number of instances and attributes. All the attributes used in this study are numerical.

3 Experimental Design

This section details the process followed for this experiment. As shown in Fig. 1, it consists mainly of four phases: data removal, missing data imputation, generating classifiers and performance evaluation. Each phase is detailed in the following subsections.

Table 1. Datasets description

Database	Instances	Attributes	Attributes type	Source
Wisconsin breast cancer original	194	35	Numeric	[48]
Wisconsin breast cancer prognosis	683	10	Numeric	[48]

3.1 Data Removal

This study aims to evaluate the impact of different imputation methods on the classification of breast cancer datasets. For this purpose, the datasets should be complete to work with, that is why all the missing data already existed were discarded. Thereafter, 18% of MD were randomly induced. The MD are not related to any other value of the existing attributes. Moreover, according to Peng and Lei [25] more than 15% of MD impact severely any interpretation and must be handled using sophisticated techniques, which explain the choice of 18% of MD. It's noteworthy, that the impact of MD percentage on imputation was discussed in a previous article [49]. The findings confirmed that the MD percentage affects negatively the classifier performance.

3.2 Missing Data Imputation

For this step, four imputation techniques were applied to handle the missing values on the datasets resulted from the data removal step.

- Statistical imputation techniques: two statistical techniques were used. The mean imputation which impute using the mean value, and the Expectation-Maximization which apply the Maximum Likelihood estimation method.
- Machine learning imputation techniques: two regression techniques were used. The KNN imputation which is the most famous algorithm used for imputation and SVR imputation which proved to be helpful in effort estimation [19]. Grid search (GS) was used to vary the parameter configuration for each technique according to Table 2.

At the end of this step, we obtained 276 complete datasets: by combining 2 incomplete datasets * (100 complete datasets using SVR (10 variations of C and 10 variations of G) + 36 complete datasets using KNN (4 distance metrics and 9 variations of K) + 1 complete dataset using mean + 1 complete dataset using EM).

3.3   Generating Classifiers

Five classifiers (C4.5, CBR, RF, SVM and MLP) were applied on the generated complete datasets, in order to evaluate and compare the influence of the different imputation techniques used. To fulfill this task, 10-fold cross validation method was used to divide the test and training test. Moreover to guarantee high performance, parameter tuning is used [50]. We opted for GS method to choose the optimal configuration parameter according to Table 2, the best variant with the highest value of the balanced accuracy criterion was retained for the comparison.

At the end of this step, we obtained 1380 classification experiments (276 * 5 = 1380).

3.4   Performance Evaluation

Three different evaluation metrics were considered to evaluate the classifiers and study the convenience of imputing data using both statistical and ML imputation techniques:

- The balanced accuracy rate: it equally weights the value of making accurate predictions in each class in order to avoid bias results caused by imbalanced data [51]. The balanced accuracy rate was evaluated using the Eq. (1).

$$Balanced\ accuracy = \frac{\frac{TN}{FP+TN} + \frac{TP}{TP+FN}}{2} \tag{1}$$

- Kappa value: it represents the pairwise agreement between two different observers (observed accuracy and expected accuracy) [52]. Observed Accuracy is simply the number of instances that were correctly classified, while the expected accuracy is the number of instances of each class along with the number of instances that the classifier classified as true. Its upper limit is +1.00, and its lower limit falls between zero and −1.00 [53]. The kappa statistic value was evaluated using the Eq. (2) [52].

$$K = pA - PE/[1 - PE] \tag{2}$$

$$PA = (TP + TN)/N \tag{3}$$

$$PE = \frac{(TP + FN) * (TP + FP) + (TN + FP) * (TN + FN)}{N^2} \tag{4}$$

- Area Under an ROC Cover (AUROC): mostly known as AUC. The Receiver Operating Characteristics (ROC) is a plot of the true positive as a function of the false positive. the AUC is defined as the area under the ROC curve and it is equal to the probability that the classifier will rank a randomly chosen positive example higher than a randomly chosen negative example [54].

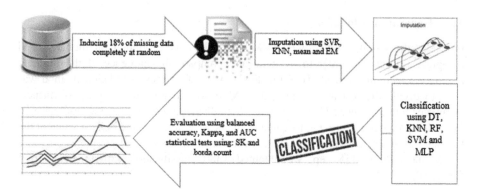

Fig. 1. Experimental design

Table 2. Parameters ranges and optimal configuration of each classifier

MD technique	Parameter ranges	Classifier	Parameter ranges	Optimal configuration for imputation	Optimal configuration for classification
KNN imputation	K = {2 -> 10, increment = 1} Distance metrics: Euclidean, Manhattan, Chebyshev, Minkowsk	C4.5	C = {0.1 -> 1, increment = 0.05}; M = {1 -> 20, increment = 1};	K = 5	C = 0.25 M = 1
		CBR	K = {1 -> 12, increment = 1);	K = 5	K = 9
		RF	I = {10 -> 100, increment = 10); K = {1 -> 10, increment = 1};	K = 5	I = 50 K = 2
		SVM	Kernel = RBFKernel; C = {1 -> 10, increment = 1}; G = {0.01 -> 0.1, increment = 0.01};	K = 7	C = 3 G = 0.01
		MLP	L = {0.1 -> 1, increment = 0.1}; M = {0.1 -> 1, increment = 0.1};	K = 5	M = 0.1 L = 0.1
SVR imputation	Kernel = RBFKernel; C = {1 -> 10, increment = 1}; G = {0.01 -> 0.1, increment = 0.01};	C4.5	C = {0.1 -> 1, increment = 0.05}; M = {1 -> 20, increment = 1};	C = 2 G = 0.01	C = 0.25 M = 1
		CBR	K = {1 -> 12, increment = 1);	C = 5 G = 0.01	K = 9
		RF	I = {10 -> 100, increment = 10); K = {1 -> 10, increment = 1};	C = 2 G = 0.01	I = 80 K = 2
		SVM	Kernel = RBFKernel; C = {1 -> 10, increment = 1}; G = {0.01 -> 0.1, increment = 0.01};	C = 3 G = 0.01	C = 1 G = 0.01
		MLP	L = {0.1 -> 1, increment = 0.1}; M = {0.1 -> 1, increment = 0.1};	C = 2 G = 0.01	M = 0.5 L = 0.1

3.5   Significance Tests

Several evaluation metrics have been used to select the best technique that achieved the highest results. However, different metrics can yield to different conclusions (i.e., if one metric prove that method A is better than method B, another metric can prove that method B is better than method A). Subsequently, two additional methods were used to significantly compare the imputation techniques used:

– Scot-Knott (SK): It's a hierarchical clustering algorithm that permits to distinguish groups with significant F-test [55]. SK is the most frequently used test among those designed for similar purposes [56]. We used SK based on the balanced accuracy rates.
– Borda count method: It's a voting system based on computing the mean rank of each candidates over all voters [57]. We used borda count method based on the three evaluation metrics mentioned above (balanced accuracy, AUC, Kappa).

4   Results and Discussion

This section evaluates and compares the influence of four imputation techniques based on both statistical and ML imputation techniques on the performance of five classifiers, over 18% of MCAR missing data in two Wisconsin breast cancer datasets.

To investigate whether the use of ML imputation techniques (i.e. SVR and KNN) outperform the use of statistical imputation techniques (i.e. mean and EM), Fig. 2, 3 and 4 presents respectively the mean balanced accuracy rates, the mean Kappa and the mean AUC for five classifiers (DT, CBR, SVM, RF and MLP) applied to two breast cancer datasets.

– Based on balanced accuracy rates, ML imputation techniques achieved the highest results compared to statistical imputation techniques for all the five classifiers. SVR and KNN proved to be more efficient for enhancing the classifiers balanced accuracy rates (the mean balanced accuracy rates achieved using RF are for SVR: 88%, for KNN: 84%, for EM: 83% and for mean: 83%). Moreover, SVR outperformed KNN for all the five classifiers (the mean balanced accuracy rates achieved using CBR are for SVR: 83%, for KNN: 81%). While, the results achieved by EM and mean are slightly the same for all the classifiers (the mean balanced accuracy rates achieved using CBR are for EM: 80% and for mean: 80%)
– Based on Kappa rates, ML imputation techniques outperformed once again the statistical imputation techniques for almost all the classifiers, while when using CBR the results were the same for the four imputation techniques (the mean kappa rates achieved using RF are for SVR: 57%, for KNN: 51%, for EM: 45% and for mean: 46%). Furthermore, SVR achieved highest results compared to KNN for C4.5 and RF, while for CBR, MLP and SVM the results were the same (the mean kappa rates achieved using C4.5 are for SVR: 60%, for KNN: 59%). Besides, mean imputation surpassed EM when using RF and SVM, while for C4.5 EM achieved higher results (the mean kappa rates achieved using RF are for EM: 46% and for mean: 45%).

- Based on AUC rates, mean imputation outperformed other techniques when using C4.5, CBR and MLP followed by KNN imputation (the mean AUC rates achieved using C4.5 are for SVR: 78%, for KNN: 77%, for EM: 75% and for mean: 81%). While when using SVM, SVR achieved the highest AUC rate (the mean AUC rates achieved using SVM are for SVR: 81%, for KNN: 80%, for EM: 79% and for mean: 80%). Furthermore, when using RF all the techniques achieved the same AUC rate.

Afterwards, we used SK algorithm to cluster the results based on the balanced accuracy rates. According to Fig. 5, it's observed that the best cluster is the one composed of ML imputation techniques. Next, we applied the borda count voting system based on three evaluation metrics, to rank the techniques belonging to the best SK cluster. From Table 3, it can be seen that SVR obtained the highest number of votes.

To summarize the findings, ML imputation techniques yield to best results compared to statistical imputation techniques. Although implementing ML imputation techniques may be costly, and may need more effort and time, our finding suggest that the performance of classifiers will be improved significantly using ML for MD imputation compared to statistical imputation. Our results align with previous experiments conducted by Perez et al. [12] using ML techniques for MD imputation to improve the prediction accuracy. SVR imputation proved to be more efficient to enhance the performance compared to other techniques [58] not only for breast cancer classification but also in many fields such us software development effort estimation. According to Idri et al. [19] the use of SVR imputation rather than KNN imputation enhance the performance of the prediction performance of both fuzzy and classical analogy-based techniques.

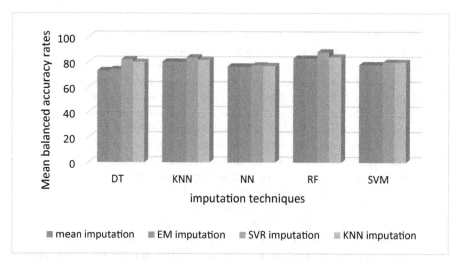

Fig. 2. Mean balanced accuracy rates of C4.5, CBR, RF, MLP and SVM when using mean, EM, KNN and SVR imputation

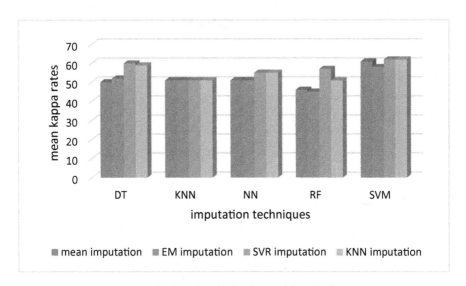

Fig. 3. Mean kappa rates of C4.5, CBR, RF, MLP and SVM when using mean, EM, KNN and SVR imputation

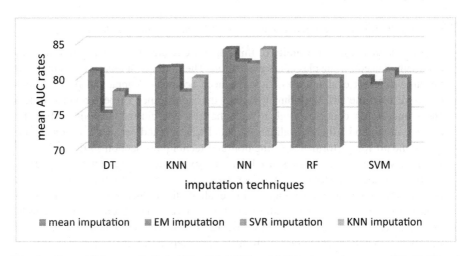

Fig. 4. Mean AUC rates of C4.5, CBR, RF, MLP and SVM when using mean, EM, KNN and SVR imputation

Table 3. Rankings of ML imputation techniques of SK best clusters based on Borda Count

Votes	Rank		
	9	2	4
1	SVR	KNN	SVR/KNN
2	KNN	SVR	

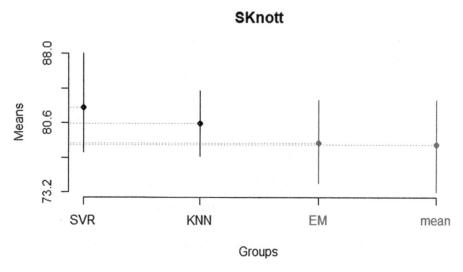

Fig. 5. Plot SK test of imputation techniques used

5   Threats to Validity

This section highlights the internal and external threats of this article.

- Internal validity: Internal validity of this paper are related to the evaluation metrics and method used for the classifiers evaluation. The findings of this study were based on three different evaluation metrics: balanced accuracy, Kappa and AUC. Moreover, we used the SK algorithm to assess the significance of performance differences and Borda count method to rank the best SK cluster techniques. For the evaluation method, 10 cross-validation model was adopted because it is considered as a standard for performance estimation and technique selection [59].
- External validity: The datasets used for this experiment only contain numerical attribute. Further investigations on other datasets are required to discuss categorical attributes. Five classifiers were applied to evaluate the influence of MD imputation techniques in breast cancer classification. Furthermore, the present study only used two statistical (Mean and EM) and two ML (SVR and KNN) imputation techniques, yet other imputation techniques with other classifiers can achieve better results.

6   Conclusion and Future Work

In this study, the impacts of statistical/ML imputation techniques on the five classifiers: C4.5, CBR, RF, SVM and MLP were evaluated over two datasets from the UCI repository: Wisconsin breast cancer original and prognosis datasets. Four imputation techniques: Mean, EM, SVR and KNN were applied on 18% MD.

RQ1: Does ML imputation techniques significantly outperform statistical imputation ones?

Our findings confirm that using ML imputation techniques improved the classifiers performance. However, they are difficult to implement and costly.

RQ2: Among the ML imputation techniques used, which one achieve the highest performance?

The experiments proved that the performance of SVR imputation is slightly superior compared with KNN.

Ongoing research intends to carry out more empirical evaluations of the impact of MD on the performance of breast cancer classification in order to refute or confirm the findings of the present study. Moreover, we intend to investigate other imputation ensembles: homogenous and heterogeneous [60, 61] based on other single imputers such as decision trees [62] and other statistical imputation techniques. Since the present study only deals with numerical attributes, it would be of great interest to deal with missing categorical data too [63].

References

1. Oskouei, R.J., Kor, N.M., Maleki, S.A.: Data mining and medical world: Breast cancers' diagnosis, treatment, prognosis and challenges. Am. J. Cancer Res. **7**, 610–627 (2017)
2. Garg, B.: Optimizing number of inputs to classify breast cancer using artificial neural network. J. Comput. Sci. Syst. Biol. **02**, 247–254 (2009). https://doi.org/10.4172/jcsb.1000037
3. Sibbering, M., Courtney, C.A.: Management of breast cancer: basic principles. Surg. (United Kingdom) **34**, 25–31 (2016). https://doi.org/10.1016/j.mpsur.2015.10.005
4. Morimoto, L.M., et al.: Obesity, body size, and risk of postmenopausal breast cancer: the women's health initiative (United States). Cancer Causes Control **13**, 741–751 (2002). https://doi.org/10.1023/A:1020239211145
5. Schafer, J.L., Graham, J.W.: Missing data: our view of the state of the art. Psychol. Methods **7**, 147–177 (2002). https://doi.org/10.1037/1082-989X.7.2.147
6. Bhat, V.H., Rao, P.G., Krishna, S., Shenoy, P.D., Venugopal, K.R., Patnaik, L.M.: An efficient framework for prediction in healthcare data using soft computing techniques. In: Abraham, A., Mauri, J.L., Buford, J.F., Suzuki, J., Thampi, S.M. (eds.) ACC 2011. CCIS, vol. 192, pp. 522–532. Springer, Heidelberg (2011). https://doi.org/10.1007/978-3-642-22720-2_55
7. Idri, A., Benhar, H., Fernández-Alemán, J.L., Kadi, I.: A systematic map of medical data preprocessing in knowledge discovery. Comput. Methods Programs Biomed. **162**, 69–85 (2018)
8. Albayrak, M., Turhan, K., Informatics, M., Introduction, I.: A missing data imputation approach using clustering and maximum likelihood estimation. In: IEEE (ed.) 2017 Medical Technologies National Congress (TIPTEKNO), Trabzon, Turkey, pp. 1–4 (2017)
9. Kadi, I., Idri, A., Fernandez-Aleman, J.L.: Knowledge discovery in cardiology: a systematic literature review. Int. J. Med. Inform. **97**, 12–32 (2017). https://doi.org/10.1016/j.ijmedinf.2016.09.005
10. Lang, K.M., Little, T.D.: Principled missing data treatments. Prev. Sci. **19**(3), 284–294 (2016). https://doi.org/10.1007/s11121-016-0644-5
11. Idri, A., Abnane, I., Abran, A.: Missing data techniques in analogy-based software development effort estimation. J. Syst. Softw. **117**, 595–611 (2016). https://doi.org/10.1016/j.jss.2016.04.058

12. Jerez, J.M., et al.: Missing data imputation using statistical and machine learning methods in a real breast cancer problem. Artif. Intell. Med. **50**, 105–115 (2010). https://doi.org/10.1016/j.artmed.2010.05.002
13. Gayathri, B.M., Sumathi, C.P.: Mamdani fuzzy inference system for breast cancer risk detection. In: 2015 IEEE International Conference on Computational Intelligence and Computing Research, ICCIC 2015, Madurai, Tamilnadu, India, pp. 1–6 (2016)
14. Myers, T.A.: Goodbye, listwise deletion: presenting hot deck imputation as an easy and effective tool for handling missing data. Commun. Methods Meas. **5**, 297–310 (2011). https://doi.org/10.1080/19312458.2011.624490
15. Barzi, F., Woodward, M.: Imputations of missing values in practice: results from imputations of serum cholesterol in 28 cohort studies. Am. J. Epidemiol. **160**, 34–45 (2004). https://doi.org/10.1093/aje/kwh175
16. Liu, Y., Gopalakrishnan, V.: An overview and evaluation of recent machine learning imputation methods using cardiac imaging data. Data (2017). https://doi.org/10.3390/data2010008
17. Penone, C., et al.: Imputation of missing data in life-history trait datasets: which approach performs the best? Methods Ecol. Evol. **5**, 961–970 (2014). https://doi.org/10.1111/2041-210X.12232
18. Vateekul, P., Sarinnapakorn, K.: Tree-based approach to missing data imputation. In: ICDM Workshops 2009 - IEEE International Conference on Data Mining, pp. 70–75 (2009)
19. Idri, A., Abnane, I., Abran, A.: Support vector regression-based imputation in analogy-based software development effort estimation. J. Softw. Evol. Process. **30**, 1–23 (2018). https://doi.org/10.1002/smr.2114
20. Wu, X., Akbarzadeh Khorshidi, H., Aickelin, U., Edib, Z., Peate, M.: Imputation techniques on missing values in breast cancer treatment and fertility data. Health Inf. Sci. Syst. **7**(1), 1–8 (2019). https://doi.org/10.1007/s13755-019-0082-4
21. Acuña, E., Rodriguez, C.: The treatment of missing values and its effect on classifier accuracy. In: Banks, D., McMorris, F.R., Arabie, P., Gaul, W. (eds.) Classification, Clustering, and Data Mining Applications. STUDIES CLASS, pp. 639–647. Springer, Heidelberg (2004). https://doi.org/10.1007/978-3-642-17103-1_60
22. Chlioui, I., Idri, A., Abnane, I.: Data preprocessing in knowledge discovery in breast cancer: systematic mapping study. Comput. Methods Biomech. Biomed. Eng. Imaging Vis., 1–15
23. Musil, C.M., Warner, C.B., Yobas, P.K., Jones, S.L.: A comparison of imputation techniques for handling Missing data. West. J. Nurs. Res. **24**, 815–829 (2002). https://doi.org/10.1177/019394502762477004
24. Santos, M.S., Soares, J.P., Henriques Abreu, P., Araújo, H., Santos, J.: Influence of data distribution in missing data imputation. In: ten Teije, A., Popow, C., Holmes, J.H., Sacchi, L. (eds.) AIME 2017. LNCS (LNAI), vol. 10259, pp. 285–294. Springer, Cham (2017). https://doi.org/10.1007/978-3-319-59758-4_33
25. Peng, L., Lei, L.: A review of missing data treatment methods. Int. J. Intell. Inf. Manag. Syst. Technol. **1**, 412–419 (2005)
26. Moon, T.K.: The expectation-maximization algorithm (1996)
27. Chlioui, I., Idri, A., Abnane, I., de Gea, J.M.C., Fernández-Alemán, J.L.: Breast cancer classification with missing data imputation. In: Rocha, Á., Adeli, H., Reis, L.P., Costanzo, S. (eds.) WorldCIST 2019. AISC, vol. 932, pp. 13–23. Springer, Cham (2019). https://doi.org/10.1007/978-3-030-16187-3_2
28. Vapnik, V.: The Nature of Statistical Learning Theory (2013)
29. Debasish, B., Srimanta, P., Dipak Chandra, P.: Support vector regression. Neural Inf. Process. Lett. Rev. **11**, 699–708 (2007)

30. Drucker, H., Surges, C.J.C., Kaufman, L., Smola, A., Vapnik, V.: Support vector regression machines. In: Advances in Neural Information Processing Systems (1997)
31. Smola, A.J., Schölkopf, B.: A tutorial on support vector regression (2004)
32. Müller, K.-R., Smola, A.J., Rätsch, G., Schölkopf, B., Kohlmorgen, J., Vapnik, V.: Predicting time series with support vector machines. In: Gerstner, W., Germond, A., Hasler, M., Nicoud, J.-D. (eds.) ICANN 1997. LNCS, vol. 1327, pp. 999–1004. Springer, Heidelberg (1997). https://doi.org/10.1007/BFb0020283
33. Quinlan, J.R.: C4.5: Programs for Machine Learning. Elsevier, Amsterdam (1992)
34. Witten, I.H., Frank, E., Hall, M.A.: Data Mining. Elsevier, Amsterdam (2011)
35. Alpaydın, E.: Introduction to machine learning, London (2014)
36. Cristianini, N., Shawe-Taylor, J.: An Introduction to Support Vector Machines and Other Kernel Based Learning Methods. Cambridge University Press, Cambridge (2000)
37. Burges, C.J.C.: A tutorial on support vector machines for pattern recognition. Data Min. Knowl. Discov. 2, 121–167 (1998). https://doi.org/10.1023/A:1009715923555
38. Marsilin, J.R.: An efficient CBIR approach for diagnosing the stages of breast cancer using KNN classifier. Bonfring Int. J. Adv. Image Process. 2, 01–05 (2012). https://doi.org/10.9756/bijaip.1127
39. Odajima, K., Pawlovsky, A.P.: A detailed description of the use of the kNN method for breast cancer diagnosis. In: 2014 7th International Conference on BioMedical Engineering and Informatics, BMEI 2014, Dalian, China, pp. 688–692 (2014)
40. Kowarik, A., Templ, M.: Imputation with the R Package VIM. J. Stat. Softw. 74, 1–16 (2016). https://doi.org/10.18637/jss.v074.i07
41. Hu, S., Liang, Y., Ma, L., He, Y.: MSMOTE: improving classification performance when training data is imbalanced. In: 2nd International Workshop on Computer Science and Engineering, WCSE 2009, Qingdao, China, pp. 13–17 (2009)
42. Breiman, L.: Random forests. Mach. Learn. 45, 5–32 (2001). https://doi.org/10.1023/A:1010933404324
43. Pavlov, Y.L.: Random forest. In: Probabilistic Methods in Discrete Mathematics, pp. 11–18 (2000)
44. Ghosh, S., Mondal, S., Ghosh, B.: A comparative study of breast cancer detection based on SVM and MLP BPN classifier. In: 1st International Conference on Automation, Control, Energy and Systems, ACES 2014, Hooghly, West Bengal, India, pp. 1–4 (2014)
45. Brockmann, D., Hufnagel, L., Geisel, T.: Data Mining and Knowledge Discovery Handbook. Springer, Boston (2006)
46. Jhajharia, S., Varshney, H.K., Verma, S., Kumar, R.: A neural network based breast cancer prognosis model with PCA processed features. In: 2016 International Conference on Advances in Computing, Communications and Informatics, ICACCI 2016, Jaipur, India, pp. 1896–1901 (2016)
47. Song, Q., Shepperd, M., Chen, X., Liu, J.: Can k-NN imputation improve the performance of C4.5 with small software project data sets? A comparative evaluation. J. Syst. Softw. 81, 2361–2370 (2008). https://doi.org/10.1016/j.jss.2008.05.008
48. Dua, D., Graff, C.: UCI Machine Learning Repository. http://archive.ics.uci.edu/ml
49. Chlioui, I., Idri, A., Abnane, I., de Gea, J.M.C., Fernández-Alemán, J.L.: Breast cancer classification with missing data imputation (2019)
50. Idri, A., Hosni, M., Abnane, I., Carrillo de Gea, J.M., Fernández Alemán, J.L.: Impact of parameter tuning on machine learning based breast cancer classification. In: World Conference on Information Systems and Technologies, Galicia, Spain, pp. 115–125 (2019)

51. García, V., Mollineda, R.A., Sánchez, J.S.: Index of balanced accuracy: a performance measure for skewed class distributions. In: Araujo, H., Mendonça, A.M., Pinho, A.J., Torres, M.I. (eds.) IbPRIA 2009. LNCS, vol. 5524, pp. 441–448. Springer, Heidelberg (2009). https://doi.org/10.1007/978-3-642-02172-5_57

52. Jonsdottir, T., Hvannberg, E.T., Sigurdsson, H., Sigurdsson, S.: The feasibility of constructing a Predictive Outcome Model for breast cancer using the tools of data mining. Expert Syst. Appl. **34**, 108–118 (2008). https://doi.org/10.1016/j.eswa.2006.08.029

53. Cohen, J.: A coefficient of agreement for nominal scales. Educ. Psychol. Meas. **20**, 37–46 (1960). https://doi.org/10.1177/001316446002000104

54. Cortes, C., Mohri, M.: AUC optimization vs. error rate minimization. In: Advances in Neural Information Processing Systems, pp. 313–320 (2004)

55. Jelihovschi, E., Faria, J.C., Allaman, I.B.: ScottKnott: a package for performing the Scott-Knott clustering algorithm in R. TEMA (São Carlos) **15**, 003 (2014). https://doi.org/10.5540/tema.2014.015.01.0003

56. Hosni, M., Idri, A., Abran, A., Nassif, A.B.: On the value of parameter tuning in heterogeneous ensembles effort estimation. Soft. Comput. **22**(18), 5977–6010 (2017). https://doi.org/10.1007/s00500-017-2945-4

57. Vuurpijl, L., Schomaker, L.: An overview and comparison of voting methods for pattern recognition. In: IEEE (ed.) Proceedings Eighth International Workshop on Frontiers in Handwriting Recognition, pp. 195–200 (2002)

58. García-Laencina, P.J., Sancho-Gómez, J.L., Figueiras-Vidal, A.R.: Pattern classification with missing data: a review. Neural Comput. Appl. **19**, 263–282 (2010). https://doi.org/10.1007/s00521-009-0295-6

59. Salzberg, S.L.: On comparing classifiers: pitfalls to avoid and a recommended approach. Data Min. Knowl. Discov. **1**, 317–328 (1997). https://doi.org/10.1023/A:1009752403260

60. Hosni, M., Abnane, I., Idri, A., de Gea, J.M.C., Alemán, J.L.F.: Reviewing ensemble classification methods in breast cancer. Comput. Methods Programs Biomed. **177**, 89–112 (2019). https://doi.org/10.1016/j.cmpb.2019.05.019

61. Abnane, I., Hosni, M., Idri, A., Abran, A.: Analogy software effort estimation using ensemble KNN imputation. In: IEEE (ed.) 2019 45th Euromicro Conference on Software Engineering and Advanced Applications (SEAA), Kallithea, Greece, pp. 228–235 (2019)

62. Twala, B.: An empirical comparison of techniques for handling incomplete data using decision trees. Appl. Artif. Intell. **23**, 373–405 (2009). https://doi.org/10.1080/08839510902872223

63. Abnane, I., Idri, A.: Improved analogy-based effort estimation with incomplete mixed data. In: Proceedings of the 2018 Federated Conference on Computer Science and Information Systems, FedCSIS 2018, Poznań, Poland, pp. 1015–1024 (2018)

Exploring Algorithmic Fairness in Deep Speaker Verification

Gianni Fenu, Hicham Lafhouli, and Mirko Marras$^{(\boxtimes)}$

{fenu,h.lafhouli,mirko.marras}@unica.it

Department of Mathematics and Computer Science, University of Cagliari,
Via Ospedale 72, 09124 Cagliari, Italy

Abstract. To allow individuals to complete voice-based tasks (e.g., send messages or make payments), modern automated systems are required to match the speaker's voice to a unique digital identity representation for verification. Despite the increasing accuracy achieved so far, it still remains under-explored how the decisions made by such systems may be influenced by the inherent characteristics of the individual under consideration. In this paper, we investigate how state-of-the-art speaker verification models are susceptible to unfairness towards legally-protected classes of individuals, characterized by a common sensitive attribute (i.e., gender, age, language). To this end, we first arranged a voice dataset, with the aim of including and identifying various demographic classes. Then, we conducted a performance analysis at different levels, from equal error rates to verification score distributions. Experiments show that individuals belonging to certain demographic groups systematically experience higher error rates, highlighting the need of fairer speaker recognition models and, by extension, of proper evaluation frameworks.

Keywords: Speaker recognition · Algorithmic fairness · Deep learning

1 Introduction

More and more systems and platforms are profiling individuals based on physical and behavioral characteristics. The resulting applicative scenarios range from accessing to smartphones to checking identities in online exams, from controlling autonomous vehicles to interact with robots, from assisting lawyers to delivering personalized services [6,7,23,28]. In these situations, where characterizing the current user is critical, one of the most prominent biometrics finding application across industries is based on human voices. The corresponding market is set to grow at a very high rate of 19.4% by 2021 [1]. Enabling voice commands into automated systems may support people to manage sensitive data (e.g., messages) or complete actions (e.g., shopping online) in a more natural way. However, handing over this responsibility to automated systems implies that they must be able to match the speaker's voice to a unique digital representation for identification or authentication, guaranteeing the security of the related applications [16].

© Springer Nature Switzerland AG 2020
O. Gervasi et al. (Eds.): ICCSA 2020, LNCS 12252, pp. 77–93, 2020.
https://doi.org/10.1007/978-3-030-58811-3_6

Speaker recognition has been actively studied over the years, and has recently undergone a revolution thanks to deep-learned acoustic representations. The latter outperformed hand-crafted features based on Gaussian mixture models [29], joint factor analysis [10], or i-Vectors [21]. Modern systems extract fine-grained acoustic feature representations from pre-trained deep neural networks. State-of-the-art solutions include x-Vector [31] and ResNet [25] models, among others. Despite high overall accuracy, speaker verifiers may be influenced by the inherent characteristics of the individuals[1], and suffer from demographic bias that causes certain populations to experience higher error rates than others. This deficiency can even put certain groups more at risk than others against impostors attacks [24]. While such a bias could be attributed to the lack of diverse training data, it nevertheless brings into question the unfairness of speaker recognition models and its mitigation, also going beyond gender (e.g., age, nationality).

In this paper, we seek to analyze speaker recognition models, using a fairness-aware perspective, in order to understand how demographic characteristics affect model performance. We conducted an offline evaluation of different speaker verification models based on *ThinResNet* [25], currently considered among the state-of-the-art models for speaker recognition in the wild. We compared the performance against algorithmic biases, by assessing: (i) how the equal error rates vary when considering models trained for different languages, (ii) how algorithmic bias affects verification score distributions and the related false acceptance and false rejection rates, and (iii) how biases related to language, gender, and age of a user propagate in the performance achieved by the considered speaker verification models. These biases involving legally-protected classes of people might have operational implications (e.g., a language bias might affect speaker verification adoption in certain geographical areas, while a gender bias might limit men or women in using this technology). Our contribution is threefold:

- We propose a general framework for inspecting algorithmic bias in machine-learning tasks tailored to the context of deep speaker verification[2].
- We perform a fairness-aware analysis of speaker verification based on a new benchmark setup, with identities coming from 16 demographic groups.
- We assess the impact of demographic attributes (i.e., language, gender, and age) in the feature representation of deep speaker verification models.

The rest of this paper is structured as follows. Section 2 depicts the related work in speaker verification and fairness-aware machine learning. Then, Sect. 3 defines the components of a general speaker verification systems, data, protocols, and models, while Sect. 4 provides a performance analysis, with results and discussion. Finally, Sect. 5 states final remarks and insights for future research.

2   Related Work

The research presented in this paper relies on literature from both the speech community and the machine learning community.

---

[1] In this paper, we will use the terms "individuals" and "users" interchangeably.

[2] Code, data, and models are available at https://mirkomarras.github.io/fair-voice/.

2.1 Deep Speaker Verification

Traditional speaker recognition systems based on hand-crafted solutions relied on *Gaussian Mixture Models* (GMMs) [29] that are trained on low dimensional feature vectors, *Joint Factor Analysis* (JFA) [10] methods that model speaker and channel subspaces separately, or *i-Vectors* [21] that attempt to embed both subspaces into a single compact, low-dimensional space.

Modern systems leverage deep-learned acoustic representations, i.e., embeddings, extracted from one of the last layers of a neural network trained for standard or one-shot speaker classification [20, 22]. The most prominent examples include *d-Vectors* [34], *c-Vectors* [8], *x-Vectors* [31], *VGGVox-Vectors* [26] and *ResNet-Vectors* [9]. Furthermore, deep learning frameworks with end-to-end loss functions have recently drawn attention to train speaker discriminative embeddings [19]. Their results proved that end-to-end systems with embeddings achieved better performance on short utterances, which are common in several contexts (e.g., robotics and proctoring), compared with traditional systems.

Speaker verification aims to confirm or refute the identify of a speaker based on an enrolled speech model. The user is asked to provide several samples of his speech, and the utterances are stored as a collection of acoustic feature vectors. Depending on the policy, the presented vocal input may be compared with all the vectors or with a single combined vector to make the verification decision.

2.2 Fairness in Machine Learning

Research on fairness in machine learning has been growing rapidly, as more and more automated decision systems are being deployed in highly sensitive areas that affect human lives and society [33]. The decisions have prediction problems at their core, and machine learning models have been used to maximize prediction performance in all these contexts. Generally, a decision is considered fair if it does not discriminate against people on the basis of their membership to a legally-protected group, such as sex or race [4]. For instance, the right to non-discrimination is embedded in the European normative framework, such as *Art. 21* of the *EU Charter of Fundamental Rights*, *Art. 14* of the *European Convention on Human Rights*, and *Artt. 18–25* of the *Treaty on the Functioning of the European Union* [15]. Ensuring that these models are less biased and adhere to the respective standards of fairness is difficult. There is overwhelming evidence showing that they can inherit or even perpetuate human biases in their decision, when trained on data that contain biased human decisions [27, 30].

In practice, there are several definitions of algorithmic fairness that try to achieve this goal, mainly classified in individual fairness and group fairness. In addition, two categories of statistical fairness definitions are based on predicted classifications and a combination of predicted classifications or risk scores and actual outcomes. The first definition, i.e., demographic parity, is based on predicted classifications [12]. Demographic parity is fulfilled if people from different protected groups has on average equal classifications. Another definition implies that, if the classifier gets it wrong, it should be equally wrong for all protected groups, since being more wrong for one group would result in harmful outcomes for this group compared to the other ones [17]. Hence, false negative and false positive rates should be equal across different protected groups.

Soft biometrics received increasing attention from the predictive perspective over the past decade [3,5]. Only relatively recently, bias- and fairness-oriented perspectives have emerged as an important research area, mainly focusing on face recognition systems [11]. For instance, the authors in [32] proposed a novel fair score normalization approach that is specifically designed to reduce the effect of bias in face recognition, and subsequently lead to a significant overall performance boost. Similarly, the authors in [2,14] showed the existence of demographic bias in the face representations returned by deep-learning-based face recognition models. These studies exposed concrete situations that may lead to a systematic discrimination of certain demographic groups. Moreover, other researchers analyzed the demographic bias in iris presentation attack detection algorithms, and showed that female users are significantly less protected by the attack detector in comparison to male users [13]. While bias and fairness in biometrics are receiving more and more attention, their impact on speaker verification is currently under-explored, motivating us to conduct this study.

3   Methodology

In this section, we formalize an experimental framework, including the speaker verification task, data, protocols, models, and their implementation details, underlying our research on bias and fairness in speaker verification.

3.1   Preliminaries

Let $A \subset \mathbb{R}^*$ denote the domain of audio waveforms with unknown length. We consider a traditional two-step processing pipeline with an intermediate visual acoustic representation $S \subset \mathbb{R}^{k \times *}$ (e.g., a spectrogram or a filterbank), and an explicit feature extraction step carried out by a speaker verification model θ, which produces fixed-length representations in $D \subset \mathbb{R}^e$. We denote the respective stages as $\mathcal{F} : A \to S$ and $\mathcal{D}_\theta : S \to D$. Given a *verification policy* p, a *decision threshold* τ, a speaker verification model θ, and N *enrolled utterances* per user, a speaker verification system can be defined as a function:

$$v_{p,\tau,\theta} : D \times D_u^N \to \{0,1\} \tag{1}$$

which compares an input feature vector d from an unknown user with a set of enrolled feature vectors $d_u^1, ..., d_u^N$ from user u to confirm or refute the speaker's identity (1 and 0, respectively). We mainly consider a verification policy, which rely on a similarity function $\mathcal{S} : D \times D \to [0,1]$, defined as follows:

$$v_{p,\tau,\theta} = any\left(\{\mathcal{S}(d, d_u^i) > \tau : i \in 1, ..., N\}\right) \tag{2}$$

where the identity of the current user is confirmed if any of the enrolled speech vectors has a similarity with the probe vector higher than the threshold. Our study considers $N = 1$ (one-shot setup), i.e., one vector as enrolment for a user.

3.2   Data

In this study, we leveraged speakers' data collected from Common Voice[3], one of the largest corpora including unconstrained speech of people, extracted from real-world scenarios, and featuring diverse acoustic environments. All waveforms were single-channel, 16-bit recordings sampled at 16 kHz. Such data was initially collected by the Mozilla Foundation in order to train an open source Speech-to-Text engine, and for this reason was not suitable for fairness analysis in speaker verification. However, to the best of our knowledge, except Common Voice, there is no other public dataset which comprises voice data coming from a range of languages and labelled with sensitive attributes, such as gender, accent, and age. Hence, after performing some modifications, which are detailed in the next subsection, we arranged Common Voice data to fit with our purposes.

The data we collected included individuals who declare sensitive attributes suitable for fairness analysis and span different languages (i.e., Chinese, French, German, English, and Kabyle). Even though Common Voice includes data from a wider range of languages, we selected the aforementioned languages since they are composed by enough utterances to conduct a statistically-relevant fairness analysis on verification models. Figure 1a shows the distribution of speakers across languages. Each speaker declared some sensitive attributes, i.e., his/her accent, age, and gender. Since these attributes are not declared by all the speakers, we filtered out the speakers who have not provided any sensitive attribute.

In numbers, we manipulated $1,046,078$ utterances coming from $12,057$ speakers. On average, each speaker contributed with around 80 utterances. Figure 1b plots the distribution of utterances per speaker. Furthermore, it can be observed that, while we did our best to keep the dataset balanced in terms of demographic groups, the dataset is still unbalanced with respect to the sensitive attributes (i.e., age and gender) and the corresponding demographic groups. The gender attribute[4] is labelled by the platform with *male* or *female*, while the age attribute is a categorical label identifying the age range, with a step of 10 years (e.g., teens, twenties). Figure 1c and d provide the individual distribution across gender and age. Please note that, while training and testing, we ensured that the representation of individuals with respect to their gender was balanced, and we kept comparable the individual distribution across ages for each gender-based group. This can represent a first pre-processing countermeasure against unfairness in speaker verification, as part of the contributions of this study.

3.3   Methodological Protocol

In this section, we detail the protocol we followed to perform the analysis presented in this paper, going from data collection to training and test procedures.

---

[3] https://voice.mozilla.org/it/datasets.

[4] While the gender is by no means a binary construct, to the best of our knowledge no dataset for speaker recognition with non-binary genders exists. What we are considering is a binary feature, as the current publicly available datasets offer.

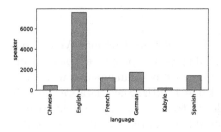

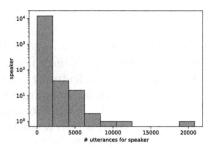

Speaker distribution across languages.   Utterance distribution across speakers.

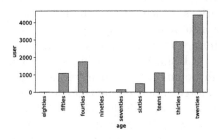

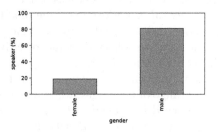

Age distribution across speakers.   Gender distribution across speakers.

Fig. 1. Data Statistics. Representative distributions of individuals and utterances along languages, ages, and genders in the data leveraged by this study.

Utterances Download. The first step served to download the utterances from the Common Voice website. More precisely, we downloaded data coming from Chinese, French, German, English and Kabyle languages. To this end, for each language, we selected the corresponding language label from the dropdown list of languages, and we clicked on the download button to start collecting data.

Data Cleaning and Conversion. The second step implied to remove, from the datasets we downloaded, all the speakers who do not declare any sensitive attribute. Moreover, since all the utterances were originally coded in *MP3*, we leveraged FFMpeg[5] to convert each utterance into a *WAV* file. This would allow us to easily manipulate utterances with existing Python audio libraries. During this conversion process, all the utterances identified as corrupted were removed.

Data Organization. Then, we organized our data in five different folders, each corresponding to a certain language among Chinese, French, German, English, and Kabyle. Then, within each language folder, we created a folder for each user speaking that language, and stored his/her utterances inside. User's folders were identified with the format *id00000*, *id00001*, and so on. To take note of the demographic groups, a file lists language, id, gender, and age for each user.

---

[5] https://www.ffmpeg.org/.

Based on gender, we grouped users in male users (G_m) and female users (G_f). In the context of this paper, we also created two age-based user's groups, balancing their representation in the dataset. The first one included users who are less than 40 years old (A_y). The remaining users were included in the second group (A_o).

Train-Test Split. This step was dedicated to identify users and corresponding utterances to be used for training and testing speaker verification models. The goal was to create training and testing sets balanced in terms of gender and age representation, so that we could then test whether the model emphasized unfairness across demographic groups, even though it received properly-balanced training data. To this end, for training a model for a certain language, we identified the less represented gender, and then we randomly selected users from the other gender in order to meet the following properties: (i) the number of male and female users in the sampled data is equal, and (ii) the number of individuals per age range for each gender is equal. Chinese and Kabyle were excluded from the experiments since they had no enough users for properly training and testing the corresponding speaker verification model. To ensure reproducibility, we stored the list of sampled users into a training file for each considered language.

Regarding the trial testing verification pairs, for each language, we considered 40 speakers, including 10 users in $G_f \cap A_y$, 10 users in $G_f \cap A_o$, 10 users in $G_m \cap A_y$, and 10 users in $G_m \cap A_o$. For each speaker, we randomly chose his/her 10 utterances and, for each sampled utterance, we compared it with 4 randomly-sampled utterances of the same speaker (i.e., to create genuine comparisons) and 4 randomly-sampled utterances from other speakers (i.e., to create impostor comparisons). For impostor comparisons, we selected the probe speaker, so that we were able to test impostor matches with an individual with the same gender and age range, same age range but different gender, same gender but different age range, and different gender and age range of the current speaker. To ensure reproducibility, for each language, we stored the trial pairs into a test file.

Model Train. In this step, we dealt with the procedure followed for training the considered speaker verification models. More precisely, we trained a different instance of the deep speaker verification architecture for each considered language (i.e., one for English, one for Spanish, one for French, and one for German). Given the training file created for a certain language in the previous step and the set of training parameters (e.g., batch size, learning rate, and so on), we first loaded the file paths corresponding to all the utterances belonging to the users listed in the training file, and we assigned a label to each utterance based on the speaker who produced it. Then, we set up a batch generator which returned (spectrogram, label) pairs to be fed into the model while training. The speaker verification architecture was instantiated, and compiled according to the training parameters passed to the script. Finally, the instantiated architecture was trained with data returned by the batch generator. Implementation details about the architecture and the training procedure are provided in the next sections[6].

Model Test. Finally, we followed a detailed procedure in order to test a pre-trained speaker verification model. More precisely, we first loaded the pre-trained model, and we removed the top layers used for aggregation and speaker classification while training, so that the top layer of the model was the fully-connected layer from which the speaker embeddings were extracted. Then, we loaded the list of trial verification pairs created in the previous steps for a given language. For each trial pair, we loaded the corresponding two audios, we computed their acoustic representations (e.g., spectrograms), and we fed them into the pre-trained model in order to extract the corresponding speaker embeddings. Then, we compared the two speaker embeddings by measuring their cosine similarity, and we saved such a value for each pair in a resulting CSV file. Given the sensitive attribute labels associated to users in the trial pairs, the related matching scores (i.e., cosine similarities), and the ground-truth labels (i.e., 1 if the two audios of a pair come from the same speaker, 0 otherwise), we computed the false acceptance rates and the false rejection rates for different demographic groups.

3.4   Experimented Speaker Verification Architecture

In this section, we describe the studied deep speaker verification architecture, namely Thin-ResNet, considered the state-of-the-art implementation for speaker verification in the wild [25]. This kind of architecture made it possible to leverage a convolutional-based architecture trainable end-to-end for the task of speaker recognition. The architecture expected to receive magnitude spectrograms extracted directly from raw audio waveforms, with no other pre-processing. Then, the deep neural network was used to extract utterance-level speaker embeddings. We treated spectrograms as single-channel images, and exploited the fact that deep networks can learn frequency-based filters, if needed for the speaker recognition task (e.g., filters can detect patterns in low-frequency regions).

Thin-ResNet is obtained from the ResNet-34 [18] architecture, known for high efficiency and good classification performance on image data. Residual-network (ResNet) architectures are based on standard multi-layer convolutional neural networks, but with added skip connections such that the layers add residuals to an identity mapping on the channel outputs. Original layers were modified to adapt to the spectrogram input, and we applied batch normalization before computing Rectified Linear Unit (ReLU) activations. Moreover, the fully-connected layer from the original ResNet-34 can be replaced by one of the following aggregation strategies, namely *NetVLAD*, *GhostVLAD*, or *Average Pooling Aggregation*.

---

[6] In the context of our work, where we are more interested in understanding algorithm characteristics beyond overall accuracy, the small further accuracy improvements that can probably be achieved through intensive hyper-parameter tuning would not substantially affect the main outcomes of our analyses.

For the latter, it was needed to replace the first fully-connected layer with two layers: a fully-connected layer of 9×1 (working on the frequency domain), and an aggregation layer (e.g., average pooling) working on $1 \times n$, where n depends on the length of the input audio (i.e., $n = 4$ for a 2-s segment). In this way, the network becomes invariant to temporal patterns but not to frequency patterns, that are the main source of information in speech, and made it possible to reduce network parameters.

3.5   Implementation Details

The different Thin-ResNet instances were implemented in Keras, with a Tensor-flow backend. Both models and training code are made publicly available. During training, we randomly sampled segments from each utterance. We used 512-point (Fast Fourier Transforms) FFTs giving us spectograms of size 257×200 (frequency x temporal). Each model was trained using a fixed-size spectrogram corresponding to a 2-s interval. If the utterance was marked as shorter, we padded it with zeros to reach the targeted 2-s length. All audio waveforms were converted to single-channel, 16-bit streams at a 16 kHz sampling rate for consistency. Spectrograms were then generated in a sliding window fashion using a hamming window of width 25 ms and step 10 ms. Each spectrogram was normalized by subtracting the mean and dividing by the standard deviation of all frequency components in a single time step. No voice activity detection or automatic silence removal was applied. Each model was trained for speaker classification using standard *Softmax*, and served with batches of size 32. We used the Adam optimizer, with an initial learning rate of 0.001, and decreased the learning rate by a factor of 10 after every 10 epochs, until 30 epochs. On top of each Thin-ResNet instance, we used a *GhostVLAD* aggregation layer [35], with 10 clusters plus 2 ghost clusters. For testing, we considered speaker embeddings of size 512, extracted from the second fully-connected layer *fc2* of each Thin-ResNet. The implementation was built on top of the work proposed in [25].

4   Results and Discussion

In this section, we empirically evaluate the considered speaker verification models with respect to their performance on different demographic groups. We aim to answer three key research questions:

1. Are equal error rates influenced by the individual demographic membership?
2. How does the demographic group impact on verification score distributions?
3. Do models fail uniformly across users or concentrate errors on specific users?

4.1   RQ1: Effect on Equal Error Rates

In this subsection, we run experiments on our data to assess whether the considered speaker verification models treated demographic groups differently. We assumed that there was a corresponding demographic group for any combination of language (i.e., English, Spanish, French, German), gender (i.e., G_m, G_f), and age (i.e., A_y, A_o). To this end, we trained four speaker verification models, one model per considered language. Then, we measured the Equal Error Rates (EERs) achieved on the trial pairs defined in Sect. 3.3 for different demographic groups, depending on language, gender, and age. Please note that the EER refers to the configuration at which the false acceptance rate and the false rejection rate are equal to each other. The lower the better.

Table 1 showed the EERs obtained for each language, grouping individuals per gender and age. It can be observed that the speaker verification architecture introduced significant differences in performance among demographic groups, even though each demographic group was equally represented in the training data. There was no clear pattern that emerged across languages, but we observed an undesired behaviour varying in scale and attributes across languages. To have a more detailed picture, the speaker verification model trained on English utterances generally performed better for females than males. More precisely, we measured a gap of 4.25%-points between performance on users in G_f (no matter the age) and on users in $G_m \cap A_y$. The gap was reduced up to 0.75%-points when we compared users in G_f with users in $G_m \cap A_o$. Considering the speaker verification model trained on Spanish utterances, it can be observed that no discrimination across gender is introduced when we considered individuals in A_o (i.e., 7.38% against 7.37%). Conversely, statistically-significant differences were introduced between users in $G_m \cap A_y$ and in $G_f \cap A_y$, with a gap of 3.75%-point in favor of the first group. This tendency of the model to discriminate individuals in A_y across genders emerged on both English and Spanish models at different extent. Furthermore, the speaker verification model trained on French utterances showed slightly different performance. Overall, this model tended to perform better for males than females, and there was a clear intra-gender gap of around 0.80%-points for both males and females. The French speaker verification model confirmed also that there was a higher difference among individuals in A_y across genders (i.e., 3.75%-points), while the difference for individuals in A_o across gender was smaller (i.e., 1.75%-points). Finally, the speaker verification

Table 1. EER per demographic group. For each language, we conducted a statistical analysis on verification scores based on a Paired Student's t-test, at 5% level. Statistically-significant differences were detected in all cases, except for ($G_f \cap A_y$ and $G_f \cap A_o$) in English and ($G_f \cap A_o$ and $G_m \cap A_o$) in Spanish.

Gender group	Age group	Language			
		English	Spanish	French	German
G_f	A_y	2.00	5.50	8.38	10.25
G_f	A_o	2.00	7.38	7.13	4.75
G_m	A_y	6.25	1.75	4.63	7.50
G_m	A_o	2.75	7.37	5.38	2.00

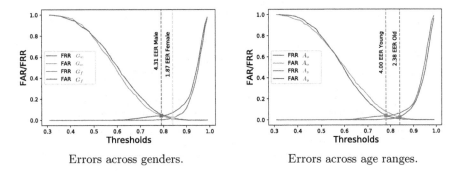

Errors across genders.   Errors across age ranges.

Fig. 2. Error Statistics. False Acceptance Rates (FARs) and False Rejection Rates (FRRs) across gender- and age-based demographics groups. (Color figure online)

model trained on German utterances exhibited more noisy patterns across genders and ages. Fixed the age, the model performed better for males than females, introducing a difference of around 2.75%-points across groups. When we fixed the gender, the best performance were measured for individuals in $G_f \cap A_o$ and in $G_m \cap A_o$.

In the context of our study, it can be concluded that the considered models tended to perform better for male individuals than female individuals, when the age range was the same. Exception was made for the English model. Similarly, when the gender was the same, we observed a tendency of the speaker verification model to foster better performance for individuals in A_o than individuals in A_y.

4.2   RQ2: Influence on Verification Score Distributions

We next compare the considered speaker verification models trained on the four different languages to assess how they perform in terms of false acceptance rates and false rejection rates in comparison to each other. The goal here is to understand whether the speaker verification models introduced differences among demographic groups in terms of security (i.e., depending on false accepts) or usability (i.e., depending on false rejections). For conciseness, we report results on the English model, but the results on other languages showed similar patterns.

Figure 2 depicts the false acceptance rates and false rejection rates at various thresholds for individuals in G_m and G_f (left) and individuals in A_y and A_o (right)[7]. From Fig. 2a, it can be observed a difference on false accepts and false rejections across genders. More precisely, individuals in G_f (red line) tended to experience higher false accepts than individuals in G_m (orange line). Conversely, individuals in G_m (blue line) were more exposed to false rejects than individuals in G_f (green line). It follows that a common setup that implies a unique verification threshold across users would result in less security for female users and less usability for male users. It should be noted also that it would not

---

[7] Please note that the figures in this manuscript are best seen in color.

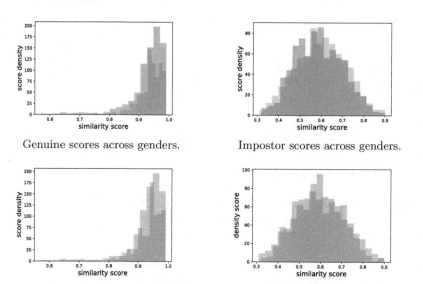

Genuine scores across genders.   Impostor scores across genders.

Genuine scores across age ranges.   Impostor scores across age ranges.

Fig. 3. Matching Score Distributions. Matching score distributions for genuine and impostor pairs between G_m (blue) and G_f (pink) individuals on the top, and between A_y (grey) and A_o (green) individuals on the bottom. (Color figure online)

be acceptable to setup different thresholds based on the gender due to privacy constraints. Moreover, it would not be scalable, since an increasing number of thresholds would be needed as more and more demographic groups are taken into account. Considering demographic groups based on the age range (Fig. 2b), similar observations could be made for individuals in A_y and A_o. Surprisingly, individuals in A_o (orange line) suffered from higher false accepts than individuals in A_y (red line). To the same extent, individuals in A_y (green line) got more false rejects than individuals in A_o (blue line). This resulted in less security for individuals in A_o and less usability for individuals in A_y.

To have a more detailed picture, we resorted our analysis to the distribution of matching scores for both genuine and impostor trial pairs. In Fig. 3, we reported such distributions along gender- and age-based demographic groups. Figure 3a highlighted that genuine matching scores over male individuals tended to fall into higher similarity values than those for female individuals. Conversely, Fig. 3b showed a more equal distribution of impostor matching scores along genders. It can be just observed that female individuals tended to have higher impostor matching scores, leading to more false accepts (i.e., less security). Similar patterns appeared in Fig. 3c and d across age ranges. Our analysis thus uncovered the need of creating speaker verification models that equally distribute matching scores, so that the same distribution pattern is measured on different demographic groups. We argue that this point is crucial to achieve higher fairness, since the verification threshold is unique among groups.

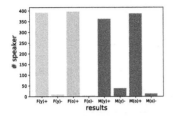 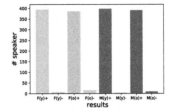

Genuine matching performance.   Impostor matching performance.

Fig. 4. Verification Errors. The verification performance in terms correct and incorrect matches across gender- and age-based demographic groups.

To provide more evidence on the above point, we considered a unique verification threshold computed on the user population as a whole (i.e., this practice is common on most of the biometric studies), and we counted in Fig. 4 the number of genuine and impostor matches that were correctly or incorrectly classified for each demographic group. Each demographic group result was identified by a gender label (F: G_f, M: G_m), an age-range label (y: A_y, o: A_o), and a classification result (+:correct, −:incorrect). Hence, for instance, the label "$F(y)+$" identified the number of matches correctly classified for individuals in $G_f \cap A_y$. From Fig. 4a, it can be observed the number of genuine matches correctly (true accepts) and incorrectly (false rejects) classified. Overall, there is a clear trend showing less rejection errors for female individuals (i.e., $F(y)-$ and $F(o)-$) than male individuals (i.e., $M(y)-$ and $M(o)-$). Regarding age ranges, individuals in A_y (i.e., $F(y)-$ and $M(y)-$) experienced more rejection errors than individuals in A_o (i.e., $M(o)-$ and $F(o)-$). Similar patterns were observed when we considered impostor matching performance. Figure 4b reported the number of impostor matches correctly (true reject) and incorrectly (false accepts) classified. These results confirmed that individuals in G_f and in A_o suffer from more false accepts.

Overall, it can be concluded that both genuine and impostor verification scores were strongly influenced by the demographic group, and the models tended to give less security or less usability to certain demographic groups.

4.3   RQ3: Errors per User Concentration

Finally, we investigated how speaker verification models performed on each of the considered users. To this end, we measured the total number of false accepts and false rejects for each user, and we reported the number of errors per user into plots to assess whether the speaker verification models made errors uniformly across users or concentrated errors to specific users and/or demographic groups.

Figure 5 showed the number of verification errors per user, with users sorted by decreasing number of errors. Considering the gender-based membership, Fig. 5a and b highlighted the fact that the errors were well-distributed within male users. Exception was made for a male user who resulted in 26 verification errors.

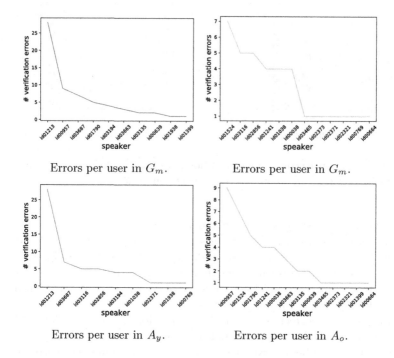

Errors per user in G_m.   Errors per user in G_m.

Errors per user in A_y.   Errors per user in A_o.

Fig. 5. Errors per User. Representative distribution of errors per user made by the speaker verification model, grouped by demographic group membership.

We further checked this result, and we found out that such a user recorded his audios in very challenging conditions, making it difficult the verification process, independently from the demographic group. This observation points to the fact that speaker verification is influenced by various co-variants (e.g.., spoken words, utterance length, noise) that, by extension, may complicate isolating the differences across demographic groups that derive from the user's membership to that group. Conversely, around half of the female users collected most of the errors among users from the same gender. Similar patterns were also observed when we considered the age-based membership in Fig. 5c and d. Overall, the number of errors per user was satisfactory, with less than 10% of errors per user.

In the context of our study, models tended to make errors uniformly across users in case of G_m and A_y. However, errors were more frequent for a subset of individuals in $G_f \cap A_y$, uncovering the need of fine-grained individual analysis.

5   Conclusions and Future Work

In this paper, we proposed a framework for analyzing deep speaker verification models in terms of their predictive accuracy, false positive rate, and false negative rate across demographic groups. Through a series of experiments, we showed that, despite a balanced representation of the demographic groups in the underlying training data, the models can be quite different in terms of performance based on the demographic group, exhibiting undesired consequences. Our work provides a better understanding on how generalizable speaker verification models are to diverse demographic groups (i.e., language, gender, age), and fosters more fairness-oriented evaluations in speaker verification research.

In next steps, we plan to investigate bias and fairness on other models, beyond *ThinResNet*, and trace these biases back to some particular patterns of training data and acoustic representations. Moreover, we will consider other types of bias, and we will design proper countermeasures to the biases we uncovered.

References

1. Global voice recognition market 2017–2021 (2019). https://www.reportlinker.com/p04338419/Global-Voice-Recognition-Biometrics-Market.html. Accessed 30 Sept 2019
2. Alasadi, J., Al Hilli, A., Singh, V.K.: Toward fairness in face matching algorithms. In: Proceedings of the 1st International Workshop on Fairness, Accountability, and Transparency in MultiMedia, pp. 19–25 (2019)
3. Anzalone, L., Barra, P., Barra, S., Narducci, F., Nappi, M.: Transfer learning for facial attributes prediction and clustering. In: Wang, G., El Saddik, A., Lai, X., Martinez Perez, G., Choo, K.-K.R. (eds.) iSCI 2019. CCIS, vol. 1122, pp. 105–117. Springer, Singapore (2019). https://doi.org/10.1007/978-981-15-1301-5_9
4. Barocas, S., Hardt, M., Narayanan, A.: Fairness in machine learning. In: NIPS (2017)
5. Barra, P., Bisogni, C., Nappi, M., Freire-Obregón, D., Castrillón-Santana, M.: Gender classification on 2D human skeleton. In: 2019 3rd International Conference on Bio-engineering for Smart Technologies (BioSMART), pp. 1–4. IEEE (2019)
6. Boratto, L., Carta, S.: Modeling the preferences of a group of users detected by clustering: a group recommendation case-study. In: 4th International Conference on Web Intelligence, Mining and Semantics, WIMS, pp. 16:1–16:7. ACM (2014)
7. Boratto, L., Manca, M., Lugano, G., Gogola, M.: Characterizing user behavior in journey planning. Computing **102**(5), 1245–1258 (2020). https://doi.org/10.1007/s00607-019-00775-8
8. Chen, Y.h., Lopez-Moreno, I., Sainath, T.N., Visontai, M., Alvarez, R., Parada, C.: Locally-connected and convolutional neural networks for small footprint speaker recognition. In: Proceedings Interspeech 2015, pp. 1136–1140 (2015)
9. Chung, J.S., Nagrani, A., Zisserman, A.: Voxceleb2: deep speaker recognition. In: Proceedings Interspeech 2018, pp. 1086–1090 (2018)
10. Dehak, N., Kenny, P.J., Dehak, R., Dumouchel, P., Ouellet, P.: Front-end factor analysis for speaker verification. IEEE Trans. Audio Speech Lang. Process. **19**(4), 788–798 (2011)
11. Drozdowski, P., Rathgeb, C., Dantcheva, A., Damer, N., Busch, C.: Demographic bias in biometrics: a survey on an emerging challenge. arXiv:2003.02488 (2020)
12. Dwork, C., Hardt, M., Pitassi, T., Reingold, O., Zemel, R.: Fairness through awareness. In: Innovations in Theoretical Computer Science Conference, pp. 214–226 (2012)
13. Fang, M., Damer, N., Kirchbuchner, F., Kuijper, A.: Demographic bias in presentation attack detection of iris recognition systems. arXiv:2003.03151 (2020)

14. Garcia, R.V., Wandzik, L., Grabner, L., Krueger, J.: The harms of demographic bias in deep face recognition research. In: 2019 International Conference on Biometrics (ICB), pp. 1–6. IEEE (2019)
15. Goodman, B., Flaxman, S.: European union regulations on algorithmic decision-making and a "right to explanation". AI Mag. **38**(3), 50–57 (2017)
16. Hansen, J.H., Hasan, T.: Speaker recognition by machines and humans: a tutorial review. IEEE Signal Process. Mag. **32**(6), 74–99 (2015)
17. Hardt, M., Price, E., Srebro, N.: Equality of opportunity in supervised learning. In: Advances in neural information processing systems, pp. 3315–3323 (2016)
18. He, K., Zhang, X., Ren, S., Sun, J.: Deep residual learning for image recognition. In: IEEE Conference on Computer Vision and Pattern Recognition, pp. 770–778 (2016)
19. Heigold, G., Moreno, I., Bengio, S., Shazeer, N.: End-to-end text-dependent speaker verification. In: 2016 IEEE International Conference on Acoustics, Speech and Signal Processing (ICASSP), pp. 5115–5119. IEEE (2016)
20. Hershey, S., et al.: CNN architectures for large-scale audio classification. In: 2017 IEEE International Conference on Acoustics, Speech and Signal Processing (ICASSP), pp. 131–135. IEEE (2017)
21. Kanagasundaram, A., Vogt, R., Dean, D.B., Sridharan, S., Mason, M.W.: I-vector based speaker recognition on short utterances. In: Proceedings Interspeech 2011, pp. 2341–2344 (2011)
22. Lukic, Y., Vogt, C., Dürr, O., Stadelmann, T.: Speaker identification and clustering using convolutional neural networks. In: 2016 IEEE 26th International Workshop on Machine Learning for Signal Processing (MLSP), pp. 1–6. IEEE (2016)
23. Mahfouz, A., Mahmoud, T.M., Eldin, A.S.: A survey on behavioral biometric authentication on smartphones. J. Inform. Secur. Appl. **37**, 28–37 (2017)
24. Marras, M., Korus, P., Memon, N., Fenu, G.: Adversarial optimization for dictionary attacks on speaker verification. In: Proceedings Interspeech 2019, pp. 2913–2917 (2019)
25. Nagrani, A., Chung, J.S., Xie, W., Zisserman, A.: VoxCeleb: large-scale speaker verification in the wild. Comput. Speech Lang. **60**, 101027 (2020)
26. Nagrani, A., Chung, J.S., Zisserman, A.: VoxCeleb: a large-scale speaker identification dataset. In: Proceedings Interspeech 2017, pp. 2616–2620 (2017)
27. Ramos, G., Boratto, L.: Reputation (in)dependence in ranking systems: demographics influence over output disparities. CoRR abs/2005.12371 (2020)
28. Reforgiato Recupero, D., Dessì, D., Concas, E.: A flexible and scalable architecture for human-robot interaction. In: Chatzigiannakis, I., De Ruyter, B., Mavrommati, I. (eds.) AmI 2019. LNCS, vol. 11912, pp. 311–317. Springer, Cham (2019). https://doi.org/10.1007/978-3-030-34255-5_21
29. Reynolds, D.A., Quatieri, T.F., Dunn, R.B.: Speaker verification using adapted Gaussian mixture models. Digit. Signal Process **10**(1–3), 19–41 (2000)
30. Selbst, A.D.: Disparate impact in big data policing. Ga. L. Rev. **52**, 109 (2017)
31. Snyder, D., Garcia-Romero, D., Sell, G., Povey, D., Khudanpur, S.: X-vectors: robust DNN embeddings for speaker recognition. In: IEEE International Conference on Acoustics, Speech and Signal Processing, pp. 5329–5333. IEEE (2018)
32. Terhörst, P., Kolf, J.N., Damer, N., Kirchbuchner, F., Kuijper, A.: Post-comparison mitigation of demographic bias in face recognition using fair score normalization. arXiv preprint arXiv:2002.03592 (2020)
33. Tolan, S.: Fair and unbiased algorithmic decision making: current state and future challenges. arXiv preprint arXiv:1901.04730 (2019)

34. Variani, E., Lei, X., McDermott, E., Moreno, I.L., Gonzalez-Dominguez, J.: Deep neural networks for small footprint text-dependent speaker verification. In: International Conference on Acoustics, Speech and Signal Processing, pp. 4052–4056. IEEE (2014)

35. Zhong, Y., Arandjelović, R., Zisserman, A.: GhostVLAD for set-based face recognition. In: Jawahar, C.V., Li, H., Mori, G., Schindler, K. (eds.) ACCV 2018. LNCS, vol. 11362, pp. 35–50. Springer, Cham (2019). https://doi.org/10.1007/978-3-030-20890-5_3

DECiSION: Data-drivEn Customer Service InnovatiON

Dario Esposito[1]([⊠]), Marco Polignano[2], Pierpaolo Basile[2],
Marco de Gemmis[2], Davide Primiceri[2], Stefano Lisi[1],
Mauro Casaburi[3], Giorgio Basile[3], Matteo Mennitti[4],
Valentina Carella[4], and Vito Manzari[4]

[1] Polytechnic University of Bari, Bari, Italy
dario.esposito@poliba.it
[2] University of Bari Aldo Moro, Bari, Italy
[3] Planetek Italia, Bari, Italy
[4] Sud Sistemi, Bari, Italy

Abstract. The paper presents DECiSION, an innovative framework in the field of Information Seeking Support Systems, able to retrieve all the data involved in a decision-making process, and to process, categorize and make them available in a useful form for the ultimate purpose of the user request. The platform is equipped with natural language understanding capabilities, allowing the interpretation of user requests and the identification of information sources from which to independently retrieve the information needed for the sensemaking task. The project foresees the implementation of a chatbot, which acts as a virtual assistant, and a conversational recommender system, able to dialogue with the user to discover their preferences and orient their answers in a personalized way. The goal is therefore to create an intelligent system to answer autonomously and comprehensively questions posed in natural language about a specific reference domain, to support the decision-making process. The paper describes the general architecture of the framework and then focuses on the key component that automatically translate the natural language user query into a machine-readable query for the service repository.

Keywords: Information Seeking Support Systems · Natural language processing · Information Filtering

1 Introduction

Decision-making involves identifying the various possibilities of alternative actions and choosing one or more of these through an evaluation process which should be sensible, rational and based on evidence. Thus, decision-making is a complex process that requires the integration of different information generated by different sources which must be interpreted to build useful knowledge. Moreover, in complex decision-making situations, problems are not well structured or clearly defined and these conditions can produce uncertainty. In particular, one key issue is to retrieve the information needed to solve the decision problem.

O. Gervasi et al. (Eds.): ICCSA 2020, LNCS 12252, pp. 94–103, 2020.
https://doi.org/10.1007/978-3-030-58811-3_7

However, there are information seeking scenarios that cannot be solved merely through a straightforward matching of queries and documents When information is sought for learning, decision making and other complex mental activities, retrieval is necessary but not sufficient. According to Pirolli, many information search tasks are part of a broader class of tasks called sensemaking [1]. Such tasks involve finding information from large document collections, categorizing and understanding that information, and producing some product, such as an actionable decision. Examples of such tasks include understanding a health problem in order to make a medical decision or deciding which laptop to buy. Information seeking support systems (ISSSs) provide search solutions that empower users to go beyond single-session lookup tasks and aim at serving the more complex requirement: "Tell me what I don't know that I need to know". They provide services that aid people in managing and analyzing sets of retrieved information [2].

The DECiSION project therefore aims to create a framework to build Decision Support Systems that can be used through an artificial dialogue system able to query heterogeneous data sources and to provide relevant and complete answers to the user's needs. These responses are customized according to user interaction habits. The DECiSION project was proposed to overcome the lack of tools for accessing structured and unstructured data services and archives that can provide an effective support to decision-making processes.

The project developed knowledge, technologies, algorithms and interfaces. These were organized in a software technology to query, interact and consult heterogeneous data sources, obtaining information and suggestions compatible with the user-citizen-organization profile that required information. Starting from the natural language requests that users make, the process of interpretation of the expressed need and the process of generating multi-format answers are activated. For example, the system is able to cross several databases in order to provide technical users with an answer which combines natural language and graphic visualization tools, allowing them to find answers to requests such as: "Which pipelines are at risk according to the weather conditions and the stability of the territory? Which of these have a greater impact on users in the event of an accident?". A distinctive feature of DECiSION is the adoption of strategies that prioritize responses favoring sustainable choices in the user's decision-making process, taking into account the time and space constraints which the user faces.

The system is composed of various modules that allow the semantic analysis of the request. Then, through the analysis of heterogeneous data sources, the system synthesizes the answers in dynamic, personalized and contextualized formats. These answers contain information "enriched" by new knowledge, generated through intelligent automatic reasoning processes. In Sect. 2, we review some related work in the area of Information Filtering, Sect. 3 describes the framework, while in Sect. 4 we focus on the key feature of DECiSION, the capability of understanding the user request and turning it into queries for system knowledge base. Section 5 describe some preliminary experiments with the natural language component of the framework, before concluding the paper with some final comments.

2   Motivations and Related Research

When a user faces a decision, he has to evaluate many options, for example a set of items from an Internet store. Often he hasn't all the necessary knowledge to choose the best option. A support system is necessary for evaluating all the options available and for helping the user to choose the best option, by taking into account preferences and behaviors. Information Filtering are appropriate for this task, because they are able to select a set of items considering different relevant personalized aspects for every single user, using the information stored usually in a user profile. Modern filtering systems, called recommender systems, can adopt different strategies for selecting relevant items for the user such as collaborative, content-based, knowledge based, context-aware techniques [3]. In particular, content-based approached exploits item descriptions in order to infer general properties of preferred that can be used to support the user in future choosing tasks. For instance, a movie recommender could learn user preferences from the content of items the user has liked in the past in order to provide suggestions based on preferred movie genres, actors or directors. Research in this area has many practical applications. Here we discuss emerging applications or new trends in traditional domains, usually aiming at improving commercial systems.

IP television (IPTV) services provide users with multimedia content (movies, news programs, documentaries, TV series) via broadband Internet networks. Bambini in a remarkable paper describes the adoption of both content and collaborative recommendation methods in the production environment of the one of the largest European IPTV providers [4]. News recommendation is a domain where content-based methods find their natural application. MESH (Multimedia sEmantic Syndication for enHanced news Services) is a research project that designed a framework for intelligent creation and delivery of semantically-enhanced multimedia news information [5]. Another interesting domain of application is recommendation of financial investment strategies, a complex and knowledge-intensive task where filtering techniques are recently used [6]. In the DECiSION project, we try to design a general framework that can be used in different domains. The proposed framework integrated several features:

1. Interpretation of the needs expressed by the user request;
2. Searching into heterogeneous sources of both structured and unstructured data;
3. Providing personalized answers based on the user profile and contextual information.

In this paper we focus on item 1. and 2., by describing the solutions adopted in the framework for the comprehension of the user need and automated query of the service catalog of the system.

3   The DECiSION Framework

The architecture of the framework is described in Fig. 1, which shows the logical-functional model, further developed and detailed through the different project research activities. The process which accounts for the system's ability to interpret data and requests is managed in block "a". It involves the processing of heterogeneous data sources in order to extract the content necessary for the semantic interpretation of the data. The key idea here is to include in a knowledge base all the services which could provide data useful for the decision-making task. All these services are enriched by the indexing component (block "b") which is a layer that operates "normalization" and "enrichment" of annotations built to provide the semantic interpretation.

Actually blocks "a" and "b" are builds the semantically-annotated catalog service which will be the target of the query component (block "c").

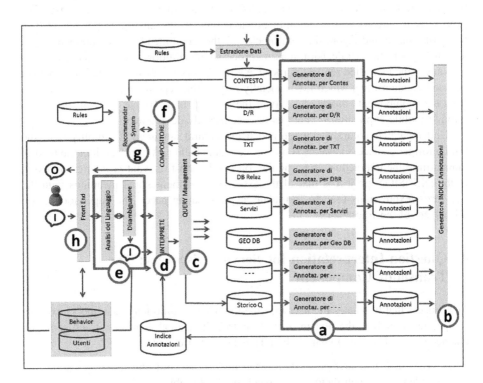

Fig. 1. DECiSION logical-functional architecture

For the implementation of these blocks, a specific module has been developed, which allows to store the OWL-S annotations in a graph database Neo4j (www.neo4j. com).

For instance, if a service that provides demographic data about customers must be included in DECiSION, it is described by OWL-S annotations, then indexed and included in Neo4j. In the same way, if traffic statistics or any statistics about other phenomena that fall within the scope of the decision must be included in the system, some services that provide this kind of data must be added to the knowledge base. In other works, blocks "a" and "b" are wrappers that connect the framework with data sources. The problem is how to understand, from the user query, which data sources contain the data needed to solve the decision task.

Components "c", "d" and "e" manage this processes, which is devoted to the interpretation of the user request (i.e. understanding the intent of the user query) and its automated translation into queries on the available data sources. In this paper, we refer to this process as "service discovery", which will be described in more detail in the next section.

The aim of the language analysis, disambiguation and interpretation processes is to extract the information required. Once this has been done, the query management module automatically builds queries to obtain useful information for the composition of the answer. Block "f" collects the results of queries to provide the response. The process is integrated with a recommendation. Indeed, the answer is personalized in terms of content and layout through block "g", the recommendation component [7]. It aims to support the user decision-making process with additional suggestions which are relevant to the identified request purpose, e.g. more services available. This component is based on algorithms which favor socially responsible recommendations. Finally, the front-end component, block "h", gives the answer in a simple and effective way through mobile applications, chatbots or user-friendly device interfaces.

Understanding natural language and using natural language to simplify dialogue with information access systems is one of the main challenges of research in the field of human-machine interaction. In particular, one of the most relevant problems addressed in the DECiSION project is that of the association of themes and meanings with the keywords /expressions used to formulate an information need. The paper focuses on this aspect of the framework.

4 Question Interpretation for Service Discovery: The Translator Component

The process that translates the user information need (natural language query) exploits a pipeline to analyze the text in order to extract its lexical, syntactical and semantic characteristics. The component, called Translator, carries out:

- A syntactical text analysis, where each node is a word and the edges show the dependency between them, e.g. subject, predicate, object;
- A disambiguation of the text, assigning correct meaning to each word;
- The recognition within the text of entities with a proper noun (people, places, organizations and so on);
- An entity annotation, exploiting of their relations and linking it to a concept contained in the database.

First, the user query (e.g. "find customers in London that might leave our company next year") is processed by basic NLP operations (tokenization, stopword elimination, named entity recognition). Semantic interpretation of word is performed by word embeddings, a set of modeling techniques in which words of a vocabulary are mapped into vectors of real numbers. This makes it possible to store both semantic and syntactical information of words [8] starting from a non-annotated corpus and building a vector space in which word vectors are closer if words occur in the same linguistic contexts, that is, if they are recognized as semantically more similar.

To learn the embedding the most used techniques are Word2Vec [9] and GloVe [10]. We don't need to train our model, as there are many models already trained on different corpus. We used Italian word embeddings trained on Wikipedia (http://hlt.isti.cnr.it/wordembeddings), and for English the embeddings are obtained with GloVe, trained on Wikipedia as well (nlp.stanford.edu/projects/glove). Then, we need to combine word embeddings in order to obtain a vector that identifies an entire sentence. This task is known as sentence embedding. Several methods are available for obtaining the vector of a sentence, ranging from simple additional composition of the word vectors to sophisticated architectures such as convolutional neural networks and recurrent neural networks.

Here the one proposed by Arora et al. is used, as it provides better performance than baselines on various textual similarity tasks and can even overcome other sophisticated methods [11]. This method represents the sentence by a weighted average of the word vectors. Once all the NLP steps are applied, we can move on the definition of the service discovery process.

All descriptions of services and output parameters are processed in the same way as the user request. From the descriptions of the output parameters it is possible understand what a service precisely provides: these textual descriptions are useful because they can be matched against what the user expects to get. The identification of a service takes place through three phases:

1. Computation of semantic similarity between request and service description;
2. Computation of semantic similarity between request and descriptions of the output parameters of a service;
3. Increase of the similarity score based on the number of recognized input parameters.

Let's consider the following query: "find places to enjoy in London"; suppose we have two services in the target repository (Table 1).

Table 1. Service descriptions

Service	Description
Service (s1)	searchTourism
Description	Search attractions to have fun near a specified place
Output description	Name and address of the attraction
Input	City (LOCATION), country (COUNTRY_CODE)
Service (s2)	searchBank
Description	Search a bank near a specified location
Output description	Name and address of the bank
Input	City (LOCATION), country (COUNTRY_CODE)

The first step applied is the computation of cosine similarity between sentence embeddings of service description and query.

After the first calculation we move on the descriptions of the output parameters of each service. We may have a service that meets the request, but that returns many different outputs. In the above example, both services return name and address of a place, but the term "attraction" is more similar to "enjoy" than the term "bank". As for the input parameters, we simply match the number and type of parameters are taken into account.

In the above example, both services have same similarity with the user request. In fact, only one parameter (type: location) is found in the user request and matched against parameter descriptions of the services. From these services, we expect the module to return search Tourism as a suitable service to satisfy the request.

5   Preliminary Experiments

In this section, we evaluate the effectiveness of the service discovery component compared with a simple keyword-based approach. An extended experiment will be performed that will involve all the DECiSION components.

We build a dataset of 64 user queries, 32 in English, 32 in Italian, in order to assess the effectiveness of the component in different languages. For each user query, a set of relevant services that we expect to be identified was defined. Table 2 shows some examples of entries in the dataset.

Table 2.   User request and relevant services

Request	Relevant services
Tell me current weather in Florence	GetWeather, GetWeatherByZip, GetWeatherLatLng
Find a station in Milan	SearchStation
What should I visit in London	SearchTourism

As a baseline, we consider the simple keyword search approach implemented by Lucene (lucene.apache.org). We used Lucene to index service descriptions in the dataset. The result of a search on a Lucene index is a list of documents, previously indexed, that contain one or more words constituting the search query.

As for the metrics, we used two common metrics in the area of Information Retrieval: Mean Average Precision (MAP) and Mean Reciprocal Rank (MRR). To understand how to calculate MAP we first define Precision, P@k and Average Precision. Precision is the fraction of the documents retrieved that are relevant to the user's information need:

$$Precision = \frac{|\{relevant\ documents\} \cap \{retrieved\ documents\}|}{|\{retrieved\ documents\}|}$$

P@k is Precision that takes into account only the top-k results returned by the system.

Average Precision is the average of P@k, defined as follows:

$$AveP = \frac{\sum_{k=1}^{n} P@k \cdot rel(k)}{|num\ relevant\ documents|}$$

where rel(k) = 1 if the document k is relevant, 0 otherwise.

MAP is the Average Precision across multiple queries:

$$MAP = \frac{\sum_{k=1}^{|Q|} AveP_{Qk}}{|Q|}$$

where Ave P_{Qk} is the average precision of query Q_k.

An example of MAP computation on two queries follows.

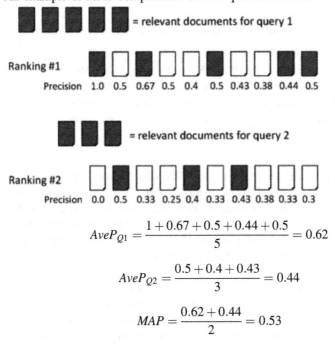

$$AveP_{Q1} = \frac{1 + 0.67 + 0.5 + 0.44 + 0.5}{5} = 0.62$$

$$AveP_{Q2} = \frac{0.5 + 0.4 + 0.43}{3} = 0.44$$

$$MAP = \frac{0.62 + 0.44}{2} = 0.53$$

MRR metric is based on the idea that the system gets a score for each query, which is the reciprocal of the position (in the ranked list of results) of the service correctly returned:

$$MRR = \frac{\sum_{i=1}^{N} \frac{1}{pi}}{N}$$

For instance, suppose we have 3 queries in the evaluation set; suppose that the correct answer s returned in position #3 for the first query, position #2 for the second query and position #1 for the third query. Then

query 1: ⬛⬛⬜⬛⬛ $pi = 3$
query 2: ⬛⬜⬛⬛⬛ $pi = 2$
query 3: ⬜⬛⬛⬛⬛ $pi = 1$

$$MRR = \frac{\frac{1}{3} + \frac{1}{2} + 1}{3} = 0.61$$

We compare the results of the Translator with those of Lucene, as well as with a those obtained by a different version of the Translator which does not consider input / output parameters when computing query-service similarity. Results are reported in the following Table 3:

Table 3. Comparison of results.

	English		Italian		Overall	
	MAP	MRR	MAP	MRR	MAP	MRR
Lucene	0.61	0.64	0.54	0.57	0.58	0.61
Translator (no input)	0.79	0.81	0.85	0.86	0.82	0.84
Translator	0.89	0.91	0.86	0.88	0.88	0.90

From the results, we can see that the reduced version of the Translator, although working on the same data as Lucene (only textual description of the services), achieves much better performances. The reason for the improved performance is the adoption of a semantic-based approach that allows us to compute a more precise similarity between sentences than simple keyword-based search. We can see also that better results are obtained on English. This is probably due to the better accuracy of the English NLP pipeline.

The main outcome of the evaluation is that the full version of the Translator achieves a MAP value of 0.88, which shows that it is able to identify in a very good way most relevant services. Also, MRR value is high, which shows that the system is able to identify in most cases in the first position of the ranking a service able to satisfy the request. This aspect is very interesting for the overall performance of the framework, because it is more likely that the services retrieved first will be invoked.

6   Conclusions and Outlook

This paper describes the DECiSION framework, an innovative information-seeking system capable of supporting users in a decision-making process, integrating different heterogeneous data sources. The framework is able to interact with the user by using natural language.

The paper focused on the Natural Language component of the platform, the Translator, which is the key to understand the user information need and to invoke the services, available in the catalog of platform, which can support the decision task. Although the project is still an ongoing work, the preliminary evaluation shows promising results. As a future work, we will integrate in the framework the component devoted to combine the results retrieved by the translator and to answer to the user request. Furthermore, we will design an extended in-vivo evaluation with specific decision-making task that will be performed by real users by exploiting the DECiSION system in order to assess if the system actually support the decision-making process.

Acknowledgments. The research described in this paper has been funded by Regione Puglia under the programme INNONETWORK - POR Puglia FESR-FSE 2014–2020, Project "DECi-SION" (code: BQS5153).

References

1. Pirolli, P.: Powers of 10: modeling complex information-seeking systems at multiple scales. Computer (Long Beach, California) **42**: 33–40 (2009). https://doi.org/10.1109/MC.2009.94
2. Marchionini, G., White, R.W.: Information-seeking support systems. Computer (Long Beach, California) **42**, 30–32 (2009). https://doi.org/10.1109/MC.2009.88
3. Ricci, F., Rokach, L., Shapira, B.: Recommender systems: introduction and challenges. In: Ricci, F., Rokach, L., Shapira, B. (eds.) Recommender Systems Handbook, pp. 1–34. Springer, Boston, MA (2015). https://doi.org/10.1007/978-1-4899-7637-6_1
4. Bambini, R., Cremonesi, P., Turrin, R.: A recommender system for an IPTV service provider: a real large-scale production environment. In: Ricci, F., Rokach, L., Shapira, B., Kantor, Paul B. (eds.) Recommender Systems Handbook, pp. 299–331. Springer, Boston, MA (2011). https://doi.org/10.1007/978-0-387-85820-3_9
5. Picault, J., Ribière, M., Bonnefoy, D., Mercer, K.: How to get the recommender out of the lab? In: Ricci, F., Rokach, L., Shapira, B., Kantor, Paul B. (eds.) Recommender Systems Handbook, pp. 333–365. Springer, Boston, MA (2011). https://doi.org/10.1007/978-0-387-85820-3_10
6. Musto, C., Semeraro, G., Lops, P., De Gemmis, M., Lekkas, G.: Personalized finance advisory through case-based recommender systems and diversification strategies. Decis. Support Syst. **77**, 100–111 (2015). https://doi.org/10.1016/j.dss.2015.06.001
7. de Gemmis, M., Lops, P., Musto, C., Narducci, F., Semeraro, G.: Semantics-aware content-based recommender systems. In: Ricci, F., Rokach, L., Shapira, B. (eds.) Recommender Systems Handbook, pp. 119–159. Springer, Boston, MA (2015). https://doi.org/10.1007/978-1-4899-7637-6_4
8. Bengio, Y., Ducharme, R., Vincent, P., Jauvin, C.: A neural probabilistic language model. J. Mach. Learn. Res. **3**, 1137–1155 (2003)
9. Mikolov, T., Chen, K., Corrado, G., Dean, J.: Distributed representations of words and phrases and their compositionality (2013)
10. Pennington, J., Socher, R., Manning, C.D.: Glove: global vectors for word representation. In: Proceedings of the 2014 Conference on Empirical Methods in Natural Language Processing (EMNLP), pp. 1532–1543 (2014)
11. Arora, S., Liang, Y., Ma, T.: A simple but tough-to-beat baseline for sentence embeddings (2016)

A Comparative Analysis of State-of-the-Art Recommendation Techniques in the Movie Domain

Dalia Valeriani, Giuseppe Sansonetti$^{(\boxtimes)}$ [ID], and Alessandro Micarelli

Department of Engineering, Roma Tre University, Via della Vasca Navale,
79, 00146 Rome, Italy
dal.valeriani@stud.uniroma3.it, {gsansone,micarel}@dia.uniroma3.it

Abstract. Recommender systems (RSs) represent one of the manifold applications in which Machine Learning can unfold its potential. Nowadays, most of the major online sites selling products and services provide users with RSs that can assist them in their online experience. In recent years, therefore, we have witnessed an impressive series of proposals for novel recommendation techniques that claim to ensure significative improvements compared to classic techniques. In this work, we analyze some of them from a theoretical and experimental point of view and verify whether they can deliver tangible real improvements in terms of performance. Among others, we have experimented with traditional model-based and memory-based collaborative filtering, up to the most recent recommendation techniques based on deep learning. We have chosen the movie domain as an application scenario, and a version of the classic MovieLens as a dataset for training and testing our models.

Keywords: Machine learning · Recommender systems · Collaborative filtering · Matrix factorization · Deep learning

1 Introduction and Background

Every day, Artificial Intelligence (AI) redesigns our lives [33] and spaces around us [8]. Without even realizing it, we interact - anytime and anywhere - with systems based on AI models and techniques [24]. One of the most popular examples is represented by recommender systems (RSs) [1]. In the research literature, a recommender system is defined as a decision strategy for users in complex information environments [18]. Examples of applications of RSs are in several domains: e-commerce [4], news articles [6], research papers [15], music [25], and movies [3]. RSs assist users in the fruition of cultural heritage resources [30] and points of general interest [28] as well. They also suggest personalized itineraries [12] based on the user's interests and the context of use [2]. With the spread of RSs over the years, we have witnessed more and more proposals of recommendation techniques that show off better results compared to classic approaches. The goal

© Springer Nature Switzerland AG 2020
O. Gervasi et al. (Eds.): ICCSA 2020, LNCS 12252, pp. 104–118, 2020.
https://doi.org/10.1007/978-3-030-58811-3_8

of our research activities is to verify the extent of such performance improvements. To this aim, we have implemented and tested some recommendation models starting from more classic techniques up to more innovative and timely approaches.

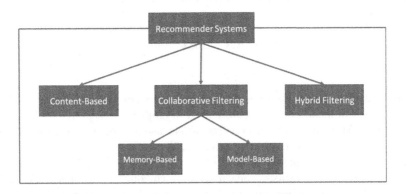

Fig. 1. A classification of recommendation techniques.

Several classifications of recommendation techniques have been proposed in the literature (see, e.g., [5,7,26,27]). According to the most general possible (see Fig. 1), RSs can be classified into three major categories based on how the recommendation is generated: content-based, collaborative filtering, and hybrid approaches. In the research work described in this paper, we mainly explored the collaborative filtering (CF) technique, with reference to two different types of approaches: memory-based (which takes advantage of all available data) and model-based (which exploits abstract representation of data) [19]. The CF technique exploits collaborative information starting from the rating matrix (i.e., user-item interactions). It can perform two types of tasks:

– prediction;
– recommendation.

In this work, we focus on the prediction task in which we want to estimate a utility function f to predict each user's preference for a new item. Typically, the set of ratings (i.e., the user-item matrix R) is divided into a training set (R_{train}) used to learn the function f, and a test set (R_{test}) used to evaluate the prediction accuracy. To assess the performance of RSs, several evaluation metrics have been proposed [32]. In this work, we consider the *root mean square error (RMSE)* to express the performance of the different models. RMSE can be defined as follows:

$$RMSE(f) = \sqrt{\frac{1}{|R_{test}|} \sum_{r_{ui} \in R_{test}} (f(u,i) - r_{ui})^2} \tag{1}$$

where $f(u, i)$ and r_{ui} are, respectively, the predicted recommendation scores and the actual rating values for all evaluated users $u \in U$ and all items $i \in I$ in the test set R_{test}.

Table 1. Statistics of the MovieLens 100K dataset.

	Users	Movies	Ratings	Sparsity
MovieLens 100K	943	1682	100,000	93.7%

The dataset chosen for experimentation purposes is *MovieLens 100K*[1], a movie dataset built ad hoc and widely used in empirical research. Table 1 shows its statistics. More precisely, it consists of 943 users, 1682 movies, and 100,000 explicit ratings with a value in the range $[1, 5]$.

The rest of this paper is structured as follows. In Sect. 2, we explore the characteristics of the dataset chosen to perform our experimental tests. We, also, describe the preprocessing steps we made on it to apply the different recommendations techniques tested. Section 3 illustrates the experimental sessions carried out and the relative results obtained. In Sect. 4, we draw our conclusions and outline some possible future developments of the work presented herein.

2 Dataset

2.1 Analysis

Before testing the different RSs, we performed an initial exploration of the dataset, in order to better understand the available data and the most interesting features for its use. A first analysis of the dataset concerned the *movies* belonging to it. Figure 2a highlights the terms that most appear in movie titles, using a larger size for those with a higher frequency. We also extracted the genres of the most popular movies in the dataset, obtaining the following list in descending order:

- Drama
- Comedy
- Thriller
- Action
- Romance
- ...

Such genres are shown in Fig. 2b, where the more popular genres are displayed with a larger size. Figure 3 shows the number of movies belonging to each genre. It can be noticed that most movies belong to the Drama category, the most popular genre, followed by the categories highlighted in the previous list.

---

[1] grouplens.org/datasets/movielens/100k/ (Accessed: June 23, 2020).

(a) Movie titles.

(b) Movie genres.

Fig. 2. Tag clouds related to the movies in the MovieLens 100K dataset (larger size means higher frequency).

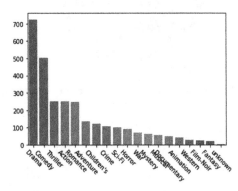

Fig. 3. Number of movies for each genre.

The subsequent analysis concerned the *users* belonging to the dataset. Specifically, we analyzed their age distribution, which led to identify the highest number of them (i.e., 35.2%) aged between 20 and 29 years, followed by a lower percentage (i.e., 25.6%) of adult users, up to the lowest percentage (i.e., 0.1%) under ten years (see Fig. 4).

After the first phase of exploration, more attention was paid to the study of the rating distribution of the whole dataset. In Fig. 5a, users appear to have been generous in their rating behavior: the average rating was 3.52 in the range $[1, 5]$, with half of the movies that received a rating value between 4 and 5. It can be also noted that the rating distribution illustrated in Fig. 5a is more on the positive side, which suggests that users are more likely to watch movies they like. The total number of users is shown in Fig. 5b, where users are represented on the y-axis and the possible rating values on the x-axis. It can be noted that almost 35,000 users gave a rating of 4, more than 25,000 users gave 3, and so on up to a rating of 1 expressed by over 5,000 users.

We also wanted to investigate the rating distribution over all movies and users. In Fig. 6a, the number of ratings is shown on the y-axis, while the movie IDs are reported on the x-axis. It can be noticed that few films have been evaluated more frequently, representing the most popular items according to the classic *long tail* style curve. The same behavior occurs in Fig. 6b, where the user IDs are displayed on the x-axis. A small proportion of users gave most of the ratings.

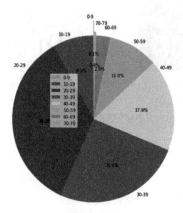

Fig. 4. Age distribution of the users in the dataset.

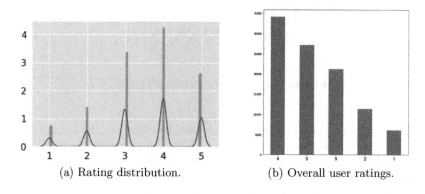

(a) Rating distribution.   (b) Overall user ratings.

Fig. 5. Ratings reported in the dataset.

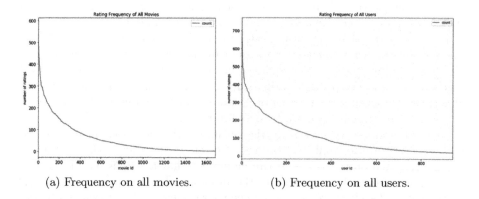

(a) Frequency on all movies.   (b) Frequency on all users.

Fig. 6. Statistics on ratings.

The last analysis of the dataset involved a key aspect to fully understand the recommendation scenario: the dataset *sparsity*. Sparsity is a common challenge to overcome in many CF applications [17]. This term denotes the lack of available ratings in the R user-item matrix. If we consider a R matrix with dimensions $(n_{users} \times m_{movies})$, where each element r_{ij} represents the rating value assigned by the user i to the movie j, this matrix will likely have a very small number of entries, since most users usually rate only a few of the available movies. In the MovieLens 100K dataset, the sparsity of the R matrix can be calculated as follows:

$$\frac{n_{ratings}}{n_{users} \cdot m_{movies}} = 0.063 \tag{2}$$

which means that only 6.3% of matrix entries have a value and 93.7% of the remaining data is missing, thus making it a very sparse dataset.

2.2 Preprocessing

For experimental purposes, we carried out a preprocessing of the dataset to build the recommendation models in offline mode. Specifically, for the memory-based technique, we explored the user-based and item-based approaches with k-nearest-neighbor algorithms. These algorithms take advantage of the overall rating matrix to generate a prediction based on a set of neighboring users/items, called "neighbors" or "peer users/items", who share similar ratings with the target user. Differently, for realizing model-based RSs, we made use of:

- a simple but effective technique, named *Slope One* [23], which relies on the average rating difference between users;
- techniques based on matrix factorization [21], which map users and items in a space with reduced dimensionality by building a latent factor model necessary for predicting the rating;
- methods based on Deep Learning [22], which through deep neural networks can be used to add nonlinear transformations to existing RS approaches and interpret them in neural extensions to generate predictions.

3 Experimental Evaluations

3.1 First Experimental Session

In the first experimental session, we created models based on user-based (UB) and item-based (IB) approaches by applying different techniques known in the literature, such as filtering neighbors and normalizing the rating. The dataset was divided into 80% training set and 20% test set. In the training dataset, we determined the similarity weights for generating the prediction. Similarity weights play a double role in the neighborhood-based recommendation methods:

- they allow for the selection of neighbors;
- they provide the means to give more or less relevance to those neighbors in the prediction process.

Calculating similarity weights is one of the most critical aspects of building a recommender system as it can have a significant impact on accuracy. The similarity metrics considered in this study are the *cosine similarity* and the *Pearson's correlation coefficient*.

Cosine Similarity. This metric consists of a vector approach: users and items are represented as dimensional vectors, and similarity is measured by means of the cosine distance between these two rating vectors, respectively. The function then measures the cosine of the angle to quantify their similarity. The calculation can be performed efficiently by taking their scalar product and dividing it by the product of their L2 (Euclidean) norms. The maximum value it assumes is 1, which indicates the maximum similarity between the two vectors of users or items. For the user-based approach, the equation is as follows:

$$s(u, v) = \frac{\sum_{i \in I_{uv}} r_{ui} \cdot r_{vi}}{\sqrt{\sum_{i \in I_u} r_{ui}^2 \sum_{i \in I_v} r_{vi}^2}} \tag{3}$$

where $s(u, v)$ represents the similarity between the user u and the user v on all items evaluated. In particular, I_{uv} denotes the set of items $i \in I$ *corated*, that is, evaluated by both the user u and the user v. For the item-based approach, the equation is as follows:

$$s(i, j) = \frac{\sum_{u \in U_{ij}} r_{iu} \cdot r_{ju}}{\sqrt{\sum_{u \in U_i} r_{iu}^2 \sum_{u \in U_j} r_{ju}^2}} \tag{4}$$

where $s(i, j)$ represents the similarity between the item i and the item j on all users who rated them. In particular, U_{ij} represents the set of users $u \in U$ who evaluated both the item i and the item j.

Pearson's Correlation Coefficient. This method, unlike the cosine similarity, relies on a statistical approach that computes the correlation between the common ratings given by two users to determine their similarity. When using the Pearson's correlation, the similarity is expressed in a range $[-1, +1]$, where a high positive value suggests a high correlation, a high negative value suggests an inversely high correlation, and a zero value suggests no correlation. For the user-based approach, the equation is as follows:

$$s(u, v) = \frac{\sum_{i \in I_{uv}} (r_{ui} - \bar{r}_u)(r_{vi} - \bar{r}_v)}{\sqrt{\sum_{i \in I_{uv}} (r_{ui} - \bar{r}_u)^2 \sum_{i \in I_{uv}} (r_{vi} - \bar{r}_v)^2}} \tag{5}$$

where $s(u, v)$ represents the similarity between users u and v, r_{ui} and r_{vi} represent the respective user's ratings for the item i, and $\bar{r}_u$ and $\bar{r}_v$ represent the average rating of the user u or v on all items evaluated. For the item-based approach, the equation is as follows:

$$s(i,j) = \frac{\sum_{u \in U_{ij}} (r_{ui} - \bar{r}_i)(r_{ui} - \bar{r}_j)}{\sqrt{\sum_{u \in U_{ij}} (r_{ui} - \bar{r}_i)^2 \sum_{i \in U_{ij}} (r_{ui} - \bar{r}_j)^2}} \tag{6}$$

where, likewise, $s(i,j)$ represents the similarity between items i and j, and $\bar{r}_i$ and $\bar{r}_j$ represent the average rating on the respective items, rated by users who evaluated both of them.

Table 2. Results of the first experimental session.

	Cosine similarity	Pearson's correlation coefficient	Cosine similarity neighbor fine tuning	Mean centering neighbor fine tuning
RMSE user-based	2.88 ($N = 943$ users)	2.91 ($N = 943$ users)	2.41 ($N = 40$ users)	2.63 ($N = 50$ users)
RMSE item-based	3.37 ($N = 1682$ items)	3.37 ($N = 1682$ items)	2.71 ($N = 40$ items)	2.85 ($N = 15$ items)

Experimental Results. The rating prediction was then performed on the training dataset and evaluated on the test dataset with and without filtering peer users or items. Table 2 shows the results in terms of RMSE when the configurations for both techniques vary. The most significant results were obtained with a pre-filtering of 40 most correlated neighbors, which led to an RMSE value of approximately 2.41 for the UB approach and 2.71 for the IB approach. Higher values were obtained through the rating normalization using the mean centering (MC) technique. The idea behind MC is to determine whether a rating is positive or negative by comparing it with the average rating. Therefore, this technique remaps a user's ratings by subtracting the average value of all its ratings, indicating whether the particular rating is positive or negative compared to the average. Values above the average rating represent positive ratings, values below the average ratings represent negative ratings. Actually, the rating normalization through MC does not improve the accuracy of the model despite a fine-tuning of the neighbors involving 50 users and 15 items in the prediction task, respectively. Furthermore, the use of both similarity metrics proved to be interchangeable for the purposes of the predictive capacity by the model itself.

3.2   Second Experimental Session

In the second experimental session, we experimented with different prediction algorithms based on collaborative filtering and matrix factorization [11], using a k-fold cross-validation technique with $k = 5$. The most significant results we obtained are shown in Table 3. For the user-based and item-based approaches, a sensitivity analysis was performed on the number of neighbors, showing a better value of RMSE for $N = 50$ and $N = 10$ neighbors, respectively. The Slope One technique, instead, registered a RMSE value of around 0.94. The more complex Singular Value Decomposition (SVD) and SVD++ algorithms obtained satisfactory RMSE values equal to 0.9343 and 0.9166 with $L = 50$ and $L = 10$ latent factors, respectively. The central point of these algorithms is to best approximate the initial matrix by learning the linear user-item interactions through stochastic gradient descent. It can be noted in Table 3 that SVD++ obtained better performance than SVD. The main difference compared to the simple SVD is that SVD++ can exploit implicit ratings for the prediction task, taking into account only which items users have evaluated, regardless of their rating values.

Table 3. Results of the second experimental session.

	KNN-UB	KNN-IB	Slope One	SVD	SVD++
RMSE	1.0158 ($N = 50$)	1.0256 ($N = 10$)	0.94	0.9343 ($L = 50$)	0.9166 ($L = 10$)

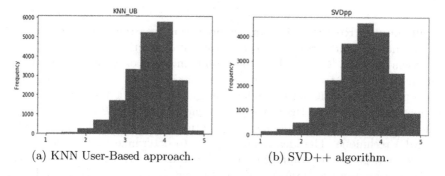

(a) KNN User-Based approach.   (b) SVD++ algorithm.

Fig. 7. Distribution of predicted ratings through two different recommendation techniques.

A key aspect to understand the predictive capacity and behavior of a recommendation model is to analyze its rating distribution. Figure 7 shows the distribution of ratings predicted by the tested algorithms by comparing a more classic technique such as the user-based approach with a more complex technique such as SVD++. The rating values are represented on the x-axis, the number of predictions for each considered rating value is represented on the y-axis. The user-based algorithm concentrates its predictions around the average, showing a high number of predictions for rating values between 3 and 4, and a low number of predictions for the extreme values of the considered rating range. The behavior is different for the SVD++ algorithm, where the rating frequency is well distributed along the extreme values of the ratings considered. Such a distribution reflects the most accurate performance of the SVD++ model.

3.3   Third Experimental Session

In the third experimental session, we experimented with three different predictive models based on feed-forward neural architectures. Figure 8 shows the architecture of the *neural collaborative filtering (NCF)* framework [34] we tested. This architecture can generate the predicted scores with the output layer through a preprocessing of the features in dense embedding vectors and the use of neural CF layers. The two first architectures created had the following structure. For the input layers, we chose the user ID and the movie ID as unique features. In the first model (NCF_1), a CF layer and an output layer were used choosing $N = 20$ latent user/item factors. In the second model (NCF_2), the same architecture is employed with an additional CF layer.

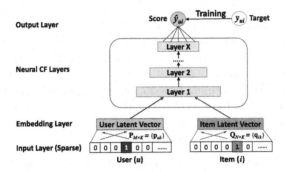

Fig. 8. Neural collaborative filtering (NCF) architecture [34].

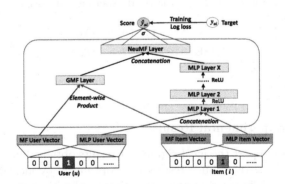

Fig. 9. Neural matrix factorization (NMF) architecture [16].

Finally, a further model [16] was implemented based on a more complex architecture, called *neural matrix factorization (NMF)*. Its architecture is depicted in Fig. 9. The main difference of this model compared to the previous two frameworks is that it combines two different neural networks:

- a standard matrix factorization network (GMF) that performs a linear modeling of the user-item features by running a simple scalar product among the latent factors of users and movies;
- a multilayer feed-forward network (MLP) that models non-linear user-item interactions to compute the final prediction score.

The key idea behind this model is to concatenate the prediction outputs from the single networks, thus creating an entirely unified network that can represent a more robust predictive structure.

Experimental Results. The three proposed architectures shared the following properties:

- The 60% of the dataset used as a training set;
- The 20% of the dataset used as a validation set;
- The 20% of the dataset used as a test set;
- Optimization function *Adam* [20] with a learning rate $\lambda = 0.0002$;
- 1875 instances per batch;
- 20 epochs with early stopping function set to 4 epochs in the training phase;
- Use of dropout layers to prevent overfitting;
- Evaluation metric for model accuracy: RMSE;
- Network loss function: mean square error.

Table 4 shows the performance of all the tested neural approaches, from the less complex neural architecture to the more structured one. It can be seen that the best result, in terms of RMSE, was achieved by the NMF model.

Table 4. Results of the third experimental session.

	NCF_1	NCF_2	NMF
RMSE	0.9327	0.9285	0.8680

3.4 Overall Experimental Results

In this section, we report the most significant results obtained in the second and third experimental session. Such results were optimized by identifying the best parameters of the different recommenders. Specifically, the algorithm specifications were as follows:

1. **KNN_IB** with $N = 10$ neighbors;
2. **KNN_UB** with $N = 50$ neighbors;
3. **SLOPE_ONE**;
4. **SVD** with $L = 50$ latent factors;
5. **SVD++** with $L = 10$ latent factors;

6. **NCF_1** with $L = 20$ latent factors (MLP);
7. **NCF_2** with $L = 20$ latent factors (MLP);
8. **NMF** with $L = 20$ latent factors (MLP) and $L = 10$ latent factors (GMF).

For the choice of the graph, we opted for a logarithmic representation capable of capturing in a more significant way the sensitive variations and the significant differences between the different RMSE values. Figure 10 summarizes all the obtained findings. The empirical results show that memory-based approaches

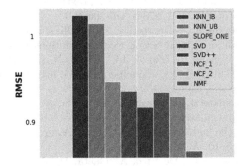

Fig. 10. Results of the second and third experimental sessions in terms of root mean square error (RMSE).

ranked in the last place in terms of predictive capacity, although they have the advantage of being able to take full advantage of user and movie data. Differently, more accurate models starting from Slope One up to SVD++ obtained more satisfactory results by addressing in the best way the typical data sparsity problem, present in the used dataset as well as in many real applications. Finally, the deep learning models proved to be accurate and robust in terms of predictive capacity, with particular reference to the NMF model, which achieved the lowest RMSE score among all the tested algorithms, thanks to the flexibility of its architecture. In order to verify the statistical significance of our experimental tests, we performed one-sample paired t-tests on the results, finding that all differences in accuracy were statistically significant for $p < 0.05$.

4 Conclusions and Future Works

In the research activities presented herein, different predictive models have been compared, thus highlighting the natural convergence to more innovative approaches that are increasingly considered in the application of RSs. Thanks to their flexibility, deep neural networks have been shown to better model user-item interactions to capture increasingly complex patterns for the benefit of the model accuracy.

In the future, it would be interesting to evaluate the behavior of architectures such as Recurrent Neural Networks (RNN) [31], and the use of unsupervised approaches such as autoencoders [14] for modeling the recommendation task. We also plan to employ different datasets (e.g., linked open data [9]), experiment with further recommendation techniques, and integrate the simple ratings provided by users with data of different nature such as attitudes [10], temporal dynamics [29], and web browsing activities [13].

References

1. Aggarwal, C.C.: Recommender Systems: The Textbook, 1st edn. Springer, Cham (2016). https://doi.org/10.1007/978-3-319-29659-3
2. Biancalana, C., Flamini, A., Gasparetti, F., Micarelli, A., Millevolte, S., Sansonetti, G.: Enhancing traditional local search recommendations with context-awareness. In: Konstan, J.A., Conejo, R., Marzo, J.L., Oliver, N. (eds.) UMAP 2011. LNCS, vol. 6787, pp. 335–340. Springer, Heidelberg (2011). https://doi.org/10.1007/978-3-642-22362-4_29
3. Biancalana, C., Gasparetti, F., Micarelli, A., Miola, A., Sansonetti, G.: Context-aware movie recommendation based on signal processing and machine learning. In: Proceedings of the 2nd Challenge on Context-Aware Movie Recommendation. CAMRa 2011, pp. 5–10. ACM, New York (2011)
4. Bologna, C., De Rosa, A.C., De Vivo, A., Gaeta, M., Sansonetti, G., Viserta, V.: Personality-based recommendation in e-commerce. In: CEUR Workshop Proceedings, Aachen, Germany, vol. 997. CEUR-WS.org (2013)
5. Burke, R.: Hybrid web recommender systems. In: Brusilovsky, P., Kobsa, A., Nejdl, W. (eds.) The Adaptive Web. LNCS, vol. 4321, pp. 377–408. Springer, Heidelberg (2007). https://doi.org/10.1007/978-3-540-72079-9_12
6. Caldarelli, S., Feltoni Gurini, D., Micarelli, A., Sansonetti, G.: A signal-based approach to news recommendation. In: CEUR Workshop Proceedings, Aachen, Germany, vol. 1618. CEUR-WS.org (2016)
7. Colombo-Mendoza, L.O., Paredes-Valverde, M.A., Salas-Zárate, M.P., Bustos-López, M., Sánchez-Cervantes, J.L., Alor-Hernández, G.: Recommender systems in the offline retailing domain: a systematic literature review. In: García-Alcaraz, J.L., Sánchez-Ramírez, C., Avelar-Sosa, L., Alor-Hernández, G. (eds.) Techniques, Tools and Methodologies Applied to Global Supply Chain Ecosystems. ISRL, vol. 166, pp. 383–409. Springer, Cham (2020). https://doi.org/10.1007/978-3-030-26488-8_17
8. D'Aniello, G., Gaeta, M., Orciuoli, F., Sansonetti, G., Sorgente, F.: Knowledge-based smart city service system. Electronics (Switzerland) 9(6), 1–22 (2020)
9. De Angelis, A., Gasparetti, F., Micarelli, A., Sansonetti, G.: A social cultural recommender based on linked open data. In: Adjunct Publication of the 25th Conference on User Modeling, Adaptation and Personalization. UMAP 2017, pp. 329–332, ACM, New York (2017)
10. Gurini, D.F., Gasparetti, F., Micarelli, A., Sansonetti, G.: iSCUR: interest and sentiment-based community detection for user recommendation on Twitter. In: Dimitrova, V., Kuflik, T., Chin, D., Ricci, F., Dolog, P., Houben, G.-J. (eds.) UMAP 2014. LNCS, vol. 8538, pp. 314–319. Springer, Cham (2014). https://doi.org/10.1007/978-3-319-08786-3_27
11. Feltoni Gurini, D., Gasparetti, F., Micarelli, A., Sansonetti, G.: Temporal people-to-people recommendation on social networks with sentiment-based matrix factorization. Future Gener. Comput. Syst. 78, 430–439 (2018)

12. Fogli, A., Sansonetti, G.: Exploiting semantics for context-aware itinerary recommendation. Pers. Ubiquit. Comput. **23**(2), 215–231 (2019). https://doi.org/10.1007/s00779-018-01189-7
13. Gasparetti, F., Micarelli, A., Sansonetti, G.: Exploiting web browsing activities for user needs identification. In: 2014 International Conference on Computational Science and Computational Intelligence, vol. 2, pp. 86–89, March 2014
14. Hassan, H.A.M., Sansonetti, G., Gasparetti, F., Micarelli, A.: Semantic-based tag recommendation in scientific bookmarking systems. In: Proceedings of the 12th ACM Conference on Recommender Systems. RecSys 2018, pp. 465–469. ACM, New York (2018)
15. Hassan, H.A.M., Sansonetti, G., Gasparetti, F., Micarelli, A., Beel, J.: BERT, ELMo, USE and InferSent sentence encoders: the panacea for research-paper recommendation? In: Tkalcic, M., Pera, S. (eds.) Proceedings of ACM RecSys 2019 Late-Breaking Results, vol. 2431, pp. 6–10. CEUR-WS.org (2019)
16. He, X., Liao, L., Zhang, H., Nie, L., Hu, X., Chua, T.: Neural collaborative filtering. CoRR abs/1708.05031 (2017)
17. Idrissi, N., Zellou, A.: A systematic literature review of sparsity issues in recommender systems. Soc. Netw. Anal. Min. **10**(1), 1–23 (2020). https://doi.org/10.1007/s13278-020-0626-2
18. Isinkaye, F., Folajimi, Y., Ojokoh, B.: Recommendation systems: principles, methods and evaluation. Egypt. Inform. J. **16**(3), 261–273 (2015)
19. Jannach, D., Zanker, M., Felfernig, A., Friedrich, G.: Recommender Systems: An Introduction, 1st edn. Cambridge University Press, New York (2010)
20. Kingma, D.P., Ba, J.: Adam: a method for stochastic optimization. In: Proceedings of the 3rd International Conference on Learning Representations (ICLR) (2015)
21. Koren, Y., Bell, R., Volinsky, C.: Matrix factorization techniques for recommender systems. Computer **42**(8), 30–37 (2009)
22. LeCun, Y., Bengio, Y., Hinton, G.: Deep learning. Nature **521**(7553), 436–444 (2015)
23. Lemire, D., Maclachlan, A.: Slope one predictors for online rating-based collaborative filtering. In: Proceedings of SIAM Data Mining (SDM 2005) (2005)
24. Micarelli, A., Neri, A., Sansonetti, G.: A case-based approach to image recognition. In: Blanzieri, E., Portinale, L. (eds.) EWCBR 2000. LNCS, vol. 1898, pp. 443–454. Springer, Heidelberg (2000). https://doi.org/10.1007/3-540-44527-7_38
25. Onori, M., Micarelli, A., Sansonetti, G.: A comparative analysis of personality-based music recommender systems. In: CEUR Workshop Proceedings, Aachen, Germany, vol. 1680, pp. 55–59. CEUR-WS.org (2016)
26. Ricci, F.: Recommender systems in tourism. In: Handbook of e-Tourism, pp. 1–18 (2020)
27. Saha, J., Chowdhury, C., Biswas, S.: Review of machine learning and deep learning based recommender systems for health informatics. In: Dash, S., Acharya, B.R., Mittal, M., Abraham, A., Kelemen, A. (eds.) Deep Learning Techniques for Biomedical and Health Informatics. SBD, vol. 68, pp. 101–126. Springer, Cham (2020). https://doi.org/10.1007/978-3-030-33966-1_6
28. Sansonetti, G.: Point of interest recommendation based on social and linked open data. Pers. Ubiquit. Comput. **23**(2), 199–214 (2019). https://doi.org/10.1007/s00779-019-01218-z
29. Sansonetti, G., Feltoni Gurini, D., Gasparetti, F., Micarelli, A.: Dynamic social recommendation. In: Proceedings of the 2017 IEEE/ACM International Conference on Advances in Social Networks Analysis and Mining 2017. ASONAM 2017, pp. 943–947. ACM, New York (2017)

30. Sansonetti, G., Gasparetti, F., Micarelli, A., Cena, F., Gena, C.: Enhancing cultural recommendations through social and linked open data. User Model. User Adap. Inter. **29**(1), 121–159 (2019). https://doi.org/10.1007/s11257-019-09225-8
31. Sherstinsky, A.: Fundamentals of recurrent neural network (RNN) and long short-term memory (LSTM) network. Physica D Nonlinear Phenom. **404**, 132306 (2020)
32. Silveira, T., Zhang, M., Lin, X., Liu, Y., Ma, S.: How good your recommender system is? a survey on evaluations in recommendation. Int. J. Mach. Learn. Cybern. **10**(5), 813–831 (2019). https://doi.org/10.1007/s13042-017-0762-9
33. Tegmark, M.: Life 3.0: Being Human in the Age of Artificial Intelligence. Knopf Publishing Group, New York City (2017)
34. Zhang, S., Yao, L., Sun, A., Tay, Y.: Deep learning based recommender system: a survey and new perspectives. ACM Comput. Surv. **52**(1), 1–38 (2019)

Automated Machine Learning: Prospects and Challenges

Lorenzo Vaccaro, Giuseppe Sansonetti$^{(\boxtimes)}$ (iD), and Alessandro Micarelli

Department of Engineering, Roma Tre University,
Via della Vasca Navale 79, 00146 Rome, Italy
lor.vaccaro1@stud.uniroma3.it, {gsansone,micarel}@dia.uniroma3.it

Abstract. The State of the Art of the young field of Automated Machine Learning (AutoML) is held by the connectionist approach. Several techniques of such an inspiration have recently shown promising results in automatically designing neural network architectures. However, apart from back-propagation, only a few applications of other learning techniques are used for these purposes. The back-propagation process takes advantage of specific optimization techniques that are best suited to specific application domains (e.g., Computer Vision and Natural Language Processing). Hence, the need for a more general learning approach, namely, a basic algorithm able to make inference in different contexts with distinct properties. In this paper, we deal with the problem from a scientific and epistemological point of view. We believe that this is needed to fully understand the mechanisms and dynamics underlying human learning. To this aim, we define some elementary inference operations and show how modern architectures can be built by a combination of those elementary methods. We analyze each method in different settings and find the best-suited application context for each learning algorithm. Furthermore, we discuss experimental findings and compare them with human learning. The discrepancy is particularly evident between supervised and unsupervised learning. Then, we determine which elementary learning rules are best suited for unsupervised systems, and, finally, we propose some improvements in reinforcement learning architectures.

Keywords: Automated Machine Learning · Meta Learning · Neural Architecture Search · Reinforcement learning

1 Introduction and Background

Artificial Intelligence (AI) is increasingly part of our lives. It organizes the services of our cities [7], suggests which points [28] are likely to be of interest to us (e.g., artistic and cultural resources [29] or restaurants [2]) and how to reach them [11]. It recommends us which news articles [4] or research papers [16] to read, which movies to watch [1], which products to buy [3], which music artists and songs to listen to [26], and even which people to attend [10]. To do this,

© Springer Nature Switzerland AG 2020
O. Gervasi et al. (Eds.): ICCSA 2020, LNCS 12252, pp. 119–134, 2020.
https://doi.org/10.1007/978-3-030-58811-3_9

however, more and more efficient *algorithms* are required, to obtain which we need an ever-deeper understanding of the theory behind them.

David Hilbert [18], Alan Turing [32], and Alonzo Church [6] were the first to formalize logic and automatic reasoning through algorithms. Since then, human and machine learning have been studied, analyzed, and classified. The first criterion with which we will analyze AI algorithms is a classification of the reasoning process into two categories. Such a criterion is reflected in Psychology and AI. In particular, two types of reasoning were found in the functions associated with the various areas and components of the brain: *top-down* and *bottom-up*. They were associated with the perception of sensory inputs and the imagination of these, respectively. In [17], the authors hypothesize that the activity of the central nervous system reflects the process of bringing together internally generated predictions and external sensory perceptions. According to this theory, our brain learns by generating predictions and comparing them with the perceived reality. In AI, however, bottom-up reasoning refers to the process of inferring a value, a function, or an algorithm through a learning method. A series of *input-output* example pairs is provided and the program searches for the algorithms that relate them. Differently, with the top-down approach, we designate the algorithms coded with a priori knowledge of the problem. The reasoning is implemented in a well-defined algorithm that transforms inputs into outputs. Automated Machine Learning (AutoML) is the process that autonomously reshapes top-down knowledge into bottom-up reasoning.

Fig. 1. The five paradigms of Machine Learning.

To classify the Machine Learning (ML) methods, we follow the following definition that incorporates the one proposed in [8] (see Fig. 1). It starts by defining the five lines of thinking that form the basis for ML methods. Pedro Domingos defines the *master algorithm* as the algorithm behind learning and identifies this component for the five paradigms. For each of them, it defines how information is represented and inferred. In the *symbolist* paradigm, the rigorous syntax and the specific representation adopted make it difficult to model the learning method. In this paradigm, it is easy to understand and model bottom-up reasoning and apply it to learning itself. However, the efficiency of these systems is highly dependent on the specific formulation. The *connectionist* paradigm has recently gained the interest of many researchers. The main advantage of these architectures is efficiency. In the training phase of neural networks, the parameters are inferred through bottom-up reasoning by induction. The trained network can quickly classify the test samples through deductive top-down reasoning. In these architectures, the structure choice is fundamental and directly shapes the limits of the solution complexity. The Neural Architecture Search (NAS) [9] science shows an example of learning application to the search for neural architectures through the connectionist paradigm. This example shows that connectionist learning can be applied to itself. However, the most successful NAS models jointly apply different learning paradigms. One of the major limitations of connectionist approaches is the modeling of discrete values and ordinal variables. The *Bayesian* paradigm introduces uncertainty. This powerful tool allows for a more realistic representation of learning. It also enables the direct modeling of understanding. It independently carries out the distinction between known and uncertain information. Among the hybrid learning methods applied to the research on neural architectures, the Bayesian paradigm has proven to be very efficient. The *evolutionary* paradigm is likely to be the most complete for the potential proposed solutions. This method is the most permissive for defining the solution space. For this reason, it generally takes more time and is subject to a higher risk of getting stuck in a local minimum. Compared to the one proposed in [8], our definition of ML paradigms differs as follows. Domingos attributes the *analogizer* paradigm only to kernel machines. Differently, we consider it present in every learning method that applies reasoning by analogy. Any ML algorithm that applies a direct or indirect similarity measure between two elements can be considered part of the analogizer paradigm as it introduces a similarity criterion.

The rest of this paper is structured as follows. In Sect. 2, the three experimental phases that constituted our research path are described in detail. In particular, the first phase focused on the implementation of an inference model based on the symbolist paradigm. In the second phase, the search algorithms for neural architectures were analyzed. The search for neural architectures was then compared with other known ML problems. In the third experimental phase, an architecture including some hybrid learning methods was proposed. During this phase, three ML models were deeply analyzed, which introduce inference through reasoning by analogy in connectionist systems. In Sect. 3, we draw our conclusions and outline some possible developments in our research activities.

2   The Experimental Path

2.1   First Experimental Phase

The first experimental phase focused on defining a symbolist model. The proposed architecture was implemented starting from an article[1] in which evolutionary learning is applied to the symbolist paradigm. This article describes an experiment that leverages an *evolutionary algorithm* to generate a Turing Machine able of correctly transforming the empty input into the requested output. To simulate the behavior of a Turing Machine without however having to generate code in a verbose programming language, the article proposes to use the BrainF*ck (BF) language designed in 1993 by Urban Müller. A useful feature of BF is the very small set of instructions sufficient to make the language Turing complete. BF is an esoteric language, it is difficult to program, however, both the instructions and the code have a common format: the ASCII coding. The input, the output, and the code are strings and the instructions consist of a single character. To avoid having to also generate the keyboard output, the "," character was removed from the instructions in the experiment of the aforementioned article. Also for this experiment, the output of the program is considered what it prints, not what remains on the tape at the end of the program. To demonstrate the potential of this system, the article shows some experiments that generate words or sentences in English. This forced approach allows for limited efficacy, several generations in the order of magnitude of one million are needed to generate a program capable of writing a sentence. In general, applying random generation to code increases the risk of running into syntax errors. To improve the ability of the system to generate the correct code, we considered several alternatives. To check the code it is sufficient to use a type-2 grammar, to generate the code we need a pushdown automaton (PDA).

$$S \rightarrow SS| + | - | < | > |[S]|\varepsilon$$

The proposed model generates solutions of increasing complexity, sequentially, until a valid solution is reached. Instead of randomly drawing a new instruction at each step, as in the aforementioned article, the algorithm explores breadth-first the tree of possible codes. In this tree, each node represents a different code. Each arc represents a choice (using the type-2 grammar of the original BF language is an unbalanced 7-ary tree). The height of a node in the tree is a direct measure of the code complexity. Exploring the tree of possible programs is an algorithm. In this model, there is no distinction between code and data. The relationship between input and output is treated in the same way as the relationship between the previously generated code and the current code. The architecture is organized in layers (see Fig. 2). All information inferred into a layer is coded and learned from the upper level. From this starting point, we experimented with different ways of evolving the model. In particular, we paid attention to trying

---

[1] www.primaryobjects.com/2013/01/27/using-artificial-intelligence-to-write-self-modifying-improving-programs/ (Accessed: June 23, 2020).

to evolve the architectures *vertically*, to ensure that the inference process took place upstream of the pile of architectures. The reason is simple: if we consider an architecture capable of generating the algorithm of the sum, for example, we can expect that this architecture is also capable of generating the code for subtraction. A higher layer architecture, if properly trained, can generalize learning outside the problems already addressed. Alternatively, it is also possible to make inference in the model by backtracking the code. The hypothesis of such a system has already been formulated by Jürgen Schmidhuber in his paper entitled "Optimal Ordered Problem Solver (OOPS)" [30]. In this experimental phase, we focused on the search for learning algorithms capable of scaling in complexity. The architecture expands dynamically, with each step the original problem is converted into the search for a learning algorithm specific to that problem. The dimensionality explosion of the research space introduces a computation overhead that makes the method inefficient.

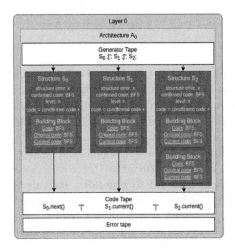
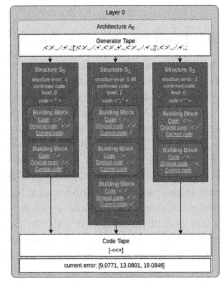

Fig. 2. High-level scheme of a hierarchically organized generator architecture.

2.2 Second Experimental Phase

In the second experimental phase, we collected and tested many NAS algorithms. This discipline proposes a connectionist approach to the problem of learning to learn. The different architectures are distinguished by the upstream learning process. With this method, the parameters of the underlying connectionist model are inferred. Early attempts model the system as a reinforcement learning (RL) problem [33]. The problem definition was then mathematically formalized.

The search space is composed of all the combinations of possible parameters of the connectionist network to be modeled. Starting from this definition, in the Bayesian paradigm Autokeras [22] and NASBOT [23] are proposed. Evolutionaries contribute with Hierarchical Evo [24] and AmoebaNet [27]. We have not found any symbolist NAS applications. For the analogizer paradigm, on the other hand, we have found a strong relationship with the most successful algorithms in this discipline. The first problem we faced in the application of connectionist techniques to NAS is raised by the discrete nature of the research space. This problem, common also to unsupervised and reinforcement learning, is solved by techniques attributable to reasoning by analogy. Among the most common and exhaustively studied applications, which require an elementary inference mechanism similar to that necessary for the search for neural architectures, we find automatic text translation, game solving, and many other complex tasks. Therefore, in the subsequent experimental phase, we analyzed RL architectures and some models that jointly exploit the connectionist, Bayesian, and analogizer paradigms.

2.3   Third Experimental Phase

The initial goal of the third experimental phase was to overcome the limitations of the connectionist models in the application context of complex tasks. In particular, we found two models of interest in this respect: Differentiable Neural Computer (DNC) [13] and Neural Arithmetic Logic Units (NALU) [31]. Linear activation functions are known to produce linear output. It is also known that to overcome this limitation it is possible to adopt non-linear functions with properties that make derivation simple. However, it is less known that these functions introduce another limitation. Neural networks tend not to generalize for values outside the range of training examples. If an artificial neural network is trained with data contained within a range to approximate a certain algorithm, such as the sum of its inputs, it will not be able to generalize this sum outside that range. Figure 3 shows the validation error for the addition algorithm with various activation functions. NALU was created to remedy this limitation. The concept behind this architecture is to model a set of arithmetic operations on the inputs and to assign each one a *learning gate*. In our first experiment on this model, we introduced a *bias* (see Fig. 4). Through this modification, it is possible to carry out several further operations. For example, the system without this foresight would not be able to double the input or add it to a constant. Starting from this model, we wondered why in the article they had not generalized the concept of exponential and logarithmic space. In practice, moving from a representation of the inputs in one space to the next logarithmic space, the effect of the addition operation is first elevated to the product, then to power, to power towers, and so on. If the gate could model an arbitrary integer n, apply the operations to the n-th logarithmic space, and raise to power the results n times, we could model any arithmetic operation and approximate any function. Looking for an architecture that models n as a discrete value, we come across the problems of reinforcement learning. However, there is a continuous mathematical function that models n

with continuous values: *tetration*. Tetrations are repeated or iterative exponentiation functions. The definition we adopted in our solution is iteratively defined as follows:

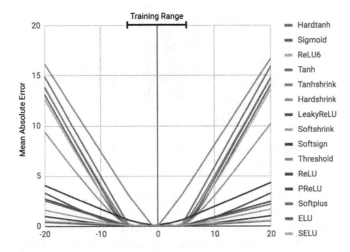

Fig. 3. The generalization problem outside the range of the training values [31].

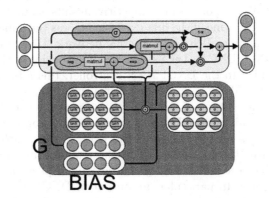

Fig. 4. First model: NALUB.

$$^x a \approx \begin{cases} \log_a \left(^{x+1} a \right) & x \le -1 \\ 1 + \dfrac{2\ln(a)}{1 + \ln(a)} x - \dfrac{1 - \ln(a)}{1 + \ln(a)} x^2 & -1 < x \le 0 \\ a^{\left(^{x-1} a \right)} & x > 0 \end{cases}$$

Experiments have shown that using this function always causes the algorithm to diverge. However, we tried to influence the choice of the parameter

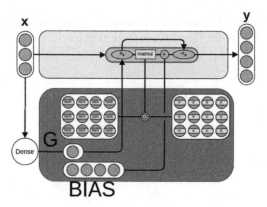

Fig. 5. Second and third model: NALUBTC.

n of the network so that the results remain correct. A valid alternative found was to approximate this parameter through a simple artificial neural network. The network also proved to be useful in alleviating the task of the NALU learning gates, leading it to converge in acceptable times. The controlled model that makes use of the tetration function and includes the bias is shown in Fig. 5. As a last experiment on the models of this architecture, we tried to define a recurrent neural network (RNN) that adopted NALU as a cell. In the scheme of the long short-term memory (LSTM) [21], we have replaced the activation functions with NALUBTC cells. We did not obtain competitive results, so we tried to integrate this model into a DNC. One of the first experiments was the implementation of a DNC grafted into another DNC. The internal network (DNC1) is the controller of the external DNC (DNC2). Let us observe the behavior of this architecture: the input is provided to the DNC1 RNN controller, this returns a set of read and write keys, the DNC1 accesses and writes into memory using the key as the instructions. The output of DNC1 is made up of the concatenation of the read cells and the reading keys. Being the output of the controller, this is interpreted by DNC2 as a set of read and write keys. In turn, DNC2 accesses the memory and returns the concatenation of the readings and output of DNC1. In this way, an indirect addressing system can be implemented, however not necessarily biunivocal. In particular, an output of DNC1 (the reading key for DNC2) points to a set of cells, a portion of memory. Therefore, while DNC2 infers several specific problem-solving algorithms, the DNC1 controller will tend to implement a problem classification algorithm. This model works particularly well for tasks where complex structures need to be modeled. In the research literature, it has been shown that DNCs can be used for information storage, graph research, Natural Language Processing (NLP), and text understanding and reasoning (bAbI Task[2]). Through the grafting of DNCs, we managed to improve the accuracy in the bAbI task, however, this increase was at the expense of effi-

---

[2] research.fb.com/downloads/babi/ (Accessed: June 23, 2020).

ciency. The grafted DNC model introduces a computation overhead that slows the convergence of the architecture. As for reinforcement learning, the slowdown is even more evident, especially if we compare the computational times with the classic architectures. We believe that the reason for this inefficiency lies in the fact that the RL models do not need a particular computational complexity, often the architectures with simple policies work better. In other terms, the best RL algorithms return the simplest possible solutions through complex inference systems. Furthermore, it is not clear to us which role the analogizer paradigm plays in the inference of politics. If the reasoning by analogy can influence the choice of policy, we would have expected a positive result for the integration of DNC into a classic architecture. To eliminate any doubt, we studied the ML methods that adopt reasoning by analogy, trying to figure out why it cannot be applied in certain circumstances. The initial experimentation of this research phase is present in the GitHub repository of the research work[3]. In the third experimental phase, we identified three ML mechanisms, commonly used in the aforementioned applications of automatic text translation and learning by reinforcement, which are at least in part the result of reasoning by analogy. The attention mechanism suggests an "algorithmic path" to the network on which it is applied. It hides unnecessary information and highlights useful information. By influencing the inference in the underlying network, this method could also be considered a *routing* algorithm. Routing in neural networks generally occurs on computation, in particular, it can help decide whether or not to move through a sub-network of the network. Under the forced assumption that attention is a routing algorithm, routing occurs for inputs, not on edges.

Much research has been done on the application of routing in neural networks. In particular, a publication caught our attention because of the simplicity, efficiency, and accuracy of the proposed method. Geoffrey Hinton (known also for his collaboration with Yoshua Bengio and Yann LeCun in founding *deep learning*) and his colleagues published a paper entitled "Transforming Autoencoders" [19] that has been very successful in Computer Vision (CV). The architecture proposed by Hinton *et al.* makes use of *capsules*. They suggest that artificial neural networks must use local capsules that perform complex computations on their inputs and encapsulate the result of these computations in compact and highly informative vectors. Each capsule learns to recognize an implicitly defined graphic entity on a limited visual domain. The proposed architecture is called *CapsNet* because of the capsules that define the hierarchical structure and the relationships between the objects in the scene. The process of breaking down an image into graphic sub-components is called *inverse 3D rendering*. From the capsules of the final layer, the vectors can be used to reconstruct the images. CapsNet introduces an auxiliary *decoder* responsible for the rendering of the capsules. This foresight, borrowed from the Generative Adversarial Network (GAN) [12] architecture, allows us to keep high the coupling between the capsules and the relative representations of the entities in the image. This type of routing is called *routing by agreement* underlining the inclusion/composition

---

[3] github.com/lorenzoviva/tesi/tree/master/recurrent/ (Accessed: June 23, 2020).

relationship between the capsules of consecutive layers. The article points out how much this method should be more effective than the more primitive form of *max-pooling* routing implemented by modern CV algorithms. Furthermore, the article shows the first successful application to the classification of "highly overlapping objects" (images with different shapes and overlapping figures). Through the routing by agreement, it is possible to model the inclusion/composition relationships among the searched objects. It is possible to recognize and model hierarchies in the structure of examples. Therefore, it becomes clear that this type of architecture can be used to model any hierarchical structure, including the structure of software, algorithms, or choices in an unsupervised system. The concept of *dynamic routing* is not new in connectionist models. The paper entitled "Deciding How to Decide: Dynamic Routing in Artificial Neural Networks" [25] shows a dynamic routing model in neural networks. Routing in networks, like the attention mechanism [15], allows for the definition of functional units specialized in a specific task, by dividing the problem into several sub-problems with analogizer techniques and solving the sub-problems through the connectionist learning method. We were interested in the possibility of using the capsules to model the actions of an RL system. In this architecture, the solution is provided with a set of additional information, a sort of explanation of the solution. The output vector maps the distinctive properties of possible solutions. These properties are recognized in all the subcomponents of the chosen solution (e.g., in Computer Vision they can be orientation, pose, scale, or others). Capsule networks have had some success recently, inspiring researchers to develop further models [5,14,20]. In an RL system, solutions are actions, by modeling them through a vector in a network of capsules it provides us with distinctive properties that represent explanations of the solution. If the final capsules represent the action, the daughter capsules, to be recognized as belonging to the solution, must represent the motivation behind a choice. Following this logic, we tried different approaches, each of which mainly differs in the *decoder* component. The interpretation of the solution varies according to how this component is defined. In the first experimental phase, we introduced the routing mechanism in the DQN algorithm for the game environment *CartPole-v1* (from OpenAI Gym[4]). Figure 6 shows the high-level architecture of this experiment. Specifically, we used a capsule network as a policy, then we assigned the decoder the task of reconstructing the *transaction* that follows a choice. The system receives as input an image section of the current frame in the game containing the pole to be balanced, this goes through a convolutional network, a network of capsules, and the capsule related to the chosen action is returned. Starting from the capsule, the decoder reconstructs the difference between the image of the current frame and the next one. Figure 7 describes some steps of the experiment. The results show that this architecture cannot converge. As it was conceived, this architecture models only one step of the environment, it is difficult to encapsulate information that is distributed over multiple transactions. Therefore, it models a very limited prediction of action consequences. We tried several alternatives in modeling transitions (see Fig. 8).

---

[4] gym.openai.com/ (Accessed: June 23, 2020).

Later, we changed the DQN model replacing it with the Advantage Actor-Critic (A2C) architecture (see Fig. 9). The main advantage introduced by this architecture is to distinctly model the potential reward value associated with the state and the potential gain associated with the actions. Again, we tried to associate a capsule of the final layer with each action. We also tried several other capsule models but, among all, one method stood out for its effectiveness. The potential of the state is modeled in a single capsule of the final layer, the vector instead represents the action potentials. In a subsequent model, we introduced a further dense layer that is applied to the capsule and returns the action (see Fig. 10). The capsule vector is also used to reconstruct the original image through a decoder. This caution pushes the network to encode a system state in the vector and not to lose useful information content. In the GitHub repository of our research work, a folder (RL_routing[5]) stores the code of these models. Results in a graphical format of many experiments are also saved on Google Drive[6]. For some experiments, we also saved a dynamic image, in GIF format, which displays the capsule values over the course of an episode. The model proposed in the third experimental phase obtained competitive results with the State of the Art in learning by reinforcement. However, the motivation that encouraged us to model the choices of an agent through a network of capsules has not been reflected in practice. The most successful formulations are those that do not model the inclusion/composition relationship of the system choices through the capsules. From an intuitive point of view, it is difficult to explain the effectiveness of this method. The capsule returned by the system is a vector of magnitude equal to the state potential and the orientation defined in the action space.

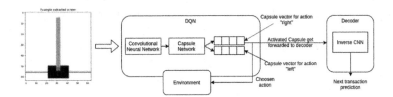

Fig. 6. A diagram showing the high-level functioning of the routing-based reinforcement learning architecture implemented on the DQN model.

[5] http://www.github.com/lorenzoviva/tesi/tree/master/RL_routing/ (Accessed: June 23, 2020).

[6] drive.google.com/drive/folders/1n74hoJ1K0hg0SQc18y7PCH1h9w6dqFJP?usp= sharing (Accessed: June 23, 2020).

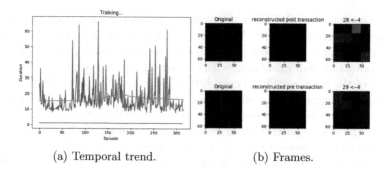

(a) Temporal trend.   (b) Frames.

Fig. 7. (a) A graph showing the duration of the experiments in steps for the *CartPole-v1* environment during the training for the first experiment on routing applied to reinforcement learning. (b) On the top left the current transaction, in the center the prediction of the transition and on the right the four capsules of the first layer each consisting of four values. The first row displays the current transaction, the second row represents the previous transaction.

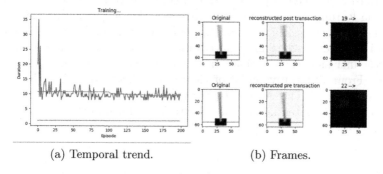

(a) Temporal trend.   (b) Frames.

Fig. 8. A different representation for transactions.

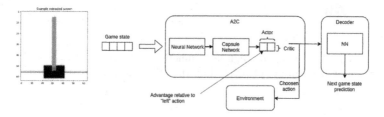

Fig. 9. A diagram showing the high-level functioning of the first reinforcement learning architecture with routing implemented on the A2C algorithm.

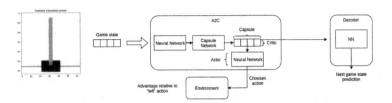

Fig. 10. A diagram showing the high-level functioning of the second reinforcement learning architecture with routing implemented on the A2C algorithm.

3 Conclusions and Future Works

The ultimate goal of our research work was to define new methods and techniques to improve the state-of-the-art models in the emerging fields of Automated Machine Learning (AutoML) and Meta Learning. Initially, we adopted a naïve approach, then we formalized the conditions for achieving the objective and, finally, we proceeded under the point of view of the *master algorithm* [8]. In the first experimental phase, we analyzed several models of the symbolist paradigm. We theorized a critical point in the development of a General Artificial Intelligence and a definitive master algorithm. We formulated criteria that allowed us to evaluate whether this goal could be achieved by certain inference algorithms. In the implementation of the symbolist ML models, we tried to structure the inference process as defined by our theory. In the development of this architecture, we introduced additional master algorithms, namely, different approaches to the inference that highlight complementary learning properties. The structural complexity and the solution specificity did not allow us to compare this system with other experiments. The symbolist models depend on the specific representation chosen. The domain in which the solutions of this method are defined is unique to this paradigm. In order to compare the experimental results, we left the symbolist paradigm for the connectionist models. Therefore, the subsequent experimentation phase focused on Meta Learning in artificial neural networks. More specifically, we experimented with different models in the Machine Learning branch called Neural Architecture Search (NAS). We compared several NAS algorithms and analyzed how they work. Finally, we tried to apply new methods and techniques to the architecture that seemed more promising to us (i.e., AutoKeras). This experimental phase led us to conclude that the connectionist paradigm alone is not sufficient to solve the NAS problem. It also allowed us to recognize that the reinforcement learning (RL) method has already addressed the problem of modeling complex dynamic structures. In the third experimental phase, we looked for learning characteristics and properties that could scale in complexity to model complex systems such as the Neural Architecture Search. In particular, we found the RL approach interesting from this point of view. In this phase, we integrated, combined, and tested RL models based on each of the five paradigms of Machine Learning. We managed to obtain competitive results with the State of the Art by applying the analogizer and the connectionist paradigms together. A possible key for reading our results is that the combination of such paradigms makes reasoning complex enough to model the learning of the system itself.

As a first future development, we wish to focus on a framework for General Artificial Intelligence which would allow us to express all the other learning algorithms in a unique, unambiguous, formal language capable of modeling uncertainty. Pedro Domingos' Markov Logic Networks could represent a good starting point for the development of this framework. We also plan to work on the alternative use of learning in the evolutionary paradigm, not for the definition of structures, but the specification of learning algorithms. This paradigm is successful in the definition of structures since it can model the presence of discrete variables better than the connectionist paradigm. Therefore, our idea is to extend the originality of the solutions proposed by the evolutionary paradigm to the definition of algorithms. Further future development could concern reinforcement learning techniques. More specifically, after successfully applying the routing to reinforcement learning, we are currently exploring a Machine Learning branch known as Auxiliary Learning. In this application scenario, we believe that the system we designed (A2C with routing) may provide noteworthy results since the capsule routing allows us to model the hierarchical relationships present in these systems.

References

1. Biancalana, C., Gasparetti, F., Micarelli, A., Miola, A., Sansonetti, G.: Context-aware movie recommendation based on signal processing and machine learning. In: Proceedings of the 2nd Challenge on Context-Aware Movie Recommendation, CAMRa 2011, pp. 5–10. ACM, New York (2011)
2. Biancalana, C., Gasparetti, F., Micarelli, A., Sansonetti, G.: An approach to social recommendation for context-aware mobile services. ACM Trans. Intell. Syst. Technol. 4(1), 10:1–10:31 (2013)
3. Bologna, C., De Rosa, A.C., De Vivo, A., Gaeta, M., Sansonetti, G., Viserta, V.: Personality-based recommendation in e-commerce. In: CEUR Workshop Proceedings, vol. 997. CEUR-WS.org, Aachen (2013)
4. Caldarelli, S., Gurini, D.F., Micarelli, A., Sansonetti, G.: A signal-based approach to news recommendation. In: CEUR Workshop Proceedings, vol. 1618. CEUR-WS.org, Aachen (2016)
5. Choi, J., Seo, H., Im, S., Kang, M.: Attention routing between capsules. In: Proceedings of the IEEE International Conference on Computer Vision Workshops (ICCVW), pp. 1981–1989 (2019)
6. Church, A.: An unsolvable problem of elementary number theory. Am. J. Math. 58(2), 345–363 (1936)
7. D'Aniello, G., Gaeta, M., Orciuoli, F., Sansonetti, G., Sorgente, F.: Knowledge-based smart city service system. Electronics (Switzerland) 9(6), 1–22 (2020)
8. Domingos, P.: The Master Algorithm: How the Quest for the Ultimate Learning Machine Will Remake Our World. Basic Books, New York (2015)
9. Elsken, T., Metzen, J., Hutter, F.: Neural architecture search: a survey. J. Mach. Learn. Res. 20, 1–21 (2019)

10. Feltoni Gurini, D., Gasparetti, F., Micarelli, A., Sansonetti, G.: Temporal people-to-people recommendation on social networks with sentiment-based matrix factorization. Future Gener. Comput. Syst. **78**, 430–439 (2018)
11. Fogli, A., Sansonetti, G.: Exploiting semantics for context-aware itinerary recommendation. Pers. Ubiquit. Comput. **23**(2), 215–231 (2019). https://doi.org/10.1007/s00779-018-01189-7
12. Goodfellow, I., et al..: Generative adversarial nets. In: Advances in Neural Information Processing Systems, pp. 2672–2680 (2014)
13. Graves, A., et al.: Hybrid computing using a neural network with dynamic external memory. Nature **538**(7626), 471–476 (2016)
14. Hahn, T., Pyeon, M., Kim, G.: Self-routing capsule networks. In: Advances in Neural Information Processing Systems, pp. 7656–7665 (2019)
15. Hassan, H.A.M., Sansonetti, G., Gasparetti, F., Micarelli, A.: Semantic-based tag recommendation in scientific bookmarking systems. In: Proceedings of ACM RecSys 2018, pp. 465–469. ACM, New York (2018)
16. Hassan, H.A.M., Sansonetti, G., Gasparetti, F., Micarelli, A., Beel, J.: BERT, ELMo, USE and infersent sentence encoders: the panacea for research-paper recommendation? In: Tkalcic, M., Pera, S. (eds.) Proceedings of ACM RecSys 2019 Late-Breaking Results, vol. 2431, pp. 6–10 (2019). CEUR-WS.org
17. Heekeren, H.R., Marrett, S., Ungerleider, L.G.: The neural systems that mediate human perceptual decision making. Nat. Rev. Neurosci. **9**(6), 467–479 (2008)
18. Hilbert, D.: Die grundlagen der mathematik. In: Die Grundlagen der Mathematik, pp. 1–21. Springer, Wiesbaden (1928). https://doi.org/10.1007/978-3-663-16102-8
19. Hinton, G.E., Krizhevsky, A., Wang, S.D.: Transforming auto-encoders. In: Honkela, T., Duch, W., Girolami, M., Kaski, S. (eds.) ICANN 2011. LNCS, vol. 6791, pp. 44–51. Springer, Heidelberg (2011). https://doi.org/10.1007/978-3-642-21735-7_6
20. Hinton, G.E., Sabour, S., Frosst, N.: Matrix capsules with EM routing. In: International Conference on Learning Representations (2018)
21. Hochreiter, S., Schmidhuber, J.: Long short-term memory. Neural Comput. **9**(8), 1735–1780 (1997)
22. Jin, H., Song, Q., Hu, X.: Auto-Keras: an efficient neural architecture search system. In: Proceedings of the 25th ACM SIGKDD International Conference on Knowledge Discovery and Data Mining, pp. 1946–1956 (2019)
23. Kandasamy, K., Neiswanger, W., Schneider, J., Poczos, B., Xing, E.P.: Neural architecture search with Bayesian optimisation and optimal transport. In: Advances in Neural Information Processing System, vol. 31, pp. 2016–2025. Curran Associates, Inc. (2018)
24. Liu, H., Simonyan, K., Vinyals, O., Fernando, C., Kavukcuoglu, K.: Hierarchical representations for efficient architecture search. In: Proceedings of the 6th International Conference on Learning Representations (ICLR), Vancouver, BC, Canada (2018)
25. McGill, M., Perona, P.: Deciding how to decide: dynamic routing in artificial neural networks. In: Proceedings of the 34th International Conference on Machine Learning, vol. 70, pp. 2363–2372 (2017). JMLR.org
26. Onori, M., Micarelli, A., Sansonetti, G.: A comparative analysis of personality-based music recommender systems. In: CEUR Workshop Proceedings, vol. 1680, pp. 55–59. CEUR-WS.org, Aachen (2016)

27. Real, E., Aggarwal, A., Huang, Y., Le, Q.V.: Regularized evolution for image classifier architecture search. In: Proceedings of the Thirty-Third AAAI Conference on Artificial Intelligence (AAAI), 27 January–1 February 2019, Honolulu, Hawaii, USA, pp. 4780–4789 (2019)
28. Sansonetti, G.: Point of interest recommendation based on social and linked open data. Pers. Ubiquit. Comput. **23**(2), 199–214 (2019). https://doi.org/10.1007/s00779-019-01218-z
29. Sansonetti, G., Gasparetti, F., Micarelli, A., Cena, F., Gena, C.: Enhancing cultural recommendations through social and linked open data. User Model. User Adap. Inter. **29**(1), 121–159 (2019). https://doi.org/10.1007/s11257-019-09225-8
30. Schmidhuber, J.: Optimal ordered problem solver. Mach. Learn. **54**(3), 211–254 (2004)
31. Trask, A., Hill, F., Reed, S., Rae, J., Dyer, C., Blunsom, P.: Neural arithmetic logic units. In: Proceedings of the 32nd International Conference on Neural Information Processing Systems, NIPS 2018. Curran Associates Inc., New York (2018)
32. Turing, A.M.: On computable numbers, with an application to the entscheidungsproblem. Proc. Lond. Math.Soc. **2**(1), 230–265 (1937)
33. Zoph, B., Le, Q.V.: Neural architecture search with reinforcement learning. arXiv:abs/1611.01578 (2016)

Contextualized BERT Sentence Embeddings for Author Profiling: The Cost of Performances

Marco Polignano[(✉)], Marco de Gemmis, and Giovanni Semeraro

Department of Computer Science, University of Bari Aldo Moro,
Via E. Orabona 4, 70125 Bari, Italy
{marco.polignano,marco.degemmis,giovanni.semeraro}@uniba.it

Abstract. The necessity to know information about the real identity of an online subject is a highly relevant issue in User Profiling, especially for analysis from digital sources such as social media. The digital identity of a user does not always present explicit data about her offline life such as age, gender, work, and more. This problem makes the task of user profiling complex and incomplete. For many years this issue has received a considerable amount of attention from the whole community, which has developed several solutions, also based on machine learning, to estimate user characteristics. The increasing diffusion of deep learning approaches has allowed, on the one hand, to obtain a considerable increase in predictive performance, but on the other hand, to have available models that cannot be interpreted and that require very high computational power. Considering the validity of new pre-trained language models on extensive data for resolving many natural language processing and classification tasks, we decided to propose a BERT-based approach (BERT-DNN) also for the author profiling task. In a first analysis, we compared the results obtained by our model with them of more classical approaches. As a follow, a critical analysis was carried out. We analyze the advantages and disadvantages of these approaches also in terms of resources needed to run them. The results obtained by our model are encouraging in terms of reliability but very disappointing if we consider the computational power required for running it.

Keywords: Language model · Author profiling · Classification · Machine learning · Deep learning · BERT

1 Introduction and Motivation

Social media plays a fundamental role in everyone's life nowadays. Our digital identity is vast and rich in details due to the many online platforms used to share information with other users about interests, places visited, or, more generally, what we are doing. This interesting data source has been extensively used to perform different types of analysis [15], such as sentiment analysis [19,25,26],

© Springer Nature Switzerland AG 2020
O. Gervasi et al. (Eds.): ICCSA 2020, LNCS 12252, pp. 135–149, 2020.
https://doi.org/10.1007/978-3-030-58811-3_10

preference extraction [38], and holistic user profiling in general [18]. As a result of the increasingly stringent laws regarding the privacy of users GDPR [35], it is always less possible to access and use the data provided directly by users such as date of birth, gender, working position. As a consequence, it is coming to gain new interest in the task of estimating personal user information directly from the public content produced by them. This task is commonly known as author profiling and aims to make estimations of users descriptive data [20]. Just think of a company that wants to carry out a market survey about its products. It will require information such as age, gender, and other personal and social data about its buyers. Knowing these user details, it can be possible to imagine how targeted advertising campaigns, corrective actions of products, or a better segmentation of the target market can be carried out. Since 2013 [28], the relationship between user characteristics and the language used on social media [20] is widely addressed in PAN campaigns [29] promoted by CLEF (Conference and Labs of the Evaluation Forum). Solutions based on probabilistic representations of text and classic machine learning approaches have proven to be effective in resolving this task. Concurrently, new language model-based linguistic approaches have emerged for many classification and inference tasks [11]. Among them, BERT [6] has proven to be the current state of the art for solving many natural language processing tasks. Given the wide diffusion of these natural language models, the importance of the author profiling task, and the small use of complex deep neural network solutions in this domain, it was decided to propose a deep learning model based on the text representations generated by BERT. We decided to compare the results obtained by our approach with them of SVM, Linear Regression, and Random Forest. Moreover, we compare the computational power required and the execution time of the evaluated approaches to estimate if the differences in predictions justify the high training cost of novel models.

2   Related Work

The author profiling task was widely addressed, each method with a specific focus on some descriptive aspects of the user. Starting from the works in the psychological field [20] that correlated the style of writing with the personality traits of the users, we defined more solutions able to explore more varied connections among written text and user such as related to age, gender, education, and more. Numerous datasets have been released since 2006 [32], starting from data about Emails [8] and Blog articles [31], up to data extracted from social media such as Twitter [3] and Facebook [33]. In particular, since 2013 [28], the number of datasets and solutions released has significantly increased, thanks to the PAN evaluation campaign promoted by CLEF. Looking at the task of author profiling celebrities proposed for PAN 2019 [5] it is possible to observe that although the amount of data available was very large, the number of solutions based on deep neural networks was extremely low (only three experiments with negative results) compared to the number of solutions based on classic machine learning approaches (Support Vector Machines, Logistic Regression, Random Forests). This observation is a strong indicator of the great difficulty in using deep learning solutions that are scalable in case of big data such as for this task. The winning solution of the 2019 challenge [27] reports the use of SVM and TF-IDF as the most effective solution to predict the traits of fame and occupation, while using logistic regression to predict the year of birth and gender. This approach is considered in this work as a baseline to compare the efficacy of BERT-DNN approach. Moreover, as proposed by Petrik and Chuda [23], we will also evaluate the performances of a random forest classifier with 200 decision trees on TF-IDF vector of the top 10,000 n-grams with the value from one to three. Considering the difficulties in using deep learning approaches in the task, we decided to investigate the issue by using approaches already proven to be effective for other Natural Language Processing tasks [24]. Specifically, the new task-independent language models pre-trained on large amounts of data have proved to be the right way to get a context-aware and efficient word representation for classification tasks. A Task-Independent Language Model is based on the idea of creating a deep learning architecture, particularly an encoder and a decoder, so that the encoding level can be used in more than one NLP task. In this way, it is possible to obtain a decoding level with weights optimized for the specific task (fine-tuning). Following this basic idea BERT (Bidirectional Encoder Representations from Transformers) [7] was trained on a Transformer network with 12 encoding levels, 768-dimensional states and 12 heads of attention for a total of 110M of parameters trained on BooksCorpus [40] and Wikipedia English for 1M of steps. The learning phase is performed by scanning the span of text in both directions, from left to right and from right to left, as was already done in BiLSTMs. Moreover, BERT uses a "masked language model": during the training, random terms are masked in order to be predicted by the net. These peculiarities allow BERT to be the current state of the art language model. We are going to use BERT in its large version to produce contextual word embeddings used as input of our designed deep neural network.

3   BERT-SE: Language Model for Sentence Embeddings

A general-purpose encoder should be able to provide an efficient representation of the terms, their position in the sentence, context, the grammatical structure of the sentence, semantics of the terms. The idea behind language models is that if a model can predict the next word that follows in a sentence, then it is able to generalize the syntactic and semantic rules of the language. In a different way from classic probabilistic word embeddings like word2vec, BERT is developed for the context-aware encoding of terms. Approaches as Word2Vec [17], Glove [21], and FastText [2] suffer from the problem that multiple concepts, associated with the same term, are not represented by different word embedding vectors in the distributional space (the representation is *context-free*). This means that each term has only a single word embedding representation in the distributional space, and different concepts of the same term are not represented. The word embedding created by BERT is dependent on the position of the term in the sentence (positional embedding), the sentence in which it occurs (sentence embedding), and the co-occurrences of the terms in a window with a bidirectional span (term embedding). Considering this approach, it is therefore clear that in order to embed a single term, it is necessary to encode the entire sentence through the entire BERT encoding pipeline.

Since at the end of each encoding phase, BERT generates a word embedding of the input phrase, it is necessary to decide which one of them to use. In order to solve this problem, several solutions have been proposed in the literature. One of them is to use a strategy similar to the established one for the ELMo language model [22]. Specifically, we will concatenate the results of the last n encoding layers of the model, for example, the last 2. The selection of how many layers to use is a parameter to estimate according to the application domain. Another strategy, proposed in [16] is to use as embedding representative of the whole sentence the value assigned by the model to the $[CLS]$ token, that is the token used as a separator between the sentences adopted in the model for the training phase "next sentence to predict". This solution brings with it the loss of information and does not respect the properties of similarity such that semantically similar sentences have similar representations.

To solve the problems highlighted, we shared the idea of using the approach proposed in [30] based on the use of siamese networks for the generation of semantically meaningful sentence embeddings. The solution proposed by Reimers [30] is based on the use of a modified version of BERT ($BERT$-SE), able to tune the weights of the model so that the sentence embeddings are comparable through a measure of cosine similarity. The model was fine-tuned on the SNLI task (sentences entailment and contradictions) using an objective function able to maximize the similarity among entailed sentences followed by a task of poly-encoders to compute a mean score between all output vectors. In our approach, we used the sentence-transformers library[1] with "bert-large-nli-stsb-mean-tokens" model for the generation of 1024 size sentence embeddings for sentences not longer than 128 tokens. If we incur in phrases longer than this limit, the sentence will be truncated.

4   BERT-DNN for Author Profiling

The model of author profiling proposed in this study ($BERT$-DNN) is based on the synergy between two deep learning classification approaches, the long-short-term memory networks (LSTM) [10] in their bi-directional variation and the convolutional neural networks [13] (CNN) mediated by a max-pooling approach as already adopted in [24]. Moreover, we decided to include, after the Bi-LSTM, a self-attention layer to allow the system to capture distant relationships among words with different weights depending on their contribution to the classification. Figure 1 shows the complete stack of the proposed model.

The first layer of the model has the purpose of accepting as input a set of 150 BERT-SE sentences embeddings representing the last contents generated

---

[1] https://github.com/UKPLab/sentence-transformers.

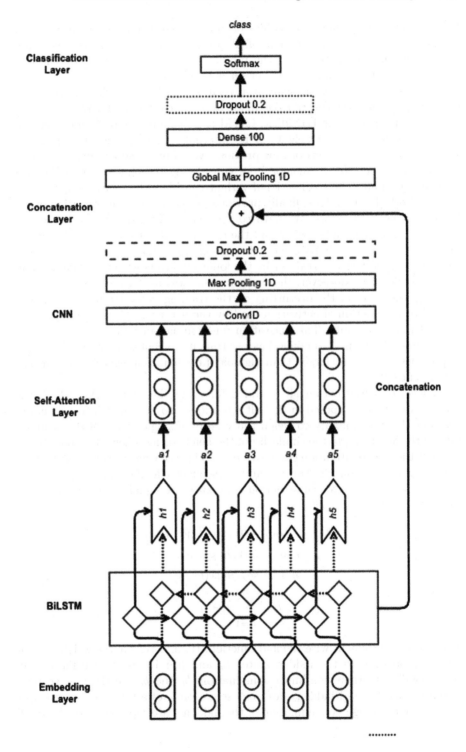

Fig. 1. The architecture of the classification model based on Bi-LSTM, CNN and Self-Attention

by the user. Since some user profiles do not contain enough content, padding with arrays of 1024 zeros will be applied in order to reach the designated input dimension. On the contrary, for the profiles with more content, only the first contents up to the maximum number set will be considered.

Considering the intrinsic sequential relationship between the contents produced sequentially, the contribution made by a recurrent neural network in order to grasp this relationship is evident. LSTM uses the forget gate (hidden neuron) to dynamically scale the weights of its internal "self-loop" depending on the weights learned by the network for previous words provided as input [10]. This step provides the layer a "memory" for considering the relations with the past elements in input. The bi-directional variant considers the relationships among data by both the directions, finally provided as output the concatenation of the links from both the sides. We have configured the LSTM network by setting the value of hidden units to 512 and the dropout value to 0.3. This choice was motivated by the need to reduce the dimensionality of the output of the network so that the operations carried out by the following layers were not computationally too expensive. Moreover, the dropout value was used to reduce, during the learning, the effect of the overfitting on the training data. We have decided to vary also the function of activation used by the net setting it to the hyperbolic tangent function (tanh). This activation function has an S-Shape and produces values among -1 and 1, making layer output more center to the 0. Moreover, it provides a gradient larger than sigmoid function, helping to speed up the convergence [9].

A level of self-attention [4] is added following the LSTM. As well as the attention strategy proposed in [1], self-attention, also known as intra-attention, provides the model ability to weigh the vectors of single words of the sentence differently, according to the similarity of the neighboring tokens. It is possible to say that the level of attention can provide us an idea of what features the network is looking at most during learning and subsequent classification. In particular, we consider an additive self-attention context-aware equal to the whole set of words in input (Eq. 1) [39].

$$h_{t,t'} = tanh(x_t^T W_t + x_{t'}^T W_{t'} + b_t)$$
$$e_{t,t'} = \sigma(W_e h_{t,t'} + b_e)$$
$$a_{t,t'} = softmax(e_{t,t'}) \tag{1}$$
$$l_t = \sum_{t'=1}^{n} a_{t,t'} x_{t'}$$

where, σ is the element-wise sigmoid function, W_t and W_t' are the weight matrices corresponding to the hidden states h_t and $h_{t'}$; W_e is the weight matrix corresponding to their non-linear combination; b_t and b_e are the bias vectors. The attention-focused hidden state representation l_t of a token at timestamp t is given by the weighted summation of the hidden state representation $h_{t'}$ of all other tokens at timesteps t. We use the last self-attention implementation for Keras[2].

CNN is a robust neural network ideal for working on data with a shape of grid [12] as a consequence of the convolutional operations performed by the algorithm over adjacent cells. The result of the convolution is a grid more dense and smaller than the previous that captures the hidden relations among cells that fall in the kernel dimension. In our specific case, we applied the CNN layer on the result of the attention algorithm. Such hidden level has a matrix form as a consequence of the vectorial representation supplied by the word embeddings on the tokens in input. In detail, it has the form 150×1024, which allows us to apply a 1D Convolutional network with 1024 filters and 5×5 kernel. We used, as activation function, ReLu that unlike the hyperbolic tangent is faster to calculate [9].

On the top of the CNN layer, we added a Max Pooling function for subsampling the values obtained, reducing the computational load and, the number of parameters of the model. In particular, we used a small 2×2 kernel. On the output of the last max-pooling layer, we applied a dropout function and a dense layer of size for reducing the number of connections inside the model and limiting the effect of overfitting [9]. Dropout is a common regularization technique that, for a defined value of p, sets p fraction of units to 0 at each update during training time. The hidden model obtained until this step has been merged with the output of the previous Bi-LSTM. We apply this operation for letting the model conceptualize both local and long-term features better. After that, we used a max-pooling layer for 'flatten' the results and reduce the model parameter. An analog function of dimensionality reduction is performed by the consequent dense layer and the following dropping function. Finally, another dense layer with a soft-max activation function has been applied for estimating the probability distribution of each class of the dataset.

The model has been trained using the categorical cross-entropy loss function [9], and Adam optimizer for 20 epochs and best models have been used for the classification phase. For the regression task, we substitute the last layer of the model with one using the linear activation function, and the root means squared error as a loss function.

5   Evaluation

The aim of the experimental session is twofold:

- evaluate the efficacy of the here proposed BERT-DNN classification model;
- study the computational cost of BERT-DNN and to compare it with classical machine learning algorithms.

More specifically, in order to achieve the first experimental goal, we performed an experiment where we compare the results obtained by BERT-DNN with them of the two best models presented during the PAN 19 evaluation campaign [5][3].

---

[2] https://github.com/CyberZHG/keras-self-attention.

[3] https://pan.webis.de/clef19/pan19-web/celebrity-profiling.html.

Moreover, we added another baseline changing the input of our proposed model. In particular, we substitute the BERT-SE embeddings with the TF-IDF vectors of each document considering the most frequent 10000 n-grams of size from one to three, in order to evaluate the contribution of the BERT-SE embeddings to the model. This model is from here referred as TFIDF-DNN.

Our first baseline is the model proposed by Radivchev et al. [27], the winner of the challenge, reports the use of *SVM* and TF-IDF as the most effective solution to predict the traits of fame and occupation, while using *logistic regression* to predict the year of birth and gender. The authors reported the use of a pre-processing pipeline that consists of removing retweets, all symbols except letters numbers, @ and #; replacing URLs, mentions; remove multiple spaces. The user tweets were transformed with a TF-IDF vectorizer, taking into account the top 10,000 features from single words and bigrams. Moreover, they use different *class_weights* depending on the number of labeled examples for each class. During the phase of tuning of hyper-parameters of the classification models, Radivchev et al. report the best performances using the SVM with a *rbf* kernel and $c = 0.1$ for the "fame" aspect and $c = 0.5$ for the "occupation" aspect. Regarding the "gender" aspect, a logistic regression was used with $solver = nnewton\_cg$", while a version with standard with $solver = "lbfgs"$ was used for the "age" aspect[4].

The second model used as a baseline is the one proposed by Petrik and Chuda [23]. A Random forest with 200 decision trees was chosen as a final classification model. They started with a preliminary pre-processing phase that consists of removing from tweets mentions, letters repeated more than two times, accented letters, and stop-words; URLs have been replaced with a standard <url> tag; emoji have been translated into their word description. Petrik and Chuda us n-grams of size from one to three, as it is commonly and successfully used in a high number of natural language tasks.

The investigation of our second experimental goal has been performed analyzing some simple performance metrics. We measured them during the standard steps performed to create a classification model. First of all, we measure the time in seconds and the need of RAM in MB required by the algorithms to perform pre-processing and sentence encoding. In particular, for these two metrics, we performed a more in-depth analysis varying the amount of data provided as the input of the encoding processes. The same metrics have been also used for the training phase and the prediction of the model on the test set.

Dataset. The evaluation of the model has been performed on the dataset released by Wiegmann et al. [37] for the author profiling competition at PAN 19 [5]. The distinctive characteristic of this dataset is the presence of a new user feature, *the fame of social networks*, that has been added at the list of the other more common user descriptive features. Moreover, this dataset has been robustly validated through Wikidata. The user profiles have been linked with it, thank the peculiarity that they were referring to the profiles of famous people

---

[4] https://scikit-learn.org/stable/modules/generated/sklearn.linear_model. LogisticRegression.html.

(celebrities). The dataset contains 33,836 celebrities with up to 3,200 tweets each and 156,411,899 tweets in total (around 3 billion words). The task organizers do not publicly provide the dataset used for the testing phase during the challenge. Consequently, we started with the idea to split the whole dataset into portions 70% training, 10% validation set, 20% test set. Unfortunately, starting the process of sentence conversion into word-embeddings, using the BERT-SE strategy described in Sect. 3, we noted that the processing took a too long time (around 50000 tweets/hour). As a consequence, we randomly selected 6000 celebrities for the training phase, 1500 for the validation and 2250 for the test, limiting the number of tweets for each account at 150, for a total number of tweets equal to 1462500.

Into the dataset, the following values are possible for each of the user traits to predict:

```
fame          := {rising , star , superstar}
occupation    := {sports , performer , creator ,
                  politics , manager , science ,
                  professional , religious}
birthyear     := {1940, ... , 2012}
gender        := {male , female , nonbinary}
```

The prediction performance for $T \in \{gender, fame, occupation\}$ is measured using the macro-averaged multi-class F1-score. The *"birtyear"* is considered as correct if it is within an m-window of the true year, where m increases linearly from 2 to 9 years with the true age of the celebrity in question: $m = (-0.1 * truth + 202.8)$ as described in the official competition [5].

The code[5] has been run on a Google Colab[6] Python 3 environment equipped with 25 GB of RAM, a GPU (a single 12 GB NVIDIA Tesla K80 GPU) and unlimited disk space on Google Storage Bucket Platform.

Discussion of Results. The results in Table 1 shows how the approach BERT based (BERT-DNN) is the best compared with the three baselines. As described in Sect. 2, the approaches we are comparing are the two best results during the PAN 2019 celebrity profiling competition and a variation of the here proposed BERT-DNN method that uses documents TF-IDF as input. For all the four classification tasks the F1 score obtained by BERT-DNN is around 2% better than the one of competitors. This result highlights the optimal performance of the neural model compared with the traditional machine learning approach. The differences in scores have been statistically validated for each pair of models using Wilcoxon Signed-Ranked Test. We obtain that the differences among BERT-DNN and all the other approaches are statistically significant for p <0.05. The best performances of BERT-DNN are not surprising. It is well known in the literature that the new language models such as BERT, RoBERTa [14], ERNIE [34], are actually the best resources to use for formalizing the relations among

---

[5] The source code of the project can be found at the following GitHub repository: https://github.com/marcopoli/ICCSA2020_author_profiling.
[6] https://colab.research.google.com/.

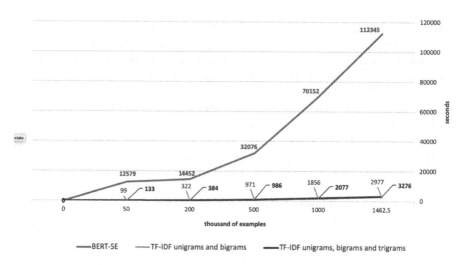

Fig. 2. In the figure it is reported the variation of the encoding time varying the number of examples provided to the function.

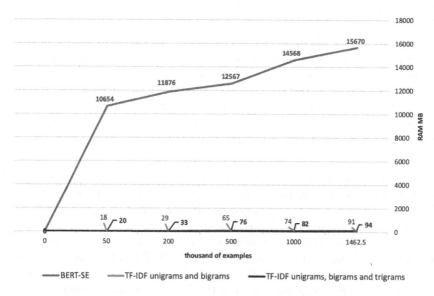

Fig. 3. In the figure it is reported the variation of the RAM need for encoding phrases varying the number of examples provided to the function.

words and their semantical meaning. Analogs results have been obtained in many other tasks of natural language understanding [36]. In particular, in our experiment, the relevance of BERT based embeddings has been demonstrated by the differences obtained in our model using the TF-IDF strategy as the input of the DNN. Indeed, it is possible to observe that these results obtained by the TFIDF-DNN are always lower of them of BERT-DNN. This encouraging results

Table 1. F1 scores obtained for the prediction of each of the author's descriptive features. Results market with a ∗ are statistically significant for p <0.05 using a Wilcoxon Signed-Ranked Test.

Task	BERT-DNN	TFIDF-DNN	SVM (rbf) + LinearRegression [27]	Random Forest trees = 200 [23]
Gender F1-score	**0.89415**∗	0.87523	0.86738	0.65980
Age F1-score	**0.83221**∗	0.813452	0.80489	0.69784
Fame F1-Score	**0.77840**∗	0.75712	0.74420	0.67321
Occupation F1-Score	**0.72733**∗	0.71095	0.70871	0.65978

Table 2. In the table are reported some statistics about the computational cost of the three approaches here discussed.

Metric	BERT-DNN	SVM (rbf) + LinearRegression [27]	Random Forest trees = 200 [23]
Text encoding time (s)	BERT-SE 112345	TF-IDF n-grams; n = 1, 2 **2977**	TF-IDF n-grams n = 1, 2, 3 3276
Text encoding space (MB)	BERT-SE 15670	TF-IDF n-grams; n = 1, 2 **91**	TF-IDF n-grams n = 1, 2, 3 94.7
Learning Time (s)	TPU-V2 934	CPU 1084	CPU **669**
Learning Space (MB)	RAM 18346	RAM **789**	RAM 922
Prediction Time (s)	TPU-V2 **12**	CPU 185	CPU **125**
Prediction Space (MB)	RAM 12561	RAM **649**	RAM 856

support our hypothesis about the importance of using a BERT based approach for sentence embedding, such as BERT-SE, for obtaining more accurate results when we deal with a text classification task, e.g., author profiling.

On the other hand, observing the analysis of complexity described in Table 2, it is easy to note how the computational time and space of the BERT-DNN model are very high in total compared with those of SVM and Random Forest. Classical models can be run on a standard computer with few RAM (8GB are more than enough) and a standard CPU. A BERT-based approach requires, instead, a TPU (patented by Google) and a much high performer machine. Moreover, using a classic SVM approach, it could be possible to train the model on a much larger dataset without encounter the problems observed using BERT-DNN.

Moreover, observing the Fig. 2 it is possible to note how the BERT-SE encoding takes a quite flat time of execution until it reaches a threshold of about 200,000 examples. After that, the time of encoding is increasing linearly. This behavior is due to the time necessary at the startup to load into the computer memory the BERT-SE pre-trained model. After that, the model starts to work on the sentences encoding normally, showing an increase of time of execution proportionally to the number of sentences to process. A slight reduction of performances is observable in the same figure when the model overcomes the threshold of 1,000,000 examples. In this scenario, the large amount of memory required for storing temporal data negatively affects also the execution time. The behavior of the TF-IDF vectorizer is quite constant without significant differences when working with only unigrams and bigrams or also with trigrams. The behavior of BERT-SE is easier to observe in Fig. 3 where it is shown the variation in consumption of RAM during the encoding phase. In an initial step, BERT-SE consumes a large amount of RAM for loading into the computer memory its pre-trained model. After that, the amount of ram required is increasing linearly. Also in this case, the behaviour of the TF-IDF vectorizer is constant requiring a low amount of RAM without significant distinction if it is working with unigrams, bigrams or trigrams.

Taking into consideration both the aspects, the model performances in complexity and accuracy, we can consider the increment in performances of the BERT-based approach too much low to be justified by the enormous quantity of computational power need for running it. Our hypothesis about the increase in performances using a BERT based approach is confirmed, but the large amount of computational power need for running it is still not convincing. This can cause significant limits in research about the topic forcing those who do not have the appropriate resources to settle for reduced datasets or lower precision of the model. In this regard, we would like to suggest to the community a further research effort to make these models more straightforward and more affordable for everyone in a future perspective of using deep learning in everyday activities of common use.

6   Conclusion

The prediction of descriptive features of a digital profile is a task of author profiling that is continuously gathering increasing attention. In this work, we proposed an approach based on the latest natural language model, i.e., BERT-SE and an LSTM-CNN deep neural network. We compared the accuracy of this model with classic approaches of machine learning that won the PAN 19 competition about author profiling. The results are encouraging if we only consider the F1 score obtained on the celebrity profiling dataset, but are very disappointing if we also consider the computational power need for running the BERT-DNN model. Novel strategies that consume less computational power should be investigated more in the future, and when less complex strategies could obtain similar performances in the scenario of application, these should be adopted. In this regard, we would like to encourage the further analysis of trade-off between accuracy and performances because a small improvement could, very often, be not justified by the high increase of computational power need for running the model. Moreover, we would like to support the idea that BERT is not always the best solution for any application scenario, as often claimed. In particular, a trade-off analysis should always be reported into new researches when a new state of the art result is claimed.

Acknowledgment. This research has been funded by Regione Puglia under the programme "INNOLABS" Sostegno alla creazione di soluzioni innovative finalizzate a specifici problemi di rilevanza sociale. POR Puglia FESR – FSE 2014-2020. Asse prioritario 1 – Ricerca, sviluppo tecnologico, innovazione. Azione 1.4.b - Project: Feel@Home cod. UIKTJF3.

References

1. Bahdanau, D., Cho, K., Bengio, Y.: Neural machine translation by jointly learning to align and translate. arXiv preprint arXiv:1409.0473 (2014)
2. Bojanowski, P., Grave, E., Joulin, A., Mikolov, T.: Enriching word vectors with subword information. Trans. Assoc. Comput. Linguist. **5**, 135–146 (2017)
3. Burger, J.D., Henderson, J., Kim, G., Zarrella, G.: Discriminating gender on twitter. In: Proceedings of the Conference on Empirical Methods in Natural Language Processing, pp. 1301–1309. Association for Computational Linguistics (2011)
4. Cheng, J., Dong, L., Lapata, M.: Long short-term memory-networks for machine reading. arXiv preprint arXiv:1601.06733 (2016)
5. Daelemans, W., et al.: Overview of PAN 2019: author profiling, celebrity profiling, cross-domain authorship attribution and style change detection. In: Crestani, F., et al. (eds.) 10th International Conference of the CLEF Association (CLEF 2019). Springer, September 2019. http://ceur-ws.org/Vol-2380/
6. Devlin, J., Chang, M.W., Lee, K., Toutanova, K.: Bert: Pre-training of deep bidirectional transformers for language understanding. arXiv preprint arXiv:1810.04805 (2018)
7. Devlin, J., Chang, M.W., Lee, K., Toutanova, K.: BERT: pre-training of deep bidirectional transformers for language understanding. In: Proceedings of the 2019 Conference of the North American Chapter of the Association for Computational Linguistics: Human Language Technologies, Volume 1 (Long and Short Papers), pp. 4171–4186. Association for Computational Linguistics, Minneapolis, Minnesota, June 2019. https://www.aclweb.org/anthology/N19-1423
8. Estival, D., Gaustad, T., Pham, S.B., Radford, W., Hutchinson, B.: Author profiling for English emails. In: Proceedings of the 10th Conference of the Pacific Association for Computational Linguistics, pp. 263–272 (2007)
9. Goodfellow, I., Bengio, Y., Courville, A., Bengio, Y.: Deep Learning, vol. 1. MIT Press, Cambridge (2016)
10. Hochreiter, S., Schmidhuber, J.: Long short-term memory. Neural Comput. **9**(8), 1735–1780 (1997)
11. Jing, K., Xu, J., He, B.: A survey on neural network language models. arXiv preprint arXiv:1906.03591 (2019)
12. Kalchbrenner, N., Grefenstette, E., Blunsom, P.: A convolutional neural network for modelling sentences. arXiv preprint arXiv:1404.2188 (2014)

13. LeCun, Y., et al.: Generalization and network design strategies. In: Connectionism in Perspective, pp. 143–155 (1989)
14. Liu, Y., et al.: Roberta: a robustly optimized Bert pretraining approach. arXiv preprint arXiv:1907.11692 (2019)
15. López-Monroy, A.P., Montes-y Gómez, M., Escalante, H.J., Villasenor-Pineda, L., Stamatatos, E.: Discriminative subprofile-specific representations for author profiling in social media. Knowl. Based Syst. **89**, 134–147 (2015)
16. MacAvaney, S., Yates, A., Cohan, A., Goharian, N.: Cedr: contextualized embeddings for document ranking. In: Proceedings of the 42nd International ACM SIGIR Conference on Research and Development in Information Retrieval, pp. 1101–1104 (2019)
17. Mikolov, T., Sutskever, I., Chen, K., Corrado, G.S., Dean, J.: Distributed representations of words and phrases and their compositionality. In: Advances in Neural Information Processing Systems, pp. 3111–3119 (2013)
18. Musto, C., Semeraro, G., Lovascio, C., de Gemmis, M., Lops, P.: Myrror: a platform for quantified self and holistic user modeling. In: Adjunct Publication of the 26th Conference on User Modeling, Adaptation and Personalization, pp. 215–216 (2018)
19. Pang, B., Lee, L., et al.: Opinion mining and sentiment analysis. Found. Trends® Inf. Retrieval **2**(1–2), 1–135 (2008)
20. Pennebaker, J.W., Mehl, M.R., Niederhoffer, K.G.: Psychological aspects of natural language use: our words, our selves. Annu. Rev. Psychol. **54**(1), 547–577 (2003)
21. Pennington, J., Socher, R., Manning, C.: Glove: global vectors for word representation. In: Proceedings of the 2014 Conference on Empirical Methods in Natural Language Processing (EMNLP), pp. 1532–1543 (2014)
22. Peters, M.E., et al.: Deep contextualized word representations. arXiv preprint arXiv:1802.05365 (2018)
23. Petrik, J., Chuda, D.: Twitter feeds profiling with TF-IDF notebook for PAN at CLEF 2019, vol. 2380 (2019)
24. Polignano, M., Basile, P., de Gemmis, M., Semeraro, G.: A comparison of word-embeddings in emotion detection from text using BiLSTM, CNN and self-attention. In: Adjunct Publication of the 27th Conference on User Modeling, Adaptation and Personalization, pp. 63–68 (2019)
25. Polignano, M., Basile, P., Rossiello, G., de Gemmis, M., Semeraro, G.: Learning inclination to empathy from social media footprints. In: Proceedings of the 25th Conference on User Modeling, Adaptation and Personalization, pp. 383–384 (2017)
26. Polignano, M., de Gemmis, M., Narducci, F., Semeraro, G.: Do you feel blue? Detection of negative feeling from social media. In: Esposito, F., Basili, R., Ferilli, S., Lisi, F. (eds.) Conference of the Italian Association for Artificial Intelligence, pp. 321–333. Springer (2017)
27. Radivchev, V., Nikolov, A., Lambova, A.: Celebrity profiling using TF-IDF, logistic regression, and SVM notebook for pan at CLEF 2019, vol. 2380 (2019)
28. Rangel, F., Rosso, P., Koppel, M., Stamatatos, E., Inches, G.: Overview of the author profiling task at pan 2013. In: CLEF Conference on Multilingual and Multimodal Information Access Evaluation. pp. 352–365. CELCT (2013)
29. Rangel, F., Rosso, P., Potthast, M., Stein, B.: Overview of the 5th author profiling task at pan 2017: gender and language variety identification in Twitter. In: Working Notes Papers of the CLEF, pp. 1613–1673 (2017)
30. Reimers, N., Gurevych, I.: Sentence-BERT: sentence embeddings using Siamese BERT-networks. arXiv preprint arXiv:1908.10084 (2019)

31. Rosenthal, S., McKeown, K.: Age prediction in blogs: a study of style, content, and online behavior in pre-and post-social media generations. In: Proceedings of the 49th Annual Meeting of the Association for Computational Linguistics: Human Language Technologies-Volume 1, pp. 763–772. Association for Computational Linguistics (2011)

32. Schler, J., Koppel, M., Argamon, S., Pennebaker, J.W.: Effects of age and gender on blogging. In: AAAI Spring Symposium: Computational Approaches to Analyzing Weblogs, vol. 6, pp. 199–205 (2006)

33. Schwartz, H.A., et al.: Personality, gender, and age in the language of social media: the open-vocabulary approach. PLoS ONE **8**(9), e73791 (2013)

34. Sun, Y., et al.: Ernie 2.0: a continual pre-training framework for language understanding. arXiv preprint arXiv:1907.12412 (2019)

35. Wachter, S.: Normative challenges of identification in the internet of things: Privacy, profiling, discrimination, and the GDPR. Comput. Law Secur. Rev. **34**(3), 436–449 (2018)

36. Wang, A., Singh, A., Michael, J., Hill, F., Levy, O., Bowman, S.R.: Glue: a multitask benchmark and analysis platform for natural language understanding. arXiv preprint arXiv:1804.07461 (2018)

37. Wiegmann, M., Stein, B., Potthast, M.: Celebrity profiling. In: Proceedings of the 57th Annual Meeting of the Association for Computational Linguistics. pp. 2611–2618 (2019)

38. Zhang, Y., Pennacchiotti, M.: Predicting purchase behaviors from social media. In: Proceedings of the 22nd international conference on World Wide Web, pp. 1521–1532 (2013)

39. Zheng, G., Mukherjee, S., Dong, X.L., Li, F.: OpenTag: open attribute value extraction from product profiles. In: Proceedings of the 24th ACM SIGKDD International Conference on Knowledge Discovery & Data Mining, pp. 1049–1058. ACM (2018)

40. Zhu, Y., et al.: Aligning books and movies: towards story-like visual explanations by watching movies and reading books. In: Proceedings of the IEEE International Conference on Computer Vision, pp. 19–27 (2015)

Expressive Analysis of Gut Microbiota in Pre- and Post- Solid Organ Transplantation Using Bayesian Topic Models

Luigi Santacroce[1,2]([✉]) [iD], Sara Mavaddati[2] [iD], Javad Hamedi[3] [iD],
Bahman Zeinali[4], Andrea Ballini[5] [iD], and Massimo Bilancia[1] [iD]

[1] Ionian Department (DJSGEM), University of Bari Aldo Moro, Taranto, Italy
[2] Microbiology and Virology Laboratory, Policlinico University Hospital of Bari,
Bari, Italy
luigi.santacroce@uniba.it
[3] Department of Microbial Biotechnology, School of Biology and Center of
Excellence in Phylogeny Living Organisms, College of Science, University of Tehran,
Tehran, Iran
[4] Department of Biology, Faculty of Basic Sciences, Tehran University, Tehran, Iran
[5] Department of Biosciences, Biotechnologies and Biopharmaceutics,
University of Bari Aldo Moro, Bari, Italy

Abstract. There is a growing evidence that variation in gut microbial communities has important associations with overall host health, and that the diversity and the richness of such communities is helpful in distinguishing patients at high risk of life-threatening post-transplantation conditions. The aim of our paper is to provide an expressive and highly interpretable characterization of microbiome alterations, with the goal of achieving more effective transplantations characterized by a rejection rate as low as possible, and to avoid more severe complications by treating patients at risk in a timely and effective way. For this purpose, we propose using topic models to identify those bacterial species that have the most important weight under the two different experimental conditions (healthy and transplanted patients, or patients whose fecal microbiota has been sampled both in pre- and post-transplantation phases). Topic models are Bayesian statistical models that are not affected by data scarcity, because conclusions we can draw borrow strength across sparse gut microbiome samples. By exploiting this property, we show that topic models are expressive methods for dimensionality reduction which can help analyze variation and diversity in gut microbial communities. With topic models the analysis can be carried out at a level close to natural language, as the output can be easily interpreted by clinicians, since most abundant species are automatically selected and the microbial dynamics can be tracked and followed over time.

Keywords: Solid-organ transplantation · Liver Transplantation · Gut microbiota · Topic models · Latent Dirichlet Allocation · Translational medicine

© Springer Nature Switzerland AG 2020
O. Gervasi et al. (Eds.): ICCSA 2020, LNCS 12252, pp. 150–165, 2020.
https://doi.org/10.1007/978-3-030-58811-3_11

1 Introduction

One of the most reliable but extreme treatment options for the end stage disease (ESD) patients is solid organ transplantation (SOT)[1,2]. It is well known that immunosuppression is a major treatment to prevent acute and chronic rejection, which unfortunately can lead to serious toxic side effects [3]. Similarly, infections [4], graft-versus-host disease (GVHD) and other post transplantation complications are frequent adverse events in the clinical practice [5,6]. In this context, there is a growing evidence that variation in gut microbial communities has important associations with overall host health, and that the diversity and the richness of such communities is helpful in distinguishing patients at high risk of life-threatening post-transplantation conditions, such as infections by multidrug-resistant bacteria (MDRB), from patients with less severe side effects [7].

It is well known that gut microbiota plays an essential role in promoting intestinal inflammation through the 'intestinal microbiota-immunity' axis, impacting on distal immune response and affecting other gut-organ axes, as well as in modulating disease in distant tissues by releasing metabolites such as short-chain fatty acids (SCFAs), tryptophan, phenylalanine and tyrosine [8–10]. Based on those physiological pathways, intestinal microbiota alterations in patients after transplantation have been recently investigated, demonstrating a significant shift in the intestinal microbiome composition and diversity compared to pre-transplantation condition [11,12]. However, it would be useful to have a broader view, in order to provide accurate and personalized host trait prediction based on microbiome alterations, with the goal of achieving a more effective transplantation characterized by a rejection rate as low as possible, treating patients at risk in a timely and effective way in order to avoid more severe complications.

If we limit ourselves to analyze the relationship between the microbiome and human disease, the wealth of available high-throughput 16 S ribosomal RNA data has allowed the publication of several excellent meta-analyses, which are likely to play a significant role in clinical practice over the next years [13]. However, if our objective is that of analyzing the dynamics of microbiota before or post transplantation, having in mind to compare gut bacterial populations between healthy patients and ESD patients candidate for transplantation or, for example, to study the associations existing between gut microbiota alterations and the onset of potentially life-threatening complications, difficulties arise because we do not have, at present, a large amount of published data. To give an idea, we searched PubMed using the MeSH thesaurus and a suitable query, with which we retrieved 276 relevant papers dealing with microbiota and SOT. However, when we re-analyzed this collection only two papers, both of them dealing with liver transplantation (LT), had abundance data published and readily available in their supplementary sections. With such a scarcity of data a classical meta-analysis would be impossible to conduct. However, we postulate that an expressive analysis of composition, diversity and richness of microbial communities is still feasible using suitable Bayesian topic models that have been introduced for dealing with automatic text analysis and classification, but that are well suited to microbiome analysis and have potential for providing clinically meaningful summaries.

To be more specific, the class of Bayesian topic models has been introduced for discovering the abstract 'topics' that occur in a collection of documents [14,15], even though the class of such statistical models can be readily adapted to microbiome data in a simple and meaningful way. Using topic models, we are able to identify those bacterial species that have the most important weights under different experimental conditions. Most importantly, Bayesian topic models are not affected by data scarcity, because conclusions we can draw borrow strength across sparse microbiome samples, allowing expressive comparison with a baseline or a pre-transplantation condition.

2   Related Work

The details of correspondence between microbiome data and text data have been explained by [16], which review a few statistical modeling techniques used in text categorization and explore how to transfer them to the microbiome. A similar approach is followed by [17], where the microbial community structure across multiple samples is inferred based on topic models. Similarly, [18] show how each microbial sample can be considered as a 'document', which has a mixture of functional groups in the human gut microbiome, while each functional group can be seen as a latent topic, that is a weighted mixture of taxonomic levels. A somewhat more technical introduction is reported by [19], which explores a difficult arising from the fact that the number of topics (functional groups) of the topic models must be pre-specified, and if the pre-specified number of topics is changed then the number of topics to be interpreted also changes. As a solution to the problem a Bayesian nonparametric model is proposed, by developing a hierarchical specification that can mitigate the parametric assumptions underlying a traditional Bayesian topic model, and can automatically decide the number of topics from the data.

In this paper we considered useful to avoid unnecessary complexity, trying to to keep the analysis pipeline structure as simple as possible, favoring therefore the interpretability of the results. Based upon these principle, we used Latent Dirichlet Allocation (LDA) to collapse together taxonomic levels that had the same expression. LDA was first introduced in [14] as a form of dimension reduction that uses a probabilistic model to find the co-occurrence patterns of terms that correspond to semantic topics in a collection of documents. Latent topics have a simple interpretation in terms of microbial communities harbored by the human gut, as described in Subsect. 3.2. To decide on a suitable number of topics, the measure traditionally used for topic models is the perplexity of held-out documents, which is a decreasing function of the log-likelihood of the unseen documents; the lower the perplexity, the better the model [20]. However, we considered multiple indices to attenuate the effect of sampling variation, calculating all metrics at once over multiple LDA models with varying number of topics.

3   Materials and Methods

3.1   Datasets

The first dataset we analyzed in this paper is reported in [7]. The study recruited 177 adult patients undergoing LT. In total $c = 723$ fecal samples spread across the sampling time-points (pre-LT, peri-LT – weeks 1, 2, and 3 after LT, and post LT – months 1, 2, 3, 6, 9, and 12) were sequenced (16S V3-V4 rRNA, with a median of 4 samples per patient). After quality filtering the dataset included 703 samples from 175 patients (spread across the sampling time points). We considered pre-LT data (83 samples on 83 patients) and post-LT data, from months 6 to 12 after transplantation (207 samples on 118 unique patients). For each sample, most of identified operational taxonomic units (OTUs) were classified at the Genus-Species level, while some OTUs were classified at the Genus species only, and a few OTUs were neither classified at the Genus or Species Level, nor assigned to any known taxon. For both pre- and post-LT data, we had 878 OTUs in the taxonomy table. Therefore, for pre-LT the dimension of the abundance matrix was 878×83, and the post-LT matrix had dimension 878×207. Each cell of the abundance matrices contains the count of OTU abundances. For shortness, from this point on this dataset will be referred to as DATASET1.

The second dataset is contained in [21]. In the treatment group were enrolled 90 LT recipients, versus 61 healthy controls in the control sample, with no significant difference existing between the two groups in terms of age, sex distribution and body mass index. For each patient and healthy control 588 OTUs were clustered from fecal samples (1 fecal sample for each patient and 1 sample for each healthy control). Hence, the abundance matrices had dimension 588×90 and 588×61, respectively. Most of OTUs were classified at the Family and Genus levels, whereas some OTUs were assigned at the Genus level only. From this point on this dataset will be referred to as DATASET2.

3.2   Statistical Analysis

Latent Dirichlet Allocation (LDA) model discovers the different topics that the documents represent and how much of each topic is present in a given document. We now briefly introduce the necessary notation to LDA, and we provide an interpretation in terms of microbiome data. The generative model of LDA can be graphically represented as the following oriented graph (Fig. 1):

In a more descriptive way (for notational simplicity, the indicator d is suppressed):

- A document d is a stream of N terms (or words), $d = (w_1, \ldots, w_N)$. Using superscripts to denote components, the νth term in $|V|$ is represented as a unit-basis vector w such that $w^\nu = 1$ and $w^u = 0$ for $u \neq \nu$.
- For each document we have K underlying semantic themes (topics), $\beta_{1:K} = (\beta_1, \ldots, \beta_K)$, where each β_k is a $|V|$-dimensional vector of probabilities over the elements of V, for $k = 1, \ldots, K$.

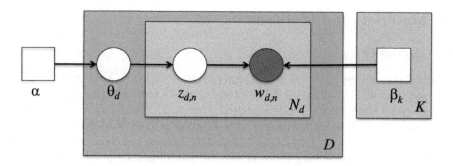

Fig. 1. A graphical model representation of Latent Dirichlet Allocation (LDA). Parameters α and $\beta_{1:K}$ are treated as unknown hyper-parameters to be estimated.

- $z_{1:N} = (z_1, \dots, z_N)$ is a vector of K-dimensional vectors indicating, for $n = 1, \dots, N$, the topic which has generated term w_n in document d. The indicator z of the k-th topic is represented as a K-dimensional unit-basis vector such that $z^k = 1$ and $z^j = 0$ for $j \neq k$.

The topic indicator uniquely selects a probability distribution in $\beta_{1:K}$, as $\beta_{z_n} \equiv \beta_k$ when $z_n^k = 1$. Independently of each other, the generative process of each pre-processed document d is the following:

1. Draw topic proportions from a symmetric Dirichlet distribution over the K-dimensional simplex, $\theta|\alpha \sim \mathsf{Dirichlet}_K(\alpha)$.
2. For each term w_n, $n = 1, \dots, N$, and independently of each other:
   (a) Choose a topic from a Multinomial distribution with probabilities θ, $z_n|\theta \sim \mathsf{Multinomial}_K(\theta)$.
   (b) Choose a term from a Multinomial distribution with probabilities dependent on z_n and $\beta_{1:K}$, $w_n|z_n, \beta_{1:K} \sim \mathsf{Multinomial}_{|V|}(\beta_{z_n})$.

The main input to LDA is the term-document matrix. The term-document matrix describes the frequency of terms that occur in a collection of documents (a corpus). In a term-document matrix, rows correspond to terms in the collection and columns correspond to documents (Fig. 2). The data matrix containing OTUs abundances has essentially the same structure, provided that we interpret rows and columns in the following way [16,17]:

- OTUs → rows → terms.
- Samples → columns → documents. In this particular case, each document has the same number of terms.
- Corpus → the set of all fecal samples associated with the environment (gut). The dimension c of the corpus (number of columns) represents the number of fecal samples.

Each column (fecal sample) contains some microbial species and does not contain others (those OTUs with null abundance in that fecal sample). A topic can be thought as a community of bacteria that share similar roles and biological

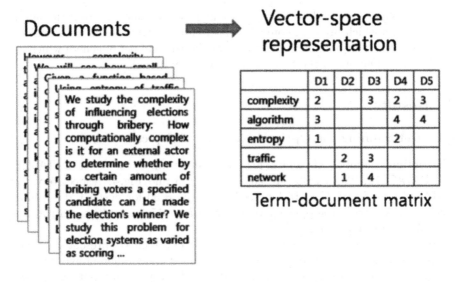

Fig. 2. The term-document matrix describing the frequency of terms that occur in a collection of documents. In a term-document matrix, rows correspond to terms in the collection and columns correspond to documents.

effects. Each fecal sample contains a mixture of topics (a mixture of bacterial communities) that LDA may contribute to disentangle. Parameters of the model were estimated using an empirical Bayes approach, following variational inference methods reliably implemented implemented in the `topicmodels` package [22], under R 3.6.1.

3.3   Choosing the Number of Topics

Setting the number of topics is the most computationally intensive part. We used three methods to compare the goodness-of-fit of the LDA model fit with varying number of topics K (K ranging between 2 and 60 with a step of 2 – 2, 4, 6, ..., and so on). All the computations were implemented in R 3.6.1 using specialized routines [23]. A sensible interpretation of the number of topics used for describing the gut microbial community is still unclear, an issue we discuss further in next section.

3.4   Assigning Terms to Topics

First, topics were sorted according their probabilities in the entire collection of samples. Alternatively, topics were sorted by counting how often a topic appeared as a primary topic. This alternative method is also known as Rank-1 [24]. Subsequently, for each of the 5-top topics, we plotted the 10-top terms (OTUs) in terms of their probability of occurrence. In this way, bacterial community associated with each topic could be further analyzed and characterized at a very high expressivity level, close to natural language, far different from the aggre-gated results which are commonly obtained through traditional meta-analyses (for example, traditional meta-analysis provides the number of genera which are significantly different in the two experimental conditions).

4   Results

4.1   Determining the Optimal Number of Topics

The optimal number of topics has been determined for both DATASET1 and DATASET2. The results are shown in Fig. 3 and Fig. 4, respectively. For DATASET1 we found $K = 15$ for pre-LT and $K = 30$ for post-LT data. Simi-larly, for DATASET2 the optimal values were $K = 15$ for healthy controls and $K = 35$ for transplanted patients.

It is interesting to note that, in both cases, the two curves presented a quali-tatively similar aspect, although they were obtained under different experimental designs (in fact, in the second case, we do not have partially matched pre-LT data, but healthy control subjects). In addition, both for ESD patients in the liver recipient waiting list and for healthy control subjects, the optimal number of topics is much lower than that determined for transplanted patients. If we interpret a topic as a microbial community sharing similar roles and biological effects in terms of overall host health, it is tempting to argue that LT always increases the diversity and richness of microbial communities. This hypothesis is only partially confirmed by computing classical diversity measures; for example, using alpha-diversity, for DATASET1 we had that the median alpha was equal to 2.94 for pre-LT data and 3.33 for post-LT, whereas for DATASET2 we had 3.37 for healthy subjects and 3.08 for transplanted patients.

4.2   Determining the 5-Top Topics

The 5-top topics for DATASET1 were labeled (13, 7, 6, 15, 3) for pre-LT data, while the corresponding Rank-1 5-top topics were (13, 15, 3, 7, 1), with four con-cordances (Fig. 5). The 5-top topics for DATASET1 for post-LT data were (13, 14, 29, 16, 19) and (13, 14, 19, 22, 1) using Rank-1, with three concordances. Similarly, the 5-top topics for DATASET2 were (5, 7, 2, 3, 9) and (3, 5, 2, 7, 9) for healthy subjects, with five concordances, using the two methods respectively (Fig. 6). For post-transplanted patients we had (11, 21, 33, 10, 6) and (11, 21, 12, 25, 6), respectively, with two concordances. For example, relative frequencies associated with the 5-top topics (13, 7, 6, 15, 3) (DATASET1 with the standard method) were respectively: $13 \to 18.21\%$, $7 \to 9.04\%$, $6 \to 8.04\%$, $15 \to 7.44\%$, $3 \to 6.97\%$. In other words, topic (microbial community) labeled as '13' is preva-lent in about 18% of fecal samples, topic (microbial community) labeled as '7' is prevalent in about 9% of samples, and so on. It is also worth noting that, at this level, the analysis has a low grade of expressivity, as topics (microbial communities) are nothing but 'labels'.

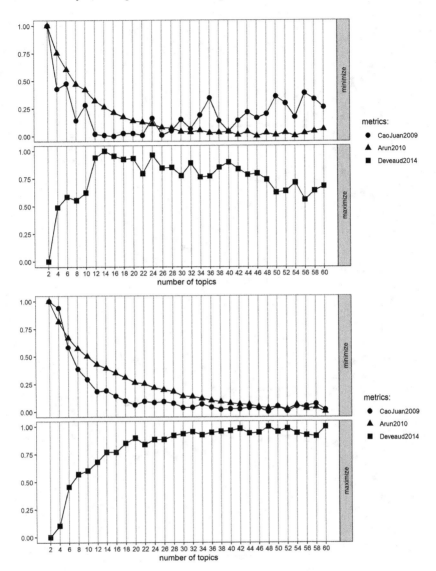

Fig. 3. Choosing the number of topics for **DATASET1**. The optimal choice was $K = 15$ for pre-LT (upper panel) and $K = 30$ for post-LT data (lower panel). We used three methods to compare the goodness-of-fit of the LDA model fit with varying number of topics K, with K ranging between 2 and 60 with a step of 2 (2, 4, 6, ..., and so on).

4.3   Determining the 10-Top OTUs for Each Top-Topic

An expressive analysis could be obtained by plotting, for each top-topic, the 10-top terms (OTUs) ranked according to their probability of occurrence. Figure 7 shows the 10-top OTUs of **DATASET1**, for both pre-LT and post-LT abundances

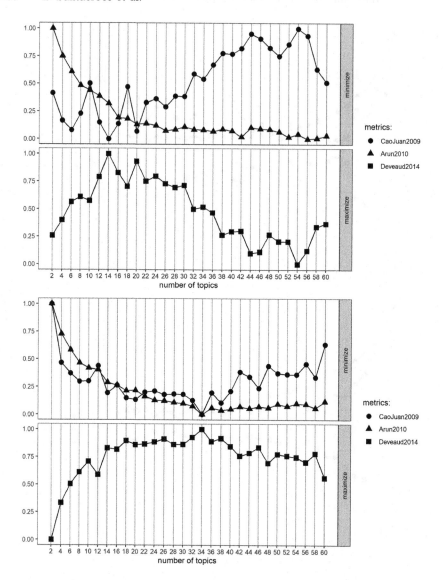

Fig. 4. Choosing the number of topics for DATASET2. The optimal choice was $K = 15$ for pre-LT (upper panel) and $K = 35$ for post-LT data (lower panel). We used three methods to compare the goodness-of-fit of the LDA model fit with varying number of topics K, with K ranging between 2 and 60 with a step of 2 $(2, 4, 6, \ldots,$ and so on).

respectively. In the same way, Fig. 8 contains the 10-top OTUs of DATASET2, for healthy control subjects and transplanted patients respectively. To make the analysis expressive, each OTU was mapped onto its Genus-Species taxon (when available), or its Genus or Family (when Species and/or Genus were not available). OTUs that could not be mapped onto any known taxon were denoted

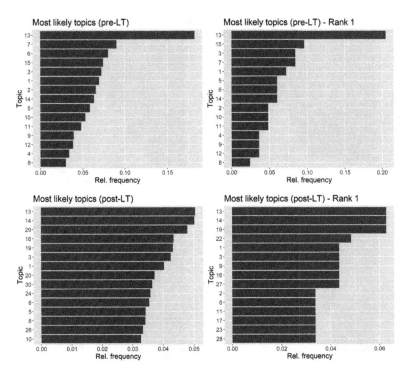

Fig. 5. Top-topics for **DATASET1**, using the two methods described in the text. With the first method, topics were sorted according their probabilities in the entire collection of samples. Using the second method, known as Rank-1, topics were sorted by counting how often a topic appeared as a primary topic.

as NA. It is worth noting that different OTUs may be assigned to the same Genus or Family (particularly when a precise Genus-Species classification was not determined). For example, for topic 15 in Fig. 7 (Rank-1 method, pre-LT) we had 6 OTUs that have been assigned to Genus *Bacteroides*. In this case, the probability that is plotted on the graph is collapsed at Genus level over the corresponding probabilities ($0.0596 + 0.0373 + 0.0335 + 0.0299 + 0.0288 + 0.0270 = 0.2161$).

5   Discussion and Conclusion

The importance and role of personalized medicine in a successful SOT cannot be neglected. Alteration of intestinal microbiome in patients after transplantation has been extensively investigated. Although there is specific microbiome in each of organ eligible for transplantation (for example liver, kidney, heart lung and pancreas), gut microbiome seems to play the most important role for overall host health through the various axes existing between solid organs and the gut microbiome itself. However, a broad view of associations between intestinal

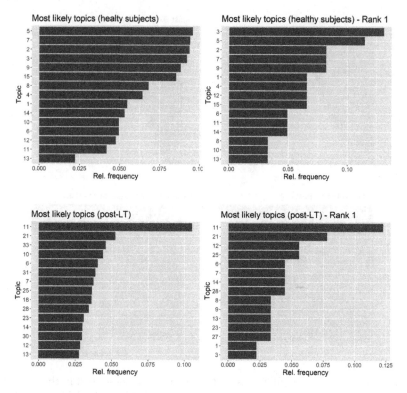

Fig. 6. Top-topics for DATASET2, using the two methods described in the text. With the first method, topics were sorted according their probabilities in the entire collection of samples. Using the second method, known as Rank-1, topics were sorted by counting how often a topic appeared as a primary topic.

microbiome and disease in the pre- and post-transplantation phases is obscured by many factors, such as the highly variable individual response to an invasive transplantation.

From this point of view, meta-analysis is the best instrument to achieve a broader view and to arrive at sound conclusions. At present, the wealth of available high-throughput 16 S ribosomal RNA data has allowed the publication of a number of excellent meta-analyses analyzing the relationship between gut microbiome and human disease. However, in a broad collection of 276 relevant papers dealing with microbiota and SOT, only two papers had microbial abundance data published readily available in the supplementary section, both of them dealing with LT. Such a lack of data makes it impossible to construct ensemble-based analyses, or to carry out host-trait prediction based on microbial abundance. However, in this paper we suggest that an expressive comparative analysis of composition, diversity and richness of microbial communities is still feasible using suitable Bayesian models, that have been introduced for dealing

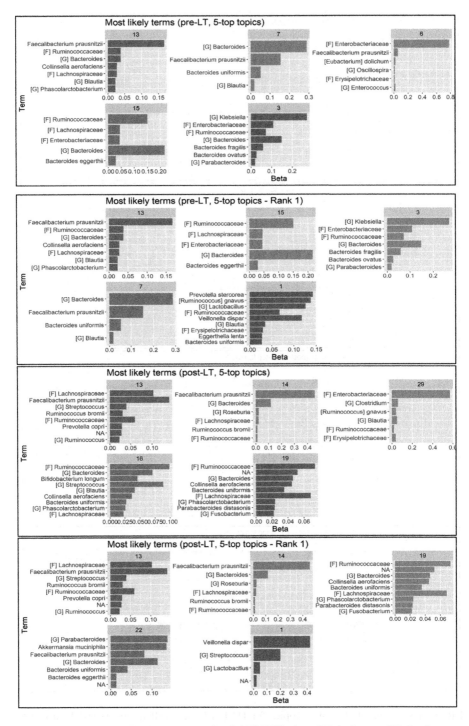

Fig. 7. Top-terms of the 5-top topics for DATASET1 (pre-LT and post-LT, both standard and Rank-1 methods) ranked according to their probability of occurrence.

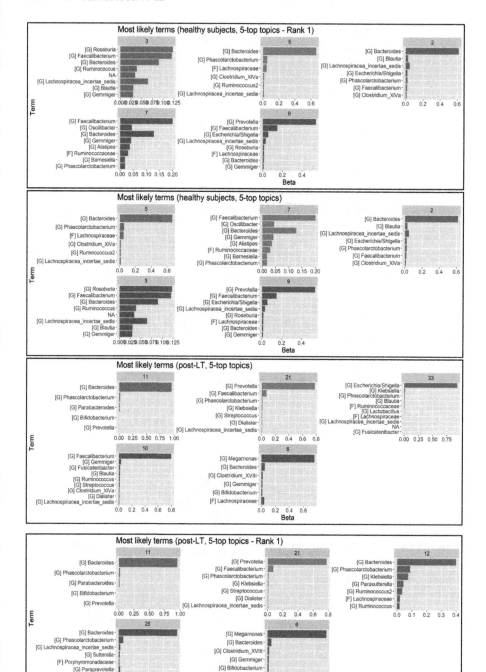

Fig. 8. Top-terms of the 5-top topics for DATASET2 (healthy and post-LT subjects, both standard and Rank-1 methods) ranked according to their probability of occurrence.

with automatic text analysis and classification, but that are well suited to microbiome analysis and have potential for providing clinically meaningful summaries.

The expressivity of topic models can lead to some interesting conclusions. For example, post-LT gut microbiomes in DATASET1 were rich in beneficial commensal bacteria such as *Faecalibacterium prausnitzi, Lachnospiraceae* and *Ruminococcacae*, whereas less abundance of *Ruminococcacae* and *Lachnospiraceae* was found in DATASET2, with a significant coexistence of opportunist pathogens such as *Streptococcus* and *Veillonella dispar*. In general, pre-LT ESD patients have a lower abundance of healthy commensal species in comparison to the post-LT phase. Moreover, after LT an increase in diversity is observed in most of the cases, due to a greater diversification in composition and abundance of both healthy and pathogen species. In DATASET1 there was a high abundance in pre-LT patients of both commensal healthy and pathogen bacteria, such as *Faecalibacterium prausnitzi, Bacteroides, Klebsiella, Enterobacteriaceae* and *Ruminococcacae*. This is consistent with previous studies, that have noted that patients with liver ESD have a decrease in non pathogenic bacteria, including *Lachnospiraceae, Ruminococcaceae,* and *Clostridium XIV* and a concomitant increase in pathogenic bacteria such as *Enterococcus, Enterobacteriaceae,* and *Bacteroidaceae* [25]. However, we realized a controversial result since pre-LT ESD patients exhibited high levels of *Ruminococcaceae* (using the rank-1 method). In addition, post-LT patients of DATASET1 had higher level of *Lachinospiraceae, Faecalibacterium prausnitzi, Ruminococcacae, Bacteroides, Enterobacteriacea* and *Streptococcus*. As long as DATASET2 is analyzed, healthy control subjects had high abundances of *Roseburia, Faecalibacterium, Bacteroides, Prevotella, Lachnospiracea*. Furthermore, whereas post-LT data demonstrated high abundances of *Bacteroides, Faecalibacterium, Prevotella* and *Megamonas* but lesser *Bacteroides, Lachnospiraceae, Blutia* and *Streptococcus*.

In conclusion, it seems even with the same SOT, there is a high variation in OTU levels. Topic models are expressive methods for dimensionality reduction, that can help to analyze variations in gut microbial communities. With topic models the analysis can be carried out at a level close to natural language that can be easily interpreted by clinicians, because most abundant species are automatically selected, and the microbial dynamics can be tracked and followed over time. This objective could be greatly facilitated by the availability of dynamic versions of topic-based models [26], which could help in monitoring post-SOT phase for prescribing the best treatment option. Future research could take these questions as the point of departure to narrow down the focus.

Author contributions. Conceptualization, LS, MB and SM; methodology, LS and MB; validation, JH, BZ and AB; investigation, LS, MB and SM; resources, LS; data curation SM; statistical analysis MB; visualization, JH, BZ and AB; supervision, MB; project administration, LS, MB and SM; writing–original draft preparation, LS, MB and SM; writing–review and editing, JH, BZ and AB. The authors declare that they have no conflicts of interest. No additional data are available.

References

1. Black, C.K., Termanini, K.M., Aguirre, O., Hawksworth, J.S., Sosin, M.: Solid organ transplantation in the 21st century. Ann. Transl. Med. **6**(20), 409 (2018). https://doi.org/10.21037/atm.2018.09.68
2. Stehlik, J., Kobashigawa, J., Hunt, S.A., Reichenspurner, H., Kirklin, J.K.: Honoring 50 years of clinical heart transplantation in circulation. Circulation **137**(1), 71–87 (2018). https://doi.org/10.1161/CIRCULATIONAHA.117.029753
3. Gurley, K.E., Lowry, R.P., Clarke Forbes, R.D.: Immune mechanisms in organ allograft rejection: II. T helper cells, delayed-type hypersensitivity, and rejection of renal allografts. Transplantation. **36**(4), 401–405 (1983)
4. Fishman, J.A.: Infection in organ transplantation. Am. J. Transplant. **17**(4), 856–879 (2017). https://doi.org/10.1111/ajt.14208
5. Chong, A.S., Alegre, M.-L.: The impact of infection and tissue damage in solid-organ transplantation. Nat. Rev. Immunol. **12**(6), 459–471 (2012). https://doi.org/10.1038/nri3215
6. Mori, D.N., Kreisel, D., Fullerton, J.N., Gilroy, D.W., Goldstein, D.R.: Inflammatory triggers of acute rejection of organ allografts. Immunol. Rev. **258**(1), 132–144 (2014). https://doi.org/10.1111/imr.12146
7. Annavajhala, M.K., et al.: Colonizing multidrug-resistant bacteria and the longitudinal evolution of the intestinal microbiome after liver transplantation. Nat. Commun. **10**, 4715 (2019). https://doi.org/10.1038/s41467-019-12633-4
8. Maynard, C.L., Elson, C.O., Hatton, R.D., Weaver, C.T.: Reciprocal interactions of the intestinal microbiota and immune system. Nature **489**(7415), 231–241 (2012). https://doi.org/10.1038/nature11551
9. Atarashi, K., et al.: Induction of colonic regulatory T cells by indigenous Clostridium species. Science **331**(6015), 337–341 (2011). https://doi.org/10.1126/science.1198469
10. Dodd, D., et al.: A gut bacterial pathway metabolizes aromatic amino acids into nine circulating metabolites. Nature **551**(7682), 648–652 (2017). https://doi.org/10.1038/nature24661
11. Bajaj, J.S., et al.: Liver transplant modulates gut microbial dysbiosis and cognitive function in cirrhosis. Liver Transpl. **23**(7), 907–914 (2017). https://doi.org/10.1002/lt.24754
12. Chalmers, J.D.: Microbial dysbiosis after lung transplantation. Am. J. Respir. Crit. Care Med. **194**(10), 1184–1186 (2016). https://doi.org/10.1164/rccm.201606-1178ED
13. Duvallet, C., Gibbons, S.M., Gurry, T., Irizarry, R.A., Alm, E.J.: Meta-analysis of gut microbiome studies identifies disease-specific and shared responses. Nat. Commun. **8**, 1784 (2017). https://doi.org/10.1038/s41467-017-01973-8
14. Blei, D.M., Ng, A.Y., Jordan, M.I.: Latent dirichlet allocation. J. Mach. Learn. Res. **3**, 993–1022 (2003)
15. Blei, D.M.: Probabilistic topic models. Commun. ACM. **55**(4), 77–84 (2012). https://doi.org/10.1145/2133806.2133826
16. Sankaran, K., Holmes, S.P.: Latent variable modeling for the microbiome. Biostatistics **20**(4), 599–614 (2019). https://doi.org/10.1093/biostatistics/kxy018
17. Yan, J., et al.: MetaTopics: an integration tool to analyze microbial community profile by topic model. BMC Genomics **18**(Suppl. 1), 962 (2017). https://doi.org/10.1186/s12864-016-3257-2

18. Chen, X., He, T., Hu, X., Zhou, Y., An, Y., Wu, X.: Estimating functional groups in human gut microbiome with probabilistic topic models. IEEE Trans. Nanobiosci. **11**, 203–215 (2012). https://doi.org/10.1109/TNB.2012.2212204

19. Okui, T.: A Bayesian nonparametric topic model for microbiome data using subject attributes. IPSJ Trans. Bioinform. **13**, 1–6 (2020). https://doi.org/10.2197/ipsjtbio.13.1

20. Wallach, H.M., Murray, I., Salakhutdinov, R., Mimno, D.: Evaluation methods for topic models. In: Proceedings of the 26th Annual International Conference on Machine Learning (ICML 2009), pp. 1–8. ACM Press, New York, USA (2009). https://doi.org/10.1145/1553374.1553515

21. Lu, H.-F., et al.: Fecal microbiome data distinguish liver recipients with normal and abnormal liver function from healthy controls. Front. Microbiol. **10**, 1518 (2019). https://doi.org/10.3389/fmicb.2019.01518

22. Grün, B., Hornik, K.: `topicmodels`: an R package for fitting topic models. J. Stat. Softw. **40**(13) (2011). https://doi.org/10.18637/jss.v040.i13

23. Nikita, M.: `ldatuning`: Tuning of the Latent Dirichlet Allocation Models Parameters (2019). https://cran.r-project.org/package=ldatuning

24. Boyd-Graber, J., Mimno, D., Newman, D.: Care and feeding of topic models: problems, diagnostics, and improvements. In: Airoldi, E.M., Blei, D., Erosheva, E.A., Fienberg, S.E. (eds.) Handbook of Mixed Membership Models and Their Applications, pp. 225–274. CRC Press, Boca Raton (2014)

25. Punzalan, C., Qamar, A.: Probiotics for the treatment of liver disease. In: Floch, M.H., Ringel, Y., Walker, W.A. (eds.) The Microbiota in Gastrointestinal Pathophysiology, pp. 373–381. Elsevier, Amsterdam (2017). https://doi.org/10.1016/B978-0-12-804024-9.00040-9

26. Jahnichen, P., Wenzel, F., Kloft, M., Mandt, S.: Scalable generalized dynamic topic models. In: Storkey, A., Perez-Cruz, F. (eds.) Proceedings of the Twenty-First International Conference on Artificial Intelligence and Statistics PMLR 2018, vol. 84, pp. 1427–1435 (2018)

Detection of Thyroid Nodules Through Neural Networks and Processing of Echographic Images

Alex R. Haro$^{(\boxtimes)}$ ⓘ, Julio C. Toalombo ⓘ, Eddie E. Galarza ⓘ, and Nancy E. Guerrón ⓘ

Universidad de las Fuerzas Armadas ESPE, Sangolquí 170501, Ecuador
{arharo, jctoalombo, eegalarza, neguerron}@espe.edu.ec

Abstract. The abnormal functioning of hormones produces the appearance of malformations in human bodies that must be detected early. In this manuscript, two proposals are presented for the identification of thyroid nodules in ultrasound images, using convolutional neural networks. For the network training, 400 images obtained from a medical center and stored in a database have been used. Free access software (Python and TensorFlow) has been used as part of the algorithm development, following the stages of image preprocessing, network training, filtering and layer construction. Results graphically present the incidence of people suffering from this health problem. In addition, based on the respective tests, it is identified that the system developed in Python has greater precision and accuracy, 90% and 81% respectively, than TensorFlow design. Through neural networks, the recognition up to 4 mm thyroid nodules is evidenced.

Keywords: Computer vision · Convolutional neural networks · Thyroid nodule · Ultrasound image

1 Introduction

The development of technology and engineering techniques have allowed the dissemination of knowledge in all fields of science [1–5]. Its application in medicine has increased with the aim of improving human health, in the treatment of diseases, making prostheses, developing rehabilitation sessions, during surgeries or in the resuscitation of patients [6–9]. Interesting proposals have been generated using informatics, instrumentation, robotics, automation, image and signal processing, among others [10–14]. Image processing as a tool for information and computation is the basis of a growing variety of applications including medical diagnosis, remote sensing, space exploration, computer vision, etc. [15].

As part of medical examinations, medical imaging procedures are performed such as: ultrasound, radiography, tomography, Magnetic Resonance Imaging (MRI), etc. [16, 17]. Imaging has become an essential component in many fields of medical research as well as in laboratory and clinical practice. Radiologists identify and

© Springer Nature Switzerland AG 2020
O. Gervasi et al. (Eds.): ICCSA 2020, LNCS 12252, pp. 166–178, 2020.
https://doi.org/10.1007/978-3-030-58811-3_12

quantify tumors and skeleton scans on MRI and computed tomography (CT) scans [18]. Neuroscientists detect regional metabolic brain activity from positron emission tomography (PET) and functional MRIs [19]. Until recently, 3D image viewing and quantitative analysis could only be performed using expensive workstations and custom software [20]. Today, much of the visualization and analysis can be done on a budget desktop computer. After receiving an initial medical evaluation, tests are carried out to determine the disease and establish an adequate diagnosis and treatment.

Ultrasonography can evaluate the appearance of the thyroid, a gland located in the neck that regulates the human metabolism [21, 22]. However, metabolism does not always work correctly. Thus, Thyroid nodules can be defined as an abnormal development in thyroid cells forming an internal tumor. Despite most are benign, other have treatment when they are identified in early stages of cancer. Although in terminal phases, doctors cannot assure that a treatment can combat this health problem, causing the patient death [23]. As can be seen in [24], the incidence of thyroid cancer has increased in adults over 65 years, demonstrating that the proper use of ultrasound contributes as a tool for its early detection. In Ecuador, approximately 10% of the adult population has thyroid nodules, 8 to 12% of them are cancerous, and therefore the use of technological tools for their early detection are of great relevance.

The purpose of this research is to prepare two proposals that allow detection of thyroid nodules in ultrasound using image processing. Through neural networks, segmentation and classification tasks are carried out to better break down the information for its respective analysis. Two user interfaces are created where results obtained from samples entered are presented to the user. It reduces the generation of false positive results.

The article is organized as follows: in Sect. 1 the introduction and in Sect. 2 the materials and methods. In Sect. 3 the implementation of the proposal is described and in Sect. 4 tests and results obtained. Finally, the conclusions and future work are presented in Sect. 5.

2   Materials and Methods

Specialist performs the ultrasound on a patient, then images obtained are analyzed visually and virtually for the detection of nodules. Each image is stored in a database (DB) and will be used to carry out the preprocessing (only in Python) and subsequent treatment of this information. Figure 1 presents a general diagram of all phases.

Once the preprocessing has been done, detection of nodules is carried out by using a convolutional neural network (CNN) strategy that mimics the visual cortex of the human eye to identify objects. The better the capacity of the computer, the better functionality is obtained.

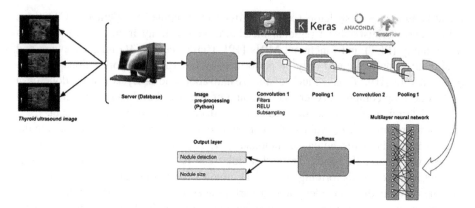

Fig. 1. System general scheme.

2.1 Definition of Requirements and Parameters

Neural network development requires the use of Python 2 or 3.7 software and TensorFlow configured and installed correctly. Subsequently, the import of images stored in the DB consisting of 500 ultrasounds captured in a period of 12 months is performed. 400 images are used for network training and 100 for experimental tests. It must be considered the same directory of the images in order to be able to execute in the code.

Regarding the parameters, it must specified the number of times the data set will be repeated during training (iteration = 20); image size, height = 100 pixels and length = 100 pixels; the number of images, in this case the processing is carried out one by one; preprocessing steps, refers to the number of times the information will be processed (steps = 1000); validation, allows at the end of each iteration to execute a certain number of steps to visualize the learning of the algorithm (validation = 200 steps); and the convolution filters A and B (filter A = 32 and filter B = 64) shown in Fig. 2 which are small squares that help to detect shapes by relating them to the pixels in the image.

2.2 Preprocessing

The preprocessing stage consist in resize every ultrasound image given from DB, i.e., since the image comes from 0 to 255 pixels, it must be rescaled to an interval between 0 and 1 (1/255) in order to make a more efficient network training. The ultrasound images will be varied, since it can be a man, woman, boy or girl. For this reason, it is necessary to generate an image that has displacement (equal to 0.3), being able to detect the nodules in different positions. When validating, it can be obtained the same image as at the beginning, but now ready to be analyzed in the CNN. This preprocessing is only developed in Python while TensorFlow does it directly.

3 Proposal Implementation

3.1 Software

SPYDER IDE must have been configured for the algorithm development in Python. It allows creating scientific packages and is available for Windows, Linux and MacOS. TensorFlow was operated as an open source platform to express machine learning algorithms and Anaconda Navigator is used as a graphical user interface (GUI), to easily start and manage packages, environments and command channels. JupyterLab was used for the development environment due to its excellent flexibility in autonomous learning tasks. Keras took advantage of TensorFlow's high-level API (Application Programming Interface) that was applied to build and train learning models.

3.2 Neural Network Development

The preprocessed image (Python case) is used in the neural network to develop its training through the IDE. Neural networks are mathematically represented in (1). Where: x_i = input data; w_i = synaptic weights; w_0 = b is the polarization factor and m = number of filters in layer $n - 1$. The result (r) is obtained with the processing of the binary function, i.e., the value of zero or one. In (2) the one and only output generated from the sum between the input vector $x = (x_i, \ldots, x_m)$ and the weight vector $w = (w_i, \ldots, w_m)$ is presented.

CNNs consist of three fundamental layers which are: input, hidden and output layers. The image is entered (input layer) to extract each of the pixels of the image by applying the different processing phases (hidden layers) and then results are obtained (output layer). Based on them, the thyroid status analysis can be run to determine the presence of nodules and their size. Results are shown in a graphical interface for each software. Mathematical representation of the convolution performed on the network is described in (3).

$$r = \sum_{i=1}^{m} x_i w_i + b \tag{1}$$

$$y = \gamma \left(\sum_{i=1}^{m} x_i w_i + w_0 \right) \tag{2}$$

$$net_j^n = \sum_{k=1}^{K} x_k^{n-1} * w_{kj}^n + b^n \tag{3}$$

Figure 2 shows the general scheme of a CNN. It consists of 6 several stages: 1) The selection of the preprocessed image described above; 2) The convolution stage. There are two types of convolution: convolution A generally detects contrasts, lines, color changes while convolution B detects more outlined elements as image forms.

3) The pooling 1 stage. It reduces the number of parameters selected with the most common feature of the image, in order to avoid over-fitting, the model. 4) The total

connectivity stages. There are the output characteristics that connect to 5) the pooling 2 stage. Characteristics contain trainable connections previously developed in the adaptive programming algorithm on CNN. Finally, in 6) the binary classification stage, results generated after processing are obtained. It details whether there is the presence of thyroid problems in the patient.

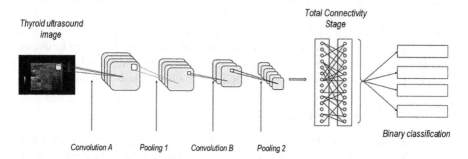

Fig. 2. General scheme of the detection of thyroid nodule by CNN.

3.3 Neural Network Training

Once the code is debugged, training and validation begin selecting several images, which will be rescaled to pixels and to all the stages previously described. CNN will be automatically learning. Then the trained network is stored in default format, so that it can be used at any time without having to train it again. The training quality is linked to the size of the database, i.e., the more images are presented to the network, the better it will be for its training and learning parameters.

3.4 Layer Construction

In TensorFlow, the layer construction stage is considered as the fundamental part for neural networks. They are layers that extract information from database to solve problems. First layer performs the transformation of the image format to a two-dimensional arrangement, keeping in mind that this layer has no parameters to learn. Next two layers are connected to each other, the first providing 128 nodes and the other with 10 nodes which allows network learning. Subsequently, the database consisting of 400 grayscale ultrasound images of thyroid with 255 pixels is loaded.

3.5 Image Processing

In TensorFlow, image processing is done while CNN is running and as the training is done, values of the Kernel parameters, filters, their learning and activation are adjusted. All these values are saved and are also transparent.

Kernel. Kernel parameters or weights are the values of a matrix that has different resignations depending on each CNN. This is a great advantage at the time of the learning process since each Kernel has a reduced size. An example may be having a

3×3 matrix; there are only 9 parameters that must be adjusted and having 32 filters gives a total of 288 parameters.

$$h * f(u, v) = \sum_{x}^{n} \sum_{y}^{n} h(x, y) * f(x - u, y - v) \tag{4}$$

Figure 3 shows the convolution performed between an image and a Kernel matrix. If Kernel is an h(x) of dimensions' $n \times n$ and the object matrix $f(x, y)$ is of size $n \times n$, using the definition of the 2D convolution for a point of the resulting matrix, we obtain (4).

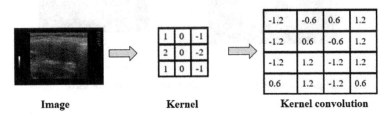

| Image | Kernel | Kernel convolution |

Fig. 3. The image performs a convolution with a Kernel.

It is easy to see that to calculate the convolution of a single point (u, v) of the matrix resulting from the convolution, n^2 products are required, as should be done for each of the N^2 elements of $f(x, y)$. In total, $n^2 \times N^2$ is required.

Filters. First filter is responsible for eliminating noise to have a clean image. It eliminates excess brightness, reduces lighting and shapes that alter the image, etc. Second filter is in charge of detecting similarities of circular shapes and making the relation of the area with the pixels, to determine the size of the nodule. The third is a classifier filter that, with data from previous ones, agrees to classify the image in which there are nodules.

Learning and Activation. Learning parameters are the system reliability, they are measured in percentage. Recommended values for these parameters must be at least 70%, considering that these values increase the more the network is trained. Activation parameters allow CNN to be activated and deactivated appropriately and are very significant for testing and exposing the results obtained.

3.6 Interface Development

To expose the results to the user, an interface is designed with the objective of showing clearly what CNN identified. For this, a main window is used that contains a Frame where all the widgets of the interface are organized. Python contains several libraries for GUI development, these are: Tkinter, WxPython, PyQT, PyGTk, Matplotlib, etc. In this case, Tkinter library was used to allow Python to be linked with the TCL/TK library, Python GUI is shown in Fig. 4. On the other hand, TensorFlow uses Anaconda

Navigator for the development of the GUI that, through the execution of Jupyter Notebook, two programs are created: 1) For network training and 2) To show the results obtained as shown in Fig. 5.

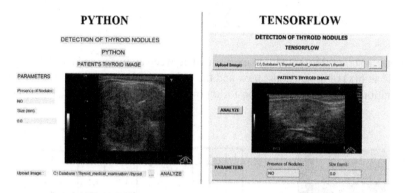

Fig. 4. Graphical User Interface for each software used.

4   Experimental Results

Due to the visual and technological analysis of the specialist, it was possible to separate cases with nodular presence both by age and gender. Cases with the presence of thyroid nodules are encapsulated in age ranges for classification into: young people (<24 years old), adults (25–59 years old) and older adults (>60 years old). With a lower percentage of 3.6% they occur in young population. This inclination is due to cases that are hereditary and no longer provoked. The appearance in the adult population is increasingly frequent with 44%. This incidence has increased each year due to the population type of diet with iodine deficiency which is the main cause in formation of thyroid nodules. The majority trend occurs in older adults with 52.4%, it is an aggravating factor the low frequency they visit the endocrinologist for preventive control and relevant examinations. These trends can be seen reflected in Fig. 5.

Another important categorization to analyze the presence of malformations in the thyroid is according to gender. Men with just 10.8%, is understandable since men are hormonally more stable. In women with 89.2% the trend is predominant, since it is more prone to hormonal imbalance. These values are shown in Fig. 6. It should be clarified that these global data (by age and by gender) have already been defined by the specialist since patients do not allow to show specific data regarding the ultrasounds obtained.

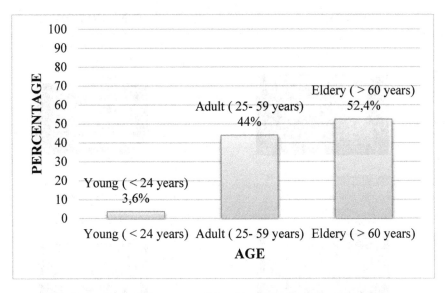

Fig. 5. Percentage of presence of thyroid nodules according to age range.

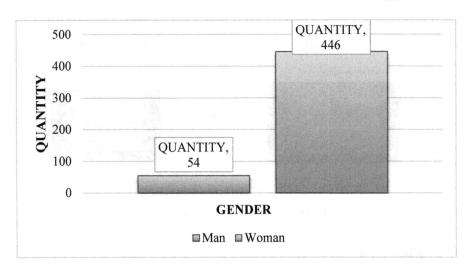

Fig. 6. Percentage of presence of thyroid nodules according to gender.

There are only two types of thyroid nodules that people can have: malignant and benign. The size of a nodule indicates its degree of danger, 10 mm being the most desirable for early treatment. For its phases determination, three parameters are considered: size (T), spread to nodes (N) and spread to other nearby organs (M). In Fig. 7. several thyroid nodules are detected in each software evidencing differences when showing its size. It allows authors to determine an accuracy test per software to define which one is the best option as a complementary tool for specialists.

PYTHON   **TENSORFLOW**

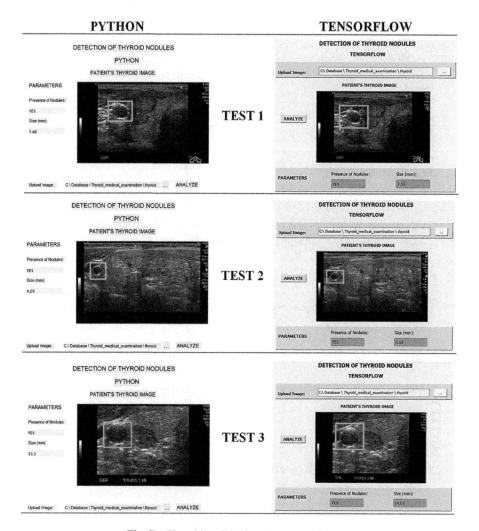

Fig. 7. Thyroid nodule detection per software.

4.1 Python Tests

To obtain a correct validation, sensitivity (SENS), specificity (ESP) and an external validity corresponding to the positive predictive value (PPV) and negative predictive value (NPV) must be analyzed. This analysis is performed to demonstrate the tool ability to detect the presence and absence of thyroid nodules. For the set of tests carried out (100 images) Python tool gave the following results as shown in Table 1.

Table 1. Test results from Python with 100 images (True diagnosis)

Results	Presence	Absence	Total
True positive	50	4	54
True negative	2	44	46
Total	52	48	100

The programming algorithm correctly classified 50 from 52 images containing thyroid nodules, obtaining a SENS of 96.15%. On the other hand, it classified 44 from 48 images with the absence of thyroid nodules, obtaining an ESP of 91.67%. The SENS and ESP are obtained by (5) and (6).

$$SENS = \frac{TP}{TP + FN} * 100\% \qquad (5)$$

$$ESP = \frac{TN}{TN + FP} * 100\% \qquad (6)$$

Where:

TP: True Positive
TN: True Negative
FP: False Positive
FN: False Negative

To obtain PPV and NPV, data is analyzed horizontally. In this way, the probability is obtained that the patient does or does not have thyroid nodules. To calculate these values, it should be followed the expressions:

$$PPV = \frac{TP}{TP + FP} * 100\% \qquad (7)$$

$$NPV = \frac{TN}{TN + FN} * 100\% \qquad (8)$$

The probability that a patient with positive results (PPV) complies with the pathology is 92.59% and the probability of not containing the pathology when the test result is negative (NPV) is 95.65%.

4.2 TensorFlow Tests

Table 2 shows the results with respect to TensorFlow, which correctly classified 49 images from the 52 that contained thyroid nodules, it allows to obtain a SENS of 94.23%, and from 48 images, the algorithm classified 42 with the absence of thyroid nodules, obtaining an ESP of 87.50%. Values in this analysis are substantiated by using recursively Eqs. (5–8).

Table 2. Test results from TensorFlow with 100 images (True diagnosis)

Results	Presence	Absence	Total
True positive	49	6	55
True negative	3	42	45
Total	52	48	100

Examining the obtained calculations, it can be mentioned that TensorFlow has a 94.23% of SENS to detect thyroid nodules. Additionally, it has an 87.50% of ESP to correctly classify patients who do not have nodules. It is also important to mention that the probability that a patient with positive results has the pathology (PPV) is 89.09% and the probability of not containing the pathology when the test result is negative (NPV) is 93.33%.

5   Conclusions and Future Work

Within the diagnosis of thyroid nodules, the pathological phase consists of the analysis of the extracted tissue and the clinical phase consists of the execution of a medical examination and an imaging study. The system has been designed to be able to identify nodules up to 4 mm in size, these can be malignant or benign. When a nodule is detected, it must be followed up and analyzed to determine if it is malignant. Antecedents that can lead to a malignant nodule are: rapid growth of the nodule, sudden and recent change in voice, difficulty swallowing or breathing, palpation of the nodule as a hard mass or enlarged neck nodes.

Women are more likely to have this pathology compared to men due to the existing variation in hormonal stability caused by two factors: 1) hormonal disturbances and 2) iodine deficiency in daily diet. Similarly, it has been identified that older adults have a higher incidence of suffering from these hormonal problems.

In this application, Python is the programming tool that offers greater reliability with a sensitivity of 96.15% and a specificity of 91.67%. TensorFlow reach less values, 94.23% of sensitivity and 87.50% for specificity. However, it should be considered that the application was developed with only 500 images, 100 of them were destined for tests this investigation, so if the CNN is trained with a larger database, the result may vary. The objective of this research is not to establish a direct diagnosis in patients, but to provide a useful tool for specialists to allow them to determine with greater certainty the presence of thyroid nodules and additionally to provide approximate information on their size.

Applications developed with TensorFlow that use CNN require immense DB to improve its training and provide higher quality results. This is why authors of this document establish this particular as a proposal for future work. Additionally, a greater number of filters could be implemented, since in the development of this investigation a notable improvement was evident when increasing them. Another improvement which should be incorporated is the detection of the number of nodules present in the echography. To accomplish this, image processing should be improved.

Acknowledgments. The authors thank the Universidad de las Fuerzas Armadas ESPE for the approval of the research project entitled: "Redes neuronales para la detección de nódulos de tiroides mediante procesamiento de imágenes de ecografías" for supporting the development of this work and especially to Jorge Buele and Esteban X. Castellanos.

References

1. Brodski-Guerniero, A., Paasch, G.F., Wollstadt, P., Özdemir, I., Lizier, J.T., Wibral, M.: Information-theoretic evidence for predictive coding in the face-processing system. J. Neurosci. (2017). https://doi.org/10.1523/JNEUROSCI.0614-17.2017
2. García, C.A., Buele, J., Espinoza, J., Castellanos, E.X., Beltrán, C., Pilatasig, M., Galarza, E., García, M.V.: Fuzzy control implementation in low cost CPPS devices. In: IEEE International Conference on Multisensor Fusion and Integration for Intelligent Systems, pp. 162–167 (2017). https://doi.org/10.1109/MFI.2017.8170423
3. Petersen, F., Brown, A., Pather, S., Tucker, W.D.: Challenges for the adoption of ICT for diabetes self-management in South Africa. Electron. J. Inf. Syst. Dev. Ctries. (2019). https://doi.org/10.1002/isd2.12113
4. Buele, J., et al.: Interactive system for monitoring and control of a flow station using LabVIEW. In: Rocha, Á., Guarda, T. (eds.) ICITS 2018. AISC, vol. 721, pp. 583–592. Springer, Cham (2018). https://doi.org/10.1007/978-3-319-73450-7_55
5. Chen, G.: Research on fuel supply intelligent monitoring system design based on PLC. J. Comput. Theor. Nanosci. (2017). https://doi.org/10.1166/jctn.2017.6932
6. Buele, J., Varela-Aldás, J., Salazar, F.W., Soria, A., Andaluz, V.H.: wheelchair controlled by eye movement using raspberry Pi for ALS patients. In: Fonseca C, E., Morales, G.R., Cordero, M.O., Botto-Tobar, M., Martínez, E.C., León, A.P. (eds.) TICEC 2019. AISC, vol. 1099, pp. 124–136. Springer, Cham (2020). https://doi.org/10.1007/978-3-030-35740-5_9
7. Albiol-Pérez, S., Palacios-Navarro, G., Guerrón-Paredes, N., Gil-Gómez, J.A., Quilis, J.A. L., Gil-Gómez, H., Manzano, P.: The perfetti method, a novel virtual fine motor rehabilitation system for chronic acquired brain injury. In: Proceedings - REHAB 2014 (2014). https://doi.org/10.4108/icst.pervasivehealth.2014.255251
8. Andrea Sánchez, Z., et al.: Virtual rehabilitation system using electromyographic sensors for strengthening upper extremities. In: Rocha, Á., Pereira, R.P. (eds.) Developments and Advances in Defense and Security. SIST, vol. 152, pp. 231–241. Springer, Singapore (2020). https://doi.org/10.1007/978-981-13-9155-2_19
9. Galarza, E.E., et al.: Virtual reality system for children lower limb strengthening with the use of electromyographic sensors. In: Bebis, G., et al. (eds.) ISVC 2018. LNCS, vol. 11241, pp. 215–225. Springer, Cham (2018). https://doi.org/10.1007/978-3-030-03801-4_20
10. Rybarczyk, Y., Deters, J.K., Gonzalvo, A.A., Gonzalez, M., Villarreal, S., Esparza, D.: ePHoRt Project: a web-based platform for home motor rehabilitation. In: Rocha, Á., Correia, A.M., Adeli, H., Reis, L.P., Costanzo, S. (eds.) WorldCIST 2017. AISC, vol. 570, pp. 609–618. Springer, Cham (2017). https://doi.org/10.1007/978-3-319-56538-5_62
11. Quezada, A., Juárez-Ramírez, R., Jiménez, S., Ramírez-Noriega, A., Inzunza, S.: An empirical study on usability operations for autistic children. In: Rocha, Á., Correia, A.M., Adeli, H., Reis, L.P., Costanzo, S. (eds.) WorldCIST 2017. AISC, vol. 570, pp. 628–638. Springer, Cham (2017). https://doi.org/10.1007/978-3-319-56538-5_64

12. Salazar, F.W., Núñez, F., Buele, J., Jordán, E.P., Barberán, J.: Design of an ergonomic prototype for physical rehabilitation of people with paraplegia. In: Nummenmaa, J., Pérez-González, F., Domenech-Lega, B., Vaunat, J., Oscar Fernández-Peña, F. (eds.) CSEI 2019. AISC, vol. 1078, pp. 341–353. Springer, Cham (2020). https://doi.org/10.1007/978-3-030-33614-1_23

13. Pilatásig, M., et al.: Interactive system for hands and wrist rehabilitation. In: Rocha, Á., Guarda, T. (eds.) ICITS 2018. AISC, vol. 721, pp. 593–601. Springer, Cham (2018). https://doi.org/10.1007/978-3-319-73450-7_56

14. Buele, J., et al.: Interactive system to improve the skills of children with dyslexia: a preliminary study. In: Rocha, Á., Pereira, R.P. (eds.) Developments and Advances in Defense and Security. SIST, vol. 152, pp. 439–449. Springer, Singapore (2020). https://doi.org/10.1007/978-981-13-9155-2_35

15. Fernández-S., Á., Salazar-L., F., Jurado, M., Castellanos, E.X., Moreno-P., R., Buele, J.: electronic system for the detection of chicken eggs suitable for incubation through image processing. In: Rocha, Á., Adeli, H., Reis, L.P., Costanzo, S. (eds.) WorldCIST'19 2019. AISC, vol. 931, pp. 208–218. Springer, Cham (2019). https://doi.org/10.1007/978-3-030-16184-2_21

16. Spaide, R.F., Fujimoto, J.G., Waheed, N.K., Sadda, S.R., Staurenghi, G.: Optical coherence tomography angiography. Progr. Retinal Eye Res. (2018). https://doi.org/10.1016/j.preteyeres.2017.11.003

17. Koo, T.K., Silvia, N.: Actuator-assisted calibration of freehand 3D ultrasound system. J. Healthc. Eng. **2018**, 9314626 (2018). https://doi.org/10.1155/2018/9314626

18. Debette, S., Schilling, S., Duperron, M.G., Larsson, S.C., Markus, H.S.: Clinical significance of magnetic resonance imaging markers of vascular brain injury: a systematic review and meta-analysis. JAMA Neurol. (2019). https://doi.org/10.1001/jamaneurol.2018.3122

19. Thomas, H.M.T., Devakumar, D., Sasidharan, B., Bowen, S.R., Heck, D.K., James Jebaseelan Samuel, E.: Hybrid positron emission tomography segmentation of heterogeneous lung tumors using 3D Slicer: improved GrowCut algorithm with threshold initialization. J. Med. Imaging **4**, 011009 (2017). https://doi.org/10.1117/1.jmi.4.1.011009

20. Dou, Q., Yu, L., Chen, H., Jin, Y., Yang, X., Qin, J., Heng, P.A.: 3D deeply supervised network for automated segmentation of volumetric medical images. Med. Image Anal. **41**, 40–54 (2017). https://doi.org/10.1016/j.media.2017.05.001

21. Dighe, M., Barr, R., Bojunga, J., Cantisani, V., Chammas, M.C., Cosgrove, D., Cui, X.W., Dong, Y., Fenner, F., Radzina, M., Vinayak, S., Xu, J.M., Dietrich, C.F.: Thyroid ultrasound: State of the art part 1 - Thyroid ultrasound reporting and diffuse thyroid diseases (2017). https://doi.org/10.11152/mu-980

22. Chi, J., Walia, E., Babyn, P., Wang, J., Groot, G., Eramian, M.: Thyroid nodule classification in ultrasound images by fine-tuning deep convolutional neural network. J. Digit. Imaging **30**(4), 477–486 (2017). https://doi.org/10.1007/s10278-017-9997-y

23. Mazzaglia, P.J., Muraveika, L.: Normal thyroid appearance and anatomic landmarks in neck ultrasound. In: Milas, M., Mandel, S.J., Langer, J.E. (eds.) Advanced Thyroid and Parathyroid Ultrasound. AISC, pp. 77–86. Springer, Cham (2017). https://doi.org/10.1007/978-3-319-44100-9_9

24. Haymart, M.R., Banerjee, M., Reyes-Gastelum, D., Caoili, E., Norton, E.C.: Thyroid ultrasound and the increase in diagnosis of low-risk thyroid cancer. J. Clin. Endocrinol. Metab. **104**, 785–792 (2018). https://doi.org/10.1210/jc.2018-01933

A Novel Algorithm to Classify Hand Drawn Sketches with Respect to Content Quality

Ochilbek Rakhmanov[(✉)] [ID]

Nile University of Nigeria, Plot 681, Cadastral Zone C-OO,
Research and Institution Area, Jabi, Abuja, Nigeria
ochilbek.rakhmanov@nileuniversity.edu.ng

Abstract. In this paper, the methodology of a novel algorithm called Counting Key-Points algorithm (CKP) is presented. The algorithm can be used during classification of same type of hand drawn sketches, where content quality is important. In brief, the algorithm uses reference pictures set to form vocabulary of key points (with descriptors) and counting how many times those key points appeared on other images, to decide the image content quality. CKP was tested on Draw-a-Person test images, drawn by primary school students, and reached 65% of classification accuracy. The results of the experiment show that the method is applicable and can be improved with further researches. The classification accuracy of CKP was compared to other state-of-art hand drawn image classification methods, to show superiority of the algorithm. As the dataset needs further studies to improve the prediction accuracy, it would be released to the community.

Keywords: Classification · Sketches · Bag of visual words · Machine learning · Draw-a-Person test

1 Introduction

Sketch can be defined as a freehand drawing, which can be done by professionals, amateurs, adults and even children. With the development of touch screen digital devices like tablets and phones, sketch research has become an active and popular field in computer vision. Many users will sketch shapes on electronic device screens, which can create tremendous amount of the data for further researches. For instance, once of such recently released datasets contains more than 50 million free-hand sketches [1], which was collected during a mobile game Quick Draw by Google. The front-runner in this field was the research and the dataset released by Eitz et al in 2012, with 20,000 sketches [2].

Aforementioned publicly accessible datasets triggered many researchers to conduct machine learning classification experiments on hand-drawn sketches [2–4]. Unlike the ordinary photographic images, hand-drawn sketches differ in three main aspects: (i) they can be very abstract and deformed and still represent the same object, (ii) some people may draw all features of the object others may miss them, and lastly, (iii) sketches lack colors as they are usually black and white only [5].

© Springer Nature Switzerland AG 2020
O. Gervasi et al. (Eds.): ICCSA 2020, LNCS 12252, pp. 179–193, 2020.
https://doi.org/10.1007/978-3-030-58811-3_13

The drawings of the children have high importance on their mental development, educational performance and can reflect inner world of the child [6]. For this purpose, researchers have developed many different types of cognitive tests, which require a child to draw a shape of particular object, and later can be used for evaluation of various mental and physical conditions [6–9]. Thus, hand-drawn sketches have high importance in the fields of education and healthcare. Cognitive drawing tests proved to be effective tool for adults with mental disorders as well [9–11]. Many different types of drawing test were developed, and several studies been done on their reliability and validity. As this research addresses the issue of classification of hand drawn sketches with respect to content quality, one particular cognitive test were chosen in this context, DAPT – Draw-a-Person test [7].

All of the datasets released to community [1, 2, 12] have one thing in common, they are useful to classify different objects; cup from plate, lion from horse, cat from dog etc. A computational device should be trained to find difference between objects to classify them. But this is not same if one decides to train computational device using the images collected from DAPT, because in this case the important feature for classification are not the differences, but common features and how frequently they are appearing in the image. In other words, the content quality of the image is important in the classification procedure.

1.1 Content Quality

At this point, a new field should be addressed, the content quality of hand-drawn images. Content quality might be defined as content that delivers value, that solves a problem. In this, if an image contains more of main features of the object in comparison to other image of the same object, then it should be classified as higher class. For instance, Fig. 1 shows 3 different level of 2 different objects, face and bicycle. If they need to be classified with respect to image quality, definitely the content of the image would carry high importance. Type C is better drawn in comparison to Type B, while Type B is better than Type A, thus, they need to be classified accordingly.

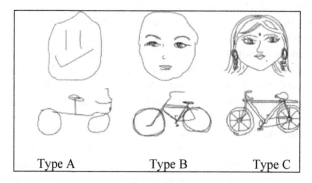

Fig. 1. Different representation of the face and bicycle [4]

Just like in Fig. 1, content quality is becoming main actor in classification of images, collected during DAPT procedure. Figure 2 present some sample images from DAPT test, drawn by children which belong to 3 different age categories. From Fig. 2, it is clearly evident that content quality of images was main actor in manual classification of the pictures to different classes (Fig. 3).

Fig. 2. DAPT sketches which belong to different categories [13].

2   Background of the Study

2.1   Machine Learning and Computer Vision Methods for Hand Drawn Sketch Classification

K-means, KNN, SVM [14] and CNN [15] are mostly used machine learning algorithms for classification of hand-drawn sketches, while computer vision algorithms like SIFT-Scale-Invariant Feature Transform [16], HOG – Histogram of Oriented Gradients [17] and BoVW – Bag of Visual Words [18] are extremely helpful for researches during future extraction, alongside with commonly used image processing operations like contour detection and convolution of the image [19].

In 2012, Eitz et al collected 20,000 original sketches of 250 different objects [2] and released this dataset to community, before testing it for classification with HOG and SVM, to reach 56% of accuracy. Year later, Li et al used several techniques like Ensemble matching, Star graph with KNN to improve classification accuracy to 62% [20]. Next promising research was conducted by Schneider et al in 2014, where they employed SIFT and SVM alongside with Fisher vectors [3] to reach accuracy of 67%. Several progressive researches were conducted by the same group Yu et al in 2015 and 2017 [4, 21], and CNN was successfully tested for Eitz et al dataset to reach 74% and 77% classification accuracy. CNN seemed to be an acceptable tool, but in 2016, Ballester and Araujo trained two state-of-art CNN structures, AlexNet and GoogleNet, and observed that those CNN structures are resulting with unacceptable accuracies, below 50% [22], when they were trained with hand-drawn sketches from Eitz et al dataset. This issue needs a further clarification in future researches. In one of recent studies, Rakhmanov tested the aforementioned classification algorithms (SVM, ANN) without computer vision algorithms (SIFT, HOG,BoVW), just using pixel values, on dataset provided by Eitz et al [5]. He stated that existing methods' results are reasonable to accept.

Fig. 3. Sample pictures from Eitz et al dataset (chair, butterfly, bicycle and pigeon) [6].

In 2017 a research group from Google [1] released a dataset of hand-drawn sketches, which is presently appears to be world largest doodling dataset, with more than 50 million samples. They used RNN to produce a software which completes the sketch from initial strokes. This triggered more researches; Xu et al [23] and Bensalah et al [24] used GNN (Graph Neural Network) in combination with CNN to classify the images. Still the highest classification accuracy is remaining in region of 77%.

Table 1 presents researches and used techniques in chronological order. While Eitz et al dataset was employed mostly, future researches may concentrate to Ha et al dataset, as it is a relatively new dataset.

Table 1. Chronological development table

Used technique	Publication	Dataset used	Accuracy
HOG + SVM	[2]	[2]	56%
KNN+Star graph+ SVM	[20]	[2]	62%
Fisher + SIFT + SVM	[3]	[2]	67%
CNN+ Stroke removal	[21]	[2]	74%
CNN + Data Augm.	[4]	[2]	77%
GNN + CNN	[24]	[1]	77%

2.1.1 Observations

Following observations can be done from Table 1:

a) If deep learning is employed to classify hand-drawn sketches, then it should be combined with some different techniques, to avoid biased results, as Balester and Araujo stated that implementing CNN straight, may result with unexpected low accuracy.

b) If the technique used is not of deep learning type, SVM can serve as good classifier.
c) BoVW uses HOG during methodology, and HOG uses SIFT. It appears that BoVW – HOG – SIFT can be also employed as reliable tools to classify hand-drawn sketches, and results can be promising.

2.2   Draw-a-Person Test (DAPT)

First conceived by Dr. Florence Goodenough in 1926 [7], the Draw-a-Person test is a skill test that is designed to measure a child's mental age through a figure drawing task. It estimates the progress of learning visual, cognitive, and motor skills by having the candidate draw a human figure, scoring the drawing for presence and quality of figure features, and comparing the score to children's typical rate of acquisition of figure features [7]. Throughout the years, this test underwent many discussions, whereby the researchers tested the validity and reliability of the test, usually resulting in supportive conclusions. The instrument is among the top 10 tools used by practitioners, according to Yama et al [25]. It is widely used in early childhood education; primary school counselors can use it to monitor children's mental development. In Psychology, for instance, it has been used during comparison between healthy patients and those with mental disorders. There are many supportive researches and case studies for these aforementioned fields, summarized by Naglieri et al [26]. Due to the wide adoption and use of DAPT, there was a need to conduct some experiments on DAPT sketches, to see if we can develop a model to classify images automatically. Evaluation of DAPT can be done only by professional psychologist or practitioner. But there are very few schools in low income countries (including both private and public) who have a psychologist as working personal, because it is too expensive for them. Thus, development of such automatic tool can help to millions of schools, guidance-counsellors and teachers around the world.

2.2.1   How the DAPT Scored?

This section will provide a brief explanation of the DAPT picture (as it was proposed by Goodenough [7]). In the DAPT image evaluation, we count the number of features, like eyes, nose, mouth, hair, hands, shoulder, fingers, etc. Yet, some more scores come from the comparison of the geometrical positioning of the features. For instance, a child can draw one leg short and other long or provide a sketch of eyes whose proportion on the face is abnormal. The sum of these scores results in a total score (minimum 0, maximum 51 points). We look up for corresponding mental age from score ~ mental age scale proposed by Goodenough [7]. This mental age is compared to biological age, and if the difference is high, then counselor or practitioner advices that the child needs special assistance or training on recognizing the functions of the objects surrounding him or her in his or her daily life [7]. Figure 4 shows some pictures from our dataset and their corresponding mental ages.

Figure 5 demonstrates some human figures which belong to the same class, even though they are drawn in very different ways. Thus, the biggest challenge in this dataset as it can be observed from Fig. 5 is that sketches may appear in very different shapes. Unlike in most common image classification tasks, we are not actually looking for the difference between the images, but for the common features and how frequently they appear. The exploration of any possible solution for this challenge is the main goal of this research.

Fig. 4. Sample sketches of the students.

Fig. 5. Different human shapes from same group.

Another important difference is that the Eitz et al dataset was collected through touch screen devices and mostly participants were adults. All pictures are clear and sharp. However, it was impossible to do so in our case as we had kids aged 4–7 years who were unfamiliar with touch screens or other electronic devices. Thus, our dataset consists of sketches drawn on a plain sheet. Each student tried to draw his or her best picture; so, there are many pictures where students tried to erase previous sketches and replace them with new ones. They also tried to draw extra elements and the lines in their drawings were clashing or not straight. All this created significant noise on images which affected prediction accuracy in some manner.

As from computer science aspect, it is very important to mention that a child's picture can be only in one highest class. In other words, a picture can only have highest class, like picture of 5 years old child, or picture of 9 years old child, with respect to content quality. This is advantage of the scoring system of DAMT, it cannot be misclassified between 4 years old and 8 years old, or 5 and 10. We only must identify what is the highest class the image belongs, which is making this challenging task easier to approach. In other words, we don't have to predict exact class of the picture, we need to predict what is the highest class it can belong.

3   Purpose of the Study

The main objective of this study is to present the methodology on how to develop and apply CKP algorithm for image classification of hand drawn sketches with respect to their content quality and to present comparative results with respect to other existing methodologies to prove the superiority of the CKP algorithm, as this type of sketches require extra-ordinary approach. A unique dataset of DAPT images (with more than 1000 images) was collected in order to conduct this experiment.

An early preliminary version of this work was published by Rakhmanov et al [27], where initial results of the experimentations on DAPT images were published. However, this paper presents complete guide on how the methodology of the CKP works, and presents a complete comparative study on results.

4   Instruments

We used 2 important concepts in machine learning and computer vision to establish CKP algorithm, they are K-means and BoVW. We also compared the prediction accuracy of CKP to other widely used algorithms. In this context, we compared CKP results with SVM+HOG sketch classification method [2], and with CNN [4]. We described the complete development process of CKP in Sect. 5, while SVM+HOG and CNN were only briefly described in methodology section, as they are already explained in the literature.

- *K-means.* K-means algorithm is an iterative algorithm that tries to partition the dataset into K pre-defined distinct non-overlapping subgroups (clusters) where each data point belongs to only one group. It tries to make the inter-cluster data points as similar as possible while also keeping the clusters as different (far) as possible. It assigns data points to a cluster such that the sum of the squared distance between the data points and the cluster's centroid (arithmetic mean of all the data points that belong to that cluster) is at the minimum [28].
- *Bag of Visual Words.* Another important algorithm for image feature detection is BoVW [18]. The general idea of BoVW is to represent an image as a set of features. These features consist of key-points and descriptors. Key points are the points in an image; so, no matter how much the image is rotated, shrunk, or expanded, its key points will always be the same. The descriptor is the description of the key point. We used the key points and descriptors to construct vocabularies and represented each image as a frequency histogram of features that are in the image. From the frequency histogram, we can find other similar images or predict the category of the image. To calculate key points and descriptors, we used ORB [29].
- *Programming instruments.* We used Python programming language, as it is one of most popular programming languages for image classification. Image processing

and computer vision algorithms were implemented by using open source library OpenCV [30]. While Scikit-Learn was our main library during machine learning training [31], Keras and Tensorflow were used during deep learning training [15].

5 Data Collection and Dataset Formation

5.1 Data Collection

- *Ethics and regulations.* We followed all ethics and regulations during data collection. All parents were properly informed of test regulations and their consents were obtained. Students were guided by their teachers during process. It was an extra-curricular activity for students with minimum level of stress.
- *Participants.* Students from private educational institution were selected. They were aged from 4 to 11 years, from Nursery 1–2 and Primary 1–2–3–4 grades. More than 1000 pictures were collected, and some meaningless sketches were eliminated, resulting with almost 1000 pictures remaining.
- *Process.* Students were given a plain sheet and told to sketch a man. No further assistance was given as the sketch required the authentic work of the child. About 10–15 min were given to the children to finish the job. After the sketching process was completed, all pictures were collected and passed for further steps.
- *Manual classification.* A consensus of three trained persons (one school counselor, one PhD student and one Physiology Professor) followed Goodenough's 51-point scoring criteria to calculate the score of every picture (Goodenough, 1926). Once scoring was done, we classified them according to mental ages, from 4 to 11 years, resulting a total of 8 classes. Below, in Table 2 we present total numbers of images for every class.

Table 2. Number of images in each class for All_8 dataset.

Class	4	5	6	7	8	9	10	11
No of images	142	131	152	160	125	124	79	38

5.2 Dataset Formation

To make our work diverse and to find best possible option, we created three versions of the dataset.

a) *All_8*: this is primer dataset, all sketches divided to 8 classes, according to the ages, from 4 to 11 years. Pictures were cropped and resized to 120 × 240 pixels.
b) *Double*: in this dataset, we merged the adjacent age groups; 4 with 5, 6 with 7, 8 with 9 and 10 with 11. This resulted in a total of 4 classes.
c) *Reference*: this is small dataset, where we joined classes 10 and 11. This dataset was used during the CKP experiment to propose a novel method.

The formation of different datasets is not a desirable condition and our expectation is to get the best possible result on All_8 dataset. However, during the experiment we discovered that the classification of All_8 is a very difficult task, which forced us to look for different methods of classification.

As a rule of thumb, we used 75% of the data for training and the remaining 25% for testing. We used training and testing dataset for other classification methods. In CKP, you do not need such partition of data. In CKP, we need only Reference dataset for formation of vocabulary and rest of data was used for testing.

6 Methodology

6.1 Counting Key Points (CKP) Algorithm

Firstly, we followed the process described in Fig. 6. During each experiment we have chosen different values for X and Y, to see how good the prediction accuracy would be. So, the set of pairs we selected for (X, Y) = {(200, 50), (800, 250), (1000, 400), (2000, 800)}.

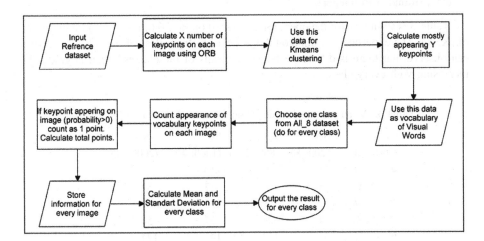

Fig. 6. CKP algorithm process scheme, first stage.

For instance, assume that (X, Y) = (1000, 400). We proceed with followings steps:

1. Step1. First, we used the Reference dataset to calculate 1000 key points and their descriptors from each picture, using ORB. Figure 7 displays some of selected images and their respective key points (1000) with red circles.
2. Step2. Next, we used K-means to find the 400 most likely descriptors to appear in every picture. We formed a vocabulary of visual words from these 400 descriptors.
3. Step3. We used matching method to determine if these vocabulary elements are appearing in other classes of All_8, and how frequently they appeared. If a descriptor was appearing on picture (probability of appearing is bigger than zero) we counted it as 1 point.

Fig. 7. Sample pictures and their key-points for BoVW.

4. Step 4. We calculated the total points for each picture.
5. Step 5. Lastly, we produce summary of the mean and standard deviation for every class (rounded to integer).

Table 3 is summary for the operation presented on Fig. 6 (after Step 5) for every set of (X, Y). The experiment is done on All_8 dataset. Regardless of the selected set, we can observe that there is difference between means of the classes and it is gradually increasing with every class.

Table 3. Mean and standard deviation for each class and set for All_8.

Class	Stats.	Set 1 (200; 50)	Set 2 (800; 250)	Set 3 (1000; 400)	Set 4 (2000; 800)
4	*Mean*	35	95	113	134
	Std.	5	27	37	53
5	*Mean*	35	109	135	161
	Std.	4	26	37	54
6	*Mean*	37	114	141	174
	Std.	7	24	36	56
7	*Mean*	37	121	152	187
	Std.	4	22	34	52
8	*Mean*	38	122	158	195
	Std.	3	20	33	57
9	*Mean*	38	132	170	217
	Std.	3	19	30	53
10	*Mean*	38	139	183	250
	Std.	3	20	32	64
11	*Mean*	40	145	192	268
	Std.	3	15	30	62

Hypothetically, we can assume that we can classify the sketches with respect to their means. But, biggest challenge in this case is the standard deviation, it is very high. Next, we applied same operation on Double dataset. Table 4 is summary of the experiment on Double dataset.

Table 4. Mean and standard deviation for each class and set, for Double.

Class	Stats.	Set 1 (200; 50)	Set 2 (800; 250)	Set 3 (1000; 400)	Set 4 (2000; 800)
45	*Mean*	35	101	118	147
	Std.	4	27	36	55
67	*Mean*	37	118	141	181
	Std.	4	23	36	54
89	*Mean*	38	127	156	206
	Std.	4	20	35	56
1011	*Mean*	39	141	180	256
	Std.	3	18	33	64

If we compare results on Tables 3 and 4, we can observe that average standard deviation for every set of (X, Y) is not changing, but still very high. Definitely, this will cause a serious challenge during prediction operation. At this point, we strongly encourage some further researches in order to reduce the value of standard deviation to improve classification accuracy. But, the margins between means are wider in Table 4, which would directly affect the classification accuracy in positive manner.

Next, we aimed to use information from Tables 3 and 4 to develop an image classification methodology. Figure 8 is process chart to develop this methodology.

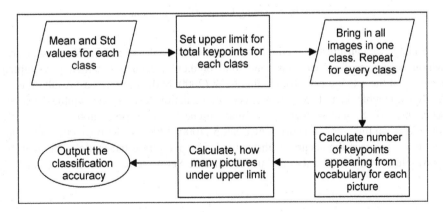

Fig. 8. methodology for development of prediction of image class

As standard deviation is too high for every class, we were careful with selection of upper limit for every class. The limits should be reasonable with respect to mean and deviation of two neighbor classes. Table 5 is the summary and limits we have chosen for every class in All_8 and Double dataset.

The rest of operation in Fig. 8 can be completed and described with algorithm presented in Fig. 9. This operation should be done for every class and accuracy should be recorded.

Table 5. Upper limit for each class in both All_8 and Double dataset.

	All_8								Double			
Set No.	4	5	6	7	8	9	10	11	45	67	89	1011
Set 1 (200; 50)	34	35	36	37	38	39	40	40+	35	37	38	38+
Set 2 (800; 250)	102	112	118	123	128	136	142	142+	109	123	132	132+
Set 3 (1000; 400)	127	138	145	155	163	177	188	188+	130	148	168	168+
Set 4 (2000; 800)	145	165	181	191	206	229	264	264+	164	194	231	231+

Algorithm   Counting Keypoints

1: $A \leftarrow$ all images in class B
2: $C \leftarrow$ upper limit for class B
3: $t \leftarrow$ total number of images in class B
4: $0 \leftarrow$ sum
5: **for** every image in A **do**
6:     $D \leftarrow$ Count total key point appearance form vocabulary
7:     **if** $D \leq C$ **then**
8:         $sum \leftarrow sum + 1$
9: $accuracy \leftarrow sum/t$
10: **return** $accuracy$

Fig. 9. Counting key-points pseudocode

Finally, we can present prediction accuracies in Tables 6 and 7. We present prediction accuracies for each class and total prediction accuracy, which is weighted accuracy of the set. We can observe that Set 4 (2000; 800) is giving best result on both All_8 and Double dataset. As it was expected, prediction accuracy on Double dataset is better than All_8, and we managed to reach highest 65% of prediction accuracy. We could keep on this version and produce Set 5 (4000; 1200) or Set 6 (6000; 2000), but this didn't increase the accuracy, instead it led to overfitting the model. This may be applicable on very large datasets, but for our case Set 4 seems to be most optimal.

Table 6. Prediction accuracy for All_8 dataset.

Class	No of images	Set 1	Set 2	Set 3	Set 4
4	142	*0.42*	*0.64*	*0.63*	*0.62*
5	131	*0.49*	*0.48*	*0.52*	*0.56*
6	152	*0.46*	*0.5*	*0.52*	*0.55*
7	160	*0.44*	*0.45*	*0.52*	*0.55*
8	125	*0.45*	*0.6*	*0.58*	*0.59*
9	124	*0.44*	*0.5*	*0.51*	*0.58*
10	79	*0.54*	*0.42*	*0.47*	*0.56*
11	38	*0.1*	*0.65*	*0.63*	*0.5*
Total accuracy	**951**	***0.443***	***0.522***	***0.543***	***0.57***

Table 7. Prediction accuracy for Double dataset

Class	No of images	Set 1	Set 2	Set 3	Set 4
45	273	*0.42*	*0.57*	*0.6*	*0.65*
67	312	*0.45*	*0.5*	*0.56*	*0.63*
89	249	*0.4*	*0.55*	*0.6*	*0.67*
1011	117	*0.75*	*0.75*	*0.7*	*0.66*
Total accuracy	**951**	***0.465***	***0.564***	***0.6***	***0.65***

6.2   Comparison of CKP Algorithm with Other Classification Methods

We developed one-to-one models of two milestone research papers for classification of hand drawn sketches; Eitz et al [2] and Yu et al [4]. In brief, Eitz et al firstly calculated Histogram of Oriented Gradients for each sketch than feed this data to SVM, while Yu et al developed a Convolutional Neural Network model to classify hand drawn sketches. Table 8 is summary of classification accuracies for aforementioned two milestone models and CKP algorithm. We can clearly observe that other two methods struggled to understand the dataset, as it needs special approach, while CKP overperformed both.

Table 8. Prediction accuracies three different methods

Method	All_8	Double
SVM + HOG	*22%*	*48%*
CNN	*32%*	*52%*
CKP	*57%*	*65%*

7 Discussion of the Results

In this paper, we aimed to conduct some classification experiments on DAPT images and we presented the methodology for CKP algorithm. Throughout the experimentation, we discovered that this kind of images should use some specific way of approach, rather than common classification methods. We observed that the All_8 dataset is difficult to classify with high accuracy, while joining 2 classes like in Double, can minimize this burden. However, our primary goal should be to develop a method to classify All_8 dataset.

We introduced a novel method, CKP algorithm, which seems to be simple but achieved good results with this type of dataset. As we have tested a unique dataset, which was not tested before for classification by computational device, we believe that our resulted prediction accuracy, 65%, is worthy finding and can be improved with further studies. We also presented comparative results on Table 8, proving that CKP is superior with comparison to existing state-of-art sketch classification methods.

The main shortcoming of the algorithm is, as we stated several times before, the standard deviation of the classes is very high. Prediction accuracy might improve if future studies can lower the standard deviation.

References

1. Ha, D., Eck, D.: A neural representation of sketch drawings (2017). arXiv preprint arXiv: 1704.03477
2. Eitz, M., Hays, J., Alexa, M.: How do humans sketch objects? ACM Trans. Graph. 31(4), 1–10 (2012)
3. Schneider, R.G., Tuytelaars, T.: Sketch classification and classification-driven analysis using fisher vectors. ACM Trans. Graph. (TOG) 33, 1–9 (2014)
4. Yu, Q., Yang, Y., Liu, F., Song, Y.-Z., Xiang, T., Hospedales, T.M.: Sketch-a-Net: a deep neural network that beats humans. Int. J. Comput. Vis. 122, 411–425 (2017). https://doi.org/10.1007/s11263-016-0932-3
5. Rakhmanov, O.: Testing strength of the state-of-art image classification methods for hand drawn sketches. In: 2019 15th International Conference on Electronics, Computer and Computation (ICECCO), pp. 1–3. IEEE (2019)
6. Jolley, R.P.: Children and Pictures: Drawing and Understanding. Wiley (2009)
7. Goodenough, F.L.: Measurement of intelligence by drawings (1926)
8. Rey, A.: L'examen psychologique dans les cas d'encephalopathie traumatique. Arch. Psychol. 28, 112 (1942)
9. Wolf-Klein, G.P., Silverstone, F.A., Levy, A.P., Brod, M.S., Breuer, J.: Screening for Alzheimer's disease by clock drawing. J. Am. Geriatr. Soc. 37, 730–734 (1989)
10. Fastenau, P.S., Denburg, N.L., Hufford, B.J.: Adult norms for the Rey-Osterrieth Complex Figure Test and for supplemental recognition and matching trials from the Extended Complex Figure Test. Clin. Neuropsychologist 13, 30–47 (1999)
11. Naglieri, J.A., MacNeish, T.J., Bardos, A.: Draw a person: screening procedure for emotional disturbance. dap: sped. Pro-Ed (1991)
12. Sun, Z., Wang, C., Zhang, L., Zhang, L.: Query-adaptive shape topic mining for hand-drawn sketch recognition. In: Proceedings of the 20th ACM International Conference on Multimedia, pp. 519–528 (2012)

13. Rakhmanov, O., Dane, S.: Correlation between vanderbilt ADHD diagnostic scale and the draw-a-man test in school children. J. Res. Med. Dent. Sci. **7**, 77–81 (2019)

14. Hastie, T., Tibshirani, R., Friedman, J.: The Elements of Statistical Learning. SSS. Springer, New York (2009). https://doi.org/10.1007/978-0-387-84858-7

15. Gulli, A., Pal, S.: Deep Learning with Keras. Packt Publishing Ltd (2017)

16. Lowe, D.G.: Distinctive image features from scale-invariant keypoints. Int. J. Comput. Vis. **60**, 91–110 (2004)

17. Dalal, N., Triggs, B.: Histograms of oriented gradients for human detection. In: 2005 IEEE Computer Society Conference on Computer Vision and Pattern Recognition (CVPR'05) 2005 Jun 20, vol. 1, pp. 886–893. IEEE (2005)

18. Yang, J., Jiang, Y.-G., Hauptmann, A.G., Ngo, C.-W.: Evaluating bag-of-visual-words representations in scene classification. In: Proceedings of the International Workshop on Workshop on Multimedia Information Retrieval, pp. 197–206. ACM, New York, NY, USA (2007). https://doi.org/10.1145/1290082.1290111

19. Baxes, G.A.: Digital Image Processing: Principles and Applications. Wiley, New York (1994)

20. Li, Y., Hospedales, T.M., Song, Y.-Z., Gong, S.: Free-hand sketch recognition by multi-kernel feature learning. Comput. Vis. Image Underst. **137**, 1–11 (2015)

21. Yu, Q., Yang, Y., Song, Y.-Z., Xiang, T., Hospedales, T.: Sketch-a-Net that Beats Humans (2015). arXiv:1501.07873 [cs]

22. Ballester, P., Araujo, R.M.: On the performance of GoogLeNet and AlexNet applied to sketches. In: Thirtieth AAAI Conference on Artificial Intelligence (2016)

23. Xu, P., Joshi, C.K., Bresson, X.: Multi-graph transformer for free-hand sketch recognition (2019). arXiv preprint arXiv:1912.11258

24. Bensalah, A., Riba, P., Fornés, A., Lladós, J.: Shoot less and sketch more: an efficient sketch classification via joining graph neural networks and few-shot learning. In: 2019 International Conference on Document Analysis and Recognition Workshops (ICDARW), pp. 80–85. IEEE (2019)

25. Yama, M.F.: The usefulness of human figure drawings as an index of overall adjustment. J. Pers. Assess. **54**, 78–86 (1990)

26. Naglieri, J.A., McNeish, T.J., Achilles, N.: Draw a person test. In: Tools of the Trade: A Therapist's Guide to Art Therapy Assessments, p. 124 (2004)

27. Rakhmanov, O., Agwu, N.N., Adeshina, S.A.: Experimentation on hand drawn sketches by children to classify Draw-a-Person test images in psychology. In: The Thirty-Third International Flairs Conference (2020)

28. Tan, P.-N.: Introduction to Data Mining. Pearson Education, India (2018)

29. Rublee, E., Rabaud, V., Konolige, K., Bradski, G.R.: ORB: An efficient alternative to SIFT or SURF. In: ICCV, p. 2. Citeseer (2011)

30. Gary, B., Adrian, K.: Learning OpenCV: Computer Vision with the OpenCV Library. O'Reilly Media, Inc. (2008)

31. Pedregosa, F., Varoquaux, G., Gramfort, A., Michel, V., Thirion, B., Grisel, O., Blondel, M., Prettenhofer, P., Weiss, R., Dubourg, V.: Scikit-learn: machine learning in python. J. Mach. Learn. Res. **12**, 2825–2830 (2011)

International Workshop on Future Computing System Technologies and Applications (FiSTA 2020)

Using Market Basket Analysis to Find Semantic Duplicates in Ontology

Irina Astrova[1(✉)], Arne Koschel[2], and Su Ling Lee[2]

[1] Department of Software Science, School of IT, Tallinn University of Technology, Akadeemia tee 21, 12618 Tallinn, Estonia
irina@cs.ioc.ee
[2] Faculty IV, Department of Computer Science, University of Applied Sciences and Arts Hannover, Ricklinger Stadtweg 120, 30459 Hannover, Germany
akoschel@acm.org

Abstract. This paper proposes a novel approach to detecting semantic duplicates in an ontology that was integrated from many other ontologies. The proposed approach is based on using: (1) a query log that was issued against the ontology; and (2) the Apriori and FP algorithms from market basket analysis, where sales transactions are viewed as queries and items in a sales transaction are viewed as search terms in a query. To prove the viability of the proposed approach, the paper also presents the results of four experiments that were conducted on the OntoLife ontology.

Keywords: Ontolgy · Semantic heterogeneity · Market basket analysis · Apriori algorithm · FP Growth (Frequent-Pattern Growth) algorithm · ICD (Iterated Contextual Distance) algorithm · Similar attributes · OntoLife ontology

1 Introduction

The main purpose of ontology-based data integration is to solve the semantic heterogeneity problem in data integration. Semantic heterogeneity refers to the ambiguous interpretation of similar terms, which are being used to describe the meaning of data in heterogeneous resources such as websites or databases. However, during an ontology-based data integration, the newly merged ontology can contain semantic duplicates, e.g., similar attributes. These attributes can cause incomplete query results.

As an example, consider a user who submits the following query against the Wikipedia ontology: *"Which performers were born in Chicago?"* In response to this query, the query-answering system will return only one result (viz. Michael Ian Black). However, if it were known that *actor* and *comedian* are subclasses of *performer* and that their attributes *birthplace*, *birth place*, *city of birth*, *place of birth* and *origin* are semantic duplicates of performer's location, the query-answering system could return 163 additional results [1]. Thus, the recall of query results can be greatly improved by finding similar attributes.

In this paper, we propose to use market basket analysis to find similar attributes. In market basket analysis, two items (or products) are considered to be similar if the purchase patterns of their customers are similar. Analogously, two attributes are

© Springer Nature Switzerland AG 2020
O. Gervasi et al. (Eds.): ICCSA 2020, LNCS 12252, pp. 197–211, 2020.
https://doi.org/10.1007/978-3-030-58811-3_14

considered to be similar if the querying patterns of their users are similar [2]. Continuing the example with the Wikipedia ontology: If it were known that there are many users who have asked about the actor's *birth place* together with the actor's *name* and *birth date*, and that there are many users who have asked about the actor's *origin* together with the actor's *name* and *birth date*, we could conclude that attributes *birth place* and *origin* in a class *actor* are similar to each other.

2   Market Basket Analysis

Baskets are defined as sets of products bought together by customers in sales transactions during their visits to supermarkets or online shops. Market basket analysis examines the buying behaviour of customers and it is used to identify similar products based on the purchase patterns. A typical example of similar products are Becks and Heineken beers. At the first sight, these two products may appear dissimilar as they do not have many common customers: the customers buy either Becks or Heineken, but not both. However, it was observed that together with Becks and Heineken, many of the customers buy the same products such as chips, sausages and pretzels. Based on this observation, a similarity measure is defined as two products are found to be similar, if the purchase patterns of their customers are similar.

The aim of market basket analysis is that of finding sets of items (products) that appear together in (are related to) many baskets. Let products be attributes in an ontology (search terms in queries issued against the ontology), baskets be queries and a sales transaction database be a query log. While market basket analysis aims at finding frequent itemsets, this information is often presented as a set of "if–then" rules called association rules. For example, *if customers buy Heineken, then they also buy chips, sausages and pretzels.*

To prove the applicability of market basket analysis to finding similar attributes in an ontology, we experimented with three algorithms:

- **ICD (Iterated Contextual Distance) algorithm** [17]: This is an array-based algorithm, which returns the distances between attributes.
- **Apriori algorithm** [3]: This is an array-based algorithm, which returns association rules.
- **FP (Frequent Pattern) Growth algorithm** [15]: This is a tree-based algorithm, which returns association rules.

In our experiments, we looked for sets of attributes that appear together in many queries, by analysing many-to-many relationships between the querying patterns and the user behaviours. We assumed that users who have similar questions in mind tend to submit similar queries, which have similar querying patterns.

In our previous work [2, 16], we used the ICD and Apriori algorithms to detect semantic duplicates in an ontology. In this paper, we employ the FP Growth algorithm, which is an improvement of the Apriori algorithm. The Apriori algorithm finds frequent itemsets and consequently querying patterns, by generating candidate itemsets. In contrast, the FP Growth algorithm finds querying patterns without the need for candidate generation, rather by constructing an FP tree, which maintains the associations between frequent itemsets.

3   OntoLife

OntoLife [4] is an ontology for semantically managing personal information. This ontology has 110 attributes called datatype properties in the OWL terminology. It was developed by Intelligent System and Knowledge Processing Research Group (ISKP) by merging 10 other ontologies:

1. **Person** [5]: This ontology provides a formal vocabulary description of people. Furthermore, it defines constraints (e.g., a person should have exactly one name). It does not have any attributes.
2. **Friend of a Friend (FOAF)** [6]: This ontology describes the people's activities and the relationships such as friendships between them. It does not have any attributes.
3. **Family Tree** [7]: This ontology models the application domain of family that defines people's relationships such as children and parents. It does not have any attributes.
4. **Relationship** [8]: This ontology defines other relationships between people such as friends, colleagues and tutors. It does not have any attributes.
5. **ISO lists for Countries and Languages** [9]: This ontology models the application domain of people's countries and their languages. It does not have any attributes.
6. **Project** [10]: This ontology describes research projects and people who are involved into those projects. It has 6 attributes such as project title, start and end dates.
7. **Research** [11]: This ontology describes the hierarchy of research projects (e.g., related projects can include cloud computing and data mining). It does not have any attributes.
8. **Publication** [12]: This ontology models the application domain of people's publications. It has 27 attributes such as book title, edition of publication and publication date.
9. **PersonProjectAssociation** [13]: This ontology models the relationships between people and publications or research projects. Furthermore, it defines constraints (e.g., a person should have at least one role in a research project). It does not have any attributes.
10. **Biography** [14]: This is the largest ontology. It has 77 attributes. It describes the people's demographics, their profiles and contacts. Furthermore, it describes the CV-related information such as people's education and qualifications, skills and working experiences as well as injuries that people have got at work.

We selected OntoLife for our experiments because it is from an easy-to-understand application domain. Furthermore, the ontology has many attributes and is merged out of many other ontologies from the same application domain. Thus, it is likely to have semantic duplicates.

4 Experiment Results

4.1 Assumptions

To run the Apriori and FP Growth algorithms against the OntoLife ontology, we made a number of assumptions about how data are stored and manipulated when searching for frequent itemsets (similar attributes):

- In market basket analysis, a basket contains only a small set of products from all products available in the supermarket or online shop. Similarly, it is also assumed that users do not inquire about all attributes in the ontology at once in a single query.
- In market basket analysis, a basket can contain any number of products. Similarly, it is also assumed that a query can contain any number of attributes (i.e., the query can be of any size).
- In market basket analysis, the details on sales transactions such as the date of purchase, product price and product quantities are ignored. Similarly, the values of attributes in the ontology are ignored.
- In market basket analysis, the order of products in a sales transaction is ignored. Similarly, the order of attributes in a query is ignored.
- In market basket analysis, sales transactions are mined for a long period of time (at least for 6 months). As a result, the sales transaction database is large. Similarly, it is also assumed that the log of queries issued against the ontology is large.
- All queries are taken into account, regardless of whether they return results or not.

4.2 Query Log

As input, the Apriori and FP Growth algorithms took the query log. This log was the result of the past user interactions with the OntoLife ontology. Figure 1 shows an excerpt of the query log, which comprises 30 queries. These queries are written in SPARQL and contain 41 attributes, which constitute approximately 37% of the total attributes in the ontology. The shortest query has one attribute, whereas the longest query has 5 attributes. Not only can queries be distinguished by their size, but also by their frequency occurrence in the query log. A unique query appears only once in the query log. An example of a unique query is: *"Who have "rain man" as their nick-name?"* In contrast, repeated queries are the queries, which appear more than once in the query log. They queried on the same attributes but possibly with different values or in a different order. An example of repeated queries is: *"Who were injured on November 22, 2009, were 50% disabled by that injury and worked in the public sector?"* and *"Who were injured on January 2, 1989, worked in the government sector and were 20% disabled by that injury?"*.

The query log was converted into a sales transaction database, which contains 30 sales transactions (one sales transaction per query) represented as rows. Figure 2 shows an excerpt of the sales transaction database. In this database, each query is identified by TID (transaction identifier). For each row, if an attribute does not appear in the query, it will not appear in the corresponding row either.

4.3   Minimum Support Threshold and Minimum Confidence Threshold

The Apriori and FP Growth algorithms find frequent itemsets, by pruning those itemsets whose support is lower than a user-defined minimum support threshold. After that, the algorithms generate strong association rules from the frequent itemsets, by pruning those association rules whose confidence is lower than a user-defined minimum confidence threshold. We conducted four experiments with different values for the minimum support threshold and the minimum confidence threshold because these values had impact on the results of our experiments.

A support reveals the probability of occurrence of an attribute set X in queries. A frequent itemset has a support, which is greater than or equal to the minimum support threshold, where P denotes the probability. A confidence refers to a conditional probability. This is the probability that an attribute set Y occurs in queries given that an attribute set X has already occurred in the same queries. A confidence is used to generate strong association rules from the frequent itemsets that meet the minimum confidence threshold.

$$\textbf{Confidence } (X \Rightarrow Y) = \textbf{Support}(X \Rightarrow Y)/\textbf{Support}(\mathbf{X}) = \mathbf{P}(X \cap Y)/$$
$$\mathbf{P}(\mathbf{X}) = \mathbf{P}(Y|X)$$

Like in market basket analysis, false positives and false negatives are inevitable when the thresholds are set either too low or too high, respectively. For example, when the minimum support threshold was too low, false positives tended to occur as those originally infrequent attributes were falsely found as frequent. When the minimum support threshold was too high, false negatives tended to occur where those originally frequent attributes were falsely found as infrequent.

4.4   Experiment 1

Figure 3 shows the results of our first experiment, where the minimum support threshold was 12% and the minimum confidence threshold was 55%. In this experiment, 24 strong association rules were generated by the algorithms. Two pairs of attributes were found similar:

1. *specificDate* and *sickness_injuryDesc*;
2. resource's *title* and resource's *name*.

Among the strong association rules, we looked for sets of attributes that frequently appeared together in the consequents (right-hand sides) of those rules. When we found such rules, we had candidates for similar attributes that appeared in the antecedents (left-hand sides) of those rules. For example, the consequents of Rule 17 and Rule 20 (marked in blue in Fig. 3) suggested a pair of similar attributes: resource's *title* and resource's *name*. Furthermore, the consequents of Rule 11 and Rule 14 (marked in red in Fig. 3) suggested another pair of similar attributes: *specificDate* and *sickness_injuryDesc*. However, intuitively these attributes were not similar and thus, such a finding was a false positive. One possible reason for this false positive was the small size of the query log (which contained only 30 queries).

The size of the query log was a crucial factor that could affect the experiment results. This is because the two algorithms assume that a sales transaction database is large. It was observed that there was yet another pair of similar attributes but it was not found (false negative): publication's *description* and biography's *description*. Again, due to the small size of the query log, there were no common query patterns, which inquired both attributes.

There was no significant difference in the runtime between the algorithms, as both took about 16 ms, but in the made count. In particular, the Apriori algorithm made 70 counts on the itemsets, whereas the FP Growth made 30 counts.

In summary, using the first experiment results, the OntoLife ontology could be refined. In particular, OWL has a construct *owl:equivalentProperty* to specify that resource's *title* is a semantic duplicate of resource's *name*.

4.5   Experiment 2

Figure 4 shows the results of our second experiment, where the minimum support threshold was 12% and the minimum confidence threshold was 90%. In this experiment, 16 strong association rules were generated by the algorithms. One pair of attributes was found similar: *specificDate* and *sickness injuryDesc*. However, it was the same false positive discovered before.

Since the minimum support threshold was still 12%, the algorithms showed the same runtime and made the same count on the itemsets as they did in the first experiment.

4.6   Experiment 3

Figure 5 shows the results of our third experiment, where the minimum support threshold was 10% and the minimum confidence threshold was 90%. In this experiment, 51 strong association rules were generated by the algorithms. Four pairs of attributes were found similar:

1. *specificDate* and *sickness injuryDesc*;
2. *disab percentage* and *hasGovernmentalInvolvement;*
3. *hasGovernmentalInvolvement* and *sector;*
4. *disab percentage* and *sector.*

However, all these pairs were false positives. The first pair was caused by the small size of the query log. The second pair was caused by redundant association rules: Rule 13 and Rule 30. (An association rule is redundant if a more general rules with the same or a higher confidence exists, i.e., if it has the same consequent but one or more items were removed from the antecedent.) The third pair was also caused by redundant association rules: Rule 17 and Rule 33. The fourth pair was discovered due to the transitivity. Since *disab percentage* is similar to *hasGovernmentalInvolvement* and *hasGovernmentalInvolvement* is similar to *sector*, so is *disab percentage* similar to *sector*.

In the third experiment, the FP Growth algorithm was again faster than the Apriori algorithm. In particular, the former ran 16 ms, whereas the latter ran about 31 ms.

During its run, the Apriori algorithm made 131 counts on the itemsets, whereas the FP Growth made 30 counts.

4.7 Experiment 4

In the fourth experiment, the minimum support threshold was 28% and the minimum confidence threshold was 55%. Here no strong association rules were generated by the algorithms. Therefore, we concluded that this minimum support threshold was too high – it pruned all the frequent itemsets.

In the fourth experiment, the FP Growth algorithm was again faster than the Apriori algorithm. In particular, the former ran about 1 ms, whereas the latter ran about 3 ms. During its run, the Apriori algorithm made 3 counts on the itemsets, whereas the FP Growth made 30 counts.

5 Related Work

Different approaches to finding similar attributes in an ontology have been proposed in the literature [18]. These approaches fall into four main categories:

- **Term-based approach:** In this approach, two attributes are considered to be similar if their names are similar. However, many false negatives and false positives can be found in the presence of synonyms and homonyms. Synonyms are different terms used to name same attributes (e.g., "bear" and "support"). Homonyms are same terms used to name different attributes. They have the same spelling but different meanings (e.g., "bear" can refer to an animal or can mean "support", depending on the contexts they are used in).
- **Value-based approach:** In this approach, two attributes are considered to be similar if their values are similar. This approach can detect semantic duplicates in an ontology more accurately than the term-based approach. However, without information about data instances, this approach is not feasible.
- **Structure-based approach**: In this approach, two attributes are considered to be similar if their structures are similar. Structures can be either internal or external. Examples of internal structures are data types, cardinalities, domains and transitivity of the attributes. However, internal structures are the subject of false negatives and false positives. For example, many attributes can have the same data types, but they are not necessarily similar. In case of external structures, an ontology is viewed as a graph, where vertices represent concepts and edges represent semantic relations between those concepts. This approach attempts to find similar classes and attributes, by identifying the structural isomorphism between sub-graphs of an ontology. For example, three types of relations can be identified between classes: taxonomic, mereologic and all the involved relations. In the taxonomic structure, the graph depicts the subClassOf relations. These relations indicate that the connected concepts are similar. One of the common similarity measures is to count the number of edges in the taxonomy between two classes to determine their similarity. In the mereologic structure, the graph depicts the PartOf relations. In all the

involved relations structure, classes are related via their attribute definitions. External structures are also the subject of false negatives and false positives. For example, it is difficult to distinguish the PartOf relations from the subClassOf relations.

- **Context-based approach:** In this approach, two attributes are considered to be similar if the contexts of their usage are similar. However, it can be difficult to identify similar contexts. In this paper, we proposed to use market basket analysis to solve this problem.

6 Conclusion

During an ontology-based data integration, the newly merged ontology such as OntoLife can contain semantic duplicates (e.g., similar attributes). These attributes can cause incomplete query results. In this paper, we focused on finding semantic duplicates in the OntoLife ontology. The approach we proposed is as follows: (1) the Apriori or FP Growth algorithm is applied to find strong association rules derived from a query log, where each query is a set of search terms being attributes in the ontology, and (2) candidates for semantic duplicates are determined as antecedents of the strong association rules having similar consequents.

In addition, we conducted a number of experiments on the query log, which was a list of queries posed by users to inquire the OntoLife ontology. The Apriori algorithm scanned the query log multiple times for generating candidate itemsets. In contrast, FP Growth algorithm scanned the query log only twice for constructing an FP tree. In all our experiments, the FP Growth algorithm made a constant of 30 counts on the itemsets. In contrast, the Apriori algorithm made a number of counts, which varied from 3 to 131 counts, depending on the minimum support threshold. The more counts the Apriori algorithm made, the longer time it ran. Despite the different runtime (the FP Growth algorithm was faster than the Apriori algorithm), it was observed that the algorithms returned the same results.

Overall, the results of our experiments showed that market basket analysis in general and the Apriori and FP Growth algorithms in particular are capable of finding similar attributes in an ontology, although user involvement is required to identify the optimal values for the minimum support threshold and the minimum confidence threshold.

Acknowledgement. Irina Astrova's work was supported by the Estonian Ministry of Education and Research institutional research grant IUT33-13.

Appendix

Nr.	Query in SPARQL:

01	PREFIX bio:≺"http://users.auth.gr/ elkar/thesis/Biography.owl#" ≻
	SELECT ?name
	WHERE {
	?person bio:awardTitle ?awardTitle .
	?person bio:awardDate ?awardDate .
	?person bio:shipmentDate ?shipmentDate.
	?person bio:internationalName ?internationalName .
	FILTER ((?awardTitle = "Best Bookseller") ||
	(?awardTitle="Oddest Booktitle Prize")
	&& (?awardDate = 2012-02-24)
	& (?shipmentDate = 10-Sept-2012) &&
	(?internationalName = "Springer"))
	}

02	PREFIX bio: ≺"http://users.auth.gr/ elkar/thesis/Biography.owl#" ≻
	SELECT *
	WHERE {
	?person bio:disab_type ?disab_type .
	?person bio:weight ?weight .
	FILTER ((?disab_type = "persistent delusion" &&
	?disab_type = "depression") && ?weight ≻ 80)
	}

03	PREFIX bio: ≺"http://users.auth.gr/ elkar/thesis/Biography.owl#" ≻
	SELECT ?name, ?nickname
	WHERE {
	?person bio:nickname ?nickname .
	FILTER (?nickname = "rain man")
	}

04	PREFIX bio: ≺"http://users.auth.gr/ elkar/thesis/Biography.owl#" ≻ SELECT ?name, ?nationality WHERE { ?person bio:nationality ?nationality . ?person bio:dateofBirth ?dateofBirth . ?person bio:militaryUnit ?militaryUnit . ?person bio:militaryGrade ?militaryGrade . FILTER (?nationality = "French" && ?dateofBirth = "2000-03-29" && militaryUnit = "Eagle" && militaryGrade = "Corporal")

Fig. 1. Query log for OntoLife.

05	PREFIX bio: ≺"http://users.auth.gr/ elkar/thesis/Biography.owl#" ≻ SELECT ?name WHERE { ?person bio:name ?name . ?person bio:height ?height . ?person bio:disab_type ?disab_type . ?person bio:weight? weight . ?person bio:selfGrade? selfGrade . ?person bio:eyecolor? eyecolor . FILTER (?height ≺ "1.0 metres" && weight ≻= 80 kg && (eyecolor = "hazel" || eyecolor = "blue") && disab_type = "depression" && selfGrade = "good") } ORDER BY ?name
06	PREFIX bio: ≺"http://users.auth.gr/ elkar/thesis/Biography.owl#" ≻ SELECT ?name WHERE { ?person bio:name ?name . ?person bio:journal ?journal . ?person bio:note ?note . FILTER ((?journal = "Newsweeks") || (?journal="Times") && note = "Fifty cents") } ORDER BY ?name
....	....
....	....

30	PREFIX bio: ≺"http://users.auth.gr/ elkar/thesis/Biography.owl#" ≻
	SELECT *
	WHERE {
	?person bio:nickname ?nickname .
	?person bio:specificDate ?specificDate .
	?person bio:disab_percentage ?disab_percentage .
	?person bio: hasGovernmentalInvolvement
	?hasGovernmentalInvolvement .
	?person bio:sector ?sector .
	FILTER ((?specificDate = "2009-11-23" && sector ="private non-business" && disab_percentage = 10 && hasGovernmentalInvolvement = 0 && nickname = "flowerpot"))
	}

Fig. 1. (*continued*)

TID:	Items:
001	{awardTitle, awardDate, shipmentDate, internationalName}
002	{disab_type, weight}
003	{nickname}
004	{nationality, dateOfBirth, militaryUnit, militaryGrade}
005	{height, disab_type, weight, selfGrade, eyecolor }
006	{journal, note}
...	...
...	...
030	{nickname, specificDate, disab_percentage, governmentInvolvement, sector}

Fig. 2. Query log converted to sales transaction database.

Nr.	Association rules:	Confidence:
Support: 13.3%		
1)	$(specificDate \Rightarrow sector)$	100%
2)	$(specificDate \Rightarrow disab\_percentage)$	100%
3)	$(sickness\_injuryDesc \Rightarrow sector)$	100%
4)	$(sickness\_injuryDesc \Rightarrow disab\_percentage)$	100%
5)	$(resource'sname \Rightarrow isAlive)$	80%
6)	$(resource'sname \Rightarrow nickname)$	80%
7)	$(resource'stitle \Rightarrow isAlive)$	57%
8)	$(resource'stitle \Rightarrow nickname)$	57%
9)	$(specificDate, sector \Rightarrow disab\_percentage)$	100%
10)	$(specificDate, disab\_percentage \Rightarrow sector)$	100%
11)	$(specificDate \Rightarrow disab\_percentage, sector)$	100%
12)	$(sickness\_injuryDesc, sector \Rightarrow disab\_percentage)$	100%
13)	$(sickness\_injuryDesc, disab\_percentage \Rightarrow sector)$	100%
14)	$(sickness\_injuryDesc \Rightarrow disab\_percentage, sector)$	100%
15)	$(nickname, resource'sname \Rightarrow isAlive)$	100%
16)	$(isAlive, resource'sname \Rightarrow nickname)$	100%
17)	$(resource'sname \Rightarrow nickname, isAlive)$	80%
18)	$(nickname, resource'stitle \Rightarrow isAlive)$	100%
19)	$(isAlive, resource'stitle \Rightarrow nickname)$	100%
20)	$(resource'stitle \Rightarrow nickname, isAlive)$	57%
Support: 26%		
21)	$(sector \Rightarrow disab\_percentage)$	100%
22)	$(disab\_percentage \Rightarrow sector)$	100%
23)	$(isAlive \Rightarrow nickname)$	88%
24)	$(nickname \Rightarrow isAlive)$	66%

Fig. 3. Experiment 1 results. (Color figure online)

Nr.	Association rules:		Confidence:
Support: 13.3%			
1)	$(specificDate \Rightarrow sector)$		100%
2)	$(specificDate \Rightarrow disab\_percentage)$		100%
3)	$(sickness\_injuryDesc \Rightarrow sector)$		100%
4)	$(sickness\_injuryDesc \Rightarrow disab\_percentage)$		100%
5)	$(specificDate, sector \Rightarrow disab\_percentage)$		100%
6)	$(specificDate, disab\_percentage \Rightarrow sector)$		100%
7)	$(specificDate \Rightarrow disab\_percentage, sector)$		100%
8)	$(sickness\_injuryDesc, sector$ $disab\_percentage)$	$\Rightarrow$	100%
9)	$(sickness\_injuryDesc, disab\_percentage$ $sector)$	$\Rightarrow$	100%
10)	$(sickness\_injuryDesc$ $disab\_percentage, sector)$	$\Rightarrow$	100%
11)	$(nickname, resource'sname \Rightarrow isAlive)$		100%
12)	$(isAlive, resource'sname \Rightarrow nickname)$		100%
13)	$(nickname, resource'stitle \Rightarrow isAlive)$		100%
14)	$(isAlive, resource'stitle \Rightarrow nickname)$		100%
Support: 26%			
15)	$(sector \Rightarrow disab\_percentage)$		100%
16)	$(disab\_percentage \Rightarrow sector)$		100%

Fig. 4. Experiment 2 results.

Nr.	Association rules:		Confidence:
Support: 10%			
1)	(*hasGovernmentalInvolvement* ⇒ *sector*)		100%
2)	(*hasGovernmentalInvolvement* *disab_percentage*)	⇒	100%
3)	(*hasGovernmentalInvolvement* ⇒ *nickname*)		100%
4)	(*publication'sdescription* ⇒ *cert_date*)		100%
5)	(*biography'sdescription* ⇒ *cert_date*)		100%
6)	(*biography'sdescription* ⇒ *resource'stitle*)		100%
7)	(*sector, hasGovernmentalInvolvement* *disab_percentage*)	⇒	100%
8)	(*disab_percentage, hasGovernmentalInvolvement* ⇒ *sector*)		100%
9)	(*hasGovernmentalInvolvement* *disab_percentage, sector*)	⇒	100%
10)	(*nickname, hasGovernmentalInvolvement* *sector*)	⇒	100%
11)	(*nickname, sector* *hasGovernmentalInvolvement*)	⇒	100%
12)	(*sector, hasGovernmentInvolvement* ⇒ *nickname*)		100%
13)	(*hasGovernmentalInvolvement* *nickname, sector*)	⇒	100%
14)	(*nickname, hasGovernmentInvolvement* *disab_percentage*)	⇒	100%
15)	(*nickname, disab_percentage* *hasGovernmentInvolvement*)	⇒	100%
16)	(*disab_percentage, hasGovernmentInvolvement* *nickname*)	⇒	100%
17)	(*hasGovernmentInvolvement* *nickname, disab_percentage*)	⇒	100%
18)	(*resource'stitle, cert_date* *biography'sdescription*)	⇒	100%
19)	(*biography'sdescription, cert_date* *resource'stitle*)	⇒	100%
20)	(*resource'stitle, biography'sdescription* *cert_date*)	⇒	100%
21)	(*biography'sdescription* *resource'stitle, cert_date*)	⇒	100%
22)	(*nickname, nationality* ⇒ *isAlive*)		100%
23)	(*nationality, isAlive* ⇒ *nickname*)		100%
24)	(*nickname, sector* ⇒ *disab_percentage*)		100%
25)	(*nickname, disab_percentage* ⇒ *sector*)		100%

Fig. 5. Experiment 3 results.

26)	$(nickname, sector,$ $hasGovernmentalInvolvement \Rightarrow$ $disab\_percentage)$	100%
27)	$(nickname, disab\_percentage,$ $hasGovernmentalInvolvement \Rightarrow$ $sector)$	100%
28)	$(nickname, disab\_percentage, sector \Rightarrow$ $hasGovernmentalInvolvement)$	100%
29)	$(disab\_percentage, sector,$ $hasGovernmentalInvolvement \Rightarrow$ $nickname)$	100%
30)	$(disab\_percentage,$ $hasGovernmentalInvolvement \Rightarrow$ $nickname, sector)$	100%
31)	$(nickname, sector \Rightarrow$ $disab\_percentage, hasGovernmentalInvolvement)$	100%
32)	$(nickname, disab\_percentage \Rightarrow$ $sector, hasGovernmentalInvolvement)$	100%
33)	$(sector, hasGovernmentalInvolvement \Rightarrow$ $nickname, disab\_percentage)$	100%
34)	$(nickname, hasGovernmentalInvolvement \Rightarrow$ $disab\_percentage, sector)$	100%
35)	$(hasGovernmentalInvolvement \Rightarrow$ $nickname, disab\_percentage, sector)$	100%

Support: 13.3%

36)	$(specificDate \Rightarrow sector)$	100%
37)	$(specificDate \Rightarrow disab\_percentage)$	100%
38)	$(sickness\_injuryDesc \Rightarrow sector)$	100%
39)	$(sickness\_injuryDesc \Rightarrow disab\_percentage)$	100%
40)	$(specificDate, sector \Rightarrow disab\_percentage)$	100%
41)	$(specificDate, disab\_percentage \Rightarrow sector)$	100%
42)	$(specificDate \Rightarrow disab\_percentage, sector)$	100%
43)	$(sickness\_injuryDesc, sector \Rightarrow disab\_percentage)$	100%
44)	$(sickness\_injuryDesc, disab\_percentage \Rightarrow sector)$	100%
45)	$(sickness\_injuryDesc \Rightarrow disab\_percentage, sector)$	100%
46)	$(nickname, resource'sname \Rightarrow isAlive)$	100%
47)	$(isAlive, resource'sname \Rightarrow nickname)$	100%
48)	$(nickname, resource'stitle \Rightarrow isAlive)$	100%
49)	$(isAlive, resource'stitle \Rightarrow nickname)$	100%

Support: 26.6%

50)	$(sector \Rightarrow disab\_percentage)$	100%
51)	$(disab\_percentage \Rightarrow sector)$	100%

Fig. 5. (*continued*)

References

1. Astrova, I., Koschel, A.: Automatic detection of duplicated attributes in ontology. In: Cordeiro, J., Filipe, J. (eds.) ICEIS 2009: Proceedings of the 11th International Conference on Enterprise Information Systems, INSTICC, 2009, vol. DISI, pp. 283 – 286 (2009)
2. Astrova, I.: Improving query results with automatic duplicate detection. In: Ioannidis, Y., Manghi, P., Pagano, P. (eds.) Proceedings of the Second Workshop on Very Large Digital Libraries, VLDL 2009: A Workshop in conjunction with the European Conference on Digital Libraries 2009. Institute of Information Science and Technology, DELOS Association (2009)
3. Agrawal, R., Srikant, R.: Fast algorithms for mining association rules. In: Stonebraker, M., Hellerstein, J.M. (eds.) Readings in Database Systems, 3rd edn., pp. 580 – 592. Morgan Kaufmann Publishers Inc., San Francisco, CA, USA (1998)
4. Kargiot, E., Kontopoulos, E.: OntoLife: An Ontology for Semantically Managing Personal Information. http://lpis.csd.auth.gr/ontologies/ontolist.html#ontolife
5. Person Ontology. http://ebiquity.umbc.edu/ontology/person.owl
6. Friend of a Friend (FOAF) Ontology. http://xmlns.com/foaf/spec/
7. Family Tree Ontology. http://users.auth.gr/elkar/thesis/FamilyTree.owl
8. Relationship Ontology. http://purl.org/vocab/relationship/
9. ISO lists for Countries and Languages Ontology. http://psi.oasis-open.org/iso/639/#
10. Project Ontology. http://ebiquity.umbc.edu/ontology/project.owl
11. Research Ontology. http://ebiquity.umbc.edu/ontology/research.owl
12. Publication Ontology. http://ebiquity.umbc.edu/ontology/publication.owl
13. PersonProjectAssociation Ontology. http://ebiquity.umbc.edu/ontology/association.owl
14. Biography Ontology. http://users.auth.gr/elkar/thesis/Biography.owl
15. Han, J., et al.: Mining frequent patterns without candidate generation: a frequent-pattern tree approach. Data Min. Knowl. Discov. **8**(1), 53–87 (2004)
16. Astrova, I., Koschel, A., Lee, S.L.: How the Apriori Algorithm can help to find semantic duplicates in ontology. In: Knowledge-Based Software Engineering. Springer Nature (2020). to appear
17. Das, G., Mannila, H.: Context-based similarity measures for categorical database. In: Proceedings of PKDD, 2000, pp. 201–210 (2000)
18. Shvaiko, P., Euzenat, J.: Ontology Matching 2007. Springer, Heidelberg (2007)

IoT Software by Dataflow Programming in Mruby Programming Environment

Kazuaki Tanaka[✉], Chihiro Tsujino, and Hiroyuki Maeda

Kyushu Institute of Technology, Fukuoka 820-8502, Japan
kazuaki@mse.kyutech.ac.jp

Abstract. In IoT software development, a method to implement software by focusing on data flow has been proposed, which is called dataflow programming. On the other hand, sensor devices are generally implemented in microcontrollers with limited resources for compactness, power savings and costs, so sensor devices are not suitable for executing data flow programs.

In this paper, an environment running the scripting language mruby is described to execute a dataflow program on a small microcontroller. The execution of the data flow program is performed asynchronously by multiple nodes, which handle the sensor data. The execution environment of a dataflow program must support this style of execution. Since mruby can execute multiple programs concurrently, it is well suited to implement dataflow programs. By generating mruby code from a program developed in Node-RED, one of the popular dataflow programming environments, the mruby program is executed on a single-chip microcontroller, which includes mruby virtual machine.

Keywords: IoT · Dataflow programming · Node-RED · Mruby

1 Introduction

One of the challenges in realizing an IoT-based system is the implementation of a series of data processing from data input to output. The IoT system is realized through the procedure of sending the data obtained from the IoT device to the cloud via the network. It is complex to implement each procedure in programs and to define the interface between them.

Dataflow programming has been proposed as a means of adequately describing the flow of such sensor data. Dataflow programming is an effective programming tool to implement IoT systems.

Open source software such as Node-RED has been released and adopted for dataflow description in the cloud [4]. However, Node-RED is implemented in JavaScript, which requires much resources not only during development but also during execution. In addition, because the dataflow implemented in JavaScript is executed sequentially by an interpreter, it becomes a dynamic execution environment and cannot be installed in a small microcontroller.

In this paper, a development environment and an execution environment are proposed to solve this problem.

© Springer Nature Switzerland AG 2020
O. Gervasi et al. (Eds.): ICCSA 2020, LNCS 12252, pp. 212–220, 2020.
https://doi.org/10.1007/978-3-030-58811-3_15

2 Mruby

Mruby is a programming language optimized to execute programs on embedded systems, based on the object-oriented programming language Ruby. Ruby is widely used as a standard development language for web applications because of its high readability, maintainability and development efficiency. Mruby was released as open source software in 2012 and is used in embedded systems such as network routers, consumer games, and so on [1,2].

2.1 Mruby Execution Environment

Mruby consists of a mruby compiler and a mruby virtual machine (mrubyVM). The mruby compiler compiles the mruby source code and generates mruby byte-code. The mruby bytecode is a device-independent and intermediate binary code that runs on mrubyVM (Fig. 1). Since mrubyVM requires less memory at execution time, it can be executed on small microcontrollers. The smallest mrubyVM configuration executes a program within 20 KB of memory.

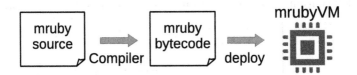

Fig. 1. mruby compiler and mrubyVM

The mruby compiler compiles mruby source code and generates bytecode. Bytecode is device-independent, and you can run the mruby program in the target device simply by porting mrubyVM. Porting mrubyVM to the target device is easy since mrubyVM is implemented in C99 standard.

2.2 Mruby/c

Mruby was released in 2012 and is now being used in a variety of commercial products. The most frequent feedback from mruby application developers was about execution on smaller microcontrollers. To achieve this goal, we developed mruby/c as another implementation derived from mrubyVM. While mruby provides a mruby compiler and mrubyVM, mruby/c only provides mrubyVM. That is, mruby and mruby/c execute the exactly same bytecodes. It is designed to support execution on small microprocessors, so it consumes less memory when running mruby/c. Mruby/c can execute the meuby bytecode within about 1/8 of the memory that mruby requires.

Also, mruby/c targets small microcontrollers (e.g., single-chip microcontrollers) that do not have an OS. For this reason, mruby/c provides memory management (dynamic memory allocation), task management, and file system functions that are usually provided by the OS. However, these features are the minimum configuration required to run mruby/c. As a result, mruby/c can be ported to a variety of microcontrollers, regardless of OS or CPU architecture. Mruby/c supports PIC32, ARM Cortex-M, RISC-V and ESP32 by default, as well as x64 and x32.

2.3 Concurrent Execution

Mruby/c can also execute multiple programs concurrently [3]. Small microcontrollers may not support an operating system due to processor performance and memory limitations. However, developers wish to use the feature of the OS to process multiple programs in parallel (e.g., tasks and processes).

Mruby/c has a task control block (TCB) for concurrent execution. The mruby compiler compiles each program that should execute concurrently and generates mruby bytecode. Bytecode is a sequence of intermediate code, and the VM fetches instruction words from bytecode and executes them sequentially. The TCB holds the execution state of the program and the next execution point in the bytecode. Since the VM executes byte code based on TCB information, concurrent execution of multiple programs can be realized by switching multiple TCBs (Fig. 2).

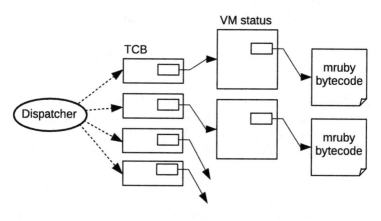

Fig. 2. TCB

The VM dispatches TCBs at fixed time intervals (1[ms] by default). The TCB is associated with a VM status that holds the execution state, such as the execution position of the executing bytecode. When the VM switches the TCB, the running bytecode is switched, allowing multiple programs to be executed concurrently. Note that when running a single program in mruby/c, TCB is not needed, so the mruby/c VM refers directly to the VM status.

3   Implementing a Dataflow Program in mruby

A dataflow program consists of nodes that process data and wires that connect the nodes to each other. Figure 3 shows the programming environment of Node-RED. Nodes are divided into those that generate data, those that process data, and those that output data. The sensor is considered to be the node that generates the data and the data transmission to the cloud is considered to be the node that outputs the data. A wire connects the nodes.

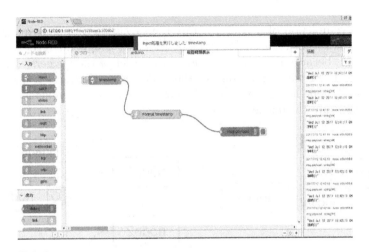

Fig. 3. Node-RED, a dataflow programing environment. Some nodes and wires are placed.

The processing of each node is executed asynchronously. dataflow programs, unlike procedural programs, cannot specify the order of execution. All nodes are triggered to start execution, although the execution of the node is different depending on the type of node. When a node's processing is complete, it generates and outputs data. The output data is sent to a node in the subsequent node connected by a wire, and the processing of that node begins.

Since the execution time of a node is non-deterministic, the order of execution cannot be determined in a prior. Therefore, the nodes must be executed asynchronously. For example, in the case of a dataflow program like the one shown in the Fig. 4, the completion time of node 1 and node 2 is uncertain, so the timing of data being passed to the wire is also uncertain. Therefore, node 3 starts execution, triggered by the completion of execution of node 1 or node 2.

3.1   Wires

The wires that connect the nodes are implemented by the data structure of the queue. For a simple one-to-one wire that connects nodes, it is enough to

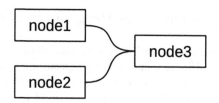

Fig. 4. Simple nodes and wires. This case contains three nodes and two wires. Output data from node 1 and node 2 will flow into node 3 through wires.

trigger the completion of a node to start the execution of a subsequent node. However, when connecting nodes to many-to-many, a simple trigger cannot be implemented, because it cannot determine the order of the triggers. Therefore, we implement the wires that connect the nodes in an abstraction queue (Fig. 5). With each node holding a queue, the flow of data can be implemented as an input of data into the queue.

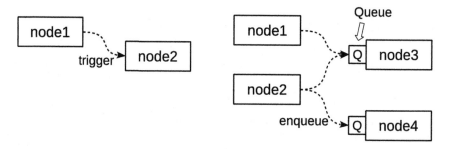

Fig. 5. Implementation of wires. (left) one-to-one wire between nodes, using trigger (right) many-to-many wire between nodes, using queue

Since data input to the queue (enqueue) is done asynchronously, exclusion processes are necessary. Mruby provides a Mutex class for exclusion processing. Mutual exclusions can be implemented by simply protecting operations on the queue with a Mutex instance, while keeping concurrency intact.

3.2 Nodes

Since node processing must be executed asynchronously, all nodes are implemented as programs that are executed concurrently. The wires connecting the nodes are implemented as queues that can support concurrent processing, so the execution and output of the nodes can be executed asynchronously (i.e., independently). The node receives input from the previous node by queue. Therefore, the processing of each node is implemented as Listing 1.1.

Listing 1.1. Generated mruby source code from node2

```
1 while true
2   if $Q_node2.size == 0 then
3     sleep 0.005
4     next
5   end
6   # Enqueue
7   data = $Q_node2.shift
8   #
9   # procedure in this node
10  #
11 end
```

The Listing 1.1 shows an example of the mruby source code generated from a node named **node2**. Since multiple programs can be executed concurrently, the processing of nodes can be implemented as a permanent loop. If there is no data in the queue (**$Q_node2**) associated with this node, processing of the node is not necessary. In order to keep fairness of concurrent execution through multiple programs, the small period sleep is executed. The sleep in mrubyVM is pass the execution period to other programs for smooth concurrent execution. On the other hand, if there is data in the queue, it is taken out of the queue (dequeue) and processed in the node.

3.3   Automatic Generation of mruby/c Programs

In this study, the development environment for the dataflow program is Node-RED. mruby/c program is generated from the node and wire information created in Node-RED (Fig. 6). Node-RED is both a development environment and a program execution environment. However, it is not possible to run Node-RED on small microcomputers because of the CPU power and small on-board memory. To solve this problem, a mechanism to convert Node-RED dataflow programs into multiple mruby programs (mruby/c dataflow program generator) has been developed.

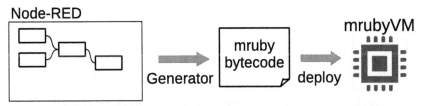

Fig. 6. deploy mruby program into targetdevice, by using mruby/c dataflow program generator

As described above, the nodes and wires of the dataflow program can be implemented by several mruby programs and queues. The dataflow programs developed in Node-RED (i.e., node and wire information) can be exported as JSON format files. The mruby/c dataflow program generator parses this file and generates a program corresponding to the node and an initialization program for the queue corresponding to the wire.

4   Execution Environment and Results

To test the mruby/c dataflow program generator, we generated mruby bytecode from a Node-RED dataflow program and ran it on a microcontroller. The microcontroller board RBoard executes the mruby bytecode. The RBoard has one-chip microcontroller, CY8C5888AXI-LP096 (Cypress Semiconductor, ARM Cortex-M3) (Fig. 7). RBoard is a general-purpose microcontroller board commercially available at Shimane Information Processing Center, and its onboard memory is 64 KB, and it is a microcontroller that assumes an execution environment without an OS.

Fig. 7. RBoard; microcontroller with mruby/c VM. ARM Cortex-M3 with 64 KB RAM/256 KB flash memory, GPIO, USB and Grove system interface (by Speed) are equipped.

4.1   Mruby Bytecode Generation

The program using the input node from the temperature sensor and the output node to the console is shown in Fig. 8.

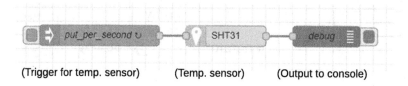

Fig. 8. Example of sensing temperature. Nodes for trigger, temperature sensor and console output are placed.

Three nodes and two wires are implemented in the data flow program shown in Fig. 8. Node-RED programs can be written using a drawing editor, which can also be output as a JSON file. The mruby/c dataflow program generator generates multiple mruby source codes from JSON files.

4.2   Bytecode Execution

Transfer multiple mruby bytecodes generated by the mruby/c dataflow program generator to the microcontroller board. Since RBoard has a USB-serial interface, it can be transferred directly from the development environment (the environment for developing Node-RED dataflow programs). The transferred mruby bytecodes will start execution in the microcontroller board.

At the start of execution, all the queues, which are wires in the dataflow program, are empty, so the program is in a suspended state. The first node in the dataflow, which is called the data source, generates the data and puts the data into the queue. Since the queue for the following node is no longer empty, the program for this node will be executed. After this, the execution propagates in the same way.

The last node outputs the data to the external. In this experiment, the data is output to the console. The last node does not generate any data, and when the processing at all nodes is finished, all queues are emptied, and the dataflow program goes into a suspended state.

4.3   Result of an Experiment

A data flow program including conditional branching is shown in Fig. 9. This data flow program obtains the value of the temperature sensor and flashes four LEDs according to the value of the temperature.

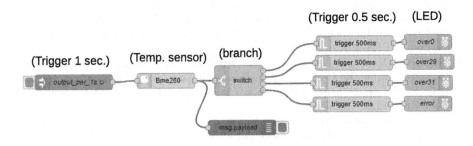

Fig. 9. Example of sensing temperature and blinking LEDs.

To ensure that the program is running asynchronously, a temperature sensor value is obtained every 1 s and the LED is blinking every 0.5 s. The mruby data flow generator also generates an mruby case statement (which is equivalent to a C switch statement) from the branch node of the multi-conditions.

Figure 9 is a data flow program consisting of 12 nodes and 11 wires. This mruby data flow generator generates 13 mruby programs. They are 12 nodes and one program to initialize the queue. All these programs were transferred to the RBoard microcontroller board and executed. As a result of the experiment, it was confirmed that the LED corresponding to the value obtained from the temperature sensor blinked.

5   Conclusion

In this paper, we describe a mechanism for executing dataflow programming for IoT software development on a small microcontroller. The execution of a dataflow program requires a lot of resources at runtime, so it is not suitable for small microcontrollers. We solved this problem by generating the mruby bytecode using the connection information of the nodes and wires in the dataflow. The mrubyVM, which runs mruby bytecode, is small enough to run on a single-chip microcontroller and supports concurrent execution of multiple programs, making it suitable for implementing dataflow program.

As IoT applications become more widespread in society, the weight of the data flow programming environment in IoT software development is expected to increase. There is also a need to combine traditional procedural programs and use data flow programs to build IoT systems. Mruby is able to remove the barriers between these two programming environments. Mruby, and the mruby bytecode generator developed in this study, are open source software[5,6]. We hope that mruby can contribute to solving this problem. The source code of this work will release at https://github.com/mruby-lab.

References

1. Maeda, H., Tanaka, K.: Hardware acceleration of language processing in scripting programming languages. In: Misra, S., et al. (eds.) ICCSA 2019. LNCS, vol. 11621, pp. 407–416. Springer, Cham (2019). https://doi.org/10.1007/978-3-030-24302-9_29
2. Nagumanthri, A.D., Tanaka, K.: Internet of Things with mruby. In: International Conference on Information Technology, Next Generation Information Technology Summit (InCITe-2016) (2016)
3. Tanaka, K., Maeda, H., Higashi, H.: Concurrent execution in scripting programming language 'mruby'. In: Gervasi, O., et al. (eds.) ICCSA 2018. LNCS, vol. 10962, pp. 136–146. Springer, Cham (2018). https://doi.org/10.1007/978-3-319-95168-3_9
4. Node-RED. https://nodered.org/
5. mruby. https://github.com/mruby/mruby
6. mruby/c. https://github.com/mrubyc/mrubyc

A Cloud VM Migration Control Mechanism Using Blockchain

Toshihiro Uchibayashi[1(✉)], Bernady Apduhan[2(✉)], Takuo Suganuma[3(✉)], and Masahiro Hiji[3(✉)]

[1] Kyushu University, Fukuoka, Japan
uchibayashi.toshihiro.143@m.kyushu-u.ac.jp
[2] Kyushu Sangyo University, Fukuoka, Japan
bob@is.kyusan-u.ac.jp
[3] Tohoku University, Sendai, Japan
{suganuma,hiji}@tohoku.ac.jp

Abstract. In the current cloud, VM migration that moves VMs between physical host machines is indispensable. For cloud providers, before shutting down the physical host machines for maintenance, migration is used to temporarily save VMs to other physical host machine. For the cloud user, migration is used to move a VM to a location which is geographically close to the end user. These VM migrations can be performed very easily and are only limited by the scope of the VM administrator's contract. However, the problem lies on the permission of the data in VM. In recent years, with the widespread use of IoT, various types of data can be stored in cloud's VMs through web services. The huge amount of data collected by IoT devices requires close attention to manage because it could be very closely related to the information of an individual. However, there is no mechanism for checking data permission in VM during VM migration, and there is concern that inappropriate data movement may occur. This includes the unintended risky movement of inappropriate data which could be malicious data. Therefore, we proposed a mechanism to ensure compliance with the conditions granted by the data owner, the country regulations, and the organization regulations during VM migration. By constructing the proposed mechanism in blockchain, we can prevent malicious tampering and thus enable robust VM migration control.

Keywords: Cloud computing · VM migration · Audit system · Privacy policy · Data protection · Blockchain

1 Introduction

With the widespread use of the Internet of Things (IoT), it has become common to store in the cloud a huge amount of data collected from various sensors that measures the health of an individual and the environment linked to that particular individual [1–3]. This huge amount of data collected by IoT devices

© Springer Nature Switzerland AG 2020
O. Gervasi et al. (Eds.): ICCSA 2020, LNCS 12252, pp. 221–235, 2020.
https://doi.org/10.1007/978-3-030-58811-3_16

reveals not only the individual's personal values but also multiple data relations that likewise reveal useful means in predicting personal preference and behavior, intervention in behavior, etc. This data analysis is performed by the service provider. These data are closely related to individuals and require careful management. Appropriate management and use in compliance with the regulations of the country or region like General Data Protection Regulation (GDPR) [4], as well as the regulations of the organization, and the conditions granted by the data owner are essentials.

Moreover, not only IoT, but also services using a cloud environment are generally used to operate applications and services via networks, and the operations in a cloud environment are already pervasive in our current world. As the demand for cloud services increases, businesses providing cloud environments is explosively increasing and are developing various services. In particular, operators providing large-scale cloud services such as AWS [5] and Azure [6] are deploying services on a global scale, and cloud users can select a data center or service that suits them. In recent years, by combining serverless cloud services, various web services can be deployed without building servers. However, serverless environments have various limitations, and traditional methods of building servers on VMs are indispensable. Among them, Infrastructure as a Service (IaaS), a cloud service that provides Virtual Machine (VM), is widely used because it can be used for general purposes. Businesses that provide IaaS are widely provided not only by large-scale businesses such as AWS, but also by small and medium-sized businesses.

What needs special attention when using the IaaS cloud is the inappropriate data movement. In the current cloud, using VM migration to move between physical host machines is indispensable. For cloud service providers, before stopping the physical host machine for maintenance, disaster recovery, etc., migration is used to temporarily store applications in VMs and move to other physical host machines. For cloud users, migration is used to move VM to a location geographically close to the end user. These VM migrations can be performed very easily and are only limited by the scope of the VM administrator's contract. Therefore, the problem is the permission of data in VM.

What needs special attention is the unintended movement of inappropriate data. VM is deployed and running on host machines in the cloud environment. It is easy for VM to migrate between host machines, and the administrator of VM can change the host machine on which VM runs as needed [7]. There is no problem if the host machines are all in the same place, but if the host machines are installed in different countries, it may cause violations of regulations and organizational rules. However, there is no mechanism yet for checking the permission of data in VM at VM migration, and there is concern that inappropriate data movement may occur. This includes the risks of unintended movement of inappropriate data which may include the movement of malicious data. Therefore, we propose a mechanism to ensure compliance with the conditions granted by the data owner and the regulations of the country, regulatory, and organization during VM migration. By constructing the proposed mechanism in blockchain, we can prevent malicious tampering and enable robust VM migration control.

In this paper, after demonstrating the mechanism of VM migration control, we implement and evaluate the proposed mechanism with blockchain to the existing cloud environment. Section 2 introduces related work and explain the difference from this research. Section 3 shows VM migration and its problems. Section 4 proposes a policy control mechanism using blockchain. Section 5 implements the proposed mechanism. Section 6 evaluates the proposed mechanism using the implemented environment, and Sect. 7 is the conclusion.

2   Related Work

The research on migration security for cloud environment [8–11] discusses security risks. They investigate attacks against live migration of VM and introduce research and examples for securing live migration. In conclusion, in current systems, there exists no integrated approach to address trust establishment, confidentiality and integrity of migration data, authentication and approval of migration operations required for secure migration. A comprehensive framework that addresses these security aspects of live migration of VM is desired. This paper falls under the certification and approval of migration operation that is necessary for safe migration. By applying the mechanism proposed in this paper to the existing cloud, it is possible to perform safe migration.

The policy control using role-based for cloud infrastructure operation [12–15], assumes all hardware in the cloud environment is safe, and adds the ability to control the user to safely perform the migration. This prevents information leakage due to the live migration of unauthorized users. In addition, load balancing policies are used to effectively balance the workload of the entire data center.

Likewise, the research efforts to perform data protection of IoT [16–21] tries to ensure the safety of data collected by IoT using blockchain technology.

Here, studies on migration control and data protection are being conducted, and security warnings for migration, policy control, and securing of data safety by blockchain are desired. However, there exists no cloud mechanism for data migration. Therefore, we propose a secure mechanism to prevent unintended data movement and inappropriate data movement triggered by malicious tampering.

In the model of storing and delivering data on the Web [22], it propose the use of IPFS's distributed file storage system and the integrity retention characteristics of the blockchain. In the P2P file system called IPFS, which enables files to be stored in a distributed system, by storing files on a distributed network, it is possible to search packets from multiple sources, thus bandwidth savings. Security is ensured by placing the time stamp on the data rather than putting it on the chain itself.

3   VM Migration

There are two types of VM migration: live migration (hot migration) and cold migration (offline migration). Live migration can be executed without stopping the running VM, so it can be moved live without stopping the service in the VM. The entire memory image on the VM running on the physical host machine is transferred to another physical host machine, and does not stop or freeze the operation of the OS, application software, network connection, etc., while the migration is carried out. Strictly speaking, a momentary interruption in a millisecond occurs at the switching moment. However, there is no disconnection of the network session, etc., and the VM user does not know that the movement has been performed. Major hypervisors such as KVM [23] and XEN [24] are already supported, and are already in practical use. In cold migration, the VM is shut down and then migrated to another host machine. The VM running on a physical host machine is temporarily stopped, and the memory image is transferred to another physical host machine via storage, etc. The operation is then resumed on the migration destination host machine. The operating status of the software is inherited without shutting down or restarting the OS.

VM migration is an indispensable technology for cloud operation. However, challenges arise to simplify the migration execution and to be easily performed whenever the cloud authorization is satisfied. When performing a migration with GCEE [25] or OpenStack [26], it can execute with one command line or one button. This only determines the cloud's authority and whether it can be physically migrated, and does not take into account the VM's internal data at all. Therefore, the problem is the unintended move destination mistake of VM and the malicious move of VM (Fig. 1). For example, suppose that VM contains personal data that cannot cross the country. And, according to internal regulations, this personal data can be stored only in Region A and Region B. There is no problem when migrating to a host machine of a region B in County X. However, if a VM is migrated to Region C by the VM manager's mistake, it will be a violation of the company policy. Also, if a malicious person migrates a VM to Region D in Country Y, it may violate the laws of the Country X. This is a very serious problem, and it is necessary to have a control mechanism that decides whether to migrate or not, considering not only the authority and physical availability of the cloud, but also the data contained in the VM.

4   Proposal of Control Mechanism

4.1   Blockchain Technique

Blockchain is a technology that records transaction data in units of blocks on nodes and records them in a distributed manner and manages the same block information. It is also called distributed management ledger technology. It is called a blockchain because the blocks are connected chronologically, like a chain. Blockchain consist of P2P networks, consensus algorithms, electronic signature and hash functions, and smart contracts. A P2P network provides a method of connecting computers for the same purpose to form a network. The consensus algorithm provides an algorithm for consensus building on distributed networks. Digital signatures and hash functions provide security mechanisms, such as a mechanism that guarantees the legitimacy of the person issuing a transaction. A

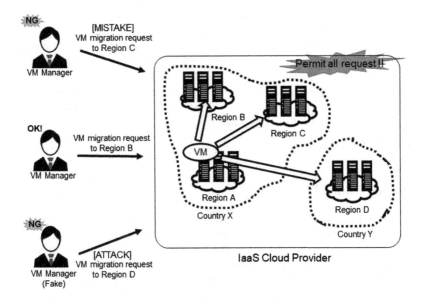

Fig. 1. VM migration problems.

smart contract refers to a program that operates on a blockchain network. Also, blockchain infrastructure can be divided into public type, consortium type and private type (Table 1). The public type, as represented by bitcoin, does not have a centralized management period, and an unspecified number of users can freely participate and participate in mining. Consortium type and private type are characterized by having a manager. Consortium types operate in multiple organizations, whereas private types operate in a single organization. Since mining can be controlled by the permission of the manager, it can be used for enterprise use such as financial system management.

Also, Blockchain was developed to support cryptocurrencies which can be used for all forms of trading without mediation. Transaction data is recorded as transaction content data and becomes a block. This data is open and anyone can check it. Also, the specific transaction content of the transaction is encrypted by the hash function. Hash functions have the irreversibility that the original data cannot be read from the generated string. Furthermore, the block data contains the transaction encrypted by the hash function and the hash value of the previous block data. This has the advantage that an attacker must compromise 51% of the system to exceed the hashing capability of the target network. Therefore, attacking blockchain networks is not computationally practical. In addition, there is a smart contract as one of the blockchain mechanism. Smart contracts, as the name implies, are protocols that can make contracts smart. It can automatically execute contract condition confirmation and fulfillment.

Table 1. Blockchain infrastructure types

	Public	Consortium (Multiple organizations)	Private (Single organization)
(Mining) Node type	No limit	Restrictable	Restrictable
Blockchain view	No limit	Restrictable	Restrictable
At block generation	High difficulty mechanism required	Any	Any
Mining reward	Necessary	Any	Any

4.2 Policy Control

We propose a policy based control mechanism to solve the problem of improper migration of data contained in VM. The control mechanism method is shown in Fig. 2. The VM manager describes the REGULATION that identifies the list of available countries and organizations based on the data regulations in the VM. The country and organization identifiers described in REGULATION are CountryCode and OrganizationCode. CountryCode indicates a country where data movement is permitted based on regulations. OrganizationCode represents an organization that instantiates and uses virtual machines. For example, if the host machine location is Japan and the organization is Company A, it described as "JP. Company A". If the data can be moved to all countries, CountryCode value is "All". If data is available to all organizations, OrganizationCode value is "All". If restrictions on the data in VM are changed, it calculates the difference between the list of country and organization identifiers added to the newly acquired data and the list of already described identifiers, and describe the values. Also, the host machine manager describes COUNTRY that identifies the country based on the physical area where the host machine is located. The country identifier described in the COUNTRY is CountryCode. If the host machine is located in Japan, it is described as "JP" Furthermore, the host machine manager describes ORGANIZATION as the organization that manages the host machine. The identifier of the organization described in ORGANIZATION is OrganizationCode. If Company B is the organization that manages the host machine, it described as "Company B".

When the migration is performed, compare the moving VM's REGULATION and the destination host machine's COUNTRY and REGULATION. First, check whether CountryCode of REGULATION is included in CountryCode of COUNTRY. Similarly, check whether the OrganizationCode of REGULATION is included in the OrganizationCode of ORGANIZATION. If both checks passed, migration is performed because the data acquired by the migrating VM can be migrated to the country or organization in which the migration destination host machine exists. The migration execution is the same as the conventional migration process. If it is not included, migration cannot be performed because it cannot move to the country where the destination host machine exists. By these mechanisms, we avoid the unintended data infringement caused by the migration of the terms and conditions of the state, the regulations of the country, and the permission from the owner of various data with different owners.

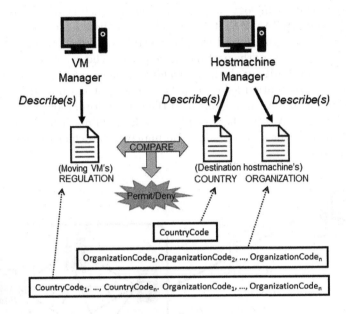

Fig. 2. Policy based control mechanism.

4.3 Control Mechanism Using Blockchain

The proposed mechanism could prevent the migration of inappropriate data, however if a malicious manager tampered with REGULATION, COUNTRY, or ORGANIZATION on a host machine running various VM, unintended migration is triggered and improper data movement occurs. Therefore, in order to prevent malicious falsification of data, we propose a method to prevent falsification using blockchain technology with a strong data protection mechanism.

The example environment using the proposed mechanism is shown the Fig. 3. Store REGULATION, COUNTRY, and ORGANIZATION in a blockchain. Only authorized VM managers and host machine managers can add or change these data. The VM manager registers REGULATION in the blockchain when the VM is newly deployed or the permission condition of the data in the VM is changed. The host machine manager registers COUNTRY and ORGANIZATION in the blockchain when a new host machine is installed or when the host machine affiliation is changed. In addition, the control mechanism using policy is implemented in the smart contract. The flow when the VM manager requests migration is shown below (Fig. 4).

1. VM manager requests migration to the blockchain.
2. Compare the moving VM's REGULATION and the destination host machine's COUNTRY and ORGANIZATION in the blockchain's smart contract.

3. If both checks pass, it requests the cloud to execute VM migration. If it does not pass the check, VM migration will not be performed.

The blockchain technology preserves the change history of REGULATION, COUNTRY, and ORGANIZATION, and checks if there is any tampering with past data. Since it is guaranteed that the current data has not been tampered based on the hash value of the past data, the person who is not the VM manager with the proper authority or the host machine manager cannot change the data. The blockchain distribution ledger is held by one host machine in each region, and the host machines in all regions hold the same information. For example, if a region exists from A to F, there will be 5 nodes holding the dispersion ledger. Only the VM manager and host machine manager can change the data in the distributed ledger.

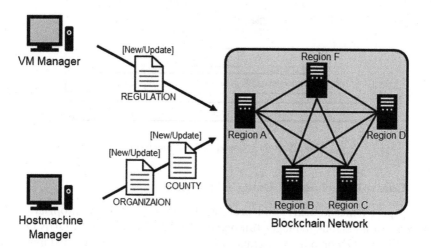

Fig. 3. Registers to blockchain.

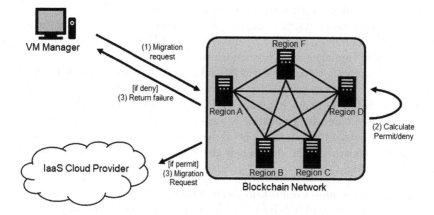

Fig. 4. Migration request process.

5 Implementation

5.1 OpenStack

On July 19, 2010, Rackspace and NASA announced the start of the project and released the initial version of OpenStack in October 2010. It features a completely open development style that follows the Ubuntu development style. It provides a multi-tenant type Infrastructure as a Service (IaaS) environment and can perform various operations on the IT infrastructure, such as creating virtual machines, creating networks, changing firewall policies, and so on. In addition, it supports cold migration and live migration, and can automatically move a VM running on a physical host machine to another physical host machine by typing a single command line or with a few mouse clicks on Horizon.

5.2 Hyperledger Fabric

In this paper, we focus on Hyperledger Fabric, which is a private type blockchain. Hyperledger Fabric is a foundation of blockchain developed by open source community about blockchain technology promoted by the Linux Foundation. In particular, it focuses on enterprise level usage, and each component can be customized freely. Figure 5 shows the configuration of Hyperledger Fabric. A control mechanism using the proposed policy is implemented in chaincode (smart contract), and a secure control mechanism is realized by storing data in PeerLedger in KVS format.

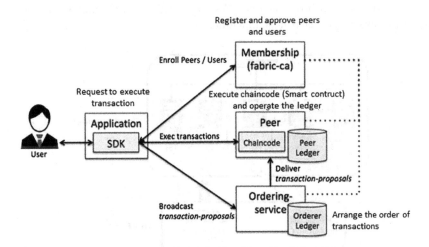

Fig. 5. Hyperledger Fabric configuration.

5.3 Constitution

In this section, we implemented the control mechanism using blockchain which we proposed in Sect. 4. This mechanism can be applied to various types of cloud environments without changing the migration process.

The configuration of the implementation environment is shown in Fig. 6. The data protection mechanism consists of "VM Manager", "FrontEnd" and "Cloud Provider". "Cloud Provider" consists of 5 host machines with 3 regions. BCMH (Blockchain Management Host) is installed on HostMachine01, HostMachine03, and HostMachine04, and has two roles for cloud's host machine and blockchain node. Also, VM1 is running on HostMachine02. "FrontEnd" performs operations on blockchain environment and operations on the cloud environment. The migration execution request is not made by the "VM Manager" directly to "Cloud Provider" but by the migration request to "FrontEnd". "FrontEnd" consists of a blockchain client and a cloud management client. Blockchain clients form a blockchain network with BCMH in "Cloud Provider". The cloud management client can operate the SDK of "Cloud Provider" and creates a migration request to "Cloud Provider". Specifically, it is used to manipulate the OpenStack API.

Also, the configuration of each host machine and VM1 is shown in Table 2. "Cloud Provider" uses the one built with OpenStack Tika. The blockchain uses Hyperledger Fabric 1.2 and Hyperledger Composer 0.20.1. The host machine and VM1's OS use CentOS7. The host machine consists of 4 core CPU, 12 GB memory, and 100 GB storage. VM1 consists of 1 core virtual CPU, 2 GB virtual memory, and 20 GB virtual storage. Also, it is assumed that Apache 2.0 and MySQL are installed in VM1, and simple web service is running. Table 3 shows the attributes of each host machine. Assign 3 regions, 3 CountryCodes, and 2 OrganizationCodes to each host machine.

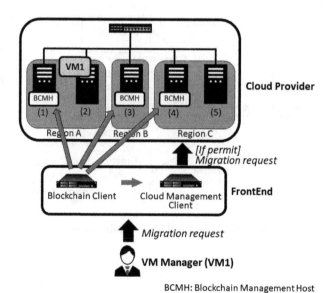

Fig. 6. Implementation environment configuration.

Table 2. Hostmachine and VM1 configurations.

Name	OS	CPU	Memory	Storage	IP address
Host Machine(1)	CentOS7	4 core	12 GB	100 GB	10.0.0.161
Host Machine(2)	CentOS7	4 core	12 GB	100 GB	10.0.0.162
Host Machine(3)	CentOS7	4 core	12 GB	100 GB	10.0.0.163
Host Machine(4)	CentOS7	4 core	12 GB	100 GB	10.0.0.164
Host Machine(5)	CentOS7	4 core	12 GB	100 GB	10.0.0.165
FrontEnd	CentOS7	4 core	12 GB	100 GB	10.0.0.170
VM1	CentOS7	1 core	2 GB	20 GB	10.0.0.7

Table 3. Hostmachine attributes.

Host name	Region	CountryCode	OrganizationCode
Host Machine(1)	A	JP	CompanyA CompanyB
Host Machine(2)	A	JP	CampanyA
Host Machine(3)	B	DE	CompanyA CompanyB
Host Machine(4)	C	GB	CompanyC
Host Machine(5)	C	GB	CampanyB

6   Evaluation

We evaluate the overhead cost of the mechanism in migration using an environment that implemented control mechanisms using policy in Sect. 5. In addition, since cold migration has fewer time constraints, this evaluation covers live migration.

6.1   New/Update Register Request

This measures execution time when new/update REGULATION, COUNTRY, or ORGANIZATION to a blockchain is performed. The Listing 1.1 below shows the JSON when a VM1 manager register a policy to a blockchain. The policy type is REGULATION, the name of the VM targeted by the policy is VM1, the country in which the VM permits are JP and GB, and the organization in which the VM is permitted CompanyA and CompanyB. Listing 1.2 and Listing 1.3 below shows the JSON when the hostmachine(1) manager registers the policy to the blockchain. In the case of COUNTRY, the type of policy is COUNTRY, the name of the hostmachine is hostmachine01, and the country in which the hostmachine is located is JP. In the case of ORGANIZATION, the type of policy is ORGANIZATION, the hostmachine name is hostmachine(1), and the hostmachine organization is CompanyA and CompanyB.

The time taken for registration to the blockchain was measured. Information on different values was registered twenty times for each policy, and the average time was examined. It took 2210 ms on average from when the VM manager or hostmachine manager made a request for policy registration to the blockchain and before processing completion notification was returned. Since these policies are not updated frequently, it takes more than 2 sec, but there is no problem.

Listing 1.1. Register REGULATION policy in VM1

```
{
    "type": "REGULATION",
    "vmName": "vm1",
    "country": "JP,GB",
    "organization": "CompanyA,CompanyB"
}
```

Listing 1.2. Register COUNTRY policy in Hostmachine(1)

```
{
    "type": "COUNTRY",
    "hmName": "hostmachine(1)",
    "country": "JP"
}
```

Listing 1.3. Register ORGANIZATION policy in Hostmachine(1)

```
{
    "type": "ORGANIZATION",
    "hmName": "hostmachine(1)",
    "organization": "CompanyA,CompanyB"
}
```

6.2   Live Migration Request

Here, we evaluate the overhead cost of the mechanism in VM migration. In addition, live migration is targeted in this evaluation. The behavior when the VM1 manager request a live migration to a different region's hostmachine, and the time required for processing the blockchain when live migration is permitted and the time required for live migration is measured.

First, we evaluate live migration (Table 4). The manager of VM1 running on the hostmachine(1) request live migration to hostmachine in other regions. When live migration is requested to the hostmachine(3), deny is returned and live migration is not performed. This is because the country where VM1 have permits are JP and GB, whereas the hostmachine(3) is located in DE, which is not permitted. Next, when the live migration request to the hostmachine(4), deny is returned and live migration is not performed. This is because the organization that VM1 have permits are CompanyA and CompanyB, and none of them is included in the organization of the hostmachine(4). Next, when live migration is requested to the hostmachine(5), permit is returned and live migration is executed. This is because all the countries and organizations that VM1 permits are included in the hostmachine(5).

Next, measure the time when the manager of VM1 that is running on hostmachine(1) requests live migration to hostmachine(5) shown Fig. 7. As mentioned above, live migration is permitted by the proposed mechanism in blockchain. The request for live migration was made 20 times and the average time was examined under the same conditions. After VM1 manager requested live migration to the blockchain, it took 15633 ms on average before processing completion notification is returned. The breakdown was 91 ms for blockchain processing and 15542 ms for live migration processing. Compared to the processing time of live migration, the processing time in the blockchain is 0.58%, and there is almost no overhead cost.

Table 4. Evaluate live migration request of VM1.

	Hostmachine(1)	Hostmachine(2)	Hostmachine(3)	Hostmachine(4)	Hostmachine(5)
Hostmachine(1)	Permit	Permit	Deny	Deny	Permit
Hostmachine(2)	Permit	Permit	Deny	Deny	Permit
Hostmachine(3)	Deny	Deny	Deny	Deny	Deny
Hostmachine(4)	Deny	Deny	Deny	Deny	Deny
Hostmachine(5)	Permit	Permit	Deny	Deny	Permit

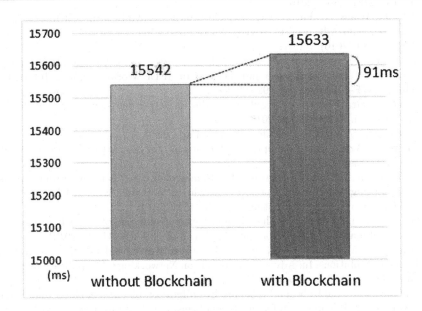

Fig. 7. Measure the VM live migration time when hostmachine(1) to hostmachine(5)

7   Conclusion

We proposed a mechanism to ensure compliance with the conditions granted by the data owner, the country's laws and regulations, and the regulations of the organization during VM migration. By constructing the proposed mechanism in a blockchain, it is possible to prevent unintended data movement and malicious tampering and enable robust VM migration control. We implemented the proposed mechanism to the existing cloud environment together with the blockchain. Policies on VM and hostmachines were registered in the blockchain, and it was evaluated whether the decision of VM live migration based on the policy was correctly performed. We also measured the execution time of live migration using the proposed mechanism and showed that there was almost no overhead cost.

Acknowledgements.. This work was supported by JSPS KAKENHI Grant Number JP20K19778.

References

1. Atzori, L., Iera, A., Morabito, G.: The Internet of Things: a survey. Comput. Netw. **54**(15), 2787–2805 (2010)
2. Tan, L., Wang, N.: Future internet: the Internet of Things. In: 3rd International Conference on Advanced Computer Theory and Engineering (ICACTE), pp. V5-376–V5-380 (2010)
3. Dhananjay, S., Tripathi, G., Jara, A.J.: A survey of Internet-of-Things: future vision architecture challenges and services. In: IEEE World Forum on Internet of Things (WF-IoT), pp. 287–292 (2014)
4. General Data Protection Regulation: GDPR. https://eur-lex.europa.eu/eli/reg/2016/679/oj. Accessed Jun 2019
5. AWS. https://aws.amazon.com/. Accessed Jun 2019
6. Microsoft Azure Cloud Computing Platform & Service. https://azure.microsoft.com/. Accessed Jun 2019
7. Khajeh-Hosseini, A., Greenwood, D., Sommerville, I.: Cloud migration: a case study of migrating an enterprise IT system to IaaS. In: IEEE 3rd International Conference on Cloud Computing, pp. 450–457 (2010)
8. Shetty, J., Anala, M.R., Shobha, G.: A survey on techniques of secure live migration of virtual machine. Int. J. Comput. Appl. (IJCA) **39**(12), 34–39 (2012)
9. Aiash, M., Mapp, G., Gemikonakli, O.: Secure live virtual machines migration: issues and solutions. In: Advanced Information Networking and Applications Workshops (WAINA), pp. 160–165 (2014)
10. Upadhyay, A., Lakkadwala, P.: Secure live migration of VM's in cloud computing: a survey. In: Reliability, Infocom Technologies and Optimization (ICRITO), pp. 1–4 (2014)
11. Rathod, N., Chauhan, S.: Survey: secure live VM migration in public cloud. Int. J. Sci. Res. Dev. (IJSRD) **2**(12), 271–274 (2015)
12. Gutierrez-Garcia, J.O., Ramirez-Nafarrate, A.: Policy-based agents for virtual machine migration in cloud data centers. In: Services Computing (SCC), pp. 603–610 (2013)

13. Koto, A., Kono, K., Yamada, H.: A guideline for selecting live migration policies and implementations in clouds. In: Cloud Computing Technology and Science (CloudCom), pp. 226–233 (2014)
14. Cui, L., Tso, F.P., Pezaros, D.P., Jia, W.: PLAN: a policy-aware VM management scheme for cloud data centres. In: Utility and Cloud Computing (UCC), pp. 142–151 (2015)
15. Papadopoulos, A.V., Maggio, M.: Virtual machine migration in cloud infrastructures: problem formalization and policies proposal. In: Decision and Control (CDC), pp. 6698–6705 (2015)
16. Xu, X., et al.: A taxonomy of blockchain-based systems for architecture design. In: IEEE International Conference on Software Architecture (ICSA 2017), pp. 243–252 (2017)
17. Dorri, A., Kanhere, S., Jurdak, R., Gauravaram, P.: Blockchain for IoT security and privacy: the case study of a smart home. In: The 2nd IEEE Workshop on Security, Privacy, and Trust in the Internet of Things (PERCOM), pp. 618–623 (2017)
18. Gaetani, E., Aniello, L., Baldoni, R., Lombardi, F., Margheri, A., Sassone, V.: Blockchain-based database to ensure data integrity in cloud computing environments. In: Italian Conference on Cyber security (ITASEC 2017), pp. 146–155 (2017)
19. Liang, X., Shetty, S., Tosh, D., Kamhoua, C., Kwiat, K., Njilla, L.: ProvChain: a blockchain-based data provenance architecture in cloud environment with enhanced privacy and availability. In: The 17th IEEE/ACM International Symposium on Cluster, Cloud and Grid Computing, pp. 468–477 (2017)
20. Xu, C., Wang, K., Guo, M.: Intelligent resource management in blockchain-based cloud datacenters. IEEE Cloud Comput. 4(6), 50–59 (2017)
21. Sharma, P.K., Chen, M., Park, J.H.: A software defined fog node based distributed blockchain cloud architecture for IoT. IEEE Access 6, 115–124 (2018)
22. Rahalkar, C., Gujar, D.: Content addressed P2P file system for the web with blockchain-based meta-data integrity. In: 2019 International Conference on Advances in Computing, Communication and Control (ICAC3), pp. 1–4 (2019)
23. KVM. https://www.linux-kvm.org. Accessed Jun 2019
24. Xen Project. https://xenproject.org/. Accessed Jun 2019
25. Compute Engine - IaaS—Compute Engine. https://cloud.google.com/compute/. Accessed Jun 2019
26. Build the future of Open Infrastructure. https://www.openstack.org/. Accessed Jun 2019

Extended RTS/CTS Control Based on Transmission Request Distribution in Wireless Ad-Hoc Networks

Momoka Hara and Hiroaki Higaki[✉]

Department of Robotics and Mechatronics, Tokyo Denki University, Tokyo, Japan
{hara,hig}@higlab.net

Abstract. In a wireless ad-hoc network where wireless nodes exchange data messages without help of stationary base stations, collisions of control and data messages are reduced and/or avoided by CSMA/CA and RTS/CTS control of wireless LAN protocols. Random backoff timers for avoidance of collisions among RTS control messages provides equally opportunities to transmit data messages to neighbor wireless nodes since the value of the backoff timer monotonically decreases. In usual wireless ad-hoc networks, wireless nodes are not equally distributed and frequency of transmission requests in wireless nodes is also not the same. Thus, especially in a region with high density of transmissions and receipts requests for data messages, it is not always possible to receive a response CTS control message even though a wireless node has an opportunity to transmit an RTS control message. Hence, the equal opportunities to transmit an RTS control message is not enough to realize the equal opportunities to transmit a data message. In order to solve this problem, this paper proposes a novel RTS/CTS control to equally provide opportunities to transmit data messages whose receiver node is hard to transmit a CTS control message on response to an RTS control message. Here, a transmission of a CTS control message precedes a transmission of an RTS control message in cases that transmissions of a CTS control message fail repeatedly.

Keywords: Wireless ad-hoc communication · Wireless LAN protocol · RTS/CTS control · Feasibility

1 Introduction

In wireless ad-hoc networks, data messages are transmitted between two neighbor wireless nodes which are included in a wireless signal transmission range each other. Since wireless signals are broadcasted in a wireless signal transmission range, they reach all neighbor wireless nodes. That is, all data and control messages transmitted by a sender wireless node N_s reach not only a receiver wireless node N_s but also all neighbor wireless nodes of N_s. When multiple neighbor wireless nodes transmit wireless signals concurrently, their common neighbor wireless

© Springer Nature Switzerland AG 2020
O. Gervasi et al. (Eds.): ICCSA 2020, LNCS 12252, pp. 236–245, 2020.
https://doi.org/10.1007/978-3-030-58811-3_17

nodes fail to receive messages carried by the wireless signals since collisions occur at these wireless nodes. In order to reduce or avoid such collisions of wireless signals, CSMA/CA (Carrier Sense Multiple Access with Collision Avoidance) is introduced in wireless LAN protocols such as IEEE 802.11. Hence, collisions caused by wireless signals transmitted by multiple exposed wireless nodes are reduced or avoided. In addition, RTS/CTS control is also introduced in wireless LAN protocols for reduction or avoidance of collisions of wireless signals concurrently transmitted by hidden wireless nodes. In RTS/CTS control, all neighbor wireless nodes of a sender wireless node N_s and a receiver wireless node N_r suspend their transmissions of any data and control message, collisions of messages at N_s and N_r can be avoided during transmissions of a data message from N_s to N_r and an *ACK* control message from N_r to N_s.

Here, among multiple neighbor wireless nodes which has requests for data message transmissions, i.e., which has transmission requests of *RTS* control messages, only one of the wireless nodes should transmit an *RTS* control message mutual-exclusively for avoidance of collisions among multiple *RTS* control messages. Hence, a randomly determined backoff timer is introduced in each wireless node. On an expiration of its own backoff timer without receiving any data and control message, a wireless node transmits an *RTS* control message for its mutually exclusive transmission of a data message without collisions. Since the expiration period is determined randomly, chances of transmissions of multiple *RTS* control messages simultaneously by multiple neighbor wireless nodes are reduced, i.e., collisions caused by multiple *RTS* control messages are reduced. In addition, since the rest time duration of a timer for its expiration is carried over without resetting it, the timer value is monotonically decrease and all wireless nodes surely transmit *RTS* control messages at some future time. Hence, each wireless node has equal opportunities to transmit an *RTS* control message for a data message transmissions and various extended method for realize more equal transmission opportunities have been proposed.

A data message transmission from a sender wireless node N_s to its neighbor wireless node N_r is allowed only after an *RTS* control message from N_s to N_r and a *CTS* control message from N_r to N_s are successfully transmitted. For transmissions of these messages, both N_s and N_r do not set any NAV (Network Allocation Vector) which represents time duration while they are prohibited to transmit any data and control message, i.e., they do not received any *RTS* and *CTS* control message from their neighbor wireless node. That is, neighboring sender wireless nodes and receiver wireless nodes contend for communication opportunities. However, currently available wireless LAN protocols do not provide equal opportunities for communication to such neighboring sender and receiver wireless nodes. Hence, if the density of communication requests around N_r is high, N_r receives many *RTS* and *CTS* control messages from its neighbor wireless nodes and it does not have equal opportunities to transmit a *CTS* control message in response to an *RTS* control message from N_s since N_r transmits the *CTS* control message passively. In order to solve this problem, this paper proposes an extended RTS/CTS control where N_r transmits a preceding *CTS* control message to N_s after multiple abandonments of transmissions of a CTS control message in response to receipt of an RTS control message from N_s and design a novel data message transmission protocol with the receiver-initiated RTS/CTS control.

2 Related Works

In wireless LAN protocols such as IEEE 802.11, for collision-free transmissions of a data message and a corresponding ACK control message between neighbor wireless nodes, an RTS and a CTS control messages are broadcasted by a sender wireless node N_s and a receiver wireless node N_r, respectively, within their wireless signal transmission range in advance. All neighbor wireless nodes receiving one of these control messages should suspend their data and control message transmissions during NAV interval included in these control messages. For transmissions of an RTS and a CTS control messages by N_s and N_r respectively, N_s and N_r should not set their NAV in response to receipts of other RTS or CTS control messages from their neighbor wireless nodes. An RTS control message from N_s is transmitted after randomly determined backoff time interval without receipt of another RTS control message from its neighbor wireless node for avoidance of concurrent transmissions of data messages causing their collisions in CSMA/CA. In addition, even if a backoff timer of another neighbor wireless node expires in advance, the rest time duration of backoff timer for its expiration is carried over without resetting it. In result, the timer value monotonically decreases and the timer surely expires in some future time. This means that each wireless node has transmission opportunities of an RTS control message equally (Fig. 1).

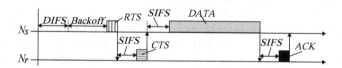

Fig. 1. RTS/CTS control for collision avoidance.

In cases that wireless nodes are not evenly distributed but their distribution is geographically localized and/or that their communication requirements are so frequent, many neighbor wireless nodes simultaneously have their transmission requests of data messages. In such cases, multiple neighbor wireless nodes may have the same randomly determined backoff timer value and transmit their RTS control messages simultaneously just after expiration of the timers, which results in a collision of the RTS control messages. In the original CSMA/CA control, in order to reduce the probability of the occurrence of such collisions, the range of the randomly determined backoff timer value is expanded. However, each wireless node locally adjusts its backoff timer range without cooperation among neighbor wireless nodes, that is, a wireless node detecting a collision unilaterally expands its backoff timer range to reduce the probability to cause such collisions for all its neighbor wireless nodes, the opportunities to transmit RTS control messages are unevenly provided among neighbor wireless nodes. In [1,2,6,8], various extended methods to improve such uneven provision of opportunities to transmit RTS control messages have been proposed. Here, histories of transmissions of RTS control messages are exchanged among neighbor wireless nodes to flatten opportunities to transmit RTS control messages, i.e., to transmit data messages. In addition, WLPB [7] provides a wireless node with less data message transmissions additional opportunities to transmit data messages by frame bursting. Here, a wireless node continuously transmits data messages by a transmission of an RTS control message with a $SIFS$ interval after a receipt of an ACK control message.

Even if a sender wireless node N_s sends an RTS control message on expiration of its own backoff timer, it is not always possible for a receiver wireless node N_r to send back a CTS control message. Here, all the neighbor nodes of N_s suspend their data and control message transmissions by setting their NAV due to receipts of the RTS control message from N_s. In case with no transmission of a CTS control message from N_r to N_s, this suspension does not contribute for avoidance of collisions with an ACK control message from N_r to N_s in response to a data message transmitted from N_s to N_r and is only takes away transmission opportunities of data and control messages from the neighbor wireless nodes of N_s. RTS Invalidation [5], NAV Reduction [5] and Cancel RTS (CRTS) [3] have been proposed to solve this problem.

3 Proposal

3.1 Problem

In a wireless ad-hoc network, a wireless node communicates with any neighbor wireless node within its wireless signal transmission range without help of a stationary wireless base station. Wireless nodes are not always distributed evenly as in Fig. 2 (a) but are localized usually as in Fig. 2 (b) due to geographical features, existence of roads and buildings, various environmental conditions and requirements for node locations by applications. Especially, in wireless ad-hoc networks with mobile wireless nodes, node distribution is not stable but time-variable due to their mobility. In addition, communication requests are also not distributed evenly and frequency of transmission requests of data messages are different in every pair of neighbor wireless nodes. For example, in wireless sensor networks, sensor nodes located in an area with frequent event occurrences have much more transmission requests of sensor data messages carrying observation data, i.e., communication requests are unevenly distributed geographically. In addition, in wireless multihop networks, some wireless nodes are required to serve a role of intermediate wireless nodes of a lot of wireless multihop transmission routes and these wireless nodes have so frequent transmission requests of data messages as a result.

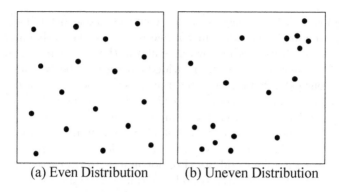

(a) Even Distribution   (b) Uneven Distribution

Fig. 2. Wireless node distribution.

For transmissions of data messages from a sender wireless node N_s to a neighbor receiver wireless node N_r, a data message from N_s to N_r and a corresponding ACK control message from N_r to N_s are required to be transmitted without collisions with any data and control messages at N_r and N_s, respectively. This is realized by RTS/CTS collision avoidance control in wireless LAN protocols such as IEEE 802.11. For avoidance of collisions with the ACK control message at N_s, N_r should transmits the ACK control message mutually exclusively among the neighbor wireless nodes of N_s. Hence, N_s broadcasts an RTS control message to all neighbor wireless nodes within a wireless signal transmission range of N_s and all the neighbor wireless nodes of N_s receiving the RTS control message are required to suspend their transmissions of data and control messages during NAV interval specified by the RTS control message. Even opportunities to transmit RTS control messages among neighbor wireless nodes are realized by monotonically decreasing backoff timer values. Initial backoff timer value which represents a waiting interval for a transmission of an RTS control message is determined randomly for collision avoidance and the rese backoff timer value is carried over even if backoff timer of another neighbor wireless node expires earlier. Hence, all the backoff timer values monotonically decrease to zero, i.e., they surely expire, and all the wireless nodes have opportunities to transmit RTS control messages at some future time.

On the other hand, in order to avoid collisions with a data message at N_r, N_s should also transmit the data message mutually exclusively among the neighbor wireless nodes of N_r. Hence, N_r broadcasts a CTS control message to all neighbor wireless nodes within a wireless signal transmission range of N_r and all the neighbor wireless nodes of N_r receiving the RTS control message are required to suspend their transmissions of data and control messages during NAV interval specified by the CTS control message. Different from RTS control messages, even opportunities to transmit CTS control messages are not provided to a wireless node among neighbor wireless nodes contending for communication requirements. In order for N_r to transmit a CTS control message to N_s, N_r should not have set its NAV interval due to receipt of an RTS or a CTS

control message from another neighbor wireless node for collision avoidance at the instance when it receives an *RTS* control message from N_s. Hence, if the neighbor wireless nodes of N_r often transmits *RTS* and *CTS* control messages due to high density of wireless node distribution and their highly frequent communication requests, N_r should set its NAV for collision avoidance so frequently. As a result, as shown in Fig. 3, time duration for suspension of data and control messages including *CTS* control messages determined by the NAV becomes longer and the opportunities to send back a *CTS* control message to N_s in response to receipt of an *RTS* control message from N_s decrease. Since times when N_r receives an *RTS* control message from N_s are independent of NAV intervals set in N_r determined by receipts of *RTS* and *CTS* control messages from its neighbor wireless nodes, opportunities of transmissions of the *CTS* control message from N_r is not even with opportunities of transmissions of *RTS* and *CTS* control messages from the neighbor wireless nodes of N_r different from colliding transmission requests of *RTS* control messages regulated by CSMA/CA collision avoidance control. Therefore, N_s does not have equal opportunities to transmit data messages to N_r and the waiting time duration for data message transmission is postponed in N_s irrationally.

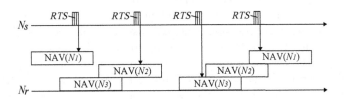

Fig. 3. Unequal transmission opportunities for CTS due to high density transmission/receipt requests.

It is considerable that N_r notifies its NAV interval to N_s in advance in order for N_s to send an *RTS* control message to N_r when N_r can send back a *CTS* control message to N_s. However, since its NAV interval is set just after receipt of an *RTS* or a *CTS* control message from its neighbor wireless node, it is impossible for N_r to transmit a control message for the notification; this is contradiction. If the NAV interval is delayed for the transmission of the additional control message for the notification, additional time overhead is required, i.e., the additional interval for RTS/CTS collision avoidance control before transmission of a data message becomes longer, and the performance of the data message transmission should become lower. On the other hand, just after the expiration of a NAV interval, N_r may send a *CTS* control message to N_s in response to the *RTS* control message which N_r receives during its NAV interval. However, the NAV interval set in the other neighbor wireless nodes of N_s has already been consumed before the transmission of delayed *CTS* control message and this may cause collisions of an *ACK* control message from N_r to N_s and another message at N_s.

3.2   Receiver-Initiated RTS/CTS Control

In order to solve the problem discussed in the previous subsection, i.e., the problem that a receiver wireless node has less opportunities to send back a *CTS* control message to a sender wireless node N_s, this paper proposes a novel receiver-initiated RTS/CTS collision avoidance control which works supplementary.

In cases that in spite of receipt of an *RTS* control message from N_s, N_r suspends transmissions of data and control messages due to its NAV interval set by receipt of a preceding *RTS* or *CTS* control message from its neighbor wireless node, N_r cannot send back a *CTS* control message to N_s. As a result, a timeout interval expires in N_s and it is impossible for N_s to send a data message to N_r. In order to solve this problem, this paper proposes a receiver-initiated RTS/CTS collision avoidance control. Here, if N_r fails to send back a *CTS* control message to N_s due to its NAV interval repeatedly more times than predetermined threshold, N_r sends a *CTS* control message to N_s antecedently to an *RTS* control message from N_s to N_r. That is, an *RTS* and a *CTS* control messages are exchanged between N_s and N_r in a reverse order to the original RTS/CTS control. As mentioned in the previous subsection, though N_r has less opportunities to send back a *CTS* control message to N_s due to higher distribution density of wireless nodes and higher frequency of communication requests for data message transmissions, N_r passively sends back a *CTS* control message in response to an *RTS* control message from N_s in the original RTS/CTS control. This is the reason of uneven distribution of transmission opportunities to send the control messages, i.e., *RTS* and *CTS* control messages among the neighbor wireless nodes of N_r. As shown in Fig. 4, in our proposal, after some continuous receipt of *RTS* control messages from N_s to which N_r fails to send back a corresponding *CTS* control message, N_r sends a *CTS* control message to N_s precedingly to an *RTS* control message from N_s. That is, just after all its NAV intervals expire, N_r sends a *CTS* control message to N_s. After receipt of the *CTS* control message, N_s sends an *RTS* control message with *SIFS* interval to all its neighbor wireless nodes including N_r for notification of receipt of the *CTS* control message to N_r and mutually exclusive transmissions of a data message to N_r and of an *ACK* control message from N_r to N_s. Same as the original RTS/CTS control, if a NAV interval has already been set by N_s due to receipt of another *RTS* or *CTS* control message from its neighbor wireless node, N_s does not send the *RTS* control message in response to the *CTS* control message from N_r. By receipt of the *RTS* control message, N_r is notified that N_s sends a data message to N_r and all neighbor wireless nodes of N_s suspends their transmissions of data and control messages to avoid collisions at N_s with an *ACK* control message from N_r. Therefore, collision-free transmissions of a data message and a corresponding *ACK* control message are realized between N_s and N_r.

In our proposed method, on expiration of all NAV intervals set by N_r due to receipts of *RTS* or *CTS* control messages from its neighbor wireless nodes, N_r should immediately send a *CTS* control message to N_s not to lose the

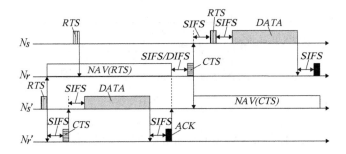

Fig. 4. Receiver-initiated RTS/CTS control.

opportunity to transmit it. That is, before a receipt of any *RTS* or *CTS* control message from its neighbor wireless nodes, N_r should send the preceding *CTS* control message to N_s. Though the *CTS* control message should be sent with a *DIFS* interval after expiration of all the NAV intervals, it is sent with a *SIFS* interval [7] or with a *DIFS* interval with zero backoff timer value [4] in our proposal. In either method of them, the transmission of the *CTS* control message from N_r to N_s precedes other *RTS* or *CTS* control messages transmitted from neighbor wireless nodes of N_r.

In our proposal, since a *CTS* control message is transmitted preceding to an *RTS* control message, different NAV values are carried by these control messages from the original RTS/CTS control. In the original RTS/CTS control, as shown in Fig. 5, the NAV interval value carried by an *RTS* control message is a summation of required time durations for a *CTS* control message transmission, a data message transmission, an *ACK* control message transmission and triple of a *SIFS* interval. The NAV interval carried by a *CTS* control message is a summation of required time durations for a data message transmission, an *ACK* control message transmission and double of a *SIFS* interval. Here, a data message transmission time depends on its size that only N_s can calculate. However, the transmission time duration of each control message and a *SIFS* interval are constant. Hence, the NAV interval carried by the *CTS* control message is calculated by N_r by subtracting the required time durations for an *RTS* control message transmission and single *SIFS* interval from that carried by an *RTS* control message.

On the other hand, as shown in Fig. 6, in our proposed receiver-initiated RTS/CTS control, the NAV interval carried by a preceding *CTS* control message is a summation of required time durations of an *RTS* control message transmission, a data message transmission, an *ACK* control message transmission and triple of a *SIFS* interval. The NAV interval carried by a corresponding *RTS* control message is a summation of required time durations for a data message transmission, an *ACK* control message transmission and double of a *SIFS* interval. Since the data message is going to be transmitted not by N_r but by N_s, N_r does not know the size of the data message. However, N_r has surely received an *RTS* control message for the same data message from N_s before this

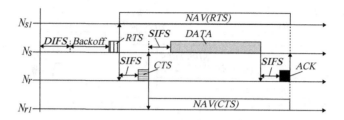

Fig. 5. NAV values in RTS/CTS control.

transmission of a preceding *CTS* control message, the required time duration for the data message transmission can be calculated by N_r even though it does not know the message size. That is, the NAV interval carried by a preceding *CTS* control message is achieved by subtracting required transmission time duration for a *CTS* control message from the NAV interval carried by an already received *RTS* control message from N_s and adding required transmission time duration for an *RTS* control message. In addition, the NAV interval carried by an *RTS* control message transmitted in response to the preceding *CTS* control message is achieved by subtracting required transmission time duration for a *CTS* control message and a *SIFS* interval from that carried by the *CTS* control message.

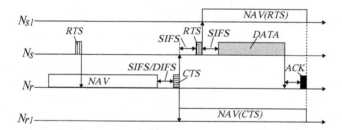

Fig. 6. NAV values in receiver-initiated RTS/CTS control.

4 Concluding Remarks

This paper pointed out the problem that *CTS* control messages are not transmitted evenly due to lack of contention mechanism with *RTS* control message transmissions. In order to solve this problem, this paper proposed the receiver-initiated RTS/CTS control where a receiver wireless node actively transmits a preceding *CTS* control message to an *RTS* control message from a sender wireless node. In future work, the authors evaluate the performance improvement in simulation experiments.

References

1. Cali, F., Conti, M., Gregori, E.: Dynamic turning of the IEEE 802.11 protocol to achieve a theoretical throughput limit. IEEE/ACM Trans. Netw. **8**, 785–799 (2000)
2. Crow, B., Widjaja, I., Kim, J., Sakai, P.: IEEE 802.11 wireless local area network. IEEE Commun. Mag. **35**(9), 116–126 (1997)
3. Harada, T., Ohta, C., Morii, M.: Improvement of TCP throughput for IEEE 802.11 DCF in wireless multi-hop networks. IEICE Trans. **85**(12), 2198–2208 (2002)
4. Ikuma, S., Li, Z., Pei, T., Choi, Y., Sekiya, H.: Rigorous analytical model of saturated throughput for the IEEE 802.11p EDCA. IEICE Trans. Commun. **E102-B**(4), 669–707 (2019)
5. Inoue, D., Shigeyasu, T., Matsuno, H., Morinaga, N.: A Proposal of IEEE802.11DCF with cancel CTS for avoiding unnecessary transmission deferment. In: Proceedings of the 18th IPSJ DPS Workshop, pp. 129–134 (2007)
6. Kwon, Y., Fang, Y., Latchman, H.: A Novel MAC protocol with fast collision resolution for wireless LANs. In: Proceedings of IEEE INFOCOM, vol. 2, pp. 853–862 (2003)
7. Shigeyasu, T., Matsuno, H., Morinaga, N.: Proposal of a method for improving mac level fairness in the coexisting environment with legacy IEEE802.11DCF terminals. IPSJ J. **50**(3), 1156–1169 (2009)
8. Tian, X., Chen, X., Ideguchi, T., Fang, Y.: Improving throughput and fairness in WLANs through dynamically optimizing backoff. IEICE Trans. Commun. **E88-B**(11), 4328–4338 (2005)

Interference of Overhearing by Eavesdropper Nodes for Secure Wireless Ad-Hoc Networks

Hinano Amano and Hiroaki Higaki[✉]

Department of Robotics and Mechatronics, Tokyo Denki University, Tokyo, Japan
{amano,hig}@uni-heidelberg.de

Abstract. In ad-hoc networks, data messages are transmitted from a source wireless node to a destination one along a wireless multihop transmission route consisting of a sequence of intermediate wireless nodes. Each intermediate wireless node forwards data messages to its next-hop wireless node. Here, a wireless signal carrying the data message is broadcasted by using an omni directional antenna and it is not difficult for an eavesdropper wireless node to overhear the wireless signal to get the data message. Some researches show that it is useful to transmit a noise wireless signal which collides to the data message wireless signal in order for interfering the overhearing. However, some special devices such as directional antennas and/or high computation power for complicated signal processing are required. For wireless multihop networks with huge number of wireless nodes, small and cheap wireless nodes without such special devices are mandatory for construction of the network. This paper proposes a novel method for interfering the overhearing by the eavesdropper wireless nodes by a routing protocol and a data message transmission protocol with cooperative noise signal transmissions by 1-hop and 2-hop neighbor wireless nodes of each intermediate wireless node. The results of simulation experiments show that the proposed intentional collision method provides enough coverage of noise wireless signals especially by help of part of 2-hop neighbor wireless nodes.

Keywords: Wireless multihop communication · Overhearing avoidance · Jamming wireless signals · Collisions · Routing protocol

1 Introduction

In wireless ad-hoc networks and wireless sensor networks, data messages are transmitted along a wireless transmission route from a source wireless node to a destination one. A wireless transmission route consists of a sequence of intermediate wireless nodes each of which forwards data messages from its previous-hop wireless node to its next-hop one. Each intermediate wireless node broadcasts a wireless signal for the data message transmission by using an omni directional antenna. Hence, it is possible for all its neighbor wireless nodes within its wireless

© Springer Nature Switzerland AG 2020
O. Gervasi et al. (Eds.): ICCSA 2020, LNCS 12252, pp. 246–260, 2020.
https://doi.org/10.1007/978-3-030-58811-3_18

transmission range to overhear the data message signal. That is, the neighbor wireless node, even if it is an eavesdropper one, receives the data message.

Usually, the data messages are securely transmitted by cryptography. The source wireless node encrypts a clear text and the data message carries a cryptogram. In order for achieving the clear text from the cryptogram in the overheard data message, a cryptography key is required for both the destination wireless node and an eavesdropper wireless node. Especially, in sensor networks where sensor data messages initiated by source sensor nodes with sensor and wireless communication devices are transmitted to a wireless sink node connected to a high performance sensor database computer, it is impossible for each sensor node to implement highly secure cryptography methods since its implementation, operation and maintenance costs are high. Thus, even in sensor networks with simple and facile cryptography methods, the sensor data is required to be transmitted securely.

For this requirement, some secure wireless transmission methods have been proposed as described in the next section. One method requires each intermediate wireless node to devise a directional antenna and wireless signals are required to be transmitted only in the specified direction by using a beam-forming method. Another one requires each intermediate wireless node to support high performance signal processing with complex calculation. However, it is difficult to introduce these conventional methods to wireless multihop networks consisting of small, light and cheap wireless nodes such as sensor nodes. Therefore, this paper proposes a novel secure wireless multihop transmission method without special hardwares such as directional antennas and/or processors supporting high performance signal processing in each intermediate wireless node. That is, under an assumption that wireless signals are transmitted according to the unit disc model [8] by using an omni directional antenna by each intermediate wireless node, it makes difficult for eavesdropper wireless nodes to overhear the data messages transmitted along a wireless multihop transmission route.

The next section overviews related works. Our proposal for interfering the overhearing by eavesdropper wireless nodes by cooperation with neighbor wireless nodes of each intermediate one is shown in Sect. 3. Both the routing and the data message transmission protocols are proposed. Section 4 evaluates our proposed method by simulation experiments.

2 Related Works

There are various security problems in wireless multihop networks and a lot of solutions have been discussed and proposed. The selfish wireless node problem and the black-hole attack problem are well known peculiar problems in wireless multihop networks. On the other hand, a so-to-speak eavesdropper problem is a common one for wired and wireless networks and a countermeasure solution is mandatory. Especially in wireless networks, since all the data messages are carried by wireless signals which are inherently broadcasted and are easily overheard by any neighbor wireless node, much more advanced method has been required to be developed. The dominant technology is an cryptography. Due to the characteristics of the mobile wireless nodes, simple and facile encryption/decryption methods have been proposed for achieving enough security with reasonably low computational complexity.

However, the cryptography is only a method which makes difficult for eavesdroppers to achieve the clear text from the cryptogram carried by the data message. That is, it may fall behind. Thus for taking the initiative, a method to make difficult or impossible for eavesdropper wireless nodes to overhear the data messages carrying the cryptograms is much effective. Combination of the method interfering the overhearing and the cryptography for wireless multihop networks is expected to provide an acceptable tradeoff between required security and inevitable overhead. In wireless multihop sensor networks and IoT (Internet of Things) consisting of huge number of low-power wireless nodes without computational power enough to support highly secure communication methods, a novel secure communication method not depending only on the cryptography is required.

One of such methods makes difficult for eavesdropper wireless nodes to overhear the transmitted data messages by intentional collisions with noise wireless signals [2,6]. Paper [2] proposes a method for secure wireless data message transmissions under an assumption that beam forming by using directional antennas is available for all the wireless nodes (at least all the wireless nodes which is possible to transmit data messages to their neighbor nodes). A sender wireless node N_s transmits a wireless signal carrying a data message to a receiver wireless node N_r by using beam forming such that N_r and only its limited neighbor wireless nodes receive it. Concurrently with the transmission of the wireless signal, N_r also transmits a noise wireless signal called a jamming wireless signal to all its neighbor wireless nodes by its omni directional antenna. Since the wireless signal transmission range of the noise wireless signal covers the wireless signal transmission range of the wireless signal carrying the data message, no wireless nodes can receive the data message itself without any collision. Here, one of the neighbor wireless nodes N_f of N_r forwards its receiving collided wireless signal which is the superposition of these wireless signals to N_r. On receipt of the collided wireless signal from N_f, N_r removes the original noise wireless signal from the received wireless signal and achieves the original wireless signal carrying the data message since the noise signal was transmitted by N_r itself. This signal processing is only possible by N_r since no other wireless nodes have the original noise wireless signal transmitted by N_r.

This method by using the intentional collisions with the noise wireless signals seems excellent for secure communication. However, the assumptions of the directional antennas for beam forming and high performance processors for complex signal processing to remove a noise wireless signal from a collided wireless signal are not reasonable to apply to the wireless multihop networks such as sensor networks and IoT. This is because the sensor nodes and the IoT devices may be so small, light and cheap and their networks consist of huge number of such wireless nodes that it is difficult or impossible to have such functionalities.

3   Proposal

This section proposes a novel method for secure wireless multihop transmissions
of data messages which interferes eavesdropper wireless nodes achieving the clear
texts carried by the data messages. Our method makes difficult for the eavesdropper wireless nodes to overhear the data message signals which are broadcasted
by intermediate wireless nodes in a wireless multihop transmission route. Here,
no additional special hardware such as directional antennas for beam forming
and high performance processors to support highly complex signal processing
is needed in the intermediate wireless nodes. That is, the transmissions of the
wireless signals from omni directional antennas of the wireless nodes are modeled
by the unit disc model [4].

3.1   Noise Signal Transmission for Ad-Hoc Wireless Communications

This section discusses the method for secure wireless transmissions of data messages in wireless ad-hoc communication between neighbor wireless nodes, i.e.,
only 1-hop wireless transmissions. Wireless nodes N_s and N_r are a sender and a
receiver ones, respectively. N_r is in the wireless signal transmission range of N_s.
A data message m is broadcasted by N_s to all the neighbor wireless node of N_s
in the wireless signal transmission range of N_s. Hence, N_r surely receives m. At
the same time all the neighbor wireless nodes including a possible eavesdropper
wireless node N in the wireless signal transmission range of N_s receives m as
shown in Fig. 1. In order to prevent N to receive m, noise wireless signals are
introduced same as the related works discussed in the previous section. Only
noise wireless signals transmitted by wireless nodes whose wireless signal transmission ranges cover at least a part of the wireless signal transmission range of
N_s contribute to the secure wireless transmission of m from N_s to N_r. At the
same time, the noise wireless signals never reach N_r. If N_r is in one of the noise
wireless signal transmission ranges, N_r cannot receive m due to the collision
caused by m and the noise wireless signal.

   This paper proposes the following conditions for a wireless node N_j to transmit a noise wireless signal to prevent a possible eavesdropper wireless node to
receive the data message transmitted from a sender wireless node N_s to a receiver
one N_r.

[Noise Wireless Signal Transmitting Node N_j]

(1) N_j is a neighbor wireless node of N_s. N_j is in the wireless signal transmission
    range of N_s.
(2) N_j is not a neighbor wireless node of N_r. N_j is out of the wireless signal
    transmission range of N_r.

   The condition (1) is a sufficient condition for the wireless signal transmission
range of N_j to cover a part of the wireless signal transmission range of N_s. Since
both m and the noise wireless signal reach the wireless nodes in the common
area of both the wireless signal transmission ranges, a collision of them occurs at

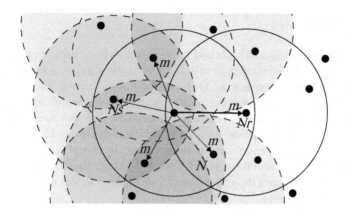

Fig. 1. Noise wireless signal transmissions by neighbor nodes.

the wireless nodes. Hence the possible eavesdropper wireless nodes are prevented to receive m by the collision. In addition as discussed in the later subsection, the wireless nodes satisfying the condition (1) does not require any additional control message transmission to synchronously transit the noise wireless signals with m from N_s to N_r. Thus, this subsection proposes that the 1-hop neighbor wireless nodes of N_s transmit the noise wireless signals.

The condition (2) is a necessary condition for the wireless signal transmission range of N_j not to include N_r. Because of the assumption of the unit disc model for the wireless signal transmission range, N_r is also out of the wireless signal transmission range of N_j. Thus, the noise wireless signal from N_j never reaches N_r and no collisions of m and the noise wireless signal occur at N_r. Thus, this subsection proposes that the neighbor wireless nodes of N_r do not transmit the noise wireless signals.

3.2 Extended Noise Signal Transmission for Ad-Hoc Wireless Communications

The previous subsection proposes a method to prevent eavesdropper wireless nodes to overhear the data message transmitted between neighbor wireless nodes. Here, secure ad-hoc wireless communication is realized by noise wireless signals transmitted by the neighbor wireless nodes of a sender wireless node out of the wireless signal transmission range of a receiver wireless node. The wireless nodes and the time duration required to transmit the noise wireless signals are also specified by the RTS/CTS control message transmissions and no additional control messages are required to be transmitted.

However, the existence probability of the neighbor wireless nodes transmitting the noise wireless signals preventing the overhearing of possible eavesdropper wireless nodes depends on the distribution of the wireless nodes, i.e., the density of the wireless nodes, and the distance $|N_s N_r|$ between the sender wireless node

N_s and the receiver one N_r. As shown in Fig. 2, if the distance $|N_sN_r|$ is relatively long, the common area of the wireless signal transmission ranges of N_s and N_r is small and the area including the wireless nodes satisfying the conditions in the previous subsection is large. Hence, the coverage of the noise wireless signals overlapping the wireless signal transmission range of N_s in which possible eavesdropper wireless nodes overhear the data messages is relatively high. On the other hand as shown in Fig. 3, if $|N_sN_r|$ is relatively short, the common area of the wireless signal transmission ranges of N_s and N_r is small. Since the wireless nodes in this area cannot transmit the noise wireless signals which reach N_r, the coverage of the noise wireless signals overlapping the wireless signal transmission range of N_s is relatively low and it is difficult to prevent eavesdropper wireless nodes to overhear the data message.

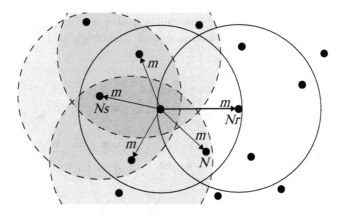

Fig. 2. Eavesdropper interfering for far sender/receiver wireless nodes.

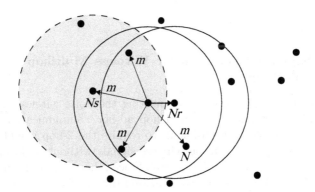

Fig. 3. Eavesdropper interfering for near sender/receiver wireless nodes.

In order to solve the problem, additional wireless nodes are required to transmit the noise wireless signals to improve the coverage, i.e., the area where wireless nodes does not receive the noise wireless signals though they receive the data message from N_s is required to be reduced. It is clear that no wireless nodes in the wireless signal transmission range of N_r can transmit the noise wireless signals without collisions at N_r, noise wireless signal transmissions by the wireless nodes out of the wireless signal transmission ranges of both N_s and N_r are expected to be efficient. Therefore, wireless nodes out of the both wireless transmission ranges of N_s and N_r are required to transmit the noise wireless signals if its wireless signal transmission range covers even a part of the wireless signal transmission range of N_s. Such wireless nodes are 2-hop neighbor wireless nodes of N_s and are not 1-hop neighbor wireless nodes of N_r. This paper proposes that transmissions of noise wireless signals are required to be common 2-hop neighbor wireless nodes of N_s and N_r as shown in Fig. 4. By this extension, even if $|N_sN_r|$ is relatively short, the coverage of transmission ranges of noise wireless signals overlapping the wireless transmission ranges of N_s is improved.

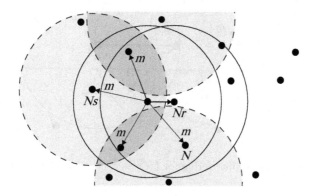

Fig. 4. Coverage improvement with help of common 2-hop neighbor wireless nodes.

3.3 Noise Signal Transmission for Wireless Multihop Communications

Different from the wireless nodes transmitting the noise wireless signals for a secure data message transmission in 1-hop ad-hoc communications discussed in the previous subsection, it is difficult to require the 2-hop neighbor wireless nodes of N_s to transmit the noise wireless signals without additional control messages to the original RTS/CTS control. Since 2-hop neighbor wireless nodes are both out of the wireless signal transmission ranges of N_s and N_r, additional control messages are required to be transmitted to notify them to transmit the noise wireless signals. In addition, it is impossible for 1-hop neighbor wireless nodes of N_s to transmit the additional control message concurrently with the

CTS control message from N_r after receipt of the RTS control message since the transmitted control message collides with the CTS control message at N_s. Therefore, the 2-hop neighbor wireless nodes of intermediate wireless nodes being required to transmit the noise wireless signals are determined in a routing protocol which detects the wireless multihop transmission route $||N_0 \ldots N_n\rangle\rangle$ which is a sequence of intermediate wireless nodes from a source wireless node $N^s = N_0$ to a destination wireless node $N^d = N_n$. Since a certain control messages is transmitted along the detected wireless multihop transmission route in most of the ad-hoc routing protocols, 1-hop neighbor wireless nodes of each intermediate wireless node can transmit some control messages to notify a part of its 2-hop neighbor wireless nodes to be required to transmit the noise wireless signals simultaneously with the data message transmissions.

The 2-hop neighbor wireless nodes of N_s selected to transmit the noise wireless signals according to the conditions for 1-hop ad-hoc communications described in the previous subsection are also required to transmit the noise wireless signals for secure wireless multihop communications. That is, 1-hop neighbor wireless nodes of an intermediate wireless node N_i out of the wireless signal transmission range of its next-hop wireless node N_{i+1} is required to transmit the noise wireless signals concurrently with the data message transmissions from N_i to N_{i+1}. In addition to cover wider part of the wireless signal transmission range of N_i by the noise wireless signal transmission ranges to prevent eavesdropper wireless nodes to overhear the data message, a part of the 2-hop neighbor wireless nodes are also required to transmit the noise wireless signals. Though the transmission ranges of the 2-hop neighbor nodes of N_i surely overlap the wireless signal transmission range of N_i, they do not transmit the noise wireless signals if N_{i+1} is their 1-hop neighbor wireless node for avoidance the collisions with the receiving data message transmissions at N_{i+1}.

Therefore, for wireless multihop data message transmissions from a source wireless node $N^s = N_0$ to a destination one $N^d = N_n$ along the wireless multihop transmission route $||N_0 \ldots N_n\rangle\rangle$, the wireless nodes N_j satisfying either of the following conditions transmits the noise wireless signals to prevent the data messages to be overheard by possible eavesdropper wireless nodes in the wireless signal transmission range of N_i (Fig. 5).

[Noise Wireless Signal Transmitting Node N_j]

(1) A wireless node N_j is a 1-hop neighbor wireless node of N_i and in not a 1-hop neighbor wireless node of N_{i+1}.
(2) N_j is not a 1-hop neighbor wireless node of N_i and N_{i+1} either and a 2-hop neighbor wireless node of both N_i and N_{i+1}.

3.4 Routing and Noise Wireless Signal Transmission Protocol

As mentioned in the previous subsection, a wireless signal transmission range of an intermediate wireless node N_i is covered by wireless signal transmission ranges of 1-hop neighbor wireless nodes of N_i out of the wireless signal transmission rage

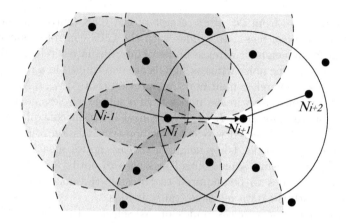

Fig. 5. Noise wireless signal transmissions for wireless multihop communication.

of N_{i+1} and of common 2-hop neighbor wireless nodes of N_i and N_{i+1} to prevent possible eavesdropper wireless nodes by noise wireless signal transmissions. In order to determine the common 2-hop neighbor wireless nodes, certain control messages are required to be transmitted by 1-hop neighbor wireless nodes of both N_i and $Ni + 1$. It is realized by forwarding of both an RTS and a CTS control messages by 1-hop neighbor wireless nodes of N_i and N_{i+1}, respectively. Though these forwarded RTS/CTS control messages might be collide to the original RTS/CTS control messages. Hence, the method results in longer transmission delay of data messages.

Different from this dynamic determination of 2-hop neighbor noise wireless signal transmission nodes, this paper proposes the method by which they are determined in a flooding based routing protocol such as AODV. Same as in [3], in addition to a flooding of an $Rreq$ control message and a unicast transmission of an $Rrep$ control message along a detected wireless multihop transmission route, additional control messages are transmitted during the transmission of the $Rrep$ control message to the 2-hop neighbor noise wireless signal transmission nodes.

Figure 6 shows an overview of the proposed protocol based on AODV. When an intermediate wireless node N_{i+1} transmits an $Rrep$ control message to its previous-hop intermediate wireless node N_i, a 1-hop neighbor wireless node N_{i+1}^n of N_{i+1} overhears the $Rrep$ control message. Just after this reception of $Rrep$, N_{i+1}^n broadcasts a noise wireless signal transmission request control message $Jreq(i + 1)$ in its wireless signal transmission range. By this extended routing protocol, 1-hop neighbor wireless node of N_i out of the wireless signal transmission range of N_{i+1} receives $Rrep$ control message from N_i but does not receive $Rrep$ control message from N_{i+1} transmits a noise wireless signal while N_i transmits data messages to N_{i+1}. On the other hand, common 2-hop neighbor wireless nodes of N_i and N_{i+1} receive $Jreq(i)$ and $Jreq(i+1)$ from 1-hop neighbor wireless nodes of N_i and N_{i+1}, respectively. These wireless nodes transmit noise wireless signals while a data message is transmitted from N_i to N_{i+1}.

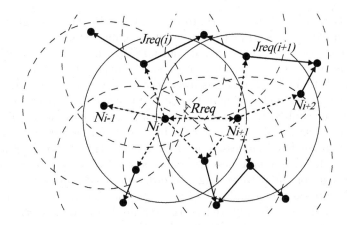

Fig. 6. Routing protocol with selection of 2-hop neighbor wireless nodes transmitting noise wireless signal.

[Noise Signal Transmitting Wireless Node Determination]

(1) On receipt of an *Rrep* control message from an intermediate wireless node N_i, a neighbor wireless node N_i^n broadcasts a *Jreq(i)* control message in its wireless signal transmission range.

(2) A wireless node N which has received *Rrep* control message not from N_{i+1} but from N_i transmits a noise wireless signal while a data message is transmitted from N_i to N_{i+1}.

(3) A wireless node N which has received both *Jreq(i)* and *Jreq(i + 1)* control messages from its neighbor wireless nodes transmits a noise wireless signal while a data message is transmitted from N_i to N_{i+1}.

A wireless node N which has received *Rrep* control message not from N_{i+1} but from N_i, i.e., which is a 1-hop neighbor wireless node of N_i and is not a 1-hop neighbor wireless node of N_{i+1} identifies the time duration when it transmits a noise wireless signal while a data message is transmitted from N_i to N_{i+1} by receipt of an RTS control message as discussed in the previous subsection. On the other hand, a wireless node N which has received both *Jreq(i)* and *Jreq(i + 1)* control messages from its neighbor wireless nodes does not receive either an RTS control messages from N_i or a CTS control messages from N_{i+1} since N is out of the wireless signal transmission ranges of both N_i and N_{i+1} and N cannot identify the time duration when it transmits a noise wireless signal while a data message is transmitted from N_i to N_{i+1}. As also discussed in the previous subsection, if the RTS and the CTS control messages are forwarded to N, though N can identify the time duration, it requires higher communication overhead, i.e., longer transmission delay for a 1-hop data message transmission from N_i to N_{i+1}, which results in longer end-to-end transmission delay of the data message along a wireless multihop transmission route from its source wireless node to its destination one. Hence, this paper proposes another simple way for N to identify the time duration. That is, N starts to transmit a noise wireless signal when it receive any noise wireless signal from one of its neighbor node. Since it is satisfied one of the conditions of a noise signal transmission wireless node mentioned in the previous subsection in advance, N is surely required to transmit a noise wireless signal. In addition, if N has received a noise wireless signal from one of its neighbor wireless nodes, it may be the 1-hop neighbor wireless node of N_i and N may be required to start to transmit a noise wireless signal. Even if N receives a noise wireless signal transmitted by its different neighbor wireless node from the 1-hop neighbor wireless node of N_i, a noise wireless signal transmitted from N never disturbs a data message transmission if N has not received a CTS control message for the data message. In order to avoid unnecessary collisions of the noise wireless signal and a data message, the time duration of the noise wireless signal from N is adjusted to the required transmission time for the shortest data message since N cannot achieve the NAV information for the data message carried by the RTS and the CTS control messages.

3.5 Notification of Noise Signal Transmission Time

In order to solve this problem, this paper proposes a method to notify the initiation time and duration of noise signal transmission to common 2-hop neighbor wireless nodes of an intermediate wireless node N_i and its next-hop intermediate wireless node N_{i+1}. Since N_i is an intermediate wireless node of a wireless multihop transmission route, N_i surely receives a data message from its previous-hop intermediate wireless node N_{i-1} before sending it to N_{i+1}. In the RTS/CTS collision avoidance control for a data message transmission from N_{i-1} to N_i, a common neighbor wireless node N_i' of N' and N_i receives a *CTS* control message from N_i. By referring NAV contained in the *CTS* control message, N_i' gets required time duration of a data message transmission. N_i' transmits an *NTTN* (Notification of Transmission Time of Noise Signal) control message containing the required time duration of a data message transmission to N' which becomes possible to transmit noise signal for the required time duration to interfere eavesdropper wireless node trying to overhear a data message transmitted from N_i to N_{i+1}. Though N_i' should suspend transmission of any message due to receipt of the *CTS* control message from N_i for avoidance of collision with the data message from N_{i-1} to N_i at N_i, N_i' transmits the *NTTN* control message to N' concurrently with an *ACK* control message from N_i to N_{i-1}. This is because both the *ACK* and the *NTTN* control messages are correctly received without any collisions by N_{i-1} and N', respectively as shown in Fig. 7.

4   Evaluation

This section evaluates the coverage of the wireless signal transmission ranges of the intermediate wireless nodes of the wireless multihop transmission routes by the noise wireless signals transmitted in accordance with the proposed method in simulation experiments (Fig. 8).

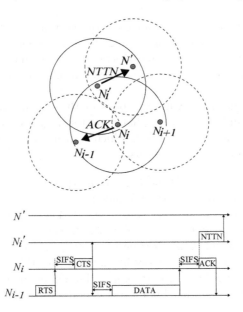

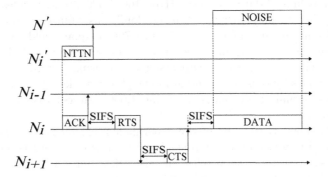

Fig. 7. Notification of time for noise signal transmission by NTTN control message.

Fig. 8. Time starting transmission of noise signal by common 2-hop neighbor node N'.

A wireless transmission range of a wireless node is 100 m and its 1-hop and 2-hop neighbor nodes are randomly distributed according to the unique distribution randomness. Here average numbers of neighbor wireless nodes are 0–20 and the distance between an intermediate wireless node and its next-hop wireless node is 0–100 m. For each density of the wireless nodes and the distance between the successive intermediate wireless nodes, the coverage is evaluated for 1,000 different distributions of the wireless nodes. For each distributions of the wireless nodes, the coverage of the wireless signal transmission ranges of the intermediate wireless nodes along the wireless multihop transmission routes by the noise wireless signal transmission ranges for the following three cases:

(1) Only 1-hop neighbor wireless nodes of the intermediate wireless nodes satisfying the proposed conditions transmit the noise wireless signals.

(2) All the 1-hop neighbor wireless nodes of the intermediate wireless nodes and the 2-hop ones satisfying the proposed conditions transmit the noise wireless signals.

(3) All the 1-hop neighbor wireless nodes of the intermediate wireless nodes and only the limited 2-hop neighbor wireless nodes which is a neighbor of the 1-hop neighbor wireless nodes which transmit the noise wireless signals transmit the noise wireless signals.

Figure 9 shows the results of the simulation experiments. The coverage monotonically increases according to the average numbers of neighbor wireless nodes, i.e., the total numbers of wireless nodes in simulation and the distance between the source and the destination wireless nodes. In the case (1), the coverage for the low density of neighbor wireless nodes and the short distance between the successive intermediate wireless nodes is relatively low. However, in the case (3), the coverage is sufficiently improved by introduction of the noise wireless signal transmissions by the 2-hop neighbor wireless nodes of the intermediate wireless node.

Next, we evaluate the performance of the proposed method in wireless multihop transmissions of data messages. Here, 100–1,000 wireless nodes with 50 m wireless signal transmission ranges are randomly distributed according to the unique distribution randomness in a 700 m × 700 m square field. A source and a destination wireless nodes are fixed at locations of (200, 200) and (500, 500), respectively. The coverage of the wireless signal transmission area of intermediate wireless nodes by those of 1- and 2-hop neighbor wireless nodes transmitting noise wireless signals is evaluated by using 1,000 different distribution of the wireless nodes.

Figure 10 shows the results of the experiments. (1) represents the coverage by the method in which only 1-hop neighbor wireless nodes of the intermediate wireless nodes transmit noise wireless signals and (2) represents the coverage by the proposed method in this paper in which part of 2-hop neighbor wireless nodes also transmit noise wireless signals to improve the coverage. Averagely, about 11% higher coverage is realized by (2) in comparison with (1). In addition, though the coverage is sensitive to the locations of wireless nodes, i.e., the coverage highly depends on length and angle of successive wireless communication links in (1), by introduction of the help of part of 2-hop neighbor wireless nodes, the coverage becomes more stable in (2) than in (1). Therefore, additional wireless noise transmitted by part of 2-hop neighbor wireless nodes of the intermediate wireless nodes highly contributes to more secure wireless multihop transmissions of data messages against silent eavesdropper wireless nodes.

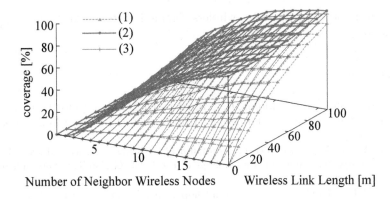

Fig. 9. Noise wireless signal coverage in 1-hop ad-hoc communication.

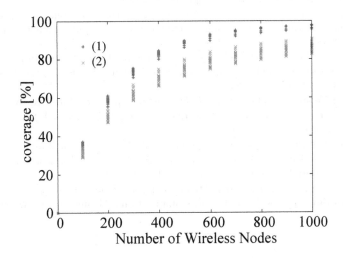

Fig. 10. Noise wireless signal coverage in wireless multihop communication.

5   Concluding Remarks

This paper proposes a novel secure wireless multihop data message transmissions by the intentional collisions with the noise wireless signals. Here, the noise wireless signals are transmitted by a part of the 1-hop and 2-hop neighbor wireless nodes of the intermediate wireless nodes to make difficult for possible eavesdropper wireless nodes to overhear the data messages. To select the neighbor wireless nodes transmitting the noise wireless signals, we extends AODV routing protocol with additional control messages. The results of the simulation experiments show that the coverage of the noise wireless signals is reasonably high. In future work, we will design an extended method to make better trade-off between coverage of the noise wireless signals, i.e, degree of security and transmission power consumption of the noise wireless signals in 1-hop and 2-hop neighbor wireless nodes.

References

1. Boneh, D., Dunworth, C., Lipton, R.J.: Breaking DES Using a Molecular Computer. In: Proceedings of the 1st International Workshop on DNA Based Computers, pp. 37–66 (1995)
2. He, X., Yener, A.: Two-hop secure communication using an untrusted relay: a case for cooperative jamming. In: Proceedings of the IEEE Global Telecommunications Conference 2008 (2008)
3. Kanachi, T., Higaki, H.: Wireless multihop transmissions for secret sharing communication. In: Proceedings of the 14th IEEE International Conference on Scalable Computing and Communications, pp. 808–813 (2014)
4. Kranakis, E., Singh, H., Urrutia, J.: Compass routing on geometric networks. In: Proceedings of the 11th Canadian Conference on Computational Geometry, pp. 51–54 (1999)
5. Shigeyasu, T., Matsuno, H., Morinaga, N.: Proposal of a method for improving MAC level fairness in the coexisting environment with legacy IEEE802.11DCF terminals. IPSJ J. **50**(3), 1156–1169 (2009)
6. Tekin, E., Yener, A.: The general Gaussian multiple-access and two-way wiretap channels: avhievable rates and cooperative jamming. IEEE Trans. Inf. Theory **54**(6), 2735–2750 (2008)
7. Toh, C.K., Vassiliou, V., Guichal, G., Shih, C.H.: MARCH: a medium access control protocol for multihop wireless ad hoc networks. In: Proceedings of IEEE/AFCEA Military Communication Conference, pp. 512–516 (2000)
8. Urrutia, J.: Two problems on discrete and computational geometry. In: Proceedings of Japan Conference on Discrete and Computational Geometry, pp. 42–52 (1999)

Towards Ontology Based Data Extraction for Organizational Goals Metrics Indicator

Tengku Adil Tengku Izhar[1(✉)] and Bernady O. Apduhan[2(✉)]

[1] Faculty of Information Management, Universiti Teknologi MARA,
UiTM Selangor, Shah Alam, Malaysia
tengkuadil@yahoo.co.uk
[2] Department of Information Science, Faculty of Science and Engineering,
Kyushu Sangyo University, Fukuoka, Japan
bob@is.kyusan-u.ac.jp

Abstract. In this paper, we proposed a measurement framework to evaluate the quality of results at organizational goals level. We proposed metrics indicators to guarantee and optimize the usage of data to extract useful information in organization. The framework is flexible to change without affecting things around because the framework is applicable in any domains. We discuss the review of the problems, proposed solution to the problems and draw a conclusion of this paper.

Keywords: Big data · Data extraction · Data analysis · Metrics · Ontology

1 Introduction

Organizational goals ontology focus on the usage of organizational data instead of knowledge, information or tools because organizational data is a major resource in every organization and it is important to evaluate the relevance of this organizational data in achieving the organizational goals. We also suggest organizational data is important as information and knowledge to assist the decision-making process [11–13]. In an organization, it is extremely important for the manager to have access to the most relevant organizational data in relation to the organizational goals. It's pointed out that sharing important data and information can provide the required knowledge to assist successful decision-making. It is crucial for organizations to create and generate new data and evaluate it to enhance decision-making. Different ways of generating new ideas, information and knowledge will help in terms of decision-making and will enable teams within the organization to use the most relevant organizational data to successfully achieve the organizational goals [1–5].

2 Literature Review

Most of the recent studies focus on the development of systems ontologies and enterprise ontologies [12, 13]. However, not many studies have been conducted on organizational goals developed an organizational ontology but this study discussed the

© Springer Nature Switzerland AG 2020
O. Gervasi et al. (Eds.): ICCSA 2020, LNCS 12252, pp. 261–276, 2020.
https://doi.org/10.1007/978-3-030-58811-3_19

development of knowledge mapping based on ontology. Previous study did not evaluate any organizational resources such as data, information or knowledge in their model, rather, they developed an ontology to show the relationship between the organizational role and organizational activity. ontology. There are a very limited number of studies which evaluate organizational resources, such as data, in relation to the organizational goals. An ontology shows the relationship between the knowledge domains within the organization. This domain knowledge is important for any future domain expert and entrepreneur to identify the goal elements in their organization. It is important for them to recognize the relevant data in relation to the organizational goals. In order to evaluate the organizational data, metrics is used. We suggest that a metrics model is important in measuring the extent to which the organization data are consistent with the organizational goals. The purpose of the organizational goals ontology is to improve the understanding of the organizational structure and the relationship between the organizational goals. Recent studies focus on the framework and the integration of ontology [3–5]. These two aspects are very important in the development of every ontology. However, an ontology also needs to focus on relationships and structure, especially in relation to organizational goals. Thus, other aspects that need to be considered are relationships and structure. Relationships and structure are important aspects in the achievement of the organizational goals. Therefore, an ontology is important to improve the common understanding of the structure and relationships in the achievement of the organizational goals.

3   Ontology

In organization, it is extremely important for the manager to have access to the most relevant organizational data in relation to the organizational goals. Sharing important data and information can provide the required knowledge to assist successful decision-making [11]. It is crucial for organizations to create and generate new data and evaluate it to enhance decision-making. Different ways of generating new ideas, information and knowledge will help in terms of decision-making and will enable teams within the organization to use the most relevant organizational data to successfully achieve the organizational goals. Data is presented in many forms such as documents and statistics. These data are the most important resources in relation to the organizational goals.

In this paper, the first step to identify the relevant organizational data is to recognize the matching set of organizational data to identify which organizational data relate to the organizational goals. A large body of existing work uses the terms record linkage, data linkage, record matching, and data matching. We use the term data dependency in an effort to identify the dependency relationship between the organizational data and organizational goals because we attempted to identify dependency for all organizational data that relate to organizational goals (Fig. 1).

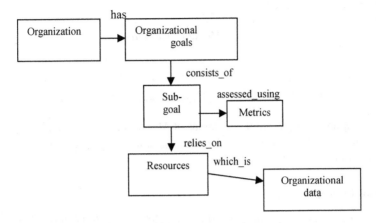

Fig. 1. Organizational goals ontology

3.1   Metric Rules

Metrics models are designed to address organization process which include organization objective and to assist the decision making process. Metric must be clarified.

Metrics. A verifiable measurement used to measure both quantitative and qualitative. As the volume of data increase, metric provide data refinement.

Metrics Requirement. Metric design of what need to be accomplished during the metrics process. Specific team attempts to identify the needs toward organization objective.

Verifiable: Set of data that has been agreed for converting process into measure.
Measure: Characteristics in a numerical or nominal form.

Metrics Analysis. Requirement must be fulfilled.

Control: Metrics enable to evaluate and control the source they are measures.
Communication: Communicate externally and internally for the purpose of control.
Improvement: Identify gaps for improvement.

Let's denote that metrics requirement clarify as verifiable and measure as $V_{erifiable}$ and M_{easure}

$$MetReq : (V_{erifiable}, M_{easure}) \tag{1}$$

and denote control, communication and improvement as C_{ontrol}, $C_{ommunication}$ and $I_{mprovement}$.

$$MetAna : (C_{ontrol}, C_{ommunication}, I_{mprovement}) \tag{2}$$

Above may also be written as

$$Met : (MetReq)(MetAna) \qquad (3)$$

so,

$$Met : \left(V_{erifiable}, M_{easure} \right) \left(C_{ontrol}, C_{ommunication}, I_{mprovement} \right) \qquad (4)$$

where *MetReq* and *MetAna* are the variables of *Met* which $V_{erifiable}$ and M_{easure} are the characteristics for *MetReq* and C_{ontrol}, $C_{ommunication}$ and $I_{mprovement}$ are the characteristics for *MetAna*.

3.2 Data Concepts

Collection of raw resources and converting this data into useful information. Organization relies on data in every aspect of their actions. It is important for organization to identify, create, store and analyse this data. Data must be clarified.

Data. Organization relies on this data toward organization objective and action. Specific team use data and convert it into valuable information.

Quality Data. Data must be in parallel with the organization's needs. Data in organization need to be subject-oriented such component of subject matter and improve the effectiveness in responding to queries. Thus, data must be,

Complete: Complete presence of the corresponding data records. Data completeness refer to the lack of needed fields.
Accurate: Data is correct and set a context for further analysis.
Current: Data is up to date to organization need.

We denote that complete, accurate and current as $C_{omplete}$, $A_{ccurate}$ and C_{urrent}. Thus,

$$Data : (QD) \qquad (5)$$

so,

$$Data : \left(C_{omplete}, A_{ccurate}, C_{urrent} \right) \qquad (6)$$

where data must be quality to support future need and performance. Data must be $C_{omplete}$, $A_{ccurate}$ and C_{urrent} in order to become quality.

3.3 Organizational Process

Organization process ($Org_{process}$) can be partitioned into several processes. However, organization process can be very large, so in this paper, the focus of organization process is on their existing data. The algorithms are defined based on the organization goals and to show the entire relationship of the organization goals rather than looking at the relationship between business side and data side. Our approach is to look at the organization data flow and the impact of data toward organization goals. Our approach is also intended to look at the relationship between the organization goals.

Process Input. During processing, the involved data called process input (P_i), where $\rightarrow$ is an involvement process. So decide,

$$\text{Org}_{\text{process}} \rightarrow P_i \tag{7}$$

Process Output. Every process generate output, so decide which organization process involve process output (P_o) where $\rightarrow$ also is an involvement process.

$$\text{Org}_{\text{process}} \rightarrow P_o \tag{8}$$

3.4   Data Process

Data process (D_{process}) can also be partitioned into several process. Here, process shows the flow of data within the organization.

Data Input. Every stage of the process involves data input. Every organization created data almost every day and this data is stored in data storage such as database. So data process involve data input (IN).

$$D_{\text{process}} \rightarrow IN \tag{9}$$

Data Output. Process generated output. Data stored in data storage need to be evaluated to make sure that the data is valuable for certain action. So decide which data process involve data output (OT)

$$D_{\text{process}} \rightarrow OT \tag{10}$$

Let, $\text{Org}_{\text{process}} = P_i, P_o$, where ϵ is a characteristic x can find in P_i. For example y is an output of x

$$\text{Org}_{\text{process}} = \left\{ \text{Org}_{\text{process}}(x, y) | x \in P_i, y \in P_o \right\}. \tag{11}$$

Then organization process can summarize as

$$\text{Org}_{\text{process}} = \left\{ \text{Org}_{\text{process}}(IN, OT) | IN \in P_i, OT \in P_o \right\}. \tag{12}$$

It shows the entire *Org*$_{process}$ rely on *IN* and *OT*. Here, P_i rely on *IN* and P_o rely on *OT*. The process define as y depend on x and it concludes as *OT* rely on *IN*. Objective and action are the main requirement to achieve the develop target within the organization. Develop target is organization main goals. Objective here can be assumed as sub-goals in order to assist the achievement of main goals.

Here, we already defined organization requirement as

$$Org_{requirement} : (Org_{objective})(Org_{actions}) \qquad (13)$$

and organization process, as Eq. (14), and assuming organization requirement as goal and objective as sub-goals

$$Org_{goal} = (Sub_{goals}, A_{ctions}) \qquad (14)$$

So, full relationship can be develop here as

$$Org_{goal} = (Sub_{goals}, A_{ctions}), \ Org_{process} = \{Org_{process}(IN, OT)| \ IN \in P_i, \ OT \in P_o\}. \qquad (17)$$

Summarized as,

$$Org_{goal} = \{Org_{goal}(x, y)| x \in A_{ctions}, y \in Sub_{goals}\} \qquad (15)$$

So,

$$Org_{goal} = \{Org_{goal}(IN, OT)| IN \in A_{ctions}, OT \in Sub_{goals}\}. \qquad (16)$$

It summarizes the entire relationship as Org_{goal} rely on Sub_{goals} and A_{ctions}. But as we understand, organization relies on data to support achieving the goals. Therefore, full relationship is defined as Sub_{goals} is an OT of Act where Sub_{goals} and A_{ctions} are the requirement for Org_{goal}. Ontology has a set of organization goal OG elements.

$$Ontology \ (O) = Organizational \ goals \ (OG) \qquad (17)$$

a set of sub-goal SG, action A and task T relation on the elements of OG, respectively.

For 2 ontologies O_1 and O_2, the set of possible pair of element is defined as

$$OG = (SG_1 \times SG_2) \cup (A_1 \times A_2) \cup (T_1 \times T_2) \qquad (18)$$

with SG_1, A_1 and T_1, the sets of elements of OG in O_1, and SG_2, A_2 and T_2, the sets of elements of OG in O_2.

Then, denote pair of elements (e_1, e_2) refers to the same elements. In other words, each elements $e_1 \equiv SG_1 \cup A_1 \cup T_1$, corresponds to on elements $e_2 \equiv SG_2 \cup A_2 \cup T_2$, and vice versa.

On the other issue, some issue may occur with the OG elements. "A" may have sub-action SA, and "T" may have a sub-task ST. Thus,

$$SG = (A_1 \times A_2) \cup (SA_1 \times SA_2) \tag{19}$$

$$A = (T_1 \times T_2) \cup (ST_1 \times ST_2) \tag{20}$$

with A_1 and SA_1, the set of element of SG_1, and A_2 and SA_2, the set of element of SG_2. T_1 and ST_2, the set of element of A_1, and T_2 and ST_2, the set of element of A_2. The elements of the relationship implies as:

Organization element
OE $\equiv$ {Set of all possible organization elements}
G $\equiv$ {Set of goal}
SG $\equiv$ {Set of sub-goal}
A $\equiv$ {Set of action}
T $\equiv$ {Set of task}

$$OE \equiv G \cup SG \cup A \cup T \tag{21}$$

Variables
V $\equiv$ {Set of all possible variables}
$V_x \equiv$ {Set of all dependent variables}
$V_y \equiv$ {Set of all independent variables}

$$V : x = (n) \text{ with } n \in V_x \tag{22}$$

$$V : y = (n) \text{ with } n \in V_y \tag{23}$$

Relationship

R $\equiv$ {Set of possible relationship}
OR $\equiv$ {Set of organization relationship}
VR $\equiv$ {Set of variables relationship}
R $\equiv f$ (OE(G(SG(A(T)))))
OE $\equiv f$ (G(SG(A(T))))
G $\equiv f$ (SG(A(T)))
SG $\equiv f$ (A(T))
A $\equiv f$ (T)

Define as

$$x \equiv f(y) \tag{24}$$

Therefore, we show the entire relationship as

$$OE \equiv f(G(SG(A(T)))) \tag{25}$$

where OE is a relationship between G, SG, A and T. In order to look at the possible variable, we define the relationship based on several factor where sum of $\sum$ and number of size n. The factors are:

if sub-goal implies
cause goal

$$\frac{SG(n)}{(\sum SG)} = G \tag{26}$$

if action implies
cause sub-goal

$$\frac{A(n)}{(\sum A)} = SG \tag{27}$$

if task implies
cause action

$$\frac{T(n)}{(\sum T)} = A \tag{28}$$

Based on the factor definition, we defined the variable as

$$x \equiv f(y) \tag{29}$$

where, variable x depend on variable y. Based on the variables, we define G as

$$G \equiv f(y) \tag{30}$$

$$G \equiv f(SG) \tag{31}$$

$$G \equiv f(SG_i \wedge SG_n) \tag{32}$$

where, G depend several number of SG. For example SG1 and SG2, SG2 and SG3. Thus, we assume G depend on the number of SG as written below

$$G = \frac{\sum G}{n} \tag{33}$$

$$G = \frac{SG(n)}{(\sum SG)} \tag{34}$$

If we define SG, then

$$SG \equiv f(y) \tag{35}$$

$$SG \equiv f(A) \tag{36}$$

$$SG \equiv f(A_i \wedge A_n) \tag{37}$$

where, SG depend several number of A. For example A1 and A2, A2 and A3. Thus, we assume SG depend on the number of A as written below

$$SG = \frac{\sum SG}{n} \tag{39}$$

$$SG = \frac{A(n)}{(\sum A)} \tag{40}$$

If we define A, then

$$A \equiv f(y) \tag{41}$$

$$A \equiv f(T) \tag{42}$$

$$A \equiv f(T_i \wedge T_n) \tag{43}$$

Where, A depend several number T. For example T1 and T2, T2 and T3. Thus, we assume A depend on the number of T as written below

$$A = \frac{\sum A}{n} \tag{44}$$

$$A = \frac{T(n)}{(\sum T)} \tag{45}$$

The other situation, if organization only require one of the variable between SG and A, then we define the relationship as

$$G \equiv f(SG_i \vee SG_n | SG_i \supset SG_n) \tag{46}$$

where, G rely on several number of SG. For example, G relies on SG1 or SG2, where SG2 depend on SG1. We define SG as

$$SG \equiv f(A_i \vee A_n | A_i \supset A_n) \tag{47}$$

where, SG rely on several number of A. For example, SG relies on A1 or A2, where A2 depend on A1. Then we define A as

$$A \equiv f(T_i \vee T_n | T_i \supset T_n) \tag{48}$$

where, A rely on several number of T. For example, A relies on T1 or T2, where T2 depend on T1.

4   Metric Requirement

We define metric requirement as a metric design of what needs to be accomplished during the metrics process. Specific team attempts to identify the needs toward organization objective. Thus, we identify two variables toward metric requirements which are verifiable and measure. Verifiable: a set of data that been agreed for converting process into measure. Measure: characteristics in a numerical or nominal form.

4.1   Metric Analysis

Metric analysis is defined as a requirement that must be fulfilled toward metric development. We identify three variables toward metric analysis which are control, communication and improvement.

Control: The ability of metric to evaluate and control the source that they measure.
Communication: The ability of metric to communicate externally and internally for the purpose of control.
Improvement: The ability to identify the gaps for improvement.

Based from the discussion of metric requirement and metric analysis, the metric can be written as
Metric: (MetReq)(MetAna)
and
Metric: ($V_{erifiable}$, M_{easure}) (C_{ontrol}, $C_{ommunication}$, $I_{mprovement}$)
where, the metric requirement and metric analysis are the variables of metric model. Verifiable and measure are the characteristics for metric requirement. Control, communication and improvement are the characteristics for metric analysis. Metric model in this paper allow the evaluation of organization data toward gaps, setting and change. We denote sub-goal as SG, action as A, sub-action as SA, task as T and sub-task as ST for our proposition example. We assume that

$$SG \rightarrow (A \rightarrow SG) (SA \rightarrow A)$$
$$(T \rightarrow A) (ST \rightarrow T) \text{ and}$$
$$(SG \rightarrow \ulcorner A) \rightarrow (SA (SG \rightarrow \ulcorner A)$$

SG is implied if $\ulcorner A$ is true and SA is implies to achieve SG and A
$(A \rightarrow \ulcorner SA) \rightarrow (T (A \rightarrow \ulcorner SA)$
A is implied if $\ulcorner SA$ is true and T is implies to achieve A and SA
$(SA \rightarrow \ulcorner T) \rightarrow (ST (SA \rightarrow \ulcorner T) \rightarrow (T \rightarrow \ulcorner ST)$
SA is implied if $\ulcorner T$ is true and ST is implies to achieve SA and T. T is implies if $\ulcorner ST$ is true.

5   Case Study

5.1   The World Bank

Most data in the World Bank dataset comes from the governments of individual countries. The World Bank collects data on living standards and debt, but not much else. Some also comes from various international and national agencies with which World Bank partners (see http://ucatlas.ucsc.edu/data.html). These data are grown from the commitment of the member countries that participate with the development projects since early 1950s. The variety of data types is also diverse and data are not just created in spreadsheets or tables but also in charts, maps and audio/video. Therefore, managing and analyzing these data can be very challenging.

The World Bank collects and processes large amounts of data and generates them on the basis of economic models. These data have gradually been made available to the public in a way that encourages reuse. The World Bank stores data of reconstruction and development for 188 countries on 20 different topics. The topics incorporate different data indicators that store data from 1960 to 2014. For example, one of the data indicators for economic growth is agriculture (value added). The data are collected from 1960–2014 for 188 countries. This dataset create large amount of data only for one indicator under one topic.

The World Bank provides an analysis and visualisation tool that contains collections of time series data on a variety of topics that allow us to create our own queries. Therefore, we can generate tables and dashboards as new knowledge to be shared. In this case study, we present queries as the goals. Then we capture relevant data from huge amount of the datasets in relation to the goals. We define the metrics to analyse this data and present it in the dashboard to support decision-making in light to the goals.

5.2   An Ontology for the World Bank

In this paper, the queries are created from the topics. We define these queries as goals. In order to evaluate these topics, we develop an ontology for the World Bank to filter large collection of data. Therefore, we can identify the relationship between the topics and data indicators. An ontology creates knowledge to helps us to define the goals that we want to evaluate. We can make a decision on which goals we want to evaluate and which data are relevant to the goals.

The amount of data stores in the World Bank make it difficult for us to identify the goals that we want to evaluate. Based on the World Bank's website, data can be identified from the topics and data indicators. Figure 2 shows the relationship based on an ontology that classifies the topics.

Based on these topics, there are few data indicators that can be identified. Figure 3 shows some examples of data indicators that relate to the certain topics. This ontology helps us to create any query.

In this paper, we refer ourselves as information professional. Using the information that we have, we set the goals that we want to evaluate. Based on the goals, we can capture relevant data that relate to the goals.

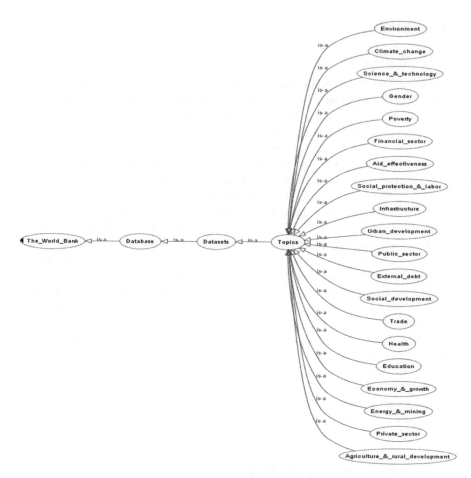

Fig. 2. Data are extracting the topics from the World Bank using Protégé OntoGraf.

5.3   Identify the Goals for the World Bank

In this case study, we aim to analyse the level of the economic growth in South East Asia in 2013. We decide to analyse the development in Indonesia, Cambodia, Malaysia, Philippines and Singapore. According to the World Bank, economic growth is central to economic development. When national income grows, real people benefit. Data can help policy-makers better understand their countries' economic situations and guide any work toward improvement. Data here covers measures of economic growth that includes indicators representing factors known to be relevant to economic growth, such as industry, manufacture, services, agriculture and household.

In order to achieve this aim, we analyse these five indicators that we believe is important to evaluate the development level of the economic growth in South East Asia. This is how we want to define the goals in this paper. We are mindful of the fact that information professionals might define the goals in a different way to the way we

Fig. 3. Data are extract using Protégé OntoGraf to shows the indicators from four different topics.

have undertaken to define the goal, which would require a different approach to evaluate the goals.

Economic growth is central to economic development. When national income grows, real people benefit. While there is no known formula for stimulating economic growth, data can help information professionals to assist the policy-makers with better understand the economic situations in South East Asia and guide any work toward improvement. Data here covers measures of economic growth based on the value added for industry, agricultural, manufacturing, service and household.

According to the World Bank website, value added is the net output of a sector after adding up all outputs and subtracting intermediate inputs. It is calculated without making deductions for depreciation of fabricated assets or depletion and degradation of natural resources. The origin of value added is determined by the International Standard Industrial Classification (ISIC), revision 3. In this case study, data are in current U.S. dollars.

- Five goals in relation to the economic growth, as shown in Fig. 3.

Goal 1: Development of services for wholesale and retail trade
Services correspond to ISIC divisions 50–99. They include value added in wholesale and retail trade (including hotels and restaurants), transport, and government, financial, professional, and personal services such as education, health care, and real estate services. Also included are imputed bank service charges, import duties, and any statistical discrepancies noted by national compilers as well as discrepancies arising from rescaling.

Goal 2: Development of agricultural production
Agriculture corresponds to ISIC divisions 1–5 and includes forestry, hunting, and fishing, as well as cultivation of crops and livestock production.

Goal 3: Development of manufacturing to supports industries growth
Manufacturing refers to industries belonging to ISIC divisions 15–37.

Goal 4: Development of industry to supports sustainable growth
Industry corresponds to ISIC divisions 10–45 and includes manufacturing (ISIC divisions 15–37). It comprises value added in mining, manufacturing (also reported as a separate subgroup), construction, electricity, water, and gas.

Goal 5: Development of household value for goods and services
Household is the market value of all goods and services, including durable products (such as cars, washing machines, and home computers), purchased by households. It

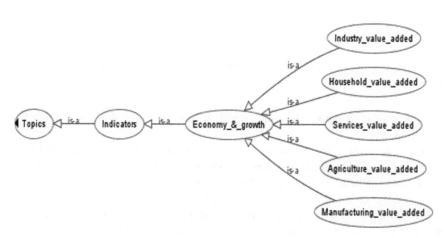

Fig. 4. Protégé OntoGraf for the World Bank to evaluate the development of economic growth in South East Asia.

excludes purchases of dwellings but includes imputed rent for owner-occupied dwellings (Fig. 4).

6 Conclusions

The discussion include how the organizational goals are identified, the possible sub-goals and variables that relate to the organizational goals, how to identify data that has been presented to the organizational goals, how to analyze organizational data and use this analysis results as a feedback to evaluate the level of the organizational goals achievement.

This paper discussed on how the framework aims to be applicable, repeatable, flexible and configurable in many domains. Big data analytics could be used to examine large amounts of data of a variety of types to discover useful information. Such information can provide a competitive advantage to help better decisions be made in relation to the organizational goals. The primary goal of big data analytics is to help companies make better business decisions by enabling data analyst to analyze huge volumes of transaction data which remains an unresolved challenge for conventional business intelligence programs.

The challenge in terms of big data analytics includes how the framework searches, transfers, captures and analyze the data from the vast collection of datasets. Due to the flexibility of the framework, it can capture large sets of data that relate to the organizational goals. This data will be analyzed and the results can assist the decision-making process in relation to the organizational goals.

References

1. Ordonez, C., Zhang, Y.Q., Cabrera, W.: The gamma matrix to summarize dense and sparse data sets for big data analytics. IEEE Trans. Knowl. Data Eng. **28**, 1905–1918 (2016)
2. Ortega, F.M., Subias, J., Cassany, D.: An ethnographic approach to digital literacy in a Compulsory Secondary Education Institute in Barcelona. CPU-E Revista De Investigacion Educativa, pp. 190–215, July–December 2016
3. Papakonstantinou, P.A., Woodruff, D.P., Yang, G.: True Randomness from big data. Sci. Rep. **6**, 33740 (2016)
4. Park, E.-M., Seo, J.-H., Ko, M.-H.: The effects of leadership by types of soccer instruction on big data analysis. Cluster Comput. **19**(3), 1647–1658 (2016). https://doi.org/10.1007/s10586-016-0609-2
5. Phuapan, P., Viriyavejakul, C., Pimdee, P.: An analysis of digital literacy skills among Thai University Seniors. Int. J. Emerg. Technol. Learn. **11**, 24–31 (2016)
6. Kobayashi, K., Kaito, K.: Big data-based deterioration prediction models and infrastructure management: towards assetmetrics. Struct. Infrastruct. Eng. **13**, 84–93 (2017)
7. Broderick, S.R., Santhanam, G.R., Rajan, K.: Harnessing the big data paradigm for ICME: shifting from materials selection to materials enabled design. JOM **68**(8), 2109–2115 (2016). https://doi.org/10.1007/s11837-016-2019-6
8. Puthal, D., Nepal, S., Ranjan, R., Chen, J.J.: A dynamic prime number based efficient security mechanism for big sensing data streams. J. Comput. Syst. Sci. **83**, 22–42 (2017)

9. Wikibon. Big data vendor revenue and market forecast 2013–2017, 2014, 26 June 2015. http://wikibon.org/wiki/v/Big_Data_Vendor_Revenue_and_Market_Forecast_2013-2017
10. Sharma, S., Osei-Bryson, K.-M.: Organization-ontology based framework for implementing the business understanding phase of data mining projects. In: International Conference on System Sciences, Hawaii, p. 27 (2008)
11. Izhar, T.A.T., Torabi, T., Bhatti, M.I., Liu, F.: Recent developments in the organization goals conformance using ontology. Expert Syst. Appl. **40**, 4252–4267 (2013)
12. Schoeneborn, D., Kuhn, T.R., Kärreman, D.: The communicative constitution of organization, organizing, and organizationality. Organ. Stud. **40**, 475–496 (2019)
13. Wu, B.: The semantic retrieval system for learning resources based on subject knowledge ontology. Adv. Comput. Sci. Res. **80**, 467–469 (2018)

International Workshop on Geodesign in Decision Making:Meta Planning and Collaborative Design for Sustainable and Inclusive Development (GDM 2020)

Geodesign as Co-creation of Ideas to Face Challenges in Indigenous Land in the South of Brazil: Case Study Ibirama La Klano

Ana Clara Mourão Moura[1]([⊠]) [iD], Francisco Henrique de Oliveira[2] [iD],
Thobias Furlanetti[3] [iD], Regina Panceli[3] [iD],
Elna Fatima Pires de Oliveira[3], and Carl Steinitz[4]

[1] Escola de Arquitetura, Universidade Federal de Minas Gerais (UFMG),
Rua Paraíba 697, Belo Horizonte, Brazil
anaclara@ufmg.br
[2] Universidade do Estado de Santa Catarina (UDESC), Av. Me. Benvenuta,
Florianópolis 2007, Brazil
chico.udesc@gmail.com
[3] Defesa Civil do Estado de Santa Catarina (DCSC), Av. Gov. Ivo Silveira,
Florianópolis 2320, Brazil
{thobias,reginapanceli}@spg.sc.gov.br,
elna@defesacivil.sc.gov.br
[4] Harvard University, Massachusetts Hall, Cambridge, USA
csteinitz@gsd.harvard.edu

Abstract. Strong development pressures affect areas in South American countries, resulting in conflicts of interests in land use and ownership, and problems of environmental protection and anthropization. Geodesign proved to be a robust systematic methodological framework to guide a workshop in which the actors are real people of the place, professionals from public administration and the academy. The paper presents a case study about an indigenous land in Santa Catarina, South of Brazil, called Ibirama La Klano, the territory of Xokleng indigenous group. In 1970 a huge dam was constructed in their land to control flooding downstream in the Itajaí valley, but it ended up causing the flooding of their place. The goal of the Geodesign workshop was to support a meeting in which different actors could co-create ideas to face vulnerabilities and to develop potentialities of the area. To prepare Geodesign workshop the academic group from UFMG and UDESC worked with the Civil Defense of the State of Santa Catarina, constructing maps about the place and evaluations about suitable areas to receive proposals. The indigenous main executive chief and regional chiefs were invited to Geodesign workshop, which resulted in ideas representing values of different sectors of society, arriving to a negotiated design.

Keywords: Geodesign · Geoprocessing · Territorial planning · Co-creation

© Springer Nature Switzerland AG 2020
O. Gervasi et al. (Eds.): ICCSA 2020, LNCS 12252, pp. 279–295, 2020.
https://doi.org/10.1007/978-3-030-58811-3_20

1 Introduction

Strong development pressures affect urban and rural areas in South American countries, as the population grows and people migrate from the countryside, resulting in conflicts of interests in land use and land ownership, and problems related to environmental protection and anthropization of the territory. Design to accommodate these conflicts and challenges is often guided solely by economic factors and implemented without consideration of social and environmental factors and, mainly, without considering the opinion of people of the place and the actors involved in the process. This approach risks unsustainable forms of land use and territorial planning.

Investment in new methodologies, procedures, collaborations and technology are needed, and Geodesign proved to be a robust systematic methodological framework to guide a workshop in which the actors are real people of the place, professionals from public administration and the academy.

Geodesign is design "with" the territory and "for" the territory. It aims at the contextualized transformation of the landscape, respecting nature and culture. Geodesign can provide a systematic methodological framework for regional, urban and local planning, aiming at the sustainable integration of human activities with the natural environment, respecting cultural peculiarities and enabling a democratic decision-making process.

It is a method of collective construction of alternative futures for a landscape or territory, which can be applied at any scale, in which citizen listening is fundamental to the construction of opinions and decision-making. It is largely based on geo-visualization applications, even if they are analog. The principle is to inform the participant about the main characteristics of the place, and for this it is necessary to provide a set of thematic information and its syntheses in main systems, which will be the basis for the co-creation of policies and projects.

Important authors such as Dangermond [1], Ervin [2], Flaxman [3], Miller [4] have already written about the theme, presenting their contributions, but the work of Steinitz [5] stands out, who structured the procedures through a methodological framework, a work framework. This methodological framework was expanded and disseminated throughout the world through the use of the web-based platform GeodesignHub that favors the development of the collaborative workshop, developed by Ballal under the supervision of Steinitz [6, 7].

Steinitz [5] presents a work structure in the form of a framework with six steps to be followed, composed of six models. The paths in these six models must be done three times, in what he calls three iterations, for adjustments and adjustments to the requirements of the case study (Fig. 1).

The case study developed was about an indigenous land in Santa Catarina, South of Brazil, called Ibirama La Klano. It's an area of 37018 km². The indigenous group called "Xokleng" had the first contact with the white men just 105 years ago, so they keep important values about land use and territory (Fig. 2).

In the 1970's, without any previous consultation on the opinion of the Indians, a huge dam was constructed, with the goal to control flooding downstream in the Itajaí valley. According to Fraga [8, 9], the dam stated to be constructed in 1976 and was

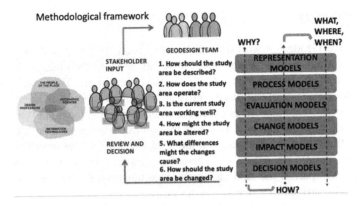

Fig. 1. Geodesign framework proposed by Steinitz [5].

Fig. 2. Images of the place: (a) the colonizer house; (b) the point where the Indians met the first white man; (c) Indigenous Land Ibirama La Klano; (d) Municipality of José Boiteux, in the State of Santa Catarina, where the area is located. Source: Organized by the authors from CDSC Report and Wikipedia.

finished in 1992. The intention was to protect the medium and low part of the valley, but it ended up causing the flooding of the high valley, in 900 hectares of Ibirama land, especially the most productive land, which influenced their livelihood. There are movies that tell about the issue, presenting their challenges and difficulties: https:// youtu.be/VCM5yu56Gzk and https://youtu.be/_awC-Ri1aa0.

The goal of the Geodesign workshop was to support a meeting in which different actors could co-create ideas to face vulnerabilities and to develop potentialities of the area.

2 Methodology

To prepare the Geodesign workshop the academic group, composed by the Federal University of Minas Gerais and the State University of Santa Catarina, worked with the Civil Defense of the State of Santa Catarina. They constructed Thematic Maps about the main characteristics of the place and Evaluation Maps about the suitable areas to receive proposals. The indigenous executive chief (sagamore, the main "cacique") and regional chiefs were invited and took part in the Geodesign workshop, together with technicians from the Civil Defense and the academic group. The meeting resulted in designs representing the values of different sectors of society and portions of the territory, as each part of the land, downstream or upstream of the dam has its expectations, but also arrived in a negotiated design.

Just after defining the main challenges to be faced, discussing vulnerabilities and potentialities, the conductor group prepares data about the case study, which are Representation Models, to answer how the area should be described. In this step happened many important meetings with the academic group and the Civil Defense of Santa Catarina State, mainly with the technicians that work with indigenous case studies and could tell us about their culture, their land, their way of living. Expressive efforts were done to get data and to construct georeferenced information.

The data organized was transformed in the spatial distribution of occurrences and phenomena's, resulting in Process Models to answer about how does the study area operates. Geoprocessing models were applied, as slope models, satellite classification to map land cover, calculation of NDVI (Normalized Difference Vegetation Index) to map vegetation and their characteristics, buffers of hot-spot elements, buffers of roads, concentration of houses, areas of influence of elements like the dam, and so one. The academic group using geoprocessing knowledge conducted the works.

The third step was based in the definition of main systems, which are the main research themes on which they want to listen to citizens and promote the co-creation of policy and project ideas for the area. The systems legend must be divided into the classes: very indicated (feasible), adequate (suitable), possible (capable), inappropriate (inappropriate) and resource that already exists or already solved (existing). These systems, as the name implies, are compositions of sets of variables of interest to the theme, which can be integrated by Combinatorial Analysis or by Weights of Evidence, presenting to users, a previous judgment or an opinion of the workshop conductors about the most suitable places to propose ideas. The combination of variables analyzing if the area is working well results in Evaluation Models. These models are uploaded in the platform to be used in the Geodesign workshop, as bases to guide the users about the suitability for change of each part of the territory.

The organizers also have to suggest targets, investigate costs and define a matrix of conflicts of interests. This information will be used in Impact Models, which tells about what differences might the changes proposed by the participants in the workshop can cause.

With Representation, Process, Evaluation and data to Impact Models already constructed, it was time to conduct the presential workshop. The workshop was held in UDESC, during "Geodesign South America 2019", as part of the conference activities.

The workshop received numerous participants, and it was necessary to distribute them to two computers' laboratories, placed side-by-side. Carl Steinitz conducted the workshop, with the support of Ana Clara Moura.

The participants were composed by professors of public and private universities, technicians from public administration, Civil Defense group, undergraduate and post-graduate students, indigenous representatives. It's important to highlight that the main hierarchy of the Indians came to the workshop.

The participants, representing actors of the society, were divided in two rooms and were asked to propose and defend ideas of teams established according to territorial divisions and social divisions: Public Administration, Civil Defense, Non-Adopters (people that was not willing to propose changes), Down (people from low part of the valley), Low (people from the medium valley) and Up (the high part of the stream).

They were asked to draw diagrams about policies and projects to the 10 systems, that are the main thematic discussion considering vulnerabilities and potentialities of the area: displacement, risk, new houses, area of operation (also corresponding to the hydro), accessibility, agriculture, vegetation, tourism and culture, entrepreneurship, others. Each team proposed at least one idea of a project or policy for each system.

After drawing the diagrams, they were asked to select, from all the systems, the ideas they approved, among all of those proposed by them and by the other teams, and to save the first design, that is a Master Plan to the territory. They defended orally their ideas and had the opportunity to construct a second design because Steinitz [5] explains that the first design is not the best one, so it's a way to make them prepare a better proposal.

They were asked to analyze the proposals of the all the teams, and were asked to compose one proposal per room, based on negotiation: in room 1, conducted by Steinitz, the group was composed by the teams Down, Low and Up; in room 2, conducted by Ana Clara Moura, the group was composed by the teams Civil Defense, Public Administration, and Non-Adopters.

Two designs resulted from the previous step, one per room, and all the participants went to the auditorium, where the last and final design was composed based on negotiation. The steps of the process can be summarized in the framework (Fig. 3):

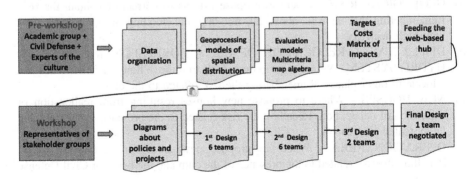

Fig. 3. Main steps in methodological framework. Source: The authors.

3 Development and Analysis

The development of any spatial analysis as a basis for proposing territorial planning actions requires clear knowledge about the object under study and the research objectives. This stage consists of the definition of the systems' analysis, which is chosen according to the main themes for the demands or needs of discussions.

In the case study of the Indigenous Land, based on the videos watched and interviews with experts on the topic and on the region, the main problems were the conflicts resulting from the construction of the dam and the flooding of the lands upstream resulted from that intervention. Added to these problems there is also the responsibility of the Civil Defense to serve the people of the place and, therefore, to negotiate emergency access and risk protection areas.

On the other hand, in order to guarantee indigenous peoples' survival resources on the lands, it would also be necessary to discuss potentialities related to cultural tourism, sustainable agriculture, improvements in infrastructure conditions related to accessibility, possible diversification in land use considering protection and requalification of vegetation cover, choices of strategic locations for new housing or for the eventual displacement of units at risk of flood impacts.

From the problematization, the production of data was started, transformed into information by geoprocessing models, and prepared for use during the workshop. The investment time in this stage was about 40 h spread over 2 months, in weekly meetings by videoconference and development in a geoprocessing laboratory.

3.1 Representation Models

Once the main characteristics of the place were identified, it resulted in the definition of the 10 systems: tourism/culture; displacement/relocation related to hydro system; geological risks; places for new houses; operation area to be protected against use; accessibility; sustainable agriculture; vegetation protection or requalification; possible entrepreneurship; other ideas. The system "other ideas" was proposed to receive ideas that were not considered in the previous systems. The goals of the systems were:

a) GEOLOGICAL RISK - Where to propose actions to correct or contain the risk. Remembering that there is, above all, flooding and flooding, in addition to areas with high declivity.
b) DISPLACEMENT/RELOCATION OF USE – CORRESPONDING ALSO TO HYDRO SYSTEM - Where to propose actions to remove housing or activities and relocate to other places. Remembering the risk related to the dam.
c) NEW HOUSES - Where to propose new houses resulting from reallocation or expansion of occupation. Recalling the risk related to the presence of the dam and the potential for growth.
d) OPERATION AREA - Where to propose new areas for operational safety. Recalling the risk related to the presence of the dam and the need for Civil Defense action.
e) VEGETATION - Where to propose new areas for protection or requalification of vegetation. Remembering the expressive vegetation to be protected, since the fact of

being an indigenous reserve does not eliminate the possibility of suppression of vegetation cover.

f) ACCESSIBILITY - Where to propose new accesses or qualify existing ones. Recalling the need to integrate areas to favor services, assistance and entrepreneurship.

g) AGRICULTURE - Where to propose new areas of activity or increase existing ones. Recalling the need for production for subsistence, but also the possibilities of entrepreneurship.

h) TOURISM AND CULTURE - Where to propose areas for exploration or increased visitation activities. Recalling the possibility of receiving interested in knowing the activities of the local culture and way of life, in ecological and adventure tours, among others.

i) ENTREPRENEURSHIP - Where to propose new areas of activity or increase existing ones. Recalling the possibility of making culture and way of life sources of entrepreneurship, related to products and interest in visits.

j) OTHERS - Free system to receive proposals that do not fit in the previous systems. It only blocks the Integral Protection Conservation Unit and authorizes proposals in any part of the territory, since they can be of any nature.

Some images of the main representation models, that tells about "how should the area be described" are presented. To construct them we used satellite images (Sentinel 2A, from Copernicus Program) that was classified according to land use and NDVI (Normalized Difference Vegetation Index); collection of data by field camp made by the Civil Defense (touristic attractions, roads, dam limits, and existing houses); DEM data (Alos Palsar from Alaska Satellite Facility, about Digital Elevation Data) to calculate slopes; and official data from the public administration (administrative limits and Conservation Units of sustainable use and of permanent protection) (Fig. 4).

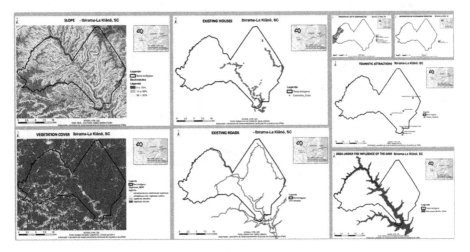

Fig. 4. Some thematic cartographic data produced: slope, vegetation cover, existing houses, existing roads, conservation units, tourist attractions, area of influence of the dam. Source: The authors.

3.2   Processes Models

With the goal to understand how the area operates, the data produced was classified according to the interest of each system, and received colors according to Geodesign semiotics proposed by Steinitz [10]:

- Dark green – "Feasible" for the best condition to receive ideas of projects and policies,
- Medium green – "Suitable" for not the best but a very good place to receive ideas of projects and policies,
- Light green – "Capable" for not a very good but an acceptable area to receive ideas of projects and policies,
- Yellow – "Not appropriate" for areas not indicated for projects or policies of that thematic,
- Red – "Existing" for areas in which the problem as already solved and it was worthless for projects or policies.

To each system was defined a set of maps and they were processed according to the specific needs of the thematic. For example: a Slope Map in the system Risks could be organized in the legends defining the most fragile areas to be protected and the areas to which it was not necessary to do an intervention (more than 47% - most fragile in terms of risks, 30–47% - medium risks, 0–30% not in risks of slope); but the same map, when used in the system Agriculture presented the legends defining areas that were most suitable for agriculture and specifying those that were not good due to topographic difficulties (0 to 5 – excellent, 5 – 15 – acceptable, more than 15% not suitable). In this sense, what is dark green (feasible) is the opposite in each case (Fig. 5).

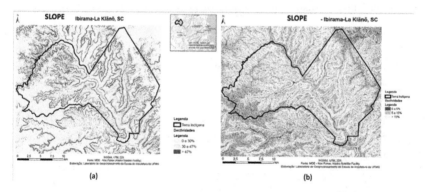

Fig. 5. Slope Map presenting different legends and semiotics, according to the system it's going to be used: (a) Slope Map in Risks System; (b) Slope Map is Agriculture System. Source: The authors.

3.3   Evaluation Models

The evaluation models have the goal to indicate if the area is working well, presenting those that are most suitable for proposals of projects or policies. It is constructed as support to participants of the Geodesign workshop, presented as a background map, to guide them where to put their contribution.

It is a result of a map algebra in which the organizers select the main variables to be combined and classify them according to their opinion of suitability to the thematic. Even when the organization group listen to people's opinion and apply methods to do a more democratic decision about the evaluation, it is still a qualitative map based on opinions. Therefore, they will never consider all possible variables (because anytime someone can arrive with a new suggestion of map to be included), and they will never feet all the possible opinions about what is more important.

Evaluation Maps have a great level of uncertainty that it is more representative if the thematic goes from technical subjects to cultural subjects. Risks Map can have less uncertainty than New Housing Map because the first one is based on quantitative parameters while the second one is based on qualitative parameters that change with local culture and even change among individuals. The problems related to the use of Evaluation Maps were observed in many workshops conducted by UFMG group because in Brazilian culture people don't accept very well the pre-defined map telling where is the best place for something, or they don't feel comfortable until its explained how the map was created, or them just don't care about the Evaluation maps during the workshop and prefer to use a general base map to draw their ideas [11–13].

Evaluation Maps results from the combination of selected variables, which can be characterized as an overlay of levels in Multicriteria Analysis (MCA). There are two methods of combining variables in MCA: based on Weighted Sum and based on Combinatorial Analysis [14]. When the relationship among the variables can result in an index, classified in a ranking and resulted from different weights applied to define the hierarchical importance of each variable, the method is the Weighted Sum [14, 15]. However, when the relationship among the variables must be decided defining which is the most important and must be on top of decisions, and then continue this definition changing levels positions of variables, the method is the Combinatorial Analysis [14].

The majority of Evaluation Maps used in Geodesign workshops are more robust if constructed according to Combinatorial Analysis. It is necessary to previously classify each layer of variables according to the Geodesign semiotics (dark green, medium green, light green, yellow and red), and it's not sad that all colors will be used, because they are definitions of conditions that may not exist. The user takes first the green elements from all variables and combines them, and if he uses transparency, the greener he can see the more expressive is the spatial combinations of suitability conditions. Then the user takes the yellow elements, but all of them must be together overlaying the previous combination because even if it considered "not appropriate" in just one layer, the area is undoubtedly not appropriate. Finally, he uses the red elements overall, defining areas in which the resources already exist and is useless to receive more projects or policies. The combinations are tested in geovisualization, but must be constructed in map algebra of addition and subtraction (Fig. 6). The conductor can share decisions with a group.

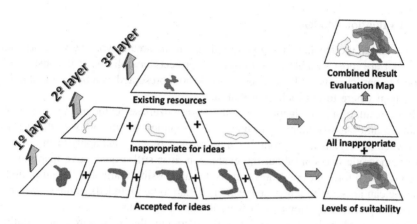

Fig. 6. Combinatorial Analysis classifying the territory according to levels of suitability: from accepted areas for ideas, to inappropriate areas for ideas, to areas already with existing resources. Source: The authors.

As an example is presented the construction of Evaluation Map to the system "Tourism and Culture", to which it was decided to work with the variables area of influence of the dam, area of influence of existing roads, indigenous houses, trails, touristic attractions, and conservation unit of permanent protection. From this 6 variables, 5 of them are potentialities and 1 is vulnerability (conservation unit of permanent protection), what means that the 5 potentialities are colored in green and combined, while the vulnerability defines an area that is not appropriate for tourism (Fig. 7, Fig. 8).

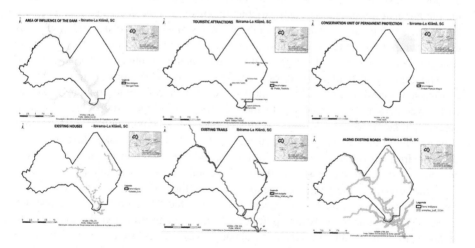

Fig. 7. Combinatorial Analysis classifying the territory according to levels of suitability, example of "Tourism and Culture": the variables classified. Source: The authors.

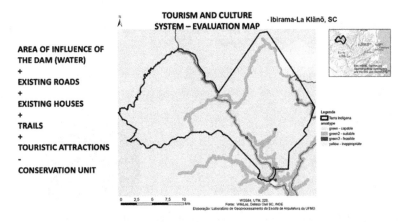

Fig. 8. Combinatorial Analysis classifying the territory according to levels of suitability, example of "Tourism and Culture": the Evaluation Map produced. Source: The authors.

All the Evaluation Maps were created the same way to be used as systems during the workshop (Fig. 9). It was also necessary to prepare external layers, that are data to be visualized as a spatial reference to recognize places and territorial characteristics (Fig. 10).

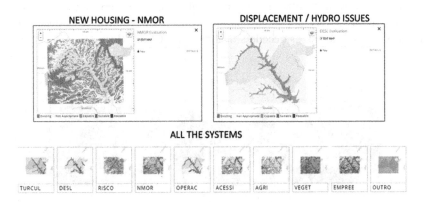

Fig. 9. All the Evaluation Maps used as systems and examples of two of them: New Housing (with the goal to discuss where to build new houses) and Displacement/Hydro Issues (with the goal to discuss what to do in areas under risk of flood). Source: The authors, using GeodesignHub.

3.4   The Workshop: Co-creation of Ideas

Once all the information to the workshop was constructed, it was organized to be held in "Geodesign South America 2019", that happened in the end of 2019 in Florianópolis, UDESC. The workshop started in the auditorium, with the Indigenous Chiefs presenting their problems and conditions of life. After watching a video about

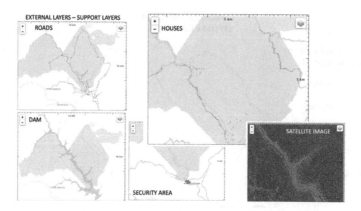

Fig. 10. External layers: roads, house, dam, security area, and satellite image. Source: The authors, using GeodesignHub.

the place, people were divided into groups to start working. The participants were divided into teams according to territorial representation (low valley, medium valley, and high valley, called UP, LOW and DOWN) and according to actors of the society (Civil Defense, Public Administration, and Non-Adopters Stakeholders). These teams were defined by Carl Steinitz. The indigenous representatives were invited to take part as consultants from their values and culture, which means two of them were in one room and one was in the other room, and people asked their opinion to construct the proposals. It was a very important opportunity to listen to them, to understand their point of view, and to ask as decoders of their expectations (Fig. 11).

Fig. 11. Teams developing their proposals consulting the Indians' opinion: (a) The main Indigenous Chief explains their problems; (b) People constructing the proposals in co-creation of ideas; (c) Working on teams. Source: The authors.

The teams were asked to design diagrams with proposals of projects and policies to all systems. Once good amounts of diagrams were inserted in the web-based platform, each team (they were 6) was asked to construct the first design, which was presented in oral defense to everybody. They learned how to calculate impacts of their proposals, to verify if they had reached the targets in ha expected per system, and to analyze possible costs (Fig. 12). This means to use Impact Models that calculate the suitability of proposing each idea in the place they were planned to be and to arrive to that result the organizers of the workshop had to prepare a matrix of possible impacts among systems (Fig. 13).

They understood that the first design is never the best one, and every 6 teams elaborated a new design. After that, they were organized in two teams per room and construct one design per team. The new teams were: Civil Defense + Public Administration + Non-Adopters; Low + Up + Down. The method to construct a common design is to use the tools to compare the proposals, finding agreements and disagreements, discussing possible adaptations to make some ideas acceptable to all the teams, co-creation of new ideas. Finally, two new designs were constructed, one per room, all the participants went to the auditorium to compose together the last design, the negotiated design (Fig. 14).

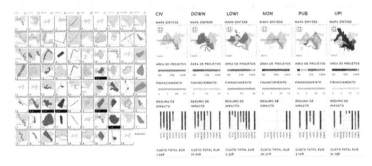

Fig. 12. Construction of diagrams about projects and policies and the selection of diagrams to compose the first design per team. Analysis of impacts (purple positive, yellow neutral, orange negative impact). Source: The authors, using GeodesignHub. (Color figure online)

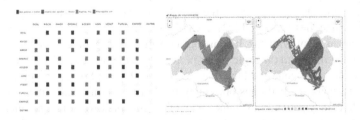

Fig. 13. Impact Matrix proposed by the organizers and example of calculation of impacts in maps representation. Positive impacts are purple, yellow are neutral and orange are negative impacts. Source: The authors, using GeodesignHub. (Color figure online)

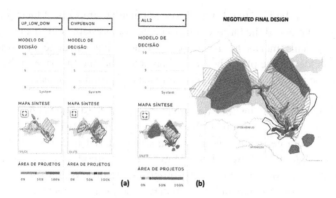

Fig. 14. Negotiated designs: (a) Two designs resulted from negotiation in each room; (b) Final negotiated design. The authors, using GeodesignHub.

The method used to arrive at the final design was: the main important system was selected to be the first one, as once it was decided it could define important decisions in the other systems. The most important system selected was "displacement", because it was on this system that issues related to the dam were proposed. They decided not for constructing anything else in indigenous territory, not to remove the dam, but mainly to do works of conservation in the existing dam, facing the problems of silting around it. After this, they discussed where to put new housings, where to construct monitoring points, rescue meeting points, escape routes. They discussed about agriculture and areas to recover the vegetation. They planned entrepreneurship activities and the possibilities of tourism.

4   Conclusions and Discussions

The main lesson learned in the experience was about how to listen to people that come from different territories and cultures and transform their expectations in diagrams of policies and projects, as well as how can the conductor group give support to the co-creation the final design respecting the indigenous knowledge of local reality and the discussion guidelines presented by the Civil Defense.

We learned a lot with the Indians because they stating observing the process to understand the rules and the logic under it, mainly on the first day of the workshop. On the second day, they controlled the final decision with equilibrium, accepting the good ideas and refusing the bad ones presenting their justifications. Since the beginning of the workshop, they patiently explained about their life, their way of being, their relation with the territory. Sometimes, when the proposal of a project or policy was not appropriate to their values and culture, or even to conditions of the geography of the place, they were able to explain the reasons in detail, demonstrating knowledgeable about laws, risks, and potentialities.

They had all the reasons to be reactive, as we were talking about their life and the big impact they suffered from the construction of the dam. But, instead of that, they were gentle, collaborative, and all the negative presented to bad ideas were followed by an explanation about why they could not be approved. It was a great opportunity for all members from different academic group to learn diplomacy and negotiation with them. And it's important to register that the main issues were all considered, contemplating the needs of Civil Defense to develop their work in operating in risk occurrences or demands.

As feedback to Geodesign method, we observed and controlled the use and the utility of each step in the process, in order to adapt them to local culture. The first observation was about the data prepared for the workshop, organized in Representation, Process and Evaluation Models. They had an importance to the conductor group as it was an opportunity to get together in video-conference meetings to learn more about the place. While we were doing the classification of satellite image and calculating the conditions of vegetation cover we stated to construct an image of the territory. While constructing the 3D representation and calculating slopes we understood the water network and the impacts of the dam. While getting official data about conservation units we identified the conflicts of interests due to the presence of agriculture areas in an area classified as of sustainable use but located in springs of the water basin, responsible for chemical pesticide pollution in the area. Nevertheless, we also understood that conservation unit classified as of permanent protection was an important landmark in the territory, in a high position, but also related to spiritual values to the Indians. While mapping the existing roads and houses we understood the risks, because most of them are in the flood areas. Summarizing, it was important for those that do not live in the territory to identify the vulnerabilities and main values of the place and to arrive in the workshop with minimum knowledge about the case study. But it's important to say that all this information was produced and constructed in Representation and Process Models.

The Evaluation Models are understood as opinions from a group about the suitability of parts of the territory to receive proposals of projects or policies. It's more a personal exercise of combining data, generalizing information and constructing a model that, as models, is a simplification of reality providing reductions in place, time, methodological framework and conceptual definitions [16]. To those that don't know the territory, as the academics that took part in the workshop, the use of Evaluation Models are a question of faith, because they just trust on them as a basis to put their ideas in a suitable place. To people of the place they are useless, because they know their territory better than anyone, and most time they do not agree with the judgment of those who construct the models. Finally, even to the group of conductors that constructed them, as it is an opinion, the judgment can change in time and conceptual evolution.

During the workshop, the Evaluation Models and Impact Models had their importance very reduced. The Impact Models are strongly related to the Evaluation Models, as they inform if the ideas of projects were drawn in suitable places according to cross-combination. As it was not an academic experiment of a theoretical place, but was a real case study, all the questions about suitability were answered by the experts: people from the place and civil defense, using their knowledge and a satellite image as a base map.

The models that worked well during the workshop were Change Models and Decision Models. In that sense, we may say we could work just with some Representation Models, a minimum list, some Process Models and develop Change and Decision Model during the workshop. The facility to draw ideas of projects and policies was much appreciated, what is Change Model. The easygoing negotiation was also much appreciated, what is Decision Model (Fig. 15).

As Geodesign is design with the territory and for the territory, the case study resulted to be very realistic and dealing with the expectations and cultural values of the participants. The final design, constructed from the agreements in a process of democratic decision making, resulted to be a sustainable integration of human activities with the natural environment, respecting cultural peculiarities, both nature and culture.

Fig. 15. Participants from the workshop that was held on Geodesign South America 2019, UDESC, Santa Catarina, Florianópolis, Brazil. The authors.

Acknowledgments. The authors thank CNPq support through the project 401066/2016-9, FAPEMIG PPM-00368-18, FAPESC/PRO2019071000025 and NPGAU/UFMG – Post Graduation Program in Architecture for the support to taking part in the conference.

References

1. Dangermond, J.: GIS: Designing Our Future. ArcNews, Summer (2009)
2. Ervin, S.: A system for Geodesign. Keynote, pp. 158–167 (2011). Abstract
3. Flaxman, M.: Geodesign: Fundamental Principles and Routes Forward. Talk at GeoDesign Summit 2010 (2010)
4. Miller, W.R.: Introducing Geodesign: The Concept. Esri Press, Redlands (2012)
5. Steinitz, C.: A Framework for Geodesign: Changing Geography by Design. ESRI Press, Redlands (2012)
6. Ballal, H., Steinitz, C.: A workshop in digital geodesign synthesis. In.: Buhmann, E., Ervin, S.M.E., Pietsch, M. (eds.) Peer Reviewed Proceedings of Digital Landscape Architecture at Anhalt University of Applied Sciences. Herbert Wichmann Verlag, Berlin (2015)
7. Ballal, H.: Collaborative planning with digital design synthesis. Doctoral dissertation. University College London (2015)

8. Fraga, N.C.: Obras Por Mais de Uma Década, estudos do processo de construção da Barragem Norte no município de José Boiteux/SC. Relatório UDESC – CNPq (1997)

9. Fraga, N.C.: As Enchentes do Vale do Itajaí-Açu, SC: das obras de contenção à indústria da enchente. Dissertação de mestrado – PPGEO/UEM, Maringá (2000)

10. Pettit, C., et al.: Breaking down the silos through geodesign – Envisioning Sydney's urban future. Environ. Plann. B. **46**, 1387–1404 (2019)

11. Moura, A.C.M.: O geodesign como processo de co-criação de acordos coletivos para a paisagem territorial e urbana. In.: Ladwig, N.I., Campos, J.B. (eds.) Planejamento e Gestão Territorial: O Papel e os Instrumentos do Planejamento Territorial na Interface entre o Urbano e o Rural, pp. 16–69, Livros Ediunesc, Criciúma (2019). https://doi.org/10.18616/pgtur01

12. Moura, A.C.M., Tondelli, S., Muzzarelli, A.: Complementary web-based geoinformation technology to geodesign practices: strategic decision-making stages of co-creation in territorial planning. In: Leone, A., Gargiulo, C. (eds.) Environmental and Territorial Modelling for Planning and Design. pp. 643–664. FedOAPress, Naples (2018)

13. Paula, P.L., Camargos, L.M., Moura, A.C.M., Freitas, C.R.: WebGIS como suporte à visualização de informações para processos de Geodesign: estudo de caso Pampulha Patrimônio da Humanidade. GeoSIG (Revista Geografía y Sistemas de Información Geográfica), Luján, vol. 10, pp. 184–208 (2018)

14. Rocha, N.A., Casagrande, P.B., Moura, A.C.M.: Análise Combinatória e Pesos de Evidência na produção de Análise de Multicritérios em modelos de avaliação. GEOSIG - Geografía y Sistemas de Información Geográfica (Argentina) **11**(10), 49–74 (2018)

15. Jankowski, P.: Mixed-data multicriteria evaluation for regional planning: A systematic approach to the decision-making process. Environ. Plann. A **21**, 349–362 (1989)

16. Moura, A.C.M.: Geoprocessamento na gestão e planejamento urbano, 3rd edn. Interciência, Rio de Janeiro (2014)

Aerial Images and Three-Dimensional Models Generated by RPA to Support Geovisualization in Geodesign Workshops

Danilo Marques de Magalhães[1](✉) [ID]
and Ana Clara Mourão Moura[2](✉) [ID]

[1] Instituto de Geociências, Universidade Federal de Minas Gerais, Av. Antônio Carlos 6627, Belo Horizonte, Brazil
danilommagalhaes@gmail.com
[2] Escola de Arquitetura, Universidade Federal de Minas Gerais (UFMG), Rua Paraíba 697, Belo Horizonte, Brazil
anaclaramoura@yahoo.com

Abstract. Remotely Piloted Aircraft (RPA) are geotechnological instruments with good cost-benefit, as they provide quick spatial data capture with satisfactory accuracy and resolution, affording the creation of three-dimensional products and aerial photographs from different perspectives. These data have been used to support geovisualization in geodesign workshops held in socially fragile and poor communities, in which people of the place have a vast knowledge about their territory but difficulties in working with cartographic representation and maps products. This study, therefore, presents the experiences earned in three geodesign workshops held in Belo Horizonte, Brazil, when aerial images in an oblique perspective and three-dimensional models with interactive navigation were used. The results allow us to conclude that the use of fields of view with an oblique perspective to the objects of analysis promotes a link between the zenithal cartographic expression and the immersive view in the landscape, which is a way for the formation of the mental maps. That is understood as an essential condition for the promotion of citizen participation in co-design processes, based on geovisualization and the sense of digital inclusion.

Keywords: Geovisualization · Geodesign · Remotely Piloted Aircraft

1 Introduction

According to the latest demographic census conducted in Brazil, 6% of the country's population resides in subnormal agglomerations, which are the places popularly known as "favelas" (slums) that are socially fragile and poor communities. These are defined based on the precarious condition of the household's infrastructure, and the data show that in the subnormal agglomerates only 67.3% had sewage collection, 72.5% installed electricity, and 88.3% piped water supply. Most of these households (49.8%) are in the metropolitan regions of the Brazilian southeastern, and frequently these areas are inappropriate to housing, such as steep slopes, caves, riversides, among others [1].

© Springer Nature Switzerland AG 2020
O. Gervasi et al. (Eds.): ICCSA 2020, LNCS 12252, pp. 296–309, 2020.
https://doi.org/10.1007/978-3-030-58811-3_21

In the Metropolitan Region of Belo Horizonte (MRBH), which has 5.4 million inhabitants, 9.1% of the population lives in subnormal agglomerations, that is, approximately 491 thousand people. In other Brazilian regions the condition is even more severe, for example, Belém, which has 53.9% (1.1 million people) of the population living in slums; Salvador with 26.1% (932,000 people); São Paulo 11% (2.16 million people); and Rio de Janeiro 14.4% (1.7 million people) [1].

Considering only the city of Belo Horizonte (BH), the total population is 2.4 million inhabitants, and according to the Brazilian census data, 307 thousand people are in subnormal agglomerates, that is, 12.96% of the people. However, the municipality officially considers 209 villages and slums in the city, which means 714 thousand people (27.4%) living with poor access to basic sanitation and urban infrastructure [2].

In order to promote faster improvement at these locations, the municipality is using the geodesign methodology to hold hearings with the population as a basis of citizen's participation in planning and decisions [3]. However, the experience in conducting geodesign workshops in these places has shown us that the use only of thematic maps and evaluation maps as a way to represents the information and characteristics of the study areas have not been successful in communicating spatial information. Although people of the place present a vast knowledge about the territory where they live, they commonly have issues in understanding maps because the zenith cartographic view is unusual for them, there are many generalizations and conventions which require a capacity of abstraction and the spatial analysis models used to generate the evaluation maps are too complicated for this audience.

These empirical perceptions led us to propose other methods of visualizing the territory in order to improve the condition of geovisualization and, from that, provide a shared basis for the discussion of the proposals resulting from the geodesign workshop. Another issue inherent to this situation is the lack of spatial data to work in these areas that present intense dynamics of territorial transformation since each day new families are installed in and, in most cases, without planning and basic needs of infrastructure.

It is worth mentioning that the local population is undoubtedly the group most directly interested in the projects and discussions and that the promotion of geovisualization, in this case, has a crucial role in including them with similar conditions of debate for the proposals and policies presented in order to compose a final design. However, what we notice, in practice, is that the use of only standard cartographic language has promoted an alienation and even omission of people who do not fully understand this language. Therefore, leaving the speech power and the design drawings for those who demonstrate broader knowledge in maps or GIS resources.

2   Use of RPA for Data Collection and 3D Modeling

Based on the issues raised, the proposal is to use Remote Piloted Aircraft (RPA) for the collection of spatial data in order to develop an updated database for conducting the geodesign workshop, as well as to perform 3D modeling and photo captures with oblique angles for geovisualization purposes.

The RPAs have as advantages the high spatial and temporal resolution of the images, the possibility of capturing data flying close to the obstacles, and with different positions of the camera for taking images and the reduction of the operation cost. The work can be carried out in a very agile way, which allows a quick action in critical situations or for constant updating, as in multitemporal monitoring [4]. Besides that, multi-rotor aircraft can take off and land vertically, without a runway, facilitating the process in places with a high density of buildings and steep relief, which are usual features in slums in southeastern Brazil.

Another advantage of the RPA aerial survey is the possibility of defining different levels of image overlap, as well as different camera positions and angles. It allows the generation of georeferenced products even with irregular overlapping of the images, that is, collecting images in complex situations that may not be covered by traditional aero photogrammetry procedures. Besides, it is possible to collect information from the sides of objects, such as building facades or on steep slopes, which allows the generation of realistic three-dimensional models that are quite similar to the object's real morphology.

By using high-precision GNSS receivers combined with data capture with RPA, it is possible to achieve positional accuracy altimetric and planimetric matches with LiDAR data, which opens up possibilities for integration and updating the database in an agile and less costly condition [5].

In this study, we highlight that the use of image captures for 3D representation of the landscape and its elements, as well as the cadastre making, has significantly expanded the conditions for building models that expand the users' view of their territorial realities. It is, therefore, an interest in exploring these geotechnological resources as a support for geovisualization, favoring the establishment of a common language to support the discussions between the parties involved in geodesign workshops.

3 Geovisualization

Geovisualization derives from cartography, and, in this sense, maps must be understood as a visualization tool and not as a simple accessory for communication. Therefore, the map must be understood as an expression of geographical and, thereby, contributing to the identification of patterns that guide new understandings [6]. The tools for visualizing spatial information have to allow us to ask questions about what we do not yet know, and the quality of the visualization is considered a critical component for the promotion of knowledge.

According to MacEachren (2005, 445), *first, visual representations can act as the object of collaboration, thus as an entity to discuss, create, or manipulate. Second, visualization can provide support for dialogue (about information, plans, methods, strategies, or decisions). Third, visual representation can provide support for coordinated activity (thus for compiling information, carrying out plans, or executing decisions)* [7].

We understand that geovisualization should serve to build a link between reality and the mental maps that a user has about reality and, in the context of participatory planning, it should act as a bridge for users to be, increasingly and better, involved in the planning and management of the territory.

It is necessary to create shareable mental models for everyone involved in the process, otherwise, processes that involve many subjects cannot obtain a joint basis for achieving an objective [8]. This concept has been treated as people interoperability, which is linked to the use of geovisualization resources that favor communication between different actors involved in collaborative planning and decision-making processes [9]. It allows the search for protocols that can establish a common language, which is the basis for sharing decisions, for co-creation, and culminate in an effective co-design.

The use of RPA, in this sense, aims to build representative models of reality that provide the actors involved in the process the ability to explore, recognize, analyze, propose, synthesize and present their opinions about the analyzed territory. It is a fundamental condition for citizen participation on an equal basis in co-design processes and, therefore, it is understood here as a valuable resource of geovisualization that can support these processes.

When geovisualization is effectively used, it offers the possibility of engagement, considering that a wide range of users will be able to participate in activities that require or reside on the spatial component [10]. We highlight the ability to change the 3D point of view in real-time as essential to create a sense of virtual reality. It opened up new approaches to visualization that is related to a new degree of cartographic freedom for visual representation [11].

We must keep in mind that the transformation from the real 3D world to the 2D map implies a loss of details and that the elements that make up the territory are represented by generic symbols that do not necessarily have scales relative to the real world, such as point features for example, [12]. In this sense, how data is presented can condition (or even compromise) its interpretation and, in turn, maps have disadvantages to digital models, as it is the reduced interaction between readers and data [13].

Currently, technologies for capturing, modeling, and presenting data assisted by RPA have changed the paradigm of visual representations of territorial information and allow to reduce some communication noises since they reduce subjectivity in the construction of the image through the presentation of realistic models. They use dynamic and interactive platforms that allow navigation in different perspectives, ranging from the zenith that allows a synthetic view to the azimuth that represents human immersion in the landscape, passing through the oblique perspective that allows connections between the navigation axes (Fig. 1).

Currently, we have the opportunity to recreate high-definition three-dimensional virtual spaces that allows us free interaction for choosing the fields of view, such as the human perspective – immersed in the landscape –, the bird's view – which flies overhead but with the freedom to move and to get closer to objects – and from the infinite – with the possibility of understanding the spatial arrangement of the elements. The bird's view, which concerns the oblique perspective, has the potential to combine the centrality of the observer (man immersed in the landscape) with the univocity of the maps (zenithal, synthetic view) [8].

Therefore, these new tools for communicating spatial information, when used creatively, can improve the quality and efficiency of public discussions and debates and

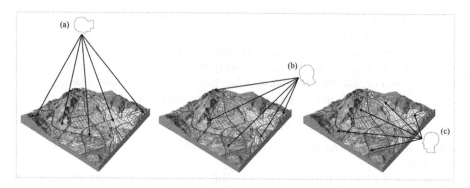

Fig. 1. Viewing Perspectives. (a) Zenithal Perspective: technical view, remote sensing; (b) Oblique Perspective: technical view & human view, technical data capture & human comprehension; (c) Azimuthal Perspective: human view, immersive, in sensing. Source: the authors.

help build community consensus around specific planning issues [14]. It should also be considered that the use of photography for situations in which communication between users is vital for decision-making. It is more significant than the use of cartography because the map is a synthetic decomposition, while photography is closer to user reality [15].

4   Study Areas

This study presents experiences of geodesign workshops with a focus on three distinct communities that present social fragility, located in BH, Brazil, which are the communities: Dandara, Conjunto Paulo VI, and Confisco (Fig. 2). These areas have in common the fact that they are considered as illegal settlements with different morphology and history in comparison to slums: these areas are invaded as they do not own the land, and they do not have official infrastructure installed (sanitation, transportation, water, energy and so one), but they had a kind of a social organization before the invasion (conducted by a group). The result is a more regular distribution of streets and lots, even without following urban planning rules of dimensions, slopes, geometry. Also, two of the areas were identified as of high vulnerability in the face of estimated climate change until the year 2030 [16].

4.1   Dandara Case Study

The illegal settlement of Dandara community is located in the northwest of Belo Horizonte and is one of the largest and in the city. The area was initially occupied in April 2009 by 150 families, but currently, more than 1,200 families are residing there (4,000 people). The support of social movements and other professional and academic groups provided that occupation took place in a very orderly manner, with an urban plan drawn up collectively for invasion, which considers the topographic and

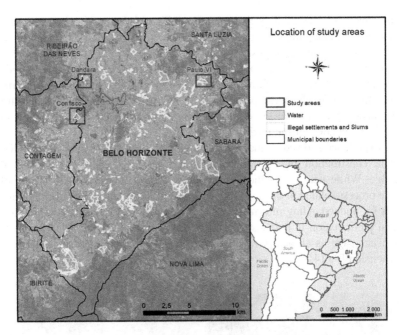

Fig. 2. Location of study areas. Source: the authors

environmental characteristics of the area for proposing the subdivision in streets and lots [3]. However, the place is still undergoing a process of urban regularization and, consequently, the installation of necessary sanitary infrastructure.

From 2016 the area begins to receive investments for urban regularization and provision necessary sanitation infrastructure and other public services, and the geodesign methodology was chosen in order to optimize the discussion process with the local population since the methodology applied previously could take up to two years to complete the study.

Then, data surveys and three-dimensional modeling were carried out with the support of a multi-rotor RPA to update the existing database as well as to test the use of a three-dimensional model of the area as a geovisualization resource. Considering that it was an extremely needy community and that some people were not wholly literate, the use of this model was proposed as a means so that all participants could have the same conditions to understand the information worked on.

Before the workshop, training was conducted with young people from the community to use digital platforms, using the computer laboratory of a public school in the area and, during the workshop, they could act as resources for their parents or other adults and elderly in the community.

It was evident that since the first contact with the 3D model and the digital data displayed on a web map, the local population tended to use them, at the expense of the maps printed on paper and the systems made available on the *geodesignhub* platform. The participants received printed materials, a web-based platform with information, and the 3D models, and we were able to observe and compare their performance. The dynamic data visualization, as well as the possibility of alternating perspectives, were identified as the main gains in geovisualization that contributed to the local population to recognize the territory features.

As the geodesign team has to propose diagrams on a two-dimensional geodesign platform, an effort was made to link map and 3D model orientation using the north as a reference. In this way, the participants started to use, to understand, and even to trust in the information presented in the evaluation maps, since there was the support of the realistic representation of the territory.

This experience showed us that the dynamic and intuitive tools of geovisualization favor the construction of mental models, self-learning, and the construction of knowledge. While using only thematic maps of defined systems, skip stages of the cognitive process related to the abstraction of spatial information, and does not provide the basis for understanding information effectively. Thus, geovisualization contributes to citizen participation in debates for co-design, as they favor the establishment of a common language as all actors can interpret spatial information at a similar level os comprehension [9, 14] (Fig. 3).

Fig. 3. Geodesign workshop in Dandara community, BH, Brazil. Source: Monteiro et al. (2018) [3].

4.2   Conjunto Paulo VI Case Study

Based on the experience in the Dandara community, a method was sought to measure whether the use of three-dimensional models elaborated with RPA, in fact, provides gains in geovisualization. For this, during the geodesign activities scheduled for the Conjunto Paulo VI illegal settlement, children were invited to participate in the activities with the proposal to raise their awareness of the existing problems in the neighborhood and to include them in listening processes about the current demands and proposals. For us, it was an opportunity to work with a layperson in cartography and observe how the process of understanding spatial information takes place. In this location, there is the presence of irregular settlements under a huge line of electric power transmission from Companhia Energética de Minas Gerais (CEMIG), an area at risk of landslides, as well as other environmental and lack of infrastructure problems.

Data collection with RPA in the area and three-dimensional modeling for viewing on computers were performed. The children participating in the workshop were divided into three groups, been Group A working with printed maps only, Group B working with printed maps and 3D model, and Group C working with 3D model only. In short, children should use the resources provided to answer questions that demanded spatial reasoning by drawing on a blank map (Fig. 4).

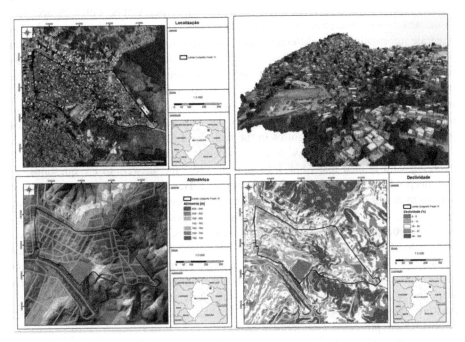

Fig. 4. Maps and 3D model used during the workshop with children. Source: the authors

The first question asked sought to identify the basic levels of spatial reasoning. Children were asked to draw an "X" on the answer sheet to indicate where their home is, an "O" to indicate the location of the Sobral Pinto Municipal School (SPMS) – the place where the workshop was held –, and a line to indicate the location and direction of the existing power transmission line in the neighborhood. This question worked only at the *description level* of spatial information, that is, without involving analysis or inference skills, but only of recognition and understanding of location [17]. *Representational correspondence* is also assessed, which refers to the ability to recognize on the map what is seen in the real world [18].

The second question worked on slightly more advanced levels of abstraction of spatial concepts. Children were asked that, understanding that a watercourse will flow from the highest parts of the land towards the lowest parts, draw a double line to indicate the position and the probable path of the stream that exists in the neighborhood. This question makes it possible to assess the ability to reason Source-Path-Goal demands [17], which involves the perception of movement, the starting point, the way forward, and the destination. This understanding is linked to *directional correspondence*, which relates to the ability to interpret directions and, thus, link the map azimuth with that of the real world [18]. Besides, for displacement reasoning, children needed to analyze the data they had access to and interpret the hypsometric map or the 3D model.

The third and last question worked on the most advanced levels of spatial abstraction. Children were asked to identify on the blank map using hatches where the places at risk of landslides involving victims were. The children were informed that the places at risk are those with houses installed on steep slopes, that is, with high declivity associated with the presence of buildings. The intention was to evaluate their ability to integrate information from different maps comparing to the use of the 3D model that presents the same content, but with another type of visualization. This question required children to analyze different data and reason about consequences from the interaction of information [17]. The solution to this kind of problem is the establishment of *configurational correspondence*, which is the understanding that the relationships between the features present on the map correspond to the relationships between the corresponding features in the real world [18].

As a result of this process, it can be mentioned that the children in Group A (working with printed maps only), in general, knew the answers to the questions, as they deeply knew the territory in which they live. However, the printed maps did not help them to materialize the answers on the answer sheet. In comparison with the other groups, it is clear that this concerns the rigidity imposed by the scale and fixed orientation of the printed map, making it impossible to choose other viewing perspectives or even to change the scale, to enlarge the elements on the map. It requires a higher capacity for spatial abstraction, for recognizing patterns and shapes of objects in an image with a zenith perspective that demands the ability to make associations between map and reality mentally. In summary, the most straightforward questions were answered consistently, but questions 2 and 3, which required a more sophisticated level of abstraction, presented more critical errors.

Children in Group B (working with printed maps and 3D model), were the ones who had the best performance in the activity. It was evident that children were more motivated to search for answers using the 3D model, which indicates that the investigative process and the formation of mental maps could be more consistent. Children who were dealing only with printed maps, although they were motivated to participate in the activity, more quickly exhausted the search options on the map, dispersing from the investigation.

In general, it was noticed in this group that the 3D model provided work in the visual field, that is, easier recognition of information due to its proximity to reality. Moreover, from this recognition, children began to use maps in the search to answer questions correctly, establishing correlations between the 3D model and the map, sometimes counting the number of blocks on the map and in the model, or recognizing some form or specific color identified in the model and on the map with the orthography. All showed comprehension of the terrain shape and obeyed the logic that the watercourse flows from the top to the bottom of the slope, and the drawings, although showing rivers in places where there are no watercourses, followed this premise (Fig. 5). Is was a significant gain because Group A showed inconsistencies in the drawing of watercourses. The children of Group B were also able to correctly identify the places with the most considerable risk of sliding in inhabited places and, also, they had a better sense of the dimension (scale) of the drawings, creating hatches with high precision in terms of area and position. Comparing with other groups, we understand that the quality of the answers of this group is not only in the use of the 3D model but also in its association with the printed maps. The printed maps contributed to consolidate the notion of scale, completing the flow of the abstraction process from the real world, passing through the virtual model, being synthesized by the 2D map and, thus, reaching the ability to express their thinking and understanding in a spatially coherent way and assertive.

The children in Group C (working only with 3D model) presented exciting results concerning the requested three-dimensional analysis, whereas they presented some difficulties for simple localization operations. It was possible to notice during the activity that the children were able to find the answers in the 3D model easily but had

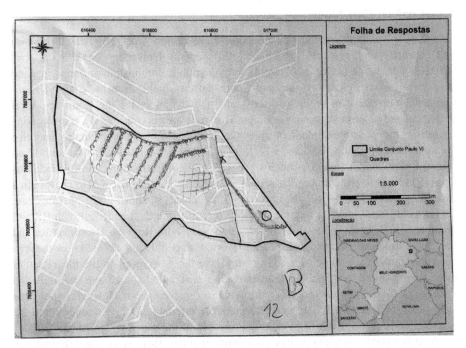

Fig. 5. Sample answer from a Grou B child. The circle represents the School, the "X" represents its home, the hatch represents the risk area, and the spiral lines represent the water flow. All the answers are right or at least coherent with reality.

great difficulty in transposing what they visualized into the model to the blank answer sheet. In this sense, it is understood that the direct transfer from the 3D model to a clean 2D environment is also an incomplete process, with no improvement in the ability to reason spatially through the use of the 3D model alone.

It was evident that only the 3D model, as well as using only the map, does not favor a better understanding of spatial information. However, the concomitant use of complementary information, which is seen in both the 3D model and the printed map, stands out as the best option. In this way, it is possible to recognize the elements in the 3D model initially and then, in a second moment, the use of support maps to enable the conversion of 3D information into 2D.

After this first activity, all children were invited to work with all available resources (maps and 3D model), and, from this moment, the evaluation maps were presented according to the systems established for the workshop. Children were asked to try to associate the information presented on the maps with the other available resources. And then, a geodesign workshop was started with them in order to produce ideas for an alternative future in the neighborhood where they live. It was noticed that they presented a clear understanding of the basic information treated, and, from that, they were able to propose diagrams with an appropriate location, orientation, and scales, showing that the geovisualization process was effective.

4.3 Confisco Case Study

In order to validate previous experiences, a geodesign workshop was held with undergraduate and graduate students in the Federal University of Minas Gerais (UFMG) with the participation of people from the public administration (municipal and state levels, from Belo Horizonte and Contagem city halls, from the State of Environmental Secretary) in order to discuss alternative futures for the Confisco illegal settlement and its immediate surroundings. The study area is considered a fragility zone concerning the possible climatic changes that may occur in the municipality and also the metropolitan region. Besides, it is located on the border between BH with Contagem, a peripheral area where there is a lack of urban infrastructure, and in conditions flood risks, as it is also an irregular settlement area. The initial goal was to analyze in a case study with students from the university if the results obtained in the previous case studies could be similar, testing the methodology of using data collected with RPA to promotes a better geovisualization in geodesign workshops (Fig. 6). The difference and the task in this academic experiment are to work with people that do not know the area but know how to use digital tools. In contrast, in the workshops in the illegal settlements, we worked with people that know the area but do not have the skill and knowledge to use digital tools or cartographic representation. However, soon, the analysis of the results will help to select and represent data in a better condition to the geodesign workshop that will be held with people of the place.

As it is a borderline area between two municipalities, there is an initial difficulty in integrating the existing database, since the municipal governments do not work with an integrated database, but they are raised separately. The mapped area totals 340 ha and surface and terrain, orthomosaic, aerial photographs, and 3D models were generated to represent the area.

Fig. 6. Participants in the workshop, composed of students from the University and representatives of local governments. Source: the authors

The workshop participants did not know the study area, and during the activity, it became evident that the materials complementary to the maps, such as the 3D model (Fig. 7) and aerial photographs, were essential for understanding the characteristics of the place. It was noticed that the use of these resources to promote geovisualization contributes not only to enable the layperson in cartography to be included in the discussion process. Nevertheless, it also enables experts to recognize the territory more effectively, giving greater clarity to the content expressed in the form of an evaluation map.

Fig. 7. 3D model from Confisco neighborhood and surroundings. Source: the authors

In this sense, the impressions already obtained in the other mentioned workshops were corroborated, validating the proposal to use dynamic visualization platforms that allow scale and perspective free adjustments to support geovisualization, and the formation of shared codes for promoting a shared design.

5 Conclusions

Following the participatory planning processes in Brazil has shown us the relevance of geovisualization resources to support geodesign workshops, especially when working in more needy communities or involving people with little knowledge in cartography. These processes demand not only the understanding of information displayed on maps but also using the spatial information creatively to propose new ideas, that is, the ability to reason spatially is essential for active citizen participation.

All actors involved in the co-creation process must have equivalent conditions of participation and then is recommended to use technological resources for the promotion of geovisualization, which can favor more effective communication between the parties.

It is noticed that in the 3D model, there is immersive navigation that favors recognition and awareness. However, the maps, with synthesis and analytical language, remain essential for thematization of information and planning. In this sense, the oblique view provided by the 3D model bridges the gap between immersion (of the body) and distancing (zenith) and is, therefore, a link of communication between these two perspectives of analysis.

The experiences presented were also successful in terms of capturing spatial data, since it enabled the creation of an updated database through a quick survey, of satisfactory accuracy and low cost. It reinforces that the use of RPA can also favor the autonomy of public agents and researchers to carry out studies.

Acknowledgments. The authors thank CNPq support through the project Process 401066/2016-9, FAPEMIG PPM-00368-18, FAPESC/PRO2019071000025, and CAPES 88887.474274/2020-00 for the support for taking part in the conference.

References

1. Instituto Brasileiro de Geografia e Estatística (IBGE) Homepage. https://agenciadenoticias. ibge.gov.br/agencia-sala-de-imprensa/2013-agencia-de-noticias/releases/14157-asi-censo-2010-114-milhoes-de-brasileiros-60-vivem-em-aglomerados-subnormais. Accessed 5 Mar 2020
2. Prefeitura Municipal de Belo Horizonte (PBH) Homepage. https://prefeitura.pbh.gov.br/urbel/pge-planejamento. Accessed 5 Mar 2020
3. Monteiro, L.O., Moura, A.C.M., Zyngier, C.M., Sena, I.S., Paula, P.L.: Geodesign facing the urgency of reducing poverty: the cases of belo horizonte. DisegnareCon **11**(20), 6.1–6.25 (2018)
4. Nex, F., Remondino, F.: UAV for 3D mapping applications: a review. Appl. Geomatics **6**(1), 1–15 (2013). https://doi.org/10.1007/s12518-013-0120-x

5. Marotta, G.S., Cicerelli, A.M.R., Roig, H.L., Abreu, M.A.: Avaliação posicional de um modelo digital de superfície derivado de câmera de pequeno formato. Revista Brasileira de Cartografia. **67**(7), 467–1477 (2015)
6. MacEachren, A.M., Ganter, J.H.: A patter identification approach to cartographic visualization. Cartographica **27**(2), 64–81 (1990)
7. MacEachren, A.M.: Moving geovisualization toward support for group work. In: Dykes, J., MacEachren, A.M., Kraak, M.-J. (eds.) Exploring Geovisualization. International Cartographic Association. Elsevier, Amsterdam (2005)
8. Massala, E., Pensa, S.: O papel da visualização no planejamento urbano: uma abordagem a partir dos conceitos por trás da imagem espacial. In. Moura, A.C.M. (ed.) Tecnologias de geoinformação para representar e planejar o território urbano. Interciência, Rio de Janeiro (2016)
9. Moura, A.C.M.: Geoprocessing Technologies for cultural landscape management: support to decision-making process based on characterization, management and studies of alternative futures. In: Unesco Chair. New Paradigms and instruments for bio-cultural landscape management. SITI, Torino (2017)
10. Dykes, J., MacEachren, A.M., Kraak, M.-J.: Exploring Geovisualization. Elsevier, Amsterdam (2005)
11. Wood, J., Kirschenbauer, S., Döllner, J., Lopes, A., Bodum, L.: Using 3D visualization. In: Dykes, J., MacEachren, A.M., Kaak, M.-J. (eds.) Exploring Geovisualization. Elsevier, Amsterdam (2005)
12. Monmonier, M.S.: How to Lie with Maps, 2nd edn. The University of Chicago Press, Chicago (1996)
13. Wood, M.: Visualization in historical context. In: MacEachren, A.M., Taylor, D.R.F. (eds.) Visualization in Modern Cartography. Pergamon, New York (1994)
14. Zyngier, C.M.: Paisagens urbanas possíveis: códigos compartilhados na construção coletiva de cenários. In: Moura, A.C.M. (ed.) Tecnologias de geoinformação para representar e planejar o território urbano. Interciência, Rio de Janeiro (2016)
15. Moura, A.C.M.: Geoprocessamento na gestão e planejamento urbano. 2nd edn. Ed. da autora, Belo Horizonte (2005)
16. Carbon, W.: Análise de vulnerabilidade às mudanças climáticas no município de Belo Horizonte. Prefeitura Municipal de Belo Horizonte, Belo Horizonte (2016)
17. Ishikawa, T., Kastens, K.A.: Why some students have trouble with maps and other spatial representations. J. Geosci. Educ. **53**(2), 184–197 (2005)
18. Merwe, F.: Concepts of space in spatial thinking. In: International Cartographic Association (ICA) CONFERENCE 2009, ICA, vol. 24, pp. 1–13. ICA, Santiago de Chile (2009)

Training Decision-Makers: GEODESIGN Workshop Paving the Way for New Urban Agenda

Francesco Scorza[(⊠)] [iD]

School of Engineering, Laboratory of Urban and Regional Systems Engineering
(LISUT), University of Basilicata, Viale dell'Ateneo Lucano 10,
85100 Potenza, Italy
francesco.scorza@unibas.it

Abstract. GEODESIGN represents an effective framework promoting collaborative planning and decision-making as an incremental process based on robust methodological guidance. In this application, GEODESIGN had been adopted as a tool for training decision makers in "facing planning challenges deriving from ITI Urban Agenda development" according to "sustainability" and "climate responsive principles". The case study represents a joined activity realized by the Municipality of Potenza (member of the EU Climate Adaptation Partnership) and the LISUT Laboratory (Engineering School at UNIBAS). The results regard the comprehensive approach in terms of participation capacity of decision makers without any background in planning disciplines and unveiled the weaknesses of traditional approach mainly based on "building agreements" without any measurements of spatial evidences or scenarios comparisons.

Keywords: GEODESIGN · New Urban Agenda · Decision making · Political Academy

1 Introduction

GEODESIGN represents a suitable framework in order to develop "urban vision" in urban planning practices. It is an effective way to organize and deploy participatory planning according to the negotiation approach according to numbers of experiences reported in scientific literature [1–7].

GEODESIGN represents relevant research focus for LISUT laboratory and several experiences had been conducted in recent years on selected case studies [8–10]. Mainly we included GEODESIGN among those technical tolls necessary to support planning processes at different scales [11] especially promoting the methodological integration of GEODESIGN with Logical Framework Approach (among others [12]).

According to C. Steinitz [1] GEODESIGN represents an inclusive approach (it involves not only technicians but all actors involved in decision making processes) supporting *"informed negotiation"*.

Concerning negotiation we address this concept in a positive procedural vision of building agreements: GEODESIGN it is not a way to aggregate some strong individual

O. Gervasi et al. (Eds.): ICCSA 2020, LNCS 12252, pp. 310–316, 2020.
https://doi.org/10.1007/978-3-030-58811-3_22

interests against other weakest groups of participants, but mainly a way in which the spatial evidences of decisions (namely "designs" in GEODESIGN taxonomy) becomes a way to make more and more explicit the evidences of individual proposals contributing to the strategic decision making process.

The huge demand for training people, citizens, technicians and politicians in participatory planning represents the basic step of this work. In facts, we adopted GEODESIGN in order to simulate a process of urban design according to the rules of ITI planning (Integrated Territorial Investments procedure promoted by EU Operative programs 2014-2020). Through this simulation and the active participation of politicians and technicians of the Municipality of Potenza (Basilicata Region Capital city) the basic learning by doing approach had been developed.

This papers reports general consideration concerning the advantages in adopting GEODESIGN for New Urban Agenda development. Then the "Potenza Political Academy" case study is described, reporting details about GEODESIGN workshop organization and conduction. Finally the discussions and conclusions section reports main evidences of the learning by doing process re-launching research perspectives in GEODESIGN applications in urban sustainable development planning.

2 Geodesign: Background for NUA Visioning

The UN New Urban Agenda [13–16], based on its five main pillars of implementation[1]: lays out standards and principles for planning, aiming at making cities a more livable place according to a shared vision of development.

We are in the era in which City Development planning becomes a challenge in order to face world population growth oriented, according to main trends, to concentrate in the huge metropolitan areas. And great efforts are driven in this domain of Urban transformation facing urban growth according to sustainable criteria (one of the key domain is represented by Smart City studies [17–20]). But the NUA deals with growing urban areas as much as with declining rural context. It is evident that while traditional planning provided models. Methodologies and approaches in order to deal with urban expansion, not enough tools are available to tackle sustainable solution in order to manage urban decline. It is the case small and medium-small size town competing with metropolitan areas.

As discussed in previous works [15, 21, 22], we may put effort in such secondary challenges considering that in such declining context the following principles has to be adopted in order to change planning approach according to NUA common perspective and local needs:

1. Planning "goes toward" Governance
2. Planning Performance has to be assessed
3. Inclusive, equitable, effective and sustainable strategies has to be designed

---

[1] National urban policies, urban legislation and regulations, urban planning and design, local economy and municipal finance, and local implementation.

The process of developing a "vision" for a place and therefore to define a long term strategy is far to be an easy matter. Generally such approach, in a multi-agents framework, delivers conflicts among groups, it takes time, it needs huge technical resources (especially constructing knowledge of the place).

GEODESIGN drives such processes in a framework reducing time for decisions and actions, comparing different interests and priorities, towards feasible decisions.

3 Potenza Political Academy Geodesign Workshop

The application proposed in this work lays to deliver main components of an urban development strategy according with EU ITI rules ITI promotes, within the complex procedures of Regional Operative Program implementation, a way to give local authorities tools to self define integrated investments programs implementing thematic objectives adopted for regional development strategies. It becomes a critical stage of planning implementation where a Municipality can get the resources to realize its planning previsions. In current practice it becomes a political decision frame in which daily issues mainly prevail on pre-determined planned strategies for urban development and therefor a way to neglect urban planning. The results could be a list of investments, infrastructures, public aids, not balances, un-effective in a long term strategy, oriented fix specific urban criticality without any systemic view of the whole urban structure.

In order to avoid this scenario in urban ITI delivering process, some methodological issues has to be talked: decision makers needs methodologies in order to actively participate in the process, time has to be controlled in order to balance the intensity of discussion among the ITI, experience and competences to contribute in decision making process has to be owned by stake-holders.

Therefore we decided to organize a training session for decision makers and technicians based on GEODESIGN workshop experience

The workshop preparation had been delivered by the research team at LISUT lab, involving engineering master students. The selection of relevant systems, the territorial analysis and the land suitability evaluation maps was prepared at technical level and then proposed to the workshop participants.

The Workshop was organized by the Potenza Municipality in the frameworks of a broader transnational cooperation activities conducted at EU level: namely Climate Adaptation Partnership. One full day of activities had been performed in Potenza (17th January 2020) according to the main topic of the event: Political Academy.

The invited participants to the workshop were policial representative of the town council of Potenza, including the Mayor, plus technical staff of the main municipal departments dealing with ITI planning and management. Researchers, PhD students and master students in engineering participated to the workshop as mentors, guiding actors through the methodological stages of the GEODESIGN and explaining technical analysis and the use of the online platform GeodesighHUB[2].

---

[2] https://www.geodesignhub.com/ by Geodesign Hub Pvt. Ltd., Dublin, Ireland.

Posters in the room documented the evaluation maps and become discussion generator among technicians and politicians (Fig. 1).

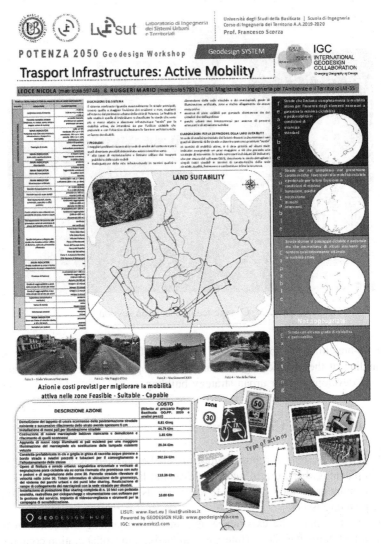

Fig. 1. An example of the poster dealing with the system: "Transport infrastructures: active mobility".

The design phase and the change teams' design selection was facilitated by a positive interaction between politicians and technicians. During the presentations of the synthesis some political conflicts arose between majority and minority groups.

Finally the negotiations payed the bill of a simulated discussion delivered in a learning event. The level of interactions becomes not effective in terms of conflicts resolution and agreement reinforcement among participants (Fig. 2)..

Fig. 2. Change team discussion session.

The de-breathing session produced numbers of interactions showing a general understanding of the methodological framework adopted and the usefulness in a process of ITI development for urban strategy building

4   Discussions and Conclusions

GEODESIGN represents a robust framework to be adopted as a Decision Support System in planning. Far from to match its essential linked broad cathegories [23] to a specific planning procedures, we have to recognize its horizontal applicability to a huge scope of planning issues.

If we want to place the experience held in Potenza among the common process types identified in the IGC 2019 (International Geodesign Collaboration conference), it represents a "multiparticipant workshop-style engagement" [23], oriented to show the methodological advantages of GEODESIGN application and starting a learning by doing process in local decisionmakers group.

The level of personal-learning derived from the participation in the workshop has not been measured by specific survey, but in the final discussion session several positive remarks had been declared by participants (mainly politicians). Their appreciation toward the experience mainly focusses on the applicability on the approach in real-case decision making concerning urban transformations. They expressed a quite evident understanding of the GEODESIGN taxonomy, remarking properly the stages of the workshop. Those are the elements that allowed us to assess the effectiveness of knowledge transfer even if limited to the essential concepts.

This application is close to the general assessment of the learning experience reported by Albert and Ott [24] for the IGC 2019. Participants learned a lot both concerning the understanding of the case study features and of the methodological background.

What was not fully discussed during the workshop (mainly due to the simulated approach adopted) is the implicit process connecting "identified problems" with "explicit assumptions" leading to effective "design" proposed as potential solutions. This is a conceptual framework strongly influenced by the messiness of the design actions [25]. It should be assess at individual level and elicited in the change team approach to synthesis building during GEODESIGN sessions. This is a critical element connecting knowledge of the place with problems detections and consequent assumptions identification (so called "wicked" problems [26]).

The "acceptability of geodesign method" was demonstrate during the experience: participants followed the workshop process and easily adapted their way to consider the city and its development perspective according to the GEODESIGN steps.

References

1. Steinitz, C.: A frame work for Geodesign. Changing geography by design (2012)
2. Fisher, T., Orland, B., Steinitz, C. (eds.): The International Geodesign Collaboration. Changing Geography by Design. ESRI Press, Redlands (2020)
3. Campagna, M.: Metaplanning: about designing the geodesign process. Landsc. Urban Plan. **156**, 118–128 (2016). https://doi.org/10.1016/J.LANDURBPLAN.2015.08.019
4. Nyerges, T., et al.: Geodesign dynamics for sustainable urban watershed development. Sustain. Cities Soc. **25**, 13–24 (2016). https://doi.org/10.1016/j.scs.2016.04.016
5. Cocco, C., Rezende Freitas, C., Mourão Moura, A.C., Campagna, M.: Geodesign process analytics: focus on design as a process and its outcomes. Sustainability **12**, 119 (2019). https://doi.org/10.3390/su12010119
6. Campagna, M., Di Cesare, E.A., Cocco, C.: Integrating green-infrastructures design in strategic spatial planning with geodesign. Sustainability **12**, 1820 (2020). https://doi.org/10.3390/su12051820
7. Cocco, C., Jankowski, P., Campagna, M.: An analytic approach to understanding process dynamics in geodesign studies. Sustainability **11**, 4999 (2019). https://doi.org/10.3390/su11184999
8. Padula, A., Fiore, P., Pilogallo, A., Scorza, F.: Collaborative approach in strategic development planning for small municipalities. Applying geodesign methodology and tools for a new municipal strategy in Scanzano Jonico. In: Leone, A., Gargiulo, C. (eds.) Environmental and Territorial Modelling for Planning and Design, pp. 665–672. FedOApress (2018). https://doi.org/10.6093/978-88-6887-048-5
9. Fiore, P., Padula, A., Angela Pilogallo, F.S.: Facing urban regeneration issues through geodesign approach. The case of Gravina in Puglia. In: Leone, A., Gargiulo, C. (eds.) Environmental and Territorial Modelling for Planning and Design. FedOAPress (2018). https://doi.org/10.6093/978-88-6887-048-5

10. Scorza, F.: Sustainable urban regeneration in Gravina in Puglia, Italy. In: Fisher, T., Orland, B., Steinitz, C. (eds.) The International Geodesign Collaboration. Changing Geography by Design, pp. 112–113. ESRI Press, Redlands (2020)
11. Casas, G.L., Scorza, F.: Sustainable planning: a methodological toolkit. In: Gervasi, O., et al. (eds.) ICCSA 2016. LNCS, vol. 9786, pp. 627–635. Springer, Cham (2016). https://doi.org/10.1007/978-3-319-42085-1_53
12. Vagnby, B.H.: Logical framework approach. 64 (2000)
13. UN HABITAT: New Urban Agenda. United Nations (2017)
14. Las Casas, G., Scorza, F., Murgante, B.: New urban agenda and open challenges for urban and regional planning. In: Calabrò, F., Della Spina, L., Bevilacqua, C. (eds.) ISHT 2018. SIST, vol. 100, pp. 282–288. Springer, Cham (2019). https://doi.org/10.1007/978-3-319-92099-3_33
15. Casas, G.L., Scorza, F.: From the UN new urban agenda to the local experiences of urban development: the case of potenza. In: Gervasi, O., et al. (eds.) ICCSA 2018. LNCS, vol. 10964, pp. 734–743. Springer, Cham (2018). https://doi.org/10.1007/978-3-319-95174-4_56
16. Las Casas, G., Scorza, F., Murgante, B.: Razionalità a-priori: una proposta verso una pianificazione antifragile. Ital. J. Reg. Sci. 18, 329–338 (2019). https://doi.org/10.14650/93656
17. Murgante, B., Borruso, G.: Cities and smartness: a critical analysis of opportunities and risks. In: Murgante, B., et al. (eds.) ICCSA 2013. LNCS, vol. 7973, pp. 630–642. Springer, Heidelberg (2013). https://doi.org/10.1007/978-3-642-39646-5_46
18. Batty, M., et al.: Smart cities of the future. Eur. Phys. J. Spec. Top. 214, 481–518 (2012). https://doi.org/10.1140/epjst/e2012-01703-3
19. Garau, C.: Smart paths for advanced management of cultural heritage. Reg. Stud. Reg. Sci. 1, 286–293 (2014). https://doi.org/10.1080/21681376.2014.973439
20. Garau, C., Pavan, V.M.: Evaluating urban quality: indicators and assessment tools for smart sustainable cities. Sustainability 10, 575 (2018). https://doi.org/10.3390/su10030575
21. Scorza, F., Saganeiti, L., Pilogallo, A., Murgante, B.: GHOST PLANNING: the inefficiency of energy sector policies in a low population density region. Arch. DI Stud, URBANI E Reg (2020)
22. Scorza, F., Pilogallo, A., Saganeiti, L., Murgante, B., Pontrandolfi, P.: Comparing the territorial performances of Renewable energy sources' plants with an integrated ecosystem services loss assessment: a case study from the Basilicata region (Italy). Sustain. Cities Soc. 56, 102082 (2020). https://doi.org/10.1016/J.SCS.2020.102082
23. Campagna, M., Ervin, S., Sheppard, S.: How geodesign processes shaped outcomes. In: Fisher, T., Orland, B., Steinitz, C. (eds.) The International Geodesign Collaboration. Changing Geography by Design, pp. 145–148. ESRI Press, Redlands (2020)
24. Albert, C.: IGC 2019: What we learned. In: Fisher, T., Orland, B., Steinitz, C. (eds.) The International Geodesign Collaboration. Changing Geography by Design, Redlands, California, pp. 139–144 (2020)
25. Shearer, A.: Design assumptions. In: Fisher, T., Orland, B., Steinitz, C. (eds.) The International Geodesign Collaboration. Changing Geography by Design, pp. 15–20. ESRI Press, Redlands (2020)
26. Rittel, H.W.J., Webber, M.M.: Dilemmas in a general theory of planning. Policy Sci. 4, 155–169 (1973). https://doi.org/10.1007/BF01405730

Opportunities and Challenges of a Geodesign Based Platform for Waste Management in the Circular Economy Perspective

Maria Cerreta$^{(\boxtimes)}$, Chiara Mazzarella, and Maria Somma

Department of Architecture, University of Naples Federico II, Via Toledo 402,
80134 Naples, Italy
{cerreta, chiara.mazzarella, maria.somma}@unina.it
c.mazzarella@tudelft.nl

Abstract. In the framework of the circular economy, the operational integration of metabolic flows management and co-planning of waste territories, also defined *wastescapes*, has been implemented by the Geodesign Decision Support Environment (GDSE) platform, a tool developed in the H2020 REPAiR project. The GDSE can be described as a Decision Support System (DSS) to manage metabolic flows in a spatial GIS-based environment. Born as a tool for the resources management in peri-urban areas, the GDSE was also configured as a repository of multiple information. By comparing the main steps of the Geodesign Hub software and the GDSE platform, the paper intends to highlight the results obtained so far from the implementation of the GDSE and the main future development hypotheses. The primary purpose is to integrate wastescapes regeneration with the management of metabolic flows by realising evaluation maps, required by Geodesign Hub software, in the GDSE to trigger a holistic regenerative process for the circular city.

Keywords: Geodesign Decision Support Environment (GDSE) · Geodesign process · Circular economy · Evaluation maps · Wastescapes

1 Introduction

The circular economy is one of the central themes of new sustainable territorial development policies [1–4]. Today cities are mostly complex in terms of tangible and intangible infrastructures, need cyclical planning processes capable of promoting collaboration between the parties concerned to reach a shared agreement. Current tools and processes tend to follow their linearity, and as a result, there is a loss of collective knowledge that would facilitate an efficient and effective planning process at the same time. Moreover, collaboration becomes essential, especially in large-scale planning processes [5]. In this perspective, there is a need to identify which decision-support tools can improve evaluation and planning processes, at different scales [6]. An attempt is being made to screen out current tools and methods that allow integrating collaboration and participation into evaluation and planning processes for design new circular economy models.

The concept of circular economy was born in the context of industrial ecology, about the use and manufacture of products, as material resources of urban metabolism.

© Springer Nature Switzerland AG 2020
O. Gervasi et al. (Eds.): ICCSA 2020, LNCS 12252, pp. 317–331, 2020.
https://doi.org/10.1007/978-3-030-58811-3_23

The optimisation of the production chains from a linear to a circular model aims to cancel the production of waste, recovering any waste that can take on new value through circular recovery processes [7] and the most of the circularity indicators of a product concern strategies for preserving materials [8].

Moving from the production chains to the built environment that organises these chains, the implications of the circular economy extend, and the city itself, as a human product, can embrace the challenge of circularity. The visions for the future of the circular city are not clearly defined but include looping actions through reuse recycle and recovery [9]. Circularity is multiscalar, multidimensional and place-specific [10] and the management of urban metabolic flows and land use planning affect and produce impacts on each other.

Considering the challenge of managing urban metabolism and land use at the same time, integration of methods and tools for policy and design strategies is required to support decision-makers in such a multi-disciplinar approach. Moreover, circular looping strategies must be regenerative, and a regenerative development considers the interaction among community engagement, resources, and territories.

According to the above purpose, Spatial Decision Support Systems (SDSS) are among the most effective tools of DSS and allow to face complex novel problems as emergency response and public participation [11]. Geodesign process [12–14] can be considered a SDSS. It represents an emerging methodological approach to spatial planning and design, able to address many of the problems encountered in urban and regional planning practices. Step by step, through a series of evaluation and design phases, the Geodesign methodological process allows multidisciplinary groups to interact and collaborate in the creation of alternative scenarios. Cooperation is a fundamental feature for a sustainable and circular economy-oriented transformation, that affect the future of communities and territories [13].

The term *geodesign* was introduced in 2005 by Jack Dangermond [15] who defined it as a multidisciplinary and synergistic approach useful to solve complex problems involving not only territorial and environmental issues but also social and economic concerns [15]. In this sense, the Geodesign methodology represents a useful framework to address the complex spatial issues related to the circular economy challenges and the reuse of cities and territories [16], as it integrates multidisciplinary knowledge with the technologies of Geographic Information Sciences [17].

Urban unsustainable scenarios are spread all over the world, and often they are related to linear economy models. Take-make-dispose model corresponds to extraction-production-consumption actions that have huge impacts on lands. For instance, if material loops are not closed, waste can be disposed of in the landfill, large parts of territories can be consumed, and at the same time, many materials that are obtained from non-renewal resources are extracted. Many materials like sand and gravels can be recycled, avoiding quarries and environmental depletion.

Each human activity is deeply connected to territories. As well as products can become waste, lands or sites turn into unsolved territories in between [18], when abandonment, degradation and pollution become dominant. Wasted lands are a consequence of different drivers. Succeeding the concept of drosscape [19, 20], *wastescapes* are considered those parts of cities as a result not necessarily polluted - but where risk exposure is high - like ghettos, abandoned areas [18, 21], and those places where social risk caused segregation. The transition of cities toward regenerative circular scenarios needs to bond the resource management, starting from the reduction, reusing and recycling of waste streams and the wastescapes regeneration through land-use planning. In this path, the integration of approaches and tools to support a collaborative decision-making process is proposed following the Geodesign methodology. The paper describes the research purpose and the methodological approach in Sect. 2; the Geodesign Decision Support Environment (GDSE), conceived as a collaborative decision-making process for resource management, is introduced in Sect. 3, and the Geodesign Hub platform is analysed in Sect. 4; the interaction between Geodesign Hub and GDSE by the evaluation maps is presented in Sect. 5; the discussion of results and conclusions are the content of Sect. 6.

2   Research Purpose and Methodological Approach

This paper illustrates the methodological process and the main outcomes of the Geodesign Decision Support Environment (GDSE) [22], to highlight its innovative aspects and critical issues that can be implemented to operationalise resource management and wastescape regeneration. The Geodesign platform has been developed as part of the H2020 REPAiR - Resource Management in Peri-Urban Areas: Going beyond the Urban Metabolism research project, to support collaborative planning processes in the transition to the circular economy. Geodesign process can be considered as a spatial-decision support system (SDSS) to facilitate circular co-design strategies of urban metabolic resources. In an attempt to pursue this goal, the GDSE implemented new types of evaluation maps of waste flows, necessary to support the knowledge of metabolic status quo and to guide the choices for closing the loops.

Starting from a methodological comparison of the GDSE with the Geodesign Hub (Fig. 1), both open-access web-based collaborative decision support systems, we intend to identify the main common ground in the Geodesign process and the main crucial differences with GDSE, for future integrations.

The highlights of the GDSE process are compared to that of Geodesign Hub to identifies the fundamental steps where landscape and wastescape evaluation maps can be made operative by integrating the eco-innovative solutions and land use policies or projects. In both systems, the Geodesign approach [12] is used, with six questions referred to six models [12] (Fig. 1):

1. How should the study area be described in content, space, and time? To answer this question, reference is made to the data collected for the study and therefore to the representation model.
2. How does the study area operate? What are the functional and structural relationships among its elements? In this case, on the other hand, through process models, knowledge about the territory under examination is outlined.
3. Is the current study area working well? That is where evaluation models come in.
4. How might the study area be altered? By what policies and actions, where and when? Change models try to answer this question. Once developed, they are compared and then used to represent future conditions.

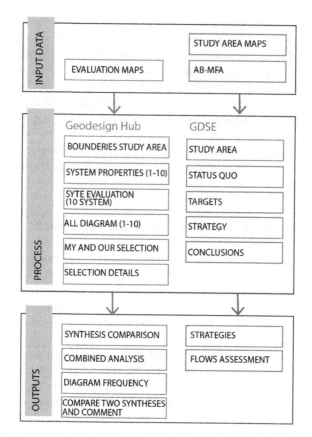

Fig. 1. GDH and GDSE methodological workflow compared (Elaboration of the authors).

5. What difference might the changes cause? It is possible to answer the question through impact models.
6. How should the study area be changed? Through decision models, how the area under consideration can change.

The Geodesign Hub platform allows different stakeholders to be involved and collaborate to reach one or more negotiated design strategy. Conceived at the Centre for Advanced Spatial Analysis at University College London by Hrishikesh Ballal [23], this platform is based on the Geodesign framework designed by Carl Steinitz [24].

This GIS-based tool incorporates planning, landscape architecture, geography, and engineering in a combination of disciplines that constitutes an SDSS, that combine local knowledge and information technologies.

To carry out a process in Geodesign Hub, three main phases are required: 1. pre-workshop; 2. workshop; 3. post-workshop. The first phase refers to the evaluation of the selected area and is based on representation models, process models and evaluation models. The second phase refers to the intervention based on change models, impact models and decision models [12]. This phase is where the Geodesign laboratory takes place. The third phase refers to the ex-post elaboration of a report. Both the first and the third phase are developed by the researcher who plays the role of facilitator in the second phase. In a similar way, the GDSE process needs a preparation phase before the workshop and a successive phase to analyse the obtained results.

Referring to the Geodesign framework, it is possible to define similarities and differences between the two open platforms, in their basic data and concerning the interactions of input data, process data and output data.

In Geodesign Hub as input data, ten evaluation maps present the status quo of the systems considered. In the software, the maps become interactive and at a later stage, and work together with the different diagrams.

In the GDSE the interface presents the wastescape maps at the actual state and an Activity-Based Material Flow Analysis (AB-MFA) of material and waste flows. These two maps, however, do not fully interact in the GDSE process.

Besides, the evaluation maps in the Geodesign Hub allow defining those optimal locations where an intervention could be expected. This is especially important in the third phase, where stakeholders, by mutual agreement, choose one preferred scenario among the proposals defined in the second phase of the workshop.

In the GDSE process, there is no real construction of possible proposals, but the qualified researcher proposes upstream, possible places where to implement the eco-innovative solutions already known at an early stage.

Following, the methodological structure and the steps that constitute the GDSE are presented. Subsequently, a comparison with the Geodesign Hub workflow allows presenting the hypotheses for the implementation of wastescape management in the GDSE, having a unique SDSS that connect material flow and land use management in circular strategies.

3 The Geodesign Decision Support Environment: A Collaborative Decision-Making Process for Resource Management

The Geodesing-based GDSE methodology has been developed in the H2020 REPAiR project as an open-source DSS tool to improve resource management in the transition toward a circular economy [18, 25–28]. Mapping material and waste flows the first step to understanding their dynamics and implementing solutions and strategies to improve urban metabolism. The REPAiR project methodology is based on the co-creation framework that is structured in five phases and uses three interactive methodologies: Geodesign Decision Support Environment (GDSE), Peri-Urban Living Lab (PULL), and Life Cycle Assessment (LCA).

The five phases Co-Exploring, Co-Design, Co-Production, Co-Decision, and Co-Governance are performed in PULLs and lead by the Geodesign team. PULLs have been activated by workshops with stakeholders and actors involved in each phase of the project [29]. LCA has been externally developed to assess the sustainability of impacts related to status quo and eco-innovative solutions on each key flow supply chain selected. In the Naples case study, two LCA have been done for organic waste and construction and demolition waste status quo and for an alternative scenario.

In REPAiR project, the methodology has been developed and tested in two pilot cases, and four follow-up cases. In Naples, the key flows considered are organic waste and constructions and demolition waste, and both relevant wastes flow with different significant impacts in their life cycles and with high impacts on territories and wastescapes. In the methodological framework, PULLs identify the opportunity to let decision-makers know the status-quo, ranking objectives and targets and to enable cooperation for territorial transformations, within a collaborative and adaptive decision-making process.

The GDSE workflow is composed of five sections. It can be managed in setup mode by researchers and in workshop mode for the public sessions. The workflow is here presented as stakeholders can use the tool in a Geodesign session.

The first step presents the study area. It is composed of:

1. the wastescape mapping elaborated in pre-workshop phases; according to the REPAiR framework, implemented by the research group and in PULLs with citizens and local actors (Table 1);

Table 1. Wastescapes layers mapped in Naples study area (REPAiR, D.3.3, 2018)

Wastescapes categories	Layers in legend
Degraded lands	nsw_1_1 Polluted Soils
	nsw_1_2 Artificial Soils
Degraded water	nsw_2_1 Degraded water bodies
	nsw_2_2 Elements linked to degrades waters
	nsw_2_3 Flooding zones
Declining fields	nsw_3_1 Abandoned agricultural fields
Settlements and buildings in crisis	nsw_4_1 Vacant underused buildings and settlements
	nsw_4_2 Urban settlements suffering from fatigue
	nsw_4_3 Poor housing conditions
	nsw_4_4 Informal settlements
	nsw_4_5 Urban lots in trasformation tampered
	nsw_4_6 Unauthorised buildings and settlements
	nsw_4_7 Confiscated assets
Dross of facilities and infrastructures	nsw_5_1 Neglected dismissed underused infrastructures
	nsw_5_2 Dismissed underused public facilities
	nsw_5_3 Interstitial spaces of infrastructures networks
	nsw_6_3 Storage facilities
Operational landscape of waste	nsw_6_4 Waste recovery
	nsw_6_10 Incinerators
	nsw_6_11 Vehicle dismantling

2. some relevant charts elaborated in PULLs;
3. lists of stakeholder groups;
4. descriptions of the waste key flow.

In the second step, the status quo is described by:

1. flows maps (Fig. 2) and Sankey diagrams of the key flows (Fig. 3);
2. some flow indicators of selected waste key flow on inhabitants or spatial units;
3. map of the study area and wastescape layers;
4. reports of the sustainability assessment on both waste key flows;
5. some lists of general and specific challenges and objectives on local flows.

Status quo of the key flow presents the activity-based material flow analysis, a flow assessment process steps and primary outcomes. In the target section, the objective presented in the status quo can be ranked. Based on some flow indicators defined by the research group, the team of Geodesign can identify the targets for increasing or reducing each significant flow indicator (Fig. 4) per key flow.

The strategy section is the step where stakeholders' groups can build the change model, and it is composed of a set of sub-steps:

1. The eco-innovative solutions (EISs) previously elaborated and implemented in the system are presented. EISs are actions that enable reduction of waste flow.
2. The elaboration of more strategies is activated with the cooperation of stakeholders by selecting the EISs and their implementation area (Fig. 5). These areas will activate a place-based solution, then on specific key flows and actors involved, classified per activity group with the NACE code.

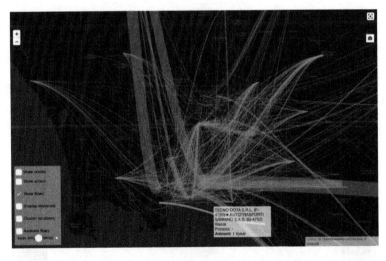

Fig. 2. Activity based-material flow map of mixed construction and demolition waste (EWC 170904) produced in Naples focus area in 2015 (source: Screenshot from GDSE. Elaboration of the authors)

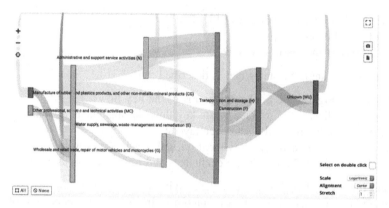

Fig. 3. Sankey diagram at the activity level of AB-MFA mixed construction and demolition waste (EWC 170904) produced from Naples focus area in 2015 (source: Screenshot from GDSE. Elaboration of the authors)

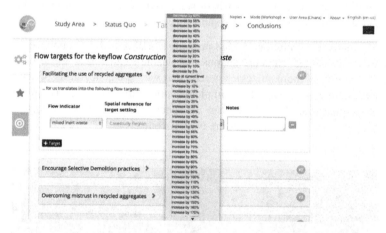

Fig. 4. Flow target selection for key flow (source: Screenshot from GDSE. Elaboration of the authors)

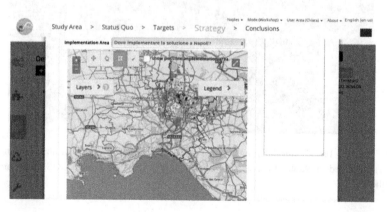

Fig. 5. Strategy elaboration: the selection of an implementation area for an EIS (source: Screenshot from GDSE. Elaboration of the authors)

3. The presentation of modified flows as results of combined EISs in strategies.
4. The control of flow target allows stakeholders to check the effectiveness of their choices.

In the last step of conclusions, results are presented by answering the following questions:

1. How to rank the alternatives per group?
2. Which flow indicators were used for target settings on which objectives?
3. Which target values were set?
4. Which EISs were selected for the strategies? How where the questions answered?
5. Where were the solutions applied?
6. Which actor groups are involved by the selected solutions and which most often?
7. Which stakeholders were chosen for implementing solutions?
8. How much do the strategies modify the flows?
9. Which strategy can meet which own target?

The GDSE workflow activates a decision-making process for the management of metabolic flows only considering the AB-MFA. The wastescape that are presented in the first section remains exclusively in the cognitive context of the co-exploring phase, but do not become operational in the elaboration of the strategies, or models of change. Therefore, the results of the process are based on the knowledge of the wastescape, but they do not give the opportunity to hypothesise policies or projects together with the management of the supply chains. For an integrated circular city strategy, it is necessary to integrate land management. For this purpose, the possibilities offered by the Geodesign Hub platform are analysed below.

4 Geodesign Hub Platform

The Geodesign Hub PSS [23] is an open-source platform mainly used to manage and organise complex problems, mainly related to the territory, promoting a collaborative decision-making process between the different actors involved. Developed to implement the Geodesign framework [12, 22] and to foster participatory and interactive planning [30], it combines the concepts of the planning support system [31, 32] with the principles of web 2.0 [32], which includes and allows different types of activities involving the public to participate in data collection, problem definition and decision-making [33, 34]. The platform is used to support planning processes allowing the different actors involved to interact. Through workshops, the actors engaged are led to define strategies in a collaborative way supported by some tools within the Geodesign Hub [30]. As for the GDSE, there is a configurational management model used by the expert researchers and a laboratory mode implemented in public sessions by the different participants involved. It is also composed of seven sections. The first section is dedicated to the visualisation of evaluation maps related to 10 priority systems (Fig. 6). These represent vulnerabilities and attractiveness for the territory. They are defined in the start-up phase of a project and after consultation with the main contract holders. Usually, 10 are defined, but they can be integrated in relation to the study area characteristics. Some model systems refer to cultural heritage, ecology, tourism and agri-food sector, green and blue infrastructure, transport, soft mobility, low and high-density housing or trade and industry. Each of these is fundamental to the definition of objectives. They are indicated by acronyms in the platform. Their definition starts with the analysis of the status quo to the elaboration of evaluation maps, which are then provided to the participants during the workshop. The second section (Fig. 6) of the Geodesign Hub interface allows the different actors involved to outline geo-referenced project proposals on an interactive map for each of the different coloured systems. These different project ideas can then be selected and visualised in a third section, where it is possible to view a summary map of the interventions and details about hectares and costs for the whole project. The fourth section is dedicated to the verification of impacts and subsequent comparison (fifth section) (Fig. 7), where workshop participants, divided into teams with the relative objectives to be pursued, select the different diagrams and compare them. In the sixth section, it is possible to compare the teams' proposals by a pairwise comparison and then reach the last section where a joint strategy between the stakeholders is defined through a negotiation phase (Fig. 8). Indeed, the Geodesign Hub platform allows the actors involved in a decision-making process to define a common agreement by reasoning through spatial analysis [30].

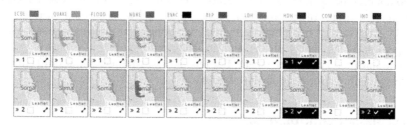

Fig. 6. Designing with diagrams: simple diagrams across systems synthesised into designs (source: Screenshot from Geodesign Hub platform https://www.geodesignhub.com/. Courtesy of Hrishikesh Ballah)

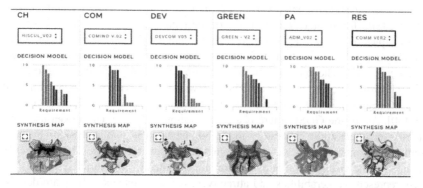

Fig. 7. Synthesis comparisons design: compare decision model and negotiations table (source: Screenshot from Geodesign Hub platform https://www.geodesignhub.com/. Courtesy of Hrishikesh Ballah)

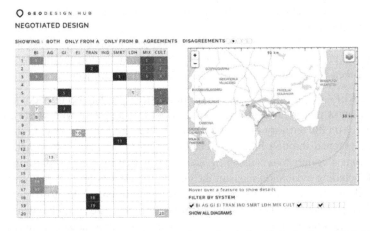

Fig. 8. Negotiation design (source: Screenshot from Geodesign Hub platform: DLA Geodesign workshop 2020 https://www.geodesignhub.com/. Courtesy of Hrishikesh Ballah)

5 Geodesign Hub and GDSE Interplay: Evaluation Maps

Each territory inherently has its vocation [14], and consequently, to define the evaluation maps, it is necessary to consider every aspect of the territory in question. The evaluation maps within the Geodesign Hub platform are built at an early stage by expert researchers who spatially analyse each phenomenon starting from the description of its conditions in the status quo. Evaluation maps can be constructed in three main ways:

1. Sketching by hand using printed maps and red, yellow, green markers and digitising the sketched maps directly on Geodesign Hub.
2. Using the GIS software where to insert the various existing data to analyse it then spatially.
3. Using automatic sprits, but, in this case, it is necessary to have previous knowledge in programming languages.

In the Geodesign Hub software are loaded in the pre-workshop phase the evaluation maps that are represented with a standard colour gradation (from red to green) defining the parts of the territory more attractive or vulnerable for given land use. The maps are elaborated for all the systems taken as reference for the study of the selected area. The researchers of the Geodesign Hub articulate the process of creating such maps in 10 systems that describe the main characteristics of the territory [14]. Each system corresponds to an evaluation map. The colours to be used can be either three (red, yellow, and green) or five (red, yellow, light green, green, dark green) and is specifically related to technical knowledge of the study area.

Each of these five colours represents a fundamental characteristic:

1. Red (Existing): Better not compromise the system.
2. Yellow (Not Appropriate): it is not a good idea to act in that place.

3. Light green (Capable): interventions can only be identified if the right tools are available to support them.
4. Green (Suitable): it is possible to define the project in this area because the territory is already provided with appropriate technologies to support the project.
5. Dark Green (Feasible): the area is feasible to define a project.

In the REPAiR project, a mapping of the wastescapes has been made, in order to identify them as places to be redeveloped and put into a system with waste conceived as a resource on the territory in the perspective of the circular economy. In the process, they were mapped through hard data elaborated by the research group and soft data derived from a collaborative mapping activated in PULLs [35]. Regarding the relevance of including evaluation maps in the GDSE, the Geodesign Hub platform helps to reflect and reason on some issues not to be underestimated. In itself, wastescapes represent critical areas or critical elements of the territory. These can be identified such as: disused buildings, places to be reclaimed, interstitial areas of infrastructure, buildings to be demolished that produce waste (Table 1), and their regeneration represents one of the objectives to be pursued on which it is necessary to develop eco-innovative considerations and solutions. By reasoning with respect to the Geodesign Hub, wastescapes become subsystems of the ten main systems. For example, since they represent highly critical areas in the status quo, they should be assessed individually according to the criteria that make them suitable or not suitable for transformative planning actions. The ten reference systems suitable to pursue the regeneration objective, also defining in the function of eco-innovative solutions, could be:

1. Environmental system;
2. Green infrastructure system;
3. Blue infrastructure system;
4. Transport system;
5. Soft mobility system;
6. Cultural system;
7. Functional mixing system;
8. Agricultural system;
9. Industrial system;
10. Energy system;

For each of these systems, as described in detail above, it is necessary to create evaluation maps on which to reason in order to identify and define both governance and planning strategies. All this can simplify the participatory process and the active involvement of the different actors not only in the analysis phase, developed during the PULLs, but also in a preparatory phase of solutions and decision-making.

A further challenge is to identify which criteria and indicators need to be considered in order to converge the evaluation of the interactive waste stream with the evaluation maps for each of the systems. The idea could be to display in single screen waste streams and evaluation maps both in the first phase of the analysis and in the impact and final transformation phases. In this way, the regeneration of territories through planning tools in a virtual environment acquires greater importance because it also evaluates waste management and considers every aspect of it, thus determining cyclical and sustainable processes for territories.

6 Discussion and Conclusions

In recent years, the research towards a successful model design of circular economy implementation included different studies and scientific publications, concentrating on business model, product design and process individually [36]. At the same time, the circular economy is seen as an opportunity to conciliate the competing objectives of economic, environmental and social benefits [37].

According to Velte et al. [36] circular economy can be described with a hierarchy of objectives, based on the value-focused thinking approach for widening the decision context and exploring the consistency of the decision-maker purposes and the strategic decision context. This means that, for a decision-maker, the context-specific alternatives need to be elaborated and evaluated considering an integrated, dynamic and open decision-making process. Indeed, a decision-making process can be defined as a procedure of learning and negotiation between a multiplicity of actors and the decision-maker, where mutual interaction allows to improve the decision.

Implementing the Geodesign process as a dynamic methodology means encouraging interaction and collaboration between all actors who are involved in a decision-making process. At the same time, GDSE starts considering wastescapes and waste flows as a whole system, but in eco-innovative strategies design, wastescape is just a layer to select the implementation area of the solutions. Territorial and spatial planning is not part of the capability of the platform. It allows us to have a dynamic view of the status quo of waste and material flows and to have an interactive material mass balance according to the selected solutions.

The Geodesign process enables a collective DSS, that involves and activate a public, private, people partnership making operative the decision-making process. It can support planning oriented to circular economy process, by considering waste flows as resources for eco-innovative strategies in the landscape regeneration. The integration between the Geodesign Hub maps management and the GDSE process allows to combine the opportunities of each of the two approaches and to structure a Decision Support System suitable for making the circular economy model operational, applying the value-focused thinking approach. This paper presents the first step of a methodological process and some considerations for integrating active management of territorial, metabolic and social resources through planning and evaluation tools.

Author Contributions. The authors jointly conceived and developed the approach and decided on the overall objective and structure of the paper. In particular, conceptualisation and methodology, M.C.; formal analysis, data curation and software, investigation and validation, writing original draft, writing, review and editing, C.M. and M.S. All authors have read and agreed to the published version of the manuscript.

Funding. This research has received funding from the European Horizon 2020 funded research "REPAiR: REsource Management in Peri-urban AReas: Going Beyond Urban Metabolism", Grant Agreement No 688920. This article reflects only the author's view. The Commission is not responsible for any use that may be made of the information it contains.

References

1. Geissdoerfer, M., Savaget, P., Bocken, N.M.P., Hultink, E.J.: The circular economy – a new sustainability paradigm? J. Clean. Prod. **143**, 757–768 (2017). https://doi.org/10.1016/j.jclepro.2016.12.048

2. Korhonen, J., Honkasalo, A., Seppälä, J.: Circular economy: the concept and its limitations. Ecol. Econ. **143**, 37–46 (2018). https://doi.org/10.1016/j.ecolecon.2017.06.041

3. Kirchherr, J., Reike, D., Hekkert, M.: Conceptualizing the circular economy: an analysis of 114 definitions. Resour. Conserv. Recycl. **127**, 221–232 (2017). https://doi.org/10.1016/j.resconrec.2017.09.005

4. Rodriguez-Anton, J.M., Rubio-Andrada, L., Celemín-Pedroche, M.S., Alonso-Almeida, M. D.M.: Analysis of the relations between circular economy and sustainable development goals. Int. J. Sustain. Dev. World Ecol. **26**, 708–720 (2019). https://doi.org/10.1080/13504509.2019.1666754

5. Fischer, J.-G., Gneiting, P.: Collaborative planning processes. In: Parry, G., Graves, A. (eds.) Build to Order: The Road to the 5-Day Car, pp. 181–207. Springer, London (2008). ISBN 978-1-84800-225-8

6. Girard, L.F., Nocca, F.: Moving towards the circular economy/city model: Which tools for operationalizing this model? Sustainability **11**, 1–48 (2019). https://doi.org/10.3390/su11226253

7. Farooque, M., Zhang, A., Thürer, M., Qu, T., Huisingh, D.: Circular supply chain management: a definition and structured literature review. J. Clean. Prod. **228**, 882–900 (2019). https://doi.org/10.1016/j.jclepro.2019.04.303

8. Moraga, G., et al.: Circular economy indicators: What do they measure? Resour. Conserv. Recycl. **146**, 452–461 (2019). https://doi.org/10.1016/j.resconrec.2019.03.045

9. Williams, J.: Circular cities: challenges to implementing looping actions. Sustainability **2019**, 11 (2019). https://doi.org/10.3390/su11020423

10. Marin, J., De Meulder, B.: Interpreting circularity. Circular city representations concealing transition drivers. Sustainability **2018**, 10 (2018). https://doi.org/10.3390/su10051310

11. Keenan, P.B., Jankowski, P.: Spatial decision support systems: three decades on. Decis. Support Syst. **116**, 64–76 (2019). https://doi.org/10.1016/j.dss.2018.10.010

12. Steinitz, C.: Which Way of Designing? In: Lee, Danbi J., Dias, E., Scholten, Henk J. (eds.) Geodesign by Integrating Design and Geospatial Sciences. GL, vol. 111, pp. 11–40. Springer, Cham (2014). https://doi.org/10.1007/978-3-319-08299-8_2

13. Campagna, M.: Metaplanning: About designing the Geodesign process. Landsc. Urban Plan. **156**, 118–128 (2016). https://doi.org/10.1016/j.landurbplan.2015.08.019

14. Di Cesare, E.A., Cocco, C., Campagna, M.: Il Geodesign come metodologia per la progettazione collaborativa di scenari di sviluppo per l'Area Metropolitana di Cagliari. In: ASITA 2016 Proceedings 2016, pp. 333–340 (2016)

15. Dangermond, J.: GeoDesign and GIS-designing our futures. In: Proceedings of the Peer Reviewed Proceedings of Digital Landscape Architecture; Anhalt University of Applied Science, Germania (2010)

16. Campagna, M., Di Cesare, E.A.: Geodesign: lost in regulations (and in practice). In: Papa, R., Fistola, R. (eds.) Smart Energy in the Smart City. GET, pp. 307–327. Springer, Cham (2016). https://doi.org/10.1007/978-3-319-31157-9_16
17. Goodchild, M.F.: Towards geodesign: repurposing cartography and GIS? Cartogr. Perspect. **2010**, 7–21 (2010). https://doi.org/10.14714/cp66.93
18. REPAiR. PULLs Handbook REPAiR Deliverable 5.1. EU Commission Participant Portal: Brussels, Belgium (2017)
19. Berger, A.: Drosscape. Wasting land in urban America; Princeton.; New York, USA (2006)
20. Gasparrini, C., Terracciano, A.: Drosscity. In: Ed, L. (ed.) Metabolismo, resilienza e progetto di riciclo dei drosscape, Trento (2016). ISBN 9788899854232
21. Amenta, L., van Timmeren, A.: Beyond wastescapes: towards circular landscapes. addressing the spatial dimension of circularity through the regeneration of wastescapes. Sustainability **2018**, 10 (2018). https://doi.org/10.3390/su10124740
22. Arciniegas, G., et al.: A geodesign decision support environment for integrating management of resource flows in spatial planning. Urban Plan. **4**, 32 (2019). https://doi.org/10.17645/up.v4i3.2173
23. Ballal, H.: Collaborative Planning with Digital Design Synthesis (2015)
24. Steinitz, C: A Framework for Geodesign: Changing Geography by Design. ESRI Press, Redlands California (2012). PRESS, E., Ed.
25. Ellen MacArthur Foundation Growth within: a circular economy vision for a competitive europe. Ellen MacArthur Found. 2015, 100
26. Cerreta, M., Inglese, P., Mazzarella, C.: Wastescapes sustainable management: enabling contexts for eco-innovative solutions. In: GAR 2019 (2019)
27. Cerreta, M., Inglese, P., Mazzarella, C.: A hybrid decision-making process for wastescapes remediation. Geodesign, LCA, urban living lab interplay. Environ. Territ. Model. Plan. Des. **2018**, In A. Leon, 603–610. https://doi.org/10.6093/978-88-6887-048-5
28. Amenta, L.,et al.: Managing the transition towards circular metabolism: Living labs as a co-creation approach. Urban Plan. **4**, 5–18 (2019). https://doi.org/10.17645/up.v4i3.2170
29. Cerreta, M., Panaro, S.: From perceived values to shared values: a Multi-Stakeholder Spatial Decision Analysis (M-SSDA) for resilient landscapes. Sustainability **2017**, 9 (2017). https://doi.org/10.3390/su9071113
30. Cocco, C., Freitas, C.R., Moura, A.C.M., Campagna, M.: Geodesign process analytics: Focus on design as a process and its outcomes. Sustainability **2020**, 12 (2020). https://doi.org/10.3390/su12010119
31. Harris, B.: Beyond geographic information systems: computers and the planning professional. J. Am. Plan. Assoc. **55**, 85–90 (1989). https://doi.org/10.1080/01944368908975408
32. Campagna, M., Steinitz, C., Di Cesare, E.A., Cocco, C., Ballal, H., Tess, C.: Collaboration in planning: the geodesign approach. Rozw. Reg. i Polityka Reg. **35**, 55–72 (2016)
33. Haklay, M.: Volunteered Geographic Information and Citizen Science (2017)
34. Nov, O., Arazy, O., Anderson, D.: Scientists@Home: what drives the quantity and quality of online citizen science participation? PLoS ONE **9**, e90375 (2014). https://doi.org/10.1371/journal.pone.0090375
35. Kørnøv, L., Thissen, W.A.H.: Rationality in decision- and policy-making: implications for strategic environmental assessment. Impact Assess. Proj. Apprais. **18**, 191–200 (2000). https://doi.org/10.3152/147154600781767402
36. Velte, C.J., Scheller, K., Steinhilper, R.: Circular economy through objectives - development of a proceeding to understand and shape a circular economy using value-focused thinking. Procedia CIRP **69**, 775–780 (2018). https://doi.org/10.1016/j.procir.2017.11.031
37. Cerreta, M., Poli, G., Regalbuto, S., Mazzarella, C.: A Multi-dimensional Decision-Making Process for Regenerative Landscapes: A New Harbour for Naples (Italy), pp. 156–170 (2019)

Brazilian Geodesign Platform: WebGis & SDI & Geodesign as Co-creation and Geo-Collaboration

Ana Clara Mourão Moura$^{(\boxtimes)}$ ⓘ and Christian Rezende Freitas ⓘ

Escola de Arquitetura, Laboratório de Geoprocessamento, Universidade Federal de Minas Gerais (UFMG), Rua Paraíba 697, Belo Horizonte, Brazil
anaclara@ufmg.br,
christianrezende@alomeioambiente.com.br

Abstract. The paper presents the main motivations for the development of a Brazilian platform for Geodesign, based on adaptations of observed needs, review of processes and facilities to face the challenges of spatial inequalities and complexity. The study is motivated by the analysis of difficulties and criticisms on the applied framework tested in robust number of workshops developed. It starts by the literature review in order to understand the main values and keywords that were constructed along time in the use of technologies of geospatial information in planning and, as a result, defines the main resources and facilities that should be considered to a new format of Geodesign. The new platform itself is presented, and the paper illustrates and discusses the proposed framework according to four steps: Reading Enrichment, Dialogues as Creation of Ideas, Voting as Selection of Ideas, and Statistics as Final Decision. It compares and justifies a new framework in Geodesign in face to main models generally used and discusses possible development to a close future.

Keywords: Spatial inequalities · Framework · Participatory planning

1 Introduction

Based on experiences developed by Geoprocessing Laboratory from the School of Architecture in the Federal University of Minas Gerais, Brazil, in case studies in Geodesign since 2015, when we first tested the framework proposed by Steinitz [1] in a local case study [2, 3], we analyzed results and understood we had to review the framework and platforms to face the challenges of complex areas of spatial inequalities.

Steinitz stablishes a framework of 6 models, 3 of them are constructed before the workshop to answer the questions: "How should the study area be described?" (Representation Models), "How does the study area operate?" (Process Models) and "Is the studying area working well?" (Evaluation Models). During the workshop the participants construct the other 3 models: the Change Models to answer "How might the study area be changed?", and the system calculates the "Impact Models" answering "What differences might the changes cause", and finally participants construct "Decision Models" to answer "How should the study area be changed".

© Springer Nature Switzerland AG 2020
O. Gervasi et al. (Eds.): ICCSA 2020, LNCS 12252, pp. 332–348, 2020.
https://doi.org/10.1007/978-3-030-58811-3_24

We worked on 43 experiences of Geodesign workshop in 35 projects. From these, 28 were proposed and conducted by the coordination of the laboratory, 4 were proposed by other researchers with our support and in 3 we acted as participants. Of the 35 experiences one was developed in analogical method, one in ArcGis, one in CityEngine, and 32 in GeodesignHub [4], a web-based platform developed by Ballal based on Steinitz framework [5, 6]. After each workshop we applied questionnaires or did notes about performances. The main difficulties and criticism we had to face were about Evaluation Models (92% of participants were not happy with using them), about time (98% of participants noted the importance of extending the time for interpretation and decision) and about the ambiguity in the use of Impact Models (85% didn't use them with knowledge and consciousness). They had difficulty to understanding the difference between policies and projects (observed in 90% of the studies).

The main difficulties in the use of Evaluation Models were about opinions and judgments, because they are a combination of spatial information resulting in a map in which the legend is: feasible (for the very best places to draw ideas of policies and projects), suitable (for the good places to draw proposal), capable (for the acceptable places to draw ideas, even if they were not the best), inappropriate (places not indicated to receive the proposals) and existing (places in which the potentialities or vulnerabilities are already solved). The model presents a scale from the most important to the last important place for proposals, what is an opinion, even if it was constructed by an expert or by stakeholders. We had experiences in which participants took part in the construction of the models, and even in those case studies there was criticism about Evaluation Maps, considered reductionist and inductors of decisions. To solve this problem, we started to include a broader collection of maps, presenting initial information about the place to the participants, using platforms of WebMaps and WebGis in parallel to GeodesignHub platform [7–9].

The main difficulties about Impact Models where about targets, costs and the matrix of impacts itself. While deciding about the ideas of projects to compose a design, the participants must analyze if they are achieving the targets (the amount of area in hectares they are expected to propose per system), the cost of their design and also if the proposals of projects are in the "right" place according to Evaluation Models. The Impact Analysis screen presents a scale from deep purple to deep orange indicating if the impact is positive, positive, neutral, negative or extremely negative. The first problem is that these calculations of impacts (targets, costs and spatial analysis impacts) are presented just for projects, and not for policies, and this is quite confusing for participants to understand. Most of them declared they selected some diagrams just to meet the target. Others declared they were not considering the Impact Model results because they did not agree with the judgment about the best place to put contributions, a problem that was also related to Evaluation Models.

Among the critics there was also a problem about time, that even when we did all the activities in a more slowly process and giving the participants more time between the meetings, they complained about that [9]. So, the question could be not exactly "time", but more possibilities of constructing an understanding, of presenting their considerations, of registering their ideas. In few words, to really be part of it. We understood we had to review the participation framework. But we had to study from the beginning, understanding deeper the sense of Geodesign and trying to get, from literate review, some keywords that should be considered in a new proposal.

2 Methodology - Reviewing Concepts and the Role of Geodesign

Studies in spatial analysis, since the 1970s, have been based on the systemic scientific approach, which proposes that the investigation of a reality happens through the decomposition in the main variables that characterize it, and in the study of the relations between them [10]. In this sense, the advent of geoinformation technologies, more specifically the use of Geographic Information Systems, have a wide association with systemic approach, as they represent reality in layers of information, which are combined in interpretative syntheses that favor diagnostic and prognostic studies. It is possible not only to consult a geographic database, but also to generate new information from the inclusion of new actors and new points of view in the process.

When using the potentiality of GIS (Geographic Information System), Cowen [11] argues that there are steps related to "database approach", "toolbox approach", "application approach" and "process-oriented approach". The data-base approach fulfills the function of dissemination and consumption of geographic information. The toolbox approach allows that users of different knowledge to apply algorithms and perform the production of information from the data. The application approach studies information consumption that meet the uses and praxis established by specialist knowledge. Finally, the process-oriented approach establishes a work framework to be followed to accomplish a mission.

In this sense, it can be said that the advent of GIS has expanded from the production and consumption of data to the support of information construction and the inclusion of new actors. In parallel to GIS development the recognition of different stakeholders in a planning process started to have the support of a PSS (Planning Support System), based on clear definition of actors, tasks, responsibilities, flow of use and production of geographic data. The PSS is designed to address complex planning problems by associating three general components according to a systemic planning approach: GIS, models and visualization instruments [12–14]. The PSS employment proposals already include discussions on the collaborative aspect [16].

Parallel to technological development, interest in the territory also expands, from the point of view of its physical and anthropic values, its environmental resources and its potentialities and vulnerabilities, especially in face of the awareness of its limitations. The regulations on the obligation of citizen consultation in decisions that are of collective interest are published for different planning scales. In Brazil, the defense of this inclusion of new actors and collective decisions in planning begins with the Federal Constitution of 1984, called "citizen's constitution", whose principles related to regional and urban planning are concretized in the City Statute, law 10.257 of 2001, which defines that citizens' participation and shared decisions in planning are mandatory.

However, there was still a challenge to be faced: the production and consumption of data could be favored by GIS, the planning process could be structured according to a PSS, but there was a lack of investments in information visualization resources, more specifically on geovisualization. Visualization is defined in science as the condition that allows users to "see the unseen" which, by representing the main components, favors the understanding of complex elements [15]. When the geographical attribute is included, the expansion of the condition of geovisualization aims to provide a way to reveal the unknown, through self-learning in a dialogue between the subject and the represented object, passing through the stages of presentation, synthesis, analysis and construction of knowledge [16].

In this sense, studies were carried out to favor the creation of representations of spatial reality that would be useful to create a common understanding of planning issues, improve communication between different actors in multidisciplinary participations [17]. Proposals related to the term Geodesign emerged along this line of using geoinformation technology resources and expanding geovisualization conditions to get together different actors for participatory and shared planning.

The term Geodesign was used for the first time in 2008 at the NCGIA Specialists Meeting on Spatial Concepts and GIS and Design, based on a methodological reference framework for planning and territorial design of urban and environmental landscape, applying an integrated process [1]. It is supported by the use of spatial information systems that favor the analysis, the construction of alternatives, the participation and collaboration of different actors, followed by the evaluation of the possible impacts of the choices made and the wide communication of partial and final results.

But should Geodesign be understood as something new, or a result from previous studies in the use of Technologies of Geoinformation that were developing some facilities to consider new values from society in a general sense, and not only among GIS people?

Trying to answer that, we found a paper that helped us to construct a timeline and to define the main values that stated to be part of the interests in scientific production, that could be the basis for the emergence of Geodesign [18]. The authors presented a descriptive picture of the evolution of principles that were incorporated into the use of geoinformation technologies, more specifically the GIS, from 1958 to 2006, and demonstrated which and how the interests start. They presented the scientific publications and their authors according to a chronological evolution and, from that, we extracted the main ideas that emerged along time. They did not quote Geodesign because they published the review in 2006, but we included the term in their timeline, created a list of keywords that could synthetize the evolution, and aggregated them in the main ideas of: process/procedures, GIS resources, geovisualization, citizens' participation and, finally, Geodesign (Table 1).

Table 1. Timeline in technologies of geoinformation and planning - constructed from the review and adapted from Balram and Dragicevic [18]:

TIME	MOTIVATIONS / ROLES	RESOURCES
1958	Expansion of the argument	Representation
1960	Insertion of sketches and modeling	Precursors of the Planning Support System (PSS)
1960	Consensus maximization	Delphi Method
1963	Produce, manage and transform data	GIS (Geographic Information Systems)
1966	Interest in thought processes and structuring	Mental Maps
1969	Judgment of potentialities and vulnerabilities	Overlay of variable layers
1969	Interest in expanding participation	Definition of actors, tasks, stages
1971	Interest in decision-making processes	Decision Matrix, precursors to DSS (Decision Support Systems)
1982	Interest in the man / machine interface	Visualization and interface
1985	Shared decision processes	Framework decision support
1985	Maps based on the World Wide Web	Hypermaps
1989	Combining variables	Multicriteria Analysis
1992	Expansion of GIS as a structure of thought	Geographic Information Science
1992	Decision support	Communication in planning
1993	Argumentation	Citizens' participation
1993	From technical representation to local tradition	Incorporation of the citizens' vision
1994	Geographic information on the web	Web Geographic Information Systems
1994	Virtual reality and scenarios	Visualization and geovisualization
1996	Deliberation of the participants	Citizens' participation
1997	Citizen participation	Collaborative Spatial Decision Making
1997	Citizen empowerment	Ladder of empowerment
2001	Expansion of geographic data visualization	Geovisualization
2002	Scenarios and simulations	Agent interactions
2003	Geospatial technologies for group processes	Geocollaboration
2008	The term Geodesign appears	Geovisualization, Geocollaboration, Citizen participation, Web-based platform for consumption and production of information.

Colors according to classification:

	Process/procedures
	GIS resources
	Geovisualization
	Citizens' participation
	Geodesign

From this table we understood how the idea of Geodesign was been developed in scientific production and that it was supposed to be based on geovisualization, geo-collaboration, citizens' participation, web-based platform for consumption and production of information. From this understanding we decided that Brazilian platform of Geodesign was going to be a support to connect SDI & WebGis & Geodesign in order to provide integrated and georeferenced information, enabling a wide availability of data to support discussions about the territory. We decide to name it: "GISCOLAB - WebGis & SDI: Geodesign as cocreation and geocollaboration".

3   Development and Analysis - Brazilian Platform of Geodesign

The Brazilian platform of Geodesign was developed in the PhD thesis of Christian Rezende Freitas, under the supervision of Prof. Ana Clara Mourão Moura [19]. The logic of the platform was constructed in Laboratory of Geoprocessing and Christian Freitas presented his ideas about the new tendencies in the use of Geoinformation Technologies in territorial planning: new forms of production, sharing and use of spatial data. The idea is to use the structure of SDI (Spatial Data Infrastructure) with the complete services of access and production of data in a process of Geodesign negotiation (Fig. 1).

In the platform the thematic maps are distributed according to "Contexts", that are the main axis of discussion in the workshop. It is noteworthy, however, that the user can search layers from one context to another and, mainly, as it is a SDI (Spatial Data Infrastructure), the user can search layers through the Metadata Catalog (data about data). In the example, the main Contexts are "Production", "Inhabit", "Culture" and "Environment", and there is also the context of "Decision" for viewing partial and final results of the negotiation process (Fig. 2).

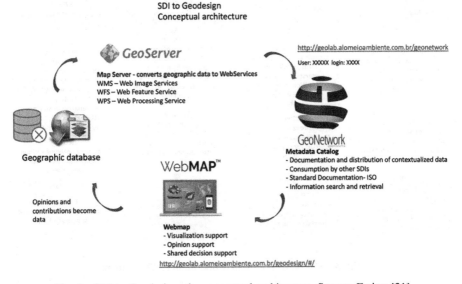

Fig. 1. SDI to Geodesign: the conceptual architecture. Source: Freitas [21]

Fig. 2. Brazilian Geodesign platform. Examples of thematic maps that are in the "Contexts". Source: The authors

The platform is developed from the logic of SDI following the patterns of data production and consumption, although it should be recognized as a "Thematic" SDI, as the data are not only the institutional ones, but those produced by the conductors of the workshop according to the main characteristics of the case study, not only representation models but also process models. When an institutional data is used directly, it is consumed via service (WMS – web map service) through a link for its visualization as a cartographic support. All thematic layers made available went through technical elaboration of content production, so even if they have references of data origin, they are new maps.

Once the platform is structured, the framework is based in 4 steps: "Reading Enrichment", "Dialogues as Creation of Ideas", "Voting as Selection of Ideas" and "Statistics as Final Decision" (Fig. 3).

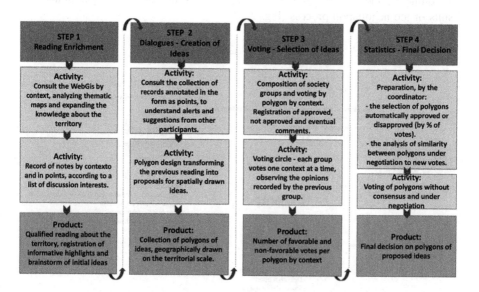

Fig. 3. The workshop framework. Source: The authors

The goal of Step 1, "Reading Enrichment", is to make the participant use the WebGis resources to read data about the place, to inform himself about the main characteristics of the place, and to be an active participant presenting notes based on what he knows about the territory: alerts and suggestions to many different themes of the case study. The goal of Step 2, "Dialogue – creation of ideas" is to make the participant draw polygons of proposals, to import existing polygons, or even to analyze the polygons that different actors presented (i.e.: proposals presented by institutions or public administration). The goal of Step 3, "Voting - Selection of Ideas" is to make the participant analyze and write comments to the list of proposals presented in the dialogues, that is a way to create a debate of ideas, presenting technical arguments and opinions that can be read by everyone, and mainly to register the individual vote about "like" or "don't like". The goal of Step 4, "Statistics as Final Decision" is to run statistical analysis about percentage of votes and to separate the proposals that are automatically disapproved, approved, and those that must go under negotiation. To give support to the negotiation it is used the analysis of topological similarity of polygons, to inform participants about each polygon and its topological relation with all other polygons.

3.1   Step 1 - Reading Enrichment

The participant receives the task to do this step before the first meeting with the group, by himself, with enough time to use the WebGis platform and open the contexts, visualize each map, to select layers and change the position of them, to apply transparencies and to change the referential base map. He takes his time to study the data. He can include more data from other platforms (using WMS – web map services) and recover data from one Contexts to another.

The participants receive a pdf explaining how to develop this first activity, with the link and the login information to use the platform. It is quite easy to be used, very intuitive. We tested this step in three opportunities: in two of them we sent the pdf instruction to participants and stablished a time to receive the doubts in the laboratory, and in one of them we created a WhatsApp group to put ourselves at their disposal to any doubt. Just one person (in a total amount of around 56 person considering the three experiences) had doubts in the very first contact with the tools, what is less than 2% of the participants, but the difficulties were solved with our help and the person was able to take part on all the steps.

After analyzing the data (representation and process maps) the participant can contribute inserting a pin (a point element) following a list of standardized symbols and colors presented by the conductor, in each context. They use the "Annotation" interface so that the point elements are geographic records of ideas, suggestions, alerts, opinions, new information about the place. Dynamically all the participants have access to the set of points and can be informed about what other people say, before the second step. It works like a brainstorm of initial ideas (Fig. 4).

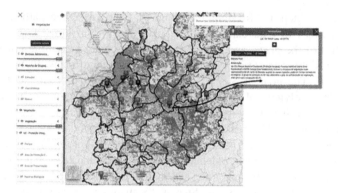

Fig. 4. Step 1 – Annotations using standardized symbols and colors. Source: The authors

3.2   Step 2 – Dialogues – Creation of Ideas

The participant, individually or in a group (what must be decided by the coordinator, as each workshop can have a dynamic composition of actors in different steps), analyzes the general ideas in the collection of points and draws polygons of those ideas that he or his working group deems relevant. The expectation is that the proposal polygons are elaborated by those who know the territory, for geographical assertiveness in terms of position, scale and content (Fig. 5).

It's also possible to import polygons designed by others, or even to draw the polygons using the tool of preference (i.e. Google Earth) and import them as contributions. They use the " Dialogues" interface and it's very easy to use the tools to draw and save, but it's important to highlight that polygons are representations of ideas that must come with the identification of the author, its name and a good description of the proposal. While in other systems the idea is based on graphic representation, this application was planned to encourage not only the drawing, but mainly the description, because it will be seriously be taken into account in the next step of voting.

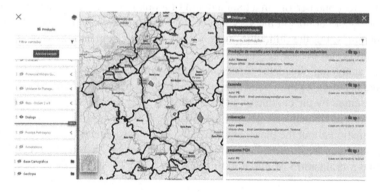

Fig. 5. Step 2 – Elaboration of polygons of ideas in the form of dialogues, containing graphic representation, author, title and description. Source: The authors

3.3   Step 3 – Voting – Selection of Ideas

The voting process can be conducted based on individual manifestation or group manifestation, according to the decision of the conductor. In the last experiments we decided by individual voting in this step and group voting in step 4. We understood that it was particularly important to make people really take a position and to feel they were listened and considered.

In this step we asked the participants to open the "Dialogues", analyze the polygons of ideas and write comments about them. They are not obliged to write comments, but they are very encouraged to do it, because this step is developed in presential workshop or in a session of a videoconference, in which they are separated by groups, according to their expertise and interests, and could call for debates or sharing opinions with other participants from his group, although when registering the own comments or votes each participant has to manifest individually on the platform (Fig. 6).

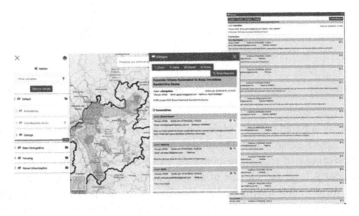

Fig. 6. Step 3-Dialogues–registration of comments with opinions, doubts, technical information, suggestions. Source: The authors

Before this presential or virtual meeting we consult the participants about their expertise or preferences in the main thematic of the workshop, so that they are separated in groups representing interests (i.e. production, inhabit, environment and culture).

The work in groups followed the logic of registering notes and voting in cycle. This means that a participant starts to contribute in context "A", that was the one he was first selected to, but must go the other contexts, like "B" and "C", in the sequence. For example, someone that was initially part of "inhabit" group starts by registering comments and voting ideas of this context, but after that he goes to "culture" context, after that to "environment" context, and finally to "production" context. While he is following this cycle, another participant that has expertise or more interest in "culture" starts by registering comments in this context and in the sequence, he goes to "inhabit", "environment" and "production" contexts. The logic for this cycle process of writing comments and voting is because when you know better about a context, you are the first one to register your observations that will be read by other participants (Fig. 7).

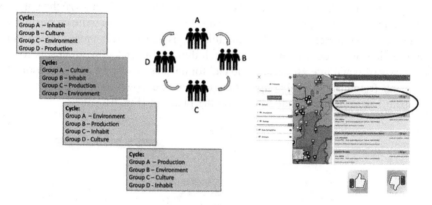

Fig. 7. Dialogues – groups voting in cycle, even in individual voting. Source: The authors

The process is based on the Delphi method, proposed in the 1950s by the American military industry Research and Development (RAND) with the objective of making structured listening and sharing responsibilities by maximizing consensus of opinions. The name comes from the Oracle of Delphi, as the objective is to issue opinions or suggestions for decision making. The procedure is made up of rounds of opinions, in which partial responses about what the majority thinks are shown to participants who have the chance to adjust their opinions [20, 21]. We observed numerous comments in each polygon of the Dialogues, what is an indication of interest and participation, motivated by the process.

3.4 Step 4 – Statistics and Final Decision

After the step of individual comments and voting, the conductor runs a script based on ETL (Extract Transform and Load) that calculates the votes and the percentages. The scripts separate those diagrams that are automatically rejected, those that are automatically selected and those that are under negotiation and must be analyzed again in another round of discussion and voting. The rating ranges can be decided by the conductor, and we used the limits of under 40% for not selected, over 60% for selected and from 40 to 60% of voting to be reconsidered and analyzed again. The ETL tool interacts with the platform and, after running it, the polygons to be negotiated are highlighted to the participants (Fig. 8).

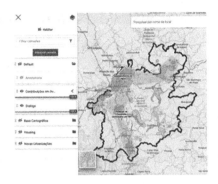

Fig. 8. Polygons to be discussed highlighted in the context. Source: The authors

Also, to give support to decision making in the second voting of polygons that are under negotiation, another ETL script (Extract Transform and Load) is used to identify similarity of polygons [22]. We applied the rule of topological similarity which checks for each polygon under negotiation whether it is within, intercepts or contains other polygons of the theme itself or of other themes, to check for possible conflicts or confluences of interests. The script is run by the coordinator before the final negotiation phase and the algorithm interacts with the platform, resulting in the visualization of results, what can be an additional support for the decision.

Working on groups and again in cycle voting using the same sequence of voting and comments, the polygons that are under negotiation are analyzed, but this time the comments and voting are not individual, but one for the entire group. The participants must declare which polygons they want to discuss about, and the decision of the group can be selected, not selected or selected under conditions. In case of approved under conditions the terms must be written in the description of the idea.

After this second round of voting another ETL script is used again to select those polygons that were voted by most of the groups, and we arrive to the final decision.

During all the process the participants have the support of a dashboard to control the performances, the partial and final results. This dashboard is based on dynamic cartography, what means that each time a data is changed, the visualization of graphics and numbers are updated. This resource of dynamic cartography also allows that while selecting a portion of the place in the map (zooming in or zooming out) the results in graphics and numbers are recalculated and presented according to the selected area: if the user wants to know about an area specifically, zooming in the screen he gets the data from that portion of the case study.

From the dashboard the participant is informed about the number of polygons (contributions) approved per context, the number of contributions that are still under negotiation, the number of contributions in that specific screen, the area in hectare, the media of voting and the highest vote among all contributions. All the process is based on geovisualization as support to opinion and decision making (Fig. 9).

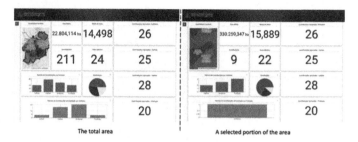

Fig. 9. Dashboard in dynamic information, according to selected area. Source: The authors

It is also important to register the possibilities of interoperability presented in the platform. The participant can upload polygons as contributions in the step of Dialogues but can also download polygons with their attributes (shapes and tables) to be used in any other system. The logic of interoperability is to make the participant feel comfortable to use the resources the way he prefers [23]. In the example, the user is downloading the list of contributions because he is interested in analyzing the polygon in some other application (QGis, ArcGis, Google Earth, and so one), or if he prefers he can download only the data table (CSV).

4   Results of the New Framework

It is important to highlight that all the steps we proposed in the new Brazilian platform attend to criticisms that we had in previous experiences, so that they are adjustments to Geodesign framework to face spatial inequalities and complexities. Now that the web-based platform and the first experiments are published and tested, to each case study and depending on the capacities and necessities of the stakeholders it can be used in different ways or to receive further resources, based on ETL tools and it's connection with the SDI & WebGis & Geodesign. Each new proposal of a step or a support to decision or opinion making can be planned as an ETL script that has interoperability with the systems that are already operative.

The goal of this new framework, the steps and procedures answered to changes to better fit our culture, based on the previous models of the traditional framework [1]:

A) Criticism of the Representation and Process Models

Representation and Process Models are carefully prepared by the organizers, using their expert knowledge in the elaboration of the geographical data, but there is a risk that they will be underutilized in the process, because the participants do not always have access to the previous cartographic collection. When they do, they are often static maps or at most as records of the elaboration of Evaluation Maps (i.e. History Maps), but they are not, in general, presented as a cartographic collection that can be more deeply interpreted in the form of enrichment of reading.

In this new platform they are presented and consumed as SDI (Spatial Data Infrastructure), what means the user has a collection of data organized according to themes and using Metadata Catalog he is able to combine themes the way he prefers and can also add new data from web-services.

B) Criticism of the Evaluation Models

Evaluation Maps in the previous framework have the standardized scales of "feasible", "suitable", "capable", "inappropriate" and "existing" [1]. The participants expressed it is reductionist to present a synthesis map that is a judgment, even if elaborated with technical justifications, as there are disagreements about the classifications performed.

In this new framework these synthesis maps are not mandatory, but if the conductor wants to have them as an additional layer in the contexts, it is up to him. In this new proposal the user selects, by himself, the layers he thinks are important as support his analysis, and he works with overlay and transparency to compose a dynamic synthesis. Each user does his analysis and synthesis.

Moreover, we observed (and had the registration in questionnaires applied after the workshops) that when a participant knows the place and the problem he doesn't use the Evaluation Maps, and instead of this he gets those information to help him just to find "where" and "what". But it is also true that when the participant does not know the area very well, he uses the Evaluation Maps indication to find a place, what means he is not totally conscious, but conducted by someone's else judgment.

C) Criticism of the Change Models

Change Models are characterized by the elaboration of polygons related to policy and project ideas for the area. It is observed the lack of perception of scale and the lack of connection between the world of ideas and reality, without saying that the ideas are inadequate, but rather that they often present detachments in relation to space reality, which is a result of fragility in spatial reading and geovisualization.

With the new framework before drawing polygons there is a brainstorm of initial ideas, suggesting "where" and "what", composed by a cloud of points symbolized according to themes, that helps the participant to draw a polygon or to analyze a contribution. The drawing or the importation of polygons comes in a second step, when the participant can count on a broader collection of base maps and is encouraged to construct a more robust contribution, as he will have to fill description boxes and some more data.

D) Criticism of the Impact Models

Impact Models assess whether the selected proposals (the diagrams or contributions) are in areas classified as some level of adequacy in the Evaluation Maps. When the proposals are not located in an appropriate area on the maps (remembering that this classification of wrong or right is according to Evaluation Map, a judgment, one point of view, even if technical point of view), the system presents a classification from most negative to most positive impact. There are no impediments to propose it, but alerts are generated.

In our opinion, alerts are not instructive in favoring the discussion of alternatives or in supporting decision-making, but comparative diagram analysis can be a way to favor the evolution of the decision in a shared way. In the new framework, instead of classifying from positive to negative, from right to wrong, the juxtaposition of comments helps participants to understand each other's reasons, to change or not change their minds.

E) Criticism of the Decision Models

Decision Models, which are the processes of composing groups and their groupings in the Geodesign workshop, have the goal to arrive, by negotiation, at a final proposal. As the negotiation process in the previous framework happens by observing the frequency table of selected diagrams (the diagrams that are common decision to the groups are chosen as select, and those with the most frequency are negotiated), there is a risk that good ideas will be lost because they have not been properly observed. There is a reduction in the choices and, often, some important themes of the work are not properly contemplated.

In this new proposal of voting based on cycles, the person not only votes but also presents comments about the polygon or contribution, according to his expertise, knowledge or main interest. This means that those who know more than others about a theme writes comments that are going to be read by others. This logic of voting on cycles is an opportunity to register technical information, alerts, additional information, cultural information. The final voting is much more robust and qualified.

5   Discussions

The Brazilian platform of Geodesign, GISCOLAB, is an adaptation of traditional Geodesign framework [1] based on scientific studies and bibliography review to understand the main keywords correlated to the term, to be applied in complex case studies of spatial inequalities. Before developing the platform, we analyzed the results of 35 workshops, based on qualitative and quantitative questionaries' applied to participants or even in not structured interviews developed during the activities. To change the steps and facilities we went back in literature review to understand the main values and concepts that were connected to the emergency of technologies of geoinformation in spatial planning, to understand which were the achievements developed and adopted in science, in order to restore them in the proposed framework.

We understood that our keywords are process and procedures, GIS resources, geovisualization and citizens' participation. These values could be part of the scope of Geodesign framework if it is based on SDI (Spatial Data Infrastructure) in all its facilities, if it favors geovisualization and usability based on WebGis, if it dialogues with other systems based on interoperability. With these resources the platform is a robust tool for cocreation and geocollaboration. New adaptations in a close future will be done according to requirements of each case study, as it is an "Open work" [24].

Acknowledgments. The authors thank CNPq support through the project 401066/2016-9, FAPEMIG PPM-00368-18 and NPGAU-UFMG for the support of taking part in the conference.

References

1. Steinitz, C.: A Framework for Geodesign: Changing Geography by Design. ESRI Press, Redlands (2012)
2. Cocco, C., Fonseca, B., Campagna, M.: Applying geodesign in urban planning case study of pampulha. In: Horizonte, B. (ed.) Revista Brasileira de Cartografia, Brazil, pp. 929–940 (2015)
3. Campagna, M., Moura, A.C.M., Borges, J., Cocco, C.: Future scenarios for the pampulha region: a geodesign workshop. J. Digital Landscape Archit. 1, 292–301 (2016)
4. Geodesignhub. https://www.geodesignhub.com. Accessed 10 March 2020
5. Ballal, H.: Collaborative planning with digital design synthesis. Doctoral Dissertation. University College London (2015)
6. Ballal, H., Steinitz, C.: A workshop in digital geodesign synthesis. In: Buhmann, E., Ervin, S.M., E. Pietsch, M. (eds.) Peer Reviewed Proceedings of Digital Landscape Architecture at Anhalt University of Applied Sciences. Herbert Wichmann Verlag, Berlin (2015)
7. Moura, A.C.M., Tondelli, S., Muzzarelli, A.: Complementary web-based geoinformation technology to geodesign practices: strategic decision-making stages of co-creation in territorial planning. In: Leone, A., Gargiulo, C. (eds.) Environmental and Territorial Modelling for Planning and Design, pp. 643–664. FedOAPress, Naples (2018)
8. Paula, P.L., Camargos, L.M., Moura, A.C.M., Freitas, C.R.: WebGIS como suporte à visualização de informações para processos de Geodesign: estudo de caso Pampulha Patrimônio da Humanidade. GeoSIG 10, 184–208 (2018)
9. Monteiro, L.O., Moura, A.C.M., Zyngier, C.M., Sena, I.S., Paula, P.L.: Geodesign facing the urgency of reducing poverty: the cases of Belo Horizonte. DisegnareCon, 11/20, 6.1–6.25 (2018)
10. Huggett, R.: Systems Analysis in Geography; Contemporary Problems in Geography, 208 p. Clarendon Press, Oxford (1980)
11. Cowen, D.: GIS versus CAD versus DBMS: what area the differences? In: Peuquet, D., Marble, D. (eds.) Introductory Readings in Geographic Information Systems, pp. 52–61. Taylor & Francis, London (1990)
12. Harris, B., Batty, M.: Locational models, geographic information and planning support systems. J. Planning Educ. Res. 12, 184–198 (1993)
13. Geertman, S.: Planning support systems (PSS) - a planner's perspective. In: Brail, R.K. (ed.) Planning Support Systems for Cities and Regions, pp. 213–274. Lincoln Institute, Cambridgde (2008)
14. Klosterman, R.E.: New perspectives on planning support systems. Environ. Planning B: Planning Des. 26, 317–320 (1999)
15. McCormick, B.H., De Fanti, T.A., Brown, M.D.: Visualization in scientific computing. Comput. Graph. 21(6), 1–21 (1987)
16. MacEachren, A., et al.: Geovisualization for knowledge construction and decision-support. Comput. Graph. Appl. 24(1), 13–17 (2004)
17. Zhou, M., Nemes, L., Reidsema, C., Ahmed, A., Kayis, B.: Tools and methods for risk management in multi-site engineering projects. In: Arai, E., Kimura, F., Goossenaerts, J., Shirase, K. (eds.) Knowledge and Skill Chains in Engineering and Manufacturing. IFIP, vol. 168, pp. 217–224. Springer, Boston (2005). https://doi.org/10.1007/0-387-23852-2_25
18. Balram, S., Dragicevic, S.: Collaborative Geographic Information Systems: Origins, Boundaries, and Structure. Idea Group Publishing, Hershey (2006)

19. Freitas, C.R.: Tecnologias de Geoinformação no planejamento territorial: novas formas de produção, compartilhamento e uso de dados espaciais. Doctoral Dissertation, Universidade Federal de Minas Gerais, Programa de Pós-Graduação em Arquitetura e Urbanismo (2020)
20. Dalkey, N., Helmer, O.: An experimental application of the Delphi method to the use of experts. Manage. Sci. **9**(3), 351–515 (1963)
21. Linstone, H.A., Turoff, M.: The Delphi Method: Techniques and Applications. Addision-Wesley, Reading (1975)
22. Freitas, C.R., Moura, A.C.M.: ETL tools to analyze diagrams' performance: favoring negotiations in geodesign workshops. DisegnareCon, **11/20**, 15.1–15.23 (2018)
23. Moura, A.C.M., Marino, T.B., Ballal, H., Ribeiro, S.R., Motta, S.R.F.: Interoperability and visualization as a support for mental maps to face differences in scale in Brazilian Geodesign processes. Rozwój Regionalny i Polityka Regionalna **35**, 89–102 (2016)
24. Eco, U.: Opera Aperta, 370 p. Milano, Bompiani (1962)

International Workshop
on Geographical Analysis, Urban
Modeling, Spatial Statistics
(GEOG-AND-MOD 2020)

A Text Mining Analysis on Big Data Extracted from Social Media

Gabriella Schoier[(✉)], Giuseppe Borruso, and Pietro Tossut

DEAMS – Department of Economic, Business, Mathematic and Statistical Sciences "Bruno de Finetti", University of Trieste, Tigor 22, 34100 Trieste, Italy
{gabriella.schoier,giuseppe.borruso}@deams.units.it

Abstract. The aim of this paper is to analyze data derived from Social Media. In our time people and devices constantly generate data. The network is generating location and other data that keeps services running and ready to use in every moment. This rapid development in the availability and access to data has induced the need for better analysis techniques to understand the various phenomena. We consider a Text Mining and a Sentiment Analysis of data extracted from Social Networks. The application regards a Text Mining Analysis and a Sentiment Analysis on Twitter, in particular on tweets regarding Coronavirus and SARS.

Keywords: Text Mining · Sentiment analysis · Big data · SARS · Coronavirus

1 Introduction

Nowadays a huge amount of data i.e. big data are collected and stored in several Data Warehouses by different public and private organizations. The analysis of big data is becoming more and more useful.

In this paper an analysis based on a Text Mining and Sentiment Analysis semi-automated approach is presented [5]. This approach is useful in several exploratory pattern-analysis, grouping, decision-making and machine-learning situations [13], including Data Mining, Web Mining and Spatial Data Mining(see e.g. [4, 12]).

The new Industry 4.0 paradigm, with digitalization, big data analytics, and so on, is heavily influencing different aspects of human being. Big data analytics could provide opportunities to develop new knowledge to reshape our understanding of different fields and to support decision making. Even though Internet has a great impact on information search behavior, several aspects of online user are not yet clear and need further investigation. Moreover there is a growing interest in utilizing user-generated data.

Computational aspects and the visual representation are becoming attractive tools in big data analysis. This paper is related to Social Network Analysis; in more details we focused our analysis on findings relevant terms and topics related to tweets on Coronavirus and SARS with the goal of identifying the trend of international opinions and preoccupations. In this analysis the *R* language has been used.

© Springer Nature Switzerland AG 2020
O. Gervasi et al. (Eds.): ICCSA 2020, LNCS 12252, pp. 351–364, 2020.
https://doi.org/10.1007/978-3-030-58811-3_25

2 Text Mining and Sentiment Analysis of Social Media

2.1 Big Data Characteristics and Methods of Analysis

In our age there has been an increase in the accessibility of data; this has created a real revolution in the organization of these data for instance those coming from social networks. The study of big data plays an important role not only in the field of computer science, but also in the socio-economic one, for this reason the extraction of information from them is very useful (see [8, 9, 11]).

A very important characteristic of big data is the size but it is not the only one as the rapid evolution of the phenomenon has highlighted other characteristics.

In 2001 Laney identified three dimensions: volume, variety, velocity, called the three V's [6]. In support of this Gartner defines big data with this expression: "Big data is high-volume, high-velocity and high-variety information assets that demand cost-effective, innovative forms of information processing for enhanced insight and decision making".

In addition to these big data have other features which are becoming important: veracity, visibility and value. In the majority of cases big data are presented in a heterogeneous, redundant and unstructured form so traditional tools do not allow a proper analysis of this type of data, a solution is given by Text Mining.

2.2 Text Mining and Sentiment Analysis

Text Mining aims to study methods and algorithms to automatically extract information from text and to classify documents on the base of the content. If one want to give a definition, one could say that Text Mining is "the discovery by a computer of new, previously unknown, information through the automatic extraction of different written documents" [1]. Text Mining is similar to Data Mining, even if it focuses on text, which is usually unstructured.

In recent years Text Mining has increased its importance due to the development of big data platforms and Deep Learning algorithms able to analyze enormous series of unstructured data. Text Mining is often used in conjunction with Text Analytics, or Text Analysis, so sometimes they are considered as synonyms. According to this approach, text data (keywords, concepts, verbs, names, adjectives, etc.) are derived from the text extraction process and are subsequently used in the Text Analytics phase to produce useful information.

Text Mining techniques try to find the thematic information hidden in a text to facilitate the process of archiving and building a logical map of knowledge. These techniques are based on algorithms that select the relevant parts of a document.

Among the most popular there are the categorization of texts, the extraction of information, the recovery of information, the processing of analyzing natural language, clustering, the summary of text and the Sentiment Analysis also known as Opinion Mining [3]. This last method is used to extract subjective information from the content. As the term suggests, it has to do with emotion and feeling. It is used to understand a subject's emotional response in a given context.

In recent years it has become an indispensable tool for companies that want to know the so-called *brand perception* taking advantage of the interaction of users of Social Networks or more in general of the web.

Since the information available on the Internet is constantly growing, it is very easy to access texts that express opinions in sites, forums, blogs and social media.

Fig. 1. Sentiment analysis: Emoticon [7]

The subjects that produce these 'judgements' are called opinion holders; they are authors of posts or reviews and users of social media. The expressed opinion, on a characteristic of an object, has an orientation indicating whether it is positive, negative or neutral. This orientation can also be defined as sentiment orientation (see Fig. 1).

In general, Sentiment Analysis is mainly structured on three levels:

- *document*: often known as document-level sentiment classification, it classifies the whole document investigating the positivity or negativity of the opinion;
- *phrase*: the analysis is focused on phrases to determine the feeling/sentiment of each of them, it requires more precision because it is necessary to identify objective, subjective and neutral phrases;
- *target*: consists in the analysis of feelings on entities and not necessarily on the whole sentence.

The analysis of opinion detection is based on the use of opinion words recognized by the machine and classified under the aspect of the positivity or negativity of the feeling.

A further classification problem occurs when there are not opinion words but emoticons that represent the feeling of the user. For these reasons, at this stage more than in others it is indispensable human work that is able to understand better the tone of a comment, to contextualize a message and recognize whether what one wanted to communicate was, for example, a real positive feeling or, on the contrary, sarcasm.

3 The Methodology and the Application

3.1 Social Network: The Case of Twitter

Social Networks, like any other tool have strengths and weaknesses depending on its the way they are used (see [14]). The advantages are many for example [7]: *global communication*, you can, with a click, communicate in real time with the rest of the world; *the convenience of use*, they are accessible by anyone just an email address or a phone number, and a password and one is immediately connected with virtual reality; *share and publish everything*, Social Networks allow everyone to express passions and thoughts so one can find a comparison with its contacts;. *social media marketing*, companies increasingly use them to communicate as they are incredibly effective for the online promotion of a large number of products, activities and services. Since social media are free their campaigns have absolutely competitive prices compared to traditional advertising.

Some defects of Social Network usage are: *alienation* if used recklessly, Social Networks can lead to estrangement from reality; d*ependence* can compromise work productivity; *privacy*: often the subject of discussion is whether there is privacy on social networks. The most important Social Networks provide the possibility to set up profiles in order to choose what you want to make public or keep private; but one must be careful and remember that sharing content on major social networks is on default public; *fakenews*: information and news circulating on Social Networks are not always true.

Twitter is a free Social Network platform or, to be more precise, is a very popular micro-blogging service that allows one to communicate with other users through the publication of tweets, i.e. short messages (the maximum number of characters allowed until 07/11/2017 was 140, now it is 280), photos or videos and all posts are freely readable. It is an excellent environment for social analysis, as there are around 220 million active users, out of 500 million subscribed users, creating over 500 million tweets every day.

The structure of Twitter is represented by two social groups: *followers* and *following*. The platform was born as a one-sided communication tool but over time the concept of conversation has been integrated. One can now mention or answer to a user through the use of the @ symbol before the user's name. When one reads a tweet published by one of the people one follows, one has three actions that allow to interact with that tweet: *answer*: clicking on reply can replicate that tweet, sending a mention to the author of the tweet; *retweet*: clicking on retweet gives the opportunity to share that tweet with all the followers; *like*: clicking on like, the tweet is put in the collection of the favorite tweets.

Through the Twitter search system one can search for tweets based on a single word that must be preceded by the symbol "#". This can be useful for searching for tweets about a single concept.

3.2   The Objective of the Analysis

In this period, a virus is creating great agitation and its spreads frightens millions of people: it is the Cornavirus [10] (see Fig. 2). The coronavirus belongs to a large family of viruses known to cause diseases ranging from common colds to more serious diseases such as Middle Eastern Respiratory Syndrome (MERS) and Severe Acute Respiratory Syndrome (SARS) [2].

Fig. 2. Coronavirus (www.ilmessaggero.it/salute/focus/coronavirus_termini_usati_a_z_alfabeto-. html)

They are positive filament RNA viruses with similar appearance to a *corona* as seen using an electron microscope. The subfamily Orthocoronavirinae of the family Coronaviridae is classified in four genera of coronavirus (cov): Alpha-, Beta-, Delta-, and Gamma coronavirus. The genus of the betacoronavirus is further separated into five sub-genera (including Sarbecovirus).

The coronaviruses have been identified in the mid-1960s and are known to infect humans and some animals (including birds and mammals). The primary target cells are the epithelial cells of the respiratory and gastrointestinal tracts. Up to date, seven coronaviruses have been shown to be able to infect humans. The coronavirus (COV-19) is a new strain of coronavirus that has never been previously identified in humans. In particular, the one called COV-19, has never been identified before being reported in Wuhan, China, in December 2019.

On the contrary SAR means the Severe Acute Respiratory Syndrome, first detected in China at the end of 2002 (see [2]). In mid-2003, there has been a worldwide epidemic that has caused a lot of cases and deaths worldwide, including Canada and the United States. It is believed that the source of infection derived from animals infected with contact with a bat carrying the virus before being sold to a slaughter market.

SARS is caused by a coronavirus; it is much more serious than most other coronavirus infections which generally only cause flu-like symptoms. In addition, coronavirus may also cause Middle Eastern Respiratory Syndrome (MERS). SARS is transmitted from person to person through direct contact with infected persons or through droplets dispersed in the air by coughing or sneezing of an infected person [2]. SARS symptoms resemble those of other more common viral respiratory infections, but are more severe. They include fever, headache, chills and muscle pain, followed by dry coughing and sometimes difficulty in breathing. Most patients recovered in a week or two. Some, however, have developed severe respiratory difficulties and in about 10% of cases death has occurred.

The first symptoms of COVID-19 and SARS are very similar and this has led to a medical glitch in the early stages of spreading the virus because the new disease has been cured as SARS, even if it was not.

It is interesting to check out what results the search of these two words will bring on Twitter.

3.3   The Preliminary Phase

One of the principal objective of Text Mining and Sentiment Analysis is the acquisition of information from the net and the extraction of the sentiment expressed.

In order to this the *R* language, that has made possible to extract tweets in which the keywords coronavirus and SARS appears, has been used. The preliminary step has been to register in the Social Network, to create an *Application Programming Interfaces* (API), to extract tweets and to create a *corpus*.

Twitter allows to discover in real time what users write about. One can access the social media via Web or via a mobile device. For companies, developers or users, an organized access to data is also available through the use of API. The method requires an authentication through the protocol "OAuth6" which, once authenticated, releases a token without expiration, to be used for all future connection requests.

An API is created in the developer section of the site. Access codes are divided into Consumer API keys (API key and API secret key), Access Token and Access Token Secret (Access Token and Access Token Secret).

In this way one is enabled to download tweets to *R*, using the twitter and RCurl packages. We downloaded 500 tweets in English each containing the word "coronavirus", the same operation has been carried out with the word SARS, the operation has been repeated in different days. Given the worrying situation in Italy regarding coronavirus, 500 tweets have been downloaded in Italian each containing the word "coronavirus", the same operation has been carried out with the word SARS, the operation has been repeated in different days.

At this point the data downloaded from Twitter have been transformed in a Data Frame. Before the representation through word clouds and other graphical methods and the application of sentiment Analysis, it has been necessary to use the *tm* package to create a *corpus*. At this step the *corpus* has been cleaned eliminating characters and words that are not of interest such as: punctuation, emoticon, adverbs, conjunctions and from the link to the tweet. At the end one gets a "clean" matrix.

3.4   Word Clouds and Other Graphical Analysis

After cleaning the texts one can proceed to the creation of the so-called clouds of words. As the name implies, Word Cloud is a visual representation of keywords used in a text. In general, it is similar to a list with the peculiar characteristic of assigning a font of larger dimensions to the words most cited by the users. For this operation the wordcloud function of the same package has been used; in addition, a maximum limit of 500 words has been chosen, a scale of 3 for the most relevant words up to 0.5 for the least frequent. As far as regards the order the words more frequently are put in the middle.

The analysis have been carried out in different days. We reported the results referred to tweets of 10/02/2020 (See Figs. 3 and 4).

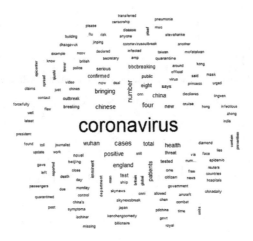

Fig. 3. Word cloud Corona virus 10-2-20 (English)

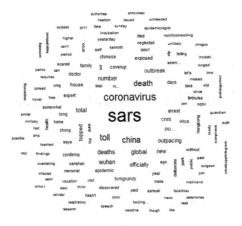

Fig. 4. Word cloud sars 10-2-20 (English)

As regards the graphical representation of the words with higher frequency the barplot command has been used. Only words with a frequency greater or equal to 5 have been represented. This choice was made taking into account the number of words that have been returned for each topic (See Figs. 5 and 6).

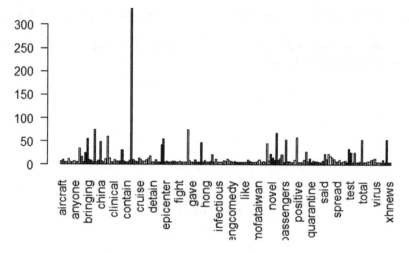

Fig. 5. Barplot Coronavirus 10-2-20 (English)

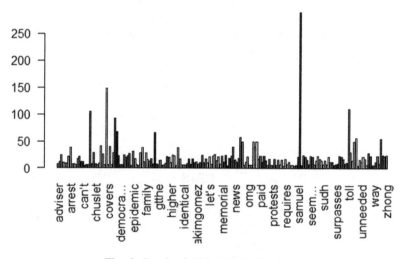

Fig. 6. Barplot SARS 10-2-20 (English)

At this point as the spread of Coronavirus in Italy has increased very much we have considered tweets both in English and in Italian. Data referred to the 11, March 2020. As one can see there are changes both in the word clouds and in the bar plots (See Figs. 7, 8, 9 and 10).

The graphical representation of the words with higher frequency has been proposed using the barplot. Only words with a frequency greater or equal to 5 have been represented. This choice was made taking into account the number of words that have been returned for each topic.

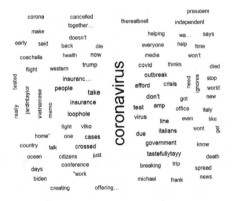

Fig. 7. Word cloud Coronavirus 11-3-20 (English)

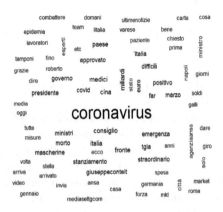

Fig. 8. Word cloud Coronavirus 11-3-20 (Italian)

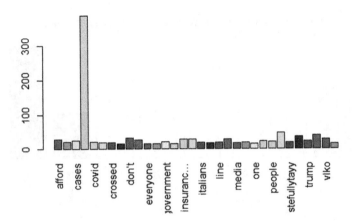

Fig. 9. Barplot Coronavirus 11-3-20 (English)

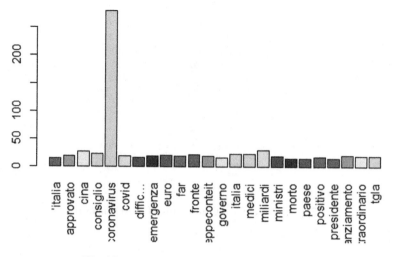

Fig. 10. Bar plot Coronavirus 11-3-20 (Italian)

3.5 A Sentiment Analysis

This phase is characterized by a first analysis carried out by the machine using *R* language and a second manual analysis.

We proceed to carry out an Opinion Analysis/Sentiment Analysis of the tweets obtained by classifying them in 8 categories: anger, anticipation (anticipation is considered as an emotion that causes different feelings thinking of unexpected events), disgust, fear, joy, sadness, surprise, trust; the following categories are provided by default by *R* and the tweets are classified according to the words used by the users.

To perform this classification, the command *get_nrc_sentiment* of the *syuzhet* package of *R* has been used and then the data obtained using the barplot command has been represented.

The reported results refer to di tweet of the 03/02/2020.

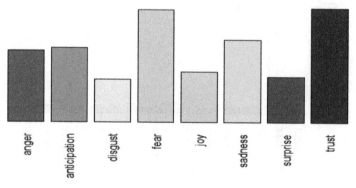

Fig. 11. Sentiment analysis Coronavirus 10-2-20 (English)

Sentiment Scores for sars Tweets

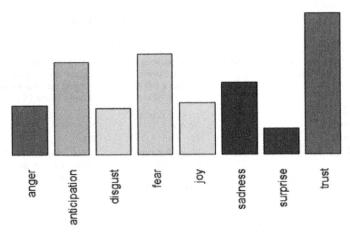

Fig. 12. Sentiment analysis Sars 10-2-20 (English)

In Figs. 11 and 12 you can see how tweets are divided by R into different groups according to the feeling that the function can determine based on the text.

Next Table 1 show the division in groups: in the first line there are the values related to coronavirus and in the second to SARS.

Table 1. Different groups for Coronavirus and SARS 10-2-20 (R analysis)

Anger	Anticipation	Disgust	Fear	Joy	Sadness	Surprise	Trust
47	72	31	89	40	51	27	82
40	76	30	88	35	45	24	80

As far as the manual analysis has been concerned, the tweets have been read one by one and classified them in three macro categories: positive, negative and non-concerning or non containing opinions or neutral. The data thus obtained have been summarized in Tables giving back, some examples for each of the categories and the retweets that are most frequently presented within the data frame obtained in the previous phases (Table 2).

Table 2. Different groups for Coronavirus and SARS 10-2-20 (manual analysis)

CORONAVIRUS 10-02-20

	Positive	Neutral	Negative
	112	98	229
example	We appreciate India for extending support in China's battle against the coronavirus	Coronavirus: Turn off air-conditioners and open windows to reduce risk of being infected, say experts	Four further patients in England have tested positive for #coronavirus, bringing the total number of cases in the UK to eight

SARS 10-02-20

	Positive	Neutral	Negative
	101	89	228
example	It's more deadly than SARS	Plagur Epidemics Crona 2020- Ebola 2014 Swine 2009-Bird 2005 SARS 2002	Doctor who exposed Sars cover-up under house arrest in China, family confirms

At this point as the spread of Coronavirus in Italy has increased very much we applied a Sentiment Analysis both to tweets in English language and in Italian language. Data referred to the 11, March 2020. The results are presented in Fig. 13 and in Fig. 14, as one can see the difficult situation is highlight much more than before.

Sentiment Scores for coronavirus Tweets

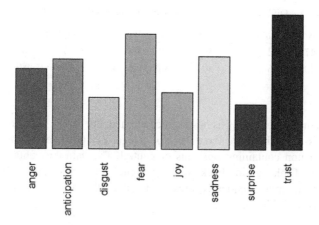

Fig. 13. Sentiment analysis Coronavirus 11-3-20 (English)

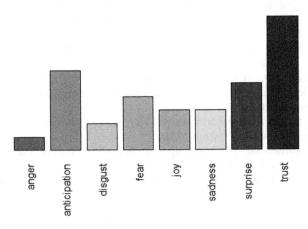

Fig. 14. Sentiment analysis Coronavirus 11-3-20 (Italian)

4 Conclusions

In this paper we have analyzed from a theoretical point of view definitions and properties of big data, we have also illustrated processes of extraction of information from the data. Processes of machine learning text mining and sentiment analysis have been analyzed in a specific area such as that of Social Network analysis. Finally, an example of these types of analysis has been given using the "R" software and its various packages in the context of Twitter. The results for the keywords coronavirus (COVID-19) and SARS have been analysed, highlighting how sentiment analysis can be useful for monitoring people's emotional situation.

References

1. Bolasco, S.: Statistica testuale e Text Mining: Alcuni Paradigmi Applicativi, Quaderni di Statistica, vol. 7 (2005)
2. Branda, L.: Sindrome respiratoria acuta (SARS) (2018). https://www.msdmanuals.com/it-it/casa/infezioni/virus-respiratori/sindrome-respiratoria-acuta-grave-SARS. Accessed March 2020
3. Inside Marketing pull information: Sentiment Analisis (2017). http://insidemarketing.it/glossario/definizione/sentiment-analysis/. Accessed March 2020
4. Jan, A.K.: Data clustering. 50 years beyond K-means. Pattern Recogn. Lett. **31**, 651–666 (2010)
5. Govoni, L.: Text mining: il processo di estrazione del testo (2019). https://lorenzogovoni.com/text-mining/. Accessed March 2020. Hearst
6. Laney, D.: 3D data management: controlling data volume, velocity and variety, application delivery strategies META GROUP (2001). https://blogs.gartner.com/. Accessed March 2020
7. Lucarini, L.: (2020). https://giacomolucarini.it/sentiment-analysis-ci-aiuta-lintelligenza-artificiale/. Accessed March 2020

8. Manhika, J., Chui, M., Brown, B., et al.: Big data: the next frontier for innovation, competition, and productivity. McKinsey Global Institute (2011). www.mckinsey.com/Insights/MGI/Research/Technology_and_Innovation/Big_datathe_next_frontier. Accessed February 2018

9. Mayer-Schonberger, V., Cukier, K.: Big Data: A Revolution That Will Transform How We Live, Work, and Think. Mariner Books, Boston (2013)

10. Ministero della salute: "FAQ - Nuovo Coronavirus COVID-19" (2020). http://www.salute.gov.it/portale/nuovocoronavirus/dettaglioFaqNuovoCoronavirus.jsp?lingua=italiano&id=228. Accessed March 2020

11. Piva, A.: Le 5 V dei Big Data: dal Volume al Valore (2019). https://blog.osservatori.net/it_it/le-5v-dei-big-data. Accessed March 2020

12. Schoier, G., Borruso, G.: A methodology for dealing with spatial big data. Int. J. Bus. Intell. Data Mining **12**(1), 1–13 (2017)

13. Software Testing Help: Data Mining Vs Machine Learning Vs Artificial Intelligence Vs Deep Learning (2019). http://www.intelligenzaartificiale.it/data-mining/. Accessed March 2020

14. Wasserman, S., Faust, K.: Social Network Analysis: Methods and Applications. Cambridge University Press, New York (1994)

Daily Spatial Footprint of Warsaw Metropolitan Area (Poland) Commuters in Light of Volunteered Geographic Information and Common Factors of Urban Sprawl. A Pilot Study

Veranika Kaleyeva[1] and Piotr A. Werner[2]([envelope]) [iD]

[1] Institute of Urban and Regional Development, Targowa 45,
03-782 Warsaw, Poland
v.kaleyeva@gmail.com
[2] Faculty of Geography and Regional Studies, University of Warsaw,
Krak. Przedm. 30, 00-927 Warsaw, Poland
peter@uw.edu.pl

Abstract. Urban sprawl directly affects on length of commuting. Acquisition of commuting data is based on theoretical (deductive) approaches, limited individual small observation samples or indirect phenomena like e.g. remote sensing night light data images. Volunteered Geographic Information (VGI) make possible deeper insight into the daily spatial footprint of commuting and is related to urban sprawl. Data acquired during the collection of VGI data reveal some new aspects of spatial phenomena, which can be additionally analyzed. VGI data concerning spatial phenomena involve both geotagging as well time stamps of acquisition, which in turn make possible indirectly inferring about spatial and temporal move of people. Analysis of the available spatial and temporal VGI data in context of national surveying acquired resources (INSPIRE) and confronted to modelling approach of commuting is the subject of pilot study of Warsaw functional urban area. The results are promising due to inter alia, generalization of huge volume real data observations set unlike to formerly used theoretical modelling.

Keywords: Volunteered Geographic Information (VGI) · Urban sprawl · Commuting patterns · Spatial behavior

1 Introduction

Urban sprawl (suburban sprawl) is defined as "the rapid expansion of the geographic extent of cities and towns, often characterized by low-density residential housing, single-use zoning, and increased reliance on the private automobile for transportation." [1]. Urban sprawl is perceived as an inherently dynamic spatial phenomenon [2] and is the subject of huge number of research papers and books and recognized and studied in numerous regions of the world due to growing interest since the introduction of the term in 1937 [3] in processes of suburbanization due to observed general tendencies of

© Springer Nature Switzerland AG 2020
O. Gervasi et al. (Eds.): ICCSA 2020, LNCS 12252, pp. 365–377, 2020.
https://doi.org/10.1007/978-3-030-58811-3_26

urban growth (and decline) during (at least) last century. Primarily, it is the outcome of people individual decisions where to live and work, which in turn have implication on different social, economic and environmental spatial phenomena processes. The first, direct implication of urban sprawl is spatial and temporal configuration of commuting to the centers of cities. The main presented problem in this pilot study touches the problem of relation of urban sprawl, understood as a state of spatial extent of metropolitan area, and its relation to commuting, assuming that urban sprawl directly affects on length of commuting. Reconstruction of spatial and temporal daily commuting within the boundaries of functional urban area was studied for the case of Warsaw Metropolitan Area from 2008 until 2018. This new insight was possible using Volunteered Geographic Information (VGI) data sets in context of official collected and shared statistical and geospatial data collected by surveying services (thereafter in paper termed as INSPIRE in international context). Assumption hypothesized that VGI make possible deeper insight into the spatial and temporal pattern of commuting and reconstruction of daily spatial footprint of commuting, which in turn is related to actual state of urban sprawl. The main question under study was where and, at what time the prevailing number of people: inhabitants and/or visitors were during the day (24 h) within the boundaries of metropolitan zone. However, analyzed data are only the sample, the subset of the whole phenomenon, although certainly pinpoints statistically the fragment of commuting in Warsaw Metropolitan Area.

Short synopsis of the thereafter threads of study involve state-of-art discussion concerning common factors of urban sprawl as well as advantages and weakness of use of different VGI data, characteristics and spatial extent of study area, more detailed discussion of methods used and rational of application. Next, there are presentation of the results of pilot study, discussion and conclusions. The proposed approach is the first step of supplementary studies related to former studies concerning spatial interactions and urban sprawl processes in the context of land use change.

Use of VGI data is nowadays the expanding way of the scientific approaches due to dissemination of ICT smartphones applications using geospatial technologies. However, they are usually strictly defined and related to geoportals and/or spatial databases aimed usually precisely defined scope of data like e.g. monitoring some elements of natural environment, people movements (e.g., GPS sport applications) as well as monitoring traffic of cars, airplanes, trains, ships. These data involve also a lot of additional information concerning also date and time of acquisition and technical features of ICT personal devices (e.g. tags, saved metadata of photos) and sometimes the metadata features of the elements of ICT nearby (e.g. in case of used in this study OpenCellId spatial database). This pilot study is trying to use this additional data.

Finally, the aim of the study has been defined as the reconstruction of commuters' daily footprint. However, there is hidden assumption in the research investigation, that the greatest part acquired database is just the result of commuters recorded observations, but it is also possible that the results were recorded by other visitors or inhabitants taking also part in the traffic.

2   Common Factors of Urban Sprawl and Impacts on Daily Behavior of Inhabitants and/or Visitors

"A variety of definitions for sprawl have been put forth that describe sprawl as a specific form of urban development with low-density, dispersed, auto-dependent and environmentally and socially-impacting characteristics" [1]. The term can be used to describe both a state of landscape as well as process. The evaluation of the existing definitions for urban sprawl reveals that most of them involve three spatial aspects: the expansion of urban area, the increase of dispersion of build-up area and low-density development in suburbia with a high land take per person [2]. The shift in population and employment density from city core to suburbia has been identified as a main characteristic associated with spatial expansion of urban area [4]. Distribution of settlement area and communing are interdependent in a complex way. Residents make choices between settlement areas taking into consideration the cost of housing and commuting between homes and work places, consequently in areas where incomes are high and travel costs are low the sprawl is more common [5]. Availability of roads, private car ownership, low cost of fuel and poor public transport in city core drive urban sprawl. In contrast, development of rail transportation raises residential density around access points [6]. At the same time, urban sprawl influences mobility patterns.

The consequences of urban sprawl include a variety of responses concerning, inter alia, landscape quality, loss of arable soil, recreation areas, shrinking open spaces, functional and spatial separation of places for living and working, and (last but not least) large numbers of commuters [2].

Commuting, making up a large part of all journeys worldwide and many resource-demanding transport investment, is important for the overall economy and for the everyday life of many people. It is related to spatial division of labor and relay on spatial structure: housing market, technical and social infrastructure and employment conditions. Commuting is perceived generally as substitute of migration and is joint or sequential decision where to live and/or to work [3]. The phenomenon is related to labor mobility and is also the consequence of different factors affecting the labor market conditions, especially for the countries characterize 4th stage of demographic transition.

However, some recent studies recognized the problem of commuting time, which will subside as these sprawled housing boom areas age and try to re-conceptualize "low density, auto-dependent urban form as a normal part of the urban growth process" [7]. The huge number of researcher approaches focused on analysis of urban form and function aimed monitoring and modelling of urban dynamics developing urban growth models [8]. Urban growth models relay on changes of land use maps including (not rarely) sparse time-intervals and subjective interpretation in documentation of urban growth [9]. The new approach postulate use of spatial metrics for quantifying key morphological characteristics of the urban fabric from profile- and patch-based metrics, originating from the field of landscape ecology, and introducing also building-based metrics aimed machine-learning-based land use and urban form classification [8]. Appreciating these geodata, they are obtained usually from officially collected and shared state – or enterprise, commercial resources. However, this concerns infrastructure, not the people and their spatial behavior, which can be only inferred about.

Another possibility is to use common, volunteered socially collected data, aimed, inter alia, easing every day life in metropolitan areas or solving defined, ad hoc, social as well scientific problems. These crowdsourcing geodata sets, VGI expose, sometimes, unexpected values added despite of obvious assumed targets.

3 Advantages and Weakness of Use of Different VGI Data

"The convergence of newly interactive Web-based technologies with growing practices of user-generated content disseminated on the Internet is generating a remarkable new form of geographic information. Citizens are using handheld devices to collect geographic information and contribute it to crowd-sourced data sets, using Web-based mapping interfaces to mark and annotate geographic features, or adding geographic location to photographs, text, and other media shared online. These phenomena, which generate what we refer to collectively as volunteered geographic information (VGI), represent a paradigmatic shift in how geographic information is created and shared and by whom, as well as its content and characteristics" [10].

VGI may suffer from different quality. Given the tremendous flow of VGI, the problem of information quality is of increasing importance. The reasons for this could be: data is generated by heterogeneous actors using different technologies and tools that have different levels of detail and precision, serve heterogeneous purposes, and have no systemically defined quality control measures [11]. It is crucial to realize that people do have perception bias. They perceive and consequently define imprecisely geographical regions and spatial relations. Moreover "people typically think and communicate about the world in terms of vague concepts" [12 p. 185]. Volunteers involved in collecting data lack a coherent conceptualization of their activities; mostly they do not follow "sharp semantic boundaries". Thus, differences in the quality of the data they collect are also determined by limited knowledge of the space being studied [13]. At the same time, it worth to emphasize that the most VGI sites require very little expertise in order to participate, except for Internet and mobile phone literacy [14]. It worth to mention also that volunteers sometimes more frequently reach to faraway locations and collect various data about them, than officially registered or surveyed information or by use and interpretation of remote sensing acquired data.

Lack of knowledge refers also to the traditional geographic information (GI) quality criteria. International Organization for Standardization (Technical Committee, ISO/TC 2117) developed a set of international standards that define such a quality (standard 19138, as part of the metadata standard 19115): completeness, consistency, positional accuracy, temporal accuracy, and thematic accuracy.

On the other hand, there is no objective measures of the accuracy. Some authors [15] point out although users of Google's search do not have any benchmarks to which they could compare the results they obtain, yet people continue to rely on google. In such a case people tend to make their assessment based on own judgment whether google results fit their search purpose at a given time. Considering this, if a substantial group of people find some VGI fit for their purpose, then VGI becomes of higher quality compared to other information sources (at least for a given purpose in a well-defined context). The volunteers providing VGI may be treated as "markers for the quality of their contributions". If the volunteers are perceived as trustworthy, then VGI becomes perceived as trustworthy too. Researchers suggest that integration of the spatial and temporal dimensions of trust may generate a new form of reputation which they call "event-reputation of volunteers using distance and time" [15]. It means that volunteers that are close to an event (spatial dimension) at the time of the event occurrence (temporal dimension) are given an event-reputation for a given time concerning reporting about this particular event. Such a reputation of VGI may not only be constituted for a time being of event, but can also be extended further through continuous reporting from those concrete volunteers through the whole course of the event, and in this way to result in establishing kind of permanent reputation for these volunteers about a certain local area, and the data they collect. In this way, a progression of trust in VGI can be anticipated over time. One must admit that VGI have unique propagation channels of informational trust, which can be treated as a feature that distinguishes VGI from other data sources.

New elements were added to the discussion of geospatial data quality in the 21st century through the development of Web 2.0 and the availability of Global Positioning System (GPS). The interactivity of the new web technology helped create a large amount of user-generated content (UGC). Scientists [16] analyze the specific example of cutting-edge VGI usage and compares it to traditional way of data gathering project by national surveying offices (INSPIRE). There is no doubt that the combination of geospatial information extracted from the two aforementioned different initiatives is truly beneficial to several stakeholders: public authorities, professionals, businesses, researchers, and NGOs. VGI based project has its advantages and disadvantages. It has full license interoperability and is founded on modern technologies. However, by its very flexible nature it suffers from the lack of rigorous data specifications, since contributors are free to use tags different from those agreed by the community. It seems the challenges of that particular VGI project play a part in broader VGI data classification problems such as:

- data is likely prone to subjective classification,
- remote contributions and flexible contribution mechanisms in most projects,
- uncertainty of spatial data and non-strict definitions of geographic features.

Guiding implementation of VGI projects using data collection protocols could help in reducing its potential drawbacks [16].

In many aspects VGI may be considered a significant innovation [17] in view of social, economic and scientific as well as educational aspects, notwithstanding the fact that it generates additional data, additional information, which is not usually recorded by the statistical and/or surveying services. Particularly noteworthy is its cultural dimension. VGI is a phenomenon of user-generated content that has fairly recently led to the adoption of open access and a collaborative approach and sharing of information resources. Nevertheless, the user-generated data are often viewed as a by-product, however it is hard not to appreciate its up-to-date dynamic and collective environment in which diverse information, opinions, experiences, and skills can be aggregated to offer extensive brand new data sources. Today it is difficult to imagine - in the era of growing internet and technology - not to see the potential that lies in the use and development of VGI, which, along with its increasing legitimization and verification - may even begin to incline the official registrars to complement official (traditional) databases with these new information.

4   Data Resources and Methodology of Pilot Study

Sources of data used in pilot study involve both official INSPIRE data sets shared publicly as well as VGI data. The spatial extent of data cover the sheet as minimum bounding rectangle of boundaries of functional urban area of Warsaw metropolis, i.e. between the coordinates (in decimal degrees): +19.8 and +22.5 longitude and +51.6 and +53.1 latitude.

To reveal the location of people: inhabitants and/or visitors – the subset of OpenCellID database has been used. Source of presented data is subset of database acquired from opencellid.org [18] (accessed Feb. 2019), which counted over 40 million records identifying base transceiver stations (BTS) and, inter alia, timestamp of the acquisition. In fact, BTS information is derived from voluntary crowdsourcing reports and later verified. OpenCellID is actively updated crowdsourcing database collecting GPS location data for cell identifiers. It had already been previously used in scientific research and its advantages and disadvantages are recognized [19, 20]. However, the volume of stored data since 2008 lets assume, that is close to real current situation at the global scale.

Records of data involve geolocation and (UNIX Epoch) timestamp. This information, due to fact, that UNIX time is not a true representation of Coordinated Universal Time (UTC), made possible to define the local time of reported acquisition. It means that the approximate local time (as well the day, month and year) and geolocation of smartphone user reporting his/her position is possible to define using this timestamp. The procedure is similar to `mapscaping` the geotagged tweets.

Additionally the maps of spatial extent of built-up areas [21], as well as, roads and railways maps have been used from Polish INSPIRE data resources [22]. These maps were used clipped to the aforementioned spatial extent.

4.1   Spatial Extent: Warsaw Metropolitan Area (Poland)

Warsaw (Polish: Warszawa - is the capital and largest city of Poland. The metropolis stands on the Vistula River in east-central Poland and its population is officially estimated at 1.791 million residents within a greater metropolitan area of 3.33 million residents, which makes Warsaw the seventh most-populous capital city in the European Union. The city limits cover 517.24 sq.km, while the metropolitan area (MA) covers 6,100.43 sq.km. Warsaw is an alpha global city, a major international tourist destination, and a significant cultural, political and economic hub. Its historical Old Town was designated a UNESCO World Heritage Site. Statistically Warsaw has the largest number of connections with neighboring cities in Poland (905) [23, 24]. Location of study area covering both Warsaw MA and city limits is presented in Fig. 1.

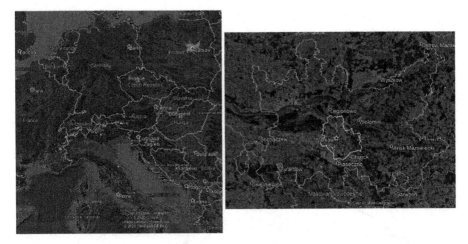

Fig. 1. Warsaw Metropolitan Area 2020; left: in Europe; right: WMA and city administrative boundaries.

The Warsaw MA is the core part of the rural-urban region of Masovian voivodship in Poland and can itself be considered as a rural-urban region of smaller scale [25]. The spatial distribution of acquired BTS data is presented on top of built-up areas layer of WMA (including height of buildings in meters, Fig. 2) according to acquired geodata subsets: OpenCellId [18] and GHSL Data Package [21]. The aim was visual comparison of spatial distribution of the observations with spatial location of possible origins and destination of moving people.

The recent, actual spatial extent of research pilot study is defined according to Eurostat Geoportal [26]; The subset of dataset contains urban clusters, based on local population data. Urban clusters are defined as groups of contiguous raster cells of 1 sq. km size, having a population density of at least 300 inhabitants/sq. km and a total population of at least 5000. The definition of urban clusters underpins the urban/rural typology of NUTS3 regions and the degree of urbanization classification of local administrative (LAU2) units. The boundaries of WMA are delimited based on Polish INSPIRE resources [22].

4.2 Warsaw MA Urban Sprawl and Projections

The movement of people, especially commuting, was indirectly taken into account, and treated as the factors of two (recently) observed main urban processes: urban sprawl and land uses change. Former studies of spatial land uses change simulations often included suitability and zoning layers created based on different evaluation of spatial accessibility (roads), maps of different types of land use (at the starting point of time) treated as prohibited zones or planned zones of change, as well as population distribution.

After 1989 suburbanization, and the transformation of peri-urban areas in the region of Warsaw MA have been characterized by spatially varying intensity, with high

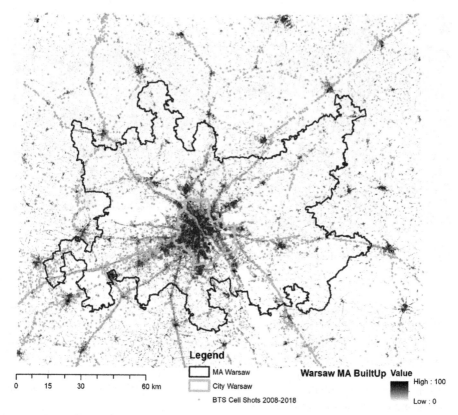

Fig. 2. Spatial distribution of acquired subset of BTS data presented on top of built-up areas layer of Warsaw Metropolitan Area WMA (including height of buildings in meters [21]).

overall dynamics accompanied by lack of spatial order, i.e. by typical urban sprawl phenomena. The previous existing zone of second homes from the 1970s has been partly invaded by new residential, as well as some commercial and industrial functions, connected with the globalized economy, while the prime recreational activities have moved further out into the region's rural hinterland. Simulation of different scenarios, generated using the application of Metronamica ML (multiple layer) framework, reveal noticeable distribution of both residential, as well as industrial and commercial land uses [25] (Fig. 3).

Prospective use of acquired real observations of population movement in space, with the set of continuously recorded data during time, create the possibility to verify the results of past models of urban sprawl and urban land use change simulations. However, for the moment, it is only the strategic aim. The hereafter-described procedure is only the proposed method, looking for the appropriate way to include VGI data into the set of future tools to be possibly developed.

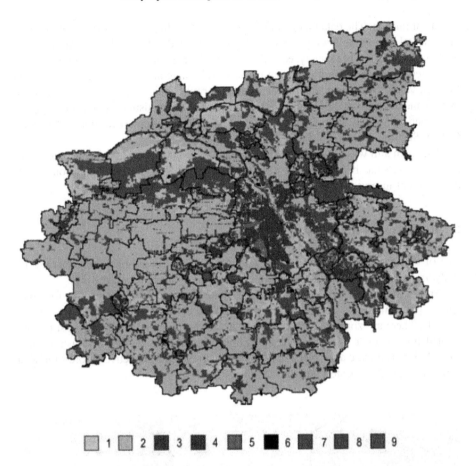

Fig. 3. Simulated land use in Warsaw MA 2025. (Limits to growth scenario Metronamica ML) [25]. Boundaries of WMA: 2012; legend of map: (1) green urban areas, (2) agricultural areas, (3) urban fabric, (4) industrial or commercial units, (5) transport areas, (6) mineral extraction or dump or construction sites, (7) standing forests, (8) natural and semi-natural vegetation, (9) water courses and bodies. (Color figure online)

4.3 VGI Insight and Methodology

Up to now the prevailing inferring concerning urban sprawl are based on registered statistical geodata and population (INSPIRE). However, it is possible to depict the spatial and temporal aspects of commuting people, using aforementioned VGI geodata.

The approach use Data Metrics method to map statistical parameters of a data set under study. Data Metrics method is used to gain information about data points in the form a grid, however it does not interpolate the data to obtain a Z Order Statistics. The data is divided into search sections where the calculation will be performed. The Z Order Statistics provide specific statistical information about the data that is specified within the search radius. The Z grid node values will have the same units as the original data file. These data values can be significant to calculate if the goal is to demonstrate areas of statistical interest. The data that is found in the search radius will be sorted from least to greatest and then the following statistics can be calculated [27]. For the pilot study, the Z median statistics has been analyzed and mapped. The median absolute deviation value is calculated by determining the median in the search range and then deviations are taken for each value. Once the deviation values are determined, then the median is taken from that set and assigned as the Z value for that grid node. The statistics for data locations are concerned with the location of the data points. All procedures have been completed using Golden Software Surfer and ESRI ArcGIS software.

The main aim was to reveal the time of the day (hour, not minutes) when the report of certain BTS has been acquired. This meant that the VGI – reporting person was in this moment in given location.

5   Results of Pilot Study

One of the purposes of social and economic geography is indirect understanding by analyzing spatial patterns and inferring spatial and temporal processes [28].

Approach using Data Metrics Z Order Statistics reveal typical picture for commuting phenomena, i.e. concentric rings around the boundaries of capital city – WMA (Fig. 4). There are zones more active early in the morning and contrary – destinations located further down – active in the evening, when people starting or finishing their daily duties. There are also 'black holes' – where the people are active before sunrise or long after sunset – located far from the city.

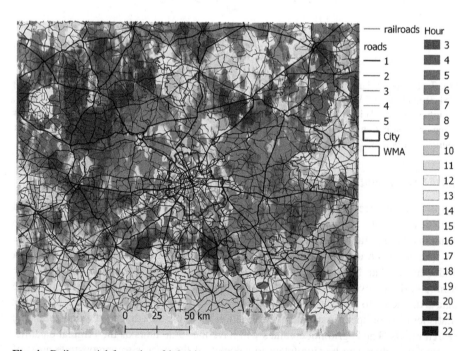

Fig. 4. Daily spatial footprint of inhabitants/visitors/commuters of Warsaw Metropolitan Area. Data Metrics Z Order Statistics (Median). Integer values represent hours of the day (24 h).

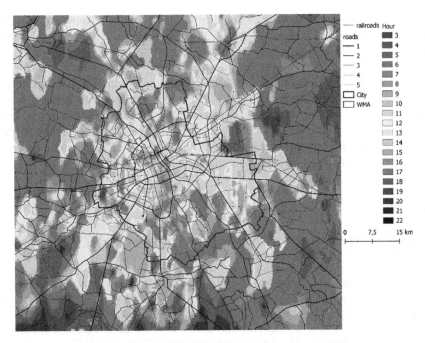

Fig. 5. Daily spatial footprint of inhabitants/visitors/commuters of Warsaw City. Data Metrics Z Order Statistics (Median). Integer values represent hours of the day (24 h).

Interesting phenomena reveal inset, containing zoom of Warsaw city itself (Fig. 5). The main activity of people in center of Warsaw City (business district) falls at noon and afternoon hours. The map shows, of course, the median hours of main (suspected) activity. Also reveals some areas, which are inside the administrative zone of the city characteristics of residential areas – active in the morning and late evening. Zooming the map shows when and where these activities are more intensive inside the administrative region of city itself.

The possible next steps for this study would be zoning procedure, evaluating of different regions of spatial and temporal intensity of VGI observations and comparison to observed qualitative and quantitative changes of land use, as well as estimation of urban sprawl. This is a far-reaching objective, and this examination is only the first step of a possible future procedures.

6 Conclusions

Some depicted observations and mapping human activity based on reports of timestamps of generalized subset of OpenCellId reports confirm spatial and temporal regularity, which shows well-known facts concerning the commuting. In fact, these VGI geodata may be possible tool to confirm some spatial and temporal models of urban activity. Especially taking into account some specific time intervals, e.g. weekends or differences for typical seasons (winter and/or summer). These time ranges seems interesting in context of planned development of the rail and road networks as well as prospective locations of residential areas. The reported results are only the pilot study aimed to verify the usefulness of VGI data.

Later it has been found out fact just after completing this pilot study that there are different versions of OpenCellId database available in the internet for several past subsequent years. For the moment in this pilot study, the studied data aimed to present daily spatial footprint (idealistically) are in fact rather an average spatial footprint for every hour of day during a period of 10 years. This discovery makes possible not only spatial but also the temporal comparisons, evaluating the dynamics of these footprints not only for urban sprawl or land use changes.

References

1. Hasse, J.E., Lathrop, R.G.: Land resource impact indicators of urban sprawl. Appl. Geogr. **23**, 159–175 (2003). https://doi.org/10.1016/j.apgeog.2003.08.002
2. Jaeger, J.A.G., Bertiller, R., Schwick, C., Kienast, F.: Suitability criteria for measures of urban sprawl. Ecol. Ind. **10**, 397–406 (2010). https://doi.org/10.1016/j.ecolind.2009.07.007
3. Haas, A., Osland, L.: Commuting, Migration, Housing and Labour Markets: Complex Interactions. Urban Stud. **51**, 463–476 (2014). https://doi.org/10.1177/0042098013498285
4. Guastella, G., Oueslati, W., Pareglio, S.: Patterns of urban spatial expansion in European cities. Sustainability **11**, 2247 (2019). https://doi.org/10.3390/su11082247
5. Wu, J.: Environmental amenities, urban sprawl, and community characteristics. J. Environ. Econ. Manage. **52**, 527–547 (2006). https://doi.org/10.1016/j.jeem.2006.03.003
6. Handy, S.: Smart growth and the transportation-land use connection: what does the research tell us? Int. Reg. Sci. Rev. **28**, 146–167 (2005). https://doi.org/10.1177/0160017604273626
7. Sultana, S., Weber, J.: The nature of urban growth and the commuting transition: endless sprawl or a growth wave? Urban Stud. **51**, 544–576 (2014). https://doi.org/10.1177/0042098013498284
8. Vanderhaegen, S., Canters, F.: Mapping urban form and function at city block level using spatial metrics. Landscape Urban Planning **167**, 399–409 (2017). https://doi.org/10.1016/j.landurbplan.2017.05.023
9. Herold, M., Scepan, J., Clarke, K.C.: The use of remote sensing and landscape metrics to describe structures and changes in urban land uses. Environ. Plan. A. **34**, 1443–1458 (2002). https://doi.org/10.1068/a3496
10. Elwood, S., Goodchild, M.F., Sui, D.Z.: Researching volunteered geographic information: spatial data, geographic research, and new social practice. Ann. Assoc. Am. Geogr. **102**, 571–590 (2012). https://doi.org/10.1080/00045608.2011.595657
11. Senaratne, H., Mobasheri, A., Ali, A.L., Capineri, C., Haklay, M.: (Muki): A review of volunteered geographic information quality assessment methods. Int. J. Geogr. Inf. Sci. **31**, 139–167 (2017). https://doi.org/10.1080/13658816.2016.1189556
12. Montello, D.R., Goodchild, M.F., Gottsegen, J., Fohl, P.: Where's downtown?: behavioral methods for determining referents of vague spatial queries. Spatial Cogn. Comput. **3**, 185–204 (2003). https://doi.org/10.1080/13875868.2003.9683761
13. Hollenstein, L., Purves, R.: Exploring place through user-generated content: Using Flickr to describe city cores. JOSIS, 21–48 (2010). https://doi.org/10.5311/JOSIS.2010.1.3

14. See, L., et al.: Crowdsourcing, citizen science or volunteered geographic information? the current state of crowdsourced geographic information. IJGI **5**, 55 (2016). https://doi.org/10. 3390/ijgi5050055
15. Bishr, M., Janowicz, K.: Can we trust information? - the case of volunteered geographic information. In: Towards Digital Earth Search Discover and Share Geospatial Data Workshop at Future Internet Symposium, vol. 640. CEUR-WS (2010)
16. Minghini, M., Kotsev, A., Lutz, M.: Comparing INSPIRE and Open Street Map data: how to make the most out of the two worlds. Int. Arch. Photogramm. Remote Sens. Spatial Inf. Sci. **XLII-4/W14**, 167–174 (2019). https://doi.org/10.5194/isprs-archives-XLII-4-W14-167-2019
17. Capineri, C., Haklay, M., Huang, H., Kettunen, J., Ostermann, F., Purves, R. (eds.): European Handbook of Crowdsourced Geographic Information. Ubiquity Press (2016). https://doi.org/10.5334/bax
18. OpenCelliD - Largest Open Database of Cell Towers & Geolocation - by Unwired Labs. http://www.opencellid.org. Accessed 02 Jan 2019
19. Ricciato, F., Widhalm, P., Craglia, M., Pantisano, F.: Estimating population density distribution from network-based mobile phone data. Publications Office of the European Union (2015)
20. Werner, P.A., Porczek, M.: Spatial patterns of development of mobile technologies for 5G networks. In: Misra, S., et al. (eds.) ICCSA 2019. LNCS, vol. 11621, pp. 448–459. Springer, Cham (2019). https://doi.org/10.1007/978-3-030-24302-9_32
21. Florczyk, A.J., et al.: European Commission, Joint Research Centre: GHSL data package 2019: public release GHS P2019 (2019)
22. Geoportal.gov.pl. http://geoportal.gov.pl. Accessed 26 Feb 2020
23. Warsaw (2020). https://en.wikipedia.org/w/index.php?title=Warsaw&oldid=962362880
24. Statistics Poland. https://stat.gov.pl/en/. Accessed 13 June 2020
25. Korcelli, P., Grochowski, M., Kozubek, E., Korcelli-Olejniczak, E., Werner, P.: Development of urban-rural regions: from European to local perspective. IGiPZ PAN, Warszawa (2013)
26. Glossary: Urban cluster - Statistics Explained. https://ec.europa.eu/eurostat/statistics-explained/index.php/Glossary:Urban_cluster. Accessed 14 Mar 2020
27. Golden Software, Inc.: Surfer. Contouring and 3D Surface Mapping for Scientists and Engineers. Golden Software, Inc. (2003)
28. Werner, P.: Simulation of changes of the Warsaw Urban Area 1969-2023 (Application of Cellular Automata), Miscellanea Geographica. 329–335 (2006). https://doi.org/10.2478/mgrsd-2006-0037

A Framework for Sustainable Land Planning in ICZM: Cellular Automata Simulation and Landscape Ecology Metrics

Andrea Fiduccia[1](✉) ⓘ, Luisa Cattozzo[2] ⓘ, Leonardo Filesi[2] ⓘ,
Leonardo Marotta[3] ⓘ, and Luca Gugliermetti[1] ⓘ

[1] Department of Astronautical Electrical and Energy Engineering (DIAEE),
Sapienza, University of Rome, Via Eudossiana 18, 00184 Rome, Italy
andrea.fiduccia.mobile@gmail.com
[2] Department of Architecture and Arts, IUAV University, Santa Croce 1957,
Ca' Tron, 30135 Venice, Italy
[3] Studio Associato Entropia, via F. Corridoni 3, 62019 Recanati, Italy

Abstract. In the paper, we present a Planning Framework for Integrated Coastal Zone Management (ICZM). The points of strength of the framework are the following:

- It is an iterative and participatory process;
- It is scenario-based and model-based;
- It uses a Spatial Decision Support System (SDSS) as enabling infrastructure;
- The SDSS is "powered" by open data and data systematically updated by public bodies.

The theoretical starting point is ICZM requires decision support tools to cope with knowledge from multiple sources, interdisciplinarity and multiple scales (e.g., spatial, temporal or organizational) [1]. The 2007 Integrated Maritime Policy for the European Union [2] is a key document to understand the relationship between coastal and marine information and policy implementation. It shows that it is necessary to develop a marine-coastal Decision Support System [3, 4] based on indicators and indices (aggregations of indicators into a synthetic representation), use of Geographic Information Systems, models and multicriteria assessment of scenarios [5, 6]. The system of indices is used to describe the complexity of a coastal system: geo-ecological level, land processes, human society, economy, and coastal uses at multiple scales [5, 7]. Multicriteria assessment is a tool to support social and environmental decisions in the perspective of sustainability and strategic planning [8–11].

During the design phase of the SDSS components (basic data, indicators and models), it was performed a review of the Land Use/Land Cover change simulation models. The output of the review was the choice of SLEUTH model [12]. The framework was tested on a study area (Veneto Region - Italy). In the test we coupled SLEUTH with Fragstats [13] for the analysis of landscape ecology metrics.

Keywords: ICZM · Landscape ecology metrics · LUCC models

© Springer Nature Switzerland AG 2020
O. Gervasi et al. (Eds.): ICCSA 2020, LNCS 12252, pp. 378–393, 2020.
https://doi.org/10.1007/978-3-030-58811-3_27

1 Introduction

From a methodological point of view, the research continues the work started by two previous researches.

The PhD thesis *"Indices and indicators for Integrated Coastal Zone Management with a Landscape Approach. Application to the Adriatic Sea"* [14] by Dr. Leonardo Marotta PhD carried out at the Universitat Politecnica de Catalunya (Doctorado de Ciencias del Mar - Escuela Técnica Superior de Ingenieros de Caminos, Canales y Puertos) (Supervisor: Prof. Joan Pau Sierra) shows an exhaustive analysis of the literature about ICZM and about the indicators applied to it. Marotta identified a multiscale ICZM model, based on the concepts of sustainability and landscape, to implement the resilience of the coastal socio-ecological system. The model uses a SDSS. Marotta applied his framework starting from the scale of the Mediterranean basin arriving at the detailed analysis of three sites on the upper Adriatic coast: the Venice lagoon, the Conero (Ancona) and Rimini.

The PhD thesis *"From linearity to circularity. A regenerative model applied to a coastal landscape"* [15] by Dr. Luisa Cattozzo PhD carried out at the Doctoral School in Architecture, City and Design of the IUAV University of Venice (Supervisor: Prof. Domenico Patassini; Co-tutors: Prof Leonardo Filesi, Dr. Leonardo Marotta PhD) has simplified Marotta's ICZM model by focusing it on the circular economy in the coastal area of the Po delta and introducing a new indicator of land eco-biodiversity.

The thesis of Dr. Cattozzo has highlighted it is appropriate to simplify the system of indicators in order to have an effective planning framework. It has to be exploitable at the level of a small dimension Territorial Body such as the Municipality.

This consideration led our choice of sustainability and landscape indicators with a high rate of update by Italian (e.g. ISPRA, Istat) or European (e.g. EUROSTAT, GMES - Copernicus) public bodies. The indicators are mainly available using Spatial Data Infrastructures for data sharing promoted and managed in the frame of the INSPIRE Directive (2007/2/CE) [16]. Otherwise, the indicators can be easily obtained starting from Open Data.

In reviewing the overall methodology, the EU DPSIR Model [17] was also considered as a reference. This model, in fact, places the problems of interest of the ICZM on a more general level (using the concepts of Land System and Land Process) and offers a systemic, multidimensional and integrated approach that takes into account space and time dimensions and relevant aspects of sustainability.

2 The Planning Framework

In Table 1 we compare the ICZM Methodology of Marotta *et al.* [18] with the EEA DPSIR Framework [17] using three macro-steps.

The two methodologies have wide possibilities of integration.

Since the ICZM Methodology of Marotta et al. [18] is targeted to the ICZM, it has a unique and explicit goal in the macro-step A.

The EEA DPSIR Framework [17] was set up with reference to a virtuous process of production and systematic updating of territorial information in which the Copernicus

Table 1. Comparison between ICZM methodologies

	Methodology for ICZM by Marotta et al. [18]	EEA DPSIR framework [17]
A	1. *Goal:* to implement the resilience of the coastal socio-ecological system from a sustainability perspective	1. *Formulation of goals as policy-relevant question*
B	2. *Definition of homogeneous environmental management units, and analysis of spatial and temporal structure, hierarchy and dynamics over multiple scales.* Deliverable: Map of Habitats 3. *Analysis of land-use changes in the coastal system* 4. *Implementation of spatial indices* characterizing each patch type and state 5. *Conservation-Strategies gaps analysis* 6. *Assessment of coastal conflicts* using a coastal conflict index following the work of Vallega [5]	2. *Identification of **Drivers** and mapping of **Pressures** (land processes)* 3. *Territorial assessment (**States**)* • Analysis of the LU/LC spatial distribution • Land management practices • Soil sealing and soil consumption • Existence of conservation areas and non-conservation areas 4. *Dynamic assessment (changes of state)* • LU/LC flows • Identification of hot spots 5. *Functional assessment (**Impacts**)* • Measurement of the effects of Land Processes on environmental functions
C	7. *Multi Criteria Analysis (MCA) in order to minimize conflicts over a set of values and constraints*	6. *Key policy message and **Responses** to specific pressures on the land system*

System plays a fundamental role and explicitly considers the dynamics of Land Take/Soil Sealing.

The Methodology of Marotta et al. [18] requires the Map of Habitats, a specific cartography with a high-specialized effort of production and not homogeneously available in all European countries, and it uses a scenario approach and MCA as well as a specific tool for analyzing coastal conflict dynamics.

However, both methodologies are not suitable for direct application in a planning process, as they do not include the Land Plan in their basic elements.

Macro-step B is the Knowledge Base of the Plan.

The macro-step C of the Methodology of Marotta et al. [18] is a system for the assessment of scenarios, but it is too complex to be used in a real urban-territorial planning process.

To overcome this difficulty, we have designed a Planning Framework that integrates the two aforementioned methodologies. The steps of the Planning Framework are shown in Table 2 according to the logic of the macro-steps.

The proposed Planning Framework (Fig. 1) is an iterative model. The zoning of a Plan (or the zoning of a territorially extended project intervention in the coastal area) has alternative hypotheses (Scenarios). Scenarios are evaluated using indices and indicators of fragmentation of the eco-mosaic, of soil consumption and urban sprawl/urban sprinkling.

Table 2. Planning framework steps

Step	Description	Notes
A	Goal: to implement the resilience of the coastal socio-ecological system from a sustainability perspective	Sources of sustainability goals • International conventions • EU and national regulations • Guidelines • Good practices • Scientific literature
B1	Knowledge Base. Annual-updated items. • Baseline data – Land Covermaps (EEA - Copernicus) – Soil Consumption (ISPRA) – Demographic and socio-economic statistical data (Eurostat, Istat, regional demographic offices) • Data Analysis Layers produced by processing of baseline data – Land Use fragmentation indices and indicators – Urban Sprawl/Urban Sprinkling analysis	The baseline data are cartographies and data systematically produced by national and European bodies
B2	Knowledge Base. Items with variable time interval of updating • Land Use maps produced from the Territorial and Sector Plans • Cartography of environmental constraints and protections • Geo-environmental maps • Map of Habitats	Maps and data produced by the competent bodies
B3	Analysis of the cartographies, indices and indicators of steps B1 and B2 to understand the ongoing Land Processes to support the Plan	
C1	Hypothesis of Land Plan • Land Use Scenarios (Zoning)	
C2	Analysis of the Land Cover and Land Use of Plan Scenarios using the indices and indicators of step B1 • Land Use fragmentation indices and indicators • Urban Sprawl/Urban Sprinkling analysis	
C3	Medium-term Land Use/Land Cover change simulation model starting from Plan Scenarios The simulation outputs will be evaluated using the indicators of step B1	SLEUTH model [12] with multi-criteria analysis of the constraints system (identified using the data of steps B1 and B2)
C4	Steps C1, C2 and C3 will be repeated iteratively based on feedback from the actors of the decision-making process until reaching an agreed scenario	

The assessment of the scenarios is carried out both against the configuration of the land use of the current state, and against scenarios forecasting the medium (and long-term) effects of zoning. The forecasts are the output of a simulation model of the evolutionary dynamics of LU/LC. Compared to the original Marotta model, a different modeling framework has been adopted to simulate the evolution of the Land Cover suitable for giving medium and long-term qualitative and quantitative perspectives to the scenarios of the Plan.

The Planning Framework is a methodology that produces cartographic outputs. Therefore, it is suitable for participatory planning [19].

The Actors (the Decision-makers, the Technicians, the Stakeholders and the Communities) will thus be able to evaluate the different scenarios. They will consider acceptable only a scenario verifying well-defined values of the set of indices and indicators. Such values will be obtained from good practices and from international and national guidelines about sustainability.

The Knowledge Base of the Planning Framework is made up of data and GIS layers having different frequencies of updating and elaborations carried out by the SDSS.

3   A Test for the Setup of the Planning Framework

3.1   The Overall Test Strategy

The overall strategy of the test is to verify whether the proposed indices, indicators and models are able to capture and assess the land dynamics in progress. A critical point of the test is the use of available datasets.

The study area is the coast of the Veneto Region (Italy) which extends for about 160 km, between the mouth of the Tagliamento river and the mouth of the Po in Goro. This area belongs to the provinces of Venice and Rovigo and administratively is divided into 11 municipalities from north to south: San Michele al Tagliamento, Caorle, Eraclea, Jesolo, Cavallino - Treporti, Venice, Chioggia, Rosolina, Porto Viro, Porto Tolle, Ariano nel Polesine.

3.2   Urban Sprawl/Urban Sprinkling

According to Merriam-Webster Dictionary, the definition of Urban Sprawl is *"the spreading of urban developments (such as houses and shopping centers) on undeveloped land near a city"*. Urban Sprawl is a disordered and rapid growth of the city, mostly concentrated in suburban areas with low settlement density against the surrounding rural areas [20].

The concept of Urban Sprinkling was subsequently proposed in the literature to account for the pulverization of this projection of the city on the rural territory: "a small quantity distributed in drops or scattered particles" [21]. It is a typical Italian phenomenon [22], but with presence also in other European territories [23].

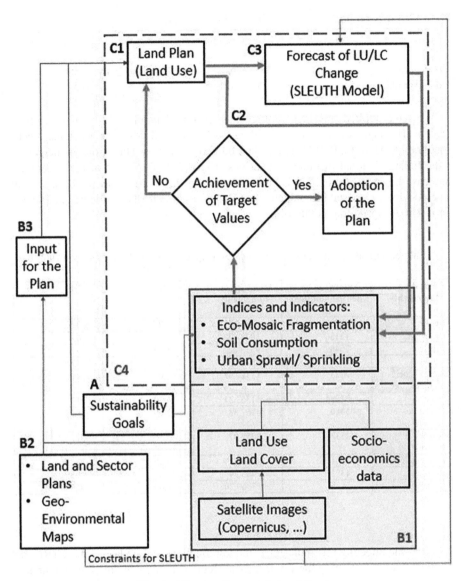

Fig. 1. Planning framework (workflow)

The two phenomena can be identified using specific indicators [24]

$$D_p = \frac{Inhabitant}{Area} \left[\frac{number}{Ha}\right] \tag{1}$$

$$D_b = \frac{Residential\ Building}{Area} \left[\frac{number}{Ha}\right] \tag{2}$$

In [24] it is proposed the following grid of criteria:

	D_b	D_p
Urban sprawl	$12 \geq D_b \geq 6$	$150 \geq D_p \geq 20$
Urban sprinkling	$0,8 \geq D_b \geq 0,1$	$2 \geq D_p \geq 0,2$

We have applied this methodology to the coastal municipalities of the Veneto Region. The layer of residential buildings was extracted from the Regional Vector Topographic Map (CTRN) [25]. The datasource for the area (Ha) of the municipalities is the Italian National Institute of Statistics (Istat) [26]. The result of the experimentation is shown in Table 3. With reference to the threshold values of [24], we can conclude that six coastal Municipalities of Veneto Region (cells highlighted in Table 3) are in Urban Sprinkling conditions.

Table 3. Urban Sprinkling in the coastal municipalities of the Veneto Region (Italy)

Coastal Municipality	Number of residential buildings	Area (Ha) of Municipality	Dp	Db
Caorle	8053	15359,45	0,77	0,52
Chioggia	12186	18782,72	2,65	0,65
Eraclea	7646	9533,02	1,32	0,80
Jesolo	8221	9628,68	2,55	0,85
San Michele al Tagliamento	7223	11420,43	1,05	0,63
Venezia	31984	41563,31	6,24	0,77
Cavallino-Treporti	5480	4467,38	2,99	1,23
Ariano nel Polesine	2132	8057,97	0,56	0,26
Porto Tolle	3841	25667,79	0,39	0,15
Rosolina	4373	7465,24	0,87	0,59
Porto Viro	5029	13369,20	1,09	0,38

The issue affecting this indicator is the low frequency of update of the CTRN and the strategy of not covering the whole Veneto Region at the same time stamp of update.

3.3   Land Fragmentation Indices and Indicators. Scenarios: Year 2007, Year 2012

Fragmentation is defined as *"the process that generates a progressive reduction of the surface of natural environments and an increase in their isolation: in this way, natural surfaces are to constitute spatially segregated and progressively isolated fragments, inserted in a territorial matrix of anthropic origin"* [27].

A first group of land fragmentation indices and indicators [28] is shown in Table 4.

Table 4. Land Fragmentation Indices and Indicators [28]

Denomination and Description	Formula
Infrastructural density: indicates the extension of the multimodal mobility system in relation to the size of the reference area. This extension is proportional to the action of environmental fragmentation deriving from the physical breakdown of the eco-mosaic and the associated disturbing factors (noises, pollution, vibrations).	$DI = \frac{\sum l_i}{Au}$ (m/kmq) l_i = length of the road sections Au = area of the reference land unit
Infrastructure fragmentation: the road sections, which already appear in the DI index formula, are weighted by means of a coefficient that takes into account the occlusion effect (physical interruption or disturbances) that the particular types of road network create towards potential flows of terrestrial fauna.	$IFI = \frac{\sum l_i * o_i}{Au}$ (m/kmq) l_i = length of the individual road sections (excluding discontinuities such as viaducts, bridges and tunnels) o_i = ecosystem occlusion coefficients of road types Au = area of the reference land unit
Urbanization Density: indicates the extent of the urbanized area for each square kilometer of reference area. Using the definition of Urbanized soil in [33], Aurb is modeled with the Land Use categories of the Veneto Region having first code 1.	$DUu = \frac{\sum Aurb_i}{Au}$ (mq/kmq) $Aurb_i$ = area of the urbanized surfaces Au = area of the reference land unit
Per capita urbanized surface for the year XXXX: indicates the size of the urbanized area for each resident (according to an official data source) and is aimed at providing information on local land use for urban purposes.	$SUpc = \frac{\sum Aurb_i}{Au}$ (mq/ab) $Aurb_i$ = area of the urbanized surfaces Nab = resident inhabitants (year XXXX)
Widespread Urbanization Fragmentation: it appears as a density of urbanized surface weighted through a form factor. The first term of the expression provides the incidence of urbanized surfaces in the reference surface, while the second term represents the relationship between the overall perimeter of the urbanized parts and the perimeter that urbanized parts would have if they were all concentrated in a single aggregation having circular shape.	$UFI = \frac{\sum Aurb_i}{Au} * \frac{\sum p_i}{2\sqrt{\pi \sum Aurb_i}}$ $Aurb_i$ = area of the urbanized surfaces Au = area of the reference land unit p_i = perimeters of urbanized areas
Biopermeability rate: indicates the percentage of biopermeability surfaces on the reference area. Biopermeability surfaces are those that are not affected by urbanization or intensive productive land use The classification of biopermeable land use shown in [28] has been "mapped" on the Legend of the Land Use Map of the Veneto Region.	$Tbiop = \frac{\sum Abiop_i}{Au}$ $Abiop_i$ = area of biopermeability surfaces Au = area of the reference land unit

The indices and indicators were calculated for two reference scenarios: year 2007 and year 2012. The choice is the consequence of the fact that in 2007 and 2012 an updated version of the Land Cover Map of the Veneto Region was released [25]. The Land Cover Map of the Veneto Region (scale 1: 10000), has a very detailed legend, made up of 174 classes, and provides for a classification of the territory according to the legend of the European CORINE Land Cover program deepened locally up to the fifth level.

The DBPrior10K was the datasource for the infrastructural network (roads and railways). DBPrior10K is a vector GIS dataset created as part of the Agreement between the State - Regions - Local Authorities on Geographic Information Systems ("Intesa GIS") on a scale of 1: 10000. The original dataset [29] has been updated using conflation procedures with the OpenStreetMap data [30].

The resident population (2007 and 2012) of the Veneto Region is available as open data on the website of the Statistical Department of the Veneto Region [31]. The dataset is available in various formats including MS Excel. The GIS dataset of the boundaries of administrative units for statistical purposes (reference year 2012) can be downloaded from the Istat website [32].

We can see in Table 5 coastal Municipalities with ongoing fragmentation dynamics (cells highlighted).

Table 5. Analysis of the 2007–2012 variation of the fragmentation indices and indicators for the coastal Municipalities of the Veneto Region (Italy). Comp "index X" is the difference between the delta 2007–2012 for "index X" in the municipality and the average delta 2007–2012 for "index X" in the coastal Municipalities of the Veneto Region

Municipality	Comp DI	Comp DUu	Comp UFI	Comp IFI	Comp Supc	Comp Tbiop
Caorle	1,21	-2653,33	-0,04	-3,66	30,41	0,19
Chioggia	7,28	-3585,13	0,00	-1,25	-6,57	0,14
Eraclea	-21,28	-1319,90	0,02	-9,31	21,89	0,02
Jesolo	91,99	8403,22	0,19	27,26	30,85	0,23
San Michele al Tagliamento	-19,91	-3595,55	-0,07	-11,59	-8,33	0,30
Venezia	39,48	-2309,64	0,02	32,86	-4,23	-0,15
Cavallino-Treporti	12,76	-4432,50	-0,06	-1,85	-49,51	1,03
Ariano nel Polesine	-21,46	-1702,18	0,01	-12,10	109,78	-0,58
Porto Tolle	-21,47	-5003,62	-0,06	-12,12	25,87	0,44
Rosolina	-8,12	-4216,75	-0,01	-8,29	-25,89	0,64
Porto Viro	-21,47	-4127,51	-0,16	-12,48	-4,50	0,42

3.4 Ecomosaic Fragmentation Indicators. Scenarios: Year 2006, Year 2012

A second set of fragmentation indicators of the Planning Framework originated in the disciplinary context of Landscape Ecology. *"Using some metrics of Landscape*

Ecology, we can analyze two of the main features of a landscape: composition and configuration. The composition of a landscape refers to the richness and abundance of the different elements that are part of it, without however considering their spatial distribution; even if the composition metrics are not explicitly spatial, they also have important consequences in terms of spatial effects. The landscape configuration, instead, applies to the spatial properties of the elements, such as their distribution, position, orientation and shape" [34].

The Planning Framework uses the following indicators according to a methodology of ISPRA [35]:

- *"Composition:*

  - *Patch Richness (PR) describes the number of different types of land cover in the land unit of analysis;*
  - *Percentage of Landscape (PLAND), describes in percentage terms the composition of a given landscape;*

- *Configuration:*
  - *Patch Density (PD) indicates the degree of subdivision of a specific class of land cover typology, related to the entire extent of the landscape;*
  - *Mean Patch Size indices (AREA_AM) expresses the average size of the elements of a given type of land cover in terms of weighted average;*
  - *Shape (SHAPE_AM) is a measure of the geometric complexity of the landscape elements of a given land cover category;*
  - *Edge Contrast (ECON_AM) measures the length of the edge shared between two types of land cover in a given landscape;*
  - *Patch Compaction (GYRATE_AM), expresses the average distance between the various cells of a single spatial unit of the same class of land cover, reported in the total area of the land cover class;*
  - *Contagion (CONTAG) measures the level of aggregation of the land cover classes and it is calculated at the landscape level;*
  - *Cohesion (COHESION) indicates the tendency of land cover types to aggregate;*
  - *Aggregation index (AI), as the previous one indicates the tendency of the types of coverage to aggregate;*
  - *Simpson Diversity Index (SIDI) is a measure of the diversity of homogeneous spatial units"* [34].

The analysis for Veneto Region (Italy) was carried out using the CORINE Land Cover 2006 and 2012 [36] level 2 classes (Table 6). Landscape ecology indicators were calculated using the Fragstats software [13].

Table 6. Assessment of the 2006–2012 dynamics of ecomosaic fragmentation indicators in Veneto Region (Italy)

Indicator	CLC2006	CLC2012	Delta 2006–2012	Assessment
PD	0,2967	0,308	0,0113	Fragmentation increased
AREA_AM	139928,8	135888,5	−4040,2369	Weighted average patch size decreased: fragmentation increased
GYRATE_AM	17527,31	17008,72	−518,5869	Fragmentation increased
SHAPE_AM	17,7269	17,1849	−0,542	The geometric complexity of the elements of the landscape has decreased
ECON_AM	97,8449	97,8732	0,0283	Increased the contrast
CONTAG	64,0012	63,6536	−0,3476	Disaggregation of landscape elements
COHESION	99,941	99,939	−0,002	Disaggregation of landscape elements
PR	15	15	0	Constant (are the CLC classes)
SIDI	0,771	0,776	0,005	Very slight increase in landscape diversification
AI	98,8462	98,8471	0,0009	Aggregation value very high and increasing

3.5 Ecomosaic Fragmentation Indicators. Scenarios: CLC Year 2012, SLEUTH Year 2040

Understanding the processes that generate the changes in land use/land cover and their patterns at a geographical level is fundamental for the design of effective policies for the management of the lands without altering the relationships that define their structure.

The claims of precision of mathematical models for the territory of the sixties and seventies have now disappeared. The consequences of Douglas Lee's Requiem of 1973 [37] is a more realistic approach to models: the aim of the model is not the exact prediction of *how much*, but to be a stimulus for reasoning and discussion with the awareness of the importance of *where*. The model illustrates the alternatives, the effects on the complexity of the territory-environment-society system. The model does not provide the "optimal" solution: the model is the tool for the construction of scenarios and to agree a common vision.

After a survey on the Land Use/Land Cover change (LUCC) models, we chose to use the SLEUTH model [12]. SLEUTH is a representative model of cellular automata models with explicit rules and it has an extensive application in different countries of the world at different scales [38, 39]: it can be considered a model with general applicability [40].

The GIS information layers used for the model were the CORINE Land Cover (CLC), the DBPrior10K infrastructure network, and the information layers of the SDI of the Veneto Region. The simulation workflow adopted in [41] was replicated to identify two scenarios for the year 2040 of the Veneto Region (Italy). As part of the simulation, the CORINE Land Cover 2012 was rasterized with a 500 × 500 m grid and reclassified into 8 classes (Fig. 2).

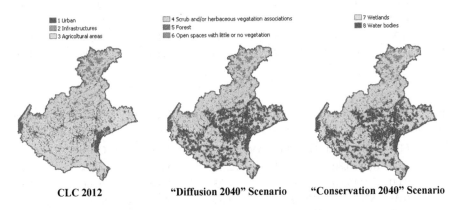

CLC 2012   "Diffusion 2040" Scenario   "Conservation 2040" Scenario

Fig. 2. SLEUTH Simulation for Veneto Region (Italy)

The landscape ecology indicators have been calculated using Fragstats [13] and applied at both landscape level (Table 7) and class level (Tables 8, 9 and 10) obtaining values consistent with a dynamic of pervasive urban expansion.

Table 7. SLEUTH 2040 simulations for Veneto Region (Italy). Landscape level fragmentation indicators

Indicator	CLC 2012	"Diffusion" scenario	"Conservation" scenario
PD	0,1439	0,1169	0,1208
AREA_AM	580814,2657	214596,151	265360,8484
GYRATE_AM	34040,9176	24989,76	27222,4472
SHAPE_AM	17,4721	14,6184	15,9773
ECON_AM	95,8565	96,4181	96,4533
CONTAG	52,9234	48,7178	49,0507
COHESION	99,0337	98,6739	98,8402
PR	9	9	9
SIDI	0,6232	0,7266	0,7227
AI	76,9824	75,5639	75,9248

Table 8. CORINE land cover 2012 of Veneto Region (Italy). Class level fragmentation indicators

TYPE	PD	AREA_AM	GYRATE_AM	SHAPE_AM	ECON_AM	COHESION	AI
1	0,06	1138,22	1415,18	2,10	99,14	74,86	45,02
2	0,01	196,47	603,66	1,35	96,68	51,49	32,10
3	0,02	912751,65	44529,78	21,90	96,54	99,72	85,76
4	0,01	299581,39	38842,37	21,52	96,77	99,23	75,66
5	0,02	1661,60	1893,44	2,31	92,71	80,71	54,11
6	0,01	2451,62	2292,26	2,26	87,78	83,70	62,69
7	0,00	5908,40	4137,15	3,09	97,95	90,44	71,17
8	0,01	20950,06	8241,47	3,59	84,41	93,06	74,86

Table 9. SLEUTH Scenario "2040 Diffusion" for Veneto Region (Italy). Class level fragmentation indicators

TYPE	PD	AREA_AM	GYRATE_AM	SHAPE_AM	ECON_AM	COHESION	AI
1	0,03	180570,80	21870,94	12,85	98,04	98,64	77,98
2	0,00	115,66	463,76	1,23	95,05	40,06	24,51
3	0,03	252627,20	27478,59	17,54	97,77	98,96	75,43
4	0,01	306920,90	36120,43	18,48	95,90	99,21	78,85
5	0,02	1307,94	1621,02	2,10	92,78	77,14	50,86
6	0,01	2479,86	2292,99	2,25	87,62	83,83	63,12
7	0,00	5178,33	3714,93	2,85	97,95	89,57	70,66
8	0,01	21577,47	8707,71	3,74	84,28	94,04	77,64

Table 10. SLEUTH scenario "2040 Conservation" for Veneto Region (Italy). Class level fragmentation indicators

TYPE	PD	AREA_AM	GYRATE_AM	SHAPE_AM	ECON_AM	COHESION	AI
1	0,03	138783,40	16778,25	10,61	98,38	98,14	76,74
2	0,00	81,67	375,19	1,11	93,87	32,00	22,31
3	0,03	379742,60	32618,70	21,25	97,78	99,28	76,85
4	0,01	354027,30	42419,47	20,26	95,74	99,34	79,53
5	0,02	1226,40	1596,60	2,03	92,66	76,17	50,30
6	0,01	2476,41	2289,56	2,25	87,65	83,80	63,03
7	0,00	5966,61	4179,04	3,06	98,11	90,67	72,08
8	0,01	21497,21	8652,60	3,65	84,17	93,81	77,33

4   Conclusions

In this work, a Planning Framework and a set of indices and indicators in the frame of Integrated Coastal Zone Management (ICZM) is presented.

The methodology identified and tested is "lean", but focused on addressing the core of the contemporary dynamics of coastal systems: anthropogenic actions are producing soil consumption with a reduction in sustainability and environmental quality and an increase in the risks due to climate change.

The "backbone" datasets, Land Use/Land Cover, are systematically updated using Earth Observation products and other data that are institutional output of public bodies. Therefore, the indices and indicators of ecosystem ecology and landscape can be "easily" calculated and mapped. This type of maps, indices, indicators and methodology are the basis of the coastal SDSS necessary for decision makers and stakeholders for the ICZM.

The path of evolution of the methodology can be identified in the following topics:

- exploitation of different implementations of the SLEUTH model;
- exploitation of a different LUCC model;
- expansion of the set of assessment models;
- exploitation of both institutional/industrial (IoT paradigm) and social and voluntary real-time data sources.

References

1. Marotta, L.: ICZM Technologies for integrating data and support decision making, Instrumentation Viewpoint, n. 8 (2010)
2. EU: Communication from the Commission to the European Parliament, the Council, the European Economic and Social Committee and the Committee of the Regions - An Integrated Maritime Policy for the European Union {COM(2007) 574 final)} {SEC(2007) 1278} {SEC(2007) 1279} {SEC(2007) 1280} {SEC(2007) 1283}(2007)
3. Van Kouwen, F., Dieperink, C., Schot, P., Wassen, M.: Applicability of decision support systems for integrated coastal zone management. Coast. Manage. 36, 19–34 (2008)
4. Fabbri, K.P.: A strategic decision support framework for integrated coastal zone management. Int. J. Environ. Technol. Manage. 6, 206–217 (2006)
5. Vallega, A.: Fundamental of Coastal Zone Management, p. 263. Kluwer, Dordrecht (1999)
6. Soncini Sessa, R.: MODSS Per Decisioni Integrate e Partecipate, p. 512. Mc Graw-Hill, Milano (2004)
7. Pearce, D.: Blueprint 3. Measuring Sustainable Development, p. 224. Earthscan, London (1993)
8. Munda, G.: Multicriteria assessment, international society for ecological economics. Internet Encyclopaedia Ecological Economics, p. 10 (2003). http://www.ecoeco.org/education_encyclopedia.php. Accessed 29 June 2008
9. Munda, G.: Social multi-criteria evaluation: methodological foundations and operational consequences. Eur. J. Oper. Res. 158, 662–677 (2004)
10. Ceccaroni, L., Cortés, U., Sànchez-Marrè, M.: OntoWEDSS: augmenting environmental decision-support systems with ontologies. Environ. Model Softw. 19, 785–797 (2004)

11. Ortolano, L.: Environmental Regulation and Impact Assessment, p. 620. Wiley, New York (1997)

12. Clarke, K.C., Hoppen, S., Gaydos, L.J.: A self modifying cellular automaton model of historical urbanization in the San Francisco Bay area. Environ. Planning B **24**, 247–261 (1997)

13. McGarigal, K., Cushman, S.A., Neel, M.C., Ene, E.: FRAGSTATS: Spatial Pattern Analysis Program for Categorical Maps. University of Massachusetts, Amherst (2002)

14. Marotta, L.: Indices and indicators for Integrated Coastal Zone Management with a Landscape Approach. Application to the Adriatic Sea, Ph.D. thesis, Universitat Politecnica de Catalunya (Doctorado de Ciencias del Mar - Escuela Técnica Superior de Ingenieros de Caminos, Canales y Puertos), supervised by Prof. Joan Pau Sierra (2012)

15. Cattozzo, L.: Dalla linearità alla circolarità. Un modello rigenerativo applicato ad un paesaggio costiero, Tesi di Dottoato, Scuola di Dottorato in Architettura, Città e Design dell'Università IUAV di Venezia (Relatore: Prof. Domenico Patassini; Co-relatori: Prof. Leonardo Filesi, Dott. Leonardo Marotta PhD) (2019)

16. EU: Directive 2007/2/EC of the European Parliament and of the Council of 14 March 2007 establishing an Infrastructure for Spatial Information in the European Community (INSPIRE) (2007)

17. EEA (European Environment Agency): Land systems at European level – analytical assessment framework. EEA Briefing no. 10/2018 (2018). https://doi.org/10.2800/141532. ISBN 978-92-9213-988-9, ISSN 2467-3196

18. Marotta, L., Ceccaroni, L., Matteucci, G., Rossini, P., Guerzoni, S.: A decision-support system in ICZM for protecting the ecosystems: integration with the habitat directive. J. Coastal Conserv **15**, 393–415 (2010)

19. Bastiani, M.: Pianificazione territoriale. Pianificazione partecipata in AA.VV, Atelier del Futuro, CUEN, Napoli (1999)

20. Romano, B., Zullo, F.: The urban transformation of Italy's adriatic coastal strip: fifty years of unsustainability. Land Use Policy **38**, 26–36 (2014)

21. Romano, B., Zullo, Ciabò, S., Fiorini, L., Marucci, A.: Geografie e modelli di 50 anni di consumo di suolo in Italia. Sci. Ric **5**, 17–28 (2015)

22. Romano, B., Zullo, F., Fiorini, L., Ciabò, S., Marucci, A.: Sprinkling: an approach to describe urbanization dynamics in Italy. Sustainability **9**, 97 (2017)

23. Romano, B., Zullo, F., Fiorini, L., Marucci, A., Ciabò, S.: Land transformation of Italy due to half a century of urbanization. Land Use Policy **67**, 387–400 (2017)

24. Saganeiti, L., Favale, A., Pilogallo, A., Scorza, F., Murgante, B.: Assessing urban fragmentation at regional scale using sprinkling indexes. Sustainability **10**, 3274 (2018)

25. SDI of Veneto Region (Regione del Veneto - Infrastruttura dei Dati Territoriali), https://idt2. regione.veneto.it/en/. Accessed 09 May 2019

26. Istat (Italian National Institute of Statistics), Main geographical statistical information about Municipalities. https://www.istat.it/it/archivio/156224. Accessed 10 June 2019

27. APAT: Gestione delle aree di collegamento ecologico funzionale. Manuali e linee guida 26/2003 (2003)

28. Romano, B., Paolinelli, G.: L'interferenza insediativa nelle infrastrutture ecosistemiche – Modelli per la rete ecologica del Veneto. Gangemi, Roma (2007)

29. CISIS – CPSG: Progetto DBPrior10K. http://www.centrointerregionale-gis.it/DBPrior/ DBPrior1.html. Accessed 10 Jan 2019

30. OpenStreetMap. https://www.openstreetmap.org. Accessed 09 July 2019

31. Veneto Region Statistic Department. http://statistica.regione.veneto.it/. Accessed 09 May 2019

32. Istat (Italian National Institute of Statistics), GIS datasets of Administrative Units. https://www.istat.it/it/archivio/222527. Accessed 09 Aug 2019
33. Romano, B., Zullo, F.: Models of urban land use in Europe. Assessment tools and criticalities. Int. J. Agric. Environ. Inf. Syst. (IJAEIS) **4**(3), July 2013. ISSN 1947-3192 (2013)
34. Fiduccia, A., Cattozzo, L., Marotta, L., Filesi, L., Gugliermetti, L.: Ecosystem indicators and landscape ecology metrics as a tool to evaluate sustainable land planning in ICZM. In: Misra, S., et al. (eds.) ICCSA 2019. LNCS, vol. 11621, pp. 561–576. Springer, Cham (2019). https://doi.org/10.1007/978-3-030-24302-9_40
35. ISPRA (Istituto Superiore per la Protezione e la Ricerca Ambientale): TERRITORIO. Processi e trasformazioni in Italia. ISPRA. Rapporti 296/2018 (2018)
36. Copernicus Land Monitoring Service. https://land.copernicus.eu/. Accessed 10 Jan 2019
37. Lee Jr., D.B.: Requiem for Large-scale models. J. Am. Inst. Planners **30**, 163–178 (1973)
38. Santé, I., García, A.M., Miranda, D., et al.: Cellular automata models for the simulation of real-world urban processes: a review and analysis. Landsc. Urban Plan. **96**, 108–122 (2010)
39. Clarke, K.C., Gaydos, L.: Loose-coupling a cellular automaton model and GIS: long-term urban growth prediction for San Francisco and Washington/Baltimore. Int. J. Geo. Inf. Sci. **12**, 699–714 (1998)
40. Chaudhuri, G., Clarke, K.C.: The SLEUTH land use change model: a review. Int. J. Environ. Resour. Res. 1(1) (2013)
41. Martellozzo, F., Amato, F., Murgante, B., Clarke, K.C.: Modelling the impact of urban growth on agriculture and natural land in Italy to 2030. Appl. Geogr. **91**, 156–167 (2018)

SPACEA: A Custom-Made GIS Toolbox for Basic Marine Spatial Planning Analyses

Miriam von Thenen[1,2(✉)] ⓘ, Henning Sten Hansen[2] ⓘ,
and Kerstin S. Schiele[1] ⓘ

[1] Leibniz Institute for Baltic Sea Research Warnemünde,
Seestraße 15, 18119 Rostock, Germany
{miriam.thenen,kerstin.schiele}@io-warnemuende.de
[2] Aalborg University, A. C. Meyers Vænge 15, 2450 Copenhagen, Denmark
hsh@plan.aau.dk

Abstract. Marine Spatial Planning (MSP) requires the analysis of the spatial distribution of marine uses and environmental conditions. Such analyses can be carried out with GIS, but standard GIS programs do not feature a toolbox that combines the most needed functionalities for such analyses. The SPACEA toolbox presented here was created to bundle and adapt existing functionalities in one toolbox. SPACEA consists of several script tools that have been designed to be user-friendly and applicable to different analyses for MSP. This includes the processing of different input layers with regard to marine uses and environmental conditions. The main functionalities of SPACEA are exemplified in a fictional case study in the Baltic Sea, where the tools are applied to find potentially suitable areas for mussel farming. The tools feature a user-friendly interface and more experienced users may also use the provided sample codes to run it from the python window or as a stand-alone script. As such, the tools can be applied by users with different levels of GIS knowledge and experience.

Keywords: Marine Spatial Planning · GIS analyses · Toolbox

1 Introduction

Marine Spatial Planning (MSP) is a public process to analyze and allocate the distribution of marine uses over space and time with the aim of achieving economic, social and ecological objectives [1]. MSP was originally developed as a nature conservation measure in the Great Barrier Reef Marine Park in the 1970/80s, which established different zones for marine uses, resource exploitation, and nature conservation to avoid both user-user and user-environment conflicts [2]. Nowadays, MPS is understood as an iterating process, which includes different steps, such as pre-planning, organization of stakeholder involvement, defining and analyzing existing as well as future conditions, drafting and approving the spatial plan, and implementation, evaluation, and adaptation [1]. In Europe, the establishment of maritime spatial plans until 2021 is a legal requirement for all Member States adjacent to the sea [3].

Spatial data analyses for MSP include the mapping of existing marine uses as well as the physical, chemical and biological features in a planning area. The analysis of

© Springer Nature Switzerland AG 2020
O. Gervasi et al. (Eds.): ICCSA 2020, LNCS 12252, pp. 394–404, 2020.
https://doi.org/10.1007/978-3-030-58811-3_28

future conditions includes the prediction of changes in the marine environment and the trends for marine uses [4]. Both traditional and emerging marine uses are expected to increase in the future due to a shift to blue growth and blue economy [5]. Such developments in the seas and oceans will increase the pressure on marine ecosystems and thus require careful planning to ensure sustainable development. This includes the selection of appropriate sites for different marine uses. Site selection for marine uses should take into account the spatial distribution of other uses, environmental conditions on which the use may depend, and sensitive or threatened habitats. In an MSP process, it can be decided that such vulnerable areas should be protected and that all activities are excluded from those areas.

The spatial analyses for MSP can be accomplished by GIS software, such as ArcGIS or QGIS. This can support the decision-making process for choosing appropriate sites for aquaculture, for example [6]. GIS analyses for site selection can furthermore be combined with Multi-Criteria Evaluation methods, sustainability indices, the use of parameter-specific suitability functions or modelling approaches [7–10]. The underlying methods in these studies are well described and the analyses can be implemented with the tools offered in standard GIS software. However, so far and to our knowledge, there is no toolbox specifically designed for MSP analyses for use in standard GIS software.

The aim of the current research was, therefore, to develop a toolbox that simplifies essential GIS analyses for MSP and bundles them in one toolbox with user-friendly documentation. In the next chapter, it is described how the tools were developed and which analyses they can perform. Subsequently, an example of the functionalities of the toolbox is provided. The paper discusses the application of the toolbox and further research needed.

2   Implementation

The "suitable space in the sea (SPACEA)" toolbox consists of five tools and the overall structure of the toolbox is presented in Fig. 1. The main output is a raster that shows the potential sites, where a maritime activity could be placed from an environmental and spatial perspective.

2.1   System Design

The starting point for the development of the SPACEA toolbox was existing functionalities in ArcGIS that have been used previously for the identification of suitable aquaculture sites [11]. These functionalities have been bundled and adapted to create a user-friendly toolbox targeted at spatial analyses for MSP (going beyond aquaculture site selection). SPACEA is based on custom-made script tools using ArcPy, a Python site package for ArcGIS.

The development of SPACEA is focused on two major aspects: User-friendliness and flexibility in the sense of multi-purpose use.

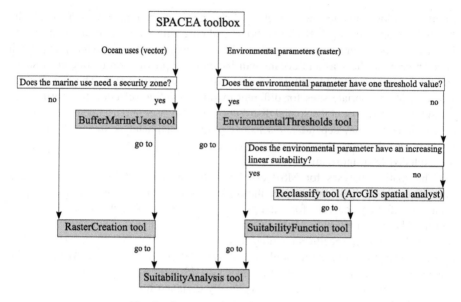

Fig. 1. Structure of the SPACEA toolbox

User-Friendliness. The user-friendliness was achieved through three different aspects. The tools are designed such that only a minimum input by the user is required. For most of the tools, the users only have to locate the input files and the output folder. Additional entries, such as a threshold value or cell size, are kept to the minimum. The output file names, for example, are created automatically by the tools and consist of the original file names with tool-specific naming attributes.

The naming conventions are clearly documented in the tool window. Transparency and clear documentation is another important aspect of user-friendly tools. The tools and their functioning are described in the tool window and in the item description, which also contains sample codes. The underlying Python scripts are furthermore annotated to disclose the purpose of each function (Fig. 2).

The tools can be accessed in three ways for different kinds of users. The least experienced user can use the tool window, which resembles the interface of standard ArcGIS tools. More advanced users may use the provided sample codes to run the tools in immediate mode (in the ArcGIS Python window) or access and modify the python scripts as they see fit.

Flexibility. Flexibility is achieved at the level of the toolbox and individual tools. SPACEA is a modular toolbox, i.e., the tools can be used independently from one another and for different purposes (Table 1). For suitability analyses, the tools build upon each other (Fig. 1), alternatively the tools can also be used as stand-alone tools. At the level of individual tools, the focus was on the combination of several functionalities within one tool. The SPACEA tools can process multiple input layers at the same time. The tool BufferMarineUses can assign individual buffer zones to multiple input layers and also the EnvironmentalThresholds tool matches individual threshold

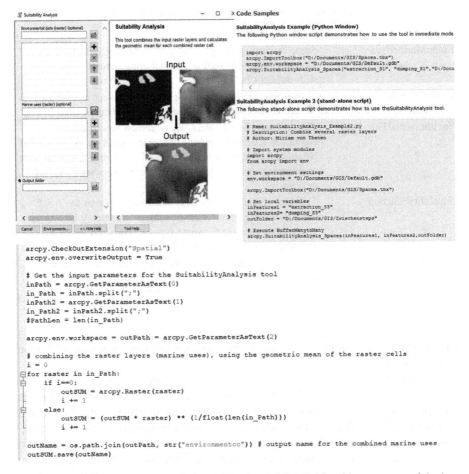

```
arcpy.CheckOutExtension("Spatial")
arcpy.env.overwriteOutput = True

# Get the input parameters for the SuitabilityAnalysis tool
inPath = arcpy.GetParameterAsText(0)
in_Path = inPath.split(";")
inPath2 = arcpy.GetParameterAsText(1)
in_Path2 = inPath2.split(";")
#PathLen = len(in_Path)

arcpy.env.workspace = outPath = arcpy.GetParameterAsText(2)

# combining the raster layers (marine uses), using the geometric mean of the raster cells
i = 0
for raster in in_Path:
    if i==0:
        outSUM = arcpy.Raster(raster)
        i += 1
    else:
        outSUM = (outSUM * raster) ** (1/float(len(in_Path)))
        i += 1

outName = os.path.join(outPath, str("environmentcc")) # output name for the combined marine uses
outSUM.save(outName)
```

Fig. 2. The user-friendly tool interface on the upper left hand side with an excerpt of the item description showing the code samples on the right. At the bottom, an excerpt of the python script with annotation for the tool "Suitability Analysis" is shown.

values to multiple layers. This is accomplished by using the MultiValue parameter option in the script tool properties and the zip() function in Python. At the same time, the tools can assign one buffer or threshold value to multiple layers or one input layer with multiple values. This is also the case for the SuitabilityAnalysis tool, which can be used to combine only environmental input raster into one output suitability raster or both marine use and environmental input raster into one overall suitability raster.

2.2   Structure and Application

SPACEA features two tools each to process data on marine uses and the marine environment (Table 1). The fifth tool (SuitabilityAnalysis) combines both types of data and requires raster layers with values of "zero" and "one" as input. Both the

Table 1. Application areas of the tools in SPACEA

Tool	Application
BufferMarineUses	Some marine uses (e.g., wind parks and pipelines) have official security zones. The tool allows buffering several input layers with different buffer distances at the same time
RasterCreation	This tool is used to turn vector layers into raster layers based on the presence/absence of marine uses in a planning area
EnvironmentalThresholds	The tool can identify areas where certain environmental conditions are met for marine uses that depend on environmental parameters. The tool can also be used to identify risk areas with regard to environmental parameters, e.g., areas with oxygen deficiency
SuitabilityFunction	This tool applies a continuous suitability function to environmental parameters, e.g., current speed may be increasingly suitable for some types of aquaculture due to decreased impacts on benthic fauna and flora
SuitabilityAnalysis	This tool combines several raster layers and can be used to identify suitable areas for marine uses based on spatial availability and environmental suitability

RasterCreation tool and the SuitabilityFunction tool can be used to prepare such input raster layers (Fig. 1).

The underlying principle is the analysis of different input data with respect to their suitability on a scale between "zero" and "one". It is assumed that some of the data need pre-processing, such as creating security zones or threshold values in case of environmental data. Some of the marine uses and infrastructures do exclude other uses from their immediate location and from adjacent areas. Wind parks, for example, have a security zone of 500 m, which precludes any other activities [12]. In other planning areas, oxygen conditions may be close to hypoxia, and a goal of MSP could be to exclude any activities, which aggravate the situation, from these areas.

The analysis is based on a study area extent (the planning area), which combines all marine uses, and provides output maps indicating the available space. The output is in raster format, where values of "zero" indicate the area of marine uses and security zones (not suitable for other uses) and values of "one" show areas suitable from a spatial perspective. The tools for the environmental input data follow the same principle and provide output raster with values of "zero" and "one" (not suitable/suitable, tool: EnvironmentalThresholds) or between "zero" and "one" (increasingly suitable, tool: SuitabilityFunction). The SuitabilityFunction tool assumes increasing linear suitability, which may require additional pre-processing of the input data by using the ArcGIS Reclassify tool (Fig. 1).

The SuitabilityAnalysis tool combines all raster data, applying raster calculation and using the geometric mean, which results in three output raster indicating spatial availability, environmental suitability, and overall suitability.

3 Example

The SPACEA toolbox is based on generalized functionalities so that it can be applied to various geographical areas, multiple scales, and for different purposes. Here, we show an application in the Baltic Sea. Publicly available data for the Baltic Sea can be obtained from the HELCOM[1] Map and Data Service.

To demonstrate the functionalities of SPACEA, we use a fictional case of site selection for mussel farming, taking into account several selection criteria. These include wind parks, cables, and Nature 2000 areas as constraining factors and salinity and water depth as enabling factors. The required tools and inputs are illustrated in Fig. 3. The first step is to determine if the marine uses need a security zone. This is the case for wind parks and cables according to national regulations (e.g., [12]). Natura 2000 areas may not be a direct marine use as such but it is a man-made boundary "drawn" on the sea. Here, it is treated as a constraining factor, without an additional security zone. Nature 2000 areas do not necessarily exclude aquaculture activities [13], but here we take a conservative approach.

The BufferMarineUses tool is used to create buffers around wind parks and cables simultaneously and subsequently, the RasterCreation tool is applied to turn all three input layers of marine uses into raster layers with values of "zero" and "one". The first questions that should be answered for the environmental parameters is whether one threshold value can be applied (Fig. 1). Such a case could occur when the objective is to mark all areas with oxygen deficiency as unsuitable.

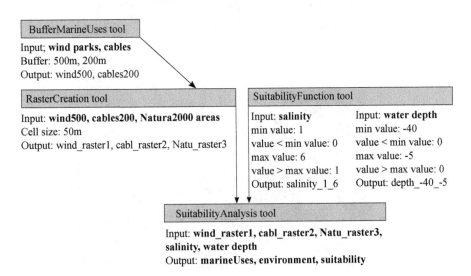

Fig. 3. The step-wise process that was applied to the fictional case study on Baltic-wide site selection for mussel farming.

---

[1] The Baltic Marine Environment Protection Commission, also known as Helsinki Commission (HELCOM).

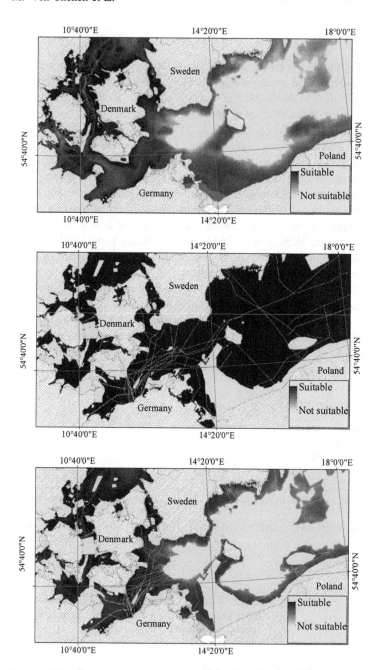

Fig. 4. The SuitabilityAnalysis tool produces three outputs: a map of environmental suitability (top), spatial availability (middle), and overall suitability (bottom). Excerpt from the south-western Baltic Sea.

In the case of salinity and water depth, however, continuous suitability is more appropriate. The salinity data from HELCOM is already classified with six classes, ranging from very low salinities (<5 PSU, class 1) to high salinities (>30 PSU, class 6). Blue mussels show a growth response to salinity, where low salinities result in decreased size and speed of growth. In the Baltic Sea, mussel farming is not feasible in waters with salinity below 5 PSU [14]. Therefore, a continuous suitability curve can be assumed (from class 1 to 6), where class 1 is assigned with "zero", class 6 obtains the highest score, and the classes in-between show increasing suitability. In case of water depth, the same tool is used to restrict the suitability curve between −5 m depth and −40 m depth, with increasing suitability the shallower the water becomes. Mussel farms are typically located in the upper water column and increasing water depth makes the anchoring of the farm more difficult. Applying the suitability analysis tool combines the input layers and results in three different output maps concerning spatial availability (output layer: marine uses), environmental suitability (output layer: environment), and overall suitability (output layer: suitability) (Fig. 4).

The three outputs enable a quick visual analysis which factors (environmental or marine use) contribute the most to the overall suitability or non-suitability. The stepwise approach, furthermore, allows to retrace also individual contributions from the factors and changes can be made at each step. For example, it could be investigated how the extent of the suitable area changes if security zones around wind parks substantially increase or projections of salinity changes are included.

4 Discussion

The example shows that SPACEA can be used to provide a quick analysis and overview of spatial availability and environmental suitability in a planning area. The HELCOM data is suitable to illustrate the functionalities and main outcomes of the tools. The data used in the example are already pre-processed and feature, e.g., an appropriate coordinate reference system and can thus be directly used as input to the tools. The HELCOM data come, however, in a relatively low resolution, which is suitable for Baltic-wide assessments, but generally too low for detailed regional or local analyses. In current planning scenarios, the planning area would be at national, regional, or even local scale. A thorough site selection analysis furthermore takes into account additional criteria; the criteria in the example above were chosen to illustrate the main functionalities of SPACEA but do not constitute a complete list of criteria for aquaculture site selection. Since the SPACEA tools do not require a certain quality or quantity of input data, it is possible to carry out the analyses even in data-scarce regions or with low-resolution data. However, care needs to be taken when analyzing these data as the results of the analysis are only as good as the quality of the input data.

The tools offer a 2-dimensional analysis of marine uses and environmental conditions. The marine environment, however, is a 3-dimensional space, and marine uses can exist at the sea bottom, in the water column, on the sea surface, and can also extend above the sea surface [15]. A 2-dimensional overlap of marine uses, therefore, does not necessarily result in conflicts, and co-location and synergies are possible [16]. The SPACEA tools do not take this into account directly but it is possible to include such considerations. As mentioned above, Natura 2000 areas and mussel farms are not necessarily mutually exclusive, i.e., the Natura 2000 areas could be removed from the analysis. Also, cables may not be restrictive for certain marine activities taking place at the surface, in which case they could also be excluded from the raster overlay. A fourth dimension in the marine environment is the temporal variability. The environment undergoes seasonal and annual variations and marine uses may change, too (e.g., ferry routes that are only frequented in the summer months) [15, 17]. With the tools provided in SPACEA, such variations can be taken into account by running scenarios with input data from different seasons, for example. It is also possible to make assumptions about future conditions and consider these in the analyses.

When all tools are applied, the final outcome is a raster showing which areas might be suitable for a specific marine use. The SuitabilityAnalysis tool is based on raster data and uses raster calculation to combine the input data. The input raster are treated as equally important, there is thus an equal weighing of the criteria. In Multi-Criteria Analyses (MCA), it is common to apply priority weights to the criteria, e.g., through pairwise comparison of the criteria by experts or stakeholders using the Analytical Hierarchy Process [9, 18]. This has not yet been implemented in SPACEA and presents an area for future improvement.

5 Conclusion

There is an increasing demand for the seas' resources and space due to a focus on blue growth and blue economy. Inevitably, this will lead to conflicts between different users and between users and the environment. MSP is a process that aims at allocating space sustainably, avoiding conflicts and creating synergies. During the process, data related to the marine environment needs to be analyzed. Both on a spatial level – where are existing and planned marine uses located? – and from an environmental perspective. The environmental perspective can include the analysis of environmental data with regard to enabling conditions for a marine use, or with regard to critical conditions that should restrict uses from an area, e.g. when that area is in a bad environmental status. Such data analysis can be carried out with SPACEA, a custom-made GIS toolbox, which is presented in this paper.

SPACEA offers a user-friendly interface, which only requires to locate the input files and a few additional parameters for the least experienced user. MSP planers are not necessarily GIS experts and therefore it is important that such tools are easy to use and well-described. Depending on prevailing planning practices, however, GIS experts may be tasked with data analyses as input to the MSP process. In such a case, the more advanced users may use the provided sample codes to run the tools in immediate mode or modify the python scripts to adapt them to their needs.

SPACEA includes several tools that can process both data related to marine uses and environmental data in a fast way through multi-value input options. The tools build upon each other if the purpose is a suitability analysis but they can also be used as stand-alone tools. This flexibility allows the user to explore data on marine uses and environmental conditions in more detail and to retrace individual contribution to the overall suitability. It facilitates scenario building, which is an important part of

MSP. The tools may be used to explore the effects on spatial availability when security zones around uses increase, or on environmental suitability, e.g. when shifts in temperature occur. SPACEA furthermore allows the consideration of vertical overlaps between different uses and the temporal variability of uses and environmental parameters. In the MSP context, this consideration of vertical and temporal dimensions is in particular important for avoiding conflicts and creating synergies. The raster overlay on which the suitability analysis rests furthermore inherently offers the opportunity to include different weighs to the input data. This form of MCA has not yet been included in SPACEA but currently presents the next step in the development.

As it is a modular toolbox, SPACEA is designed to be extended and to include more functionalities if needed. While SPACEA was developed for MSP analyses, the current functionalities are generic and may also be applied in terrestrial planning. The spatial suitability analyses can provide useful input for the management of both terrestrial and marine areas.

Acknowledgements. The research has been carried out within the BONUS BASMATI project, which has received funding from BONUS (Art. 185), funded jointly by the EU, Innovation Fund Denmark, Swedish Research Council Formas, Academy of Finland, Latvian Ministry of Education and Science, and Forschungszentrum Jülich GmbH, Germany.

References

1. Ehler, C., Douvere, F.: Marine Spatial Planning. A Step-by-Step Approach toward Ecosystem-based Management. Intergovernmental Oceanographic Commission and Man and the Biosphere Programme. UNESCO, Paris (2009)
2. Hassan, D., Alam, A.: Marine spatial planing and the Great Barrier Reef Marine Park Act 1975: an evaluation. Ocean Coast. Manag. **167**, 188–196 (2019). https://doi.org/10.1016/j.ocecoaman.2018.10.015
3. EC: Directive 2014/89/EU establishing a framework for maritime spatial planning. Off. J. Eur. Union. L257, 135–145 (2014)
4. von Thenen, M., Frederiksen, P., Hansen, H.S., Schiele, K.S.: A structured indicator pool to operationalize expert-based ecosystem service assessments for marine spatial planning. Ocean Coast. Manag. **187**, 105071 (2020). https://doi.org/10.1016/j.ocecoaman.2019.105071
5. van den Burg, S.W.K., Aguilar-Manjarrez, J., Jenness, J., Torrie, M.: Assessment of the geographical potential for co-use of marine space, based on operational boundaries for Blue Growth sectors. Mar. Policy **100**, 43–57 (2019). https://doi.org/10.1016/j.marpol.2018.10.050
6. Nath, S.S., Bolte, J.P., Ross, L.G., Aguilar-Manjarrez, J.: Applications of geographical information systems (GIS) for spatial decision support in aquaculture. Aquac. Eng. **23**, 233–278 (2000). https://doi.org/10.1016/S0144-8609(00)00051-0
7. Benassai, G., Mariani, P., Stenberg, C., Christoffersen, M.: A Sustainability Index of potential co-location of offshore wind farms and open water aquaculture. Ocean Coast. Manag. **95**, 213–218 (2014). https://doi.org/10.1016/j.ocecoaman.2014.04.007
8. Longdill, P.C., Healy, T.R., Black, K.P.: An integrated GIS approach for sustainable aquaculture management area site selection. Ocean Coast. Manag. **51**, 612–624 (2008). https://doi.org/10.1016/j.ocecoaman.2008.06.010

9. Gimpel, A., et al.: A GIS modelling framework to evaluate marine spatial planning scenarios: Co-location of offshore wind farms and aquaculture in the German EEZ. Mar. Policy. **55**, 102–115 (2015). https://doi.org/10.1016/j.marpol.2015.01.012

10. Bricker, S.B., Getchis, T.L., Chadwick, C.B., Rose, C.M., Rose, J.M.: Integration of ecosystem-based models into an existing interactive web-based tool for improved aquaculture decision-making. Aquaculture **453**, 135–146 (2016). https://doi.org/10.1016/j.aquaculture.2015.11.036

11. von Thenen, M., Maar, M., Hansen, H.S., Friedland, R., Schiele, K.S.: Applying a combined geospatial and farm scale model to identify suitable locations for mussel farming. Mar. Pollut. Bull. **156**, 111254 (2020). https://doi.org/10.1016/j.marpolbul.2020.111254

12. Wulf, S., Säbel, A.: Marine Vorrang- und Vorbehaltsgebiete für Windenergieanlagen - Risikoanalyse (marine priority and reservation areas for offshore wind energy) (2016)

13. EC: Guidance document on aquaculture activities in the context of the Natura 2000 Network (2012)

14. Baltic EcoMussel: Mussel Farming: The New Baltic Sea Aquaculture Industry (2013). https://doi.org/10.13140/2.1.4849.0561

15. Holzhüter, W., Luhtala, H., Hansen, H.S., Schiele, K.S.: Lost in space and time? A conceptual framework to harmonise data for marine spatial planning. Int. J. Spat. Data Infrastruct. Res. **14**, 108–132 (2019). https://doi.org/10.2902/1725-0463.2019.14.art05

16. Bonnevie, I.M., Hansen, H.S., Schröder, L.: Assessing use-use interactions at sea: a theoretical framework for spatial decision support tools facilitating co-location in maritime spatial planning. Mar. Policy **106**, 103533 (2019). https://doi.org/10.1016/j.marpol.2019.103533

17. Hansen, H.S.: Cumulative impact of societal activities on marine ecosystems and their services. In: Misra, S., et al. (eds.) ICCSA 2019. LNCS, vol. 11621, pp. 577–590. Springer, Cham (2019). https://doi.org/10.1007/978-3-030-24302-9_41

18. Gagatsi, E., Giannopoulos, G., Aifantopoulou, G., Charalampous, G.: Stakeholders-based multi-criteria policy analysis in maritime transport: from theory to practice. Transp. Res. Procedia **22**, 655–664 (2017). https://doi.org/10.1016/j.trpro.2017.03.062

A Method of Identification of Potential Earthquake Source Zones

K. N. Petrov[ID], V. G. Gitis[ID], and A. B. Derendyaev[(✉)][ID]

The Institute for Information Transmission Problems, Moscow, Russia
stranger12@list.ru, gitis@iitp.ru, wintsa@gmail.com

Abstract. We propose a machine learning method for mapping potential earthquake source zones (ESZ). We use two hypotheses: (1) the recurrence of strong earthquakes and (2) the dependence of sources of strong earthquakes on the properties of the geological environment. To solve this problem, we know the catalog of earthquakes and a set of spatial fields of geological and geophysical features. We tested the method of identification of the potential ESZ with $m \geq 6.0$ for the Caucasus region. The map of the potential earthquake source zones and a geological interpretation of the decision rule are presented.

Keywords: Earthquake prediction · Spatial grid fields of features · Machine learning · One-class classification · Potential Earthquake Source Zones

1 Introduction

In areas of natural risk, a mapping of potential hazards of geological processes and phenomena is carried out. The level of danger depends on the energy characteristics of the source of exposure, the distance to it, and the attenuation parameters. This article discusses the problem of zone identification of potential sources of earthquakes. The complexity of the task lies in need to assess the places of the possible occurrence of rare events, and the importance is associated with social and economic consequences due to errors in missing the target and adding false zones to the analyzed territory on the map.

To construct a map of the earthquake source zones (ESZ), we use two hypotheses: (1) the recurrence of strong earthquakes and (2) the dependence of sources of strong earthquakes on the properties of geological environment. The first hypothesis is based on the known facts of an earthquake repetition. But the history of seismic observations is very short with respect to the speed of tectonic processes, and strong earthquakes occur relatively rarely. Therefore, the use of only the first hypothesis can lead to omissions of the zones due to the relatively short observation period [4,13,17]. The second hypothesis compensates for the effect of insufficient representativeness of existing seismic observations

The paper is supported by the Russian Science Foundation, project No20-07-00445.

[3,7,21]. However, usually, the data of the geological environment are incomplete and indirectly associated with the magnitude of the strong earthquakes. Incomplete information dramatically complicates the search for patterns based on empirical data. Besides, this makes it difficult to choose a reasonable model for the statistical estimation of the accuracy of a solution. Therefore, the result of solving the problem should allow specialists in the field to interpret the obtained forecasting rule.

In solving the problem, we are aware of the epicenters of the occurrence of targeted earthquakes with magnitudes above a certain threshold and a set of spatial grid based fields of geological and geophysical features. We suggest that the target earthquakes may recur in the vicinity of the earlier earthquake epicenters. The rest of the region is a mixture of points at which the possibility of the appearance epicenters of target earthquakes has not been established. The challenge is to map the zones in which epicenters of the targeted earthquakes are possible and provide a geological interpretation of the solution. In machine learning, this task is called a one-class classification task [2,12,15].

A method for identifying potential ESZ is discussed in Sect. 2. It generalizes two one-class classification algorithms: the algorithm of the method of the minimum area of alarm [9] and the algorithm of the preference method [10]. Section 3 discusses the verification of this method for determining ESZ with $m \geq 6.0$ for the Caucasus region.

2   Method

Let the seismotectonic properties of the analyzed zone be represented by a catalog of earthquakes and a set of geological and geophysical spatial fields. The challenge is to use this data for identifying potential earthquake source zones (ESZ) with target magnitudes that exceed a certain threshold. We suggest a recurrence of strong earthquakes, as well as the possibility of the emergence of new sources of earthquakes in areas with similar geological properties. Following the hypothesis of an earthquake recurrence, the potential ESZ should cover all the epicenters of the target earthquakes in the catalog. In order to extrapolate the area of ESZ to the territory where target earthquakes were not observed, it is necessary to determine the decision rule based on the hypothesis that zones with strong earthquakes depend on the properties of the geological environment. For this, machine learning methods are used.

The difficulty in finding a decision rule lies in incomplete data. Our set of examples of targeted earthquakes is not full due to the relatively short observation period. In addition, among the target earthquakes presented in the catalog, there are examples in which available geological and geophysical fields do not have geological and geophysical properties that explain their high magnitudes. In the first case, examples of environmental properties inherent in the areas of target earthquakes are not included in the training set. In the second case, examples of target earthquakes do not have properties that would distinguish places of their source zones from areas where target earthquakes are impossible. This explains the errors in decision-making: errors in missing places where targeted earthquakes are possible, and errors in the reassessment of danger due to an incomplete description of the properties of the geological environment.

The method of identifying the potential ESZ consists of 3 stages.

1. Calculate a decision rule and select a target earthquakes for which the values of the feature fields adequately represent the seismotectonic features of the focal zones.
2. Calculate potential ESZ and generate a text explanation of the decision rule.
3. Supplement potential ESZ with remaining epicenters of target earthquakes.

The method uses decision rules based on monotonic functions. These rules can be applied in problems in which there is reason to assume that for a certain range of values the dependence of the predicted property on the features or the degree of confidence in the belonging of the objects in question to a certain class changes monotonously when the value of the function changes. Without loss of generality, we assume that the predicted property $S(\mathbf{x})$ increases or does not change (but does not decrease) with an increase in the value of any of the characteristics of the object, i.e., $\frac{\partial S(\mathbf{x})}{\partial x_i} \geq 0, i = 1 \dots I$. For example, earthquake-risk zones are often characterized by heterogeneity of the geological environment, closeness to zones of active geological faults, abnormal velocities of modern vertical movements, high gradients of gravitational anomalies, etc. It can be assumed that the reliability of the fact that a map point belongs to a seismic zone is greater, all other things being equal, the greater the value of at least one of the listed feature fields.

Let the seismotectonic properties of the analyzed area are represented by spatial grid-based fields of features $\mathbf{F}_i, i = 1, \dots, I$, in a single coordinate grid with a step $\Delta x \times \Delta y \times \Delta t$ and a sample of earthquakes $q = 1, \dots, Q$ with the target magnitudes $m \geq M$. The values of these fields at the nodes of the grid $n = 1, \dots, N$ correspond to the vectors of the I-dimensional feature space $\mathbf{f}^{(n)} = \{f_i^{(n)}\}$. The points of the feature space $\mathbf{f}^{(n)} = \{f_i^{(n)}\}$, which correspond to the nodes of the grid of feature fields closest to the epicenters of the target earthquakes, will be called precedents. The task is to find the field $\mathbf{\Phi}(\mathbf{F}_i)$, which determines the potential ESZ.

The data model contains two assumptions.

1. *Anomalilty condition*: epicenters of earthquakes with target magnitudes relate to zones in which the values of the feature fields are improbable and close to maximum (or minimum). To simplify the explanation, we assume that the anomalies refer only to the *largest* values of the features fields.
2. *Monotonicity condition*: points of the feature space that are componentwise greater than or equal to the precedent $\mathbf{f}^{(q)}$ of the earthquake q can also be the precedents for similar target events, that is, if $\mathbf{f}^{(n)} = \{f_i^{(n)}\} \geq \{f_i^{(q)}\}$, then $\mathbf{f}^{(n)}$ is also a precedent for a similar event.

Points of the feature space $\mathbf{f}^{(n)}$ which are componentwise greater than or equal to the precedent $\mathbf{f}^{(q)}$, will be called the *base* points of the event q. This points belong to the half-interval $O^{(q)}$ with the vertex at the point $\mathbf{f}^{(q)}$. Each point $\mathbf{f}^{(n)}$ corresponds to one of the grid nodes of the features fields. Denote by $W^{(q)}$ a set of all grid nodes corresponding to the base points of the event q. The number of such nodes is denoted by $L^{(q)} = |W^{(q)}|$. We will call the ratio $v^{(q)} = L^{(q)}/L$ the alarm volume of the event q, where $L^{(q)}$ is the number of grid nodes of the potential ESZ field corresponded to the base points of the q event, L is the number of all grid nodes of the area of analysis.

The quality of the solution is determined by two indicators: (1) probability of detection U which is equal to the share of correctly detected epicenters of target earthquakes Q^* from all Q target events, $U = Q^*/Q$ and (2) alarm volume which is equal to the share of the number of grid nodes, falling in the alarm area L^*, from the number of all grid nodes L of the analyzed area $V = L^*/L$. Often the quality of the forecast is determined by the dependence $U(V)$, which practically coincides with the error curve represented by the ROC curve [5].

Algorithm [9] allows for any given alarm volume V to find optimal potential ESZ zones in which the maximum number of epicenters of target earthquake fall. We are considering a version of the algorithm that provides a solution close to optimal.

To begin to solve the problem, one should determine the magnitude of the target earthquakes and the alarm volume V_0 equal to the fraction of the analysis zone that the potential ESZ may occupy. We are not aware of the mathematically reasoned answers to both of these questions. Our model assumes that potential ESZ refer only to areas with anomalous geological and geophysical properties. As for the alarm volume V_0, here we can proceed from the fact that it's equal to the probability of detecting the epicenters of target earthquakes in random zones consisting of $L^* = VL$ grid nodes. Given this, the alarm volume V_0 can be determined empirically from the ratio $U(V_0) \geq (1.5 - 2.0)V_0$, which shows that the source zones of the target earthquakes were not randomly selected and are well represented by fields of features.

The algorithm.

1. Generate a training sample $\{\mathbf{f}^{(q)}, v^{(q)}\}$, in which the precedents $\mathbf{f}^{(q)}$ represent all the epicenters of the target eartquakes $q = 1, \ldots, Q$.
2. Arrange the precedents $\mathbf{f}^{(q)}$ in accordance with the increase in alarm volumes: $v^{(1)} \leq v^{(2)} \leq, \ldots, \leq v^{(q)} \leq, \ldots, \leq v^{(Q)}$.
3. Set all the grid nodes of the potential ESZ field the value 1. Change the value 1 of potential ESZ field to $V(1) = v^{(1)}$ at the grid nodes corresponding to the base points of the precedent $\mathbf{f}^{(1)}$; replace the value 1 with $V(2) = |W^{(1)} \cup W^{(2)}|/L$ in the grid nodes belonging to the base points of the precedent $\mathbf{f}^{(2)}$ and then, successively to replace the values of 1 with the corresponding sizes of the union of alarm volumes. We obtain the sequence $V(1), \ldots, V(q), \ldots, V(Q)$. This sequence uniquely determines the relationship $U(V)$, and V_0 determines a set of the target earthquakes $q = 1, 2, \ldots, Q_0 \leq Q$, for which the values of the feature fields distinguish the places of their source zones from the regions where target earthquakes are impossible. The precedents $\mathbf{f}^{(1)}, \mathbf{f}^{(2)}, \ldots, \mathbf{f}^{(Q_0)}$ define a domain A in the feature space consisting of the union of Q_0 half-intervals with vertices at the points $\mathbf{f}^{(q)}$.

4. Calculate for the feature fields $\mathbf{F}_i$ the standard deviations in the analysis area: $\sigma_1, \sigma_2, \ldots, \sigma_i, \ldots, \sigma_I$.

5. Calculate the domain B that covers the domain A. The domain B consists of the union Q_0 of the half-intervals with vertices at the points $\mathbf{g}^{(q)} = \{g_i^{(q)}\} = \{f_i^{(q)} - \mu \sigma_i\}$, where μ is a parameter that determines the accuracy of the approximation of the area A.

6. Build the membership matrix (P_{qr}). The row of the matrix denotes the vertex of the half-interval $\mathbf{g}^{(q)}$, and the column denotes the target event r. An element of the matrix $P_{qr} = 1$ if the point r belongs to the half-interval with the vertex $\mathbf{g}^{(q)}$, that is, if $g_i^{(r)} \leq f_i^{(q)}$ for all $i = 1, 2, \ldots, I$.

7. Find the subset of the minimum number of half-intervals that contain all the use case points. For this, it is necessary to find in the membership matrix (P_{qr}) a subset of the minimum number of rows for which at least one unit remains in each column of the matrix. For this, standard methods of minimizing the disjunctive normal forms of Boolean functions are used [19].

It's seen that the conditions $P_{qr} = 1$ if $g_i^{(r)} \leq f_i^{(q)}$ for all $i = 1, 2, \ldots, I$ are conjunctions. All rows of the matrix (P_{qr}) correspond to a disjunction from Q_0 conjunctions. Covering the domain A by the domain B simplifies this expression. Obviously, the larger value μ, the less accurate the approximation of the domain A by the domain B and the smaller the number of conjunctions needed to represent B. Further, the resulting logical expression is easily represented as a text expression. For this, you can use pre-prepared linguistic variables and templates.

At the last stage, we added to the potential ESZ the sites with target earthquake epicenters that were not detected using the decision rule.

3   Testing

Dynamic processes in the Caucasus region are determined by the convergence of the Arabian and Eurasian plates [16]. The seismicity of the region is largely determined by the zones of development of thrusts, shifts, and faults. Work [20] shows on models that strain to cause shifts in overthrusts, shifts, and faults are related approximately as 15:5:1. These zones can display the distribution of tectonic strains, and one can use them as a geological interpretation of the cause-effect regional model of strong earthquakes [8]. According to the model, it can be assumed that strong earthquakes are localized in the regions of the intersection of the inhomogeneities of the earth's crust. Let us consider an example of finding potential ESZ with target magnitudes $m \geq 6.0$. There are 20 epicenters with $m \geq 6.0$ in the area of analysis. Following to formula of Yu.V. Riznichenko [18], we assume that the projection of the target earthquake source zone onto the earth's surface is a circle with a radius of 16 km. We get that the area occupied by the centers of 20 earthquakes amounts to 15.5% of the analysis area. We will look for potential ESZ, which make up 25% of the analysis area.

The following primary data were used to solve the problem [11]: heights of the surfaces of the day relief, the consolidated foundation and Mohorovicic, the amplitude of neotectonics movements, isostatic, and deep gravity anomalies in the Bouguer reduction, the velocity gradient of vertical tectonic movements in the post-Sarmatian time (T = 17 million years), deviation of the travel times of the first primary waves and secondary waves in the upper mantle, heat flow, magnetic field anomalies, faults ranked by age, by the age of the last activation, by the type of movements and by the tectonic significance, as well as catalogs of earthquakes [1,14].

We analyzed the effectiveness of the solution using the primary fields listed above and a series of secondary fields. During the analysis, we compared the quality indicators of the solution obtained by the training sample and obtained through cross-validation. The best match of the indicators was shown by two calculated from primary fields of features: $\mathbf{F}_1$ is the field of absolute values of the velocity gradient of vertical tectonic movements in the post-Sarmatian time [1/year], and $\mathbf{F}_4(\mathbf{F}_2, \mathbf{F}_3)$, where $\mathbf{F}_2$ is the field of absolute values of the gradient of gravity anomalies in the Bouguer reduction, $\mathbf{F}_3$ is the field of absolute values of the gradient of the digital elevation model, the values of the field $\mathbf{F}_4$ grid nodes are $f_4 = \min\{(f_2 - \overline{f_2})/\sigma_2, (f_3 - \overline{f_3})/\sigma_3\}$, where f_2, f_3 are the values of the fields $\mathbf{F}_2$ and $\mathbf{F}_3$ in grid nodes, $\overline{f_2}$, $\overline{f_3}$ and σ_2, σ_3 mean and standard deviations within the area of analysis. The fields $\mathbf{F}_1$ and $\mathbf{F}_4$ are shown in Fig. 1.

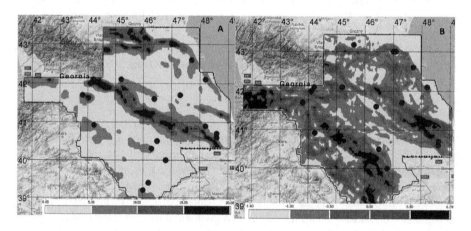

Fig. 1. Fields of features selected for the solution. (A) $\mathbf{F}_1$ is the field of absolute values of the velocity gradient of vertical tectonic movements in the post-Sarmatian time [1/year], (B) $\mathbf{F}_4$ is the field of a minimum of absolute values of the gradient of gravity anomalies in the Bouguer reduction and absolute values of the gradient of the digital elevation model.

Figure 2 shows the dependence $U(V)$ obtained by the training sample. It can be seen that with the alarm volume of 25%, the probability of hit of the target earthquakes epicenters in the potential ESZ is 80%. The following logical rule corresponds to the resulting solution:

IF
$$(f_1 \geq 3.37 \wedge f_4 \geq -0.36) \vee (f_1 \geq 10.07 \wedge f_4 \geq -1.11), \tag{1}$$

THEN

the earthquake sources with the magnitudes $m \geq 6.0$ are possible.

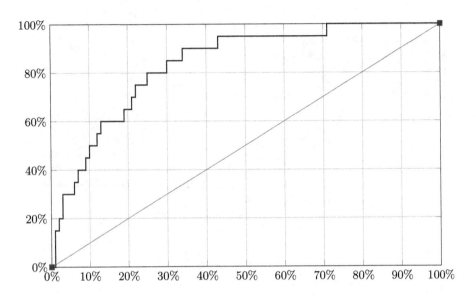

Fig. 2. The dependence $U(V)$ obtained by the training sample.

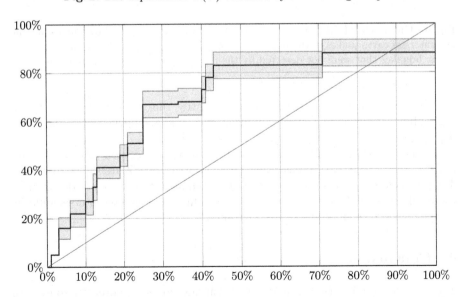

Fig. 3. The results of 5-fold cross-validation tests to verify the result with $k = 2$: mean and standard deviations of the $U(V)$ dependence.

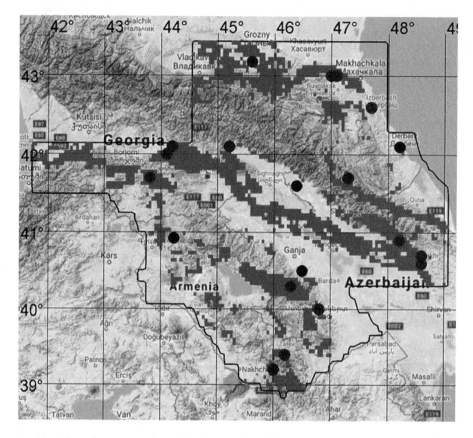

Fig. 4. The potential ESZ obtained by the decision rule 1. The yellow circles are the epicenters of earthquakes in the potential ESZ. The blue circles indicate the epicenters of earthquakes that were not detected by the resulting rule. (Color figure online)

We use k-fold cross-validation tests to verify the result with $k = 2$ [6]. In Fig. 3 shows the result for five tests: mean and standard deviations of the $U(V)$ dependence.

Figure 4 shows the potential ESZ obtained by the decision rule 1. The epicenters of the target earthquakes that hit the potential ESZ are shown in yellow. The blue color indicates the epicenters of earthquakes that were not detected by the resulting rule. The source areas corresponding to these epicenters should be complementary to those discovered by potential ESZ.

4   Conclusion

The data for solving the problem of identifying zones of potential sources of earthquakes consists of earthquake epicenters with target magnitudes and a set of grid-based spatial geophysical and geological fields. In our solution we use the assumptions about the repeatability of strong earthquakes and the existence of a relationship between the properties of the geological environment and the locations of the earthquake epicenters. It follows that potential ESZ include places where earthquakes with target magnitudes were recorded, and areas identified by the found dependence. Errors arise due to the small number of examples of target earthquakes and due to the incomplete representation of the seismotectonic properties of the geological environment by the available feature fields.

In the article, we propose the method as a tool that can help a specialist to solve this important practical problem. The decision is divided into three stages. First, using the machine learning method proposed in the article, examples of target earthquakes that occurred in zones that differ in geological and geophysical data from other places in the region are selected. Then for these examples, a logical decision rule is calculated, which determines potential ESZ by the attribute fields. After that, the resulting map of potential ESZ are supplemented by the sources of the remaining target earthquakes. The decision rule allows specialists to give a geological interpretation of the solution.

Examples of the application of the method are performed for constructing zones with magnitudes $m \geq 6.0$ in the Caucasus region. We used the cross-validation procedure to select feature fields. The article provides two examples for which the quality of the forecast for cross-validation and training sample are the most successful.

We were not able to obtain convincing results when identifying potential ESZ with magnitudes $m \geq 5.5$. Possible reasons are the high magnitude of the background earthquakes in the Caucasus, which are possible anywhere in the analyzed area, and the lack of data on the properties of the geological environment.

References

1. Ananin, I.: European part of the USSR, Ural, West Siberia. In: A New Catalog of Strong Earthquakes in the USSR from Ancient Times to 1975, pp. 465–470 (1975). (in Russian)
2. Bishop, C.M.: Machine Learning and Pattern Recognition. Information Science and Statistics. Springer, Heidelberg (2006)
3. Bune, V., Gorshkov, G.: Seismic zonation of USSR, p. 307. Nauka, Moscow (1980)
4. Burton, P.W.: Seismic risk in southern Europe through to India examined using Gumbel's third distribution of extreme values. Geophys. J. Int. **59**(2), 249–280 (1979)
5. Fawcett, T.: An introduction to ROC analysis. Pattern Recogn. Lett. **27**(8), 861–874 (2006)
6. Geisser, S.: Predictive Inference, vol. 55. CRC Press, Boca Raton (1993)
7. Gelfand, I., et al.: Pattern recognition applied to earthquake epicenters in California. Phys. Earth Planet. Inter. **11**(3), 227–283 (1976)
8. Gitis, V., Ermakov, B.: Fundamentals of spatiotemporal forecasting in geoinformatics, p. 256. FIZMATGIS, Moscow (2004)
9. Gitis, V.G., Derendyaev, A.B.: Machine learning methods for seismic hazards forecast. Geosciences **9**(7), 308 (2019)

10. Gitis, V., Andrienko, G., Andrienko, N.: Exploration of seismological information in analytical web GIS. Izvestiya. Phys. Solid Earth **40**(3), 216–225 (2004)

11. Gitis, V., Ermakov, B., Ivanovskaya, L., Osher, B., Trofimov, D., Shchukin, Y.K.: The GEO expert system: application for seismic hazard analysis of the caucasus region. In: Cahiers du Centre Europeen de Geodynamique et de Seismologie. Centre européen de géodynamique et de séismologie (1992)

12. Khan, S.S., Madden, M.G.: A survey of recent trends in one class classification. In: Coyle, L., Freyne, J. (eds.) AICS 2009. LNCS (LNAI), vol. 6206, pp. 188–197. Springer, Heidelberg (2010). https://doi.org/10.1007/978-3-642-17080-5_21

13. Kijko, A.: Estimation of the maximum earthquake magnitude, m_{max}. Pure Appl. Geophys. **161**(8), 1655–1681 (2004)

14. Kondorskaia, N., Shebalin, N.: New Catalog of Strong Earthquakes in the USSR from Ancient Times Through 1977, vol. 31. World Data Center A for Solid Earth Geophysics (1982)

15. Kotsiantis, S.B., Zaharakis, I., Pintelas, P.: Supervised machine learning: a review of classification techniques. Emerg. Artif. Intell. Appl. Comput. Eng. **160**, 3–24 (2007)

16. Philip, H., Cisternas, A., Gvishiani, A., Gorshkov, A.: The Caucasus: an actual example of the initial stages of continental collision. Tectonophysics **161**(1–2), 1–21 (1989)

17. Pisarenko, V.: Statistical evaluation of maximum possible earthquakes. Phys. Solid Earth **27**(9), 757–763 (1991)

18. Riznichenko, Y.V.: The source dimensions of the crustal earthquakes and the seismic moment. In: Issledovaniya po fizike zemletryasenii, pp. 9–27 (1976)

19. Sapozhenko, A., Chukhrov, I.: Boolean function minimization in the class of disjunctive normal forms. J. Sov. Math. **46**(4), 2021–2052 (1989)

20. Sibson, R.H.: Frictional constraints on thrust, wrench and normal faults. Nature **249**(5457), 542–544 (1974)

21. Soloviev, A., Novikova, O., Gorshkov, A., Piotrovskaya, E.: Recognition of potential sources of strong earthquakes in the Caucasus region using GIS technologies. Dokl. Earth Sci. **450**(2), 658 (2013). https://doi.org/10.1134/S1028334X13060159

Variography and Morphometry for Classifying Building Centroids: Protocol, Data and Script

Joan Perez[1](✉) 🆔, Alexandre Ornon[1] 🆔, and Hiroyuki Usui[2] 🆔

[1] Université Côte-Azur, CNRS, ESPACE, Nice, France
{joan.perez,alexandre.ornon}@univ-cotedazur.fr
[2] Department of Urban Engineering, Housing and Urban Analysis Laboratory,
The University of Tokyo, Tokyo, Japan
usui@ua.t.u-tokyo.ac.jp

Abstract. Different spatial patterns of urban growth exist such as infill, edge-expansion and leapfrog development. This paper presents a methodology, and a corresponding script, that classify new residential buildings as patterns of urban growth. The script performs a combination of variography and morphometry over building centroids on two different dates. The test data is made of the building centroids of 2002 and 2017 for Centre-Var, a region located in southern France. The different bounding regions, yield from series of morphological closings, allow classifying the building centroids that appeared between 2002 and 2017 into different categories of spatial patterns of urban growth. The final classification is made according to the degree of clustering/scattering of new centroids and to their locations regarding existing urban areas. Preliminary results show that this protocol is able to provide useful insights regarding the degree of contribution of each new residential building to the following patterns of urban growth: clustered infill, scattered infill, clustered edge-expansion, scattered edge-expansion, clustered leapfrog and scattered leapfrog. Open access to the script and to the test region data is provided.

Keywords: Classification · Morphology · Geoprocessing · Variography · Geostatistics

1 Introduction

Nowadays, a growing number of sources are directing the attention on the urgency of transforming the way urban spaces are built and managed [1–3]. Amongst these sources, a recurring issue is sprawl, which is deemed has a non-sustainable dynamic regarding environmental issues [2–4]. Yet, the literature on urban sprawl and its different patterns is ambiguous, or even confusing since no consensus is emerging in the academics [5–7]. This is without mentioning other patterns of growth which are not directly related to sprawl, such as redevelopment of existing urban areas, urban scattering, leapfrog urbanization, etc. Numerous denominations of somewhat similar

© Springer Nature Switzerland AG 2020
O. Gervasi et al. (Eds.): ICCSA 2020, LNCS 12252, pp. 415–424, 2020.
https://doi.org/10.1007/978-3-030-58811-3_30

patterns also exist in the literature such as central-city revival and urban regeneration for urban redevelopment [8]; edge-expansion for continuous sprawl [9], etc. Even if sprawl remain the main scapegoat, other patterns of urban development are also pointed out as hardly sustainable [10]. As suggested by Liu *et al.,* [9], urban growth spatially operates following three main possibilities: infill, edge-expansion and leapfrog. Solely focusing on sprawl, Galster *et al.,* [6] proposes a conceptual definition based on eight dimensions. Among them, one is of particular interest in this research: clustering. It is defined as the degree to which development is tightly bunched together. The degree of clustered development appears not only relevant for edge-expansion patterns, but also for infill and leapfrog. Based on these observations, it should be possible to classify new residential buildings into the aforementioned patterns of urban growth focusing on location and clustered measures of both long-standing and new building centroids. Since certain patterns are deemed more sustainable than others, such as compact or resilient models of development [10, 11], such a classification could provide useful insights regarding into which pattern new building falls. Various methods have been proposed in the literature for measuring, quantifying, and/or delineating urban growth [5, 7, 12–15]. Yet, to the authors' knowledge, no methods are evaluating both urban development and redevelopment from the building scale.

The goal of this paper is to present a protocol, developed within the R platform, that classify spatiotemporal patterns of residential urban growth within a region located in southern France named Centre-Var. The protocol can be described as a location-based morpho-structural approach which combines variography analysis and morphometry (mathematical morphology analysis applied to vector objects). It first detects thresholds of residential building agglomerations in 2002 and 2017 and then performs several morphological closings according to building locations. The bounding regions obtained through the morphological closings then allow classifying the new residential buildings into six different spatial patterns of urban growth: clustered infill, scattered infill, clustered edge-expansion, scattered edge-expansion, clustered leapfrog, and scattered leapfrog. The script makes use of easily accessible data: GIS layers of residential building footprints. Open access to the source code and to the test region data is provided.

This paper is organized as follows. Section 2 introduces the test region and the primary data. Section 3 presents and details each step of the script. Section 4 presents the preliminary results obtained on the test region. Section 5 concludes the paper with a discussion on future applications and developments of the protocol.

2   Test Region and Data Presentation

The region in which the method is applied is the center of the Var department in southern France. The extent of the case study goes from the cities of Brignoles to Le Muy and also includes Draguignan, Vidauban and Le Luc. This area, named

Centre-Var, is located close to three major cities: Marseille, Toulon and Nice. Due to the proximity of these metropolitan areas, this region is sustaining fast processes of urbanization (increase of population, sprawl, urban redevelopment, etc.). According to INSEE[1], Centre-Var population in 1999 was 157.919 inhabitants and 210.071 in 2016, thus showing an impressive growth of 33.02% (Fig. 1).

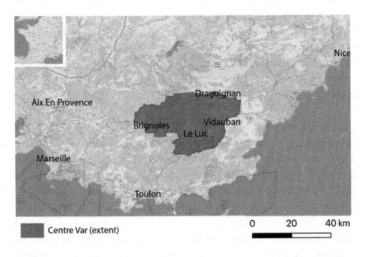

Fig. 1. Centre-Var presentation. Background: OpenStreetMap, 2020.

The BD TOPO® datasets from the French National Geographic Institute (IGN) are extracted and filtered according to the Centre-Var boundaries. BD TOPO® are GIS layers of building footprints (polygons that represent building shapes on a two-dimensional plane) where buildings are digitized as single-part polygons. Two dates are retained: 2002 and 2017. Buildings not possessing any residential functions are filtered out of the datasets using the specialization attribute included in the primary data. Since these data includes small polygons usually associated to residential buildings (garage, pergola, sheds, etc.), light buildings and small structures below 20 m^2 are filtered out. Data are finally harmonized into a single point feature class (centroids of polygons) possessing two attribute columns indicative of the building presence for each period: *pres2002* and *pres2017* (modalities: "1" for building presence; "0" otherwise). The prepared dataset is ultimately made of 82.249 centroids of residential buildings in 2017, from which 63.238 were also present in 2002. Data are compiled into a GeoPackage file named *CV_PT_Ext_0217*, itself containing two layers: the centroids, named *CV_Building_PT* and the boundaries of Centre-Var, named *Centre_Var_extent*.

---

[1] French national institute for statistical and economic studies.

3   Script Presentation and Application

The script starts with a subsection that provides information on the R session and packages versions. Necessary packages are then loaded. A second subsection loads the GeoPackage and subsequently divides the centroids into three simple feature geometry objects: the centroids present in 2002 (*Pt_2002.sp*), those present in 2017 (*Pt_2017.sp*) and the new centroids that appeared between 2002 and 2017 (*Pt_2017_new.sp*). The script is then organized in three parts, as follows:

Part one of the script creates a *RasterLayer* object of 50 m of resolution within the case study boundaries using the "raster" function from the *raster* package. The grid, superimposed on the sampling area *Extent.sp*, allows counting the number of building centroids inside each cell for 2002 and 2017 using the "cellFromXY" function. The average number of centroids for non-zero cells is 1.77 in 2002 and 1.87 in 2017, with an increase of occupied cells from 35.722 to 43.829, thus showing both a concentration and an expansion of urban development.

A cross-variogram is calculated for these two variables using the "variogram" function of the *gstat* package [16]. Variography allows exploring the spatial structure inherent to the point distributions by computing the square difference between the values of all the couples of pairs at given distances [17]. The main way to interpret a variogram is to observe where the breaks occur, in order to detect structures at a varying distance. When performed on density grids, the variations of autocorrelation explain a local change in the way that buildings are structured. In a cross-variogram, the first variation is considered as a micro-structure: the first pattern of point agglomeration. It is detected through the local R, which is a local correlation coefficient computed by the cross-variogram values divided by the product of the square roots of both regular variograms [18]. It sets the threshold of the agglomeration distance within the point distribution, which is going to be used in the morphometry section of our protocol. As displayed in Fig. 2, the first micro-structure threshold is identified at 227 m, which is rounded according to the grid resolution at 250 m.

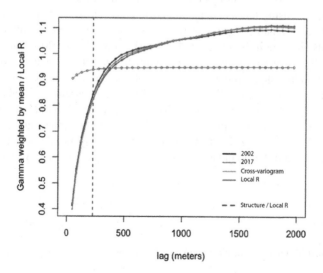

Fig. 2. Cross-Variogram for 2002 and 2017 residential buildings (50 by 50 m)

Offsets around the 2002 and 2017 point features are then created in order to extract built-up areas using the "buffer" function of the *raster* package. These operations, named morphological closings [14], are composed of a dilatation followed by an erosion algorithm. They allow linking close by centroids, ignoring small holes and interstices. The micro-structure threshold of 250 m detected by the analysis of the cross-variogram sets the buffering distance from each point (radius r = 250/2). For both closings, a filter is applied in order to remove the small isolated surfaces artificially generated by the dilation algorithm, which are the surfaces below the lower limit of πr^2. The last section of part one performs the difference between the closings of 2017 and 2002 and the difference between the extent of the case study and the closing of 2017 using the "gDifference" function from the package *rgeos*.

Part two of the script divides the new centroids *Pt_2017_new.sp* into three subsets through basic operations of intersect using the "st_intersection" function of the *sf* package. *Point_evo_inside_2002* are the centroids within the 2002 morphological closing, *Point_evo_outside_2017* are the centroids outside the 2017 closing and *Point_evo_diff_0217* are the centroids located both outside 2002 and inside 2017 closings. A downscaling is performed through the creation of a *RasterLayer* object of 25 m of resolution. The number of new building centroids is then counted, using once again "raster" and "cellFromXY" functions. Performing a downscaling is relevant since, at this stage, the focus of the study is no more on the inclusion/exclusion of new buildings within existing urban areas but rather on their clustered/scattered properties. Since each subset is representative of a peculiar trajectory, regular variograms are calculated within each subset (instead of a cross-variogram). As displayed in Fig. 3, they yield thresholds of 113 m for *Point_evo_inside_2002* (rounded at 125 m), 161 m for *Point_evo_diff_0217* (rounded at 150 m), and 238 m for *Point_evo_outside_2017* (rounded at 225 m). Morphological closings are once again performed for each subset using the different identified thresholds as buffering radiuses.

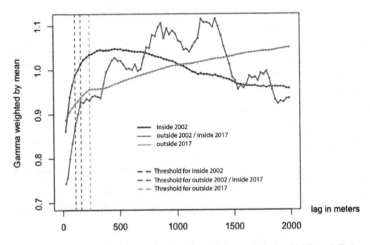

Fig. 3. Variograms for *Point_evo_inside_2002*, *Point_evo_outside_2017* and *Point_evo_diff_0217* (25 by 25 m)

Part three performs the final classification by selecting the building centroids encroaching upon the different buffers, ultimately yielding the following categories: clustered infill, scattered infill, clustered edge-expansion, scattered edge-expansion, clustered leapfrog and scattered leapfrog. The different geometries are also clipped together once again using the function "gDifference". Several plots and maps are displayed and results are recorded, including the variogram samples. Result layers are added within the original GeoPackage file. Figure 4 summarizes the different steps of the protocol. Open access to the script and to the test region data is provided (Appendix).

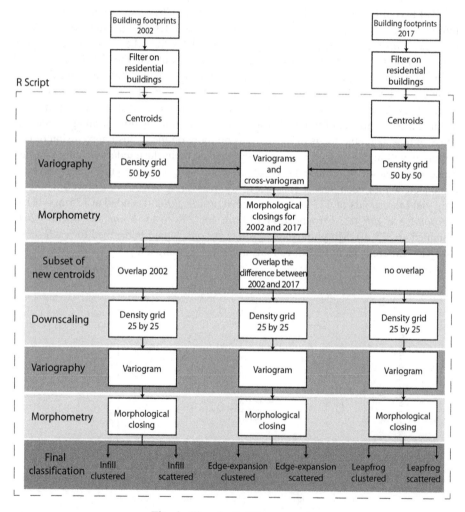

Fig. 4. Flowchart of the protocol

4   Preliminary Results

New residential buildings have been successfully classified into three categories: infill, edge-expansion, and leapfrog; each of the latter further subdivided into clustered and scattered patterns.

As Fig. 5 shows, the three categories, as well as their subdivisions, clearly stand out. Both Brignoles and Le Luc are mostly concerned by infill and edge-expansion patterns. They are both gaining a lot of ground on non-urban spaces from existing urban structures, whereas leapfrogs exist but remain limited comparing to the other patterns.

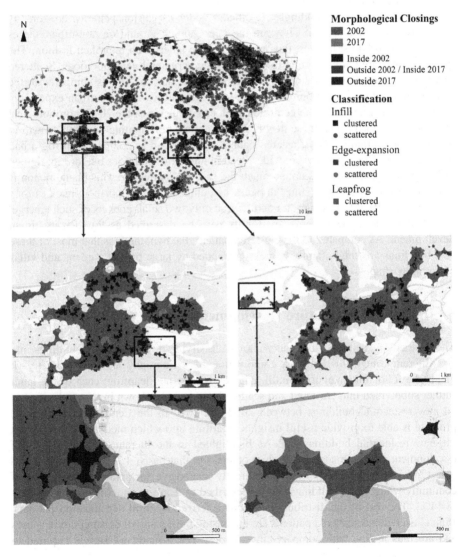

Fig. 5. Morphological closings and classification results. Focus on Brignoles (left) and Le Luc (right). Background: OpenStreetMap, 2020.

66.71% of the new buildings are located within urban structures that were already present in 2002. These buildings are infill patterns of urban growth directly contributing to urban densification. Among this group, the clustered pattern corresponds to the infilling of urban vacuities at the scale of urban blocks or strips of land that were previously not constructed, or at least not fully occupied by residential buildings. This category is also corresponding to various projects of urban redevelopment and regeneration of old urban fabrics. The scattered pattern can however be described as additions of adjacent buildings or infillings of urban vacuities at the scale of the plot, within existing urban blocks. It can be safely assumed that these new buildings are not planned nor coordinated by administrative authorities and promoters, but rather the outcome of individual initiatives.

24.85% of the new buildings, classified as edge-expansion patterns, are directly responsive for urban sprawl. They are the ones gaining ground on non-urban spaces from existing urban structures, thus prolonging the latter in an unbroken fashion. The clustered ones are corresponding to compact new peripheral neighborhoods. Scattered urban development are also contributing to urban expansion. Yet, as compared to the former, this pattern is not compact, thus contributing to low-density urban expansion.

8.44% of the new building centroids are located outside of the 2017 morphological closing, which means that these new buildings are not contributing to urban growth in the sense of continuity. The clustered pattern be described as compact leapfrog urban developments. These patterns are widespread in numerous countries but, as highlighted in Fig. 4, it appears that it is not so much the case in Centre-Var. This phenomenon is often described in the academic literature as compact but yet not continuous urban development [19, 20]. In Brignoles and Le Luc only two small pockets of such emerge. The scattered leapfrog pattern can, for its part, be described as low-density urban development. As compared to the clustered pattern, the hypothesis is that most of these new buildings are single family homes surrounded by large private gardens and villas of complex shapes.

5 Discussion and Future Developments

The protocol presented in this paper allows classifying new residential buildings into six different categories though a combination of variography and morphometry. It yields the following categories: infill, edge-expansion and leapfrog; each of the latter further subdivided into clustered and scattered patterns. As shown in the application to all new residential buildings between 2002 and 2017 in the Centre-Var region, this protocol is able to provide useful insights regarding into which model of development the new residential buildings fall. As highlighted in the literature, some models of development are more sustainable than others. On that basis, 4.726 residential buildings (24.85% of the distribution) are directly responsive for sprawl in the sense of continuity while 1.603 buildings can be described as leapfrog patterns of development (8.44%). The rest of the distribution are characterized by infill densification patterns. Both clustered and scattered patterns are increasing the density of existing urban spaces and are thus in line with compact city theories. Yet, a fieldwork step is required to validate these preliminary results. The protocol also must be tested in other areas, notably within more urbanized regions such as metropolitan areas.

The script will be improved in several directions. First, alternatives will be sought for some functions that are time-consuming regarding computation, such as "variogram" and "gDifference". Parallel computing is also considered. Second, the script will be simplified to make it reproducible to any area. Since it only requires GIS layers of residential building footprints, it could evolve into a decision tool for the evaluation and quantification of spatial patterns of urban growth.

Appendix: Data and Script

Files
- CV_PT_Ext_0217.gpkg (9.8 MB)
- PT_Classification (v.1.2 - 13.6 kB)
- CV_PT_Ext_0217_RES.gpkg (48.9 MB)
- README.txt (2.9 kB)

Title

Variography and Morphometry for Classifying Building Centroids as Patterns of Urban Growth v1.2

Link

https://zenodo.org/record/3899981

Description

This upload contains a dataset ready to be processed, an R script (v1.2) and a dataset with the associated results of the processing steps. The dataset is a GeoPackage file (EPSG:2154 - RGF93/Lambert-93 - Projected) named "CV_PT_Ext_0217.gpkg" containing two layers (1) "CV_Building_PT": a point feature class made of the centroids of residential buildings in 2002 and 2017 extracted from the French BD TOPO® (National Geographic Institute). This layer possesses two attribute columns indicative of the building presence for each period: "Pres_2002" and "Pres_2017" (modalities: "1" for building presence; "0" otherwise). (2) "Centre_Var_ext": a polygon feature class related to the extent of the case study: a region in southern France named Centre-Var. The script performs a combination of variography analysis and morphological closings over the building centroids. The different bounding regions then allow classifying new residential buildings (the ones that appeared between 2002 and 2017) into different categories of patterns of urban growth according to their degrees of clustering/scattering and to their locations regarding existing urban areas. The GeoPackage associated with the results "CV_PT_Ext_0217_RES.gpkg" contains two additional layers (3) "PT_CLASS" a point feature class made of the new building centroids with an attribute column "cat" related to the classification outputs. The categories are as follows: 1 - clustered infill, 2 - scattered infill, 3 - clustered edge-expansion, 4 - scattered edge-expansion, 5 - clustered leapfrog and 6 - scattered leapfrog. (4) "BR_Clipping": a polygon feature class made of the different bounding regions clipped together.

References

1. United Nations: Transforming our World: The 2030 Agenda for Sustainable Development. United Nations, New York (2015)
2. European Environment Agency. Urban sprawl in Europe, The ignored challenge. European Commission report, p. 60 (2006)
3. Verderber, S.: Sprawling Cities and Our Endangered Public Health. Routledge, London (2012)
4. Brueckner, J.K.: Urban sprawl: diagnosis and remedies. Int. Reg. Sci. Rev. **23**(2), 160–171 (2000)
5. Bhatta, B., Saraswati, S., Bandyopadhyay, D.: Urban sprawl measurement from remote sensing data. Appl. Geogr. **30**(4), 731–740 (2010)
6. Galster, G., Hanson, R., Ratcliffe, M., Wolman, H., Coleman, S., Freihage, J.: Wrestling sprawl to the ground: defining and measuring an elusive concept. Hous. Policy Debate **12**(4), 681–717 (2001)
7. Bhatta, B.: Analysis of Urban Growth and Sprawl from Remote Sensing Data. Advances in Geographic Information Science, p. 172. Springer, Berlin (2010). https://doi.org/10.1007/978-3-642-05299-6
8. Smith, N.: The New Urban Frontier, Gentrification and the Revanchist City. Routledge, New York (1996)
9. Liu, Z., He, C., Wu, J.: General spatiotemporal patterns of urbanization: an examination of 16 world cities. Sustainability **8**, 41 (2016)
10. Jenks, M., Burton, E., Williams, K.: The Compact City: A Sustainable Urban Form? Spon Press, London, p. 360 (1996)
11. Burdett, R., Philipp, R.: Shaping Cities in an Urban Age, p. 448. Phaidon Press, New York (2018)
12. Tannier, C., Thomas, I., Vuidel, G., Frankhauser, P.: A fractal approach to identifying urban boundaries. Geogr. Anal. **43**(2), 211–227 (2011)
13. Chaudhry, O., Mackaness, W.A.: Automatic identification of urban settlement boundaries for multiple representation databases. Comput. Environ. Urban Syst. **32**(2), 95–109 (2008)
14. Perez, J., Fusco, G., Moriconi-Ebrard, F.: Identification and quantification of urban space in India: defining urban macro-structures. Urban Stud. **56**(10), 1988–2004 (2019)
15. Usui, H.: A bottom-up approach for delineating urban areas minimizing the connection cost of built clusters: comparison with top-down-based densely inhabited districts. Comput. Environ. Urban Syst. **77**, 101363 (2019)
16. Pebesma, E.: Multivariable geostatistics in S: the GSTAT package. Comput. Geosci. **30**, 683–691 (2004)
17. Armstrong, M.: Experimental variograms. In: Basic Linear Geostatistics, pp. 47–58. Springer, Berlin, Heidelberg (1998). https://doi.org/10.1007/978-3-642-58727-6_4
18. Dauphiné, A., Voiron Canicio, C.: Variogrammes et structures spatiales, Collection Reclus Modes d'Emploi no 12, GIP Reclus (1988)
19. Mills, D.E.: Growth, speculation and sprawl in a monocentric city. J. Urban Econ. **10**(2), 201–226 (1981)
20. Zang, W., Wrenn, D.H., Irwin, E.G.: Spatial heterogeneity, accessibility, and zoning: an empirical investigation of leapfrog development. J. Econ. Geogr. **17**(3), 547–570 (2017)

Analyzing the Driving Factors of Urban Transformation in the Province of Potenza (Basilicata Region-Italy)

Amedeo Ieluzzi, Lucia Saganeiti[✉], Angela Pilogallo,
Francesco Scorza, and Beniamino Murgante

School of Engineering, University of Basilicata, 85100 Potenza, Italy
lucia.saganeiti@unibas.it

Abstract. The main transformation dynamics in the province of Potenza territory (Basilicata region in the south of Italy) correspond to those of urban sprinkling. The urban sprinkling phenomena is typical of mainly mountainous internal areas with indices of settlement density and artificial coverage ratios very low. The temporal and spatial analysis of the urban sprinkling phenomenon gives a picture of the transformation dynamics of the territory, i.e. the phenomena of fragmentation and compaction of the urban territory. Through a logistic regression, the driving factors that have affected the dynamics of urban transformation and specifically the phenomena of fragmentation and compaction between 1998 and 2013 will be analyzed. The two transformation phenomena (dependent variables Y), will be analyzed separately and built on the basis of the variation of the sprinkling index in the analyzed period. In the model, eleven independent variables concerning physical characteristics, proximity analysis, socioeconomic characteristics and the urban policies or constraints, have been considered.

The result of the logistic regression consists of two probability maps of change of the dependent variable Y from non-urban to fragmented or compacted. The indexes of the relative operational characteristic (ROC) of 0.85 and 0.84 respectively for compaction and fragmentation, testify the goodness of the model.

Keywords: Urban sprinkling · Logistic regression · Fragmentation · Low-density

1 Introduction

Land take is the phenomenon of land area conversion from its original (natural) to its anthropic (urban) use [1, 2]. The phenomenon of soil consumption is becoming more and more widespread all over the world despite the implementation of various policies to contain its consumption [3–5]. European commission has legislated for soil protection by setting a target of zero net land consumption by 2050 (EU Environment Action Programme to 2020 (7th EAP)). This can be achieved by aligning soil consumption growth with real population growth by 2030. The demographic trend is crucial in the urban expansion process of a territory. In Italy, but also in other European

© Springer Nature Switzerland AG 2020
O. Gervasi et al. (Eds.): ICCSA 2020, LNCS 12252, pp. 425–434, 2020.
https://doi.org/10.1007/978-3-030-58811-3_31

countries, more and more often urban expansion is not justified by real settlement demand [6, 7]. In many contexts of low density and continuous depopulation, urban expansion is coupled with a negative demographic trend (decoupled growth) [8–10].

The phenomenon of land take in Europe, assumes more relevance considering that since the 1950s it has been largely driven by urban expansion characterized by a sharp decrease in urban density with decentralization of urban areas [11, 12]. This has led to changes in the shape of urban settlements from compact to fragmented and dispersed around the territory. The urban expansions in the last fifty years have detached from the more traditional and recognized dynamics of urban sprawl acquiring different forms and very low settlement indexes. Characteristic of internal Mediterranean areas is the phenomenon of urban sprinkling [13] recognized in Italy, Spain and Africa [9, 14–16].

Urban sprinkling is a transformation phenomenon different from that of urban sprawl [17] and characterized by a sporadic, pulverized and scattered diffusion of urban settlements on the territory. It has very low-density indices compared to those of urban sprawl, resulting in urban and landscape fragmentation [18]. The urban sprinkling phenomenon is measured by SPrinkling IndeX (SPX) which is a geometric indicator that through the subdivision of the study area into homogeneous territorial units measures the dispersion of urban settlements on the basis of Euclidean distance. The SPX index, analyzed in the temporal dimension, returns a picture of the transformation dynamics of a territory in terms of fragmentation and compaction.

The case study analyzed is the territory of the province of Potenza, in the Basilicata region (southern Italy) where, as demonstrated by previous studies [9, 19, 20], the urban transformations from the 1950s to the present day have occurred on the basis of urban sprinkling rules. Therefore, on the basis of the sprinkling index the processes of fragmentation and compaction on the territory of the province of Potenza have been analyzed.

The aim of this article is to model the factors determining the dynamics of transformation (fragmentation and compaction) with a logistic regression in the period between 1998 and 2013. Analyzing all these factors is of fundamental importance in order to understand what are the driving forces behind the dynamics of transformation of the territory and also to obtain information about future transformations to be used as a support in the work of policy makers. The determining factors (driving forces) considered include physical factors, socio-economic factors, proximity factors to road infrastructure and major urban centers, factors concerning urban legislation on the transformability of territories. Logistic regression will be carried out once considering the phenomenon of compaction and once considering the phenomenon of fragmentation. The results of the logistic regression are probability maps of change of the dependent variable Y (fragmentation or compaction) from the initial state "untransformed" to the subsequent state "fragmented" or "compacted".

2 Study Area

The territory of the Province of Potenza in the Basilicata region presents a significant orographic range with the presence of many mountain peaks, especially in the southern part of the territory where there is the Pollino massif where the maximum provincial and regional altimetry is reached (2238 m above sea level). The province of Potenza has a territorial extension of 6594 km², includes 100 municipalities and has a total population of 368,251 inhabitants (ISTAT 2019 [21]).

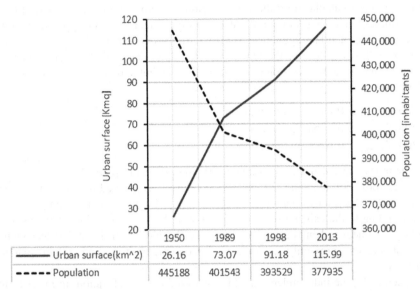

	1950	1989	1998	2013
Urban surface(km^2)	26.16	73.07	91.18	115.99
Population	445188	401543	393529	377935

Fig. 1. Comparison from demographic trends and urban surface (in square kilometers) from 1950 to 2013 in the Province of Potenza.

The largest city for population is the municipality of Potenza (67168 inhabitants) which is also the regional capital. The other municipalities are small in size. Specifically, 6 municipalities on 100 have population between 10000 and 20000 inhabitants, 12 municipalities on 100 have population between 5000 and 10000 inhabitants and the rest (81 municipalities on 100), representative of the majority of the provincial municipalities, has population less than 5000 inhabitants. The graph in Fig. 1 shows a comparison between population growth and urban expansion measured in square kilometers of urban area from 1950 to 2013. The urban area in this case is defined as the surface occupied by buildings and road infrastructure. A disaggregated trend of the two variables emerges: as the population decreases, the urbanized area increases. This trend is still active all over the region, which, in the face of a negative demographic trend and a high rate of depopulation, sees its urban areas increase. Land take is therefore unsustainable in the absence of demand for settlement.

3 Materials and Methods

The aim of this study is to model the determinants of urban transformation dynamics (fragmentation and compaction) with two logistic regressions in the time interval 1998–2013 considering 11 driving forces as independent variables (X). The dependent variables (Y) will be derived from the sprinkling index and will be in a first case fragmentation and in a second case compaction.

3.1 Dataset

The dependent variables include the dynamics of urban transformation and specifically: fragmentation and compaction. These layers were obtained from the analysis of the sprinkling index calculated on the whole regional territory in previous studies [9, 20]. The sprinkling index has a range of values between 0 and $+\infty$ and is an expression of the distribution of urban aggregates on the territory divided into homogeneous territorial areas. Large values of the index indicate a high degree of fragmentation of the territory. Analyzing the variation of the index from an initial time t_0 to a final time t_1 we obtain:

- $\Delta SPX_{(t_1 - t_0)} > 0$ Urban fragmentation
- $\Delta SPX_{(t_1 - t_0)} < 0$ Urban compaction
- $\Delta SPX_{(t_1 - t_0)} = 0$ No transformation

The index was calculated on a 200×200 m grid for the years 1998 and 2013. For each transformation dynamic, 2 binary rasters have been created in which the value 0 corresponds to no transformation and the value 1 to fragmentation or compaction.

According to the existing scientific literature [22–24] and the characteristics of the territory, 11 independent (predictive) variables (X) have been identified that include physical factors, proximity factors, socioeconomic factors and urban planning legislation.

Specifically, the independent variables analyzed are: X_1 elevation, in raster format and with pixels at 5×5 m resolution; X_2 slope in percentage obtained from elevation; X_3 proximity to highways; X_4 proximity to secondary roads; X_5 proximity to local roads; X_6 proximity to railway stations; X_7 proximity to big cities, i.e. those with a population greater than 50000 inhabitants (Potenza city); X_8 proximity to medium-sized cities, i.e. those with a population between 10000 and 50000 inhabitants (Avigliano, Venosa, Lauria, Rionero in Vulture, Lavello and Melfi municipalities); X_9 population density in 2001 at municipal level; X_{10} employment rate (source: Urbistat [25]); X_{11} raster of transformability containing all the constraints of inedificability present in the territory. Except for variable X_{11}, all variables have been rasterized with 200×200 resolution pixels and standardized. The X_{11} variable is categorical (0–1) and the other variables are continuous, in meter, percentual or number.

3.2 Logistic Regression

Logistic regression is a statistical method used to analyze a dataset in which there are one or more independent variables that determine a result [26]. Logistic regression can also be considered as a special case of linear regression when the result variable is categorical, so it predicts the probability of an event occurring by adapting the data to a logit function. Logistic regression is usually used in estimating a model that describes the relationship between one or more continuous independent variables and binary dependent variables. The dependent variable can only assume two values: 0 and 1. The basic assumption is that the probability of the dependent variable assumes value 1 (positive response) following the logistic curve. The probability of the dependent variable assuming value 1 is expressed by the formula (1):

$$P(Y = 1|X) = \frac{\exp(\sum \beta x)}{1 + \exp(\sum \beta x)} \tag{1}$$

Where: P is the probability that the dependent variable Y becomes 1; X are the independent variables; β are the estimated parameters, the regression coefficients for each independent variable X.

The goodness of fit of the model calibration is estimated by *Pseudo R_square* which estimates the goodness of setting the logistic regression model. *Pseudo R_square* equal to 1 indicates a perfect fit, *Pseudo R_square* equal to 0 indicates no relationship.

As mentioned in [27], pseudo R_square greater than 0.2 is considered a relatively good fit. To verify the absence of multi-collinearity between the independent variables, the Variance Inflation Factor (VIF) was calculated. VIF values less than 5 show the absence of multi-collinearity while VIF values greater than 5 indicate the presence of multi-collinearity between the independent variables [28, 29]. The overall adaptive fit of the model is assessed using the Relative Operative Characteristic (ROC) index which must be greater than 0.5 [30].

4   Results

The results of the logistic regression carried out first for the dependent variable fragmentation and then compaction for the period 1998–2013 are shown below. The Fig. 2 shows the regression coefficients of the two transformation dynamics. The independent variable X1 has a negative correlation coefficient for both transformation dynamics and is more influential for the compaction phenomenon. The negative correlation indicates that the probability of the cell becoming 1 (compaction/fragmentation) increases as the elevation decreases. The variable X2 shows negative correlation with a higher coefficient for the fragmentation process which, compared to compaction, tends to occur more as the slope decreases. The probability that a cell changes its state from non-urban to compact increases with increasing distance from highways (variable X3). Compact urban centers, in fact, are located far away from highways. The variables X4 and X5 have a negative correlation index with both transformation phenomena. The probability of finding compacted or fragmented cells increases as the distance from secondary and local roads decreases. The variable X6 is among the most influential variables and shows positive correlation. The probability of finding compacted cells increases as the distance from railway stations increases. Usually urban transformations take place near railway stations, this anomalous behavior is justified by the concentration of railway stations mainly in the northern part of the study area. The variable X7 shows a strong negative correlation. It represents the distance from large cities, i.e. the city of Potenza. The probability that a cell undergoes transformation increases as the distance from large cities decreases.

Differently, for variable X8 the correlation is positive and higher for the compaction process. The transformations take place, therefore, far from medium-sized cities.

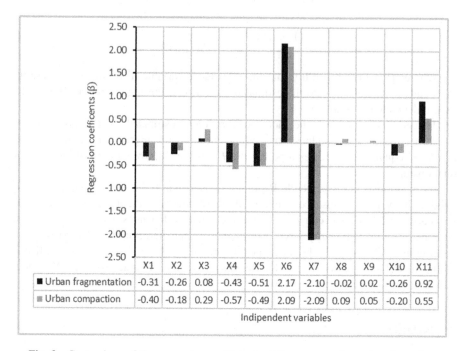

	X1	X2	X3	X4	X5	X6	X7	X8	X9	X10	X11
■ Urban fragmentation	-0.31	-0.26	0.08	-0.43	-0.51	2.17	-2.10	-0.02	0.02	-0.26	0.92
▪ Urban compaction	-0.40	-0.18	0.29	-0.57	-0.49	2.09	-2.09	0.09	0.05	-0.20	0.55

Indipendent variables

Fig. 2. Comparison of the regression coefficients of the two transformation dynamics.

The coefficient of variable X_9 is very small, which shows that in the case study urban transformations are not driven by a real settlement demand. The variable X_{10} shows negative correlation: the probability that a cell undergoes transformation increases as the employment rate decreases. This correlation is quite unusual because the employment rate is an expression of the economic level of an area and it is quite irrational to build in areas where the employment rate is low. Finally, for the last variable X_{11} the correlation is positive, transformations increase near transformable territories and the greatest correlation is for the fragmentation process.

The *Pseudo R_square* for the fragmentation process was 0.25 and for compaction process 0.23; these coefficients, according to [27], show a good adaptation of the regression model.

The maps in Fig. 3 shows the final result of logistic regression: the change probability maps for both dependent variables: fragmentation and compaction. The maximum probability of change for fragmentation is 69% and for compaction 52%. This shows that the territory will be more subject to transformation dynamics regarding fragmentation. The ROC indices of 0.85 and 0.84 for compaction and fragmentation, respectively, testify to the goodness of the model.

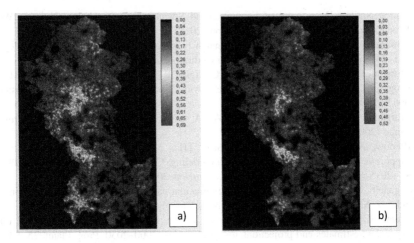

Fig. 3. Predicted dependent variables: a) fragmentation, b) compaction.

5 Conclusions

The objectives target of zero net land consumption by 2050 (EU Environment Action Programme to 2020 (7th EAP) of the European Community are fundamental especially for territories that are fragile and critical, among them there is undoubtedly the Italian territory [31–33]. The definition and implementation of such policies, rules and actions aimed at reducing soil consumption are urgent [34]. The results of this study show that the likelihood of land change will generate more fragmentation processes. In the case analyzed but, more generally, in the Basilicata region, fragmentation has also been caused, in recent years, by other components of the settlement system such as renewable energy installations [19, 35] and oil wells [20]. Urban transformations have a significant impact on the quality of the landscape, the ecosystem services provisioning [36–38] and the costs to the population of transforming the city in no sustainable way [39, 40]. More generally, the dynamics of urban transformation can have a significant impact and cause considerable damage to cultural heritage, and due to the dynamics that develop following an uncontrolled transformation of the territory (landslide movements) can be a cause of risk to human life [41–43].

The results shown in this work are preliminary and will provide a model for predicting the dynamics of urban transformation in the future.

References

1. European Commission: Guidelines on best practice to limit, mitigate or compensate soil sealing (2012). https://doi.org/10.2779/75498
2. European Union: FUTURE BRIEF: No net land take by 2050? (2016). https://doi.org/10.2779/537195
3. Brown, L.A.: The city in 2050: a kaleidoscopic perspective. Appl. Geogr. **49**, 4–11 (2014). https://doi.org/10.1016/j.apgeog.2013.09.003

4. United Nations Department of Economic and Social Affairs/Population Division: World Urbanization Prospects The 2018 Revision (2018)

5. Cobbinah, P.B., Aboagye, H.N.: A Ghanaian twist to urban sprawl. Land Use Policy **61**, 231–241 (2017). https://doi.org/10.1016/j.landusepol.2016.10.047

6. Murgante, B., Borruso, G., Balletto, G., Castiglia, P., Dettori, M.: Why Italy first? Health, geographical and planning aspects of the Covid-19 outbreak. Preprints (2020). https://doi.org/10.20944/preprints202005.0075.v1

7. Murgante, B., Las Casas, G., Sansone, A.: A spatial rough set for locating the periurban fringe (2007)

8. Rienow, A., Goetzke, R.: Supporting SLEUTH - enhancing a cellular automaton with support vector machines for urban growth modeling. Comput. Environ. Urban Syst. **49**, 66–81 (2015). https://doi.org/10.1016/j.compenvurbsys.2014.05.001

9. Saganeiti, L., et al.: Assessing urban fragmentation at regional scale using sprinkling indexes. Sustainability **10**, 3274 (2018). https://doi.org/10.3390/su10093274

10. Angel, S., Parent, J., Civco, D.L., Blei, A., Potere, D.: The dimensions of global urban expansion: estimates and projections for all countries, 2000–2050. Prog. Plann. **75**, 53–107 (2011). https://doi.org/10.1016/j.progress.2011.04.001

11. Siedentop, S., Fina, S.: Monitoring urban sprawl in Germany: towards a gis-based measurement and assessment approach. J. Land Use Sci. **5**, 73–104 (2010). https://doi.org/10.1080/1747423X.2010.481075

12. Nolè, G., Lasaponara, R., Lanorte, A., Murgante, B.: Quantifying urban sprawl with spatial autocorrelation techniques using multi-temporal satellite data. Int. J. Agric. Environ. Inf. Syst. **5**, 19–37 (2014). https://doi.org/10.4018/IJAEIS.2014040102

13. Romano, B., Zullo, F., Fiorini, L., Marucci, A., Ciabò, S.: Land transformation of Italy due to half a century of urbanization. Land Use Policy **67**, 387–400 (2017). https://doi.org/10.1016/j.landusepol.2017.06.006

14. Xu, G., et al.: Urban expansion and form changes across African cities with a global outlook: spatiotemporal analysis of urban land densities. J. Clean. Prod. **224**, 802–810 (2019). https://doi.org/10.1016/j.jclepro.2019.03.276

15. Urbieta, P., Fernandez, E., Ramos, L., Méndez Martínez, G., Bento, R.: A land-cover based urban dispersion indicator suitable for highly dispersed, discontinuously artificialized territories: the case of continental Portugal. Land Use Policy **85**, 92–103 (2019). https://doi.org/10.1016/J.LANDUSEPOL.2019.03.048

16. Romano, B., Zullo, F., Fiorini, L., Ciabò, S., Marucci, A.: Sprinkling: an approach to describe urbanization dynamics in Italy. Sustainability **9**, 97 (2017). https://doi.org/10.3390/su9010097

17. Nechyba, T.J., Walsh, R.P.: Urban sprawl. J. Econ. Perspect. **18**, 177–200 (2004). https://doi.org/10.1257/0895330042632681

18. Saganeiti, L., Pilogallo, A., Scorza, F., Mussuto, G., Murgante, B.: Spatial indicators to evaluate urban fragmentation in Basilicata region. In: Gervasi, O., et al. (eds.) ICCSA 2018. LNCS, vol. 10964, pp. 100–112. Springer, Cham (2018). https://doi.org/10.1007/978-3-319-95174-4_8

19. Saganeiti, L., Pilogallo, A., Faruolo, G., Scorza, F., Murgante, B.: Territorial fragmentation and renewable energy source plants: which relationship? Sustainability **12**, 1828 (2020). https://doi.org/10.3390/SU12051828

20. Scorza, F., Saganeiti, L., Pilogallo, A., Murgante, B.: Ghost planning: the inefficiency of energy sector policies in a low population density region. Arch. DI Stud. URBANI E Reg. (2020). (in press)

21. Istat.it. https://www.istat.it/. Accessed 05 Apr 2019

22. Traore, A., Watanabe, T.: Modeling determinants of urban growth in Conakry, Guinea: a spatial logistic approach. Urban Sci. **1**, 12 (2017). https://doi.org/10.3390/urbansci1020012
23. Salem, M., Tsurusaki, N., Divigalpitiya, P.: Analyzing the driving factors causing urban expansion in the peri-urban areas using logistic regression: a case study of the greater Cairo region. Infrastructures **4**, 4 (2019). https://doi.org/10.3390/infrastructures4010004
24. Martellozzo, F., Amato, F., Murgante, B., Clarke, K.C.: Modelling the impact of urban growth on agriculture and natural land in Italy to 2030. Appl. Geogr. **91**, 156–167 (2018). https://doi.org/10.1016/J.APGEOG.2017.12.004
25. Statistiche economicheProvincia di POTENZA. https://ugeo.urbistat.com/AdminStat/it/it/economia/dati-sintesi/potenza/76/3. Accessed 08 May 2020
26. Aldrich, J., Nelson, F.: Linear Probability, Logit, and Probit Models. SAGE Publications, Inc. (2011). https://doi.org/10.4135/9781412984744
27. Clark, W.A., Hosking, P.L.: Statistical Methods for Geographers (Chapter 13). Consortium Erudit, New York (1986). https://doi.org/10.7202/021850ar
28. Kock, N., Lynn, G.S.: Lateral collinearity and misleading results in variance-based SEM: an illustration and recommendations. J. Assoc. Inf. Syst. **13**, 546–580 (2012). https://doi.org/10.17705/1jais.00302
29. Belsley, D.A.: A Guide to using the collinearity diagnostics. Comput. Sci. Econ. Manag. **4**, 33–50 (1991). https://doi.org/10.1007/BF00426854
30. Walsh, S.J.: Goodness-of-fit issues in ROC curve estimation. Med. Decis. Mak. **19**, 193–201 (1999). https://doi.org/10.1177/0272989X9901900210
31. Las Casas, G., Murgante, B., Scorza, F.: Regional local development strategies benefiting from open data and open tools and an outlook on the renewable energy sources contribution. In: Papa, R., Fistola, R. (eds.) Smart Energy in the Smart City. GET, pp. 275–290. Springer, Cham (2016). https://doi.org/10.1007/978-3-319-31157-9_14
32. Las Casas, G., Scorza, F., Murgante, B.: Razionalità a-priori: una proposta verso una pianificazione antifragile. Ital. J. Reg. Sci. **18**, 329–338 (2019). https://doi.org/10.14650/93656
33. Scorza, F., Grecu, V.: Assessing sustainability: research directions and relevant issues. In: Gervasi, O., et al. (eds.) ICCSA 2016. LNCS, vol. 9786, pp. 642–647. Springer, Cham (2016). https://doi.org/10.1007/978-3-319-42085-1_55
34. Murgante, B., Borruso, G., Lapucci, A.: Sustainable development: concepts and methods for its application in urban and environmental planning. Stud. Comput. Intell. **348**, 1–15 (2011). https://doi.org/10.1007/978-3-642-19733-8_1
35. Saganeiti, L., Pilogallo, A., Faruolo, G., Scorza, F., Murgante, B.: Energy landscape fragmentation: Basilicata region (Italy) study case. In: Misra, S., et al. (eds.) ICCSA 2019. LNCS, vol. 11621, pp. 692–700. Springer, Cham (2019). https://doi.org/10.1007/978-3-030-24302-9_50
36. Pilogallo, A., Saganeiti, L., Scorza, F., Murgante, B.: Ecosystem services' based impact assessment for low carbon transition processes. TeMA - J. L. Use Mobil. Environ. **12**, 127–138 (2019). https://doi.org/10.6092/1970-9870/6117
37. Scorza, F., Pilogallo, A., Saganeiti, L., Murgante, B., Pontrandolfi, P.: Comparing the territorial performances of renewable energy sources' plants with an integrated ecosystem services loss assessment: a case study from the Basilicata region (Italy). Sustain. Cities Soc. **56**, 102082 (2020). https://doi.org/10.1016/J.SCS.2020.102082
38. Scorza, F., Pilogallo, A., Saganeiti, L., Murgante, B.: Natura 2000 areas and sites of national interest (SNI): measuring (un)integration between naturalness preservation and environmental remediation policies. Sustainability **12**, 2928 (2020). https://doi.org/10.3390/su12072928

39. Manganelli, B., Murgante, B., Saganeiti, L.: The social cost of urban sprinkling. Sustainability **12**, 2236 (2020). https://doi.org/10.3390/SU12062236

40. Dvarioniene, J., Grecu, V., Lai, S., Scorza, F.: Four perspectives of applied sustainability: research implications and possible integrations. In: Gervasi, O., et al. (eds.) ICCSA 2017. LNCS, vol. 10409, pp. 554–563. Springer, Cham (2017). https://doi.org/10.1007/978-3-319-62407-5_39

41. Lasaponara, R., et al.: Spatial open data for monitoring risks and preserving archaeological areas and landscape: case studies at Kom el Shoqafa, Egypt and Shush, Iran. Sustainability **9**, 572 (2017). https://doi.org/10.3390/su9040572

42. Pascale, S., et al.: Landslide susceptibility mapping using artificial neural network in the urban area of Senise and San Costantino Albanese (Basilicata, Southern Italy). In: Murgante, B., et al. (eds.) ICCSA 2013. LNCS, vol. 7974, pp. 473–488. Springer, Heidelberg (2013). https://doi.org/10.1007/978-3-642-39649-6_34

43. Elfadaly, A., Attia, W., Qelichi, M.M., Murgante, B., Lasaponara, R.: Management of cultural heritage sites using remote sensing indices and spatial analysis techniques. Surv. Geophys. **39**(6), 1347–1377 (2018). https://doi.org/10.1007/s10712-018-9489-8

Designing a Semi-automatic Map Construction Process for the Effective Visualisation of Business Geodata

Marion Simon[1(✉)] and Hartmut Asche[2(✉)]

[1] Institute of Geosciences, University of Potsdam, Potsdam, Germany
marion.simon@uni-potsdam.de
[2] Computer Graphics System Group, Hasso Plattner Institute,
University of Potsdam, Potsdam, Germany
hartmut.asche@hpi.de

Abstract. This paper proposes a map construction process for the semi-automatic construction of thematic maps from business information data. Addressing a non-specialist user audience, the map construction process will allow a correct, at the same time effective cartographic visualisation for further (geo)visual analysis. Utilising the frequently disregarded geospatial component of existing business mass data, quality map representations facilitate the visual exploration, detection, and analysis of relevant spatial data distributions and structures hitherto unseen in the data. Presently, neither operational procedures nor appropriate software systems, such as BIS, DDS or GIS, are available in the industry for an effective map representation of the geocoded data. To put economic and business experts into a position to make full use of the geo coordinates present in the data, an easy-to-handle map construction process is required to exploit the full semantic and spatial potential of business data. Exemplified for an area diagram map, the map construction process discussed here provides the relevant tools and methods for the targeted audience.

Keywords: Geocoded business data · Geovisualisation · Map construction · Quality map representation · Geovisual analysis · Modular process design

1 Introduction

Most data in company databases possess a spatial reference. Hamilton [1] estimates a spatial reference in about 95 percent of all data; that is, 95 percent of all data is geospatial. Nevertheless, the use of spatial attributes is not fully exploited for a number of reasons. However, many connections, dependencies and interrelations are only expressed through the geo-component of the data. Potential further insights gained from the analysis of the spatial component of corporate (geo)data constitute a new and valuable contribution to corporate decision-making. Communication of spatial reference and their visual analysis is most effective through the visual channel, i.e. by visualisation, e.g. through map representations. Such maps also serve as a means of communication for these very decisions [2]. From a business perspective, it can be assumed that integration of the geo-component will result in all assessments for value

© Springer Nature Switzerland AG 2020
O. Gervasi et al. (Eds.): ICCSA 2020, LNCS 12252, pp. 435–447, 2020.
https://doi.org/10.1007/978-3-030-58811-3_32

creation and employment being approximately two times higher [3]. Nevertheless, the expert effort and cost expenditure for the economic production of effective thematic maps need to be taken into account [4].

This article presents a solution approach that enables companies to visually analyse existing company (geo)data not only according to their semantic content but also with regard to their spatial reference. Up to now, there has been little research on the methods, processes and analyses that deals with both the expressive and effective graphic representation [5] as well as use of geocoded business data in the industry. Our focus in this presentation is on the effective representation of spatially related quantitative information in segmented proportional area symbols. Related issues of professional cartographic symbolization will be dealt with elsewhere.

2   Solution Approach

To empower corporate businesses to visualise their data expressively and effectively, it is necessary to make available the existing knowledge for the creation of professional, meaningful map graphics in the form of easy-to-use digital production processes. This enables even non-expert users to create effective map graphics from non-graphic company data. The basis of the solution approach is an executable visualisation process (Fig. 1), based on the classical visualisation pipeline [6]. The design and implementation of this principally scalable process is described below for the generation of small-scale map representations.

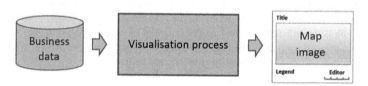

Fig. 1. Principle to convert non-graphic company data into graphic map representations

Explorative data analysis (EDA), also known as data mining, includes the special form of explorative spatial data analysis (ESDA) [7]. The process to be developed enables companies to extend the previously graphics-free data evaluation by analyses of the spatial distribution of the data based on their spatial attributes that have been left unused so far.

The way to design and develop an executable construction process for the production of effective cartographic visualisations from geodata consists of three essential stages:

a) formalisation of the map construction,
b) design a map construction process and
c) process automation.

In order to provide cartographic expertise for the visualisation of enterprise data, it is necessary to formalise this expertise. On the one hand this requires the identification of the relevant map construction steps, including the definition of the spatial reference, the selection of adequate map types, generalisation measures and the definition of the presentation form. On the other hand, it is necessary to define of the target group for which the map results are to be made available. In the course of this formalisation, the entire map production process is broken down into a finite number of content-defined modules that can be executed separately.

Initially, the design of such modular map construction process for the professional visualisation of spatial (mass) data is done on a semantic (external) and logical level. For this purpose, the classical visualisation pipeline with its modules is adapted. The map construction process is also modular, consisting of a fixed number of micro-modules. Depending on the application, these micro-modules can be combined flexibly to process chains via defined connectors. They are assembled semantically and logically into a dedicated card design process. The linking of the micro-modules by means of corresponding connectors depends on a company's analysis objectives defined in terms of data content. Map construction rules define the dependencies between the micro-modules. These interrelations are then graphically represented by process flow diagram elements.

To automate the cartographic expertise mentioned above, the process is first outlined with UML and SysML for a better understanding, and then graphically modeled with the jABC software [8]. This software system offers capabilities to generate Java code directly from graphic modelling. It can be determined which micro-modules do run automatically and for which modules user interaction is required or useful. Automation of the micro-modules will enable the user to generate alternative visualisation results with a higher degree of user control instead of default map graphics. It has to be noted that more user control is only possible to the extent that the quality criteria for the output of map visualisations implemented in the process modules are met. Finally, servicification of selected micro-modules is implemented. Existing open source tools and applications are into the map construction process integrated, such as the well-known ColorBrewer colour definition system [9].

The stages described provide a picture of the automation scope of the application.

3   Implementation Strategy

Taking the data analysis module as an example, the solution approach presented above will be dealt with in more detail (see Fig. 2). This module incorporates an automated process for the selection of the adequate map type, based on the analysis of the existing source data.

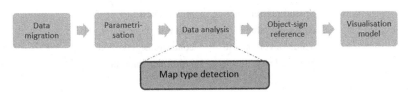

Fig. 2. Map construction pipeline (section, modified from [6])

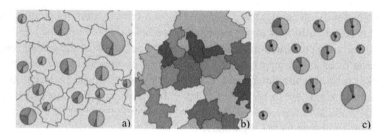

Fig. 3. Selection of map types relevant for business data: a) area diagram map, b) choropleth map, c) positional diagram map. Source: [10, 11]

Starting from the database, the possibility of a spatially related visualisation of the dataset in question is examined in a first step. If thre generation of a map graphic turns out to be feasible, the map type optimally representing the available geodata is identified. To do so, the selection process for choosing the appropriate map type is formalised. Map types are described based on their presentation characteristics. Selection of the appropriate map type is from about a dozen of different map types widely accepted in cartographic theory and applications (see Fig. 3). The optimal map type is one that is best fitting the geographic and semantic characteristics of the data to be mapped.

It has already been mentioned that an analysis of the source data is essential to determine the selection process for the dataset to be mapped. This is performed in a second component. To set up a selection process, an analysis of the data to be visualised in relation with the data characteristics is required for the creation of the adequate map type. Based on the definition of the relevant map types in cartographic literature, all map types representing quantitative data are identified. Suitable map types are characterised by the geometric and semantic components of the data that constitute the thematic content as well as the geographic reference of the map to be constructed. The focus of this paper is on the quantitative semantic content for thematic maps. The thematic content refers to the semantic information of a particular dataset expressed numerically [12]. Requirements of the data characteristics essential for visualisation (spatial reference, attribute value, value development and scaling level) are listed separately for each map type. Table 1 gives as an example for area diagram maps which are described below.

Table 1. Formalisation of map type characteristics of the area diagram map (modified after [10, 13])

Map type characteristics	Area diagram map
Spatial reference	area-related
Attribute value	absolute
Value development	continuous/classified
Scaling level	ratio oder interval

Because of its spatial reference, the quantitative content of the map presentation is always linked to specific geographic units. Areas (e.g. administrative units), lines (e.g. traffic routes) or points (e.g. settlements) are possible. For example, quantitative data of the consumption behaviour of a particular country's population has an area reference (because the population is related to a national territory). The representation of the reference unit (here: the delimitation of the corresponding country, the highest-level administrative unit) is in the base map. The corresponding diagram is then placed in the administrative unit to show the spatial reference of the respective data [14]. The semantic reference is further differentiated in the attribution as an attribute value. Thus, the absolute value and the relative or ratio value are assigned to the quantitative attribute data category. Options for further processing depend on the relations between the attributes, which are determined by the attribute value [11].

The value range can be separated into continuous (i.e. unstructured) attributes as well as discrete (i.e. structured) attributes. This describes a characteristic of the relationship between the attributes, which, in turn, determines their further processing options and the selection of the optimal map type [11].

The level of measurement characterises the information content of the data. It defines possible transformations of attribute values and describes the graphical relational properties of characters that make these transformations visible on the map. A total of four levels are distinguished to which the semantic attributes of the geodata can be assigned: nominal scale, ordinal scale and metric scale, which can be further subdivided into interval and ratio scales [11, 15].

In the following, the formal data characteristics relevant for the selection of the adequate map type are subsequently combined in a structured way to form a subprocess of the map type selection process source data analysis. The decision tree for the selection of the optimal map representation for the respective data is derived from this. A detail is shown in Fig. 4.

The sequence of the individual process steps of the map type selection component begins by checking the spatial reference of the existing business statistics to be mapped. Spatial reference provides "the geometrical information about the location and shape of the individual objects necessary for any digital modelling and cartographic representation [...]" [12]. Examples are postal codes, telephone area codes or even place names.

Export datasets can contain, for example, country names or customer locations to which export quantities listed in the dataset are delivered. Country names or place names can be automatically extracted from the selected data lists (e.g. table schemata of a database). These geographic names are then compared with digital directories of geographic names, so-called gazetteers. This process is limited to fields of the 'TEXT' data type, so that not every field entry is checked for matching and thus affects the performance of the service. Finally, non-matches are displayed for manual error correction of the geographic names. This procedure can be used to check location-based (point-referenced place names) and area-related data (country names) for their spatial reference.

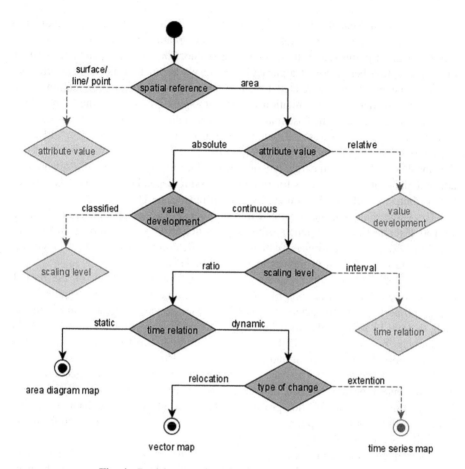

Fig. 4. Decision tree for selecting a map type (section)

Relative attribute values are generally expressed in percent or per thousand [14]. Absolute values characterise a quantity starting from a zero point. They are specified by value unit. It is possible to automate this sub-module that differentiates relative from absolute values by reading out field types (percentage or currency formats), field contents (% or currency symbol or weight unit addition) or column headings (entries in % or 'percent' or €/t or 'Euro'/'tons').

An unclassified value progression is assumed when specifying export volumes or export revenues. It is further assumed that the company's interest in data analysis is based on data that are as accurate as possible. Classified values are data already stored in a classified form.

In the case of quantitative data, options to select the scaling level are limited to the values of ratio and interval scale attributes. Weight data or sales revenues belong to the group of ratio-scaled data, which have a natural zero point. The system can use the results of attribute value determination for evaluation purposes.

To find out the time reference, interaction with the user is necessary. The system can make suggestions to the user on the basis of existing temporal attributes or time stamps read (date formats of various specifications).

Dynamics in the data can be expressed in two ways depending on the type of change (vector or time series map). Whether a representation of changing target regions of exported products is desired can be inquired. If the wish does not exist, a static temporal reference is assumed and the corresponding map type area diagram map is selected in the result.

4   Applying the Map Construction Process: A Use Case

To illustrate what has been presented, we take the use case a spread-producing company from a particular country. We assume this company exports its products Europe-wide. In order to be able to analyse its export data both in terms of content and region, an easy-to-comprehend graphic representation of the market penetration on the European market for spreads is required. The most effective way to do this is by a map graphic.

We also assume that the company aims at further market development by observing the European consumption behaviour of bread and cereals. For this purpose, sales managers extract the current figures from European databases and compare the numerical values with their own export figures using a so-called map construction assistant, which generates an effective map display from this geodata.

Our exemplary spread company keeps its own export data in table form under the file name 'ExportsSpreads.xls'. It contains annual export values (weight in tons-t and currency in euro-EUR) of the product category spreads to, say, the Scandinavian countries (Denmark, Finland, Norway, Sweden) (Fig. 5).

	A	B	C	D
1			export: weight	export: value
2	Year	NAME_ENGL	t	thsd. EUR
3	2018	Denmark	1390.8	4890
4	2018	Finland	328.5	787
5	2018	Sweden	927.6	2937
6	2018	Norway	265.0	749

(C)opyright Statistisches Bundesamt (Destatis), 2019

Fig. 5. Exemplary export figures of a product category of a manufacturing industry from Germany to Scandinavia

This export table forms the starting point for a data analysis to feed the described map type selection process. For the selection of the optimal map type, the decision tree presented in Sect. 3 is run through semi-automatically. For this data example the following can be determined: The available geodata

a) refer to state territories (selected Scandinavian countries are available in the digital GeographicNamesIndex),

b) are available in absolute values in the units t (tons) and Eur (euro) (no percentage signs in column headings),
c) are not broken down,
d) are ratio-scaled (identifiable by the system from the units t and Eur - conclusion: scale with natural zero = ratio-scaled),
e) refer to the year 2018 (static).

Thus, after having traversed the decision tree, the map type of the area diagram map to be implemented is selected. In order to go through this selection process on a technical level, the individual intermediate steps need to be described in more detail. As an example, the procedure for the first step, the detection of the spatial reference in the geodata set to be mapped, is presented here.

The tool-based determination of the geodata reference is carried out by searching for place or country names. First, the column must be identified, which holds a corresponding spatial reference. Since column designations are not titled in a standardised way and a certain range of names (e.g. country, city, name) exists, it is advisable to start with the selection procedure in the first or second line (depending on the table structure). It is also assumed at this point that export data is stored country- or location-wise and that these spatial data are listed at the beginning of the table for easier reading. For this reason, the search for country designations is started in column A.

```
/* Identification of the column with spatial reference data */
if field A2 formatted as text;
do check string compatibility to members of 'GeographicNamesIndex';
else if field B2 formatted as text;
    do check string compatibility to members of 'GeographicNamesIndex';
    else if field C2 formatted as text;
    do check string compatibility to members of 'GeographicNamesIndex';
    else break;
```

This loop is repeated over all contents contained in the table section (here: country names). A digital, internationally recognised index of names (Gazetteer Service) is fictitiously constructed here and shown as an example in Fig. 6. It represents the data basis for the spatial reference check within the source data analysis.

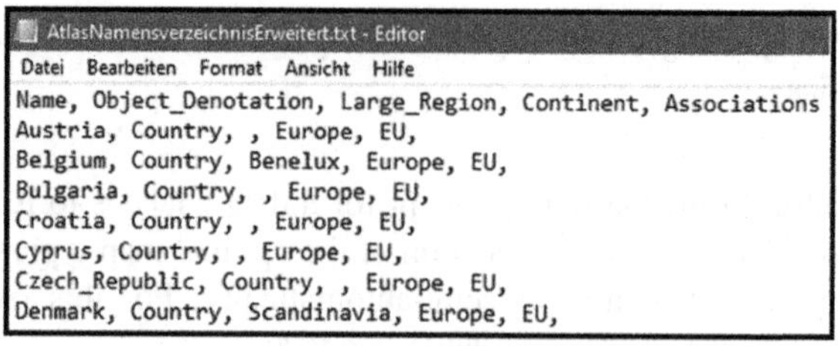
AtlasNamensverzeichnisErweitert.txt - Editor
Datei Bearbeiten Format Ansicht Hilfe
Name, Object_Denotation, Large_Region, Continent, Associations
Austria, Country, , Europe, EU,
Belgium, Country, Benelux, Europe, EU,
Bulgaria, Country, , Europe, EU,
Croatia, Country, , Europe, EU,
Cyprus, Country, , Europe, EU,
Czech_Republic, Country, , Europe, EU,
Denmark, Country, Scandinavia, Europe, EU,

Fig. 6. Geographic names index (section)

The execution order (do) required in pseudocode is integrated into a separate micro-module and is described as follows:

```
/* Check for compatibility with the 'GeographicNamesIndex' */
Gazetteer Compatibility Check

{
    initialize x = read string;
    initialize y = read string from 'GeographicNamesIndex.txt' in (column
A, row 2);
    if (x unequal y);
    do initialize y = read string from 'GeographicNamesIndex.txt' in (col-
umn A, row 3);
    else    check    in    'GeographicNamesIndex.txt'    if    Object-
Denotation = country or city and load geometry data for base map via API
}
```

Based on this pseudo code description, the module description shown in Fig. 7 can be expected for the first segment of the bipolar decision tree "spatial reference". The coding of the other elements of the decision tree is also carried out according to this scheme. The decomposition and combination results in micro-modules such as the 'Gazetteer Checker'.

With the development and coding of the decision tree, the resulting micro-modules as well as their superordinate modules, shown here as roles in the SysML activity diagram, can now be described.

The coded and modularised decision tree will propose an area diagram map to represent the example data set of the selected export data. In the process module of object-sign reference, the design elements are assigned to the geodata to be displayed (Fig. 8).

After further execution of the map construction process (see Sect. 3), this map type, which has been identified as adequate, is implemented as standard output. In this example, the diagram type 'bar chart' is assigned as standard. To represent comparative export figures of the EU, the bar chart can be segmented at the users' request. The larger column represents the EU export figures for comparison with the embedded smaller column of the company's own export figures. The 'visualisation model' module displays the initial graphical design on a canvas, based on decisions made or predefined by the user, taking into account the output characteristics defined in the initial 'parameterization' module, i.e. the display of the base map and the embedding of the segmented bar charts, see Fig. 9.

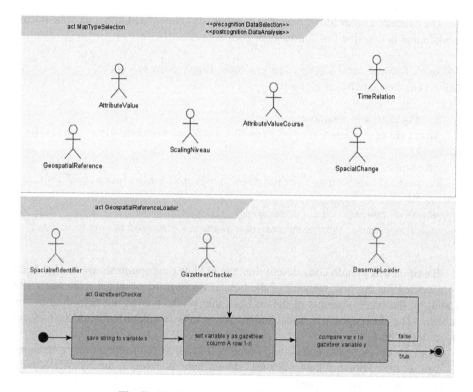

Fig. 7. Decision tree as SysML activity diagram

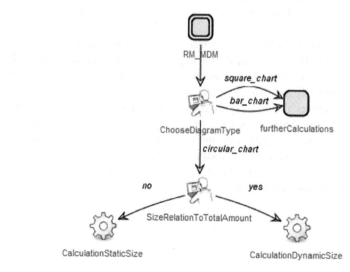

Fig. 8. Process model for diagram type selection in jABC (section, [16])

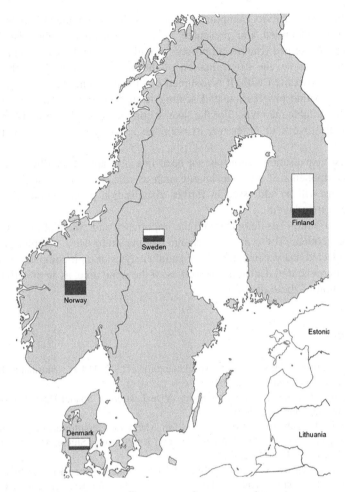

Fig. 9. Area diagram map for use case data set

5   Conclusion

This contribution presents a semi-automated design process for the generation of effective map visualisations from company databases with a spatial reference.

In order to incorporate the existing expertise of effective map visualisation into algorithms, the relevant map construction steps have been identified and broken down into executable steps that can be run separately. The semantic and logical linking of modules and micro-modules completes the step of formalisation. To facilitate the automated selection of the optimal map type a decision tree has been developed. By means of programming and servicification, users can access this expertise. The solution approach was explicitly exercised with an example data set. The data analysis module from the adapted visualisation pipeline has been used and enriched with systematically arranged expertise to identify the optimal map type for the example data. The modules are described using activity components from SysML. A suitable map type for the use case has been identified and presented in a non-generalised map visualisation. It remains to be examined whether all process modules are mandatory for data analysis or whether, for example, the determination of the measurement scale of the processed dataset can be dispensed with. It is assumed that the micro-modules for examining the data for their value progression and scaling level will provide similar results when selecting the suitable map type. For the sake of completeness, they have been taken into account in this work in order not to prejudge a possible extension of the overall process.

The first visualisation result has not been free of graphical conflicts. Furthermore, essential components of the map layout such as title, legend and scale are missing. These deficits will be addressed in further visualisation process modules for georeferencing and map layout.

This contribution has demonstrated the importance and potential of spatial analysis of business geodata. These methods enable companies to use a completely new, previously neglected analysis method. The spatial analysis of their company data supports efficient entrepreneurial decisions and serves, at the same time, as an effective means of communication of these decisions.

References

1. Perkins   (2010).   http://computerworld.com/article/2549741/have-you-mapped-your-data-today-.html. Accessed 15 Mar 2020
2. Kraak, M.J., Ormeling, F.J.: Cartography. Visualization of Spatial Data. Addison Wesley Longman Ltd., Harlow (1996)
3. Fornefeld, M., Oefinger, P., Rausch, U.: Der Markt für Geoinformationen: Potentiale für Beschäftigung, Innovation und Wertschöpfung. Kurzfassung. Studie. MICUS-Management Consultig GmbH, Düsseldorf (2003)
4. Asche, H., Herrmann, C.: Desktop Mapping in der thematischen Kartographie. Stand der Technik und Marktübersicht. In: Deutsche Gesellschaft für Kartographie (DGfK) (edt.): Kartograpisches Taschenbuch 1994/95, 4th edn. Kirschbaum, Bonn (1994)
5. Mackinlay, J.: Automating the design of graphical presentations of relational information. ACM Trans. Graph. **5**, 110–141 (1986)
6. Haber, R.B., McNabb, D.A.: Visualization idioms: a conceptual model for scientific visualisation systems. In: Shriver, B., Nielsen, G.M., Rosenblum, M. (eds.) Visualization in Scientific Computing, Los Alamitos (1990)
7. Slocum, T.A., McMaster, R.B., Kessler, F.C., Howard, H.H.: Thematic cartography and geovisualization. In: Series in Geographic Information Science, 3rd edn. Prentice-Hall, Upper Saddle River, NJ. (2009)
8. Technische Universität (TU) Dortmund: jABC Link (2020). http://ls5-www.cs.tu-dortmund.de/projects/jabc/index.php. Accessed 13 May 2020
9. Harrower, M., Brewer, C.: ColorBrewer.org: an online tool for selecting color schemes for maps. Cartographic J. **40**(1), 27–37 (2003)
10. Bollmann, J., Koch, W.G. (eds.): Lexikon der Kartographie und Geomatik, vol. 1. Spektrum Akademischer Verlag, Heidelberg (2001)
11. Bollmann, J., Koch, W.G. (eds.): Lexikon der Kartographie und Geomatik, vol. 2. Spektrum Akademischer Verlag, Heidelberg (2002)

12. Hake, G.: Grünreich, D., Meng, L.: Kartographie. Visualisierung raum-zeitlicher Informationen, 8th edn. Walter de Gruyter & Co., Berlin, New York (2002)
13. Arnberger, E.: Thematische Kartographie. Westermann, Braunschweig (1997)
14. Witt, W.: Thematische Kartographie. Methoden und Probleme, Tendenzen und Aufgaben, 2nd edn. Gebr. Jänecke, Hannover (1970)
15. Kucharczyk, C.: Konzeption, Entwicklung und Implementierung eines regelbasierten Kartenkonstruktionsassistenten zur fachgerechten Visualisierung statistischer Massendaten. Masterthesis (2013). Unpublished
16. Simon, M., Asche, H.: Automated spatial data processing and refining. In: Lamprecht, A.-L. (ed.) ISoLA 2012/2014. CCIS, vol. 683, pp. 38–49. Springer, Cham (2016). https://doi.org/10.1007/978-3-319-51641-7_3

Constructing Geo-Referenced Virtual City Models from Point Cloud Primitives

Andreas Fricke[✉] and Hartmut Asche

Hasso Plattner Institute, Digital Engineering Faculty, University of Potsdam,
Prof.-Dr.-Helmert-Str. 2-3, 14482 Potsdam, Germany
{andreas.fricke,hartmut.asche}@hpi.uni-potsdam.de

Abstract. This paper presents a novel approach to construct spatially-referenced, multidimensional virtual city models from remotely generated point clouds for areas that lack reliable geographical reference data. A multidimensional point cloud is an unstructured array of single, irregular points in a spatial 3D coordinate system plus time stamp. If geospatial reference points are available, a point cloud is geo-referenced. Geo-referenced point clouds contain a high-precision reference dataset. Point clouds can be utilised in a variety of applications. They are particularly suitable for the representation of surfaces, structures, terrain and objects. Point clouds are used here to generate a virtual 3D city model representing the complex, granular cityscape of Jerusalem and its centre, the Old City. The generation of point clouds is based on two data acquisition methods: active data capture by laser scanning and passive data collection by photogrammetric methods. In our case, very high-resolution stereo imagery in visible light and near infrared bands have been systematically acquired an aerial flight campaign. The spatio-temporal data gathered necessitate further processing to extract the geographical reference and semantic features required in a specific resolution and scale. An insight is given into the processing of an unstructured point cloud to extract and classify the 3D urban fabric and reconstruct its objects. Eventually, customised, precise and up-to-date geographical datasets can be made available for a defined region at a defined resolution and scale.

Keywords: Point cloud · Object reconstruction · Data acquisition

1 Introduction

It is a fundamental human need to appropriate one's immediate environment. A prerequisite to do so is positioning and orientation in space. The term space here refers both to physical reality and to virtual, i.e. modelled and generalised spaces, which either depict abstracted reality or create an artificial cyberspace. Orientation and positioning as well as direction and movement in space requires data gathered in one's environment to establish a spatial reference. Such data can, e.g., be landmarks, stars and physical or temporal distance measurements between them and one's position. It is obvious that in addition to the classical

© Springer Nature Switzerland AG 2020
O. Gervasi et al. (Eds.): ICCSA 2020, LNCS 12252, pp. 448–462, 2020.
https://doi.org/10.1007/978-3-030-58811-3_33

spatial reference, time reference of geospatial data is equally important. This applies not only to everyday applications but also to scientific work in modern geographic information science [11]. Spatial data with explicit temporal reference are therefore referred to as spatio-temporal data. Without exception, geographic data have one or more temporal reference. This can, e.g., either be the acquisition, storage or processing time. Because of these different time stamps, the temporal validity of geospatial data can be assessed. Focusing on the acquisition date, the majority of geodata are considered static and are processed accordingly. This contrasts markedly with the constant dynamics of our natural environment. Hence the need to update geographical data has to be considered when it comes to processing the data for a topical or near real-time application [4,5].

Today, establishing a valid spatio-temporal reference is no longer a specialis's task. Anyone using a mobile device, such as a smartphone or GPS watch, is able to acquire geodata in the form of, e.g., a geocoded photo or GNSS track. Open-source geo databases like OpenStreetMap (OSM) database are compiled and updated by using such crowd-sourced geodata largely collected by volunteers with their smartphones. Thanks to systems like OSM geodata of good to sufficient quality are now globally available. However their regional coverage, scale, precision and topicality varies considerably according to the numbers and efforts of the data acquisition volunteers. Official geodata can compensate that disadvantage only to a certain degree due to access restrictions, the geopolitical environment or outdated data. As a consequence, it remains inevitable to collect up-to-date geodata of a specific area for specific application purposes. Starting from the 1960s, the method of choice for the acquisition of precise, scalable geodata for global, regional and local area coverages is remote sensing from aircraft, satellite and, lately, drone platforms. A variety of sensor technologies is employed for data capture, staring from high resolution aerial survey cameras to multi-spectral sensors, radar and lidar sensors. The spatio-temporal data gathered by any of these systems necessitate further processing to extract the geographical reference and semantic features required in a specific resolution and scale [14]. Eventually, customised, precise and up-to-date geographical datasets can be made available for a defined region at a defined resolution (and scale).

This article presents an innovative approach to construct spatially-referenced, multidimensional virtual city models from photogrammetrically generated point clouds for areas that lack reliable geographical reference data. Here we focus on the processing of the unstructured point cloud to extract and classify the urban fabric and its objects. The work presented here is part of a wider international R+D project on a 3D geovirtual decision support system for community development in East Jerusalem.

2   Use Case: The Complex Cityscape of Jerusalem

The centre of the urban agglomeration of Jerusalem is the ancient, walled Old City. Prototypical of an Oriental City, the East Jerusalem cityscape is characterised by a complex, granular buildup of houses of various dimensions and heights and an irregular network of streets, paths and lanes (see Fig. 2). Buildings usually house multiple functions, e.g. commercial and residential use. The 3D image depicting part of the Old City represents a very high resolution point cloud providing a pseudo-realistic visualisation of the area (see Fig. 1).

2.1 Lacking Geospatial Database Due to Complex Geopolitical Situation

The agglomeration of Jerusalem, and East Jerusalem in particular, is an area where precise and reliable geotopographic data are not easily available or accessible, respectively. This is a result of an ongoing complex geopolitical situation in which Israel has annexed East Jerusalem to its territory contrary to international law. Crowd-sourced geodata, such as the OSM database, cannot compensate for the lack of official survey data, since the OSM system does not enforce a strict, authoritative geometric and semantic quality control of the data largely gathered by non-specialist volunteers [4,5]. In addition, the cityscape of Jerusalem is exposed to very high dynamics in the built-up area and infrastructure development. As a consequence, taking account of all relevant circumstances, a realistic, practicable way to access and process high-resolution, up-to-date geodata of East Jerusalem is the acquisition by an airborne multi-spectral digital camera system [15]. The data stock used in the project presented here has been collected in autumn 2019.

2.2 Applications

The geospatial data stock forms a uniform, topical high-resolution basis to construct a virtual 3D city model of East Jerusalem dedicated to the web-based use by the civil society and its institutions in the area. The virtual city model will come with easy-to-use GIS functionalities, facilitating a range of spatio-temporal applications, such as information and documentation, urban land use and land management, education and health infrastructure, technical infrastructure, tourism, planning purposes and decision making.

3 Approach

This paper deals with a novel approach to construct a geo-referenced virtual city model of East Jerusalem from unorganised, unstructured point clouds. As we deal with a granular cityscape, a particular focus is on the classification and extraction of building models [6,7,10]. The novelty of our approach is the fact that we adapt the processing of invariant point data in terms of spatio-temporal reference to the construction of multidimensional city models. In that way, a generic processing (and acquisition) technique is made available for the construction of both geospatial cityscapes and landscapes in areas where no reliable reference data are available. During the construction process, an elastic grid is generated by means of voxels in different levels of resolution and hierarchy,

Fig. 1. Old City of East Jerusalem: overview, point cloud representation

which represents and maps the point cloud [2,17]. Applying established methods of computer graphics, object surfaces are then projected and constructed using iterative resampling methods [1,13]. Particular attention is paid to the point consolidation process, with respect to uniform point distribution as well sufficient sampling density at minimum distance from point to voxel. In addition, the requirements point clouds need to comply with in order to perform the process in multidimensional point clouds, are checked during pre-processing [16]. The solution approach outlined above is developed within the scope of a wider R+D effort that deals with the with the creation, (re-)construction, administration and maintenance of virtual 3D city models in constantly changing urban environments [4,5]. An essential prerequisite for this work is the volume and quality of the geospatial source data. The more precise the source data record or map geographical reality, i.e. spatio-temporal object features or geometric and multi-spectral resolution, the higher the degree of the pseudo-realistic visualisation of the resulting city model can be [12].

3.1 Point Clouds as a Comprehensive Basic Data Set

To date, remotely sensed point clouds can best meet the above requirements. Point clouds can also easily capture the spatio-temporal dynamics typical of urban environments. Point clouds easily map 3D surfaces and objects by a densely spaced sequence of points storing the detected geometry of objects and surfaces point-wise. Thus the totality of points, the point cloud, is a versatile geospatial data representation of complex terrestrial surfaces, such as cityscapes [12]. Because of their geometric nature, point clouds are particularly well-suited for the derivation and subsequent visualisation of geospatial phenomena and artefacts. Other than classical vector and raster data, point clouds facilitate the extraction of a regional, spatially invariant, geometric base structure [3,14].

Fig. 2. Old City of East Jerusalem: spatial structures, point cloud representation

Any processing of point cloud data requires to solve a twofold problem: How can addressable objects from any kind of geodata be connected in a meaningful way, and how can these objects be analysed for their potential added value? Solving these R+D issues is considered a major challenge in the interdisciplinary field of spatial sciences [7, 11]. Based on the lowest common denominator, the space-time reference, two possible solutions can be identified to model high to very-high resolution 3D geo-objects: schematisation and reconstruction.

Schematisation. This research field deals with the procedures required to schematise available geodata. To link existing data with or without a spatial reference a scheme is essential to do this in a meaningful way. A common scheme is therefore mandatory to facilitate successful harmonisation and fusion of data [14]. Schematisation of different input data is hampered by the data reference which is both spatial and semantic. When source data have different spatial as well as semantic references, which generally is the case, schematisation may result in a loss of reference accuracy. In addition, data schematisation, like, e.g., interpolation, is a one-way process. As a result, the original source data are irreversibly altered. This is compensated by the fact that geospatial data different sources can successfully be processed jointly and stored in uniform datasets. Today, structured schematisation, harmonisation and integration of different data forms and formats is implemented in the quasi-standard Feature Manipulation Engine (FME) or in the INSPIRE Guidelines of the EU. In contrast, schematisation of references is a somewhat disregarded R+D field as it directly affects the accuracy of geodata.

Reconstruction. This research field investigates the use of computational engineering methods to approximate an artefact or semantics by constructing both virtually. Hence, an artificial reconstruction of the original data is carried out without directly manipulating them, thus creating new data while leaving the source data unaltered. This is the rationale behind machine learning and artificial intelligence in general. Although both schematisation and reconstruction are roughly based on the same principle, they differ in their handling of source data. This is apparent when it comes to the application of 3D building models which have massively increased in importance far beyond simple visualisations in times of so-called digital twins [5]. One driving factor behind this development is the rapidly growing availability of high-resolution input data. What is lacking, however, is an executable generic process applicable to all current domains and solutions. For the time being, only domain-specific approaches can be found. Consequently, the level of abstraction is currently limited to the domain and therefore increasingly schematised.

3.2 Acquisition of Uniform Geodata Base

It has been pointed out that the availability and quality of source data is an essential prerequisite for the construction of a virtual 3D city model of the Jerusalem agglomeration. The ideal database would be a uniform data with identical spatial resolution and parametrisation that covers the entire study area [5]. As has been mentioned, such spatio-temporal data are not readily available, neither from topical official survey data nor from crowd-sourced OSM data or other regional data pools. There is also a lack of high-resolution regional reference data. To generate a uniform high-resolution geo database as the single source used throughout the R+D project, an aerial flight campaign was commissioned to systematically acquire very high-resolution stereo imagery in visible light and near infrared bands. Figure 3 illustrates the flight campaign of September 2019 with flight strips and study area. In the area where flight strips are orthogonally overlaid the Old City of Jerusalem can be found. It goes without saying that the acquired database bears a time stamp of the collection time. All of its data represent the real-world status at the time of acquisition. This is important to note, since cityscapes such as Jerusalem are subjected to permanent spatial change over time. However, such urban dynamics are not mirrored in the available static data pool [7]. The time stamp attached to the geo-objects captured serves as an independent, invariant variable specific to each object. Each new recording of the same object at a particular time comes with a new time stamp making it possible to distinguish the same object over different points in time and trace its spatio-temporal development. The following time is relevant to geospatial databases: Real time refers to a fully synchronised digital replica of present reality with events, people, places and spatial processes, future time relates to modelling, simulation or projection of future spatial scenarios, and past time is used for the documentation and interpretation of historical events, places and processes. To keep an acquired geospatial database up-to-date and usable over time, updating of the data either at defined points in time or permanently is essential.

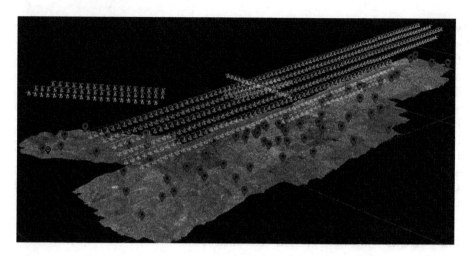

Fig. 3. Overview of flight campaigns and study area East Jerusalem; source Bentley ContextCapture (v15)

4   Generation of Geo-Referenced Point Clouds

Characteristics. A multidimensional point cloud is a 3D or 4D data set of a single, irregular and unstructured point array in a spatial 3D coordinate system defined by x, y, z coordinates and the time component [16]. The result is a registered point cloud. If reference points are available, a point cloud is geo-referenced. Assuming a spatial reference, point clouds contain an high-precision reference dataset, since every single point has a very high position accuracy and fidelity compared with classical vector and raster spatial models. Therefore, referenced point clouds are often used for secondary referencing of other geodata. Point clouds can be employed in a variety of applications. They are particularly suitable for the representation of surfaces, structures, terrain and objects [15]. Point clouds are used for documentation purposes or further processing in, e.g., CAD, BIM or in 3D rendering software for 3D modelling or 3D visualisation [12].

Generation. The generation of primary point clouds is based on two data acquisition methods: Active data capture by laser scanning and passive data collection by photogrammetric methods [10]. 3D laser scanning is based on the principle of beam tracing or distance measurement using a laser beam. The scanner emits laser pulses at extremely short intervals. The pulsed photons have a high energy. They are reflected by the objects targeted, and the returned beams are detected again in the transmitter. Based on the speed of light, from the transit time measurement the object distance can be calculated. Similarly, the spatial coordinates of a targeted point, relative to the scanner position, can easily be calculated, since horizontal and elevation angles are implicitly measured. Photogrammetric point clouds, in contrast, are based on the image-based evaluation of co-existing object-image points in at least two different image data. Their accuracy depends on the inner orientation (camera calibration) and outer orientation (camera orientation), as well on as potential reference points. Corresponding image points are mathematically mapped using a bundle block adjustment. This method to calculate 3D points is known as stereo-photogrammetric processing. It allows to calculate all unknown parameters of the collinearity equations. In addition, an near-reality colour value can be extracted by means of photogrammetric processing. Active laser scanning allow the registration of one coded colour value only per point [16].

4.1 Data Acquisition, Database

Implementing the approach detailed above, aerial imagery obtained from a flight campaign is evaluated photogrammetrically to generate a point cloud for the study area of East Jerusalem. A total of 571 RGBI (red, green, blue, near infrared) nadir aerial images are available acquired in two flight campaigns of 23.09.2019 with a ground resolution of (minimum) 10 cm GSD, taken with a camera system of the Z/I DMC 250 II e type (see Fig. 3). The first campaign covers the entire investigation area of East Jerusalem with 525 images (forward overlap 80%, side overlap 60%). The imagery covers an area of nearly 190 km^2, corresponding to a data volume of almost 135 gigapixels. The second campaign covers the Old City of Jerusalem only with 46 images (forward overlap 80%, side overlap 80%) encompassing an area of nearly 13.5 square kilometres, which corresponds to a data volume of almost 11 gigapixels. This campaign is located within the area covered by the first Campaign. Corresponding pixels have been recorded in at least 10 different aerial images in the entire study area, with exceptions in the peripheral areas. In the area of the Old City, corresponding pixels are present in at least 30 different images due to the overlay of the flight campaigns. A total of 70 ground reference points (differential GPS), equally distributed across the study area, are available for geo-reference. All aerial images are referenced by GPS and INS. Bentley's ContextCapture (v14) software system is used to perform referencing of the input imagery as well as of 69 out of 70 ground points, and is also employed for bundle block adjustment (see Fig. 3). Essential parameters are the collinearity equations at pixel level and to maximally increase the quality of matching. The processing is performed on a mini-cluster consisting of two identical workstations. An AMD Ryzen 9 3900X 12-core processor, 64 GB, NVMe memory and NVIDIA GeForce RTX 2080Ti are used for the calculation. The mini-cluster allows, among other things, parallel computation and simultaneous use of several graphics cards. It shows that a very consistent dataset or bundle block is provided, since the global error with ground reference points is about half a pixel; the median is even slightly below. Turning to the point clouds generated, it can be seen that these cover massive volume of data and, with more than 100 points per square meter, represent the full pixel density of the source data. Note that this number refers to a 2D reference surface only. However, it includes all points of the surface, i.e. the 3D points, too. also. The theoretical maximum for photogrammetric processing in the reference plane X & Y is 100 points per square meter (image data 10 cm GSD), or 91 points in the computed block.

4.2   Structuring of Point Clouds

Within the framework described above, 3D respectively 4D point clouds are photogrammetrically generated in the pre-processing. Subsequently, the data space is subdivided by hierarchical methods, such as octree or n-tree. Octree, for example, defines a hierarchy that can be used to inspect large point clouds and interact with them with high performance [12,14]. An octree is a data structure for indexing three-dimensional data. It extends the concept of binary trees and quadtrees, which structure 1D or 2D data. Each node of an octree represents a volume as a cuboid. Furthermore, these cubes are often aligned with axes of the coordinate system. Each octree node has up to eight subnodes. If a node has no subnodes, the corresponding cube can be represented uniformly and no further subdivision is necessary. Each node of the spatial system with associated subnodes is characterised by the presence or absence of points. In the representation of volumetric data, such as building objects, a further subdivision of a node is not necessary if the mapped volume is completely uniform and a reference plane is known. Nodes that have points will become part of a spatially adaptive, elastic hierarchical voxel grid in the further process. Elasticity includes the possibility to use different resolutions in a grid in an advantageous way.

Volume graphics is a different method of modeling as a voxel data set [1]. Here a value is recorded at a single point from the object at regular intervals. The result is a cube-shaped 3D grid of voxels. These voxel models can easily be converted into images, which, depending on the minimum resolution, can be extremely pseudo-realistic and detailed [2]. This type of modelling requires significantly higher resources in direct comparison to triangle-based polygonal meshes and has a performance loss in visualisation compared to a polygonal surface model of similar size. In addition, the manipulation of these data is much more complex [1]. The ultimale goal of all algorithms briefly touched on here is to model 3D objects. This is usually done, even on the most modern graphics hardware, by means of simple triangular structures, which in mass reproduce and represent complex polygonal surfaces [13]. Also, despite the inclusion of complex 3D textures in the volume graphics, the hardware acceleration is still focused on triangle computation. Hence a combination of both approaches proves to be expedient, as the example of the Marching Cubes algorithm from 1987 in imaging medicine proves [9]. For the first time it was possible to approximate inefficient volume models by efficient polygonal surface models, to visualise them effectively and to combine the advantages of both approaches [2].

4.3   Generation of Urban 3D Objects Using the Marching Cube Algorithm

The core idea of Marching Cubes is to decompose a given voxel model of an object into small cubes and then march from one cube to the next and determine how the surface of the object intersects the respective cube [9]. A selected threshold value regulates which parts of the relevant cube lie inside or outside the object. The distinction between solid and transparent is fundamental to the procedure. It affects the normal calculation of the surface, since the slope of the scalar field at each voxel point is also the normal vector of a hypothetical iso surface running from that point. There are 256 possibilities of how an arbitrarily shaped surface can divide a voxel into interior and exterior areas, as, based on combinatorics, there are 2 to the power of 8 possibilities to divide the eight corners of a voxel into two disjoint sets inside and outside [9]. Due to symmetry effects, however, the number is reduced to only 15 different variants. The so-called Triangle Lookup Table contains all these possibilities. The runtime of the classical marching cube algorithm depends significantly on the number of voxels considered. An optimisation is based on the hierarchical investigation beforehand, as described, to use only voxels as input that contain points and thus represent an object [8,17].

It emerges that the Marching Cube algorithm represents an effective technique for the calculation of iso-surface and object modelling in 3D [17]. Consequently, a combination of volume graphics and triangle-based polygonal meshes based on a well-established algorithm can be used to approximate and reconstruct the surface and thus the hull of an object [8]. Finally, this geometry requires to be characterised and extracted as an object in order to enrich it with spatially referenced semantics for use in a spatial information system of the entire study area.

The essential work steps in this context include a meaningful subdivision of a point cloud [16]. This has to be manageable for algorithms working on it. The subdivision can be based on either the data structure, as described, using a hierarchical tree structure, or with spatial or structural filtering within the process. Similar to a segmentation, this reduction represents an adjustment factor, since an object can occur in several areas, nodes or tiles [14]. An overlapping of areas to be processed also needs to be considered so that no break between regions occurs. Similarly, it has to be made sure that an object has identical characteristics across regions. In other words, voxels or horizontal slices of a point cloud, as familiar from imaging medicine, are fed into an algorithm [2]. The algorithm reconstructs an object from them bit by bit, as one would do with, say, with a finite number of small Lego bricks. Depending on the resolution, i.e. how high the layers and the voxel are, an object image, for example of a building, is gradually created. If the process is repeated and parameters of resolution are changed, there is also an incremental approach that can model an object in its entirety or in a spatio-temporal manner. This results is a volume model of an object as well as a polygonal triangular model that can be stored in a database. Depending on the process, different levels of detail are conceivable for one and the same object.

Fig. 4. Point cloud (point spacing 30 30 cm)

Fig. 5. Point cloud (point spacing 50 50 cm)

5   Implementation Issues

In a nutshell, the methodological concept of this approach addresses the research question of how accurately and precisely multidimensional virtual spatial models correspond to the complex reality they present. It challenges the widespread approach to different virtual models by different levels of detail (LOD) [14]. Since the availability of high-resolution output data such as point clouds has increased significantly, it can be assumed that the concept of static LOD degrees is less appropriate to represent very-high resolution complex objects. In addition, discretisation of the source data is always applied when preparing a LOD inventory. It is important to consider the geometric tolerances of existing LODs with regard to quality assurance. In this context, discretisation of the source data to known LODs is possibile but not mandatory. Even without discretisation, the full data depth available can be utilised. The above issues need further analysis and evaluation. Tests have shown that the approach outlined here includes some open issues that need to be addressed. Figure 6 shows derived and extracted two-dimensional rings generated with a provisional version of the layer algorithm. It is important to note that this layer is based on the terrain's reference plane only. In the area of each outline, mean heights for the individual object areas can be derived from the point cloud and added to the data as a semantic feature. As shown in Fig. 7, the result is a 2.5 D data set containing extruded building outlines, which can be semantically augmented with further attributes. Both Figs. 6 and 7 show the current status quo of point cloud processing.

Another issue to be addressed when implementing the algorithm is the reduction of objects to two dimensions. Without exact segmentation and classification of a 2D slice of a point cloud's reference plane, it is sometimes problematic to derive the exact extent and position of an outline generated [6]. This may result in a wrong rotation or over-extraction of an object. A point cloud can also have

Fig. 6. 2D building outlines from point clouds

Fig. 7. Extruded building outlines in 2.5D

a too high resolution for an algorithm (see Figs. 2 and 1). Likewise, photogrammetric point clouds of building facade elements may contain few or no points due to missing corresponding pixels. Contrary to that, the Marching Cube algorithm requires a consistent database. Hence, no values can be generated where no values are available. At this point, one option is the reconstruction of buildings by means of voxels. Buildings usually have a cubic or cuboid shape, hence it can be assumed that facades can be reconstructed in a simple geometric way (see Fig. 5). In contrast, if an object is represented in a point cloud of a very high resolution, and this resolution is not required to represent this object distinctly, resources are wasted (see in contrast Figs. 1 and 5). It is therefore a matter of the correct dimension and an incremental and interactive approach to extract the most realistic object from the point cloud. Potential applications are, for example, the analysis of the deviation between vector, raster and point cloud representations that map a building object. Differences can reveal geometric accuracies between the different representations, but also show structural changes. Typically, objects are analysed by algorithms, especially in machine learning, with the help of similarities, and are successively derived and constructed. Consequently, a building model is broken down into its components (i.e. walls and roof) and then, by means of trained similarities, it is determined which part of the object is to be represented and how [3,6,10]. This requires a substantial number of potential object components that can be compared to automatically derive the required object component. Overall, the mathematical morphology of point clouds is highly suitable to be processed in this context, since the most versatile objects from a comprehensive, invariant 4D data set are available in a complete and simple form. With machine learning methods, as with the marching cube algorithm, considerable added value can be gained from geodata with an ever-present link to the original data.

6   Conclusion

This article presents an innovative approach to construct spatially referenced multidimensional virtual city models from photogrammetric point clouds for areas where no reliable geographic reference data are available. The work presented here is part of a larger international R+D project that investigates the generation, (re-)construction, management and maintenance of virtual 3D city models in a constantly changing urban environment. To date, the project work carried out has shown that the generation and processing of point clouds can provide quality geodata to create and maintain a uniform, fully referenced 3D geodata base in a limited period of time, if not on an ad-hoc basis. In the study area of East Jerusalem, the lack of precise, up-to-data geospatial data necessitates the airborne acquisition of geospatial point data conforming to the key requirements of resolution, data quality and topicality. The resulting high-resolution point cloud can be used for a variety of applications. One relevant usage is the extraction of virtual building models from high-resolution point clouds. The use of point clouds is of crucial importance in East Jerusalem, where no primary data source is able to provide geospatial data representing the complex urban reality and its spatio-temporal dynamics. Because of their purely geometric content, point clouds are especially suitable for the derivation and visualisation of geospatial phenomena and artefacts. To extract building models from point clouds, a procedure originating from the field of imaging medicine is adapted, allowing for the modelling of 3D objects in (very) high resolution. Drawing on methods of volume graphics (voxel grids) and classical computer graphics (polygonal triangular meshes), this novel approach facilitates the effective processing of point clouds. In that context, the structuring of the source data is given special attention. Preliminary applications of the approach discussed here prove that extruded building outlines can successfully be extracted and visualised.

Acknowledgements. The work discussed here is part of a larger R+D project on East Jerusalem with Palestinian, East Jerusalem, and NGO partners funded by the European Union. Part of this research work is supported by a PhD grant from the HPI Research School for Service-Oriented Systems Engineering at the Hasso Plattner Institute for Digital Engineering, University of Potsdam. The funding of both institutions is gratefully acknowledged.

References

1. Akenine-Möller, T., Haines, E., Hoffman, N.: Real-Time Rendering. CRC Press, Boca Raton (2019)
2. Ashburner, J., Friston, K.J.: Why voxel-based morphometry should be used. Neuroimage **14**(6), 1238–1243 (2001)
3. Brenner, C.: Building reconstruction from images and laser scanning. Int. J. Appl. Earth Obs. Geoinf. **6**(3–4), 187–198 (2005)
4. Fricke, A., Döllner, J., Asche, H.: Servicification – trend or paradigm shift in geospatial data processing? In: Gervasi, O., et al. (eds.) ICCSA 2018. LNCS, vol. 10962, pp. 339–350. Springer, Cham (2018). https://doi.org/10.1007/978-3-319-95168-3_23
5. Fricke, A., Asche, H.: Geospatial database for the generation of multidimensional virtual city models dedicated to urban analysis and decision-making. In: Misra, S., et al. (eds.) ICCSA 2019. LNCS, vol. 11621, pp. 711–726. Springer, Cham (2019). https://doi.org/10.1007/978-3-030-24302-9_52
6. Haala, N., Kada, M.: An update on automatic 3D building reconstruction. ISPRS J. Photogrammetry Remote Sens. **65**(6), 570–580 (2010)
7. Hall, T., Barrett, H.: Urban Geography. Routledge, Abingdon (2018)
8. Huang, M., Wei, P., Liu, X.: An efficient encoding voxel-based segmentation (EVBS) algorithm based on fast adjacent voxel search for point cloud plane segmentation. Remote Sens. **11**(23), 2727 (2019)
9. Lorensen, W.E., Cline, H.E.: Marching cubes: a high resolution 3D surface construction algorithm. ACM Siggraph Comput. Graph. **21**(4), 163–169 (1987)
10. Mayer, H.: Object extraction in photogrammetric computer vision. ISPRS J. Photogrammetry Remote Sens. **63**(2), 213–222 (2008)
11. Seymenov, K.: Climate elasticity of annual streamflow in Northwest Bulgaria. In: Nedkov, S., et al. (eds.) Smart Geography. KCG, pp. 105–115. Springer, Cham (2020). https://doi.org/10.1007/978-3-030-28191-5_9

12. Richter, R., Discher, S., Döllner, J.: Out-of-ccore visualization of classified 3D point clouds. In: Breunig, M., Al-Doori, M., Butwilowski, E., Kuper, P., Benner, J., Haefele, K. (eds.) 3D Geoinformation Science. LNGC, pp. 227–242. Springer, Cham (2015). https://doi.org/10.1007/978-3-319-12181-9_14
13. Szeliski, R.: Computer Vision: Algorithms and Applications. Springer, London (2010). https://doi.org/10.1007/978-1-84882-935-0
14. Tolpekin, V., Stein, A.: The Core of GIScience: A Process-Based Approach. University of Twente, Faculty of Geo-Information Science and Earth Observation (ITC) (2012)
15. Vosselman, G., Dijkman, S.: 3D building model reconstruction from point clouds and ground plans. Int. Arch. Photogrammetry Remote Sens. Spat. Inf. Sci. **34**(3/W4), 37–44 (2001)
16. Weinmann, M.: Preliminaries of 3D point cloud processing. In: Reconstruction and Analysis of 3D Scenes, pp. 17–38. Springer, Cham (2016). https://doi.org/10.1007/978-3-319-29246-5_2
17. Zhou, Y., Tuzel, O.: Voxelnet: end-to-end learning for point cloud based 3d object detection. In: Proceedings of the IEEE Conference on Computer Vision and Pattern Recognition, pp. 4490–4499 (2018)

Seismic Assessment of Reinforced Concrete Frames: Influence of Shear-Flexure Interaction and Rebar Corrosion

Alessandro Rasulo[1(✉)] ⓘ, Angelo Pelle[2] ⓘ, Davide Lavorato[2] ⓘ,
Gabriele Fiorentino[2] ⓘ, Camillo Nuti[2] ⓘ, and Bruno Briseghella[3] ⓘ

[1] Department of Civil and Mechanical Engineering, University of Cassino
and Southern Lazio, 03043 Cassino, FR, Italy
alessandro.rasulo@unicas.it
[2] Department of Architecture, Roma Tre University, Largo G. B. Marzi 10,
00153 Rome, Italy
{angelo.pelle,davide.lavorato,gabriele.fiorentino,
camillo.nuti}@uniroma3.it
[3] College of Civil Engineering, Fuzhou University, Fuzhou 350108, China
bruno@fzu.edu.cn

Abstract. The stock of existing buildings across most of the European earthquake-prone countries has been built before the enforcement of modern seismic design codes. In order to assure uniform levels of safety and reduce the social and economic impact of medium to high earthquakes costly seismic intervention plans have been proposed. But their application, in order to define which building should primarily be retrofitted, requires adequate vulnerability assessment methodologies, able to model the effective non-linear response and to identify the relevant failure modes of the structure. In the case of reinforced concrete (RC) buildings, due to the lack of application of capacity design principles and the aging effects due to exposition to an aggressive environment, existing structures can exhibit premature failures with a reduction of available strength and ductility. In the last couple of decades some state-of-the-art simplified models aiming at capturing the complex interaction between shear and flexural damage mechanisms as well as behavior of rebar corrosion have been proposed in specialized literature and, in some cases, implemented in regulatory building codes and guidelines. The present paper presents how those phenomena that have a significant impact in reducing the element capacity in term of strength and energy dissipation can be implemented in the assessment of the structures.

Keywords: Earthquake engineering · Seismic assessment · Reinforced concrete · Shear-flexure collapse · Rebar corrosion

© Springer Nature Switzerland AG 2020
O. Gervasi et al. (Eds.): ICCSA 2020, LNCS 12252, pp. 463–478, 2020.
https://doi.org/10.1007/978-3-030-58811-3_34

1 Introduction

The seismic vulnerability of the existing building stock in Italy and in most of the others earthquake-prone European countries is a topic of serious economic and social concern [5, 32, 35]. The need for the adoption of a systematic retrofitting or rebuilding intervention scheme grows as time progresses and existing structures become older and degrade further [9–11].

Existing buildings have been conceived when many sites were not classified as seismically prone and therefore neglecting in the design process the seismic action at all; even if the site was recognized as subject to earthquakes, the level of seismic demand was much lower than the one currently adopted [27, 28, 33, 34].

Furthermore the design standards enforced at the time of their construction relied on the admissible stress method, and, therefore, the resulting structures where designed to respond in the elastic range, leaving a false sense of security that the actual resistances (well beyond the nominal ones considered in the design process) would be assured by the adopted safety coefficients and by the inelastic behavior of materials and structures. On the contrary, the lack of a hierarchy of strengths that would be lately assured by the implementation, in modern codes, of capacity design principles, would not prevent the occurrence of non-ductile failure modes reducing the extent of the inelastic response.

Finally, many existing buildings are affected by significant structural degradation which leads to a decrease in their performance, especially in terms of safety requirements. This is either due to the neglecting during their conception of durability features or the premature natural decay of mechanical characteristics of materials and elements. One of the most dominant deterioration mechanisms of reinforced concrete structures is corrosion of reinforcement.

The situation of Italy is emblematic: less than 23% of buildings have been built after 1980 (when a major revision of the seismic code was implemented as a consequence of the Irpinia earthquake), but this case is absolutely not isolated across Europe as shown in a recent survey of building seismic exposure [29].

2 Objectives and Methods

The present study aims at contributing to the modeling capability of reinforced concrete (RC) frame elements under seismic loading. To pursue this objective, a comprehensive models has been developed, considering the most relevant damage modes affecting the response of existing RC frame elements.

After an examination of the general characteristics of the Italian building stock, the research has focused on the older RC structures designed and constructed between 1950–1960. The scope is modeling the seismic response of significant elements and sub-assemblages, considering the presence of corroded reinforcements.

During hydration of cement, an alkaline pore solution (pH up to 13.5) is obtained and in such environment a protective oxide film is formed spontaneously around the steel rebars embedded in RC elements. Passive film prevents damage of steel surface from corrosion phenomena, however, carbon dioxide or the presence of chloride ions on the steel surface could destroy the protective oxide film so that corrosion could initiate.

Carbon dioxide produces the carbonation of cover concrete and it generally takes place on whole surface of steel resulting in a uniform corrosion, instead when the aggressive ions exceeds a critical threshold value, the protective passive layer on the rebar surface breaks down initiating the corrosion process giving as a result a localize corrosion, indicated as pitting corrosion. The later phenomenon is more relevant than the first one.

Those ions are generally present in the environment and are capable to reach the interior of the concrete element thanks to different penetration mechanisms, such as diffusion, capillary suction, permeation, migration or a combination of those mechanisms. Hence, the capability of a concrete to prevent or make negligible corrosion phenomena is due to concrete cover which represents a sound protection for the reinforcement acting like a physical barrier that prevents the chemicals (chloride ions, carbon dioxide, etc.) from reaching the reinforcement, but also, as already said, thanks to the natural alkalinity of the concrete that helps forming a passive film on the steel surface, thus chemically protecting the embedded bar against corrosion.

Since the corrosion products formed at the steel/concrete interface have a mass density lower than steel, a volume expansion is obtained associated to tensile stresses and the cracking of the concrete cover, thus favoring further the ingress of the aggressive agent from outer environment [1].

The corrosion process is associated to the formation of different damage in structural elements, such as the loss of cross-sectional area of the reinforcing bars, the reduction of bond between bars and surrounding concrete and the crack propagation into the cover ultimately producing spalling and delamination of the concrete protective layer.

Particular emphasis in the development of the model has been given to the study of the shear-flexure interaction, that is deemed a pivotal issue for the assessment of existing buildings. A typical characteristic of existing buildings columns is the presence of low percentage of transversal reinforcement (poorly detailed and highly spaced stirrups).

According to the experimental evidence, structures with those characteristics, that would be considered substandard according the construction practice adopted today can show essentially two types of failure: a premature buckling of the steel rebars under compression or a premature shear failure, limiting the capacity to undergo inelastic deformation and therefore dissipate energy. Indeed the widening of flexural–shear cracks due to cyclic inelastic deformations, especially in the plastic-hinge region, reduce the ability of concrete to transfer the shear action through mechanisms relying on aggregate interlock. As a consequence there is a sectional shear capacity reduction, showing that under cyclic loading the shear strength of columns can be heavily dependent on the inelastic deformations and that shear strength degrades with ductility more quickly than flexural strength. Thus, it is important, when assessing the seismic response of existing structures to take into consideration in the numerical model the insurgence of those complex interaction phenomena affecting the overall response of the building structures. Instead, with regards to a premature shear failure, several researches and studies on shear strength have evidenced that, even in the case those columns have been initially designed with nominal shear capacity exceeding the shear in equilibrium with flexural yielding, those piers could still fail early in shear due to the detrimental action of inelastic flexural deformations on the shear strength.

Furthermore, one of the most common failure mode of RC elements, observed in existing structures after an earthquake, is due to the buckling of longitudinal reinforcement [16]. Several researchers have investigated this problem analytically through either Euler theory of elastic buckling [2] or FEM modeling [6, 21] as well as experimentally [4, 12, 16, 25, 37].

Essentially, the instability of a longitudinal reinforcement under compression involves in a decrease of stress with an increase of strain (i.e. the post-yielding slope is negative), contrary to what happens in tension. An accurate knowledge of the stress-strain relationship of reinforcing steel is needed to provide the capability to model the inelastic buckling of rebars.

3 The Italian Building Stock

In Italy the general characteristics of the building stock at nationwide level can be obtained by the Census campaigns. The Census is conducted and elaborated by Italian National Institute of Statistics (ISTAT) every ten years to screen important information about the state of population and dwellings [13–15].

The Census data are collected and aggregated at different geographical levels. The basic unit for data collection is the single household and dwelling, but each dwelling is classified as being located within a building, of given characteristics as explained below.

In particular for each census tract is specified the number of buildings, the occupancy type (e.g. residential or not), the state of conservation, the number of stories, the construction year, the main structural typology (Reinforced Concrete or Masonry). A list of available information that are useful for an evaluation of the state of conservation and of the seismic vulnerability of the residential building stock is reported in Table 1. For sake of exemplification in Table 1 the variables have been taken from the 2001 census, but the data structure has been kept essentially the same throughout the subsequent campaigns.

In Table 2 an overview of the whole Italian stock is given: the number of buildings belonging to each age of construction and structural typology class is reported. As shown, many buildings belong to the "before 1919" class (more than 20%). In terms of typology, masonry buildings are the more numerous in absolute value (about 65%), but RC buildings (26% in total) become the prevalent typology in more recent years (starting from the 1981). Buildings belonging to "other" category are much less numerous. In order to protect privacy, the collected data are released by ISTAT only in aggregated format.

The publicly available database is organized for the entire nation adopting as minimum territorial extension the Census tract. A Census tract is a small, relatively permanent statistical geographical subdivision of a territory, designed to be relatively homogeneous with respect to population characteristics, economic status and living conditions. In highly urbanized areas, a census tract generally has the dimensions of a building block. In Fig. 1 is mapped the percentage of structural type at municipality level.

Table 1. Residential building Census variables

Structural typology
Masonry (M)
Reinforced Concrete (RC)
Other
Number of stories
1
2
3
4 or more
Construction time
Before 1919
From 1919 to 1945
From 1946 to 1961
From 1962 to 1971
From 1972 to 1981
From 1982 to 1991
From 1992 to 2001

Table 2. Number of residential buildings in Italy per construction time and structural typology.

Construction time	Masonry	Reinforced concrete	Other
Before 1919	2'026'538	–	123'721
From 1919 to 1945	1'183'869	83'413	116'533
From 1946 to 1961	1'166.107	288'784	204'938
From 1962 to 1971	1'056'383	591'702	319'872
From 1972 to 1981	823'523	789'163	370'520
From 1982 to 1991	418'914	620'698	250'890
From 1992 to 2001	228'648	394'445	167'934
Total	**6'903'982**	**2'768'205**	**1'554'408**

As it is clear from the construction period break-down in Table 1, the Italian building stock has been built mostly after the II World War, during or right after the decade of the so-called 'Italian economic miracle' (from late 50' through early 60') and it is formed by buildings that often show low standards of quality.

The need of a strategic renovation of the built environment represents a crucial issue to assure the safety of population and the resilience of communities, to improve the quality of life and to foster the recovery of the construction sector.

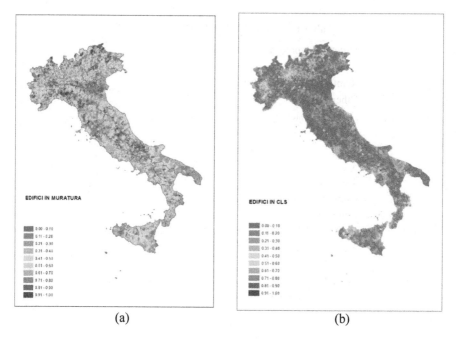

(a)   (b)

Fig. 1. Exposure: percentage of number of buildings for structural type aggregated at municipality level. (a) masonry buildings and (b) RC (reinforced concrete) buildings.

In the last years, the attention of public policies, thanks to the impulse of the European Union, has been driven mainly to the aspects of energy efficiency. However, a significant portion of Italian territory is earthquake-prone, as it has been unfortunately shown by recent events, so that, the possibility to combine energy and seismic retrofitting turns out to be a crucial opportunity.

The classification of the Italian territory in zones, recognized to be seismically prone and where special earthquake-resistant measures have to be adopted when constructing a building, started in 1909, after the devastating earthquake that in 1908 hit the cities of Messina and Reggio Calabria. The subsequent classification of the Italian territory, with the creation of new seismic areas, followed the major seismic events. Generally their occurrence, anticipated the creation of new seismic areas and the enforcement of new seismic regulations. Nowadays, after a revision of seismic zonation based on a site specific probabilistic seismic hazard analysis, the whole Italian country, with just the exception of Sardinia, is considered earthquake prone. Unfortunately, most of the building stock dates to periods when the application of seismic provisions was not mandatory in most of the country.

As a consequence, even the buildings with a structure supported by a RC frame, have been conceived without considering seismic provisions and are affected by important structural defects. In these buildings, designed mainly for gravity loads only, the resisting elements are arranged in just one direction, leaving the structure weak and flexible in the orthogonal direction. Furthermore, the structural codes neglected the basics of the capacity design and proper detailing, producing low ductile elements both at global and at local level, with for instance the potential formation of story collapse mechanisms.

Finally, the situation may be aggravated by the use of low quality or time degradation of materials. Indeed, together with the seismic risk, corrosion is one of the main factors causing deterioration of reinforced concrete buildings.

A periodic monitoring of structural condition would be required to assess the state of advancement of the corrosion phenomena and eventually repair their adverse effects. However, this task is judged too expensive to be conveniently undertaken over a large populations of buildings, distributed over large areas.

4   Numerical Model for the Seismic Assessment

The seismic response of a reinforced concrete frame element can be studied through a numerical model based on a componential approach, in which three main response mechanisms coexists: flexure, shear and bonding. As schematically depicted in Fig. 2, the lateral displacement of a frame column can, indeed, be theoretically seen as the sum of the displacements produced by those three components.

Flexure is by far the most relevant of those mechanisms and it is also the most investigated. The bonding is essentially responsible for the additional displacement due to the slippage of the longitudinal reinforcing bars in the anchoring concrete.

Finally, regarding shear deformation, it is admitted that in slender columns the contribution due to shear is relatively small, compared to flexure, so that in professional practice the shear influence has been generally neglected.

Despite this, shear deformations have a significant effect if the reinforced concrete element experiences damage in shear especially after diagonal cracking.

4.1   Flexural Behavior

The flexural behavior has been modeled with a distributed plasticity approach. In order to analyze the non-linear response of the element cross-section, it has been discretized in fibers, as depicted in Fig. 3.

A reinforced concrete section is essentially composed by:

- Unconfined concrete (in the cover)
- Confined concrete (in the core) and
- Steel reinforcing bar.

Three different kinds of constitutive relationship have been used to model the mechanical behavior of those materials and assigned to relevant fibers within the element sections.

The concrete has been modeled using the Popovics constitutive law [31]. The effect of stirrup lateral confinement on the core concrete has been considered adopting the Mander et al. model [20]. The longitudinal steel reinforcement has been modeled by the Menegotto and Pinto [24] constitutive law.

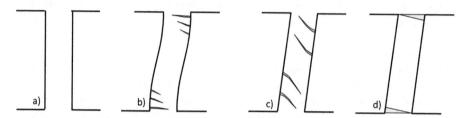

Fig. 2. Components of horizontal displacement. a) original configuration; b) bending deformation; c) shear deformation and d) bonding deformation.

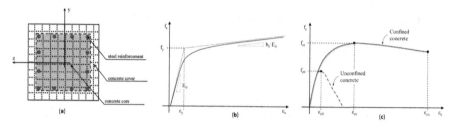

Fig. 3. Properties of a RC section: (a) fiber discretization of the section (y and z are the element local axis); (b) steel reinforcement and (c) cover (unconfined) and core (confined) concrete constitutive law.

The effect of corrosion over the steel rebar has been considered through the reduction of the nominal diameter:

$$D' = D \cdot \sqrt{\left(1 - \frac{m_0 - m}{m_0}\right)} \tag{1}$$

where D' and D are the diameter of the corroded and uncorroded rebar, respectively, m_0 is the mass of the uncorroded rebar and m is the mass of the corroded rebar. The ratio $(m_0 - m)/m_0$ measures the amount of corrosion in terms of mass.

Generally speaking, any mechanical property $X'i$ (i = stress/force/strain) of the corroded rebar in case of pitting corrosion may be calculated by:

$$X'_i = X_i \cdot \left(1 - \beta'_i \cdot \Psi\right) \tag{2}$$

where Xi (i = stress/force/strain) is the mechanical property of the uncorroded rebar and $\beta'i$ is the coefficient which takes into account the pitting corrosion and can be evaluated as in Fig. 4.

A calibration of the coefficient $\beta'i$ can be performed based on experimental data by Meda et al. [23] for i = f_y, f_{max}, f_u, ε_{max} and b. The parameter $\beta'i$ is obtained starting from Eq. 2 for given experimental corrosion percentage, uncorroded and corroded rebar properties i. These values are the red crosses in Fig. 4. Ψ is the corrosion percentage which can be evaluated by:

$$\Psi = 100 \cdot \left(\frac{m_0 - m}{m_0}\right) \tag{3}$$

The experimental effect of corrosion over the behavior of the rebar in tension and in compression is reported in Fig. 5.

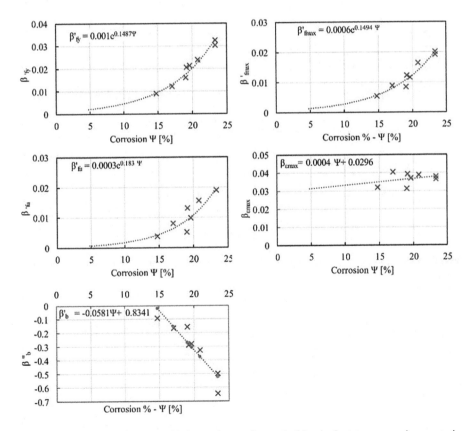

Fig. 4. Calibration of $\beta'i$ for yield f_y, maximum f_{max} and ultimate f_u stresses; maximum strain ε_{max}; hardening ratio b. Red crosses represent the experimental data, whilst the black dot lines the analytical interpolation curves [17].

In compression, buckling behavior can arise when the slenderness of the longitudinal rebar λ is greater that the critical value of the slenderness λ_{cr}, where λ is the slenderness of the longitudinal rebar defined as the ratio between the free length of the longitudinal rebar L and its diameter D, according to the Monti and Nuti constitutive relationship [25, 26] depicted in Fig. 6.

Indeed, regarding the instability of compressed steel rebars, transverse reinforcements is required not only to prevent the shear failure or to provide the confinement of concrete, but should also provide the lateral support to prevent early buckling phenomena in reinforcing steel under compression [30].

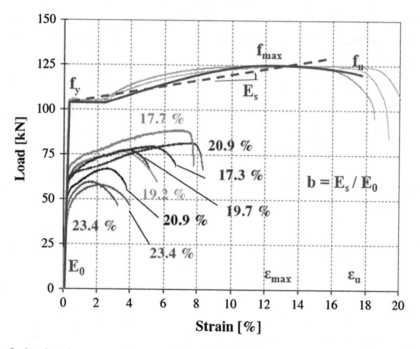

Fig. 5. Load-strain curves for corroded rebars in RC members for different corrosion percentages [18].

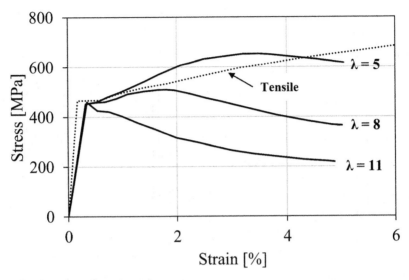

Fig. 6. Monotonic compressive stress-strain response with different slenderness ratio ($\lambda = L/D$ where L is the free length of longitudinal rebar and D is the diameter of longitudinal rebars) [26].

4.2 Slippage Behavior

The slippage of the reinforcing bars will cause rigid-body rotation of the column, that produces an additional source of the deformation, that can be significant, as depicted in Fig. 7 [3, 7, 36]. The slippage has been implemented in the numerical model through a couple of rotational slip springs at the top and bottom of the element with a linear constitutive relationship.

4.3 Shear Behavior

The conceptual model accounting for the flexure-shear coupling follows the formulation codified in the ATC seismic design guidelines. In this model a shear-capacity curve degrades with displacement ductility.

In this study the phenomenological model illustrated in Fig. 8 and 9 has been adopted for modelling the shear spring, accounting for both strength and deformation components due to shear action.

As interaction model the one contained in OpenSEES (named Limited State Material) was used [8, 22].

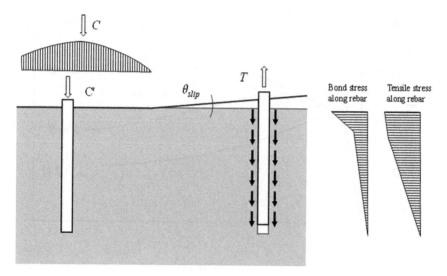

Fig. 7. Slippage model of the rebar. In figure C is the compression acting on the concrete and T is the tension on the steel bar.

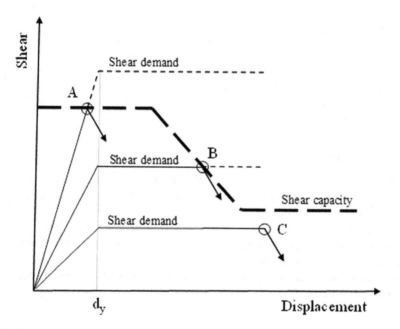

Fig. 8. Conceptual model for shear-strength degradation (dy: yielding displacement). Three cases are considered: (A) shear failure before flexural yielding (pure shear failure); (B) shear failure after flexural yielding (shear-flexural failure); (C) flexural failure.

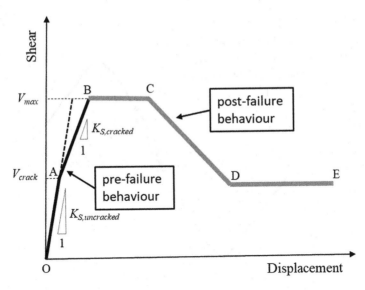

Fig. 9. Phenomenological model for the shear spring.

5 Numerical Validation

Using the model explained in previous chapter, the experimental response of a series of full-scale columns tested by Lynn 2001 [19] was simulated analytically by OpenSEES. The tested columns have a double cantilever configuration (they are fixed at top and bottom edges). The section as square shape of dimensions 457×457 mm^2, the longitudinal steel reinforcement was placed uniformly around the perimeter of the columns and they were #10 as nominal diameter while the transversal reinforcements were hoop with #3 and 457 mm respectively as nominal diameter and spacing (ρ" = 0.001), axial force was equal to P = 503 kN and concrete compressive strength was equal to fc = 26 MPa.

In Fig. 10 the experimental behaviour of the specimen marked as 3CLH18 is shown. The experimental response demonstrates a clear shear strength degradation after the formation of the flexural plastic hinge. The shear failure occurs immediately after flexural yielding. The numerical monotonic (black line) and cyclic (red line) response are investigated and the numerical curves approach well the experimental one, above all the monotonic response.

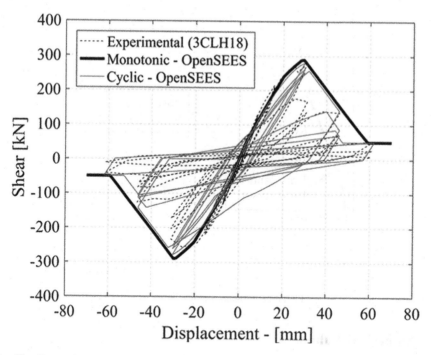

Fig. 10. Comparison of numerical cyclic response with experimental results after the calibration of some parameters.

6 Conclusions

A finite element modelling technique has been presented for the assessment of the seismic performance of ageing reinforced concrete structures, considering the deterioration of longitudinal and shear reinforcement due to corrosion. The effect of corrosion has been taken into account by the using of both corroded diameter and corroded mechanical proprieties, while the shear-flexural interaction phenomena has been introduced, in the FE model, through the incorporation of a zero-length shear spring in series with a flexural column element and a rotational slip spring.

The accuracy of the modelling has been tested on different case studies. Strengths and drift capacities of some column tested cyclically have been compared with the numerical OpenSEES model and a good agreement between the numerical prediction and experimental data can be observed.

References

1. Bertolini, L., Elsener, B., Pedeferri, P., Redaelli, E., Polder, R.: Corrosion of Steel in Concrete, 2nd edn., vol. 392. Wiley-Vch, Weinheim, Germany (2013)
2. Bresler, B., Gilbert, P.H.: Tie requirements for reinforced concrete columns. ACI J. Proc. **58**(11), 555–570 (1961)

3. CEB-FIB: Model Code 2010-Final Draft. The International Federation for Structural Concrete (FIB CEB-FIP), Lausanne, Switzerland (2010)
4. Cosenza, E., Prota, A.: Experimental behaviour and numerical modelling of smooth steel bars under compression. J. Earthquake Eng. **10**(03), 313–329 (2006)
5. Decanini, L., De Sortis, A., Goretti, A., Langenbach, R., Mollaioli, F., Rasulo, A.: Performance of masonry buildings during the 2002 Molise, Italy, earthquake. Earthquake Spectra **20**(S1), 191–220 (2004)
6. Dhakal, R.P., Maekawa, K.: Modeling for postyield buckling of reinforcement. J. Struct. Eng. **128**(9), 1139–1147 (2002)
7. Eligehausen, R., Bertero, V.V., Popov, E.P.: Local bond stress-slip relationships of deformed bars under generalized excitations: tests and analytical model. In: Report No EERC, 83-23, Earthquake Engineering Research Center, University of California: Berkeley, CA, USA (1983)
8. Elwood, K.J., Moehle, J.P.: Drift capacity of reinforced concrete columns with light transverse reinforcement. Earthquake Spectra **21**(1), 71–89 (2005)
9. Grande, E., Imbimbo, M., Rasulo, A.: Experimental response of RC beams strengthened in shear by FRP sheets. Open Civ. Eng. J. **7**, 127–135 (2013)
10. Grande, E., Rasulo, A.: A simple approach for seismic retrofit of low-rise concentric X-braced steel frames. J. Constr. Steel Res. **107**, 162–172 (2015)
11. Grande, E., Rasulo, A.: Seismic assessment of concentric X-braced steel frames. Eng. Struct. **49**, 983–995 (2013)
12. Imperatore, S., Rinaldi, Z.: Experimental behavior and analytical modeling of corroded steel rebars under compression. Constr. Build. Mater. **226**, 126–138 (2019)
13. Istituto Nazionale di Statistica: L'Italia in 150 anni. Sommario di statistiche storiche 1861–2010. Roma (2011)
14. Istituto Nazionale di Statistica (ISTAT): 14° Censimento della popolazione e delle abitazioni 2001, Roma (2005). (in Italian)
15. Istituto Nazionale di Statistica (ISTAT): 15° Censimento della popolazione e delle abitazioni 2011 – Dati definitivi, Roma (2012). (in Italian)
16. Kashani, M.M.: Size effect on inelastic buckling behavior of accelerated pitted corroded bars in porous media. J. Mater. Civ. Eng. **29**(7), 04017022 (2017)
17. Lavorato, D., et al.: A corrosion model for the interpretation of cyclic behavior of reinforced concrete sections. Struct. Concr. (2019). https://doi.org/10.1002/suco.201900232
18. Lavorato, D., Pelle, A., Fiorentino, G., Nuti, C., Rasulo, A.: A nonlinear material model of corroded rebars for seismic response of bridges. In: Papadrakakis, M., Fragiadakis, M. (eds.) 7th ECCOMAS Thematic Conference on Computational Methods in Structural Dynamics and Earthquake Engineering (COMPDYN 2019), pp. 24–26, Crete Island, Greece (2019)
19. Lynn, A.: Seismic Evaluation of Existing Reinforced Concrete Building Column. Ph.D. Thesis, University of California at Berkeley, Berkeley, CA, USA (2001)
20. Mander, J.B., Priestley, M.J., Park, R.: Theoretical stress-strain model for confined concrete. J. Struct. Eng. **114**(8), 1804–1826 (1988)
21. Mau, S.T., El-Mabsout, M.: Inelastic buckling of reinforcing bars. J. Eng. Mech. **115**(1), 1–17 (1989)
22. McKenna, F., Fenves, G.L., Scott, M.H., Jeremic, B.: Open System for Earthquake Engineering Simulation (OpenSEES). University of California, Berkeley, CA, USA (2000)
23. Meda, A., Mostosi, S., Rinaldi, Z., Riva, P.: Experimental evaluation of the corrosion influence on the cyclic behaviour of RC columns. Eng. Struct. **76**, 112–123 (2014)

24. Menegotto, M., Pinto, P.E.: Method of analysis of cyclically loaded RC plane frames including changes in geometry and non-elastic behavior of elements under normal force and bending. In: International Association for Bridge and Structural Engineering, vol. 11, pp. 15–22 (1973)

25. Monti, G., Nuti, C.: Nonlinear cyclic behavior of reinforcing bars including buckling. J. Struct. Eng. **118**(12), 3268–3284 (1992)

26. Monti, G., Nuti, C.: Un modello analitico del comportamento ciclico di barre in acciaio con svergolamento post-elastico. Dipartimento di ingegneria strutturale e geotecnica, Università degli studi di Roma "La Sapienza", Report No. 6 (1991)

27. Nuti, C., Rasulo, A., Vanzi, I.: Seismic safety evaluation of electric power supply at urban level. Earthquake Eng. Struct. Dyn. **36**(2), 245–263 (2007)

28. Nuti, C., Rasulo, A., Vanzi, I.: Seismic safety of network structures and infrastructures. Struct. Infrastruct. Eng. Maintenance Manag. Life-Cycle **6**(1–2), 95–110 (2010)

29. Palermo, V., Tsionis, G., Sousa, M.L.: Building stock inventory to assess seismic vulnerability across Europe, EUR 29257 EN, Publications Office of the European Union, Luxembourg (2018). https://doi.org/10.2760/530683. ISBN 978–92-79-86707-1. PUBSY No 112031

30. Paulay, T., Priestley, M.N.: Seismic Design of Reinforced Concrete and Masonry Buildings, 1st edn. Wiley, Hoboken (1992)

31. Popovics, S.: A numerical approach to the complete stress-strain curve of concrete. Cem. Concr. Res. **3**(5), 583–599 (1973)

32. Rasulo, A., Fortuna, M.A., Borzi, B.: A seismic risk model for Italy. In: Gervasi, O., et al. (eds.) ICCSA 2016. LNCS, vol. 9788, pp. 198–213. Springer, Cham (2016). https://doi.org/10.1007/978-3-319-42111-7_16

33. Rasulo, A., Goretti, A., Nuti, C.: Performance of lifelines during the 2002 Molise, Italy, earthquake. Earthquake Spectra **20**(S1), 301–314 (2004)

34. Rasulo, A., Pelle, A., Lavorato, D., Fiorentino, G., Nuti, C., Briseghella, B.: Finite element analysis of reinforced concrete bridge piers including a flexure-shear interaction model. Appl. Sci. **10**(7), 2209 (2020). https://doi.org/10.3390/app10072209

35. Rasulo, A., Testa, C., Borzi, B.: Seismic risk analysis at urban scale in Italy. In: Gervasi, O., et al. (eds.) ICCSA 2015. LNCS, vol. 9157, pp. 403–414. Springer, Cham (2015). https://doi.org/10.1007/978-3-319-21470-2_29

36. Sezen, H., Setzler, E.J.: Reinforcement slip in reinforced concrete columns. ACI Struct. J. **105**(3), 280 (2008)

37. Zhou, Z., Nuti, C., Lavorato, D.: Modeling of the mechanical behavior of stainless reinforcing steel. In: Proceedings of the 10th fib International PhD Symposium in Civil Engineering, pp. 21–23. Québec, QC, Canada (2014)

Geovisualization for Energy Planning

Luigi Santopietro[1]([✉]), Giuseppe Faruolo[1], Francesco Scorza[1],
Anna Rossi[2], Marco Tancredi[3], Angelo Pepe[3],
and Michele Giordano[3]

[1] Laboratory of Urban and Regional Systems Engineering (LISUT),
School of Engineering, University of Basilicata, Potenza, Italy
luigi.santopietro@studenti.unibas.it,
giuseppe.far88@gmail.com, francesco.scorza@unibas.it
[2] Potenza Municipality, Potenza, Italy
anna.rossi@comune.potenza.it
[3] Lucana Energy Company (SEL), Potenza, Italy
{marco.tancredi,angelo.pepe,
michele.giordano}@selspa.it

Abstract. In 2018 across 885 urban areas of the EU-28 only 66% of EU cities have, according to Reckien et al. classification a A1 (autonomously produced plans), A2 (plans produced to comply with national regulations) or A3(plans developed for international climate net- works) mitigation plan, 26% an adaptation plan, and 17% a joint adaptation and mitigation plan, while about 33% lack any form of stand-alone local climate plan [1]. Local climate plans are a new emerging field of application for urban planning and, in this sector appropriate geovisualization techniques could be useful tool in supporting make decisions about actions for local energy and climate plans. Geovisualization can help decision makers or researchers to transfer information to stakeholders and people. In this work we discuss geovisualization approach for energy consumptions and renovation scenarios for private and public buildings delivered in a specific case study: Potenza Municipality. This tool allows to visualize energy consumptions at urban scale thorough a geo- database including individual buildings information with several functions: i.e. to identify urban areas where take action with higher priority. The application to case study of Potenza Municipality is a component of a wider process of developing the Sustainable Energy and Climate Action Plan (SECAP). It shows the potential of geovisualization as a tool to support decisions making and monitoring of actions to be included in the plan.

Keywords: Geovisualization · Visualization · SEAP/SECAP · Local climate plans

1 Introduction

The Covenant of Mayors [2] was launched in 2008 in Europe with the ambition to gather local governments voluntarily committed to achieving and exceeding the EU climate and energy targets. On October 2015, the new Covenant of Mayors for Climate & Energy has been launched. Its goals were defined with cities through a consultation

O. Gervasi et al. (Eds.): ICCSA 2020, LNCS 12252, pp. 479–487, 2020.
https://doi.org/10.1007/978-3-030-58811-3_35

process and are ambitious and broad-ranging: signatory cities now pledge to actively support the implementation of the EU 40% GHG-reduction target by 2030 and agree to adopt an integrated approach to climate change mitigation and adaptation and to ensure access to secure, sustainable and affordable energy for all. In the same year 2015, EU submitted the Paris Agreements [3]. This strategy involved energy and climate policy including the so-called 20/20/20 targets [4], namely the reduction of carbon dioxide (CO_2) emissions by 20%, the increase of renewable energy's market share to 20%, and a 20% increase in energy efficiency. In June 2016, the Covenant of Mayors entered a major new phase of its history when choosing to join forces with another city initiative, the Compact of Mayors. The resulting "Global Covenant of Mayors for Climate and Energy" is the largest movement of local governments committed to going beyond their own national climate and energy objectives. Fully in line with the UN Sustainable Development Goals and climate justice principles [5], the Global Covenant of Mayors will tackle three key issues: climate change mitigation, adaptation to the adverse effects of climate change and universal access to secure, clean and affordable energy. When officially joining the Covenant of Mayors, signatories commit to developing a Sustainable Energy and Climate Action Plan (SECAP) within two years. New SECAP opposite to Sustainable Energy Action Plan (SEAP), adds to the reduction of CO_2, adaptation and mitigation to climate change.

In Italy at this moment, the most adopted strategic energy plan at Municipal level is SECAP. These plans, with a bottom-up process, are structured on a numbers of local scale actions, policies and transformations directed to improve the performance of the territorial systems addressing energy efficiency objectives and interested in climate change mitigation/adaptation processes.

The SECAP development process, is based on a very synthetic table of contents and, in the perspectives of the authors, could reveal several weaknesses in the comprehensive structure linking objectives to actions and indicators.

The aim of this work is to experiment an effective way to collect and evaluate energy consumption about public and residential sectors related to the case study of Potenza Municipality as a supporting tool for SECAP development. The issue to reinforce the geovisualization tools connected with SECAP allowed us to test technologies for the visualization of geographic information (spatial, temporal, or attribute, or a combination of all three) in order to create interactive visualizations for geographic analysis, using maps, map-like displays, multimedia, plots and graphs (also in combination) to aid visual thinking and insight/hypotheses generation, and a perspective on cartography [6].

2   Energy Consumption and Case Study of Potenza Municipality

Potenza Municipality in the 2009 became signatory of Covenant of Mayors and drew up its SEAP[7]. At this moment is developing the SECAP with new updated BEI (the previous was referred to SEAP 2009). The core of SECAP is Baseline Emission Inventory (BEI), and in the emission inventories part, it reports data concerning final energy consumption, local energy production (if applicable), and the emission factors used to calculate CO_2 emissions.

From a methodological point of view, the first inventory year refers to declared baseline year. It represents the year against which the achievements of the emission reductions in your target year are measured. On the bases of BEI data, every four years, Covenant Signatories compile Monitoring Emission Inventory (MEI) to evaluate progresses in terms of emissions reductions. In this way, subsequent inventories may be compared with the BEI and progress to achieve goals, can be monitored.

Collecting or estimate energy consumption is not very easy, only for public sectors, there are (or there should be) open data easily assessable but for residential buildings and other private sectors those data are not available, especially at the single building scale. For the purposes of this study, we collaborate with SEL (Basilicata Region Energy Company) that is responsible of public procurement for local municipalities and public bodies in the sector of energy provisioning. SEL developed a platform (SELBench) to manage energy consumptions and bills in partnership with final users (i.e. local administrations).

To elaborate data concerning BEI (including relevant SECAP sectors) about energy consumption, in this work data comes from:

- SELBench, the SEL database, which collects thermic and electric consumption data by institutions or municipalities in agreement with SEL;
- Statistic benchmark based on mean statistic value about a sample of buildings similar to building interested, the chosen benchmark are processed by Milan Polytechnic, Energy Strategy Group [8]. After selecting the benchmark, the consumption is obtained as:

$$\text{Energy consumption data} = \text{bemchmark } [kWh/m^2 * \text{year}]^* \text{area}[m^2]$$

- Application of archetypes of project TABULA [9] (Typology Approach for BUiLding stock energy Assessment) where every building represents a specific construction age and specific dimension. To obtain the energy performance (expressed in kWh/m^2), it needs four steps:

a. Select the period of construction between seven different periods ranging from 1900 (including buildings built before 1900) to 2005,
b. Select the building size class between four classes: detached houses, terraced houses, multifamily buildings and blocks of flats,
c. Select energy performance between three different building conditions: original state, standard requalification and advanced requalification,
d. Obtained the energy performance, the energy consumption is calculated as:

$$\text{Energy consumption} = \text{energy performance } [kWh/m^2] * \text{area}[m^2]$$

Collection of data allows us to fill SECAP BEI for the year 2019, as shown in the following Figure (Fig. 1):

Sector		FINAL ENERGY CONSUMPTION [MWh]			
				Fossil fuels	
		Electricity	Heat/cold	Natural gas	Total
BUILDINGS, EQUIPMENT/FACILITIES AND INDUSTRIES					
Municipal buildings, equipment/facilities		3605,938		10526,32786	14132,2659
Tertiary (non municipal) buildings, equipment/facilities		22775,752		53326,36441	76102,1164
Residential buildings		85600		2660	88260
Public lighting		8154,445			8154,445
Industry	Non-ETS	35600		35600	71200
	ETS (not recommended)				0
Subtotal		155736,135	0	102112,6923	257848,827

Fig. 1. Final energy consumption for sectors (adapted from SECAP template)

The results are compared with electric and thermic consumption of SEAP referred to 2009 and PEAC (Energetic and Environmental Municipality Plan) referred to 1997.

Table 1 Final electric consumption for different sectors for years 1997, 2009 and 2019

Final electric consumption [MWH]			
Sector	1997	2009	2019
Municipal buildings	$4.24 * 10^3$	$4.41*10^3$	$3.6*10^3$
Tertiary	$5.59 *10^4$	$2.06*10^5$	$2.2*10^4$
Residential buildings	$5.43 *10^4$	$3.59*10^5$	$8,56*10^4$
Public lighting	N.a.	$1.04*10^4$	$8.48*10^3$
Industry	$2.70*10^5$	$3.31*10^5$	$3.5*10^4$

Some differences come out. From our point of view and on the basis of the analysis of previous plans (SEAP and PEAC), we believe that the proposed estimation gained an advanced level of accuracy.

Table 2. Final thermic consumption for different sectors for years 1997, 2009 and 2018

Final natural gas consumption [MWH]			
Sector	1997	2009	2018
Municipal buildings	$1.98*10^7$	$2,06*10^7$	$2.6*10^6$
Tertiary	$5.9 *10^7$	N.a.	
Residential buildings	$2.6 * 10^5$	N.a.	$2,66* 10^3$
Industry	$2.7 *10^6$	N.a.	$4,63* 10^4$

Comparing the data in Table 1 and 2 between different years, in this work we focus our studies on some actions about energy efficiency, reduction energy consumption and building renovation of Municipal and Residential buildings. The choice of these two sectors is based on the evidence that they are main contributors to BEI as shown both PEAC and SEAP. Some actions have been undertaking by Potenza Municipality with the PAES from 2009 and haven't completed yet. Two of these actions to achieve 20-20-20 goals [4], are related to municipal and residential building renovation respectively with a CO_2 estimated reduction of 3130 ton/year and 16453 ton/year. The actions will concern substitution of window frames, boilers and installation of RES technologies. In 2020, Potenza Municipality will be a signatory of new COM for Climate and Energy, with a SECAP, so it's a chance to improve reduction of CO_2, reduction of energy consumption and fight against climate change.

3 Geovisualization System for Energy Data

Around 1990 s, were proposed important conceptual frameworks as "Swoopy" framework proposed by DiBiase [10] that offers a continuum in which we see both visual thinking and visual communication, and as such, it provides foundations as to how we think about geovisualization today. In 1994 MacEachren [11], proposed a defining theoretical framework on geovisualization with MacEachren's Cartography. The Cartography framework extends the Swoopy framework, essentially adding the interaction (low vs. high) as a dimension and mapping its relationship to users (public vs. expert), and tasks (communication vs. exploration), in a continuum. MacEachren et al. [12], further developed the Cartography later, slightly adjusting Swoopy's "idealized" research steps exploration, confirmation, synthesis, and presentation by replacing confirmation step with analysis. The updated framework sums up the core functions of geovisualization: with the support from geovisualization software environments, the public (e.g., non-expert users) or specialists (e.g., researchers, decision makers) can discover patterns and form informed questions (exploration), conduct analyses to confirm or reject individual hypotheses (analysis/confirmation), generalize the findings (synthesis), and present/communicate these findings. In this way, we propose geovisualization as fundamental tool for the decisional making of the SECAP actions. The framework developed, is based on two output tools that display collected information about energy consumption for every building using:

1. CityEngine Software (A framework)
2. ArcGIS Earth (B framework)

The choice about technologies is based on comparison between commercial and free software available, related to them has expressed a technical judgment with the aim of the work.

3.1   Geovisualization Framework A

Esri CityEngine is a three-dimensional (3D) modeling software application developed by Esri R&D Center Zurich and is specialized in the generation of 3D urban environments. It improves the shape generation via the rule-based system and data sets similar as the Geographic Information System (GIS). The choice of this software is based on the fully implementation with GIS software and the next possibility of export 3D models to the web, VR experiences, or a geodatabase but it requires expert users or specialist. Starting from footprints of public, residential and industrial buildings, with the rule "*Building_From_Footprints*" have been obtained 3D models related to energy consumption (Fig. 2). In particular, for thermic consumption have been obtained 3D models of energy consumption for every scenario (actual conditions, standard requalification and advanced requalification).

Fig. 2. 3D models of electric energy consumption buildings

3.2   Geovisualization Framework B

ArcGIS Earth, is a free software developed by ESRI to understand spatial information, with World Map. This program, is friendly-user and accessible from all users and not only from specialists as the previous CityEngine. 3D models representing the energy consumption for every scenario are imported as KML files into ArcGIS Earth and the results are shown in Figs. 3 and 4. This representation of 3D models, opposite to previous into CityEngine is more intuitive and understandable for not expert people. This feature could be useful to involve citizen to became active part into decision – making and empowerment them to reduction energy consumption.

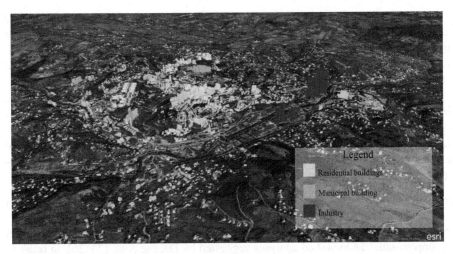

Fig. 3. 3D models of electric consumption in ArcGIS earth

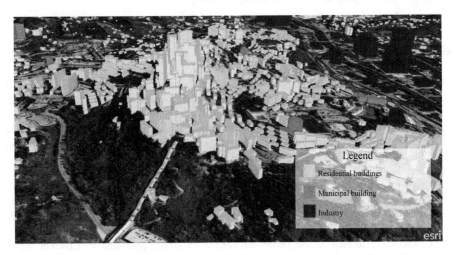

Fig. 4. Particular of 3D models of electric consumption in ArcGIS earth

4   Conclusion

As seen, geovisualization fits as support in decision-making or comparing different energy requalification scenario and a tool to share information/decisions to stakeholders or citizen. Those applications of advanced geovisualization tools are very rare in the SECAP and COM development, while they could represents the effective application of a collaborative approach oriented to include stakeholders and decision makers, but also citizens, in a collaborative elaboration process [13–17]. This assumption goes in the direction to establish a common awareness facing those challenging issues of energy efficiency and climate change mitigation/adaptation.

In order to improve energy efficiency, urban transformations could be monitored and checked any possible overlay between different instruments able to produce impacts and consequences to territory, in a uniform framework [18–21].

We are in the domain of new rational planning for sustainable development, and such tools integrates the existing toolbox for planners and decision makers [22, 23].

As future developments, the choice of open geovisualization tools (available on the internet) can be used to analyze and compare deeper the data organized into GIS, i.e. comparing energy consumption between different archetype or age of construction. Individual citizens, decision makers, investors and operators will easily find spatial explicit opportunities to realize energy renovations in urban context. Other developments are related to:

- improve the visualization of the data, in particular when attributes to display are not closely related to 2D objects (i.e. energy consumption of public lighting).
- compare the 3D visualization obtained in this work, choosing other visualization opportunities as viewshed analyses suggested by Danese et al. [24–26], in order to improve the awareness of citizen to reduce energy consumption and support the detection of highly energy-consuming buildings.

References

1. Reckien, D., et al.: How are cities planning to respond to climate change? assessment of local climate plans from 885 cities in the EU-28. J. Clean. Prod. **191**, 207–219 (2018). https://doi.org/10.1016/j.jclepro.2018.03.220
2. Covenant of Mayors – Home. https://www.covenantofmayors.eu/en/, Accessed 13 Mar 2020
3. UNFCC: Adoption of the Paris agreement. In: United Nations Framework Convention on Climate Change (UNFCCC), Paris, France, p. 31 (2015)
4. Commission, E.: Europe 2020: A strategy for smart, sustainable and inclusive growth: Communication from the commission. Publications Office of the European Union (2010)
5. Transforming our world: the 2030 Agenda for Sustainable Development.: Sustainable Development Knowledge Platform. https://sustainabledevelopment.un.org/post2015/transformingourworld, Accessed 20 Apr 2020
6. Cöltekin, G.: Journal Article Published Version Originally published at: Cöltekin, Arzu, Janetzko, Halldór; Fabrikant. Geovisualization. Geogr. Inf. Sci. (2018). https://doi.org/10.22224/gistbok/2018.2.6
7. SEAP Potenza Municipality. https://www.covenantofmayors.eu/about/covenant-community/signatories/action-plan.html?scity_id=13874, Accessed 18 Apr 2020
8. Energy & Strategy Group|Energy & Strategy Group. http://www.energystrategy.it/, Accessed 17 Apr 2020
9. Corrado, V., Ballarini, I., Corgnati, S.P., Talà, N.: Typology Approach for Building Stock Energy Assessment: Building Typology Brochure – Italy (2011)
10. DiBiase, D.: Visualization in the earth sciences. Earth Min. Sci. **59**, 13–18 (1990)
11. Maceachren, A.M.: Visualization in modern cartography: setting the agenda. In: Modern Cartography Series, pp. 1–12. Academic Press, Cambridge (1994). https://doi.org/10.1016/B978-0-08-042415-6.50008-9
12. Rhyne, T.M.: Geovisualization for knowledge construction and decision support. IEEE Comput. Graph. Appl. (2004). https://doi.org/10.1109/MCG.2004.1255801

13. Dvarioniene, J., Grecu, V., Lai, S., Scorza, F.: Four perspectives of applied sustainability: research implications and possible integrations. In: Gervasi, O., et al. (eds.) ICCSA 2017. LNCS, vol. 10409, pp. 554–563. Springer, Cham (2017). https://doi.org/10.1007/978-3-319-62407-5_39

14. Scorza, F., Grecu, V.: Assessing sustainability: research directions and relevant issues. In: Gervasi, O., et al. (eds.) ICCSA 2016. LNCS, vol. 9786, pp. 642–647. Springer, Cham (2016). https://doi.org/10.1007/978-3-319-42085-1_55

15. Pontrandolfi, P., Scorza, F.: Sustainable urban regeneration policy making: inclusive participation practice. In: Gervasi, O., et al. (eds.) ICCSA 2016. LNCS, vol. 9788, pp. 552–560. Springer, Cham (2016). https://doi.org/10.1007/978-3-319-42111-7_44

16. Murgante, B., Botonico, G., Graziadei, A., Sassano, G., Amato, F., Scorza, F.: Innovation, technologies, participation: new paradigms towards a 20 citizenship. Int. J. Electron. Gov. 11, 62–88 (2019). https://doi.org/10.1504/IJEG.2019.098814

17. Scorza, F., Pontrandolfi, P.: Citizen participation and technologies: the C.A.S.T. architecture. In: Gervasi, O., et al. (eds.) ICCSA 2015. LNCS, vol. 9156, pp. 747–755. Springer, Cham (2015). https://doi.org/10.1007/978-3-319-21407-8_53

18. Saganeiti, L., Pilogallo, A., Faruolo, G., Scorza, F., Murgante, B.: Territorial fragmentation and renewable energy source plants: which relationship? Sustainability 12, 1828 (2020). https://doi.org/10.3390/SU12051828

19. Scorza, F., Pilogallo, A., Saganeiti, L., Murgante, B., Pontrandolfi, P.: Comparing the territorial performances of renewable energy sources' plants with an integrated ecosystem services loss assessment: a case study from the Basilicata region (Italy). Sustain. Cities Soc. 56, 102082 (2020). https://doi.org/10.1016/J.SCS.2020.102082

20. Scorza, F., Pilogallo, A., Saganeiti, L., Murgante, B.: Natura 2000 areas and sites of national interest (SNI): measuring (un) integration between naturalness preservation and environmental remediation policies. Sustainability 12, 2928 (2020). https://doi.org/10.3390/su12072928

21. Scorza, F., Saganeiti, L., Pilogallo, A., Murgante, B.: Ghost planning: the inefficiency of energy sector policies in a low population density region. Arch. DI Stud. URBANI E Reg. (2020)

22. Las Casas, G., Scorza, F., Murgante, B.: Razionalità a-priori: una proposta verso una pianificazione antifragile. Sci. Reg. 18, 329–338 (2019). https://doi.org/10.14650/93656

23. Las Casas, G., Scorza, F., Murgante, B.: New urban agenda and open challenges for urban and regional planning. In: Calabrò, F., Della Spina, L., Bevilacqua, C. (eds.) ISHT 2018. SIST, vol. 100, pp. 282–288. Springer, Cham (2019). https://doi.org/10.1007/978-3-319-92099-3_33

24. Danese, M., Nolè, G., Murgante, B.: Visual impact assessment in urban planning. In: Geocomputation and Urban Planning, pp. 133–146. Springer, Heidelberg (2009). https://doi.org/10.1007/978-3-540-89930-3_8

25. Danese, M., Las Casas, G., Murgante, B.: 3D simulations in environmental impact assessment. In: Gervasi, O., Murgante, B., Laganà, A., Taniar, D., Mun, Y., Gavrilova, M.L. (eds.) ICCSA 2008. LNCS, vol. 5072, pp. 430–443. Springer, Heidelberg (2008). https://doi.org/10.1007/978-3-540-69839-5_32

26. Danese, M., Nolè, G., Murgante, B.: Identifying viewshed: new approaches to visual impact assessment. Stud. Comput. Intell. 348, 73–89 (2011). https://doi.org/10.1007/978-3-642-19733-8_5

Studying the Spatial Distribution of Volunteered Geographic Data Through a Non-parametric Approach

Giorgia Bressan[1]([⊠]) [iD], Gian Pietro Zaccomer[1] [iD],
and Luca Grassetti[2] [iD]

[1] Department of Languages and Literatures, Communication, Education and
Society (DILL), University of Udine, Via Petracco 8, 33100 Udine, Italy
{giorgia.bressan, gianpietro.zaccomer}@uniud.it
[2] Department of Economics and Statistics (DIES), University of Udine,
Via Tomadini 30, 33100 Udine, Italy
luca.grassetti@uniud.it

Abstract. Nowadays, new knowledge on the immaterial characteristics of surrounding landscapes can easily be produced by relying on volunteer contributions. However, the spatial distribution of the collected data may be influenced by the contributor's location. Using data sets derived from the administration of a map-based survey, aimed at collecting explicit spatial information on sites perceived as having positive and negative qualities in Friuli Venezia Giulia (Italy), a descriptive analysis and a non-parametric procedure are employed to study the relevance of a respondent's municipality of reference on the mapping activity.

The findings indicate that the volunteered geographic data collected in the survey are not uniformly distributed across the study area and that a different spatial relationship exists between mapped elements and a respondent's residence when the two different attributes of interest are considered. The results underline the importance of considering volunteers' characteristics when engaging local populations in participatory initiatives.

Keywords: Map-based survey · Landscape judgments · Spatial distributions · Simulations · Volunteers

1 Introduction

In the European context, consideration of the importance of direct engagement of local communities in the study of the conditions of everyday landscapes has become increasingly common in research. The European Landscape Convention acknowledges the importance of public participation for landscape planning as a way to capture local knowledge; unravel sensitive issues and conflicts; and promote the exchanges of information [15]. Undoubtedly, it is politically desirable to use a participatory process to collect landscape judgments of those who directly observe and experience local landscapes. However, the involvement of the public in such processes gives rise to a series of issues, such as identifying a suitable spatial data collection method and

O. Gervasi et al. (Eds.): ICCSA 2020, LNCS 12252, pp. 488–504, 2020.
https://doi.org/10.1007/978-3-030-58811-3_36

correctly interpreting the new knowledge produced. Map-based surveys, where people can directly input geographic information, can be an effective tool to democratize landscape planning. They are in fact a means to collect spatial data on topics that, given their subjective nature, are not possible to analyze using other available data sources. However, how do respondents' characteristics influence mapping results?

The main goal of this study is to evaluate participatory data bias in online map-based surveys. This is done by demonstrating that respondents tend to identify sites as having certain attributes of interest near their municipality of residence rather than expressing judgments on the spatial distribution of the same attributes on locations that are far away from their home. Moreover, we want to verify that the attributes of interest are differently distance-sensitive, i.e. the mean distance (between the respondents' home and the mapped element) varies according to the attribute considered. Some descriptive information on the spatial databases created through the map-based approach is also provided in this paper in order to deepen further aspects of the mapping activity conducted by respondents.

The research has been conducted by using results collected in 2018 during the administration of an online map-based survey as an empirical base. This survey aimed to study citizens' perceptions of the quality of the regional landscape in the Italian Friuli Venezia Giulia region (7,924 km^2). Volunteers were invited to fill in a questionnaire and, along with traditional multiple-choice questions, they were given the opportunity to identify places on maps that they perceived to be of high landscape quality and others seen as degraded. The evaluation of participatory data bias is possible as the collected spatial data were accompanied by information describing participants' characteristics. In particular, the existence of a question on respondents' residence allow us to quantify the distance between the centroid of the municipality of reference for each respondent and the mapped elements.

This paper intends to contribute to the literature on the participant and sampling bias of public participatory GIS (PPGIS) applications. Specifically, it aims to expand the empirical research that recognizes that the domicile of a participant influences the mapped locations of the spatial attributes of interest. Moreover, it argues for the existence of a different relationship between respondents' residence and the type of spatial attribute being mapped. Brown and Reed [5] show that respondent characteristics such as gender, age, level of education and knowledge of the landscape can affect mapping results. However, scarce empirical evidence exists on the impact of a participant's domicile on the typology of landscape judgment expressed.

2 Past Work

A variety of approaches that fall into the category of PPGIS methods are being used in the most diverse geographic contexts and fields to bring out citizens' opinions on the conditions of their surrounding environments [16]. The key feature of these approaches is that participants are asked to identify the geographic locations that in their view are characterized by certain selected attributes of interest. Despite being a very exciting idea – producing new knowledge by relying on user-generated content – there are several problems when involving citizens in such initiatives and dealing with data that have not been filtered through peer review. Specifically, Brown and Kytta [6] warn that spatial data might be biased by the effect of participant variables such as the geographic location of participants. This element, together with variables concerning participants' socio-demographic characteristics, their beliefs, values, ideology, and familiarity with the study area, are identified as potential sources of bias and as such need to be considered to ascertain the characteristics (and quality) of the data collected. A consequence of the influence of the location of PPGIS participants is well exemplified in Brown [4]. If a PPGIS application is used for future decisions on land planning, then the participants most connected to the study area will probably have a different mapping behavior to those who live further away. Only the first group is likely to perceive greater gains or losses as a result of the PPGIS process, as the impacts of possible land-use changes would affect them more directly.

A theory studying the relationship between the assignment of values and preferences across landscapes and the commitment to a place of people making such evaluations has been advanced in Norton and Hannon [12]. At the basis of the theory is the testable scientific hypothesis that 'the intensity of one's opposition to unpopular industries and the strength of approbation for desirable land uses, vary inversely with the distance of that activity from one's own geographic "place"' (Norton and Hannon [12], 230). Despite the reference to geographical distance, the authors argue that changes in environmental valuation cannot simply be attributed to distance. In fact, two individuals who live at the same distance from the same point of reference may value a location very differently in light of distinctive historical, cultural and personal factors. In this view, environmental values have a cultural dimension and are the result of a perspective defined in spatial and temporal terms; in addition, the intensity of environmental valuation is discounted from the home perspective across both time and space. This theory is an extension of the concept of geographic discounting [10] which suggests that people (and, similarly, animals and plants) prefer to be close to what they consider good and maintain distance between themselves and what they dislike (fear).

Interest in the impact of where people live on their mapping patterns has already emerged in some PPGIS applications. In the research presented in Brown, Reed and Harris [7] respondents were asked to map where a series of environmental values were located and to express the importance assigned to the point locations in order to investigate the spatial distribution of environmental values and their relationship to place attachment. In their work, a tendency emerges of mapped environmental values to cluster, even if the distances vary according to the type of selected attribute: values associated with direct or active human uses are located closer to communities than those involving indirect or passive human uses. Their findings also highlight the existence of an inter-community variation in distance, pinpointing that the different locations involved in the study have peculiar spatial profiles. Pocewicz and Nielsen-Pincus [13] empirically assessed whether people, when asked to state their preferences for locating energy and residential development sites, wish to be close to what they consider "good" and further away from what they think is "bad". The analysis revealed that on average participants mapped perceived positive biological conditions closer to home than negative conditions. Moreover, the distance between a participant's home and their mapped preferences for wind development versus the distance from their homes to projected turbines differed, as these latter were located much closer to their homes. As for mapped oil and gas developments, participants' mapped preferences were located much further from their home then either existing or projected oil and gas wells. Residential development preferences were mapped in the respondents' surroundings (that is, the town and neighboring areas) in 70% of cases. Together, these results suggest a reduced spatial discounting rate for residential developments than for a wind energy development. In de Vries et al. [17] the focus is on the influence of a respondent's origin on where they placed their markers. In their research, the spatial questions consisted of asking respondents to indicate which places they found highly valuable or attractive at the national level and where they lived. The findings indicate that a participant's region of residence influenced which places were marked, and, excluding the reports made for some nationally well-known localities (i.e. in four hotspots), the pattern of a marker's density exhibited a clear decay with distance, for all regions of origin.

The interest in how residents perceive natural resources is not a prerogative of geographic literature; on the contrary, there is a long tradition in this area of research in the field of environmental psychology. Brody et al. [3], for example, produce quantitative evidence on the importance of a study participant's physical proximity to specific environmental features for their knowledge and perception of such features.

As emerges from the reviewed articles, there are many approaches to studying the influence of respondents' spatial location on mapped values and preferences. Our data allow us to explore how the mapping behavior, interpreted as the distance between a respondent's reference municipality and the mapped elements, changes in relation to the selected attributes of interest. A density of mapped elements near a respondent's home would testify to the existence of a relationship between the intensity of environmental valuation and the individual's (spatial) perspective. Given that the spatial data collected through the map-based approach are a subjective truth, the context in which they are gathered matter. For example, Klonner et al. [11] in their work on flood risk perceptions well exemplify this issue by underling that while a participant may be motivated to identify a certain site because his/her property has been heavily affected, another neighbor might not have the same incentive, despite the original problem being the same. Similarly, in our research, the information reported is based on everyday living experience and so the participant's context should be accounted.

3 The Survey Instrument

The following section presents the map-based approach which served for the collection of volunteer geographic data and carries out a first analysis of the spatial data. These reflections assist in illustrating the potential of PPGIS applications in the collection of subjective data and to justify the non-parametric procedure used in Sect. 4 below.

3.1 Data Collection

The spatial data analyzed in this research derive from the administration of an online map-based survey, in the period June–November 2018, to a group of volunteers familiar with the Friuli Venezia Giulia region (Italy's north-easternmost region, near Austria and Slovenia). What is relevant to highlight in this section are the parts of the questionnaire essential to the study of the spatial discounting effect[1].

The core component of the map-based survey, which was developed using the platform Enketo, was two optional questions requiring respondents to use maps to indicate their reply. The first question asked respondents to identify a maximum of three sites in the Friuli Venezia Giulia region that in their view were of particular value/quality; and a second question where respondents were required to identify a maximum of three sites that they perceived to be particularly critical/degraded in the same region. The respondents could answer the spatial questions by drawing points, lines and polygons on maps, which were saved in the form of coordinates, if the survey was correctly submitted. Given that there was room to identify a maximum of three sites per attribute of interest, the number of total sites submitted could range from zero to six. When points were selected as spatial features to make the report, the output file directly contained the latitude and longitude of the respondent-selected localities; with lines and polygons, the output was a sequence of coordinates corresponding to the mapped element. As the final objective of the project, for which this map-based survey was administered, was to create a spatial database containing the various reports by aggregating various data sources (see, [2]), a decision was made to transform lines and polygons into points by calculating the centroids of such geometries.

Another important point to make is that each spatial question was accompanied by another two asking that respondents describe textually the site drawn on the map and explain the reason for the selection. The existence of the open, free text permits us to verify the correspondence of the intended mapped element with the geometry drawn. In other cases, it allowed us to gather further replies from people who were probably not very comfortable with online maps. However, these textual replies were generally very vague in spatial terms, and for now, we preferred to exclude them from this analysis.

In the demographic section of the survey, besides traditional questions such as the age class, sex, occupation, and education qualification of participants, there was also a question asking respondents to indicate their place of residence. Specifically, the question required respondents to select an option from a multiple-choice list containing either the complete list of municipalities in the region, or the options "abroad" and "in another Italian region". If respondents selected these last two replies from the list, some further questions were asked. The first asked respondents to select the specific region or the foreign country of residence; the second asked about the reason for attending/visiting the study area; and the third asked about the municipality attended in the region. For simplicity, from now on we will use the expression "municipality of reference" to identify both the municipalities where respondents lived, for those who

---

[1] An exhaustive account of the survey is present in the conference proceedings authored by Bressan and Amaduzzi [1]. Besides the characteristics of the survey, the paper presents a detailed analysis of participants' profiles and a general description of the results.

stated that they resided in the Friuli Venezia Giulia region, and the municipality attended, when they declared that they resided outside the study area. The municipality of reference is assumed to be, for both cases, the geographic area for which each respondent is most familiar with and has the most knowledge[2].

On a final note before proceeding with the empirical analysis, it is worth briefly outlining the structure of the shapefiles that were used in this research. The output of the survey is a spreadsheet containing the respondents' replies. In this file, the first column contains the ID of each respondent, while the other columns store the various spatial and non-spatial answers that each participant gave. The first element to point out is that two final databases served the empirical analysis (and, consequently the shapefiles), one gathering the sites perceived as 'of beauty' (that is, of particular value/quality), the other concerning the degraded sites. Each shapefile is made up of point features: despite respondents having the opportunity to draw not only points but also lines and polygons, a decision was made to represent the spatial replies using only the point geometry. Each shapefile has the same structure: each row corresponds to a different respondent-selected location and the columns have various information concerning such sites: identification code of the volunteer who made the report; the name of his/her municipality of reference; and the latitude and longitude of the centroid of such municipality. The other columns contain information about the report. These consist of the indication of the original geometry used to make the report; the order in the map-based survey (i.e. if the respondent drew that site in the first, second or third map provided); the geographic coordinates of such points; and the municipality in which the point falls[3].

3.2   A Descriptive Analysis of the Spatial Datasets

As illustrated earlier, the spatial data collected through the map-based survey has been organized into two separate datasets: the first gathers the respondent-selected locations of the sites perceived as of beauty, the second collects the spatial data concerning degraded sites. The following descriptive analysis separately studies the two datasets. Another preliminary note concerns the fact that, as previously observed, the reports considered in this paper are only those made by participants through their mapping activity, i.e. by drawing points, lines or polygons on the online maps integrated in the survey.

---

[2] We would like to point out that we had considered asking respondents to indicate their home's coordinates by including an additional online map in the survey. However, this feature would have meant gathering data that would reveal private information about the respondents, so the option was discarded. In the PPGIS application developed in Pocewicz and Nielsen-Pincus [13], there is no difference in the results when an individual's home addresses or population centers are respectively considered.

[3] The identification of the centroid for the municipalities of residence, as well as for the reports made with lines and polygons, was made using the Feature To Point (Data Management) tool in ArcGIS 10.2.1. An overlay operation was carried out in order to identify in which municipality (polygon layer) each respondent-selected location (point layer) was falling. In this way, we were able to confront the municipality where the spatial attribute was located and the municipality of residence/attendance of the corresponding individual that mapped it.

The first element to consider is the participation of the volunteers in the initiative. The first dataset concerns 126 citizens who provided 279 reports for an average of 2.2 reports of beauty per participant. The second dataset is the result of the contribution of 92 volunteers who mapped 196 sites for an average of 2.1 reports of degradation per participant. Although the second dataset is smaller compared to the first, both in terms of citizens involved and reports collected (27% and 30% less, respectively), the averages of spatial responses in per capita terms are quite similar.

Before analyzing the distribution of the two spatial attributes, we want to return to the concept of "municipality of reference". This defines the geographical unit to which each participant is in principle more connected, and is used both for participants living within the study area and also people who are resident outside the regional border but cross regional borders for study or work reasons, for example. In reality, looking at the first dataset on reports concerning perceived sites of beauty, only four volunteers out of 126 declared that they resided in another Italian region, mostly in the nearby Veneto region, and one respondent was from Slovenia. As regards the second dataset, no respondent was resident outside the region. Although in this latter case we might refer exclusively to the municipality of residence to describe where a participant lives, for convenience we will continue to use the generic expression explained before.

An illustration of the spatial distribution of the volunteers, according to the spatial attribute considered, is proposed in Fig. 1. Specifically, it represents the number of participants by municipality of reference. It should be noted that the coverage of the regional territory is not homogeneous as participants mainly come from the hilly and plain areas of the Friuli Venezia Giulia region. This result is in line with the demographic distribution of the population in the region. In fact, the northern part of the region, constituted by a mountainous area, is highly depopulated. The highest concentration of respondents was found in the major urban centers, namely Pordenone, Gorizia, Trieste and Udine. As highlighted by the darkest color in the legend of Fig. 1, this latter municipality is the only one that, for both spatial attributes, hosted more than 10 respondents.

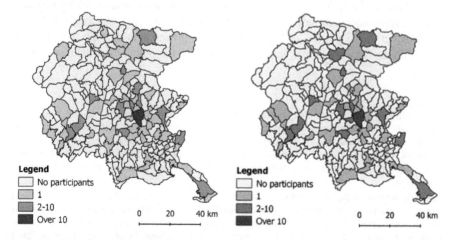

Fig. 1. Spatial distribution of participants in the map-based survey who identified sites perceived as of beauty (left) and of degradation (right).

Recalling the fact that participants could select up to three reports per attribute of interest, it is worth analyzing how respondents reacted to the opportunity of drawing, using the maps, for one, two, or three sites. 43.7% of the reports in the first dataset corresponded to the first report, 30.8% to the second, and 25.5% to the third. In the second dataset, the order of completion was 45.4%, 32.7% and 21.9%. The respondent-selected locations concerning degraded sites were slightly more concentrated than in the first dataset, meaning that less respondents used all the possibilities.

The second aspect of the analysis considers the distance[4] of the centroids of the respondents' municipality of reference from the sites reported. Such distance in the first dataset varied between 0.6 (within Udine's municipality) and 121.8 km (between Trieste and Forni di Sotto) with a mean value of 22.2 km; in the second dataset the range was between 0.1 km (within Spilimbergo's municipality) and 102.8 km with a mean value of 17.8 km (between Moggio Udinese and Trieste).

In addition, we calculated the arithmetic mean of the Great Circle Distances of the first reports and those for the second and third reports, these two latter reports were considered jointly. This distinction is relevant because we can assume that the order used by participants to identify the locations of the attributes matters. In fact, the sites mentioned in the first map provided were likely to be those that came immediately to the respondents' mind. In the first dataset, the average was 20.4 km for the first report, and 23.6 km for the second and third reports; in the second dataset such arithmetic means were respectively 16.4 km and 19 km. If we move on to the percentage values, the results were similar in both datasets: the mean distance of the first report was about 8% less than that overall, while the mean distance of the second and third report was slightly less than 16% of that of the first report. It is therefore possible to affirm that there was a tendency to map first the place, both of beauty or degradation, closest to where the respondents lived/attended.

As is evident from the analysis of both the maximum and mean distances, in the sample the sites of beauty were further away from one home's location than degraded ones. In this sense, it seems probable that while the area characterized by notable positive features were more easily remembered by individuals even if they visited them only once, the degraded sites were remembered because, being closer, they are seen more often.

As will be made clear in the next section, it is crucial to differentiate the reports made inside and outside the respondents' reference municipality. In the first dataset, the reports within the municipality of reference amounted to 29.4%, while for the second dataset to 35.7%. In other words, for the sites characterized by positive features, for

---

[4] We would like to point out that the computation of other distance measures would have been more straightforward using the default functions in R, the environment for statistical computing and graphics used to make the following simulations; however, we preferred to opt for a more sophisticated measure that took into account the earth's curvature. Despite the nice feature, this distance has some limitations, as for example it does not take into consideration accessibility issues. However, as the introduction of the driving distance to study the effect of location-based variables on environmental concerns and attitudes (see [3]) is not without drawbacks (for instance, which track to follow when calculating road distances), the orthodromic distance can be regarded as a satisfactory solution.

each "domestic" report there were 2.4 external reports, while for the second spatial attribute (degradation) the ratio was 1.8. These results highlight how, in this survey, the volunteers identified without hesitation degraded places that were inside their municipality of reference, even if this behavior could contribute to giving a negative image of the place where they lived/attended. When the dichotomous classification of distances is examined in the first dataset, the mean distance of the respondent-selected locations with the centroid was 2.6 km when "domestic" reports are considered. In comparison, the mean distance for the sub-sample of reports referring to locations outside the municipality of reference was 30.3 km. For the second dataset, the mean distances were 2.2 km and 26.5 km respectively. As expected, not only were the values of the mean distances lower in responses referring to the sites of degradation, but in both cases the differences between the two means were quite high, i.e. 27.8 km (beauty) and 24.2 km (degradation).

If together with the internal and external nature of the reports we also consider their order, the mean distance for the external reports in the first dataset was 28.4 km for the first reports and 31.8 km for the second and third reports (the total value was, as shown earlier, 30.3 km). It is therefore verified that the first reports had an average distance less than those for the second and third reports, even considering only the reports outside of the municipality of reference. As for the second dataset, however, the values were very close, 27 km and 26.1 km (the total value is 26.5 km). Given the smaller number of cases on which these mean values were calculated (there were only 51 first reports on degraded sites outside the municipality of reference), these results should be considered with some prudence.

Roughly one-third of the reports concerned sites within the respondent's municipality of reference. This particular spatial structure of the sample cannot be overlooked during the subsequent simulation exercise. In fact, the preference of respondents for identifying domestic sites impacts on the overall average distance.

The last section of this descriptive analysis of the datasets concerns the spatial distribution of the respondent-selected locations (Fig. 2).

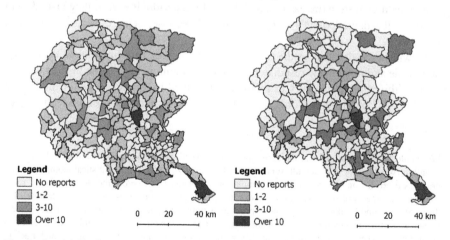

Fig. 2. Spatial distribution of the reports made for locations perceived as of beauty (left) and of degradation (right).

The possibility given to respondents to report more than one location per spatial attribute is evident in Fig. 2. In the previous maps concerning participants' distribution (Fig. 1) the number of municipalities in white (corresponding to "no participants") is rather large. Here it is evident that there are more colored municipalities, especially in the map on the left, as a consequence of the presence of at least one attribute in that geographic unit. This confirmed that people mapped more than one site and the reports concerned sites inside their municipality of reference. The second insight is that not only is the distribution of mapped elements is rather widespread but that the reports are particularly concentrated in some geographic areas of the region. The cities of Udine and Trieste are the municipalities that received most reports, both when the attribute of interest was perceived to be of beauty and of degradation; however, the other two main urban centers in the region, Pordenone and Gorizia, also received a relatively high number of reports. Some unexpected data – the rather high number of degraded sites in Tarvisio, which is widely known internationally for its majestic forest – derive from the mapping behavior of a single participant who decided to map three degraded sites in her municipality of residence. This result suggests once again the exigence of analyzing the impact of the resident's characteristics on the mapping activity.

To sum up, from the joint analysis of the maps presented in Figs. 1 and 2, we can highlight two general insights. The first is that there is a strong relationship between the municipality of residence and the sites reported, an aspect that makes one think of the existence of some form of relationship between geographic locations of participants and participant-selected sites. The second, linked to the previous insight, pertains to the fact that spatial data do not have a homogeneous distribution in the study area: data were mainly concentrated in the major urban centers of the region.

4   A Non-parametric Comparison Procedure

To check the null hypothesis, that states that the sites of interest (i.e. the respondent-selected locations perceived as of beauty and degradation) are reported independently from a respondent's municipality of reference, we considered a non-parametric comparison procedure based on the bootstrap approach (see [8] and [9] for a full review).

From an operative point of view, the null hypothesis of independence between the reported sites and the place of reference for each respondent corresponds to the idea that the full set of identified sites can be considered as reportable by the whole sample of citizens, regardless of their municipality of reference.

As highlighted in the descriptive analysis of the spatial datasets, the empirical evidence suggests a strong relationship between the places of reference and the reported sites. Moreover, the spatial distribution of the collected sample data is highly irregular within the region. This characterization of the observed data relates to sites both considered of beauty and degraded.

For this reason, the development of a formal comparison procedure based on a full resampling approach would be useless. A more reliable comparison can be obtained by relaxing the working hypothesis introducing a constraint in the bootstrap procedure. In particular, splitting the observed sample into homogeneous sub-samples, the comparison procedure adopted considers a reshuffling process based on two separate approaches for people reporting sites in their municipality of reference and for those indicating locations outside their community. Formally, the bootstrap replications are obtained by fixing the records where the stated sites are within the municipality of reference and resampling the remaining sites considering a uniform distribution. For instance, if a respondent residing in Udine mapped three degraded sites and two are within Udine, the only record that is resampled is that which refers to the place outside the borders of the municipality.

The following naïve procedure is used for the approximation of the reference distribution of the mean distance under the null of independence between the reported sites and the place of reference (all the reported sites can be reported by each inter-viewed person). The algorithm considers a resampling procedure regarding the cited sites based on the spatial permutation of the subsample of sites obtained excluding those reported within the municipality of residence. The algorithm we considered can be summarized as follows.

- Considering the observed sample, compute the sample mean of the distances between the reference municipality and reported sites.
- Identify the sub-sample of records regarding sites reported within the municipality of residence.
- For enough replications (for example, 100,000):

  a) consider the records identified in the previous step as fixed (i.e. "structural constraint");
  b) reassign the other sites considering a resampling procedure (the samples are generated with or without replacement, even though only the first mode guar-antees independence);
  c) for each observation in the simulated samples, compute the new distances, and, finally, calculate their average; and
  d) save the obtained measures in the vector of simulated means.

- Determine the empirical distribution of the resampled means and consider such distribution to verify the null hypothesis.

The decision regarding the acceptance or rejection of the null hypothesis can be based on the empirical significance level (p-value) computed as the proportion of resampled means presenting a value more extreme than the "observed" sample mean.

As will be illustrated later, all the simulated datasets are less extreme than the observed sample, and for this reason, the p-values are empirically equal to 0. This result is connected to the peculiar structure of the observed data, which undoubtedly contrasts with the null hypothesis. The obtained replications are not strictly independent, but, as we will analyze later, the empirical results are so clear that it is useless to discuss the theoretical properties of the procedure for verification. A possible solution to the described issue is to ignore the records related to people indicating locations inside their area of residency.

The described procedure has been separately applied to the samples regarding the sites of beauty and degradation, respectively. The non-parametric testing procedure is coded in R language [14] defining the resampling procedure (with and without constraints; and with and without replacement) and the distance computation in kilometers based on the Great Circle Distance for decimal degrees coordinates.

5 Empirical Results

The second part of the empirical analysis concerns the analysis of the results obtained through the non-parametric comparison procedure introduced in Sect. 4. The four simulations made for both datasets allowed a better understanding of which was the most appropriate approach to compare the simulated data with the observed sample. The distributions were achieved through the generation of 100,000 random samples.

In the first stage, the simulations were made considering the whole set of respondent-selected locations for both datasets, without taking into account the peculiar spatial structure of the sample. This decision was taken to legitimize the introduction of the so-called "structural constraint" since the conduct of simulations on all the collected spatial data was based on the hypothesis that there is a homogeneous distribution of the reports within the regional territory. This assumption has already been refuted by the analysis of the geographic distribution of the spatial data provided in Sect. 3.2.

The first part of the analysis concerns the distributions relating to the first dataset on the sites perceived as of beauty. The mean of the simulated distances, in this case, was 42.1 km, which is almost twice the value obtained for the observed sample (22.2 km). Clearly, the problem is that if the structural constraint is not introduced, the probability of obtaining a sample that has a third of reports within the respondent's reference municipality is rather small. The introduction of the constraint, which breaks the sample into two sub-samples, keeps the mean of the distances constant for the reports within the municipality of reference, while it varies the mean distance for the reports outside the respondents' municipality of reference, according to the procedure described in Sect. 4.

Besides the problem of the geographic distribution of user-generated content, the second issue to be considered is whether the simulation must be made with or without replacement. In other words, should the respondent-selected localities outside the municipality of reference, which serve to calculate distances, be extracted with or without considering the previous extracted places? From a purely statistical perspective, it would be preferable to generate the 100,000 samples with replacement. However, when considering the comparison of such simulated distribution with the observed sample, the solution without replacement seems more suitable, which corresponds to a permutation of sites outside the municipality of reference. In order to understand how this decision can affect the results, both simulations have been carried out.

The first result regards the fact that two kinds of simulations (with and without replacement) with the structural constraint returned a distribution with almost the same mean of 30.3 km. However, as evident in Fig. 3, the standard deviation is slightly higher in the case with replacement, as it is equal to 1.07, against the value 0.85 of the simulation without replacement. The result seems plausible since the reintroduction of already extracted locations can lead to the extraction of more "extreme simulated samples", even though with a low probability. Another difference between the two simulations concerns the form of the distribution. The Jarque-Bera test, which is used to verify the hypothesis of normality, highlights the acceptance of this hypothesis for the only case with replacement (chi-square 3.0; df 2; p-value 0.222).

As for the comparison between mean values, the mean of the simulated distributions is 30.3 km which, compared with the value of the sample (22.2 km), entails a difference of 8.1 km. Considering that the maximum distance in the dataset is 121.8 km, this difference is not an extremely high value, but it is statistically significant. In fact, in terms of non-parametric tests, the p-value referred to the average of the original reports is null, as it is possible to observe from Fig. 3. This result, therefore, demonstrates the presence of the spatial discounting effect in the case of sites perceived as of beauty. The relevance of geographic proximity however is not limited to this result. As highlighted before, in fact, the mean distance between the report made with the first map and the Municipality of residence is 20.4 km. Respondents tended to report places that are near home first, even if they were outside the limits of the municipality of reference.

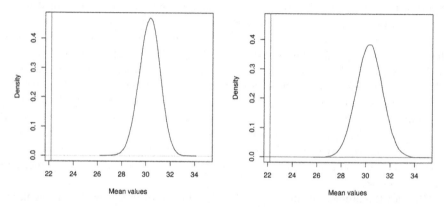

Fig. 3. Simulated distributions of the respondent-selected locations concerning sites having positive features using the structural constraint without replacement (left, st. dev. 0.85) and with replacement (right, st. dev. 1.07). The red vertical line indicates the mean value of the observed distances (22.2 km). (Color figure online)

The dataset concerning perceptions on degraded sites differs from the first dataset both because it involves smaller distances and because there are about 30% fewer respondent-selected location reports than those of beauty. However, the main results do not differ greatly from the previous case, even if the results are less pronounced.

The simulations without the inclusion of the structural constraint lead to a mean of the simulated distances of 38.7 km. This value is always more than double the average value of the original reports (17.8 km). By introducing the constraint, however, the value drops to 26.4 km. As one can see in Fig. 4, the standard deviation in case with replacement is higher than the one observed in the data simulated without replacement. The standard deviations are 1.24 and 0.90, respectively. In this case, however, neither of the two distributions passed the Jarque-Bera normality test.

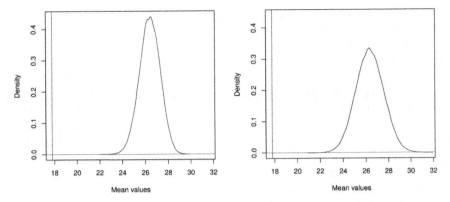

Fig. 4. Simulated distributions of the respondent-selected locations concerning sites having negative features using the structural constraint without replacement (left, st. dev. 0.90) and with replacement (right, st. dev. 1.24). The red vertical line indicates the mean value of the observed distances (17.8 km). (Color figure online)

As for the comparison between means, the difference is 8.6 km. This is slightly higher than the corresponding value in the case of reports of sites perceived as having positive features. However, considering that the maximum distance in the sample is 102.8 km, this difference continues to be a relatively low but statistically significant value. This result still demonstrates the presence of the spatial discounting effect in the case of reports of degraded sites. In addition, when looking at the mean distance of the first reports, which in this case is 16.4 km, the conclusions are very similar to those obtained for the previous dataset: respondents tended to report places which are the nearest to them first.

Finally, it seems important to underline the fact that, both in the case of reports concerning sites with positive features and degraded ones, the simulations lead to the same results regardless of the choice of the extraction sample scheme (with or without replacement). This empirical result (i.e. the mean is always the same) suggests that the main findings are invariant to the extraction sample scheme.

6   Conclusions

Internet participatory mapping initiatives are gaining increasing popularity as a tool to collect citizens' knowledge of the territories that surround them. Despite having the undeniable advantage of permitting the involvement of citizens regardless of their specific geographic location, this feature is not enough to guarantee the spatial representativeness of respondents. For a better interpretation of participants' mapping activity and a potential use of such spatial data as a source of political reflection, it is also necessary to take into account, besides the response of the target population to such initiatives, how participants' characteristics can affect outcomes. This paper aimed to provide a methodological contribution to the study of participatory data bias in

PPGIS applications by studying the relationship of a respondent's reference municipality with the position of the mapped elements.

In this work, the tendency of respondents to map places within their reference municipality and its close proximity has emerged. Moreover, the mapping outcome also suggests that people identify as a first report a place that is closer to their home, if compared to the second and third reports which are generally further away. These results highlight the limitations associated with the recruitment of volunteers and the dissemination of the initiative via the internet. As people tended to map places near their home, it is necessary, if the objective is to carry out an analysis of the entire regional territory, to implement a dissemination strategy that takes into account the spatial distribution of the participants. The use of the Internet as a mean to interact with participants impacted on the ability to control their spatial distribution. One of the consequence of such choice is that the mapping output is not evenly distributed throughout the region but it is concentrated on areas close to the actual respondents.

We also provided empirical evidence that degraded sites are more distance-sensitive than sites of beauty. The attribute of interest constituted by degraded sites, which in this research is the attribute given the most attention as they constitute areas most in need of change, is the landscape attribute that (unfortunately) received fewer reports and which was generally closer respondents' location. These results suggest the need to plan a data collection scheme that takes into account the thematic content of the spatial attribute. The fact that people tended to remember and map beautiful places further away from home means that a participants' home is less likely to affect mapping outcome, compared to degraded sites.

Despite the strong evidence in this paper for participatory data bias, further research is needed to increase our understanding of the impact of respondents' domicile. One priority is to identify the geographic space that best approximates the area with which people have strong knowledge, as using the municipality as a reference, that is an administrative unit, could be oversimple. In our view, it would also be relevant to study the intensity of the report in order to unravel if all reports have equal importance in the eyes of the respondents or if there are sites that are perceived as more worthy of attention than others. We found evidence of a difference between the first report made and the others, in terms of distance from a participant's home. However, further analysis is needed to assess whether the order of the reports also corresponds to a sort of hierarchy of attention. Another crucial issue is to consider whether the spatial distribution of the attributes of interest is linked with the absence/presence of the built environment. One would expect that more high-quality sites would be found in natural areas, while degraded sites are linked to the presence of abandoned buildings. The physical geography of the study area, plus the demographic distribution of the population, are likely to affect the mapping activity. Furthermore, the inclusion in the analysis of additional variables on the geographical setting (such as living in an urban or rural area) can contribute to understanding the impact of place-specific factors on the mapping results.

Before user-generated content (such as in our research) can substitute expert views and rigorous data collection methods based on statistical sampling, which are extremely difficult to implement in this context, important issues such as the impact of participants' location on their mapping activity need to be addressed.

Acknowledgments. This contribution is the result of the work carried out for the project "VGI and the Landscapes of Risk and Degradation", conducted at the University of Udine, which especially from a quantitative perspective deepens the research carried out for the departmental project PaRiDe. The authors thank Mauro Pascolini, Andrea Guaran, and Salvatore Amaduzzi, who are the other members of the PaRiDe research group. Some preliminary results of the map-based approach that allowed the collection of the spatial data analyzed in this paper were presented at the seminar "Dalla mappa al GIS 2019" (Rome, 17-18 April 2019).

References

1. Bressan, G., Amaduzzi, S.: Map-based surveys for mapping high-quality and degraded sites. In: Gallia, A. (ed.) Territorio: rischio/risorsa. Labgeo Caraci, Rome, pp. 197–213 (2020)
2. Bressan, G., Pascolini, M.: Dalle percezioni della popolazione al dato georiferito: studio quali-quantitativo del paesaggio del Friuli V.G. In: 23a Conferenza Nazionale ASITA, Asita, Trieste, pp. 115–122 (2019)
3. Brody, S.D., Highfield, W., Alston, L.: Does location matter? measuring environmental perceptions of creeks in two san antonio watersheds. Environ. Behav. **36**, 229–250 (2004). https://doi.org/10.1177/0013916503256900
4. Brown, G.: A review of sampling effects and response bias in internet participatory mapping (PPGIS/PGIS/VGI). Trans. GIS **21**, 39–56 (2017). https://doi.org/10.1111/tgis.12207
5. Brown, G., Reed, P.: Public participation GIS: a new method for use in national forest planning. For. Sci. **55**, 166–182 (2009). https://doi.org/10.1093/forestscience/55.2.166
6. Brown, G., Kyttä, M.: Key issues and research priorities for public participation GIS (PPGIS): a synthesis based on empirical research. Appl. Geogr. **46**, 122–136 (2014). https://doi.org/10.1016/j.apgeog.2013.11.004
7. Brown, G., Reed, P., Harris, C.C.: Testing a place-based theory for environmental evaluation: an Alaska case study. Appl. Geogr. **22**, 49–76 (2002). https://doi.org/10.1016/s0143-6228(01)00019-4
8. Davison, A.C., Hinkley, D.V.: Bootstrap Methods and Their Application. Cambridge University Press, Cambridge (1997)
9. Efron, B., Tibshirani, R.J.: An Introduction to the Bootstrap. Chapman & Hall/CRC Press, Boca Raton (1998)
10. Hannon, B.: Sense of place: geographic discounting by people, animals and plants. Ecol. Econ. **10**, 157–174 (1994). https://doi.org/10.1016/0921-8009(94)90006-x
11. Klonner, C., Usón, T.J., Marx, S., Mocnik, F.-B., Höfle, B.: Capturing flood risk perception via sketch maps. ISPRS Int. J. Geo-Inf. **7**(9), 359 (2018). https://doi.org/10.3390/ijgi7090359
12. Norton, B.G., Hannon, B.: Environmental values: a place-based theory. Environ. Ethics **19**, 227–245 (1997)
13. Pocewicz, A., Nielsen-Pincus, M.: Preferences of Wyoming residents for siting of energy and residential development. Appl. Geogr. **43**, 45–55 (2013). https://doi.org/10.1016/j.apgeog.2013.06.006
14. R Core Team, R.: A language and environment for statistical computing. R Foundation for Statistical Computing. R-project.org, Vienna, Austria (2019)
15. Santé, I., Fernández-Ríos, A., Tubío, J.M., García-Fernández, F., Farkova, E., Miranda, D.: The landscape inventory of galicia (NW Spain): GIS-web and public participation for landscape planning. Landscape Res. **44**, 212–240 (2018). https://doi.org/10.1080/01426397.2018.1444155

16. Sieber, R.: Public participation geographic information systems: a literature review and framework. Ann. Assoc. Am. Geogr. **96**, 491–507 (2006). https://doi.org/10.1111/j.1467-8306.2006.00702.x

17. de Vries, S., Buijs, A.E., Langers, F., Farjon, H., van Hinsberg, A., Sijtsma, F.J.: Measuring the attractiveness of Dutch landscapes: Identifying national hotspots of highly valued places using Google Maps. Appl. Geogr. **45**, 220–229 (2013). https://doi.org/10.1016/j.apgeog.2013.09.017

Describing the Residential Valorisation of Urban Space at the Street Level. The French Riviera as Example

Alessandro Venerandi[1]([⊠]) and Giovanni Fusco[2]

[1] Université Côte-Azur, ESPACE, Nice, France
alessandro.venerandi@univ-cotedazur.fr
[2] Université Côte-Azur, CNRS, ESPACE, Nice, France
giovanni.fusco@univ-cotedazur.fr

Abstract. There is a growing concern regarding the use of relatively coarse units for the aggregation of various spatial information. Researchers thus suggest that the street segment might be better suited than areal units for carrying out such a task. Furthermore, the street segment has recently become one of the most prominent spatial units, for example, to study street network centrality, retail density, and urban form. In this paper, we thus propose to use the street segment as unit of analysis for calculating the residential valorisation of urban space. To be more specific, we define a protocol that characterises street segments through a measure of central tendency and one of dispersion of prices. Moreover, through Bayesian clustering, it classifies street segments according to the most probable combination house type-valuation to provide a picture of local submarkets. We apply this methodology to the housing transactions exchanged in the French Riviera, in the period 2008–2017, and observe that outputs seem to align with local specificities of the housing market of that region. We suggest that the proposed protocol can be useful as an explorative tool to question and interpret the housing market, in any metropolitan region, at a fine level of spatial granularity.

Keywords: House prices · Street network · Summary statistics · Bayesian clustering · French Riviera

1 Introduction

The scale at which socioeconomic indicators are computed is of paramount importance, especially if they then guide urban interventions. In France, social mix policies have been harshly criticized because they targeted spatial units that were too coarse (i.e., entire municipalities) and seemed to produce segregation at a smaller level of spatial granularity [1]. In studying the relationship between poverty and accessibility in Atlanta (GA, US), Carpenter and Peponis [2] highlighted how even census tracts and city blocks could hid differences, which became apparent only when considering street segments[1].

---

[1] A street segment is the line connecting two intersections in a street network.

© Springer Nature Switzerland AG 2020
O. Gervasi et al. (Eds.): ICCSA 2020, LNCS 12252, pp. 505–520, 2020.
https://doi.org/10.1007/978-3-030-58811-3_37

In the last 60 years, the street segment has gained recognition as one of the most relevant spatial units of analysis because is the physical component at the basis of the functioning of urban systems [3–6]. Thus, several indicators were computed at such level of spatial granularity. In Urban Design, for example, researchers defined and computed several street-based metrics of network centrality (e.g., betweenness, closeness) [5]. Similarly, in the field of Geography, academics quantified several aspects of urban form and commerce at the street level and summarised this information through Bayesian clustering [7, 8]. However, to the best of the authors' knowledge, street-based indicators of the housing market have never been defined. Aggregations of such information are usually made at areal level or through surface interpolation [9]. However, such aggregations never concerned street segments.

In this paper, we propose a novel protocol to aggregate information on house prices for street segments, to study the relative residential valorisation of urban space, street by street. To be more specific, such protocol, firstly, renders house prices comparable across different years and house types; secondly, it aggregates such information for streets segments by means of a measures of central tendency and one of dispersion; thirdly, it uses Bayesian clustering to categorise streets based on their most probable price range-house type. To test the protocol, we implemented it on the housing transactions exchanged in the French Riviera, in the period 2008–2017, and observed that patterns of value and dispersion at the street level and clusters of price range and house type seem to correspond to current real estate and socioeconomic dynamics. For example, the outputs of the proposed protocol well identify historically well-off sets of streets (e.g., Promenade des Anglais and Carré d'Or in Nice and the eastern part of Cannes) as well as more popular ones (e.g., Vieux-Nice, Grasse and Vallauris).

We argue that the protocol presented in this paper might be useful to realtors and public officials to obtain an alternative reading of the housing market, which, in turn, might inspire innovations in sales strategies and policy making. Furthermore, it might be helpful to researchers who want to analyse the relationship between any kind of street-based phenomenon and the housing market. Related to this, our protocol would also avoid statistical issues associated with the aggregation of data computed for different spatial units. Several studies explored the relationship between housing transactions and street network centrality, for example Chiaradia et al. [10] and Narvaez et al. [11], but their focus was still on transactions seen as points in urban space, overlooking data aggregation issues at the level of street segments.

The reminder of this paper is structured as follows: we firstly present related works, pointing out the relevance of the street segment as spatial unit of analysis; secondly, we illustrate the methodology to characterise the housing market at the street level; thirdly, we present the data used to test the methodology and its pre-processing; fourthly, we lay out the results; finally, we conclude with final remarks and possible future work.

2   Related Works

This section firstly provides a brief excursus on the relevance of the street segment as spatial unit of analysis in various fields. Secondly, it presents previous works that focused on the computation of street-based measures of several urban phenomena. Thirdly, it illustrates known aggregation techniques of house prices, at different spatial resolutions.

2.1   The Street Segment: A Brief Retrospective

The street segment has for long been considered one of the most relevant spatial units by several researchers. Conzen [3], one of the founders of the Anglo-German school of Urban Morphology, theorised a technique of town plan analysis focused on three main components: the streets and their organisation into a street system (i.e., street network); the plots and their arrangement into street blocks; buildings as block plans. In his view, these three elements were keys to understand the form and dynamics of urban settlements. The Italian school of Urban Morphology developed a similar theory and much of its research on the form and evolution of settlements focused on the "fascia di pertinenza" ("pertinent strip"), that is the street with all the plots that abut on it [12]. Several influential works that focused on the role of streets in cities were also developed in US context, in the second half of the XXth century. Jacobs [4], renown urban theorist and activist, considered streets as the most important spatial entities in cities as their form and configuration not only affected human interactions, but also the success of neighbourhoods, in terms of liveability and economic prosperity. Lynch [13] based much of his imageability theory on the visual perception that pedestrians have at the street level. More recently, an entire new branch of quantitative research focused on the analysis of streets, and the network they create, from a graph theory perspective [5, 6, 14].

2.2   Examples of Street-Based Measures

Several works in different domains focused on the definition and implementation of street-based measures. Porta et al. [5], for example, formalized a set of centrality measures to study the configuration of street networks. Such measures are based on the assumption that a street could be central, with respect to all the other streets in a network, in different ways: being central as being characterized by through-movement (i.e., betweenness centrality) or by high interconnectedness in a small space (i.e., closeness centrality). These very same measures, however with different names (i.e., choice for betweenness and integration for closeness), are also at the basis of the Space Syntax methodology [6].

Researchers in the field of Urban Geography defined several street-based measures to quantify aspects of urban form and commerce [7, 8]. The former are, for example, the fragmentation of street fronts and canyon effect [7]. Measures of commerce at the street level were, for example, the richness of retail categories within 300 m of a store location or the ratio between the number of stores belonging to a specific category and the total number of stores within the same radius [8]. Here again, retail becomes a street-dependent phenomenon, both for its description and understanding.

2.3 Spatial Aggregation of House Prices

Classic techniques for the aggregation of house prices focus on areal units (e.g., census areas). In France, for example, Meilleurs Agents (i.e., a private company that offers real estate services) and Notaires de France (i.e., the French association of notaries) provide the average[2] and median price[3] per square meter, respectively, for official administrative boundaries called IRIS. In England, the London Datastore provides information on the average and median house prices[4] for census areas of various sizes, the finest of which is at the intra-neighbourhood scale, i.e. Lower Layer Super Output Area (LSOA).

A more advanced technique of aggregation of house prices is the Kernel Density Estimation (KDE), which interpolates values, usually through a Gaussian function, at a chosen resolution. McMillen [9], for example, used such a technique to pre-process 25,633 housing transactions of single-family homes in Chicago (IL, US), before testing different modelling solutions.

In this section, we illustrated that there exist different types of aggregation methods of house prices, however, none of them focused on the street segment. In the next section, we present a novel protocol to carry out this task and provide not only information on a measure of central tendency, but also on dispersion of values and on the belonging to a given residential submarket.

3   Method

To characterise the housing market at the street level, our methodology requires three subsequent steps:

- data pre-processing;
- aggregation of house prices at the street level through a measure of central tendency and one of dispersion;
- application of Bayesian clustering to classify each street based on its most probable price range and house type.

We provide more details on each of these steps in the following subsections.

3.1   Data Pre-processing

The study of the relative valorisation of subspaces, being them districts, census tracts, city-blocks, or streets always needs aggregation of house prices. However, such data

---

[2] https://www.meilleursagents.com/prix-immobilier/provence-alpes-cote-d-azur/.

[3] https://www.immobilier.notaires.fr/fr/prix-immobilier?periodeReferences=1ettypeLocalisation=
COMMUNEetcodeInsee=06088.

[4] https://data.london.gov.uk/dataset/average-house-prices.

for different house types and years are not directly comparable for two main reasons. Firstly, each calendar year has specific economic trends, namely inflation and housing market cycles (i.e., recession or upturn), which affect the prices of properties on a yearly basis. Secondly, different house types have different markets and this unevenly affects the valuations. For example, small flats tend to be sold more frequently than larger homes because they usually have higher demand and involve short term investments. On the contrary, larger properties tend to be sold less frequently than smaller homes because they typically have lower demand and they are associated with long term investments. The average price per square meter tends also to be structurally higher for smaller flats due to very technical reasons (i.e., even the smallest flat needs sanitary and cooking equipment, which proportionally weigh more on the average price per surface unit compared to larger properties). The very notion of an average price per square meter can thus be challenged when applied to such diverse sections of the housing market. To address these issues and have prices comparable across several years and house types our method requires three subsequent steps:

- segmenting the data by year of transaction;
- segmenting the data by house type;
- computing ventiles and deciles of house prices for each subset year of transaction-house type.

At the end of this process, the valuations are comparable as they have been segmented by typology and year and are expressed in relative terms, that is they are no longer nominal values but classes of prices (i.e., ventiles and deciles). We will explain the use of such classes of prices in the next paragraphs.

3.2 Computation of Median and Dispersion

To obtain information on the central measure and dispersion of prices at the street level, the next step of our protocol requires to, firstly, associate each data point to the street segment to which they belong and, secondly, aggregate such information at the street level, through the computation of a measure of central tendency and one of dispersion. The first of such measures is the median of the ventiles, which provides information on the mid-point of the local distribution of the relative housing valuation, for each street. The second measure is the difference between the 9th decile (D9) and the 1st decile (D1) of the distribution of the ventiles. This provides information on the range of valuations in each street. Our method requires to compute these statistics for the ensemble of each street segment and its immediate neighbouring segments, directly connected to it. This provides a smoothing of local statistics, which takes into account the morphological impact of closely connected street segments and the "hybrid" situation of properties laying on street corners. Since our protocol requires the computation of the D9-D1 statistic, street segments with too few transactions should not be considered. We thus propose to consider only those – and relative neighbouring streets – with at least 10 transactions. This also recognises the limits, in terms of statistical knowledge, of the relative valorisation of street segments when using transaction data: below a certain threshold, our knowledge is too limited and, as we will see in the Conclusions, issues of uncertainty might arise.

3.3   Identifying Classes of Housing Market

To identify different classes of housing markets at the street level, the last step of our methodology requires the application of a well-known technique for classification purposes (i.e., Bayesian Networks) to the double description (i.e., house type and value) associated to each street segment. More specifically, we describe each of these spatial elements with a total of 17 variables: 10 correspond to the percentages of properties falling in each decile of the distribution of house prices; 7 represent the percentages of properties for each house type.

Several statistical and machine learning methods can cluster instances into classes. However, we argue that Bayesian Networks are better suited, in this specific case, for two main reasons. They can identify subsets of records presenting a precise pattern on a limited number of features whereas other methods usually look for homogeneous behaviour of records across all features [15]. A further advantage is that the clustering uses probabilities defined on a finite probability space. We can thus identify elements which belong to a given cluster with low uncertainty (for example, when the probability of assignment is higher than 0.9) and more "hybrid" ones, which have a higher probability of belonging to other clusters.

Operationally, Bayesian Networks work as follows. A star-shaped network is built between all the measured variables and a newly implemented non observable node, which plays the role of a cluster variable. Such variable is linked to each individual variable through oriented arcs, in what is called a naive Bayes classifier [16]. In such a network, each variable becomes independent of the value of every other knowing the cluster, hence the name "naive". The conditional probability tables linking the cluster variable to each observed variable are determined through an Expectation-Maximisation (EM) algorithm [17]. These probabilistic parameters are recursively used to assign to each given record its most probable cluster. Two different schemes can guide the EM algorithm. The easiest one consists in predetermining the number of clusters required, as in k-means clustering. The EM algorithm is here guided by likelihood maximisation of the clustering model, given the data. By repeating the clustering process for different number of clusters, the algorithm obtains a series of optimal solutions. A more computationally intensive scheme consists in applying a random walk among all possible solutions, considering different number of clusters. The EM algorithm is, in this case, guided by a Minimal Description Length score [18], which combines clustering likelihood to a penalisation factor for the number of clusters used in the model (to avoid overfitting), and its result is a unique optimal solution. Both schemes were applied within our research.

4   Application to the French Riviera

The French Riviera is a coastal metropolitan area in South-Eastern France, stretching over 60 km from the French-Italian border to the Esterel mountains. It includes several towns and cities, namely, from East to West, Menton, Monaco, Nice, Antibes and Cannes. After being the birthplace of aristocratic tourism in the XIX century, and of mass tourism since the 1930s, this metropolitan area of more than 1 million people has presently one of the tensest real estate markets in France, after the one of Paris, the capital city. The Principality of Monaco is one of the most expensive markets in the whole of Europe, but it will be excluded from our analysis, given its fiscal and regulatory specificity. The municipalities of the French Riviera are required by law to favour residential mix through their social housing projects, but they are all far from attaining the 25% threshold imposed by the ALUR Law for 2025 [19]. Lack of generational mix is also becoming a concern on the French Riviera. Because of the high demand for small secondary homes, the coastal cities seem increasingly unable to cater for families with children. These are thus leaving the most central areas and moving to suburban and exurban areas in the hinterland which, in turn, have difficulties in coping with the sudden increase of demand for day-care and schooling. Gentrification of city-centres and further development of the tourism economy through Airbnb add to this trend. If issues of social and generational mix were to be addressed (as the public policies state), then it is fundamental to understand the spatial logic of the private housing sector in this area.

We thus applied the methodology presented above to the housing transactions exchanged in the French Riviera, between 2008 and 2017. To carry out our study, we accessed two official data sources: PERVAL, which contains information on housing transactions, and BD TOPO, which contains the street network of the study area, in vector format. We provide more details on these next.

4.1   Datasets

PERVAL

The PERVAL is a proprietary dataset containing recorded housing transactions in France[5]. It is curated and kept updated by the association Notaires de France, the French association of notaries. PERVAL is a very rich geo-referenced dataset containing tens of features for each transaction. The information provided goes from the habitable surface to the energetic label, from the number of rooms to the presence of a basement, from the condition of properties to the number of toilets. For the purpose of this study, we obtain PERVAL data for the French Riviera and its close hinterland, for the period 2008–2017. This resulted in a total of 150,116 transactions, 124,236 of which are flats, while 25,880 are single houses. The average price (taxes included) of a flat is €205,075, that of a single house is €711,747.

BDTOPO

The DB TOPO is an official dataset, provided in shapefile format, that contains vector representations of multiple elements of the landscape and the built environment, such as, streets, natural features, and buildings[6]. It is issued and kept constantly updated by the Institute National de l'Information Geographique et Forestiere (the French national institute of Geography and Forestry). For the purpose of our study, we obtain the BD TOPO dataset for the area under study, which contains 98,297 junction-to-junction street segments, with an average length of 131 m.

---

[5] https://www.perval.fr/.

[6] http://professionnels.ign.fr/bdtopo.

4.2   Pre-processing

A first analysis of the PERVAL dataset revealed some issues, for example, spatial inaccuracies were present for some housing transactions. Moreover, it did not include housing typologies, a requirement of our methodology. A pre-processing has thus been necessary before proceeding further. Such procedure mainly included: performing a new geocoding based on the addresses provided with PERVAL; cleaning and repairing the dataset; and assigning housing typologies to each transaction. We provide more details on each step next.

To perform the new geocoding, we matched the addresses of each housing transaction contained in PERVAL with the ones contained in the Base Address Nationale (BAN), the official dataset of French addresses. At the end of this process, each transaction had a set of geographic coordinates derived from BAN, which was then used to re-geocode the entire dataset. Although BAN is accurate, the spatial precision was particularly low for 25,078 transactions (e.g., some transactions were geo-coded at the municipal level). We thus filtered them out.

Having carried out this step, we performed some further cleaning and repairing. The PERVAL dataset included transactions of properties that were not the subject of this study, that is retirement homes and properties under special contractual agreements. The values of such properties could be quite different from the ones sold at normal market prices and could thus bias the analysis. For this reason, we discarded them. At the end of this process, the total number of transactions was 113,781, 95,556 of these were flats, while 18,225 were single houses.

As we mentioned above, the PERVAL dataset did not include information on the house type of each transaction, a datum required by our protocol. However, it contained information on the broad category of each property (i.e., single house or flat) and the number of rooms. We thus assigned a house type to each transaction based on this information and created the following categories: T1 for studios and 1-bedroom flats, T2 for 2-bedroom flats, T3 for 3-bedroom flats, T4 for 4-bedroom flats, T5 for flats with 5 bedrooms or more, small houses (PM, petites maisons in French) for single houses with up to 4 rooms, and big houses (GM, grandes maisons in French) for single houses with 5 or more rooms. For 1,770 transactions, typology had to be estimated from dwelling surface since the number of rooms was not available in the original database.

5   Results

5.1   Median and Dispersion of House Prices in the French Riviera

Having assigned a dwelling type to each transaction, we segmented the PERVAL dataset by year and house type. We thus obtained 60 separate datasets, one for each combination year of transaction - house type. Following the proposed protocol, we computed ventiles of house prices for each subset. To then aggregate the information at the street level, we firstly assigned to each transaction the ID of the closest street segment and, secondly, we computed median and dispersion of ventiles for units comprising each street segment and its directly linked segments, whenever a minimum of 10 transactions were found in such spatial unit.

We present the median of ventiles of prices for the whole study area and a zoom on the city of Nice in Fig. 1. The information provided by these maps reveals the overall valorization-devalorization of the street segments within the study area. Furthermore, we present the dispersion of ventiles of prices for the whole study area and a zoom on the city of Nice in Fig. 2. This latter set of maps visualize a less explored aspect of housing prices, that is the capacity of streets to support a wide variety of values (streets that tend to red) or to specialize in a specific market segment (streets that tend to blue).

A visual inspection of these maps allows several considerations on the relationship between the outputs and the current socioeconomic as well as real estate market conditions in the French Riviera. By taking Nice as example, we note that the historically well-off neighborhood of Cimiez, characterized by villas and detached blocks of flats, has many streets in the top three classes of ventiles (i.e., 14–16, 16–18, 18–20). We observe a similar pattern in the Carre d'Or, a very central neighborhood built in the XIX century, with elegant blocks of 5–6 floors. For what concerns devalued streets (i.e., streets in classes 1–2, 2–4, 4–6), the output seems to correctly identified those of the historic core of Nice (i.e., Vieux-Nice), which is a heritage district but lacks, at times, of contemporary living standards (e.g., more generous habitable surfaces, natural light). The very same reason probably holds true also for the devalued streets of some ancient settlements outside of Nice, such as Grasse, Vence, and Vallauris.

For what regards the dispersion of ventiles of prices (Fig. 2), the outputs of our method show that the traditional centers of the coastal cities, characterized by short street segments, are more capable of supporting ranges of house prices (i.e., classes 14–16, 16–18, 18–19) than the peripheral and suburban areas, which, conversely, are characterized by longer street segments. This holds true for Nice, Menton, Antibes and even Cannes, with the exception of the luxurious Boulevard de La Croisette and nearby streets, which tend to have a more homogeneously highly priced housing market. By allowing a greater mix of housing valuations, the streets of the coastal city-centers might thus favor more socioeconomic mix. However, there are also sets of central streets that tend to more stably retain high or low valuations and thus probably attract the same population segments. The former are, for example, the above mentioned Boulevard de La Croisette and nearby streets in Cannes, the latter can be found around the main train station of Nice. For what concerns more peripheral/suburban streets, we observe homogeneously high valorization in the capes (Cap Ferrat, Cap-d'Ail, Cap Martin, Cap d'Antibes), coastal areas of outstanding scenic beauty and homogenous devalorization in the streets near the two above mentioned social housing estates (i.e., Ariane and Les Moulins) and at the bottom of valleys, such as Route de Canta Galet and Boulevard de la Madeleine in Nice, which tend to have unfavorable micro-climatic conditions (i.e., lower amount of day-light, higher levels of pollution).

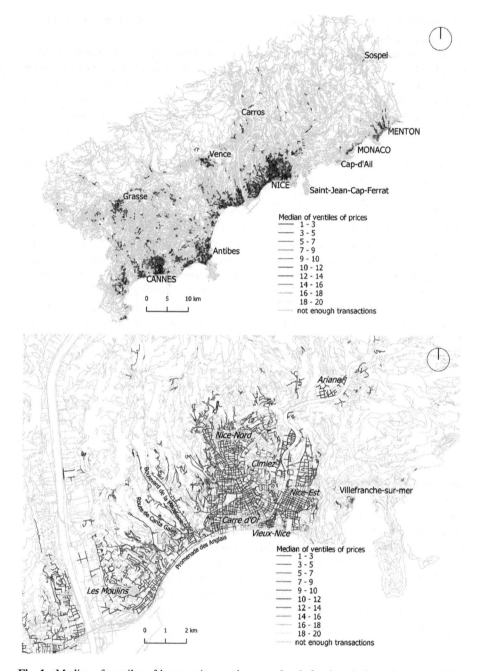

Fig. 1. Median of ventiles of house prices at the street level, for the whole study area and the city of Nice.

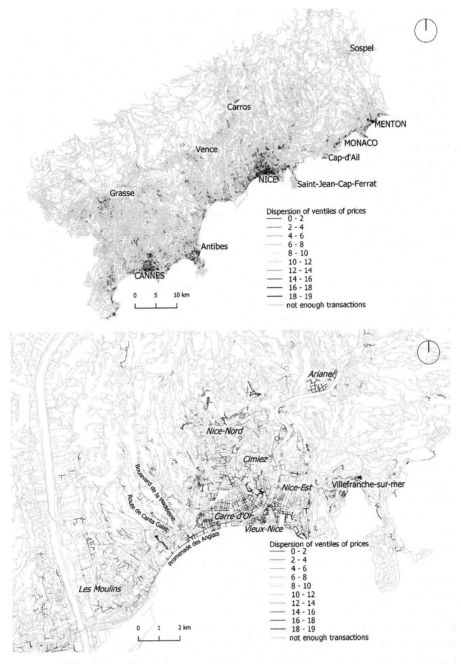

Fig. 2. Dispersion of ventiles of house prices at the street level, for the whole study area and the city of Nice. (Color figure online)

5.2   Classes of Housing Markets in the French Riviera

The analyses conducted so far allow a fine description of the spatial logic of housing valorization and devalorization on the French Riviera, which is potentially very relevant in terms of social mix. However, generational mix (or lack of) cannot be understood only in terms of valorization, but has to addressed also from the perspective of house types. To have a description of the housing market at the street level that integrates both value and house types, we applied Bayesian Networks to the previously computed 10 variables of deciles of prices and the 7 variables of house types (i.e., T1, T2, T3, T4, T5, PM, and GM). However, before performing the computation we weighted each of the house type variable 1.5 to balance the amount of information provided by the 10 variables associated with the deciles of prices. The random walk search for the best clustering, output by the Bayesian Network, converged to a solution with 10 classes. The final output had a contingency table fit score of 27% (i.e., the amount of information contained in the 17 variables which was captured by the cluster variable). We interpreted the probabilistic profiles of the 10 clusters and defined the following labels:

- Cluster 1 (C1): small to medium flats with value above average;
- Cluster 2 (C2): very small flats with mixed values;
- Cluster 3 (C3): medium to big flats with medium value;
- Cluster 4 (C4): big flats and houses with very high value;
- Cluster 5 (C5): small flats with value above average;
- Cluster 6 (C6): flats of mixed sizes with low value;
- Cluster 7 (C7): flats and houses with mixed values;
- Cluster 8 (C8): flats of mixed sizes with very high value;
- Cluster 9 (C9): medium to big flats with very low value;
- Cluster 10 (C10): houses with low value.

In Fig. 3, we map the clusters output by the Bayesian Networks on the street segments of the whole study area and the city of Nice. By visually inspecting these maps, we observe that the output of the Bayesian Networks seems to add a layer of information to the results for median and dispersion previously showed. More specifically, we observe that the groups of streets uniformly characterized by above average valuations in Fig. 1 (i.e., the eastern part of Cannes, the city center of Nice, and the area around Menton) are actually more nuanced, if housing typologies are accounted for. The eastern part of Cannes is characterized by very expensive flats, however of mixed sizes (i.e., C8). In the city center of Nice and in Menton, flats are moderately expansive, but also small to medium-sized (i.e., C1 and C5). There are also differences in groups of streets evenly characterized by low and median values in Fig. 1. For example, in Nice-Nord and Nice-Est, the housing market is relatively devalorized. However, there are notable changes within these submarkets, namely the presence of sets of streets with medium to big flats (i.e., C9), very small ones (i.e., C2), and flats of mixed sizes (i.e., C6). Interestingly, higher dispersion of prices, which tends to be more present in central areas (see Fig. 2), seems to affect streets characterized by very diverse housing typologies and not only small flats.

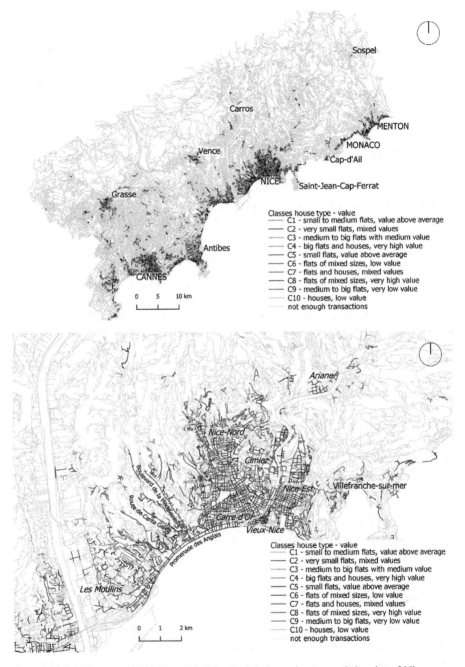

Fig. 3. Classes value - house type, for the whole study area and the city of Nice.

We also remark the peculiarity of clusters C2 and C7 as they both offer a wide range of valuations, with C7 also offering a mix of house types. Due to these characteristics, we suggest that streets belonging to C7 and, to a lesser extent C2, are likely to be more prone to generational and socioeconomic mix, an aspect which is considered fundamental for promoting a more equal society and thriving neighborhoods by several urbanists and researchers. See, for example, the works by Matan and Newman [20] and Andersson [21].

6 Conclusions

In the last 60 years, the street segment has gained recognition as one of the most relevant spatial units of analysis in different fields (e.g., Urban Morphology, Urban Design). Several street-based measures have been defined at this level of spatial granularity. However, as of today, a street-based measure of house prices has yet to be defined. In this paper, we proposed a protocol to carry out precisely this task by aggregating information on housing transactions at the street level in three ways: through a measure of central tendency (i.e., median of prices), through a measure of dispersion of prices, and through classes value-house type. We implemented such protocol on the housing transactions occurred in the French Riviera, in the period 2008–2017, and found patterns that seemed to correspond to current socioeconomic and real estate market specificities. For example, the patterns of high and low median valuations seem to match the urban landscapes of better-off and less-advantaged neighbourhoods, respectively. The dispersion of prices seem, instead, to be especially concentrated in areas more intensely urban, regardless of the house types. Finally, the classes value-house types seem to add further knowledge to the characterisation provided by the median and dispersion of prices. For example, although both the eastern part of Cannes and the centre of Nice are characterised by medium to high median values, they can be seen as different local markets. The former tends to have flats of different sizes, while the latter only small to medium sized ones. We suggest that the protocol proposed in this paper might be useful to a wide range of actors, from realtors, who might want to explore alternative readings of the housing market, to public officials, who might desire to use its outputs in policy making. Finally, academics might want to analyse the relationship between the outputs of our protocol and existing or novel street-based measures.

7 Future Work

We consider the outputs presented in this paper only the first phase of a wider research endeavour on urban housing markets. In fact, we envision three main research directions. Firstly, our protocol was able to identify streets with greater dispersion of prices. We thus hypothesised that such dispersion was associated with more socioeconomic mix. Future work might test: whether this pattern is confirmed through quantitative analysis, for example, through the analysis of the relationship between dispersion of prices and socioeconomic indicators extracted from census data. Secondly, since our methodology ignores street segments with a limited number of housing transactions, we envision to use uncertainty-based methodologies to infer the housing market characteristics of streets with partial information. Thirdly, the interpretations of the outcomes presented in this paper were based on expert knowledge. Future work should ascertain whether such interpretations hold from a quantitative standpoint, for example, through the implementation of linear or non-linear models that explore the relationship between the proposed street-based measures of housing values and morphological, positional and configurational characteristics of the built environment. Comparison with other approaches like Geographically Weighted Regression [22] could also be carried out, as long as the street segment is kept as the spatial unit of analysis.

Acknowledgements. This research was funded by the French Government, through the National Research Agency, under the Investissements d'Avenir IDEX UCA JEDI, with reference number ANR-15-IDEX-01. The authors would like to thank Pr. Andrea Tettamanzi, at I3S Laboratory in Université Côte d'Azur, and Dr. Denis Overal, director of the R&D at Kinaxia, for their support and insightful suggestions.

References

1. Jaillet, M.C., Perrin, E., et Ménard, F.: Diversité sociale, ségrégation urbaine, mixité. Research report Plan Urbanisme Construction Architecture (PUCA) (2008)
2. Carpenter, A., Peponis, J.: Poverty and connectivity. J. Space Syntax **1**(1), 108–120 (2010)
3. Conzen, M.R.G.: Alnwick, Northumberland: a study in town-plan analysis. Trans. Papers (Inst. Brit. Geogr.) **27**, iii–122 (1960)
4. Jacobs, J.: The Death and Life of Great American Cities. Random House, New York (1961)
5. Porta, S., Crucitti, P., Latora, V.: The network analysis of urban streets: a primal approach. Environ. Plan. B Plan. Des. **33**(5), 705–725 (2006)
6. Hillier, B.: Space is the Machine: a Configurational Theory of Architecture. Space Syntax, London (2007)
7. Araldi, A., Fusco, G.: Decomposing and recomposing urban fabric: The city from the pedestrian point of view. In: Gervasi, O., et al. (eds.) ICCSA 2017. LNCS, vol. 10407, pp. 365–376. Springer, Cham (2017). https://doi.org/10.1007/978-3-319-62401-3_27
8. Araldi, A., Fusco, G.: Retail fabric assessment: describing retail patterns within urban space. Cities **85**, 51–62 (2018)
9. McMillen, D.P.: Changes in the distribution of house prices over time: structural characteristics, neighborhood, or coefficients? J. Urban Econ. **64**(3), 573–589 (2008)
10. Chiaradia, A., Hillier, B., Barnes, Y., Schwander, C.: Residential property value patterns in London: space syntax spatial analysis. In: Proceedings to the 7th International Space Syntax Symposium, Stockholm, Sweden (2009)
11. Narvaez, L., Penn, A., Griffiths, S.: Space syntax economics: decoding accessibility using property value and housing price in Cardiff, Wales. In: Proceedings of the Eighth International Space Syntax Symposium, Santiago, Chile (2012)
12. Caniggia, G., Maffei, G.L.: Architectural composition and building typology: interpreting basic building. Alinea Editrice, Florence, Italy (2001)
13. Lynch, K.: The Image of the City. MIT press, Cambridge (1960)

14. Batty, M.: Cities as Complex Systems: Scaling, Interaction, Networks, Dynamics and Urban Morphologies. Research report Centre for Advanced Spatial Analysis (CASA), no. 131 (2009)
15. Fusco, G., Perez, J.: Bayesian Network clustering and self-organizing maps under the test of Indian districts. A comparison. Cybergeo Eur. J. Geogr. (2020). https://doi.org/10.4000/cybergeo.31909. http://journals.openedition.org/cybergeo/31909
16. Duda, R., Hart, P.: Pattern Classification and Scene Analysis. Wiley, New York (1973)
17. Dempster, A., Laird, N., Rubin, D.: Maximum likelihood from incomplete data via the EM algorithm. J. Roy. Stat. Soc. Ser. B 39(1), 1–38 (1977)
18. Rissanen, J.: Information and Complexity in Statistical Modeling. Springer, New York (2007)
19. Levasseur, S.: La loi SRU et les quotas de logements sociaux 15 ans après, quel bilan? Research report OFCE (Sciences Po) no. 54 (2015)
20. Matan, A., Newman, P.: People Cities: The life and Legacy of Jan Gehl. Island Press, Washington (2016)
21. Andersson, C.: Public space and the new urban agenda. J. Public Space 1(1), 5–10 (2016)
22. Manganelli, B., Pontrandolfi, P., Azzato, A., Murgante, B.: Using geographically weighted regression for housing market segmentation. Int. J. Bus. Intell. Data Min. 9(2), 161–177 (2014)

A Toolset to Estimate the Effects of Human Activities in Maritime Spatial Planning

Henning Sten Hansen[(⊠)] and Ida Maria Bonnevie

Aalborg University Copenhagen, A.C. Meyers Vænge 15,
2450 Copenhagen, Denmark
hsh@plan.aau.dk

Abstract. Marine space is overall under increasing pressures from human activities. Traditionally, the activities taken place in oceans and seas were related to fishery and transport of goods and people. Today, offshore energy production – oil, gas, and wind, aquaculture, and sea-based tourism are important contributors to the global economy. This creates competition and conflicts between various uses and requires an overall regulation and planning. Maritime activities generate pressures on the marine ecosystems, and in many areas severe impacts can be observed. Maritime spatial planning is seen as an instrument to manage the seas and oceans in a more sustainable way, but information and tools are needed. The current paper describes a tool to assess the cumulative impacts of maritime activities on the marine ecosystems combined with a tool to assess the conflicts and synergies between these activities.

Keywords: Maritime spatial planning · Maritime activities · Cumulative impact assessment · Conflict and synergies · Multi-use · Decision-support tools

1 Introduction

In the Blue Growth initiative from 2012 [1], the European Commission (EC) identifies a potential for further job-creation and innovative technology development in the sea area, like new offshore renewable energy technologies, sustainable aquaculture, maritime coastal and cruise tourism, marine mineral resources, and biotechnology utilising marine organisms. With expanding human uses at sea, the objective of EU maritime spatial planning (MSP) to promote sustainable coexistence between marine uses becomes an increasingly important task. On one hand, human activities are not always compatible with the needs of nature, and may lead to several threats like eutrophication, habitat damage, and proliferation of invasive species, especially if they are more spatially-temporally concentrated [2]. On the other hand, marine activities in close spatial-temporal proximity and with an area interest overlapping with many other marine activities might conflict with each other to a high degree, if they are not located in a manner that increase use-use synergies and decrease use-use conflicts [3].

Thus, to assess potential locations for new maritime activities, both use-use interactions and use-environment interactions need to be explored and the costs and benefits in broad terms balanced against each other.

© Springer Nature Switzerland AG 2020
O. Gervasi et al. (Eds.): ICCSA 2020, LNCS 12252, pp. 521–534, 2020.
https://doi.org/10.1007/978-3-030-58811-3_38

In the sea, everything is connected. Fish, nutrients, and hazardous substances move from one location to another without barriers. The marine space is characterised not only by a three-dimensional water column supporting multi-functional use (different uses at the same location but at different depths) but is strongly four-dimensional (seasonal and diurnal cycles appears in many forms in the marine environment). Hence, Maritime Spatial Planning (MSP) needs to be based on this context different from terrestrial planning which traditionally only needs to address two dimensions – the earth surface. Accordingly, the EC launched a new directive on maritime spatial planning which entered into force in 2014. It requires its member states to establish maritime spatial plans by 2021 [4].

According to the MSP Directive, the member states are required to follow an ecosystem-based and thus holistic approach to marine spatial planning. Such an approach can also be linked to the UN Sustainable Development Goals. In 2015, the United Nations adopted the 2030 Agenda for Sustainable Development and its 17 Sustainable Development Goals (SDG), and they entered into force by 1st January 2016[1]. Number 14 of the 17 SDG's concerns the *conservation and sustainable use of the oceans, seas and maritime resources*. Careful management and regulation of the global marine resources is a key element in obtaining a sustainable future. To make this operational, a set of ten targets for Goal 14 are defined with deadlines. Target 14.2 urges EU to already by 2020 sustainably manage and protect marine and coastal ecosystems to avoid significant adverse impacts, strengthening their resilience, and act for their restoration in order to achieve healthy and productive oceans.

In order to follow an ecosystem-based approach and avoid too much pressures on the environment, impacts from maritime human activities and their options for co-location need to be investigated as part of MSP. For this purpose, open-source, free spatial decision support tools are needed. Therefore, the aim of the current research has been to develop a comprehensive package of spatial tools to assess the environmental impacts and use-use interactions of societal activities under different maritime spatial planning proposals. First, a description will be given of the background and theory behind cumulative environmental impact assessment and use-use interactions. Next, follows the design and implementation of the new toolbox, and some examples of its use. The paper ends with a discussion of the proposed approach to tools targeted towards cumulative impacts assessment on marine ecosystems from anthropogenic activities and targeted towards co-location.

2   Theory

Ecosystem-based maritime spatial planning (MSP) is a complicated process comprising several steps - including identification of the planning needs, pre-planning, and stakeholder engagement, defining and analysing existing and future conditions, preparing and approving the spatial management plan, implementation of the plan, and finally, monitoring and evaluating the performance [5]. MSP is characterised by being a

---

[1] https://www.un.org/sustainabledevelopment/development-agenda/.

continuing and iterative process adapting over time to adapt to new realities and visions. Practical tools supporting MSP and supporting cross-border coordination and participation are still limited, and spatial tools should always be designed to be used at specific stages of the MSP process, and they are more likely to be used if they have a clear, task-limited functionality, and if their methods are transparent, and they are open-source [6]. The tools in this article, have been designed with such guidelines in mind.

An ecosystem-oriented maritime spatial planning support tool needs to respond to a number of challenges to integrated planning and management, including to consider effects on the ecosystems of various and/or alternative economic/recreational/cultural activities in the maritime space – and to communicate benefits and trade-offs of different alternatives with stakeholders in the planning phases. This requires a framework for assessment of effects that can: a) integrate societal effects of multiple human activities, b) integrate the impacts of spatially explicit maritime human activities on multiple ecosystem services related to the sea and coastal ecosystems, c) address ecosystem services related to waters, seabed, sub-seabed, as well as to coastal ecosystem services, d) point out economic and social impacts related to involved and affected stakeholders, e) ensure conservation of biologically and ecologically sensitive marine areas, and f) support governance of maritime activities at various governance levels and between horizontal authorities and stakeholders. A large number of impact assessment frameworks for terrestrial activities exist along lines of Environmental Impact Assessment (EIA) [7], Strategic Environmental Assessment (SEA) [8] or sustainable development criteria [9]. At the top level of many of the frameworks you find the driving forces representing different kinds of needs for humans [10]. Examples are more basic needs e.g. for food, for water, for shelter, and more advanced needs e.g. for transport, for culture, etc. The number of people, their age structure, and their education levels are important factors, affecting the total strength of each driver. The driving forces lead to human activities like food production (e.g. fishery) or transportation (e.g. sailing). These human activities exert pressures on the environment – often trough emission of substances, noise, radiation, etc. The pressures subsequently change the state of the environment e.g. reduce biodiversity in the seas and oceans or cause fewer fish due to overfishing. If the impacts on the ecosystems go beyond what is acceptable by the societies, some response is required in order to reduce the pressures on the ecosystems. This may be done by regulation e.g. through higher taxation of the human activities being the reason to the adverse effects, or by maritime spatial planning dictating what is allowed and what is forbidden in specific sea areas.

2.1 Assessing the Effects on the Marine Environment

Although the aim of the MSP Directive from 2014 is to facilitate the Blue Growth vision, it is emphasized that this should be done without harming the environment and the ecosystems providing services for maritime activities. Prior to the MSP Directive, the European Union back in 2008 adopted the Marine Strategy Framework Directive (MSFD) [11]. It marked an important step forward in the EU marine environmental policy. MSFD was the first legal framework, which specifically aimed at protecting and preserving the marine environment by setting rather precise criteria and methodological standards for the implementation of the Directive. To better link the ecosystems and the anthropogenic pressures the Annex III MSFD Directive was amended in 2017 [12]. Thus, proper regulation of maritime activities is a prerequisite for reaching the goals on Good Environmental Status of the Ecosystems.

Like the MSP Directive, the MSFD directive requires the EU member states sharing the same marine region (i.e., Baltic Sea, and the North Sea) to collaborate to develop marine strategies and plans in order to ensure coherence in the environmental assessments, setting environmental targets, and monitoring efforts. The regional platforms for developing coherent marine strategies are the Regional Sea Conventions[2], which are mandatory regional coordination structures under the UN Environment Programme. Furthermore, the MSFD states that the marine strategies shall apply an ecosystem-based approach to the management of human activities.

Achieving a Good Environmental Status in the European marine regions require appropriate planning decisions which furthermore requires the comprehensive knowledge of the impacts induced by different anthropogenic activities and natural changes. Therefore, methods and techniques are required to efficiently estimate the cumulative impacts from multiple and interactive human activities and their pressures enabling planners and decision makers to apply science-based information to assess different efforts in marine management by using scenarios.

Most often the impacts on marine ecosystems is not only the result of a single human activity but of cumulative effects of several human activities.

The concept of cumulative impact assessment (CIA) on the marine environments was originally defined by Halpern et al. [13] and has since inspired further research. Halpern et al. [13] developed an index to assess the cumulative impact on the marine environment at a rather high spatial resolution in a global perspective.

According to Halpern et al. [13], cumulative impacts are determined from three components: maps of pressures from different human activities; maps over different ecosystems, and a matrix describing the sensitivity of each ecosystem to each pressure. Thus, the cumulative impact (I_a) on the environment within a square pixel can be estimated by multiplying the values for each pressure (P) with the values for each ecosystem component (E) and its specific sensitivity μ. Finally, these impacts are summarised over all pressures and ecosystems:

$$I_a = \sum_{i=1}^{n} \sum_{j=1}^{m} P_i \times E_j \times \mu_{i,j} \tag{1}$$

Here n is the number of pressure layers and m is the number of ecosystems. The sensitivity variable μ represents the sensitivity of ecosystem j to pressure i and are most often derived by expert judgment in a rather complicated process – see for example the way this is done in HELCOM's assessment of the cumulative impacts in the Baltic Sea [14].

---

[2] https://www.unenvironment.org/explore-topics/oceans-seas/what-we-do/working-regional-seas/ regional-seas-programmes/regional-seas.

2.2 Use-Use Conflicts and Synergies

For co-location options to be considered in MSP, it is important to supplement a cumulative environmental impact focus with knowledge about use-use interactions. Therefore, one needs to know the types of interactions that can take place between different marine human activities. The co-location concept highlights the situations with positive use-use links where marine uses successfully can be located close to each other without too high a cumulative environmental impact [15]. However, marine uses can both experience negative and positive links with each other, and often they experience negative links. If one marine activity benefits from an interaction with another marine activity, it is not necessarily a synergic relation. To be a synergic interaction, no marine use should experience overall negative impacts due to that interaction. That conclusion can be deduced from the scale by Klinger et al. [3] that describes use-use interactions as a spectrum from *competition* (negative impacts to all interacting activities), *antagonism* (benefits to one activity on behalf of another activity), *amensalism* (negative impacts to one interacting activity), *commensalism* (positive impacts to one interacting activity without harmfully affecting other activities) to *mutualism* (benefits to all marine activities). Thus, only commensalism and mutualism constitute synergies, since antagonism, even though it provides benefits to one marine use, is not without harmful impacts. An antagonistic relation could be when either fishers or sand extraction ships exclude the other from a fish- and sand-rich seamount [3].

Four types of spatial-temporal links have been found to exist individually or in groups for closely located marine activities: location links, environmental links, technical links, and user attraction links. Location links are connections between the extents and duration of marine activities. The spatial-temporal attributes of marine uses such as their horizontal and vertical location, and whether they are fixed, mobile and/or seasonal influence location links. Environmental links are when marine activities are positively or negatively affected by environmental processes or environmental by-products from other marine activities. Technical links are links that concern safety zones, shared infrastructure and/or shared tools. User attraction links are when nearby marine activities affect the user attraction of other marine activities [15].

Not much knowledge is available about how synergic different marine activity combinations are. Many studies only examine the compatibility degree between marine activities, meaning their ability to be located together [15], without diving into the actual benefits that co-location can provide to marine activities. Studies that only consider compatibility include Kannen [16], Baltic SCOPE [17], Plan Bothnia [18], and the UNESCO-step-by-step MSP guide [5]. However, the Horizon 2020 Multi-Use in European Seas (MUSES) project is an exception, since it has put a focus on opportunities, advantages, and challenges for combining activities into multi-use in Europe. MUSES should thus be acknowledged for its systematic research on promising multi-use constellations in Europe (https://muses-project.com). To synthesis all knowledge about potential use-use conflicts and synergies into a table, knowledge from all the previously mentioned compatibility studies, the MUSES project [19], as well as findings from the PartiSEApate project [20] and the AquaSpace project [21] have been systematically gathered. The information has been used to estimate conflict-synergy degrees for pairwise use-use combinations in a matrix on a scale from -3 to 3. The scores are not actual scores estimated by experts but are based on ordering the different marine use combinations after their compatibility degree, their number of potential conflicts and synergies, and their multi-use potentials according to existing literature. When use-use synergy-conflict knowledge improves over time as current best knowledge gets updated, the categorisation of individual pairwise combinations might change. However, a systematic, matrix-based, and iterative approach to existing knowledge can help planners visualise current known trends.

By providing the matrix with a spatial dimension by summing up potential conflict-synergy scores on maps based on the distribution of maritime activities, it is possible to gain an overview over spatial patterns of potential use-use conflicts and synergies. Such maps are useful in MSP processes to enable co-location where use-use synergies are highest and use-use conflicts lowest, and to separate very conflicting marine uses. Combined with the cumulative environmental impact approach, co-location can be decided to take place only when the cumulated negative impacts on the environment is not too high.

For a given spatial distribution of marine activities, the total conflict-synergy score (S) within a square pixel can be estimated by multiplying the presence of each marine activity category (A_1) with the presence of each different marine activity category (A_2, $A_1 \neq A_2$) and with the specific conflict-synergy score input ($s_{A1, A2}$) belonging to each activity pair, and then by summarizing these multiplications for all unordered, unique pairwise activity combinations:

$$S = \sum\nolimits_{A_1=1}^{n} \sum\nolimits_{A_2=A_1+1}^{n} A_1 \times A_2 \times s_{A_1,A_2} \qquad (2)$$

Here, n is the number of unique marine human activity combinations. The pairwise activity conflict-synergy input score is derived from the previously mentioned conflict-synergy matrix. The formula and the conflict-synergy matrix inputs are further introduced in [22].

3   Implementation

During the last few years several tools have been developed to calculate the cumulative impact on ecosystems and assessing conflicts between different human activities in the marine space. They are all based on the principles on cumulative impact assessment as described by Halpern et al. [13] but typically adding some additional features. The most well-known software packages for cumulative impact assessments are EcoImpactMapper [23], Tools4MSP [24], Symphony [25], and MYTILUS [26] with different advantages and disadvantages, and although most of the tools are freely available they cannot be considered as traditional software with user guides, and other kinds of support. Rather, they are all developed under research and development projects, with limited further development after project ends. However, the source code is typically available for further development. The current research has used the MYTILUS software as a basic container.

The overall aim of developing this new extended toolbox is to provide a more comprehensive set of tools to assess the effects of maritime activities on the ecosystems – but also to assess potential conflicts and synergies between human activities. Maritime spatial planning aims to organise the use of the marine space, considering as well the interactions among human uses (e.g., fisheries, aquaculture, shipping, tourism, renewable energy production), for which reason it is a needed tool improvement to add options to also explore potential use-use interactions, based on the inputted use-use synergy-conflict score matrix presented in Sect. 2.2.

3.1 Systems Design

The modelling system applies native ESRI ASCII raster data facilitating an easier exchange of data between MYTILUS and GIS software like ArcGIS and QGIS. In this way, MYTILUS can be used as a decision-support tool while doing data preparation and advanced visualisation in general purpose GIS-packages. The cumulative impact tool contains several options to assess the impacts on the ecosystems [26]. The conflict-synergy score tool contains several options to assess areas with overall high/low potential synergies and conflicts. The calculations are carried out according to Eq. (2) with the options to select all activities or selected sets of activities, the latter to provide more detailed information of the potential conflicts and synergies from just one activity. This is particularly relevant when looking for an appropriate synergic or neutral area for locating new activities with known high conflict potential that needs to be minimised. The user interface is illustrated on Fig. 1.

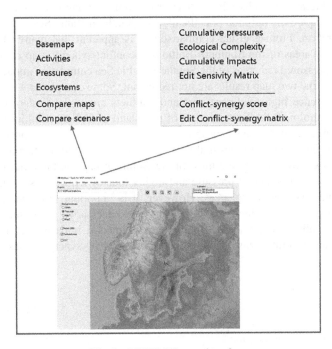

Fig. 1. MYTILUS user interface.

4 Examples from the Baltic Sea

The MYTILUS toolbox is being tested in the Baltic Sea, where HELCOM[3] provides freely available Baltic Sea wide data on human activities, pressures, and ecosystems. The activity layers from the HELCOM portal used for conflict-synergy analysis are transformed into a binary raster-format where the value 1 indicates that the specific activity exist in a raster cell. Otherwise the value is 0. The pressure layers available from HELCOM's data portal are used for their own assessment of the Baltic Sea Environment and follows the pressure layers mentioned in the Marine Strategy Framework Directive (MSFD) [11]. The following examples illustrate the flexibility and analytical capacity of the MYTILUS toolset. Figure 2 visualises the spatial distribution of the cumulative impact from all pressures on all ecosystems. The maximum cumulative impacts are observed in the South-Western Baltic Sea and along the Southern coast of Finland and around Stockholm. In addition, the user can also select a single pressure or groups of pressure layers and combine with a single ecosystem or groups of ecosystems thus getting possibilities for better understanding cause-effect relationships. Finally, the user can calculate the max-pressure index – i.e. the pressure in each grid cell providing the highest impact (Fig. 3). This is important in identifying needed actions regarding reducing pressures from human activities in certain areas. Such reduction strategies have to be considered in maritime spatial plans. Figure 3 illustrates that the heavy impacts in South-Western Baltic Sea as well as along the Southern coast of Finland are mainly due to phosphorus emissions.

With the MYTILUS extension in the form of the conflict-synergy score tool, it is possible to compare cumulative environmental impact maps with total synergy-conflict score maps. Figure 4 visualises how a user can zoom in on the same area for both tool outputs to compare the outputs. Specifically, the Southern Baltic Sea is used in Fig. 4 as demonstration. From a visual comparison, it is apparent that many of the highly conflicting red areas of the Southern Baltic Sea conflict-synergy map do not overlap with highly pressured red areas of the Southern Baltic Sea cumulative impact map. This illustrates that the two map results are not redundant. Some exceptions where both map outputs experience high total pressures and conflicts are at the Eastern coast of the island of Bornholm, at the Eastern coast of the island of Gotland, and in the Northern end of the inner Danish waters. In these areas, ecosystems are extra pressured at the same time as the marine activities in these areas might experience high competition and negative impacts from other activities. In the Bothnian bay, on the other hand, many areas with less environmental pressure and higher total synergies exist, indicating less pressured and less conflicting areas. However, it is important to emphasize that the green-coloured areas in the two maps are not necessarily environmentally and socioeconomically thriving areas. Smaller environmental impacts are still negative impacts in an absolute sense, and green-coloured total synergy areas might still

---

[3] HELCOM (Helsinki Convention).

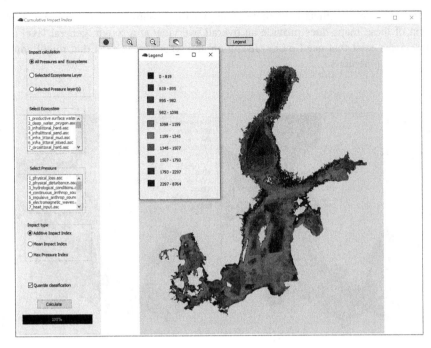

Fig. 2. Cumulative impact assessment from all pressures on all ecosystems

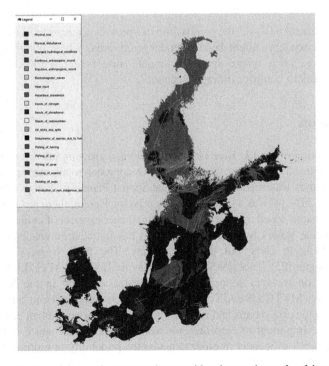

Fig. 3. Identifying each pressure that provides the maximum local impact

experience many conflicts (just more synergies than conflicts). However, the combination of these maps does provide an overall overview at a rough, general level over where areas exist that need more precaution and where areas exist that might contain co-location potentials.

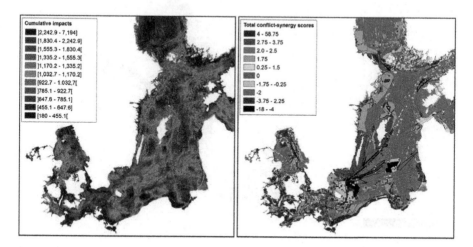

Fig. 4. Comparing the cumulative impact on the marine environment (left map) with potential conflict-synergies between human activities (right map).

Used in scenario analysis, the comparison can provide a means to spatially visualise areas where ecosystems might become endangered, areas where competition/conflict might arise, and areas where synergies might cause potential for co-location; all important factors to compare different scenarios.

5   Discussion

Since the adoption of the EU Blue Growth initiative, a growing interest of investing in maritime activities has emerged. Therefore, a new approach to allocate space to various maritime activities was needed. The Maritime Spatial Planning Directive by the European Union in 2014 [4] was a first step in this process. Herein, there is a requirement to adopt an ecosystem-based approach. Particularly, the assessment of cumulative impacts on global marine waters by Halpern et al. [13] has initiated an academic interest in developing tools to carry out the assessments. The tools being developed like EcoImpactMapper [23], Tools4MSP [24], Symphony [25], and MYTILUS [26] are all fine examples on tools to support the ecological assessment in the MSP process. However, except MYTILUS and Tools4MSP all of them have until now only considered the impacts on the ecosystems and not the interactions between human activities. Such interactions are important to consider in a world where marine space is increasingly becoming sparser – especially in order to assess the possibility of multi-use.

By combining conflicts and synergies between human activities with impacts on the ecosystem from the same activities into one toolbox such as done in this MYTILUS update, marine spatial planners have the possibility to generate maps illustrating:

- The overall impact on the ecosystems from all (or selected) activities and pressures on all ecosystems within the study area
- The overall potential conflict-synergy) score between all (or selected) activities for the same area
- Options to compare the two maps within the same tool in order identify areas with a) high environmental impact and high conflict; b) high environmental impact and synergy; c) low environmental impact and high conflict; d) high environmental impact and synergy;

The main challenges with such tools are the quality of the data and particularly the values in the sensitivity matrix for the cumulative impact tool and in the conflict-synergy matrix related to the conflict-synergy score tool. The values used in the ecological sensitivity matrix are typically science-based and created by ecology experts, while the values in the conflict-synergy matrix can be assessed by literature reviews or through interviews with spatial planners and relevant stakeholders representing the various activities. MYTILUS provides input schemes for easily changing values for the sensitivity matrix as well as for the conflict-synergy matrix. Especially, it makes sense to discuss and potentially improve the values in the conflict-synergy matrix – partly because they are not evidence-based in the same way as the sensitivity matrix (it is a relatively new focus area), and partly because the technological development may change the conflict or synergy potential between various human activities in marine space. Technological advances may also have an effect on the impact of maritime activities on the ecosystems – for example by introducing new kinds of feed in fish farms, and therefore all the score inputs should be updated when best available knowledge is updated. The MSP Directive requires all marine plans to be based on best available knowledge.

The concerns about uncertainty may be the reason why only very few maritime authorities have used cumulative impact assessment of the ecosystems or conflict-synergy analysis in the preparations of their maritime spatial plans. One example regarding cumulative impact assessment is the Swedish Agency for Marine and Water management, who have carried out extensive analysis of the cumulative impacts on the ecosystem of the marine activities [25]. Another reason may be the lack of appropriate and up-to-date data and information. One approach could be to apply a distributed database structure instead of the centralised database currently being applied for example by HELCOM. The Baltic Lines project developed a prototype for such a distributed database solution for the Baltic Sea [28].

6   Conclusion

Maritime spatial planning (MSP) is a rather new discipline, which in most European countries mainly has received attention due to the adoption of the MSP Directive in 2014. Use of marine space has until recently mainly been regulated by various sector plans without mutual coordination. The new maritime spatial plans have to be implemented before 2021, and they have to allocate marine space without harming the ecosystems and avoiding conflicts between uses. This require up-to-date information and tools to assess the current status as well as the future situation whether or not the marine space will be used according to the plan.

Recently, several tools have been developed to estimate the cumulative impacts from various anthropogenic pressures on the ecosystems. Various tools like EcoImpactMapper, Tools4MSP, and MYTILUS are good examples of tools for cumulative impact assessments. However, human activities do not only provide pressures on ecosystems, they also interact with other human activities – generating conflicts or synergies. The current paper has described the further development of the MYTILUS toolset by adding capacity to carry out conflict-synergy analysis, thus facilitating the allocation of activities to marine space considering not only the impact on the ecosystems but also how they interact with other activities. Hereby, the decision-making processes can be based on a more holistic approach and provide support for discussing multi-use options of marine space. It is expected that the updated MYTILUS toolset can contribute to more knowledge-based maritime spatial plans among the EU Member States, as well as contribute to the process of aiming to reach the targets set by the UN SDG goal 14 on the marine environment.

The next step in the development of MYTILUS will be to address the concerns regarding uncertainty by introducing uncertainty maps in order to support the decision-makers in the discussion with stakeholders, who often raise question about the validity of the analysis and modelling results.

Acknowledgement. The current research has been carried out under the BONUS BASMATI project[4], which has received funding from BONUS (art. 185), funded jointly by the EU, Innovation Fund Denmark, Swedish Research Council Formas, Academy of Finland, Latvian Ministry of Education and Science, and Forschungszentrum Jülich GmbH (Germany).

References

1. European Commission: Report on the Blue Growth Strategy – Towards more sustainable growth and jobs in the blue economy. Commission Staff Working Document, Brussels 31.3.2017 (2017)
2. Blaesbjerg, et al.: Marine Spatial Planning in the Nordic Region. TemaNord, 2009:525. Nordic Council of Ministers (2009)
3. Klinger, et al.: The mechanics of blue growth: management of oceanic natural resource use with multiple, interacting sectors. Mar. Policy **87**, 356–362 (2018)
4. European Commission: Directive 2014/89/EU of the European Parliament and of the Council of 23 July 2014 establishing a framework for maritime spatial planning. The Official Journal of the European Union, L 257/135 (2014)

---

[4] https://bonusbasmati.eu.

5. Ehler, C., Douvere, F.: Marine spatial planning: a step-by-step approach toward ecosystem-based management. Intergovernmental Oceanographic Commission and Man and the Biosphere Programme. In: OC Manual and Guides No. 53 IDNPU, editor (2009)

6. Pinarbaşi, K., et al.: Decision support tools in marine spatial planning: present applications, gaps and future perspectives. Mar. Policy **83**, 83–91 (2017)

7. European Commission: Directive 2014/52/EU of the European Parliament and of the Council of 16 April 2014 amending Directive 2011/92EU on the assessment of the effects of certain public and private projects on the environment. Official Journal of the European Union L 124/1 (2014)

8. European Commission: Directive 2001/42/EC of the European Parliament and of the Council of June 2001 on the assessment of the effects of certain plans and programmes on the environment. Official Journal of the European Communities L 197/30 (2001)

9. Hacking, T., Guthrie, P.: A framework for classifying the meaning of triple bottom-line, integrated, and sustainability assessment. Environ. Impact Assess. Rev. **28**, 73–89 (2008)

10. Kristensen, P.: The DPSIR framework. Paper Presented at the 27–29 September 2004 Workshop on a Comprehensive/Detailed Assessment of the Vulnerability of Water Resources to Environmental Change in Africa Using River Basin Approach. UNEP Headquarters, Nairobi, Kenya (2004)

11. European Commission: Directive 2008/56/EC of the European Parliament and of the Council of 17 June 2008 establishing a framework for community action in the field of marine environmental policy (Marine Strategy Framework Directive). The Official Journal of the European Union, L 164/19 (2008)

12. European Commission: Commission Directive (EU) 2017/845 of 17 May 2017 amending Directive 2008/56/EC of the European Parliament and of the Council as regards the Indicative lists of elements to be taken into account for the preparation of marine strategies. Official Journal of the European Union L 125/27 (2017)

13. Halpern, B.S., et al.: A global map of human impact on marine ecosystems. Science **319**, 948–952 (2008)

14. HELCOM: The assessment of cumulative impacts using the Baltic Sea Pressure Index and the Baltic Sea Impact Index - supplementary report to the first version of the HELCOM 'State of the Baltic Sea' report 2017 (2017). http://stateofthebalticsea.helcom.fi/about-helcom-and-the-assessment/downloads-and-data/

15. Bonnevie, I.M., et al.: Assessing use-use interactions at sea: a theoretical framework for spatial decision support tools facilitating co-location in maritime spatial planning. Mar. Policy **106**, 1–12 (2019)

16. Kannen, A.: Challenges for marine spatial planning in the context of multiple sea uses, policy arenas and actors based on experiences from the German North Sea. Reg. Environ. Change **14**(6), 2139–2150 (2012). https://doi.org/10.1007/s10113-012-0349-7

17. Veidemane, et al.: Development of a maritime spatial plan: the Latvian recipe (2017). http://www.balticscope.eu/events/final-reports/

18. Backer, et al.: Planning the Bothnian Sea: Outcome of Plan Bothnia – a transboundary Maritime Spatial Planning pilot in the Bothnian Sea (Digital Edition 2013) (2013). https://www.helcom.fi/wp-content/uploads/2019/08/Planning-the-Bothnian-Sea.pdf

19. Depellegrin, D., et al.: Exploring multi-use potentials in the Euro-Mediterranean Sea space. Sci. Total Environ. **635**, 612–629 (2019)

20. PartiSEApate Project: Flyer on Workshop Results: Stakeholder Dialogue on Maritime Spatial Planning (2014). https://www.partiseapate.eu/results/

21. Gimpel, et al.: A GIS-based tool for an integrated assessment of spatial planning trade-offs with aquaculture. **627**, 1644–1655 (2018). https://doi.org/10.1016/j.scitotenv.2018.01.133

22. Bonnevie, I.M., Hansen, H.S., Schrøder, L.: SEANERGY - a spatial tool to facilitate the increase of synergies and to minimise conflicts between human uses at sea. Environ. Modell. Softw. (2020, submitted)

23. Stock, A.: Open source software for mapping human impacts on marine ecosystems with an additive model. J. Open Res. Softw. **4**, 1–7 (2016)

24. Menegon, S., Sarretta, A., Depellegrin, D., Farella, G., Venier, C., Barbante, A.: Tools4MSP: an open source software package to support Maritime Spatial Planning. PeerJ Comput. Sci. (2018). https://doi.org/10.7717/peerj-cs.165

25. Swedish Agency for Marine and Water Management: Symphony - integrated planning support for national maritime planning from an ecosystem approach, Gothenburg (2018). (in Swedish)

26. Hansen, H.S.: Cumulative impact of societal activities on marine ecosystems and their services. In: Misra, S., et al. (eds.) ICCSA 2019. LNCS, vol. 11621, pp. 577–590. Springer, Cham (2019). https://doi.org/10.1007/978-3-030-24302-9_41

27. European Commission: Directive 2007/2/EC of the European Parliament and of the Council of 14 March 2007 establishing an Infrastructure for Spatial Information in the European Community (INSPIRE). Official Journal of the European Union (2007)

28. Hansen, H.S., Reiter, I.M., Schrøder, L.: A system architecture for a transnational data infrastructure supporting maritime spatial planning. In: Kő, A., Francesconi, E. (eds.) EGOVIS 2017. LNCS, vol. 10441, pp. 158–172. Springer, Cham (2017). https://doi.org/10.1007/978-3-319-64248-2_12

Towards a High-Fidelity Assessment of Urban Green Spaces Walking Accessibility

Ivan Blečić[1]([⊠]), Valeria Saiu[1] (ID), and Giuseppe A. Trunfio[2] (ID)

[1] Department of Civil and Environmental Engineering and Architecture,
University of Cagliari, 09129 Cagliari, Italy
{ivanblecic,v.saiu}@unica.it
[2] Department of Architecture, Design and Urbanism, University of Sassari,
07041 Alghero, Italy
trunfio@uniss.it

Abstract. Urban Public Green Spaces (UPGS) *available at walking distance* are a vital component of urban quality of life, of citizens' health, and ultimately of the right to the city. Their demand has suddenly become even more ostensive due to the measures of "social distancing" and the restrictions of movement imposed in many countries during the COVID-19 outbreak, showing the importance of the public urban parks and green open spaces located near homes and accessible by foot. Hence, the idea of "green self-sufficiency" at the local, neighbourhood and sub-neighbourhood level has emerged as a relevant objective to pursue. For this purpose, we have constructed a high-fidelity evaluation model to assess the walking accessibility of UPGS at the highly granular spatial scale of street network nodes. The evaluation procedure is based on a novel index constructed around the concept of distance-cumulative deficit, scoring nodes with respect to all the available UPGS within their catchment area of slope-corrected walking distance of 2 km. To showcase the possible outputs of the evaluation procedure and their exploratory analyses, we present an application on the city of Cagliari, Italy. In doing that, we argue that the proposed evaluation approach is an advancement over the traditional (density-based) approaches of assessment of green area availability, and that it provides an intuitive, flexible and extendable tool useful to better evaluate and understand the current and the potential accessibility of urban green space, and to support urban planning, policy making and design.

Keywords: Urban Public Green Spaces · Accessibility · Walkability · Evaluation model

1 Introduction

The rapid and intensive urbanisation of the last decades adversely affects the environment, impoverishes ecosystems, causes climate change and major problems in citizens' health and quality of life. In light of these impacts, Urban Public Green Spaces (UPGS) are increasingly recognised as essential elements for improving urban quality of life, especially in the large and medium size cities where the densification process causes a loss of green space per capita and, consequently, a decrease in daily exposure

O. Gervasi et al. (Eds.): ICCSA 2020, LNCS 12252, pp. 535–549, 2020.
https://doi.org/10.1007/978-3-030-58811-3_39

for many citizens [1–3]. According to the "three pillars of sustainable development", the UPGS provide an array of services and potential benefits, from the environmental, social, and economic standpoints [e.g. 4–8]. This view has been strengthened recently by the principles of the UN's *New Urban Agenda* [9] and the Sustainable Development Goals [10], and in particular by the Goal 11 to "build cities and human settlements inclusive, safe, resilient and sustainable", which states the objective «to provide universal access to safe, inclusive and accessible, green and public spaces» by the year 2030 (SDG 11, Target 11.7).

This objective has suddenly become even more apparent and vital due to the "social distancing" measures imposed in many countries during the COVID-19 pandemic. As observed by the 2020 special report on *Parks and the pandemic* published by the Trust for Public Land, during the pandemic crisis the role of the close-to-home parks and green spaces has proven crucial for the community wellbeing, but at the same time «the pandemic highlights that in too many communities, access to the outdoors is considered a privilege when it should be a right» [11: 2]. Notwithstanding the waning of the acute phase of the pandemic in many places at the time of this writing, accompanied by the relaxation of stringent restrictions on movement, the experience has left scars, will likely produce durable changes, and has rekindled a debate on the spatial reorganisation and distribution of activities in cities.

The 2018 Working Paper of the European Union *A walk to the park? Assessing access to green areas in Europe's cities* [12] reports the results of a recent study conducted in a sample of 400 cities that assessed the total surface of green areas that can be reached within 10 min walking time. The findings show the differences in the distribution of the green accessible areas between cities and, within cities, between different neighbourhoods. Similarly, numerous other recent studies underline the uneven distribution and accessibility of green areas within cities, and how this condition generates notable socio-spatial inequalities [13–16]. It follows that an equitable accessibility of UPGS is one of the main objectives to be addressed to develop more secure, fair, and sustainable urban development patterns.

Among the necessary directions of work to pursue this goal and to support a better UPGS provision, one is the advancement of evaluation models and operational assessment tools. The conventional planning practice usually employs indicators of density, i.e. the per capita availability of green spaces within predetermined areas (zones, neighbourhoods), as factors of city's liveability [2]. Along this approach, different standards were established in the past by the regional planning and regulatory agencies; for example, in Europe the standard ranges from 6 to 50 m^2 per person [17, 18]. Numerous studies have been conducted to measure and assess such densities at the neighbourhood and urban scale, employing different methods and data sources, from those using remote sensing coupled with GIS [19–23] to those, more recently, taking advantage of the freely available geographic data such as OpenStreetMap [e.g. 24–26].

However, such density-based measures may be spatially imprecise, may fail to capture the differences in scale and nature of different green areas, and risk concealing important constraints and factors limiting the real capability to access the green areas. Indeed, the per capita availability does not provide enough precise and adequate information on the effective accessibility of public green spaces and on which urban areas and citizens can best benefit from the available UPGS.

More accurate analyses go beyond mere indicators of densities, and evaluate the UPGS accessibility taking into account different modes of transportation to reach those spaces [27–29] and different functional levels of public green spaces related to different uses which these fulfil at different scales, from neighbourhood to metropolitan, typically based on the green space size [30–32]. Furthermore, there are various attempts to establishing typologies of parks and green areas, each related to different walkable catchment area and on distance-decay functions associated with distinct types of parks [27, 31, 33–35].

Furthermore, to assess the accessibility, many evaluation models employ an inadequate representation of the key variable of distance/proximity [36]. Among these, the Euclidean buffer (the minimum as-the-crow-flies distance between points of origin and destination) is still frequently adopted [e.g. 30, 37–40]. As Unal et al. [41] note, this approach shows at least three critical elements. First, it uses circular buffer zones, created around all destination points, without considering the effective street connectivity and the distance that must be crossed along a transportation network (walking routes). In this way, it does not account the impedance elements, such as barriers (e.g. rivers, railways) and terrain characteristics (slope) that may alter the acceptable distances. Second, it considers all parks as open spaces, fully accessible along their boundaries without consider the effective access points. Third, by measuring the distance from the centre of the park it does not allow to consider irregular park's shapes, leading to an inaccurate representation of the site catchment zone.

Some studies are based on street network analysis which should provide a more realistic representation of the available access routes [e.g. 37, 38, 42], access points [e.g. 43, 44] and impedance elements [e.g. 45, 46].

However, most of the cited studies do not consider all these elements simultaneously. Therefore, the main purpose of this paper is to propose a high-fidelity evaluation model, and the respective UPGS capability index, designed to overcome limitations mentioned above. The model produces evaluations (scores) at every street node, effectively obtaining assessments at the micro-urban level. It employs a novel index based on the cumulative computing of the UPGS deficit at different distances. To test and showcase the effectiveness of the evaluation procedure, we conducted an application on the city of Cagliari (Italy) which we present here as a case study.

2 Evaluation Model

2.1 Definition

For assessing the level of capability to access UPGS, we have devised a novel index based on the idea of "distance-cumulative" deficit. Intuitively, the model is grounded on a normatively predefined benchmark establishing the cumulative amount of green areas deemed as sufficient *at each* distance from the node in the street network under evaluation. By comparing these benchmark levels with the observed availability of green areas at different distances from the node, the model assigns the index value from 0 (minimum) to 1 (maximum level of capability).

In our application, the index is computed at every node of the street network, producing highly detailed and spatially granular evaluations.

To compute the UPGS *distance-cumulative deficit index* (UPGS-DCD index), the required data are:

- the set of the available UPGS (in short parks) together with their access points and sizes in terms of surface area (for simplicity, the size is assumed as a proxy of the salience and the level of services provided by the parks);
- the graph of the street network, with the set of nodes, for which the shortest-path distances from all the available parks are preliminarily computed; importantly, to add to the fidelity of the modelling, the walking distances have been corrected for slope (following the procedure suggested in [47]), modelled as a dilation of distances increasing with the steepness of the path.

Given a sequence of n available parks ($i = 1, \ldots, n$) – each with surface area p_i, at the walking distance δ_i from the node – indexed in non-decreasing order of distance (i.e. $\delta_i \leq \delta_{i+1}$), we define the *distance-cumulative curve* (DCC) of park areas at the distance $\dot{\delta}$ as:

$$C\left(f\left(\dot{\delta}\right)\right) = \sum_{0 \leq \delta_i \leq \dot{\delta}}^{n} s(p_i)$$

where:

- $f\left(\dot{\delta}\right) \in [0, 1]$ is a distance scale transformation function which, besides rescaling distances from 0 to 1, allows for modelling of possible decay with distance of park's salience for the residents at the origin node;
- $s(p_i)$ is an area transformation function which, besides possible measurement scale conversions, allows for modelling of variable park unit-area salience depending of the park's size (the form of f and s may both also depend of the purpose and scope of the specific application and evaluative question addressed).

We further define a *benchmark distance-cumulative profile* (BDCP) $X(f(\delta))$, which designates the benchmark value of the distance-cumulative park area at each distance, deemed to be fully adequate to satisfy a (normatively defined) required level of UPGS availability. Hence, being the benchmark distance-cumulative profile the upper-limit frontier at each distance, beyond which any further cumulative availability is irrelevant for the sake of computing the deficit index, we can define a *trimmed version of the distance-cumulative curve* (tDCC) as:

$$\bar{C}(f(\delta)) = \begin{cases} C(f(\delta)), & \text{if } C(f(\delta)) \leq X(f(\delta)) \\ X(f(\delta)), & \text{if } C(f(\delta)) > X(f(\delta)) \end{cases}$$

Having established the above, we define the UPGS *distance-cumulative deficit index* (Δ) geometrically, as the area between the BDCP and the tDCC divided the entire area under the BDCP. That is:

$$\Delta = \frac{\int_0^1 [X(f(\delta)) - \bar{C}(f(\delta))]d\delta}{\int_0^1 X(f(\delta))d\delta}$$

The logic of this index can perhaps best be understood with a visual example. The following Fig. 1 represents the distance-cumulative profile for a node in our dataset.

The distance-cumulative curve (DCC) indicates the cumulative park area (transformed by the function s) of all the UGPS at the (scale-transformed) distances from 0 to 1. The bisecting diagonal line represents the predefined benchmark profile (BDCP). Given this profile, the resulting trimmed DCC (tDCC) is shown as the thicker dashed line. The difference between the benchmark profile and the tDCC gives rise to the two "deficit" areas marked in the figure. Thus, following the definition from above, the value of the *distance-cumulative deficit index* Δ is the sum of the two deficit areas divided by the total area under the benchmark profile (which equals 0.5 by definition). In the example in Fig. 1, this calculation yields approximately $\Delta = 0.92$.

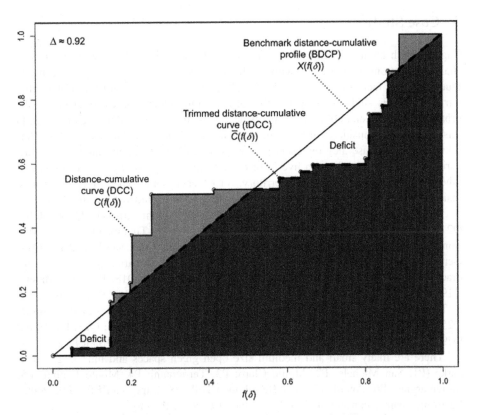

Fig. 1. Distance-cumulative deficit index, a geometrical illustration.

2.2   Specification

For the example application on the city of Cagliari presented in this paper, we have established the maximum walking range of 2 km, or roughly 20 min on a moderate pace. To model the distance decay, assuming the maximum walking distance at which we consider a green area reachable by foot of $\delta_{max} = 2000$ m, we have used the following distance scale transformation function:

$$f(\delta) = \sqrt{\frac{\delta}{\delta_{max}}}$$

Assuming the area threshold of $p_{max} = 10$ ha (hectares) as yielding the maximum possible benefit for a single park (i.e. beyond which we assume no additional benefit from a single park area), for the area transformation function we employ $s(p) = (p/p_{max})^2$. Finally, for the BDCP, we posit $X(f(\delta)) = f(\delta)$. These specifications have yielded the results for the node in Fig. 1.

As the final phase in the assessment procedure, the values computed at each node get interpolated to obtain a value at each point in urban space.

3   Case Study

Cagliari, with about 150.000 inhabitants, is the largest city of the island of Sardinia (Italy) and among Italian cities with the largest green and blue coverage. Green and blue spaces, in fact, occupy 55 of 85 km^2 of the total surface, about 65% of the entire territory. In this study we consider the Urban Public Open Spaces, referring to the urban parks and open public spaces freely accessible for everyone during entire year. In this respect, we considered the Poetto seafront, the Cape Sant'Elia and the San Bartolomeo Hill because they represent two areas of environmental and landscape value, variously used by people who live in or close to them, but also by the inhabitants of other neighbourhoods and wider territory. Vice versa, some types of green spaces, mainly private, informal, or abandoned area, have been excluded from the dataset.

Figure 2 show the UPGS distribution across 31 city neighbourhoods (Q1. Castello; Q2. Villanova; Q3. Marina; Q4. Stampace; Q5. Tuvixeddu-Tuvumannu; Q6. Is Mirrionis; Q7. La Vega; Q8. Fonsarda; Q9. Sant'Alenixedda; Q10. San Benedetto; Q11. Genneruxi; Q12. Monte Urpinu; Q13. Monte Mixi; Q14. Bonaria; Q15. Sant'Avendrace- Santa Gilla; Q16. Mulinu Becciu; Q17. San Michele; Q18. Barracca Manna; Q19. Is Campus - Is Corrias; Q20. Villa Doloretta; Q21. Monreale; Q22. S. Giuseppe, S. Teresa, Parteolla; Q23. Is Bingias–Terramaini, Q24. Monteleone - Santa Rosalia; Q25. Quartiere Europeo; Q26. CEP; Q27. Poetto - Medau su Cramu; Q28. La Palma; Q29. Quartiere del Sole; Q30. Borgo Sant'Elia; Q31. Nuovo Borgo Sant'Elia).

There are many small and medium size open green spaces and nine large urban parks (P1. San Michele; P2. Monte Claro; P3. Terramaini; P4. Monte Urpinu; P5. Molentargius; P6. Anelli; P7. San Bartolomeo Hill; P8. Cape Sant'Elia; P9. Poetto Seafront), mainly concentrated in the southeast areas of the city.

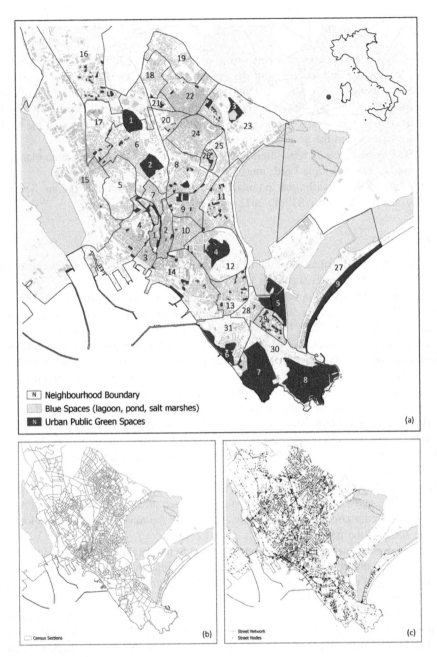

Fig. 2. The distribution of Urban Public Green Spaces in Cagliari and the boundaries of the 31 city neighbourhoods (a); Population Census Tracts (b); Street Network with the over 6.500 Street Nodes used in the assessment.

The data for the assessment were collected from various sources and further processed as follows:

– the city's street network was obtained from the OpenStreetMap (OSM), using urban roads, walking pathways and all the available street nodes (Fig. 2c);
– the geographical distribution of the UPGS and their related data were digitised starting from the OSM data and verified by comparing the satellite imagery (Google Earth), to check, and, if necessary, to correct the discrepancies between the OSM classification and the ground truth;
– UPGS access points were digitised starting from the OSM data and manually corrected using Google Earth imagery for validation;
– the geographic distribution population was obtained from the Italian National Institute of Statistics (ISTAT) 2011 residential population census.

3.1   Results

The geographical distribution of the UPGS *distance-cumulative deficit* index calculated for the city of Cagliari is shown in Fig. 3.

The index has shown a notable variability for the 31 city neighbourhoods (Figs. 3 and 4). The highest score is obtained from the neighbourhoods located in the south-east area of the city (N30, N27, N31) where the spatial proximity to the large parks corresponds to a high accessibility, due to the fact that the majority of UPGS analysed have open access (P6, P7, P8, P9), and that the relatively flat terrain allows for easy pedestrian mobility. A similar observation can be made for the more central neighbourhoods (N12, N7, N9), which are also located near large urban parks (P2, P4) and where the increase in the terrain slope is compensated by the greater choice offered by various parks of different sizes situated in the surroundings. Three of the 31 neighbourhoods analysed (N8, N11, N13) show a large variability in the scores. In particular, the index value of N8 and N11 varies from 0.30 to 0.50 points. The northern area of these two neighbourhoods shows a lower score than the southern one, due to the presence of a large road infrastructure which represents an impediment to pedestrian accessibility, and to the scarcity of open public green areas in the surrounding urban tissues. A similar condition characterises N13 where the road infrastructure is located to the south of the neighbourhood.

The lowest values of the index were assigned to the neighbourhoods located in the north western suburbs of the city (N16, N15, N4, N5) and in the peripheries of the Pirri municipality, in the north-west urban areas, at the borders on large road-infrastructures (N18, N19, N21, N20, N24, N25, N26).

The four neighbourhoods of the historic centre (N1, N2, N3, N4) have markedly different index values, largely dependent on the different type-morphological characteristics and terrain slopes. In decreasing order of score, N2 has the highest values especially in the northern area, where there are numerous public open green spaces; N1 has good scores for the presence of a system of green areas along the north-eastern

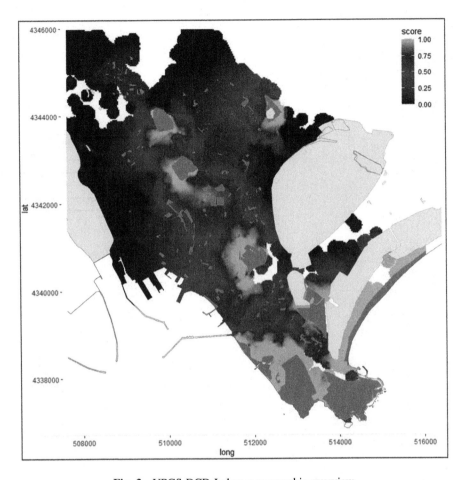

Fig. 3. UPGS-DCD Index: a geographic overview.

rampart/bastion; low indices values of N3 are affected by the scarce endowment of UPGS and by the great distance from large urban parks; finally, N4 shows low indices values especially in the peripheral areas, outside the boundary of the historic centre, also due to the impediments related to the terrain slope which make accessibility to the surrounding large urban parks more difficult (Fig. 5).

The analysis of the index values in relation to the residential population has shown (Fig. 4) that approximately 45,396 inhabitants out of the 149,855 total (30%) live in urban areas characterised by a very low index value (<0.2), while only about half of that, 26,303 people (17.5%), live in areas with a high index (score between 0.8 and 1). Most of the population 78,156 (52.5%) live in areas with intermediate values (score between 0.2 and 0.8). For the purposes of the analysis, it is important to note that some of the neighbourhoods with low index score are among the most densely populated (N16, N17, N4; N18, N19; N26 and the part of N13 with low score).

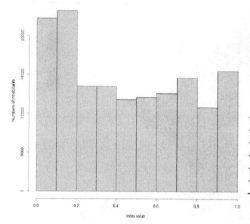

Index value range	N. of inhabitants
0.0 – 0.2	45.396
0.2 – 0.4	27.073
0.4 – 0.6	23.899
0.6 – 0.8	27.184
0.8 – 1.0	26.303

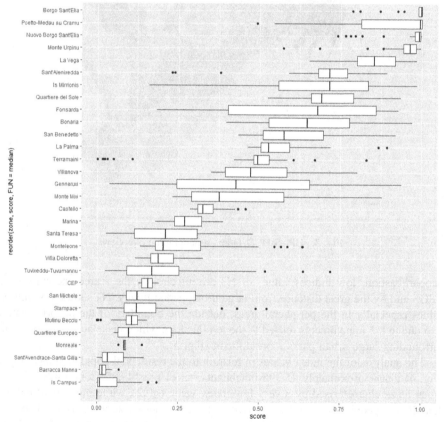

Fig. 4. Distribution of the UPGS-DCD index values among the city population (above) and within each neighbourhood.

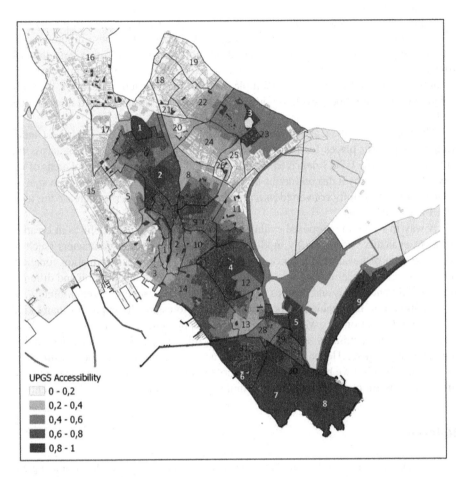

Fig. 5. UPGS-CD Index: map of the calculated values for each census tract (the numbers indicate the neighbourhoods and major parks, according to the Fig. 2).

4 Conclusions

The evaluation model and the related assessment procedure presented in this study allow to assign a UPGS capability index to each node, evaluating its pedestrian connectivity with the set of available public green spaces. The model is based on the idea of UPGS distance-cumulative deficit, and was developed specifically to obtain a better, more detailed and a high-fidelity understanding of different degrees of UPGS accessibility at a spatially granular level, allowing subsequent aggregation at the neighbourhood level for comparison.

The application on the city of Cagliari showed that the neighbourhoods have a high internal variability in accessibility characteristics, which can easily be overlooked by the traditional evaluation procedures. For instance, as can be seen results in Fig. 3, nodes and areas apparently close to large urban parks may obtain low index value due to the presence of impedance elements such as the high terrain slop, lack of nearby park access/entrance points, or due to inadequate street connectivity. These differences are also found within the same neighbourhood, so policies aimed at improving the distribution and accessibility of UPGS cannot be exclusively based on neighbourhoods boundaries, but must work on multiple scales, from strictly local, at the sub-neighbourhood and block level, to wider spatial scenarios, at the city and metropolitan scale.

The results from the Cagliari case study also show the areas with the lowest index values, suggesting places for planning interventions to reduce inequalities across the city. Many of these UPGS-deprived areas are located in the most peripheral areas of the city, characterised by a discontinuous urban fabric, with many abandoned open spaces, which could be usefully converted into public green areas in order to increase the level of UPGS accessibility.

A way in which the proposed evaluation model can also prove useful is in creating different evaluative scenarios by modifying reference values and parameters (such as the maximum distance, the distance decay and the park-size-transformation function, among others), in order to take into account other modes of transportation and different uses by different groups and profiles of users (e.g. children, senior citizens). Finally, as a simulation tool, the evaluation model can be used to assess the impact of many kind of urban interventions to which the traditional approaches are insensitive, such as adding new park entrances, removal of barriers, improvements of street connectivity, among many others. Hence, although there are still steps to be made, with these possibilities in mind we believe that the proposed approach is a promising candidate to grow into a useful planning and urban design support at different scales of intervention.

References

1. Artmann, M., Inostroza, L., Fan, P.: Urban sprawl, compact urban development and green cities. How much do we know, how much do we agree? Ecol. Indic. **96**, 3–9 (2019)
2. Fan, P., Ouyang, Z., Basnou, C., Pino, J., Park, H., Chen, J.: Nature-based solutions for urban landscapes under post-industrialization and globalization: Barcelona versus Shanghai. Environ. Res. **156**, 272–283 (2017)
3. James, P., Tzoulas, K., Adams, M.D., Barber, A., et al.: Towards an integrated understanding of green space in the European built environment. Urban For. Urban Gree. **8**, 65–75 (2009)
4. Braubach, M., Egorov, A., Mudu, P., Wolf, T., Ward Thompson, C., Martuzzi, M.: Effects of urban green space on environmental health, equity and resilience. In: Kabisch, N., Korn, H., Stadler, J., Bonn, A. (eds.) Nature-Based Solutions to Climate Change Adaptation in Urban Areas. TPUST, pp. 187–205. Springer, Cham (2017). https://doi.org/10.1007/978-3-319-56091-5_11
5. Byrne, J., Sipe, N.: Green and open space planning for urban consolidation. A review of the literature and best practice. Urban Research Program Issue Paper 11, Griffith University Brisbane (2010)
6. Kabisch, N., Korn, H., Stadler, J., Bonn, A. (eds.): Nature-Based Solutions to Climate Change Adaptation in Urban Areas: Linkages between Science, Policy and Practice. TPUST. Springer, Cham (2017). https://doi.org/10.1007/978-3-319-56091-5

7. Lyytimäki, J., Sipilä, M.: Hopping on one leg. The challenge of ecosystem disservices for urban green management. Urban For. Urban Gree. **8**, 309–315 (2009)
8. Sadeghian, M.M., Vardanyan, Z.: The benefits of Urban Parks, a review of urban research. J. Novel Appl. Sci. **2**(8), 231–237 (2013)
9. UN: New Urban Agenda. Resolution Adopted by the General Assembly on 23 December 2016. United Nations A/RES/71/256 (2017)
10. UN: Transforming Our World: The 2030 Agenda for Sustainable Development. Resolution Adopted by the General Assembly on 25 September 2015. United Nations A/RES/70/1 (2015)
11. Trust for Public Land: Parks and the pandemic, special Report. https://www.tpl.org/sites/default/files/Parks%20and%20Pandemic%20-%20TPL%20special%20report.pdf. Accessed 20 Apr 2020
12. Poelman, H.: A walk to the park? Assessing access to green areas in Europe's cities. https://ec.europa.eu/regional_policy/sources/docgener/work/2018_01_green_urban_area.pdf. Accessed 20 Apr 2020
13. Hoffimann, E., Barros, H., Ribeiro, A.: Socioeconomic inequalities in green space quality and accessibility. Evidence from a Southern European city. IJERPH **14**, 916 (2017)
14. Rigolon, A., Browning, M., Jennings, V.: Inequities in the quality of urban park systems: an environmental justice investigation of cities in the United States. Landscape Urban Plan. **178**, 156–169 (2018)
15. Ruijsbroek, A., et al.: Does the health impact of exposure to neighbourhood green space differ between population groups? An explorative study in four European cities. IJERPH **14**, 618 (2017)
16. Shanahan, D.F., Lin, B.B., Gaston, K.J., Bush, R., Fuller, R.A.: Socio-economic inequalities in access to nature on public and private lands: a case study from Brisbane, Australia. Landscape Urban Plan. **130**, 14–23 (2014)
17. Cvejic, R., et al.: Typology of Urban Green Spaces, Ecosystem Services Provisioning Services and Demands. Report: D3.1, GREEN SURGE Project 2013–2017 (2015)
18. Kabisch, N., Strohbach, M., Haase, D., Kronenberg, J.: Urban green space availability in European cities. Ecol. Ind. **70**, 586–596 (2016)
19. Beirevant, A., Bonyad, A.E., Sousani, J.: Evaluation of changes in per capita green space through remote sensing data. Int. J. Adv. Biol. Biomed. Res. **1**(4), 321–330 (2013)
20. Gupta, K., Kumar, P., Pathan, S.K., Sharma, K.P.: Urban Neighborhood Green Index. A measure of green spaces in urban areas. Landscape Urban Plan. **105**, 325–335 (2012)
21. Lahoti, S., Kefi, M., Lahoti, A., Saito, O.: Mapping methodology of public urban green spaces using GIS: an example of Nagpur City, India. Sustainability **11**, 2166 (2019)
22. Yan, W.Y., Shaker, A., El-Ashmawy, N.: Urban land cover classification using airborne LiDAR data: a review. Remote Sens. Environ. **158**, 295–310 (2015)
23. Tian, Y., Jim, C.Y., Wang, H.: Assessing the landscape and ecological quality of urban green spaces in a compact city. Landscape Urban Plan. **121**, 97–108 (2014)
24. Jokar Arsanjani, J., Mooney, P., Zipf, A., Schauss, A.: Quality assessment of the contributed land use information from OpenStreetMap versus authoritative datasets. In: Jokar Arsanjani, J., Zipf, A., Mooney, P., Helbich, M. (eds.) OpenStreetMap in GIScience. LNGC, pp. 37–58. Springer, Cham (2015). https://doi.org/10.1007/978-3-319-14280-7_3
25. Lopes, P., Fonte, C., See, L., Bechtel, B.: Using OpenStreetMap data to assist in the creation of LCZ maps. In: Joint Urban Remote Sensing Event (JURSE), pp. 1–4 (2017)
26. Schultz, M., Voss, J., Auer, M., Carter, S., Zipf, A.: Open land cover from OpenStreetMap and remote sensing. Int. J. Appl. Earth Obs. Geoinformation **63**, 206–213 (2017)

27. Dony, C.C., Delmelle, E.M., Delmelle, E.C.: Re-conceptualizing accessibility to parks in multi-modal cities: a variable-width floating catchment area (VFCA) method. Landsc. Urban Plan. **143**, 90–99 (2015)
28. Li, L., Du, Q., Ren, F., Ma, X.: Assessing spatial accessibility to hierarchical urban parks by multi-types of travel distance in Shenzhen, China. Int. J. Environ. Res. Public Health **16** (1038), 1–23 (2019)
29. Xing, L., Liuab, Y., Liu, X.: Measuring spatial disparity in accessibility with a multi-mode method based on park green spaces classification in Wuhan, China. Appl. Geogr. **94**, 251–261 (2018)
30. Breuste, J., Rahimi, A.: Many public urban parks, but who profits from them? The example of Tabriz, Iran. Ecological Processes **4**(1), 1–15 (2015). https://doi.org/10.1186/s13717-014-0027-4
31. Van Herzelele, A.V., Wiedemann, T.: A monitoring tool for the provision of accessible and attractive urban green spaces. Landscape Urban Plan. **63**, 109–126 (2003)
32. Iraegui, E., Augusto, G., Cabral, P.: Assessing equity in the accessibility to urban green spaces according to different functional levels. Int. J. Geo-Inf. **9**(308), 1–17 (2020)
33. Almohamad, H., Knaack, A.L., Habib, B.M.: Assessing spatial equity and accessibility of public green spaces in Aleppo City, Syria. Forests **9**(706), 1–22 (2018)
34. Giles-Corti, B., Broomhall, M.H., Knuiman, M., Collins, C., Douglas, K., Donovan, K.R.J.: Increasing walking: how important is distance to, attractiveness, and size of public open space? Am. J. Prev. Med. **28**(2), 169–176 (2005)
35. Guan, C.H., Song, J., Keith, M., Akiyamad, Y., Shibasakid, R., Satoe, T.: Delineating urban park catchment areas using mobile phone data: a case study of Tokyo. Comput. Environ. Urban Syst. **81**, 101474 (2020)
36. La Rosa, D.: Accessibility to greenspaces: GIS based indicators for sustainable planning in a dense urban context. Ecol. Ind. **42**, 122–134 (2014)
37. De Sousa, C., Viegas, I., Panagopoulus, T., Bell, S.: Environmental justice in accessibility to green infrastructure in two European cities. Land **7**(4), 134 (2018)
38. Fan, P., Lee, Y.C., Ouyang, Z., Huang, S.L.: Compact and green urban development. Towards a framework to assess urban development for a high-density metropolis. Environ. Res. Lett. **14**, 1–17 (2019)
39. Atikur Rahman, K.M., Zhang, D.: Analyzing the level of accessibility of public urban green spaces to different socially vulnerable groups of people. Sustainability **10**, 1–27 (2018)
40. Rigolon, A.: Parks and young people: an environmental justice study of park proximity, acreage, and quality in Denver. Colo. Landsc. Urban Plan. **165**, 73–83 (2017)
41. Unal, M., Uslu, C., Cilek, A.: GIS-based accessibility analysis for neighbourhood parks: the case of Cukurova district modelling accessibility to urban greenspaces. J. Digit. Landsc. Archit. **1**, 46–56 (2016)
42. Martins, B., Pereira, A.N.: Index for evaluation of public parks and gardens proximity based on the mobility network: a case study of Braga, Braganza and Viana do Castelo (Portugal) and Lugo and Pontevedra (Spain). Urban For. Urban Gree. **34**, 134–140 (2018)
43. Comber, A., Brunsdon, C., Edmund, G.: Using a GIS-based network to determine urban greenspace accessibility for different ethnic and religious groups. Landscape Urban Plan. **86** (1), 103–114 (2008)
44. Handley, J., et al.: Providing Accessible Natural Greenspace in Towns and Cities: A Practical Guide to Assessing the Resource and Implementing Local Standards for Provision. http://www.english-nature.org.uk/pubs/publication/PDF/Accessgreenspace.pdf. Accessed 20 Apr 2020
45. Gilderbloom, J.I., Riggs, W.W., Meares, W.L.: Does walkability matter? An examination of walkability's impact on housing values, foreclosures and crime. Cities **42**, 13–24 (2015)

46. Hsu, C.I., Tsai, Y.C.: An energy expenditure approach for estimating walking distance. Environ. Plan. **41**, 289–306 (2014)
47. Daniel, P., Burns, L.: How steep is that street? Mapping 'real' pedestrian catchments by adding elevation to street networks. Radic. Stat. **121**, 26–48 (2018)

Count Regression and Machine Learning Approach for Zero-Inflated Over-Dispersed Count Data. Application to Micro-Retail Distribution and Urban Form

Alessandro Araldi[1]([⊠]) [ID], Alessandro Venerandi[1] [ID],
and Giovanni Fusco[2] [ID]

[1] Université Côte-d'Azur, ESPACE, Nice, France
{alessandro.araldi,
alessandro.venerandi}@univ-cotedazur.fr
[2] Université Côte-d'Azur, CNRS, ESPACE, Nice, France
giovanni.fusco@univ-cotedazur.fr

Abstract. This paper investigates the relationship between urban form and the spatial distribution of micro-retail activities. In the last decades, several works demonstrated how configurational properties of the street network and morphological descriptors of the urban built environment are significantly related to store distribution. However, two main challenges still need to be addressed. On the one side, the combined effect of different urban form properties should be considered providing a holistic study of the urban form and its relationship to retail patterns. On the other, analytical approaches should consider the discrete, skewed and zero-inflated nature of the micro-retail distribution. To overcome these limitations, this work compares two sophisticated modelling procedure: Penalised Count Regression and Machine Learning approaches. While the former is specifically conceived to account for retail count distribution, the latter can capture non-linear behaviours in the data. The two modelling procedures are implemented on the same large dataset of street-based measures describing the urban form of the French Riviera. The outcomes of the two modelling approaches are compared in terms of prediction performance and selection frequencies of the most recurrent variables among the implemented models.

Keywords: Retail distribution · Urban form · Street-network configuration · Feature selection · Penalised models · Machine Learning

1 Introduction

Distribution of micro-retail is one of the most studied phenomena in urban space: the presence of stores is traditionally associated with socioeconomic dynamics and attractiveness of urban spaces [1]. Understanding the relationship between retail distribution and urban form, also named 'the morphological sense of commerce' [2], might provide academics and practitioners with evidence on how urban systems work and, ultimately, nourish the discussion on how to improve quality of life in urban areas through design and planning.

© Springer Nature Switzerland AG 2020
O. Gervasi et al. (Eds.): ICCSA 2020, LNCS 12252, pp. 550–565, 2020.
https://doi.org/10.1007/978-3-030-58811-3_40

In the last two decades, a large number of empirical works investigated the association between store distribution and specific aspects of urban form [3]. Within the theoretical framework of Hillier's Movement Economy Theory (MET) [4, 5], the street-network represents the most extensively explored aspect of the urban environment. MET explains how the spatial configuration of public spaces influences movement patterns and indirectly the location of stores. Inspired by this theory, several works investigated the relationship between store distribution and street-network configuration in different urban and socioeconomic contexts, for example, through the metrics of integration in Space Syntax-SSx [5] and Betweenness in Multiple Centrality Assessment (MCA) [6].

While an overall agreement on the importance of street-network properties in relation to the location of stores might be found in this specific literature, several criticisms were raised by other authors. The configurational analysis did not account, in fact, for additional aspects of urban form, such as building distribution and heights, site morphology, built-up density, which might also participate to the description of the relationship between urban form and retail distribution [3]. Together with configurational approaches, researchers have been gradually introducing additional descriptors, for example, street-based urban design qualities [7], skeletal streetscape [8], street-block typologies and built-up density [9, 10], and plot system [11]. Moreover, they started to investigate how the importance of each descriptor of urban form might play different roles depending on the relative morphological context: different aspects of urban form might be associated with the presence of retail in different typo-morphological regions, such as urban fabrics [8], centre-periphery [12], the extent of the urban centre or the different morphogenetic processes (spontaneous or planned) underlying urban grids [13].

Beyond the theoretical and methodological discussion underlying the identification and conceptualisation of variables of urban form, two aspects related to the modelling procedures should be highlighted. Firstly, the aforementioned proliferation of approaches and features of urban form investigated in relation to retail distribution results in a rich yet fragmented literature. Despite evidence about the individual importance of specific aspects of urban form on store distribution, we still miss an overall picture. Assessing the combined and relative importance of a large number of urban form descriptors with innovative data analysis and feature selection procedures might provide further evidence about the relative importance of each component.

Secondly, the techniques of data analysis utilised in previous works tend to be overly simplistic [14]. Indeed, while important efforts have been devoted to the conception and implementation of sophisticated computer-aided procedures for the description of different aspects of urban form, the choice and implementation of statistical and modelling procedures have received less attention [8]. Relationships are often checked through visual inspection of maps [10], simple bivariate correlation [6, 12], or Multiple Linear Regressions (MLR) [13, 14]. However, the assumption of normality of residuals underlying MLR is hardly met given the usually *very skewed* and *zero-inflated* distribution of number/density of stores in the spatial unit. Only very few works considered these two specificities of the retail distribution: log-transformation of the dependent variable [15] or count regressions approaches [9] for the former, suppression of spatial units without retail for the latter [6].

Nonetheless, the absence of retail should be considered as much informative as its presence and ignoring this specific aspect would hide important evidence on the phenomena under study. The retail distribution might be explained as the combined result of a twofold generative process defining presence/absence and number of stores, each one associated with different combinations of urban form features. Zero-Inflated Negative Binomial (ZINB) technique [16] has been shown to better perform when compared to traditional MLR and count regression [8, 17], with the only downside of not being able to capture non-linear behaviours in data.

To overcome the limitations stated above and provide a more robust description of the relationship between features of urban form and retail distribution, the ZINB model developed by Araldi [17] is here compared to Gradient Boosting (GB) [18]. The former is a count regression model, part of the larger family of Generalised Linear Models (GLM) providing a built-in variable selection solution. The latter is a recently developed Machine Learning (ML) algorithm, combined with a forward feature selection, which proved to be a very versatile and robust technique of data analysis based on train and test and cross-validation [19].

These two methodologies are here compared to analyse the relationship between a large set of urban features and retail distribution in the French Riviera, a large metropolitan area located in the south of France. Outcomes, both in terms of prediction performance and selected variables, are compared and discussed. Findings show that ZINB is, in general, better than canonical GB. However, a specific nested modelling architecture combining Boolean and regressive GBs approaches to model respectively absence/presence and retail count provides higher performance levels.

The paper is structured as follows: Sect. 2, specifies the goal of the paper. Section 3 presents the methodology under investigation: we briefly describe the study area, data sources, the set of urban form descriptors and the two modelling procedures under analysis. Outcomes of the two modelling procedures are presented and compared in Sect. 4, focusing both on predictive potential and the selected variables. Conclusion and perspectives of future work conclude the paper.

2   Objective

As introduced in the previous section, the major challenge in this work is how to deal with zero-inflated and highly skewed distribution characterising the retail distribution along streets. ZINB regressions were shown to handle both skewness and inflation in the data distribution in the case of retail distribution modelling, better perform among other statistical regressive approaches [8, 17]. Nonetheless, an important limitation still persists: count data models might not be able to detect the presence of complex non-linear interactions between the predictors and the response variable. To overcome this problem, GB is here implemented and compared to ZINB. GB is an improved version of Random Forests (RF), a technique of data analysis based on multiple decision trees. However, while the prediction output by RF is the average of the predictions of each of such trees, the one made by GB is obtained through an iterative process that, each time, fits new decision trees to improve predictions, and thus reduce errors [18].

However, despite a high predictive capacity, two main limitations are traditionally associated with ML (and therefore GB) approaches: firstly, the interpretation of the parameters is less straightforward. Secondly, the sample size for each class or range to be predicted should roughly be similar. When this assumption is not met, the application of a canonical ML might produce biased results focusing on the prediction of the class/range with the highest number of samples [20]. Data imbalance/skewness represents a non-trivial problem that has received growing attention in the last two decades within the ML community [20, 21]. To overcome these limitations, numerous solutions have been proposed in the ML literature. Three groups might be recognised [22]: i) ad-hoc modification at the data level (i.e. over/under-sampling techniques); ii) variation at the algorithm level removing the bias towards the majority class (i.e. cost-sensitive approaches); iii) hybrid approaches combining both data and algorithm modifications.

Although many efforts targeting imbalanced distributions are regularly proposed in the community, these procedures are mainly based on heuristics aimed at the improvement of the prediction performance. Moreover, they lack relevant insights/basis on the generating process(es) underlying the phenomena to be modelled, that might guide the development of systematic imbalanced learning approaches. As recently observed by Kravzczyk [22], many shortcomings in existing methods and problems still need to be addressed appropriately. Furthermore, alterations of canonical procedures might also be associated with degradation of model performances.

For these reasons, in this work, rather than focusing on procedures that could handle imbalanced models, we propose a theory/process-based solution combining canonical well-established ML approaches. Starting from the same hypothesis underlying traditional zero-inflated regression approaches, we propose to study the retail distribution with a decomposition of the original problem into a set of two sub-problems: absence/presence and amount of stores. These two aspects are investigated with canonical classificatory (Boolean) and regressive GB, both in a disconnected and combined/nested fashion. This approach allows a straightforward comparative assessment of the two modelling approaches investigated in this paper (ZINB and RF). Moreover, feature selection procedures can be easily implemented through shrinkage (or penalised) regressions [23] and Sequential Forward Selection (SFS) [24] for ZINB and RF, respectively.

The implementation of these procedures on the same study area provides important empirical evidence about specificities of these two methodological approaches and on two major challenges: on the one side, the ability to deal with zero-inflated and highly skewed distribution characterising the retail distribution along streets, on the other, the need to identify a subset of meaningful variables from a large set, characterised by high multicollinearity. Comparing the selected variables from the two methods allows understanding whether the underlying assumptions of traditional modelling approaches might influence the results of the analysis and if non-linearity might better explain the relationship between urban spaces and retail distribution.

Both procedures are applied to a vast metropolitan region and on nine sub-regions defined for their different morphological/contextual characteristics and degrees of skewness and zero-inflation. The spatial decomposition of the models allows assessing performances and selected variables in different contexts, providing information on the scale/contextual independence/dependency of each variable and possible non-linear behaviours between descriptors of urban form and retail.

3   Methodology

3.1   Study Area and Data Sources

In order to assess the modelling protocols under analysis, we implement them on a real case study, that of the French Riviera, an extensive metropolitan area, including 88 coastal and inland municipalities of the department of the Alpes-Maritimes, in the southern French region Provence Alpes Côte d'Azur (PACA). Six main urban centres structure the French Riviera (Fig. 1). In its western part, we find the inland town of Grasse and the two coastal cities of Cannes and Antibes, counting respectively 51, 74.2, and 73.8 thousand inhabitants. Nice, with its 343 thousand inhabitants, represents the largest municipality of the French Riviera and the administrative centre of the department. The enclave of Monaco and the border city of Menton have respectively 38 and 28 thousand inhabitants. Spread around these main centres, 295 thousand people find their home in smaller cities, villages, and hamlets. With a total of more than 1 million inhabitants, the French Riviera is the seventh most populated conurbation in France.

The combination of all these elements produces a sequence of urban centres and peripheral areas of different sizes and urban forms. Considering such a variety might help to overcome the limitation of traditional works investigating only urban cores [3]. Furthermore, the high heterogeneity of urban forms present in this study area allows a more thorough assessment of the outcomes of our two modelling approaches as different zero-inflation and overdispersion of the micro-retail distributions are observed.

Two sources of data have been used in this work. The official data on retail distribution has been provided by the local Chamber of Commerce of Nice Cote-d'Azur. Urban form descriptors are based on the geographic databases (BD TOPO®, 2017) from the French National Institute of Geographical and Forest Information. Four layers of urban morphological elements have been used: building, street-network, parcel and digital terrain model-DTM. While GIS-based protocols have been implemented for computing the different descriptors of urban forms, open-source Python and R libraries were used to implement GB (scikit-learn) and ZINB models (mpath).

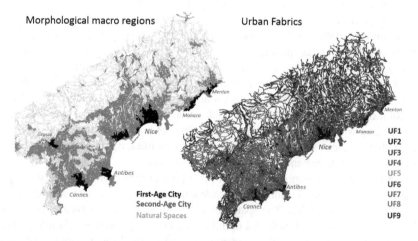

Fig. 1. The study area and the morphological regions at the macro- (First/Second-Age Cities, left) and meso-scale (the nine Urban Fabrics, right), considered in this work. Source: [8].

3.2   The Variables Under Investigation

The spatial unit of analysis considered in this work is the street segment. It represents one of the most used spatial units and has attracted the attention of urban designers, morphologists, and geographers in the last twenty years, [25]. The street is also considered the bridging element between different theoretical backgrounds and methodological approaches [26].

The output variable was computed by assigning to each street segment, belonging to the study area under exam, the number of small stores (surface < 300 m^2) lying on it. In order to describe different aspects of urban form, several computer-aided procedures, extracted from established scientific literature, were applied to our study region. Once excluded empty streets segment,[1] our dataset had 63 thousand elements, described by more than one-hundred street-based indicators of urban form.

Such descriptors can be categorised in four main subsets. Forty indicators describe street network configurational properties and were computed through the MCA protocol [27]. Four traditional configurational indices, Reach, Straightness, Closeness and Betweenness centralities were implemented at different radii and impedances (metric and temporal, corresponding to pedestrian movement and vehicular mobility). Thirty-six indicators describe the street-network accessibility towards public squares, coastline and Anchor Stores (e.g., shopping centres, arcades etc. with an overall surface > 2000 m^2, AS), considered as influential components in the commercial fabric of cities [28]. As for the previous metrics, different radii and impedances were considered. Thirty indicators measure various aspects of urban form and were implemented through GIS procedures. These indicators describe the layout of the built form along street edges (also named skeletal streetscape [29]). Examples of such indicators are: façade alignment, set-back of buildings, average building height, distribution of plots, etc.

Finally, street-based contextual variables are obtained through the implementation of the Multiple Fabric Assessment procedure [30, 31]. Each street segment is associated with twelve values, each describing the probability of association to nine families of urban fabrics and three morphological regions, respectively, at the neighbourhood and district level (Fig. 1). These two typo-morphological partitions of the space also define the subareas where count regression and GB models were separately applied.

3.3   Modelling Approaches

Based on the thematic and methodological literature previously discussed, this paper investigates the relationship of micro-retail distribution and urban form as generated by a double process (store presence and quantity), through count regression and GB. For each study (sub)region, we implement at first two couples of models exploring the aforementioned processes separately: Binomial (B) regression and GB Boolean classification for the former, Negative Binomial (NB) regression and regressive GB for the latter. The separation of these two processes requires the manipulation and separation of the original dataset that corresponds, in other terms, to an artificial introduction of

---

[1] Defined as those street segment where no built-up elements are observed within a radius of 50 m from its edges.

expert-based knowledge in the modelling procedure. Consequently, the models of presence/absence of retail do not consider the number of stores observed along each street and their outcomes only describe streets with favourable or hostile conditions to the presence of at least one store. Contrarily, in the case of count models, outcomes describe those features of urban form which are best associated with greater/smaller numbers of stores on street segments, when/if observed. To model the combined effect of these two processes without their manual separation, specific procedures are therefore implemented.

In the GML count regression methodological framework, the Zero-Inflated Negative Binomial regression (ZINB) provides a built-in solution for the simultaneous implementation of a Binomial and a Negative Binomial regression. In such an approach, zeros are originated by two simultaneous processes: structural zeros (or true zeros) and random zeros (or false zeros). ZINB is a well-established statistical procedure already tested and implemented in several disciplines and, more recently, demonstrated to well perform when investigating retail distribution.

On the contrary, for what concerns the GB methodological framework, the absence of a specific acknowledged procedure able to consider the two processes requires us to test two different solutions. The first consists in implementing the canonical algorithm, where no difference between the two processes is made. Canonical GB is a versatile and robust technique of data analysis that combines several weak models to output a stronger overall prediction [18]. As mentioned above, the prediction made by GB is based on an iterative process that fits new decision tree models to improve predictions, and thus reduce errors, at each iteration. The minimisation of such errors is based on a loss cost function pointing in the negative gradient direction. To avoid overfitting, the original dataset is divided in train and test subsets. First, the model is trained on a random subset of the dataset. Second, its performance is evaluated on the part of the dataset that was not used in the previous step. This procedure must be combined with the k-fold cross-validation, which consists in dividing the dataset into k folds and using each fold k − 1 times as train set and once as test set to be predicted. The number of folds considered is this work is 10.

The second solution within the GB methodological framework accounts for the two processes in retail distribution (store presence and quantity) and uses several ML algorithms in a nested fashion. Firstly, to identify the best predictors of presence/absence of retail, a GB classifier is fitted in a cross-validated regime. Having obtained the model, this must be used to predict presence/absence of retail across all observations in the study area. Subsequently, a regressive GB is implemented again, in a cross-validated regime, to predict retail count where the previous model predicted presence. The presented nested solution allows to specifically consider the two process of retail presence/absence and count without manual separation of the two subsets.

In order to deal with the redundant and highly correlated information originated by the large number of variables,[2] both GLM and GB procedures are combined with specific variable selection procedures to allow the identification of the most significant

---

[2] Which might especially affect the GLM based on the assumption of independent regressors.

variables of urban form related to retail distribution. In the case of count regressions (B, NB and ZINB), penalised regression approaches are applied: the notion underlying this procedure is to shrink the regressive coefficients toward zero. The coefficients associated with the variables with a minor contribution to the outcomes of the model are close or equal to zero. In this way, the complexity of the model is reduced. The specific ElasticNet (Enet) procedure [32] is implemented in this work. For what concerns the ML approach, GB models (both classificatory and regressive) are all preceded by a Sequential Forward Selection (SFS). SFS identifies the best predictors of the output variable through an iterative process based on a regressor performance that adds one variable at the time until an optimal subset of features is reached [19].

The implementation of Enet and SFS procedures, allow us to identify those subsets of variables associated with retail presence/absence and count separately, within each sub-region. To compare the outcomes of all modelling solutions (ZINB, canonical GB, and nested GB), F1 scores must be computed to evaluate their performances. The F1 score measures a model's accuracy as the harmonic mean of precision and recall [33]. The former represents the number of correct positive predictions divided by the total number of all positive predictions output by the model. The latter is the number of correct positive predictions divided by the number of all samples that should have been identified as positive. F1 scores range between 1 (perfect accuracy) and 0 (worst accuracy). These performance measures describe the combined effect of the variable selection and modelling procedures within the GLM and ML approaches where specific subset of selected variables underlies each model. We will, however, remark that F1 scores are better suited to compare the zero-part of the models (presence/absence of stores) than the count part. For the latter, any predicted value differing from the observed one will contribute equally to lowering the F1 score, regardless of the magnitude of the difference. More specific measures, like the area under the Count-REC (Regression Error Characteristic) curve [8] could be used to compare the quality of the count models. As for the GM models, F1 scores are always calculated as an average of the 10 test subsets within the k-fold procedure.

The outcomes of the variable selection procedures are finally presented in terms of selection frequency. Comparing the selected variables from each couple of models (B vs Boolean GB, zero-truncated NB vs regressive GB, ZINB vs canonical/nested GB) allows identifying the degree of similarity of the GLM and ML modelling approaches.

4   Results

4.1   Comparing Model Goodness of Fit Values

In Table 1, the outcomes of all 81 models are collected and compared. For each study (sub)region, zero rates and variances of the count part are provided. By visually inspecting Table 1, we note that higher zero-inflation is associated with lower overdispersion in non-dense sub-regions while dense urban fabrics are associated with lower zero-inflation and higher variability. F1 scores are separately evaluated for the zero and count parts allowing a direct comparison and evaluation of the different modelling procedures in relation to conditions of zero-inflation and overdispersion.

Before discussing performances, we remind the reader that each model is based on different subsets of variables, since different feature selection procedures had to be used in GLM and ML. The performances showed in Table 1 are to be considered the combined result of such feature selections and modelling, implemented on the same original dataset of 105 descriptors of urban form and optimised for each sub-region under analysis.

Depending on the process(es) under analysis and judging solely from F1 scores, different outcomes can be outlined: when focusing on the presence/absence prediction of stores (zero part), both Binomial and GB Boolean models show better performances for sub-regions with more zero-inflation. F1 scores of the two modelling approaches converge for sub-regions with higher zero-inflation (less than 1,5% of variation), although traditional Binomial regressions tend to perform slightly better than GB Boolean classifiers. On the other hand, the latter tends to perform better than Binomial regressions in cases with less zero-inflation.

When modelling the number of stores (count part) with zero-truncated Negative Binomial regressions and regressive GB, the latter approach is consistently associated with higher predictive capacity, with an improvement of the F1 scores between 25% and 125%. Furthermore, stronger improvements seem to be associated with larger subsets rather than with smaller ones, which also tend to be more zero-inflated and/or overdispersed.

When the two processes of presence/absence and quantity of retail are modelled with ZINB and canonical GB, we observe that: i) F1 scores of both zero and count parts are lower than the ones obtained through models that considered the two processes separated; ii) canonical GB performs slightly better for both zero and count parts, when considering the entire dataset; iii) in compact/planned urban fabrics, where greater numbers of stores can be found, the ZINB outperforms the canonical GB for both zero and count parts; vi) in the remaining subspaces, GB performs better in the zero part, while ZINB provides better predictions for the count part.

The proposed nested GB protocol, inherit the higher predictive performance from the separate implementation of Boolean and regressive GB. We observe that the nested GB always performs better than the canonical GB, in both zero and count parts. When comparing nested GB to ZINB, we observe that: i) F1 scores of the zero parts for the former are always greater than the ones for the latter, although the improvement decreases in those cases with stronger zero-inflation; ii) F1 scores relative to the count part of the nested GB are greater than the ones for ZINB, with the exception of those urban fabrics with grater variability of values. Finally, in UF2 (traditional planned urban fabrics with adjoining buildings), nested GB and ZINB show similar predictive performances, while, in UF4 (modern discontinuous urban fabrics with big and medium-sized buildings), ZINB outperforms the nested GB approach.

Table 1. Performance of models subdivided for morphological contexts/regions. Count variance and zero-inflation are reported in the first row. F1 scores are provided separately for the zero and count parts. The darker the red, the stronger the improvement in performance of GB approaches over GLM ones. The darker the green, the stronger the improvement in performance of regressive GLM over GB ones.

Modelled process		Dependent Variable (stores per street)	Study Region	Global	First	Second	UF1	UF2	UF3	UF4	UF5	UF6
			Variance (count part)	28,40	40,62	16,55	11,86	50,62	5,00	27,66	2,38	1,30
			% zeros	77,4	63,1	85,7	74,9	52	81,8	80,5	88,7	89,6
Separate models for micro-retail Presence/Absence and Count	Zero Model	Binomial		0,911	0,830	0,924	0,872	0,763	0,902	0,893	0,943	0,948
		GB Boolean		0,913	0,843	0,923	0,874	0,758	0,896	0,896	0,942	0,947
		±		0,26%	1,54%	-0,07%	0,21%	-0,62%	-0,63%	0,37%	-0,12%	-0,16%
	Count Model	NB		0,170	0,123	0,239	0,195	0,110	0,285	0,155	0,399	0,484
		GB Regressive		0,366	0,224	0,408	0,312	0,148	0,452	0,218	0,585	0,618
		±		115,34%	81,64%	70,50%	59,63%	34,43%	58,77%	40,55%	46,57%	27,68%
Combined model for micro-retail Presence/Absence and Count	Zero Part	ZINB		0,883	0,764	0,909	0,843	0,676	0,885	0,863	0,934	0,948
		GB Regressive		0,903	0,812	0,906	0,853	0,696	0,892	0,875	0,944	0,949
		±		2,25%	6,36%	-0,25%	1,16%	2,98%	0,82%	1,40%	1,11%	0,14%
		GB nested		0,913	0,843	0,923	0,874	0,758	0,896	0,896	0,942	0,947
		±		3,4%	10,4%	1,6%	3,6%	12,1%	1,2%	3,9%	0,9%	-0,1%
	Count part	ZINB		0,102	0,157	0,154	0,214	0,133	0,220	0,169	0,145	0,180
		GB Regressive		0,106	0,115	0,084	0,174	0,108	0,117	0,028	0,000	0,000
		±		4,55%	-27,04%	-45,47%	-18,81%	-18,94%	-46,85%	-83,65%	-100,00%	-100,00%
		GB nested		0,209	0,216	0,337	0,290	0,134	0,412	0,126	0,367	0,705
		±		105,8%	37,5%	119,2%	35,3%	0,7%	86,9%	-25,2%	153,8%	291,1%

To conclude, when retail absence/presence and count are modelled separately, Boolean GB and the traditional Binomial model show similar results for absence/presence, while GB outperforms zero-truncated NB in predicting the number of stores. Nested GB outperforms canonical regressive GB when the output variable shows skewed and zero-inflated distributions, both in zero and count processes. When comparing nested GB and ZINB regressive approaches, the former outperforms the latter, especially in those cases with stronger zero-inflation. Conversely, in cases with less 0s and stronger dispersion, the two modelling approaches output similar results.

4.2   Comparing Outcomes of Feature Selections

The attentive interpretation of regression coefficients and feature importance output by each model goes beyond the goals (and limits) of this work. In this section, we will focus instead only on checking similarities and differences between the indicators of urban form selected by the two feature selection procedures (Enet and SFS), in each model.

The number of selected indicators varies between few, in the case of non-compact peripheral regions, to many in compact urban areas (up to 30 variables, a third of the input variables). The nested GB approach displays the greatest number of selected indicators in the overall study area and in compact regions (i.e. between 18 and 30), due to the double selection procedure for each retail distribution process under analysis (presence/absence and quantity). To summarise and assess the importance of each of the chosen indicators, the frequency of their presence in the models is evaluated. Tables 2 and 3 show such frequencies for the different modelling approaches, retail distribution processes, and spatial subsets.

The first column of Table 2 reports those indicators with the highest frequencies (>30%), across all 63 models. Among the ten most selected indicators, seven describe morphometric properties of the skeletal streetscape: Street Length, Building Coverage Ratio, Street Acclivity, Street Corridor Effect, Built-up Fragmentation, Average Building Height and Street Open Space. Local Betweenness at different scales (1,200 m, 5 and 20 min) are the most selected variables among the configurational descriptors. In the next two columns of Table 2, frequencies are separately reported for the two modelling approaches, GLM and GB techniques. Five of the aforementioned indicators are found relevant for retail distribution independently by the modelling procedure (Street Length, Corridor Effect, Coverage Ratio, Built-up Fragmentation, Betweenness at 1,200 m). However, we observe higher selection frequencies in the GLM approaches compared to GB ones. The former identifies a similar subset of variables for the different spatial partitions. The latter tends instead to select more diverse sets of variables for each model, seizing distinctive characteristics in each morphological sub-region. Moreover, GB approaches tend to select variables with a regionalised distribution such as Slope, contextual morphometric partitions (UFs and morphological regions) and proximity to specific features (coastline and AS). They also tend to select variables describing punctual/discrete occurrences (i.e. cul-de-sac). Here again, the reason underlying these outcomes might be related to the ability of GB approaches to model non-linear relationships. In the last two columns of Table 2, frequencies are reported considering zero/count models for compact (First Age City, UF1-3) and sprawled/modernist (sub)regions (Second Age City, UF4-6), separately. We observe how the same indicators of urban form might play different roles in the two retail distribution processes. For instance, Street Corridor Effect appears to have a relatively higher importance in defining the number of stores rather than their presence/absence, in compact contexts; however, the opposite behaviour is observed in non-compact regions. Similar presence of configurational and morphometric indicators is as influencing the retail presence/absence independently by the urban context; nonetheless, count process in compact areas seems to be more importantly influenced by morphometric streetscape descriptors than configurational ones.

In Table 3, we report the top 30 most selected features of urban form (the stronger the red, the greater the frequency of a feature). Models are divided only by considering the study (sub)regions. In this case, higher values describe greater importance of the variable in relation to retail, independently by the modelling procedure and by the separation of the zero and count processes. Among the top 10 most selected indicators, we still find the indicators mentioned in the previous paragraph (i.e. Street Length, Building Coverage Ratio, Street Acclivity, Street Corridor Effect, Built-up Fragmen-tation, Average Building Height and Street Open Space, Local Betweenness at 1,200 m, 5 and 20 min). Nonetheless, when considering each sub(region), different frequencies can be observed: for instance, in compact city centres (First-Age city), together with the ten aforementioned indicators, Standard Deviation of the Building

Table 2. Outcomes of feature selection procedures. Selection frequencies of the most recurrent descriptors of urban form, in relation to micro-retail spatial distribution. Frequencies are here reported considering all 63 models under analysis, grouped by modeling approach (GLM/ML), Zero/Count Parts, in Compact and Sprawled/Modernist morphological regions. Background colors identify groups of urban form descriptors: yellow- street-network configuration, light-green - skeletal streetscape, green - urban fabrics, blue - directional descriptors.

ALL (63)		Modeling approach				Compact		Sprawled/Modernist	
		Regression (27)		Machine Learning (36)		Zero Parts (18)		Zero Parts (18)	
Street Length	75%	Street Acclivity	85%	Street Length	72%	Build. Coverage Ratio	100%	Street Corridor Effect	88%
Street Corridor Effect	70%	Street Corridor Effect	81%	Street Corridor Effect	61%	Street Length	100%	Street Length	88%
Build. Coverage Ratio	67%	Build. Coverage Ratio	78%	Build. Coverage Ratio	58%	Betweenness 1200m	75%	Betweenness 1200m	75%
Street Acclivity	63%	Street Length	78%	Slope	56%	Betweenness 5min	75%	Betweenness	63%
Betweenness 1200m	60%	Betweenness 1200m	74%	Cul de sac	53%	Street Corridor Effect	75%	Street Acclivity	38%
Betweenness 5min	54%	Avg Build. Height	67%	Reach AS 300m	53%	Straightness 5min	75%	Avg Open Space	38%
Built-up Fragmentation	54%	Betweenness 5min	67%	UF9	53%	Straightness 1200m	75%	Betweenn GS	38%
Avg Open Space	48%	Built-up Fragmentation	59%	Betweenness 1200m	50%	Street Acclivity	63%	Betweenness 20min	38%
Avg Build. Height	41%	Avg Open Space	52%	Built-up Fragmentation	50%	Betweenness 20min	63%	First Age City	38%
Betweenness 20min	41%	Small Houses (<125m²)	52%	Build.Specialisation	50%	Built-up Fragmentation	63%	Built-up Fragmentation	38%
Cul de sac	40%	Straightness 5min	52%	Street Acclivity	47%	Avg. HW ratio	50%	Straightness 5min	38%
Straightness 5min	40%	Betw.AS 1200m	48%	Betw. AS 300m	47%	Avg Open Space	50%	Avg Build. Height	25%
Betw. Coast 2400m	37%	Straightness 20 min	48%	Avg Open Space	44%	Reach1200m	50%	Small Build. (250-'000m²)	25%
Build.Specialisation	35%	Betweenness 20 min	44%	Betweenness 5min	44%	Straightness 300m	50%	Build. Coverage Ratio	25%
UF9	34%	Freq Parc	44%	Clos. Coast 1200m	44%	Avg Build. Height	38%	Cul de sac	25%
Reach AS 600m	32%	Sd. Building Set-back	44%	UF1	44%	**Count Parts (18)**		**Count Parts (18)**	
Slope	32%	Straightness 600m	41%	Closeness 1200	42%	Street Corridor Effect	88%	Street Acclivity	50%
UF2	30%	Straigh. AS 1200m	41%	Reach AS 600m	42%	Street Length	88%	Betweeness 300m	50%
Betw.AS 1200m	30%	Betw. Coast 2400m	37%	Betw. Squares 300m	39%	Street Acclivity	75%	Betweenness 5min	50%
Reach AS 300m	30%	Straigh. Coast 600m	37%	Betweenness 20min	39%	Avg Build. Height	63%	Small Build. (250-'000m²)	50%
Straightness 300m	30%	Sd. Build. Height	33%	Betw. Coast 2400m	36%	Betw. Coast 2400m	63%	Street Corridor Effect	50%
Straightness 600m	30%	Straightness 1200m	33%	Closeness AS 300m	36%	Betweenness 20min	63%	Build.Specialisation	50%
Straigh. AS 1200m	30%	Reach 20 min	30%	First Age City	36%	Build. Coverage Ratio	63%	Straightness 20min	50%
		Straightness 300m	30%	Natural Spaces	36%	Cul de sac	63%	Betw. Coast 2400m	38%
		Straigh. AS 600m	30%	Second Age City	36%	Built-up Fragmentation	63%	Betw. Squares 300m	38%
				Straight. AS 300m	36%	Sd. Building Set-back	63%	Ave. Build. ('000-4000m²)	38%
				Straight.Squares 300m	36%	Straightness 600m	63%	Large Build. ('>4000m²)	38%
				Clos.Squares 300m	33%	Avg. Open Space	50%	Build. Coverage Ratio	38%
				Reach Squares 600m	33%	Betw. AS 1200m	50%	First Age City	38%
				Closeness 20min	31%	Betweenness 1200m	50%	Reach AS 600m	38%
				Reach AS 1200m	31%	Betweenness 5min	50%	Second Age City	38%
				Reach Squares 300m	31%	Small Houses (<125m²)	50%	Straight. Coast 600m	38%
				Straightness 5min	31%	Closeness Coast1200m	50%	Straight. Coast 2400m	38%
				Straightness 300m	31%	Reach 20 min	50%	Street Length	38%
				UF2	31%	Reach Squares 1200m	50%	UF1	38%
				UF7	31%	Sd. Open Space	50%	UF6	38%

Legend:
- Street-based indicator group
- Skeletal streetscape
- Typo-morphological context
- Street-Network Configuration
- Proximity towards Coastline, Anchor Stores (AS) and Squares

Set-back and Straightness centrality at 1,200 m also play important roles in the definition of retail distribution.

We finally compared the sets of variables selected by the two modelling approaches implemented in each region. For each couple of models (B vs Boolean GB, NB vs regressive GB, ZINB vs canonical/nested GB), we considered the number of variables found in common and computed a Similarity Index as the harmonic mean of the rate of the shared variables. This indicator describes the degree of resemblance of the selected variables between GLM and ML approaches (thorough Enet and SFS, respectively).

The sets of selected variables tend to show greater Similarity Indexes in larger regions (Global, First/Second Age city with values between 0.31 and 0.49). Conversely, values are lower in smaller partitions (each single UF, with the exception of

Table 3. Outcomes of feature selection procedures. Selection frequencies (highlighted in red) of the most recurrent descriptors of urban form, in relation to micro-retail spatial distribution, in the French Riviera (Global), in the context-based partitions at the district scale (Fist/Second Age City), and at the neighbourhood scale (UF1-6). Background colors identify groups of urban form descriptors: yellow- street-network configuration, light-green - skeletal streetscape, green - urban fabrics, blue - directional descriptors.

	Global	First Age City	Second Age City	UF1	UF2	UF3	UF4	UF5	UF6
Street Length	100%	100%	86%	71%	86%	86%	71%	57%	14%
Street Acclivity	100%	100%	71%	71%	86%	29%	57%	29%	29%
Build. Coverage Ratio	86%	100%	86%	57%	100%	86%	29%	29%	29%
Betweenness 1200m	100%	100%	57%	57%	57%	43%	57%	57%	14%
Street Corridor Effect	86%	71%	86%	57%	86%	71%	71%	29%	71%
Built-up Fragmentation	86%	100%	57%	43%	86%	29%	71%	14%	
Betweenness 5min	71%	71%	43%	29%	71%	71%	71%	57%	
Avg Building Height	86%	71%	57%	43%	43%	43%		14%	14%
Betweenness 20min	71%	57%	43%	14%	86%	71%	29%		
Avg. Open Space	57%	100%	57%	29%	29%	71%	43%	29%	14%
Straight. AS 1200m	86%	29%	43%		57%	29%	14%	14%	
Betw. Coast 2400m	43%	57%	57%	57%	43%	43%	29%		
Straightness 5min	43%	57%	43%	57%	43%	71%	29%	14%	
Straightness 600m	57%	57%	29%	29%	43%	43%		14%	
Straightness 20min	57%	29%	57%		57%	14%	14%	14%	14%
UF2	86%	43%	29%	14%				29%	43%
Cul de sac	29%	43%	57%	29%	57%	43%	43%	43%	14%
Straightness AS 600m	43%	29%	43%	29%	57%		29%	14%	14%
Small Houses (<125m²)	29%	43%	57%	29%	57%	29%		14%	
Reach 20min	43%	29%	29%	43%	57%	14%	14%	29%	
Straightness Coast 600m	43%	29%	57%	29%	43%		14%		
Large Houses (125-250m²)	57%	29%	57%		14%				
Build. Specialisation	29%	29%	71%	29%	29%	57%	43%	14%	14%
Sd. Building Set-back	14%	71%	14%	29%	57%	14%	29%		
Closeness 1200m	43%	43%		14%	43%	29%	43%		
Straight. Coast 1200m	57%	43%	29%	29%					
Betweenn AS 1200m	29%	43%	57%	29%	14%	29%	29%		43%
Straightness 1200m	14%	71%	71%	43%		43%	14%		
Straightness 300m	14%	29%	43%	100%	57%		29%		
Reach 600m	43%		29%	43%	57%	14%			14%

UF2, for which values are still between 0.30 and 0.36). Higher similarity can also be observed for the absence/presence models between Binomial regression and Boolean GB approaches. In general, the harder the task (count vs absence/presence) and the smaller the spatial domain, the more specific the models produced by the different approaches.

5   Conclusion and Discussion

In this work, we proposed a comparative study between GLM and ML approaches to explain the relationship between descriptors of urban form and number of stores, along street segments. Following previous works by Araldi [8, 17], retail distribution was modelled in two ways: firstly, by applying separate models on the presence/absence and quantity of retail and, secondly, by using specific solutions able to model the two processes conjointly. To assess the two modelling procedures, implemented in these two different manners, we applied them on the same dataset, describing 105 different street-based aspects of the urban form of the French Riviera, a large coastal conurbation located in the south of France. The two modelling approaches were tested on the whole study area, but also on smaller morphological sub-regions, with different conditions of zero-inflation and overdispersion.

For what concerns model performances, similar outcomes between GLM and GB approaches were observed when modelling presence/absence; the latter proved more successful when describing the number of stores. When modelling the combined effect of the presence/absence and count processes, the canonical GB model showed lower performance compared to the ZINB model. On the contrary, the nested GB proposed in this paper proved to be a better modelling solution for dealing with the zero-inflation of retail distribution. Just like ZINB, the nested GB approach does not inject any expert knowledge in data partitioning and is not prone to survivorship biases. Nonetheless, when modelling highly skewed distribution in specific urban fabrics (UF2-4), the nested GB did not outperform ZINB.

For what concerns the outcomes of the feature selection, similarities among sets of variables were stronger in larger and central (sub)regions, while they were weaker in smaller and peripheral urban fabrics. The most recurrent variables tended to be street properties (Length and Acclivity), streetscape descriptors (Building Coverage Ratio), and aspects related to the layout of buildings (i.e. Corridor Effect, Built-up Fragmentation, Building Height and Open Space). A key role was also found to be played by local Betweenness centrality, while other configurational indices were found to be important only in specific urban contexts.

The work proposed in this paper lies the basis for more advanced comparative studies that would provide better descriptions – linear and non-linear – of the relationship between features of urban form and retail distribution. We argue that this could be very helpful to confirm or reformulate previous theories, but also to propose new ones.

In this work, we only evaluated the frequencies of the variables selected in the different models. Future work will focus on interpreting the behaviours and relative magnitudes of such variables in light of further aspects of urban morphology and concurrent urban phenomena acting on the study area.

For what concerns the approaches presented in this paper, future work might develop improvements to classic GB algorithms that would allow a better modelling of zero-inflated/skewed distributions, for example through the combination of weak (i.e. decision trees) and strong estimators (i.e. models for count data) as proposed by [34] or with multi-output modelling approaches [35]. Advanced cross-validation techniques specifically conceived for highly spatially correlated data [36] might be also considered.

Intelligibility of model results is also an issue [37]. Statistical models are easier to interpret: the signs of coefficients indicate whether regressors contribute positively or negatively to the target variable. The same cannot be said for ML approaches, and more sophisticated techniques are needed to help the understanding of model results [19]. Finally, future research might focus on the implementation of the same procedures to analyse the relationship between urban form and other urban phenomena, such as the number of traffic accidents, tweets, etc.

References

1. Chiaradia, A., Hillier, B., Schwander, C., Wedderburn, M.: Spatial centrality, economic vitality/viability. In: Proceedings of 7th International SSx, KTH Royal Institute of Technology, Stockholm, Sweden, pp. 16.1–16.19 (2009)
2. Saraiva, M.: The morphological sense of commerce: symbioses between commercial activity and the form and structure of portuguese medium-sized cities. Ph.D., Univ. of Porto, Porto (2013)
3. Saraiva, M., Marques, S.T., Pinho, P.: Vacant shops in a crisis period – a morphological analysis in portuguese medium-sized cities. Plann. Pract. Res. 34(3), 255–287 (2019)
4. Hillier, B.: Space is the Machine. Cambridge University Press, Cambridge (1996)
5. Hillier, B., Iida, S.: Network and psychological effects in urban movement. In: Cohn, A.G., Mark, D.M. (eds.) COSIT 2005. LNCS, vol. 3693, pp. 475–490. Springer, Heidelberg (2005). https://doi.org/10.1007/11556114_30
6. Porta, S., et al.: Street centrality and densities of retail and services in Bologna, Italy. Environ. Plann. B: Plann. Des. 36(3), 450–465 (2009)
7. Remali, A.M., Porta, S., Romice, O.: Correlating street quality, street life and street centrality in Tripoli, Libya. The past, present and future of high streets, pp. 104–129 (2014)
8. Araldi, A.: Retail distribution and urban form: street-based models for the French Riviera. Doctoral dissertation, Université Côte d'Azur, Nice (2019)
9. Ye, Y., Li, D., Liu, X.: How block density and typology affect urban vitality: an exploratory analysis in Shenzhen. China. Urban Geogr. 39(4), 631–652 (2018)
10. Joosten, V., Van Nes, A.: How block types influence the natural movement economic process: micro-spatial conditions on the dispersal of shops and Café in Berlin. In: 5th International SSx, Delft, The Netherlands (13) (2005)
11. Bobkova, E., Marcus, L., Berghauser Pont, M., Stavroulaki, I., Bolin, D.: Structure of plot systems and economic activity in cities: linking plot types to retail and food services in London, Amsterdam and Stockholm. Urban Sci. 3(3), 66 (2019)
12. Saraiva, M., Pinho, P.: Spatial modelling of commercial spaces in medium-sized cities. GeoJournal 82(3), 433–454 (2015). https://doi.org/10.1007/s10708-015-9694-7
13. Omer, I., Goldblatt, R.: Spatial patterns of retail activity and street network structure in new and traditional Israeli cities. Urban Geogr. 37(4), 629–649 (2016)
14. Sevtsuk, A.: Path and place: a study of urban geometry and retail activity in Cambridge and Somerville. Doctoral dissertation, Massachusetts Institute of Technology (2010)
15. Cutini, V.: Centrality and land use: three case studies on the configurational hypothesis. Cybergeo: Eur. J. Geogr. (2001). document 188. Accessed 31 December 2019. http://journals.openedition.org/cybergeo/3936. https://doi.org/10.4000/cybergeo.3936
16. Greene, W.H.: Accounting for excess zeros and sample selection in Poisson and negative binomial regression models (1994). https://archive.nyu.edu/bitstream/2451/26263/2/94-10.pdf
17. Araldi, A.: Towards an integrated methodology for model and variable selection using count data. Application to micro-retail distribution. Urban Sci. 4(2), 21 (2020)
18. Friedman, J.H.: Greedy function approximation: a gradient boosting machine. Ann. Stat. 29, 1189–1232 (2001)
19. Venerandi, A., Fusco, G., Tettamanzi, A., Emsellem, D.: A machine learning approach to study the relationship between features of the urban environment and street value. Urban Sci. 3(3), 100 (2019)
20. He, H., Garcia, E.A.: Learning from imbalanced data. IEEE Trans. Knowl. Data Eng. 21(9), 1263–1284 (2009)

21. Japkowicz, N., Stephen, S.: The class imbalance problem: a systematic study. Intell. Data Anal. **6**(5), 429–449 (2002)
22. Krawczyk, B.: Learning from imbalanced data: open challenges and future directions. Prog. Artif. Intell. **5**(4), 221–232 (2016). https://doi.org/10.1007/s13748-016-0094-0
23. Tibshirani, R.: Regression shrinkage and selection via the lasso. J. Roy. Stat. Soc.: Ser. B (Methodol.) **58**(1), 267–288 (1996)
24. Raschka, S.: MLxtend: providing machine learning and data science utilities and extensions to Python's scientific computing stack. J. Open Source Softw. **3**(24), 638 (2018)
25. Fleury, A.: La rue: un objet géographique? Tracés. Revue de Sci. Hum. (5), 33–44 (2004)
26. Kropf, K.: Bridging configurational and urban tissue analysis. In: Proceedings of 11th Space Syntax Symposium, Lisbon, pp. 165.1–165.13 (2017)
27. Sevtsuk, A., Mekonnen, M.: Urban network analysis. Revue Int. de Géom. **287**, 305 (2012)
28. Brown, S.: Retail location at the micro-scale. Serv. Ind. J. **14**(4), 542–576 (1994)
29. Harvey, C., Aultman-Hall, L., Troy, A., Hurley, S.E.: Streetscape skeleton measurement and classification. Environ. Plann. B: Urban Anal. City Sci. **44**(4), 668–692 (2017)
30. Araldi, A., Fusco, G.: From the built environment along the street to the metropolitan region. Human scale approach in urban fabric analysis. Environ. Plann. B: Urban Anal. City Sci. **46**(7), 1243–1263 (2019)
31. Fusco, G., Araldi, A.: The nine forms of the French riviera: classifying urban fabrics from the pedestrian perspective. In: 24th ISUF International Conference. Book of Papers, pp. 1313–1325. Editorial Universitat Politècnica de València (2017)
32. Zou, H., Hastie, T.: Regularization and variable selection via the elastic net. J. Roy. Stat. Soc.: Ser. B (Stat. Methodol.) **67**(2), 301–320 (2005)
33. Van Rijsbergen, C.J.: Information retrieval (1979)
34. Garcia-Marti, I., Zurita-Milla, R., Swart, A.: Modelling tick bite risk by combining random forests and count data regression models. PLoS ONE **14**(12), e0216511 (2019)
35. Roberts, D.R., Bahn, V., Ciuti, S., et al.: Cross-validation strategies for data with temporal, spatial, hierarchical, or phylogenetic structure. Ecography **40**(8), 913–929 (2017)
36. Borchani, H., Varando, G., Bielza, C., Larrañaga, P.: A survey on multi-output regression. Wiley Interdisc. Rev.: Data Mining Knowl. Discov. **5**(5), 216–233 (2015)
37. Hofman, J.M., Sharma, A., Watts, D.J.: Prediction and explanation in social systems. Science **355**, 486–488 (2017)

Modeling the Determinants of Urban Fragmentation and Compaction Phenomena in the Province of Matera (Basilicata Region - Italy)

Giorgia Dotoli, Lucia Saganeiti$^{(\boxtimes)}$, Angela Pilogallo, Francesco Scorza, and Beniamino Murgante

School of Engineering, University of Basilicata, 85100 Potenza, Italy
lucia.saganeiti@unibas.it

Abstract. The main objective of the present study was to integrate a logistic regression (LR) model and a geographic information system (GIS) technique to analyze the urban transformations patterns and investigate the relationship between urban transformation dynamics and its various determinant forces.

The case study concerns the territory of the province of Matera, in the region of Basilicata (southern Italy) where the main transformation phenomenon corresponds to the dynamics of urban sprinkling. The definition of the variables, corresponding to the dynamics of urban fragmentation and compaction, will be carried out through spatial analyses concerning the temporal variation of the sprinkling index.

The relationships between the dependent variables (Y) fragmentation and compaction and the independent variables (X) referring to different factors will be analyzed through two logistic regressions. The time interval considered is 1998-2013 and the determining factors (driving forces) refer to physical characteristics, proximity analysis to roads or cities, socioeconomic factors and land use policies. The results consist of two maps showing the probability of variation of the dependent variables whose accuracy will be evaluated using the Relative Operational Characteristic Index (ROC).

Keywords: Urban sprinkling · Logistic regression · Fragmentation

1 Introduction

This article shows the preliminary results for the construction of an urban transformation prediction model. The target of zero net land consumption by 2050 (EU Environment Action Programme to 2020 (7th EAP) [1–3] of the European Community are fundamental for fragile and critical territories, among them is undoubtedly the Italian territory [4–7]. The definition and implementation of such policies, rules and actions aimed at reducing soil consumption are urgent. To the phenomenon of land take are strongly linked the dynamics of urban transformation of fragmentation and compaction. In this study we will analyze the main factors that drive these dynamics.

© Springer Nature Switzerland AG 2020
O. Gervasi et al. (Eds.): ICCSA 2020, LNCS 12252, pp. 566–574, 2020.
https://doi.org/10.1007/978-3-030-58811-3_41

Over the last 50 years, land occupation in Europe has become more important, leading to the formation of low-density, fragmented settlements. Urban expansions have therefore moved away from the more traditional and recognized dynamics of urban expansion, acquiring different forms and very low settlement rates [8–10]. Characteristic of the internal areas of the Mediterranean is the urban sprinkling phenomenon [11].

The urban sprinkling phenomenon is a transformation dynamic different from that of urban sprawl [12] and characterized by a sporadic, pulverized and dispersed diffusion of urban settlements on the territory. It has very low-density indexes compared to those of urban sprawl, with consequent urban and landscape fragmentation [13]. The phenomenon of urban sprinkling is measured by SPrinkling IndeX (SPX) which is a geometric indicator that, through the subdivision of the study area into homogeneous territorial units, measures the dispersion of urban settlements on the basis of Euclidean distance.

The case study analyzed in this paper includes the territory of the province of Matera, in the region of Basilicata (southern Italy) where, as shown by previous studies [14–16], urban transformations from the 1950s to the present day have occurred on the basis of the urban sprinkling target. Therefore, on the basis of the sprinkling index, the processes of fragmentation and compaction on the territory of the province of Matera have been analyzed. The objective of this article is to model the factors that determine the dynamics of transformation (fragmentation and compaction) with a logistic regression in the period between 1998 and 2013. Among the determining factors (driving forces) considered are physical factors, socio-economic factors, factors of proximity to road infrastructure and main urban centers, factors concerning urban legislation on the transformability of territories. Logistic regression will be carried out once the phenomenon of compaction and the phenomenon of fragmentation have been considered. The results of logistic regression are maps of probability of change of the variable dependent on Y from the initial state "untransformed" to the subsequent state "fragmented" or "compacted".

2 Study Area

The case study concerns the territory of the province of Matera, located in the eastern part of the Basilicata region in southern Italy (Fig. 1). It borders to the west with Calabria, in particular with the province of Cosenza, to the south it is washed by the Ionian Sea, and to the east it borders with Puglia, and in particular with the province of Taranto and Bari. It has a variable orography where plains and hills alternate and slope down towards the sea.

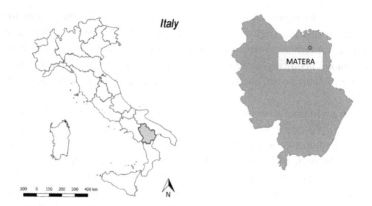

Fig. 1. Geographical context: on the left the location of the Basilicata region in Italy, while on the right the territory of the province of Matera.

The provincial territory includes three regional nature reserves, the Natural Park of Gallipoli Cognato, the Archaeological and Historical Natural Park of the Rupestrian Churches of Matera, also known as the Murgia Materana Park, and finally a small portion of the Pollino National Park. Basilicata includes a total of 131 municipalities, 31 of which reside in the province of Matera. The largest city is Matera, also capital of the province, with 60351 inhabitants [17]. Three municipalities have a population between 10000 and 50000 inhabitants: Bernalda, Pisticci and Policoro. The remaining part has a population of less than 10000 inhabitants.

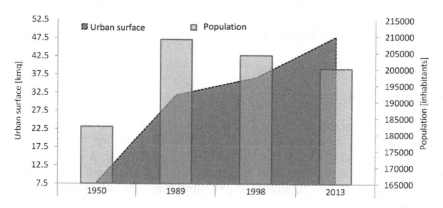

Fig. 2. Comparison from demographic trends and urban surface (in square kilometers) from 1950 to 2013 in the Province of Matera.

The graph in Fig. 2 shows the dynamics of urban expansion and population growth from the 50s to 2013 in order to highlight the general growth trend of the territory. From 1950 to 1989 the demographic trend is positive, in the following years a decrease in population starts instead. The urban expansion, after a strong increase between 1950 and 1989, continues to grow until 2013 in contrast with the demographic trend. This decoupled growth trend is characteristic of the all regional territory [16].

3   Materials and Methods

The aim of this study is to model the determinants of urban transformation dynamics (fragmentation and compaction) with two logistic regressions in the time interval 1998-2013 considering 10 driving forces as independent variables (X). The dependent variables (Y) will be derived from the sprinkling index (analyzed in previous studies at regional level [14, 16]), as reported in the Table 1, and will be in a first case fragmentation and in a second case compaction.

Table 1. Urban transformation dynamics.

SPX	Urban transformation dynamics
$\Delta SPX_{(2013-1998)} > 0$	Urban fragmentation
$\Delta SPX_{(2013-1998)} < 0$	Urban compaction
$\Delta SPX_{(2013-1998)} = 0$	No transformation

The index was calculated on a 200×200 m grid for the years 1998 and 2013. For each transformation dynamics, 2 binary rasters were created in which the value 0 corresponds to no transformation and the value 1 to fragmentation or compaction.

According to the existing scientific literature [18–20] and the characteristics of the territory, 10 independent (predictive) variables have been identified (X).

Variable X_1: elevation, in raster format and with pixels at a resolution of 5×5 m; variable X_2 slope in percentage obtained from the elevation; X_3 proximity to secondary roads; X_4 proximity to local roads; X_5 proximity to railway stations; X_6 proximity to large cities, i.e. those with a population of more than 50000 inhabitants (city of Matera); X_7 proximity to medium-sized cities, i.e. those with a population between 10000 and 50000 inhabitants (municipalities of Montescaglioso, Bernalda, Policoro and Pisticci); X_8 population density in 2001 at municipal level; X_9 employment rate (source: Urbistat [21]); X_{10} raster of transformability containing all the constraints of inedificability present in the territory. All variables have been rasterized with 200×200 pixel resolution and standardized, with the exception of variable X_{10} which is categorical (0–1).

Logistic regression can be considered as a special case of linear regression when the result variable is categorical, so it predicts the probability of an event occurring by adapting the data to a logit function [22]. Logistic regression is usually used in the estimation of a model that describes the relationship between one or more continuous independent variables and binary dependent variables. The dependent variable can only assume two values: 0 and 1. The basic assumption is that the probability of the dependent variable assumes the value 1 (positive response) following the logistic curve.

Pseudo R_square estimates the goodness of the logistic regression model setting. *Pseudo R_square* equal to 1 indicates a perfect fit, *Pseudo R_square* equal to 0 indicates no relationship. According to [23], the *Pseudo R_square* greater than 0.2 is considered a relatively good fit. The multi-collinearity test between the independent variables will be done with the Variance Inflation Factor (VIF). VIF values below 5 show the absence of multi-collinearity, while VIF values above 5 indicate the presence of multi-collinearity between the independent variables [24, 25]. The overall adaptive fit of the model is evaluated using the Relative Operative Characteristic Index (ROC) which must be greater than 0.5 [26].

4 Results and Conclusions

Below are the results of the logistic regression carried out first for the fragmentation of the dependent variable and then for the compaction for the period 1998-2013. The multicollinearity test has a VIF less than 5 so all variables were considered in the logistic regressions. Figure 3 shows the regression coefficients of the two transformation dynamics.

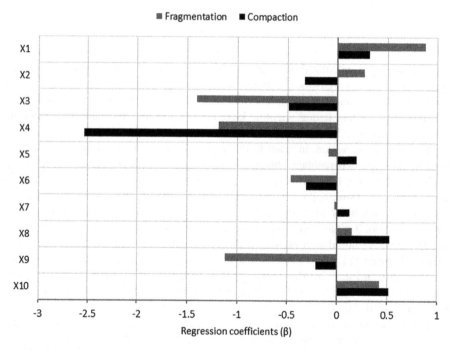

Fig. 3. Comparison of the regression coefficients of the two transformation dynamics.

The dependent variable X_1 has a positive coefficient for both transformation dynamics and is more influential for the fragmentation phenomenon. The positive correlation indicates that the probability that the cell becomes 1 (compaction/fragmentation) increases with increasing elevation. Variable X_2 has negative correlation for compaction dynamics and positive correlation for fragmentation dynamics. The processes of urban transformation concerning fragmentation occur, therefore, at greater slopes than those of compaction. The variables X_3 and X_4 have a negative correlation index with both transformation phenomena and are the most significant factors for both processes. The correlation coefficients are the highest and show that the transformations in this territory are strongly influenced by the proximity of roads. The probability that a cell changes its state from untransformed to fragmented or compacted increases as the distance from secondary and local roads decreases. The probability for a cell to change its state from untransformed to fragmented increases near train stations (variable X_5) while the probability for a cell to change its state from untransformed to compacted increases as the distance from train stations increases. Transformation processes take place more in the vicinity of large cities (variable X_6) and away from medium-sized municipalities (variable X_7). Transformations are positively correlated with population density (variable X_8). The variable X_9 shows a negative correlation: the probability that a cell undergoes a transformation increases as the employment rate decreases. Finally, for the last variable X_{10} the correlation is positive, the transformations increase near the transformable territories and the greatest correlation is for the compaction process.

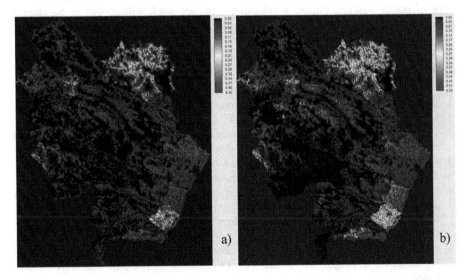

Fig. 4. Predicted dependent variables: a) Compaction, b) Fragmentation.

The *Pseudo R_square* for the fragmentation process was 0.26 and for the compaction process 0.23; these coefficients, according to [23], show a good adaptation of the regression model.

The maps in Fig. 4 show the final result of the logistic regression: the change probability maps for both dependent variables: fragmentation and compaction. The maximum probability of change is 54% for fragmentation and 42% for compaction.

This shows that the territory will be more subject to transformation dynamics with regard to fragmentation. The ROC indices of 0.87 and 0.84 for compaction and fragmentation, respectively, demonstrate the goodness of the model.

This article shows the preliminary results for the construction of an urban transformation prediction model. The results show that the probability of transformation of the territory is more related to processes of urban fragmentation. In the case study analyzed but, more generally, in the whole Basilicata's regional territory, urban fragmentation is the main dynamics of transformation and, in recent years it has also been caused by other components of the settlement system such as renewable energy plants [15, 27] and oil wells [16]. It is crucial to analyze and model urban transformation dynamics as they have a significant impact on the quality of the landscape, the supply of ecosystem services [28–30] and the costs to the population of transforming the city in an unsustainable way [31, 32]. For these and other reasons, analyzing the dynamics of urban transformation is of fundamental importance since they can have a significant impact and cause significant damage to cultural heritage and, because of the dynamics that develop as a result of uncontrolled land transformation (landslide movements) can be a risk to human life [33–35].

The analysis of all these factors is of fundamental importance to understand what are the driving forces of the transformation-transformation dynamics of the territory and also to obtain information on future transformations to be used as a support to the work of policy makers. Future developments of this work will consist in building a model for predicting the dynamics of urban transformation in the future.

References

1. Brown, L.A.: The city in 2050: a kaleidoscopic perspective. Appl. Geogr. **49**, 4–11 (2014). https://doi.org/10.1016/j.apgeog.2013.09.003
2. United Nations Department of Economic and Social Affairs/Population Division: World Urbanization Prospects The 2018 Revision (2018)
3. Cobbinah, P.B., Aboagye, H.N.: A Ghanaian twist to urban sprawl. Land Use Policy **61**, 231–241 (2017). https://doi.org/10.1016/j.landusepol.2016.10.047
4. Las Casas, G., Scorza, F., Murgante, B.: New urban agenda and open challenges for urban and regional planning. In: Calabrò, F., Della Spina, L., Bevilacqua, C. (eds.) ISHT 2018. SIST, vol. 100, pp. 282–288. Springer, Cham (2019). https://doi.org/10.1007/978-3-319-92099-3_33
5. Las Casas, G., Scorza, F., Murgante, B.: Razionalità a-priori: una proposta verso una pianificazione antifragile. Ital. J. Reg. Sci. **18**, 329–338 (2019). https://doi.org/10.14650/93656
6. Scorza, F., Grecu, V.: Assessing sustainability: research directions and relevant issues. In: Gervasi, O., et al. (eds.) ICCSA 2016. LNCS, vol. 9786, pp. 642–647. Springer, Cham (2016). https://doi.org/10.1007/978-3-319-42085-1_55
7. Murgante, B., Borruso, G., Balletto, G., Castiglia, P.D.: Why Italy First? Health, Geographical and Planning aspects of the Covid-19 outbreak. Preprints (2020). https://doi.org/10.20944/preprints202005.0075.v1

8. Nolè, G., Lasaponara, R., Lanorte, A., Murgante, B.: Quantifying urban sprawl with spatial autocorrelation techniques using multi-temporal satellite data. Int. J. Agric. Environ. Inf. Syst. **5**, 19–37 (2014). https://doi.org/10.4018/IJAEIS.2014040102

9. Las Casas, G., Murgante, B., Scorza, F.: Regional local development strategies benefiting from open data and open tools and an outlook on the renewable energy sources contribution. In: Papa, R., Fistola, R. (eds.) Smart Energy in the Smart City. GET, pp. 275–290. Springer, Cham (2016). https://doi.org/10.1007/978-3-319-31157-9_14

10. Murgante, B., Las Casas, G., Sansone, A.: A spatial rough set for locating the periurban fringe (2007)

11. Romano, B., Zullo, F., Fiorini, L., Marucci, A., Ciabò, S.: Land transformation of Italy due to half a century of urbanization. Land Use Policy **67**, 387–400 (2017). https://doi.org/10.1016/j.landusepol.2017.06.006

12. Nechyba, T.J., Walsh, R.P.: Urban sprawl. J. Econ. Perspect. **18**, 177–200 (2004). https://doi.org/10.1257/0895330042632681

13. Saganeiti, L., Pilogallo, A., Scorza, F., Mussuto, G., Murgante, B.: Spatial indicators to evaluate urban fragmentation in Basilicata region. In: Gervasi, O., et al. (eds.) ICCSA 2018. LNCS, vol. 10964, pp. 100–112. Springer, Cham (2018). https://doi.org/10.1007/978-3-319-95174-4_8

14. Saganeiti, L., et al.: Assessing urban fragmentation at regional scale using sprinkling indexes. Sustainability **10**, 3274 (2018). https://doi.org/10.3390/su10093274

15. Saganeiti, L., Pilogallo, A., Faruolo, G., Scorza, F., Murgante, B.: Territorial fragmentation and renewable energy source plants: which relationship? Sustainability **12**, 1828 (2020). https://doi.org/10.3390/SU12051828

16. Scorza, F., Saganeiti, L., Pilogallo, A., Murgante, B.: Ghost Planning: the inefficiency of energy sector policies in a low population density region. Arch. DI Stud. URBANI E Reg. (2020, in press)

17. Istat.it. https://www.istat.it/. Accessed 05 Apr 2019

18. Traore, A., Watanabe, T.: Modeling determinants of urban growth in Conakry, Guinea: a spatial logistic approach. Urban Sci. **1**, 12 (2017). https://doi.org/10.3390/urbansci1020012

19. Salem, M., Tsurusaki, N., Divigalpitiya, P.: Analyzing the driving factors causing urban expansion in the peri-urban areas using logistic regression: a case study of the Greater Cairo region. Infrastructures **4**, 4 (2019). https://doi.org/10.3390/infrastructures4010004

20. Martellozzo, F., Amato, F., Murgante, B., Clarke, K.C.: Modelling the impact of urban growth on agriculture and natural land in Italy to 2030. Appl. Geogr. **91**, 156–167 (2018). https://doi.org/10.1016/J.APGEOG.2017.12.004

21. Statistiche economicheProvincia di MATERA. https://ugeo.urbistat.com/AdminStat/it/it/economia/dati-sintesi/matera/77/3. Accessed 07 July 2020

22. Aldrich, J., Nelson, F.: Linear Probability, Logit, and Probit Models. SAGE Publications, Inc. (2011). https://doi.org/10.4135/9781412984744

23. Clark, W.A., Hosking, P.L.: Statistical Methods for Geographers (Chapter 13). Consortium Erudit, New York (1986). https://doi.org/10.7202/021850ar

24. Kock, N., Lynn, G.S.: Lateral collinearity and misleading results in variance-based SEM: an illustration and recommendations. J. Assoc. Inf. Syst. **13**, 546–580 (2012). https://doi.org/10.17705/1jais.00302

25. Belsley, D.A.: A guide to using the collinearity diagnostics. Comput. Sci. Econ. Manag. **4**, 33–50 (1991). https://doi.org/10.1007/BF00426854

26. Walsh, S.J.: Goodness-of-fit issues in ROC curve estimation. Med. Decis. Mak. **19**, 193–201 (1999). https://doi.org/10.1177/0272989X9901900210

27. Saganeiti, L., Pilogallo, A., Faruolo, G., Scorza, F., Murgante, B.: Energy landscape fragmentation: Basilicata region (Italy) study case. In: Misra, S., et al. (eds.) ICCSA 2019. LNCS, vol. 11621, pp. 692–700. Springer, Cham (2019). https://doi.org/10.1007/978-3-030-24302-9_50

28. Pilogallo, A., Saganeiti, L., Scorza, F., Murgante, B.: Ecosystem services' based impact assessment for low carbon transition processes. TeMA J. L. Use Mobil. Environ. **12**, 127–138 (2019). https://doi.org/10.6092/1970-9870/6117

29. Scorza, F., Pilogallo, A., Saganeiti, L., Murgante, B., Pontrandolfi, P.: Comparing the territorial performances of Renewable Energy Sources' plants with an integrated Ecosystem Services loss assessment: a case study from the Basilicata region (Italy). Sustain. Cities Soc. **56**, 102082 (2020). https://doi.org/10.1016/J.SCS.2020.102082

30. Scorza, F., Pilogallo, A., Saganeiti, L., Murgante, B.: Natura 2000 areas and sites of national interest (SNI): measuring (un)integration between naturalness preservation and environmental remediation policies. Sustainability **12**, 2928 (2020). https://doi.org/10.3390/su12072928

31. Manganelli, B., Murgante, B., Saganeiti, L.: The social cost of urban sprinkling. Sustainability **12**, 2236 (2020). https://doi.org/10.3390/SU12062236

32. Dvarioniene, J., Grecu, V., Lai, S., Scorza, F.: Four perspectives of applied sustainability: research implications and possible integrations. In: Gervasi, O., et al. (eds.) ICCSA 2017. LNCS, vol. 10409, pp. 554–563. Springer, Cham (2017). https://doi.org/10.1007/978-3-319-62407-5_39

33. Lasaponara, R., et al.: Spatial open data for monitoring risks and preserving archaeological areas and landscape: case studies at Kom el Shoqafa, Egypt and Shush, Iran. Sustainability **9**, 572 (2017). https://doi.org/10.3390/su9040572

34. Pascale, S., et al.: Landslide susceptibility mapping using artificial neural network in the urban area of Senise and San Costantino Albanese (Basilicata, Southern Italy). In: Murgante, B., et al. (eds.) ICCSA 2013. LNCS, vol. 7974, pp. 473–488. Springer, Heidelberg (2013). https://doi.org/10.1007/978-3-642-39649-6_34

35. Elfadaly, A., Attia, W., Qelichi, M.M., Murgante, B., Lasaponara, R.: Management of cultural heritage sites using remote sensing indices and spatial analysis techniques. Surv. Geophys. **39**(6), 1347–1377 (2018). https://doi.org/10.1007/s10712-018-9489-8

Geoprofiling in the Context of Civil Security: KDE Process Optimisation for Hotspot Analysis of Massive Emergency Location Data

Julia Gonschorek[(✉)] [iD]

German Aerospace Center, Rutherfordstr. 2, 12489 Berlin, Germany
julia.gonschorek@dlr.de

Abstract. In the performance of their duties, authorities and organisations with safety and security tasks face major challenges. As a result, the need to expand the knowledge and skills of security forces in a targeted manner through knowledge, systemic and technological solutions is increasing. Of particular importance for this inhomogeneous end user group is the time factor and thus in general also space, distance, and velocity. Authorities focus on people, goods, and infrastructure in the field of prevention, protection, and rescue. For purposive tactical, strategic, and operational planning, geodata and information about past and ongoing operations dispatched and archived at control centers can be used. For that reason, a rule-based process for the geovisual evaluation of massive spatio-temporal data is developed using geoinformation methods, techniques, and technologies by the example of operational emergency data of fire brigade and rescue services. This contribution to the extension of the KDE for hotspot analysis has the goal to put the professional and managerial personnel in a position to create well-founded geoprofiles based on the spatial-temporal location, distribution, and typology of emergency mission hotspots. In doing so, significant data is generated for the neighborhood of the operations in abstract spatial segments, and is used to calculate distance measures for the Kernel Density Estimation (KDE) process. At the end there is a completely derived rule-based kde process for the geovisual analysis of massive spatio-temporal mass data for hotspot geoprofiling.

Keywords: Civil security · KDE · Geoprofiling · Hotspots · Geovisual analytics

1 Hotspot Analysis of Spatio-Temporal Mass Data

1.1 About Geoprofiling

In principle, the tasks and competences of the fire brigade and rescue service in the Federal Republic of Germany are regulated at state level. The range of tasks extends from fighting fires, providing assistance in the event of accidents and public emergencies caused by natural events, explosions, and similar occurrences, through to involvement in the rescue service. In addition, fire protection requirement plans and plans for the deployment of the fire brigade must be drawn up and updated annually.

© Springer Nature Switzerland AG 2020
O. Gervasi et al. (Eds.): ICCSA 2020, LNCS 12252, pp. 575–589, 2020.
https://doi.org/10.1007/978-3-030-58811-3_42

This includes emergency response plans for major emergencies and special protection plans for particularly endangered objects.

Geoprofiling, also known as geographic profiling or geographic profiling analysis, should be understood as a bundle of methods. "[The] geographic locations of an offender's crimes [...] are used to identify and prioritize areas where the offender is likely to live." [1] Geoprofiling in the context of civil security was first adopted by Rossmo in the 1990s as a theme in perpetrator identification. The main function of this investigative methodology is "to prioritise suspects and assist in investigative information management." [2] The differences between the requirements of geoprofiling for police applications and for the fire brigade and rescue services are based on the respective area of responsibility and competence. Emergency location and time are known very precisely; it is not a matter of identifying offenders or reconstructing the course of events or estimating possible further victims in the case of serial offenders. Also in the field of responsibility of the fire brigade and the rescue service there are usually no spatio-temporal connections to preceding or subsequent emergencies. An exception includes "fire devils" and vandalism as well as domestic violence. However, the police investigate this. Fire and rescue services provide care for injured persons in such situations and secure the infrastructure in the event of fire or possibly leaking hazardous substances. Geovisual analysis with geoprofiles in the non-police control centres are used to plan requirements and deployment of forces. A typical question aims at the change of hotspots, e.g. regarding their spatio-temporal stability.

Figure 1 shows emergency event's spatial association and aggregation mapped in field cartograms for geoprofiling (a model space) with temporal variances and classified into different density intensity levels.

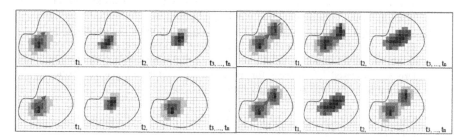

Fig. 1. Extracts of the exemplary hotspot typology taking into account possible behaviour characteristics over time (t1, t2, ..., tn) [3].

Detailed predictive information based on spatio-temporal data analyses can help to plan efficiently, demand- and focus-oriented. The visualisation of spatio-temporal peculiarities represents a value in itself, because humans perceive the predominant part of information optically. In addition, the visualisation can lead to the sensitisation of practitioners in control centres for certain, if necessary, recurring and associated plannable deployment strategies. The mass data analysed for this purpose are past emergencies, i.e. operations involving the fire and rescue services. The mission data are available in their entirety. The aim is to identify significantly spatial, temporal or spatio-temporal aggregations of emergencies visually, and neither to calculate possible nor statistically probable event locations in space (e.g. by using methods of the Kriging family) [4].

Aggregations need to be defined and a distinction must be made here between hotpoints and hotspots.

Hotpoints mark punctual locations where emergencies occur repeatedly within a defined temporal interval and which show significantly strong event intensities in their neigbourhood [3]. In contrast to hotpoints, hotspots describe areas. This is often formulated imprecisely in the literature. Hotspots can be understood as concentration or clustering of events in space. In criminalistics, these spaces are regarded as high crime areas [5]. It is often assumed that there is a connection between aggregations of events and their spatial association. It is likely that events of this kind will occur again in the space identified as a hotspot. However, not every location in a hotspot becomes a scene of such an event [5]. These definitions have in common that they assume the totality of all events would describe a hotspot. This means that every event, even a statistically random one, is taken into account when determining the hotspot and thus contributes to the hotspot's profile (appearance, form and expression, cf. Fig. 1, 2). These assumptions are factually unfounded and mathematically incorrect.

Here the problem is described and a process is developed, which exclusively feeds the hotspot-characterizing events, namely hotpoints, into the analysis and thus allows more objective, because rule-based, visualizations of spaces of high event densities. Therefore it is defined:

Hotspots mark areas based on the existence of hotpoints. Hotspots consist of a high density of hotpoints. Each hotspot has at least one density center, i.e. an area of highest event density [3].

Depending on predefined time intervals, such as time of day or month, hotspots can be determined and statements can be made about the behavior of hotspots in terms of permanence or periodicity, mobility or movement patterns and aggregation or dissimilation [6, 7]. The results can be used for the purpose of more detailed situation assessments and form a basis for prognostic and geovisual analyses. Long-term hotspots become visible and analyzable for strategical and operational tasks. This makes it possible to identify performance and weaknesses in previous implementation practice and subsequently adaption of identified needs. The aim is to support fire brigades and rescue services in the planning of their means required with data analyses that go beyond descriptive statistics and to make mission-relevant information visible and communicable. In this way, together with the longterm experience of the emergency forces, a set of instruments is created that strengthens the ability to act, and supports adaptation processes to changing hazard situations.

1.2   Mapping Significant Neighbours: From Single Events to Hotspots

Related work presents a large variety of different methods that are often presented one after the other, their respective advantages and disadvantages being pointed out. The connecting elements between the approaches are rarely pointed out. As a result, separate analyses and visualizations are produced, whose individual expressiveness is limited [1, 2, 5, 8–10]. On the other hand, methods are combined in so many ways, for example in the approach of software systemically linked views, that the multiple visual representations of one or more variables are not always easy to interpret and can sometimes lead to the viewer being overwhelmed [12].

A central element of most authors is the neighbourhood of the events to be investigated - usually reduced to their density. The understanding of neighbourhood underlying this work is based on the spatial and temporal proximity of events or hotpoints and hotspots. Tobler's first law of geography describes this connection in general terms: "Everything is related to everything else, but near things are more related than distant things." [13] In this field of application, emergencies that are several kilometres apart cannot be described as spatially close. This is a scale problem in cartographic representation. It should be noted that events that are spatially distant from each other are not adjacent. The spatial distance has to be taken into account and separate events should not be combined into one area. HENGL is convinced: "[Standard] grid resolutions (20–200 m in most cases) with which we work today, will soon shift towards finer and finer, which means that we need to consider grid resolution in time context also." [14] In the real world, 20 m street length, for example in real-estate areas, means one to three single-family or terraced houses, whereas in the city centre it means several business floors and numerous residential units in vertical construction. Therefore, even shorter distances are not recommended if the information is to be generated on a large scale. Furthermore, this is a not insignificant data protection issue: identity-exact data analyses are not permitted in Germany in the non-police use. Furthermore, they are not relevant for the questions and methods presented here. These values were verified in the course of our own unpublished calculations and discussed with the control services of the professional fire brigades of Cologne and Berlin. The resources, i.e. vehicles of the emergency services, report the geo-coordinate of the operation. This is usually not congruent with the actual location of the operation. A 20 to 40 m walk is quite common, in some cases even more. With a minimum mesh size, as proposed by HENGL, misinterpretations of the field cartograms can therefore occur. In order to counteract this problem, it is recommended here to set the minimum edge length of the grid cell at 50 m.

Larger distances or cell sizes, as they are often found in US-American crime analyses, for example, should also be critically evaluated. Due to the method of representation, field cartograms with coarsely meshed grid cells give the impression that events are homogeneously distributed in this large area. In the real world this can include two to three street crossings, shopping arcades and high-rise commercial buildings. The importance of cell sizes and search radii is a considerable one for KDE, which is realized in field cartograms. It should be noted here that the mesh or cell size of 50 m × 50 m to 200 m × 200 m is recommended for this field of application as a sensible distance measure for neighbourhood, i.e. the distance between events.

In addition, spatial distances must be delimited from each other in case of semantic proximity. This is possible in urban areas by abstract segmentation of space and is based on the functional selection of subspaces even before geo and statistical analyses are applied. In the transition from model space to representation space the scale is introduced. Each representation space is scaled, this effect does not exist in the data space. In addition, the treated facts are scaled spatially-semantically. The considered data have semantic information and spatial coordinates. The former can be classified into categories. These categories were taken and analysed with respect to their spatial distribution in order to identify patterns. Territorial units such as street sections, building blocks, statistical and administrative units are deliberately avoided. Spatial units consist of semantic categories. These are based on the function of space. Examples of this are public playgrounds, railways, airports, industrial areas, bridges and residential areas. This cannot be mapped onto territorial units without causing misinterpretations.

The semantic facts are categorized and space is defined from them. This does not correspond to the conventional way of first defining the room reference and then mapping the data to it. The transformation from model to real space is data-driven by focusing on the point position in the surface. The common denominator is formed by field cartograms as a special form of area cartograms. In concrete terms, regular square grids are formed. Thus a common area reference is available, in which different semantic and spatial questions can be processed.

After analysis, the segments formed are reassembled in the final field map. In this way it is possible to reduce the amount of data (segmentation by selection) and to increase the information content in the result (aggregation).

2   Optimisation of the KDE Process for Geoprofiles

2.1   KDE in the Context of Hotspot Analyses

Similar to the determination of hotpoints, various methods of cartography and statistics can be used to calculate and visualize hotspots. The aim of the approach presented here is to extend the spatial reference from single point to area information. Therefor a transformation of the point geometry into a surface geometry is necessary.

Known methods among others are interpolation by isolines, cluster analyses like NNH and K-Means, creation of choropleth maps in which the point information is related to areas as densities. Kriging and Inverse Distance Weighting are able to estimate intensities between known points and output them as area information.

However, if a geoprofile is needed, the methods mentioned are not suitable. When choosing a method, the objective is of central importance. This involves the development of hotspot maps in which the location, distribution, density values and movement patterns of deployment hotspots in urban space become visible. Based on the real distribution of events both in space and time, the basic assumption is valid: fire and rescue operations do not take place everywhere in the entire urban area and are often not homogeneously distributed - neither in space nor in time. Furthermore, the focus is not on estimating the probability of occurrence of events, but rather on the information about neighbourhoods contained in the data in the form of spatio-temporal event densities. One method that has proven to be suitable and has been accepted in criminology over the past 30 years is the KDE. With respect to Nadaraya, a sufficiently large sample and a correspondingly selected bandwidth allow an arbitrary good estimation of the unknown event distribution by kernel density estimation [15]. This is a non-parametric estimation method for density interpolation. A pioneer in this field is PARZEN, who worked continuously on a probability density function since the 1950s

[16, 17]. The prerequisite for the application of the continuous estimator for the density of the distribution of the individual events are random variables independent of each other. It is generally true that the deployments of the fire brigade and the rescue service are not interdependent and that random samples from the deployment database are unrelated.

2.2   KDE Parameter Specification

How KDE works: first of all, in a GIS a uniform grid is laid above the study area. The spatial reference is provided by the georeferenced base map data of the study area (e.g. UTM). The grid has a maximum north-south and west-east extension according to the boundaries of the investigation area. Starting from the cell center x the kernel function K moves from cell to cell and searches for events X_i within the fixed bandwidth d. The events that lie within this window are weighted according to their distance from the cell center. The cell center is therefore the point at which the density is estimated. The following applies: Events that lie closer to the center point receive a greater weight than events that lie further away. Finally, the summed up and averaged density value is transferred to the raster cell. The set screws of the KDE are the parameters kernel function, cell size and bandwidth.

Kernel functions, or kernels, are estimation functions that work like normal weighting functions. There are numerous functions that can be used for this purpose. SILVERMAN has shown in empirical studies that the differences in the estimation results are minor depending on the choice of the core function: "It is quite remarkable that the efficiencies obtained are so close to one [...]." [15] LEVINE confirms this in principle, but shows depth-differentiated effects for geospatial application: "Each method of interpolation will produce slightly different results. Triangular and negative exponential functions tend to produce and emphasize many small hot [...] spots and thus produce a "molted" appearance on [...] [the] map. Quartile, uniform, and normal distribution functions tend to smooth the data more." [10]

The choice of cell size influences the calculation of density values and the visual granularity, i.e. the graphical output of density values into the field cartogram. If one compares different cell sizes with the same data basis, the cartographic results sometimes differ considerably. Smaller cell sizes cause a smooth surface. Larger cell sizes produce a more granular surface in which hotspots can disappear. For comparability between hotspots of different time intervals, uniform cell sizes should always be chosen [7, 15]. The discussion about a fitting cell size was already conducted above. The results are applied here.

The third parameter is the bandwidth (syn.: smoothing parameter, search radius). The bandwidth is fixed during the entire process and must be determined before use. It is generally agreed that the choice of this parameter represents the greatest challenge in KDE. Figure 2 illustrates the effects of different cell size and bandwidth on KDE geoprofiles. Each geoprofile allows different conclusions. A well-founded decision support and planning basis for authorities and organisations with safety and security tasks has to be done differently, because this scope for interpretation is not scientifically acceptable [7].

Hotspots based on the conventional bandwidth selection for KDE are usually created by the mass of data, i.e. by quantity [1, 2, 5, 8, 9, 20, 22–24]. The aggregation of the mass data, its weighting and neighborhood analysis by the GETIS-ORD Gi* [18, 19] statistics for bandwidth selection, which is anchored in the concept presented here, defines a quality. This enables the classification of the geodata into non-significant events as well as weakly significant, significant, high and highly significant hotpoints. This smaller subset of the original sample is fed into the KDE. It follows that each hotspot identified by the KDE is based on at least one weakly significant hotpoint in the center. By applying the Gi* test statistics and calculating the mean distances between the hotpoints, the spatial proximity is taken into account directly at KDE. As a result, the hotspots are more sharply (mutually) distinguishable.

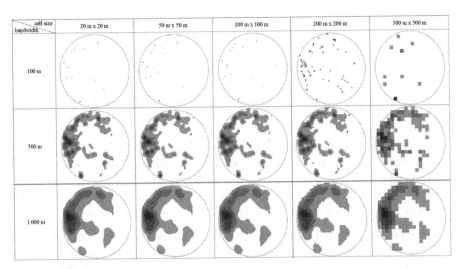

Fig. 2. Influence of the kde-relevant parameters *cell size* and *bandwidth* on hotspot field cartograms and their effects on the interpretability of geoprofiles [3].

2.3 Generating Geoprofiles via KDE

The preceding discussion of methods and parameter problems points out interfaces from which a complete process for the rule-based generation of geoprofiles can be derived, which can be automated to a large extent. A new way to set parameters of the KDE process is defined here. This is done by means of a Gi* test statistic preceding the KDE, taking into account the adapted cell size approach of HENGL, in combination with an extension of the distance approach of Williamson et al. [20, 21] by masking the investigation area into segments. The analysis is described conceptually as follows. Figure 3 shows the whole process modelled in UML.

1. Preparation: The analysis setting is defined:
    a. Data pre-processing: a data set to be analysed is selected from the data set. The selection is based on the operation type or several operation types of one or several time intervals. This new dataset is used for the upcoming analysis.
    b. Spatial pre-processing: The expert in the control centre has a thorough knowledge of study areas. He is able to divide the total space for the analysis into abstract segments, which can be delimited from other/adjacent spaces, e.g. by spatial-structural elements (e.g. streets, fences, water bodies or by functions of spaces), and to generate masks.
2. Hotpoint analysis: For this purpose, a new data set must be generated. Based on 1. a., all operations that are located at the same location are summarized. The number is saved as new attribute weight. This data set is fed into the Gi* test statistics and the hotpoints determined are classified.
3. Distance analysis: the distances between the hotpoints determined in step 2 within their spatial segments (masks) are calculated and the mean value d is calculated.
4. Hotspot analysis: d is now set as bandwidth. The hotpoint data are fed into the KDE procedure and classified.
5. Map products: as a result, at least two visual products are available: a hotpoint map and a hotspot map (geoprofile). This information can be displayed in a map. The interpretation of hotspots combined with the localisation of hotpoints can be important in the analysis and planning of requirements.
6. Furthermore, it is useful to create temporal hotspot series in order to carry out a change analysis. This is realized by choosing several time intervals.

For applications in civil security research, this KDE procedure is thus considerably enhanced in terms of the quality of the process and results. For the first time, it is not individual decisions or aesthetic aspects that determine the visual result, nor are there any rules of thumb or formulas without reference to geo space. When choosing the two parameters cell size and bandwidth, both the position of the data points in relation to each other and the real spatial and temporal anchoring of these events are directly taken into account: characteristics of neighbourhood relations are embedded into the KDE by hotpoint analysis, subsequent data preparation, and distance determination.

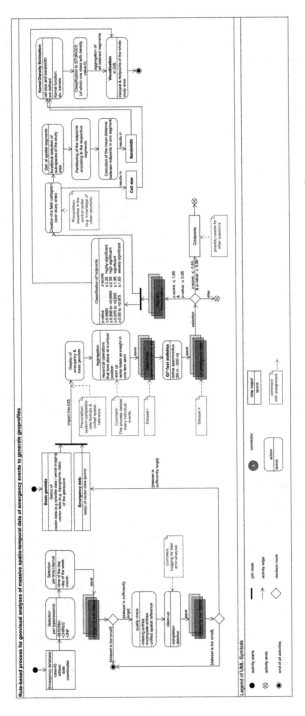

Fig. 3. Rule-based process for geovisual analyses of massive spatio-temporal data of emergency events to generate geoprofiles [3].

3   An Example for Geovisual Analysis Using the Optimised KDE Process

The functionality of the KDE process will be demonstrated by means of a case study in Berlin. For this purpose, Table 1 describes the process step-by-step in graphic and textual form on the following pages.

Table 1. The conception of the rule-based process for generating a geoprofile of massive spatio-temporal datasets using the case study (41,498 emergency alerts for rescue vehicles in an abstract space segment within one calendar year) [3]

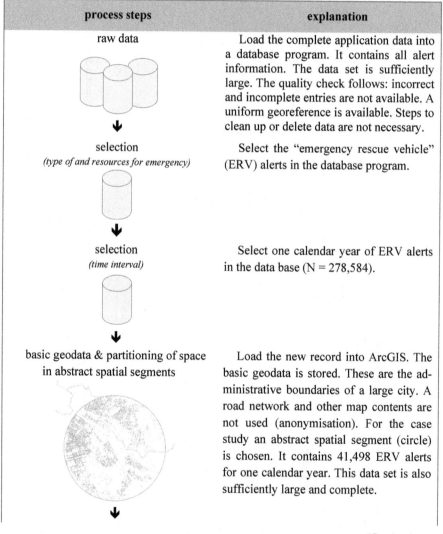

process steps	explanation
raw data	Load the complete application data into a database program. It contains all alert information. The data set is sufficiently large. The quality check follows: incorrect and incomplete entries are not available. A uniform georeference is available. Steps to clean up or delete data are not necessary.
selection *(type of and resources for emergency)*	Select the "emergency rescue vehicle" (ERV) alerts in the database program.
selection *(time interval)*	Select one calendar year of ERV alerts in the data base (N = 278,584).
basic geodata & partitioning of space in abstract spatial segments	Load the new record into ArcGIS. The basic geodata is stored. These are the administrative boundaries of a large city. A road network and other map contents are not used (anonymisation). For the case study an abstract spatial segment (circle) is chosen. It contains 41,498 ERV alerts for one calendar year. This data set is also sufficiently large and complete.

(Continue)

Table 1. *(Continue)*

aggregation

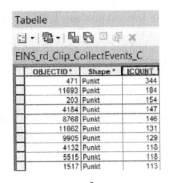

Emergencies that took place at the same location are aggregated and the number of emergencies is stored as a weight. The result is 12,156 data points with weighting. The maximum: in the selected space segment, 344 ERV alerts occurred at one location (point in space) within half of the calendar year.

Gi*-test statistics

Apply the Gi* test statistics to the data set in ArcGIS. The search radius is set to 50 m. The newly created data set is saved.

selection

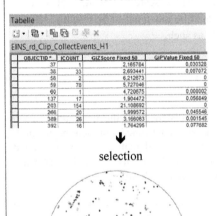

Within the new record, hot-points are selected and all other data is removed.

The applied selection rule:

z-score $\geq 1,65$ and p-value $\geq 0,95$.

A total of 379 hotpoints were identified. These can be displayed in the GIS (point map). The hotpoint data record is saved.

classification

X-Koord.	Y-Koord.	Einsätze (abs.)	Gi
...	...	45	99,9%
...	...	2	99%
...	...	73	95%
...	...	16	12%

The hotpoints of the hotpoint data record are classified.

The applied classification rules:
z-score $\geq 3,28$ and p-value $\geq 0,9995 :=$ highly significant
z-score $\geq 2,58$ and p-value $\geq 0,995$ to $< 0,9995$

(Continue)

Table 1. *(Continue)*

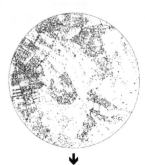

:= high significant
z-score ≥ 1,96 and p-value ≥ 0,975 to < 0,995
:= significant
z-score ≥ 1,65 and p-value ≥ 0,95 to < 0,975 :=
low significant

    The point map shows all calculated hotpoints (points in shades of red) and all non-significant data (points in black).

generating a field cartogram

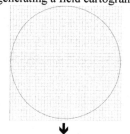

    An exemplary representation of the regular grid is shown, because at the chosen display scale the 50 m x 50 m cells would be too small to be visually detectable as such.

calculating mean distances

    The distances of the hotpoints to each other are determined and then the arithmetic mean is calculated. This value is fed into the core density estimation as bandwidth d. (d = 345 m)

KDE

    In ArcGIS the KDE is based on the hotpoint dataset with the cell size 50 m x 50 m and the bandwidth d = 345 m. The result is the hotspot field cartogram.

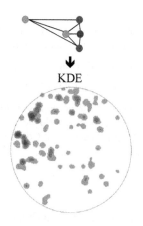

4 Discussion of Results

The central research question of this dissertation project is: How does an automatable process have to be described in order to analyse point mass data of real emergencies with regard to their location in space and time geovisually and to make them interpretable? To answer this question, a concept was developed which enables rule-based geovisual analyses of the continuous and mass data stored in the control centres of authorities and organisations with safety and security tasks. The concept is characterized by the standardization of central process steps and can be implemented in GIS, for example, via program interfaces. The goal of transforming the point into the surface in order to increase the overall informative value is achieved. The KDE procedure is discussed for this purpose and a problem solution is offered by targeted modelling of a new method process.

Neighbourhood and density are described in the geoanalytical context of space and time and the concept of horizontality and verticality of event neighbourhoods is introduced. Furthermore, methods for hotpoint and hotspot analysis are presented, their deficits were identified and a generic approach to their elimination is presented. Based on this, the experts of the control centres can formulate requirements and recommendations for strategic, operational and tactical action on deployment planning in more detail.

Through the combination of methods and the definition of comprehensible spatial and temporal variables, it has been possible to develop a process of analysis for the calculation and visualization of hotspots that is capable of standardisation and largely automated. The necessary factor expert knowledge is part of the definition of the abstract segmentation of the space for mask creation. These masks are stored in the overall process. (They can be easily adapted in case of changing spatial structures.)

The innovative, generic analytics process designed here to determine hotspots based on KDE is an extension of the optimised KDE-process. The proven benefit lies in the calculability, availability of expert knowledge in process form and in improving the quality of analysis. The concept is more comprehensive than the conventional KDE process. At the same time, the quality of the geovisual analyses increases. Not all emergency events of the entire urban space are included in the determination of hotspots. With the integration of the hotpoint determination into the overall process, a necessary selection of significant and actually significant emergency events into the hotspot calculation takes place.

This also reduces the enormous data volume and increases the physical computing power. Practice shows that the reduced data volume due to hotpoint-based selection does not always provide a sufficiently large sample for the core density estimation to be carried out. This circumstance is not to be understood as a deficit of the concept developed here. In statistics, the functionality of numerous methods is based on minimum data requirements. Test and estimation methods must not be applied without the compliance with these requirements, which is subject to proof. If these indications are ignored, the procedures may lead to erroneous results as well as misinterpretations of the real situation. If there is a complete lack of hotpoints in a spatial segment, despite a comparatively high compression of individual events, methods other than KDE must be applied in order to generate a spatial, cartographic visualization.

The result is geoprofiles in the form of maps with standardised class formation, signature and colour values. These also provide a starting point for further analyses and strategic, tactical and operational planning steps.

Acknowledgements. The work presented here is part of the dissertation entitled *"Konzeption und prototypische Umsetzung eines regelbasierten Prozesses zur geovisuellen Auswertung massiver raumzeitlicher Datenbestände von Feuerwehreinsätzen. Ein Beitrag zur Erweiterung der KDE für die Hotspot-Analyse im Kontext ziviler Sicherheitsforschung."* and was successfully completed at the University of Potsdam, Germany, in 2019. The support of his conference contribution by the German Aerospace Center, Institute of Optical Sensor Systems, Department Security Research and Applications is gratefully acknowledged.

References

1. Boba, R.: Crime Analysis and Crime Mapping. SAGE, London (2005)
2. Rossmo, K., Velarde, L.: Geographic profiling analysis: principles, methods and applications. In: Tompson, L., Chainey, S. (eds.) Crime Mapping Case Studies: Practice and Research, pp. 35–44. Wiley, Chichester, England, Hoboken (2008)
3. Gonschorek, J.: Konzeption und prototypische Umsetzung eines regelbasierten Prozesses zur geovisuellen Auswertung massiver raumzeitlicher Datenbestände von Feuerwehreinsätzen: Ein Beitrag zur Erweiterung der KDE für die Hotspot-Analyse im Kontext ziviler Sicherheitsforschung. Dissertation. University of Potsdam, Potsdam (2019)
4. Schernthanner, H., Asche, H., Gonschorek, J., Scheele, L.: Spatial modeling and geovisualization of rental prices for real estate portals. In: Gervasi, O., et al. (eds.) ICCSA 2016. LNCS, vol. 9788, pp. 120–133. Springer, Cham (2016). https://doi.org/10.1007/978-3-319-42111-7_11
5. Lersch, K.M., Hart, T.C.: Space, Time, and Crime, 3rd edn. Carolina Academic Press, Durham (2011)
6. Gonschorek, J., Räbiger, C., Bernhardt, B., Asche, H.: Civil security in urban spaces: adaptation of the KDE-method for optimized hotspot-analysis for emergency and rescue services. In: Gervasi, O., et al. (eds.) ICCSA 2016. LNCS, vol. 9788, pp. 98–106. Springer, Cham (2016). https://doi.org/10.1007/978-3-319-42111-7_9
7. Gonschorek, J.: Zivile Sicherheit in urbanen Räumen – Adaption des KDE-Verfahrens zur optimierten Hotspot Analyse für Behörden und Organisationen mit Sicherheitsaufgaben. In: Strobl, J., et al. (eds.) AGIT_2016 - Open:Spatial:Interfaces, Salzburg, 08 July 2016, pp. 364–372. Wichmann-Verlag, Heidelberg (2016)
8. Kalinic, M., Krisp, J.M.: Kernel density estimation (KDE) vs. hot-spot analysis – detecting criminal hot spots in the City of San Francisco. In: AGILE Proceedings (2018). https://agile-online.org/conference_paper/cds/agile_2018/shortpapers/66%20Kernel%20Density%20Estimation%20(KDE)%20vs.%20Hot-Spot%20Analysis%20-%20Detecting%20Criminal%20%20Hot%20Spots%20in%20the%20City%20of%20San%20Francisco_UPDATE.pdf. 16 Dec 2019
9. Chainey, S., Ratcliffe, J.: GIS and Crime Mapping. Wiley, Chichester, England, Hoboken (2005)

10. Levine, N.: CrimeStat III. A Spatial Statistics Program for the Analysis of Crime Incident Locations (v3.1), Houston, Washington (2007). https://www.icpsr.umich.edu/CrimeStat/workbook/CrimeStat_Workbook.pdf. Accessed 15 Jan 2018
11. Ratcliffe, J.: Crime mapping: spatial and temporal challenges. In: Piquero, A., Weisburd, D. (eds.) Handbook of Quantitative Criminology, pp. 5–24. Springer, New York (2010). https://doi.org/10.1007/978-0-387-77650-7_2
12. Yau, N.: Visualize This: The FlowingData Guide to Design, Visualization, and Statistics. Wiley Publishing Inc., Indianapolis (2011)
13. Tobler, W.R.: A computer movie simulating urban growth in the Detroit region. In: Clark University (ed.) Economic Geography: International Geographical Union. Commission on Quantitative Methods, pp. 234–240 (1970)
14. Hengl, T.: Finding the right pixel size. Comput. Geosci. 32(9), 1283–1298 (2006). https://pdfs.semanticscholar.org/9b60/27abf3e02bce5d5adc2764fac47fe1fcf334.pdf. Accessed 10 Feb 2018
15. Silverman, B.W.: Density Estimation for Statistics and Data Analysis. Chapman & Hall/CRC, Boca Raton (1986)
16. Parzen, E.: On estimation of a probability density function and mode. Ann. Math. Stat. (33), 1065–1076 (1962). http://bayes.wustl.edu/Manual/parzen62.pdf. Accessed 15 Jan 2018
17. Parzen, E.: Nonparametric statistical data modeling. J. Am. Stat. Assoc. 74(365), 105–121 (1979). http://www.dtic.mil/dtic/tr/fulltext/u2/a056827.pdf. Accessed 15 Jan 2018
18. Getis, A., Ord, J.K.: The analysis of spatial association by use of distance statistics. Geogr. Anal. 24(3), 189–206 (1992)
19. Ord, J.K., Getis, A.: Local spatial autocorrelation statistics: dristributional issues and an application. Geogr. Anal. 27(4), 286–306 (1995)
20. Williamson, D., McLafferty, S., Goldsmith, V., Mollenkopf, J., McGuire, P.: A better method to smooth crime incident data. ESRI ArcUser Mag., 1–5 (1999). http://www.esri.com/news/arcuser/0199/crimedata.html. Accessed 10 Mar 2018
21. Williamson, D., et al.: Tools in the spatial analysis of crime. In: Hirschfield, A. (ed.) Mapping and Analysing Crime Data: Lessons from Research and Practice, pp. 187–202. Taylor & Francis, London (2001)
22. Chainey, S.: Examining the influence of cell size and bandwidth size on kernel density estimation crime hotspot maps for predicting spatial patterns of crime. Bull. Geogr. Soc. Liege 60, 7–19 (2013)
23. Hart, T., Zandenberg, P.: Kernel density estimation and hotspot mapping: examining the influence of interpolation method, grid cell size, and bandwidth on crime forecasting. Policing Int. J. Police Strateg. Manag. 37(2), 305–323 (2014)
24. Gottlieb, S., Arenberg, S., Singh, R.: Crime Analysis: From First Report to Final Arrest. Alpha, Montclair (1994)

Assessment of Post Fire Soil Erosion with ESA Sentinel-2 Data and RUSLE Method in Apulia Region (Southern Italy)

Valentina Santarsiero[1,2(✉)], Gabriele Nolè[1], Antonio Lanorte[1],
Biagio Tucci[1], Lucia Saganeiti[2], Angela Pilogallo[2],
Francesco Scorza[2], and Beniamino Murgante[2]

[1] IMAA-CNR, C.da Santa Loja, Zona Industriale,
Tito Scalo, 85050 Potenza, Italy
{valentina.santarsiero,gabriele.nole,
antonio.lanorte,biagio.tucci}@imaa.cnr.it
[2] School of Engineering, University of Basilicata, Viale dell'Ateneo Lucano 10,
85100 Potenza, Italy
{valentina.santarsiero,lucia.saganeiti,
angela.pilogallo,beniamino.murgante}@unibas.it

Abstract. Fires are one of the main causes of environmental degradation as they have an impact on flora and fauna, can also strongly influence ecological and geomorphological processes and permanently compromise the functionality of the ecosystems and soils on which they impact. The severity of the fire event influences the superficial hydrological response and the consequent loss of soil. Precipitation on the basins recently affected by fires produces an increase in the outflow which commonly transports and deposits large volumes of sediment, both inside and downstream of the burned area. In the years following the fire, the loss of soil is very high and the degradation processes of the soils are much greater than in the pre-event. The aim of this study is to evaluate the potential annual loss due to post-fire erosion using remote sensing techniques, RUSLE (Revised Universal Soil Loss Equation) methodology and GIS tecniques in nine different event occurred in 2019 in the northern part of the Apulia Region (Southern Italy). Geographic Information System techniques and remote sensing data have been adopted to study the post-fire soil erosion risk. Satellite images are the most appropriate for environmental monitoring as they provide high resolution multispectral optical images, infact are able to monitor the development of vegetation by assessing the water content an changes in chlorophyll levels. This study can be useful to spatial planning authorities as a tool for assessing and monitoring eroded soil in areas affected by fires, representing a useful tool for land management.

Keywords: Soil erosion · RUSLE method · Geographic Information System

© Springer Nature Switzerland AG 2020
O. Gervasi et al. (Eds.): ICCSA 2020, LNCS 12252, pp. 590–603, 2020.
https://doi.org/10.1007/978-3-030-58811-3_43

1   Introduction

Since at least the second half of the 19th century, soil erosion has been recognized as one of the most significant environmental problems worldwide [1], particularly in areas having seasonally contrasted climate and a long history of human pressure.

Soil loss leads to a decrease of the water holding capacity, nutrient availability and organic matter content and to a reduction in the overall fertility of arable lands [5].

Fire represents one of the most important causes of degradation of Mediterranean area bringing important transformations at different temporal and spatial scales which affect ecosystems, landscapes and environments [9, 19].

Ongoing global climate changes are increasing the risk of fires, this risk is an effect of climate change but at the same time it is the cause. Fires cause a loss of the carbon contained in the vegetation and soils, against which it is important to evaluate the impact of the fire. Among the long-term effects of fires, which can also be found in the years following the event, there are profound alterations in the characteristics and structure of the soils.

Fire severity influences the hydrological response and soil loss [21–23]. In fact, a high severity of burned soil is generally associated with an increase in the water repellency of the soil [2, 8] and a decrease in infiltration [23]. Precipitation on recently burned areas produces a greater surface runoff which commonly transports and deposits large volumes of sediment, both inside and downstream of the burned area [2, 15, 20, 23, 24].

In the Mediterranean area, soil composition and structure have been generally strongly shaped by fires, which they tend to operate as an erosive force. The aim of this work is to understand the erosion of burned soil in Apulia Region (Southern Italy) in pre and post-fire conditions in nine different fire event occurred in 2019 in the northern part of the Region (Gargano Area). The analysis has been carried out by using satellite images derived from Sentinel 2A and Sentinel 2B satellite and geographical information systems (GIS). RUSLE (Revised Universal Soil Loss Equation) methodology has been applied to evaluate the pre-fire and post-fire soil erosion. The entire procedure was carried out with the open source QGIS software and related plugins.

This study confirm that Remote Sensing and GIS are effective tools in generating spatial and quantitative information on soil erosion studies and risk assessment mapping.

2   Material and Method

Soil erosion is one of most serious environmental problems in the Mediterranean area and is also the most intensively studied subjects in this European Region. This process is extremely variable due to the interaction with different factors such as geomorphological and geological features, type of climate and exogenous agents, fire occurrence, land use and management and type and density of vegetation cover. It includes the erosion of the washing of the slabs, the breakthrough, the trampling, the surface landslide and the development of large and active badlands both in the sub-humid and semi-arid areas [10].

Fires are a serious short-term risk of soil erosion, but can also result in land degradation and sometimes desertification over the long-term.

2.1 Study Area

The study areas are located in the northern part of Apulia Region, in Foggia Province (Fig. 1).

Foggia is one of the largest provinces in Italy, about 7000 km^2 and its dived in three areas characterized by different geomorphological and geological features: Gargano, Tavoliere of Apulia Region and Monti Dauni Area (Fig. 2).

Fig. 1. Geographical localization of study area in Apulia Region.

This area is characterized by a typically Mediterranean climate with mild and slightly rainy winters alternating with hot and dry summers. However there is a great climatic variability between the two areas, in fact the Gargano is characterized by a high rainfall while the Tavoliere plain has some of the highest temperatures in Italy.

This area lies in the northern sector of the Bradanic foredeep bounded to the west by the external sector of the southern Apennines chain ('Subappennino Dauno') and to the east by the Gargano Promontory (northern part of the Apulian foreland) (see Fig. 2) [4, 13, 21, 26].

The Tavoliere di Puglia is a large alluvial plain located in southern Italy (Foggia Province, Apulia Region) characterized by a series of low elevations, in fact large weakly inclined surfaces are well observable. From a geological perspective view, it represents the northern part of the Bradanic trough located between the southern Apennine Chain and the Apulian Foreland [9, 11, 12, 18, 19, 24, 26].

The outcrops are characterized by quaternary deposits mainly in facies alluvial and lake [10, 12, 13, 18].

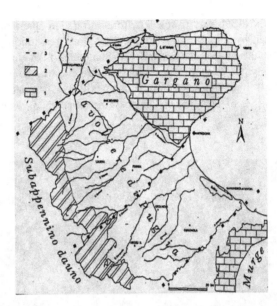

Fig. 2. Schematic geologic map of the chain-foredeep-foreland system of the southern Apennines and location of the Tavoliere di Puglia plain and Gargano horst: note that it represents the northern sector of the Bradanic trough. Rectangle 1 represents the carbonate units of the Apulian foreland. White part represents the terraced marine deposits of the Tavoliere and finally rectangle 2 represents the deposits belonging to the Appennine Chain of the Dauno Apennines [2, 4, 21, 26].

The Gargano Promontory is a carbonate horst and Monte Calvo (1056 m. asl) represents the highest part of the whole Gargano Area. Overall from geomorphological point of view, the entire territory is characterized by a succession of escarpments, isolated reliefs, depressions and small plains. Surface erosion forms are evident due to the action of morpho-climatic processes [4, 12].

To assess pre- and post-fire soil erosion we selected nine fire events that occurred in the 2019 into the study area. One of them (Lucera fire) is located within the morpho-geological unit of the Bradanic Trough. Geology of the territory is mainly constituited by Quaternary deposits like such as deposits of silty clays, sands and pebbles interspersed with clay sands [13].

The other eight fires are located in the municipalities of Ischitella, San Maro in Lamis, Carpino and Cagnano Varano, in the Gargano area. Deposits presents in this area are mainly costituited by different type of calcarenite and limestones [4, 23].

2.2 Data and Methodology

Multi-spectral and multi-temporal satellite data with medium and high spatial resolution are very appropriate to evaluate the burned soil erosion process and fire severity. In present work images of ESA (European Space Agency) Sentinel-2A and 2B satellite have been used (source: https://scihub.copernicus.eu/dhus/#/home). Sentinel 2 satellite acquired images with 13 bands (Table 1), from infrared to thermal infrared wavelengths, characterized by a mid-high spatial and temporal resolution [32, 33].

Specifically, for the events considered, two Sentinel 2 L2A images were already downloaded correctly atmospheric, pre and post fire, in which all the bands were resampled with a 10 m spatial resolution. Fire severity was stimulated using sentinel bands 2 most sensitive to changes in the post-fire reflectance value [7, 19, 27–29] (Fig. 3).

Carpino – Parco Farnese Fire (09/09/2019), Image False color pre fire (Sentinel 2Bands 8 4 3).

Carpino – Parco Farnese Fire (09/09/2019), image False color post fire (Sentinel 2Bands 8 4 3).

Carpino – Parco Farnese Fire (09/09/2019), Image RGB color pre fire (Sentinel 2Bands 4 3 2).

Carpino – Parco Farnese Fire (09/09/2019), image RGB color post fire (Sentinel 2Bands 4 3 2).

Fig. 3. Carpino – Parco Farnese fire. Sentinel 2 images before and after the fire (true colors, false colors) in black the perimeter of the polygon of the burned area.

In particular, the reflectance in the medium infrared band (band 12 - SWIR), sensitive to the knowledge content of the soil and growth, increased after the fire, while in the near infrared region (band 8A - NIR) occurs a decline in reflectance due to the demand for the chlorophyll content of the phytomass.

The Normalized Burn Ratio (NBR) index was created considering these characteristics [14, 15] and is widely used to evaluate the severity of fire [17].

Table 1. Sentinel 2A overview.

Satellite	Bands	Range wavelength (nm)	Resolution (m)
Sentinel 2	Band 1 –Coastal aereosol	443	60
	Band 2 – Blue	490	10
	Band 3 – Green	560	10
	Band 4 – Red	665	10
	Band 5 – Vegetation Red Edge	705	20
	Band 6 – Vegetation Red Edge	740	20
	Band 7 – Vegetation Red Edge	783	20
	Band 8 – NIR	842	10
	Band 8a –Vegetation Red Edge	865	20
	Band 9 – Water vapour	945	60
	Band 10 – SWIR – Cirrus	1375.3	60
	Band 11 – SWIR	1610.0	20
	Band 12 – SWIR	2190.0	20

In reference to Sentinel-2 images, the NBR is calculated as reported in Eq. 1:

$$NBR = (Band\,8A - Band\,12)/(Band\,8A + Band\,12) \tag{1}$$

In addition, in order to evaluate the difference between pre- and post-fire NBR, the dNBR index was calculated:

$$dNBR = NBR\,pre\,fire - NBR\,post\,fire \tag{2}$$

The dNBR index, being linked to the variation of the NBR values calculated before and after the event, provides a measure of the effects of the fire and can therefore be used to characterize the degree of severity of the fire (Fig. 4).

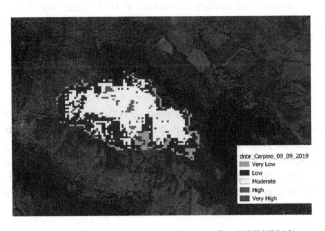

Fig. 4. dNBR Carpino – Parco Farnese fire (09/09/2019).

The QGIS software (www.qgis.org) is the tool used for all data processing and spatial analyzes. In particular, for the management of satellite images, the reference is the QGIS Semi-Automatic Classification Plugin (SCP) plugin. It allows you to download satellite images and to do their pre and post processing.

2.3 RUSLE Methodology

Several soil erosion models exist with varying degrees ofcomplexity. One of the most widely applied empirical models forassessing the sheet and rill erosion is the Universal Soil Loss Equation (USLE), developed by Wischmeier and Smith in 1965 [31, 38]. Agriculture Handbook 703 [30] is a guide to conservation planning with the RUSLE. With its revised (RUSLE) and modified (MUSLE) versions [35, 37, 38].

Pre- and post-fire soil loss have been calculated using the RUSLE (Revised Universal Soil Loss Equation) model [8, 20, 22, 23], developed from the previous USLE model [30] by resampling all parameters necessary for the spatial resolution of Sentinel 2A (10 m). The estimate of the annual loss of soil according to the RUSLE model (Eq. 3) is a function of five variables relating to the regime of rainfall, soil characteristics, topography, coverage and management of crops and crop conservation practices, according to the following formula:

$$A = R \times K \times LS \times C \times P \tag{3}$$

Where:

A = annual soil loss (Mg · ha −1 · year −1);
R = precipitation erosion factor (MJ · mm · ha −1 · h −1 · year −1);
K = soil erodibility factor (Mg · h · MJ −1 · mm −1);
LS = slope length factor and slope steepness (dimensionless);
C = crop and cover management factor (dimensionless);
P = cultivation or anti-erosion (dimensionless) practice factor.

The erosion factor of the outflow of rainfall R (MJ · mm · ha−1 · h−1 · year−1), constitutes a measure of the rain energy considered as the main erosive agent [25]. It is calculated on the basis of the average monthly cumulated rainfall and was determined using the following formula [35]

$$R = (1163, 45 + 4, 9 \times H - 35, 2 \times NRE - 0.58 \times q) \tag{4}$$

where H is mean value of annual precipitation, q is the site elevation using 5mt DTM and NRE is the mean value of rainy events per year. K factor is obtained from the "Soil Erodibility in Europe High Resolution Dataset" provided by the JRC's European Soil Data Centre (ESDAC) [30]. LS topographic factor was calculated with the support of the QGIS software starting from the DTM with a grid size of 5 mt. For the calculation of the LS factor at a point r located along a hilly slope, the following equation was used [23].

$$LS(r) = (\mu + 1)[a(r)/a0]\mu \times [sin\ b(r)/b0]^n \tag{5}$$

C factor reflects the effects of surface coverage and roofing management on soil erosion [16], where C is the cover management factor and a = 1.18.

$$C = -a \times SAVI + 1 \tag{6}$$

For both the pre-fire and post-fire scenarios, the estimate of the factor C was carried out on the basis of the calculation of vegetation indices derived from satellite. In particular, the SAVI (Soil-Adjusted Vegetation Index) was used.

$$SAVI = [(NIR - RED) \times (1 + L)]/(NIR + RED + L) \tag{7}$$

where L is a correction factor and has been assumed equal to 0.5 while NIR and RED are the reflectance values in the near infrared and red bands. SAVI is calculated using the best Sentinel 2 images acquired pre and post-fire as close as possible, temporally, to the date of the fire.

The cultivation or anti-erosion practice factor (P) is an expression of the effects of agricultural management practices aimed at reducing water runoff and consequently soil loss [18]. A is the forecast of soil lost one year after the fire.

The assessment of soil erosion before and after the fire was divided into the following three phases: (1) collection of geospatial data relating to the areas covered by the fire; (2) development of RUSLE spatial factors for pre- and post-fire conditions; (3) estimate of soil loss with RUSLE for pre and post fire scenarios (QGIS Raster Calculator) considering the variations recorded by the factors K, LS and C, influenced by the fires [19, 24, 29].

3 Result and Discussion

Applying methodology described allowed us to map fire severity for our nine study sites, which were subsequently used as input for the RUSLE model parameters estimation.

Figure 5 shows the calculation of the pre-fire RUSLE index (image on the left) and of the post-fire (image on the right) in Lucera fire. It can be seen that the second image has much larger areas (red), which indicate an increase in soil loss on areas that previously showed a low erosion index.

The pre and post-fire RUSLE maps are compared for each study area, in Fig. 6 shows some example of the nine areas analyzed.

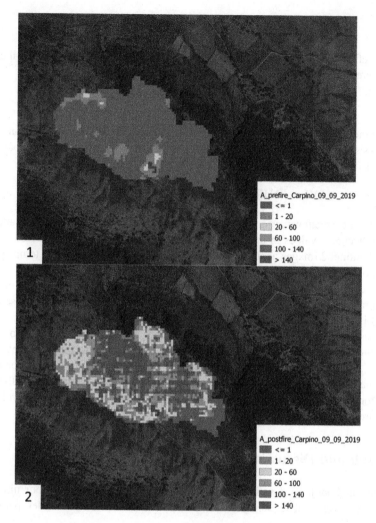

Fig. 5. Fire Lucera: RUSLE A pre and post fire factor. Annual post-fire soil erosion forecast. (Color figure online)

It is immediately evident that wildfire always increases the amount of soil loss, but there are also differences among the sites.

Thus, although the fire, according to the model, determines as expected, in all the analyzed cases, an increase in the potential soil loss, this increase shows different trends in the various sites. In relation to the high geological, geomorphological and vegetational variability, nine study sites were compared.

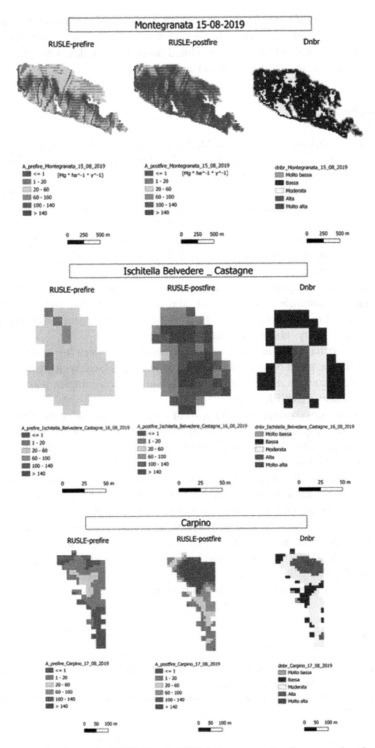

Fig. 6. Pre and post fire RUSLE and dNBR index: example of some analyzed areas.

Fire severity (estimated through the dNBR and SAVI satellite-derived indices) influences some RUSLE parameters. In the specific case, according to previous studies, the K and LS factors of RUSLE were modified using dNBR index, while the C factor was calculated as a function of the SAVI index.

4 Conclusion

Soil erosion is a serious problem in the Mediterranean area and is caused or aggravated by human activities, such as inadequate agricultural practices, industrial activities, fires or it urban and industrial development.

The result is less soil fertility and disruption of nutrient, this has direct repercussions on quality of ecosystem, biodiversity and climate change (European Commission, 2006).

This work provides a contribution to the study of the phenomenon of soil erosion caused by fires in the northern part of the Puglia Region, affected each year by incendiary phenomena.

The sites analyzed generally present themselves as areas very subject to erosive phenomena both for their geological and climatic characteristics, and for their high susceptibility to fire. In relation to the high to the geological, geomorphological and vegetational variability, nine study sites were compared.

Many authors have also investigated the relationships between fire severity and soil loss. In conclusion, it can be said that soil erosion risk maps have been created from the combination of many parameters interacting each others in a complex way generating the final quantitative RUSLE values.

The final results confirm that the loss of soil undergoes a significant increase following the fire, but also show that the intensity of this impact is different in relation to the specific properties of the nine site (from a geological, geomorphological and vegetational point of view).

This paper proved that the integration of soil erosion models with GIS and remote sensing is a simple and effective tool for mapping and quantifying areas and rates of soil erosion for the development of better soil conservation plans.

This study can be useful to spatial planning authorities as a tool for assessing and monitoring eroded soil in areas affected by fires, representing a useful tool for land management [18, 27, 28]. Future research will be aimed at validating the outputs of RUSLE and deepening the use of the parameters of the model and will explore the link between soil erosion monitoring and urban planning.

References

1. Bakker, M.M., Govers, G., Jones, R.A., Rounsevell, M.D.: The effect of soil erosion on Europe's crop yields. Ecosystems 10(7), 1209–1219 (2007)
2. Caldara, M., Pennetta, L.: Lineamenti geografici della Provincia di Foggia. Bonifica 8(3), 13–24 (1993)

3. Cannon, S.H., Gartner, J.E., Wilson, R.C., Bowers, J.C., Laber, J.L.: Storm rainfall conditions for floods and debris flows from recently burned areas in southwestern Colorado and southern California. Geomorphology **96**(3–4), 250–269 (2008)

4. Cremonini, G., Elmi, C., Selli, R.: Note illustrative della Carta geologica d'Italia alla scala 1: 100 000, foglio 156 S. Marco in Lamis (1971)

5. Csáfordi, P., Pődör, A., Bug, J., Gribovsyki, Z.: Soil erosion analysis in a small forested catchment supported by ArcGIS Model Builder. Acta Silvatica et Lignaria Hungarica **8**(1), 39–56 (2012)

6. Doerr, S.H., Woods, S.W., Martin, D.A., Casimiro, M.: 'Natural background' soil water repellency in conifer forests of the north-western USA: its prediction and relationship to wildfire occurrence. J. Hydrol. **371**(1–4), 12–21 (2009)

7. Elfadaly, A., Attia, W., Qelichi, M.M., Murgante, B., Lasaponara, R.: Management of cultural heritage sites using remote sensing indices and spatial analysis techniques. Surv. Geophys. **39**(6), 1347–1377 (2018). https://doi.org/10.1007/s10712-018-9489-8

8. Fox, D.M., Darboux, F., Carrega, P.: Effects of fire-induced water repellency on soil aggregate stability, splash erosion, and saturated hydraulic conductivity for different size fractions. Hydrol. Process. Int. J. **21**(17), 2377–2384 (2007)

9. Fu, B.J., et al.: Assessment of soil erosion at large watershed scale using RUSLE and GIS: a case study in the Loess Plateau of China. Land Degrad. Dev. **16**, 73–85 (2005). https://doi.org/10.1002/ldr.646

10. Gallicchio, S., Moretti, M., Spalluto, L., Angelini, S.: Geology of the middle and upper Pleistocene marine and continental terraces of the northern Tavoliere di Puglia plain (Apulia, southern Italy). J. Maps **10**(4), 569–575 (2014)

11. García-Ruiz, J.M., Nadal-Romero, E., Lana-Renault, N., Beguería, S.: Erosion in Mediterranean landscapes: changes and future challenges. Geomorphology **198**, 20–36 (2013)

12. Gioia, D., Gallicchio, S., Moretti, M., Tropeano, M.: STUDIO GEOLOGICO E GEOMORFOLOGICO DEL RETICOLO IDROGRAFICO DEL SETTORE PUGLIESE DEL SUBAPPENNINO

13. Jacobacci, A., Malatesta, A., Martelli, G., Stampanoni, G.: Note illustrative della Carta Geologica d'Italia. Foglio 163–Lucera (1967)

14. Key, C.H.: Landscape assessment (LA): sampling and analysis methods. In: Lutes, D.C., et al. (eds.) FIREMON: Fire Effects Monitoring and Inventory System. USDA Forest Service, Rocky Mountain Research Station. General Technical Report RMRS-GTR-164-CD, Fort Collins (2006)

15. Key, C.H., Benson, N.C.: Landscape assessment (LA) sampling and analysis methods. USDA Forest Service General Technical Report, RMRS-GTR-164-CD (2006)

16. Kuo, K.T., Sekiyama, A., Mihara, M.: Determining C factor of universal soil loss equation (USLE) based on remote sensing. Int. J. Environ. Rural Dev. **7**(2), 154–161 (2016)

17. Lanorte, A., Danese, M., Lasaponara, R., Murgante, B.: Multiscale mapping of burn area and severity using multisensor satellite data and spatial autocorrelation analysis. Int. J. Appl. Earth Obs. Geoinf. **20**, 42–51 (2013)

18. Las Casas, G., Murgante, B., Scorza, F.: Regional local development strategies benefiting from open data and open tools and an outlook on the renewable energy sources contribution. In: Papa, R., Fistola, R. (eds.) Smart Energy in the Smart City. GET, pp. 275–290. Springer, Cham (2016). https://doi.org/10.1007/978-3-319-31157-9_14

19. Lasaponara, R., et al.: Spatial open data for monitoring risks and preserving archaeological areas and landscape: case studies at Kom el Shoqafa, Egypt and Shush, Iran. Sustainability **9**(4), 572 (2017). https://doi.org/10.3390/su9040572

20. Lufafa, A., Tenywa, M.M., Isabirye, M., Majaliwa, M.J.G., Woomer, P.L.: Prediction of soil erosion in a Lake Victoria basin catchment using a GIS-based Universal Soil Loss model. Agric. Syst. **76**(3), 883–894 (2003)
21. Maggiore, M., Masciale, R., Massari, R., Pappagallo, G., Passarella, G., Vurro, M.: Caratteri idrostrutturali del Tavoliere di Puglia ed elaborazione di una carta geolitologica a finalità idrogeologiche. Geologi e Territorio-Periodico di Scienze della Terra dell'Ordine dei Geologi della Puglia **2**, 6–16 (2005)
22. Miller, J.D., Nyhan, J.W., Yool, S.R.: Modeling potential erosion due to the Cerro Grande Fire with a GIS-based implementation of the Revised Universal Soil Loss Equation. Int. J. Wildland Fire **12**(1), 85–100 (2003)
23. Mitasova, H., Hofierka, J., Zlocha, M., Iverson, L.R.: Modelling topographic potential for erosion and deposition using GIS. Int. J. Geogr. Inf. Syst. **10**(5), 629–641 (1996)
24. Moody, J.A., Martin, D.A.: Initial hydrologic and geomorphic response following a wildfire in the Colorado Front Range. Earth Surface Process. Landforms J. Br. Geomorphol. Res. Group **26**(10), 1049–1070 (2001)
25. Moody, J.A., Shakesby, R.A., Robichaud, P.R., Cannon, S.H., Martin, D.A.: Current research issues related to post-wildfire runoff and erosion processes. Earth Sci. Rev. **122**, 10–37 (2013)
26. Moretti, M., Gallicchio, S., Spalluto, L., Ciaranfi, N., Pieri, P.: Evoluzione geologica del settore settentrionale del Tavoliere di Puglia (Italia meridionale) nel Pleistocene medio e superiore. Il Quaternario **23**(2), 181–198 (2010)
27. Murgante, B., Borruso, G., Lapucci, A.: Sustainable development: concepts and methods for its application in urban and environmental planning. In: Murgante, B., Borruso, G., Lapucci, A. (eds.) Geocomputation, Sustainability and Environmental Planning. Studies in Computational Intelligence, vol. 348, pp. 1–15. Springer, Heidelberg (2011). https://doi.org/10.1007/978-3-642-19733-8_1
28. Murgante, B., Borruso, G., Balletto, G., Castiglia, P., Dettori, M.: Why Italy first? Health, geographical and planning aspects of the COVID-19 outbreak. Sustainability **12**, 5064 (2020)
29. Nolè, G., Lasaponara, R., Lanorte, A., Murgante, B.: Quantifying urban sprawl with spatial autocorrelation techniques using multi-temporal satellite data. Int. J. Agric. Environ. Inf. Syst. **5**(2), 20–38 (2014). https://doi.org/10.4018/ijaeis.2014040102
30. Nyman, P., Sheridan, G.J., Smith, H.G., Lane, P.N.: Evidence of debris flow occurrence after wildfire in upland catchments of south-east Australia. Geomorphology **125**(3), 383–401 (2011)
31. Panagos, P., Meusburger, K., Ballabio, C., Borrelli, P., Alewell, C.: Soil erodibility in Europe: a high-resolution dataset based on LUCAS. Sci. Total Environ. **479**, 189–200 (2014)
32. Pascale, S., et al.: Landslide susceptibility mapping using artificial neural network in the urban area of Senise and San Costantino Albanese (Basilicata, Southern Italy). In: Murgante, B., et al. (eds.) ICCSA 2013. LNCS, vol. 7974, pp. 473–488. Springer, Heidelberg (2013). https://doi.org/10.1007/978-3-642-39649-6_34
33. Renard, K.G.: Predicting Soil Erosion By Water: A Guide to Conservation Planning with the Revised Universal Soil Loss Equation (RUSLE). United States Government Printing (1997)
34. Riley, K.L., Bendick, R., Hyde, K.D., Gabet, E.J.: Frequency–magnitude distribution of debris flows compiled from global data, and comparison with post-fire debris flows in the western US. Geomorphology **191**, 118–128 (2013)
35. Robichaud, P.R.: Evaluating the effectiveness of postfire rehabilitation treatments (No. 63). US Department of Agriculture, Forest Service, Rocky Mountain Research Station (2000)

36. Santarsiero, V., Nolè, G., Lanorte, A., Tucci, B., Baldantoni, P., Murgante, B.: Evolution of soil consumption in the municipality of Melfi (Southern Italy) in relation to renewable energy. In: Misra, S., et al. (eds.) ICCSA 2019. LNCS, vol. 11621, pp. 675–682. Springer, Cham (2019). https://doi.org/10.1007/978-3-030-24302-9_48

37. Santi, P.M., Morandi, L.: Comparison of debris-flow volumes from burned and unburned areas. Landslides 10(6), 757–769 (2012). https://doi.org/10.1007/s10346-012-0354-4

38. Terranova, O., Antronico, L., Coscarelli, R., Iaquinta, P.: Soil erosion risk scenarios in the Mediterranean environment using RUSLE and GIS: an application model for Calabria (southern Italy). Geomorphology 112(3–4), 228–245 (2009)

39. Van Remortel, R.D., Hamilton, M.E., Hickey, R.J.: Estimating the LS factor for RUSLE through iterative slope length processing of digital elevation data within ArcInfo grid. Cartography 30(1), 27–35 (2001)

40. Wischmeier, W.H., Smith, D.D.: Predicting rainfall erosion losses - a guide for conservation planning. U.S. Department of Agriculture, Hyattsville, Agriculture Handbook No 537, p. 58 (1978)

41. Wischmeier, W.H., Smith, D.D.: Predicting rainfall-erosion losses from cropland east of the Rocky Mountains: Guide for selection of practices for soil and water conservation (No. 282). US Department of Agriculture (1965)

International Workshop on Geomatics for Resource Monitoring and Management (GRMM 2020)

Coupled Use of Hydrologic-Hydraulic Model and Geomorphological Descriptors for Flood-Prone Areas Evaluation: A Case Study of Lama Lamasinata

Beatrice Lioi$^{(\boxtimes)}$, Andrea Gioia , Vincenzo Totaro ,
Gabriella Balacco , Vito Iacobellis , and Giancarlo Chiaia

Politecnico di Bari, via Orabona 4, 70125 Bari, Italy
{beatrice.lioi,andrea.gioia,vincenzo.totaro,
gabriella.balacco,vito.iacobellis,
giancarlo.chiaia}@poliba.it

Abstract. The delineation of flood risk maps is a fundamental step in planning urban areas management. This evaluation can be carried out by hydraulic/hydrological modelling that allows obtaining water depths and related flooded areas. In this way, it is possible to mitigate and contain the catastrophic effects of floods, which become more frequent in the last decades. These events result in losses of both human lives and assets. In addition, the growing availability of high-resolution topographic data (i.e. Digital Terrain Models - DTM), due to new technologies for measuring surface elevation, gave a strong impulse to the development of new techniques capable of providing rapid and reliable identification of flood susceptibility. In this study, two methodologies for mapping flood-prone areas in karst ephemeral streams in Puglia region (Southern Italy) are compared, highlighting how DTM-based technologies are a precious source of information in data-poor environments. Results are in perfect agreement with previous studies on similar areas, showing the marked influences of topography in defining flood-prone areas. These researches can also be useful in investigating a wider gamma of hydrological-related aspects, in particular with respect to the social behavior of communities.

1 Introduction

In the last decades floods impact increased dramatically in many regions of the world, requiring a proper understanding of interactions between physical and social processes. A future worsening is expected due to the increase in alluvial phenomena and the rise of sea level [1]. Among several situations which have to be tackled in terms of flood risk, in this paper particular attention is dedicated to the ephemeral streams typical of the Apulian territory, defined as *lame* (in Italian). These karst streams convey the rainwater from the Murgia plateau towards the outlet of the watershed to which they belong, and are widespread throughout the Apulian regional territory but mainly in the metropolitan area of Bari. Lame are geomorphological structures with fertile alluvial soils [2–4] and represent a structural typology typical of the Apulian karst

© Springer Nature Switzerland AG 2020
O. Gervasi et al. (Eds.): ICCSA 2020, LNCS 12252, pp. 607–619, 2020.
https://doi.org/10.1007/978-3-030-58811-3_44

environments; more generally in this region different types of risk may coexist connected with the presence of waterways, for example in above-mentioned karst [5, 6], with respect to the type of soil [7] and in reservoirs [8]. Different approaches can be used for the management and mitigation of hydraulic risk, for example by making use of theoretical tools in the framework of derived flood frequency distributions [9, 10] or in the context of conceptual models [11]. In addition, useful support for flood management is provided by satellite data, which use is widespread in the environmental field, both for the evaluation of hydrological parameters [12–16] and for flood risk assessment [17–20]. Recent advances in the definition of high-resolution Digital Elevation Models (DEM) were carried out exploiting the use of Unmanned Aerial Vehicle (UAV) (e.g., [21]). Furthermore, an interesting application of these methodologies can be found in the field of landslide detection [22]. Flood management issues can also extend to other areas, such as damage to structures. In particular, different models can be adopted to define the levels of damage connected, among others, both to flood and seismic events [23–25].

The paper is structured as follows. In Sect. 2 details of Lama Lamasinata are illustrated, while in Sect. 3 the main features of bidimensional hydraulic/hydrological models and geomorphic descriptors are described. In Sect. 4, instead, the main results of this analysis will be highlighted. In the conclusive section, instead, some comments and operative proposals are reported.

2 Study Area

This study is focused on lama Lamasinata (Fig. 1), a karst ephemeral stream that flows through the metropolitan area of Bari (Puglia region, Southern Italy). It crosses the municipalities of Toritto, Palo del Colle, Bitonto, Binetto, Bitetto, Modugno and Bari and slopes down, channelled, to the pinewood of San Francesco, in Bari. This stream has a basin area of about 650 km^2.

The main characteristics of the basin are shown in Table 1.

Table 1. Hydro-geomorphological characteristics

Hydro-geomorphological characteristics of the Lama Lamasinata			
Average slope of the basin i_m (%)	Maximum basin height Q_{max} (m a.s. l.)	Medium basin height Q_m (m a.s. l.)	Length of the main stream network L_{max} (km)
0.9	513.46	276.19	54.14

The importance of Lama Lamasinata is mainly due to the marked interaction with the urban environments of Palo del Colle, Binetto and Bitetto.

Fig. 1. Study area (Lama Lamasinata, Bari)

3 Materials and Methods

This section illustrates the two methodologies implemented in the present study:

- the evaluation of flooded areas through a coupled hydrological-hydraulic model;
- the assessment of flood-prone areas by means of geomorphological descriptors.

The river channel as well as the digital elevation model of the area of interest, were reconstructed in a GIS environment starting from georeferenced vector cartography. This study aims to evaluate floodable areas in terms of water depth.

The Southern Apennines Hydrographic District identifies the areas with hydraulic hazard as portions of territory characterized by the same flood probability, which corresponds to the return periods of the reference flood equal to 30, 200 and 500 years, in accordance with current national legislation.

3.1 Hydrologic-Hydraulic Model

The management of hydraulic risk is carried out through the definition of maps able to highlight the areas of the territory subjected by assigned risk levels. Through the use of numerical modeling it is therefore possible to predict the areas affected by flooding after assuming all the input elements, such as morphology, land use and flood event. Currently, the determination of floodable areas can be performed through the use of coupled hydrological and hydraulic models. In the proposed work the hydraulic simulation was carried out using a two-dimensional (2D) FLO-2D software, which provide flood-prone areas delineation, starting from flood hydrographs obtained for fixed return periods.

The first step of the procedure was implemented by importing the Digital Terrain Model (DTM) in ASCII format on which the calculation grid will be subsequently built. For this purpose, it was necessary to specify the grid pixel, i.e. the size of the cell that represents the elementary unit of the model. Subsequently, the altimetric value is assigned to each cell. The creation of the grid represents a central element of the simulation as it defines the resolution with which the model will perform the simulation. Obviously, the higher the resolution, the greater the accuracy with which the flooded areas are evaluated. It is straightforward that higher resolutions (small cell size) correspond to long processing times. Therefore, the choice of the grid must be based on an adequate compromise between an accurate representation of the morphology of the soil and a maximum acceptable number of cells. Indicatively the maximum value of the ratio between the peak value of the flow rate and the area of the cell should not exceed the value of 0.3 m^3s^{-1}/m^2; beyond this value the calculation may become unstable, although the simulation may take place. For the purposes of the present study, a cell with a resolution of 10 m $\times$ 10 m was selected. The grid cell to which associate the inflow condition is identified through the use of a design hydrograph. Then, a triangular hydrograph with a flow peak rate of $Q_P = 606.64$ m^3/s, corresponding to a return period of 200 years, was selected.

The flood hydrograph is characterized by a concentration period that extends for a duration equal to the corrivation time ($t_c = 10.34$ h) and ends with the reaching of the flow peak, followed by a recession curve that has a double duration respect to the corrivation time. In this way, the hydrograph extends for a total of 31.02 h. Another parameter that influences the results of the hydraulic simulation is given by the roughness of the surfaces. The two-dimensional hydraulic model FLO 2D takes into account the roughness coefficients that must be known for each cell of the calculation domain. A Manning coefficient of 0.04 $m^{-1/3}s$ is then considered.

Similarly, the hydrological model with a return period of 30 years corresponding to the high hydraulic hazard, with a flow rate of 224.74 m^3/s, is applied.

3.2 Geomorphological Descriptors

Geomorphological descriptors represent promising tools for a rapid assessment of flood-prone areas [26, 27]. They exploit morphological features of floodplains, providing a quantitative measure for a preliminary detection of areas exposed to flood hazards. In fact, the morphology of a river basin is the basic element that allows the identification of the effects of the outflow distribution, resulting from the occurrence of meteoric events that characterize the input of the basin itself. Geomorphic descriptors analyzed in this document were obtained from a DTM compatible with the version of the basic FLO-2D open-source software, having 10 * 10 m spatial resolution. It should be remarked that the characteristics of the DTM could significantly affect descriptors performances.

3.2.1 Synthetic and Composite Descriptors

Consistently with their nature, geomorphological descriptors can be subdivided into two main categories:

Synthetic Descriptors

- upslope contributing area, A_s $[m^2]$;
- elevation to the nearest stream, H [m];
- distance from the nearest stream, D [m];
- surface curvature, $\nabla^2 H$ [-];
- local slope, S [-].

Composite Descriptors

- modified topographic index, TI_m:

$$TI_m = \ln\left[\frac{A_d^n}{\tan(\beta)}\right] \tag{1}$$

A_d is the drainage area per unit of length, $\tan(\beta)$ is the local gradient and n is a dimensionless parameter with a value less than 1.
- downslope index, DW_i:

$$DW_i = \tan(\alpha_d) = \frac{d}{L_d} \tag{2}$$

the index aims to describe the length (L [m]) of the flow path which deprives the particle of water a given amount of potential energy d [m]. We imposed $d = 5$ m.
- $\ln\left[\frac{h_l}{H}\right]$: this index relates, in each point, the water depth h with the synthetic descriptor H, where h can be defined for each basin location with the following relationship:

$$h_l \cong bA_l^n \tag{3}$$

with A_l $[m^2]$ upslope contributing area at the point of interest, b a scale factor usually set equal to 10^{-2} and n a dimensionless exponent set equal to 0.3.
- Geomorphic Flood Index (GFI) $\ln\left[\frac{h_r}{H}\right]$: this index is different from the previous, because the upslope contributing area A_r is computed on the cell belonging to the hydrographic network hydraulically nearest to the considered one.
- $\frac{[h_r - H]}{D}$: an evolution of the last index, with the introducing D into the denominator.

For a detailed overview of these indices, see [28].

3.2.2   Calibration Procedure

Calibration procedure is an important part in the implementation of geomorphic descriptors for flood-prone areas detection. In this process, each of the investigated indexes was scaled in the range [−1; 1]; then a moving threshold was applied into this interval, generating binary maps to be compared with the flooded reference map. In this respect, each cell of the descriptor matrix can be classified as True Positive (TP), False Positive (FP), True Negative (TN) and False Negative (FN). For each threshold, the following measures are computed:

True Positive Rate

$$r_{tp} = \frac{TP}{TP + FN} \tag{4}$$

False Positive Rate

$$r_{fp} = \frac{FP}{FP + TN} \tag{5}$$

All of these computed values allow to build a function able to provide a measure of error, the *objective function*:

$$OB = r_{fp} + \left(1 - r_{tp}\right) \tag{6}$$

Threshold corresponding to the minimum value of this function provides the best performing map for the analyzed descriptor.

True positive and false positive rates can be exploited for implementing another performances indicator based on the Receiver Operating Curves (ROC) [29]. In this approach, false positive rate is plotted against the true positive rate, and Area Under Curves (AUC) can be computed from this line and used as metric (closer to 1 is AUC, better is the index fit).

4   Results and Discussion

The application of the hydrologic-hydraulic model and geomorphological descriptors led to comparable results. In this paragraph a more specific discussion about the two implemented methodologies is reported.

4.1   Hydrologic-Hydraulic Model Results

In the FLO-2D two-dimensional model, the MAPPER module was used to extract the model outcomes regarding the flooded areas in terms of maximum flow depth.

In Figs. 2a and b the flooded areas corresponding to return periods of 200 (medium hazard) and 30 (high hazard) years are respectively shown:

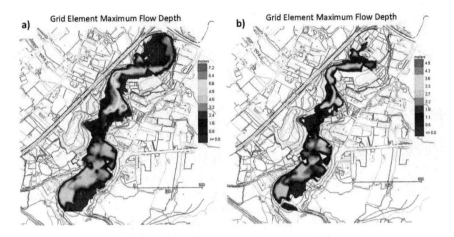

Fig. 2. Flooded areas obtained from FLO-2D simulation. Return periods are 200 (a) and 30 (b) years

It can be seen that the flooding obtained by propagation, affects the channel near the existing structures, probably due to the narrowing of the section, which determines a backwater condition, with the consequent raising of the free surface.

4.2 Results of Geomorphological Descriptors

Results obtained by applying the above-mentioned geomorphological descriptors are showed in terms of flood-prone areas and indices performances. For the sake of clarity, only floodable areas with a return period of 30 years are showed in Fig. 3, while ROC curves and calibration outputs are reported for the two investigated flood events. As it emerges from the comparison between the results of the two applied methodologies, effects of the urbanization in the investigated area with respect to flood extension led us to consider appropriate to redefine the study area. For the same reason, an excess of flooded area using the FLO-2D model was depicted (Fig. 3b).

The performances of geomorphic descriptors considering return periods of 30 and 200 years are showed below in Tables 2 and 3 respectively. The respective ROC curves are instead plotted in figures from Figs. 4, 5, 6 and 7.

Results show that better performances were obtained with the indices H, $\ln(h_r/H)$ and $\ln(h_l/H)$, highlighting the key role of the H index. This is perfectly coherent with the particular nature of lame, generally characterized by a regular rectangular section.

Furthermore, H provided the best results both in terms of true positive and false positive rate, detecting excellent abilities in interpreting flood phenomenology in this type of karst ephemeral streams. Outputs of this analysis are in accordance with the findings of other studies on similar areas [2, 4], confirming the goodness of fit of the index H when applicated to lame.

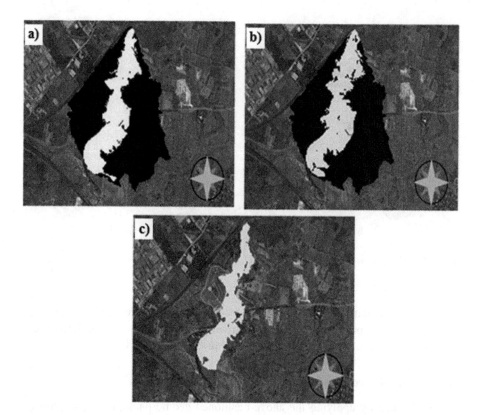

Fig. 3. a) Flood inundation identified by the descriptor H; **b)** Flood inundation identified by the descriptor $\ln\left(\frac{h_R}{H}\right)$; **c)** Flooded area obtained by hydraulic-hydrologic simulation (30 years).

Table 2. Performances of geomorphic descriptors for a return period of 30 years

	τ	r_{fp}	r_{tp}	min(ob)	AUC
As	−0.999	0.247	0.401	0.846	0.583
C	0.231	0.587	0.739	0.848	0.574
S	−0.771	0.721	0.902	0.819	0.614
D	−0.588	0.198	0.929	0.269	0.939
H	−0.801	0.076	0.968	0.108	0.986
TI_m	−0.576	0.671	0.864	0.807	0.635
DW_i	−0.917	0.083	0.708	0.375	0.849
H/D	−0.932	0.045	0.634	0.410	0.821
$\ln(h_r/H)$	−0.551	0.117	0.914	0.203	0.950
$\ln(h_l/H)$	−0.591	0.122	0.924	0.198	0.972
$(h_r - H)/D$	0.681	0.050	0.723	0.327	0.865
$(h_r - H)/DW_i$	−0.975	0.224	0.960	0.264	0.957

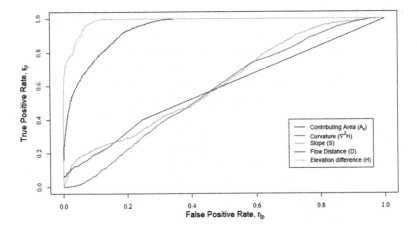

Fig. 4. ROC curves- single features (T = 30 years)

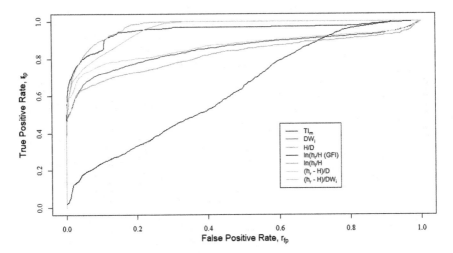

Fig. 5. ROC curves –composite indices (T = 30 years)

Table 3. Performances of geomorphic descriptors for a return period of 200 years

	τ	r_{fp}	r_{tp}	min(ob)	AUC
A_s	−0.999	0.249	0.365	0.885	0.564
C	0.231	0.592	0.698	0.893	0.565
S	−0.715	0.778	0.908	0.871	0.556
D	−0.588	0.148	0.919	0.229	0.952
H	−0.752	0.054	0.986	0.069	0.992
TI_m	−0.648	0.778	0.921	0.857	0.574
DW_i	−0.917	0.074	0.616	0.458	0.807
H/D	−0.932	0.038	0.540	0.498	0.774
$\ln(h_r/H)$	−0.579	0.099	0.912	0.187	0.951
$\ln(h_l/H)$	−0.639	0.141	0.961	0.180	0.970
$(h_r - H)/D$	0.681	0.039	0.626	0.413	0.821
$(h_r - H)/DW_i$	−0.975	0.173	0.952	0.222	0.963

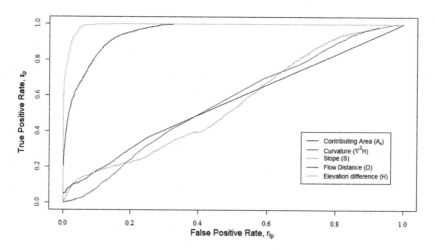

Fig. 6. ROC curves – single features (T = 200 years)

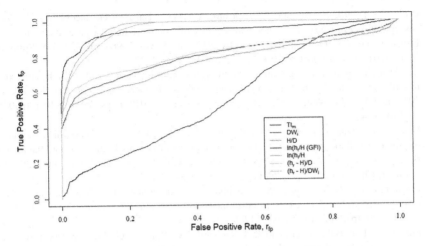

Fig. 7. ROC curves – composite indices (T = 200 years)

5 Conclusions

In this paper, two methodologies were compared for the identification of flooded areas, each one characterized by a different level of complexity and amount of *a priori* information. In the first case, a hydrological-hydraulic model was implemented using the FLO-2D software, while the second methodology is based on the use of geomorphological descriptors and requires, for calibration, a binary flooded area, obtained with numerical simulation. At the base of both approaches the DTM is required as the fundamental element, the dimension of which strongly influences the accuracy of results. For this reason, the correspondence in terms of resolution (i.e. cell size) in both models was necessary. Even if the two compared are conceptually different, they give us comparable outputs. Moreover, the obtained floodable areas are consistent with those proposed by the Southern Apennines Hydrographic District, demonstrating that, although in one case a fast method was used, the results are compatible with each other.

The outcomes of this paper provide a contribution in the field of flood-prone area delineation, highlighting that the use of geomorphic methods, at the expense of their conceptual simplicity, could give relevant information about the susceptibility of areas to flooding.

In this way, the implementation of this kind of methodologies could lead to an improvement in the updating of flood risk maps, in order to give new tools to practitioners and public authorities for a more aware management of risk.

References

1. Di Baldassarre, G., et al.: Debates - perspectives on socio-hydrology: capturing feedbacks between physical and social processes. Water Resour. Res. (2015). https://doi.org/10.1002/2014WR016416

2. Gioia, A., Totaro, V., Bonelli, R., Esposito, A.A.M.G., Balacco, G., Iacobellis, V.: Flood susceptibility evaluation on ephemeral streams of Southern Italy: a case study of Lama Balice. In: Gervasi, O., et al. (eds.) ICCSA 2018. LNCS, vol. 10964, pp. 334–348. Springer, Cham (2018). https://doi.org/10.1007/978-3-319-95174-4_27

3. Iacobellis, V., et al.: Investigation of a flood event occurred on Lama Balice, in the context of hazard map evaluation in karstic-ephemeral streams. In: Gervasi, O., et al. (eds.) ICCSA 2018. LNCS, vol. 10964, pp. 317–333. Springer, Cham (2018). https://doi.org/10.1007/978-3-319-95174-4_26

4. Balacco, G., Totaro, V., Gioia, A., Piccinni, A.F.: Evaluation of geomorphic descriptors thresholds for flood prone areas detection on ephemeral streams in the metropolitan area of Bari (Italy). In: Misra, S., et al. (eds.) ICCSA 2019. LNCS, vol. 11622, pp. 239–254. Springer, Cham (2019). https://doi.org/10.1007/978-3-030-24305-0_19

5. Apollonio, C., Delle Rose, M., Fidelibus, C., Orlanducci, L., Spasiano, D.: Water management problems in a karst flood-prone endorheic basin. Environ. Earth Sci. **77**(19), 1–15 (2018). https://doi.org/10.1007/s12665-018-7866-8

6. Fidelibus, M.D., Balacco, G., Gioia, A., Iacobellis, V., Spilotro, G.: Mass transport triggered by heavy rainfall: the role of endorheic basins and epikarst in a regional karst aquifer. Hydrol. Process. (2017). https://doi.org/10.1002/hyp.11037

7. Balacco, G.: The interrill erosion for a sandy loam soil. Int. J. Sediment Res. (2013). https://doi.org/10.1016/S1001-6279(13)60043-8

8. Apollonio, C., Balacco, G., Gioia, A., Iacobellis, V., Piccinni, A.F.: Flood hazard assessment of the Fortore River downstream the Occhito Dam, in Southern Italy. In: Gervasi, O., et al. (eds.) ICCSA 2017. LNCS, vol. 10405, pp. 201–216. Springer, Cham (2017). https://doi.org/10.1007/978-3-319-62395-5_15

9. Gioia, A., Manfreda, S., Iacobellis, V., Fiorentino, M.: Performance of a theoretical model for the description of water balance and runoff dynamics in Southern Italy. J. Hydrol. Eng. (2014). https://doi.org/10.1061/(ASCE)HE.1943-5584.0000879

10. Iacobellis, V., Fiorentino, M., Gioia, A., Manfreda, S.: Best fit and selection of theoretical flood frequency distributions based on different runoff generation mechanisms. Water (Switzerland) (2010). https://doi.org/10.3390/w2020239

11. Gioia, A.: Reservoir routing on double-peak design flood. Water (Switzerland) (2016). https://doi.org/10.3390/w8120553

12. Tarantino, E., Novelli, A., Laterza, M., Gioia, A.: Testing high spatial resolution WorldView-2 imagery for retrieving the leaf area index. In: Third International Conference on Remote Sensing and Geoinformation of the Environment (RSCy 2015) (2015). https://doi.org/10.1117/12.2192561

13. Tarantino, E.: Monitoring spatial and temporal distribution of sea surface temperature with TIR sensor data. Eur. J. Remote Sens. (2012). https://doi.org/10.5721/ItJRS20124418

14. Aquilino, M., Novelli, A., Tarantino, E., Iacobellis, V., Gentile, F.: Evaluating the potential of GeoEye data in retrieving LAI at watershed scale. In: Remote Sensing for Agriculture, Ecosystems, and Hydrology XVI (2014). https://doi.org/10.1117/12.2067185

15. Mattia, F., et al.: Time series of COSMO-SkyMed data for landcover classification and surface parameter retrieval over agricultural sites. In: International Geoscience and Remote Sensing Symposium (IGARSS) (2012). https://doi.org/10.1109/IGARSS.2012.6352738

16. Balenzano, A., et al.: A ground network for SAR-derived soil moisture product calibration, validation and exploitation in Southern Italy. In: International Geoscience and Remote Sensing Symposium (IGARSS) (2014). https://doi.org/10.1109/IGARSS.2014.6947206

17. Figorito, B., Tarantino, E., Balacco, G., Fratino, U.: An object-based method for mapping ephemeral river areas from WorldView-2 satellite data. In: Remote Sensing for Agriculture, Ecosystems, and Hydrology XIV (2012). https://doi.org/10.1117/12.974689

18. Novelli, A., Tarantino, E., Caradonna, G., Apollonio, C., Balacco, G., Piccinni, F.: Improving the ANN classification accuracy of landsat data through spectral indices and linear transformations (PCA and TCT) aimed at LU/LC monitoring of a river basin. In: Gervasi, O., et al. (eds.) ICCSA 2016. LNCS, vol. 9787, pp. 420–432. Springer, Cham (2016). https://doi.org/10.1007/978-3-319-42108-7_32

19. Totaro, V., Gioia, A., Novelli, A., Caradonna, G.: The use of geomorphological descriptors and landsat-8 spectral indices data for flood areas evaluation: a case study of Lato River Basin. In: Gervasi, O., et al. (eds.) ICCSA 2017. LNCS, vol. 10407, pp. 30–44. Springer, Cham (2017). https://doi.org/10.1007/978-3-319-62401-3_3

20. Totaro, V., Peschechera, G., Gioia, A., Iacobellis, V., Fratino, U.: Comparison of satellite and geomorphic indices for flooded areas detection in a Mediterranean River Basin. In: Misra, S., et al. (eds.) ICCSA 2019. LNCS, vol. 11622, pp. 173–185. Springer, Cham (2019). https://doi.org/10.1007/978-3-030-24305-0_14

21. Annis, A., et al.: UAV-DEMs for small-scale flood hazard mapping. Water (2020). https://doi.org/10.3390/w12061717

22. Pellicani, R., et al.: UAV and airborne LiDAR data for interpreting kinematic evolution of landslide movements: the case study of the montescaglioso landslide (Southern Italy). Geosci. (2019). https://doi.org/10.3390/geosciences9060248

23. Sangiorgio, V., Uva, G., Fatiguso, F., Adam, J.M.: A new index to evaluate exposure and potential damage to RC building structures incoastal areas. Eng. Fail. Anal. (2019). https://doi.org/10.1016/j.engfailanal.2019.02.052

24. Sangiorgio, V., Pantoja, J.C., Varum, H., Uva, G., Fatiguso, F.: Structural degradation assessment of RC buildings: calibration and comparison of semeiotic-based methodology for decision support system. J. Perform. Constr. Facil. (2019). https://doi.org/10.1061/(ASCE)CF.1943-5509.0001249

25. Sangiorgio, V., Uva, G., Adam, J.M.: Integrated seismic vulnerability assessment of historical masonry churches including architectural and artistic assets based on macro-element approach. Int. J. Archit. Herit. (2020). https://doi.org/10.1080/15583058.2019.1709916

26. Manfreda, S., et al.: Investigation on the use of geomorphic approaches for the delineation of flood prone areas. J. Hydrol. (2014). https://doi.org/10.1016/j.jhydrol.2014.06.009

27. Samela, C., Troy, T.J., Manfreda, S.: Geomorphic classifiers for flood-prone areas delineation for data-scarce environments. Adv. Water Resour. (2017). https://doi.org/10.1016/j.advwatres.2017.01.007

28. Manfreda, S., et al.: Flood-prone areas assessment using linear binary classifiers based on flood maps obtained from 1D and 2D hydraulic models. Nat. Hazards **79**(2), 735–754 (2015). https://doi.org/10.1007/s11069-015-1869-5

29. Fawcett, T.: An introduction to ROC analysis. Pattern Recogn. Lett. **27**, 861–874 (2006). https://doi.org/10.1016/j.patrec.2005.10.010

Combined Photogrammetric and Laser Scanning Survey to Support Fluvial Sediment Transport Analyses

Luigi Barazzetti[1(✉)], Riccardo Valente[1], Fabio Roncoroni[2],
Mattia Previtali[1], and Marco Scaioni[1]

[1] ABC Department, Politecnico di Milano, via Ponzio 31, 20133 Milan, Italy
{luigi.barazzetti,riccardo.valente,mattia.previtali,
marco.scaioni}@polimi.it
[2] Polo territoriale di Lecco, Politecnico di Milano,
via G. Previati 1/c, 23900 Lecco, Italy
fabio.roncoroni@polimi.it

Abstract. This paper presents the contribution of digital surveying techniques for the estimation of fluvial sediment transport. The aim is to create predictive models able to minimize or reduce the hydrogeological hazard, especially before or during critical meteorological events. The case study is the Caldone stream, a watercourse located in the municipality of Lecco (Italy). Structure-from-Motion photogrammetry and terrestrial laser scanning techniques were used to collect metric data about the morphology of the riverbed. Data acquisition was carried out to create a digital model of visible and submerged parts of the riverbed. Then, a second area with a sedimentation pool was selected to monitor the variation of the depth induced by progressive accumulation of sediments. As the pool is constantly covered by water, a low-cost bathymetric drone was used coupling the measured depth values with total station measurements to track the drone. Finally, the paper describes the implementation of an on-line data delivery platform able to facilitate retrieval of heterogeneous geospatial data, which are used in the developed numerical model for sediment transport. This service aims at providing simplified access to specific map layers without requiring knowledge about data formats and reference systems.

Keywords: Geosciences · Hydrogeology · River monitoring · Remote sensing · Structure-from-Motion · Terrestrial laser scanning

1 Introduction

1.1 General Project Framework

The activities described in this paper have been carried out within "SMART-SED: Sustainable Management of sediment transpoRT in responSE to climate change conDitions", an interdisciplinary research project that involved different research groups from Politecnico di Milano, Italy (Applied Geology, Surveying, Geophysics, Hydraulic

© Springer Nature Switzerland AG 2020
O. Gervasi et al. (Eds.): ICCSA 2020, LNCS 12252, pp. 620–633, 2020.
https://doi.org/10.1007/978-3-030-58811-3_45

engineering, Mathematics, Hydrology) and the Municipality of Lecco, a city located in northern Italy. Fondazione Cariplo funded the project.

The main aim of SMART-SED project was to address severe issues and hazards related to critical events due to hydrogeological instability, which is a major concern for a large part of the Italian territory. Indeed, some of the most critical events are often localized in mountain or hilly areas, acting as an effective threat for local populations, economical activities, and the built environment.

The project objective is mainly related to the transportation of solid sediment by rivers and streams. During acute meteorological events, the overall amount of solid sediment moved by the water flow can reach critical limits: this phenomenon dramatically increases its effects in areas characterized by hydrogeological instability.

The additional challenges introduced by climate change require urgent answers and interventions. For instance, rainfalls bring higher quantities of water into the hydrogeological basins in short periods, resulting in increased hydraulic energy able to displace high volumes of sediments.

The SMART-SED project aims at creating a feasible tool for erosion prediction within a certain hydrogeological basin. The hydraulic processes of the watercourses are analyzed and compared with data belonging to regional and national databases. Here, the morphology of the involved riverbed is one of the main data sources to be included within the final mathematical model for predictions of future hazardous events.

Nowadays, different Geomatics instruments and techniques can be used to reconstruct the geometry of rivers and streams [7, 10, 27]. Global Navigation Satellite Systems (GNSS [4]), total stations (TS) [15, 16, 19], and terrestrial laser scanning (TLS) [17, 20, 25, 26, 28] measurements are common solutions able to create accurate geometric models. Remote sensing [29] is also one of the most common tools, especially in combination with echo sounding and photogrammetry [6, 11]. The application of photogrammetry was already proposed in early research work, such as [5]. Recently some effective solutions based on digital Structure-from-Motion/photogrammetry [31, 32] were presented [9, 24]. Data from UAVs [23] were used in [12]. Echo-sounding methods were also used by several authors [7, 10].

At a different scale, airborne bathymetric laser scanners [8, 13] and Light Detection and Ranging (LiDAR) technology were also tested [14, 18, 30]. An updated review of remote sensing methods applied to watercourse surveying is presented in [29].

1.2   The Local Framework of the Project

The case study of the project is the Caldone stream in Lecco (Fig. 1). Lecco is a town in northern Italy that directly fronts onto the Lario lake. It is included within the Prealpine area, close to the first relieves belonging to the Prealps mountain range. The presence of the lake, its main emissary (the Adda river), and many minor streams made the Caldone water body an ideal case study for the analysis required in the project.

The selected observation period lasted two years. Caldone is a watercourse that springs from different minor river channels mount and ends up into the Lario lake. It is one of the three main watercourses crossing the town of Lecco along with Gerenzone and Bione. The first portion of the riverbed is mostly located in a natural environment, while the last section flows closer to the urbanized area and passes through it.

Here, the stream was highly exploited during the industrialization phases of this area during the 19th–20th Centuries to provide water energy to several mills and industries that were built along its course. The original natural banks in this area were completely transformed and substituted by artificial barriers.

During the 60s and 70s of the 20th Century, the final part of the stream was completely covered. These interventions dramatically modified the stream. In the 19th century, the deviation of the water has been already proposed for urban development of the town, reducing the risk related to sediments. The covering has increased the issues related to critical meteorological events because the water is forced into an underground culvert; as a direct consequence, floods of the Caldone are not rare events.

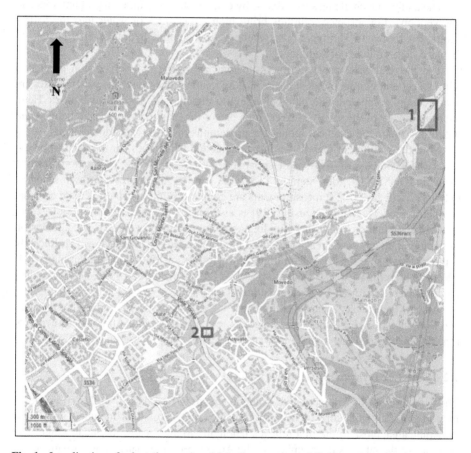

Fig. 1. Localization of selected areas 1 and 2 (red rectangles) of Caldone stream in the territory of the town of Lecco, Italy. (Color figure online)

2 Surveying Activity

2.1 Overview

The surveying activity was focused on the data acquisition of two data sets along the Caldone stream riverbed within the administrative region of the Municipality of Lecco, Italy (see Fig. 1). These areas (see Fig. 2) feature different characteristics:

- Area 1 is close to the mountain and within a quasi-natural environment included in the Bonacina district; and
- Area 2 is close to downtown, where a sedimentation pool and a weir helps to control the water flow.

Fig. 2. Views of both selected areas reported in Fig. 1: Area 1 is located in a non-urbanized environment (a); Area 2 is a sedimentation pool (b).

The main goal of the investigation carried out in Area 1 was to record the morphology of the stream during a period of shallow water. The acquired data will be successively processed and imported into the mathematic model used for erosion prediction developed in the project.

The same area had already been used for previous tests aimed to analyze different aspects of sediment transport. Several pebbles in this section of the riverbed were equipped with an RFID transponder and painted to allow for a quick recovery. The position and movements of pebbles were recorded after every rain event to assess the displacement of sediments. At the same time, selected areas within the riverbed were painted in red: the amount of displaced sediment after each rainfall was performed by comparing multitemporal information [2, 3, 21].

A section 120 m long was surveyed with an approach based on multiple geodetic instruments and techniques. Four permanent benchmarks were positioned and measured in the stream proximity with RTK-GNSS instruments to establish a reference system based on the WGS84-UTM 32N (ETRF2000) datum. These benchmarks will allow all subsequent measurements to be geo-referenced in the mapping grid. To transform the ellipsoidal elevation obtained from GNSS measurements, the mean geoid undulation in the area was derived from the national geoid model distributed by the IGMI (Istituto Geografico Militare Italiano/Italian Military Geographic Institute).

The main surveying activity was carried out with a terrestrial laser scanner (TLS) Faro Focus HDR 130 (Fig. 3). TLS instrument can measure several million points, recording not only the morphology of the stream but also the close surroundings with very high detail. 21 scans were acquired on the field, some of which directly inside the riverbed. To register single scans, checkerboard and sphere targets were also located along the riverbed. Checkerboard targets were previously measured with a total station georeferenced using GNSS benchmarks. An open traverse was established to cover the entire length of the considered section of the stream. The scans were successively registered with a precision of about ±4 mm, resulting in a single georeferenced point cloud.

Several total station stand-points were also established in the same area, from which a large number of points were measured inside the riverbed, both on dry and wet sections (475 points in submerged parts). The location of these measurements was scattered according to a random acquisition sequence, depending also on the depth of the water level. A user manually placed a pole inside the river, which is sufficiently shallow to allow operators to enter directly in the water (Fig. 3a).

The aim was to gather data sufficient to recreate a digital model of the riverbed also in those parts covered by water. Laser scanning technology cannot provide information on those areas unless a bathymetric instrument is adopted [33]. Although quite slow, manual measurements taken with the total station (Fig. 3b) were the only solution to measure the riverbed permanently covered by water. A series of measurements located along sequences of stripes perpendicular to the river flow was taken to obtain multiple sections of the bottom of the stream.

Finally, a UAV flight (Fig. 3c) has been also planned throughout the stream to integrate TLS point clouds within a photogrammetric block. A series of ground control points (GCPs) measured with both a total station and an RTK-GNSS were also measured along the course of the stream.

The flight was carried out at a fixed height of 50 m, due to the presence of trees all over the area. A total number of 115 images were acquired using a DJI Spark drone, equipped with an on-board 1280 × 960 pixel camera. Drone and laser scanning surveys were simultaneously executed on a working day.

Figure 3 depicts the point cloud obtained from drone-photogrammetry, as described in successive sections.

a   b

c

Fig. 3. Some images of 3D surveying by terrestrial laser scanning (a), total station (b), and the point cloud obtained from Structure-from-Motion photogrammetry based on UAV images (c).

2.2   Fieldwork in Area 2

Area 2 is closer to the urbanized downtown of the town of Lecco, where an artificial sedimentation pool helps to control the sediment transport. In this case, the natural course of the stream is "blocked" by a deep pool of water approximately 45 m long and 15 m wide, which is cyclically filled up by solid sediments. The aim was to estimate the volume of submerged sediments that are constantly covered by water and to monitor it over a given period to understand the process.

This task requested a different approach because the bottom of the pool was never visible. Thus, the riverbed can not be reached, even with the help of extendable poles.

Three GNSS benchmarks were measured to establish a reference system as already described in the previous sections. A floating device specifically designed for this purpose was equipped with a commercial depth sensor that could be remotely controlled. The sedimentation pool was divided into different stripes corresponding to the different areas to be covered by the sensor, moving the floating device manually along this path.

To correlate depth measurements and spatial positioning of the sensor, a total station (TS) was set up in the middle of the riverbed in correspondence of one of GNSS benchmarks. A 360° topographic reflector was fixed on the top of the floating device, to guarantee full and constant visibility from any direction between the device and the TS during measurement operations. A fully automated approach was used, i.e., automatic detection of the prism, followed by automatic tracking and automatic measuring at a rate of one second. Such a measuring rate was enough to assure redundant data that could be successively decimated. An overall number of more than 2,500 points was measured with this method (Fig. 4).

a   b

Fig. 4. Spatial distribution (a) of measured points on the riverbed in Area 2 (b): the lower part corresponds to the sedimentation pool. Red lines show hydraulic sections. (Color figure online)

Measurements by the floating device were integrated with a series of standard hydraulic sections as previously presented. This approach was applied in the sector where the riverbed can be reached with an extendable pole. An overall number of 8 hydraulic sections was recorded in addition to other single measurements of the bottom of the riverbed.

TLS was also used to record the surrounding environment and the banks; point clouds were then registered together using checkerboard targets previously measured with the TS.

3 Data Processing

3.1 Area 1

One of the aims was to generate a digital elevation model (DEM) of the selected part of the riverbed. To reach this goal, data from TLS scans were used for the area not covered by water. The UAV images were processed using Agisoft Metashape® (ver. 1.4.0) photogrammetric software, obtaining a point cloud to be integrated with laser scanning data. GCPs were also measured with a GNSS receiver to define the reference system of the project.

Besides, an orthophoto of the area covered by the UAV flight was generated. The ground sampling distance of the image was set to 15 mm, which is much higher than the resolution of the available cartographic data in the same area.

Points measured with TS instrument were used to reconstruct the profile of the submerged riverbed, whereas TLS and image-based points were used for areas above the water level instead. In the case of laser scanning measurements, a manual selection was necessary to decimate the final point cloud substantially. A subset of points was extracted to guarantee a uniform distribution in space, which is for DEM generation through interpolation. Points were selected and picked using Faro Scene® (ver. 2019.0.1.1653) software, obtaining text files of 3D coordinates that could be merged to those coordinates from TS measurements. An example showing the homogenous distribution of the selected points is shown in the left part of Fig. 5.

The set of 3D coordinates were then processed using Surfer® (ver. 14), a software for DEM generation from scattered data. Main challenges were found in the complex and irregular morphology of the riverbed, mostly due to the presence of several medium-size boulders in it, causing numerous and sudden changes in elevation compared to the relatively regular bottom of the stream made up of small pebbles.

A DEM able to describe the morphology of the stream without many details that could prevent its use within the final hydrogeological model was the main priority.

During the creation of DEM, the nearest neighborhood method was selected as the more appropriate interpolation. Indeed, other interpolation methods provided a smoothing effect of the riverbed, while we planned to preserve the typical roughness of the topographic surface.

The DEM was also superimposed to the orthoimage to check the correct georeferencing and to provide a graphic output (Fig. 5 on the right side).

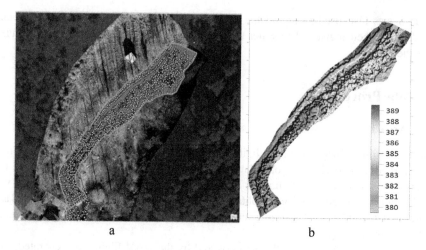

a   b

Fig. 5. Reconstruction of a digital elevation model (DEM) of Area 1: spatial distribution of points selected from TLS, drone-photogrammetry, and TS for DEM generation (a); and the final DEM (b).

3.2   Area 2

TS measurements georeferenced using GNSS points are the data used in area 2. A successive decimation and selection of data were necessary: the position of the floating device carrying the depth sensor had been measured every second, resulting in thousands of points.

The calculation of the depth value at a certain location of the sedimentation pool requires both data coming from the bathymetric sensor and the spatial coordinates measured with the TS. This approach provided the average profile of the bottom at a certain time; if repeated constantly, this approach will allow monitoring the amount of solid sediment transported by the stream at different epochs.

4   Data Sharing Platform

The availability of cartographic data is a fundamental aspect of Geosciences. Although many different institutions, such as geographic and geological institutes, public administrations, collaborative communities, and web companies, make available many open data, the availability of specific reference data for fluvial sediment transport analysis is still limited. For this reason, the authors decided to develop a novel platform to share the main data source for sediment transport evaluation in the case of the Caldone stream. The platform can be intended as a data-hub where two sets of information can be downloaded:

- novel data produced in the framework of the project; and
- existing data sets (especially open-source data) that can be retrieved from various repositories. In such a case, data harmonization procedures may be necessary to generate uniform products in terms of formats and reference systems.

In particular, the developed platform shares the DTM of a 120 m long portion of the Caldone stream, obtained by combining laser scanning and UAV data, and the orthophoto derived from UAV photogrammetry.

Other existing data can be added in the future, such as cartographic layers (both vector and raster formats) or land use data sets that need to be recovered from various services.

The developed platform represents a unique data hub where the data needed for sediment transport analysis can be retrieved, overcoming limitations related to uneven formats and reference systems. This concept could be then extended to other areas to facilitate the creation of a cartographic repository for fluvial sediment transport analysis.

Two key elements when dealing with data repository and creation of data-sharing platforms are as follow:

- user-friendly data search and retrieval; and
- data interoperability.

The implemented online data delivery platform is based on the software GET-IT (http://www.get-it.it/), which is particularly suitable for the deployment of Spatial Data Infrastructures (SDI) (see [1, 23] for more details). In particular, the platform allows for visualization, sharing, and management of different heterogeneous data types of geographic data: digital images, vector data, processed maps, data acquired by sensors (observations), or text documents.

Besides, different data formats are supported. For example, raster products can be delivered as TIFF, NetCDF, EUMETSAT archive, etc. The supported front-end for data-source access includes not only the initial data format but also OGC standard services (e.g., WMS, WFS, WCS), providing standardized access to the published data sets.

One of the most important characteristics of the platform is the possibility to act as a working environment (EDI) for the guided creation of metadata, improving search and discovery of the data and its reuse. Indeed, it is possible to create metadata compliant with the INSPIRE directive through a guided procedure. This is a fundamental aspect of data retrieval since it allows one to link the developed infrastructure to existing brokering services [22, 23].

The availability of a semantic broker automatically looks for synonyms and provides multi-language support. In this way, an automatic search can be performed in a specific language, and the broker allows to retrieve results published in a different language. For instance, after inserting the Italian word "sedimenti", the broker allows one to identify results published in another language, like the keyword "sediments" in English. Search expansion is carried out by using a set of aligned semantic instruments, which are typically controlled vocabularies, thesauri, gazetteers, and ontologies.

Figure 6 shows an example of an automatic search for the word "Caldone". The idea is to extend (in future work) the approach developed for the Caldone stream to other areas in which such data are available through various data sources.

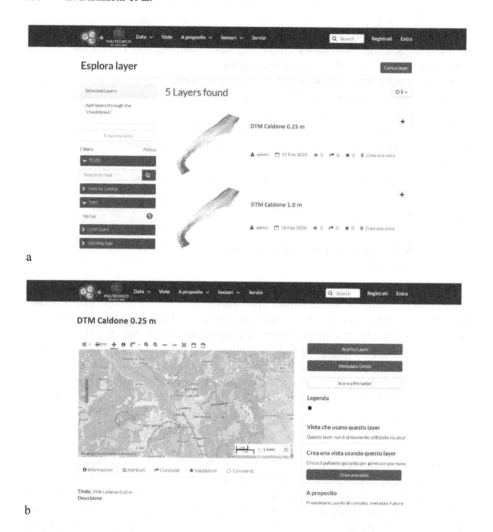

Fig. 6. The graphic interface of the developed fluvial sediment data-sharing platform: (a) results for the query with the keyword "Caldone" and (b) metadata page for the product "DTM Caldone 0.25 m")

5   Conclusions

This paper presented the work aimed at generating 3D metric products in the framework of the estimation of solid sediments in mountain rivers and streams. The knowledge of riverbed geometry is a fundamental requirement for both basic and advanced analyses.

Structure-from-Motion photogrammetry and terrestrial laser scanning were used to capture the complex and irregular geometry of a river. The integration of total station measurements was needed to survey those parts permanently covered by water (e.g., the riverbed), where the previous solutions were not able to provide any information.

The integration of data acquired with several instruments allowed one to overcome the limitations of single techniques, obtaining several final deliverables based on orthoimages, point clouds, and digital elevation models.

For what concerns the surveying of the first area, data gathered during on-field measurements were successfully used to produce numeric outputs. About the second area, the method was able to determine the depth of the sedimentation pool and it will be repeated at different epochs to understand the accumulation of materials inside the pool.

A surveying approach based on the combination of different methods (TS, TLS, UAV, and bathymetric sensor) was necessary to produce accurate metric data that will be used for the mitigation of hydrogeological hazards. Finally, the development of a data-sharing platform allowed us to publish the obtained results as Open Data allowing an easy search and discovery of data for further analysis on this topic. The inclusion of geospatial data in other sites can extend the proposed approach to national and international level, facilitating the work of operators involved in numerical simulation for hydrogeological risk assessment and mitigation.

Acknowledgments. This work has been financed by Fondazione Cariplo in the framework of the "SMART-SED project: Sustainable MAnagement of sediment transpoRT in responSE to climate change conditions," grant no. 2017–0722. The authors want to thank Laura Longoni and Davide Brambilla (Politecnico di Milano, Dept. of Environmental and Civil Eng.) for the coordination during the project and the development of the floating device used in the sedimentation pool. We want to thank you also to Valentina Conca and Claudio Sironi for their help during the on-site survey carried out for their thesis.

References

1. Bigagli, L., Santoro, M., Mazzetti, P., Nativi, S.: Architecture of a process broker for interoperable geospatial modeling on the web. ISPRS J. Geogr. Inf. **4**(2), 647–660 (2015)
2. Brambilla, D., Ivanov, V.I., Longoni, L., Papini, M.: Morphological variations in mountain streams as proxy for sediment transport: a case study. In: 19th International Multidisciplinary Scientific GeoConference SGEM 2019, pp. 411–418 (2019). https://doi.org/10.5593/sgem2019/3.1/s12.053
3. Brambilla, D., Papini, M., Longoni, L.: Temporal and spatial variability of sediment transport in a mountain river: a preliminar investigation of the Caldone River, Italy. Geosciences **8**(5), 163 (2018). https://doi.org/10.3390/geosciences8050163
4. Brasington, J., Rumsby, B.T., McVey, R.A.: Monitoring and modelling morphological change in a braided gravel-bed river using high resolution GPS-based survey. Earth Surf. Process. Landf. **25**, 973–990 (2000). https://doi.org/10.1002/1096-9837(200008)25:9%3c973:AID-ESP111%3e3.0.CO;2-Y
5. Brewer, R.K.: Project planning and field support for NOS photobathymetry. Int. Hydrogr. Rev. **56**(2), 55–66 (1979)
6. Dietrich, J.T.: Bathymetric structure-from-motion: extracting shallow stream bathymetry from multi-view stereo photogrammetry. Earth Surf. Proc. Landf. **42**(2), 355–364 (2017). https://doi.org/10.1002/esp.4060

7. Guerrero, M., Lamberti, A.: Flow field and morphology mapping using ADCP and multibeam techniques: survey in the Po River. J. Hydraul. Eng. **137**, 1576–1587 (2011). https://doi.org/10.1061/(ASCE)HY.1943-7900.0000464

8. Hillade, R.C., Raff, D.: Assessing the ability of airborne LiDAR to map river bathymetry. Earth Surf. Process. Landf. **33**, 773–783 (2008)

9. Javernick, L., Brasington, J., Caruso, B.: Modeling the topography of shallow braided rivers using Structure-from-Motion photogrammetry. Geomorphology **213**, 166–182 (2014)

10. Kasvi, E., Laamanen, L., Lotsari, E., Alho, P.: Flow patterns and morphological changes in a sandy meander bend during a flood - spatially and temporally intensive ADCP measurement approach. Water **9**, 106 (2017)

11. Kasvi, E., Salmela, J., Lotsari, E., Kumpula, T., Lane, S.N.: Comparison of remote sensing based approaches for mapping bathymetry of shallow, clear water rivers. Geomorphology **333**, 180–197 (2019). https://doi.org/10.1016/j.geomorph.2019.02.017

12. Kim, J.S., Baek, D., Seo, I.W., Shin, J.: Retrieving shallow stream bathymetry from UAV-assisted RGB imagery using a geospatial regression method. Geomorphology **341**, 102–114 (2019). https://doi.org/10.1016/j.geomorph.2019.05.016

13. Kinzel, P.J., Wrigt, C.W., Nelson, J.M., Burman, A.R.: Evaluation of an experimental LiDAR for surveying a shallow, braided, sand-bedded river. J. Hydraul. Eng. **133**, 838–842 (2007)

14. Kinzel, P.J., Legleiter, C.J., Nelson, J.M.: Mapping river bathymetry with a small footprint green LiDAR: applications and challenges. J. Am. Water Resour. Assoc. **49**, 183–204 (2013)

15. Koljonen, S., Huusko, A., Mäki-Petäys, A., Louhi, P., Muotka, T.: Assessing habitat suitability for juvenile Atlantic salmon in relation to in-stream restoration and discharge variability. Restor. Ecol. **21**, 344–352 (2012)

16. Lane, S.N., Richards, K.S., Chandler, J.H.: Developments in monitoring and modelling small-scale river bed topography. Earth Surf. Process. Landf. **19**, 349–368 (1994). https://doi.org/10.1002/esp.3290190406

17. Longoni, L., et al.: Monitoring riverbank erosion in mountain catchments using terrestrial laser scanning. Remote Sens. **8**(3), paper no. 241, 22 p. (2016). https://doi.org/10.3390/rs8030241

18. McKean, J., et al.: Remote sensing of channels and riparian zones with a narrow-beam aquatic-terrestrial LIDAR. Remote Sens. **1**(4), 1065–1096 (2009). https://doi.org/10.3390/rs1041065

19. Milne, J.A., Sear, D.A.: Modelling river channel topography using GIS. Int. J. Geogr. Inf. Sci. **11**, 499–519 (1997)

20. O'Neal, M.A., Pizzuto, J.E.: The rates and spatial patterns of annual riverbank erosion revealed through terrestrial laser-scanner surveys of the South River, Virginia. Earth Surface Process. Land. **36**(5), 695–701 (2011). https://doi.org/10.1002/esp.2098

21. Papini, M., Ivanov, V., Brambilla, D., Arosio, D., Longoni, L.: Monitoring bedload sediment transport in a pre-Alpine river: an experimental method. Rendiconti Online della Società Geologica Italiana **43**, 57–63 (2017). https://doi.org/10.3301/ROL.2017.35

22. Pavesi, F., et al.: EDI–A template-driven metadata editor for research data. J. Open Res. Soft. **4**(1), 55–66 (2016)

23. Pepe, M., Fregonese, L., Scaioni, M.: Planning airborne photogrammetry and remote-sensing missions with modern platforms and sensors. Eur. J. Remote Sens. **51**(1), 412–435 (2018). https://doi.org/10.1080/22797254.2018.1444945

24. Previtali, M., Barazzetti, L., Scaioni, M.: Accurate 3D surface measurement of mountain slopes through a fully automated imaged-based technique. Earth Sci. Inf. **7**(2), 109–122 (2014). https://doi.org/10.1007/s12145-014-0158-2

25. Resop, J., Hession, W.: Terrestrial laser scanning for monitoring streambank retreat: comparison with traditional surveying techniques. J. Hydraul. Eng. **136**(10), 794–798 (2010). https://doi.org/10.1061/(ASCE)HY.1943-7900.0000233

26. Rutzinger, M., et al.: Training in innovative technologies for close-range sensing in alpine terrain. ISPRS Ann. Photogramm. Remote Sens. Spatial Inf. Sci. **4**(2), 239–246 (2018). https://doi.org/10.5194/isprs-annals-iv-2-239-2018

27. Scaioni, M.: Remote sensing for landslide investigations: from research into practice. Remote Sens. **5**(11), 5488–5492 (2013). https://doi.org/10.3390/rs5115488

28. Starek, M.J., Mitasova, H., Wegmann, K.W., Lyons, N.: Space-time cube representation of stream bank evolution mapped by terrestrial laser scanning. IEEE Geosci. Remote Sens. Lett. **10**(6), 1369–1373 (2013). https://doi.org/10.1109/LGRS.2013.2241730

29. Tomsett, C., Leyland, J.: Remote sensing of river corridors: a review of current trends and future directions. River Res Appl. **35**, 779–803 (2019). https://doi.org/10.1002/rra.3479

30. Tonina, D., et al.: Mapping river bathymetries: evaluating topobathymetric LiDAR survey. Earth Surf. Process. Landf. **44**(2), 507–520 (2018). https://doi.org/10.1002/esp.4513

31. Westoby, M.J., Brasington, J., Glasser, N.F., Hambrey, M.J., Reynolds, J.M.: 'Structure-from-Motion' photogrammetry: a low-cost, effective tool for geoscience applications. Geomorphology **179**, 300–314 (2012)

32. Woodget, A.S., Carbonneau, P.E., Visser, F., Maddock, I.P.: Quantifying sub-merged fluvial topography using hyperspatial resolution UAS imagery and structure from motion photogrammetry. Earth Surf. Proc. Landf. **40**, 47–64 (2015)

33. Rhee, D., Kim, Y., Kang, B., Kim, D.: Applications of unmanned aerial vehicles in fluvial remote sensing: an overview of recent achievements. KSCE J. Civil Eng. 1–15 (2017). https://doi.org/10.1007/s12205-017-1862-5

Road Infrastructure Monitoring: An Experimental Geomatic Integrated System

Vincenzo Barrile[1], Antonino Fotia[1(✉)], Ernesto Bernardo[1], Giuliana Bilotta[2], and Antonino Modafferi[1]

[1] Geomatics Lab – DICEAM, Mediterranea University of Reggio Calabria, Località Feo di Vito, 89124 Reggio Calabria, Italy
antonino.fotia@unirc.it
[2] University IUAV of Venice, Santa Croce 191 Tolentini, 30135 Venice, Italy

Abstract. Road infrastructures systems are critical in many regions of Italy, counting thousands of bridges and viaducts that were built over several decades. A monitoring system is therefore necessary to monitor the health of these bridges and to indicate whether they need maintenance.

Different parameters affect the health of an infrastructure, but it would be very difficult to install a network of sensors of various kinds on each viaduct.

For this purpose, we want to finalize the use of geomatics technologies to monitor infrastructures for early warning issues and introducing automations in the data acquisition and processing phases.

This study describes an experimental sensor network system, based on long term monitoring in real-time while an adaptive neuro-fuzzy system is used to predict the deformations of GPS-bridge monitoring points.

The proposed system integrates different data (used to describe the various behaviour scenarios on the structural model), and then it reworks them through machine learning techniques, in order to train the network so that, once only the monitored parameters (displacements) have been entered as input data, it can return an alert parameter.

So, the purpose is to develop a real-time risk predictive system that can replicate various scenarios and capable to alert, in case of imminent hazards. The experimentation conducted in relation to the possibility of transmitting an alert parameter in real time (transmitted through the help of an experimental control unit) obtained by predicting the behavior of the structure using only displacement data during monitoring is particularly interesting.

Keywords: Road infrastructures · Monitoring · Models

1 Introduction

The road are the links between the cities, so the investigation of the road performance components are very important. There is system to investigate the Structural health monitoring (SHM) in short and long term. To study the safety level and the behavior of the bridge is better use long- term monitoring. Over the last 20 years, SHM is the most used technology to establish the safety condition of bridge and viaducts [1–3]. The continuously measured position data is used to estimate the status of deformation. The

© Springer Nature Switzerland AG 2020
O. Gervasi et al. (Eds.): ICCSA 2020, LNCS 12252, pp. 634–648, 2020.
https://doi.org/10.1007/978-3-030-58811-3_46

global positioning system (GPS) is widely used to measure deformation applications, also through sensor in smart structures.

Examining the movements and deformations of road infrastructures have a fundamental rule in bridge safety evaluation to know the bridges performance and to predict in the future their safety [4]. In the past, many procedures were used to predict the nonlinear GPS measurement, but, because they provide only an approximate description of movement behavior, an artificial neural networks (ANN) have been widely used to mitigate GPS error and predict the behavior of the road infrastructures [5–7].

In recent years, research has focused on identifying the response of an infrastructure as a result of damage or failure. In some research a wavelet transform of beam translation is used [8, 9] or acceleration [10] response to a moving vehicle to identify damage in a beam, while in other empirical mode decomposition to the acceleration response is applied [11, 12]. Most of these studies allow the operators to detect damage by analyzing the differences between two consecutives signals. Gonzalez and Hester investigate the damage anomaly in an acceleration response by dividing it into three components: static, dynamic and damage components, then they demonstrate and determine that the distance between the sensor and the damage is correlated to the amplitude of the anomaly [13]. He and Zhu [14] investigate the dynamic response of a supported beam as a combination of two components: the moving-frequency and the natural-frequency components;, then they use a discrete wavelet transform could localized the damage. The method is time saving and easy to implement as it utilizes single sensor measurements.

In [15], the authors apply a Moving Force Identification algorithm to the translation response and use the calculated force histories as indicators of bridge damage, this methodology is a kind of indirect approach. At the same way Li and Au [16] from multiple vehicles passes calculate the modal strain energy of the acceleration signals and localize the damage from the extracted frequencies of healthy and damaged bridges. Others use strain response to identify damage from the main beam neutral axis position's change in the position of the neutral axis of the main beams [17–20]. In [21] the authors develop a novel damage localization technique for a long suspension bridge based on stress influence lines (SILs) obtained using strain responses of a bridge to be traversing vehicles.

The aim of this research is to create a real-time risk predictive system that simulating many various scenarios on various infrastructure behaviors under investigation, it is able to provide an alert those in charge, in case of imminent hazards, through the use of the proposed system, that integrates data of a different nature (preventive used to define the various behaviour scenarios on the structural model). Then it reworks them through machine learning techniques, in order to train the network so that once inserted only the monitored parameters (displacements) as input data can return an alert parameter.

2 Materials and Methods

In this work we applied the methodology on a girder bridge with a deck in a mixed steel-concrete structure was examined in order to verify its main structural. The selected bridge elements (in order to verify through the use of this predictive system that the bridge does not enter into alert and its collapse occurs). The bridge under inspection is located in the area between Palmi and Gioia Tauro (South Italy); it has an overall length of 520 m (Fig. 1).

Fig. 1. Case study: road bridge in Reggio Calabria (between Palmi and Gioia Tauro) South Italy

A UAV survey was carried out in order to identify the geometric features of the structure. For the aerial photogrammetric survey, a UAV (or APR) was used, that is a remote piloted aircraft, model DJI Phantom 4 Pro (Fig. 2) equipped with the OcuSync high resolution transmission system, with 1″ 20 megapixel sensor capable of producing 4K video at 60 fps, and to take 14 fps photos.

Fig. 2. UAV Phantom 4 Pro

A flight height of 20 m has been set in order to obtain a GSD on the ground equal to 0.68 cm/pixel. The acquisition time was 17 min, taking 181 images overall for each survey [22, 23]. A total of 10 measurements were made.

The processing of 3D model construction, useful to extract geometry includes four standard main steps:

– Alignment of pictures, the software looks for common points on pictures to blend in.
– Generation of a dense point cloud that can be modified and classified before proceeding with the export or generation of the three-dimensional mesh model.
– Reconstruction of the surface of a 3D polygonal mesh that represents the object based on the dense cloud of points obtained from the previous phase.
– Mesh reconstruction and orthophotos restitution.

In particular, the beams have an asymmetrical double T cross section with a height of 3.0 m and a wheelbase of 4.10 m. Each beam is made up of 43 segments joined together by welded joints. For all the segments, it was decided to keep the thicknesses of the cores and platelets constant to facilitate the realization of the metal structural work. The dimensions of the beams are shown in Table 1, on each of which stiffeners have been positioned.

A long-term SHM system has been installed on the bridge to monitor its performance. The system used provides the possibility to install gps and/or accelerometric modules [24, 25]. The sensors are necessary to measure the vertical and horizontal vibrations and displacements (Gps: Static Hz 3 mm ± 0,5 ppm V 5 mm ± 0,5 ppm; Accelerometer: Sampling frequency: 1024 Hz; Minimum level measured: 0.0005 mm/s, Dynamic range: 120 dB; Frequency range: 0.8–100 Hz (315 Hz); Maximum measurable value: 8 g; Spectral noise: 1 µg/Hz-2 at 1 Hz; Cross Axis Sensitivity: <5%; Noise in the band (0–100 Hz): 15 µg; Sensitivity: 1000 mV/g; Frequency response: 0.8–600 Hz; Resonance frequency: 16 kHz; Sampling frequency: 1024 Hz; Linearity: ±1% Max; Dynamic range (of the sensor, in band): 120 dB; Dynamic range AD Converter (24 bit): 130 dB). In the specific case, only the data obtained from GPS units installed to monitor the bridge deck movements in three directions were used, and compared with those obtained from accelerometers (which are expected to be used later for subsequent dynamic analyzes). The 12 receivers are installed on the road in correspondence of the pier and in the middle of the span and on some known external points near the infrastructure [26–28].

The installation points of the sensors, (some points of the viaduct and some fixed points external to the bridge) were also measured in static mode through the use of an external GPS network consisting of 6 points capable of guaranteeing a high precision. This operation was necessary in order to mitigate the uncertainty of the sensor measurement and optimize the overall accuracy of the system by referring it to a single reference system by correlating the measurements obtained from the sensors to the measurements obtained from the instrumentation [29, 30] (Fig. 3).

Fig. 3. Sensor position

In order to investigate the stability of the slope, a (previously described) sensor system was installed on pillars and beams, and at the same time GPS measurements were made. These parameters were used to recreate the condition in the various scenarios required for neural network training.

The movements were also monitoring through the use of two GPS (rover and base).

Therefore, the coordinate's data were converted to a local bridge coordinate system for the analysis and evaluation procedures. In this coordinate system, x-axis is aligned with the traffic direction and z-axis gives the vertical direction of the viaduct.

Using the sensors previously described we obtained the accuracy deflection is on the order of 1.5 mm (horizontal) and 2 mm (vertical). The accuracy dynamic deflection is on the order of 10 mm (horizontal) and 15 mm (vertical). However, the accuracy for dynamic deflection measurement can be improved by post-processing methods [31].

3   Results and Discussion

3.1   Database for Load Actions on the Structural Model

In order to create a predictive model, it is necessary to know the response of the structural model subjected to various loading actions on the infrastructure. In this regard, in addition to the effects of the wind, the water flow rate on the batteries and the average daily traffic, we also used the deterioration parameters of the materials in order to create a structural model that varies over time.

In particular, while for the effects of wind flow and average daily traffic, the classic standard formulas for calculation have been used [32], to calculate the deterioration of the materials, we proceeded using the "mechanistic model" which allows determining the micro response of the structure, caused by the acting loads, environmental conditions that uses soft computing, and neural network techniques to obtain the variation of the parameter to be inserted in the model [33]. Such a micro-response includes the nucleation of the damage, the growth of this defect and the impact that it can have on the safety and maintenance of the structure. These models are used for the project level analysis and for the safety analysis of the structures, where the damage is described by measurable indicators such as: resistance, voltages, displacements, etc. [34]. The damage mechanisms of a bridge can be described in three types:

- Excessive damage due to total or partial collapse (ductile or fragile), yielding, instability problems (local or global), cracks and large deformations;
- Problems of wear by materials, related to problems of fatigue and corrosion;
- Combination of the two mechanisms described above.

The following are the parameters (whose values are partially imposed by legislation and other variables over time) constituting the dataset implemented for the construction of the structural model [35]. An example is shown on Table 1.

Table 1. Load examples

Wind	$F_x = 18.312$ kN/m	$F_y = 14.856$ kN/m	$M_z = 202.478$ kNm/m
Traffic	Q = 300 kN/m	$q = 9$ kN/m^2	TGM = 8659
Flow	Qin = 180 m^3/s	Qe = 0	R = R(kN) = 2483,17
Deterioration	Low = 1,1	Medium = 1	Alto 0,8

3.2   Integrated Predictive System

To detect the geometry of the viaduct in question and implement a structural model, a survey was carried out with a drone and a subsequent three-dimensional modeling as described in paragraph 2.

Once the model was obtained, the geometry was extrapolated. In Fig. 2 the longitudinal profile of the bridge is shown, its characteristics are shown in Table 2 (Fig. 4).

Table 2. Bridge metrics characteristics

Pier	High [m]	Span	[m]
P1	3.60	1	60
P2	4.70	2	80
P3	5.75	3	80
P4	7.80	4	80
P5	8.80	5	80
P6	3.60	6	60

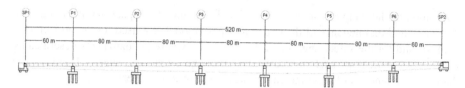

Fig. 4. Longitudinal deck profile

Therefore the infrastructure model was built (Fig. 5) applying the established loads and the failures detected (or established in the network test phase).

Fig. 5. Bridge model

A simplified Finite Element Model (FEM) using one-dimensional elements (as beams, truss, and rigid links) with properties equivalent to those of the real elements, was then used to obtain the infrastructure response to the stresses of the loads previously highlighted [36].

From the structural model, given the particular position of the building, it has been verified that the third span is the span subject to greater stresses (Fig. 6).

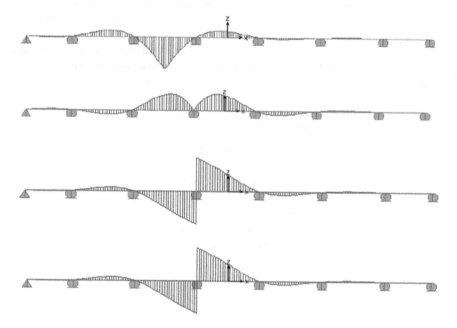

Fig. 6. Lines of influence for the maximum moment in span (a) and on the pillars (b); maximum cut in span (c) and pillars (d);

Structural monitoring of existing works is an engineering practice that, from a theoretical point of view, rediscovers the roles played by the information used at the design stage. When designing a construction, the actions (static or dynamic) are known and the structural model is possessed, this knowledge is combined to get the prediction of the structural response in the various conditions of interest (service limit of the state of interest and last state limit). In this case, then, we are aware of the response and the actions, while what we want to determine is the model. In the first case we manage a direct problem, while in the second case we deal with the reverse problem.

In the specific case, only the static model described above has been examined, it is good to observe that to better analyze elements it will be necessary to use complex models that takes into account both static and dynamic actions, which is expected to be done in a subsequent phase, not yet carried out as a test model.

In order to identify an alert signal from the FEM analysis, it is necessary to identify threshold values of the various risk classes with which to associate the response of the structural model.

Four risk classes have therefore been identified according to the various software processes, see Fig. 7:

Class A: Negligible. Infrastructures that do not show significant signs or defects, (on the calculation sheet all elements are displayed in green color).

Class B: Low. Infrastructures that manifest some elements with slight defects. (some elements with yellow coloring appear on the calculation sheet).

Class C: Moderate. The infrastructures belonging to this class show elements with significant defects (some elements with orange coloring are displayed on the calculation sheet).

Class D: High. The infrastructures belonging to this class show elements with significant defects (on the calculation sheet some elements are displayed in red color).

Fig. 7. Example verification and classification (Color figure online)

As can also be highlighted in the Fig. 7, the level of risk depends on several variables (loads, deformations, displacement, material).

The value of the proposed note lies in the possibility of evaluating, through the soft computing techniques used, the risk class and therefore predicting the behavior of the structure using only the movements and not all the parameters that in determining the level of risk, parameters which instead were used in an initial phase exclusively to train the neural network.

In this regard, it is necessary to previously train the neural network based on the back-propagation algorithm, given its easy of use and ability to implicitly store information in the form of connection weights.

The neural network was trained as follows:

- Various loading actions (wind, earthquake …) and different displacements (associated with settlements chosen for training the network) have been implemented on the structural software in different scenarios in order to highlight the different responses of the structure.
- Out of 800 implemented scenarios, 100 were used as tests to verify the correct training of the neural network by entering as input only the displacement data previously chosen set and used (Fig. 8); thus comparing the correspondence of the risk levels obtained between software and neural network in various scenarios.

At this point, once the network has been trained, the displacement (s) and rotation (r) values obtained by the sensors are applied as input (Fig. 8), using the procedure described above in order to mitigate the uncertainty of the sensor measurement. Moreover, the overall accuracy of the system is thus optimized by referring it to a single reference system, by correlating the measurements obtained by the sensors with the measurements obtained by the mode.

Profilo	s[cm]	r [°]
1-2	0,060	0,01
2-3	0,081	0,00
3-4	0,104	0,00
4-5	0,129	0,00
5-6	0,158	0,00
6-7	0,188	0,00
7-8	0,224	0,00
8-9	0,262	0,00
9-10	0,167	0,00
10-11	0,199	0,00
11-12	0,247	0,03
12-13	0,304	0,00
13-14	0,360	0,00
14-15	0,423	0,00
15-16	0,204	0,00
16-17	0,267	0,00
17-18	0,337	0,00
18-19	0,426	0,00
20-21	0,512	0,00
21-22	0,613	0,00
22-23	0,092	0,00
23-24	0,117	0,00
24-25	0,175	0,00
25-26	0,086	0,00
26-27	0,106	0,00
27-28	0,134	0,00
28-29	0,160	0,00
29-30	0,188	0,00
30-31	0,220	0,00

Fig. 8. Example displacement data input

It should be noted that unfortunately (for our research activities) or fortunately (for the viaduct stability) no displacements were measured that could test the goodness of the system.

The predictive system (presented in this note) therefore allows to know the structural behavior of the viaduct following the measurement of the displacements only, the method is therefore capable of sending an alert signal with a respective risk class of ownership each time certain movements occur, in order to provide an early warning in the event of important movements or rotations.

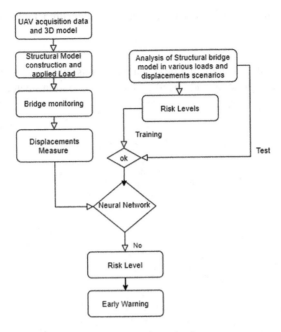

Fig. 9. Flow chart of monitoring system

Figure 9 shows how the proposed system works.

Specifically, the central part of the system concerns soft computing techniques and the implementation of the neural network. Therefore, we have implemented soft computing techniques that can provide an outbound forecast value related to load forecasting, which is necessary to know the behavior of the infrastructure in advance.

The back-propagation algorithm was used for its simplicity and its ability to extract useful information from examples. In fact, its ability to implicitly stores information in the form of connection weights and its applicability to digitally or analog models [37].

The back-propagation algorithm can understand two phases: an initial phase and a feedback phase. In the first step we have to enter the displacements x value (clearly other rotations loads and deformations can also be used) which are obtained from the structural model given the stability of the bridge under investigation and therefore the impossibility of acquiring its real data.

We inserted and propagated the displacement values x through the multilayer network; to calculate the correct output value y (displacements and risk class).

The second phase of propagation backwards, on the other hand, involved a backward path through the network, during which the error signal was calculated and, between the desired output d and the y obtained and then propagated appropriately from the output layer to the input state, in order to update the values of the weights and bases. In fact, this error signal was reported through all the layers of the network adjusting or modifying at the same time all the values of the connection between weights and bases, thus bringing current output closer to the desired output. In particular, the learning using the back-propagation algorithm takes place in the following steps (Fig. 10):

(1) initialization of weights and bases,
(2) presentation of the desired input/exit pairs. At this stage, we presented a vector with N input components and specified the desired output vector.

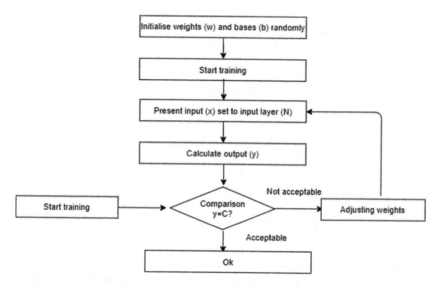

Fig. 10. Flowchart back propagation neural network

This procedure was then repeated with the presentation of new input/output pairs for a number of iterations that depend on the stop condition that is typically defined based on the difference between total errors obtained in two successive iterations until we get the weight and base values and then assigning them to the neural network.

In the testing phase, the sensor-captured data were compared (specifically, we report data acquired and calculated on the beam of the span with data obtained from the model to verify the goodness of the model itself) [38].

The network thus constructed therefore allows to obtain the desired outputs at any time (risk classes) according to the inputs (displacements) displayed on a table which is sent to a control center by means of a special control unit.

In the specific, we used a control unit to manage the output data (Fig. 11). In particular, the processed signal is sent, through communication channels, to a hardware system. It records the data and compare signal with the previous ones. If there are any change it informs the operator of possible crisis of the structure or simply change of risk class.

Fig. 11. Prototype of integrated monitoring system

The system was designed in EasyEDA® environment. The board was properly designed and integrated with components needed for data processing. Data were transmitted with 4G LTE to the monitoring platform. The simple platform is implemented in the WordPress® environment.

Specifically, the our integrated predictive system produce the displacement values measured by the sensors and the risk classes calculated by the neural network, and shown in a corresponding color, as shown in Fig. 12; from this response we can observe on the left side the sensor value monitoring during the time, and on the right side a table with the value used as input, and associated risk classes in the column C (that in our case is highlighted in green, if the displacement measured should made change the class of risk, automatically also the coulor of the correspondent value change in red, yellow orange o).

The result attests good adaptability of the model to the real state with an average error of about 10%.

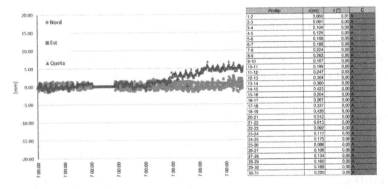

Fig. 12. Data output from sensor and neural network (Color figure online)

4   Conclusion

Note how specifically the tests carried out with a neural network on a structural model returned a correspondence of 90%, indicating a good adaptability and functioning of the system. The System is currently being tested on the real case which, however, does not present good stability and consequently does not allow a more in-depth analysis to test the goodness of the expected results.

Today, understanding the structural behavior of an infrastructure takes on a more fundamental role. Analysis of infrastructure behavior models is still under development, but by solving the reverse problem it can be used both to monitor existing structures and as a control system in newly built buildings and bridges. So that you can:

1. Evaluation of the bridge's original capacity based on the stresses induced by the loads with which it is assumed to have been designed (model realization).
2. Possible reduction of the original capacity taking into account the state of degradation of the bridge and estimation of the speed of progress of degradation (model of deterioration).
3. Determining the ratio of the original reduced capacity to the demand calculated based on real traffic data (current model).

The experimentation conducted has allowed us to highlight the potential of a speedy method for alerting. In addition, on the other, appreciate the good results achieved specifically.

In confirmation of this, it should be noted how specifically the tests carried out with neural network on a structural model returned a correspondence of 90%, indicating a good adaptability and functioning of the system.

It is clearly aware that an improvement could be achieved by including dynamic analysis.

To date, the monitoring carried out has not shown any shifts for which it was possible to test the goodness of the neural network only in relation to the structural model.

In the future, we will work in such a way as to be able to apply the same system (appropriately also modifying the structural model) on a viaduct where it is assumed that there are more deformations that are important.

In this sense, we are working to identify another case study, with possible significant failures in progress in order to carry out further checks.

References

1. Gentile, C., Cabboi, A.: Vibration-based structural health monitoring of stay cables by microwave remote sensing. Smart Struct. Syst. **16**, 263–280 (2015)
2. Harris, D.K., Brooks, C.N., Ahlborn, T.M.: Synthesis of field performance of remote sensing strategies for condition assessment of inservice bridges in Michigan. J. Perform. Constr. Facil. **30**, 04016027 (2016)
3. Vaghefi, K., et al.: Evaluation of commercially available remote sensors for highway bridge condition assessment. J. Bridge Eng. **17**, 886–895 (2012)

4. Chen, S.-E., Liu, W., Dai, K., Bian, H., Hauser, E.: Remote sensing for bridge monitoring. In: Condition, Reliability, and Resilience Assessment of Tunnels and Bridges, vol. 214, pp. 118–125. Geotechnical Special Publication, Reston (2011)
5. Rytter, A.: Vibration BASED inspection of civil engineering structures. Department of Building Technology and Structural Engineering, Aalborg University, Denmark (1993)
6. Elnabwy, M.T., Kaloop, M.R., Elbeltagi, E.: Talkha steel highway bridge monitoring and movement identification using RTK-GPS technique. Measurement **46**, 4282–4292 (2013)
7. Psimoulis, P.A., Stiros, S.C.: A supervised learning computer-based algorithm to derive the amplitude of oscillations of structures using noisy GPS and robotic theodolites (RTS) records. Comput. Struct. **92–93**, 337–348 (2012)
8. Zhu, X.Q., Law, S.S.: Wavelet-based crack identification of bridge beam from operational deflection time history. Int. J. Solids Struct. **43**, 2299–2317 (2006)
9. Zhang, W.W., Wang, Z.H., Ma, H.W.: Studies on wavelet packet-based crack detection for a beam under the moving load. Key Eng. Mater. **413–414**, 285–290 (2009)
10. Hester, D., González, A.: A wavelet-based damage detection algorithm based on bridge acceleration response to a vehicle. Mech. Syst. Signal Process. **28**, 145–166 (2012)
11. Bradley, M., González, A., Hester D.: Analysis of the structural response to a moving load using empirical mode decomposition, p. 117. Taylor & Francis, London (2010)
12. Huang, N.E., Huang, K., Chiang, W.-L.: HHT based bridge structural health-monitoring method. In: Hilbert-Huang Transform and Its Applications, pp. 263–287. World Scientific (2014)
13. González, A., Hester, D.: An investigation into the acceleration response of a damaged beam-type structure to a moving force. J. Sound Vib. **332**, 3201–3217 (2013)
14. He, W., Zhu, S.: Moving load-induced response of damaged beam and its application in damage localization. J. Vib. Control **22**, 3601–3617 (2016)
15. OBrien, E., Carey, C., Keenahan, J.: Bridge damage detection using ambient traffic and moving force identification. Struct. Control Health Monit. **22**, 1396–1407 (2015)
16. Li, Z.H., Au, F.T.K.: Damage detection of a continuous bridge from response of a moving vehicle. Shock Vib. **2014**, 1–7 (2014)
17. Park, J., Moon, D.-S., Spencer, B.F.: Neutral-axis identification using strain and acceleration measurements. In: The 2017 World Congress on Advances in Structural Engineering and Mechanics (ASEM 2017), Seoul, Korea (2017)
18. Sigurdardottir, D.H., Glisic, B.: Neutral axis as damage sensitive feature. Smart Mater. Struct. **22**, 075030 (2013)
19. Sigurdardottir, D.H., Glisic, B.: Detecting minute damage in beam-like structures using the neutral axis location. Smart Mater. Struct. **23**, 125042 (2014)
20. Sigurdardottir, D.H., Glisic, B.: The neutral axis location for structural health monitoring: an overview. J. Civ. Struct. Health Monit. **5**(5), 703–713 (2015). https://doi.org/10.1007/s13349-015-0136-5
21. Ye, X., Jin, T., Yun, C.: A review on deep learning-based structural health monitoring of civil infrastructures. Smart Struct. Syst. **24**(5), 567–585 (2019)
22. Barrile, V., Candela, G., Fotia, A.: Point cloud segmentation using image processing techniques for structural analysis. ISPRS Int. Arch. Photogramm. Remote Sens. Spat. Inf. Sci. **XLII-2/W11**, 187–193 (2019)
23. Barrile, V., Candela, G., Fotia, A., Bernardo, E.: UAV survey of bridges and viaduct: workflow and application. In: Misra, S., et al. (eds.) ICCSA 2019. LNCS, vol. 11622, pp. 269–284. Springer, Cham (2019). https://doi.org/10.1007/978-3-030-24305-0_21
24. Voutetaki, M.E., Papadopoulos, N.A., Angeli, G.M., Providakis, C.P.: Investigation of a new experimental method for damage assessment of RC beams failing in shear using piezoelectric transducers. Eng. Struct. **114**, 226–240 (2016)

25. Karayannis, C.G., Voutetaki, M.E., Chalioris, C.E., Providakis, C.P., Angeli, G.M.: Detection of flexural damage stages for RC beams using Piezoelectric sensors (PZT). Smart Struct. Syst. **15**, 997–1018 (2015)
26. Kaloop, M.R., Li, H.: Multi input-single output models identification of tower bridge movements using GPS monitoring system. Measurement **47**, 531–539 (2014)
27. Chen, Y., Xue, X.: Advances in the structural health monitoring of bridges using piezoelectric transducers. Sensors **18**, 4312 (2018)
28. Liao, W.I., Hsiao, F.P., Chiu, C.K., Ho, C.E.: Structural health monitoring and interface damage detection for infill reinforced concrete walls in seismic retrofit of reinforced concrete frames using piezoceramic-based transducers under the cyclic loading. Appl. Sci. **9**, 312 (2019)
29. Moschas, F., Stiros, S.: Measurement of the dynamic displacements and of the modal frequencies of a short-span pedestrian bridge using GPS and an accelerometer. Eng. Struct. **33**, 10–17 (2011)
30. Moschasa, F., Stiros, S.: Noise characteristics of short-duration, high frequency GPS-records. In: Advanced Mathematical and Computational Tools in Metrology and Testing. Series on Advances in Mathematics for Applied Sciences, vol. 84, pp. 284–291 (2012)
31. Matarazzo, T.J., Pakzad, S.N.: Scalable structural modal identification using dynamic sensor network data with STRIDEX. Comput. Aided Civ. Infrastruct. Eng. **33**(1), 4–20 (2018)
32. Qu, K., Tang, H.S., Agrawal, A., Cai, Y., Jiang, C.B.: Numerical investigation of hydrodynamic load on bridge deck under joint action of solitary wave and current. Appl. Ocean Res. **75**, 100–116 (2018). https://doi.org/10.1016/j.apor.2018.02.020
33. Wu, D., Yuan, C., Kumfera, W., Liu, H.: A life-cycle optimization model using semi-Markov process for highway bridge maintenance. Appl. Math. Model. **43**, 45–60 (2017)
34. Fukuda, Y., Feng, M.Q., Narita, Y., Kaneko, S., Tanaka, T.: Vision-based displacement sensor for monitoring dynamic response using robust object search algorithm. IEEE Sens. J. **13**, 4725–4732 (2013)
35. Lydon, D., Lydon, M., Taylor, S., Del Rincon, J.M., Hester, D., Brownjohn, J.: Development and field testing of a vision-based displacement system using a low cost wireless action camera. Mech. Syst. Signal Process. **121**, 343–358 (2019). ISSN 0888-3270
36. Pucinotti, R., Fiordaliso, G.: Multi-span steel-concrete bridges with anti-seismic devices: a case study. Front. Built Environ. **72**, 1–15 (2019)
37. Li, S., Zuo, X., Li, Z., Wang, H.: Applying deep learning to continuous bridge deflection detected by fiber optic gyroscope for damage detection. Sensors **20**(3), 911 (2020)
38. Matarazzo, T.J., Pakzad, S.N.: Structural identification for mobile sensing with missing observations. J. Eng. Mech. **142**(5), 04016021 (2016)

Geospatial Tools in Support of Urban Planning: A Possible Role of Historical Maps in Programming a Sustainable Future for Cities

E. Borgogno-Mondino[1](✉) and A. Lessio[2]

[1] GEO4Agri Lab, DISAFA, University of Torino, L.go Braccini 2, Grugliasco, 10095 Turin, Italy
enrico.borgogno@unito.it
[2] ITHACA, Via Pier Carlo Boggio 61, 10138 Turin, Italy

Abstract. In urban planning, a numerical and spatially based approach is expected to drive to the "best" choice. In this work a GIS-based procedure is proposed to model territorial dynamics by comparing maps of two different periods (1830 and 2000). The study area is located in the urban fringe of Torino (NW Italy) that suffered from important changes especially in the last 60 years. A workflow was defined and applied, based on a multi-criteria approach implemented by GIS. With reference to existing maps, strength and direction of forces, opposing urban to rural/semi-natural surroundings, were mapped and described operating through the following scheme: a) vectorization and qualification of both impacted (rural) and impacting (urban) landscape elements; b) implementation of spatially dependent functions representing strength and direction of urban pushes against rural; c) qualification of rural areas majorly exposed to urban growth. Accordingly, some maps, useful to read the playing urban growth dynamics, were generated and some applications proposed. Nevertheless some limitations still persist: the proposed methodology is based on simplified hypotheses, mainly related to the definition of spatial indices that somehow depend on the type of information that available maps contain. A second limitation is related to the persistence of a great component of sub-jectivity during the extraction of the starting information from the available maps and weights assignation.

Keywords: Transitional landscapes · GIS · Urban fringe · Urban pushes · Urban planning · Spatial functions

1 Introduction

GIS tools and spatial analysis techniques have already proved to be effective in urban planning [1, 2] and landscape description [3–6]. In the last few years, GIS technology and the increasing amount of free digital georeferenced data have encouraged the adoption of spatial analysis to support land planning, mainly relying on multi-criteria approaches [7, 8]. Many authors [9, 10] have investigated the spatial distribution of environmental factors, particularly to support management of metropolitan areas

© Springer Nature Switzerland AG 2020
O. Gervasi et al. (Eds.): ICCSA 2020, LNCS 12252, pp. 649–663, 2020.
https://doi.org/10.1007/978-3-030-58811-3_47

[11–13]. Highly populated peri-urban areas are very critical for different aspects, like soil sealing and degradation, urban sprawl and, in general, loss of ecosystem services [14]. Landscape metrics are widely adopted to characterize both planned [15–17] and unplanned urban areas expansion [18]. In some works remote sensing data and socio-economic factors [19, 20] were jointly used with landscape metrics. In spite of a wide literature, in the most of cases, GIS tools are used to generate mere representations by integrating data from different sources. Only in few cases, conversely, GIS-based works take into consideration quantitative concerns that are expected to increase the level of objectivity in landscape reading and future planning [21, 22]. From this point of view maps move from simple territorial representations and turn to be basic measurement tools, that planners and policy makers can adopt to base their decisions on. It is authors' conviction that, if one has to select among different planning solutions, a numerical approach, standardly adopted, can drive to the "best" choice. It is worth to remind that the concept of "best" strictly depends on the criteria used to base the choice on; therefore a choice is "the best" one only under "those" conditions. According to this operational philosophy, in this work a procedure is presented based on GIS advanced tools, specifically aimed at urban dynamics description (in space and time) for planning purposes. The initial assumption is that urban growth dynamics can be assimilated to a force balance where urban growth pushes against rural/natural areas, making desirable external landscape preservation. In a war, the programmed actions of a single battle, occurring in a specific moment of the conflict, represent "tactics"; differently, long-term decisions, possibly affecting more than one battle, define the "strategy". Transposing the same interpretation key to the urban planning context, it is easy to see that the representation of the pushing and resisting forces operated by urban growth and rural/natural surroundings, respectively, at a certain time (the one of the considered maps) is something related to "tactics". Differently, if two situations showing the same area at different times are compared, the underlying "strategy" can be guessed that planners chose to drive urban growth in the transitional period. This is the idea behind this work; consequently, GIS tools were initially used for representing the "battlefield" at two different times, i.e. the place where urban growth pushes and rural areas resist; successively, those scenarios were compared to analyze and represent the strategy that, possibly, drove urban growth in the study area.

Concerning the first task, to give a rather complete description of the field of acting forces at a certain time, methodology operated at two levels. Firstly, it gave a representation of strength and direction of the pushing forces of urban against rural/semi-natural surroundings; this was obtained through a spatial comparison of the previously represented scenarios. Then impacted areas (rural, semi-natural) were qualified with a special focus on the perceptive impact that urban growth can generate onto an observer located within a still resisting rural/semi-natural area. According to these premises, a GIS-based procedure was proposed, with the explicit goal of supporting urban planners with a tool aimed at giving a spatial representation about the on-going territorial dynamics. The presented case study has to be intended as a paradigm for readers, i.e. a place where the core item of this work (the GIS-based procedure) is tested. For this purpose, a peri-urban area located in the proximity of Torino (NW Italy) was selected and the procedure applied with reference to the territorial changes that this area suffered from in the time range 1830–2000. The following workflow was defined and applied, based on a multi-criteria approach modelled within GIS. With reference to the available maps a selection, vectorization and qualification of landscape features were done to define impacted players (rural areas) and threats (urban). According to the above mentioned philosophy some space dependent functions were designed and implemented by GIS tools to give a spatial representation of strength/direction of urban pushes against rural. Rural/semi-natural areas that were exposed, or potentially exposed, to urban growth aggression were analyzed and qualified. A discussion is finally given about results, proposing possible interpretations and deductions in terms of urban planning.

2 Materials and Methods

2.1 Study Area

The study area is located in the first urban belt of Torino (NW Italy) including the municipalities of Collegno and Grugliasco (about 32 km^2 and 80000 inhabitants, Fig. 1). This area is characterized by the permanence of historical and valuable farmhouses surrounded by agricultural pertinences which are prevailingly disused at present. The erosion of traditional rural landscape and the pressure onto farmhouses due to urban expansion after the World War II are especially evident on the North-Western fringes of the settlement. Around the middle of XX century local engineering industries and automotive factories (Pininfarina, Bertone, Westinghouse, etc.) determined radical changes that deeply modified the urban frame.

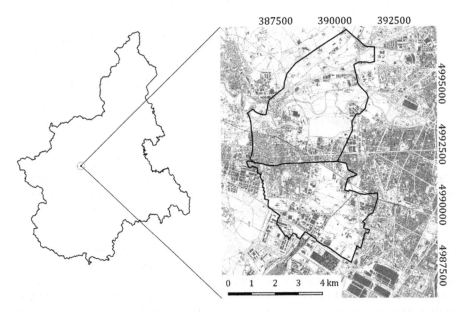

Fig. 1. Study area within Piedmont Region (NW Italy); Reference System is UTM/WGS84 32N.

Building activity frenetically increases as well: residential areas, infrastructures, industrial and commercial activities greatly affected the local rural landscape by cancelling the most of the pre-existing agriculture-devoted landmarks. Canals network for crop water supplying, service trails, rural buildings and crop fields were almost completely cancelled, finally determining the loss of the entire rural cultural background of the area. Moreover, some historical farmhouses progressively turned to dereliction and rural landscape gets more and more unreadable. In the area, urban pressure is still active making it a good laboratory to test new procedures to better manage future territorial changes instances.

2.2   Available Data

Focusing on urban growth affecting the study area, the following two periods were assessed and compared: one preceding the industrial revolution (1816–1830), hereinafter called T1; one corresponding to the present situation (2000), hereinafter called T2. As far as T1 is concerned, the reference map was the so called *"Carta topografica degli Stati di Terra-ferma di S.S.R.M. Carlo Alberto Re di Sardegna fatta dal Corpo dello Stato Maggiore Generale alla scala di 1:50,000"* (hereinafter called M1830). It is dated between 1816 and 1830 and reports continental estates (islands excluded) of the Savoia Italian Royal Family.

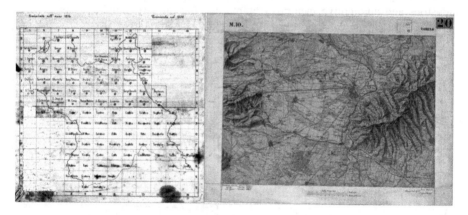

Fig. 2. (Right) A digital scanned image of the M.10 sheet obtained from the Italian Military Survey Office (Istituto Geografico Militare, IGM) used as reference for describing T1 situation (1830). (Left) Overall scheme of map sheets.

Main technical features of M1830 are the following: a) the geodetic reference frame is centred on the Real Observatory of Torino, assumed as the origin of the Cartesian system; b) adopted projection is a modified Sanson-Flamsteed one; c) the whole mapped area is covered by 112 sheets (format is about 0.42 × 0.60 m); d) planimetric positioning was derived by reduction of pre-existing maps integrated with some new surveys; e) altitude is only qualitatively reported, being obtained "by landscape visual interpretation operated by an experienced surveyor"; f) no reference grid is reported, but a scale bar is drawn in each sheet, with reference to the ancient local measurement unit of distance: the Piedmontese Trabucco (3.0864 m). For this work, a digital scanned image of the paper tile labelled as M.10 (Fig. 2) was obtained from the Italian Military Survey Office (Istituto Geografico Militare, IGM).

Scanning was performed @300 DPI (dots per inch), determining a pixel physical size of 84.6 microns that, in ground units, corresponds to 4.23 m. This value is consistent with the reference accuracy officially expected for a modern 1:50,000 scale map in the Italian cartographic context, i.e. 10 m. As far as T2 is concerned we used the present Regional technical vector map 1:50,000 (hereinafter called CTR50), obtained for free from the online Geoportal of the Piemonte Region Cartographic Office (http://www.geoportale.piemonte.it/cms/). Map metadata report that CTR50 is updated at the year 2000 and the reference frame is the WGS84 UTM 32N.

2.3   Data Pre-processing

Data processing was operated by QGIS 3.8 and SAGA GIS 7.0.0. Concerning M1830, since only a scanned image was available, it was preventively georeferenced (Fig. 3). Native map symbols were decoded, and the main local land cover classes vectorised by editing. The meaning of the vectorised land cover classes was assigned with reference to Table 1. In the proposed landscape interpretation model, urban growth was considered a threat for the rural/semi-natural areas (impacted objects); consequently, built-up classes were labelled as "impacting" and rural/semi-natural classes were labelled as "resisting".

The same classes were consequently extracted from the available CTR50 vector map by GIS attribute selection. For both the maps, a weight was assigned, depending on the considered land cover class of Table 1 with the following criteria: a) weights of built-up areas define the level of threat that a certain type of urbanization is expected to generate onto resisting rural surroundings. Higher weights were assigned to industrial areas and main roads; b) weights of rural/semi-natural areas define landscape value of local land cover. In this case, weights were assigned admitting that higher the degree of naturalness, higher the local landscape value.

Table 1. Impacting and resisting classes used in this work. They were selected/edited from the two compared maps (M1830 and CTR50). Table also shows weights whose meaning is reported in the text.

Classes	Weights		Classes	Weights	
	M_{1830}	CTR50		M_{1830}	CTR50
Impacting			Resisting		
Secondary roads	Not present	1	Other natural surfaces	Not present	1
Main roads	1	3	Agricultural land cover	1	2
Residential	2	2	Meadows	2	3
Industrial	Not present	4	Forest	3	4
			Vineyards	4	Not present

With reference to the assigned weights, two land cover maps, hereinafter called LC1830(x, y) and LC2000(x, y) were generated from M1830 and CTR50 respectively.

The analysis was conducted at two levels, to contemporarily investigate dynamics of urban growth and its impacts against surrounding rural landscape: a) firstly, a representation of strength and direction of the pushing forces of urban against rural/natural surroundings was generated; b) successively the impacted/exposed areas were qualified.

2.4   Representing Strength and Direction of Threats

Regarding representation of urban pushes, it must be admitted that they are related to the local difference of "Urban Potential", (UP). In the present work UP was computed and mapped in terms of "local urban density". Computation was achieved by rasterizing the urban class from *LC1830(x, y)* and *LC2000(x, y)* and converting the original content into the correspondent binary representation, hereinafter called *Ur(x, y, t)*, where t = [1830, 2000]. *Ur(x, y, t)* is a grid where built-up pixels were labelled as 1 (independently from building type) while all the other ones as 0. Grid resolution was set to 10 m, consistent with a 1:50000 scale map. Successively an "area of influence" (AI) was defined around each pixel of *Ur(x, y, t)* and the correspondent urban local density map, hereinafter called UDM(x, y, t), computed. It was obtained running over *Ur(x, y, t)* a 150 × 150 m sliding window (AI) in charge of locally computing the following value:

$$UDM(x, y, t) = 100 \cdot \frac{N_{urb}}{N_{tot}} \qquad (1)$$

where N_{urb} and N_{tot} are the local number of built-up pixels and the total number of pixels, respectively, within the 150 × 150 m sliding window (i.e. AI) at the generic position within the analyzed raster map. *UDM(x, y, t)* was assumed as map of the "local potential" of urban forces pushing against rural/semi-natural surrounding areas. The local difference of potential, consequently, was assumed as descriptor of the local acting force (push). The passage from the representation of the potential to the correspondent field of acting forces can be managed considering *UDM(x, y, t)* as a 3D surface, i.e. a sort of Digital Surface Model. A pre-processing step was initially achieved aimed at down-sampling *UDM(x, y, t)* from 10 m to 150 m pixel size, with the aim of cutting off high frequency components of urban density variations (micro changes), thus focusing on the low frequency ones (macro changes). The underlying hypothesis was that, at the scale of this work (1:50,000) only low frequency components of the density can be reliable enough to describe the actual urban pushes against rural.

Successively, slope, *SL(x, y, t)*, and aspect, *AS(x, y, t)* grids were computed from the down-sampled UDM(x, y, t). Slope was interpreted as measure of the local force strength; aspect was assumed as measure of its direction. To translate this disaggregated information (two independent raster layers) into a more effective representation, closer to an ordinary field of forces, *SL(x, y, t)* was vectorised, obtaining two point layers for T1 and T2, respectively. The slope local value was recorded as numerical attribute in the tables associated with the two newly-generated vector layers. The attribute table was then completed with a further field containing the aspect local value extracted from $AS(x, y, t)$. Finally, using the proper visualization tool available in QGIS (Vector Field Renderer - https://github.com/ccrook/QGIS-VectorFieldRenderer-Plugin), the field of forces was mapped for the two investigated periods. From the original 10 m $UDM(x, y, t)$ was also derived a contour line-based representation to improve readability of the vector field (Fig. 4).

2.5   Representing Landscape Exposed Values

In the proposed model both the exposed value of a rural/semi-natural areas and the degree of impact local (one can perceive looking from country to town) related to the advancing urbanization were considered. The "exposed value" was assumed depending on the type of land cover class (eventually from the shape properties of the each patch of the polygon layer). The degree of local impact, differently, was assumed to be strictly related to: a) the distance between the generic location within rural areas and the closest built-up element; b) the type of the nearest built-up element (residential, industrial, public facility, etc.). In terms of spatial analysis, the latter was represented as a grid map where the threat affecting the generic rural position is inversely proportional to the distance from the nearest urban feature and directly proportional to its impacting strength (the previously mentioned "weight").

This relationship was modelled defining the Local Pressure Index, $LPI(x, y, t)$, Eq. 2, for both the considered periods (T1 and T2).

$$LPI(x, y, t) = \frac{A(x, y, t)^-}{D(x, y, t)^-} \qquad (2)$$

where $A(x, y, t)^-$ and $D(x, y, t)^-$ are respectively the Allocation and Distance spatial operators, generated with a pixel size of 10 m, from $LC2000(x, y)$ and $LC1830(x, y)$ respectively; only the "impacting" classes were considered at this point with reference to Table 1. It is worth to remind that $A(x, y, t)^-$ defines, for each pixel, the weight value of the corresponding threatening nearest feature (road or building). Differently, $D(x, y)^-$ defines, for each pixel, the Euclidean horizontal distance that separates that specific location from the nearest threatening feature. $LPI(x, y)$ was generated under the following hypotheses: a) the contribution of the impacting factor decreases while increasing the distance from the nearest impacting feature; b) its initial (and maximum) value is the one corresponding to the weight of the nearest feature.

Successively, in order to quantify the potential depletion of the local rural landscape quality, due to the surrounding urban features, a Local Impact Index (LII) was calculated according to Eq. 3.

$$LII(x, y, t) = \frac{A(x, y, t)^+}{LPI(x, y, t)} \qquad (3)$$

where $A(x, y, t)+$ is the raster map of positive weights assigned to rural/semi-natural areas.

It is worth to remind that index maps are space-and time-dependent since they have been generated for both the periods.

3   Results and Discussion

3.1   Data Pre-processing

Concerning M1830 georeferencing, given the flatness of the area, it was successfully operated by applying a 2nd order Polynomial transformation in QGIS. Fifty-two regularly distributed GCPs were collimated with reference to CTR50 (Fig. 3) determining a RMSE (Root Mean Squared Error) of 22.1 m; this value is two times the expected value (10 m) that, however, concern maps produced by modern technical instruments. Considering the time and the type of survey, and assuming a rigorous positioning not so relevant for this type of application, this type of result was retained reasonable. Georeferenced image was consequently generated with a pixel size of 5 m.

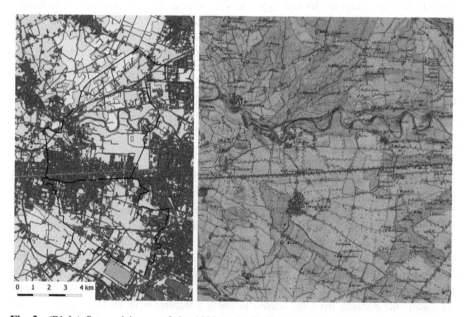

Fig. 3. (Right) Scanned image of the 1830 map. (Left) CTR50 map used as reference layer during georeferencing. Red triangles show the position of Ground Control Points. (Color figure online)

The georeferenced M1830 was interpreted to generate the *LC1830(x, y)* polygonal vector layer, mapping the recognized land cover classes at T1 (Table 1). Differently, land cover classes at T2 were selected by ordinary GIS query (select by attribute) from the available CTR50 vector map to generate *LC2000(x, y)*. This step was needed to reduce spatial content by aggregation in few classes. Both *LC1830(x, y)* and *LC2000(x, y)* were finally completed by weights assignation using newly added fields of the correspondent attribute tables.

LC1830(x, y) and *LC2000(x, y)* were used as starting point for successive selections (and rasterizations) to generate following maps needed for the goals of this work.

3.2   Strength and Direction of Threats

UDM(x, y, 1830) and *UDM(x, y, 2000)* were generated using information about built-up areas derived respectively from *LC1830(x, y)* and *LC2000(x, y)*.

In Fig. 4, a representation of *UDM(x, y, t)* is given for both the periods, adopting a contour lines visualization (lines connecting points having the same urban density level).

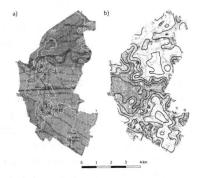

Fig. 4. Urban Density Maps generated respectively for the years 1830 (a) and 2000 (b). Contour lines join points having the same density value.

From maps, it can be noted that urban sprawl proceeded along two preferred directions: a) new residential buildings were built to close the gap between the two existing main urban agglomerates (centripetal direction); b) new industrial areas, differently, were placed in the external parts of the historical towns following a centrifugal direction. These two coupled dynamics moved the "hot spots" (highest urban density) to new positions and determined an almost completely loss of the agricultural pattern of the local landscape. To give an easiest and immediate reading key of the situation at the two compared times, a vector field representation was generated. *UDM(x, y, t)* maps were therefore down-sampled to a Ground Sample Distance (GSD) of 150 m to cut off weak local potential differences and emphasizing only the strongest ones. This simplification permitted a more efficient representation in the next step of the work, when slope and aspect information, derived from *UDM(x, y, t)*, where converted into a point vector layer to generate the vector field visualization of Fig. 5.

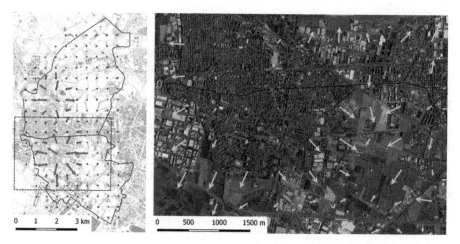

Fig. 5. Comparison between fields of pushing forces for the 1830 (red ones) and 2000 (green ones). (Left) Whole area. (Right) A detail of the squared area. (Color figure online)

As expected, pushes @T1 were stronger than @T2. Potential of urban growth was huge, in force of the enormous free space around towns potentially available to extend built areas. Nevertheless, they remained spatially constrained in a limited area (the one immediately close to the existing urban agglomerates). Differently, at T2 pushes appeared to be weaker; vector field minima are higher in respect of maxima, determining a general reduction of the strength of pushes; this can be related to the high degree of proximity between different built-up areas that makes pushing forces unable to completely exhaust their strength before entering a new built zone. The reading key is that in this situation rural landscape is too degraded by a badly managed soil sealing. In fact, resisting and occluded agricultural areas cannot be anymore perceived felt and lived by people like "true" agricultural ones. Presently, the remaining strong pushes are pointing towards the remaining agricultural context in the South-East part of the area.

Another notable aspect in 2000 is that pushing forces appear to be more diffused and poorly concentrated, confirming the idea that agricultural pattern is almost completely loss and the remaining parts are only waiting to turn to urban. The new assault to remaining agricultural areas comes from every part and no new strategy in urban planning can be imagined different from the ordinary simplest and deprecable one, i.e. to fill the gaps. In other words, these considerations confirm that pushes of the first generation are almost exhausted in the area just for an objective lack of further free space and not for a more virtuous planning strategy.

3.3   Representing Landscape Exposed Values

Once $LC1830(x, y)$ and $LC2000(x, y)$ were generated, proper weights (Table 1) were assigned to classes to describe their influence on surrounding features (Fig. 6). It is worth to remind that during weights values assignation, a high level of subjectivity is applied, since they strictly depend on the existing cultural/political situation. Weights can operate positively or negatively according to the instances expressed by local population, or urban planners, at the moment when the analysis is performed. In this work pushes of built-up areas against rural/natural ones were negatively intended. Consequently, were assumed as "threats". Oppositely, agricultural/natural areas were interpreted as landscape valorising elements. In Fig. 6, both *LC1830(x, y)* and *LC2000 (x, y)* are reported, mapping the above mentioned distinction between "threats" (negative) and "valorising elements" (positive). The latter were also interpreted as map of the "exposed landscape values" showing the resisting rural areas waiting for a new aggression by urban growth.

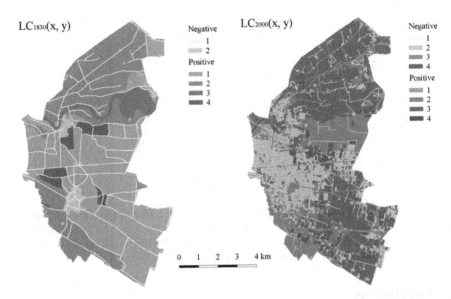

Fig. 6. Urban threats (negative) and landscape exposed values (positive) represented according to the assigned weights. (left) 1830; (right) 2000.

Successively, *LPI(x, y, t)* was calculated for both 1830 and 2000, assuming that it represents the local impact (in landscape feeling and perception) that built-up areas generate onto people. Figure 7(a, c) shows that, in both the periods, *LPI* highest values can be related to urban and peri-urban areas, gradually decreasing while moving outside. The difference between 1830 and 2000 is evident both in strength and in spatial distribution. In 1830, stronger pressures were located very closed too built-up areas, exhausting their effect immediately after a small distance. In 2000 urban pushes are diffused all around and, in general, they act more strongly everywhere.

LII(x, y, t) was generated too, assuming that natural and semi-natural areas improve landscape quality; *LII* takes contemporary into account the local landscape quality and the degree of impact given by the nearest built-up areas (synthesized by *LPI*). The lower is the distance from threat, the higher is the impact. Consequently, *LII(x, y, t)* maps can be assumed as a proxy of environmental/landscape quality as perceived by people at the generic position in the area and, consequently, as a measure of the expected impact that urban pressure generates at that position (landscape exposed value). Figure 7(b, d) shows that lowest values of *LII* are reasonably located close to built-up areas and roads network. It also shows that in 1830 *LII* values were higher and higher (maximum value is 10) than in 2000 (maximum value is 3.50); this is a further confirmation that the present situation has turned to a too compromised condition from the rural/natural landscape point of view. In fact, the expected perception of urban advancing, seen from the few (and small) resisting natural/rural patches, is lower and lower than in the past. This is the effect of the encirclement that urban achieved in respect of the remaining rural areas.

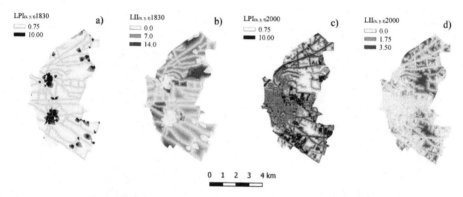

Fig. 7. Local Pressure Index (*LPI*) and Local Impact Index (*LII*) maps generated for the two periods. In *LPI* (a, c) highest values represent urban and peri-urban areas which have the greatest influence on the surrounding surfaces, gradually decreasing far from them; in *LII* (b, d) lower values represent areas where environmental/landscape quality is low.

4   Conclusions

In this work a procedure based on GIS advanced tools specifically aimed at urban dynamics description and planning (in space and time) was proposed. Native authors' assumption was that urban growth dynamics can be assimilated to a force balance where urban growth pushes against rural/natural areas. Somehow, it was admitted that in peri-urban areas a battle is continuously on, opposing urban growth instances to rural, or natural, landscape preservation ones.

As a case study we assessed and compared two extreme situations concerning urban growing in the proximity of Torino (Piemonte, NW Italy): one preceding industrial revolution (years 1816–1830) and one showing the contemporary situation (year 2000). The proposed methodology was based on space-dependent index maps specifically designed to locally measure landscape factors retained involved in urban growing processes. It is authors' opinion that a complete description of urban growth dynamics is only possible by comparison of consequent situations. Urban Density Maps were considered as the starting point to derive this information from, at the single time. Strength and direction of pushes were derived by considering slope and aspect of UDM and representing them through a vector field approach.

The reading of vector fields representing urban pushes at different times is a useful tool to interpret strategy underlying urban growth management in the assessed transitional period.

The possibility of mapping the importance of both built-up and agricultural/natural areas, by measuring their chances of advancing (urban) or resisting (rural), can give a further interpretation key for peri-urban landscape dynamics reading. Two space-dependent indices (LPI and LII) were proposed to map, at the single time, these peculiarities. The combined interpretation of these indices in time and space can support planners to recover the meaning of the hidden dynamics that drove urbanization in the area.

The same approach is expected to be adopted to compare the present situation with a planned (potential) future one to evaluate the properness, or limitations, of the suggested planning solutions. Consequently, planners will be provided of a further tool to validate their proposals and, eventually, to re-calibrate them.

Nevertheless some limitations can be still recognized in this approach: firstly, the proposed methodology is based on simplified hypotheses, mainly related to the definition of spatial indices that somehow depend on the type of information that available maps contain. A second limitation is related to the persistence of a great component of subjectivity during the extraction of the starting information from the available maps and weights assignation. A bad interpretation can lead to a wrong description of the reality. In conclusion to improve results and, in particular, to properly set land cover weights in respect of the forecasted social/economic development of an area, a strong synergy among planners, landscape experts, local administrators and population has to be activated. Moreover new professionals, well skilled in spatial analysis and GIS advanced tools have to enter the decisional process to support the above mentioned main actors. Their expected role is the numerical formalization of technical and political instances tending to effective representation in the shape of maps (of space dependent indices).

Acknowledgement. We would like to acknowledge the Italian Military Survey Office (Istituto Geografico Militare, IGM) that provided us the historical map used in this work ("Carta topografica degli Stati di Terra-ferma di S.S.R.M. Carlo Alberto Re di Sardegna fatta dal Corpo dello Stato Maggiore Generale alla scala di 1:50000"). We would like to acknowledge Prof. Barbara Drusi for her valuable suggestions concerning the history of the urban development of the area.

References

1. Dai, F.C., Lee, C.F., Zhang, X.H.: GIS-based geo-environmental evaluation for urban land-use planning: a case study. Eng. Geol. **61**, 257–271 (2001). https://doi.org/10.1016/S0013-7952(01)00028-X
2. Yeh, A.G.-O., Li, X.: Simulation of Development Alternatives Using Neural Networks, Cellular Automata, and GIS for Urban Planning. https://www.ingentaconnect.com/content/asprs/pers/2003/00000069/00000009/art00010. Accessed 20 Feb 2020. https://doi.org/10.14358/PERS.69.9.1043

3. Brown, G., Brabyn, L.: An analysis of the relationships between multiple values and physical landscapes at a regional scale using public participation GIS and landscape character classification. Landsc. Urban Plan. **107**, 317–331 (2012). https://doi.org/10.1016/j. landurbplan.2012.06.007

4. MacMillan, R.A., Jones, R.K., McNabb, D.H.: Defining a hierarchy of spatial entities for environmental analysis and modeling using digital elevation models (DEMs). Comput. Environ. Urban Syst. **28**, 175–200 (2004). https://doi.org/10.1016/S0198-9715(03)00019-X

5. Papadopoulou-Vrynioti, K., Alexakis, D., Bathrellos, G.D., Skilodimou, H.D., Vryniotis, D., Vassiliades, E.: Environmental research and evaluation of agricultural soil of the Arta plain, western Hellas. J. Geochem. Explor. **136**, 84–92 (2014). https://doi.org/10.1016/j.gexplo. 2013.10.007

6. Liu, T., Yang, X.: Monitoring land changes in an urban area using satellite imagery, GIS and landscape metrics. Appl. Geogr. **56**, 42–54 (2015). https://doi.org/10.1016/j.apgeog.2014. 10.002

7. Malczewski, J.: GIS-based multicriteria decision analysis: a survey of the literature. Int. J. Geogr. Inf. Sci. **20**, 703–726 (2006). https://doi.org/10.1080/13658810600661508

8. Rikalovic, A., Cosic, I., Lazarevic, D.: GIS based multi-criteria analysis for industrial site selection. Procedia Eng. **69**, 1054–1063 (2014). https://doi.org/10.1016/j.proeng.2014.03. 090

9. Koschke, L., Fürst, C., Frank, S., Makeschin, F.: A multi-criteria approach for an integrated land-cover-based assessment of ecosystem services provision to support landscape planning. Ecol. Ind. **21**, 54–66 (2012). https://doi.org/10.1016/j.ecolind.2011.12.010

10. Jeong, J.S., García-Moruno, L., Hernández-Blanco, J.: A site planning approach for rural buildings into a landscape using a spatial multi-criteria decision analysis methodology. Land Use Policy **32**, 108–118 (2013). https://doi.org/10.1016/j.landusepol.2012.09.018

11. Polebitski, A., Palmer, R.: Impacts of climate change and growth on water demands in the Puget Sound Region. In: World Environmental and Water Resources Congress, pp. 125–134 (2010). https://doi.org/10.1061/41114(371)15

12. Xie, D., Liu, Y., Chen, J.: Mapping urban environmental noise: a land use regression method. Environ. Sci. Technol. **45**, 7358–7364 (2011). https://doi.org/10.1021/es200785x

13. Ioja, C.I., Niță, M.R., Vânău, G.O., Onose, D.A., Gavrilidis, A.A.: Using multi-criteria analysis for the identification of spatial land-use conflicts in the Bucharest Metropolitan Area (2014). https://doi.org/10.1016/j.ecolind.2013.09.029

14. Antrop, M.: Landscape change and the urbanization process in Europe. Landsc. Urban Plan. **67**, 9–26 (2004). https://doi.org/10.1016/S0169-2046(03)00026-4

15. Weng, Y.-C.: Spatiotemporal changes of landscape pattern in response to urbanization. Landsc. Urban Plan. **81**, 341–353 (2007). https://doi.org/10.1016/j.landurbplan.2007.01.009

16. Aguilera, F., Valenzuela, L.M., Botequilha-Leitão, A.: Landscape metrics in the analysis of urban land use patterns: a case study in a Spanish metropolitan area. Landscape Urban Plan. **99**, 226–238 (2011). https://doi.org/10.1016/j.landurbplan.2010.10.004

17. Frondoni, R., Mollo, B., Capotorti, G.: A landscape analysis of land cover change in the Municipality of Rome (Italy): spatio-temporal characteristics and ecological implications of land cover transitions from 1954 to 2001. Landsc. Urban Plan. **100**, 117–128 (2011). https:// doi.org/10.1016/j.landurbplan.2010.12.002

18. Kuffer, M., Barrosb, J.: Urban morphology of unplanned settlements: the use of spatial metrics in VHR remotely sensed images. Procedia Environ. Sci. **7**, 152–157 (2011). https:// doi.org/10.1016/j.proenv.2011.07.027

19. Irwin, E.G., Geoghegan, J.: Theory, data, methods: developing spatially explicit economic models of land use change. Agric. Ecosyst. Environ. **85**, 7–24 (2001). https://doi.org/10. 1016/S0167-8809(01)00200-6

20. Schwarz, N.: Urban form revisited—Selecting indicators for characterising European cities. Landsc. Urban Plan. **96**, 29–47 (2010). https://doi.org/10.1016/j.landurbplan.2010.01.007

21. Borgogno-Mondino, E., Fabietti, G., Ajmone-Marsan, F.: Soil quality and landscape metrics as driving factors in a multi-criteria GIS procedure for peri-urban land use planning. Urban For. Urban Green. **14**, 743–750 (2015)

22. Borgogno Mondino, E., Fabrizio, E., Chiabrando, R.: Site selection of large ground-mounted photovoltaic plants: a GIS decision support system and an application to Italy. Int. J. Green Energy **12**, 515–525 (2015)

Indoor Positioning Methods – A Short Review and First Tests Using a Robotic Platform for Tunnel Monitoring

Alberico Sonnessa[1]([✉]), Mirko Saponaro[1], Vincenzo Saverio Alfio[1],
Alessandra Capolupo[1], Adriano Turso[2], and Eufemia Tarantino[1]

[1] Department of Civil, Environmental, Land, Construction and Chemistry
(DICATECh), Politecnico di Bari, Via Orabona 4, 70125 Bari, Italy
{alberico.sonnessa,mirko.saponaro,
vincenzosaverio.alfio,alessandra.capolupo,
eufemia.tarantino}@poliba.it
[2] Sipal S.p.A. S.P. 83 c/o Aeroporto "Marcello Arlotta",
74023 Grottaglie, TA, Italy
turso.adriano@sipal.it

Abstract. The aim of this work is to provide a review of the main indoor positioning methodologies, in order to evidence their strengths and weaknesses, and explore the potential of the integration in an Unmanned Ground Vehicle built for tunnel monitoring purposes. A robotic platform, named Bulldog, has been designed and assembled by Sipal S.p.a., with the support of the research group Applied Geomatic laboratory (AGlab) of the Politecnico di Bari, in the definition of the data processing pipeline. Preliminary results show that the integration of indoor positioning techniques in the Bulldog platform represents an important advance for accurate monitoring and analysis of a tunnel during the construction stage, allowing a fast and reliable survey of the indoor environment and requiring, at this prototypal stage of development, only a remote supervision by the operator. Expected improvements will allow to carry out tunnel monitoring activities in a fully autonomous mode, bringing benefit for the safety of people involved in the construction works and the accuracy of the acquired dataset.

Keywords: Indoor positioning · Indoor mapping · IP for civil engineering · Tunnel monitoring · Unmanned Vehicles · SLAM

1 Research Aims

The aim of the research presented hereafter is to provide a short review of the main indoor positioning methods, by showing the preliminary results of an industrial application in the field of civil engineering, developed by Sipal S.p.a. and coordinated by the research group AGlab at the Politecnico di Bari, aimed at exploring the opportunity to deploy Unmanned Ground Vehicles for tunnel monitoring purposes.

To achieve this, a remote-controlled prototype robotic platform, equipped with sensors, has been designed and assembled. Field tests were carried out to assess the

© Springer Nature Switzerland AG 2020
O. Gervasi et al. (Eds.): ICCSA 2020, LNCS 12252, pp. 664–679, 2020.
https://doi.org/10.1007/978-3-030-58811-3_48

performance of the system and are still ongoing. The first results indicate that the integration of indoor positioning techniques in the inspection and monitoring activities can be a valid support in the tunnel construction stages.

2 Introduction

The accurate mapping of the environment in which we live, along with the precise positioning of people and objects in it, still represents one of the most challenging issues for the scientific community.

Nowadays, high-precision mapping techniques, that encompass satellite and ground-based sensors, allow to get very detailed 3D models of the territory and the built environment. Current positioning and navigation techniques, which mainly rely on geodetic GNSS (Global Navigation Satellite System) receivers, permit to estimate positions of a sensor with near-millimeter accuracy.

As for the consumer market, mobile phones made real-time positioning within everyone's reach. Thanks to increasingly more advanced sensors and algorithms embedded in our devices and the availability of web mapping/navigation services (e.g. Google Maps, Apple Maps), we can easily locate ourselves and navigate towards every destination. Outdoor real-time precise positioning needs a good visibility of the satellite constellations (open sky conditions) and a web access.

At indoors, the level of degradation of the satellite signals makes the civilian-graded accuracy of GNSS inadequate for many purposes [1]. However, the estimation of a sensor indoor position and/or motion finds application in different contexts, such as augmented/virtual reality, autonomous robot control [2] and civil engineering.

The improvements in the reliability of outdoor positioning methodologies, do not correspond to same advances in indoor positioning systems (IPS). Simultaneous Localization And Mapping (SLAM) problem for indoor locations, that is the simultaneous estimation of the state of a platform equipped with on-board sensors and the building of a model (map) describing what is observed by the sensors [3], is still an open issue.

Consumer market solutions have been recently implemented by Apple in its high-end iPad tablet, that couple cameras and laser sensors. Interesting attempts aimed at freely making available indoor maps is the use of an Open Source platform to support indoor navigation, based on the OpenStreetMap tool, as showed in [4], and the opportunity provided by Google to its partners of integrating indoor maps in Google Maps.

3 Indoor Positioning Requirements in Underground Constructions

Many activities in the field of civil engineering requires reliable and robust IPS, as:

- Excavation and tunneling.
- Tunnel modelling and monitoring.

- Mining activities.
- Operation in dangerous environments.

With regards to the case study, in Table 1 are summarized the main positioning requirements in underground construction.

Table 1. Positioning requirements in underground construction according to [5]

Criteria	Criteria description	Value
Accuracy	For deformation analyses	1–5 mm
Accuracy	For monitoring purposes	1–5 mm
Accuracy	For machine control	1–5 cm
Range	Depending on the application	10–50 m
Positioning	Tasks requiring 3D-coordinates	Yes
Construction site-proof	Resistance against dust, emissions caused by construction machines, damages during construction works, vibrations and site deformations	Yes
Real-time availability	Survey tasks may need real-time measurements/outputs	80%
Usability	System should be operable by workers without surveying background	Yes
Costs	Cost must not exceed that of a surveying total station	5k–50k €
Operability under nonline of sight (NLoS) conditions	System should be operational under NLoS conditions; direct LoS between the reference sensors and the work site may be not available	Required

In accordance with the conditions indicated in the table it is therefore necessary to design an indoor system that guarantees the performance of the positioning. The position information of an Unmanned Vehicle can be provided by using various methodologies exploiting different sensors and technologies (or a combination of them). Main IP techniques will be shortly described in the following section along with main advantages and limitations.

4   Overview of the Main IP Techniques

IPS can be classified starting from the principles on which they are based, namely electromagnetic waves (visible, infrared, microwave and radio spectrum), mechanical waves (audible/ultra-sound) and inertial navigation (accelerometers and gyroscopes) [6]. Despite the difficulties of performing IP - especially where scenarios rapidly change for the presence of "moving things" (e.g. workers, construction machinery) – depending on possible Non-Line-of-Sight (NLoS) conditions, multipath from walls, ceilings and objects, signal attenuation/scattering - nevertheless, indoor locations can simplify navigation and positioning tasks, because of:

- Slow dynamics (with reference to the outdoor environment).
- Limited areas to be covered.
- Availability of facilities (electric power, web access, walls for target installation)
- Very limited weather effects.

Main IP techniques are listed in Table 2.

Table 2. Overview of indoor positioning methodologies by [6]

Technology	Accuracy	Coverage (m)	Measuring principle	Typical application
Cameras	0.1 mm-dm	1–10	Angle measurements from images	Automotive, metrology, robot navigation
Infrared	cm–m	1–5	Thermal imaging, active beacons	People detection and tracking
Polar Systems	μm-mm	3–4000	Time of Flight interferometry	Underground construction, automotive
Sound	cm	2–10	Distances using time of arrival	Hospitals, tracking
WLAN/WiFi	m	20–100	Fingerprinting	Pedestrian navigation
RFID	dm–m	1–50	Proximity detection, fingerprinting	Pedestrian navigation
Ultra-Wideband	cm–m	1–50	Body reflection, time of arrival	Resource management in construction projects - robotics, automation
High Sensitive GNSS	10 m	Global	Parallel correlation, assistant GPS	Navigation
Pseudolites	cm–dm	10–1000	Carrier phase ranging	GNSS challenged mines
Inertial Navigation	1%	10–100	Dead reckoning	Navigation

4.1 Cameras

Optical IP uses cameras as main sensor. With the improvement of their performances in terms of resolution of collected images/data and speed in their acquisition, the accuracy of this method has significantly improved in the last years.

The retrieving of 3D information about the investigated environment is based on a photogrammetric approach. As discussed in [7], the scale of the photogrammetric model can be obtained integrating a Time Of Flight (ToF) range camera. Different references can be used to carry out the sensor positioning, according to [6], that is:

1. **Reference from 3D Building Models**, where the detected objects are compared with a database containing building interiors dataset.
2. **Reference from Projected Targets/patterns** when mounting of reference markers is not indicated or possible.
3. **Reference from Deployed Coded Targets** aimed at a) simplifying the automatic identification of corresponding points assigning a unique code to each marker, b) providing the system scale.
4. **Systems without Reference** that relies on the direct tracking of objects. Illuminated targets are often used to improve algorithmic robustness.

Cameras can be used to simultaneously map the surrounding environment and estimate motion, i.e. performing a Visual SLAM. According to [8], this solution can rely on geometry by getting geometric constraints from images for motion estimation, or, following the recent trends, using deep learning to autonomously reconstruct and navigate in an unknown location.

An innovative approach to implement Visual SLAM, based on the integration of standard and event cameras with IMU (Inertial Measurement Unit), has been presented in [2]. This method overcomes typical limitations affecting standard cameras, (motion blur and low dynamic range) integrating event cameras, where pixels operate autonomously, transmitting their changes of intensity/time they occur/pixel space-time coordinates. These sensors produce little amount of information when motion is limited.

The authors in [2] introduced a pipeline that combines events, standard frames, and inertial measurements to compute reliable and accurate state estimation, applied for onboard state estimation of an autonomous quadrotor.

This approach led to an accuracy enhancement of 130% if compared to the use of the event camera only, and 85% over standard-frames-only visual-inertial systems, although still being computationally manageable.

Main advantages and limitations of this technique are summarized in Table 3.

Table 3. Advantages and limitations IP camera-based technique

Advantages	Limitations
No infrastructure required (1,3,4)	Need for providing a constantly updated database (1)
Accuracy	Must be generally coupled with other sensor for SLAM purposes
Cost	

4.2 Infrared

Infrared (IR) light is characterized by a wavelength longer than those of visible light, thus making this technology less invasive with respect to the IP techniques based on visible light. According to [6], the main methods of using infrared signals are: a) artificial light sources b) infrared imaging based on thermal radiation c) use of active beacons.

1. **Artificial Infrared Light sources** using active infrared sources and infrared sensitive cameras. An application in the gaming field is the Kinect (V1) embedded in the Xbox console, where the 3D shape is retrieved from the distortion of a pseudo random pattern of structured IR light dots captured with the infrared camera.

   Though developed in the video gaming world, Kinect has been wide spreadly used in the SLAM field thanks to the KinectFusion and Kintinuos algorithms [9–11].

2. **Imaging using Natural Infrared Radiation,** namely passive IR localization methods. Sensors operational in the thermography region are capable to acquire a passive image of the environment using natural thermal emissions.

3. **Active Beacons** based on infrared receivers located at known positions and mobile beacons whose positions are not known. A sub-meter precision can be reached when several receivers are employed in each room.

   Main advantages and limitations of this technique are listed in Table 4.

Table 4. Advantages and limitations IP IR-based technique

Advantages	Limitations
Low cost	Limited coverage range and accuracy
No infrastructure required (1,2)	NLoS problems between sender and receiver
	Interference of IR waves with fluorescent light/sunlight

4.3   Sound

The sound wave is a particular wave in which the perturbation is the pressure variation induced by a vibrating body in the surrounding medium (usually air or building material). The use of sound waves for IP purposes is based on locating mobile nodes through multilateration and TOA (Time of Arrival)/TDOA (Time Difference of Arrival) that is the multiple distance measurements to static nodes mounted permanently in a given environment.

Most widely known techniques are [12]:

- **Active Bat**
  A network of receivers with a centralized control unit are used to process the transmitters signal (ultrasound) and estimate their position.
- **Cricket System**
  A number of active devices (beacons, emitting ultrasound)), called 'Cricket nodes' [13], establish the positioning network and are used by the target (listener) for position determination.
- **Dolphin System**
  Mixed ultrasound-RF system, where a number of reference nodes emit in series RF and ultrasound signal, used by other nodes to compute distance to reference node.

- **Audible Sound Positioning System**

  A mobile device (transmitter) emits sound detected by acoustic receivers equipped with a CPU and a wireless network interface capable to send data to a central server, that estimates the range transmitter-receiver and send the estimated coordinates to the transmitter.

  Main advantages and limitations of this technique are evidenced in Table 5.

Table 5. Advantages and limitations IP sound-based technique

Advantages	Limitations
Low cost (at room scale)	Expensive for large environments
Accuracy (few centimeters) [14]	Variable accuracy as sound speed depends on temperature and humidity

4.4 WLAN/Wi-Fi

Due to its wide deployment in many indoor environments, WLAN (Wireless Local Area Networks), known as Wi-Fi, is employed to estimate the position of a mobile device in a range up to about 100 m.

To date, empirical models for WLAN-based indoor positioning are preferred [15], such as fingerprinting (FP) [16, 17] hereafter described.

As first step, signals are collected offline in order to build a database of discrete grid of locations, or reference point (RP), namely the radio-map. A signature is generated from the collected RF signals. The next stage, that is the online phase, make use of the radio-map for navigation via classification algorithms, or novel methodologies based on machine learning [18], and deep learning [19–22].

The accuracy of FP is strictly related to the number of calibration points, ranging from one to tens of meters.

Main FP-based IPS are:

- **FP-Based IPS Based on RSS**

  This method employs received signal strength (RSS) measurements as fingerprints for radio-map creation and online navigation.
- **FP-Based IPS Based on CSI**

  This approach is based on the channel estimate, which defines an indoor location using multipath attenuation and further physical phenomena such as refractions and reflections, characterizing this environment with detailed information [18, 19, 22]. The channel state information (CSI) can be used as FP.
- **FP-Based IPS Using FFNN**

  This innovative combined approach is proposed in [15], using WLAN signals such as CSI and RSS for fingerprint and state-of-the-art feed-forward neural network (FFNN) model for the evaluation of the IPS.

  The proposed FFNN model achieved a 1.3 m mean accuracy in an indoor setting, with 0.8 m of std. dev.

Main advantages and limitations of this technique are shown in Table 6.

Table 6. Advantages and limitations IP WLAN-based technique

Advantages	Limitations
Low cost (use existing infrastructure)	Signal power loss due to reflection, absorption, refraction, scattering, interference, and multipath
Accuracy (around meter)	

4.5 Radio Frequency Identification

RFID (Radio Frequency IDentification) IP methods relies on a reader, capable of obtaining through RF the data from active, passive or semi-passive electronic tags storing an ID, used to locate the RFID tag. A standard application able to manage a large number of tags is in the product tracking aimed at avoiding stealing in stores, with readers at known locations and tags on the product to be monitored. The accuracy and the range in RFID may vary significantly, depending on whether they are active or passive and the density of devices, with some researches achieving around-centimeters accuracies [23].

The typical case of RFID positioning using ToA, is based on measurements from a single tag; positioning is obtained combining the Angle of Arrival (AoA) measurements from that tag [1].

Main advantages and limitations of this technique are shown in Table 7.

Table 7. Advantages and limitations IP RFID-based technique

Advantages	Limitations
Accuracy (decimeter-meter)	Signal power loss due to reflection, absorption, refraction, scattering, interference, and multipath
	Privacy concern
Unique ID can be used for security purposes	Data management and configuration when a large number of devices is deployed

4.6 Ultra-Wide Band

A review of the state of the art in Ultra-Wide Band (UWB) positioning has been recently performed in [24].

UWB is defined as a RF signal characterized by a bandwidth greater than 500 MHz, usually operated in the 3.1–10.6 GHz range.

According to [25], UWB positioning methods can be grouped into two main classes, i.e. FP-based and geometric methods. Geometric methods are hereafter described, because comprehensive FP database are difficult to build.

- **TOA and TDOA-Based Methods**

  The TOA method is based on computing of the range transmitter - receiver by estimating of the Time Of Arrival of signals, thus requiring the precise synchronizations between the transmitter and receiver. The TDOA method locates the receiver using the Time Difference Of Arrival computed between the receiver and multiple transmitters, not necessitating their synchronization [26].

- **AOA-Based Methods**

  The AOA-based approaches first make use of the angle of the signal received from the transmitter, and then estimate the receiver location by using the intersection of the angle line from the transmitters [25]. Such approaches don't require clock synchronization and use a small number of anchors nodes, nevertheless necessitating the coupling of nodes with an antenna array.

- **RSSI-Based Methods**

  Geometric-RSSI (Received Signal Strength Indicator) methods relies on the measurement of the strength of the signal acquired by the receiver and transform it into a range observation between the transmitter and receiver. The performance of RSS methods is usually low if compared to TOA and TDOA approaches [27], but they are relatively low cost, and can deploy a large number of nodes.

Main advantages and limitations of this technique are summarized in Table 8.

Table 8. Advantages and limitations IP UWB-based technique

Advantages	Limitations
High data rate acquisition, multipath resolution capabilities, low energy consumption/interference with other systems	Signal power loss due to reflection, absorption, refraction, scattering, interference, and multipath
Accuracy (centimeter-meter)	
Penetration of obstacles	

4.7 High-Sensitive GNSS/Assisted GNSS

GNSS receivers hardly track signals in challenging settings such as urban canyons or at indoors, where signal fades [28]. This has boosted the research in the field of so-called highly sensitive and assisted GNSS (HSGNSS-AGNSS) receivers.

AGNSS receivers use an additional data link (e.g. internet connection) for providing information about satellite ephemeris, almanac, differential corrections and timing information, usually directly acquired from the GNSS constellations.

High-Sensitive GNSS (HSGNSS) receivers deploy further methods, not deepened here, aimed at increasing the signal reception in indoor environments.

However, performance of indoor GNSS technologies are not yet comparable to the level of accuracy reachable in outdoor settings. Even if indoor GNSS do not provide the needed accuracy for pedestrian navigation in a closed environment, this sensor can be integrated in an IPS with an inertial platform, in order to supply sparse coordinate updates.

Main advantages and limitations of this technique are showed in Table 9.

Table 9. Advantages and limitations HS-GNSS -based technique

Advantages	Limitations
Availability of an already existing infrastructures (satellite network)	Expensive
	Low accuracy

4.8   Pseudolites

The pseudolite system represents a powerful indoor positioning system, due to the capability of covering large areas and provide accurate positioning solution [29].

Pseudolites (pseudo-satellites) are basically ground-based beacons capable to generate pseudo-codes analogous to GNSS codes. This solution also embeds mobile rovers whose positions are estimated by measuring the distance between rovers and pseudolite beacons, generally positioned at known locations [6].

Pseudolites can cover wide areas (tens of kilometers); the main restriction in the yr usability is related to NLoS conditions between pseudolites and rovers. The use of a combined pseudolite receiver enables the acquiring and tracking of both GNSS and pseudolite signals, thus permitting a seamless transition from outdoor to indoor settings.

Main advantages and limitations of this technique are listed in Table 10.

Table 10. Advantages and limitations of IP pseudolites-based technique

Advantages	Limitations
Large coverage area	Multipath
	Time synchronization in deep indoor settings due to the unavailability of atomic clocks
Accuracy (centimeter-decimeter)	No easy solution for ambiguity resolution

4.9   Dead Reckoning Positioning Based on Inertial Navigation Systems

Dead Reckoning (DR) relies on the estimation of the current location of a target, computed from an already known position (fix), and taking advantages on the measurements of physical quantities used for defining its movement, (e.g. path and speed) [1].

The DR technique based on Inertial Navigation Systems (INS) encompass the integration of an Inertial Measurement Unit (IMU) with a computational platform.

An INS estimates the position, velocity and orientation quantities from the IMU, which embeds gyroscopes, accelerometers, and/or a magnetometer aimed at measuring the direction and strength of the magnetic field.

Due to significant drift problems, INS is commonly integrated with additional sensors which provide information on the system position.

Main advantages and limitations of this technique are evidenced in Table 11.

Table 11. Advantages and limitations IP INS-based technique

Advantages	Limitations
High accuracy if positions are estimated with high rate	Costs (for high precision IMUs)
No need for external reference	Drift that can lead to cumulative error

4.10   Polar Systems

Polar systems measure distance and angles, retrieving the position of a target object using the three-dimension vector between sensor and objects.

Most widely known polar systems are Total Stations (TS) and Laser Scanners (LS). Basically, TS and LS rely on the same measuring principles, where angles are measured by means of digital bar-codes embedded in the sensor, and an Electronic Distance Meter (EDM) measures the distance from the instrument to a target (typically a retroreflective prism) or a surface by timing the round-trip of a pulse of light. The signal reflected by the surface is detected by a sensor connected with the emitter. The instrument automatically scans the surfaces in its field of view and is capable to acquire millions of point per second [30].

These instruments mainly differ in terms of accuracy (TS can reach an accuracy of few millimeters) speed of acquisition and number of acquired point per seconds (LS can acquire up to one million of point/sec).

IP Polar systems-based tools, relying on high-precision rugged sensors/instruments developed for working in severe conditions, are particularly suited for civil engineering applications.

Main advantages and limitations of this technique are showed in Table 12.

Table 12. Advantages and limitations IP Polar system-based technique

Advantages	Limitations
Accuracy (around mm)	Cost
	Must be coupled with other sensors for navigation purposes
	Computational problems due to the amount of data (LS)

5   Case Study – IP for Civil Engineering Applications

An experience of IP for civil engineering applications is being jointly conducted by Sipal S.p.a, and the research group Applied Geomatic laboratory (AGlab) of the Politecnico di Bari in the frame of the innovative project "Technological Construction Site for Military and Civil Infrastructures/Cantiere Tecnologico per Infrastrutture Militari e Civili." (Unmanned Vehicles and Virtual Facilities).

The project is co-funded by the European Union-European Regional Development Fund POR Puglia 2014/2020 and the Puglia Region. A section of the project involves the development of hardware and software tools to be installed on board aerial and ground UVs, aimed at integrating or replacing traditional survey techniques used for collecting and analyzing key data in the different stages of a construction site.

Within this activity, it is being implementing a platform named Bulldog to be used for tunnel monitoring purposes [31], that is:

- The estimation of the over/under-excavated sections of the tunnel with respect to the type section.
- The survey of the excavation head, during the tunneling works, for controlling its stability and identifying the most suitable consolidation systems.
- The automatic identification of under-excavated areas that requires further work to reach the minimum theoretical tunnel section.

5.1   The Bulldog Platform

The Bulldog platform (Fig. 1) exploits IP Polar system-based techniques.
   The hardware of the platform consists of:

- A remotely controllable Unmanned Ground Vehicle (UGV), (max speed: 30 km/h, max payload: 130 kg) equipped with two Optic cameras and two IR cameras.
- A Trimble SX10 scanning station, that integrates the features of a TS (angular accuracy: 1", distance accuracy: 1 mm + 1.5 ppm) and LS (3D point position accuracy @100 m: 2.5 mm).
- A GEO-Laser AD-12 automatic tripod, for automatic levelling of the surveying instrument.

At this stage of its development, Bulldog must be remotely driven towards the target area inside the tunnel. As first step, the platform carries out high-precision localization operations computing its position by mean of the TS. The sensor position is obtained by measuring some retro-reflective prisms of known location installed in the tunnel. After the preliminary IP operations, Bulldog is able to perform a scan of the target area in LS mode, providing a point cloud with an average centimeter spacing.

The acquired data are processed and analyzed using specific tools developed on purpose in Python language, able to extract cross-sections of the tunnel and related construction characteristics and to estimate the over/under-excavated sections of the tunnel with respect to the typical section (Fig. 2).

Fig. 1. The Bulldog platform

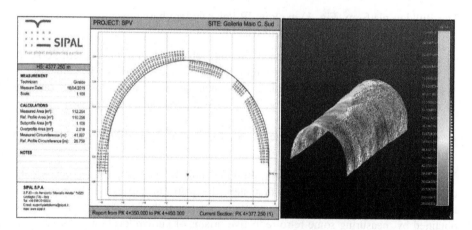

Fig. 2. Analysis tool user interface

Bulldog has been designed considering the requirements in terms of needed accuracy for the UGV positioning and reconstruction of the 3D model (some millimeters) of the surveyed area, and the possibility of easily upgrading the system by replacing or adding new SW features and/or sensors.

5.2 Expected Developments

Next steps expect the implementation of SLAM algorithms in the system, in order to make Bulldog capable of autonomously detect obstacles and move inside the construction area from its initial position, simply providing to the system the coordinates of an end point. To this aim, a Velodyne VLP-16 LS and an IMU will be integrated in the platform.

While not as accurate as SX10, Velodyne LS can be used for navigation, being able to quickly acquire a reliable (about 3 cm of accuracy) point cloud, useful for a fast and continuous mapping of the indoor environment. Therefore, the lack of efficient real-time 3D model generation methods of as-built 3D indoor environment is still an open issue.

An IMU will be also integrated to better reconstruct the Bulldog trajectories.

In this prototyping stage, SLAM algorithms are verified using ROS (Robot Operating System), a set of open source software libraries and tools for building robot applications [32], installed on TurtleBot, a low-cost robot kit with open-source software, equipped with a 2D or 3D distance sensor, a simplified IMU and microcomputer [33].

ROS+TurtleBot enable the testing and improvement of new features, allowing the speeding up of the system development.

6 Conclusive Remarks

Positioning and mapping activities in an indoor environment represent, in some cases, very difficult tasks. Nevertheless, high-accuracy IPSs have become in high demands in recent years, due to the increasing need for precise indoor localization in many sectors, ranging from the assistance for aged people to pedestrian navigation in large public buildings, to autonomous driving.

In the field of civil engineering, accurate IP and SLAM are required especially in potentially dangerous environments, as construction sites, where traditional measurement techniques could be replaced by fully automated procedures, avoiding possible injuries to operators.

In this work, different IP methodologies have been described in order to provide an overview of the main advantages and limitation of each technique, and an application of IP polar system-based method to an integrated robotic platform for monitoring tunnels has been presented.

As discussed above, the integration of IP techniques in the Bulldog platform represents an important advance for accurate monitoring and analysis of a tunnel during the construction works, allowing a fast and reliable survey of indoor environments and requiring, at this stage of development, only a remote supervision by the operator.

Expected improvements will allow to carry out monitoring activities without the need of a surveyor, bringing benefit for the safety of the construction area and accuracy of the acquired dataset by reducing possible errors due to the human factor.

Acknowledgements. This research is funded by the project "Technological Construction Site for Military and Civil Infrastructures/Cantiere Tecnologico per Infrastrutture Militari e Civili." (Unmanned Vehicles and Virtual Facilities), co-financed by the European Union-European Regional Development Fund POR Puglia 2014/2020 and Puglia Region.

References

1. Mendoza Silva, G., Torres-Sospedra, J., Huerta, J.: A Meta-Review of Indoor Positioning Systems. Sensors **19**(20), 4507 (2019)
2. Rosinol Vidal, A., Rebecq, H., Horstschaefer, T., Scaramuzza, D.: Ultimate SLAM? combining events, images, and IMU for robust visual SLAM in HDR and high-speed scenarios. IEEE Robot. Autom. Lett. **3**(2), 994–1001 (2018)
3. Cadena, C., et al.: Past, present, and future of simultaneous localization and mapping: toward the robust-perception age. IEEE Trans. Robot. **32**(6), 1309–1332 (2016)
4. Mascitelli, A.: An open source platform for indoor navigation: application to the Faculty of Civil and Industrial Engineering of Sapienza, University of Rome. Bollettino Sifet n.2-Sezione Scienza (2017)
5. Schneider, O.: Requirements for positioning and navigation in underground constructions. In: Proceedings of the 2010 International Conference on Indoor Positioning and Indoor Navigation (IPIN), 15–17 September, Campus Science City, ETH Zurich, Switzerland (2010)
6. Mautz, R.: Indoor Positioning Technologies. In: Sechsundachtzigster Band +, vol. 86 (2012)
7. Ravanelli, R., Nascetti, A., Crespi, M.: Kinect V2 and RGB stereo-cameras integration for depth map enhancement. Int. Arch. Photogrammetry Remote Sens. Spatial Inform. Sci. **XLI-B5–XXIII**, 699–702 (2016)
8. Duan, C., Junginger, S., Huang, J., Jin, K., Thurow, K.: Deep learning for visual SLAM in transportation robotics: a review. Transp. Safe. Environ. **1**, 177–184 (2019)
9. Newcombe, R.A., et al.: KinectFusion: real-time dense surface mapping and tracking. In: 10th IEEE International Symposium on Mixed and Augmented Reality, pp. 127–136. IEEE (2011)
10. Izadi, S., et al.: KinectFusion: real-time 3D reconstruction and interaction using a moving depth camera. In: Proceedings of the 24th Annual ACM Symposium on User Interface Software and Technology, pp. 559–568 (2011)
11. Whelan, T., Kaess, M., Fallon, M., Johannsson, H., Leonard, J. J., McDonald, J.: Kintinuous: Spatially extended kinectfusion. Technical report, MIT CSAIL (2012)
12. Sakpere, W., Adeyeye-Oshin, M., Mlitwa, N.B.W.: A state-of-the-art survey of indoor positioning and navigation systems and technologies. S. Afr. Comput. J. **29**(3), 145–197 (2017)
13. Priyantha, N.B.: The cricket indoor location system. Doctoral dissertation, Massachusetts Institute of Technology (2005)
14. Yassin, A., et al.: Recent advances in indoor localization: a survey on theoretical approaches and applications. IEEE Commun. Surv. Tutor. **2017**(19), 1327–1346 (2017)
15. Schmidt, E., Huang, Y., Akopian, D.: Indoor positioning via WLAN channel state information and machine learning classification approaches. In: Proceedings of ION GNSS+, pp. 355–166 (2019)
16. Bahl, P., Padmanabhan, V.: RADAR: an in-building RF-based user location and tracking system. In: Proceedings of the 19th Annual Joint Conference of the IEEE Computer and Communications Societies, vol. 2, pp. 775–784 (2000)

17. Youssef, M., Agrawala, A.: He Horus WLAN location determination system. In: Proceedings of the 3rd International Conference on Mobile Systems, Applications, and Services (MobiSys 2005), Seattle, WA, USA, pp. 205–218 (2005)
18. Schmidt, E., Akopian, D.: Fast prototyping of an SDR WLAN 802.11b Receiver for an indoor positioning systems. In: Proceedings of 31st International Technical Meeting Satellite Division Institute Navigation (ION GNSS), Miami, FL, USA, pp. 674–684 (2018)
19. Wang, X., Gao, L., Mao, S., Pandey, S.: CSI-based fingerprinting for indoor localization: a deep learning approach. IEEE Trans. Veh. Technol. 66(1), 763–776 (2017)
20. Wang, X., Gao, L., Mao, S.: CSI phase fingerprinting for indoor localization with a deep learning approach. IEEE Internet Things J. 3(6), 1113–1123 (2016)
21. Hsieh, C.-H., Chen, J.-Y., Nien, B.-H: Deep learning-based indoor localization using received signal strength and channel state information. IEEE Access 7, 33256–33267 (2019)
22. Chen, H., Zhang, Y., Li, W., Tao, X., Zhang, P.: ConFi: convolutional neural networks based indoor Wi-Fi localization using channel state information. IEEE Access 5, 18066–18074 (2017)
23. Brena, R.F.; García-Vázquez, J.P.; Galván-Tejada, C.E.; Muñoz-Rodriguez, D.; Vargas-Rosales, C.; Fangmeyer, J.: Evolution of indoor positioning technologies: a survey. J. Sens. 2017, 1–21 (2017)
24. Gabela, J., et al.: Experimental evaluation of a UWB-based cooperative positioning system for pedestrians in GNSS-denied environment. Sensors 2019, 5274 (2019)
25. Mazhar, F., Khan, M.G., Sällberg, B.: Precise indoor positioning using UWB: a review of methods, algorithms and implementations. Wireless Pers. Commun. 97(3), 4467–4491 (2017). https://doi.org/10.1007/s11277-017-4734-x
26. Xu, B., Sun, G., Yu, R., Yang, Z.: High-accuracy TDOA-based localization without time synchronization. IEEE Trans. Parallel Distrib. Syst. 24(8), 1567–1576 (2013)
27. Pittet, S., Renaudin, V., Merminod, B., Kasser, M.: UWB and MEMS-based indoor navigation. J. Navig. 61, 369–384 (2008)
28. Zhang, J., Li, B., Dempster, A.G., Rizos, C.: Evaluation of high sensitivity GPS receivers. In: International Symposium on GPS/GNSS Taipei, Taiwan. 26–28 October 2010
29. Xu, R., Chen, W., Xu, Y., Ji, S.: A new indoor positioning system architecture using GPS signals. Sensors 15, 10074–10087 (2015)
30. D'Aranno, P.J.V.: High-resolution geomatic and geophysical techniques integrated with chemical analyses for the characterization of a Roman wall. J. Cult. Heritage 17, 141–150 (2016)
31. Argese, F., et al.: Piattaforma HW/SW per la gestione dei Cantieri Tecnologici per Infrastrutture Civili. Atti Asita (2019)
32. ROS Website. http://www.ros.org. Accessed 15 Feb 2020
33. Turtlebot Website. http://www.turtlebot.com. Accessed 15 Feb 2020

Application of the Self-organizing Map (SOM) to Characterize Nutrient Urban Runoff

Angela Gorgoglione[1](✉) , Alberto Castro[1] , Andrea Gioia[2] ,
and Vito Iacobellis[2]

[1] Universidad de la República, 11300 Montevideo, Uruguay
agorgoglione@fing.edu.uy
[2] Politecnico di Bari, 70126 Bari, Italy

Abstract. Urban stormwater runoff is considered worldwide as one of the most critical diffuse pollutions since it transports contaminants that threaten the quality of receiving water bodies and represent a harm to the aquatic ecosystem. Therefore, a thorough analysis of nutrient build-up and wash-off from impervious surfaces is crucial for effective stormwater-treatment design. In this study, the self-organizing map (SOM) method was used to simplify a complex dataset that contains precipitation, flow rate, and water-quality data, and identify possible patterns among these variables that help to explain the main features that impact the processes of nutrient build-up and wash-off from urban areas. Antecedent dry weather, among the rainfall-related characteristics, and sediment transport resulted in being the most significant factors in nutrient urban runoff simulations. The outcomes of this work will contribute to facilitating informed decision making in the design of management strategies to reduce pollution impacts on receiving waters and, consequently, protect the surrounding ecological environment.

Keywords: SOM · Nutrient urban runoff · Water quality · SWMM · Diffuse pollution

1 Introduction

Urban stormwater runoff is one of the principal causes that contribute to the non-point source (NPS) (or diffuse) pollution and subsequent impairments of rivers, streams, lakes, and estuaries [1, 2]. Diffuse nutrients are challenging to manage and reduce since their quantification is difficult to evaluate. In fact, it is not possible to identify a point source, and they are generated by the contribution of many small sources [3]. Surface-water eutrophication could produce the growth of phytoplankton biomass (causing the decrease in water transparency) and toxic and irritating algal blooms (with odor and taste issues). Consequently, an increment of the costs of drinking water treatment could be registered [4]. Hence, the sustainable management of urban watersheds plays a crucial role in the protection of the quality of surface water bodies.

The dynamic nature of urban stormwater quality has been attributed to several factors. Previous researches have demonstrated that pollutant concentrations observed in stormwater were highly sensitive to local environmental conditions. The latter can be

O. Gervasi et al. (Eds.): ICCSA 2020, LNCS 12252, pp. 680–692, 2020.
https://doi.org/10.1007/978-3-030-58811-3_49

summarized as follows: *i)* temporal factors (like first flush pattern, antecedent dry period, rainfall trend) [5]; *ii)* spatial factors (like land use/land cover, watershed characteristics) [6]; *iii)* water-quality features (like pH, salinity, temperature, suspended solids) [7]; and *iv)* type of pollutants (like mass, composition, decay rates) [8]. In addition to the inherent randomness of nature, most of the works mentioned above have also shown that many multifaceted interactions among these factors have occurred in numerous dimensions [9].

During the last decade, linear multivariate statistical methods, like cluster analysis (CA) and principal component analysis/factor analysis (PCA/FA), have been well-reviewed in the evaluation and analysis of surface-water quality since their outstanding capability to process, analyze, and simplify a large amount of environmental data [3, 10, 11]. However, the linear multivariate statistical techniques are limited by the assumption of linearity, a hypothesis not verified for the process under study (pollutant build-up/wash-off).

Nowadays, the self-organizing map (SOM), a particular type of artificial neural network (ANN), has received attention from environmental researchers. SOM was proposed by Kohonen [12]. It is a competitive and unsupervised self-organizing network, formed of fully connected neuron arrays, which can produce the mapping from a multi-dimensional space to a two-dimensional space. With the pros of non-linear features, learning and induction skills, and a large number of parallel distributed structures, SOM has been successfully applied to tackle different environmental problems, such as water-quality characterization, water-area delineation with satellite images, and several other topics related to environmental engineering and water resources [13, 14].

Based on these considerations, this study aims to assess possible patterns among rainfall-runoff and water-quality variables that can help to analyze the main factors that influence nutrient build-up and wash-off from urban areas. We will take into account the non-linearity of these processes and the multidimensionality of the system involved. Therefore, to accomplish this objective, the SOM technique will be adopted.

The outcomes of this work not only will deliver useful information on emerging strategies for NPS management and regulation but also will widen the potential applications of SOM methodology in the environmental field, particularly in the water-resource engineering.

2 Materials and Methods

2.1 Methodology Description

The workflow reported in Fig. 1 summarizes the methodology adopted to accomplish the main objective of this work.

Three main phases can be identified: data set creation, data analysis, and results. More details about each of these phases can be found in the remainder of this paper. In particular, in Sect. 2.2, the data set creation is explained; in Sect. 2.4, all the techniques adopted are thoroughly described; in Sect. 3 and all its sub-sections, the results are rigorously presented and discussed.

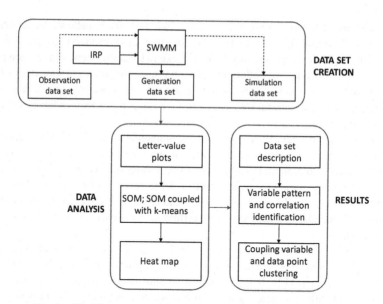

Fig. 1. Workflow summarizing the approach adopted in this study.

2.2 Study Area and Data Collection

The investigated area is represented by an urban watershed located in Sannicandro di Bari (hereafter called SB) (Puglia Region, Southern Italy). The catchment area is equal to 31.24 ha, including 21.87 ha (70%) of impervious surface. The SIT Puglia [15] land-use map indicates that the whole basin is residential, and only 3.80% of the watershed (1.20 ha) is characterized by a green area. The average slope of the catchment is equal to 1.56%, and the stormwater-drainage network is 1.96 km-long, collecting water into a concrete channel 1.20 m × 1.70 m [16]. The precipitation is recorded with a rain gauge located near the outlet of the basin. The water-quality monitoring is carried out through an autosampler with 24 bottles of 0.5 L each [16]. In Fig. 2, the watershed area, the drainage network, and the outfall are displayed.

In this work, three different datasets were used: *i) observations*: observed precipitation, flow rate, and water-quality data, used for calibrating and validating the hydrologic/hydraulic and water-quality models; *ii) generations*: flow rate and water-quality variables are obtained using generated precipitation time series, produced through numerical simulation, used as input in the hydrologic/hydraulic and water-quality models; *iii) simulations*: flow rate and water-quality data are obtained using observed precipitation as input data set in the hydrologic/hydraulic and water-quality models.

Considering the observations dataset, the monitoring campaign provided rainfall, flow rate, total suspended solids (TSS), and nutrients (N_{tot} and P_{tot}) for five rainfall events that occurred at SB (11/10/2006, 11/22/2006, 12/17/2006, 1/24/2007, and 2/10/2007). In Table 1, the observed dataset is summarized.

Fig. 2. Urban study area. Watershed surface (red area), drainage network (yellow lines), and location of the outfall (green pin). (Color figure online)

Table 1. Summary of the (a) rainfall-runoff and (b) water-quality data for the monitored events at SB watershed.

(a)	Event	ADP (days)	Total rainfall (mm)	Event duration (min)	Max. Rainfall intensity (mm/h)	Runoff volume (m³)	Runoff peak (m³/s)
	11/10/2006	6	2.40	50.00	24.00	113.49	0.04
	11/22/2006	11	4.30	112.00	6.00	148.86	0.04
	12/17/2006	18	5.90	251.00	12.00	286.88	0.05
	1/24/2007	19	1.60	37.00	12.00	111.62	0.05
	2/10/2007	6	12.90	398.00	36.00	460.11	0.05

(b)	Event	TSS (mg/L)			N_{tot} (mg/L)			P_{tot} (mg/L)		
		min	max	EMC	min	max	EMC	min	max	EMC
	11/10/2006	224.0	420.0	19.54	7.0	8.3	0.47	0.70	1.00	0.05
	11/22/2006	124.0	2160.0	86.40	3.6	14.0	0.45	0.24	2.96	0.11
	12/17/2006	6.0	217.0	6.040	NA			NA		
	1/24/2007	177.0	807.0	47.96	5.4	10.0	0.48	0.65	0.99	0.03
	2/10/2007	541.0	2090.0	40.00	6.3	13.0	0.25	2.08	3.63	0.08

Regarding the *generation* dataset, synthetic precipitation time series were produced exploiting the Iterated Random Pulse (IRP) rainfall model (proposed by Veneziano and Iacobellis [17]), providing a time series of 15 years length and 15 min of aggregation. More details regarding the model description, its parameters, and its implementation to the study area is provided in the literature [18, 19]. Taking into account the regional regulation [20], single rainfall events were defined considering a condition of 48 h of antecedent dry weather. Accordingly, 567 rainfall events were identified in the 15-years-time series.

Regarding the *simulation* dataset, observed rainfall events and simulation results of runoff and water quality were considered. A brief description of the adopted rain-fall-runoff and water quality models is reported in Sect. 2.2. The model calibration and validation was an issue already tackled in our previous work [16].

2.3 Hydrologic/Hydraulic and Water-Quality Model Implementation

The Environmental Protection Agency's Storm Water Management Model (EPA's SWMM) was adopted in this work to estimate the flow rate and water quality variables [21]. In particular, the runoff block was used to simulate water runoff, the formation of surface runoff constituent loads due to the pollutant build-up during dry weather, and pollutant wash-off during wet weather. The transport block was also used to execute the flow and pollutant routing through the drainage network. In the transport module, flow routing was accounted for utilizing the kinematic-wave; in turn, water-quality dynamics included first-order degeneration within the sewer system [22]. Furthermore, the accounted water losses are represented by the depression storage on the impervious surface of the watershed and the infiltration amount. In this work, Horton's equation was used to calculate the infiltration rate, whose parameters have been estimated considering the typical values reported in the recent literature [23].

A comprehensive explanation of the mathematical description of these physical processes is reported in the recent bibliography [16, 22]. In particular, Di Modugno et al. [16] described good performances regarding the evaluation of the water quantity response of SB by exploiting a hydrologic/hydraulic approach with several sets of input parameters; moreover, the build-up and wash-off simulations were positively performed.

2.4 Data Analysis

The SOM is a particular kind of ANN that learns in an unsupervised manner, as there is no target or objective to compare with [24]. It is conceived to self-manage similar information that has not yet been classified. In the Self-Organizing Map, neurons compete with each other in order to describe the input data, as opposed to error-correction learning (such as backpropagation with gradient descent). As an outcome, data in the multidimensional attribute space can be reorganized to a smaller number of latent dimensions, which is arranged considering a predetermined geometry in a space of lower dimensionality, usually an ordinary two-dimensional array of neurons.

K-means CA was exploited to organize the investigated variables into clusters base on their similarity. A distance function evaluates the similarity, firstly, among data points, afterward, among the groups as well [25]. This approach also needs a priori selection of an arbitrary number of groups (k). In this work, the silhouette method was employed to evaluate the most suitable k [26]. This approach measures the proximity of each point of a cluster to the points of neighboring clusters:

$$s(i) = \frac{b(i) - a(i)}{\max(b(i), a(i))} \tag{1}$$

where $a(i)$ is the average distance of the point (i) with respect to all the other points in the assigned cluster (A), $b(i)$ is the average distance of the point (i) with respect to other points belonging to its closest neighboring cluster (B). Silhouette values are within the range $[-1, 1]$; the higher the value, the better is the cluster conformation.

Heat map analysis is a pseudo-color picture, including two dendrograms for two different objects, which can be divided into several clusters [27]. The different influence characteristics in these two objects were reorganized considering their similarity based on CA.

3   Results and Discussion

3.1   Data Set Description

Figure 3 shows the distribution and quantiles of the investigated water-quality variables, obtained using the three different given datasets (generations, simulations, and observations). In particular, each variable was normalized based on its mean and standard deviation, so that the new standardized variable is characterized by mean equal to 0 and standard deviation equal to 1. This plot style is known as a "letter-value plot" because it shows a large number of quantiles. It is similar to a box-plot in plotting a non-parametric representation of a distribution in which all features correspond to actual observations [28]. In particular, the horizontal gray lines denote the median, and the colored dots correspond to extreme values.

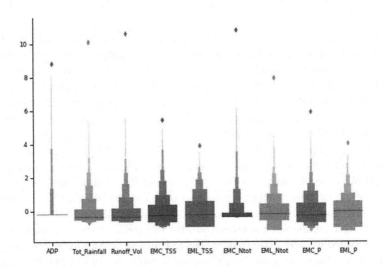

Fig. 3. Letter-value plots of the complete dataset (observations, simulations, and generations). The horizontal gray line represents the median; the colored dot corresponds to outliers.

In Table 2, the main quantiles (25, 50, and 75%) and the maximum values of the standardized variables are reported.

The letter-value plots reported in Fig. 3 are able to show the skewed tails of the investigated variables. In particular, the figure highlights the strong asymmetry of the standardized variables, except for the *EML_P* and *EML_TSS*, which show lower asymmetry.

Table 2. Statistical description of rainfall-runoff and water-quality variables.

	ADP	Tot_Rainfall	Runoff_Vol	EMC_TSS	EML_TSS	EMC_N$_{tot}$	EML_N$_{tot}$	EMC_P	EML_P
mean	0.000	0.000	0.000	0.000	0.000	0.000	0.000	0.000	0.000
sd	1.001	1.001	1.001	1.001	1.001	1.000	1.000	1.000	1.000
min	−0.177	−0.680	−0.674	−0.993	−0.968	−0.414	−1.182	−1.247	−1.227
25%	−0.176	−0.565	−0.575	−0.680	−0.959	−0.378	−0.593	−0.724	−1.005
50%	−0.175	−0.329	−0.327	−0.267	−0.198	−0.334	−0.196	−0.256	0.000
75%	−0.173	0.133	0.139	0.349	0.577	−0.138	0.407	0.438	0.565
max	8.841	10.136	10.608	5.442	3.919	10.816	7.964	5.893	4.025

3.2   Variable Correlations

The visualization of the weight maps is a useful tool to identify possible correlations of the different rainfall-runoff and water-quality variables (Fig. 4). To build the map, initially, the input data is normalized per variable. Then, the map size is evaluated by calculating the number of neurons from the number of data points in the training data using the following equation [29]:

$$M \approx 5\sqrt{N} \tag{2}$$

where M is the number of neurons, which is an integer close to the result of the right-hand side of the equation, and N is the number of data points. In this study, there are 577 input data points (N), so the number of neurons used was 121 (M), i.e., a map of 11 by 11 neurons. In this work, the implementation was coded in Python on a 2.6 GHz Intel i7 PC with 32 GB of memory using the *minisom* package for the creation of the SOM [30], and the *seaborn* package for visualization [31]. The phases of the map-weights initialization and the map training were both realized picking samples at random from the input data set. After a training phase of 10,000 epochs (all the input data samples were used 10,000 times), a quantization error of 0.095 and a topographic error of 0.067 were obtained, assuring the quality of the resulting map.

Considering the rainfall-related variables (*ADP*, *Tot_Rainfall*, and *Runoff_Vol.*), the three weight maps presented in Fig. 4 show consistent results. *Tot_Rainfall* and *Runoff_Vol.* activate the same neurons (positive neurons), which are symmetric to the neurons activated by *ADP*. The "redder" the activated neurons of *ADP* are, the greater the water loss in the system, the "bluer" are the negative neurons of runoff volume and total rainfall maps.

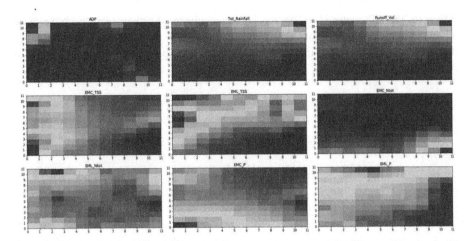

Fig. 4. Pattern evaluation of the rainfall and water-quality variables with the SOM-weight map.

Among the water-quality-related features, three map patterns can be identified: pollutant EMLs, *EMC_TSS* and *EMC_P*, and *EMC_N$_{tot}$*. One of the significant findings achieved with this analysis is the strong relationship between sediment load (*EML_TSS*) and nutrient EMLs and between the sediment and phosphorus concentration (*EMC_TSS* and *EMC_P*). This correlation suggests that sediment transport plays an essential role in the mobilization of nutrients from urban impervious surfaces. In particular, in our study area, phosphorus transport is highly correlated to the sediment wash-off. The particle-bound portion of the nitrogen is depicted by the same positive activated neurons of *EML_TSS* and *EML_N$_{tot}$*. While its dissolved portion is represented by the symmetric positive neurons between *EMC_N$_{tot}$* and *Tot_Rainfall-Runoff_Vol*. This correlation suggests that the bigger the runoff volume, the smaller the nitrogen concentration. The latter can be justified with the dilution process. Therefore, in our study area, nitrogen mobilization predominantly occurs in the dissolved form. Furthermore, it is worth remarking that the red positive neurons activated by *ADP* are located in the high-left corner, as well as those activated by pollutant EMLs. Therefore, the longer the antecedent dry weather, the higher is the amount of pollutants built up on the impervious surface, mainly sediments.

It is worth noting that the water quality-related features activate more neurons than the rainfall-related ones, that are, instead, located in a single area and not sparse all over the map. This means that the variation of the water-quality variables is higher and the neighbor region is ready to acquire their information.

3.3   SOM/Clustering Results

The analysis was performed by a SOM and k-means algorithm ensemble to group the variables into clusters based on their similarities. To identify the most representative number of clusters (*k*), the silhouette method was adopted. The average silhouette score of all the samples in the data set was calculated (Fig. 5a). This produces a value that represents the silhouette score of that particular cluster. Furthermore, the boxplot of silhouette scores was built to assess the dispersion of the data at each number of clusters taken into account. (Fig. 5b). We considered the possibility of having from 2 to 10 clusters ($k \in [2, 10]$).

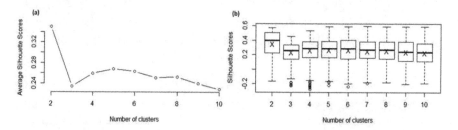

Fig. 5. (a) Average silhouette scores per k; (b) boxplot of silhouette scores per k (with $k \in [2, 10]$). The average is represented by 'X'.

In Fig. 5a, the optimum number of clusters seems to be $k = 2$. However, in Fig. 5b, we can see that the data dispersion related to $k = 2$ is higher than the rest. Moreover, the $k = 3$ and $k = 4$ have several outliers under the minimum value. Therefore, we decided to group the data points into 5 clusters, also considering that this boxplot has the highest maximum, and the average silhouette scores are the second-highest after $k = 2$. In Fig. 6(a), a matrix that shows the neighboring distances is represented (SOM-distance map). The higher the difference between one node and its neighbor, the darker the resulting color between those two neurons. The SOM outcome was coupled with k-means cluster analysis. In Fig. 6(a), the five clusters of the neurons are overlapped on top of the distance map and represented with different shapes and colors (green cross, orange x, blue circle, purple rhombus, and red square). Considering that each neuron is a vector, in Fig. 6(b), the feature with the highest value in each neuron is highlighted.

From Figs. 6(a) and (b), it is possible to see that the "green cross" group is characterized by high values of EMC_N_{tot}. The "orange x" cluster has mainly high values of EMC_P and also EMC_N_{tot} and EMC_TSS. The other three groups are more heterogeneous. The "red square" one is characterized by high values of EMC_TSS, EML_P, ADP, EML_Ntot, EML_TSS. The "purple rhombus" cluster has high values of $Tot\_Rainfall$, $Runoff\_Vol.$, EML_TSS, ADP, EMC_N_{tot}, EMC_TSS. The "blue circle" group, the biggest, is characterized by high values of all the variables.

With the aim of coupling variable-clustering and data point-clustering, a heat map analysis was run using Ward linkage and Euclidean distance (Fig. 7).

Also for the heat map, we considered 5 clusters ($k = 5$). The left dendrogram was obtained considering the original matrix (577 × 9), being 577 generated, observed, and simulated events and 9 rainfall and water-quality variables. It is possible to highlight that ADP is playing an essential role by clearly marking the 5 clusters. Furthermore, we can appreciate that for groups with high values of $Tot\_Rainfall$ and $Runoff\_Vol$, the values of EMCs are low and vice-versa. The latter is explained by the dilution process.

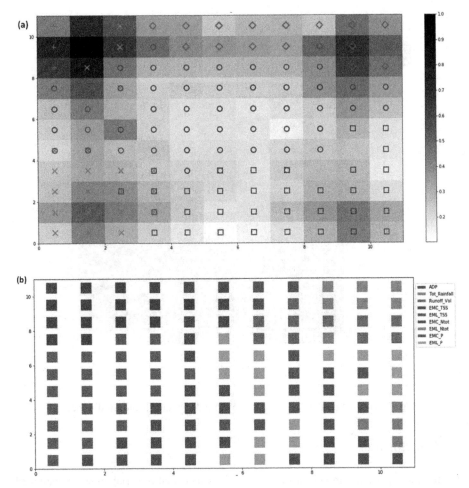

Fig. 6. (a) SOM-distance map coupled with k-means. (b) Variables with the highest value in each neuron. (Color figure online)

The top dendrogram was obtained considering the transposed of the previous matrix (9 × 577). The first cluster identified is formed by *Tot_Rainfall* and *Runoff_Vol*. *ADP* has its own cluster. EMLs are all grouped together. *EMC_TSS* and *EMC_P* are grouped, while *EMC_N$_{tot}$* forms another cluster. This portion of the heat map perfectly confirms the outcomes obtained with the SOM-weight map (Fig. 4).

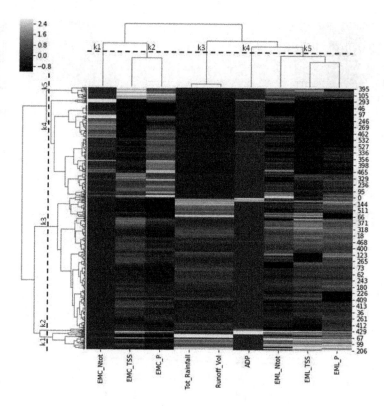

Fig. 7. Heat map analysis outcome (Ward linkage and Euclidean distance).

4 Conclusions

In this study, patterns among rainfall-runoff and water-quality variables were evaluated to identify the main factors that influence nutrient build-up and wash-off from urban areas, taking into account the non-linearity of these processes and the multidimensionality of the system involved. A study area located in southern Italy and the SOM technique were considered for this study. The main conclusions can be summarized as follows:

- Rainfall factors: *ADP*, *Tot_Rainfall*, and *Runoff_Vol.* present a reliable correlation driven by *ADP*. In fact, the "redder" the activated neurons of *ADP* are, the higher the water loss in the system, the "bluer" are the negative neurons of runoff volume and total rainfall maps.
- Water-quality factors: *EML_TSS* and nutrient EMLs present a robust correlation, confirming as appropriate the use of suspended solids as a proxy for the study of the behavior of nutrients in urban areas. Considering pollutant EMCs, a strong relationship was found only between the *EMC_TSS* and *EMC_P*, showing the high importance of the phosphorus particle-bound in the system under study.

- Interactions rainfall and water-quality factors: the nitrogen dilution process is represented by the symmetric positive neurons between EMC_N_{tot} and $Tot\_Rainfall\text{-}Runoff\_Vol$. A high correlation was also found between ADP and pollutant EMLs: the longer the antecedent dry weather, the higher is the amount of pollutants built up on the impervious surface, mainly sediments.

The outcomes of this work have proved that coupling watershed-scale studies and non-linear exploratory analysis, like SOM, can provide an adequate overview of the relationships between water-quality variables and rainfall characteristics. Furthermore, the results presented in this work are expected to assist researchers and technicians in quantifying their confidence in the water-quality assessment, which aids informed analysis and decision-making in the design of management strategies to reduce pollution impacts on receiving waters and, consequently, protect the surrounding ecological environment.

References

1. Bernhardt, E.S., Palmer, M.A.: Restoring streams in an urbanizing world. Freshw. Biol. **52**, 738–751 (2007)
2. Jiang, S.C., Lim, K.-Y., Huang, X., McCarthy, D., Hamilton, A.J.: Human and environmental health risks and benefits associated with use of urban stormwater. Wiley Interdiscip. Rev. Water **2**, 683–699 (2015)
3. Gorgoglione, A., Gioia, A., Iacobellis, V.: A framework for assessing modeling performance and effects of rainfall-catchment-drainage characteristics on nutrient urban runoff in poorly gauged watersheds. Sustainability **11**, 4933 (2019)
4. Brett, M.T., et al.: Non-point-source impacts on stream nutrient concentrations along a forest to urban gradient. Environ. Manage. **35**, 330–342 (2005)
5. Lee, H., Lau, S.L., Kayhanian, M., Stenstrom, M.K.: Seasonal first flush phenomenon of urban stormwater discharges. Water Res. **38**(19), 4153–4163 (2004)
6. Gobel, P., Dierkes, C., Coldewey, W.C.: Storm water runoff concentration matrix for urban areas. J. Contam. Hydrol. **91**(1–2), 26–42 (2007)
7. Nguyen, H.L., Leermakers, M., Elskens, M., De Ridder, F., Doan, T.H., Baeyens, W.: Correlations, partitioning and bioaccumulation of heavy metals between different compartments of Lake Balaton. Sci. Total Environ. **341**(1–3), 211–226 (2005)
8. Surbeck, C.Q., Jiang, S.C., Ahn, J.H., Grant, S.B.: Flow fingerprinting fecal pollution and suspended solids in stormwater runoff from an urban coastal watershed. Environ. Sci. Technol. **40**(14), 4435–4441 (2006)
9. Ki, S.J., et al.: Advancing assessment and design of stormwater monitoring programs using a self-organizing map: characterization of trace metal concentration profiles in stormwater runoff. Water Res. **45**, 4183–4197 (2011)
10. Varol, M.: Spatio-temporal changes in surface water quality and sediment phosphorus content of a large reservoir in Turkey. Environ. Pollut. **259**, 113860 (2020)
11. Batur, E., Maktav, D.: Assessment of surface water quality by using satellite images fusion based on PCA method in the Lake Gala, Turkey. IEEE Trans. Geosci. Remote Sens. **57**(5), 2983–2989 (2019)
12. Kohonen, T.: Automatic formation of topological maps of patterns in a self-organizing system. In: Oja, E., Simula, O. (eds.) Processing 2nd Scandinavian Conference on Image Analysis, pp. 214–220 (1981)

13. Sengorur, B., Koklu, R., Ates, A.: Water quality assessment using artificial intelligence techniques: SOM and ANN—a case study of Melen River Turkey. Water Qual. Exposure Health **7**(4), 469–490 (2015)

14. Jiang, M., Wang, Y., Tang, Q., Meng, F., Yao, Z., Cheng, P.: Assessment of surface water quality using a growing hierarchical self-organizing map: a case study of the Songhua River Basin, northeastern China, from 2011 to 2015. Environ. Monit. Assess. **190**, 260 (2018). Regional geographical information system: SIT Puglia: Available online: http://www.sit. puglia.it/. Accessed 8 Jan 2020

15. Di Modugno, M., et al.: Build-up/wash-off monitoring and assessment for sustainable management of first flush in an urban area. Sustainability **7**, 5050–5070 (2015)

16. Veneziano, D., Iacobellis, V.: Multiscaling pulse representation of temporal rainfall. Water Resour. Res. **38**, 131–1313 (2002)

17. Veneziano, D., Furcolo, P., Iacobellis, V.: Multifractality of iterated pulse processes with pulse amplitudes generated by a random cascade. Fractals **10**, 209–222 (2002)

18. Gorgoglione, A., Gioia, A., Iacobellis, V., Piccinni, A.F., Ranieri, E.: A rationale for pollutograph evaluation in ungauged areas, using daily rainfall patterns: Case studies of the Apulian region in Southern Italy. Appl. Environ. Soil Sci. 2016 (2016)

19. Regional Regulation: Stormwater runoff and first flush regulations (implementation of article 13 of Legislative Decree no 152/06 and subsequent amendments), no 26, 9 December 2013. https://www.indicenormativa.it/sites/default/files/R_26_09_12_2013.pdf. Accessed 6 Jan 2020

20. Rossman, L.A.: Storm water management model user's manual version 5.0; EPA/600/R-05/040; National Risk Management Research Laboratory-Office of Research and Development, U.S. Environmental Protection Agency, Cincinnati, OH, USA (2010)

21. Gorgoglione, A., Bombardelli, F.A., Pitton, B.J.L., Oki, L.R., Haver, D.L., Young, T.M.: Uncertainty in the parameterization of sediment build-up and wash-o processes in the simulation of sediment transport in urban areas. Environ. Model. Softw. **111**, 170–181 (2019)

22. Horton, R.E.: An approach toward a physical interpretation of infiltration capacity. Soil Sci. Soc. Am. **5**, 399–417 (1940)

23. Kohonen, T.: Self-organizing Maps, 3rd edn. Springer, Heidelberg (2001). https://doi.org/10. 1007/978-3-642-56927-2

24. Jain, A.K., Murty, M.N., Flynn, P.J.: Data clustering: a review. ACM Comput. Surv. **31**, 264–323 (1999)

25. Rousseeuw, P.J.: Silhouettes: a graphical aid to the interpretation and validation of cluster analysis. J. Comput. Appl. Math. **20**, 53–65 (1987)

26. Wei, C., Gao, C., Han, D., Zhao, W., Lin, Q., Wang, G.: Spatial and temporal variations of water quality in Songhua River from 2006 to 2015: implication for regional ecological health and food safety. Sustainability **9**, 1502 (2017)

27. Hofmann, H., Kafadar, K., Wickham, H.: Letter-value plots: boxplots for large data. J. Comput. Graph. Stat. **26**(3), 469–477 (2017)

28. Vesanto, J.: SOM implementation in SOM toolbox. SOM toolbox online help. http://www. cis.hut.fi/projects/somtoolbox/documentation/somalg.shtml. Accessed Feb 2020

29. Vettigli, G.: Minisom: minimalistic and numpy-based implementation of the self organizing map. https://github.com/JustGlowing/minisom. Accessed Feb 2020

30. Waskom, M., Botvinnik, O., O'Kane, D., Hobson, P., Ostblom, J., Lukauskas, S., et al.: mwaskom/seaborn: v0.9.0, July 2018. https://www.doi.org/10.5281/zenodo.1313201. Accessed Feb 2020

Parallel Development of Comparable Photogrammetric Workflows Based on UAV Data Inside SW Platforms

Mirko Saponaro[1](✉), Adriano Turso[2], and Eufemia Tarantino[1]

[1] Polytechnic University of Bari, Via Orabona 4, 70125 Bari, Italy
mirko.saponaro@poliba.it
[2] Sipal S.p.A., S.P. 83 c/o "Marcello Arlotta" Airport,
74023 Grottaglie, TA, Italy

Abstract. A wide range of industrial applications benefits from the accessibility of image-based techniques for three-dimensional modelling of different multi-scale objects. In the last decade, along with the technological progress mainly achieved with the use of Unmanned Aerial Vehicles (UAVs), there has been an exponential growth of software platforms enabled to return photogrammetric products. On the other hand, the different levels of final product accuracy resulting from the adoption of different processing approaches in various softwares have not yet been fully understood. To date, there is no validation analysis in literature focusing on the comparability of such products, not even in relation to the use of workflows commonly allowed inside various software platforms. The lack of detailed information about the algorithms implemented in the licensed platforms makes the whole interpretation even more complex.

This work therefore aims to provide a comparative evaluation of three photogrammetric softwares commonly used in the industrial field, in order to obtain coherent, if not exactly congruent results. After structuring the overall processing workflow, the processing pipelines were accurately parameterized to make them comparable in both licensed and open-source softwares. For the best interpretation of the results derived from the generation of point clouds processed by the same image dataset, the obtainable values of root-mean-square error (RMSE) were analyzed, georeferencing models as the number of GCPs varied. The tests carried out aimed at investigating the elements shared by the platforms tested, with the purpose of supporting future studies to define a unique index for the accuracy of final products.

Keywords: UAV data processing · MicMac · Pix4d · PhotoScan

1 Introduction

The technological trends strongly linked to the use of Information and Communications Technologies (ICT) hardware and software solutions are now an unequivocal source of development for Industry 4.0 and therefore make the development of Technological Systems totally vital for the determination of new industrial scenarios worldwide [1].

© Springer Nature Switzerland AG 2020
O. Gervasi et al. (Eds.): ICCSA 2020, LNCS 12252, pp. 693–708, 2020.
https://doi.org/10.1007/978-3-030-58811-3_50

Among all of them, it is evident how the introduction of remote control technologies has in itself revolutionized different areas of use but above all simplified, in the common vision, the obtainment of various certified products in a short time. One of the fields mostly influenced by the exponential growth of hardware and software technologies is certainly the geomatic sector, encouraged by the now widespread use of Unmanned Aerial Vehicles (UAV) equipped with simple low cost cameras for the generation of two and three-dimensional photogrammetric products [2].

Many industrial applications benefit from the accessibility of Structure from Motion (SfM) techniques, essentially based on the manipulation of 2D images for three-dimensional modelling of different objects at different scales [3, 4]. In the last decade, together with the technological evolution of aircraft components and transportable sensors, there has been an exponential growth of software platforms enabled to return photogrammetric products, but above all a sophistication of the algorithms implemented [5]. However, while it is possible for any software used with the necessary precautions to return products which are much more comparable than those obtained from much more expensive technologies (e.g. Terrestrial Laser Scanner) [6], the different levels of final product accuracy resulting from the adoption of different processing approaches in various softwares have not yet been fully understood [7]. No validation analysis has been conducted so far in literature to consider these products as repeatable and reproducible, not even in relation to the use of workflows commonly allowed inside various software platforms. In fact, in consideration of the way products are validated geometrically, as drafted by ASPRS [8] or often by national regulations, the dependence between the evaluations made and the repeatability and reproducibility of the results remains unexpressed [9, 10]. Moreover, the lack of detailed information on the algorithms implemented in the licensed platforms makes the whole interpretation even more complex. This work therefore aims to provide a comparative evaluation of three photogrammetric softwares commonly used in the industrial field, in order to obtain coherent, if not exactly congruent. In particular, three processing chains were started in parallel in Agisoft Photoscan, Pix4D Mapper and MicMac. After structuring the overall processing workflow, the processing pipelines were carefully parameterized to make them comparable in both licensed and open source softwares. For the best interpretation of the results derived from the generation of point clouds processed from the same set of image data, through statistical inference, the influence on the final product accuracy of the number of Ground Control Points (GCP) implemented in the georeferencing was then analyzed [11]. The tests carried out were aimed at investigating the elements shared by the platforms tested, with the purpose of supporting future studies to define a single index for the accuracy of final products.

2   Methods

2.1   Study Area and Field Operations

The tests were carried out on a dataset of images about the excavation area of a road section in the trench of the Pedemontana Veneta Highway. The Pedemontana Veneta Highway is a road infrastructure currently under construction that crosses Veneto (a region in Northern Italy) being developed in the context of the European Mediterranean Corridor (ex Corridor n.5). The intervention concerns the decongestion of the territorial conurbation of the central metropolitan area of the regional territory, with the creation of an overall by-pass and a foothill route for continuity. The dataset consists of 243 images acquired by a low-cost camera NIKON CORPORATION Coolpix A (focal length 18.5 mm, ISO 400, Shutter 1/1000, 4928 × 3264 pixels, 16 MP) mounted on board the professional multicopter IA-3 Colibrì of the IDS supplied by SIPAL S.p.A. This latter is a vertical take-off landing (VTOL) UAV of weight up to 5 kg and is propelled by 4 brushless rotors. Being characterized by a maximum flight time of 40 min at optimal payload (0.5 kg) as in the case study, the flight was performed at a height of about 50 m above the ground, obtaining a Ground Sample Distance (GSD) of 1.23 cm/pix, and covering an area of about 0.0853 km^2, considering a non homogeneous longitudinal overlap of 80% in the whole area.

The UAV was equipped with a high-precision GNSS rover receiver, which in continuous mode records the coordinates of the antenna phase centre in Real Time Kinematic (RTK), creating a radio-bridge with the GNSS master station on the ground in static acquisition. Thus, each image was associated with the geo-tag of the receiver at the time of shooting. The coordinates of the images were recorded and transformed into a Linear Local Reference System, useful during the road construction phase.

Finally, twenty 80 × 80 cm targets were distributed throughout the entire scene as in Fig. 1, so that they could be recognized in the images captured by UAVs. The targets were then measured in a GNSS survey using Leica GS08plus receivers in Real Time Kinematic (RTK) mode, achieving an average accuracy equal to 0.02 m along the three axes. The ground truth coordinates were consequently obtained, to be used as Ground Control Points (GCPs) or Check Points (CPs) in each test performed.

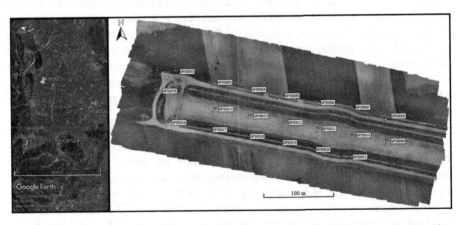

Fig. 1. On the left, in red, the road axis of the Pedemontana Veneta Highway in its extension. On the right, a detail of the road section under excavation, object of study, near km 60 and the distribution of the GCP/CP targets in the overflown area. (Color figure online)

2.2   Parallel Workflows

Based on extensive literature work and currently validated methodologies for the return of products complying with commonly accepted accuracy standards [9, 12–14], an overall processing workflow was structured (Fig. 2). Parallel processing was performed in a hardware system with ordinary performance, i.e. featuring an Intel(R) Core (TM) i7-5500U CPU @ 2.40 GHz, 8 GB RAM and an Intel(R) HD Graphics 5500 GPU.

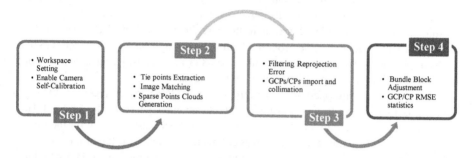

Fig. 2. General structure of a photogrammetric process workflow

The first step, which tends to be underestimated and preferred by a default parameterization, is fundamental and necessary to obtain reliable products. In any software, a reasonable setting of the workspace impacts on the plausibility of its operations, targeting to specify the workflow for each case study. In a general view, the choice of a shared reference system, both in consideration of the data acquired in the field and the factors that will intervene in the resolution of the equations at the base of the photogrammetric algorithms, establishes the coherence of the orientations and scale of the final models; lastly, the arrangement of the calibration parameters of the camera and its lever-arm optimize the estimates of the internal orientations, possibly the propagation source of a multitude of distortions in the final accuracy values. Such arrangement may be derived from rigorous operations in the laboratory or obtained through self-calibration from the acquired data, which is often preferred and returns totally reliable values compared to the former.

On the other hand, the calibration parameters of a low-cost camera cannot be considered as constant since they are subject to variations mainly related to optical-mechanical deterioration and temperatures [15]. These parameters are corrected during the processing of the acquired data, optimizing the interior orientation of the cameras from time to time. The achievable corrections will depend on the quality of the acquired images, as well as on the characteristics of the surveyed scenario, the incli-nation of the camera, the overlap between the images and above all on the presence of ground-truth points marked on the screen.

In the second step, the software enables the algorithms to search for point features image by image, i.e. based on the primitive Scale Invariant Feature Transform (SIFT) algorithms [16], characteristic and unambiguous points which are present in images invariant to scale and orientation changes and partially invariant to lighting changes.

At the end of the count, the software starts matching algorithms, i.e. the images are compared by searching for homologous points among those already recorded. Once the correspondences between the images have been defined by means of tie points, considering the interior orientation estimates of the camera assisted by the positional information of the images, the geometrical relations between the various images are constructed and then a sparse points cloud is computed.

In most cases, implemented algorithms are not public domain in commercial software platforms, whereas in clearly open-source suites users can even contribute with their intervention. The lack of this information therefore makes a comparative analysis of the achievable results more complicated.

In the next step, the sparse points cloud can preferably be filtered, reducing the amount of points characterized by a Reprojection Errors above a certain threshold, usually greater than 0.5 pixels. The Reprojection Error in pixels identifies the difference between the estimated values of the points present in an image and those projected in the sparse points cloud [14]. The software thus learns the corrections and processes the improved information about the relative orientation of the images to update the estimates made in the first phase of images alignment.

The collimation phase is the most complex and time-consuming step. In particular, when the coordinates of the points measured in the field are loaded into the workspace, they must be marked in all the images in which they are visible. The GCPs are different from the CPs, the first ones are useful for the photogrammetric block georeferencing while the others to control the accuracy.

The last but no least important phase provides that the sparse points cloud filtered and assisted by the accurate information of the ground truths is started to an adjustment of the estimates by means of the Bundle Block Adjustment (BBA) algorithms. These adjust and refine the geometry of the scene by minimizing squared reprojection errors between the points in the images and those in the photogrammetric block. Most softwares allow to also aggregate heterogeneous information to BBA compensations, such as the positional information recorded in each image by the UAV receiver. This information, although of lower accuracy than the ground truth and therefore with a lower weight in the equations, is essential in cases of Direct Georeferencing (DG) and Indirect Georeferencing (IG) with less than 3 GCPs implemented. For the remaining cases, the choice of aggregation could produce different final results, so any discrepancies will be analysed.

At the end of the processes, the model obtained can thus be considered as valid and consistent for the generation of products useful in any field.

The processing pipelines were carefully parameterized for each software, generating a sparse points cloud in each one of them. In the relative georeferencing management fields, GCPs were implemented through leave-one-out techniques [17, 18], thus generating a wide case history of 21 models for each workspace. At the end of the processes, an overall representation of any differences, in terms of mean error and root-mean-square error (RMSE) evaluated on GCPs and CPs, was built.

For the purposes of this work, the processes for obtaining the products beyond the sparse points clouds were not undertaken, these being considered as the main ones for any discussion regarding geometric accuracy.

Agisoft PhotoScan. Considering the premises described about the workflow structure, the working area of the software platform needed a suitable parameterization in order to guarantee the success of consecutive operations. In the Settings panel a window showed three areas of the settings configuration of the entire workspace. The *Reference Settings* acts on the general Coordinate System by setting a local system as described in Sect. 2.1. The other two configuration areas parameterize the field measurements accuracy of the receiver UAV on-board and the Inertial Measurement Unit (IMU), and the coordinates accuracies of the GCPs in meters when acquired. A value of 0.05 m was set in the *Camera Accuracy (m)* option, maintained at 10 deg in the *Camera Accuracy (deg)* option since the UAV did not record IMU orientation data, and 0.02 m in the *Marker Accuracy (m)* parameter. Under the Image Coordinates Accuracy title, the accuracy in pixels of the markers was parameterized, i.e. to determine how carefully the markers could be placed in the software workspace, and a fairly realistic value of 0.5 pixels was assigned. The *Tie Point Accuracy* option, instead, identifies the weight that will have to be given to the tie points in the block adjustment phases, and this was fixed as equal to about 3 pixels, as suggested in Mayer et al. [14].

In *Camera Calibration* the corrections of the camera parameters were enabled in every orientation estimation process and in *GPS/INS Offset* the Lever-Arm vector equal to [0.00, 0.00, 0.40] m was introduced with the relative accuracy of 0.01 m, having measured it in laboratory. Agisoft PhotoScan adopts Brown's model [19] for the parametric description of the camera lens.

In the second phase shown in Fig. 2, the *Align Photos* process was run, setting *High* option as execution mode and preferring to disable the automatic pre-filtering by fixing the value 0 in the *Key Point* and *Tie Point Limits* options. Considering the interior orientation estimates of the camera assisted by the positional information of the images, the geometrical relations between the various images were constructed and finally a sparse points cloud was computed.

The process launched required 5 h and 57 min of processing time in the matching phase and 20 min and 33 s in image alignment. At the end of the processing a sparse cloud of 2,284,543 points was returned, with a mean Reprojection Error of 0.452339 pixels and an average point spacing of about 27 points/m^2.

The Agisoft PhotoScan platform gives the possibility to manipulate the obtained point cloud, filtering those points characterized by conspicuous Reprojection Errors and thus obtaining a model quite consistent with reality. The *Gradual Selection* item was selected: this option contains filtering tools for sparse point clouds. Following the indications proposed in Mayer et al. [14], three filtering operations were performed:

- *Reconstruction Uncertainty*: 10 - The number of points after this first filter was 2,284,136.
- *Projection Accuracy*: 3 - The number of points after this filter was 1,517,282.
- *Reprojection Error*: 0.40 - The number of points after this last filter was 1,517,282.

The cloud thus presented an RMSE of the Reprojection Error equal to 0.307533 pixels so that it can be considered consistent and robust for subsequent processing.

Then the coordinates of the 20 GCPs acquired during the survey in the same image reference system were imported into the workspace. The GCPs thus needed to be collimated, image by image, trying to keep their reprojection value low in the model.

The 21 Chunks consequently generated by duplication represented a limited number of solutions to be adopted in the georeferencing phase as the number of GCPs implemented varies up to 0 GCP solution, i.e. by DG. In order to follow a fairly univocal methodology, starting from a number of implemented GCPs equal to 20, the case study was built using the leave-one-out technique, i.e. removing a GCP from time to time and transforming it into a Check Point (CP). The GCPs were removed in such a way to always have a homogeneous distribution between external and central zones of both GCPs and CPs.

After defining the list of Chunks, each one characterized by a number of GCP implemented from 20 to 0, for GCP cases with GCP greater than 3 the positional information of the images was removed in order to use only GCP in the adjustment. Then BBA processing was programmed for each case into a Batch Process using the *Optimize Cameras* command.

Pix4D Mapper. When the software was started, it required to load the images to be processed and then to set the workspace [20]: the *Image Properties* window is where we set the Coordinate System distinctive of the geo-tags of the images, select the source from which to extract the positional information of the images, select the relative geolocation accuracy and finally choose the model of the camera used. The choices already described in the previous paragraph were consequently followed.

The camera model was then configured. Pix4D is equipped with an internal database in which the calibration data of several commercial cameras are stored. The software recognizes the camera model from the EXIF and automatically searches for it in its database: if present, as in the case under this study, it loads the calibration values. Unlike many other softwares, Pix4D adopts a proprietary camera model, i.e. a different parametric description of the lenses but convertible to any model.

After selecting the *Output Coordinate System*, the software offered a wide choice of processing methods organized in predefined *Templates*. These templates are briefly standardized processing options that facilitate the user's work in the immediate achievement of results, without following the various processes step by step. A model (e.g. 3D maps) can be chosen and adapted to the needs of the case.

In *Advanced*, the software enables new subfolders for advanced processing parameterization. In particular, for the *Initial Processing* advanced parameters can be selected using: *Generals* panel which allows the user to modify the processing options and to select what will be displayed in the Quality Report; *Matching* panel which allows the user to modify the processing options related to the matching of the key points for the first step; and *Calibration* panel where it is possible to modify the calibration options of the camera and the desired outputs for this first step. For the purposes of this work, it was chosen to make the software work at the original image resolution with the *Full* option, indicating the *Aerial Grid or Corridor* option as the matching strategy between the corresponding images, the flight mission having been structured in swaths. While making the processing slower, a geometric verification of the correspondences was enabled, in order to discard the geometrically inconsistent correspondences. Afterwards, continuous optimization of the internal and external parameters of the camera orientations was preferred, calibrated through the *Alternative* option, recommended for images acquired by UAV.

The launched process took 1 h and 26 min of processing time for the entire first step. At the end of the processing a sparse cloud of 2,255,469 points was returned, with an RMSE value of Reprojection Error of 0.195 pixels, a relative difference of 0.42% between the optimized internal camera parameters and the initial ones and an average point spacing of about 26 points/m^2.

With *GCP/MTP Management*, Pix4D provides a worksheet for the management of important Ground Control Points (GCP) in the workspace. Using the *RayCloud Editor*, GCPs were marked on the images.

Finally, 21 projects were generated by duplication, representing the same case history as the solutions adopted in the previous case.

Once the list of 21 projects had been drawn up, the BBA processing for each of them was started with the *Re-Optimize* command, considering, in the compensation, the contribution offered by the camera's positional information.

MicMac. Unlike the other softwares seen, MicMac tends to be exclusively used from the command line, as a high-performance graphic user interface has not yet been completed [21]. Therefore, it was necessary to parameterize each command each time in order to make the processes comparable to the other two platforms.

Having available the file in which the positions of the camera were indicated at the time of acquisition, it was useful to build an.xml file helping the search algorithm and tie points matching. The *OriConvert* command generates the.*xml* file containing the appropriate pairings between the images of the entire dataset according to their position.

In the following stage, the *Tapioca File* command was started. As already done in the previous sections, among the options of the command, the value −1 has been used to indicate as image size the full resolution one. The software gives the possibility to activate the basic SIFT++ algorithms, an evolution of D. Lowe's original SIFT [16], or to choose, as in the case of this study, the DIGEO algorithms, a much faster and more efficient evolution of the SIFT algorithms.

At the end of the feature search processes and therefore of the correspondences among the various points of the images, it was necessary to introduce an orientation phase that could set preliminary geometries among all the points starting from a modelling of the camera, then passing through the relative geometries among the various acquisitions.

Tapas is the useful command for calculating purely interior and relative exterior orientation. The camera calibration mode was set to Brown's Model [19], which was known to have been adopted in Agisoft PhotoScan software.

Then the *CenterBascule* tool was started, as it allows to transform the purely relative orientation, as calculated with *Tapas*, into an absolute one. In particular, *CenterBascule* assigns a new orientation to an image dataset, characterized by an orientation of its centers, considering the actual positioning of the centers defined by the database processed in *OriConvert*.

At the end of this step the *Campari* command was used to compensate to the minimum squares the model orientation by heterogeneous measurements. Essentially, starting from the orientation obtained in *CenterBascule*, *Campari* compensates the measurements by assuming the coordinates of the GNSS-receiver of UAV-images with the relative planar and altitude accuracies. To follow, it enables the refinement of the estimates of all the parameters of the camera calibration.

Once the compensated orientation database was obtained, the *AperiCloud* command was executed with it. In *AperiCloud* the optional argument *SeuilEc = 0.4* was introduced to filter all the points with a high residual value, i.e. those that can be classified as outliers eliminated in Agisoft PhotoScan through the *Reprojection Accuracy* filter. The entire process returned a sparse cloud of 1,771,128 points with an RMSE value of 1,238 pixels and an average point spacing of about 21 points/m^2.

The processes so far analysed required a much longer processing time than those described in the other two reports. Among the subsequent operations, the *Tapioca* command took about 50% of the time taken by this first step (about 19.26 h of processing in total).

In order to import the GCPs and CPs datasets into the processing, a preliminary management of the positional information was required to obtain a.*xml* file readable by MicMac. The *GCPConvert* command was used for this purpose.

By means of the *SaisieAppuisPredicQT* command, a graphic interface was started to collimate the points, first for GCPs and then also for CPs. Considering the orientation obtained by the *Campari* command and loading the coordinates of the points, the *SaisieAppuisPredicQT* command is able to hypothesize the position of GCPs and CPs in the images indicated in the command line that must be approved by the operator. The last mandatory argument is the name of an.*xml* file in which the coordinates of the points image were stored.

As in the previous sections, the case history of 21 folders for each georeferencing case was organized and the *GCPBascule* command started for each one of them to transfer the absolute orientation inherited from the collimated GCPs to the entire photogrammetric block. Once a robust absolute orientation was transferred to the point clouds scattered by the GCPs, BBA processing was started to correct and fix the entire block. In particular, the *Campari* command was restarted by introducing the database of implemented GCPs as a useful measure for compensation. Two cases of compensation were studied, one sticking to the BBAs executed in Agisoft PhotoScan and the other keeping the positional information of the cameras as in Pix4D Mapper.

The method to verify the accuracy of the georeferencing is to use CPs to estimate the 3D similarity of the measurements between the calculated coordinates and those measured in the field. The residues on GCPs allow to qualify the accuracy of the georeferencing result. The command introduced, *GCPCtrl*, allowed to quantify these residues and then to return the degree of accuracy achieved in the processes seen.

2.3   Comparative Analysis

The values obtained from the 21 GCPs and CPs management cases implemented for each software and therefore from the related BBA processes, were analyzed and compared to the geometric standards widely accepted by the scientific community, as updated by ASPRS in 2015. These standards were developed in response to the pressing need of the GIS and mapping community to embrace the growing rise of new geospatial technologies.

The standard follows metric units of measurement in order to be consistent with international standards and practices, although it does not specify the best methodology needed to obtain values above the set thresholds. It will be the data provider's responsibility to establish the control procedures and the final quality of the geospatial product to be returned, in conjunction with the commissioned requests. The standard is independent from the technology and addressed to a broad base, while recognizing the existence of application limitations.

The ASPRS defines accuracy classes based on root-mean-square error (RMSE) thresholds evaluated on CPs for digital orthoimagery, digital planimetric data and digital elevation data [8]. The RMSE values, taken as cumulative values of systematic errors and any variances, are actually a measure of the accuracy of the referenced datum. At the same time, the absolute average errors obtained along the three axes will be analyzed, looking for possible systematisms. A control instead of the same values on the GCPs accredits the robustness and consistency of the georeferencing phases in the photogrammetric blocks.

Given the specific requirements recommended by the document, for the purposes of this work, the statistics concerning the Horizontal Accuracy Standards for Geospatial Data and the Vertical Accuracy Standards for Elevation Data were evaluated [20]. In particular, for the former, the ASPRS tables the RMSEr values in 24 accuracy classes, i.e. the planar error resulting from contributions along the x and y axes, recommended for Digital Planimetric Data produced by digital source imagery at various ranges of GSDs [8]. While the vertical one is based on 10 accuracy classes using $RMSE_Z$ statistics, i.e. exclusively along the z-axis, but differing for non-vegetable soils and for vegetated soils, in which the statistics of its 95th percentile are considered. In this case study it was possible to clearly assume the statistics for the first scenario.

3   Results and Discussion

As pointed out in the previous paragraphs, the comparisons in this study are presented regarding the results firstly obtained in Agisoft PhotoScan and MicMac by not implementing the geotags of the images in the various BBA processes; then comparisons are made with those derived in Pix4D Mapper and MicMac, however considering the BBA processes completed by the positional information of the images. Finally, the planar and Z-axis RMSE values are evaluated in an integrated analysis of the three softwares, comparing them with the thresholds established by the ASPRS standards.

Figure 3 shows the trends in $RMSE_{XYZ}$ values and average errors recorded in the various cases of georeferencing in Agisoft PhotoScan and MicMac softwares.

Analyzing the values returned in the CPs, completely equal values are presented for cases where the number of GCPs implemented is less than 3, being characterized by the positional information of geo-tags that therefore reduce the contribution of tie points in the BBA processes. This is in fact evident in subsequent cases where the BBA processes within MicMac do not support a reduced number of GCPs and reveal much larger $RMSE_{XYZ}$ values than those derived from Agisoft PhotoScan.

While in Agisoft PhotoScan the values can be considered as constant for the entire case history, in MicMac there is a downward trend to a minimum value in the

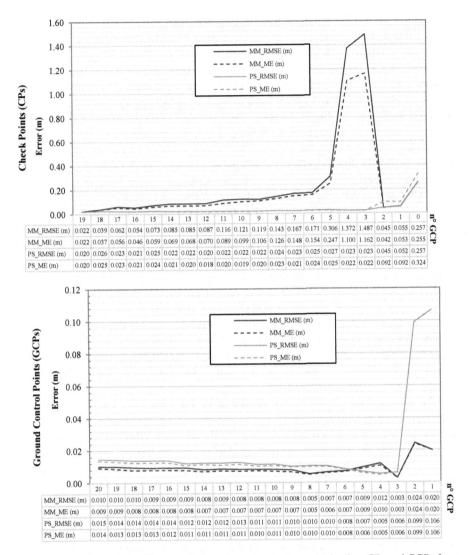

Fig. 3. Comparison of RMSE$_{XYZ}$ and Mean Error (ME) values obtained on CPs and GCPs from MicMac (MM) and Agisoft PhotoScan (PS) processes

georeferencing condition with 19 GCPs. The average errors follow the same trends, except for the cases in MicMac falling in the 3–5 GCPs range implemented, where the deviation shows systematic errors lower than the accidental ones.

On the other hand, in PhotoScan, although there are slight deviations between mean and RMSE errors below the 3 GCPs implemented, the values recorded in the GCPs show a reduced robustness of the georeferencing, which then remains constant for all other cases analyzed. MicMac, on the other hand, produces more robust georeferencing than PhotoScan ones, attesting lower values of RMSE and mean errors from the 6th GCP implemented onwards.

Figure 4 shows the trends in $RMSE_{XYZ}$ values and average errors recorded in the various cases of georeferencing in Pix4D Mapper and MicMac software.

Figure 4a shows a descending step behaviour of the Pix4D Mapper software for less than 3 GCPs implemented, unlike MicMac where, from the first implementation onwards, RMSE values and average errors are almost constant. The precariousness of georeferencing below the 3 GCPs implemented is in fact reflected in the error values recorded in Fig. 4b in the GCPs about the trend in Pix4D. In MicMac, on the other hand, the variability is negligible, showing a uniform robustness in any case of geo-referencing even if with values higher than those obtained in Pix4D. The BBA procedures in Pix4D thus benefit from a number greater than 3 GCP, giving accuracy values on CPs better than an average deviation of about 1.5 cm up to the extreme case of 19 GCP where the results between the two softwares converge.

As it can be seen in the Figs. 3 and 4 about the estimated values on CPs, regardless of the assumptions made and the software used, the maximum accuracy limit achieved of 0.02 m was inherited from the measurements on the GCPs implemented. It can therefore be ascertained that more accurate results could only be achieved by adopting more accurate GNSS measurement modes (e.g. with longer acquisition intervals in relative mode) or post-processing modes (e.g. using precise orbital ephemeris).

Figure 5a integrates the planar RMSE values obtained in the three softwares and compares them with the thresholds set by ASPRS for Digital Planimetric Data. Figure 5b shows the comparison between the RMSE values along the Z axis for each georeferencing case and the ASPRS standards for Vertical Data. In this comparison, the RMSE values obtained in MicMac by integrating positional image information into the BBA processes were considered.

The results obtained can be considered as in line with those already discussed in previous works [11, 18], in which it was possible to see a coherent trend of RMSE values for DG and complete IG cases, especially about the elbow point of the statistic curve in a range of GCPs implemented equal to 5–7. Considering a different application scenario and a flight altitude of 120 m, in Agüera-Vega et al. [17] the trends obtained in this work were confirmed by recording a reduction of both planar and vertical RMSE values around the seventh GCP implemented, while the lowest values were recorded in the configuration with 15 GCPs. Instead, observing the results obtained by Benassi et al. [9], comparing the processes in the three softwares analysed under this study, as in Fig. 5, MicMac offers a constancy of the planar RMSE values as the implemented GCPs vary, while, at the same time, Pix4D also shows a behaviour comparable to those obtained in PhotoScan even if they are considered as better.

From a summary analysis of the examination generated, it is fundamental to see that the processing in different softwares, being it carried out in accordance with a common workflow, generate results that are not congruent but in most cases coherent. In fact, as it is possible to observe, both planar and vertical RMSE values assume comparable trends, maintaining, in most cases of implemented georeferencing, the same class of accuracy set by ASPRS standards.

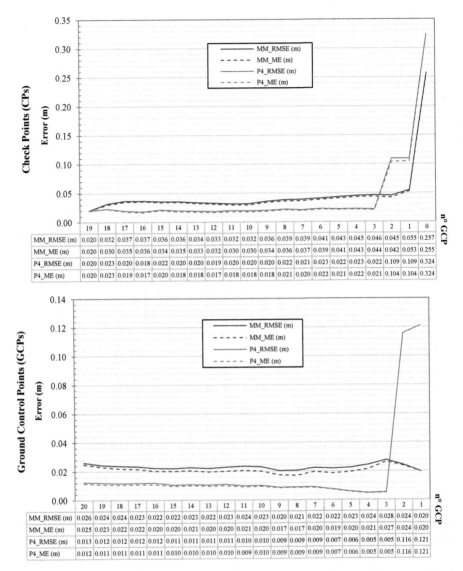

Fig. 4. Comparison of RMSE$_{XYZ}$ and Mean Error (ME) values obtained on CPs and GCPs from MicMac (MM) and Pix4D Mapper (P4) processes

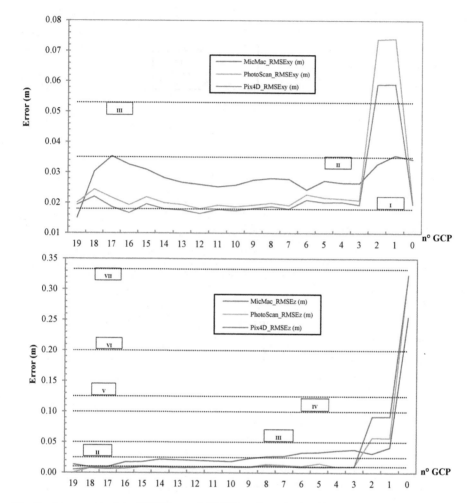

Fig. 5. Assessment of the RMSE$_{XY}$ and RMSE$_Z$ values obtained in the three softwares, as the GCPs implemented vary, with the threshold values published by ASPRS for Digital Planimetric Data and Vertical Data, respectively.

4   Conclusions

In the last decade, while hardware evolution has determined a colossal modernization of the industrial sector, there has also been an exponential development of software systems, with an increasing sophistication of the algorithms implemented, enabling users to define high-performance ICT solutions. One of the sectors mostly affected by such modernization is Geomatics, with digital photogrammetry being completely reformed by the rise of UAVs. Despite a wide utilisation of a variety of softwares for the return of the same products in high quality, no validation analysis has been conducted, in literature, to date, to determine whether such products can be considered as repeatable and reproducible regardless of the platform used.

In order to obtain consistent results, a comparative evaluation of three photogrammetric softwares, commonly used in the industrial field, was therefore carried out in this work: in particular, for the purposes of this study, three processing chains were started in parallel in Agisoft Photoscan, Pix4D Mapper and MicMac.

The tests carried out aimed at investigating the elements of shared by the platforms tested, in order to support future studies to define a unique index for the accuracy of the final products.

In particular, setting up a general workflow for the processes, the related sparse point clouds were processed within each software and then subjected to 21 georeferencing strategies, varying the number of GCPs implemented with the leave-one-out technique.

After obtaining the results from the BBA for each model, a statistical inference was generated to compare the results obtainable from the different softwares and verify them based on the accuracy thresholds established by the ASPRS.

From the analysis of the comparisons generated, it is evident that, despite sharing a common workflow, the processes analyzed generate results that are consistent, yet at the same time not congruent. Both planar and vertical RMSE values follow comparable trends, so that in most cases of georeferencing the same class of accuracy was defined, as indicated by ASPRS standards.

References

1. Argese, F., et al.: A procedure for automating earthwork computations using UAV photogrammetry and open-source software. In: AIP Conference Proceedings, vol. 2116, no. 1, p. 280008 (2019)
2. Yao, H., Qin, R., Chen, X.: Unmanned aerial vehicle for remote sensing applications—a review. Remote Sens. **11**, 1443 (2019)
3. Green, D.R., Hagon, J.J., Gómez, C., Gregory, B.J.: Using low-cost UAVs for environmental monitoring, mapping, and modelling: examples from the coastal zone. In: Coastal Management, pp. 465–501. Elsevier (2019)
4. Themistocleous, K.: The use of UAVs for cultural heritage and archaeology. In: Hadjimitsis, D.G., et al. (eds.) Remote Sensing for Archaeology and Cultural Landscapes. SRS, pp. 241–269. Springer, Cham (2020). https://doi.org/10.1007/978-3-030-10979-0_14
5. Cummings, A., McKee, A., Kulkarni, K., Markandey, N.: The rise of UAVs. Photogram. Eng. Remote Sens. **83**, 317–325 (2017)
6. Peterson, S., Lopez, J., Munjy, R.: Comparison of UAV imagery-derived point cloud to terrestrial laser scanner point cloud. ISPRS Ann. Photogramm. Remote Sens. Spatial Inf. Sci. **IV-2/W5**, 149–155 (2019)
7. Saponaro, M., Tarantino, E., Fratino, U.: Generation of 3D surface models from UAV imagery varying flight patterns and processing parameters. In: International Conference of Numerical Analysis and Applied Mathematics (ICNAAM 2018) (2018)
8. American Society for Photogrammetry and Remote Sensing (ASPRS): ASPRS positional accuracy standards for digital geospatial data (Edition 1, Version 1.0., November, 2014). Photogrammetric Engineering & Remote Sensing, vol. 81, pp. A1–A26 (2015)

9. Benassi, F., et al.: Testing accuracy and repeatability of UAV blocks oriented with GNSS-supported aerial triangulation. Remote Sens. **9**(2), 172 (2017)

10. Hendrickx, H., et al.: The reproducibility of SfM algorithms to produce detailed digital surface models: the example of PhotoScan applied to a high-alpine rock glacier. Remote Sens. Lett. **10**(1), 11–20 (2019)

11. Saponaro, M., Capolupo, A., Tarantino, E., Fratino, U.: Comparative analysis of different UAV-based photogrammetric processes to improve product accuracies. In: Misra, S., et al. (eds.) ICCSA 2019. LNCS, vol. 11622, pp. 225–238. Springer, Cham (2019). https://doi.org/10.1007/978-3-030-24305-0_18

12. Carbonneau, P.E., Dietrich, J.T.: Cost-effective non-metric photogrammetry from consumer-grade sUAS: implications for direct georeferencing of structure from motion photogrammetry. Earth Surf. Proc. Land. **42**, 473–486 (2017)

13. Gagliolo, S., et al.: Parameter optimization for creating reliable photogrammetric models in emergency scenarios. Appl. Geomat. **10**(4), 501–514 (2018). https://doi.org/10.1007/s12518-018-0224-4

14. Mayer, C., Gomes Pereira, L., Kersten, T.P.: A comprehensive workflow to process UAV images for the efficient production of accurate geo-information. In: IX National Conference on Cartography and Geodesy (2018)

15. Cramer, M., Przybilla, H.J., Zurhorst, A.: UAV cameras: overview and geometric calibration benchmark. Int. Arch. Photogramm. Remote Sens. Spatial Inf. Sci. **XLII-2/W6**, 85–92 (2017)

16. Lowe, D.G.: Distinctive image features from scale-invariant keypoints. Int. J. Comput. Vision **60**, 91–110 (2004)

17. Agüera-Vega, F., Carvajal-Ramírez, F., Martínez-Carricondo, P.: Assessment of photogrammetric mapping accuracy based on variation ground control points number using unmanned aerial vehicle. Measurement **98**, 221–227 (2017)

18. Saponaro, M., Tarantino, E., Reina, A., Furfaro, G., Fratino, U.: Assessing the impact of the number of GCPS on the accuracy of photogrammetric mapping from UAV imagery. Baltic Surv. **10**, 43–51 (2019)

19. Brown, D.: Close-range camera calibration. Photogramm. Eng. **37**, 855–866 (2002)

20. Whitehead, K., Hugenholtz, C.: Applying ASPRS accuracy standards to surveys from small unmanned aircraft systems (UAS). Photogram. Eng. Remote Sens. **81**, 787–793 (2015)

21. Rupnik, E., Daakir, M., Pierrot Deseilligny, M.: MicMac – a free, open-source solution for photogrammetry. Open Geospatial Data Softw. Stand. **2**(1), 1–9 (2017). https://doi.org/10.1186/s40965-017-0027-2

Road Cadastre an Innovative System to Update Information, from Big Data Elaboration

Vincenzo Barrile[1], Antonino Fotia[1(✉)], Ernesto Bernardo[1],
and Giuliana Bilotta[2]

[1] Geomatics Lab - DICEAM, Mediterranea University of Reggio Calabria,
Località Feo di Vito, 89124 Reggio Calabria, Italy
antonino.fotia@unirc.it
[2] University IUAV of Venice, Santa Croce 191 Tolentini, 30135 Venice, Italy

Abstract. The proposed research activity is based on the study and development of advanced monitoring techniques for the inspection and mapping of road infrastructures. Data detection (initial and periodic) is one of the most important phases of the process to be followed for the knowledge of the current state of road infrastructure and this is fundamental for the design and intervention choices. This operation can be done both through traditional (such as GNSS receivers, total motorized station and 3D laser scanner) and innovative tools (such as remote sensing, mobile mapping systems vehicles or road drones and APAs). Recently, technological development has offered the possibility to use tools that allow continuous detection of the object to be investigated, and there is the possibility to have multiple sensors at the same time that allow to make high-performance surveys. The aim of the research will be the design and implementation of an innovative measurement and component sensor system to be equipped on technological systems for data acquisition. The research also consists on the implementation of dedicated algorithms for the management of the amount of georeferenced data obtained and their representation on GIS (Geographic Information System) platforms as "open and updatable" thematic cartography. In this context, the establishment and update of the Road Cadastre is also included, intended (in our application) as a computer tool for storing, querying, managing and visualizating of all the data that the owner/manager acquired on its road network. In it will be possible to represent the elements inherent geometric characteristics elements of the roads and their relevance, as well as the permanent installations and services related to the needs of the circulation; in this way we can obtain a continuos updated database that allow rapid selective searches for topics.

Keywords: Road Cadastre · UAV · Big data

1 Introduction

For some decades now, the introduction of electronic computers has led to a substantial revolution in the capacity of analytics and data collection, trhough the latest technological advances in the digital age.

Pratically, what was once acquired in the field manually with timely surveys and consequently with relatively high time and cost it can now be acquired through a

© Springer Nature Switzerland AG 2020
O. Gervasi et al. (Eds.): ICCSA 2020, LNCS 12252, pp. 709–720, 2020.
https://doi.org/10.1007/978-3-030-58811-3_51

growing number of devices such as sensors, actuators and cameras, characterized by ever-increasing automation (also in terms of the possibility of a subsequent integrated and dynamic analysis of the data) and increasingly reduced costs.

Among the many types of sensors that can be used in the infrastructure examples of hardware systems aimed at quantifying virtually real-time, or almost, traffic flows, noise, flooring status, geometric (for example, point clouds by laser scanning, etc.), are already today consolidated.

It will be possible to carry out visual inspections of the state of an infrastructure continuously and automatically via drones, land and aircraft, using artificial intelligence for the analysis of the collected data (in the form of instrumental measurements, but also images), so exceeding in this the intrinsic limits of a human operator in terms of fallibility and the ability to compare a large amount of data varying over the time.

The very first effect of this evolution is the increase in mobility-related information that can be stored in databases, whose availability and number for stakeholders grows at an exponential rate, also introducing the new aspect of the dynamism of the data over time; At the same time, even traditional systems for analysis and management are insufficient to process such a large amount of big data.

By focusing on the operation of transport infrastructures, a Management Authority therefore has available not only the data collected by sensors distributed on the network, such as data related to the monitoring of structures, traffic data and videos collected along the roadways, but also demographic and environmental information.

The archives also contain the register of works, the history of maintenance work with the related costs and all information related to the security of the infrastructure.

One of the main elements of the management of the road network thus becomes the system (of timely and forecasting interrogation and analysis) used to manage the database in order to arrive at informed decisions about the interventions to be carried out, also implementing decisions in time as real as possible.

Although the amount of data can be considered a distinctive character, the heterogeneity and the information structure strongly characterize this type of data and it becomes essential to be able to rely on effective methods and as much as possible automated. This characterization enhances the information useful for analysis, discarding unnecessary information to avoid a burden of the system, without the risk to incurre on excessive errors' simplifications or their amplification.

The biggest challenge of managing big data is precisely in developing methods that can predict future observations, optimize the information available, and at the same time find correlations between the information collected.

In this regard (management and use of the large amount of data acquired for infrastructure monitoring), the application reported in this note can be particularly useful.

In fact, the aim of the research will be the design and implementation of an innovative measurement and component sensor system to be equipped on technological systems for data acquisition. The research also consists of the implementation of algorithms dedicated to the management of the amount of georeferenced data obtained and their representation on GIS (Geographic Information System) platforms as "open and updatable" thematic cartography. This developed system is therefore an open GIS to be considered as a valid tool also for updating the Road Cadastre; once completed and implemented it can be proposed to the Authorities responsible for its use.

2 Materials and Methods

2.1 Study Area

To test the methodology, it was decided to identify an area with a low level of traffic, and with all the necessary elements to be examined within the experiment.

The operations were tested in a road with low traffic in the territory of the city of Melito di Porto Salvo (RC), South Italy, on a low density and traffic area (Figs. 1 and 2).

It is an interurban road that connects the city center with a hamlet that develops along the bank of a river. The road reports deteriorations in some stretches, and failures, as well as stretches in which the horizontal signs are covered with brushwood of various kinds and there is also present a good number of vertical signals.

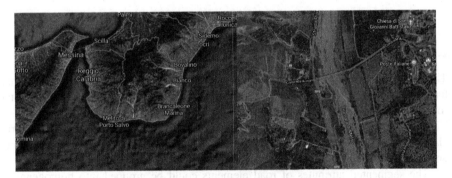

Fig. 1. Study area in Reggio Calabria South Italy

The study area can be reached through a 5-arch bridge, which crosses the Tuccio stream. It was built in 1924 during fascism and is the identifying symbol of the country of Prunella. In the first arch of the bridge, there is a concrete plaque, which recalls the construction data and the lives of the numerous workers sacrificed to build this majestic work.

Fig. 2. Case study: road and bridge in Reggio Calabria South Italy

2.2   Road Cadastre and Proposed Automatic Update Methodology

The road Cadastre represents the inventory of all public roads present in the national territory and has as its first objective the definition of the consistency of the national road network in a way compatible and integrated with the Land and Buildings [1].

Usually, the Road Cadastre must contain certain elements relating to the geometric characteristics of the roads and their relevance, as well as the permanent installations and services related to the needs of the traffic.

The segmented attributes of road elements could be grouped into homogeneous entities. Among these, the most significant are: (1) Road Element Section; (2) Road paving; (3) Road body; (4) Bridges, viaducts and underpasses; (5) Tunnel and subways; (6) Margins, gutters; (7) Road body protection; (8) Protection of the surrounding environment; (9) Lighting systems; (10) Parking pitches; (11) Retention devices; (12) Service relevance; (13) Works of hydraulic continuity; (14) Accesses; (15) Mileage signals.

For the survey of the quantities necessary for the construction of the Road Cadastre, the so-called Mobile Mapping System (MMS) [2] i.e. high-performance detector vehicles (VARs) are usually used to determine its position on time and acquire data from other different on-board sensors related to each other [3–5]. In this case, instead, an innovative procedure was tested which contemplate the use of a properly designed fleet of drones, which, proceeding from point *a* to point *b,* allows to acquire the images of the object of study. Subsequently, images are processed by suitable automated finalized algorithms to the identification of potholes, road signs, traffic lights, manholes and their subsequent visualization and updating of a basic cartography on the GIS system.

The captured data is therefore high-resolution images with high spatial sampling rates.

In this research, we focused specifically on the analysis of some of the attributes in the Database. In particular, we focalized the attention to the elements that can be identified through the classification and segmentation of the images acquired by the proposed system: the presence of deterioration of the road surface, the presence and maintenance status of the horizontal signs, vertical traffic lights and the presence of manholes.

2.3   Innovative Measurement System

We have used a fleet of automated drones connected to the cloud (or a local network) that are automatically recharged through special charging stations located in pre-established points. With the integration of the cloud platform, a real-time data feed is obtained from the drone fleet; this dataset is subsequently processed by our proposed algorithms for the selection of the images. The drones used are DJI Mavic 2 Pro, equipped with omnidirectional vision sensors and infrared sensors, DJI-branded technologies, such as obstacle detection system, intelligent features such as Hyperlapse and ability to set the flight fly points.

The data capture system planned the installation of two platforms along the path to be detected. These platforms are necessary to allow the charging of the drone battery and the transfer of data necessary for the next processing.

In this research we realized a mini light-weight unattended drone system, including a C500 charging pad, a charging landing gear, a tailored Mavic 2 Pro battery, a canopy, an OC(Embedded AI-computer), a LS (local server), an CS (internet server), a T3 (HDMI camera monitoring), a Loudspeaker and a DJI Mavic 2 10 parts.

Using this solution, we can control a fleet of automated drones connected to the cloud.

In particular, the process of this research is divided into three automated phases, schematized in the flowchart of Fig. 3 and that provide:

1. Definition of flight plan, in terms of GSD (Ground Sampling Distance), image overlay and waypoint route [6]
2. Image analysis: pre-elaboration – segmentation –classification. In order to improve the quality and precision of the images, the use of different ad hoc algorithms that involve the combination of various methodologies has been experimented (segmentation; Edge detector; Canny filter; Gaussian filter; Support Vector Machine - SVM).
3. Geo-localization data on the GIS platform in order to associate each element of the GIS with coordinates relative to the data implemented in the database [7, 8].

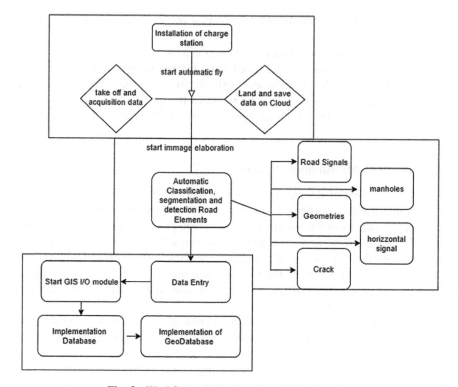

Fig. 3. Workflow automatic system Gis integration

3   Result and Discussion

3.1   Image Acquisition and Processing

In order to populate the database, we appropriately processed the images acquired through the described acquisition system, extracting the geometric characteristics of the infrastructures, the presence of deterioration of the road surface, the presence and maintenance status of the horizontal and vertical signs and the presence of manholes.

To better explain the procedure, we present the methodology applied to the classification of only a typology of crack (Fig. 4).

The acquired images (Fig. 4a) were automatically subjected to a pre-processing and enhancement process (Sobel and Prewit operator) (Fig. 4b–d), then they were segmented (edge detector, Canny filter, Gaussian filter) and classified (Segmentation and Classification (SVM)) (Fig. 4c and e) in order to be able to extrapolate the information we need (cracks, signal horizontal and vertical, light signal.. etc...).

In particular, the SVM classification was carried out in two phases [9, 10].

1) SVM Training.
2) Performance testing.

In the first phase, the geometric characteristics of the linked components assigned for SVM training were initially calculated [11–13]. Then, these features were normalized to a range. Kernel with radial base function (RBF) was chosen as a kernel trick, because the number of instances (connected regions) was not very large and the size of the space transformed with RBF is infinite.

The optimal training parameters for the SVM were found using grid search. During this operation, triple cross-validation was performed to correctly learn the different types of cracks. In this triple cross-validation, the training set was divided into 3 equal subsets. To ensure proper learning, a subset was tested using the trained classifier on the remaining two subsets. The goal was to identify good parameters in a such way that the classifier can predict exactly data test. After learning that the parameters had been determined, SVM was trained with the "One Against All" approach using the MATLAB LIBSVM library [14].

In the second phase, connected regions that were not used during SVM training were tested.

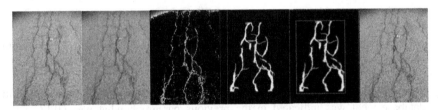

Fig. 4. (a) Input Images, (b) Enhancement, (c) Segmentation, (d) Post Processing and Image Enhancement, (e) Classification and Detected Crack Candidates, (f) Crack detection.

3.2 Database and Geodatabase

As is well known, the data in a Geographic Information System are traditionally divided into "graphs" and "attribute". The first are organized in vector or raster structures while the attribute data are made up of tables connected to the graphical data and connectable to each other through the rules of the relational databases (through the application of SQL commands on the table structures appropriately). Vector graphic structures are those that mostly use SQL commands for the connection between attribute tables ("select" and "join" commands). Generally, in this way the thematic cartography is produced, often as integral part of extensive and in-depth territorial studies. In these studies, the term "database" is sometimes used improperly, the set of tables connected to graphic layers defined as a database, often not connected to each other. A relational database, on the other hand, is a completely different thing of an archive of integrated and shared digital data, cause the relationships created by the various keys in the fields of the tables. In fact, storing a multitude of tables connected to graphic layers on hard disk does not mean building a relational database.

We can define a database as a digital data store. Generally, a software called DBMS (Database Management System) manages databases. The management of a database consists of a whole series of operations (data storage, deletion, display access to the database, updating, processing). Similar to the data, these operations are stored only through tables (generally non-square matrices made up of columns (fields) and rows (records). The data of a database must be integrated and shared. This feature is of fundamental importance for the correct and efficient functioning of the database.

As mentioned above, integration means avoiding the duplication of a data item in the archive. Integration ensures that information is managed efficiently (for example, updates are faster) and is a good premise to avoid errors within the archive. Data integration is achieved by relating the different tables that populate the database. Relationships are achieved through the equality of common fields ("key" fields).

If geometric components are also stored in the database tables, we can speak of spatial databases or geodatabases. In this way, the database structure acquires additional potential, linked to the spatial analyses (often also very advanced) made available. So, the management software becomes a "Spatial DBMS" able to perform spatial queries and geographical elaborations of the data obtained from them.

Specifically, in our appliction the database was built with:

- the trajectory graphic subsystem (in ASCII format containing trajectory information) Table 1
- photo capture units of the drone (JPEG image folders related to photographic capture, and ASCII files containing the connection information between the trajectory data and the images,) Table 2
- the connection with the elaborations of the acquired data and the information of the database what was indicated in the previous paragraph what was (JPEG image folders related to elaboration, ASCII files containing the connection information between the trajectory data and the elaborated images).

Since there are a multitude of these elements, it is necessary to put them in connection each other by populating for each of elements a table also containing a reference to an element of the upper level [15, 16].

Therefore, the data structure used consists of a set of integrated relational table, some auxiliary tables that contain the source data and the information processed in progress.

Table 1. Trajectories table

Trajectories (contains survey data and association with photograms)
Id (primary key)
Id Session (unique identifier assigned to the survey session, and the name of folders containing the image files)
Time (numeric, instant of the measure)
Distance (numeric, odometric distance detected)
Latitude (numeric, latitude)
Longitude (numeric, longitude)
Altitude (numeric)
Heading (numeric)
Frame (string, measure associated file name)

Table 2. Table frame.

Frame
(contains the pixel observations performed on the frames, the flat coordinates of the points in the map system and the classification of observations)
Id (primary key)
Id Session (foreign key to the Trajectories table)
Photogram (foreign key to the Trajectories table)
Typology (main classification numeric code)
Collocation (bin code to the axis [+ , −, NULL])
Segmentation (Segment end marking [Start, End, NULL])
Element (numeric, elements road code)

In order to relate the data described previously, an initial processing is carried out, that consists of the population of the table, using with the grids and defining the placement of the images within folders with the same name assigned to the measurement session. Moreover copies of the trajectories table, exported in XML format, and the folders containing the images are then delivered to operators to make frame observations on frames [17]. For the construction of the Geodatabase, we proceeded by creating and naming the database on pgAdmin and inside it, the PostGIS spatial extension was inserted. A connection to the database was built on QGIS in pgAdmin and through the "DB manager" plugin, PostGIS was chosen among the available spatial extensions (thus ensuring the connection between the database and the layers); thus it was created the database tables with spatial component [18]. The experimental system, using the aforementioned automations, was tested on the reference area by acquiring a number 180 frames, transferred to the cloud and processed. In the post-processing phase, the entities detected automatically were georeferenced and shown on the screen (see Fig. 5). In particular, 14 manholes, 52 between vertical and horizontal signals, and 96 cracks were detected.

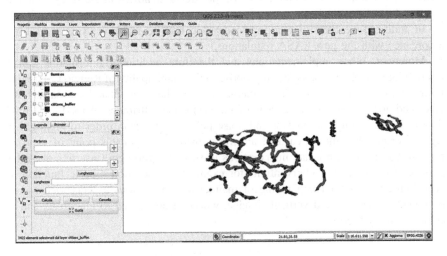

Fig. 5. Gis elaboration

We realized a first updated map showing the road network updated by the data collected by the proposed experimental system (Fig. 6). The roads are clearly visible from the images and both the presence of signs or artefacts and the conditions of the road surface can be determined. The images acquired by drone clearly show the details of the roads, and the data can be acquired regularly, without the aid of operators, thus facilitating operations and reducing costs and times.

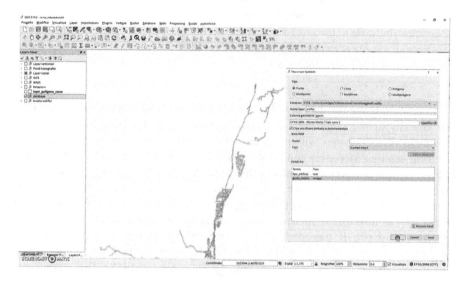

Fig. 6. Example of Gis results.

Thanks to the proposed system, through the creation of road network geodatabases the roads can then be monitored and consequently facilitate the scheduled maintenance process. The database shows the names of the streets identified in the study area, their types and conditions, etc.

In addition, we are still working to develop how to make the system usable in accordance with the new EASA regulations.

Moreover, other implementations and therefore additional information can be inserted into the Road Cadastre. To propose to the municipality of Reggio Calabria the Information System that we are implementing, we have populated the dataset with other additional information (census of the segmented attributes of road arcs, traffic flow data, air quality monitoring and noise pollution data); in order to highlight the regions within the study area, that are more distressed from this point of view and propose the most appropriate interventions to solve the problem (inserting noise barriers or traffic diversion interventions for example), in addition a basic function has been implemented for the planning of maintenance of various aspects such as road pavement, horizontal and vertical signage, works of art related to the streets and the complementary works.

For this purpose, in addition to the geometric and identifying information of the censused elements, the conservative and functional state must also be indicated, in this way it's possible to integrate the information entered in the Gis Cadastre.

4 Conclusion

In the representation of the roads Cadastre, clearly not all the roads have the same characteristics and for this they cannot be described in the same way; according to the context where they are (urban or suburban) some information are more or less useful.

From an economic point of view the construction of the Road Cadastre is very expensive; however, if implemented with road body maintenance functions, this can be a great tool for the management agencies, that can then schedule maintenance based on GIS indications.

In fact, even if the Roads Cadastre was born with the aim of surveying the existing road heritage and therefore has fundamental cognitive purposes, however, relying on the acquired data, we could extend the knowledge to elements more aimed at planning maintenance activities. Databases have been therefore enriched with a number of possible additional information that are useful for this purpose and that are not provided by the legislation. We therefore decided to analyze how to implement the Road Cadastre in order to be able to use it for planning the maintenance of horizontal road signs, through the implementation of a an Innovative System to Update Information on Road Cadastre from Big Data Elaboration.

Future developments aimed to the implementation of functions allow the planning of maintenance of additional elements such as road pavement, vertical signage and works of art related to roads.

References

1. Hinz, S., Baumgartner, A., Mayer, H., Wiedemann, C., Ebner, H.: Road extraction focussing on urban areas. In: Baltsavias, E.P, Gruen, A., Gool, L.V. (eds.) Automatic Extraction of Man-made Objects from Aerial and Space Images (III), pp. 255–265. A.A. Balkema Publishers (2001)
2. Soilán, M., Riveiro, B., Martínez-Sánchez, J., Arias, P.: Automatic road sign inventory using mobile mapping systems. In: The International Archives of the Photogrammetry, Remote Sensing and Spatial Information Sciences, 2016 XXIII ISPRS Congress, vol. XLI-B3, Prague, Czech Republic, 12–19 July 2016
3. Gruen, A., Li, H.: Road extractions from aerial and satellite images by dynamic programming. ISPRS J. Photogram. Remote Sens. **50**(4), 111–120 (1995)
4. Grüen, A., Li, H.: Linear feature extraction with 3-D LSB-snakes. In: Automatic Extraction of Man-Made Objects from Aerial and Space Images (II), pp. 287–298. BirkhäuserVerlag, Basel (1997)
5. Hatger, C., Brenner, C.: Extraction of road geometry parameters from laser scanning and existing databases. In: Proceeding of ISPRS Workshop: 3D Reconstruction from Airborne Laserscanner and InSAR DATA, Dresden, Germany, 8–10 October 2003

6. Serna, A., Marcotegui, B.: Detection, segmentation and classification of 3D urban objects using mathematical morphology and supervised learning. ISPRS J. Photogrammetry Remote Sens. **93**, 243–255 (2014)

7. Barrile V., Cotroneo F.: A software for the automatic update of the road cadastre in the GIS environment. Bull. Ital. Soc. Photogrammetry Topogr. (2006)

8. Barrile, V., Leonardi, G., Fotia, A., Bilotta, G., Ielo, G.: Real-time update of the road cadastre in GIS environment from an MMS rudimentary system. In: International Symposium on New Metropolitan Perspectives, pp. 240–247 (2018)

9. Yu, Y., Li, J., Guan, H., Wang, C., Yu, J.: Semiautomated extraction of streetlight poles from mobile LiDAR point-clouds. IEEE Trans. Geosci. Remote Sens. **53**(3), 1374–1386 (2015)

10. Cireşan, D., Meier, U., Schmidhuber, J.: Multi-column deep neural networks for image classification. Neural Netw. **32**, 333–338 (2012)

11. Huang, C., Abu Al-Rub, R., Masad, E., Little, D.: Three dimensional simulations of asphalt pavement permanent deformation using a nonlinear viscoelastic and viscoplastic model. J. Mater. Civil Eng. **23**, 56–68 (2011)

12. Bacher, U., Mayer, H.: Automatic road extraction from IRS satellite images in agricultural and desert areas. In: XXth Congress ISPRS, Istanbul, Turkey, 12–23 July 2004

13. Goeman, W., Martinez-Fonte, L., Bellens, R., Gautaman, S.: Automated verification of road network data by VHR satellite images using road statistics. In: Proceedings of IPSRS Workshop: High Resolution Earth Imaging for Geospatial Information, Hannover, Germany (2005)

14. Barrile, V., Cotroneo, F., Praticò, F.: Automatic updating processes of road surface surveys and surface defects: proposal of an innovative high-performance method. In: SIIV National Conference Cosenza, Italy (2006)

15. Wallace, S., Hatcher, M., Priestnall, G., Morton, R.: Research into a framework for automatic linear feature identification and extraction. In: Automatic Extraction of Man-Made Objects from Aerial and Space Images (III), pp. 381–390. Balkema Publishers, Lisse (2001)

16. Wiedemann, C., Ebner, H.: Automatic completion and evaluation of road networks. Int. Arch. Photogram. Remote Sens. **33**(B3/2), 979–986 (2000)

17. Zhang, C., Baltsavias, E., Gruen, A.: Updating of cartographic road databases by image analysis. In: Baltsavias, E.P, Gruen, A., Gool, L.V. (eds.) Automatic Extraction of Man-made Objects from Aerial and Space Images (III), pp. 243–253. A.A. Balkema Publishers (2001)

18. Hinz, S., Baumgartner, A.: Urban road net extraction integrating internal evaluation models. In: International Society for Photogrammetry and Remote Sensingpp, Graz, Austria, pp. 255–265 (2002)

Land-Cover Mapping of Agricultural Areas Using Machine Learning in Google Earth Engine

Florencia Hastings[1,2(✉)] , Ignacio Fuentes[3] , Mario Perez-Bidegain[1] ,
Rafael Navas[4] , and Angela Gorgoglione[5]

[1] School of Agronomy, Universidad de la República, Av. Gral. Eugenio Garzón 780,
Montevideo, Uruguay
fhastings@mgap.gub.uy
[2] Directorate of Natural Resources, Ministry of Agriculture, Livestock and Fisheries,
Av. Gral. Eugenio Garzón 456, Montevideo, Uruguay
[3] School of Life and Environmental Sciences, University of Sydney,
Sydney, NSW 2006, Australia
[4] Programa Nacional de Investigación en Producción y Sustentabilidad Ambiental,
Instituto Nacional de Investigación Agropecuaria, Montevideo, Uruguay
[5] School of Engineering, Universidad de la República, Julio Herrera y Reissig 565,
Montevideo, Uruguay

Abstract. Land-cover mapping is critically needed in land-use planning
and policy making. Compared to other techniques, Google Earth Engine
(GEE) offers a free cloud of satellite information and high computation capabilities. In this context, this article examines machine learning
with GEE for land-cover mapping. For this purpose, a five-phase procedure is applied: (1) imagery selection and pre-processing, (2) selection
of the classes and training samples, (3) classification process, (4) post-
classification, and (5) validation. The study region is located in the San
Salvador basin (Uruguay), which is under agricultural intensification. As
a result, the 1990 land-cover map of the San Salvador basin is produced.
The new map shows good agreements with past agriculture census and
reveals the transformation of grassland to cropland in the period 1990–
2018.

Keywords: Land-cover map · Supervised classification · Google earth
engine · Agricultural region

1 Introduction

Land-use/land-cover (LULC) change plays a critical role in the global change
study. Often, land cover is the result of human actions to modify the natural
environment into a "customized environment". Such customization takes place
to increase agriculture production, satisfy domestic needs, or restore ecosystem
services. In the last decade, several studies have demonstrated that environmental problems are often related to LULC change [1,2]. LULC and human/natural

O. Gervasi et al. (Eds.): ICCSA 2020, LNCS 12252, pp. 721–736, 2020.
https://doi.org/10.1007/978-3-030-58811-3_52

modification have impacted negatively on the degradation of water quality, loss of biodiversity, deforestation, and global warming [3]. Therefore, characterizing and mapping land cover is essential for planning and managing natural resources, including agricultural fields [4]. Furthermore, LULC is a major data source of hydrologic models [5,6]. For this purpose, the implementation of effective land-cover mapping requires advanced remote-sensing methodologies able to provide accurate, inexpensive, and on-demand land-cover products using free cloud-based data processing platforms and free and open-access information.

Based on these considerations, it is essential to process big earth data (e.g., satellite images) in the classification procedure over a large watershed. Numerous platforms, such as Google Earth Engine (GEE), Amazon's Web Services, Microsoft's Azure, and National Aeronautics and Space Administration (NASA) Earth Exchange have been created to tackle this issue and support processing and analysis of big earth data [7,8]. In particular, GEE is an application that processes big geospatial data and classifies land cover over vast areas [9]. In this platform, the open-source satellite images can be efficiently imported and processed in the cloud without the need for downloading the data to local computers. Furthermore, many remote-sensing algorithms (e.g., classification algorithms and cloud masking techniques) and several image-driven products are available in this platform and are included and editable in user-defined algorithms [9,10]. To date, numerous studies about classifications using GEE in large areas have been conducted. Belgiu et al. investigated the ability of a machine learning technique in land-cover mapping in different agro-ecological areas of the world [11]. Many efforts with remote sensing have been carried out to overcome the challenges of producing less costly (or free) and more time-efficient land-cover mapping around the world [12]. Project MapBiomas is a good example; it shows how collections of LULC maps could be integrated into a web platform to aid planning and managing natural resources in Brazil [13].

Based on these considerations, this study explores a methodology that uses a cloud-based free open-source database to contribute to current land-cover mapping efforts. Particularly in Uruguay, only LULC maps for the years 2000, 2008, 2011, 2015 [14] and 2018 [15] are available (online). The primary objective is to explore machine learning in GEE and its accuracy for historical land-cover mapping of areas mainly characterized by agricultural land use. The specific objectives of this study are: i) evaluate the utilization of GEE for feature extraction, with its advantages and disadvantages; ii) assess the performance of supervised machine-learning techniques to classify the land surface; iii) obtain a historical land-cover map for an agricultural watershed by coupling GEE and machine learning methods. This methodology was applied to the San Salvador watershed, an agricultural basin located in Uruguay (South America).

2   Materials

This section first presents a description of the study area, and then the data used to develop the land-cover map. The data used includes satellite data and field data from the General Census of Agriculture (GCA). The phenological data of the surveyed crops is also presented.

2.1 Study Area

The San Salvador basin is located in Uruguay, in the Soriano department, and it covers an area of 2,390 390 km^2 (Fig. 1).

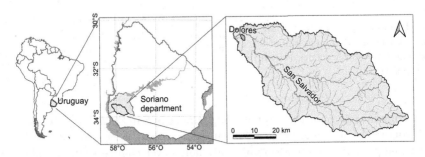

Fig. 1. Location of San Salvador basin (Soriano department, Uruguay). Coordinate reference system: world geodetic system 1984 (WGS84).

Uruguay has a humid subtropical climate. According to the Köppen climate classification, it is Cfa, C = temperate, moderate, rainy, f = fully humid, a = mean temperature in the warmest month is 22 °C or higher [16]. The mean total annual precipitation is 1100 mm and the temperature can range between –7.9 °C and 40.4 °C [16]. The region is characterized by a landscape of smooth hills and, the study area, has an average slope equal to 2.3%.

The San Salvador basin is located in the west part of the country where the most suitable soils for agriculture are [17]. In the decade of 1990, the agriculture practices included crop-pasture rotation, associated with livestock, with tillage practices[18]. Since the 21st century, agriculture suffered important changes due the incorporation of no-tillage practices, transgenic, continuous cropping, and economic freedom [18]. In a short period, soybean become the main grain crop, increasing the planted area from 12,000 ha in 2000/2001 to 1,300,000 ha in 2014/2015, total cropland extension were 426,000 ha and 1,500,000 ha respectively [19]. Also, production forest had an important increase from 186,277 ha planted in 1990 [20] to 1,000,190 ha in 2018 [21] because of the development in the forest-wood sector. Land-cover map of 2018 shows that 68% of Uruguay surface is covered with native grassland associated with livestock and 18% with croplands [15]. It is worth to mention that the 8.4% of the national gross domestic product (GDP) (2018) is from agricultural products and associated industries [22].

The above-mentioned increase in cropland also took place in the San Salvador basin. The land-cover map of 2018 shows that 62.4% of the basin is covered by cropland. Figure 2 and Table 1 show the basin land-cover of 2018.

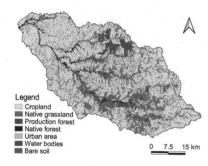

Fig. 2. Land-cover map of San Salvador basin in 2018, classification of Sentinel-2 Level 2A scenes (resolution 10m/pixel) [15].

Legend
- Cropland
- Native grassland
- Production forest
- Native forest
- Urban area
- Water bodies
- Bare soil

0   7.5   15 km

Table 1. Area of land-cover classes in 2018 in the San Salvador basin.

Class	Area (ha)	%
Cropland	149,255	62.4%
Native grassland	74,845	31.3%
Production forest	7,943	3.3%
Native forest	5,691	2.4%
Urban area	927	0.4%
Water bodies	361	0.2%
Bare soil	27	0.0%
Total	239,047	100.0%

Taking into account the strategic importance of San Salvador watershead for the economy of the country, it is fundamental to have accurate historical land-cover mapping of this area to detect any land-cover change that can affect the agricultural production. Furthermore, it is worth mentioning the importance of the distribution of croplands in 1990 to study the land-cover change in this area. Based on these considerations, we selected San Salvador and the year 1990 as our case study.

2.2 Satellite and Field Data

Surface Reflectance Tier 1 dataset, which represents the atmospherically corrected surface reflectance from the Landsat 5 Enhanced Thematic Mapper (ETM) sensor, was used in this study. Landsat 5 was operational in the '90s (launched in 1984 and decommissioned in 2013) and its images are freely available. The satellite had a 16-day repeat cycle and a spatial resolution of 30 m.

The field data available for 1990 is the database from the General Census of Agriculture (GCA) that provides aggregated data to validate the results of the imagery classification. Furthermore, the phenological data of the surveyed crops were used for the visual interpretation of the satellite images.

General Census of Agriculture
In Uruguay, the GCA is conducted by the Ministry of Agriculture, Livestock and Fisheries (MGAP) every ten years. Census data is reported, to preserve people's privacy, in aggregated geographical units called census tracts (CTs).

In 1990, for the Soriano department, the census registered an area dedicated to winter crops six times larger than the one dedicated to summer crops. The main crops are wheat in winter and sorghum in summer. Among winter crops, wheat covers 72% of the planted area, barley covers 21%, and oat (grain) 7%. The main winter forage crop is oat (sowed pasture), 80% of the oat area is for

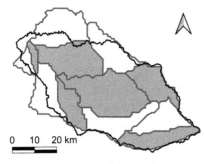

Fig. 3. Selected census tracts of the General Census of Agriculture 1990.

Table 2. Land-cover area of the selected census tracts of the General Census of Agriculture 1990.

Class	Area (ha)	%
Native grassland	73,525	51.7%
Cropland	34,563	24.3%
Sowed pasture	30,856	21.7%
Native forest	2,490	1.7%
Production forest	923	0.6%
Total	142,357	100.0%

grazing (sowed pasture) and 20% is for grain. In summer sorghum, corn, and soybean cover 54% , 33% and 12% of the planted area respectively.

The data from GCA disaggregated per CTs was obtained from the GCA database facilitated by agricultural statistics of MGAP. The database showed that some CTs had under-coverage and over-coverage of the total area. For this reason, only were considered those CTs that had a difference smaller than ± 15% in the coverage-area. So, even though the San Salvador watershed has 12 CTs in common with the Soriano department, only 6 CTs were taken into account. The selected CTs and the land-cover area obtained from GCA is presented in Fig. 3 and Table 2.

Phenological Data

The phenological data used was taken from two sources. For wheat, barley, and oat, phenological data was obtained from the reports on the evaluation of cultivars (results of 2003) [23]. In the case of sorghum, corn, and soybean, a phenologic model developed on the base of experimental data ran in 1990 [24] was considered. Table 3 presents the phenology of crops surveyed in the 1990 census. The phenological phases considered were the early growth stage (between emergence and flowering) and peak on leaf area index season (after flowering).

3   Methods

This section outlines the conceptualization of the methodology approach and the phases implemented to develop the land-cover map.

3.1   Conceptualization of the Methodology Approach

According to the major steps of image classification identified by Lu and Weng [25], in this study, five phases were implemented: (1) imagery selection and pre-processing, (2) selection of the classes and training samples, (3) classification

Table 3. Average dates of phenological phases. *Average date of harvest. **Average date of the last cut.

Crop	Sowing	Emergence	Flowering	Maturity
Wheat [23]	13-jun	23-jun	22-oct	12-dic*
Barley [23]	10-jul	19-jul	10-oct	2-dic*
Oat [23]	12-mar	18-mar		17-nov**
Sorghum [24]	15-oct	26-oct	9-ene	13-feb
Corn [24]	7-oct	17-oct	24-dic	24-feb
Soybean [24]	21-oct	2-nov	31-dic	16-abr

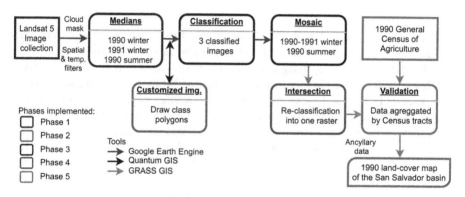

Fig. 4. Conceptualization of the methodology approach.

process, (4) post-classification process, and (5) validation. An overall flowchart of the methodology approach showing each phase is presented in Fig. 4.

GEE is a cloud-based platform that includes a wide geospatial dataset, as well as the entire Landsat archive, and algorithms that facilitate spatial analysis [10]. Image selection and supervised classification techniques were implemented in GEE which was coupled with Geographic Information Systems (GIS) environment. Quantum GIS 3.4.15 (QGIS) was used to customize images and create the polygons classes, and GRASS GIS 7.4.2 was adopted for the post-classification phase.

3.2 Phase 1: Imagery Selection and Pre-processing

The satellite images were collected between December 1989 and August 1991. The criterium adopted for imagery selection was to cover completely the study area considering the crop peak growth phenological stage of winter and summer crops. According to the wheat phenology, the main winter crop, winter peak growing season ranges from October 22nd to December 12th. Sorghum and corn were the main crops for summer season, so, in average, peak growing season ranges from December 15th to February 15th. Furthermore, a quality filter was applied to mask pixels with clouds, cloud shadows or high reflectance (reflectance greater than 6000). Considering the scarcity of quality scenes that covers the entire study area, scenes acquired in different dates were used. To minimize the phenology variation among the scenes, a period smaller than a month was chosen within each growing season. To perform the classification, the images selected were reduced to one per season by the median. Thus, when images had overlapping pixels, the median was computed independently in each band.

3.3   Phase 2: Selection of Classes and Training Samples

The supervised classification approach uses the training samples signatures to classify the image and define the land-cover categories [25]. A successful classification depends on a proper class selection and its representative sampling [25]. Considering that the classes are defined by visual interpretation of satellite images, discernible land-cover units were selected as native grasslands, croplands, and water. Cropland class was also disaggregated into a hierarchical system of subclasses by the post-classification process. Three spectral bands (red, green and near infrared) of surface reflectance were used for the class-visual interpretation.

Some other classes as urban area, production forest, and native forest were considered. These classes were not included in the classification because of mixed pixel problems in remote sensing technology within non-cropland [26]. Instead, some ancillary data were used. For urban area, from the land-cover map of Uruguay of 2000 was used [14]. For production forest, data were mapped from Landsat imagery as there were only four polygons of this class. For native forest, data from the national forest inventory (2018) [21] was used. A visual comparison between the data of the national forest inventory (2018) and aerial photos, taken in 1966 by the Military Geographic Service [27] was made, and no substantial difference was observed. Furthermore, native forest represents about 2% of the study area according to 1990 census data, so it does not represent a significant contribution to the land-cover map.

3.4   Phase 3: Classification Process

A supervised classification approach was performed using a Classification and Regression Tree (CART) classifier implemented in GEE. CART is a binary decision tree. It uses a sample of training data for which the correct classification is known. It recursively splits the data based on a statistical test ending in terminal nodes associated with entities correctly classified [28, 29]. One advantage of selecting non-parametric classifiers, like decision trees, is that they do not suppose a normal distribution of the dataset, which is difficult to achieve especially in complex landscapes [25]. Furthermore, visual interpretation-sampling data were considered.

The polygons with data classes of 1990 winter and 1990 summer were randomly split keeping on average 70% of the polygons for training and 30% for validating the classifier. Also, were consider polygons with data classes of 1991 winter and 1991 summer to perform a cross-year validation. As a result, two classified images were obtained representing 1990 winter and 1990 summer. All spectral bands were used as inputs to classification, four visible and near-infrared (VNIR) bands, two short-wave infrared (SWIR) bands processed to orthorectified surface reflectance, and one thermal infrared (TIR) band processed to orthorectified brightness temperature.

An error matrix was employed to assess the accuracy of the classification and cross-year validation. The overall accuracy (OA), Kappa coefficient (K), consumer's accuracy (CA), and producer's accuracy (PA) coefficients were calculated from the error matrix. OA is the rate of the total correctly classified field samples [30]. K is a measure of overall statistical agreement of an error matrix, which takes into account non-diagonal elements [30]. CA is the conditional probability that the pixels classified as category i was assigned as category i by the reference data [30]. PA is the conditional probability that the pixels assigned as category j by the reference data are classified as category j [30].

3.5   Phases 4 and 5: Post-classification Process and Validation

The post-classification process consisted of observing the sequence winter-summer land cover and making a re-assignment of classes resulting in the final land-cover map. For that, the two classified images were imported as a raster image into GRASS GIS. Then, the two raster images were intersected, creating a new cross-raster map representing all unique combinations of classes and its associated cross-matrix. Finally, the classes were re-assigned.

After the classes re-assignment, a comparison to census data was made to evaluate the accuracy of the resulting map. The map validation is performed since training and validating data were not surveyed in the field [25].

4   Results and Discussion

In this section, the results of each methodological phase to develop the land-cover map are presented. Furthermore, a discussion of the main findings of the study reported in this article is included.

4.1   Phase 1 Results: Imagery Selection and Pre-processing

To create a cloud-free image of 1990, winter scenes corresponding to the early growth stage of winter crops were selected due to the lack of scenes during the phenological phase of peak growth of winter crops. However, due to the quality filters (to mask pixels with clouds, cloud shadows, or high reflectance) applied to the images, the coverage of the studied area was 83% . Thus, to complete the coverage of the entire study area, images of 1991 winter were used. For summer period, scenes during the phenological phase of the peak growth of summer crops were selected. Also, images of 1991 winter and 1991 summer were selected

Table 4. Scenes used from Landsat 5 (Enhanced thematic mapper sensor, surface reflectance Tier 1 dataset). *Scene ID refers to path, row, and acquisition date from the complete ID.

	ID*	Cloud cover	Acquisition date
1990 winter	224083_19900804	0%	8/4/1990
	224084_19900804	0%	8/4/1990
	225083_19900811	28%	8/11/1990
	225084_19900811	41%	8/11/1990
	224083_19900820	0%	8/20/1990
	224084_19900820	0%	8/20/1990
	225084_19900827	58%	8/27/1990
1991 winter	224084_19910807	96%	8/7/1991
	225083_19910814	0%	8/14/1991
	225084_19910814	0%	8/14/1991
1990 summer	224083_19891223	1%	12/23/1989
	224084_19891223	0%	12/23/1989
	225083_19891230	7%	12/30/1989
	225084_19891230	27%	12/30/1989
	225084_19900115	4%	1/15/1990
	225083_19900115	0%	1/15/1990
1991 summer	224083_19910111	10%	1/11/1991
	224084_19910111	12%	1/11/1991
	225083_19910102	5%	1/2/1991
	225084_19910102	3%	1/2/1991

(a) 1990 winter

(b) 1991 winter

(c) 1990 summer

0   10   20 km

Fig. 5. Landsat median images of 1990 winter, 1991 winter and 1990 summer (false colour composite Bands 4, 3, 2).

to perform a cross-year validation. A summary of the considered scenes for each season, its cloud coverage, and acquisition date is presented in Table 4. In Fig. 5, the selected scenes, reduced by the median, representing (a) 1990 winter, (b) 1991 winter, and (c) 1990 summer are shown.

4.2 Phase 2 Results: Selection of Classes and Training Samples

A first search was made in USGS Landsatlook to recognize how crops looked during August and define the land-cover units [31]. A 1989 sequence of images showing the different phenologic phases of winter crops was found. Wheat and barley (winter crops) are discern in May image (Fig. 6a) respectively highlighted in red and yellow but not distinguished in the image from August onward (Figs. 6b–d). Figure 6c shows that winter crops achieved peak growth and Fig. 6d shows they were harvested. From August image (Fig. 6a) oat was recognized, highlighted in green, this enable to assign a subclass of winter crops to oat. Native grasslands were recognized and showed in black with no significant variation observed into the four images.

(a) Date 5/20/1989.   (b) Date 8/1/1989.   (c) Date 10/27/1989. (d) Date 11/28/1989.

Fig. 6. Landsat 5 images showing the evolution of winter crops (red circle: wheat, yellow square: barley, green square: sowed pasture, black circle: grassland). (Color figure online)

Table 5. Land-cover classification classes.

1st level	2nd level	Descriptions
Water bodies	WATB	Streams, rivers, lakes and reservoirs
Grassland	GRAS	Native grasslands or improved grasslands
	FLDP	Native grasslands placed in floodplains
Cropland	PAST, PAST2	Sowed pasture in two phenological phases (only for winter images)
	CRPw	Winter cropland. Includes: wheat and barley
	CRPs	Summer cropland. Includes: sorghum, corn and soybean
	FLLW	Summer fallow
	BARE	Bare or tilled soil

In this study, ten classes were defined to perform the classification. For floodplains (FLDP) a new class was added, as it was observed that grassland kept misclassified as cropland. A list of the defined classes with their description is presented in Table 5.

4.3   Phase 3 Results: Classification Process

For each image, an average of 20 polygons were defined per class, and area used to train and validate the classifiers. This resulted in an average of 1500 ha for training, 500 ha for validation, and 1000 ha for cross-year validation (6). The supervised classification was applied to the three median images described in Sect. 4.1. Finally, in the case of winter images, a mosaic was made to couple the missing area of the winter image of 1990 with data of the winter image of 1991.

The statistical accuracy assessment was applied to train and validate datasets of each image. Table 6 presents the results of statistics OA, K, CA and PA calculated. For the training, validating and cross-year validating dataset, OA and K vary in a range of 0.96 to 1.00 and 0.95 to 1.00 respectively. These results indicate that the three classified images achieved high overall accuracies. Furthermore, CA and PA coefficients show the performance per class. In general, PA and CA vary in a range of 0.83 to 1.00. However, floodplain class had low accuracy, PA and CA vary in a range of 0.44 to 1.00. As mentioned before, it was detected by visual inspection that grassland was misclassified as cropland by the classifier in this area. The post-classification process allowed separating cropland and grassland from the floodplain class.

Table 6. Classification performance and area used for training and validation. CA: consumer's accuracy, PA: producer's accuracy, OA: overall accuracy, K: Kappa.

	Winter						Summer					
	1990				1991		1990				1991	
	Training		Validation		Validation		Training		Validation		Validation	
	CA	PA	CA	PA	CA	PA	CA	PA	CA	PA	CA	PA
Water bodies	1.00	1.00	1.00	1.00	—	—	1.00	0.99	0.83	0.99		
Native grassland	1.00	1.00	0.99	0.98	0.99	0.95	1.00	0.97	0.99	0.97	0.99	1.00
Floodplain	1.00	0.98	1.00	0.95	0.62	0.97	0.98	0.90	0.44	0.90	1.00	0.94
Sowed pasture	1.00	1.00	0.99	1.00	0.99	0.87	—	—	—	—	—	—
Sowed pasture2	1.00	1.00	1.00	1.00	1.00	0.99	—	—	—	—	—	—
Winter cropland	1.00	1.00	1.00	0.99	0.96	1.00	—	—	—	—	—	—
Fallow	—	—	—	—	—	—	1.00	0.99	1.00	0.99	1.00	1.00
Summer cropland	—	—	—	—	—	—	1.00	0.99	1.00	0.99	1.00	0.99
Bare soil	1.00	1.00	0.97	1.00	0.96	0.98	1.00	1.00	1.00	1.00	1.00	1.00
OA	1.00		0.99		0.96		1.00		0.98		1.00	
K	1.00		0.99		0.95		1.00		0.98		0.99	
Area (ha)	1548		454		1,016		1,411		615		1,066	

4.4   Phase 4 Results: Post-classification Process

The seasonal variation of each class was taken into account to better distinguish the class of interest and do the class re-assignation. The intersection of the two classified images (winter and summer) resulted in a cross-raster map and its associated cross-matrix. The five classes considered to construct the final map are water bodies, native grassland, sowed pasture, winter croplands, summer croplands and double cropping lands.

In Table 7, the cross-matrix shows the area (ha) distribution of the intersection between the classified winter image and the classified summer image. Each row represents the area of winter classes desegregated into summer classified classes. Similarly, each column represents the area classified on summer image desegregated into winter classified classes.

The cross-matrix, presented in Table 7, shows that 84% of the area classified as GRAS on winter image stayed as GRAS on the final map, and the remaining 16% was assingned to a cropland class. Furthermore, 76% of the area classified as FLDP on winter was re-assigned to the class GRAS and the remaining 24% was re-allocated to a cropland class (CRPw). This was the main reason for defining the specific FLDP class, as discussed in Sect. 4.3.

Table 7. Cross-matrix expressing the area (ha) distribution of the intersection of the classified winter image with the classified summer image.

	Class	Area (ha) classified on summer					
		Native grassland	Flood-plain	Fallow	Summer cropland	Bare soil	Total
Area (ha) classified on winter	Native grassland	63,942	25,435	6,772	3,835	6,565	106,549
	Floodplain	12,228	29,703	9,279	5,001	5,147	61,358
	Sowed pasture	1,814	5,208	3,033	678	1,843	12,576
	Sowed pasture2	2,625	5,613	2,594	1,846	1,917	14,595
	Winter cropland	2,703	3,384	5,077	706	7,033	18,903
	Bare soil	7,203	5,174	4,634	1,405	5,551	23,967
	Total	90,515	74,517	31,389	13,471	28,056	237,948

4.5 Phase 5 Results: Validation

A comparison between 1990 GCA and the new land-cover map was made to validate the results of the final land-cover map. GCA data was grouped into classes of interest. So, the total area surveyed in GCA as vegetables, row crops, tilled soil, and fallow was compared with the total area of CRPw, CRPs and CRPWs classes; native forest was compared with MONT class area; production forest surface was compared with the FRST surface; the total area covered by pasture and annual forages was compared with the PAST area; and the total area dedicated to improved grassland and native grassland was compared with the GRAS area. The area of the six CTs selected was aggregated to reduce the geographic resolution errors and compared with the same extension of the land-cover map.

The area of the land-cover map classes is very similar to surface reported in the GCA. In Table 8 is presented the areas per class obtained from the land-cover map and from the GCA, and the difference between the two areas. In general, the area of the new-defined categories is greater than the GCA area due to the difference between the surveyed and the measured area that is equal to 6,574 ha. This difference is not valid for pasture and production forest classes. The challenge in classifying pasture class is represented by the fact that perennial pastures can be confused with grasslands. Furthermore, dairy production land use occupies an area where there are mixed portions of pasture and crop that are difficult to separate. About production forest area, an error in the CTs borders may explain the misclassified area since an area of production forest was identified next to the CTs borders.

Figure 7 shows the final land-cover map of the San Salvador basin in 1990 and, Table 9 presents the area covered by each class. The three main land covers identified in the basin were native grasslands (GRAS) with a surface equal to 56.8%, croplands (CRPw, CRPws and CRPs) with a total area of 30.0%, and sowed pastures with a surface of 9.8%.

As expected, the results showed a significant land-cover change between 1990 and 2018. Cropland surface increased from 95,258 ha to 149,255 ha (57%) and grassland reduced from 135,826 ha to 74,845 ha (45%). Also, the production forest area increased from 1,185 ha to 7,943 ha (570%). The observed trends are

Table 8. Comparison of the areas per class of the land-cover map and the General Census of Agriculture 1990 (GCA).

Class	Classified (ha)	%	GCA (ha)	%	Difference (ha)
Native grassland	84,097	57%	73,525	52%	10,572
Native forest	3,520	2%	2,490	2%	1,030
Cropland	43,805	29%	34,563	24%	9,242
Sowed pasture	17,509	12%	30,856	21%	−13,347
Production forest	0	0%	923	1%	−923
Total	148,931	100%	142,357	100%	6,574

Legend
- ■ Native grassland
- ▨ Winter cropland
- ▨ Summer cropland
- ▨ Double cropping lands
- ■ Sowed pasture
- ■ Production forest
- ■ Native forest
- ▨ Urban area

0   7.5   15 km

Fig. 7. Land-cover map of San Salvador basin in 1990.

Table 9. Area of land-cover classes of San Salvador basin in 1990.

Class	Area (ha)	%
Native grassland	135,826	56.8%
Winter cropland	66,830	28.0%
Summer cropland	4,314	1.8%
Double cropping	662	0.3%
Sowed pasture	23,452	9.8%
Native forest	5,683	2.4%
Production forest	1,185	0.5%
Urban area	991	0.4%
Water bodies	127	0.0%
Total	239,070	100.0%

related to agriculture and forestry expansion since 1990. Uruguay met a challenge for sustainable intensification as committed, in 2015, in the 21st Session of the Conference of the Parties (COP21) [32]. Since 2013, a public policy towards soil conservation, based on the Universal Soil Loss Equation (USLE), is being implemented [32]. This policy, designed by the MGAP, is recognized as a good example by the Food and Agriculture Organization (FAO) [33].

The main source of error identified in this study might be related to the scarcity of scenes on the dates and area of interest. For instance, the winter crop season was characterized only based on the available images in August, when winter crops were on an early growth stage. Another source of error may be introduced by the training and validation polygons created by the visual interpretation of images and its sampling design. The low accuracy achieved on the floodplain class may occur due to: (1) reflectance similarities between vegetation on floodplains and crops, especially in the summer season, and (2) the heterogeneity of the vegetation on the surface this class represents. However, the low accuracy in the floodplain class was improved, based on visual validation, by using a multi-seasonal post-classification approach.

The methodology of this study can be used to develop a series of historical annual land-cover maps and might be applied for mapping other basins with similar surface features. Landsat scenes are freely available since 1984. Yet, their frequency increase since 1987–1988, so temporal series from this period to the present can be achieved. For validation, data from GCA is available every ten years and data of agricultural annual surveys (DIEA-MGAP) can also be employed. Furthermore, since 2000 onwards other satellite missions, such as MODIS (2000), CEBERS-4 (2014) and Sentinel (2014), provide free satellite imagery. Therefore, the presented methodology might be improved using a multi-satellite approach.

5   Conclusions

This study presented an efficient approach to estimate the land-cover of an agricultural basin, using free open-source tools. GEE showed excellent potential in land cover mapping with high processing efficiency. Machine-learning algorithms developed in GEE are easily applied and a wide range of free satellite imagery is available.

As a case study, we estimated the land-cover in the San Salvador basin in 1990 based on Landsat 5 imagery and GEE processing platform. High accuracy was achieved in the supervised classification according to the error matrix analysis. Additionally, map validation showed good agreements with GCA data. The methodology presented was capable to deal with the scarcity of historical quality scenes.

The methodology presented in this article can be improved by a multi-satellite approach. Temporal map series of the same watershed can be developed as well as other catchments. The above mentioned are issues that can be explored in future research.

Map availability. The San Salvador basin land-cover map of 1990 can be freely downloaded from https://www.gub.uy/ministerio-ganaderia-agricultura-pesca/politicas-y-gestion/mapa-cobertura-utilizando-google-earth-engine-cuenca-del-rio-san-salvador-1990.

Funding. This research was supported by the National Research and Innovation Agency (ANII) under contract number FSA_PI_2018_1_148628.

Acknowledgements. We thank DIEA-MGAP that kindly made available the GCA data and DGRN-MGAP for their comments and suggestions.

References

1. Giri, S., Qiu, Z.: Understanding the relationship of land uses and water quality in Twenty First Century: a review. J. Environ. Manag. **173**, 41–48 (2016)
2. Rodríguez, J., Rico, A., Mendoza-Martínez, E., Gómez-Ruiz, A., Sedeño-Diaz, J., López-López, E.: Impact of changes of land use on water quality, from tropical forest to anthropogenic occupation: a multivariate approach. Water **10**, 1–16 (2018)
3. Dwivedi, R., Kandrika, S., Ramana, K.: Land-use/land-cover change analysis in part of Ethiopia using landsat thematic mapper data. Int. J. Remote Sens. **26**, 1285–1287 (2005)
4. Gomez, C., White, J., Wulder, M.: Optical remotely sensed time series data for land cover classification: a review. ISPRS J. Photogramm. **116**, 55–72 (2016)
5. Figorito, B., Tarantino, E., Balacco, G., Fratino, U.: An object-based method for mapping ephemeral river areas from WorldView-2 satellite data. Proc. SPIE **8531**, 85310B (2012)
6. Aquilino, M., Tarantino, E., Fratino, U.: Multi-temporal land use analysis of an ephemeral river area using an artificial neural network approach on Landsat imagery. ISPRS - Int. Arch. Photogramm. **XL–5/W3**, 167–173 (2013)
7. Amani, M., et al.: A generalized supervised classification scheme to produce provincial wetland inventory maps: an application of Google Earth Engine for big geo data processing. Big Earth Data **3**(4), 378–394 (2019)
8. Xiong, J., et al.: Automated cropland mapping of continental Africa using Google earth engine cloud computing. ISPRS J. Photogramm. **126**, 225–244 (2017)
9. Kumar, L., Mutanga, O.: Google earth engine applications since inception: usage, trends, and potential. Remote Sens. **10**, 1509 (2018)
10. Gorelick, N., Hancher, M., Dixon, M., Ilyushchenko, S., Thau, D., Moore, R.: Google earth engine: planetary-scale geospatial analysis for everyone. Remote Sens. Environ. **202**, 18–27 (2017)
11. Belgiu, M., Csillik, O.: Sentinel-2 cropland mapping using pixel-based and object-based time-weighted dynamic time warping analysis. Remote Sens. Environ. **204**, 509–523 (2018)
12. Mumby, P., Green, E., Edwards, A., Clark, C.: The cost-effectiveness of remote sensing for tropical coastal resources assessment and management. J. Environ. Manag. **55**, 157–166 (1999)
13. MapBiomas Project - Collection v4.0 of the Annual Land Use Land Cover Maps of Brazil. http://mapbiomas.org. Accessed 7 Feb 2020
14. National Directorate of Land-use Planning - Ministry of Housing, Land Planning and Environment (DINOT-MVOTMA): Land-cover map of Uruguay. Technical report, Montevideo, Uruguay (2014). (in Spanish)
15. Petraglia, C., Dell'Acqua, M., Pereira, G., Yussim, E.: Integrated Land Cover/Use Map of Uruguay of 2018. Gráfica Mosca, Montevideo (2019). (in Spanish)
16. Uruguay Meteorological Institute (INUMET). https://www.inumet.gub.uy/index.php/clima. Accessed 3 Jan 2020
17. Agricultural Statistics - Ministry of Agriculture, Livestock and Fisheries (DIEA-MGAP): Agricultural Regions of Uruguay. Technical report, Montevideo, Uruguay (2015). (in Spanish)
18. Arbeletche, P., Coppola, M., Paladino, C.: Analysis of agro-business as a form of business management in South America: the Uruguayan case. Agrociencia Uruguay **16**, 110–119 (2012). (in Spanish)

19. Couto, P.: Recent trends in rainfed agriculture. Plan Agropecuario **161**, 64–68 (2017). (in Spanish)
20. Agricultural Statistics - Ministry of Agriculture, Livestock and Fisheries (DIEA-MGAP): General Census of Agriculture of 1990. Editorial MGAP, Montevideo, Uruguay (1994). (in Spanish)
21. Forestry Directorate - Ministry of Agriculture, Livestock and Fisheries (DGF-MGAP): Results of the national forest mapping 2018. Technical report, Montevideo, Uruguay (2018). (in Spanish)
22. Agricultural Statistics - Ministry of Agriculture: Agricultural statistical yearbook 2019. Technical report, Montevideo, Uruguay (2019). (in Spanish)
23. Castro, M., Pereyra, S., Stewart, S., Germán, S., Vázquez, D.: Experimental results of the national cultivar evaluation. Technical report, National Institute of Agricultural Research (INIA) and National Institute of Seeds (INASE), Montevideo, Uruguay (2003). (in Spanish)
24. Fassio, A., et al.: Prediction of phenological states for soy, sunflower, corn, sorghum (grain, forage, sweet and silage). Technical report, National Institute of Agricultural Research (INIA), Montevideo, Uruguay (2014). (in Spanish)
25. Lu, D., Weng, Q.: A survey of image classification methods and techniques for improving classification performance. Int. J. Remote Sens. **28**, 823–870 (2007)
26. Liu, J., et al.: Spatial and temporal patterns of China's cropland during 1990–2000: an analysis based on landsat TM data. Remote Sens. Environ. **98**, 442–456 (2005)
27. Military Geographic Service (SGM): Aerial photographs of Uruguay 1966/67, scale 1 / 40,000. http://visualizador.sgm.gub.uy/gmaps/index.html. Accessed 3 Jan 2020. (in Spanish)
28. Bittencourt, H., Clarke, R.T.: Use of classification and regression trees (CART) to classify remotely-sensed digital images. In: IGARSS 2003, 2003 IEEE International Geoscience and Remote Sensing Symposium. Proceedings (IEEE Cat. No. 03CH37477), vol. 6, pp. 3751–3753 (2003)
29. Friedl, M., Brodley, C.: Decision tree classification of land cover from remotely sensed data. Remote Sens. Environ. **61**(3), 399–409 (1997)
30. Stehman, S.: Selecting and interpreting measures of thematic classification accuracy. Remote Sens. Environ. **62**, 77–89 (1997)
31. U.S. Geological Survey (USGS) Landsatlook. https://landsatlook.usgs.gov/viewer.html. Accessed 15 Jan 2020
32. Ministry of Agriculture: Livestock and Fisheries (MGAP): Uruguay agribusiness. The challenges for sustainable development. Technical report, Montevideo, Uruguay (2017). (in Spanish)
33. Food and Agriculture Organization of the United Nations and Intergovernmental Technical Panel on Soils: Status of the World's soil resources - main report. Technical report, Rome, Italy (2015)

A Methodological Proposal to Support Estimation of Damages from Hailstorms Based on Copernicus Sentinel 2 Data Times Series

F. Sarvia, S. De Petris, and E. Borgogno-Mondino[✉]

DISAFA, University of Torino, L.go Braccini 2, 10095 Grugliasco, TO, Italy
{Filippo.sarvia, enrico.borgogno}@unito.it

Abstract. Hail is one of the risks that most frightens farmers and one of the few currently insured climatic-related phenomena. In the last years, a significant increase occurred of adverse events affecting crops, highlighting that ordinary strategies of insurance companies should migrate to a more dynamic management. In this work a prototype of service based on remotely sensed data is presented aimed at supporting evaluation of hail impacts on crops by mapping and qualifying areas damaged by hail. Further, a comparison was done testing effectiveness of approaches based on short term (i.e. with reference to images acquired immediately after the event) and long term (i.e. with reference to images acquired close to crop harvest) analysis. Investigation was solicited by the Reale Mutua insurance company and focused on a strong hailstorm occurred on 6th July 2019 in the Vercelli province (Piemonte - NW Italy). The analysis was based on Copernicus Sentinel-2 level 2A imagery. A times series made of 29 NDVI maps was generated for the growing season 2019 (from March to October) and analyzed at pixel level looking for NDVI trend anomalies possibly related to crop damages. Phenological behavior of damaged crops (NDVI local temporal profile) was compared with those of unharmed fields to verify and assess the impact of the phenomenon. Results showed evident anomalies along the local NDVI temporal profile of damaged cropped pixels, permitting a fine mapping of the affected areas. Surprisingly, short and long term approaches led to different conclusions: some areas, appearing significantly damaged immediately after the event, showed a vegetative recover with the proceeding of the growing season (temporary damages). Differently, some others showed that damages detected after the events never turned into a better situation (permanent damages). This new information could drive to considered a revision of the ordinary insurance procedures that are currently used by companies to certify and quantify damages of crops after adverse events. It can therefore said that, the high temporal resolution of the Copernicus Sentinel 2 mission can significantly contribute to improve evaluating procedures in the insurance sector by introducing temporal variables.

Keywords: Crop insurance · NDVI · Hail in agriculture · Risk management in agriculture · Remote sensing-based services

© Springer Nature Switzerland AG 2020
O. Gervasi et al. (Eds.): ICCSA 2020, LNCS 12252, pp. 737–751, 2020.
https://doi.org/10.1007/978-3-030-58811-3_53

1 Introduction

All economic activities are exposed to risk factors, and agriculture is probably the most vulnerable one being sensitive to several exogenous events, not controllable by farmers. Hail is one of the risks that most frightens farmers and, consequently, one of the few insured climatic-related phenomena. In the last years, a significant increase occurred of adverse events affecting crops, highlighting that ordinary strategies of insurance companies should mi-grate to a more dynamic management. According to FAO, between 2003 and 2013 agriculture absorbed 25% of the total impact of climate disasters in developing countries. These numbers are significantly higher than the previously reported ones and suggest to strengthen planning actions and increase investments in disaster risk reduction. The likelihood of worsening conditions will increase if no improvement of the resilience of the agricultural sector is achieved and specific investments to strengthen food security and productivity are done [1]. Agriculture is an essential practice for growth and development of societies, but it is exposed to multiple risk factors [2]. The production risk is related to the possibility that the quantity or quality of products may be lower than expected as a result of adverse weather conditions or phytopathogens. The financial risk is related to the possibility of bankruptcy due to lack of financial reserves to repay debts or to advance expenses. The market risk is related to the possibility of not finding outlets at expected prices or of not being able to find production factors at favourable prices. The institutional risk is related to the possibility that rules and regulations may change unexpectedly as a result of certain production decisions. The personal risk is related to the ability of the farmer and other permanent employees to continue to carry out their activities effectively. Risk management tools are therefore mandatory and should be addressed to take care about crop diversification, utilization of resistant varieties, irrigation practices, adoption of anti-hail coverings, utilization of physical barriers against insects, use of chemical products (e.g. pesticides or herbicides), finalization of supply chain contracts and underwriting of insurance policies. When insurances transfer part of the income risk out of the farmers' portfolio they can afford to invest in high-risk/high-yield technologies such as improved seeds and inputs [3, 4]. The role of insurance tools for risk management in agriculture is increasing [5, 6]. The insurance is based on a contract between the insurer and the economic agent (e.g. the farmer). The latter pays a premium (i.e. a cash sum) to receive, in case of adverse events, compensation for losses due to specific risks covered by the insurance contract. Agricultural insurance is fairly well developed in US and Canada, where no shortage of issues is present related to stimulation of demand for insurance [7–9]; in Europe, although it has been growing in recent years, it still presents some limitations. The European agricultural insurance system is very diversified: different types of instruments and public intervention measures characterize the European scenario. In Italy, insurance market is still underdeveloped, despite strong political attention and large subsidies (up to 80% of the insurance premium) paid to farmers. The participation (i.e. the percentage of farmers taking out agricultural insurance contracts) is around 15%. There are different types of contracts: single risk, multiple risk and multi-risk contracts. Since 2004, single risk policies are no longer supported by state subsidies to favour multi and multi-risk policies. Multi-risk policies are also known as yield policies: farmers are compensated for yield losses with reference to historical yields calculated over previous years. These policies, despite being subsidized and more attractive, are not very widespread, even though the trend of contracts is increasing. Among the new policies there are the so called indexed ones, that operates with reference to: a) proper indices (e.g. weather related, like temperature and humidity regimes; or, possibly in future, remote sensing based); b) attribute thresholds (e.g. maximum or minimum average temperatures). Positive or negative deviations from a reference threshold will result in the payment of the premium by the insurance to the farmer. In many countries, governments are showing great interest in these new types of insurance policies, and many pilot projects are promoted worldwide [10–12]. Technologically innovative insurance programs are currently privileging "index insurances" that link payments to environmentally based proxy variables instead of losses. These are announced as promising strategies for reducing poverty and improve climate risk management and system resilience especially in countries that are heavily dependent on smallholder agriculture [13, 14]. In future, insurance policies are expected to focus on optimization of the efficiency of the company's resources for both economic performance and climate/environmental impacts mitigation [15]. In this context, some insurance companies are currently testing new strategies to increase business profitability, to attract a greater number of customers and to be competitive and innovative in the market. Satellite remote sensing is one of the new tools that can be proficiently used in agriculture. Free of charge or low price satellite data can be an excellent starting point for the analysis of large areas, especially if completed with ground data [16, 17]. Satellite images can be useful to support the estimation of damage caused by extreme weather events such as floods, hail or drought [18], to estimate the loss of agricultural production due to climate change [19, 20] and to manage risk in forested and urban green areas [21, 22]. The future potential of index-based insurance policies is very high; expectation is that insurance expert ground surveys could be activated with reference to preventive controls operated by remotely sensed data. For all of the false claims (detected by comparison between farmer's claim and satellite based information), insurance company could save the cost of the expert's report. Savings could consequently, reduce the cost of insurance fees by offering farmers better conditions than at present [23]. In this work a prototype service based on remotely sensed data is presented aimed at supporting evaluation of hail impacts on crops by mapping and qualifying areas damaged by hail. Further, a comparison was done testing effectiveness of approaches based on short term (i.e. with reference to images acquired immediately after the event) and long term (i.e. with reference to images acquired close to crop harvest) analysis. This study was suggested by the Reale Mutua insurance company and was addressed to analyze effects of a strong hailstorm occurred on 6th July 2019 in the Vercelli province (Piemonte - NW Italy), where rice is the dominating crop. Copernicus Sentinel-2 level 2A imagery was used for this purposes. It is worth to highlight that, even if the proposed methodology concerns the Vercelli province area, results can be thought globally valuable, i.e. applicable in any part of the world (cloudiness permitting).

2 Materials and Methods

2.1 Study Area

Reale Mutua insurance company reported a strong hailstorm occurred on 6th July 2019 in the Vercelli province (Piemonte - NW Italy, Fig. 1). Rice cultivation plays a leading role in the agricultural local context. The area has a typically temperate continental climate, where NW Alps gradually determines a temperature reduction while altitude rises. The entire surface affected by the hail was not known by Reale Mutua.

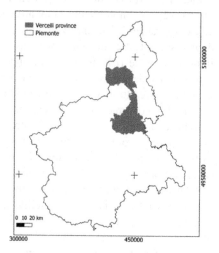

Fig. 1. The study area is located in Vercelli, NW Italy (Reference frame: WGS 84 UTM 32N).

2.2 Available Data

For this work, 29 Sentinel 2 Level-2A images were obtained from the Copernicus Open Access Hub geoportal (scihub.copernicus.eu). They are supplied as 100×100 km^2 tiles orthoprojected in the WGS84 UTM reference frame [24]. Level-2A products are supplied already calibrated in "at-the-bottom of the atmosphere" reflectance (BOA), guaranteeing immediate usability for land applications. Table 1 shows main technical specifications of S2 MSI (Multi Spectral Instrument).

Table 1. Sentinel-2 characteristics

Launch date	23/06/2015
Orbit height	786 km
Geometric resolution	b2–b4, b8: 10 m
	b5–b7, b8a, b11, b12: 20 m
	b1, b9, b10: 60 m
Radiometric resolution	12 bit
Spectral resolution	13 bands
Temporal resolution	5 days

Reale Mutua provided a vector map representing some reference fields: some damaged by hail during the event of 6th July 2019; some others unharmed (Fig. 2). Additionally some ground information were supplied too (Table 2).

Table 2. Characteristics of the unharmed and damaged fields (D = damaged; ND = not damaged)

State	Municipality	Crops	Area (ha)	ID
ND	Vercelli	Rice	6.76	–
	Prarolo	Soybean	5.08	–
	Prarolo	Soybean	7.14	–
	Prarolo	Wheat	8.21	–
	Borgo Vercelli	Corn	17.49	–
D	Vercelli	Soybean	17.46	1
	Vercelli	Soybean	13.66	2
	Vercelli	Wheat	19.99	3
	Vercelli	Rice	14.18	4
	Vercelli	Rice	7.16	5
	Vercelli	Corn	10.97	6

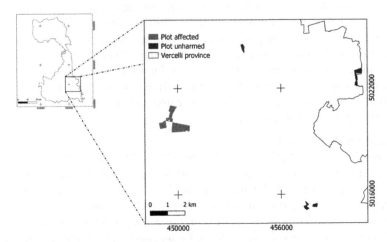

Fig. 2. Fields provided by Reale Mutua. In blue unharmed fields (ND), in red fil damaged (Reference frame: WGS 84 UTM 32N). (Color figure online)

2.3   Procedure

Many studies have already explained the importance of remote sensing in agriculture [25–29] introducing specific spectral indexes like EVI (Enhanced Vegetation Index), SAVI (Soil-Adjusted Vegetation Index), NDVI (Normalized Difference Vegetation Index) and many others [30–34]. In this work the authors choose NDVI because it is well suited to the study area proposed by the insurance company and it works better than other indices featured in literature. Reliability, convenience and ease of use of data are extremely important for external users like insurance company can be.

Leprieur affirms that NDVI (Eq. 1) is a vegetation index that can be used for retrieval of vegetation canopy biophysical properties [35]; consequently, it can be reasonably thought to be used for the new index-based crop insurance design [36, 37] being a good predictor of crop yield [38–40].

$$NDVI = \frac{\rho_{NIR} - \rho_{RED}}{\rho_{NIR} + \rho_{RED}} \tag{1}$$

where ρ_{NIR} and ρ_{RED} are respectively the NIR (band 8 of S2) and RED (band 4 of S2) at-the-ground reflectances. NDVI negative values are related to water/snow surfaces, NDVI values close between 0.1 and 0.25 refer to bare and dry soils, highly positive values (>0.4) refer to vegetated surfaces characterized by photosynthetic activity (earthobservatory.nasa.gov). With respect to vegetated surfaces (e.g. crops), comparison of NDVI values before and after an occurred catastrophic event can generate good prediction and mapping of damaged areas [41]. Nevertheless, this approach neglects the reaction of crops to the event. Some crops, in fact, that appear as damaged immediately after the event, at the end of the season can, however, provide an excellent production. Obviously, plants must have the necessary time to fully resume all their functions. In other words, the time of the damage along the growing season of crop is more important than the instantaneous intensity of the event. For example, during flowering and before harvesting crop are more sensitive event occurs damages could be highly relevant for the final production. For this reason, authors retain that remote sensing based deductions should be done with reference to different investigations: one close to the event (short term analysis) and one for the remaining time separating the date of the event from the harvest (long term analysis). According to these premises, in this work, an NDVI time series, covering the entire growing season of the investigated crops, was generated and assessed.

Damaged Fields Mapping

Hailstorm area was detected by producing NDVI difference (DM1 = after-before) calculated by grid differencing using the available "good" NDVI maps closer (before and after) to the event. NDVI maps of 16/07/2019 and 06/07/2019 were selected showing the post- and pre-event situation, respectively. Destructive action of hail on crops is expected to lower local NDVI values in damaged fields. Consequently, DM1 should show positive and negative values for unharmed and damaged fields, respectively. It is worth to remind that, only significant NDVI differences can be related to an actual occurred change. According to literature [42], only DM1 values (absolute value) > 0.02 were assumed as significant, and, consequently, reliable. To automatically map damaged and not-damaged fields, with reference to DM1 a threshold value of −0.05 was applied, admitting that values < −0.05 correspond to damaged pixels.

Level of Damage

Phenological behavior of damaged crops (averaged for each individual plot) was assumed to be well represented by the correspondent NDVI temporal profile; to verify and assess the degree of damage, it was therefore compared with the NDVI profile of close not-damaged fields looking for long-term effects on crop production. In fact, damaged crops can possibly recover, totally or partially, their health after a while moving towards a good production anyway. Degree of damage and recover can also vary in space within the same field, making damage effects not similar in spatial distribution. This is a very common situation when exploring hail damages, that are known to be very local and fast changing in space.

To answer the first question, a long-term analysis was achieved comparing by differencing the pre-event scene (6/7/2019) with one acquired one month after the event (5/8/2019). A new NDVI difference map was generated (hereinafter called DM2). Nevertheless, sometimes, long-term analysis is not enough to determine the remaining/recovered vitality of crops; it is possible that positive DM2 values are false positives; in fact, died plants can be substituted by a different vegetation type, like weeds, that can determine positive DM2 values. For this reason a "single shot" difference (even though on long-term basis) can be not enough to describe the actual occurring phenomena. Conversely, it is essential to monitor crop during along its entire phenological development, i.e. with reference to its complete NDVI local profile. An accurate analysis of NDVI profile can be greatly helpful to correctly interpret positive DM2 values.

As far as spatial distribution of damage within the field is concerned, the local anomaly of NDVI, $PA_i(t)$, was computed at field level by Eq. 2, for both the post-event dates (16/7/2019, 5/8/2019). Only damaged fields were taken into account.

$$PA_i(t) = \frac{a_i(t)}{\mu_j(t)} \tag{2}$$

where $a_i(t)$ is the NDVI value of a single pixel within the damaged field at the t day and $\mu_j(t)$ the NDVI mean value of that field at the same t day. For some of the investigated fields, a map of $PA(t)$ was therefore generated to make possible to locally tune the average damage caused by hail. Pixels showing a PA value > 1 indicates that suffered from a weak damage in respect of the others; PA value < 1 refer to those areas within the field that were heavily damaged. PA map can be therefore useful to farmer to understand how calibrate agronomic operations; to insurance company to define the compensation for the damage in case the impact of hail is only on a portion of the field. The driving value to decide if the damage is significant or not within the field is, obviously, its mean NDVI value.

3   Results and Discussion

Damaged Field Mapping

The area potentially damaged by hail during the explored event, was mapped (Fig. 5) according to DM1 (Fig. 4). Compared NDVI maps are shown in Fig. 3 (16/07/2019 and 06/07/2019). All those areas showing a DM1 value lower than −0.05 were labeled as "damaged" and resulted in 1568 ha. Results were compared with the reference fields (damaged and not-damaged) supplied by Reale Mutua showing a total consistency (Fig. 6).

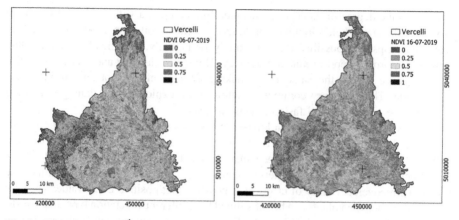

Fig. 3. NDVI map of 16th July (left) and map of 6th July (right). Reference frame: WGS 84 UTM 32N.

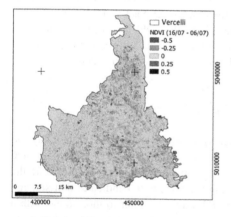
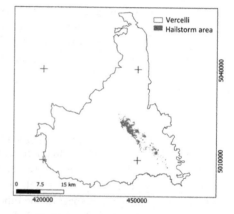

Fig. 4. NDVI difference map (DM1) obtained by differencing between the NDVI map of 16th July and that of 6th July. Reference frame: WGS 84 UTM 32N.

Fig. 5. Map of the areas damaged by the hailstorm of July 6th 2019. Reference frame: WGS 84 UTM 32N.

Level of Damage

To quantify the level of damage caused by hail the ordinary change detection approaches was adopted based on the comparison a single couple of images (after – before). DM1 and DM2 were therefore computed. With reference to DM1 all fields that, according to Reale Mutua data, were declared as damaged confirmed to fall in the "damaged" area as mapped by satellite. An exception came for the soybean field in the North side and fro the rice field in the East side (Fig. 7-left). In fact, these fields were the only ones presenting positive DM1 values (Table 3). Differently, while looking at

DM2, some differences can be observed (Fig. 7-right). On August 5th (about one month after the hailstorm) a recovery of local vegetation seemed to be occurred, corn and wheat fields excluded. With specific focus on wheat, a negative DM2 value was expects since, in the area, harvest is normally scheduled around 10th July. Consequently, the only crop that after one month from the event showed weak negative DM2 values was corn (Table 3).

Table 3. Average NDVI difference in the short (DM1) and long term (DM2) for each damaged field

Fields	Area (ha)	Average NDVI difference in the short term	Average NDVI difference in the long term
Soybean Nord	17.46	0.08	0.22
Soybean West	13.66	−0.05	0.19
Rice East	14.18	0.01	0.22
Rice in the middle	7.16	−0.06	0.09
Corn	10.97	−0.17	−0.20
Wheat	19.99	−0.07	0.03

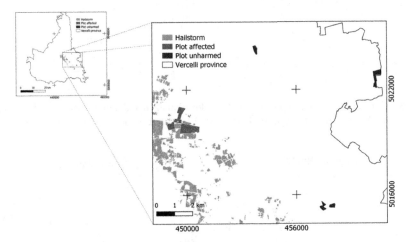

Fig. 6. Map of the fields unharmed and damaged in relation to the hailstorm area (Reference frame: WGS 84 UTM 32N).

These results could be misleading, if one assumed that all fields showing DM2 positive values recovered from damages. As previously mentioned, DM2 positive values could be related to weeds within damaged fields. To solve this doubt the mean temporal profile of NDVI was observed looking for evidences of removal of profile

Fig. 7. DM1 (left) and DM2 (right) maps. Reference frame: WGS 84 UTM 32N.

from its expected trend (crop type dependent). This was achieved by comparing the phenological behavior of damaged crop (NDVI local temporal profile) with the one expressed by a not-damaged field having the same crop (Figs. 8, 9 and 10).

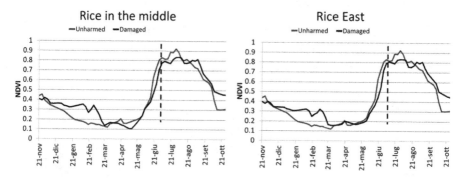

Fig. 8. Comparison of NDVI profiles of rice fields (damaged and unharmed). Left - Rice field in the middle. Right – Rice field in the East. Dotted line corresponds to the day of the hailstorm.

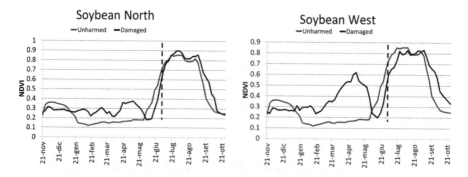

Fig. 9. Comparison NDVI profiles of soybean fields (damaged and unharmed). Left - soybean field in the North. Right-soybean field in the West. Dotted line corresponds to the day of the hailstorm.

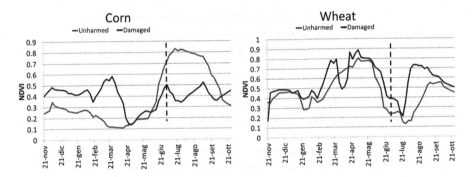

Fig. 10. Comparison of NDVI profiles for corn (left) and wheat (right) fields. Dotted line corresponds to the day of the hailstorm.

NDVI profiles of soybean and rice fields show little differences between damaged and unharmed fields: only in the very proximity of hailstorm, NDVI significantly reduced suggesting that, despite the hail, crops properly reached the harvest time. Wheat fields, differently showed a different behaviour, since harvest occurred few days after the event. In these cases NDVI values reduction was possibly related to harvest and not to hail. Corn fields instead show an evident permanent damage, never recovered. NDVI profile of corn in Fig. 10 shows, in fact, a drastic decrease of NDVI values after hail; NDVI tends to increase slowly after the event with such a trend that can be reasonably interpreted as related to weeds. In fact, the NDVI profile of corn in a not damaged field appears as completely different. Maximum NDVI value for damaged corn was around 0.5, while for not damaged corn was above 0.8.

Results showed that just one out of the reference fields was actually damaged by hail: the corn one. Consequently, a focus was done on this field aimed at mapping the spatial variation of damage within the fields. An anomaly map was therefore computed for both July 16th and August 5th (Fig. 11) with the following meaning:

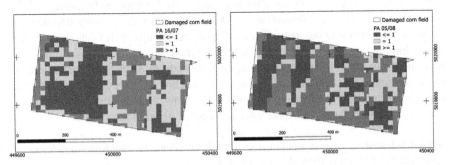

Fig. 11. Map of corn field anomalies in the short (left) and long (right) term. Reference frame: WGS 84 UTM 32N.

- PA > 1: local NDVI value greater than 1 means that in that position the damage was lower than the average one of the investigated field;
- PA < 1: local NDVI value lower than 1 means that in that position the damage was higher than the average one of the investigated field;
- PA = 1: local NDVI value correspond to the average one of the investigated field.

For the explored field it was found that in the 41.02%, 23.39% and 35.58% of the field area showed a PA value <1, >1, = 1 respectively immediately after the event. In the long-term negative anomalies (PA < 1) decreased, suggesting that weeds spread over the field or corn partially developed. Nevertheless these preliminary tests showed that, only one out of the 6 reference fields declared as damaged for insurance claims was found to be actually damaged by hail. Since it is authors' conviction that remote sensing-based information are not conclusive, ground surveys area always required, the final verdict can only come after a field survey.

4 Conclusions

In crop insurance sector remote sensing could support experts in the evaluation of crop damages after hail events. It proved to be an excellent tool that can provide proper information to insurance companies. Presently, insurance companies must operate a ground survey to evaluate each compensation request; in a not-too-far future, remote sensing systems could circumstantially explore the entire context locating those anomalies useful to better target losses appraisals. Economical and management strategies, supported by this new type of information, are expected to increase competitiveness and business income of insurance companies. Optical images from Copernicus, obtainable for free, proved to effectively support hail damage analysis in agriculture. NDVI time series showed that they can reasonably describe impacts of hail on crops. This study suggests that the use of ordinary analysis systems, integrated with the NDVI time series could drive to interesting results for insurance companies, providing more reliable information about hail damaged fields. Copernicus data are the natural tool for this type of investigation, given their temporal frequency (5 days, nominally) and geometric resolution (GSD = 10 m) and will certainly improve effectiveness, reliability and competitiveness of insurance company. It is also expected that this technology will allow companies to provide more precise and detailed information to farmers moving to a more transparent quantification of damage compensations. It is worth to remind that remote sensing-based approaches do not exclude ground survey, that are still needed to precisely interpret indications from satellite data but moving towards an easier, faster and more effective way of generating reports.

Acknowledgments. Authors would like to thank Reale Mutua for supplying all needed ground data and maps to achieve the tasks of this works.

References

1. FAO: Damage and losses from climate-related disasters in agricultural sectors (2016)
2. Santeramo, F.G., Di Pasquale, J., Contò, F., Tudisca, S., Sgroi, F.: Analyzing risk management in mediterranean countries: the Syrian perspective. New Medit **3**, 35–40 (2012)
3. Morduch, J.: Income smoothing and consumption smoothing. J. Econ. Perspect. **9**(3), 103–114 (1995)
4. Dercon, S., Christiaensen, L.: Consumption risk, technology adoption and poverty traps: evidence from Ethiopia. J. Dev. Econ. **96**(2), 159–173 (2011)
5. Smith, V.H., Glauber, J.W.: Agricultural insurance in developed countries: where have we been and where are we going? Appl. Econ. Perspect. Policy **34**(3), 363–390 (2012)
6. Glauber, J.W.: Agricultural insurance and the world trade organization (2015)
7. Goodwin, B.K.: Problems with market insurance in agriculture. Am. J. Agr. Econ. **83**(3), 643–649 (2001)
8. Serra, T., Goodwin, B.K., Featherstone, A.M.: Modeling changes in the US demand for crop insurance during the 1990s (2003)
9. Goodwin, B.K., Mahul, O.: Risk modeling concepts relating to the design and rating of agricultural insurance contracts. The World Bank (2004)
10. Jensen, N.D., Barrett, C.B., Mude, A.G.: Index insurance quality and basis risk: evidence from northern Kenya. Am. J. Agr. Econ. **98**(5), 1450–1469 (2016)
11. Greatrex, H., et al.: Scaling up index insurance for smallholder farmers: recent evidence and insights (2015)
12. Karlan, D., Osei, R., Osei-Akoto, I., Udry, C.: Agricultural decisions after relaxing credit and risk constraints. Q. J. Econ. **129**(2), 597–652 (2014)
13. Carter, M., de Janvry, A., Sadoulet, E., Sarris, A.: Index insurance for developing country agriculture: a reassessment. Ann. Rev. Resour. Econ. **9**, 421–438 (2017)
14. Kramer, B., Hellin, J., Hansen, J., Rose, A., Braun, M.: Building resilience through climate risk insurance: insights from agricultural research for development (2019)
15. Zhang, B., Jin, P., Qiao, H., Hayat, T., Alsaedi, A., Ahmad, B.: Exergy analysis of Chinese agriculture. Ecol. Ind. **105**, 279–291 (2019)
16. Brown, J.C., Kastens, J.H., Coutinho, A.C., de Castro Victoria, D., Bishop, C.R.: Classifying multiyear agricultural land use data from Mato Grosso using time-series MODIS vegetation index data. Remote Sens. Environ. **130**, 39–50 (2013)
17. Borgogno Mondino, E., Gajetti, M.: Preliminary considerations about costs and potential market of remote sensing from UAV in the Italian viticulture context. Eur. J. Remote Sens. **50**(1), 310–319 (2017)
18. Hill, R.V., et al.: Ex ante and ex post effects of hybrid index insurance in Bangladesh. J. Dev. Econ. **136**, 1–17 (2019)
19. Borgogno-Mondino, E., Sarvia, F., Gomarasca, M.A.: Supporting insurance strategies in agriculture by remote sensing: a possible approach at regional level. In: Misra, S., et al. (eds.) ICCSA 2019. LNCS, vol. 11622, pp. 186–199. Springer, Cham (2019). https://doi.org/10.1007/978-3-030-24305-0_15
20. Sarvia, F., De Petris, S., Borgogno-Mondino, E.: Remotely sensed data to support insurance strategies in agriculture. In: Remote Sensing for Agriculture, Ecosystems, and Hydrology XXI. International Society for Optics and Photonics (2019)
21. De Petris, S., Berretti, R., Sarvia, F., Borgogno-Mondino, E.: Precision arboriculture: a new approach to tree risk management based on geomatics tools. In: Remote Sensing for Agriculture, Ecosystems, and Hydrology XXI. International Society for Optics and Photonics (2019)

22. Orusa, T., Mondino, E.B.: Landsat 8 thermal data to support urban management and planning in the climate change era: a case study in Torino area, NW Italy. In: Remote Sensing Technologies and Applications in Urban Environments IV. International Society for Optics and Photonics (2019)

23. Barnett, B.J., Mahul, O.: Weather index insurance for agriculture and rural areas in lower-income countries. Am. J. Agr. Econ. **89**(5), 1241–1247 (2007)

24. European Space Agency. Sentinel-2 User Handbook. ESA (2015)

25. Colwell, H., Carneggie, D., Croxton, R., Manzer, F., Simonett, D., Steiner, D.: Applications of remote sensing in agriculture and forestry. Applications of remote sensing in agriculture and forestry (1970)

26. Steven, M.D., Clark, J.A.: Applications of Remote Sensing in Agriculture. Elsevier, Amsterdam (2013)

27. Sahoo, R.N., Ray, S.S., Manjunath, K.R.: Hyperspectral remote sensing of agriculture. Curr. Sci. **108**, 848–859 (2015)

28. Shanmugapriya, P., Rathika, S., Ramesh, T., Janaki, P.: Applications of remote sensing in agriculture. A review. Int. J. Curr. Microbiol. Appl. Sci. **8**, 2270–2283 (2019)

29. Weiss, M., Jacob, F., Duveiller, G.: Remote sensing for agricultural applications: a meta-review. Remote Sens. Environ. **236**, 111402 (2020)

30. Zhang, X., Zhang, B., Wei, Z., Chen, Z.C., Zheng, L.F.: Study on spectral indices of MODIS for wheat growth monitoring. J. Image Graph. **10**(4), 420–424 (2005)

31. Chen, P.Y., Fedosejevs, G., Tiscareno-Lopez, M., Arnold, J.G.: Assessment of MODIS-EVI, MODIS-NDVI and VEGETATION-NDVI composite data using agricultural measurements: an example at corn fields in western Mexico. Environ. Monit. Assess. **119**(1–3), 69–82 (2006). https://doi.org/10.1007/s10661-005-9006-7

32. Son, N.T., Chen, C.F., Chen, C.R., Minh, V.Q., Trung, N.H.: A comparative analysis of multitemporal MODIS EVI and NDVI data for large-scale rice yield estimation. Agric. For. Meteorol. **197**, 52–64 (2014)

33. Lu, J., Carbone, G.J., Gao, P.: Mapping the agricultural drought based on the long-term AVHRR NDVI and North American Regional Reanalysis (NARR) in the United States, 1981–2013. Appl. Geogr. **104**, 10–20 (2019)

34. Nanzad, L., Zhang, J., Tuvdendorj, B., Nabil, M., Zhang, S., Bai, Y.: NDVI anomaly for drought monitoring and its correlation with climate factors over Mongolia from 2000 to 2016. J. Arid Environ. **164**, 69–77 (2019)

35. Leprieur, C., Verstraete, M.M., Pinty, B.: Evaluation of the performance of various vegetation indices to retrieve vegetation cover from AVHRR data. Remote Sens. Rev. **10**(4), 265–284 (1994)

36. Turvey, C.G., Shee, A., Marr, A.: Addressing fractional dimensionality in the application of weather index insurance and climate risk financing in agricultural development: a dynamic triggering approach. Weather Climate Soc. **11**(4), 901–915 (2019)

37. Jensen, T.K., Johnson, R.R., McNamara, M.J.: Funding conditions and insurance stock returns: do insurance stocks really benefit from rising interest rate regimes? Risk Manag. Insur. Rev. **22**(4), 367–391 (2019)

38. Bacchini, R.D., Miguez, D.F.: Agricultural risk management using NDVI pasture index-based insurance for livestock producers in south west Buenos Aires province. Agric. Financ. Rev. **75**(1), 77–91 (2015)

39. Haghverdi, A., Washington-Allen, R.A., Leib, B.G.: Prediction of cotton lint yield from phenology of crop indices using artificial neural networks. Comput. Electron. Agric. **152**, 186–197 (2018)

40. Zambrano, F., Vrieling, A., Nelson, A., Meroni, M., Tadesse, T.: Prediction of drought-induced reduction of agricultural productivity in Chile from MODIS, rainfall estimates, and climate oscillation indices. Remote Sens. Environ. **219**, 15–30 (2018)
41. Zhou, J., Pavek, M.J., Shelton, S.C., Holden, Z.J., Sankaran, S.: Aerial multispectral imaging for crop hail damage assessment in pota-to. Comput. Electron. Agric. **127**, 406–412 (2016)
42. Borgogno-Mondino, E., Lessio, A., Gomarasca, M.A.: A fast operative method for NDVI uncertainty estimation and its role in vegetation analysis. Eur. J. Remote Sens. **49**(1), 137–156 (2016)

A Multidisciplinary Approach for Multi-risk Analysis and Monitoring of Influence of SODs and RODs on Historic Centres: The ResCUDE Project

Alberico Sonnessa[✉], Elena Cantatore, Dario Esposito, and Francesco Fiorito

Department of Civil, Environmental, Land, Construction and Chemistry (DICATECh), Politecnico di Bari, Via Orabona 4, 70125 Bari, Italy
{alberico.sonnessa, elena.cantatore, dario.esposito, francesco.fiorito}@poliba.it

Abstract. The presented paper describes the ReSCUDE project, developed by the Department of Civil, Environmental, Land, Construction and Chemistry (DICATECh) of the Polytechnic University of Bari under the grant Attraction and International Mobility, of the Italian Ministry of Education, University and Research. The project focuses on the evaluation of the effects of Slow-Onset Disasters (SODs), and Rapid Onset Disasters (RODs) on historic town centres. To this end, an integrated approach based on innovative geomatics, building techniques and advanced behavioural models, is being applied to the old town built area of Ascoli Satriano (FG) and Molfetta (BA) in the Apulia Region (Italy). Over the next three years, the ReSCUDE project will allow to perform in-depth analyses on the historic built environment of the identified case studies, fostering the processes of its knowledge, assessment, control, management and design, in connection to the risks deriving from ROD and SOD events. The expected outputs will be useful to define possible scenarios for civil defence purposes and undertake actions aimed at risk mitigation.

Keywords: Geomatics for risk management · Slow onset disaster · Rapid onset disaster · SOD · ROD · Multi-risk analysis · Retrofit building technologies · Agent-based simulation · Cultural heritage

1 Introduction

In recent decades, the increasing anthropization has considerably amplified the negative impact of critical events, both natural (earthquakes, landslide, subsidence) and/or triggered by anthropogenic causes (panic in crowded places, terrorist attacks) on the safety of the Built Environment (BE), consisting of a network of street, buildings, infrastructures, open spaces and its users.

Over the long-term period the BE is also influenced by very slow phenomena, such as the climate change, which have a direct impact on the climate of the cities, pollution and rainfall levels, energy consumption and aging of buildings. Such critical events, with reference to the disasters they can lead to and how fast they can occur, are usually referred to as Slow-Onset Disasters (SODs), and Rapid Onset Disasters (RODs), as defined by United Nation [1]. The BE (and its users) is increasingly subject to SODs and RODs, showing poor resilience as evidenced, for example, by the damages resulting from the seismic sequences that affected Central Italy in 2016–17, and the accident occurred in Turin during the 2017 UEFA Champions League Final broadcast, when about 1500 people were injured.

This is even more evident in highly valued historical-cultural contexts, such as historic centres, where the level of risk increases exponentially with the simultaneous growth of their value and vulnerability due to aging. Historic districts represent an exception in management, planning and transforming necessities. The socio-economic relevance in re-use of residential buildings stock, socio-cultural significance of historic formal and environmental values and the explication of interaction between the necessity to accommodate human needs - health, safety, self-sufficiency - and external territory conditions, constitute the basis of the cultural landscape values of historic districts [2].

According to the slow process of their generation, historic districts represent the result of a system of overlapped techniques and materials application along the time [3].

Urban morphology, spatial configuration, type, density and use, as well as the layout and the organization of the public spaces, contribute to make the access difficult to these areas characterized by multiple enclosures, narrow streets with their labyrinthine nature and a limited number of access routes, deriving from the defence strategies of ancient cities [4–6]. Moreover, old towns are affected by intense pedestrian and tourist flows [7], who may not be aware of their surroundings or how to reach a safe place, in case of evacuation [8]. This can lead to the adoption of risk-increasing behaviours by evacuees, thereby decreasing their safety. Historic building types and their constructive materials can amplify this effect, but at the same time their value needs to be preserved. As is not feasible to demolish buildings for creating new escape routes, thought must be given to innovative solutions compatible with the historic urban context [9].

These things considered, the BE is characterized by a high complexity level due to its interactions with natural components and human presence. The need of assessing and increasing the resilience of the BE and monitoring the effects of SOD and ROD over time clearly emerges. Survey and monitoring geomatics techniques can play an important role, in the frame of an integrated methodology that must necessarily include the knowledge of building performance and their opportunity in transformation for their improvement, and the modelling of human spatial and social behaviour response during emergencies.

The project AIM1871082-1, Cultural Heritage Research Line, developed by the Department of Civil, Environmental, Land, Construction and Chemistry (DICATECh), Politecnico di Bari under the call Attraction and International Mobility, of the Italian Ministry of Education, University and Research (MIUR), hereafter named ResCUDE (RESilient Cultural Urban context to Disaster Exposure), is aimed at analysing and facing these critical issues by mean of a holistic approach, that encompass the joint use of geomatics and resilient urban methodologies, land-use and managing techniques and an agent-based approach.

The project, whose description and its progress are hereafter presented, will develop over three years (from October 2019 to October 2022) and will be jointly developed by the Geomatics, Building Technologies and Urban Planning Groups.

2 The ResCUDE Project

The ResCUDE project aims at addressing the needs for a better understanding of the effects of SOD and ROD on historic town centres. To this end, a multi-risk analysis is being applied to the historical BE, in order to the define its vulnerability and exposure to critical events (and the related damage), evaluate its levels of resilience and outline targeted mitigation actions.

SODs and RODs have been usually analysed extensively in a separate way. At present, it is still necessary to deepen:

- the mechanisms of potential interaction between RODs and SODs and the increase in magnitude of the latter;
- interaction of people with the RODs;
- the intrinsic resilience of the man-made environment towards the RODs;
- the mitigation potential of the man-made environment against the negative effects caused by SODs.

Current poor BE resilience usually depends on the fact that:

- risk mitigation/prevention strategies for RODs exclude the open spaces and human/user reactions, focusing just on the building;
- interactions between buildings and surrounding areas for risk reduction seem to be ignored, although they could lead to unpredictable critical safety conditions for open urban areas (i.e. uncontrolled car parking or inaccessible streets may make inaccessible the nearby open areas);
- risk increasing conditions such as crowding, and users' types are often ignored;
- causes and effects of ROD/SODs combination are usually neglected.

Moreover, for SODs with a variable intensity over time (i.e. air pollution), risk reduction strategies marginally consider the potential of BE as a resilience-increasing element (i.e. typical strategies adopted to limit pollution are: vehicle stops, restriction of cars circulation, reduction of heating hours).

The project wants to fill the previous gaps by fostering the integration between processes of knowledge, assessment, improvement and monitoring of BE in case of risks related to ROD/SOD. In this frame, geomatics data is being collected and/or generated on purpose, with the double aim of:

1. building a comprehensive 3D database of the BE, focusing on the historical centres, the acquired dataset will enable the opportunity of applying innovative approaches for:

- Defining the performances of building aggregates to SOD, by collecting morpho-typological characters and technological features of buildings in historic districts from urban plans, usually expressed by classes of categories (e.g. building typologies, number of floors, constructive techniques, levels of conservations). These features constitute a Geographic Information System, used for the creation of main cataloguing maps in compounding the "Historic District Plan", and define a comprehensive model for assessing the potential level of resilience in response to climate change.
- Adopting human response analyses in disasters by outlining spatial cognition and social behaviour in situations of panic and simulating evacuation and interventions in case of ROD. This methodology is based on the analysis of the behaviours in outdoor scenarios, as well as the influence on human choices of gender, age, health and other features, and focus on properties of the environment as activated, perceived and cognized by humans and on critical situations produced and driven by behavioural relationships between agents and with places, both of which tend to overlap in emergency situations [10].

2. monitoring the structures over time, in order to identify potentially critical phenomena, as subsidence or landslides when present, and control they evolution and influence on the BE.

The project is organized in three work packages, better described in the following paragraphs.

2.1 WP1 - Definition of an Integrated Geomatics Monitoring System for the Definition of the Influence of SOD on ROD in Historical Centres

The activities foreseen in WP1, coordinated by the Geomatics Group, are aimed at the extraction of multi-sensor and multi-scale 3D models, both through photogrammetric techniques and Synthetic Aperture Radar Interferometry (InSAR).

WP1 will be developed as follow:

- Analysis of multi-sensor geo-spatial data for the extraction of high-precision Digital Surface Model (DSM) that will constitute the database on which three-dimensional simulations will run at predetermined time intervals. DSMs will be also deployed for delimiting areas subject to SOD and ROD in historical centres.
- Exploitation of long-term Differential Interferometry Synthetic Aperture Radar (DInSAR) time series and other ancillary information (where available), as the geological setting of the investigated areas, to highlight subsidence and/or landslide phenomena [11].
- Development of algorithms for the processing of data acquired from satellite sensors operating in the thermal band, and hyperspectral data from airborne sensors and/or Unmanned Aerial Vehicle (UAV) systems. This will allow the production of Land Surface Temperature (LST) maps to support analyses on surface urban heat islands.

- Generation of 3D models at urban scale, which can be integrated with LST data, in order to better understand the intervention areas and supporting the mitigation actions of the effects of the investigated phenomena.
- Implementation of a prototype WebGIS portal capable of providing detailed three-dimensional information aimed at identifying the portion(s) of the building needing modifications/restoration and improve its performance.

2.2 WP2 - Analysis of Resilience and Potential Mitigation in Buildings and Systems of Them

WP2 is coordinated by Building Technology Group. The activities focus on the relations between buildings in historic districts and the boundary environment in a long-term perspective in order to:

- Define a comprehensive model aimed at the assessment of potential level of resilience in historic districts exposed to climate change (SOD). The knowledge of the historic building stock, as a combination of morpho-typological characters and technological solutions, represents the starting point of the analysis [12].
- Analyse and model technologies and materials for the mitigation of negative effects of SODs [13], mainly related to the human wellbeing and the reduction of energy consumptions, solving the aesthetic normative constrain. Here, technologies and materials require a different scale of application: from the district scale to assess the outdoor comfort and the microclimate alteration, to the building scale to consider the comfort indoor and the energy needs (both as average and peak values).

2.3 WP3 - Agent Based Modelling and Simulation of Human Spatial Behaviour in Urban Historic Centres During RODs

The effort allocated in WP3 will be carried out by the Urban Planning Group. In historic centres, RODs can lead to critical disaster conditions faster, undermining the host community's safety as well as resulting in time loss, which in an emergency equates to loss of life [14]. The aim of this WP is to enhance the understanding of the effect of physical and social settings in case of RODs. This is crucial in improving the safety of individuals and groups and to plan strategies, procedures and operations for preventing, controlling and managing risks and to optimize operational decision-making in emergency responses.

More in detail, WP3 main objectives are to investigate:

- Pedestrian dynamics and flows to identify localized critical aspects, evaluating the impacts and cascade effects and analysing its re-arrangement, including the development of evacuation time maps, space utilization maps and density maps.
- Major factors of human spatial cognition and behaviour during an emergency, evaluating interactions and interference arising between people and between people/environment.
- Relation with crowd conditions and high-density built spaces, understanding at what point does a crowd emerge.

- Behaviour of key agent types, evaluating how their choices in different risk scenarios affect the whole emergency management.
- Risk level of different spatial configurations evaluating their degree of criticality and assessment of the performance of different functional areas.
- Evacuation procedures to define strategies for evacuation management, including low-level emergency service response and high-level system resilience implementation.

3 Employed Methodologies

The methodologies that are being employed in a synergic manner in the project, are briefly discussed hereafter.

3.1 Geomatics Techniques

Geomatics is widely used in the field of cultural heritage preservation, with the purpose of reconstructing the shape of structures with a high level of accuracy, investigate their conditions and monitor their stability and changes over time. Some interesting applications are discussed in [15] and [16].

At the same time, 3D geomatics data constitute the element on which to base all the activities related to the documentation, the analysis and the enhancement of the built environment, as well as an input in the human behaviour simulation tool helping the decision-maker in risk management activities.

The critical issue previously evidenced requires a number of different geomatics methodologies to be employed in the project that are:

- Survey techniques useful to acquire 3D data at different scales of investigation (ranging from the single building to the district). Satellite and aerial photogrammetry, including UAV are being used to obtain DEMs [17, 18]. A slightly different approach, included in an open source tool for DEMs generation from high resolution optical satellite imagery, will also be considered [19].
- Monitoring techniques able to identify/measure subsidence/displacement phenomena and temperatures on large areas. Multi-temporal SAR datasets, where available, will provide useful information on both the spatial and temporal patterns of displacements, if present, through the generation of time series [20] using the DInSAR technique, while thermal image acquired from satellite [21] will allow the production of Land Surface Temperature (LST) maps. Satellite dataset will be considered also to assess the albedo value at large scale [22].

Geomatics techniques suitable to be employed are listed in Table 1 and Table 2

3.2 Buildings Technologies

The assessment of cultural heritage prone to climate change (SOD) requires the quantification of resilience as the main instrument in evaluating multi-dimensional risk

Table 1. Survey methodologies employed in the project

Survey				
Photogrammetric techniques	Ground resolution	Elevation accuracy	Limitation	Advantages
Using optical satellite imagery	1–10 m	1–10 m	Fix. scheduled data acquisition	Large area coverage
Using aircraft/UAV	0.1–1 m	0.01–1.0 m	Small area coverage	On demand data acquisition

Table 2. Monitoring methodologies employed in the project

Monitoring	
DInSAR	Accuracy = cm/year
LST	Resolution = 1–30 m

assessment to SOD. However, the assessment of resilience, by definition, should involve mitigation and adaptation behaviours in a synergic way [23]. In the field of Cultural Heritage, the traditional process of recovery (knowledge – diagnosis – intervention) should be adapted to the resilient point of view [23].

Because of the cultural relevance, the methodology should include three main goals:

- The identification of inherent behaviours of the cultural heritage in decreasing the effects of climate change locally (adaptive characters).
- The detection of critical elements in the Built Environment that increase the exposure and affection to climate change, as well as the recognition of the most exposed elements to the effect of climate change (risk exposure).
- The study of opportunities offered by complex and critical systems to be transformed to increase the resilient behaviour (mitigation solutions).

As aforementioned in Sect. 2.2, the assessment of resilience should involve analysis both at district and building scale.

At district scale, local microclimate alterations have to consider geometric and physic features of buildings as well as their environmental conditions. It is the case of protocols useful in determining Urban Heat Island Intensity (UHII) according to the Oke classification in Local Climate Zones [25]. Geometric and morphological features of buildings, physic characters and anthropogenic loads represents all the characters involved in evaluating classes of exposures to local Heatwave amplification or overheating. Direct local surveys of micro-climate and Land Surface Temperature (LST) maps (by satellite acquisition) represent the main tools in exploring behavioural attitude of district to be prone to local exacerbation of heatwaves (ROD). Moreover, the quantification of albedo value or the reflectance of surfaces is also required at large scale, as the result of large-scale analysis. Albedo physic parameter contributes in modifying local conditions for energy assessment as a consequence of potential temperatures reached by exposed surfaces; for local temperatures variation, the albedo parameter represents the capacity of materials in re-emitting in the system longwave [26]. Values could be computed as their direct measures on a sample (by spectrophotometer) or comparing database and previous data collected for traditional materials.

Whereas, software-based on Computational Fluid Dynamics (CFD) (e.g. ENVI-met) support the creation of virtual models to test mitigation actions at district scale.

At building scale, morpho-construction techniques and state of maintenance support the recognition of opportunity of transformation at sub-system scale [27]. However, because of the presence of traditional techniques, direct surveys should be required in order to quantify thermal and optical parameters that can influence the assessment of comfort indoor and the energy needs at building scale. Here, dynamic simulation tools are the main instruments in correlating outdoor microclimate conditions – scaled in previous phase – and indoor energy and comfort results at building scale.

3.3   Multi-agent Simulation

The investigation of human factors is of fundamental importance in evaluating risk through emergency plans and operations. An innovative feature of the research to represent dynamic and complex social systems in case of RODs, is the scientific approach through a Multi-Agent modelling and simulation framework [28].

Multi-Agent Systems are particularly suitable for modelling cognitive processes and human interaction between people and their environment. Agent-based modelling performed in the proper manner [29], can be used to analyse emerging social phenomena at group and crowd level, in our case applied to RODs [30]. This is also the fundamental technique to build computational simulations for these case studies, in order to apply modelling of individuals and social relationships in spatially explicit virtual environments [31].

The computer-based simulation is a method of realistic replication of human activities and use of space. It allows for hypothesis testing, verification and calibration of modelling formalization, the drawing up of recommendations based on the analysis of what if scenarios and the performance analysis of different case studies [32]. The comparison of simulated scenarios will help to define solutions that can improve BE resilience. Additionally, this approach is useful for the study of worst-case scenarios and disruptions that are not directly observable. A final advantage of the proposed methodology is to support knowledge structuring, where the main problem for the decision makers is their missing knowledge and lack of functional models [33].

4   Requirements for the Geomatics Dataset

In this preliminary stage, the main requirements of the 3D dataset have been outlined. With reference to the described activities, the main requirements are:

- High resolution DSMs (around meter or better) to support the analysis of morphological features of complex urban systems at districts scale such as the historic ones; here, models support the recognition of geometric and constitutive elements of open areas and elementary linear units (streets) as well as the features of built environment as an aggregate that can modify locally inherent qualities.
- High resolution Surface Temperature models in order to support the analysis at large scale of local microclimate alterations derived from urban (inherent) constitutive features and anthropogenic heat loads derived from human activities. In detail, the model resolution should be comparable with (or lower than) the smaller element of the districts that - usually for high compact areas - is the canyon featured by 2–3 m width.

Since Multi-Agent systems develop simulations which must represent the dynamic variation of the system under study, the virtual environment built on the DSM should act a changing layer on which the social simulation takes place [34]. Thus, the main requirement for the digital layout of the area is the capacity of representing the real time evolution of risks in order to trigger agents' spatial behaviours [35]. Indeed, in accordance with its transition states, agents adapt their behaviours, e.g. movements. The digital environment not only needs to be dynamic in time, but also in space. These things considered, the digital model of the environment based on the DSM dataset should update at a pace which must fit both with:

- The temporal scale of the simulation, which will range from the immediate choices of individuals, e.g. evacuees, first responders and emergency managers, to long term decision making on design, urban regeneration and strategic planning.
- The spatial scale of the simulation, which will range from the area surrounding individuals and their behaviour in space, to the configuration of the urban neighbourhood area.

5   Case Studies – Ascoli Satriano and Molfetta Municipalities

The historic districts placed in the municipalities of Ascoli Satriano (FG) and Molfetta (BA), in the Apulia Region – Italy, have been selected as case studies, considering:

- Their peculiar location. Referring to the Koppen-Geiger classification, Apulia region has many different climates, due to its orography. The oceanic climate is associated at the promontory of Gargano, in the north-east part, and the subappennine zone, located at north-west, both featured by high altitude; whereas along the cost and hills, humid sub-tropical (Cfa) and hot-summer Mediterranean (Csa) climates are predominant. Ascoli Satriano and Molfetta are located in the Daunian sub-appennine and on the eastern coasts respectively. Consequently, they are representative of two major Apulian climates, Cfa and Csa [36]. Thus, the two municipalities differ also in terms of Heating Degree Days (HDD) as defined by Italian law: Ascoli Satriano has 1652 HDD representative of climatic zone D, while Molfetta has 1142 HDD, and is included in climatic zone C.

- The different morphology on built environment. As a clear consequence of local values and previous events, Molfetta and Ascoli Satriano show different morphologies in district arrangement. The two districts mainly include residential buildings; however, tower houses – with vertical development of dwelling on 3–4 floors – are representative for Molfetta's district, while dwellings in Ascoli Satriano are featured by two floors and a horizontal development.
- Construction materials. Molfetta is representative of the traditional use of calcareous squared stone – with regular bonds - as prevalent construction material. Here, the structures are usually associated to compounded walls made by two layers of stone (inner and outer) and an incoherent system of mortar and slices of stones in the middle. Roofs are usually flat and have a structural wooden sub-layer. In the outer part there are both traditional (calcareous stone paving) and modern (paving or bituminous layers) materials. On the other hand, buildings in the historic districts of Ascoli Satriano are featured by pitched roofs while walls are very heterogeneous. In fact, walls made by small bricks and tufa blocks were combined with or substituted the original one made by irregular bonds of calcareous stones.
- Their representativeness of two ancient towns typical of the Italian landscape. From a preliminary evaluation of their plan and topography, both case studies present interesting typological affinities and comparable differences, hereafter described, which may play a determinant role in influencing pedestrian spatial behaviour during emergencies.
  - Molfetta is a coastal town. Its origins can be traced to a small fisherman's village. The historic district is a peninsula surrounded by the Adriatic Sea on three sides. Until the 1800s, the water lapped the southern side which made the old town almost an island. The plan has the shape of an ellipse with the sites of the cathedral and the castle (destroyed in 1416, now Town Hall Square) in its vertices. Along the minor axis is the main street where 14 side streets converge. These streets run parallel and present sudden changes of section, in ancient times this had the function of trapping and disorienting enemies if they managed to enter the city.
  - Ascoli Satriano is located on the edge of the Apennines. In 1456 an earthquake totally destroyed the ancient site and forced relocation of the surviving inhabitants to the site of the current town. Since then the planimetric layout of the old town centre has remained unchanged despite it has been rebuilt many times following seismic events. This is characterized by a labyrinth of narrow alleys that climb up the hillside. This orography determines the spatial configuration and distribution of the streets of the ancient city, which is dominated by the Ducal Palace. This is a massive building placed at the highest point to protect against war attacks from the plain. On the opposite side the cathedral, as a landmark, stands out among lower buildings. The other hillside is steeper, inaccessible and with no buildings, this allows for wide views over the valley.
- The different exposure to natural disasters, both for BE and man. Figure 1 and Fig. 2 highlighted the risk exposure to earthquake, landslide for Ascoli Satriano e Molfetta respectively, as well as human and built vulnerability for classes of ages and period of construction.

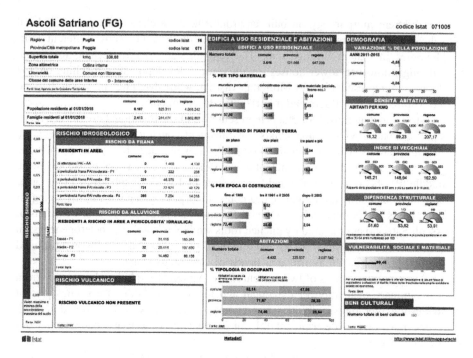

Fig. 1. Ascoli Satriano ISTAT Risk indicators [37]

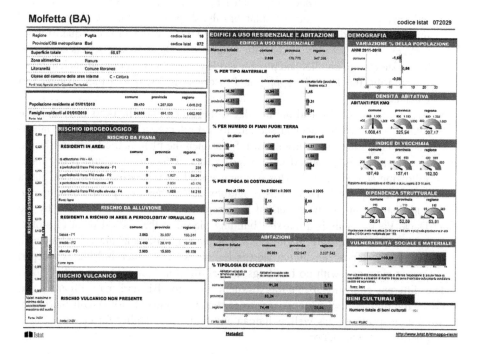

Fig. 2. Molfetta ISTAT Risk indicators [37]

Fig. 3. Subsidence phenomena evidenced By DInSAR data [38]

– Ongoing subsidence phenomena affecting Ascoli Satriano that can provide further elements to the multi risk analysis. Displacements in the satellite Line Of Sight direction, obtained from DInSAR data, are evidenced by permanent scatterers (dots in Fig. 3) that show a velocity of displacements of some centimeters per year.

Available geomatics data are listed in Table 3.

Table 3. Available geomatics data [39]

Digital terrain model	Cell size = 8 × 8 m
Ortophoto	Res. = 0,5 × 0,5
BE shapefiles	

6 Conclusive Remarks

The assessment of the consequences of SOD and ROD on the BE and its users represent a complex task, due to the difficulties in the prompt detection of critical events (both in the long and short-term period), and the proper evaluation of the human behaviour in response to such events. The particular constructive characteristics (narrow/crowded streets, presence of ancient/valuable buildings and heterogeneous constructive techniques/materials) of historical centres makes them more prone to be damaged by ROD and SOD effects.

Recent catastrophic episodes, along with the growing awareness of the increasing negative action of the weathering due to climate change, underline the need to improve the resilience of the historical BE towards these events. This problem necessarily requires an integrated approach that must take into account the topography and the constructive elements of the investigated areas and consider the human factor and its interaction with the BE during potentially critical occurrences.

As discussed in this work, geomatics methodologies applied at the high-resolution survey and monitoring of the cultural heritage provide a very useful tool for measuring and controlling the evolution of historical centres. However, a thorough assessment of the problem requires also accurate information on the efficiency of the buildings for mitigating the negative effects of SOD, as well as reliable dimensionally constrained simulation models of the human behaviour in case of ROD.

Over the next three years, the ResCUDE project will allow to carry out in-depth analyses on the identified case studies, integrating spatial, human and behavioural data, improving the processes of knowledge, evaluation, control, management and design of the BE in relation to the risks deriving from ROD and SOD events. The expected outputs will be used to define possible scenarios for civil defence purposes and undertake actions aimed at risk mitigation. Findings can be included in emergency planning for decision makers and emergency managers.

Acknowledgements. This research is funded under the project "AIM1871082-1" of the AIM (Attraction and International Mobility) Program, financed by the Italian Ministry of Education, University and Research (MIUR).

Author Contributions: Design of the geomatics research framework Alberico Sonnessa; contribution in building technologies methods and tools: Elena Cantatore; contribution in land-use and managing methods and techniques: Dario Esposito.

Paper design, investigation, methodology, formalization, identification and analysis of the case studies, writing, review and editing Alberico Sonnessa, Elena Cantatore and Dario Esposito; Project conceptualization and supervision: Francesco Fiorito.

All authors have read and agreed to the published version of the manuscript.

References

1. Assembly UNG: Report of the open-ended intergovernmental expert working group on indicators and terminology relating to disaster risk reduction (2016)

2. ICOMOS: The Valletta Principles for the Safeguarding and Management of Historic Cities, Towns and Urban Areas (2011). http://www.icomos.org.tr/Dosyalar/ICOMOSTR_0209751001353671440.pdf
3. De Tommasi, G., Fatiguso, F., De Fino, M.: Riqualificazione energetica del patrimonio edilizio storico. Studi per il geocluster dei borghi antichi in area mediterranea. EdicomEdizioni, Monfalcone (2019)
4. Hillier, B., Hanson, J.: The Social Logic of Space. Cambridge University Press, Cambridge (1984)
5. León, J., Mokrani, C., Catalán, P., Cienfuegos, R., Femenías, C.: Examining the role of urban form in supporting rapid and safe tsunami evacuations: a multi-scalar analysis in Viña del Mar. Chile. Procedia Eng. **212**, 629–636 (2018)
6. Srinurak, N., Mishima, N., Fuchikami, T., Duangthima, W.: Analysis of urban morphology and accessibility character to provide evacuation route in historic area. Procedia-Soc. Behav. Sci. **216**, 460–469 (2016)
7. Stokols, D.: A social-psychological model of human crowding phenomena. J. Am. Plan. Assoc. **38**, 72–83 (1972)
8. Esposito, D., Mastrodonato, G., Camarda, D.: The cognitive visualization of space in city walking: spacescape experimentation in Italy. In: Luo, Y. (ed.) CDVE 2017. LNCS, vol. 10451, pp. 160–167. Springer, Cham (2017). https://doi.org/10.1007/978-3-319-66805-5_20
9. Drdácký, M., Binda, L., Herle, I., Lanza, L.: Protecting the cultural heritage from natural disasters. Adv. Res. Cent. Cult. Herit. **100**, 1–106 (2007)
10. Shimura, K., Ohtsuka, K., Vizzari, G., Nishinari, K., Bandini, S.: Mobility analysis of the aged pedestrians by experiment and simulation. Pattern Recogn. Lett. **44**, 58–63 (2014)
11. Scifoni, S., et al.: On the joint exploitation of long-term DInSAR time series and geological information for the investigation of ground settlements in the town of Roma (Italy). Remote Sens. Environ. **182**, 113–127 (2016)
12. Cantatore, E., Fatiguso, F.: Riabitare il patrimonio edilizio dei centri storici come strategia di retrofit energetico – un caso studio. In: D'Andria, P.F.E. (ed.) Small Towns… From Problem to Resource Sustainable Strategies for the Valorization of Building, Landscape and Cultural Heritage in Inland Areas, pp. 1193–1201. FrancoAngeli, Milano (2019)
13. Santamouris, M., Kolokotsa, D.: Urban Climate Mitigation Techniques. Routledge, London (2016)
14. Tiernan, A., Drennan, L., Nalau, J., Onyango, E., Morrissey, L., Mackey, B.: A review of themes in disaster resilience literature and international practice since 2012. Policy Des. Pract. **2**, 53–74 (2019)
15. Margottini, C., et al.: Landslide hazard, monitoring and conservation strategy for the safeguard of Vardzia Byzantine monastery complex, Georgia. Landslides **12**, 193–204 (2015). https://doi.org/10.1007/s10346-014-0548-z
16. D'Aranno, P.J.V., et al.: High-resolution geomatic and geophysical techniques integrated with chemical analyses for the characterization of a Roman wall. J. Cult. Heritage **17**, 141–150 (2016)
17. Nex, F., Remondino, F.: UAV for 3D mapping applications: a review. Appl Geomatics **6**(1), 1–15 (2013). https://doi.org/10.1007/s12518-013-0120-x
18. Baiocchi, V., et al.: First geomatic restitution of the sinkhole known as 'Pozzo del Merro' (Italy), with the integration and comparison of 'classic' and innovative geomatic techniques. Environ. Earth Sci. **77**(3), 1–14 (2018). https://doi.org/10.1007/s12665-018-7244-6
19. Lastilla, L., Ravanelli, R., Fratarcangeli, F., Di Rita, M., Nascetti, A., Crespi, M.: Foss4g date for DSM generation: sensitivity analysis of the semi-global block matching parameters. In: The International Archives of the Photogrammetry, Remote Sensing and Spatial Information Sciences, vol. XLII-2/W13 (2019)

20. Bonano, M., Manunta, M., Pepe, A., Paglia, L., Lanari, R.: From previous C-band to new X-band SAR systems: assessment of the DInSAR mapping improvement for deformation time-series retrieval in urban areas. IEEE Trans. Geosci. Remote Sens. **51**(4), 1973–1984 (2013)

21. Ermida, S.L., Soares, P., Mantas, V., Göttsche, F.M., Trigo, I.F.: Google earth engine open-source code for land surface temperature estimation from the landsat series. Remote Sens. **12**(9), 1471 (2020)

22. Li, Z., et al.: Preliminary assessment of 20-m surface albedo retrievals from sentinel-2A surface reflectance and MODIS/VIIRS surface anisotropy measures. Remote Sens. Environ. **217**, 352–365 (2018)

23. Castellari, S., et al.: Elementi per una Strategia Nazionale di Adattamento ai Cambiamenti Climatici. Ministero dell'Ambiente e della Tutela del Territorio e del Mare, Roma (2014)

24. Fatiguso, F., De Fino, M., Cantatore, E., Caponio, V.: Resilience of historic built environments: inherent qualities and potential strategies. Procedia Eng. **180**, 1024–1033 (2017)

25. Stewart, I.D., Oke, T.R.: Thermal differentiation of local climate zones using temperature observations from urban and rural field sites. In: Preprints, 9th Symposium, on Urban Environment, Keystone, CO, pp. 2–6 (2010)

26. Santamouris, M.: Cooling the cities–a review of reflective and green roof mitigation technologies to fight heat island and improve comfort in urban environments. Sol. Energy **103**, 682–703 (2014)

27. Fatiguso, F., Cantatore, E., De Fino, M.: Strategies for energy retrofitting of historic urban districts. Prog. Ind. Ecol. Int. J. **10**(4), 334–352 (2016)

28. Ferber, J.: Multi-agent Systems: An Introduction to Distributed Artificial Intelligence. Addison-Wesley, Harlow (1998)

29. Helbing, D. (ed.): Social Self-Organization: Agent-Based Simulations and Experiments to Study Emergent Social Behavior. Springer, Heidelberg (2012). https://doi.org/10.1007/978-3-642-24004-1

30. Pan, X., Han, C.S., Law, K.H.: A multi - agent based simulation framework for the study of human and social behavior in egress analysis. In: International Conference on Computing in Civil Engineering, pp. 1–12. American Society of Civil Engineers (2005)

31. Schaumann, D., et al.: A computational framework to simulate human spatial behavior in built environments. Proc. Symp. Simul. Archit. Urban Des, pp. 121–128 (2016)

32. Rose, J.M., Ligtenberg, A., Van der Spek, S.C.: Simulating pedestrians through the inner-city: an agent-based approach. In: Proceedings of Social Simulation Conference SSC 2014, Barcelona, Catalunya (Spain), 1–5 September 2014. F.J. Miguel, F. Amblard, J.A. Barceló M. Madella Adv. Comput. Soc. Sci. Soc. Simulation, Barcelona Autònoma Unive. (2014)

33. Pawl, Z., Sets, R.: Advances in Decision Making Under Risk and Uncertainty (1992)

34. Weiss, G.: Multiagent Systems: A Modern Approach to Distributed Artificial Intelligence (2000)

35. Benenson, I., Torrens, P.M.: Geosimulation: object-based modeling of urban phenomena. Comput. Environ. Urban Syst. **28**, 1–8 (2004)

36. Koppen, W.: Das geographische system der klimat. In: Handbook der klimatologie, vol. 46 (1936)

37. www.istat.it/it/mappa-rischi/indicatori. Accessed 04 Mar 2020

38. http://www.pcn.minambiente.it. Accessed 04 Mar 2020

39. Sistema Informativo Regione Puglia. http://www.sit.puglia.it/. Accessed 23 Apr 2020

Road Extraction for Emergencies
from Satellite Imagery

Vincenzo Barrile[1] , Giuliana Bilotta[2(✉)] , Antonino Fotia[1] ,
and Ernesto Bernardo[2]

[1] DICEAM Department, Faculty of Engineering, University "Mediterranea"
of Reggio Calabria, 89100 Reggio Calabria, Italy
[2] University IUAV of Venice, Santa Croce 191 Tolentini, 30135 Venice, Italy
giuliana.bilotta@iuav.it

Abstract. After earthquakes, international and national organizations must overcome many challenges in rescue operations. Among these, the knowledge of the territory and of the roads is fundamental for international aid. The maps that volunteers make are a valuable asset, showing the roads in the area affected by the seismic events, a knowledge which is necessary to bring rescue. This was very helpful during many earthquakes as in Haiti (on 2010-01-12) and in Nepal (on 2015-04-25) to support the humanitarian organizations. Many volunteers can contribute remotely to mapping little known or inaccessible regions with crowdsourcing actions, by tracing maps from satellite imagery or aerial photographs even if staying far from the affected site.

This research, still in progress, aims at experiencing quickly obtaining roads through the so-called Object Based Image Analysis (OBIA), by extracting it from satellite data, semi-automatically or automatically, with a segmentation that starts from concepts of Mathematical Morphology. We compared it with a classification in ENVI and, using an algorithm in GIS, we verified the goodness of the method.

The good results obtained encourage further research on fast techniques for map integration for humanitarian emergencies moreover the results were implemented on open street map.

Keywords: Satellite imagery · Segmentation · OBIA · Mathematical morphology

1 Introduction

Traditional surveying methods are often time-consuming and laborious; instead, development of remote sensing technology in recent years has opened the way to an automatic road detection application.

Many are the advantages of satellite remote sensing technology: among others, it can provide nearly real-time updated maps.

Taken into consideration optical images, different types of roads (highways, rural roads or streets) are identifiable and classifiable in different areas (rural or suburbs), depending on the spatial resolution.

O. Gervasi et al. (Eds.): ICCSA 2020, LNCS 12252, pp. 767–781, 2020.
https://doi.org/10.1007/978-3-030-58811-3_55

Until a few years ago, some topographic features as shape and structure were not describable or verifiable because of the insufficient spatial resolution of the satellite imagery used for Earth Observation [1]. Thus, the application of these data was greatly limited in fields such as analysis and monitoring of the urban environment [2].

Again, the increasing resolution in the images recently available brings to an increasing ambiguity in the statistical definition of the land use classes or ground cover and, in case of application of the standard multispectral classification, pixel-based, to a decrease of the accuracy of automatic detection [3].

We have chosen to apply OBIA as an analysis capable of extracting high semantic level information from the simple radiometric data acquired by satellite sensors, thanks to the structural approach that we will illustrate later. The strength of this type of analysis in particular is in the ability to extract objects by segmenting the image according to rules that are chosen *ad hoc*, favoring for example the content of the pixel over the shape or taking into account the shape of the objects to be extracted.

In Fig. 1a we report multiresolution segmentation example, that does not take into account the shape factor.

Fig. 1. Multiresolution segmentation that does not take into account the shape factor.

2   Case Study

Our study area is in Calabria; we considered an area in the Province of Reggio Calabria (Fig. 2a): Melito di Porto Salvo (Fig. 2b), that has a population of about 11000 inhabitants.

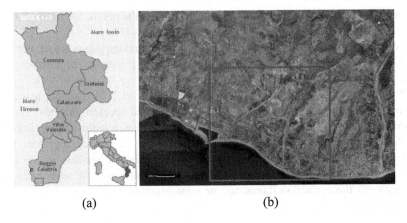

Fig. 2. (a) Province of Reggio Calabria, (b) Study area, in Melito di Porto Salvo.

Calabria, the southernmost region of the Italian peninsula, has a mainly hilly surface, which covers 49.2% of its territory, has large mountainous areas that cover 41.8% of its territory, while plains occupy 9% of the region's territory.

The province of Reggio Calabria is located in the exact center of the Mediterranean Sea and is composed almost entirely of municipalities overlooking the coasts. Streams and rivers, often seasonal, flow from the internal mountains and the Aspromonte massif. The Strait of Messina separates Reggio Calabria, its capital, from the island of Sicily. The territory of Melito di Porto Salvo is the southernmost of mainland Italy and is characterized by the presence of torrential waterways, with a pebbly bed and dry for most of the year.

As satellite imagery, we processed a GeoTIFF from IKONOS-2 acquired on 2001-07-01, 09:51 GMT, and 4.00 meters for the pixel size. It is a multispectral IKONOS image with zero as percent Cloud Cover. Spatial resolution of these images seems suitable for the purpose, considering the usual dimensions of the road network. Image was orthorectified; no further processing was therefore required.

3 Methodology

3.1 OBIA

The methodology we used is not the classic analysis pixel based of satellite data. This analysis has a limit: the recognition of a semantic information, of low-level, derived only from the energy emitted by the pixel, by measuring its amount, which does not take into account the context [4].

A structural approach like that of OBIA, instead, rises the semantic level by adding topological information and statistics, spatial relationship rules, defining the context. Very similar to this is the manual photo interpretation, but this approach overcomes the limits of a subjective classification: in fact, it is homogenous and can be reproduced. However, these analysis tools that can add the information (structural and morphological) contained in the images to the simple spectral content of the pixels, are from a long time used in other fields such as processing of medical images [5].

Concepts of Mathematical Morphology [6] lead this image analysis to a recognition of objects [7] and a classification based on Fuzzy Logic principles [8]. Furthermore, to every rule we can assign an appropriate weight [9].

We get a structural analysis with high semantic level [10] allowing a wealth of information that we cannot achieve with the pixel-based spectral analysis. Thanks to the direct extraction of vector maps from satellite imagery, it is possible an immediate and full integration in GIS. Moreover, the possibility of introducing rules for the relationships between the obtained objects [11] and the recognition of the context significantly makes the photo interpretation process reproducible, increases recognition and improves the extraction (automatic or semi-automatic) of objects that are on the Earth's surface.

3.2   Multiresolution Segmentation

OBIA operates a segmentation of the whole image by adequately setting the parameters of shape and color. In this case the appropriate choice of rules for segmentation, as a certain interval similar to perimeter/area ratio (indeed the ratio between the image object border length and, attributable to the area of the image object, the square root of the pixels number). This rule allows recognizing and extracting objects that have an elongated shape, and this will discriminate from the others the shapes of rivers and roads. The rules on spectral content, instead, easily can distinguish roads from rivers. Therefore, it is possible to export quickly the data obtained in GIS or also in Open Street Map, collaborative open source tools. This automated migration process is much faster and more efficient than manual integration which, in addition to not being homogeneous, is also subject to many variables.

By choosing an appropriate scale factor, we can size largeness of the achieved polygons, because the scale setting is related to the scale that we want to achieve in cartography. The segmentation process, as will, is multiresolution: in fact, starting from the same image, we can obtain some levels in a hierarchy of polygons at different scale factors. When we reduce the scale factor, the generated polygons are smaller and smaller; therefore, there is less color variability within the polygons, while we have the opposite by increasing the scale factor.

There is a relationship among the polygons in these hierarchical levels. All the polygons of lower hierarchical level have a geometrical relationship with polygons of higher level in the hierarchy. Every lower level polygon belongs only to one higher-level polygon. All the polygons of all segmentation levels constitute a single database in which are all the relationships between the polygons of the same and of different hierarchical levels. The adjacent polygons on a hierarchical level, as the polygons of a lower hierarchical level, as the polygon in which the examined polygon in the upper hierarchical level is contained, are therefore known for each polygon (Fig. 3, Fig. 4).

Furthermore, there is a characteristic circular interaction between processing and classification of image objects for the object-based approach. Specific information segmentation-based, image objects' shape, and scale are all useful for classification. Moreover, the classification, including semantic information and details related to the

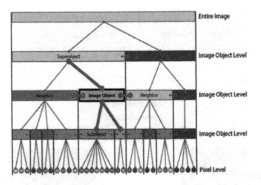

Fig. 3. Hierarchical network of the image.

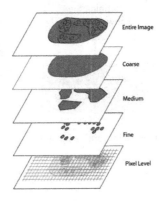

Fig. 4. Overlap of the different levels of segmentation

context, uses the attributes of the image objects as well as the relationship of image objects connected in network, resulting so in an operational classification model. The required geoinformation and required objects are gradually extracted, through classification – processing iterative cycles (Fig. 5), useful for many applications.

Therefore, processing units (image objects) are constantly changing shape, mutual relationships as, so, classification. Analogous to the processes of human understanding images, this type of circular processing translates into intermediate states that follow one another, with a growing variation of the class and information more and more abstract about the starting image.

In the example explained, we performed a segmentation of the scene on one level, but we can carry out a multiresolution and multilevel segmentation, and therefore a classification. We operate a multiresolution segmentation obtaining the automatic creation of vector polygons, extracted directly from the image and coinciding in the overlapping on raster; thus the final classification prepares a suitable class hierarchy taking into account relationships between the segmentation levels achieved.

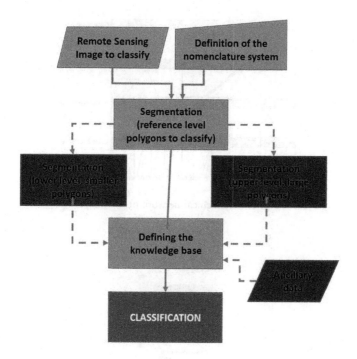

Fig. 5. Procedures diagram: green steps are mandatory, yellow steps (dashed arrows) are optional. (Color figure online)

4 The Segmentation

The segmentation technique starts with one-pixel objects: it is a technique of merging the region from the bottom up. In the following steps, segmentation produces smaller image objects increasingly merged into larger objects [12]. During the clustering process, and through the process, the optimization procedure decreases *nh*, that is the weighted heterogeneity of the image objects obtained (*n* is the segment size and *h* the definition of heterogeneity, arbitrary). For each step, adjacent image objects merge to represent the smallest growth in the chosen heterogeneity. The described process stops when this growth overcomes the threshold we defined with the scale parameter. Multiresolution segmentation is thus a procedure for optimization that acts locally.

We obtain the color (or spectral) heterogeneity by summing, in each layer, the standard deviations of the spectral values weighted with the weights we assigned to each layer:

$$h_s = \sum\nolimits_{c=1}^{q} w_c \sigma_c \tag{1}$$

where: h_s is spectral or color heterogeneity; σ_c is st. dev. of *digital number* in *c* spectral band; *q* is bands number; w_c instead is the weight we assign to c spectral band.

If we only perform a minimization of the spectral heterogeneity, however, we obtain image objects or branched segments with a fractally shaped edge [13], with a heavy effect in structured data, as in radar data.

Therefore, we consider it helpful that the spectral heterogeneity criterion is mixed with the spatial heterogeneity criterion, for reducing the deviation from a shape smooth or compact. Here, we describe heterogeneity as deviation from a compact shape as the ratio between the length l of the border and the square root of the pixels (to be precise, the number of pixels) that make up the image object.

$$h_{g\_smooth} = \frac{l}{\sqrt{n}} \tag{2}$$

where: h_{g_smooth} = fractal factor for spatial heterogeneity;
l = length of the border;
n = in the image object, the number of pixels.

The compactness factor ($h_{g\_compact}$) is the second; it depends from the ratio of polygon axis dimensions:

$$h_{g\_compact} = \frac{l}{b} \tag{3}$$

with $h_{g\_compact}$ is the factor of compactness; l is the length of the border;
b, instead, is the shortest length of the border given by the bounding box on image-object parallel to the raster.

As described, the algorithm of segmentation merges the adjoining polygons starting from each pixel of the image up to the variation of heterogeneity between the two previous polygons and therefore until the new polygon does not overcome the user-defined scale factor, that is the threshold. Until the change in heterogeneity does not overcome the defined threshold, merge is actually carried out; when the change overcomes the threshold, the two polygons stay separate. The variation in heterogeneity (overall fusion value) among the resulting object and the two starting polygons is:

$$f = w_f \Delta h_s + (1 - w_f) \Delta h_g \tag{4}$$

with f = overall fusion value;
w_f = user defined weight of color, it is against shape.

For w must be chosen a value between 0 and 1, where 0 and 1 are also possible: for $w_f = 1$ is just valued the heterogeneity of shape, while for $w_f = 0$ is valued solely the heterogeneity of color.

Δh_s is the variation in spectral or color heterogeneity between the achieved polygon and the two starting polygons:

$$\Delta h_s = \sum_{c=1}^{q} w_c \left[n_{merge} \sigma_{merge_c} - \left(n_{obj1} \sigma_{obj1_c} + n_{obj2} \sigma_{obj2_c} \right) \right] \tag{5}$$

where: n_{merge} = achieved polygon pixel number;
σ_{merge_c} = st. dev. of digital number in c -spectral band (resultant polygon);

n_{obj1} = pixel number of the first of the two starting polygons;

σ_{obj1c} = st. dev. of *digital number* in c -spectral band of the first of the polygons before that they merged;

n_{obj2} = pixel number of the second starting polygon, before the fusion;

σ_{obj2c} = st. dev. of *digital number* in c -spectral band of the second polygon before the fusion.

Moreover, the variation Δh_g in shape heterogeneity, caused by the merge, is assessed by calculating the variation between after and before the fusion. This involves the calculation methods for compactness and smoothness:

$$\Delta h_g = w_g \Delta h_{g\_compact} + (1 - w_g) \Delta h_{g\_smooth} \tag{6}$$

w_g is the user defined weight for smoothness (remember that it is against compactness). For w we must chose a value between 0 and 1, with 0 and 1 possible: if $w_f = 1$ is valued only smoothness, if $w_f = 0$ is valued only compactness.

$$\Delta h_{g\_compact} = n_{merge} \frac{l_{merge}}{\sqrt{n_{merge}}} - \left\{ n_{obj1} \frac{l_{obj1}}{\sqrt{n_{obj1}}} + n_{obj2} \frac{l_{obj2}}{\sqrt{n_{obj2}}} \right\} \tag{7}$$

$$\Delta h_{g\_smooth} = n_{merge} \frac{l_{merge}}{b_{merge}} - \left\{ n_{obj1} \frac{l_{obj1}}{b_{obj1}} + n_{obj2} \frac{l_{obj2}}{b_{obj2}} \right\} \tag{8}$$

n is the object size, l the perimeter of the object, b the bounding box perimeter.

4.1 Segmentation Process

In this case study, multiresolution segmentation created only a single level with the parameters we indicated in the following table, which takes into account the features of the IKONOS dataset (Table 1):

Table 1. Segmentation parameters.

Segmentation level	Bands				Scale	Homogeneity criteria			
						Color	Shape	Shape Settings	
	Blue	Green	Red	Near Infra-Red				Smoothness	Compactness
Single Level	1	1	1	1	40	0.1	0.9	0.9	0.1

We applied the chosen level of segmentation on the four bands of the IKONOS dataset.

Therefore, we can identify the long shapes by assigning a very high value to the form factor (0.9) and, consequently, a 0.1 value to the color content.

We also assign a minimum factor of 0.1 to compactness to identify objects which have a strong perimeter development.

The scale factor is 40 because we do not want an overly fragmented image. However, the fragmentation in some areas is quite strong.

Figure 6 shows segmentation with identification of objects.

Fig. 6. Segmentation level.

We can see some long objects matching waterways, roads and streets.

Figure 7 shows variability of the pixels intra-polygon, which would be even greater choosing a largest scale factor. We applied the method illustrated in this article with a version of the eCognition software, created by Definiens and released by Trimble in recent years.

4.2 ENVI Classification

Other commercial software for satellite image processing such as ENVI of L3Harris Geospatial can perform image segmentation similarly to what obtained with eCognition in this application. In that case, however, it is necessary to proceed first with the classification of the image and only afterwards focus on the segmentation and extraction of the objects, while in eCognition the classification is based precisely on the previous segmentation.

In ENVI, the segmentation process as Feature Extraction is based on a watershed by immersion algorithm developed by Vincent and Soille [14] that equates pixel DN values in an image with elevation points on a topographic surface. Figure 8 shows classification in ENVI, using the maximum likelihood algorithm, in Fig. 9 is the related confusion matrix.

Fig. 7. Segmentation with variability intra-polygons

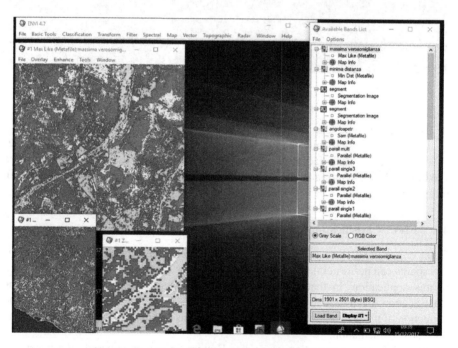

Fig. 8. Classification in ENVI and segmentation image.

Moreover, Spectral Angle Mapper (SAM) is a physically based spectral classification that uses an n-D angle to match pixels to reference spectra. The algorithm

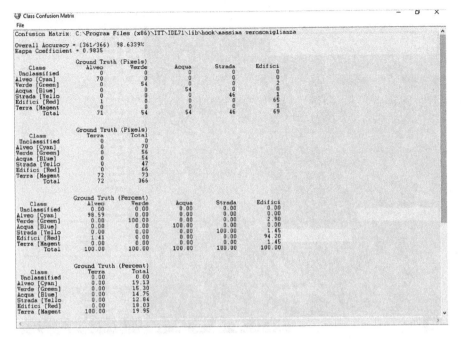

Fig. 9. Confusion matrix. Overall accuracy is 98.6339%

determines the spectral similarity between two spectra by calculating the angle between the spectra and treating them as vectors. With SAM, by varying the classification parameters, firstly the riverbeds only were identified (Fig. 10) and then the riverbeds and roads (Fig. 11).

Through a process of subtraction between the two images, we obtained the roads. However, in this classification we identified only a few larger roads.

4.3 Processing in GIS

We then superimposed on GIS the open street maps (OSM) layers, the segmentation – vector - achieved by eCognition, the classifications of ENVI and the result obtained from the aforementioned subtraction.

By comparing the distances between the lines that identify the outline of the vector layers, we can compare the results obtained.

For this reason, we implemented a function on QGIS for automating the process of calculation of the distance between the different roads, thanks to the field calculator as the starting point in the program attribute table.

Results obtained demonstrate that the object classification, compared to a pixel-based classification, gives better results because the deviation between the different layers exceeds one meter and therefore the latter cannot be used without further processing to refine the result (Fig. 12).

Next step is the import of these shapefile into Open Street Map (Fig. 13).

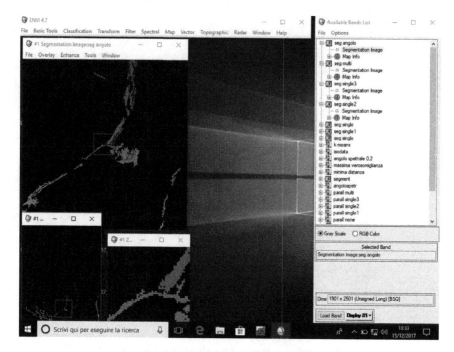

Fig. 10. Identification of the riverbeds.

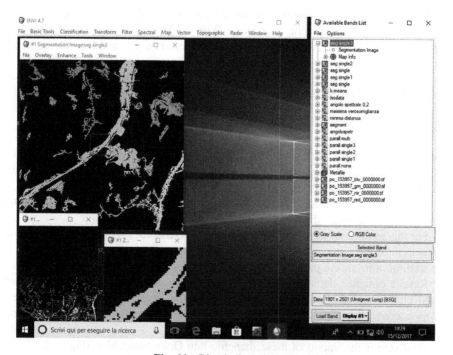

Fig. 11. Riverbeds and roads

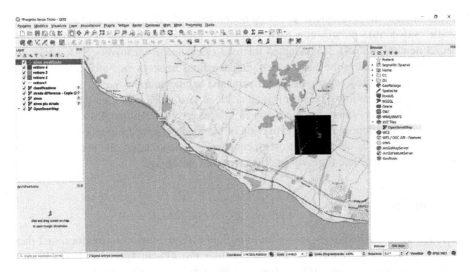

Fig. 12. Layer overlay for validation of results.

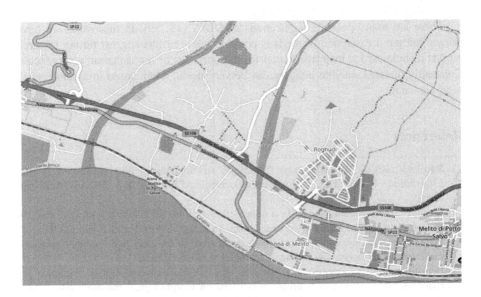

Fig. 13. Insertion in Open Street Map (OSM).

5 Results, Comparison and Discussion

Various attempts were made over time to extract road lattices from satellite images, as the need for an automatic road extraction method is also felt due to the continuous development of transport networks. Some of these have been applied to data from radar satellites, which have the advantage of being free from the influence of the weather: the satellite-mounted synthetic aperture radar (SAR). Some studies propose automatic discrimination methods based on a deep neural network (DNN) adapted for roads from single and double polarization SAR Sentinel-1 images, extending the convolutional neural network (CNN). It is adapted for road extraction from images SAR analyzing the potential of using the fully convolutional neural network or Fully Convolutional Network (FCN) [15], which works for semantic segmentation.

SWT (Stroke Width Transform) is an artificial vision algorithm (an image operator) used in Computer Vision to detect text in images. A non-traditional use of this algorithm has been proposed for the extraction of the road network from an optical satellite image [16]. Results obtained with segmentation are encouraging; the precision is very high, since we extracted the objects directly from the image.

6 Conclusions

The structural methodology (using multiresolution segmentation techniques, and then achieving a classification object-based), unlike the classic spectral or pixel-based analysis, is able to make the best use of the wealth of information detected with remotely sensed data, with rapid integration into GIS. Moreover, it allows the direct and quick production of vector maps [17].

There are many possible applications of OBIA [18, 19]. In this work, we have shown that rapid extraction of roads is possible; these results suggest further research on fast techniques for map integration for the purposes of humanitarian emergencies. Constantly updated satellite imagery can be very useful when speed in an emergency becomes vital.

References

1. Barrile, V., Bilotta, G.: Metodologie "Strutturali" su immagini Satellitari per l'analisi Urbana e Territoriale. In: Atti della XI Conferenza Nazionale ASITA, pp. 267–272. ASITA, Torino (2007)
2. Small, C.: Multiresolution analysis of urban reflectance. In: IEEE/ISPRS Joint Workshop on Remote Sensing and Data Fusion over Urban Areas, pp. 15–19. IEEE, Rome (2001)
3. Pesaresi, M.: Texture analysis for urban pattern recognition using fine-resolution panchromatic satellite imagery. Geogr. Environ. Model. 4, 43–63 (2000)
4. Benediktsson, J.A., Pesaresi, M., Arnason, K.: Classification and feature extraction for remote sensing images from urban areas based on morphological transformations. IEEE Trans. Geosci. Remote Sens. 41, 1940–1949 (2003)
5. Köppen, M., Ruiz-del-Solar, J., Soille, P.: Texture segmentation by biologically-inspired use of neural networks and mathematical morphology. In: Proceedings of the International ICSC/IFAC Symposium on Neural Computation, pp. 23–25. ICSC Academic Press, Wien (1998)
6. Serra, J.: Image Analysis and Mathematical Morphology. Theoretical Advances, vol. 2. Academic Press, New York (1998)
7. Bianchin, A., Pesaresi, M.: Approccio strutturale all'analisi di immagine per la descrizione del territorio: una esplorazione degli strumenti di morfologia matematica. Atti del V Convegno Nazionale A.I.T., pp. 25–29. AIT, Milano (1992)

8. Benz, U.C., Hofmann, P., Willhauck, G., Lingenfelder, I., Heynen, M.: Multi-resolution, object-oriented fuzzy analysis of remote sensing data for GIS-ready information. ISPRS J. Photogramm. Remote Sens. **58**, 239–258 (2004)
9. Barrile, V., Bilotta, G.: Object-oriented analysis applied to high resolution satellite data. WSEAS Trans. Signal Process. **4**, 68–75 (2008)
10. Soille, P., Pesaresi, M.: Advances in mathematical morphology applied to geoscience and remote sensing. IEEE Trans. Geosci. Remote Sens. **40**, 2042–2055 (2002)
11. Shackelford, A.K., Davis, C.H.: A hierarchical fuzzy classification approach for high resolution multispectral data over urban areas. IEEE Trans. Geosci. Remote Sens. **9**, 1920–1932 (2003)
12. Blaschke, T.: Object based image analysis for remote sensing. ISPRS J. Photogramm. Remote Sens. **65**, 2–16 (2010)
13. Barrile, V., Bilotta, G.: An application of object-oriented analysis to very high resolution satellite data on small cities for change detection. In: Proceedings of 3rd WSEAS Conference on Remote Sensing, pp. 98–103. WSEAS, Venice (2007)
14. Vincent, L., Soille, P.: Watersheds in digital spaces: an efficient algorithm based on immersion simulations. IEEE Trans. Pattern Anal. Mach. Intell. **13**(6), 583–598 (1991)
15. Zhang, Q., et al.: A new road extraction method using Sentinel-1 SAR images based on the deep fully convolutional neural network. Eur. J. Remote Sens. **52**(1), 572–582 (2019). https://doi.org/10.1080/22797254.2019.1694447
16. Zhang, X., Zhang, C., Li, H., Luo, Z.: A road extraction method based on high resolution remote sensing image. In: The International Archives of the Photogrammetry, Remote Sensing and Spatial Information Sciences, 2020 International Conference on Geomatics in the Big Data Era (ICGBD), Guilin, Guangxi, China, 15–17 November 2019, vol. XLII-3/W10 (2019)
17. Bilotta, G.: Metodologie avanzate applicate allo studio dell'uso della terra. Cartographica **12**, 21–24 (2005)
18. Barrile, V., Armocida, G., Bilotta, G.: Sistema integrato per il rilievo e la gestione del catasto delle aree incendiate. In: Atti della XII Conferenza Nazionale ASITA, pp. 293–298. ASITA, L'Aquila (2008)
19. Barrile, V., Bilotta, G., Meduri, G. M.: Individuazione di discariche mediante segmentazione del dato satellitare. In: Atti della XVI Conferenza Nazionale ASITA, pp. 137–142. ASITA, Vicenza (2012)

Extracting Land Cover Data Using GEE: A Review of the Classification Indices

Alessandra Capolupo$^{(\boxtimes)}$ ⓘ, Cristina Monterisi, Giacomo Caporusso, and Eufemia Tarantino ⓘ

Departtment of Civil Environmental, Land, Construction and Chemistry (DICATECh), Politecnico Di Bari, Via Orabona 4, 70125 Bari, Italy
alessandra.capolupo@poliba.it

Abstract. Land Use/Land Cover (LU/LC) data includes most of the information suitable for tackling many environmental issues. Remote sensing is largely recognized as the most significant method to extract them through the application of various techniques. They can be extracted through the application of many techniques. Among the several classification approaches, the index-based method has been recognized as the best one to gather LU/LC information from different images sources. The present work is intended to assess its performance exploiting the great potentialities of Google Earth Engine (GEE), a cloud-processing environment introduced by Google to storage and handle a large number of information. Twelve atmospherically corrected Landsat satellite images were collected on the experimental site of Siponto, in Southern Italy. Once the clouds masking procedure was completed, a large number of indices were implemented and compared in GEE platform to detect sparse and dense vegetation, water, bare soils and built-up areas. Among the tested algorithms, only NDBaI2, CVI, WI2015, SwiRed and STRed indices showed satisfying performance. Although NDBaI2 was able to extract all the main LU/LC categories with a high Overall Accuracy (OA) (82.59%), the other mentioned indices presented a higher accuracy than the first one but are able to identify just few classes. An interesting performance is shown by the STRed index since it has a very high OA and can extract mining areas, water and green zones. GEE appeared the best solution to manage the geospatial big data.

Keywords: Landsat images · Cloud-computing platform · Land cover/land use

1 Introduction

Every day, many new space-borne sensors are introduced in order to increase massively the earth observation (EO) datasets since, nowadays, they play a key role in landscape planning and environmental monitoring. This results in the generation of a continuous stream of geospatial data that must be stored and handled, producing, in turn, novel geospatial data to be managed. As reported by the Open Geospatial Consortium (OGC), the global EO archive exceed the one Exabyte during 2015. Therefore, geospatial data are generally considered as big data and, over the last few years, new cloud computing platforms have been introduced to overcome the limitations of

© Springer Nature Switzerland AG 2020
O. Gervasi et al. (Eds.): ICCSA 2020, LNCS 12252, pp. 782–796, 2020.
https://doi.org/10.1007/978-3-030-58811-3_56

common desktop software. In fact, such environments need an excellent computational power to integrate data acquired by different sensors and providing complementary information [1]. Thus, considering their features, these software require a great amount of time to meet the fixed operational purpose. Conversely, the cloud platforms allow to save acquisition and processing time exploiting the great potentialities of the cloud. Among them, Google Earth Engine (GEE) (https://earthengine.google.org), designed and realized by Google, is, currently, the most promising cloud computing environment [2]. This is essentially due to its main properties, enhanced by [1] and [2]:

1. the presence of an Application Programming Interface (API) aimed at helping the users to interact with the integrated data catalogue, consisting of publicly available geospatial datasets. Such catalogue is continuously updated, indeed, about 6000 scenes, acquired by several sensors, are daily uploaded;
2. the presence of a High-Performance Computing (HPC) infrastructure intended to speed the processing phase up thanks to the integration of many processors in running the algorithms. This results in solving all the issues linked to the storage and handle of geospatial big data;
3. the presence of an interactive programming environment aimed at ensuring the possibility to develop specific code to meet user's needs.

Therefore, it appears extremely useful to manage geospatial big data and, mainly, to create Land Use/Land Cover (LU/LC) map at global scale. Such thematic charts can be obtained through the application of several methods, such as classification indices [9–12, 16–80], maximum likelihood supervised classification (ML) [3], machine learning algorithms (MLAs) [4] and object-based image analysis (OBIA) approach [[5] and [6]]. Although none of the above-mentioned approaches are problems-free and able to always produce the best result, [7] demonstrated that the index-based classification technique, built on the combination of diverse spectral bands, is the best one for automatically revealing LU/LC information from satellite data in multitemporal and multisensory analysis perspectives. Therefore, over the years, several indices have been developed to quickly extract some LU/LC categories according to their specific needs. Although some review papers have been realized to describe their potentialities and limitations, currently, they are not exhaustive since the indices are continuously updated.

Therefore, this paper is aimed at exploring the potentialities of 85 indices to automatically extract LU/LC information on the pilot site of Siponto, a historical municipality in the Puglia Region (Southern Italy). Both traditional and new indices were investigated in order to assess and compare their performance and, thus, identify the optimal index to distinguish each LU/LC categories. Therefore, 59 indices developed to detect sparse and dense vegetation, 5 introduced to classify water, 7 presented to distinguish bare soil and the remaining 14 indices related to built-up areas identification were tested on twelve Landsat images, belonging to three different missions. Each considered mission is equipped with diverse sensors in order to ensure to examine their potentialities in both a multi-sensor and a multi-temporal perspective.

The paper is composed by three main sections: the first one, titled "Materials and methods", aimed at describing the selected classification indices and the applied processing environment; the second one, "Results and discussion", instead, is intended to report the obtained outcomes in order to identify the optimal index to be adopted to extract the needed LU/LC data; finally, the third section synthetizes the conclusions of the work, describing the performance of the detected optimal solution and of the platform.

2 Materials and Methods

2.1 Pilot Site and Dataset Description

The coastline of Siponto in the Puglia Region (Southern Italy) was chosen as study area (Fig. 1). Such area, indeed, has played a key role since its foundation (194 BC), inasmuch it was considered as the most considerable hub form the commercial as well as maritime perspectives. Nevertheless, because of two devastating earthquakes occurred in 1223 and 1255, this site was subjected to a gradually depopulation process and, consequently, the swamping of its seaport. From then on, it was mainly exploited to meet agricultural purposes thanks to the presence of a dense network of irrigation ditches. However, over the last few years, this issue lost its significance in favor of tourism, drove by the beauty of its landscape and the climate conditions. Therefore, it is a meaningful site to evaluate the classification indices performance due to the changes experienced by its territory over the years and the heterogeneity of its landscape.

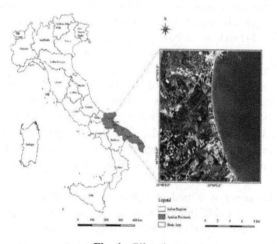

Fig. 1. Pilot site

Selected traditional indices, described in depth in the following section, were tested on twelve Landsat images, listed in Table 1. They were collected from three different Landsat missions: 5, 7 and 8, respectively, covering a period of 17 years (2002–2019). Moreover, one image for each season was acquired in order to carry out a multi-sensor, multi-temporal and multi-season evaluation. All the collected images composing the dataset were supplied in the Universal Transverse Mercator (UTM) projection and the

World Geodetic System (WGS84) datum. An additional criterion was introduced to select the data: a cloud cover threshold equal to 20% was set.

Table 1. Landsat satellite images collected by each sensor. ETM+ : Enhanced Thematic Mapper; TM: Thematic Mapper; OLI-TIRS: Operational Land Imager - Thermal Infrared.

Landsat satellite mission	Sensor	Acquisition date (mm/dd/yyyy)	Average cloud cover (%)
Landsat 7	ETM+	01/21/2002	4
		08/01/2002	6
		10/27/2002	1
		04/14/2003	4
Landsat 5	TM	02/07/2011	1
		03/27/2011	16
		08/25/2011	0
		10/05/2011	1
Landsat 8	OLI-TIRS	12/08/2017	1.69
		08/12/2018	8.1
		09/22/2018	2.41
		03/17/2019	19.46

2.2 Google Earth Engine Environment and Pre-processing Phase

Traditional desktop software, commonly involved in geospatial analysis, show numerous limitations in storage and managing geospatial big data [1]. Therefore, in the last few years, Google realized a new cloud computing platform to go beyond these issues and to optimize the processing phase: Google Earth Engine (GEE) [1]. It gives the possibility both to download the selected images and to process them exploiting the great cloud potentiality and saving acquiring and processing time [7]. Moreover, its most eligible property: satellite images can be downloaded in raw as well as pre-processed format. This implies the reduction of the time needed to acquire and process geospatial big data [2] and [1]. GEE involves a JavaScript Application Programming Interface (API) as well, allowing the users to carry out whenever operations, such as spectral bands integration to compute classification indices.

Taking advantages of GEE abilities, atmospherically corrected images were selected and all the subsequent processing steps (Fig. 1) were implemented in GEE environment and performed on cloud. Once the selected images were collected in a pre-processed format, where needed, the cloud masking procedure was conducted by adopting a proper filters, already implemented in GEE, as proposed by [8]. Such filter, based on the information provided by the quality assessment (QA) band, rends transparent cloudy pixels which will not considered in classification indices computation phase. Conversely, the ortho rectification process was not required since the USGS provided satisfying images. Classification indices were computed on the outcome of pre-processed phase (https://developers.google.com/earth-engine) (Fig. 2).

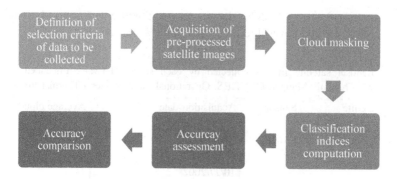

Fig. 2. Workflow of the whole procedure

2.3 Classification Indices Computation

Index-based classification approach is widely and efficient applied to quickly generate LU/LC thematic map from satellite images [7]. Such property makes it more attractive than the other classification methods both when a large volume of geospatial data should be investigated and global maps are required [7]. Therefore, an enormous number of indices have been introduced over the years. Each of them is devoted to detecting a specific LU/LC class and just few of them can simultaneously identify several categories. In fact, based on the integration of the information provided by one or more spectral bands, indices can extract Earth's features according to their spectral signature, commonly considered as a footprint since each element has a different trend, even if objects belonging to the same LU/LC class show a similar sign. This is due to features ability of absorbing, reflecting and transmitting the energy.

Thus, each band is essential to bring out specific properties, as highlighted by several research activities. For instance, [9] enhanced the relevance of Red band to discriminate vegetated areas because of its dependency by the energy absorbed by chlorophyll; conversely, [10] demonstrated the significance of TIR as well as SWIR band to classify bare soil and built-up areas [11] which is also essential to extract information related to sparse and dense vegetation thanks to its linkage with the amount of water in leaves [12].

Therefore, 85 conventional indices, listed in Table 2, were computed and their performance compared in order to bring out their potentialities in classifying Landsat satellite images. Although all of them were quickly implemented in GEE environment, just a few reported appreciable contribution: Normalized Difference Bareness Index (version 2) (NDBaI2) (Eq. 1) [13], SwirTirRed (STRed) index (Eq. 2) [14], SwiRed index [14] (Eq. 3), Composite Vegetation Index (CVI) [15] (Eq. 4) and Water index 2015 (WI2015) (Eq. 5) [16]:

$$NDBaI2 = \frac{SWIR1 - TIR1}{SWIR1 + TIR1} \qquad (1)$$

$$STRed = \frac{SWIR1 + R - TIR1}{SWIR1 + R + TIR1} \qquad (2)$$

$$SwiRed = \frac{SWIR1 - R}{SWIR1 + R} \qquad (3)$$

$$CVI = \left(\frac{NIR - G - R}{NIR + G + R} - 0.4\right)^{0.5} \qquad (4)$$

$$WI2015 = 1.7204 + 171 * Blue + 3 * Green - 70 * Red - 45 * NIR - 71 * SWIR2 \qquad (5)$$

2.4 Accuracy Assessment

The method "stratified random sampling point" was adopted to generate a multitemporal reference dataset composed by a total of 11,245 pixels, used as testing samples, as suggested by [17]. Such points were proportionally distributed in each LU/LC category according to their area. Consequently, they were allocated as following: 1328 pixels were dedicated to water class, 492 pixels to built-up areas, 151 pixels to mining areas, 3165 pixels to bare soil, and 755 and 924 pixels to sparse and dense vegetation, respectively. Overall Accuracy (OA), Producer's Accuracy (PA), and User's Accuracy (UA) were, thus, estimated for each obtained thematic map [18] and [19]. All introduced metrics show a value between 0 and 1: as closest to 1 their value is, better the accuracy is. Once classification indices performance was estimated, they were compared in order to detect the optimal indices for identifying different LU/LC classes.

3 Results and Discussion

This paper is aimed at evaluating the potentialities of 85 conventional indices (Table 2) in distinguishing LU/LC classes from Landsat satellite images using GEE platform. Therefore, twelve atmospherically corrected images, belonging to 5, 7 and 8 missions, were selected according to the criteria reported in Sect. 2.1. Selecting such missions allows to assess indices performance on a multi-sensor and multi-temporal perspective since each of them is equipped with a different sensor (Table 1) and covers a diverse historical period. Moreover, the dependency from season was explored as well by acquiring, for all the considered Landsat missions, an image for fall, spring, summer and autumn, respectively (Table 1). Indices performance was assessed on the study area of Siponto, an historical city of Puglia Region (Southern Italy).

The best Overall Accuracy (OA) of each index as well as the detected LU/LC classes were reported in Table 2. Only the Automated Water Extraction Index (AWEI) [20], Normalized Difference Bareness Index (NDBaI) [13] and Normalized Difference Bareness Index (version 2) (NDBaI2) [13] were able to extract the maximum number of categories: bare soil, built-up areas, dense and sparse vegetation, water and mining areas. Nevertheless, among them, NDBaI2 showed the highest OA (82.59%); on the contrary, AWEI had the worst OA value (68.04%). This means that, although the three mentioned indices can automatically classify the whole study area, NDBaI2 showed the best performance. Its OA was slightly reduced by its difficulties in distinguishing sparse from dense vegetation.

Totally opposite was the performance presented by the Misra Yellow Vegetation Index (MYVI) [21] and the Triangular Greenness Index (TGI) [22]. Both, indeed, cannot detect any class in the experimental site. Our considerations are supported by literature as well since [23] demonstrated that MYVI encounters some difficulties in detecting LU/LC information because it does not consider atmosphere-soil-vegetation interactions. Similarly, TGI is strongly influenced by the scale and by the chlorophyll content in leaves and, consequently, it is appropriate just in few cases. Therefore, although it is recognized as the optimal index to classify "green areas" from high-resolution images, it is completely inadequate to extract LU/LC information from medium and low resolution input data [24]. On the contrary, the other computed indices can extract just few LU/LC categories in line with the purpose of their creation. For instance, among the indices introduced to detect the water, the Water index 2015 (WI2015) [25] showed the best performance (99.81%), while Composite Vegetation Index (CVI) [15] presented the best performance (98.0) in discriminating vegetated areas and SwiRed index [14], instead, had the best OA (97.76) in detecting built-up areas. A very high accuracy (94.71%) is also obtained by calculating the SwirTiRed (STRed) index [14] which is able to assess different LU/LC categories, such as mining areas, water as well as sparse and dense vegetation.

GEE cloud computing platform played a key role in this research because it allowed to download atmospherically corrected satellite images and to automatize the processing step with a consequent reduction of acquisition and processing time. After programmed a specific code, such environment allowed to automatically extract the LU/LC information from selected satellite images which were separately analyzed. Thus, this study confirms the great ability of the GEE platform in processing geospatial big data, overcoming the limitations of commonly applied desktop software. Beyond to minimize the acquisition and processing time thanks to its eligible property to implement adapted programming code, it can exploit the cloud capacity in storing and managing a large amount of data without needing excellent computational power capacity.

Table 2. Tested classification indices listed in alphabetical order. OA column reports the best overall accuracy of each index. LU/LC column reports the Land Use/Land Cover classes detected by each index; OA: Overall Accuracy; W: water; DV: Dense Vegetation; SV: Sparse vegetation; MA: Mining areas; BS: Bare Soil; BUA: Built-up area; *: water mask is required; -: no classes were detected.

Spectral Index	LU/LC	OA (%)	Spectral Index	LU/LC	OA (%)
Aerosol Free Vegetation Index version 1.6 (AFRI1.6) [26]	DV, SV	72.24	Modified Nonlinear vegetation Index (MNLI) [27]	W, DV, SV	77.40
Aerosol Free Vegetation Index version 2.1 (AFRI2.1) [26]	DV, SV	86.02	Modified Soil Adjusted Vegetation Index 2 (MSAVI2) [28]	W, DV, SV, BUA, BS	83.30
Atmospherically resistant vegetation index (ARVI) [29]	W, DV, SV, BUA, BS	59.97	Misra Soil Brightness Index (MSBI) [21]	W, DV, SV, BUA, BS	78.56
Adjusted Soil Brightness Index (ASBI)* [30]	DV, SV	66.70	Modified Simple Ratio (MSR) [31]	W, DV, SV, BUA, BS	67.03
Ashburn Vegetation Index (AVI) [32]	W	99.78	Misra Yellow Vegetation Index (MYVI) [21]	-	-
Automated Water Extraction Index (AWEI) [20]	W, DV, SV, BUA, MA, BS	68.04	New Built-up Index (NBI)* [33]	DV, SV, BUA, MA, BS	71.46
Automated Water Extraction Index (shadow version) (AWEIsh) [20]	W, BUA	91.46	Normalized Difference Bare Land Index (NBLI)* [34]	DV, SV, BUA, MA, BS	75.51
Build-area extraction index (BAEI)* [35]	DV, SV, BUA	63.60	New Built-up Index (NBUI) [36]	W, DV, SV	76.39
Biophysical Composition Index (BCI) [37]	W, DV, SV	68.23	Normalized Canopy Index (NCI) [38]	W, BUA	78.34
Built-up Land Features Extraction Index (BLFEI) [39]	W, DV, SV, BUA, BS	72.03	Normalized Difference Bareness Index (NDBaI) [13]	W, DV, SV, BUA, MA, BS	67.93
Bare Soil Index (BSI)* [40]	DV, SV	73.62	Normalized Difference Bareness Index (version 2) (NDBaI2) [13]	W, DV, SV, BUA, MA, BS	82.59
Built-up land (BUI) [41]	W, DV, SV	69.81	Normalized Difference Built-up Index (NDBI) [42]	DV, SV	71.14
Combinational Biophysical Composition Index (CBCI) [43]	DV, SV	67.22	Normalized Difference Impervious Surface Index (NDISI) [44]	W, MA	97.60
Green Chlorophyll Index (CI) [45]	W, DV, SV	68.40	Normalized Difference Moisture Index (NDMI)* [46]	DV, SV	73.47
Composite Vegetation Index (CVI) [15]	SV, DV	98.0	Normalized Difference Tillage Index (NDTI)* [47]	DV, SV	71.57
Davies-Bouldin index (DBI) [48]	W, DV, SV, BUA, BS	70.59	Normalized Difference Vegetation Index (NDVI) [49]	W, DV, SV, BUA, BS	73.24

(continued)

Table 2. (*continued*)

Spectral Index	LU/LC	OA (%)	Spectral Index	LU/LC	OA (%)
Dry Bare-Soil Index (DBSI)* [50]	DV, SV	68.47	Normalized Difference Water Index (NDWI) [51]	W, DV, SV, BUA, BS	73.54
Simple Difference Indices (DVI) [52]	W, DV, SV	69.85	Non-Linear Index (NLI) [53]	W, DV, SV	76.63
Enhanced Built-up and Bareness Index (EBBI) [54]	W, DV, SV	64.93	Optimized Soil Adjusted Vegetation Index (OSAVI) [55]	W, DV, SV	88.84
Enhanced Normalized Difference Impervious Surfaces Index (ENDISI) [56]	DV, SV BUA, MA	67.55	Renormalized Difference Vegetation Index (RDVI) [57]	W, DV, SV	77.34
Enhanced Vegetation Index (EVI) [58]	W, DV, SV, BUA, BS	58.59	Ratio Vegetation Index (RVI) [59]	W, DV, SV, BUA, BS	72.30
Green Atmospherically Resistant Vegetation Index (GARI) [60]	W, DV, SV, BUA, BS	69.78	Soil-Adjusted Vegetation Index (SAVI) [61]	W, DV, SV	72.04
"Ghost cities" Index (GCI) [62]	W, DV, SV, BUA, BS	71.26	Soil Brightness Index (SBI) [63]	W, BUA, MA	80.27
Green Difference Vegetation Index (GDVI) [64]	W, DV, SV	70.59	Specific Leaf Area Vegetation Index (SLAVI) [65]	W, DV, SV	83.56
Global Environment Monitoring Index (GEMI) [66]	W, DV, SV	67.74	Simple Ratio (SR) [67]	W, DV, SV	68.93
Green leaf index (GLI) [68]	DV, SV	66.70	SwirTirRed index (STRed) [14]	W, DS, SV, MA	94.71
Green Normalized Difference Vegetation Index (GNDVI) [60]	W, DV, SV, BUA, BS	72.48	SwiRed index [14]	BUA	97.76
Green Optimized Soil Adjusted Vegetation Index (GOSAVI) [69]	W, DV, SV	89.89	Transformed difference vegetation index (TDVI) [70]	W	99.81
Green-Red Vegetation Index (GRVI) [71]	W, DV, SV, BUA, BS	71.26	Triangular Greenness Index (TGI) [22]	–	–
Green Soil Adjusted Vegetation Index (GSAVI) [69]	W, DV, SV, BUA, BS	73.91	Triangular Vegetation Index (TVI) [72]	W, DV, SV	74.15
Green Vegetation Index (GVI)* [73]	DV, SV, BUA	57.30	Urban Index (UI) [74]	BUA	76.66
Built-up Index (IBI) [75]	DV, SV	74.75	Visible Atmospherically Resistant Index (VARI) [76]	W, DV, SV	68.34
Infrared Percentage Vegetation Index (IPVI) [77]	W, DV, SV, BUA, BS	69.10	Visible-Band Difference Vegetation Index (VDVI) [78]	DV, SV	66.70

(*continued*)

Table 2. (*continued*)

Spectral Index	LU/LC	OA (%)	Spectral Index	LU/LC	OA (%)
Modified Bare Soil Index (MBSI) [43]	W, DV, SV	73.22	Vegetation Index of Biotic Integrity (VIBI) [79]	DV, SV	66.57
Modified Chlorophyll Absorption Ratio Index1 (MCARI1) [80]	DV, SV	64.28	Wide Dynamic Range Vegetation Index (WDRVI) [16]	W, DV, SV	78.87
Modified Chlorophyll Absorption Ratio Index (MCARI2) [80]	W, DV, SV, BUA, BS	82.24	Water index 2015 (WI2015) [25]	W	99.81
MERIS Global Vegetation Index (MGVI) [81]	W, DV, SV	76.88	Worldview Improved Vegetative Index (WV-VI) [82]	W, DV, SV, BUA, BS	75.47
Modification of Normalized Difference Snow Index (MNDSI) [83]	W, MA	76.55	Yellow Stuff Index (YVI)* [84]	DV, SV	66.70
Modification of normalised difference water index (MNDWI) [85]	W, BUA	74.62			

4 Conclusion

Over the years, several indices have been introduced to bring out LU/LC data. Currently, although each of them shows different performance, the optimal index for all LU/LC class has not been detected yet. Thus, this research explored the performance of 85 indices. All investigated indices showed the ability of automatically extracting LU/LC information in a short time independently from the size of the study area. Nevertheless, just three of them (AWEI, NDBaI and NDBaI2) were able to detect the main LU/LC categories (bare soil, built-up areas, water, mining areas, sparse and dense vegetation). Thus, the best performance, in terms of number of detected classes and Overall Accuracy, was shown by NDBaI2 index. Similarly, the optimal index for revealing each LU/LC category was assessed as well. Therefore, CVI, WI2015 and SwiRed were the best indices to detect "green areas", water and built-up areas, respectively. An interesting performance was presented by STRed index as well, since it can quickly distinguish water, vegetated and mining areas generating a really high accurate outcome.

GEE environment appeared to be the best solution to automatize the processing step, speeding up all the procedure. Therefore, this study confirms also the great potentiality of GEE in handling geospatial big data, reducing acquiring and processing time as well as operational cost.

References

1. Kumar, L., Mutanga, O.: Google earth engine applications since inception: usage, trends, and potential. Rem. Sens **10**(10), 1509 (2018)
2. Gorelick, N., Hancher, M., Dixon, M., Ilyushchenko, S., Thau, D., Moore, R.: Google earth engine: planetary-scale geospatial analysis for everyone. Rem. Sens. Environ. **202**, 18–27 (2017)
3. Susaki, J., Shibasaki, R.: Maximum likelihood method modified in estimating a prior probability and in improving misclassification errors. Int. Arch. Photogram. Rem. Sens. **33**, 1499–1504 (2000)
4. Abdi, A.: Land cover and land use classification performance of machine learning algorithms in a boreal landscape using Sentinel-2 data. GISci. Rem. Sens. **57**, 1–20 (2020)
5. Capolupo, A., Kooistra, L., Boccia, L.: A novel approach for detecting agricultural terraced landscapes from historical and contemporaneous photogrammetric aerial photos. Int. J. Appl. Earth Obs. Geoinf. **73**, 800–810 (2018)
6. Crocetto, N., Tarantino, E.: A class-oriented strategy for features extraction from multidate ASTER imagery. Rem. Sens. **1**(4), 1171–1189 (2009)
7. Patel, N.N., Angiuli, E., et al.: Multitemporal settlement and population mapping from Landsat using Google Earth Engine. Int. J. Appl. Earth Obs. Geoinf. **35**, 199–208 (2015)
8. Mateo-García, G., Gómez-Chova, L., Amorós-López, J., Muñoz-Marí, J., Camps-Valls, G.: Multitemporal cloud masking in the Google Earth Engine. Rem. Sens. **10**(7), 1079 (2018)
9. Capolupo, A., Kooistra, L., Berendonk, C., Boccia, L., Suomalainen, J.: Estimating plant traits of grasslands from UAV-acquired hyperspectral images: a comparison of statistical approaches. ISPRS Int. J. Geo-Inf. **4**(4), 2792–2820 (2015)
10. Kazakis, N., Kougias, I., Patsialis, T.: Assessment of flood hazard areas at a regional scale using an index-based approach and analytical hierarchy process: application in Rhodope-Evros region, Greece. Sci. Total Environ. **538**, 555–563 (2015)
11. Southworth, J.: An assessment of Landsat TM band 6 thermal data for analysing land cover in tropical dry forest regions. Int. J. Remote Sens. **25**, 689–706 (2004)
12. Yusuf, B.L., He, Y.: Application of hyperspectral imaging sensor to differentiate between the moisture and reflectance of healthy and infected tobacco leaves. Afr. J. Agric. Res. **6**(29), 6267–6280 (2011)
13. Li, S., Chen, X.: A new bare-soil index for rapid mapping developing areas using landsat 8 data. Int. Arch. Photogram. Rem. Sens. Spat. Inf. Sci. **40**(4), 139 (2014)
14. Capolupo, A., Monterisi, C., Tarantino, E.: Landsat images classification algorithm (LICA) to automatically extract land cover information in google earth engine environment. Rem. Sens. **12**(7), 1201 (2020)
15. Capolupo, A., Saponaro, M., Fratino, U., Tarantino, E.: Detection of spatio-temporal changes of vegetation in coastal areas subjected to soil erosion issue. Aquatic Ecosystem Health & Management. (in press)
16. Sakamoto, T., Gitelson, A.A., Wardlow, B.D., Verma, S.B., Suyker, A.E.: Estimating daily gross primary production of maize based only on MODIS WDRVI and shortwave radiation data. Rem. Sens. Environ. **115**(12), 3091–3101 (2011)
17. Pengra, B., Long, J., Dahal, D., Stehman, S.V., Loveland, T.R.: A global reference database from very high resolution commercial satellite data and methodology for application to Landsat derived 30 m continuous field tree cover data. Rem. Sens. Environ. **165**, 234–248 (2015)

18. Caprioli, M., Tarantino, E.: Accuracy assessment of per-field classification integrating very fine spatial resolution satellite imagery with topographic data. J. Geospat. Eng. **3**(2), 127–134 (2001)
19. Caprioli, M., Scognamiglio, A., Strisciuglio, G., Tarantino, E.: Rules and standards for spatial data quality in GIS environments. In: Proceedings of 21st International Cartographic Conference Durban, South Africa, 10–16 August 2003 (2003)
20. Feyisa, G.L., Meilby, H., Fensholt, R., Proud, S.R.: Automated water extraction index: a new technique for surface water mapping using landsat imagery. Rem. Sens. Environ. **140**, 23–35 (2014)
21. Misra, P.N.: Kauth-Thomas brightness and greenness axes. Contract NASA, 23–46 (1977)
22. Broge, N.H., Leblanc, E.: Comparing prediction power and stability of broadband and hyperspectral vegetation indices for estimation of green leaf area index and canopy chlorophyll density. Rem.0 Sens. Environ. **76**(2), 156–172 (2001)
23. Zhao, H., Chen, X.: Use of normalized difference bareness index in quickly mapping bare areas from TM/ETM + . In: International Geoscience and Remote Sensing Symposium, vol. 3, p. 1666 (2005)
24. Chandra, P.: Performance evaluation of vegetation indices using remotely sensed data. Int. J. Geomatics Geosci. **2**(1), 231–240 (2011)
25. Fisher, A., Flood, N., Danaher, T.: Comparing Landsat water index methods for automated water classification in eastern Australia. Rem. Sens. Environ. **175**, 167–182 (2016)
26. Karnieli, A., Kaufman, Y.J., Remer, L., Wald, A.: AFRI—aerosol free vegetation index. Rem. Sens. Environ. **77**(1), 10–21 (2001)
27. Gong, P., Pu, R., Biging, G.S., Larrieu, M.R.: Estimation of forest leaf area index using vegetation indices derived from hyperion hyperspectral data. IEEE Trans. Geosci. Rem. Sens. **40**, 1355–1362 (2003)
28. Qi, J., Chehbouni, A., Huete, A.R., Kerr, Y.H., Sorooshian, S.: A modified soil adjusted vegetation index. Rem. Sens. Environ. **48**, 119–126 (1994)
29. Kaufman, Y.J., Tanre, D.: Atmospherically resistant vegetation index (ARVI) for EOS-MODIS. IEEE Trans. Geosci. Rem. Sens. **30**(2), 261–270 (1992)
30. Jackson, R.D., Slater, P.N., Pinter, P.J.: Adjusting the tasselled-cap brightness and greenness factors for atmospheric path radiance and absorption on a pixel by pixel basis. Int. J. Rem. Sens. **4**(2), 313–323 (1983)
31. Chen, J.M.: Evaluation of vegetation indices and a modified simple ratio for boreal applications. Can. J. Rem. Sens. **22**(3), 229–242 (1996)
32. Ashburn, P.: The vegetative index number and crop identification. In: The LACIE Symposium, Proceedings of the Technical Session, USA, Houston, TX, USA (1978)
33. Chen, X.L., Zhao, H., Li, P., Yin, Z.: Remote sensing image-based analysis of the relationship between urban heat island and land use/cover changes. Rem. Sens. Environ. **104**, 133–146 (2006)
34. Li, H., et al.: Mapping urban bare land automatically from Landsat imagery with a simple index. Rem. Sens. **9**(3), 249 (2017)
35. Bouzekri, S., Lasbet, A.A., Lachehab, A.: A new spectral index for extraction of built-up area using Landsat-8 data. J. Indian Soc. Rem. Sens. **43**(4), 867–873 (2017)
36. Sinha, P., Verma, N.K.: Urban built-up area extraction and change detection of adama municipal area using time-series landsat images. Int. J. Adv. Rem. Sens. GIS **5**(8), 1886–1895 (2016)
37. Deng, C., Wu, C.: BCI: A biophysical composition index for remote sensing of urban environments. Rem. Sens. Environ. **127**, 247–259 (2012)

38. Vescovo, L., Gianelle, D.: Using the MIR bands in vegetation indices for the estimation of grassland biophysical parameters from satellite remote sensing in the Alps region of Trentino (Italy). Adv. Space Res. **41**, 1764–1772 (2008)
39. Bouhennache, R., Bouden, T., Taleb-Ahmed, A., Cheddad, A.: A new spectral index for the extraction of built-up land features from Landsat 8 satellite imagery. Geocarto Int. **34**(14), 1531–1551 (2019)
40. Luo, N., Wan, T., Hao, H., Lu, Q.: Fusing high-spatial-resolution remotely sensed imagery and OpenStreetMap data for land cover classification over urban areas. Rem. Sens. **11**(1), 88 (2019)
41. Kaimaris, D., Patias, P.: Identification and area measurement of the built-up area with the built-up index (BUI). Int. J. Adv. Rem. Sens. GIS **5**(6), 1844–1858 (2016)
42. Zha, Y., Gao, J., Ni, S.: Use of normalized difference built-up index in automatically mapping urban areas from TM imagery. Int. J. Rem. Sens. **24**(3), 583–594 (2003)
43. Zhang, S., Yang, K., Li, M., Ma, Y., Sun, M.: Combinational biophysical composition index (CBCI) for effective mapping biophysical composition in urban areas. IEEE Access **6**, 41224–41237 (2018)
44. Xu, H.: Analysis of impervious surface and its impact on urban heat environment using the normalized difference impervious surface index (NDISI). Photogram. Eng. Rem. Sens. **76**(5), 557–565 (2010)
45. Gitelson, A.A., Kaufman, Y.J., Merzlyak, M.N.: Relationships between leaf chlorophyll content and spectral reflectance and algorithms for non-destructive chlorophyll assessment in higher plant leaves. J. Plant Physiol. **160**, 271–282 (2003)
46. Jin, S., Sader, S.A.: Comparison of time series tasseled cap wetness and the normalized difference moisture index in detecting forest disturbances. Rem. Sens. Environ. **94**(3), 364–372 (2005)
47. Van Deventer, A.P., Ward, A.D., Gowda, P.H., Lyon, J.G.: Using thematic mapper data to identify contrasting soil plains and tillage practices. Photogram. Eng. Rem. Sens. **63**, 87–93 (1997)
48. Davies, D., Bouldin, D.: A clustering separation measure. IEEE Trans. Pattern Anal. Mach. Intell. **1**, 224–227 (1979)
49. Rouse Jr, J., Haas, R.H., Schell, J.A., Deering, D.W.: Monitoring vegetation systems in the Great Plains with ERTS (1974)
50. Rasul, A., et al.: Applying built-up and bare-soil indices from landsat 8 to cities in dry climates. Land **7**(3), 81 (2018)
51. McFeeters, S.K.: The use of the Normalized Difference Water Index (NDWI) in the delineation of open water features. Int. J. Rem. Sens. **17**(7), 1425–1432 (1996)
52. Tucker, C.J.: A spectral method for determining the percentage of green herbage material in clipped samples. Rem. Sens. Environ. **9**(2), 175–181 (1980)
53. Goel, N.S., Qin, W.: Influences of canopy architecture on relationships between various vegetation indices and LAI and FPAR: a computer simulation. Rem. Sens. Rev. **104**, 309–347 (1994)
54. As-syakur, A., Adnyana, I., Arthana, I.W., Nuarsa, I.W.: Enhanced built-up and bareness index (EBBI) for mapping built-up and bare land in an urban area. Remote Sensing **4**(10), 2957–2970 (2012)
55. Rondeaux, G., Steven, M., Baret, F.: Optimization of soil-adjusted vegetation indices. Rem. Sens. Environ. **55**(2), 95–107 (1996)
56. Chen, J., Yang, K., Chen, S., Yang, C., Zhang, S., He, L.: Enhanced normalized difference index for impervious surface area estimation at the plateau basin scale. J. Appl. Rem. Sens. **13**(1), 016502 (2019)

57. Roujean, J.L., Breon, F.M.: Estimating PAR absorbed by vegetation from bidirectional reflectance measurements. Rem. Sens. Environ. **51**(3), 375–384 (1995)

58. Matsushita, B., Yang, W., Chen, J., Onda, Y., Qiu, G.: Sensitivity of the enhanced vegetation index (EVI) and normalized difference vegetation index (NDVI) to topographic effects: a case study in high-density cypress forest. Sensors **7**(11), 2636–2651 (2007)

59. Pearson, R.L., Miller, L.D.: Remote mapping of standing crop biomass for estimation of the productivity of the shortgrass prairie, Pawnee National Grasslands, Colorado. In: Eighth International Symposium on Remote Sensing of Environment, University of Michigan (1972)

60. Gitelson, A.A., Kaufman, Y.J., Merzlyak, M.N.: Use of a green channel in remote sensing of global vegetation from EOS-MODIS. Rem. Sens. Environ. **58**(3), 289–298 (1996)

61. Huete, A.R.: A soil-adjusted vegetation index (SAVI). Rem. Sens. Environ. **25**(3), 295–309 (1988)

62. Zheng, Q., Zeng, Y., Deng, J., Wang, K., Jiang, R., Ye, Z.: "Ghost cities" identification using multi-source remote sensing datasets: a case study in Yangtze River Delta. Appl. Geogr. **80**, 112–121 (2017)

63. Thompson, D.R., Wehmanen, O.A.: Using landsat digital data to detect moisture stress in corn-soybean growing regions. Photogram. Eng. Rem. Sens. **46**(8), 1087–1093 (1980)

64. Wu, W.: The generalized difference vegetation index (GDVI) for dryland characterization. Rem. Sens. **6**(2), 1211–1233 (2014)

65. Lymburner, L., Beggs, P.J., Jacobson, C.R.: Estimation of canopy-average surface-specific leaf area using Landsat TM data. Photogram. Eng. Rem. Sens. **66**(2), 183–192 (2000)

66. Pinty, B., Verstraete, M.M.: GEMI: a non-linear index to monitor global vegetation from satellites. Vegetation **101**(1), 15–20 (1992)

67. Jordan, C.: Derivation of leaf area index from quality of light on the forest floor Ecology. Ecology **50**, 663–666 (1969)

68. Louhaichi, M., Borman, M.M., Johnson, D.E.: Spatially located platform and aerial photography for documentation of grazing impacts on wheat. Geocarto Int. **16**(19), 65–70 (2001)

69. Sripada, R.P., Heiniger, R.W., White, J.G., Meijer, A.D.: Aerial color infrared photography for determining early in-season nitrogen requirements in corn. Agron. J. **98**(4), 968–977 (2006)

70. Bandari, A., Asalhi, H., Teillet, P.M.: Transformed difference vegetation index (TDVI) for vegetation cover mapping. In: IEEE International geoscience and remote sensing symposium, vol. 5, pp. 3053–3055 (2002)

71. Motohka, T., Nasahara, K.N., Oguma, H., Tsuchida, S.: Applicability of green-red vegetation index for remote sensing of vegetation phenology. Rem. Sens. **2**(10), 2369–2387 (2010)

72. Hunt Jr., E.R., Doraiswamy, P.C., McMurtrey, J.E., Daughtry, C.S., Perry, E.M., Akhmedov, B.: A visible band index for remote sensing leaf chlorophyll content at the canopy scale. Int. J. Appl. Earth Observ. **21**, 103–112 (2013)

73. Jackson, R.: Spectral indices in n-space. Rem. Sens. Environ. **13**, 409–421 (1983)

74. Kawamura, M.: Relation between social and environmental conditions in Colombo Sri Lanka and the urban index estimated by satellite remote sensing data. In: Proceedings 51st Annual Conference of the Japan Society of Civil Engineers, pp. 190–191 (1996)

75. Han-Qiu, X.U.: A new index-based built-up index (IBI) and its eco-environmental significance. Rem. Sens. Technol. Appl. **22**(3), 301–308 (2011)

76. Gittelson, A.A., Stark, R., Grits, U., Rundquist, D., Kaufman, Y., Derry, D.: Vegetation and soil lines in visible spectral space: a concept and technique for remote estimation of vegetation fraction. Int. J. Rem. Sens. **23**, 2537–2562 (2002)

77. Crippen, R.E.: Calculating the vegetation index faster. Rem. Sens. Environ. **34**(1), 71–73 (1990)
78. Liu, F., Liu, S.H., Xiang, Y.: Study on remote sensing monitoring of vegetation coverage in the field. Trans. CSAM **45**(11), 250–257 (2014)
79. Stathakis, D., Perakis, K., Savin, I.: Efficient segmentation of urban areas by the VIBI. Int. J. Rem. Sens. **33**(20), 6361–6377 (2012)
80. Haboudane, D., Miller, J.R., Pattey, E., Zarco-Tejada, P.J., Strachan, I.B.: Hyperspectral vegetation indices and novel algorithms for predicting green LAI of crop canopies: modeling and validation in the context of precision agriculture. Rem. Sens. Environ. **90**, 337–352 (2004)
81. Gobron, N., Pinty, B., Verstraete, M., Govaerts, Y.: The MERIS global vegetation index (MGVI): description and preliminary application. Int. J. Rem. Sens. **20**(9), 1917–1927 (1999)
82. Wolf, A.F.: Using WorldView-2 Vis-NIR multispectral imagery to support land mapping and feature extraction using normalized difference index ratios. In: Algorithms and Technologies for Multispectral, Hyperspectral, and Ultraspectral Imagery XVIII, vol. 8390 (2012)
83. Fall, A.G.U.: Snow monitoring using remote sensing data: modification of normalized difference snow index (2016)
84. Kauth, R.J., Thomas, G.S.: The tasselled cap—a graphic description of the spectral temporal development of agricultural crops as seen by Landsat. In: Proceedings of Symposium on Machine Processing of Remotely Sensed Data, pp. 41–51 (1976)
85. Xu, H.: Modification of normalised difference water index (NDWI) to enhance open water features in remotely sensed imagery. Int. J. Rem. Sens. **27**(14), 3025–3033 (2006)

Post-processing of Pixel and Object-Based Land Cover Classifications of Very High Spatial Resolution Images

Tommaso Sarzana[1] , Antonino Maltese[1(✉)] ,
Alessandra Capolupo[2] , and Eufemia Tarantino[2]

[1] Università degli Studi di Palermo, 91011 Palermo, PA, Italy
antonino.maltese@unipa.it
[2] Politecnico di Bari, 70125 Bari, BA, Italy

Abstract. The state of the art is plenty of classification methods. Pixel-based methods include the most traditional ones. Although these achieved high accuracy when classifying remote sensing images, some limits emerged with the advent of very high-resolution images that enhanced the spectral heterogeneity within a class.

Therefore, in the last decade, new classification methods capable of overcoming these limits have undergone considerable development. Within this research, we compared the performances of an Object-based and a Pixel-Based classification method, the Random Forests (RF) and the Object-Based Image Analysis (OBIA), respectively. Their ability to quantify the extension and the perimeter of the elements of each class was evaluated through some performance indices. Algorithm parameters were calibrated on a subset, then, applied on the whole image. Since these algorithms perform accurately in quantifying the elements areas, but worse if we consider the perimeters length, hence, the aim of this research was to setup some post-processing techniques to improve, in particular, this latter performance.

Algorithms were applied on peculiar classes of an area comprising the *Isole dello Stagnone di Marsala* oriented natural reserve, in north-western corner of Si-cily, salt pans and agricultural settlements. The area was covered by a World View-2 multispectral image consisting of eight spectral bands spanning from visible to near-infrared wavelengths and characterized by a spatial resolution of two meters. Both classification algorithms did not quantify accurately object perimeters; especially RF. Post-processing algorithm improved the estimates, which however remained more accurate for OBIA than for RF.

Keywords: Random forest · Object-Based image analysis · Vector based generalization

1 Introduction

A large amount of studies compared Pixel-Based and Object-Based classification methods based on different image data sources [1–4] are present in literature. Aggarwal *et al.* [5] documented that the Object-Based methods allow achieving a higher accuracy

© Springer Nature Switzerland AG 2020
O. Gervasi et al. (Eds.): ICCSA 2020, LNCS 12252, pp. 797–812, 2020.
https://doi.org/10.1007/978-3-030-58811-3_57

than pixel-based methods, since these latter analyze only the spectral features while the former taking advantage also of the spatial features during the segmentation process. Recently, Cai *et al.* [6] proposed new similarity metrics to evaluate the accuracy of objects extraction from Earth Observation images in terms of area and perimeter.

Since pixel-based classification methods are based only spectral characteristics of single pixel produce erroneous small classes. Thus, post-classification algorithms were implemented to reduce the occurrence of these classes through majority focal filters [*e.g.*, 7, 8].

Object-based methods firstly groups neighboring pixels into objects through segmentation [*e.g.*, 9]. Thus, although errors always occur, they show up less frequently.

Jensen *et al.* [10] proposed a size-based filter to select and remove classes having areas smaller than a threshold.

However, classification output can be improved by applying both cleaning and smoothing post-processing algorithms. Snakes algorithms, in particular, represent a powerful tool to correct the pixelated edges derived from the classification of raster images. An overview of line smoothing algorithms in automated generalization is presented by Weibel [11]. The aim of this research was to reckon if smoothing and cleaning post-processing algorithms could be used to improve the classification accuracy in terms of area and perimeter.

2   Materials

2.1   Study Area

The *Stagnone di Marsala* is the largest coastal lagoon in Sicily (southern Italy). It is framed between 277400 and 274030 from West to East and 4187160 and 4199100 from South to North (UTM WGS84). The lagoon was declared a Regional Natural Reserve since it constitutes a peculiar ecosystem characterized by phanerogams such as Posidonia oceanica, Caulerpa prolifera and Cymodocea nodosa [*Ciraolo et al.* 12]. Isola Lunga is the largest island of the reserve. It results from the union of three small islands through salt pans. Indeed, historically the main activity practiced in the lagoon is the production of salt by evaporating the water channeled into the salt pans.

The salt collection begins in July and lasts until September/October. The raw salt is piled up in spaces called *arioni* and exposed to the first rains, which wash away the magnesium sulphate, then, the piles are covered with tiles.

The geomorphology of the coastal area is marked by a succession of marine terraces which gives the landscape a flat structure. The slope of this coastal plain in the EW direction is ≈1° going up towards an inland slightly hilly area at 100–150 m altitude.

Main cultivations are vineyards, often overlooking the sea and in any case exposed to intense sun exposure, growing on clayey sometimes rich in red soils and sandy soils. The climate is Mediterranean-insular, with hot dry summers, with sea breezes, sometimes hot African winds. The average yearly temperature is ≈18 °C, and the average annual rainfall ≈500 mm.

Cultivar characterized by white berried grapes are breed for the production of gold and amber wine, while cultivar with red berried grapes are breed for the production of ruby wine as regulated by the disciplinary of production of the Controlled Designation of Origin of the Marsala wine. The study area and the location of four representative plots are reported in Fig. 1.

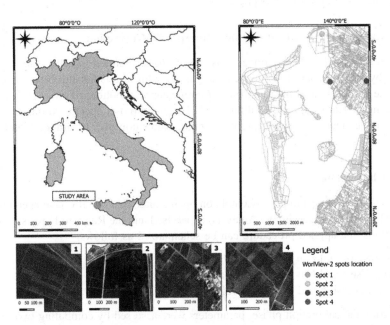

Fig. 1. Study area: location of the study area in Italy (top-left panel); map of the study area with location of the four spots (green, cyan, blue and red spots in the top right-panel) and natural color composition of the spots (lower panels). (Color figure online)

2.2 Data

Data used in this research includes satellite images and in situ spectroradiometric signatures.

Earth Observation Images. The research has been applied on a WorldView-2 (VW2) multispectral satellite image acquired on 6 August 2011 at 10/10: 30 UTC that covers a ≈58 hectares area. The multispectral image provides eight spectral bands in the visible and near infrared (NIR) parts of the spectrum: Coastal (400–450 nm), Blue: 450–510 nm, Yellow (585–625 nm), Green: 510–580 nm, Red Edge (705–745 nm), Near-IR2: 860–1040 nm, Near-IR1: 770–895 nm. The dynamic range is 11-bits per pixel.

Spectroradiometric Data. Spectroradiometric data were acquired on dark and bright natural surfaces during the satellite overpass using an ASD Field Spec Pro FR spectroradiometer covering the full solar reflected spectrum (350–2500 nm) with 10 nm spectral resolution.

3 Methodology

Smoothing and cleaning procedures were applied on classified images. Two wide-spread pixel-based and vector-based classification methods were chosen as representative of two different paradigms. Raster images were erstwhile calibrated in spectral reflectance at bottom of atmosphere.

3.1 Radiometric Calibration and Atmospheric Correction

The WorldView 02 (WV2) image was radiometric calibrated in reflectance and corrected by the atmospheric influence by setting up a linear relationship between spectral radiance at top of atmosphere and spectral reflectance at bottom of atmosphere, R_0 (−) according to Karpouzli and Malthus [13]. To this purpose, spectroradiometric signatures were collected in situ during the satellite acquisition over natural dark and bright targets.

3.2 Classification

Two classification techniques available on open-source SAGA GIS have been applied: an OBIA (Object-based Image Analysis) supervised and the Random Forests. For both algorithms, the applied procedure can be schematized as follows:

- Parameters setup on a subset of the study area;
- Land Use Land Cover (LULC) classification;
- Post-processing and accuracy evaluation.

During the calibration phase, parameters were assessed by computing two indices: the Areal Overall-Accuracy and the Perimeter Index-Accuracy.

To create a reference or ground truth layer a number of polygons for each class have been digitized on Google Earth. These polygons cover the whole image almost proportionally to the area of each class, following a random stratified criterion. The location of the ground truth polygons, indeed, was chosen for each class via random points generated by the *Random Points* tool of QGIS.

The ground truth polygonal layer was successively intersected with classification, allowing calculating the overall areal accuracy, AOA (%), as well as user and producer accuracies, *UA* (%) and *PA* (%), respectively (1).

$$AOA = \frac{\sum_i^n Aii}{A_{tot}} \times 100 \qquad (1)$$

where, n is number of classes; A_{ii} is area of the ith class correctly classified; A_{tot} is the total area.

To assess the accuracy with which the procedure reproduces the perimeters of the objects, a perimeter accuracy index, *PAI* (%), was defined as (2):

$$PAI = \left(1 - \frac{\sum_{i=1}^{n}\left|1 - \frac{\sum_{i=1}^{n_k} P_{obj_{i,k}}}{\sum_{i=1}^{n_k} P_{ref_{i,k}}}\right|}{n}\right) \times 100 \tag{2}$$

where, $P_{obj_{i,k}}$ is the perimeter of the ith object classified as class k; $P_{ref_{i,k}}$ is the perimeter of the ith object of the kth class in the ground truth layer.

The PAI was evaluated on polygons characterized by a degree of compactness less than a threshold. The compactness was evaluated via the Normalized Perimeter Index, NPI (−) [14]. The threshold has been chosen based on the NPI frequency distribution equal to 2.

$$NPI = \frac{P_{obj}}{P_{cea}} < 2 \tag{3}$$

where, P_{cea} is the perimeter of a circle with equivalent area.

Random Forest Classification. The Random Forests is among the most efficient Machine Learning pixel-based algorithms for images classification. High performances are achievable with a single calibration parameter, the $nTree$ [15]. This parameter regulates the number of trees that make up the random forest. The algorithm creates a multiple decision trees by analyzing the training dataset, so that many combinations of predictive variables are explored, by maximizing the non-correlation between trees and minimizing the over-fitting [16]. After the learning phase, the most recurrent output from the trees is chosen as predicted class. The $nTree$ parameter of the RF algorithm implemented in SAGA GIS was calibrated on the subset. The following orders of magnitude were tested for calibration: $nTree$ = 10, 100, 1000 and 10000. In addition, the computational time and the correlation increase of the probabilities of correct prediction were also evaluated. The determination coefficient, r^2, increased with the number of tree. The calibration returned $nTree$ = 1000 as the suitable value for this case study, with r^2 = 0.99%, and a computational time of one tenth of that required by 10000 trees.

OBIA Supervised Classification. The OBIA algorithm processes an image through a preliminary segmentation phase; then, classifying the segments based their spectral characteristics. A Minimum Distance method was chosen to classify the segments. The algorithm, implemented in SAGA GIS, has been calibrated by tuning the Band Width for Seed Point Generation parameter. This parameter drives the number and the size of the segments. The seeds, indeed, defines the distance within which to search for the point of minimum spectral variance [17]. The greater this distance the more hetero-geneous the spectral characteristics of the segments. The following Band Width values were chosen: 2, 4, 10 and 20 m. The Band Width achieving the best performance (10 m, AOA 91.5% PAI 41%) was chosen to classify the whole study area.

3.3   Post Processing

Algorithms of cleaning and smoothing were applied to remove small classes mainly resulting from images heterogeneities and smoothing to remove the pixelated boundary of the objects resulting from the classification of the raster images.

Smoothing. An algorithm for vector smoothing has been applied to the cleaned polygon vector. The algorithm is the *Snakes* included in the module *v.generalize* of Grass. The snakes algorithm was introduced by Kass *et al.* [18] that defined the energy of a snake [19] by considering an inner and an external energy E_I and E_{ext} with respect to arc length s.

$$E_S = \int_0^1 (E_E + E_I)ds \qquad (4)$$

The minimization of E_S allows obtaining a smoothed line or polygonal vector. Configuration parameters have been fixed to the default values ($\alpha = 1$, $\beta = 1$ and 1 iteration).

Cleaning. A cleaning tool from Grass *v.clean* with option *rmarea* to remove small polygonal areas and union with adjacent polygons sharing the longest arc. Configuration threshold has been set to 150 m^2 after visual inspection of the classifications.

4   Results

Confusion matrices summarizing user accuracy (UA %) and producer accuracy (PA %) for each class, and the areal overall accuracy of each classification method are reported in Tables 1 and 2 for RF and Tables 4 and 5 for OBIA.

The relative errors for each class and the average perimeter accuracy for each classification method are reported in Table 3 and 6 for RF and OBIA, respectively.

Some spots are also reported to exemplify the behavior of the classification and post-processing algorithms over each class.

4.1   Pixels Based

The following spot (Fig. 2) shows that the RF algorithm distinguishes bare soil from vegetation, while non dense and dense vegetation are difficult to distinguish.

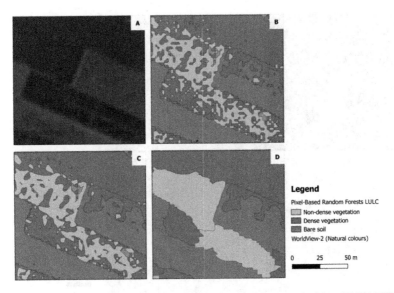

Fig. 2. Spot 1, vegetated and bare soils: A) WV2 Natural colours composition; B) RF LULC; C) after smoothing; D) after cleaning

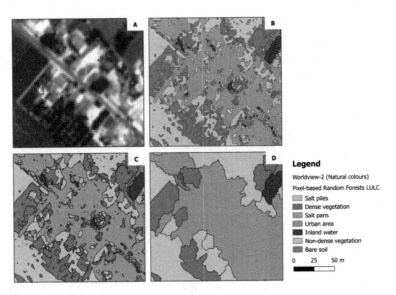

Fig. 3. Spot 2, urban area: A) WV2 Natural colours composition; B) RF LULC; C) after smoothing; D) after cleaning.

In Fig. 3 are clearly evident some classification errors, indeed urban and salt classes are confused. Omissions and commissions errors are partly reduced by applying the cleaning algorithm.

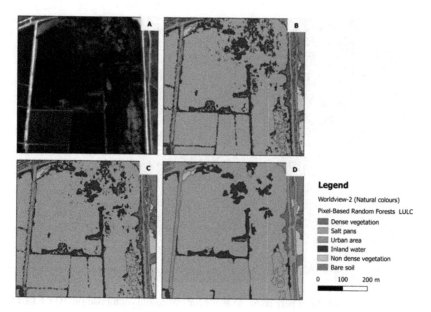

Fig. 4. Spot 3, salt pans: A) WV2 Natural colours composition; B) RF LULC; C) after smoothing; D) after cleaning.

The last spot (Fig. 4) exemplifies the behaviour of the RF classifier over salt pans. The need to remove polygons with small areas is evident. This need diminishes in OBIA classification (Fig. 7).

Table 1. RF confusion matrix with User Accuracy (*UA* %), Producer Accuracy (*PA* %) and Area overall accuracy (*AOA* %)

Ground truth → Classification ↓	Acronym	NDV	DV	BS	SPa	SPi	IW	UA	*PA*
Non-dense vegetation	NDV	7.7	1.2	0.5				0.1	**81.1**
Dense vegetation	DV	2.4	15.5	2.1			0.1		**77.1**
Bare soil	BS	0.5	2.0	11.8			0.2		**81.4**
Salt pans	SPa				33.8	0.1	3.3	0.4	**89.9**
Salt piles	SPi				0.1	5.2	0.1	1.6	**74.3**
Inland water	IW		0.8	0.1	0.3		4.3		**78.2**
Urban area	UA	0.6	0.4	1.1		0.1	0.2	3.3	**57.9**
	UA	**68.8**	**77.9**	**75.6**	**98.8**	**96.3**	**52.4**	**61.1**	OA **81.7**

Summarizing, the lowest *PA* was 57.9% for urban areas; while, the lowest *UA* was 52.4% for inland water whose ground truths are often are classified salt piles. Overall, the *AOA* was 81.7%.

Table 2. RF confusion matrix after post processing with User accuracy *UA* (%), Producer accuracy *PA* (%), Areal Overall Accuracy *AOA* (%).

Ground truth → / Classification ↓	Acronym	NDV	DV	BS	SPa	SPi	IW	UA	*PA*
Non-dense vegetation	NDV	8.1	0.6	0.4					**89.0**
Dense vegetation	DV	1.9	15.5	1.5					**82.0**
Bare soil	BS	0.4	2.1	13.0					**83.9**
Salt pans	SPa				35.1		3.2	0.2	**91.2**
Salt piles	SPi				0.1	5.1	0.1	1.4	**76.1**
Inland water	IW		0.8		0.1		4.5		**83.3**
Urban area	UA	0.4	0.5	1.0	0.0	0.1	0.1	3.7	**63.8**
	UA	**75.0**	**79.5**	**81.8**	**99.4**	**98.1**	**57.0**	**69.8**	*AOA* **85.1**

After post-processing, the *PA* for urban areas increased to 63.8%; while, the *UA* for inland water increased to 57.0% for whose ground truths are still often classified salt piles. Overall, the *AOA* increased to 85.1%. The analysis of the probability of random agreement evaluated according to the Cohen's kappa resulted in *K* equal to 0.77 after the RF classification, then, it raised to 0.81 after the post processing.

Table 3. RF relative errors ρ_E (%) of class perimeters with NPI < 2 and after post-processing

Class	Acronym	Classification ρ_E	Post-processing ρ_E
Non-dense vegetation	NDV	14	17
Dense vegetation	DV	22	19
Bare soil	BS	27	28
Salt pans	Spa	133	137
Salt piles	SPi	42	29
Inland water	IW	33	34
Urban area	UA	80	56
Perimeter accuracy index:		49.5	54.3

The accuracy in classifying the object perimeters was very low (49.51% on the average). The relative error decreased significantly after post-processing for salt piles and for urban areas (−13% and −24%, respectively). Accuracy achieved remains quite low since classification algorithms are not able to distinguish two objects belonging to the same class when the splitting element has a thickness lower that the spatial resolution of the images (for instance, two contiguous salt pans not identified as different objects since their boundary wall was smaller than half a meter).

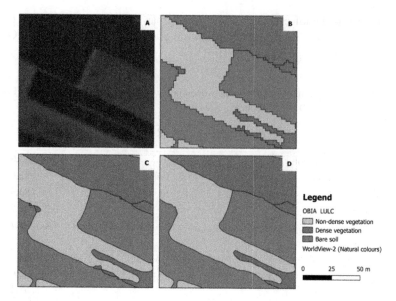

Fig. 5. Spot 1, vegetated and bare soils: A) WV2 Natural colours composition; B) OBIA LULC; C) after smoothing; D) after cleaning.

4.2 Object Based

The following spots exemplify omission and commission errors between vegetated and bare soil (Fig. 5) and among urban area, salt piles and bare soil (Fig. 6). These errors are reduced by applying the cleaning algorithm.

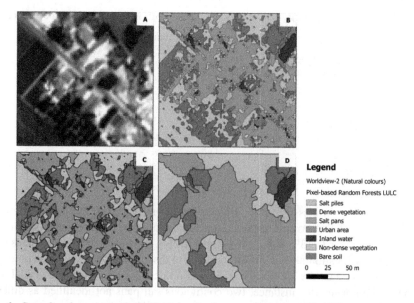

Fig. 6. Spot 2, urban area: A) WV2 Natural colours composition; B) OBIA LULC; C) after smoothing; D) after cleaning.

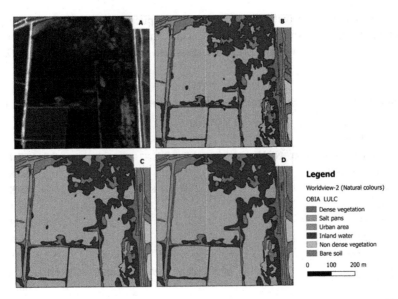

Fig. 7. Spot 3, salt pans: A) WV2 CIR composition; B) OBIA LULC; C) after smoothing, D) after cleaning.

The spot in Fig. 7 exemplifies the effects of post processing on salt pans. Differently than in RF classification, the segmentation in OBIA, incorporates in homogeneous areas adjacent pixels with some heterogeneity, thus reducing the need of post processing.

Table 4. OBIA confusion matrix with User accuracy *UA* (%), Producer accuracy *PA* (%), Areal Overall Accuracy *AOA* (%).

Ground truth → Classification ↓	Acronym	AP	DV	BS	SPa	SPi	IW	UA	*PA*
Non-dense vegetation	AP	4.0	0.8	0.1				0.9	**69.0**
Dense vegetation	DV	1.5	5.2	1.3				0.1	**64.2**
Bare soil	BS	0.3	1.4	24.3	0.2		0.2	0.7	**89.7**
Salt pans	SPa				38.8	0.5	0.6		**97.2**
Salt piles	SPi			0.2	2.1	3.1		2.5	**39.2**
Inland water	IW				0.9		3.8		**80.9**
Urban area	UA		0.1	0.6	0.2		0.1	5.7	**85.1**
	UA	**69.0**	**69.8**	**91.7**	**91.9**	**86.1**	**80.9**	**57.6**	*AOA* **84.7**

Summarizing, the lowest *PA* was 39.2% for salt piles a class, that often corresponds to salt pans and urban areas ground truths; while, the lowest *UA* was 57.6% for urban areas whose ground truths are often are classified salt piles. Overall, the *AOA* was 84.7%.

Table 5. OBIA confusion matrix after post processing with *UA* (%), *PA* (%) *AOA* (%)

Ground truth → Classification ↓	Acronym	NDV	DV	BS	SPa	SPi	IW	UA	*PA*
Non-dense vegetation	NDV	4.1	1.0	0.1				0.9	67.4
Dense vegetation	DV	1.5	5.3	1.3				0.1	64.8
Bare soil	BS	0.3	1.4	24.8	0.2		0.3	0.6	89.8
Salt pans	SPa				39.5	0.4	0.6		97.4
Salt piles	SPi			0.2	0.7	3.1		2.5	47.8
Inland water	IW				0.9		3.8		80.6
Urban area	UA			0.6	0.1			5.7	87.1
	UA	69.5	68.8	91.9	95.4	88.6	80.9	58.2	*AOA* 86.3

After the post-processing, the *PA* for salt piles increased to 47,8%, this class often corresponds to urban areas ground truths; while, the *UA* for urban areas increased to 58.2% with the urban area ground truth still sometimes classified as salt piles. Overall, the *AOA* slightly increased to 86.3% (+1.6%).

The expected agreement due to the case resulted in $K = 0.79$ after the OBIA classification, that increased to 0.81 after the post processing.

Table 6. OBIA ρ_E (%) of class perimeters with NPI < 2 and after post-processing

Class	Acronym	Classification ρ_E	Post-processing ρ_E
Non-dense vegetation	NDV	36	36
Dense vegetation	DV	39	38
Bare soil	BS	37	37
Salt pans	Spa	25	22
Salt piles	SPi	32	31
Inland water	IW	20	20
Urban area	UA	32	32
Perimeter accuracy index:		68.4	69.1

The accuracy in classifying the object perimeters was quite low (68.1% on the average). The relative error decreased slightly after post-processing (0–3%).

Accuracy in distinguish two objects belonging to a class when separated by an object having thickness lower 2 m (images spatial resolution) is enhanced by splitting the two objects during the segmentation phase. For instance, ρ_E was ∼130% for salt pans after RF classification (Table 3), while for the same class OBIA reached a $\rho_E \cong$ 25% (Table 6).

4.3   Comparison

The spot in Fig. 8 shows a comparison between OBIA and RF classification (panels B and C, respectively). It is clear that OBIA is more efficient in reducing classification errors due to spectral heterogeneity. Thus, post processing is more effective on RF (panel D) that in OBIA (panel E).

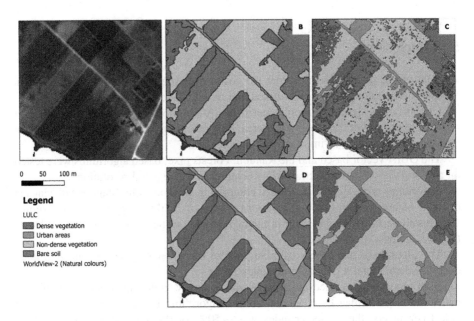

Fig. 8. Spot 4, OBIA vs. RF comparison: A) WV-2 Natural colours; B) Random Forests LULC; D) Post-processed OBIA LULC; E) Post-processed Random Forests LULC.

The comparison between the two classification methods shows that both of the classification methods accurately identified the classes and the object areas: the *AOA* were ≈81% and ≈85% for RF and OBIA, respectively (Table 7). However, RF requires a post-processing to reach accuracies comparable to that OBIA. Indeed, after post-processing, the *AOA* increased significantly for RF (up to ≈85%) while slightly increases for OBIA (≈86%). Objects perimeters were assessed with much lower accuracy. It was even lower that 50% for RF, while it was lower than 70% for OBIA. The OBIA algorithm, indeed takes is able to merge adjacent heterogeneous pixels to those characterizing a class during the segmentation process. Although the perimeter accuracy it increased significantly for RF (up to ≈55%) it remains lower than for OBIA. Differences are probably due to the classification units the pixel for the RF and the segment for the OBIA. Indeed, heterogeneity within pixels belonging to a class is higher than that of segments belonging to the same class, thus, increasing the need for a post processing of pixel-based classifications.

Table 7. RF vs. OBIA overall areal accuracy and perimeter accuracy indexes

Indexes	RF	RF post-processing	OBIA	OBIA post-processing
Area overall accuracy	81.5	85	84.7	86.3
Perimeter accuracy	49.5	54.3	68.4	69.1

5 Conclusions

The aim of this paper was to explore the post-processing techniques to improve areal and perimeter accuracy of a pixel-based and an object-based algorithm.

Classification algorithms implemented in SAGA GIS were calibrated on a subset and then applied over the whole study area. Post-processing algorithms implemented in GIS were applied then to improve the classification.

The OBIA vector based and the Random Forests pixel based algorithms were tested on a WorldView-2 multispectral image acquired at 2 m spatial resolution.

Algorithms were applied on an area comprising the Isole dello Stagnone di Marsala oriented natural reserve, in north-western corner of Sicily. In particular, algorithms were tested on Isola Lunga island in the lagoon and on the agricultural area settled in the eastern coast of the lagoon.

The algorithms parameters calibration were carried out by quantifying the areal overall accuracy and a perimeter accuracy index.

Both algorithms reached an areal overall accuracy higher than $\sim 80\%$; however, much lower performances characterized the algorithms in the quantification of the object perimeters: the perimeter index was $\sim 50\%$ for Random Forests and less than 70% for OBIA. Then, to enhance accuracies, two post-processing steps were developed: a smoothing algorithm (the Snakes algorithm implemented in *v.generalize*) to smooth pixelated polygons resulting from a raster classification; and a cleaning algorithm (*v.clean* with *rmarea* option) to remove small classes (<150 m^2) resulting from images spectral heterogeneities. The accuracy in reproducing objects perimeters increased significantly for RF (+5%) but even so remained lower than that OBIA.

We are planning to apply a machine learning classification method, such as a Random Forests, to an object-based segmentation, thus coupling the learning ability of the radiometric characteristics typical of machine learning and the minimization of the radiometric heterogeneity typical of an object based segmentation.

With the increasing availability of multispectral and hyperspectral images, as the number of spectral bands increases an analysis of spectral separability becomes progressively more necessary to assess the contribution of each band of the spectral separability.

Acknowledgments. The authors would like to thank G. Ciraolo for helping in collecting spectroradiometric data and for his technical advices.

References

1. Liu, D., Xia, F.: Assessing object-based classification: advantages and limitations. Rem. Sens. Lett. **1**(4), 187–194 (2010)
2. Tarantino, E., Figorito, B.: Mapping rural areas with widespread plastic covered vineyards using true color aerial data. Rem. Sens. **4**(7), 1913–1928 (2012)
3. Koc-San, D.: Evaluation of different classification techniques for the detection of glass and plastic greenhouses from WorldView-2 satellite imagery. J. Appl. Rem. Sens. **7**(1), 073553 (2013)
4. Tehrany, M.S., Pradhan, B., Jebuv, M.N.: A comparative assessment between object and pixel-based classification approaches for land use/land cover mapping using SPOT 5 imagery. Geocarto Int. **29**(4), 351–369 (2014)
5. Aggarwal, N., Srivastava, M., Dutta, M.: Comparative analysis of pixel-based and object-based classification of high resolution remote sensing images – a review. Int. J. Eng. Trends Technol. (IJETT) **38**(1), 5–11 (2016)
6. Cai, L., Shi, W., Miao, Z., Hao, M.: Accuracy assessment measures for object extraction from remote sensing images. Rem. Sens **10**(2), 303 (2108)
7. Tomas, I.L.: Spatial postprocessing of spectrally classified Landsat data. Photogram. Eng. Rem. Sens. **46**, 1201–1206 (1980)
8. Townshend, J.R.G.: The enhancement of computer classification by logical smoothing. Photogram. Eng. Rem. Sens. **52**, 213–221 (1986)
9. Benz, U.C., Hofmann, P., Willhauck, G., Lingenfelder, I., Heynen, M.: Multi-resolution, object-oriented fuzzy analysis of remote sensing data for GIS-ready information. ISPRS J. Photogram. Rem. Sens. **58**, 239–258 (2004)
10. Jensen, J.R., Qiu, F., Patterson, K.: A neural network image interpretation system to extract rural and urban land use and land cover information from remote sensor data. Geocarto Int. **16**(1), 1–10 (2001)
11. Weibel, R.: Generalization of spatial data: principles and selected algorithms. In: van Kreveld, M., Nievergelt, J., Roos, T., Widmayer, P. (eds.) CISM School 1996. LNCS, vol. 1340, pp. 99–152. Springer, Heidelberg (1997). https://doi.org/10.1007/3-540-63818-0_5
12. Ciraolo, G., Cox, E., La Loggia, G., Maltese, A.: The classification of submerged vegetation using hyperspectral MIVIS data. Ann. Geophys. **49**(1), 287–294 (2006)
13. Karpouzli, E., Malthus, T.: The empirical line method for the atmospheric correction of IKONOS imagery. Int. J. Rem. Sens. **24**, 1143–1150 (2003)
14. Pipitone, C., Maltese, A., Dardanelli, G., Capodici, F., Lo Brutto, M., La Loggia, G.: Detection of a reservoir water level using shape similarity metrics. In: Remote Sensing for Agriculture, Ecosystems, and Hydrology XIX, Proceedings, vol. 10421, p. 104211L (2017)
15. Duro, D., Franklin, E., Dubé, G.: A comparison of pixel-based and object-based image analysis with selected machine learning algorithms for the classification of agricultural landscapes using SPOT-5 HRG imagery. Rem. Sens. Environ. **1**(18), 259–272 (2012)
16. Breiman, L.: Random Forests. Mach. Learn. **45**, 5–32 (2001)
17. Böhner, J., Selige, T., Ringeler, A.: Image segmentation using representativeness analysis and region growing. Göttinger. Geogr. Abh. **115**, 29–38 (2006)

18. Kass, M., Witkin, A., Terzopoulos, D.: Snakes: active contour models. In: Proceedings of the First International Conference on Computer Vision, pp. 259–268. IEEE Computer Society Press (1987)
19. Burghardt, D.: Glättung mit Snakes. Festschrift zum 65. Geburtstag von Prof. Dr. Ing. habil. Siegfried Meier. TU Dresden (2002)

Evaluation of Changes in the City Fabric Using Multispectral Multi-temporal Geospatial Data: Case Study of Milan, Italy

Branka Cuca[(✉)]

Politecnico di Milano, 20133 Milan, Italy
branka.cuca@polimi.it

Abstract. In recent decades the global effects of climate change have requested for a more sustainable approach in thinking and planning of our cities, making them more inclusive, safe and resilient. In terms of consumption of natural resources and pollution, cities are seen as entities with most significant impact to the natural environment. Strategic policies focused on tackling the challenges induced by climate change suggest in fact the necessity to start from the management and operating models of the cities themselves. This study illustrates an initial evaluation of parameters for purposes of urban generation studies using optical multi-spectral satellite imagery from Landsat-5, Landsat-8 and Sentinel-2 missions. The changes in land occupation and urban density are the first aspects chosen to be examined for the period 1985–2020. The focus was given on possible modifications occurred in occasion of Milano Expo 2015. The paper firstly explores the known best band combination for observation of urban fabric. Suggestions derived have then been calibrated with reference to ground truth data, while the image pairs over the 35 years span were then build with selected bands. Finally, all image pairs have been processed for Principal Component Analysis in order to identify possible "hot-spots" of significant changes. The results found on the image pair 2006–2015 have been explored in detail and checked upon official orthophotos. Monitoring of changes in urban fabric using multispectral optical imagery can provide valuable insights for further evaluation of single urban generation interventions. Such contributions could be considered in the processes of urban planning policies in a more systematic manner.

Keywords: Earth Observation · Geospatial open data · Landsat · Copernicus programme · PCA · Urban planning · Milan

1 Introduction

In recent decades the global effects of climate change have requested for a more sustainable approach in thinking and planning of our cities and human settlements, making them more inclusive, safe and resilient as openly addressed by the Sustainable Development Goals (SDGs) number 11 of the United Nations (UN) [1]. In terms of consumption of natural resources and pollution, cities are seen as entities with most significant impact to the natural environment. Strategic policies focused on tackling the

© Springer Nature Switzerland AG 2020
O. Gervasi et al. (Eds.): ICCSA 2020, LNCS 12252, pp. 813–828, 2020.
https://doi.org/10.1007/978-3-030-58811-3_58

challenges induced by climate change suggest in fact the necessity to start from the management and operating models of the cities themselves [2]. Some studies have already investigated the relationship between land cover and the air temperature of a specific area using Earth Observation (EO) information. More specifically, in [3] Local Climate Zone (LCZ) maps depicting land cover compositions were built for the city of Milan.

The study here presented focuses on a broader issue i.e. issue of the change in urban fabric of Milan over a longer period of time (decades) as an initial input to the evaluation of parameters for purposes of urban generation studies. This paper, based on the use of Full Open and Free (FOF) optical multi-spectral satellite imagery, attempts to answer two questions:

1) What is the best combination of multispectral bands that will allow statistical analysis (such as PCA) to highlight highest changes in the urban fabric over time?
2) What are the areas where significant changes in urban fabric have occurred in the last 35 years and that are visible from freely available satellite imagery?

Firstly, the best band combination for observation of urban growth based on data provider suggestions have been explored [4]. In particular the paper has investigated pseudo-composite combinations considering short-wave infrared, near-infrared and red bands. The results were then calibrated with reference to ground truth data such as thematic map of land destination (DUSAF), an open tested layer of Topographic Database of Lombardy Region (TBD Regione Lombardia).

Successively, the changes in land occupation and urban density have been examined in the period 1985–2020, with focus on possible modifications in urban fabric occurred in occasion and after the event of Milano Expo 2015. The pairs of images were built on different thresholds over the 35 years (circa one decade period) using only three selected bands. Finally, four image pairs have been processed for Principal Component Analysis (PCA) in order to identify possible "hot-spots" of significant changes in the indicated period. The PCA is a technique used to identify common spatial patterns and it has been used on Landsat data in different application regarding cities such as urban growth [5], urban climate and spatial distribution of heat [6], as well as typology of changes in urban fabric over time [7].

Satellite imagery was chosen for this analysis having in mind possible needs of public authorities and/or experts in the urban regeneration field: (i) the sensors have high re-pass period (in case of Landsat and Sentinel circa 14–16 days) hence the imagery can possibly be used systematically and over different periods of the year (e.g. for detection of presence/absence of green areas in the urban structure); (ii) satellite imagery is highly compatible with common GIS software (both commercial and open source), hence results derived are comparable with geospatial data commonly used by public authorities such as technical territorial, urban or cadastral maps. In fact, this last characteristics was extremely important in both calibration of imagery and verification of the results.

Experts identify presence of green areas, accessibility, pollution, temperature and other as important parameters for evaluation of urban regeneration interventions in both short-term experiments and long-term strategic vision [8]. The possibility to explore and structure such changes of urban environment over almost half a century using freely available information, places the satellite imagery in high ranking position. The future implications of this work can be further explored for purposes of urban regeneration studies.

2   Data and Specific Band Combination Selection for the Analysis of Changes in Urban Texture in Milan

2.1   Study Area

The city of Milan occupies a strategic geographical position in central Europe. Milan has undergone significant urbanization during the years of "economic boom" after the second world war (WWII), expanding into predominantly agricultural lands at the outskirts of the city. In the last few decades, the changes have affected mainly the already dense urban fabric. The population of the city of Milan accounts for 1.4MIL inhabitants on an area of about 180 km^2.

2.2   Data Selection Over Time Period 1985–2020

The first feature that was going to be inspected was the change in urban fabric in past 35 years, especially in occasion of a major event that has regarded Milano's structure – Milano Expo 2015. Another factor that was considered is that the maple is the most represented spices in municipal area of Milan. Since maple trees undergo the process of leaf-fall in months of October and November, this period was evaluated as the best for observation of changes (choice towards lowering any interference with possible changes over time in urban fabric). In terms of time slots, the following year pairs have been chosen for inspection 1985–1995; 1995–2005; 2005–2015; 2015–2019 (latest data available for the chosen period).

Given that in autumn months, the area of Milan could be subjected to precipitations or cloudy weather, an additional criteria of cloud cover was added and set to less than 5% for the scene of interest. Table 1 shows the final selection of images used in this paper.

Table 1. Satellite imagery chosen for Milano case study

Year (date-month)	Satellite (Sensor)	Spatial resolution (m)	
		(VIS and VNIR)	Panchromatic
23 October 1985	Landsat 5 TM	30	NA
29 October 1993	Landsat 5 TM	30	NA
2 November 2006	Landsat 5 TM	30	NA
27 November 2015	Landsat_8 OLI_TIRS	30	15
23 December 2019	Sentinel 2A	10	NA

2.3   Spectral Resolution and Pseudo-colour Band Combination of Selected Imagery

When it comes to visibility of urban features, literature suggests some main pseudo-composite band combinations that enhance these aspects. Since the main slot of data analyzed regarded Landsat data, the following two pseudo composite band combinations (with reference to Landsat 5) were chosen:

- Combination 1: Red: Band 7; Green: Band 5; Blue: Band 3.
- Combination 2: Red: Band 7; Green: Band 4; Blue: Band 2, and

Figure 1 illustrates the two combinations for the city of Milan as seen by Landsat5 in 1985.

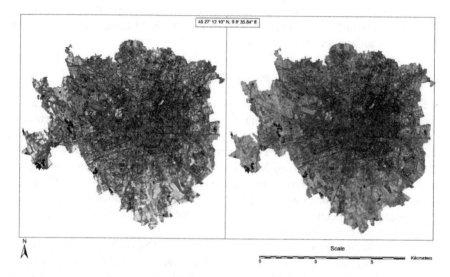

Fig. 1. Image of Milan in 1985 Combination 1 LS5 B7-5-3 (left) and Combination 2 LS5 B7-4-2. CRS:WGS84/UTM zone 32 (Color figure online)

In order to follow the correct visualization of these bands across different images acquired by different sensors, Table 2 was created by the author. In this table the bands' order in Landsat 5 and 8 has been rearranged in order to match the order of Sentinel 2A data in terms of wavelengths. The different band combinations across different sensors for two main combinations described have been summarized in Table 3. Combination 1 (LS5 B7-5-3) enhances urban features in white and light purple, while Combination 2 (LS5 B7-4-2) presents urban features in varying shades of magenta.

Table 2. Bands' wavelength and spatial resolution in Landsat 5, Landsat 8 and Sentinel 2A

Landsat 5 (USGS)			Landsat 8 (USGS)			Sentinel-2A (ESA)		
Spectral bands	Wavelength (μm)	Spatial resolution (m)	Spectral bands	Wavelength (μm)	Spatial resolution (m)	Spectral bands	Wavelength (μm)	Spatial resolution (m)
			Band 1 AEROSOL	0.43–0.45	30	Band 1 AEROSOL	442.7	60
Band 1 BLUE	0.45–0.52	30	Band 2 BLUE	0.45–0.51	30	Band 2 BLUE	492.4	10
Band 2 GREEN	0.52–0.60	30	Band 3 GREEN	0.53–0.59	30	Band 3 GREEN	559.8	10
Band 3 RED	0.63–0.69	30	Band 4 RED	0.64–0.67	30	Band 4 RED	664.6	10
						Band 5 Veg Red-Age	704.1	20
						Band 6 Veg Red-Age	740.5	20
Band 4 NIR	0.76–0.90	30				Band 7 Veg Red-Age	782.8	20
			Band 5 NIR	0.85–0.88	30	Band 8 NIR	832.8	10
						Band 8A Veg Red-Age	864.7	20
						Band 9 NIR	945.1	60
			Band 9 CIRRUS	1.36–1.38	30	Band 10 MIR	1373.5	60
Band 5 SWIR	1.55–1.75	30	Band 6 SWIR-1	1.57–1.65	30	Band 11 MIR	1613.7	20
Band 7 SWIR	2.08–2.35	30	Band 7 SWIR-2	2.11–2.29	30	Band 12 MIR	2202.4	20
Band 6 TIR	10.40–12.50	120 (30)	Band 10 TIRS 1	10.6–11.19	100			
			Band 11 TIRS 2	11.50–12.51	100			
			Band 8 Panchromatic	0.50–0.68	15			

Pseudo composite images have been built for all years chosen in Table 1 and for both Combination 1 and 2, hence considering only the three bands chosen for inspection.

3   Methodology

The work proposed in this paper was conducted in two distinct phases: (i) in the first phase the two literature-recommended band combinations have been examined and compared to ground truth data (official map of the soil use destination) in order to choose the most suitable band combination for the change detection of the urban fabric of Milan; (ii) the second phase focused on a) detection of areas subject to major changes using statistical methods and b) verification of the changes on the ground truth data (official publicly available orthophotos).

Table 3. Pseudo-composite band combinations in Landsat 5, Landsat 8 and Sentinel 2A

COMBINATION 1		
Pseudo-composite for Landsat 5	Pseudo-composite for Landsat 8	Pseudo-composite for S2A
Red: Band 7	Red: Band 7	Red: Band 12
Green: Band 5	Green: Band 6	Green: Band 11
Blue: Band 3	Blue: Band 4	Blue: Band 4
COMBINATION 2		
Pseudo-composite for Landsat 5	Pseudo-composite for Landsat 8	Pseudo-composite for S2A
Red: Band 7	Red: Band 7	Red: Band 3
Green: Band 4	Green: Band 5	Green: Band 8
Blue: Band 2	Blue: Band 3	Blue: Band 12

3.1 Comparison of the Band Combination 1 (LS5 B7-5-3) and Combination 2 (LS5 B7-4-2)

In order to evaluate the most suitable band combination for inspection over time (multi-temporal data analysis), it was chosen to examine how the information observed from satellite correspond to ground truth data. In this case, two series of information have been used as ground truth data [9]:

- For comparison and satellite imagery calibration: a DUSAF map - Intended Use of Agricultural and Forest Soils (Destinazione d'Uso dei Suoli Agricoli e forestali), produced for Lombardy Region by ERSAF, a regional body for agriculture and forests services. This database adopts a legend in accordance with the Corine Land Cover 3rd level classification;
- For results validation: Orthophotos of Lombardy Region produced by means of aero-photogrammetry for years 2003, 2007, 2012 and 2015.

2015 was chosen as the reference year as it was the year of MilanoExpo event and of the one of the most updated DUSAF maps available. 2018 DUSAF map (latest update) was not considered as it could already indicate changes occurring after 2015.

Preparing DUSAF Data for Comparison of Classified Satellite Imagery. In order to compare selected Combinations to DUSAF ground truth data, the original categories had to be re-classified. As shown in Fig. 2, the DUSAF legend categories have been combined into fewer classes in order to make the distinction between built environment (infrastructures and buildings) and green areas more straightforward. The areas for these new 5 classes were hence calculated (see Table 4 for details).

This new re-classified image of DUSAF information has enabled a better comparison with satellite imagery and its specific band combination described in the following paragraphs.

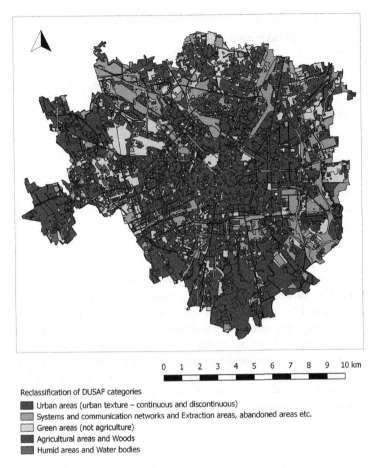

0 1 2 3 4 5 6 7 8 9 10 km

Reclassification of DUSAF categories

▨ Urban areas (urban texture – continuous and discontinuous)
▥ Systems and communication networks and Extraction areas, abandoned areas etc.
▢ Green areas (not agriculture)
▩ Agricultural areas and Woods
▦ Humid areas and Water bodies

Fig. 2. Representation of re-classified DUSAF classes: the image emphasizes the difference between urban build texture (in red) and the infrastructures (grey areas) on one side and on the other the green areas (light green) and agricultural areas (dark green). CRS:WGS84/UTM zone 32 N. (Color figure online)

Classification of Band Combinations 1 and 2. In order to make satellite imagery comparable to DUSAF data, it was chosen to classify them also into 5 classes. The supervised method was firstly tested but eventually abandoned as it was not possible to read spectral signatures of different features and create proper regions of reference with only three bands. The three band 2015 LS5 images have been hence classified using Unsupervised classification method and then converted into vector shape files (Fig. 3). The images were then inserted into a Free and Open Source Software (FOSS) QGIS environment for further analysis [10]. The use of open source GIS environment was a benefit to this paper – the environment has been tested for robustness and stability for investigation of both Landsat and Sentinel-2 satellite imagery. In fact, experts evaluate FOSS a mature and reliable technology for geo-data management [11].

Table 4. Aggregation of DUSAF legend categories into classes

Class	Colour	DUSAF legend	Area calculated (sq. km.)
Class 1	Red	1.1 Urban areas (urban texture – continuous and discontinuous);	71.63
Class 2	Grey	1.2 Systems and communication networks and 1.3 Extraction areas, abandoned areas etc.;	124.41
Class 3	Light green	1.4 Green areas (not agriculture);	29.27
Class 4	Dark green	2. Agricultural areas and 3. Woods;	65.96
Class 5	Light blue	4. Humid areas and 5. Water bodies	2.32

From the first visual investigation, first three classes seem to indicate built areas with no distinction between buildings and streets (Class 1 and 2 from Table 4), two other classes seemed to indicate better green areas respectively classes 3 and 4 of Table 4, while Class 5 was not represented (it seemed to be incorporated into Class 4). It was hence chosen to represent satellite imagery in this manner: Distinguishable classes 1, 2 and 3 were represented in three shades of red (dark red, red and orange); while Distinguishable classes 4 and 5 have been represented in light and dark green. The areas of these five distinguishable classes were hence calculated for both Combination imagery and compared to DUSAF classes as shown in Table 5.

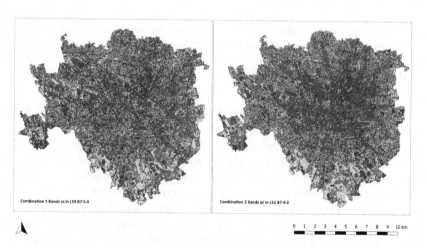

Fig. 3. Classification of the image of Milan (2015) taken by Landsat 8 in (left) Combination 1 (LS5 B7-5-3) and (right) in Combination 2 (LS5 B7-4-2). Colours of classifications classes have been attributed by the author. CRS:WGS84/UTM zone 32 N.

Table 5. Areas of specific classes as calculated within a FOSS GIS environment

	Area in Comb. 1, (LS5 B7-5-3) (sq. km)	Area in Comb. 2, (LS5 B7-4-2) (sq. km)	Areas of re-grouped DUSAF classes (sq. km)
Distinguishable class 1 (dark red)	24.23	28.76	196.04 (Total for Class 1 and Class 2)
Distinguishable class 2 (red)	48.24	47.28	
Distinguishable class 3 (orange)	56.68	49.61	29.27
Distinguishable class 4 (light green)	43.07	39.54	68.28 (Total for Class 4 and Class 5)
Distinguishable class 5 (dark green)	10.25	17.28	

From the first visual inspection, it seemed that Combination 2 i.e. the band combination with reference to Landsat 5 bands B7-6-4 (i.e. Landsat 8 B7-5-3) is a more suitable one for identification of urban changes. This was further investigated by calculating compatibility percentage with DUSAF Classes. For purposes of this comparison, the area DUSAF Class 5 Water bodies was incorporated into Class 4 Agriculture areas. Table 5 shows the areas calculated per specific distinguishable class (in satellite imageries) and for re-grouped classes of DUSAF. Given that all products were now vector shape files, all calculations have been performed within a FOSS GIS environment.

Such information enabled to proceed with error calculation of both Combination 1 and Combination 2. For the built environment the errors observed regarded Urban areas only as well Urban areas and communication networks, while for green areas errors have been observed for Agricultural areas only as well as for all green areas, comprehensive of wet areas and water bodies. Table 6 provides a summary of errors observed in both Combination 1 and Combination 2.

Table 6. Errors observed in Combinations 1 and 2 across specific re-grouped DUSAF classes

	Error in Urban areas only (Class 1) (%)	Error in Urban areas and networks (Class 1 and 2) (%)	Error in Agriculture areas only (Class 4) (%)	Error in all green areas (Classes 3, 4 and 5) (%)
Combination 1 (LS5 B7-5-3)	80.33	−34.11	−19.16	−45.34
Combination 2 (LS5 B7-4-2)	75.43	−35.90	−13.85	−41.75

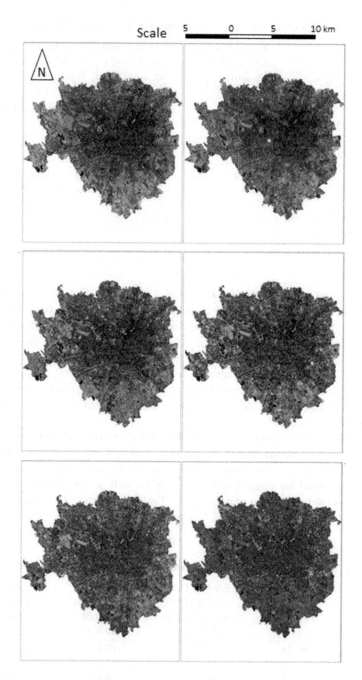

Fig. 4. Milan across band Combination 2 (LS5 B7-4-2) respectively of following years: 1985 (above left), 1993 (above right), 2006 (middle left), 2015 (middle right. LS8 B7.5.3). Sentinel 2A in 2019 across B12-8-3 (low left) and NIR-R-G (low right). CRS:WGS84/UTM zone 32 N.

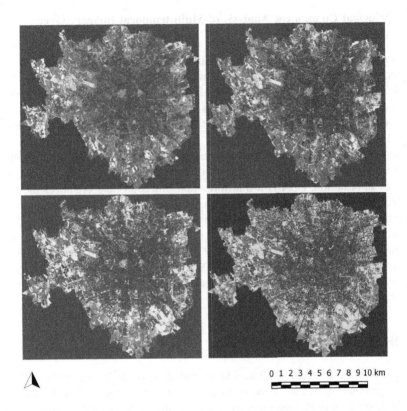

0 1 2 3 4 5 6 7 8 9 10 km

Fig. 5. Principal Component Analysis (PCA) over pair images in the following years: 1985–1993 (above left); 1993–2006 (above right); 2006–2015 (lower left) and 2015–2019 (lower right). All images are show in R: 1, B: 2 and G: 4 element combination. CRS:WGS84/UTM zone 32 N.

From Table 6 it can be observed that pixels attributed Urban area (Class 1) seem to be overestimated in both images, with a slightly better result in Combination 2, while the comparison with both Classes 1 and 2 gives an underestimation in both combination of an order of 30%. Agriculture areas are as well underestimated with pretty good results in Combination 2 (order of 10%). The high number of underestimation for all green areas (column 4 of Table 6) can be explained with the fact that Class 3 features are too small to be detected by 30 m resolution – hence while calculated in DUSAF maps because documented on a specific layer, these are not easily detected neither in Combination 1 nor 2. Considering however that agricultural areas account for two thirds of all green areas (67%), this last error could be declared as misleading and omitted from the considerations.

The first visual inspection has been thus confirmed with results presented in Table 6 leading to the choice of Combination 2 for further investigation i.e. band combination B7-4-2 as intended in Landsat 5. Figure 4 shows Milan across Combination 2 in all years considered. S2-A image in NIR-RED-GREEN pseudo-combination was inserted to facilitate observations.

3.2   Principal Component Analysis of Multi-temporal Imagery Over Milan

In order to compare images over different time period the following methodology was adopted: i) four stack pair of six (6) band images have been created i.e. combination of LS5 Bands 7-4-2 (Year 1) and LS8 Bands 7-5-3 (Year 2); ii) statistical method of Principal Component Analysis (PCA) has been conducted upon these new images. PCA is a frequently employed technique for image analysis and pattern detection applied in domains using satellite imagery and image fusion. Given the multi-spectral i.e. multi-dimensional nature of remotely sensed data, it is very often observed that the measured variables have significant level of correlation among them, causing redundancy of information. PCA is a transformation procedure that organizes the original variables (spectral bands) into a new set of variables as a novel linear combination. When the linear functions used in the process are not correlated among each, other they are called "principal components" (PCs). Such process summarizes the original information into fewer dimensions, where the most of the information is contained within first few PCs [12]. In this paper a PCA was applied on multi-temporal satellite imagery i.e. on 4 raster pairs of specifically selected bands (3 bands combination respectively in 2 different years) over five (5) components.

4   Discussion of the Results

The results of the PCA are illustrated in the Fig. 5. In order to emphasize the first two components, the images are show in the combinations as follows R: 1, B: 2 and G: 4.

The first visual inspection gives some indications on the changes in urban texture of the city of Milan over the last few decades. Excluding the error due to small cloud formation in the 1993 image (appears in the first two images above, coordinate 513084.46, 5034841.09 UTM/WGS84), it could be observed that in decade 1985–1993 there are more significant changes in the norther part of the city. Furthermore, it can be observed over the period 1993–2006 changes in urban fabric seem to be concentrated in the center area while over the period 2015–2019 they seem to be spread out over the whole area of Milan. No significant "hot-spots" can be identified in those periods.

In the period 2006–2015 however, quite a few "hot-spots" can be noticed and they have been further investigated.

The image pair 2006–2015 was firstly observed for single PCs, as shown in Fig. 6. The hotspots have then been identified over all bands using the following method: (i) a fishnet of 50 by 50 m was built (a distance comparable to city blocks of Milan urban fabric); (ii) every raster (PC band) has been inspected in order to obtain a mean value of its center; (iii) such vector file was investigated for hotspots using Hot Spots Analysis (Getis-Ord Gi*) © ESRI.

Figure 7 illustrates the hotspots analysis of PC1 where the points with high z-score i.e. high Standard deviation value (>2.58) have been highlighted (cyan colour).

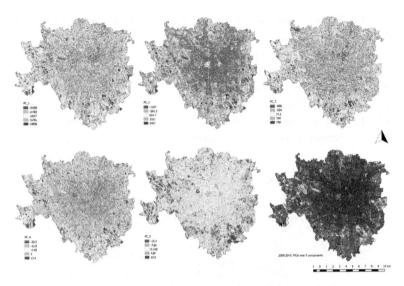

Fig. 6. Principal Component 1–5 observed in pseudo-colour with respective score values. The Principal Component Analysis (PCA) over the pair of images 2006–2015 is shown for reference at the bottom right corner. CRS:WGS84/UTM zone 32 N.

Hotspots Validation Over Lombardy Region Aero-Photogrammetric Orthophotos. An additional step consisted in validating the hotspots using orthophotos as ground-truth data. Considering the prior knowledge of the operator in the changes in urban fabric, some of the identified hotspots have been selected for further illustration. The areas considered were those possibly interested by changes in occasion of Milan Expo 2015, namely: 1. The area of ex - City Fair of Milan (Fiera MilanoCity); 2. Porta

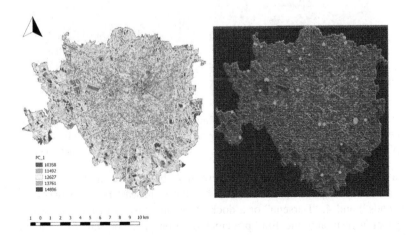

Fig. 7. PC1 of 2006–2015 PCA (left) and the result over the same band conducted with Hot Spots Analysis (Getis-Ord Gi*) © ESRI (left) (Color figure online)

Table 7. UTM/WGS84 coordinates of the four "hot-spot" areas identified in PCA over the period 2006–2015.

The "hot-spots" identified in the first class of Principal Component Analysis (PCA)	Coordinate X	Coordinate Y
"Hot-spot" 1 – ex-city fair of Milan (Fiera)	512414.52	5035946.00
"Hot-spot" 2 – Porta Nuova area	514845.00	5036715.00
"Hot-spot" 3 – Porta Vittoria railway stopover	517155.00	5034120.00
"Hot-spot" 4 – Darsena (Dock of Milano Canals)	513706.92	5033388.79

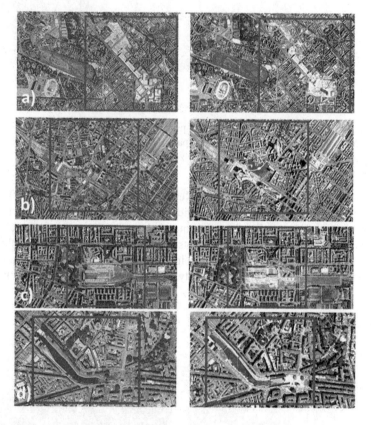

Fig. 8. Four areas identified as "hot-spots" of the first class in PCA, here seen in orthophotos in 2003 (left) and 2015 (right). Respectively these are a) Ex-City Fair Milan; b) Porta Nuova area c) Porta Vittoria railway stopover; d) "Darsena", a dock of Milan artificial water canals' system

Nuova area (literally New Gate), the new main business district of Milan; 3. Porta Vittoria railway stopover (an area located at the south-east between two main Milan "ring-roads") and 4. "Darsena" or a dock of Milano system of artificial water canals. The paper investigates the four principal locations i.e. coordinates as identified in Table 7.

All coordinates were hence verified for changes in orthophotos available for different years (2003 and 2015 were used in this paper). In Fig. 8 it can be observed in details how all four areas have undergone changes in terms of demolition/construction and urban regeneration activities in the period between 2003 (closest orthophoto available before 2006) and 2015. These can be further verified by documentation on contracting of major construction sites in the area of Milan. All of the projects, considering the four identified locations, have been initiated (or have intensified their activities) as city regeneration projects in occasion of the world fair held in Milan in 2015.

5   Conclusions

The work presented in this paper illustrates how major changes in urban fabric can be detected and identified on the multi-temporal multi-spectral optical satellite imagery. A specific band combination, referred to as Combination 2 in this paper (LS5 B7-4-2), has been calibrated and checked upon an open ground truth official data, DUSAF map. Such insight could be of help in detecting changes on a larger batch of images and for specific time periods. Furthermore, changes in the urban fabric have been clearly identified on a separate set of ground truth data of the geomatics discipline – the official orthophotos provided as Web Map Services (WMS) by the Lombardy Region Geoportal.

This kind of crossed use of freely available open geospatial information could provide suggestions on replicability and experiments to be conducted on other cities in Italy or beyond, in view of the urban regeneration parameters evaluation. The aspect of "openness", regarding both data and processing software, and their compatibility with traditionally used cartographic methods, could be an additional asset for EO derived products and services to be considered in the processes of urban planning and policy in a more systematic manner.

Acknowledgements. The author acknowledges the use of Landsat-8 image courtesy of the U.S. Geological Survey and Copernicus Sentinel-2 (ESA) image courtesy of the U.S. Geological Survey.

References

1. United Nations: Sustainable Development Goals. https://www.un.org/sustainable development/cities/. Accessed 25 Apr 2020
2. Directorate General for Research and Innovation-European Commission: Towards an EU Research and Innovation policy agenda for Nature-Based Solutions & Re-Naturing Cities. Publication Office of the European Union (2015)
3. Oxoli, D., et al.: Measuring urban land cover influence on air temperature through multiple geo-data - the case of Milan, Italy. ISPRS Int. J. Geo-Inf. 7(11) (2018). https://doi.org/10.3390/ijgi7110421. Art. no. 421

4. United States Geological Survey (USGS) - What are the best Landsat spectral bands for use in my research? https://www.usgs.gov/faqs/what-are-best-landsat-spectral-bands-use-my-research?qt-news_science_products=0#qt-news_science_products. Accessed 25 Apr 2020

5. Dhali, M.K., Chakraborty, M., Sahana, M.: Assessing spatio-temporal growth of urban sub-centre using Shannon's entropy model and principle component analysis: a case from North 24 Parganas, lower Ganga River Basin, India. Egypt. J. Remote Sens. Space Sci. **22**(1), 25–35. https://doi.org/10.1016/j.ejrs.2018.02.002. ISSN 1110-9823

6. Lemus-Canovas, M., Martin-Vide, J., Moreno-Garcia, M.C., Lopez-Bustins, J.A.: Estimating Barcelona's metropolitan daytime hot and cold poles using Landsat-8 Land Surface Temperature. Sci. Total Environ. **699**, 134307 (2020). https://doi.org/10.1016/j.scitotenv.2019.134307

7. Cuca, B., Agapiou, A., Hadjimitsis, D.G.: Observing landscape changes around the Nicosia old town center using multi-temporal datasets. In: Ioannides, M., et al. (eds.) EuroMed 2016. LNCS, vol. 10058, pp. 615–624. Springer, Cham (2016). https://doi.org/10.1007/978-3-319-48496-9_49

8. Mussinelli, E., Tartaglia, A., Fanzini, D., Riva, R., Cerati, D., Castaldo, G.: New paradigms for the urban regeneration project between green economy and resilience. In: Della Torre, S., Cattaneo, S., Lenzi, C., Zanelli, A. (eds.) Regeneration of the Built Environment from a Circular Economy Perspective. RD, pp. 59–67. Springer, Cham (2020). https://doi.org/10.1007/978-3-030-33256-3_7

9. Lombardy Region Geoportal Homepage. http://www.geoportale.regione.lombardia.it/. Accessed 25 Apr 2020

10. Open Source Geospatial Foundation: QGIS Geographic Information System. https://qgis.org/en/site/. Accessed 25 Apr 2020

11. Brovelli, M.A., Minghini, M., Moreno-Sanchez, R., Oliveira, R.: Free and open source software for geospatial applications (FOSS4G) to support Future Earth. Int. J. Digit. Earth **10**, 386–404 (2017). https://doi.org/10.1080/17538947.2016.1196505

12. Brivio, P.A., Lecchi, G., Zilioli, E.: Principi e metodi di Telerilevamento. CittàStudiEdizioni (2006)

Supporting Assessment of Forest Burned Areas by Aerial Photogrammetry: The Susa Valley (NW Italy) Fires of Autumn 2017

S. De Petris⊙, E. J. Momo⊙, and E. Borgogno-Mondino$^{(\boxtimes)}$⊙

DISAFA, University of Torino, L.go Braccini 2, 10095 Grugliasco, TO, Italy
enrico.borgogno@unito.it

Abstract. In October 2017, a large wildfire occurred in the Susa valley (Italian Western Alps) affecting wide areas of mixed forests (*Pinus sylvetris* L.; *Fagus sylvatica* L., *Quercus pubescens* Willd.) with a spot pattern. Few days after the event an aerial survey operated by an RGB camera Sony ILCE-7RM2-a7R II was done with the aim of testing a digital photogrammetry-based 3D rapid mapping of fire effects. Flight altitude was about 800 m above ground level (AGL) determining an average image GSD of about 0.2 m. Image block adjustment was performed in *Agisoft PhotoScan vs 1.2.4* using 18 ground control points that were recognized over true color orthoimages (GSD = 0.4 m). Height values of GCPs were obtained from a 5 m grid size DTM. Both orthoimages and DTM were obtained for free from the Piemonte Region Cartographic Office (ICE dataset 2010). A point cloud, having an average density of 7 pt/m^2 and covering 14 km^2 was generated, filtered and regularized to generate the correspondent DSM (Digital Surface Model) with a grid size of 0.5 m. With reference to the above-mentioned ICE DTM, a Canopy Height Model (CHM) was generated by grid differencing with a grid size of 0.5 m. A true-orthoimage was also generated having a GSD of 0.5 m. The latter was used to map burned areas by a pixel based unsupervised classification approach operating with reference to the pseudo GNDVI image, previously computed from the native red and green bands (no radiometric calibration was applied aimed at converting back the raw digital numbers to reflectance). Results were compared with 2 official datasets that were generated after the event from satellite data, one produced by the Piemonte Region and the other one by the Copernicus Emergency System. In order to test differences between burned and not-burned areas, point density, point spacing and canopy heights were computed and compared looking for evidences of geometrical differences possibly characterizing burned areas in respect of the not burned ones. Results showed that no significant differences were found between point density and point spacing in burned and not burned area. There was a significant difference in CHM minimum values distribution between burned and not-burned areas while maximum values distribution does not change significantly, proving that fire change crown structure but tree height remain unchanged. These results suggest that aerial photogrammetry could detect fire effect on forest having higher accuracy respect to ordinary approaches used in forest disturbance ecology.

Keywords: Forest fire · Photogrammetry · Forest structure

© Springer Nature Switzerland AG 2020
O. Gervasi et al. (Eds.): ICCSA 2020, LNCS 12252, pp. 829–844, 2020.
https://doi.org/10.1007/978-3-030-58811-3_59

1 Introduction

In case of forest fire, mapping and characterization of those areas that have changed has great importance for future planning and decision making. Geomatics techniques are essential for forest fire monitoring, especially in region characterized by difficult accessibility and large surfaces; they are widely used to map burned and unburned areas measuring fire severity, i.e. environmental change caused by fire and corresponding to the loss or decomposition of below- and above-ground biomass. The knowledge of temporal and spatial patterns of severity is essential to assess the ecological effects of recent fires. The creation of fire severity maps gives a valuable tool to support post-fire management and/or evaluate the success of fuel treatments [1]. In this context many approaches based on remotely sensed data are used supporting many operative protocols in response to forest fire [2, 3]. Spectral vegetation indices from optical data are used to monitor vegetation changes after fire [4]; other indices like Normalized Burn Ratio (NBR), differenced NBR (dNBR), relative dNBR (RdNBR) and MIRBI were proposed to specifically map burned and unburned areas aiming at measuring fire severity [5]. Optical remotely sensed data are widely used coupling easy accessibility and interpretability with reasonably accurate estimates of burn severity [5]. Nevertheless, spatial resolution and monoscopy of these data limit ecological description of fire effects, making them unable to describe local variations at a higher spatial scale [6]. LiDAR (Light Detection and Ranging, [7, 8]) is known to be able to, conversely, provide three-dimensional measures that can be used to estimate forest parameters as tree height, leaf area index (LAI) and above ground biomass, needed for describing forest structure and monitoring structural changes [9]. A main advantage of LiDAR technique is the capability of generating detailed DTMs (Digital Terrain Models) under forest canopy, fundamental step to normalize an image-based or point cloud respect to ground level. Nevertheless, in recent years, digital photogrammetry has been proposed as a possible alternative to LiDAR. Some studies [10] showed that photogrammetry is capable of mapping forest structure with an accuracy similar to LiDAR, but at lower cost; current image matching algorithms allow to generate point clouds with a higher density than LiDAR making possible to accurately estimate forest metrics, e.g. tree height, stem volume, basal area and biomass [11]. Consequently, photogrammetry represents an important opportunity to monitor fire severity and fire effects on forestry stands giving, possibly, estimates of stem volume lost. In this work a test concerning exploration of digital photogrammetry potentialities in mapping fire effects is presented, based on data obtained by an aerial survey operated by an RGB camera in the Susa Valley (Italian Western Alps) after a large wildfire event occurred in October 2017. In particular, authors focused on the following issues: (a) classification of burned areas; (b) characterization of burned and not-burned areas testing differences of point cloud features (point density, point spacing and canopy heights); (c) estimation of wood volume damaged/burnt by fire.

2   Materials and Methods

2.1   Study Area

The study area (AOI - Area Of Interest) is located in the municipalities of Bussoleno and Mompantero in Susa Valley (Italian Western Alps), being part of a wider area interested by a great wildfire in October 2017. AOI show a dominant south slope aspect and extends for about 14 km^2 covering a range of altitude from 450 m to 1500 m above sea level. In the area, about 920 ha are covered by forests dominated by different species such as scots pine (23% of surface), beech (15%) and other broadleaves (62%) like downy oak, chestnut, maple, ash and linden. Climatic conditions of this area are peculiar for Alps, being characterized by low annual rainfall, frequent wind and temperature rarely lower than 0 °C. October 2017 was characterized by anomalous weather conditions where high temperature and a prolonged lack of rainfall became the predisposing factors for wildfires that, in the same period, interested a lot of forests in the whole Piemonte Region. A large wildfire occurred finally in AOI in the second part of October. According to the post-fire assessment operated by the Piemonte Region [12], about 50% of the area interested by fire was characterized by a medium or high fire severity, especially in stands dominated by scots pine, beech, and, secondly, by larch and chestnut. Some beech stands were also interested by a wildfire in 2003 making them particularly critical [13] (Fig. 1).

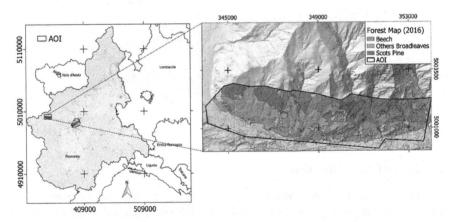

Fig. 1. (Left) Study area is located in mesalpic zone of Susa valley, Piemonte region (NW – Italy). (Right) Main forest types present in the area (Reference frame: WGS84 UTM32N).

2.2   Photogrammetric Workflow

The photogrammetric aerial survey was operated on 10th November 2017 (few days after fire stopped) by DIGISKY s.r.l. company. During the flight a Tecnam P92 JS airplane was used equipped with SmartBay©, a device for boarding up to three different sensors simultaneously on the wing lower surface (intrados) in order to quickly and efficiently reconfigure the payload and to perform complex, aerial mapping missions. SmartBay© is equipped with its own mission computer that automatically manages all remote sensing activities (Payload Control System) during the mission while providing the pilot with all needed to conduct the aircraft (Crew Operator Deck). An RGB camera Sony ILCE-7RM2-a7R II, focal length = 28 mm, CMOS full frame 42 MP, pixel size = 4.53 μm was used. Flight direction was parallel to valley and flying altitude above ground level (AGL) ranged between 500–1200 m, determining an average baseline of about 43 m. Three-hundred-one images (13 Mb per image) were acquired with GSD (Ground Sample Distance) sizing between 0.05–0.2 m. Forward overlap ranged between 90 and 97%, side overlap between 85 and 96%. Image block was processed by *Agisoft Photoscan vs 1.2.4*. Eighteen ground control points (GCPs) were collected after the flight (Fig. 2) by photointerpretation from the available AGEA True-color orthophotos (2015) having a GSD = 0.5 m. Height value was obtained from the gridded Piemonte-ICE Digital Terrain Model (DTM), having a grid size of 5 m and a height precision of 0.6 m (σ_z). After image block bundle adjustment, a dense point cloud (PPC) was generated. PPC was filtered and regularized using *LAStools* [14] in order to create a Digital Surface Model (DSM) with a grid size of 0.5 m. Finally, a true color ortho-mosaic (TCOM) having a GSD of 0.2 m (corresponding to a nominal map scale of 1:1000) was generated for the whole area.

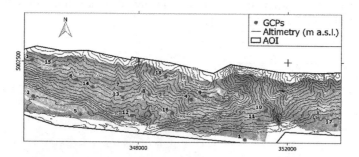

Fig. 2. GCPs location in the AOI with contour lines (Reference frame: WGS84 UTM32N).

2.3 Burned Area Detection

Available institutional Forest Map (FM) was obtained in vector format from the Piemonte region geoportal having a nominal scale 1:10000 (updated in 2016) mapping local forest types. With respect to FM all data from the photogrammetric process were masked in order to address following operation only onto forested area. From TCOM a green normalized difference vegetation index (GNDVI) was calculated according to (1) from RGB bands to minimize shadows effects across the scene. No radiometric calibration was applied to TCOM aimed at converting back the raw digital numbers to reflectance.

$$GNDVI = \frac{DN_{Green} - DN_{Red}}{DN_{Green} + DN_{Red}} \qquad (1)$$

K-means unsupervised classification with 2 clusters was applied to GNDVI map in order to detect burned (B) or not-burned (NB) forest areas. The resulting two-class map (B-NB map) was vectorized. In order to assign the right meaning to the generated clusters, the Cumulated Frequency Distribution (CFD) of GNDVI map was generated at cluster level. With respect to CFD (Fig. 3) a threshold was found to distinguish B from NB. It resulted to be located in correspondence of the CFD inflection point (second derivate equal to 0), where GNDVI value was 0. Consequently, all forested pixels with GNDVI < 0 where labeled as B, the others as NB.

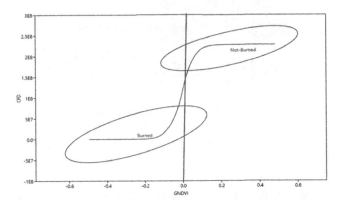

Fig. 3. CFD of GNDVI map. 95% Ellipses of two defined clusters. Redline shows the position of the selected threshold value (GNDVI = 0) used to classify B and NB forested areas. (Color figure online)

To explore the effects of fire on forest structure, two areas (burned and not burned crown, hereinafter called BC and NBC, respectively) sizing about 3.5 ha each and located over the same mountain slope were recognized on TCOM by photointerpretation (Fig. 4). According to FM, the same forest types and density were present in these areas. PPC points belonging to these areas were compared with the available DTM by differencing thus obtaining the correspondent NH value (Normalized Height, i.e. height from the ground level). Since NH values within the selected BC/NBC polygons were not normally distributed, the two statistical distribution were compared using the Kolmogorov-Smirnov non-parametric test and Mann-Whitney for equal median test. Other statistic moments like mean, median and quantiles were calculated, as well.

2.4   Damaged Trees Assessment

Photogrammetry already proved to be well performing in forest applications especially for tree counting and tree height measurement [15]. The joint use of both radiometric and geometric discriminants, possibly derived from photogrammetric survey can certainly improve tree state assessment after forest disturbance, e.g. wildfire and windstorm [16, 17]. Ordinarily, the adopted approach to derive forest parameters is based on

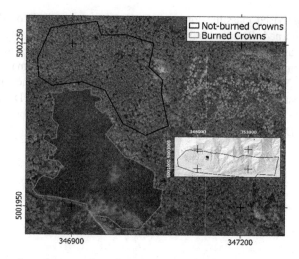

Fig. 4. Polygons show the two selected areas representing burned (BC, Red) and not burned (NBC, Black) crowns. They size approximately 3.5 ha each. According to FM the main forest type in the area is Scots Pine and tree density is similar (Reference frame: WGS84 UTM32N). (Color figure online)

Canopy Height Models (CHM) processing [15]. Consequently, in this study, a CHM was calculated by grid difference between DSM and DTM, covering the whole AOI. Tree counting (Tree Tops –TT) was performed using the Local Maxima (LM) approach operating over the CHM. This algorithm finds tree highest apex within a given crown that were assumed as representative of a single tree position. In particular, CHM analysis was performed by the Forest Tools [18] developed by using R programming language working with a Variable Window Filter algorithm (VWF); VWF is a local maxima operator [19] that changes its size according to a determinate function, that, for this work, was related to the local tree height (2). Local height values used to find the local maxima were recorded as attribute to the generated TT point vector layer. During the process points having a height local value lower than 3 m were filtered out.

$$VWF\ size = DN_{CHM}\ 0.05 + 0.6 \qquad (2)$$

An estimate of trees stem volume within the areas damaged by fire was computed using tree height information from TT, an hypsometric curve provided by the Territorial Forestry Planning – PFT [20] and the volume equation obtained from Tabacchi and his collaborators [21]. For each of the main local species (scots pine, beech and other broadleaves) a dendrometric function was calibrated, relating tree height with stem volume (Fig. 5). Once calibrated, functions were applied to all TT points to give an estimate of the amount of wood volume interested by fire.

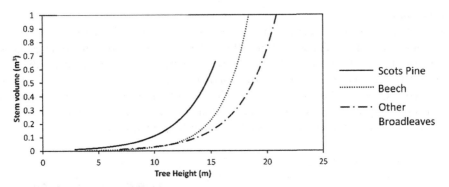

Fig. 5. Three dendrometric functions calibrated from PFT and Tabacchi [20, 21] showing relationship between single tree stem volume and tree height.

2.5   Reference Data

Burned Area

The Delineation Map (DM), nominal scale 1: 22,000, provided by Copernicus EMS – Mapping Service was obtained in vector format (Activation: EMSR253 – Susa). DM shows the fire delineation derived from post-event satellite image (Plèiades-1A/B) acquired on 30th October 2017 by photointerpretation. Piemonte Region institutional post-fire map (PFM) was also collected [12] in vector format (nominal scale 1:100,000). Metadata report that PFM was created with reference to FIREMON - Fire Effects Monitoring and Inventory System protocol [2] involving both optical remotely sensed (Sentinel-2 multispectral instrument) and ground-based data. DM and PFM (Fig. 6) were used as reference data to test relative accuracy of B-NB classes obtained by the authors.

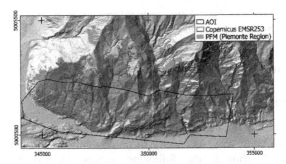

Fig. 6. Reference data used to compare classification results about B and NB areas. Black line (AOI) is the surveyed area by aerial (Reference frame: WGS84 UTM32N).

Tree Counting

Tree counting accuracy was tested by generating, randomly within burned areas, 50 virtual circular plots (VP) with 20 m radius. They were constrained to homogenously explore all the altitude zones. They sized about the 2% of total burned area. Ordinarily in forestry, tree density is estimated by counting all trees fallen in a given circular plot [22]; consequently, all crown centroids falling in each of the defined VP were counted by photo-interpretation of TCOM (Fig. 7). All trees lower than 3 m were filtered out in order to be consistent with the threshold previously defined.

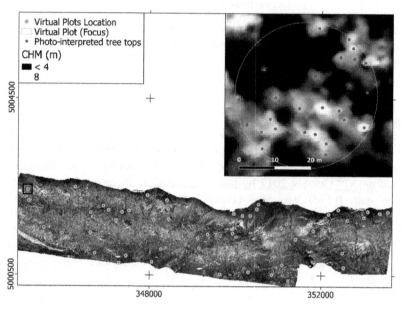

Fig. 7. VP distribution over burned area with a focus on example VP photo-interpretation procedure of tree tops (Reference frame: WGS84 UTM32N).

3   Results and Discussions

3.1   Image Bundle Adjustment and PPC

Bundle Adjustment was run using 18 GCPs having a 3D accuracy that can be estimated in 0.8 m (WGS84 UTM 32N). Accuracy of photogrammetric resection from the oriented image block showed the following values: $\sigma_x = 0.63$ m; $\sigma_y = 1.33$ m; $\sigma_z = 1.74$ m; $\sigma_{x,y,z} = 2.28$ m. The obtained dense PPC contained 94 million points resulting in a point density of about 7 pt/m^2, and an average spacing of 0.4 m. After filtering and regularization, the correspondent DSM was generated with a GSD of 0.5 m, assuming that it maintained the same Z accuracy as the one of the photogrammetric resections. TCOM was, therefore, generated with a GSD of 0.2 m assuming having same XY accuracy as the one of the photogrammetric resections. To assess the effects of fire on forest structure NH point cloud of BC (containing about 230000 points) was compared with NH point cloud of NBC (about 220000 points). BC point density and point spacing were respectively 7.62 pt/m² and 0.34 m; NBC point density and point spacing were 7.21 pt/m² and 0.37 m. In spite of these very similar results, the Kolmogorov-Smirnov test proved that the statistical distribution functions of the two areas were significantly different ($D = 0.5$, $p < 0.001$); the Mann-Whitney test proved that the two median values were different too ($U = 23292$, $p < 0.001$). Figure 8 shows the distributions of the normalized height values in BC and NBC. It can be noted that both mean and median values of BC are lower than those of NBC, proving that when fire severity is high, photogrammetry can penetrate canopy and reach the ground. As far as higher NH values are concerned, it can be noted that fire does not change significantly tree height. If we consider the previously estimated tree height measure accuracy, 1.74 m, upper NH values of BC and NBC are substantially the same. These results suggest that: (a) points resection efficiency from the oriented image block does not significantly changes in BC and NBC areas, being point spacing and density very similar; (b) high severity of fire significantly changes forest structure, but, in the short term, it doesn't affect tree height of the dominant layer; (c) photogrammetry proved to be effective to explore forest structure and assess fire severity.

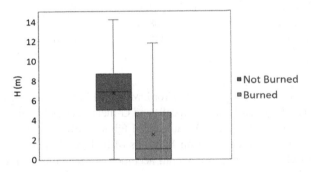

Fig. 8. CB-CNB NH distributions. Box-plot lines are respectively starting from bottom to up: minimum, Q1, median, Q3, x is mean value, maximum.

3.2   Burned Area Detection Accuracy

In Fig. 9 the produced B-NB map is reported. Statistics from classification are reported in Table 1 that shows that about 48% of the forested areas, about 447 ha, was classified as burned. Burned class equally affects main forest types in the area; in fact, about 50% of the area covered by each forest type proved to be damaged by fire (Table 1).

Classification accuracy was tested with respect to the available reference layers (DM and PFM). Classification accuracy is here defined as binary classification of imbalanced data since NB area was greater than B one [23]. Confusion matrix results and related accuracy measures are reported in Table 2. Precision and specificity were high (both 0.86) while balanced accuracy was 0.48 and 0.65 for DM and PFM respectively. Overall accuracy (defined as the ratio of correct decisions made by a

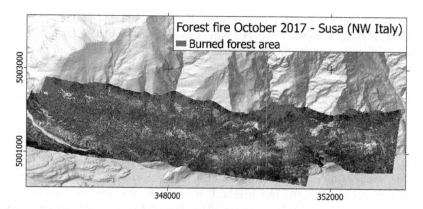

Fig. 9. B-NB map created by k-means unsupervised classification of GNDVI map (Reference frame: WGS84 UTM32N).

Table 1. Results of B-NB map reported by main forest types burned.

Forest type	Area (ha)	Burned area (ha)	Burned area (%)
Scots pine	218.18	111.04	50.89
Beech	136.14	67.41	49.52
Other broadleaves	566.81	268.68	47.40
Total	921.13	447.13	48.50

classifier) seem to be low: 0.57 and 0.47 for DM and PFM respectively, while F1 Score (harmonic mean of the precision and recall) and G-mean (geometric mean of sensitivity and precision) were high both in DM and PFM (about 0.6). These results suggest that classification of burned area based on K-means of high resolution GNDVI map is an effective approach. Regarding low overall accuracy is needed take in to account how reference data were generated.

DM was a product of rapid mapping procedure [24] therefore, since it was generated from high resolution satellite images, it suffers from the fast photointerpretation at small nominal scale (1:22000) compromising the delineation of medium/small or articulated areas. Furthermore, DM was not refined with any available forest map.

As far as PFM is concerned, it was the result of FIREMON-based protocol [12] which involved ground-based and remotely sensed data [25]. In particular, CBI - Composite Burn Index [26] was measured on ground-based plots while Sentinel-2 derived RdNBR was calculated as difference between images pre and post event and finally correlated with ground data to better calibrate a model to infer fire severity over large area. This procedure has problems related to fire severity model calibration. In fact, CBI summarizes both herbaceous/shrubs layer and tree canopy severity but, in closed forest canopy, remotely sensed data detect mainly the upper layer spectral response. Therefore, is very difficult inferring about dominated forest layers, making the calibration procedure heavily affected by this problem. Understory burns are

Table 2. Metrics derived from the confusion matrices of DM e PFM. TP (true positives): number of positive elements predicted as positive; FP (false positives): number of negative elements predicted as positive; FN (false negatives): number of positive elements predicted as negative; TN (true negatives): number of negative elements predicted as negative.

Measure	DM	PFM	Formula
Sensitivity	0.44	0.46	TPR = TP/(TP + FN)
Specificity (Producer's Accuracy)	0.86	0.50	SPC = TN/(FP + TN)
Precision (User's Accuracy)	0.86	0.83	PPV = TP/(TP + FP)
Negative Predictive Value	0.43	0.15	NPV = TN/(TN + FN)
False Positive Rate	0.14	0.50	FPR = FP/(FP + TN)
False Discovery Rate	0.13	0.17	FDR = FP/(FP + TP)
False Negative Rate	0.56	0.53	FNR = FN/(FN + TP)
Overall Accuracy	0.57	0.47	ACC = (TP + TN)/(P + N)
Balanced Accuracy	0.48	0.65	BA = TPR + TNR/2
F1 Score	0.58	0.60	F1 = 2TP/(2TP + FP + FN)
G-mean	0.62	0.61	G-mean = sqrt(TPR * PPV)

difficult to detect from satellite imagery due to interception of radiation and presence of shadows by the overstory layer especially where dense tree cover increases leaf area index (LAI) [27, 28]. Nevertheless, PFM constituted a real tool to better create priority zones where addressing restoration operations. All these considerations make clear that authors' intention was not having an absolute error estimate of their B-NB map, but comparing it with available data and measure relative correspondences.

3.3 Damaged Trees Counting Accuracy

A CHM of the area was obtained by grid differencing of DSM (from PPC) and DTM (from the Piemonte Region Geoportal). With reference to DSM and DTM height accuracies (1.74 m and 0.60 m respectively) and applying the variance propagation law CHM accuracy was found to be equal to 1.8 m. This result was similar to the one that can be obtained by ordinary forest ground-based tree height survey operated by hypsometer [29]. Starting from CHM, the TT vector layer was generated by LM approach. According to B-NB map, burned areas were considered where, reasonably, fire caused damages on trees. It is worth to remind that tree could be damaged on its trunk, the so called *"cat face"* [30], or on its crown [31]. Nevertheless, fire severity could change according to micro-station conditions [32]. Both these damages influence timber quality [33] and tree mortality [34]. Therefore, all detected trees in burned areas were considered as damaged and the corresponding biomass estimate computed (Fig. 10). Stem volume was estimated for each tree as recognized by the LM algorithm applying the correspondent dendrometric model. Results showed that about 26000 m^3 of stem biomass were damaged by the fire, distributed in the different forest type as reported in Table 3. It is possible to observe that, even though areas covered by scots pine is smaller than the one covered by broadleaves, the majority of wood volume interested by fire belong to this category.

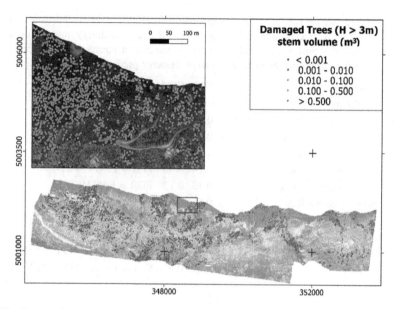

Fig. 10. Damaged trees (>3 m) as detected from the generated high-resolution CHM (Reference frame: WGS84 UTM32N). TT stems volume (m³) are represented by a color code (see legend). A focus subset is reported too, showing that B-NB map combined with TT permits to separate burned crown trees (high severity) from the other ones (low severity/not burned).

Table 3. Distribution of wood damaged by forest type.

Forest type	V (m³)	%
Scots pine	12153	46.82
Beech	2863	11.03
Other broadleaves	10937	42.14
Total	25953	

TT counting accuracy was tested with respect to tree density measured on 50 VP. A MAPE (Mean Absolute Percentage Error) equal to 30% was found proving that TT underestimated tree density. Similar results were reported by several studies [35, 36]. In particular, Pont [37] highlighted limitations of tree counting based on photo-interpretation. Nevertheless, photointerpretation of tree crowns by aerial images represents a reliable and cheaper [38] support when no ground data are available or surveyed areas are big and moving means large distances and, possibly, environmentally asper situations [39].

4   Conclusions

Susa forest fire of October 2017 was a relevant event that changed landscape and caused economic value loss of damaged trees. In general, after a fire, interactions with other natural hazards, e.g., debris flow and avalanches may delay forest regrowth and related restoring of ecosystem services [40]. Therefore, assessing and mapping fire effects is crucial to understand disturbance dynamics and to address interventions according to reliable criterion based on occurred changes. In this work authors have proposed a new approach based on low cost aerial photogrammetry (the cost can be estimated in about 2.5 euros/ha), that can be thought as alternative to a more traditional one based on satellite remote sensing or LiDAR acquisitions. Low cost aerial photogrammetry proved to be able to generated PPC, DSM and TCOM with a very high geometrical resolution and an accuracy that is comparable with the one affecting ordinary ground-based survey of forest parameters. A K-means based clustering of the obtained GNDVI map was run to classify burnt and not-burnt areas. The former, it was found, that covered about 447 ha in the area. Correspondent confusion matrix, generated after cluster interpretation and comparison with reference data, proved that this approach can be retained effective and classification accuracy (precision = 0.8) comparable with the one reported in other works about the same topic [41, 42]. A second goal of this study was to investigate effects of fire on forest structure. The comparison between NH values statistical distributions derived from PPC in B and NB areas, respectively, showed that in the short term, fire significantly changes crown structure (discovering the understory layers), but not tree height distribution in the dominant layer. Tree tops were mapped by LM showing an underestimation of about 30% of trees if compared with VP photointerpretation approach. In future it is expected that accuracy test could be referred to ground data. Detected TT were finally used to give an estimate of potentially damaged stem volume. This was achieved by applying proper dendrometric functions for the main local tree species. Potentially damaged stem volume was estimated to be approximately 26000 m^3. Finally, it can be said that the present study establishes a quantitative framework for detecting and measuring fire effects on forest structure. Future works will concern fire severity assessment through PPC local properties investigation. Unfortunately, this study did not cover the whole burned area in the Susa valley (about 2522 ha), limiting results to about the half of the area, according to the availability of aerial images. It is worth to remind that presented results cannot be completely generalized. In fact, for instance, no radiometric calibration was applied while generating TCOM. Moreover, classification of B and NB areas could fail if overstory layer shows a high LAI value or, conversely, low severity crown fire is present (mixed severity). Nevertheless, photogrammetry proved to be an effective technique to detect and characterize fire effects on forest with high geometrical resolution suggesting new research scenarios mainly related to single crown structure analysis.

Acknowledgments. We thank DIGISKY s.r.l (Strada Vicinale della Berlia, 500, 10146 Torino, Italy) for performing the aerial survey.

References

1. Arkin, J., Coops, N.C., Hermosilla, T., Daniels, L.D., Plowright, A.: Integrated fire severity–land cover mapping using very-high-spatial-resolution aerial imagery and point clouds. Int. J. Wildland Fire **28**(11), 840–860 (2019). https://doi.org/10.1071/WF19008
2. Lutes, D.C., et al.: FIREMON: fire effects monitoring and inventory system. Gen. Tech. Rep. RMRS-GTR-164. Fort Collins, CO: US Department of Agriculture, Forest Service, Rocky Mountain Research Station. 1 CD. 164 (2006)
3. De Santis, A., Chuvieco, E.: GeoCBI: a modified version of the Composite Burn Index for the initial assessment of the short-term burn severity from remotely sensed data. Remote Sens. Environ. **113**, 554–562 (2009)
4. Vo, V.D., Kinoshita, A.M.: Remote sensing of vegetation conditions after post-fire mulch treatments. J. Environ. Manage. **260**, 109993 (2020)
5. Furniss, T.J., Kane, V.R., Larson, A.J., Lutz, J.A.: Detecting tree mortality with Landsat-derived spectral indices: improving ecological accuracy by examining uncertainty. Remote Sens. Environ. **237**, 111497 (2020)
6. Hoe, M.S., Dunn, C.J., Temesgen, H.: Multitemporal LiDAR improves estimates of fire severity in forested landscapes. Int. J. Wildland Fire. **27**, 581–594 (2018)
7. Fissore, V., Mondino, E.B., Motta, R.: Limits and potentialities of gridded LiDAR data in the forest context: the case of the new Piemonte Region dataset. In: ForestSAT2014 Open Conference System, p. 1. AIT (2014)
8. Borgogno Mondino, E., Fissore, V., Falkowski, M.J., Palik, B.: How far can we trust forestry estimates from low-density LiDAR acquisitions? The Cutfoot Sioux experimental forest (MN, USA) case study. Int. J. Remote Sens. **41**, 4551–4569 (2020)
9. Su, Y., Guo, Q., Collins, B.M., Fry, D.L., Hu, T., Kelly, M.: Forest fuel treatment detection using multi-temporal airborne lidar data and high-resolution aerial imagery: a case study in the Sierra Nevada Mountains, California. Int. J. Remote Sens. **37**, 3322–3345 (2016)
10. Filippelli, S.K., Lefsky, M.A., Rocca, M.E.: Comparison and integration of lidar and photogrammetric point clouds for mapping pre-fire forest structure. Remote Sens. Environ. **224**, 154–166 (2019)
11. Bohlin, J., Wallerman, J., Fransson, J.E.: Forest variable estimation using photogrammetric matching of digital aerial images in combination with a high-resolution DEM. Scand. J. For. Res. **27**, 692–699 (2012)
12. Regione Piemonte: Piano straordinario di interventi di ripristino del territorio percorso dagli incendi boschivi dell'autunno 2017. (2019) https://www.regione.piemonte.it/web/sites/default/files/media/documenti/2019-04/Piano%20Straordinario%20interventi%20di%20ripristino.pdf
13. Ascoli, D., Castagneri, D., Valsecchi, C., Conedera, M., Bovio, G.: Post-fire restoration of beech stands in the Southern Alps by natural regeneration. Ecol. Eng. **54**, 210–217 (2013)
14. Isenburg, M.: LAStools-efficient tools for LiDAR processing (2012). http://www.cs.unc.edu/~isenburg/lastools/. Accessed 9 Oct 2012
15. Lisein, J., Pierrot-Deseilligny, M., Bonnet, S., Lejeune, P.: A photogrammetric workflow for the creation of a forest canopy height model from small unmanned aerial system imagery. Forests **4**, 922–944 (2013). https://doi.org/10.3390/f4040922
16. Chen, S., McDermid, G.J., Castilla, G., Linke, J.: Measuring vegetation height in linear disturbances in the boreal forest with UAV photogrammetry. Remote Sens. **9**, 1257 (2017)
17. Honkavaara, E., Litkey, P., Nurminen, K.: Automatic storm damage detection in forests using high-altitude photogrammetric imagery. Remote Sens. **5**, 1405–1424 (2013)

18. Plowright, A.: R package "ForestTools" (2018). https://github.com/andrew-plowright/ForestTools
19. Monnet, J.-M., Mermin, E., Chanussot, J., Berger, F.: Tree top detection using local maxima filtering: a parameter sensitivity analysis. In: 10th International Conference on LiDAR Applications for Assessing Forest Ecosystems (Silvilaser 2010) (2010). 9 p.
20. IPLA: PFT - Paini Forestali Territoriali, Regione Piemonte (2000)
21. Tabacchi, G., Di Cosmo, L., Gasparini, P.: Aboveground tree volume and phytomass prediction equations for forest species in Italy. Eur. J. Forest Res. 130, 911–934 (2011). https://doi.org/10.1007/s10342-011-0481-9
22. van Laar, A., Akça, A.: Forest Mensuration. MAFE. Springer, Dordrecht (2007). https://doi.org/10.1007/978-1-4020-5991-9
23. Zliobaite, I.: On the relation between accuracy and fairness in binary classification. arXiv preprint arXiv:1505.05723 (2015)
24. Ajmar, A., Boccardo, P., Disabato, F., Giulio Tonolo, F.: Rapid Mapping: geomatics role and research opportunities. Rendiconti Lincei 26(1), 63–73 (2015). https://doi.org/10.1007/s12210-015-0410-9
25. Morresi, D., Marzano, R., Motta, R., Garbarino, M.: Assessing fire severity through the integration of remote sensing and field burn indices: the big forest fires in North-Western Italy during autumn 2017. In: Geophysical Research Abstracts (2019)
26. Kasischke, E.S., Turetsky, M.R., Ottmar, R.D., French, N.H., Hoy, E.E., Kane, E.S.: Evaluation of the composite burn index for assessing fire severity in Alaskan black spruce forests. Int. J. Wildland Fire 17, 515–526 (2008)
27. Cocke, A.E., Fulé, P.Z., Crouse, J.E.: Comparison of burn severity assessments using Differenced Normalized Burn Ratio and ground data. Int. J. Wildland Fire 14, 189–198 (2005)
28. Rogan, J., Franklin, J.: Mapping wildfire burn severity in southern California forests and shrublands using Enhanced Thematic Mapper imagery. Geocarto Int. 16, 91–106 (2001)
29. Bragg, D.C.: Accurately measuring the height of (real) forest trees. J. Forest. 112, 51–54 (2014). https://doi.org/10.5849/jof.13-065
30. Norton, D.A.: Modern New Zealand tree-ring chronologies II: nothofagus menziesii. Tree-Ring Bull. (43), 39–49 (1983)
31. Weatherspoon, C.P., Skinner, C.N.: An assessment of factors associated with damage to tree crowns from the 1987 wildfires in northern California. For. Sci. 41, 430–451 (1995)
32. Kane, V.R., et al.: Mixed severity fire effects within the Rim fire: relative importance of local climate, fire weather, topography, and forest structure. For. Ecol. Manage. 358, 62–79 (2015)
33. Marschall, J.M., Guyette, R.P., Stambaugh, M.C., Stevenson, A.P.: Fire damage effects on red oak timber product value. For. Ecol. Manage. 320, 182–189 (2014)
34. Catry, F.X., Rego, F., Moreira, F., Fernandes, P.M., Pausas, J.G.: Post-fire tree mortality in mixed forests of central Portugal. For. Ecol. Manage. 260, 1184–1192 (2010)
35. Kattenborn, T., Sperlich, M., Bataua, K., Koch, B.: Automatic single tree detection in plantations using UAV-based photogrammetric point clouds. Int. Arch. Photogramm. Remote Sens. Spat. Inf. Sci. 40, 139 (2014)
36. Nevalainen, O., et al.: Individual tree detection and classification with UAV-based photogrammetric point clouds and hyperspectral imaging. Remote Sens. 9, 185 (2017)
37. Pont, D., Kimberley, M.O., Brownlie, R.K., Sabatia, C.O., Watt, M.S.: Calibrated tree counting on remotely sensed images of planted forests. Int. J. Remote Sens. 36, 3819–3836 (2015)

38. Eid, T., Gobakken, T., Næsset, E.: Comparing stand inventories for large areas based on photo-interpretation and laser scanning by means of cost-plus-loss analyses. Scand. J. For. Res. **19**, 512–523 (2004)

39. Avery, T.E.: Forester's guide to aerial photo interpretation. US Department of Agriculture, Forest Service (1966)

40. Conedera, M., Peter, L., Marxer, P., Forster, F., Rickenmann, D., Re, L.: Consequences of forest fires on the hydrogeological response of mountain catchments: a case study of the Riale Buffaga, Ticino, Switzerland. Earth Surf. Proc. Land. J. Br. Geomorphol. Res. Group **28**, 117–129 (2003)

41. Wing, M.G., Burnett, J.D., Sessions, J.: Remote sensing and unmanned aerial system technology for monitoring and quantifying forest fire impacts. Int. J. Remote Sens. Appl. **4**, 18–35 (2014)

42. Cruz, H., Eckert, M., Meneses, J., Martínez, J.-F.: Efficient forest fire detection index for application in unmanned aerial systems (UASs). Sensors. **16**, 893 (2016)

Urban Geology: The Geological Instability of the Apulian Historical Centers

Alessandro Reina[✉] and Maristella Loi

DICATECh, Politecnico di Bari, Bari, Italy
alessandro.reina@poliba.it

Abstract. The tourist success of the Apulian region is certainly associated with the great landscape and architectural heritage. The union of these aspects is particularly evident in the territory and in the urban centers of Salento, Murgia and the surroundings in the coastal territory.

The conservation and sustainability of these places, however, often confronts the most invasive terms of hydrogeological instability (earthquakes, floods, landslides, etc.). It is true that sometimes in the Apulian urban centers geological phenomena of instability are observed much less evident than those mentioned but more subtle and equally invasive and harmful: for example subsidence, sink holes, karst.

In order to avoid the aforementioned effects, when planning and growing an urban environment, it is necessary for decision-makers, engineers, planners and managers to take into account the physical parameters of the urban area, as well as susceptibility to dangers natural.

The geology and geomorphology of an area are crucial to guarantee the sustainable management of the territory and consequently in the protection of human life in urban areas.

With this work we illustrate some examples of hydrogeological instabilities that have been observed in the historical centers of some Apulian cities and that can significantly affect strategies for preventing damage to things and people.

The cases of the hydrogeological subsidence in Acquaviva delle Fonti, in Castellana Grotte and Cutrofiano have been described and analyzed.

Keywords: Geological instability · Geological risk · Urban planning · Sustainable development

1 Introduction

Urban sustainability can be influenced by a wide range of economic, social and environmental factors (Fedeski and Gwilliam 2007; Thapa and Murayama 2010) such as economic development, socio-economic policy, population growth, physical environment and natural risks (Xiao et al. 2006; Rozos et al. 2011; De Lotto et al. 2018; Gazzola 2019). When planning, developing and managing an urban environment, usually only the economic and social parameters are taken into consideration.

Consequently, in vulnerable places, such as areas with steep slopes and/or degraded land, the natural hazards that often occur, such as landslides, earthquakes and floods,

© Springer Nature Switzerland AG 2020
O. Gervasi et al. (Eds.): ICCSA 2020, LNCS 12252, pp. 845–857, 2020.
https://doi.org/10.1007/978-3-030-58811-3_60

can cause serious damage, disruptions to the social and economic network and lead to loss of life and property.

The choice and use of risk management strategies strongly depend on the reference context and the scope of application. The United States Department of Defence has recognized four categories of risk management intervention. ACAT is an acronym for Avoid, Control, Accept, Transfer (www.defense.gov). The "Risk Elimination" strategy is desirable, for example, in cases where, both from a management and economic point of view, other measures are not suitable for reducing the conditions of the risk. On the other hand, this type of intervention also leads to the loss of potential benefits. Instead, "Acceptance of risk" interventions are used when the assumption of risk is not considered worrying for safety or when containment strategies are deemed excessively onerous. The definition of technical measures, traditional practices and public experiences to reduce the impacts of extreme natural events can also be recognized as a valid response to risk conditions.

The evolution of the concept of risk has seen a profound change in the risk reduction strategy itself. The minimization of the factors causing disasters was contemplated, providing for action on one or more variables that contribute to the definition of the risk such as Danger, Vulnerability, Exposure and Adaptation. In recent years, from an approach that dealt with the study of the hazard factor we have gone on to determine risk prediction and prevention. The forecast is aimed at understanding the dynamics and intensity of the expected phenomena. Prevention is that set of activities aimed at avoiding or minimizing the possibility of damage resulting from calamitous events. It is believed to be in line with the philosophy of recent years to underline the importance of adopting an approach to prevent, mitigate and prepare and not only to respond to disasters.

During the World Summit on Sustainable Development WSSD in Johannesburg (2002), disaster reduction is recognized as a fundamental prerequisite for achieving sustainable development. Of the 17 Sustainable Development Goals approved by the United Nations in 2015, ten concern the challenge of reducing natural hazards. It is believed that it is impossible to plan a sustainable and lasting development of cities and territories without taking into account the negative consequences of calamitous events that have proved critical for the development of urban and territorial settlements. When planning and growing an urban environment, it is necessary for decision makers, engineers, planners and managers to take into account the physical parameters of the urban area, as well as the susceptibility.

The geology and geomorphology of an area are crucial to guarantee the sustainable management of the territory and consequently in the protection of human life in urban areas.

The conservation and sustainability of these places, however, often confronts the more invasive terms of hydrogeological instability (earthquakes, floods, landslides, etc.). It is true that sometimes in the Apulian urban centers geological phenomena of instability are observed much less evident than those mentioned but more subtle and equally invasive and harmful. For example subsidence, sink holes, karst. There is a need to convert short-term non-structural interventions which are generally characterized by post-disaster emergency periods with long-term and permanent structural prevention interventions (Mejri et al. 2017; Esteban et al. 2011).

The contribution of this work is aimed at the possibility of activating an urban functional redefinition (Gazzola V. 2019) policy as the best answer to the need for urban improvement and redevelopment in relation to safety.

The cases of the hydrogeological subsidence in Acquaviva delle Fonti, in Castellana Grotte and in Cutrofiano have been described and analysed (Fig. 1).

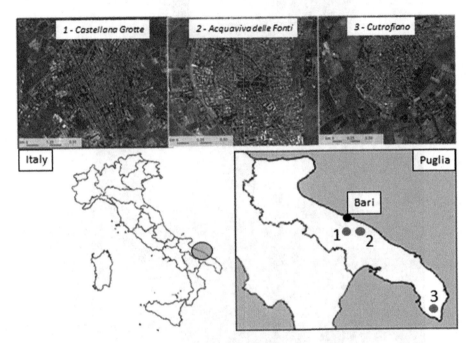

Fig. 1. Location of the historical centres of Puglia studied

2   Study Cases

2.1   Castellana Grotte

The city of Castellana Grotte is located at an altitude of about 300 m above sea level in the Murge of the south-east of Bari, about 20 km the Adriatic coast. From geological point of view, the territory is characterized by the presence in the outcrop and in the subsoil of layers of fractured and karst limestones dating back to the Upper Cretaceous.

A particularly serious event occurred in Largo Porta Grande in 1968 (Fig. 2), where following a phenomenon of subsidence, which also involved an overlying building, a pre-existing karst cavity 55 m deep was identified which in the ancient quaternary, following the collapse of the vault it was filled with red earth and continued to function as a way to dispose of rainwater. The phenomenon of opening of the cavity that it was triggered by the massive presence of water which lubricated the filling soil making it plastic and plastic-fluid consistency. Consequently, the removal of the finer particles through the joints of the limestone has led the progressive settlement of the imposing mass of earth, creating the cavity.

Fig. 2. The collapse in Largo Porta Grande in 1968

To date, 22 natural caves are known in the area of Castellana Grotte; among these, the Castellana Caves (total length over 3500 m) and the Pozzo Cucù Caves system (total length of 1200 m) stand out for their planimetric development. Some important cavities are known below the town, such as Torre del Mastro, Abate Eustasio and Voragine del Canalone (Fig. 3).

In the case of cavities, their collapse is a real calamitous event, induced by natural but also anthropic causes. In general, the natural causes that can cause collapses of karst voids are earthquakes and the same evolution of the dissolution phenomena.

The change in the use of a territory is one of the factors triggering the collapse of the cavities: the vibrations induced by vehicular traffic, the expansion of the rooms in the subsoil, the increase in the load on the ground due to the need to raise old buildings, water leaks from sewage water networks, both public and private, are anthropogenic causes of the phenomenon.

Fig. 3. Location planimetric extension of the main cavities in the urban area: *1) Grotta di Torre di Mastro, 2) Voragine del Canalone; 3) Grotte dell'Abate Eustasio; 4) Grotte di Castellana*

The main problem is due to the fact that for the city area, a specific study has never been carried out to systematically verify any other cavities present, but only emergency intervention has been carried out on the occasion of a failure.

There is a situation of difficult management of prevention as there is a practical difficulty of preventive investigation that can be carried out on the whole territory. The underground cavities determined in a karst context present an objective difficulty due to their anisotropic development and often not accompanied by evident signals on the surface of the soil. The economic commitment of a possible plan of geognostic investigations of a direct or indirect type for the entire city area is also not negligible.

2.2   Acquaviva delle Fonti

The original nucleus and consequently the name of the city are due to the easy availability of fresh water in the subsoil. Geological and hydrogeological structure is made up of quaternary sandy deposits that rest on stratified and karst limestones of the Cretaceous age (Fig. 4). Interposed between the two sedimentary terms, silty clays and red earth are observed, according to the scheme in the figure.

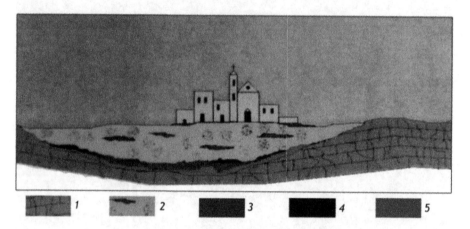

Fig. 4. Geological schematic section of the city of Acquaviva delle Fonti: 1) Cretaceous limestones; 2) Pleistocene sands and silts; 3) Pleistocene clays; 4) peat; 5) red soils (from Maggiore et al. 1995, modified) (Color figure online)

With the ban on the use of surface water, what was once a resource in the past is proving to be a failure factor. Due to the high degree of pollution, the use of the surface stratum was prohibited. The historic center currently complains about a series of failures in buildings such as cracks and rising damp, in relation to the change in the level of the water table with rainfall. The relief of the recognizable damages in the buildings of the historical center are shown in the Fig. 5.

Monitoring of groundwater levels in observation wells found that indicated the hydrogeological regime of the aquifer which is connected with the rainfall. the level of the aquifer rises almost simultaneously to coincide with rainy events. During periods of low or no rainfall (summer) there are phenomena of land subsidence probably connected with the compaction of the sands. With the rain there is an increase in the volume more clayey lithological terms.

Fig. 5. Map of the distribution of the type of damage in the buildings analysed in Acquaviva delle Fonti

The sands also have a certain degree of particle size uniformity ($D_{60}/D_{10} = 3 - 3,3$) and therefore may be susceptible to liquefaction in the event of earthquakes.

The forecast of phenomena is not accompanied by an adequate prevention policy.

2.3   Cutrofiano

The municipality of Cutrofiano rises in central-southern Salento and is about 30 km from Lecce. It occupies a territorial surface of 55.72 km^2 and is located at an average altitude of about 80 m a.s.l.

In consideration of the peculiar geological-stratigraphic constitution and for the intense anthropic activity, the territory of Cutrofiano is characterized by the diffusion of a series of phenomena about instability of the soil which cause subsidence, even of considerable entity, which can affect the functionality and the stability of infrastructure and buildings (Fig. 6).

Fig. 6. A building damaged by subsidence

The hydrogeological risk is linked to the presence of tunnels built for the underground cultivation of calcarenite (Fig. 7), a material widely used in local construction, and subsequently abandoned, from the early 1990s, due to the unsustainable increase in extraction costs.

The underground mining, which began at the time of the unification of Italy and lasted almost to the end of the last century, started from the area immediately south of the inhabited center, where the deposit was more superficial (about 6 ÷ 8 m), and it pushed southwards into the countryside at increasingly greater depths and with consequent greater costs and risks.

The underground quarries represent a particular type of quarry that is adopted when the deposits are positioned at a depth that makes the open-pit uneconomical, as long as the rock masses have good self-bearing characteristics and that are in the absence of substantial aquifers. The quarry is therefore made up of a series of underground tunnels and rooms of considerable size oriented in the direction of the bench to be quarried. The wells were used for access from the surface and for the transfer of the extracted material (Fig. 8).

Over time the tunnels and descending wells have given rise to sinkhole phenomena (sinking and subsidence of the soil) in some places, also affecting some existing buildings. The calcarenitic bank, which constitutes the cultivable field, was reached through descending wells (160 in total) that crossed the various superficial layers of the soil.

Different types of causes (stress, mechanical, geometric, karst) contribute to the manifestation of the instabilities:

- poor strength and/or reduced thickness of the reservoir roof - the low degree of compactness of the calcarenitic material is certainly one of the causes of the collapses.

Fig. 7. Images of some underground galleries. Lithostratigraphic succession with location of underground tunnels.

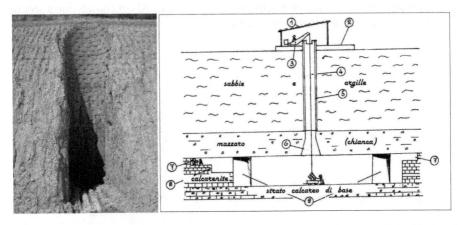

Fig. 8. Example of a well and typical section of an underground quarry (from Toni and Quartulli 1986). Sabbie = sands; argille = clays; mazzaro = hard calcarenite; strato calcareo di base = limestone

– poor strength and/or small dimensions of the pillars - the mechanical characteristics of the calcarenite to be extracted, constituting the quarry pillars and their dimensions, are fundamental for the stability of the same 5 × 5 m of the first deposits, to those of 20 × 20 m or 25 × 25 m of the more deposits recent and profound.
– tunnel size - the width and height of the tunnels affect stability
– depth of the quarry - the bank of the calcarenite deposit is at depths progressing further south towards the inhabited center.
– presence of wells - the extraction well has always been considered as the weak element of the system. The causes of collapse can be determined by various factors such as: depth of the well, with the concentric forces acting on the rings gradually increasing with depth; the development of the roots of the trees, which with time could expel segments; rainwater runoff and groundwater infiltration phenomena.

The stability conditions of the wells were analyzed. The boundary conditions can be quite variable in correspondence with the 160 wells present, therefore, for the purposes of this study, a single case has been considered in which the realization of the collapse conditions is hypothesized, in order to be able to carry out what are the induced effects on the ground following the loss of load-bearing capacity of the coating layer of the well.

The stability of the wells was investigated under axial symmetry conditions. The boundary conditions of the analyses were defined essentially on the basis of the hydro-geological structure of the modelled area. The hydro-mechanical behaviour of the materials was simulated through the use of an elastic-perfectly plastic constitutive model with a Mohr-Coulomb breakage criterion. The geometry adopted for the well is that typical of the descents used to lift the material, with a diameter of 3 m. At the mouth of the well, in the surface layer of sand, an inclined excavation profile equal to the effective friction angle of the material ($\varphi' = 28°$) was considered.

In the hypothesis of axial symmetry, the study was carried out considering a section identified by a radial abscissa of the well originating from its axis (Fig. 9).

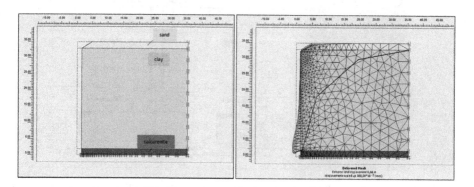

Fig. 9. Deformation associated with the collapse of the well

The analyzes highlighted the presence of subsidence in the area surrounding the well, which increase significantly when the condition of collapse of the vertical walls is reached (Fig. 9).

At the foot of the well, in contact with the reservoir, the deformations reached in the clay layer are of the order of 6 m (Fig. 9) which, in consideration of the axisymmetric condition of the model, show how, following the collapse, the well is occluded by the layers of clay, triggering a sinking of the area adjacent to the mouth of the well (surface sinkhole), as described in the analysis of the collapse phenomenon.

For the purposes of a correct risk mitigation policy for citizens, the results highlighted with this research indicate that the hydrogeological instabilities observed in the Cutrofiano area are attributable to different causes. These failures, which entail different types of phenomenology and damage to the structures (Fig. 10), cannot be attributed exclusively to sinking in correspondence with the presence of underground tunnels (De Pascalis et al. 2009), as shown by the commented analyses. The analyses have in fact shown how subsidence phenomena can also be associated in correspondence with vertical wells, in which potential collapse phenomena develop.

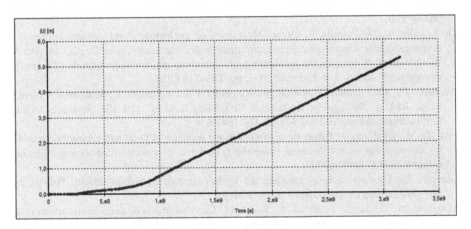

Fig. 10. Diagram of the horizontal displacements observed at the base of the well (the extent of which is limited to a few centimeters until the collapse of the vertical walls occurs).

3   Results and Discussion

The critical points of the geological instabilities that characterize some historical centers of Puglia have been illustrated. These studies aim to contribute to the evaluation of the urban recovery and enhancement capacity of Castellana Grotte, Acquaviva delle Fonti and Cutrofiano.

Due to the growing demand in the tourism sector, it is necessary to adopt mitigation intervention measures that must be targeted and adapted for a better conservation of buildings and for the safety of citizens.

It is clear that the discrepancy between the forecast of failures and prevention actions is still strong with respect to the evident increase in demand for populations in historic centers.

The historical centers of Puglia represent strategic and identity places with a difficult proposition of functional redefinition. Therefore, providing a knowledge base on geological hazards, preventive intervention policies are desirable, which above all safeguard the historical building heritage, while maintaining the destination and function.

References

Ciaranfi, N., Pieri, P., Ricchetti, G.: Nota alla Carta Geologica delle Murge e del Salento (Puglia Meridionale). Mem. Soc. Geol. It. **41**, 449–460 (1998)

De Lotto, R., Gazzola, V., Venco, E.M.: Functional change as urban regeneration and risk reduction strategy. In: Margani, G., Rodonò, G., Sapienza, V. (a cura di) Proceedings of the Seismic and Energy Renovation for Sustainable Cities (SER4SC 2018), International Conference Catania, 1–3 Febbraio 2018, pp. 319–330. EdicomEdizioni (2018). ISBN 978-88-96386-56-9

De Pascalis, A., De Pascalis, F., Parise, M.: Genesi ed evoluzione di un sinkhole connesso a cavità antropiche sotterranee nel distretto estrattivo di Cutrofiano (Lecce, Puglia). In: Atti 2° Workshop Int. "I sinkhole. Gli sprofondamenti catastrofici nell'ambiente naturale ed in quello antropizzato", Roma, 3–4 dicembre 2009, pp. 703–718 (2010)

Esteban, J.F., et al.: Current mitigation practices in the EU. In: Menoni, S., Margottini, C. (eds.) Inside Risk: A Strategy for Sustainable Risk Mitigation, pp. 129–186. Springer, Milano (2011). https://doi.org/10.1007/978-88-470-1842-6_4

Fedeski, M., Gwilliam, J.: Urban sustainability in the presence of flood and geological hazards: the development of a GIS-based vulnerability and risk assessment methodology. Landsc. Urban Plan. **83**, 50–61 (2007)

Gazzola, V.: Uso del suolo e riduzione del rischio naturale in ambito urbano. Politecnica. Maggioli Editore (2019). ISBN 978889163418

Maggiore, M., Pagliarulo, P., Reina, A., Walsh, N.: La vulnerabilità di alcuni centri urbani della Puglia in relazione ai fenomeni di instabilità dei terreni di fondazione nei depositi di copertura quaternari. Geologia Applicata e Idrogeologia **XXX**(Parte I), 471–479 (1995)

Mejri, Q., Menoni, S., Matias, K., Aminoltaheri, N.: Crisis information to support spatial planning in post disaster recovery. Int. J. Disast. Risk Re. **22**, 46–61 (2017)

Rozos, D., Bathrellos, G.D., Skillodimou, H.D.: Comparison of the implementation of rock engineering system and analytic hierarchy process methods, upon landslide susceptibility mapping, using GIS: a case study from the Eastern Achaia County of Peloponnesus. Greece. Environ Earth Sci **63**, 49–63 (2011). https://doi.org/10.1007/s12665-010-0687-z

Thapa, R.B., Murayama, Y.: Drivers of urban growth in the Kathmandu Valley, Nepal: examining the efficacy of the analytic hierarchy process. Appl. Geogr. **30**, 70–83 (2010)

Toni, L., Quartulli, S.: Coltivazione di calcareniti in sotterraneo nel comune diCutrofiano (Lecce). Quarry Constr. 23–26 (1986)

Xiao, J., et al.: Evaluating urban expansion and land use change in Shijiazhuang, China, by using GIS and remote sensing. Landsc. Urban Plan. **75**, 69–80 (2006)

Internet

Autorità di Distretto dell'Appennino meridionale. www.distrettoappenninomeridionale.it
Dipartimento di Difesa degli Stati Uniti. www.defense.gov
Comune di Acquaviva delle Fonti. www.comune.acquaviva.ba.it
Comune di Castellana Grotte. www.comune.castellanagrotte.ba.it
Comune di Cutrofiano. www.comune.cutrofiano.le.it

Satellite Stereo Data Comprehensive Benchmark for DSM Extraction

G. Mansueto[1]([✉]), P. Boccardo[2]([✉]), and A. Ajmar[2]([✉])

[1] ITHACA, Via Pier Carlo Boggio 61, 10138 Turin, Italy
giuseppe.mansueto@ithaca.polito.it
[2] DIST, Politecnico di Torino, Viale Mattioli 39, 10125 Turin, Italy
{piero.boccardo,andrea.ajmar}@polito.it

Abstract. The quite recent availability of satellite stereo pairs allows users to extract three-dimensional data that can be used in different domain of applications, such as urban planning, energy, emergency management, etc. This research paper aims to extract digital surface models (DSM) from satellite stereo pairs acquired by three different satellites (Deimos-2, Pléiades-1 and WorldView-3) over the area of the city of Turin (Italy). The results are then assessed in term of geometric accuracy comparing them with a cadastral point height dataset, used as benchmark. The comparison, in terms of difference height values (between the DSM and the benchmark), is calculated on a set of sample points. Just two of the generated DSM guaranteed a high height accuracy level useful for the domain of application, such as existing cartography update, emergency management, building damage assessment, roof slope and solar incoming radiation assessment. Further developments will investigate different blending techniques and software that could provide more accurate results.

Keywords: Satellite stereo pair · DEM/DSM extraction · Accuracy assessment

1 Introduction

The development of the very high resolution (VHR) optical sensors mounted on satellites nowadays allows to achieve a ground sample distance lower than 1 m. This increased, in the last years, the geo-referencing accuracy and the mapping capability, bringing to an improvement in resolution of digital surface models (DSMs) based on data acquired by VHR sensors [1]. Since these data models permit more precise and economically advantageous measurements of large land surfaces, they are more and more required in many different application domains and new methodologies have been implemented to improve the quality and accuracy of automatic 3D processing [2]. The capacity of acquiring high-resolution stereo couples, from which to extract accurate 3D data, is therefore considered a relevant element in new satellites.

The aim of the paper is to address the differences in resolution and accuracy of the generated DSM over the city of Turin (Italy) from a satellite stereo pair acquired by three different satellite sensors, comparing the result in term of geometric accuracy using two benchmark, a ground height points dataset of the City of Turin, constituted by geodetic heights values of ground marked points (mainstay, trustworthy, network

© Springer Nature Switzerland AG 2020
O. Gervasi et al. (Eds.): ICCSA 2020, LNCS 12252, pp. 858–873, 2020.
https://doi.org/10.1007/978-3-030-58811-3_61

vertex and stable reference points) and a cadastral gutter height points dataset, reporting the geodetic gutter heights of each building of Turin. The paper describes the common datasets and procedures for the DSM generation, exploring the potential of stereoscopic images of Deimos-2, Pléiades-1 (in two- and tri-stereo mode) and WorldView-3 satellites for this purpose and assessing them from qualitative and quantitative point of view.

The DSM is generated by collecting tie points (TPs) or ground control points (GCPs) from a stereo pair, then used to create the Epipolar images from which the automatic DSM generation is carried out.

The paper is organized as follows. After this introduction, Sect. 2 provides a description of the satellites platforms, on-board sensors and acquisition modes. Section 3 introduce the stereo imagery used dataset. In Sect. 4 it is described the processing methodology adopted to generate the satellite-based DSMs, then qualitatively analyzed in Sect. 5. Section 6 focuses on the description of benchmark data characteristics, used for accuracy verification. Section 7 assess the satellite-based DSM accuracy, discussing about the results and, in the end, chapter 8 close with conclusion and future developments.

2 Satellite and Sensor Description

The input dataset is composed by images acquired by civilian VHR stereo satellites sensors (Table 1), which allows creating first-rate quality stereo geometry thanks to a convergence angle higher than 0.5, improving the DSM vertical accuracy.

Table 1. Stereo satellites comparative table

Satellite	GSD [m] (Panchromatic)	Stereo	Tri-stereo
Deimos-2	1	y	n
WorldView-3	0.31	y	n
Pléiades-1	0.5	y	y

This sun-synchronous satellites (Deimos-2, WorldView-3 and Pléiades-1) can acquire more than one image, with a difference inclination of the platform, in a low-range acquisition time difference (1–3 min), minimizing the radiometric variation and facilitating the DSM generation [3].

2.1 Deimos-2

With a lifetime of at least seven years, Deimos-2 is a VHR stereo multispectral optical satellite (1 m GSD resolution at nadir in panchromatic), equipped with a push-broom VHR camera with 5 spectral channels (1 panchromatic, 4 multispectral), improved by the fast and precise rotation of the platform which hold it [4].

2.2   WorldView-3

WorldView-3, launched in 2016, is the latest in a constellation of commercial high-spatial resolution Earth imaging satellites developed by Maxar (DigitalGlobe Inc). It is equipped with a VHR camera with 29 spectral channel: 1 pan-chromatic (with 0.31 m GSD), 8 multispectral, 8 SWIR bands (from 1.2 to 3.7 m GSD resolution), 12 CAVIS bands ("clouds, aerosols, water vapor, ice, and snow" at 30 m GSD resolution for atmospheric compensation), improved by the fast and precise rotation of the platform which hold it [1].

2.3   Pléiades-1

Pléiades-1 is a very-high resolution stereo multispectral optical satellite constellation (0.5 m GSD resolution in panchromatic at nadir), composed by two spacecraft purchased by CNES (Space Agency of France) company. The satellite is equipped with a VHR camera with four spectral bands (blue, green, red, and IR), capable of acquiring high-resolution stereo imagery in just one pass and accommodating large areas (up to 1,000 km × 1,000 km) [5]. One of the aims of this mission is the provision of so-called "level-2 products" to customers, consisting of a panchromatic image with a merged multispectral image orthorectified on a digital terrain model (DTM) [6].

Pléiades-1 offers also a tri-stereo terrain data generation approach (Fig. 1), which differs from conventional stereo data generation through the application of two oblique and one near-nadir viewing of the terrain, as opposed to just two oblique views, which provides the ideal solution for accurate 3D modelling. This is especially relevant in areas of high relief variation, including dense, high-rise urban landscapes, where the tri-stereo image coverage image combination significantly minimizes the problem of data 'loss error' areas in the final DSM. This can result in a reduction of ±75% of "hidden area objects", which can arise with conventional 2 × oblique image coverages, as a result of object lean and view obscuring effects [7].

3   Dataset

The input dataset is composed by seven VHR stereo satellite images, two from Deimos-2, two from Worldview-3 and a triplet from the tri-stereo satellite Pléialdes-1. All the used panchromatic images have been provided with a low processing data level, with basic geometric and radiometric correction. As we can see in the Tables 2 and 3, the two/three stereoscopic images coming from the same satellite are acquired on the same date, with a difference of few minutes (the maximum difference is 9'47") in acquisition time, in order to minimize solar irradiation differences that may cause shadows-linked errors.

The chosen test area is the city of Turin, regional capital of Piedmont in Italy. Figure 2 outlines the stereo pairs orientation in the space, giving an idea of their dimension, and the chosen test area for the further accuracy assessment.

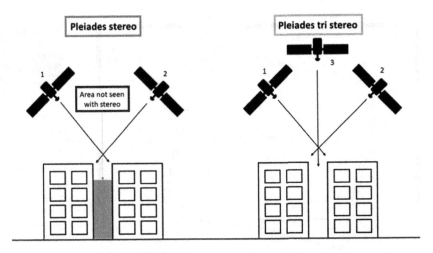

Fig. 1. Comparison between stereo and tri-stereo Pleiades acquisition [8]

Table 2. Characteristics of Deimos-2 (D2) and WorldView-3 (W3) panchromatic images

Image ID	D2 (1)	D2 (2)	W3 (1)	W3 (2)
Acquisition date	11/07/18	11/07/18	16/12/17	16/12/17
Acquisition time (GTM)	10:04:50	10:06:34	11:05:21	11:06:16
Incidence angle (DEG)	4	1.4	−25.0	−26.1
Sun azimuth (DEG)	133.93	134.68	175	175.2
Sun elevation (DEG)	60.60	60.85	21.6	21.6
Columns	11712		33333	
Rows	8604		33333	
Framed area (km^2)	196.3		99.4	

Table 3. Characteristics of Pléiades-1 (PH1) panchromatic images

Image ID	PH1 (1)	PH1 (2)	PH1 (3)
Acquisition date	27/04/2018		
Acquisition time (GTM)	13:23:08	13:24:06	13:32:55
Incidence angle (DEG)	−4.69	−5.93	−4.59
Sun azimuth (DEG)	153.99	153.99	153.99
Sun elevation (DEG)	56.02	56.02	56.02
Columns	21340	21482	21887
Rows	21296	22356	22736
Framed area (km^2)	128.3		

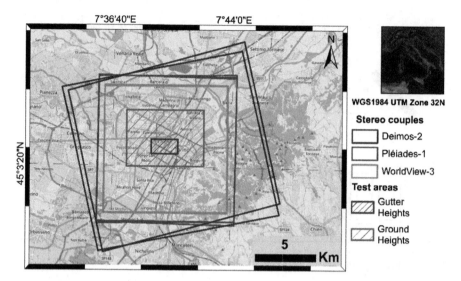

Fig. 2. Location of satellite imagery footprints and test areas in Turin, OSM Basemap in background

4   Processing Methodology

PCI Geomatica, and specifically the OrthoEngine production toolkit, has been used for stereo satellite data processing. Using this software, it is possible to generate a DSM referred to the ellipsoid height or to the geodetic elevation [9].

The steps followed in the extraction process are:

1. Creation of a new project choosing the current satellite origin of the dataset and as orientation mode the one with RPCs model (exploiting the metadata file supplied by the satellite data provider);
2. Import of the stereo pair and conversion in.pix file (PCI Geomatics internal file format);
3. Tie points (TP) collection by means of automatic extraction, imposing the following settings:
   a. Distribution Pattern: Overlap area
   b. Trial per point (number of iterations per point): 3
   c. TP per area: 50
   d. Min. acceptance score: 0.75
   e. Search radius: 100 pixels
   f. Sample source method: Susan
   g. Elevation Search Strategy: SRTM DEM with 30 m GSD extracted over the area

The residuals RMSE (average between the RMSE on the x and y axis) of each TP collected needs to be a tenth of the dimension of the sampling scheme (pixels size of the image) "to ensure that they will be completely independent of their random position and their orientation in relation to the sampling scheme (Shannon Sampling theorem)" [8].

4. Epipolar image generation
5. Automatic DEM extraction, inserting the following inputs as settings:
    a. Extraction method: Normalized cross-correlation (NCC)
    b. Elevation range: Automatic
    c. DEM detail: High
    d. Terrain type: Hilly (in this case)
    e. Output DEM vertical datum: Mean sea level
    f. Output DEM channel type: 32-bit real
    g. Pixel sampling interval 2
    h. Smoothing filter: Low
    i. Geocoded DEM resolution: double of sensor GSD (i.e. 1 m for Pléiades-1)
    j. Output option: Blending

It is important to point out that, due to the PCI Geomatics processing, the resolution of the generated DSMs is always the half of the one in the used dataset [10].

5 Qualitative Analysis

There were generated four models: one Deimos-2, one WorldView-3, one Pléiades-1 two-stereo and one Pléiades-1 tri-stereo DSM.

From a preliminary and qualitative assessment, evaluating noise, sharpness in city canyons, ability in shaping the geometries and identification of details, emerged that Deimos-2 model (with a resolution of 2 m) (Fig. 3) results very poor with respect to the others (Fig. 4 Pléiades-1 two-stereo DSM for comparison), showing an elevation accuracy that does not permit to identify or distinguish the shape of the object on the ground and presenting several issues related to noise and false elevation spikes.

Concerning the other DSM, it was found that for WorldView-3, even if presents a high GSD in the acquisition, the generated DSM quality results lower in comparison to Pléiades-1 ones. Focusing on the roof in the Fig. 5, reported as example, its shape is not represented faithfully in the WorldView-3 model. Both Pléiades-1 DSMs shows a good result; the two-stereo DSM better represents the roofs flaps, exhibiting that the external spans of it are higher than the central one. The tri-stereo one, instead, better defines the details in the North-West part.

As far as the streets and city-canyon are concerned (Fig. 6), tri-stereo Pléiades-1 DSM reach up a higher quantity of details in the scene, outlining more objects in the middle of main street. The two-stereo Pléiades DSM, instead, delineate the streets shaping them completely, without the noise founded in the other one and without the building overlaps present in WorldView-3 DSM, which also in this case looks weak in comparison to the others.

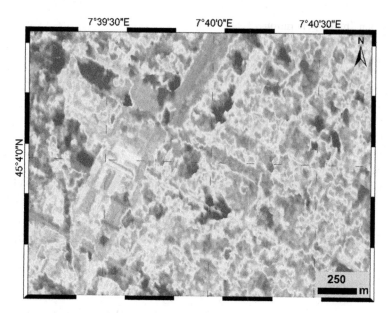

Fig. 3. Focus of Deimos-2 geoid DSM in the city area of Turin

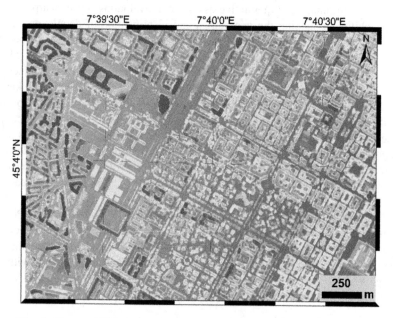

Fig. 4. Focus of Pléiadel-1 two-stereo geoid DSM in the city area of Turin

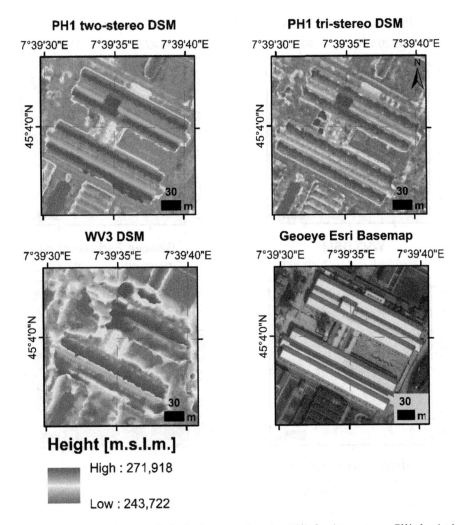

Fig. 5. Visual analysis over a limited urban area, in order: Pléiades-1 two-stereo, Plèiades-1 tri-stereo, WV-3 extracted geoid DSMs and Geoeye Esri basemap

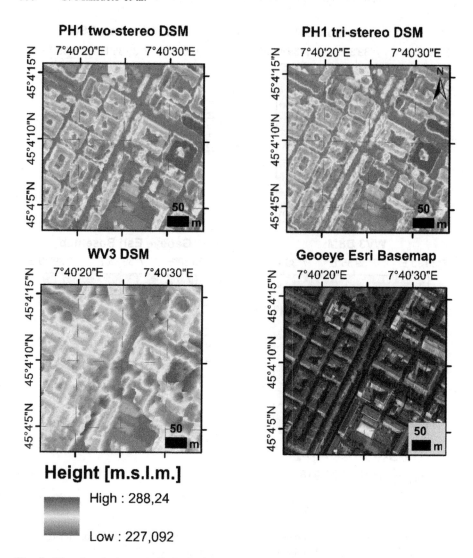

Fig. 6. Visual analysis over a limited urban area, in order: Pléiades-1 two-stereo, Plèiades-1 tri-stereo, WV-3 extracted geodetic height DSMs and Geoeye Esri basemap

6 Description of the Used Benchmark Data

The qualitative output was double checked with the quantitative analysis of the data, evaluating the altimetric accuracy of the models through the use of two benchmarks documenting the correct geoid heights of Turin: a ground height points dataset (last update 2011) of the City of Turin, constituted by geodetic heights values of a sample of ground marked points (mainstay, trustworthy, network vertex and stable reference points) and a cadastral gutter height points dataset (last update 2015), reporting the geodetic gutter heights of each building of Turin.

In order to compare them with the DSMs, these benchmarks have been converted into two raster products:

1. a raster reporting in the pixel cells the values of ground heights ("ground raster");
2. a raster reporting in the pixel cells the values of gutter heights of the buildings ("gutter raster").

The comparison was carried out in two smaller test areas, common for all the satellite acquisition frames, respectively of 27,6 km^2 for ground and 2,4 km^2 for gutter heights assessment.

At this point, the benchmark have been subtracted to the six assessed DSMs (2 DSMs for each of the three sensors used as input), obtaining three ground height difference rasters and three gutter height differences raster (as output), and then (after the subtraction) re-converted in vector products (in order to extract the statistics). The achieved vector points dataset, composed by three ground height differences and three gutter height differences, describes the accuracy in "geodetic height difference" between the DSMs data and a certain-known one.

7   Results and Discussion

As said previously, the DSMs assessment (WV3, PH1 two- and tri-stereo) has been carried out on three ground height differences and three gutter height differences. In the Fig. 7 it is reported as example the test area within the "ground height difference" points form the PH1 tri-stereo subtraction, against the back-ground of PH1 tri-stereo DSM.

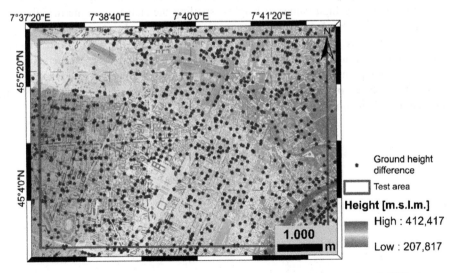

Fig. 7. Test area, inside "ground height difference" points PH1 tri-stereo referred, PH1 tri-stereo DSM on the background

From these points we have extracted the statistics for all the six outputs (count in the sample, minimum, maximum, mean and standard deviation above all samples heights). All the values are reported in the Table 4 and 6.

7.1 Results Using Ground Heights Benchmarks

The analysis on ground height differences was conduct on a sample of 2693 points for WorldView-3 and 988 points for Pléiades-1 (each representing a height difference).

Table 4. Summary table of the statistics referred to the ground height differences

GROUND HEIGHTS	WV-3	PH1 2-st	PH1 3-st
Count	2693	988	988
Min [m]	−104	−7	−21
Max [m]	50	56	47
Mean [m]	5.7	11.8	1.5
St. dev [m]	9.4	9.4	10.2

Being a difference between the heights of the DSM and the real heights, the models reach the perfection for values of difference that tends to zero.

Looking at the statistics referred to all the sample (Table 4), focusing on the standard deviation (expressing the dispersion around the mean), it is possible to notice that it is high for all the generated DSMs, meaning that outliners are present in the analyzed sample. Moreover, looking at the mean, it is visible that all the models seems to overestimate (high values of mean) the city height values, meaning that the most of the outliners present high values of heights (spoiling the statistics on the model).

The anomalies that led to these phenomena can be related to two cases:

a. High positive difference values (Fig. 8), found where the point (which in the reality is on the ground) fall in the DSM on a roof, then the DSM present the height of the roof and the point the ground one, and consequently a high height difference value; the effect is related to a perspective geometric distortions, due to the off nadir angle in the satellite acquisition.

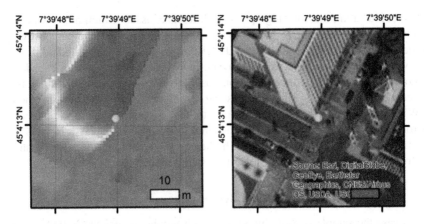

Fig. 8. Example of an "High positive difference values anomaly" in ground heights assessment (left PH1 two-stereo DSM, right Geoeye Esri basemap)

b. High negative difference values, when the DSM for the foreshortening or the presence of shadows (usually in the city canyons) has wrong digitalized the ground, underestimating the height value. In this case the DSM present a really low height and the point the real one of the ground, implying a negative height difference value.

It is observable that PH1 tri-stereo declare a low value of mean, really distant from the high standard deviation one. This is amenable to the fact that this sensor catch more details on the ground, bringing to another additional effect, that are errors caused by the presence of object on the streets (e.g. vehicles, dehors, stalls, etc.) during the acquisition of the images, bringing in this cases to an overestimation of the heights.

After this ascertainment, it was decided to restrict the sample in an acceptance range between −10 m and 10 m. In this way, deleting the systematic errors from the sample, it was obtained a more representative one.

From a first look at the new samples statistics (Table 5), we can assert that no one of the three models can be evaluated as the best one.

Table 5. Summary table of the statistics referred to the ground height differences in the range [−10, 10]

GROUND HEIGHTS	WV-3	PH1 2-st	PH1A 3-st
Points in [−10; 10]	64%	54%	76%
Mean [m]	0.3	4.3	−2.9
St. dev [m]	5	2.8	5.4

The model with the better distribution of the values in the range, presenting a Gaussian trend, is PH1 tri-stereo. It is also the model with mayor number of sample points falling in the acceptance range (76%), followed by WV3 with 64% and PH1 two-stereo with 54%. As it is possible to see the mean of the tri-stereo DSM is negative, indicating that the "high positive difference" issue is minimized with respect to the two-stereo one, due to the tri-stereo mode which reduce the perspective geometric distortions. Despite this, this model displays a high value of standard deviation, with very disperse values far from the mean. In WV3, and even more in Pléiades two-stereo, the distribution is concentrated on positive values, suggesting that these models reduce the fore-shortening effect. Discussing about these two models: even if the mean of WV3 DSM ground heights is proximal to zero the values of the samples are not approaching to the fitting one, PH1 two-stereo DSM instead display a lower value of standard deviation at the expense of a higher mean. Therefore, the analysis shows a better ground heights accuracy in PH1 two-stereo model.

7.2   Results Using Gutter Heights Benchmarks

In this case the sample is made by a really high number of points (262690 for WV3, 91835 for PH1) displaced on the gutters (perimeter walls) of the buildings. All the three models exhibit high values of standard deviation (Table 6). The mean, instead, is oriented to negative heights for WV-3 and PH1 in tri-stereo mode and to positive for the two-stereo model of PH1.

Table 6. Summary table of the statistics referred to the gutter height differences

GUTTER HEIGHTS	WV-3	PH1 2-st	PH1 3-st
Count	262690	91835	91835
Min [m]	−74	−62.7	−54
Max [m]	90	69.3	61.9
Mean [m]	−2.3	3.1	−6.6
St. dev [m]	7.5	6.2	7.7

Also, in this case the models are affected by issues related to a perspective geometric distortion, due to the off-nadir angle in the satellite acquisition:

a. High negative difference values, found where a point of the benchmark (which in the reality is on the gutter) falls in the DSM on the ground area, then the DSM present the height of the ground and the point the gutter one (Fig. 9), and consequently a negative height difference value;

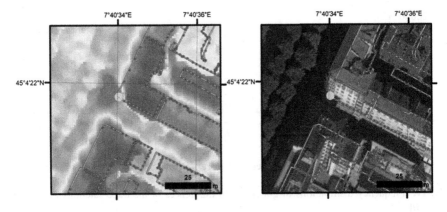

Fig. 9. Example of an "High negative difference values anomaly" in gutter heights assessment (left PH1 two-stereo DSM, right Geoeye Esri basemap)

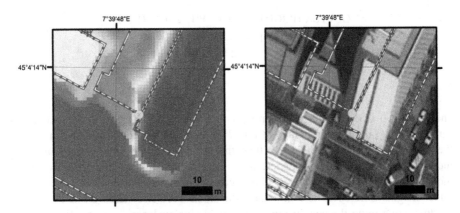

Fig. 10. Example of an "High positive difference values anomaly" in gutter heights assessment (left PH1 two-stereo DSM, right Geoeye Esri basemap)

b. High positive difference values, when the DSM has overestimated the height value. In this case the error can also be related, as it is possible to appreciate in the Fig. 10, to strong heights differences between adjacent buildings or to the presence of new constructions in the DSMs (WV3 2017, PH1 2018) not present in the benchmark dataset (2015).

Although the sample is numerous, in order to obtain a more representative sample delating the systematic errors, also in this casa it was preferred to reduce the acceptance range from −10 to 10.

All the models frequency distributions present a gaussian trend (Fig. 11). It is important to point out that the higher pecks of WV3 distribution is due to the fact that the sample is denser of points (because of the better resolution), falling in the current case in that range of values. The different position of the distribution peaks of PH1 two-

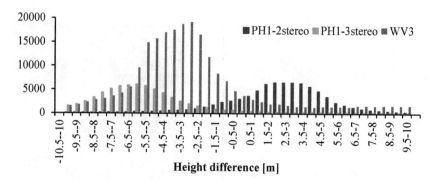

Fig. 11. Frequency distributions of gutter height differences of the three satellites in the range [−10,10]

Table 7. Summary table of the statistics referred to the gutter height differences in the range [−10, 10]

GUTTER HEIGHTS	WV3	PH1 2-st	PH1 3-st
Points in [−10; 10]	85.2%	89%	78.9%
Mean [m]	−2.5	2.3	−4.8
St. dev [m]	3.8	3	3.7

and tri- stereo DSMs confirm the previous statements. Looking at the percentage of sample points falling in this range (Table 7), it is possible to conclude that in the city the DSMs better defines the roofs than the streets, due to the fore-shortening and inclination. Analyzing the statistics, it is, once again, evident that PH1 two-stereo model guarantee the best gutter heights accuracy. At the end of this assessment of the gutter heights differences is legitimate to evaluate PH1 two-stereo DSM as the best product, confirming the conclusion of the qualitative analyses.

8   Conclusion and Future Developments

It was established that the quality of a DSM has not a resolution dependence only. Despite to what expected, concerning the other DSM, it was found that for WorldView-3, even if presents a high GSD in the acquisition, the generated DSM has lower accuracy in comparison to Pléiades-1 one, showing in particular some problems in the canyon shaping. Pléiades-1 DSMs exceed in height accuracy level WorldView-3 product. Focusing on Pléiades-1 models, the one generated in tri-stereo mode exhibit higher capacities in the identification of details, small objects on the ground (e.g. cars, vegetation, road signs), which in some case can turn into noise; the model generated in two-stereo mode, instead, demonstrate an improved sharpness in city canyons and roofs geometries shaping. Resulting more efficient in terms of both ground and building heights calculation, it is therefore legitimate to evaluate PH1 two-stereo DSM as the best product over the generated ones.

If in the next future more stereo pairs will be available over the area of Turin, it could be very interesting to investigate on them in order to find other discriminating factors, testing them with different blending techniques and more accurate bench-marks (LIDAR) for the quantitative assessment.

References

1. Hu, F., Gao, X.M., Li, G.Y., Li, M.: DEM extraction from worldview-3 stereo-images and accuracy evaluation. In: International Archives of the Photogrammetry, Remote Sensing and Spatial Information Sciences, vol. 2016, pp. 327–332 (2016)
2. Poon, J., Fraser, C.S., Chunsun, Z., Zhang, L.I., Gruen, A.: Quality assessment of digital surface models generated from ikonos imagery. Photogramm. Rec. **20**(110), 162–171 (2005)
3. Aguilar, M.Á., et al.: DSM extraction from worldview.pdf. IEEE Trans. Geosci. Remote Sens. Gener. (2013)
4. Galileo, E., Imaging, S.L.U.: DEIMOS-2 Imagery User Guide (2015)
5. Airbus Defence & Space: Pléiades Spot the Detail, Geo-Intelligence Fact Sheet (2013). https://www.intelligence-airbusds.com/files/pmedia/public/r49228_9_pleiades_product.pdf
6. Codou, G., Cubero-Castan, E., Duverger, T., Mesnard, R., Tavera, F., Casserra, C.: Operational scheduling of direct tasking innovative concept to improve reactivity on earth observation system. In: SpaceOps 2016 Conference (2016)
7. Thompson, M., et al.: High resolution landcover modelling with pléiades imagery and DEM data in support of fine scale landscape thermal modelling. In: The International Archives of the Photogrammetry, Remote Sensing and Spatial Information Sciences, vol. XLII-3/W2 (2017)
8. Blaschke, T.: Object based image analysis for remote sensing (2010)
9. Boccardo, P., Sandu, C., Ajmar, A., Perez, F.: Digital surface models extraction by Göktürk-1 satellite stereo pairs. In: 9th International Conference on Recent Advances in Space Technologies RAST (2019)
10. PCI: Geomatica OrthoEngine Pleiades 1A data – DEM extraction and DSM to DTM Conversion, pp. 1–12 (2013)

International Workshop on Software Quality (SQ 2020)

Cross-Project Vulnerability Prediction Based on Software Metrics and Deep Learning

Ilias Kalouptsoglou, Miltiadis Siavvas$^{(\boxtimes)}$, Dimitrios Tsoukalas,
and Dionysios Kehagias

Centre for Research and Technology Hellas, Thessaloniki, Greece
{iliaskaloup,siavvasm,tsoukj,diok}@iti.gr

Abstract. Vulnerability prediction constitutes a mechanism that enables the identification and mitigation of software vulnerabilities early enough in the development cycle, improving the security of software products, which is an important quality attribute according to ISO/IEC 25010. Although existing vulnerability prediction models have demonstrated sufficient accuracy in predicting the occurrence of vulnerabilities in the software projects with which they have been trained, they have failed to demonstrate sufficient accuracy in cross-project prediction. To this end, in the present paper we investigate whether the adoption of deep learning along with software metrics may lead to more accurate cross-project vulnerability prediction. For this purpose, several machine learning (including deep learning) models are constructed, evaluated, and compared based on a dataset of popular real-world PHP software applications. Feature selection is also applied with the purpose to examine whether it has an impact on cross-project prediction. The results of our analysis indicate that the adoption of software metrics and deep learning may result in vulnerability prediction models with sufficient performance in cross-project vulnerability prediction. Another interesting conclusion is that the performance of the models in cross-project prediction is enhanced when the projects exhibit similar characteristics with respect to their software metrics.

Keywords: Software quality · Security · Vulnerability prediction

1 Introduction

According to the ISO/IEC 25010 [1] International Standard on Software Quality, software security is one of the main quality characteristics of modern software products. In order to enhance the security of the produced software, software industries should ensure that their products are not bundled with critical vulnerabilities. The exploitation of a single vulnerability may lead to far-reaching consequences both for the end user (e.g., information leakage) and for the owning enterprise of the compromised software (e.g., financial losses and reputation

© Springer Nature Switzerland AG 2020
O. Gervasi et al. (Eds.): ICCSA 2020, LNCS 12252, pp. 877–893, 2020.
https://doi.org/10.1007/978-3-030-58811-3_62

damages) [2]. Hence, appropriate mechanisms are required in order to assist the identification and mitigation of software vulnerabilities as early in the Software Development Lifecycle (SDLC) of a software product as possible [3].

One such mechanism that enables the early identification and mitigation of software vulnerabilities is vulnerability prediction [3]. Vulnerability prediction, which is actually inspired by the idea of fault prediction [4] that is used for reliability assessment [5], is a subfield of software security aiming to predict software components that are likely to contain vulnerabilities (i.e. vulnerable components). Vulnerability prediction models (VPMs) are normally built based on Machine Learning (ML) techniques that use software attributes as input (e.g., software metrics [6–8]), to discriminate between vulnerable and neutral components. These models can be used for prioritizing testing and inspection efforts, by allocating limited test resources to potentially vulnerable parts [9].

Several VPMs have been proposed over the years utilizing various software factors as inputs for predicting the existence of vulnerable components, including software metrics [10], text mining [9,11], and static analysis alerts [12,13]. Although these models have demonstrated promising results in predicting the existence of vulnerabilities in the projects on which they have been trained (i.e., within-project vulnerability prediction), they failed to sufficiently predict the existence of vulnerabilities in previously unknown software projects (i.e., cross-project vulnerability prediction) [3,14]. However, the adoption of advanced ML techniques like deep learning is expected to increase the predictive performance of existing models in cross-project vulnerability prediction. Despite some initial attempts (e.g., [11,15]), more work is required in order to reach safer conclusions.

To this end, in the present paper we investigate whether the adoption of deep learning along with software metrics may lead to accurate and practical cross-project vulnerability prediction. For this purpose, we initially construct a vulnerability dataset by carefully restructuring the dataset provided by Walden et al. [16]. The resulting dataset contains 21,445 vulnerable and clean files, which were retrieved from three real-world open-source PHP applications. Subsequently, based on this dataset, several machine learning (including deep learning) models are constructed, both for the case of within-project vulnerability prediction and for the case of cross-project vulnerability prediction. In each one of these cases, the produced models are evaluated and compared with respect to their accuracy and practicality based on a set of performance metrics. Finally, feature selection is also applied in order to examine how the selected features affect the performance of the produced models.

The rest of the paper is structured as follows. Section 2 discusses the related work in the field of vulnerability prediction. Section 3 provides information about the adopted methodology, whereas Sect. 4 presents the results of our analysis. Finally, Sect. 5 concludes the paper and presents directions for future work.

2   Related Work

A large number of VPMs has been proposed in the literature over the past decade [3]. As stated in [14], the main VPMs that can be found in the literature utilize software metrics [10,17,18], text mining [9,15], and security-related static analysis alerts [12,13] to predict vulnerabilities in software products. However, as stated before, while these models have demonstrated promising results in predicting the existence of vulnerabilities in the software projects on which they have been built (i.e., within-project vulnerability prediction), they have failed to demonstrate sufficient performance in cross-project vulnerability prediction. This is a major shortcomings of existing VPMs, affecting their practicality [3].

In fact, several empirical studies have shown that that text mining-based models exhibit better predictive performance compared to other state-of-the-art techniques [16,19,20], but they perform poorly in cross-project vulnerability prediction [13]. This can be explained by the fact that that these models base their predictions on the frequencies of specific text features (i.e., keywords) extracted directly from the source code (e.g., [9]), which makes them highly project-specific. On the contrary, VPMs based on software metrics have been found to be more promising solutions in cross-project vulnerability prediction [16,19], as software metrics are able to capture more high-level characteristics of the analyzed code. Therefore, more work is required towards this direction.

Recently, several researchers have started examining whether the adoption of more advanced ML techniques, particularly deep learning, may lead to better VPMs. For instance in [15], the authors employed deep learning, and more precisely a Long-short Term Memory (LSTM) network [21], to construct new features from the vulnerability dataset provided by Scandariato et al. [9]. Subsequently, based on these features, they built both metric-based and text mining-based VPMs using Random Forest algorithm. The results of their experiments indicate that the new models are better than the models of Scandariato et al. [9], both in within-project and in cross-project vulnerability prediction. Similarly, Pang et al. [11] used deep neural networks to built text mining-based VPMs using four software projects retrieved from the dataset provided by Scandariato et al. [9]. Their results showed that deep learning-based VPMs demonstrate sufficient predictive performance in within-project vulnerability prediction.

Although these studies provide useful insights regarding the efficacy of deep learning in vulnerability prediction, they are hindered by several shortcomings. First of all, in [15], deep learning was used only for the construction of new features, while the produced models were built using the Random Forest algorithm. However, better results could have been achieved, if deep learning was adopted for the construction of the VPMs, especially in the case of cross-project vulnerability prediction. Secondly, although Pang et al. [11] built deep learning-based VPMs, they focused only on the case of within-project vulnerability prediction, not providing any insight on the performance of these models on cross-project vulnerability prediction. Finally, an important issue of both studies is that the vulnerability dataset that was utilized does not contain actual vulnerability data retrieved from real-world vulnerability databases. That is, the source code files of the software projects are marked as vulnerable (or clean), based on the outputs of a commercial static code analyzer (i.e., Fortify SCA[1]), and not based

---

[1] https://www.microfocus.com/en-us/products/static-code-analysis-sast/overview.

on actual reported vulnerabilities. As a result, due to the fact that static code analyzers are prone to false positives and false negatives [3, 20], many of the files that are marked in the dataset as vulnerable may, in fact, be clean (and vice versa), obviously affecting the correctness of the produced models.

The main goal of the present study is to examine whether the adoption of deep learning along with software metrics may lead to VPMs with sufficient accuracy and practicality, especially in the case of cross-project prediction. Contrary to the previous studies, in the present work, we put significant emphasis on the predictive performance of the produced models in cross-project vulnerability prediction, since in this case, poor performance may hinder the practicality and acceptance of the produced models, whereas it is an open issue in the related literature that remains unresolved [3]. In addition, as opposed to the previous studies that were based on static analysis to classify the source code files as vulnerable or clean, in the present work, we construct our experiments based on real-world vulnerability data retrieved from actual vulnerability databases and vendor advisories. In particular, our work is based on the vulnerability dataset provided by Walden et al. [16], which contains actual vulnerability data retrieved from three popular open-source PHP web applications.

3 Methodology

3.1 Dataset

For the purposes of the present study, the vulnerability dataset provided by Walden et al. [16] was utilized. This dataset contains real-world vulnerability information retrieved from public databases, including both vendor advisories and the National Vulnerability Database[2] (NVD) for three popular PHP web applications, namely Drupal, PHPMyAdmin, and Moodle.

More specifically, to construct the dataset, Walden et al. [16] fetched multiple versions of these three open-source applications, and for each source code file they marked its vulnerability status based on whether there were relevant reports for these files on vendor and NVD security advisories. In brief, according to this approach, files that have at least one vulnerability reported on vulnerability databases are marked as vulnerable, whereas files that do not have any reported vulnerabilities are defined as neutral. It should be noted that files with no vulnerabilities are defined as neutral, and not as clean, because they may contain potential vulnerabilities that have not been reported yet.

For each one of the source code files of the dataset, 12 software metrics were computed, using a custom static code analyzer proposed by Walden et al. [16], which is based on the PHP compiler front-end developed by Vries and Gilbert [22]. The reasoning behind the adoption of this tool is twofold. Firstly, no tools are available on the market that are capable of computing a sufficient set of coupling, complexity, and size metrics of PHP files. Secondly, using this tool could enable us more reliably compare the results of the present work to the

---

[2] https://nvd.nist.gov/.

results of the work of Walden et al. [16] on which the present study was based. The source code metrics collected for each version of every PHP file of the three selected software applications are listed below:

- **Lines of code (LoC)**: The total lines of code of the PHP file being measured, excluding lines that do not have PHP tokens.
- **Non-HTML lines of code (Nonecholoc)**: The same with the LoC metric, excluding lines containing HTML code embedded in the file being measured.
- **Number of functions (Nmethods)**: The total number of functions and methods of the PHP file being measured.
- **Cyclomatic Complexity (Ccom)**: The total number of linearly independent paths through a program's source code.
- **Maximum nesting complexity (Nest)**: The maximum nesting depth of loops and control structures of the PHP file being measured.
- **Halstead's volume (Hvol)**: An estimate of the program's size (i.e., volume) using the number of unique operators (i.e., method names and PHP language operators) and operands (i.e., parameter and variable names).
- **Internal functions or methods called (nIncomingCalls)**: The number of functions or methods defined in a PHP file that are invoked (at least once) by another method or function that belongs to the same file.
- **Fan-in (NIncomingCallsUniq)**: The number of files that invoke methods or functions of the PHP file being measured.
- **Fan-out (nOutgoingInternCalls)**: The number of files that contain methods and functions that are invoked by the PHP file being measured.
- **External calls to functions or method (nOutgoingExternCallsUniq)**: The number of files calling a particular function or method defined in the file being measured, summed across all functions and methods.
- **Total external calls (nOutgoingExternFlsCalled)**: The total number of statements that invoke functions or methods that are not defined in the PHP file being measured.
- **External functions or methods called (nOutgoingExternFlsCalledUniq)**: The total number of statements that invoke methods or functions that belong to the PHP file being measured.

The dataset that is used in the present study is based on the original dataset provided by Walden et al. [16]. However, while constructing it we followed a slightly different approach. More specifically, the original dataset consists of the computed metrics and the vulnerability status of each PHP file and version of the selected PHP applications. This results in a broader dataset of 112,947 samples. In the original study [16], the authors focused on a significantly smaller subset of the dataset, as they considered only one version of each PHP file. However, we observed that significant differences may exist in the source code of different versions of the same file. Therefore, in the present study, we decided to treat the different versions of the same file as different samples of the dataset, provided that a significant difference is observed between their computed metrics (as this indicates significant differences in their actual source code).

Hence, from the original dataset we kept only those files that were different in all the computed metrics. This ensures that the remaining samples refer to PHP files that are significantly different with respect to their source code. Even a small change in the source code of a PHP file (e.g., addition or removal of a single line of code in a function, addition or removal of a single square bracket, etc.) will lead to a difference in at least one of the file-level metrics. Requesting a difference to exist in all the studied metrics means that significant modifications need to be performed between commits in order these files to be considered different. In that way, we ensure that not only duplicates are removed, but also highly different files are considered as part of the dataset. This led to a dataset of 21,445 samples. Table 1 shows the descriptive statistics of the final dataset.

Table 1. Descriptive statistics of the final dataset

Application	Vulnerable files	Total files
Drupal	62	195
PHPMyAdmin	480	4732
Moodle	362	16536

3.2   Data Pre-processing

Sampling Techniques and Scaling. As can be seen by Table 1, the produced dataset is highly imbalanced. In particular, the number of neutral files is significantly larger compared to the number of the files that are marked as vulnerable. This observation, which is in-line with the majority of similar research endeavors that are based on real-world vulnerability data (e.g., [13, 14, 19]) can be explained by the fact that only a small number of vulnerabilities are identified and reported on public databases throughout the lifetime of software applications [14].

Classification problems with imbalanced datasets are challenging, as the skewed distribution makes many conventional ML algorithms less effective, especially in predicting minority class examples. To eliminate this risk, similarly to other studies [16, 19], we applied under-sampling to make the dataset perfectly balanced. For this purpose, we employed the *RandomUnderSampler* offered by the sklearn[3] package to reduce the neutral samples to a number equal to the number of vulnerable samples. More specifically, we retained all the samples that belong to the minority class (i.e., vulnerable files) and randomly chose N samples from the majority class (i.e., neutral files), where N is the total number of the samples of the minority class. It is worth mentioning that under-sampling was applied only to the training set, as re-sampling on test data imposes a bias on the findings. This is crucial in order to preserve the correct testing conditions.

---

[3] https://scikit-learn.org/.

In addition, we performed data normalization due to the fact that ML techniques (especially neural networks) produce better results when data are normalized. For this purpose, we used sklearn's *MinMaxScaler*, which transforms features by scaling each sample to a given range between zero and one.

Feature Selection. The selection of independent input variables (i.e., features) is a critical part in the design of ML algorithms. Each additional feature makes the model more complicated by adding an extra dimension. A large number of input variables may lead to the "curse of dimensionality", a phenomenon in which the model's performance degrades as the inputs' number increases. Feature selection is a strong weapon against the curse of dimensionality, as it reduces both the computational cost of modeling and training time. In many cases, feature selection can even improve the performance of the model, since irrelevant features can negatively affect the model performance.

In order to study the statistical significance of each file-level software metric over the existence of vulnerabilities, we applied an embedded method named Tree-based Elimination (TBE) [21]. TBE uses the built-in feature selection mechanism of the Random Forest algorithm to measure the importance of each feature. Importance provides a score that indicates how valuable each feature is in the construction of the decision trees within the model. We chose Random Forest as it is one of the most popular methods for feature selection [23].

We applied the TBE method independently on the feature set of each application of our dataset and ranked the 12 metrics (features) presented in Sect. 3.1 by the order that they were selected by the method. The results are illustrated in Fig. 1. In particular, in Fig. 1a, Fig. 1b and Fig. 1c, we present the importance of each metric in vulnerability prediction for Drupal, PHPMyAdmin and Moodle respectively, as computed by the TBE method.

By having a look at Figs. 1a, 1b and 1c, we can clearly see that the ranking of metrics is highly similar for PHPMyAdmin and Moodle, whereas the top three metrics (i.e., Hvol, nOutgoingExternCallsUniq, and Ccom) are identical for both applications. More specifically, the importance of Hvol in vulnerability prediction was found to be 0.140226 and 0.171136 for PHPMyAdmin and Moodle respectively. The importance of nOutgoingExternalCallsUniq metric equals to 0.139171 for PHPMyAdmin and 0.147026 for Moodle, while the importance of Ccom was found to be 0.118421 and 0.126714 for PHPMyAdmin and Moodle respectively. In addition to the top metrics, the rest of the ranking is also highly correlated, indicating that a model trained to predict vulnerabilities in one application, may as well perform equally good in the other. Regarding Drupal, the Hvol metric is also ranked first with an importance of 0.141249. In the second place, however, we can see the nOutgoingExternFlsCalledUniq metric (with an importance of 0.129682), while the nOutgoingExternCallsUniq metric that is ranked second for PHPMyAdmin and Moodle, in this case is ranked third (with an importance of 0.106244).

We believe that Hvol is considered the most important metric by the TBE as it indicates how many distinct operators and operands are used. Thus, if all

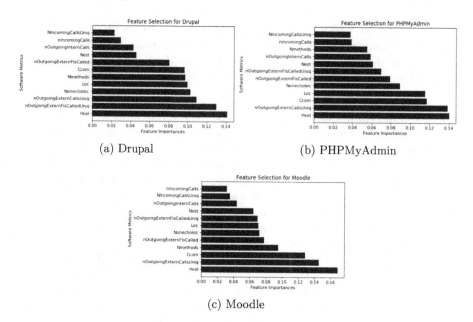

(a) Drupal   (b) PHPMyAdmin

(c) Moodle

Fig. 1. Feature selection for each one of the software applications of the selected dataset, namely (a) Drupal, (b) PHPMyAdmin, and (c) Moodle.

the operators and operands are used in a project, as opposed to only using the safe ones, the Hvol value will be directly affected. The same holds for the Ccom metric. If we use only the safe linearly independent paths instead of using all of them, it will have an important variation in Ccom's value.

It should be noted, that in the case of within-project vulnerability prediction (see Sect. 4.1), for the construction of the application-specific models, the top three features of their corresponding application are used. However, in the case of cross-project prediction (see Sect. 4.2), the top three features of the dominant projects, i.e., PHPMyAdmin and Moodle, are used (i.e., the Hvol, nOutgoingExternCallsUnique, and Ccom metrics) for each one of the three studied cases, in order to investigate whether the application of a vulnerability prediction model, which was built based on a specific application, on previously unknown applications that demonstrate similarities with respect to the importance of their features in the existence of vulnerabilities may affect its prediction performance.

3.3   Model Selection and Performance Metrics

Selection of Classifiers. In the present study different ML algorithms are used in order to build models able to discriminate between vulnerable and neutral source code files. Contrary to the previous work of Walden et al. [16], in which emphasis was given only on the Random Forest algorithm, in the present work we also investigate additional ML algorithms, including Support Vector Machine (SVM), XGBoost, and an ensemble method that combines various ML algorithms. We also examine the ability of deep learning, specifically the Multi-Layer Perceptron (MLP), to provide reliable vulnerability predictions.

For the construction of these models, hyperparameter tuning is initially employed in order to determine the optimal parameters for each model. More specifically we use the Grid-search method [24], which is commonly used to find the optimal hyper-parameters of a model, by performing an exhaustive search over specified parameter values for an estimator. Subsequently, we train the models using the dataset presented in Sect. 3.1. For instance, for the case of MLP, several models were constructed using the hyperparameters presented in Table 2. It should be noted that the same parameters were used for the MLP models that were built both for the case of within-project and cross-project vulnerability prediction. The performance of the produced models is compared using the performance parameters presented in the rest of this section. Based on these performance metrics the best model in each case is determined.

Table 2. The selected hyperparameters of the Multi-layer Perceptrons (MLPs) that are constructed in the present study.

Hyperparameter name	Value
Number of layers	4
Number of hidden layers	3
Number of hidden units (per hidden layer)	1000/500/50
Weight initialization technique	Glorot Xavier
Learning Rate	0.01
Gradient descent optimizer	Adagrad
Batch size	128
Activation function	relu
Output activation function	sigmoid
Loss function	Cross-entropy
Over-fitting prevention	Dropout = 0.15 (per layer)

Evaluation Metrics. Several performance indicators are available in the literature and are commonly used for evaluating the predictive performance of ML models. These performance indicators are normally computed based on the number of True Positives (TP), True Negatives (TN), False Positives (FP), and False Negatives (FN) that are generated by the produced models.

Similarly to previous works in vulnerability prediction [9,13–16], we put specific emphasis on the Recall (R) of the produced models, as the higher the Recall of the model, the more actual vulnerabilities it predicts. Recall is described as follows:

$$R = \frac{TP}{TP + FN} \tag{1}$$

Apart from the ability of the produced models to accurately detect the vast majority of the vulnerable files that a software product contains, it is important to take into account the volume of the produced FP, (i.e., neutral files that are marked as vulnerable by the models), since they are known to affect the models' practicality. A large number of FP forces the developers to inspect a non-trivial number of non-vulnerable files, in order to detect a file that is actually vulnerable. Hence, the number of FP is associated to the manual effort required by the developers for identifying files that actually contain vulnerabilities.

In order to measure the impact of the produced FP, similarly to [16], we use the *Inspection Ratio* (I), which is the percentage of files that one has to consider (i.e., inspect manually) to make it possible to find the TP identified by the model. This performance metric, which actually corresponds to the effort required for identifying a vulnerable file, receives values between 0 and 1, and is given by the following formula:

$$I = \frac{TP + FP}{TP + NP + FP + FN} \tag{2}$$

These two performance metrics are used as the basis for the comparison of the produced VPMs, as well as for the selection of the best model in each one of the studied cases that are presented in Sect. 4, as their combination provides a complete picture of the model performance in predicting vulnerable files. In fact, *Recall* (R) indicates how effectively the produced models detect TP, whereas the *Inspection Ratio* (I) indicates how efficient the model is in predicting TP, based on how many FP have to be triaged by the developer until a TP is detected.

3.4   Strategy

Within-Project Prediction. The first step of our study is to investigate the performance of the selected ML algorithms described in Sect. 3.3 in predicting the occurrence of vulnerabilities in the software applications on which they have been trained. To achieve this, we trained the selected models on each application of our dataset, namely Drupal, PHPMyAdmin, and Moodle, and evaluated them based exclusively on data retrieved from the corresponding application.

For the evaluation of the models we decided to employ k-fold cross-validation. In k-fold cross-validation, the dataset is split into k folds from which the k-1 participate in training and the remaining one participates in evaluation. The fold that remains for the evaluation is different every time. In this way, we have a model that is trained and evaluated k times using each time different training and testing data. The model performance is the average performance of these k models. In that way, we reduce the possibility of having biased results.

We chose to perform a 3-fold cross-validation in order to be in line with the work of Walden et al. [16]. More specifically, we used the sklearn's stratified cross-validation in order to construct folds that retain the percentage of samples for each class, thus creating realistic conditions for model training and validation. The 3-fold cross-validation was repeated 10 times for each model, after shuffling the dataset randomly before each iteration. Hence, the computed performance metrics (i.e., *Recall* and *Inspection Ratio*) of each model are the average values of 30 models trained and evaluated on the same dataset. This enhances the reliability of the produced results, as the potential bias introduced by the selection of non-representative subsets of the broader dataset is avoided.

Cross-Project Prediction. During the second part of this study, we examined the predictive performance of the software metrics-based VPMs, constructed using the ML algorithms presented in Sect. 3.3, in cross-project vulnerability prediction. In cross-project vulnerability prediction, emphasis is given on the ability of a given vulnerability prediction model to accurately predict vulnerabilities in previously unknown software projects (i.e., applications).

For this purpose, we trained several ML models based on the data of two out of the three PHP applications of the dataset (i.e., by merging their vulnerability data into a single dataset), and tested them on the vulnerability data of the remaining application. We repeated this experiment three times, covering the cases described in Table 3 (i.e., combinations of training and testing data).

Table 3. The studied cases of cross-project vulnerability prediction.

Case	Training set	Testing set
Case 1	Drupal+PHPMyAdmin	Moodle
Case 2	Drupal+Moodle	PHPMyAdmin
Case 3	Moodle+PHPMyAdmin	Drupal

The reasoning behind the decision of merging vulnerability data of two applications for constructing the training set in each one of the studied cases is twofold. Firstly, the combination of data retrieved from various software projects for training enhances the generalizability of the produced models, as the models will be able to capture patterns from several applications (instead of one), which is expected to lead to better cross-project vulnerability prediction. Secondly, by merging vulnerability data from various projects the size of the training set is increased, which is critical for the performance of deep learning models. It should be noted that in the case of cross-project vulnerability prediction, 3-fold cross-validation was not required, as a completely independent test set (i.e., the vulnerability data of the remaining application) was used for the evaluation.

4   Results and Discussion

4.1   Within-Project Prediction

In this section, we present the results of within-project vulnerability prediction. Table 4 reports the evaluation results of the classifiers that were build based exclusively on the vulnerability data of each one of the three PHP applications. These results were obtained after applying the cross-validation approach described in Sect. 3.4. In brief, the values on the Table 4 depict the average performance of the models over 10 executions of the 3-fold cross-validation experiment. As mentioned in Sect. 3.4, we considered *Recall* and *Inspection Ratio* as the main performance indicators, as they provide a complete picture of the accuracy and practicality of the produced models (see Sect. 3.3).

Table 4. Classification results of the projects.

Application	Indicator	SVM	RF	MLP	XGBoost	Ensemble
Drupal	Recall	71.17	**77.11**	75.32	76.27	75.76
	Inspection Rate	41.44	**47.64**	44.92	44.58	46.35
PHPMyAdmin	Recall	82.38	**90.25**	87.57	85.26	90.62
	Inspection Rate	17.59	**19.13**	21.47	22.84	19.77
Moodle	Recall	81.77	**92.13**	84.63	86.81	91.16
	Inspection Rate	7.78	**16.65**	17.97	19.41	15.74
Combined	Recall	78.34	**90.32**	85.25	83.54	90.45
	Inspection Rate	18.74	**17.30**	17.81	23.95	18.88

As can be seen by Table 4, in the case of Drupal, all classifiers, except for SVM have similar performance metrics, with RF being slightly better with respect to Recall. In the case of PHPMyAdmin, we notice that the RF classifier shows the best performance in terms of Recall (90.25%) and Inspection Ratio (19.13%). In the case of Moodle, RF demonstrates again the best performance, with a Recall of 92.13% and an Inspection Ratio of 16.65%, but competes closely with the stacking ensemble method (which has a Recall of 91.16% and an Inspection Ratio of 15.74%). These results are in bold font.

As can be seen by Table 4, RF is the best classifier in all the studied cases. This indicates that metric-based VPMs that are constructed using the RF algorithm exhibit sufficient predictive performance and practicality in within-project vulnerability prediction. This observation is in line with the the results of other similar studies (e.g., [9,13,15,19]), including the work of Walden et al. [16]. In all these research endeavors, RF was found to be the most promising model for the construction of project-specific VPMs. It should be noted that a direct comparison of our evaluation results with those of Walden et al. [16] would not be correct, since the original dataset was restructured (see Sect. 3.1), whereas a different pre-processing process was employed (see Sect. 3.2). Finally, another interesting observation is that the MLP-based VPMs also demonstrate sufficient predictive performance, which suggests that they may also constitute a promising solution for within-project vulnerability prediction.

4.2   Cross-Project Prediction

In this section we present the results of cross-project vulnerability prediction. As described in detail in Sect. 3.4, we investigate three individual cases (see Table 3). In each case, we merge the vulnerability data of two PHP applications and we test the produced models on the vulnerability data of the remaining one. Feature selection is also applied in order to improve the predictive performance of the produced models. It should be noted that the utilization of all the 12 features, did not lead to any good model in cross-project prediction. However, by applying feature selection (see Sect. 3.2) we achieved much better results.

More specifically, for each one of the cases presented in Table 3, we built several ML models. Emphasis was given on the RF algorithm that was found to be the best algorithm in the case of within-project vulnerability prediction, as well as on the MLP, as the specific interest of the present work is to examine whether deep learning can lead to better cross-project vulnerability prediction. As already mentioned in Sect. 3.2, for each one of the three studied cases, we took into account the top three features of the dominant projects in the training set, i.e., PHPMyAdmin or Moodle. It should be noted that in the case of PHP-MyAdmin and Moodle the top three features are exactly the same. We built the models using two projects and evaluated them using the complete vulnerability data of remaining project. In what follows, we report the performance metrics of the two best-performing models, namely RF and MLP. In particular, in Table 5 we present the results of RF and MLP for cross-project prediction after feature selection for each one of the three studied cases (see Table 3).

Table 5. The evaluation results of the classifiers that were built using the Random Forest (RF) and the Multi-layer Perceptron (MLP) algorithms in the case of cross-project vulnerability prediction.

Project	Indicator	RF	MLP
Drupal & PHPMyAdmin (train) – Moodle (test)	Recall	56	80
	Inspection Ratio	33.99	38.16
Drupal& Moodle (train) – PHPMyAdmin (test)	Recall	53	72
	Inspection Ratio	39.77	42.29
PHPMyAdmin & Moodle (train) – Drupal (test)	Recall	47	52
	Inspection Ratio	35.90	28.21

An interesting observation obtained by Table 5 is that RF, although it was found to be the best model in within-project vulnerability prediction, does not demonstrate sufficient predictive performance in cross-project vulnerability prediction (i.e., the Recall of the produced models does not exceed the value of 56% in all the studied cases). This is in line with the findings of Walden et al. [16] who also observed that the predictive performance of RF drops when it comes to cross-project vulnerability prediction. On the contrary, MLP demonstrates higher Recall than RF in all the three cases. In addition, in the case where Drupal and PHPMyAdmin were used for training and Moodle for testing, as well as in the case where Drupal and Moodle were used for training and PHP-MyAdmin for testing, the observed Recall was found to be above 70%, which is considered sufficient for cross-project vulnerability prediction. This indicates that deep learning may provide better VPMs than RF.

Focusing on the MLP models themselves, from Table 5 we can see that in the first two cases the observed Recall is higher than 70%, whereas in the third case the Recall was found to be only 52%. This can be explained by the fact that in the first two cases the models were built and subsequently tested on software projects that were similar with respect to the relevance (i.e., importance) of their features to the existence of vulnerabilities. More specifically, as was discussed in Sect. 3.2, PHPMyAdmin and Moodle had a very similar feature ranking, whereas their top three features were identical (Hvol, nOutgoingExtern-CallsUniq, and Ccom). Hence, in these two cases, both in the training set and in the testing set there were projects with similarities with respect to their feature ranking. On the contrary, in the third case, the projects in the training set (i.e., PHPMyAdmin and Moodle) and the project in the test set (i.e., Drupal), are not very similar with respect to their feature ranking, whereas their top three features (which were used as the models' inputs) are not identical. This indicates that the relative importance of the selected features (i.e., metrics) on the existence of vulnerabilities may affect the predictive performance of the produced models in cross-project vulnerability prediction.

In simple words, satisfactory cross-project vulnerability prediction can be achieved, if a model is built on a specific set of projects and applied on a previously unknown software project that exhibits similar characteristics regarding the relative importance of the selected metrics to the existence of vulnerabilities. Hence, several VPMs can be built based on the available data and then, the most suitable model can be applied to a new software project, based on whether the inputs (i.e., features) of the model are within the most important features of the new project, with respect to vulnerability identification.

Contrary to previous research endeavors in the field of vulnerability prediction [3,14] that demonstrated bad predictive performance in cross-project prediction, the results of the present work indicate that the adoption of software metrics with deep learning may lead to better results, especially when feature selection is employed. This, in fact, constitutes the main contribution of the present work.

5   Conclusion and Future Work

In this paper, we investigated the ability of software metrics to be used as the basis for the construction of VPMs, with sufficient accuracy in cross-project vulnerability prediction. For this purpose, we constructed a dataset by properly restructuring the vulnerability dataset provided by Walden et al. [16], which contains real-world vulnerability data (i.e., 21,445 files) retrieved from three popular PHP web applications, namely Drupal, PHPMyAdmin, and Moodle. Several ML, including deep learning, models were built covering both the cases of within-project and cross-project vulnerability prediction. Feature selection was also employed using the popular TBE [21] technique, in order to detect important features and to examine whether feature selection affects the performance of the produced models in the case of cross-project vulnerability prediction.

The results of our experiments showed that RF is the best model in the case of within-project vulnerability prediction, which is in line with the findings of Walden et al. [16]. On the contrary, Deep Learning was found to be the best solution in the case of cross-project vulnerability prediction, as MLP-based models demonstrated sufficient levels of recall and inspection ratio, especially compared to the RF models. This indicates that deep learning and software metrics constitute a promising solution for cross-project vulnerability prediction. Another interesting observation is that the performance of the models in cross-project vulnerability prediction tends to be affected by feature selection. In fact, models that were built based on a specific set of software projects seem to provide better results when applied to new software projects that exhibit similarities with respect to the relevance of their features to the existence of vulnerabilities.

Several directions for future work can be identified. First of all, the present study was based solely on PHP web applications. In order to investigate the generalizability of the produced results, we are planning to replicate our study using software products that are written in other programming languages (e.g., Java, C/C++, etc.) and that belong to different domains (e.g., healthcare). Secondly, although the present analysis was based on a relatively large vulnerability dataset comprising 21,445 files, these files were actually retrieved from three real-world PHP applications. Hence, in the future, we are planning to extend our analysis by enriching this dataset with vulnerability information retrieved from additional PHP applications, in order to ensure that the results are not biased towards specific applications. Finally, we are also planning to replicate our study by using metrics calculated at lower levels of granularity, such as class- or function- level, in order to further investigate the generalizability of our results.

References

1. ISO/IEC: ISO/IEC 25010 - Systems and software engineering - Systems and software Quality Requirements and Evaluation (SQuaRE) - System and software quality models. ISO/IEC (2011)
2. Gelenbe, E., et al.: NEMESYS: enhanced network security for seamless service provisioning in the smart mobile ecosystem. In: Gelenbe, E., Lent, R. (eds.) Information Sciences and Systems 2013, pp. 369–378. Springer, Cham (2013). https://doi.org/10.1007/978-3-319-01604-7_36
3. Siavvas, M., Gelenbe, E., Kehagias, D.: Static analysis-based approaches for secure software development. In: Security in Computer and Information Sciences, p. 142 (2018)
4. Kumar, L., Misra, S., Rath, S.K.: An empirical analysis of the effectiveness of software metrics and fault prediction model for identifying faulty classes. Comput. Stand. Interfaces **53**, 1–32 (2017)

5. Shukla, S., Behera, R.K., Misra, S., Rath, S.K.: Software reliability assessment using deep learning technique. In: Chakraverty, S., Goel, A., Misra, S. (eds.) Towards Extensible and Adaptable Methods in Computing, pp. 57–68. Springer, Singapore (2018). https://doi.org/10.1007/978-981-13-2348-5_5
6. Chidamber, S.R., Kemerer, C.F.: A metrics suite for object oriented design. IEEE Trans. Softw. Eng. **20**(6), 476–493 (1994)
7. Misra, S., Akman, I., Colomo-Palacios, R.: Framework for evaluation and validation of software complexity measures. IET Softw. **6**(4), 323–334 (2012)
8. Misra, S., Adewumi, A., Fernandez-Sanz, L., Damasevicius, R.: A suite of object oriented cognitive complexity metrics. IEEE Access **6**, 8782–8796 (2018)
9. Scandariato, R., Walden, J., Hovsepyan, A., Joosen, W.: Predicting vulnerable software components via text mining. IEEE Trans. Softw. Eng. **40**(10), 993–1006 (2014)
10. Zhang, M., de Carnavalet, X.D.C., Wang, L., Ragab, A.: Large-scale empirical study of important features indicative of discovered vulnerabilities to assess application security. IEEE Trans. Inf. Forensics Secur. **14**(9), 2315–2330 (2019)
11. Pang, Y., Xue, X., Wang, H.: Predicting Vulnerable Software Components through Deep Neural Network. In: Proceedings of the 2017 International Conference on Deep Learning Technologies - ICDLT 2017, pp. 6–10 (2017)
12. Tang, Y., Zhao, F., Yang, Y., Lu, H., Zhou, Y., Xu, B.: Predicting vulnerable components via text mining or software metrics? An effort-aware perspective. In: IEEE International Conference on Software Quality, Reliability and Security (2015)
13. Yang, J., Ryu, D., Baik, J.: Improving vulnerability prediction accuracy with secure coding standard violation measures. In: 2016 International Conference on Big Data and Smart Computing, BigComp 2016, pp. 115–122 (2016)
14. Jimenez, M., Papadakis, M., Traon, Y.L.: Vulnerability prediction models: a case study on the Linux kernel. In: 2016 IEEE 16th International Working Conference on Source Code Analysis and Manipulation (SCAM), pp. 1–10 (2016)
15. Dam, H.K., Tran, T., Pham, T.T.M., Ng, S.W., Grundy, J., Ghose, A.: Automatic feature learning for predicting vulnerable software components. IEEE Trans. Software Eng., 1 (2018)
16. Walden, J., Stuckman, J., Scandariato, R.: Predicting vulnerable components: software metrics vs text mining. In: 2014 IEEE 25th International Symposium on Software Reliability Engineering, pp. 23–33, November 2014
17. Ferenc, R., Hegedűs, P., Gyimesi, P., Antal, G., Bán, D., Gyimóthy, T.: Challenging machine learning algorithms in predicting vulnerable JavaScript functions. In: Proceedings of the 7th International Workshop on Realizing Artificial Intelligence Synergies in Software Engineering (2019)
18. Siavvas, M., Kehagias, D., Tzovaras, D.: A preliminary study on the relationship among software metrics and specific vulnerability types. In: 2017 International Conference on Computational Science and Computational Intelligence (2017)
19. Tang, Y., Zhao, F., Yang, Y., Lu, H., Zhou, Y., Xu, B.: Predicting vulnerable components via text mining or software metrics? An effort-aware perspective. In: Proceedings - 2015 IEEE International Conference on Software Quality, Reliability and Security, QRS 2015, pp. 27–36 (2015)
20. Jimenez, M., Rwemalika, R., Papadakis, M., Sarro, F., Le Traon, Y., Harman, M.: The importance of accounting for real-world labelling when predicting software vulnerabilities. In: 27th ACM Joint Meeting on European Software Engineering Conference and Symposium on the Foundations of Software Engineering (2019)
21. Hochreiter, S., Schmidhuber, J.: Long short-term memory. Neural Comput. **9**(8), 1735–1780 (1997)

22. de Vries, E., Gilbert, J.: Design and implementation of a PHP compiler front-end. dept. Technical report, TR-2007-47, Trinity College Dublin (2007)
23. Genuer, R., Poggi, J.M., Tuleau-Malot, C.: Variable selection using random forests. Pattern Recogn. Lett. **31**(14), 2225–2236 (2010)
24. Feurer, M., Klein, A., Eggensperger, K., Springenberg, J., Blum, M., Hutter, F.: Efficient and robust automated machine learning. In: Proceedings of the 28th International Conference on Neural Information Processing Systems (NIPS) (2015)

Software Requirement Catalog on Acceptability, Usability, Internationalization and Sustainability for Contraception mPHRs

Manal Kharbouch[1], Ali Idri[1,2(✉)], Leanne Redman[3], Hassan Alami[4],
José Luis Fernández-Alemán[5], and Ambrosio Toval[5]

[1] Software Project Management Research Team ENSIAS, Mohammed V
University, Rabat, Morocco
ali.idri@um5.ac.ma
[2] CSEHS-MSDA, Mohammed VI Polytechnic University, Ben Guerir, Morocco
[3] Pennington Biomedical Research Center, Baton Rouge, LA 70808, USA
[4] Faculty of Medicine, University Mohammed V, Rabat, Morocco
[5] Software Engineering Research Group, Department of Computing
and Systems, Faculty of Informatics, University of Murcia, Murcia, Spain

Abstract. Contraception Mobile Personal Health Records (mPHRs) are efficient mobile health applications (apps) to increase awareness about fertility and contraception and to allow women to access, track, manage, and share their health data with healthcare providers. This paper aims to develop a requirements catalog, according to standards, guidelines, and relevant literature to e-health technology and psychology. The requirements covered by this catalog are Acceptability, Usability, Sustainability, and Internationalization (i18n). This catalog can be very useful for developing, evaluating, and auditing contraceptive apps, as well as helping stakeholders and developers identify potential requirements for their mPHRs to improve them.

Keywords: Acceptability · Usability · Internationalization · Sustainability · I18n · mPHR · Contraception · SRS · eHealth

1 Introduction

Besides being important for both individuals and families, well-informed contraception is mandatory for population regulation [1], and deserves by all means high attention, since it does not only improve women's reproductive health but also their quality of life [2]. Owing to the tremendous evolution in medicine and technology, unprecedented opportunities for new progress in the field of contraception now present themselves. The development of emerging contraceptive solutions that improve the understanding and use of existing contraceptives; expanding acceptance and access to contraception, will help alleviate the growing unmet demand for satisfactory contraceptives worldwide[1]. However, the need for more theory-guided research to support the

© Springer Nature Switzerland AG 2020
O. Gervasi et al. (Eds.): ICCSA 2020, LNCS 12252, pp. 894–905, 2020.
https://doi.org/10.1007/978-3-030-58811-3_63

development of future Mobile Health (mHealth) apps to determine their clinical efficacy is highly stressed, especially in the field of contraception [3].

Addressing occasional treatment unfairness in health care, improving access to health information, reducing health system failures and remodeling primary health care, all depend on the enormous potential that the use of mobile health technologies offers nowadays [4]. These mHealth apps potentially involve reaching a wider scope with equal accessibility while keeping it a low-cost way to deliver a healthcare service, which makes these apps a vigorous public health solutions [5]. These apps are widespread, however, in-depth research addressing the effectiveness and acceptability of these apps is lacking [6]. Although there are many methods for evaluating existing systems and technologies that have already proven themselves, there is a lack of methods for evaluating innovative technologies. In this regard, systematic and scientific methods are required to evaluate innovative technologies in terms of user acceptance [7]. Of course, usability assessment is an essential feature of user-centered designs, where an iterative approach to product development is emphasized and user feedback is included at various points in the process. However, more research is needed to understand the gaps between intent and the actual and ongoing use of the application [3]. While the Human-Computer Interaction (HCI) is about usability, the Acceptability Engineering (AE) deals with acceptability. Comparative studies of usability and acceptability provided insight into the fact that acceptance can be understood as a concept of a higher level of usability, and acts as a compromise between a variety of factors that influence the adoption of new technologies [7]. For instance, there are cases when the system is easy to use, but users do not accept it. On the contrary, there may be unwieldy systems, but they are appreciated by many users. Moreover, limited reliance on Personal Health Records (PHRs) by individuals is a real problem, for several reasons such as the use of medical terms that are generally difficult to understand by users, the lack of language support, as well as social and cultural barriers [8]. Yet, having solid awareness about contraception solutions does not necessarily induce them to be used, since the bottleneck of modern contraception usage is still misconceptions entrained by social and cultural influences [9], which stress the importance of internationalization in contraception applications.

To the best of our knowledge, no software requirement catalog for contraception mPHRs has yet been developed. Therefore, this paper aims to elaborate on a requirements' catalog suited for the contraception apps with respect to IEEE 29148:2011 ISO/IEC/IEEE Standard [10]. This catalog mainly focuses on acceptability, usability, i18n, and sustainability for contraception mPHRs.

This article is structured as follows. Section 2 describes this software requirements specification (SRS) catalog, the process to obtain it, and explains the audit method to validate the catalog. The catalog validation is well explained in Sect. 3 through an application example that serves as the validation strategy for the proposed approach. Section 4 discusses the results of the audit report. Finally, Sect. 5 outlines our conclusions and further work.

2 Method

In order to identify standards and studies as resources to extract requirements related to contraception apps prior to the catalog generation, a literature review was conducted within the software engineering, psychology, and health fields. The distinguished standards and models were applied in the extraction process of requirements. Then, on the basis of the set of extracted requirements a catalog that was generated conforming to the IEEE 29148:2011 ISO/IEC/IEEE Standard [10]. Finally, the catalog is evaluated with a contraception app for audit purposes.

2.1 Requirements Specification

In the interest of including the distinguished SRS for the catalog, the present study relied upon the following: (1) previous studies concerning software quality [11, 12]. (2) research dealing with usability [3, 13, 14], acceptability[7], and the fare difference between the two aspects [15]. (3) software requirements catalogs that implement sustainability and internationalization [8, 16], and reusable catalog concerning software usability specifications [17]. Likewise, the following set of standards and models was applied in the extraction process of requirements.

- ISO/IEC 25010 is considered the cornerstone of a product quality evaluation system;
- ISO 9241-11 is a multi-part standard dealing with product usage characteristics. It offers a framework for understanding the concept of usability and its application to situations in which people use interactive systems and other types of systems;
- ISO/TR 14292 is used for the definition of the scope and context of personal health records;
- The W3C standards for Web and mobile devices;
- UTAUT stands for Unified Theory of Acceptance and Use of Technology and explains the user's intentions to use an information system and subsequent usage behavior.

2.2 Catalog Development

Geared toward ensuring a firm and reliable set of software requirements for contraception mPHRs, the development of the catalog in question is in respect to the specifications of contraception apps in the leading apps repositories. and to the former literature related to contraception. As described in Fig. 1 the generation process of the catalog consists of four steps: (1) Resources identification, which are the aforementioned related studies and standards. (2) The requirements extraction from the highlighted resources. (3) The catalog generation from the extracted requirements conforming to the IEEE 29148:2011 ISO/IEC/IEEE Standard [10], which contains a set of provisions for the processes and products related to the engineering of requirements for systems and software products and services throughout the life cycle.

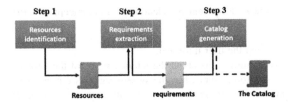

Fig. 1. The generation process of the catalog

2.3 Audit Process

In order to assess an mPHR for contraception using the catalog of requirements of the developed software, and to validate the latter, we elaborated a questionnaire that consists of 30 items based on the catalog guidelines, which is presented in Table 2. This questionnaire has been used in the evaluation of the app 'Clue Period & Ovulation Tracker' and was exclusively tailored to this app's relevant specifications. Following the app installation, the first step of the evaluation is to carry out a preliminary analysis of the application's work environment, its characteristics, and its main functionalities. The first author then conducted the assessment questionnaire on the 5th of February 2020. Then, a Checklist to evaluate the app was generated from the catalog. The Checklist was in the form of a questionnaire containing 30 questions, to facilitate the work of the evaluator, requirements that are not applicable to this app have been discarded. The answer to the questions adopted in this study has three choices, which are as follows: Yes (1 point) if the application offers this feature/functionality, No (0 points) if the application does not support this feature/functionality, and Partially (0.5 points) if the app does not fully respond to the statement detailed.

3 Results

3.1 The Identified Requirements

Based on existing contraception apps for iOS and Android platforms and scientific literature on contraception [18–23] (step 1 in Fig. 1), contraception mPHR requirements have been extracted (Step 2 of Fig. 1). Note that the requirements for i18n and sustainability and acceptability have been slightly adapted to contraception mPHRs according to [8, 16, 24, 25]. The contraception mPHR requirements are detailed in Table 1.

Table 1. Requirements identified for contraception mPHR

Usability requirements

1) The mPHR must keep the user informed

1.1) The mPHR must inform users about the internal status of the system

1.2) The mPHR must inform users when the system registers a user interaction

1.3) The mPHR must inform users of any action with important consequences

1.4) The mPHR should inform users that the system is processing an action when the action takes some time to complete

2) The mPHR must allow easy navigation and system recovery for the user

2.1) The mPHR must allow undoing system actions at several levels

2.2) The mPHR must allow canceling the execution of an action or the whole application

2.3) The mPHR must allow going back to a particular state in a command execution sequence

3) The mPHR must support user error protection

3.1) The mPHR must prevent users from data input errors

3.2) The mPHR must help users with tasks that require different steps with user input and correct such input records for each user's option

Internationalization requirements

1) The mPHR must be designed for cultural diversity and multilingual use

1.1) The mPHR must adapt its content to the user's linguistic preferences

1.2) The mPHR should be available in multiple languages, providing a simple and clear way to switch languages at multiple points while using it

1.3) The mPHR must adapt the help sections and the privacy policy to the user's linguistic preferences

1.4) The mPHR must adapt the reproductive health and contraception terms to the user's language preferences

1.5) The mPHR must display the text with the correct alignment of the text according to the user's linguistic preferences

2) The mPHR must use images to express ideas

3) The mPHR should clarify the content with icons

4) The mPHR should use graphs to display the history of measurements and period/ovulation tracking

5) The mPHR uses formats, units of measurement, and currencies appropriate for an international audience

5.1) The mPHR must adopt the digital format to the linguistic preferences of the user

5.2) The mPHR must adapt the currency to the geographic location of the user

5.3) The mPHR must adapt the units of measurement to the geographic location of the user

5.4) The mPHR must adapt the date and time format to the user's preferences

5.5) The mPHR must adapt the telephone numbers to the geographic location of the user

5.6) mPHR must adapt the address to the geographic location of the user

6) The mPHR should take into account the first day of the week depending on the geographic location

7) The mPHR should adjust the advertisements broadcast to the user to avoid cultural inconsistencies

8) The mPHR should allow the user to manage personal information, according to the laws or regulations of different countries regarding the ownership of personal information by the user

8.1) The user must be able to adjust the personal information in accordance with the laws or regulations of the different countries concerning the ownership of personal information by the user

(continued)

Table 1. (*continued*)

Internationalization requirements

8.2) The user must be able to control personal information in accordance with the laws or regulations of the various countries concerning the ownership of personal information by the user

8.3) The user must be able to process personal information in accordance with the laws or regulations of different countries regarding the ownership of personal information by the user

Sustainability requirements

1) The mPHR must have a positive individual impact

1.1) The mPHR must respect the security and confidentiality of the user

1.2) The mPHR must promote fertility and contraception awareness

2) The mPHR must have a positive social impact

2.1) The mPHR should allow interaction between users

2.1.1) The mPHR must connect to social networks

2.1.2) The mPHR should support a forum and/or chat

2.2) The mPHR should promote social solidarity and user participation

3) The mPHR must have a positive environmental impact

3.1) The mPHR should reduce transportation to restore health in Obstetrics and family planning centers

3.2) The mPHR should be convenient for frequent use

3.3) The app shall connect to other IT resources

3.3.1) The mPHR must store data in data warehouses, drivers, or cloud systems

3.3.2) The mPHR should use device functions such as Bluetooth, GPS, camera, and fingerprint sensor

3.3.3) The mPHR must communicate with mapping applications to display locations

3.4) The mPHR should be energy efficient

4) The app shall have a positive technical impact

4.1) The mPHR will easily adapt to future updates

4.2) The mPHR should stop in standby mode

Acceptability requirements

1) The mPHR should be personally relevant

2) The mPHR should be interesting

3) The mPHR should contribute to establish and maintain contraception self-monitoring

4) The mPHR should be clear and easily understandable

5) The mPHR should teach the user about contraception and reproductive health

6) The mPHR should motivate the user to keep track of her contraceptive use

3.2   The Generated Catalog

The general structure of the catalog is thus adapted to the recommended SRS structure from the standard as shown in Fig. 2. Seeking to address the most relevant software requirements for contraception mPHRs, the present catalog covers acceptability, usability, internationalization, and sustainability. As illustrated in Fig. 2, the Usability Requirements are indexed under Sect. 3.3. Three additional subsections have been integrated into the SRS structure under the Software system attributes section, which are internationalization (3.7.6) and sustainability (3.7.7) in keeping with [16], followed by acceptability (3.7.8). Each identified requirement contains a set of predefined attributes, which provide additional information about it, such as Project Unique Identification (PUID), description, and priority to cite but a few.

1. Introduction

    1.1 Purpose

    1.2 Scope

    1.3 Product overview

    1.3.1 Product perspective

    1.3.2 Product functions

    1.3.3 User characteristics

    1.3.4 Limitations

    1.4 Definitions

2. References

3. Specific requirements

    3.1 External interfaces

    3.2 Functions

    3.3 Usability Requirements

    3.4 Performance requirements

    3.5 Logical database requirements

    3.6 Design constraints

    3.7 Software system attributes

        3.7.1 Reliability

        3.7.2 Availability

        3.7.3 Security

        3.7.4 Maintainability

        3.7.5 Portability

        3.7.6 internationalization

        3.7.7 Sustainability

        3.7.8 Acceptability

    3.8 Supporting information

4. Verification (parallel to subsections in Section 3)

5. Appendices

    5.1 Assumptions and dependencies

    5.2 Acronyms and abbreviations

Fig. 2. IEEE 29148:2011 SRS outline

3.3   Illustration

In order to illustrate how to apply the developed catalog to evaluate an mPHR for contraception, we selected Clue Period Tracker, Ovulation, which is one of the most downloaded, best-reviewed mPHR in apps repositories. The number of total installs of this app exceeds ten million, and its review score on the app store is 4.8/5, which is considered a very high score.

The assessment questionnaire responses for 'Clue Period Tracker, Ovulation' evaluation, as shown in Table 2, are as follows: 22 Yes (73.33%), 1 Partially (3.33%), and 7 No (23.30%). The result for Q14 was "Partially", although the app allows adding, editing, and removing some personal data it does not allow the user to edit the current menstrual cycle nor add logs of previous menstrual cycles. Thereby, the score of this app is:

$$(22 * 1 + 1 * 0.5 + 7 * 0)/30 = 75\%$$

This score is considered as a very high score since 73.33% of the answers were positive. Yet, there is still room for improvement. Although 'Clue Period Tracker, Ovulation' recorded a perfect score of 100% in terms of usability and acceptability. However, the app scored 50% in internationalization and 63.64% in sustainability. Thereby, to improve this app, it is recommended to cover sustainability in all its dimensions (individual, social, environmental, technical, and economical) in future versions of this app, and to bridge the cultural and language barriers among women seeking contraception from different backgrounds to enhance the international aspect of the app.

4   Discussion

4.1   Main Findings

Despite the undeniable importance of user acceptability, usability, internationalization (i18n), and sustainability in today's contraception apps industry, no specific standard is found to handle such required mPHRs. Therefore, the catalog presented in this article is very useful for stakeholders of contraception apps. Developers can use some or all of the requirements in this catalog to develop international and sustainable contraceptive applications in which end users can find them both usable and acceptable.

Health organizations and/or development companies that wish to promote, improve, and facilitate access to contraceptive care through mPHRs can obtain their needs and define them from this catalog. Moreover, audit organizations or contraception apps stakeholders can use the catalog to assess and/or audit contraceptive applications. Furthermore, the content of the catalog of requirements will be continuously improved by incorporating new knowledge from additional information sources, such as recommendations, standards, or other policies.

Table 2. Assessment questionnaire

ID	Question	Result
Q1	Does the mPHR inform the user when the system registers a user interaction?	Yes
Q2	Does the mPHR inform the user of actions with important consequences?	Yes
Q3	Does the mPHR inform the user when the system is processing long actions?	Yes
Q4	Does the mPHR allow easy navigation?	Yes
Q5	Does the mPHR allow canceling the execution of an action or the whole application?	Yes
Q6	Does the mPHR support user error protection?	Yes
Q7	Does the mPHR list in its description the supported languages?	No
Q8	Does the mPHR adapt its content to the user's linguistic preferences?	No
Q9	Does the mPHR use pictures/icons to explain ideas?	Yes
Q10	Does the mPHR support the possibility to browse the history of the logs taken?	Yes
Q11	Does the mPHR use graphs to display the history of measurements and period/ovulation tracking?	Yes
Q12	Does the mPHR use formats, date/time, and units of measurement appropriate for an international audience?	Yes
Q13	Does the mPHR adjust the advertisements broadcast to the user?	No
Q14	Does the mPHR allow the user to manage personal information?	Partially
Q15	Does the mPHR support different profiles in the same device?	Yes
Q16	Is the user able to access the app without Internet connexion?	Yes
Q17	Is the user able to access the app using a login or social network account?	Yes
Q18	Does the mPHR connect to social networks?	Yes
Q19	Does the mPHR connect with maps repositories?	No
Q20	Is the user able to back up data from the mPHR?	Yes
Q21	Is the user able to find nearby obstetrics and family planning centers?	No
Q22	Is the user able to use phone resources (i.e. Bluetooth, camera, GPS..) within the mPHR?	Yes
Q23	Does the mPHR promote interaction among users via social networks?	Yes
Q24	Does the mPHR promote social solidarity among users via forums/chats?	No
Q25	Does the app shut down in idle mode?	No
Q26	Is the mPHR personally relevant?	Yes
Q27	Does the mPHR provide interesting contraception awareness content?	Yes
Q28	Does the mPHR contributes to period/ovulation tracking and contraception self-monitoring	Yes
Q29	Dos the mPHR include a Help or FAQ section to help understand it?	Yes
Q30	Does the mPHR motivate keep track of period/ovulation and contraceptive use?	Yes

4.2 Limitations

This study may contain several limitations, such as: (1) the multiple requirements that are scattered throughout different sources for the catalog generation were not harmonized; and (2) The application example that uses only one application may not be sufficient to demonstrate the applicability of the catalog. However, an example of the application is presented to give an overview of how the catalog is used to evaluate contraception apps.

5 Conclusion and Future Work

This study has presented the software requirement catalog on acceptability, usability, internationalization, and sustainability for contraception mPHRs, which is an SRS repository for contraception stakeholders to help them design, identify and verify requirements for acceptable, usable, internationalized, and sustainable contraception mPHRs. The requirements presented in this study were determined mainly from the results of literature reviews conducted in this domain and from the analysis of standards related to software engineering, psychology, and e-health.

For future work, we intend to: (1) Evaluate the moderation effect of personal innovativeness on each sub-component of acceptability requirement and its influence on the intention of use of mobile applications for contraception. (2) Make progress in improving the catalog of requirements by harmonizing the multiple requirements distributed across different sources and detailing those requirements giving various application examples resulting in a much richer catalog that would still have simple topics, but would be able to guide stakeholders into perfecting contraception mPHRs. (3) Develop a validation method called AUISC-AUDIT to determine if the contraception mPHRs meet the requirements mentioned in AUISC-CAT which evaluation will be carried out in a family planning center in Rabat (Morocco).

Acknowledgment. This work was conducted within the research project PEER 7-246 supported by the US Agency for International Development. The authors would like to thank the National Academy of Science, Engineering, and Medicine, and USAID for their support. Moreover, this research has been supported by the Spanish Ministry of Economy and Competitiveness and the European Fund for Regional Development (ERDF) under project RTI2018-098309-B-C33.

References

1. Sitruk-Ware, R., Nath, A., Mishell, D.R.: Contraception technology: past, present and future. In: Contraception, pp. 319–330. Elsevier, Amsterdam (2013)
2. Institute of Medicine: New Frontiers in Contraceptive Research. National Academies Press (2004). https://doi.org/10.17226/10905
3. Reyes, J., Washio, Y., Stringer, M., Teitelman, A.M.: Usability and acceptability of everhealthier women, a mobile application to enhance informed health choices. J. Obstet. Gynecol. Neonatal Nurs. **47**, 853–861 (2018)

4. Malvey, D., Slovensky, D.J. (eds.): mHealth: Transforming Healthcare. Springer, Boston (2014). https://doi.org/10.1007/978-1-4899-7457-0

5. Fjeldsoe, B.S., Miller, Y.D., Marshall, A.L.: MobileMums: a randomized controlled trial of an sms-based physical activity intervention. Ann. Behav. Med. **39**, 101–111 (2010). https://doi.org/10.1007/s12160-010-9170-z

6. Zhao, J., Freeman, B., Li, M.: Can mobile phone apps influence people's health behavior change? Evid. Rev. (2016). https://doi.org/10.2196/jmir.5692

7. Kim, H.C.: Acceptability engineering: the study of user acceptance of innovative technologies. J. Appl. Res. Technol., 230–237 (2015). https://doi.org/10.1016/j.jart.2015.06.001

8. Bachiri, M., Idri, A., Redman, L.M., Fernandez-Aleman, J.L., Toval, A.: A requirements catalog of mobile personal health records for prenatal care. In: Misra, S., et al. (eds.) ICCSA 2019. LNCS, vol. 11622, pp. 483–495. Springer, Cham (2019). https://doi.org/10.1007/978-3-030-24305-0_36

9. Ochako, R., et al.: Barriers to modern contraceptive methods uptake among young women in kenya: a qualitative study global health. BMC Public Health **15**, 1–9 (2015). https://doi.org/10.1186/s12889-015-1483-1

10. ISO, IEC, IEE: ISO/IEC/IEEE 29148: systems and software engineering—life cycle processes—requirements engineering (2011). https://doi.org/10.1109/IEEESTD.2011.6146379

11. Ouhbi, S., Idri, A., Aleman, J.L.F., Toval, A.: Evaluating software product quality: a systematic mapping study. In: Proceedings - 2014 Joint Conference of the International Workshop on Software Measurement, IWSM 2014 and The International Conference on Software Process and Product Measurement, Mensura 2014, pp. 141–151. Institute of Electrical and Electronics Engineers Inc. (2014). https://doi.org/10.1109/IWSM.Mensura.2014.30

12. Ouhbi, S., Idri, A., Fern, L.: Applying ISO/IEC 25010 on mobile personal health records. In: 8th International Conference on Health and Informatics, pp. 405–412 (2015)

13. Mistrik, I., Bahsoon, R., Eeles, P., Roshandel, R., Stal, M.: Relating system quality and software architecture (2014). https://doi.org/10.1016/C2013-0-00646-9

14. Ouhbi, S., Fernández-Alemán, J.L., Pozo, J.R., Bajta, M.E., Toval, A., Idri, A.: Compliance of blood donation apps with mobile OS usability guidelines. J. Med. Syst. **39**(6), 1–21 (2015). https://doi.org/10.1007/s10916-015-0243-1

15. Okumus, B., Ali, F., Bilgihan, A., Ozturk, A.B.: Psychological factors influencing customers' acceptance of smartphone diet apps when ordering food at restaurants. Int. J. Hosp. Manag., 67–77 (2018). https://doi.org/10.1016/j.ijhm.2018.01.001

16. Ouhbi, S., Fernández-Alemán, J.L., Idri, A., Toval, A., Pozo, J.R., Bajta, M.E.: A reusable requirements catalog for internationalized and sustainable blood donation apps. In: Proceedings of the 12th International Conference on Evaluation of Novel Approaches to Software Engineering, pp. 285–292 (2017). https://doi.org/10.5220/0006360202850292

17. Cruz Zapata, B., Fernández-Alemán, J.L., Toval, A., Idri, A.: Reusable software usability specifications for mHealth applications. J. Med. Syst. **42**(3), 1–9 (2018). https://doi.org/10.1007/s10916-018-0902-0

18. Egarter, C., Grimm, C., Nouri, K., Ahrendt, H.J., Bitzer, J., Cermak, C.: Contraceptive counselling and factors affecting women's contraceptive choices: results of the CHOICE study in Austria. Reprod. Biomed. Online, 692–697 (2012). https://doi.org/10.1016/j.rbmo.2011.12.003

19. Reiss, K., et al.: Using automated voice messages linked to telephone counselling to increase post-menstrual regulation contraceptive uptake and continuation in Bangladesh: study protocol for a randomised controlled trial. BMC Public Health, 1–10 (2017). https://doi.org/10.1186/s12889-017-4703-z

20. Koch, M.C., et al.: Improving usability and pregnancy rates of a fertility monitor by an additional mobile application: results of a retrospective efficacy study of Daysy and DaysyView app. Reprod. Health, 1–10 (2018). https://doi.org/10.1186/s12978-018-0479-6

21. McCarthy, O., et al.: A randomized controlled trial of an intervention delivered by mobile phone app instant messaging to increase the acceptability of effective contraception among young people in Tajikistan. Reprod. Health 15, 1–14 (2018)

22. Fruhauf, T., et al.: Measuring family planning quality and its link with contraceptive use in public facilities in Burkina Faso, Ethiopia, Kenya and Uganda. Health Policy Plan., 828–839 (2018). https://doi.org/10.1093/heapol/czy058

23. Hardon, A.: The development of contraceptive technologies: a feminist critique. Gend. Dev., 40–44 (1994). https://doi.org/10.1080/09682869308520010

24. Ouhbi, S., Fernández-Alemán, J.L., Carrillo-de-Gea, J.M., Toval, A., Idri, A.: E-health internationalization requirements for audit purposes. Comput. Methods Programs Biomed. 144, 49–60 (2017)

25. Plaete, J., De Bourdeaudhuij, I., Verloigne, M., Crombez, G.: Acceptability, feasibility and effectiveness of an eHealth behaviour intervention using self-regulation: "MyPlan". Patient Educ. Couns. 98, 1617–1624 (2015). https://doi.org/10.1016/j.pec.2015.07.014

Quantifying Influential Communities in Granular Social Networks Using Fuzzy Theory

Anisha Kumari[1], Ranjan Kumar Behera[1(✉)], Abhishek Sai Shukla[2],
Satya Prakash Sahoo[1], Sanjay Misra[3], and Sanatanu Kumar Rath[4]

[1] Department of CSE, Veer Surendra Sai University of Technology,
Burla, Odisha, India
anishamishracs@gmail.com, jranjanb.19@gmail.com,
sahoo.satyaprakash@gmail.com
[2] PwC Service Delivery Center, Bengaluru, India
deva.abhi96@gmail.com
[3] Department of Electrical and Information Engineering, Covenant University,
1023, Ota, Nigeria
ssopam@gmail.com
[4] Department of CSE, National Institute of Technology, Rourkela, Rourkela, India
skrath@nitrkl.ac.in

Abstract. Community detection and centrality analysis in social networks are identified as pertinent research topics in the field of social network analysis. Community detection focuses on identifying the subgraphs (communities) which have dense connections within it as compared to outside of it, whereas centrality analysis focuses on identifying significant nodes in a social network based on different aspects of importance. A number of research works have focused on identifying community structure in large-scale network. However, very less effort has been emphasized on quantifying the influence of the communities. In this paper, group of nodes that are likely to form communities are first uncovered and then they are quantified based on the influencing ability in the network. Identifying exact boundaries of communities are quite challenging in large scale network. The major contribution in this paper is to develop a model termed as FRC-FGSN (Fuzzy Rough Communities in Fuzzy Granular Social Network), to identify the communities with the help of fuzzy and rough set theory. The proposed model is based on a idea that, the degree of belongingness a node in a community may not be binary but can be models through fuzzy membership. The second contribution is to quantifying the influence of the community using eigenvector centrality. In order to improve the scalability, several steps in the proposed model have been implemented using map-reduce programming paradigm in a cluster-computing framework like Hadoop. Comparative analysis of FRC-FGSN with other parallel algorithms as available in the literature has been presented to demonstrate the scalability and effectiveness of the algorithm.

© Springer Nature Switzerland AG 2020
O. Gervasi et al. (Eds.): ICCSA 2020, LNCS 12252, pp. 906–917, 2020.
https://doi.org/10.1007/978-3-030-58811-3_64

Keywords: Influential community · Eigenvector centrality · Granular social network · Cluster-computing

1 Introduction

A social network can be defined as a graph structure where nodes represent the individuals and the edges within it represent the relationships among the individuals. With recent growth in the online social networking sites (OSNs) such as Facebook, Twitter, Instagram etc., the analysis of the static and dynamic features plays an important role in every aspect of human life. Real-world social networks have some distinctive characteristics like, small-world effect [1], power law degree distribution [2] and community structure [3], which make the analysis of these networks even more interesting. Small world effect and power law degree distribution basically deals with degree of association among the nodes in the network. Communities are defined as the functional units of the network which may be formed due to the mentioned features. It can also be defined as the dense subgraph which have large number of edges within themselves and less number of edges going out of them. Since the real-world social network follows power law degree distribution, some of the nodes are more significant as compared to others [4,5]. The communities having more number of influential nodes are said to have high influencing factor as compared to the communities having less significant nodes. The identification of influential communities passes through two phases:

1. **Phase I- Community detection process**: With the increase in complexity and size, exploring communities in large scale network is found to be a challenging task. Pal et al. have developed an efficient algorithm to explore the fuzzy-rough communities [6]. This algorithm has been designed to run on a granular social network model which is based on fuzzy and rough-set theory known as fuzzy-granular social network (FGSN) [7]. Unlike other community detection algorithms, this approach gives better results when the network consist of bigger number of overlapping communities [6]. The extension of the work has been implemented in the proposed work.
2. **Phase II- Influence maximization for the Communities**: Bonacich has studied the unique properties of eigenvector centrality [8]. Unlike graph-theoretic centralities like degree, betweenness, and closeness centrality, eigenvector centrality considers the centrality of its neighbors [8,9]. Thus, eigenvector centrality measure helps in estimating the influence of a certain node in a real-world scenario. In this work, eigenvector centrality has been considered to calculate the influence of the communities.

Social networks have similar characteristics of big data namely volume, variety and velocity (3 V's) [10]. Real-world social networks with number of nodes of the order $\geq 10^6$ are quite difficult to process with conventional tools. In this paper, map-reduce based community detection algorithms have been designed which is implemented in Apache Spark distributed framework. *Apache Spark* is a cluster-computing framework, widely used for processing distributed applications.

The subsequent sections of the papers are described as follows: Sect. 2 presents the motivation about fuzzy implementation of social network. Section 3 presents the literature survey of the work. The background details is discussed in Sect. 4. Section 5 presents the problem statement and the proposed algorithm of the work. Section 6 presents the implementation work of the proposed algorithms. The experimental results and the observation is presented in Sect. 7. The conclusion and future work is presented in Sect. 8.

2   Motivation

Although a good number of research works have been carried out in the literature for community detection in social networks, quantifying them in term of influential factor is still a challenging task. Each individual entity and relationship may not have significant impact in community formation. For example, if there is an edge, that exists between two entities, it is wrong to conclude that they have a strong relationship and if no edge exists between them they are totally unfamiliar with each other. Exact degree of bonding for a relationship or a node in a community is quite difficult to measure. In this paper, social network has been modeled with fuzzy relationships in order to capture the degree of fuzziness in bonding.

Analyzing social networks can be a tedious task mostly because of its larger data size [10]. Conventional tools and methods are either not scalable or consume high computational power. Apache Spark, Hadoop, Sqoop, Hive, NOSQL etc. are the few available tools in order to handle the big data applications in scalable and time efficient manner. These are the cluster-computing frameworks where the computation is distributed among several nodes in a cluster. The results from all the nodes are combined together (by the master node) in order to get the final output. In this work, we have considered Apache Spark, which is one of the popular tools for cluster computing and is nearly 100 times faster than Apache Hadoop [11].

3   Literature Survey

Girvan *et al.*, in their seminal work on community structure in biological and social networks have presented one of the most popular community detection algorithms [12]. This algorithm is based on divisive approach where, edges are removed in the order of their edge betweenness value (number of shortest paths going through them). The intuition behind the algorithm is that communities are connected through the edges with larger betweenness value. This concept is found to be widely adopted in several others methods for community detection [3, 13,14]. These algorithms may be classified into two major categories; first, those methods where a node is considered to be member of any single community at a particular instance of time and second, those where a node may belong to more than one community (overlapping communities).

Pal *et al.* came up with the idea of fuzzy-rough based communities detection algorithm [6]. In their work, social network was modeled using fuzzy-granular concepts, which is necessary to detect fuzzy-rough communities [7]. Unlike conventional social network models, in fuzzy-granular social networks (FGSN's) nodes are clustered into number of granules and the unit of processing is granules rather than nodes. This kind of modeling approach helps in calculating the influence of communities by calculating the overlap of communities (granular embeddedness) which helps us to obtain a weighted undirected graph whose eigenvector centrality can be easily calculated.

Li *et al.*, have presented a method to detect influential communities [15]. In their model of social network, each node is associated with a weight which measures the importance of node. The communities have been detected using k-cores (group of connected nodes whose degree is at least k). In their work the influence of community is defined as the minimum weight of the nodes in the community. Though a scalable version of the algorithm has been presented, but it has certain limitations. Firstly, it doesn't consider the overlapping nature of real-world communities. Secondly, the least weight of a node may not be the perfect measure for quantifying the influence of community.

Wang *et al.*, have presented a unique approach for detecting influential community in large scale networks [16]. In this approach community is detected using kr-cliques and influence is then measured using influence maximization technique. This approach evaluates the influence efficiently, but the dataset necessary for evaluating influence using this measure needs to have activation probability of every edge in the graph. Activation probability of an edge is the probability with which one node can influence its adjacent node along that edge. Obtaining these probabilities is a quite cumbersome process [17]. Thus, calculating influence using this approach is highly computational expensive which is not feasible for real world network.

4 Background Details

4.1 Fuzzy-Granular Social Network (FGSN)

Social network consists of set of entities (individual, group or organization) and relationships among the entities. As the size of the social network is obviously large in nature, real world networks have huge contribution to the era of big data world. It is quite a difficult task to investigate each individual node and relationships for large scale network. Social network can be modeled as a Fuzzy-granular social network (FGSN) where the network consists of set of macro units known as granules [7]. A granule around a node can be constructed with the help of fuzzy set [18] consisting of neighboring nodes with the degree of membership. Each granule is identified by a granule representative. A fuzzy-granular social network can be represented by four parameters as follows:

$S = (C, V, G, A_c)$ such that,
- V is the set of vertices in the network.
- C is the set of granule representatives, where $C \subseteq V$.
- G is the set of all granules around each granule representative $c \in C$
- A_c is the granule having center at c.

The membership value of a node in a granule can be obtained by various parameters associated in the network. Usually the membership value of a node should be decreased as the distance from granule representative increases. In this paper, the fuzzy membership function is defined as follows: where $\mu_c(v, r)$ is the membership value of node v with respect to granule representative c. r is the radius of the granule (Granule Radius). For the method presented in this paper, $d(c, v)$ has been considered as the minimum hop distance between the granule representative c and node v.

Few terms related to FGSN used throughout this paper are discussed below:

- **Granule Radius**: It is defined as the maximum allowable hop distance of a node from the granule center in a granule. The value of granule radius depends on the user preference and problem in hand.
- **Granule Representative**: The node around which the granule is being formed is designated as granule representative. The distance term $d(c, v)$ in Eq. 1 is calculated with respect to granule representative.
- **Granular Degree**: Granular degree of a granule centered at node c is defined as the cardinality of the fuzzy set A_c that represents the granule. Mathematically it can be expressed as follows:

$$D(A_c) = |A_c| = \sum_{v \in V} \mu_{A_c}(v, r) \tag{1}$$

where $\mu_A(v, r)$ is the membership value of node v in granule A_c and r is the granular radius for the granule A_c
- **θ-Core**: A granule A_c can be represented as θ-core, if granular degree is greater than or equals to a threshold value θ, i.e., $D(A_p) \geq \theta$
- **Neighbourhood of a granule**: Set of all granules are said to be neighborhood for A_c, if their centers lies in the support set of A_c. It can be defined as below:

$$Nb(A_c) = \{A_i | i \in Support(A_c) \text{ and } i \neq c\} \tag{2}$$

where $Nb(A_c)$ is the set of neighboring granules for A_c. The support set of A_c can be defined as follows:

$$Support(A_c) = \{v | \overline{\mu_A}(v, r) > 0\} \tag{3}$$

- **Normalized granular embeddedness**: The normalized granular embeddedness of two granules, A_p and A_q is defined as the ratio of union and intersection of the fuzzy sets that represents the granules. It can be expressed as follows:

$$\varepsilon(A_p, A_q) = \frac{|A_p \bigcap A_q|}{|A_p \bigcup A_q|} \tag{4}$$

The value of ϵ lies in the range from 0 and 1.

5 Fuzzy-Rough Community (FRC) Detection

5.1 Problem Statement

A social network may be considered, consisting of three parameters (C, V, G), and two constant θ, and, ϵ, where C is the set of communities, V is the set of users or entities and G the set of granules. The objective is to identify a community C such that it is a non-empty subset of granules G that satisfies the following constraints:

– $\forall A_p, A_q \in C, A_p$ and A_q are the community connected θ-cores.
– $\forall A_p \in C, f_{nge}(A_p, \bigcup_{A_q \in C \setminus A_p} A_q) > \epsilon$

where f_{nge} is the function that computes the normalized granular embeddedness of two granules. After obtaining the set of communities C, influential score of each community has been quantified.

5.2 Proposed Algorithm

Unlike conventional community detection methods Fuzzy-Rough Community (FRC) has the ability to capture the behavior of real world network. In this approach, the social network is modeled into a fuzzy-granular social network [6,7]. Similar to the normal perception of associating nodes with high connectivity to the same community, FRC detection considers granules with similar features belonging to the same community. Few terms as noted below help to understand the algorithm in a better way [6]:

Fuzzy-Rough Community. Let n communities to be discovered in a social network be $C_1, C_2, C_3, ..., C_n$, and the upper and lower approximation of the ith community be $\overline{C_i \theta}$ and $\underline{C_i \theta}$ respectively. Then,

$$\underline{C_i \theta} = \{x | x \in Support(A_p) \wedge x \notin Support(A_q C_i)\} \tag{5}$$

where $\forall A_p \in C_i$ and $A_q \in C_j; i \neq j$

$$\overline{C_i \theta} = \{x | x \in Support(A_p); A_p \in C_i\} \tag{6}$$

Fuzzy-Rough Membership. The membership function, that characterizes the Fuzzy-rough community C_i can be expressed as follows:

$$\delta_{C_i}^{\theta}(x, r) = \begin{cases} 1 & \text{if } x \in \underline{C_i \theta} \\ \sum_{c \in C_i \theta} \overline{\mu_c}(x, r) & \text{if } x \in \overline{C_i \theta} \setminus \underline{C_i \theta} \\ 0 & otherwise \end{cases} \tag{7}$$

For a given social network, communities are identified based on the granular computing approach. In the proposed algorithm, various communities are detected with the help of fuzzy and rough-set representation defined over a granular model of social network. The isolated node that are not included in any of

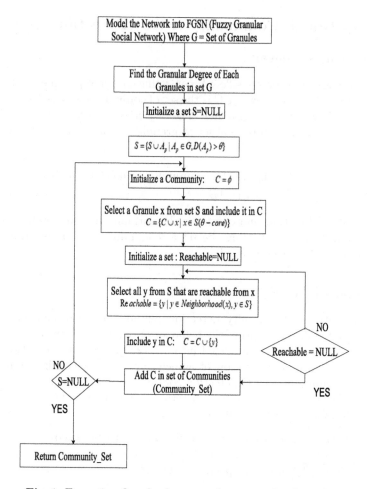

Fig. 1. Execution flow for fuzzy-rough community detection

the detected communities are being treated as outliers. The proposed algorithm i.e., FRC-FGSN is presented in Algorithm 1. For the sake of simplicity and low space, the detail map-reduce implementation of all-pair shortest path and eigen vector centrality as mentioned in step-2 and step-10 respectively in algorithm 1 is omitted. The overall execution flow for enumerating all the communities is presented in Fig. 1.

6   Implementation

6.1   Dataset Used

The proposed algorithm has been experimented on a small-scale network (<1000 nodes and <10000 edges) and three real world large-scale networks (>1000 nodes

Algorithm 1. Map-Reduce based FRC-FGSN Algorithm

1: Transform the input dataset in edge list format into adjacency list format for ease of processing in map-reduce model.
2: All pairs shortest path of the network using a modified ring-search method [22] are obtained using three pair of map-reduce functions.
3: Granular embeddedness of every pair of granule are calculated.
4: Granules with granular degree less than θ i.e. $D(A_p) < \theta$ are filtered.
5: The θ-cores which constitute communities are obtained.
6: $A_c \leftarrow \theta$-cores are initialized
7: The membership value of a node in a community, is calculated
8: The nodes which belong to the lower approximation of a community are filtered out.
9: Normalised community overlap factor is obtained.
10: Eigenvector centrality is being calculated using map-reduce based distributed algorithm.
11: Output: return the set of communities.

---

and >10000 edges). Small dataset is used to optimize the value of θ and ϵ, which are the major parameters of the FRC-FGSN algorithm. The value of θ and ϵ usually vary from dataset to dataset. However for the sake of simplicity the parameter value has been optimized for the small dataset only and the same value has been fixed for other datasets. The description of the datasets are listed in Table 1.

Table 1. Datasets used for the experiment

Dataset	No. of vertices	No. of edges	Size	Type
Dolphin	62	152	Small scale	Undirected
ego-Facebook	4039	88234	Large scale	Directed
ego-Gplus	$107,614$	$13,673,453$	Large scale	Undirected
ego-Twitter	$81,306$	$1,768,149$	Large scale	Directed

6.2 Experimental Setup

The proposed algorithm is implemented in Hadoop distributed platform. The cluster used in distributed platform consists of five nodes with symmetric configuration. Each node is of i7 processor with 3.4 GHz clock speed. The secondary memory space and main memory space in each system is 1 TB and 20 GB respectively. In the cluster, one system is dedicated for master node and rest of the node act as slave or datanode. The master node is configured as namenode as well as datanode so that it can also contribute to the data processing whenever it is required.

6.3   Normalized Community Overlap Factor

In order to quantify the influential communities we have introduced a measure known as the normalized community overlap factor, $N_{p,q}$. It is defined as the ratio between the cardinality of the fuzzy intersection and the fuzzy union of the two communities p and q.

$$N_{p,q} = \frac{|A_p \bigcap A_q|}{|A_p \bigcup A_q|} \tag{8}$$

After community detection process is completed, the network is transformed into an un-directed weighted network. In this new network the nodes are represented by the community representatives (granule representatives with highest granular degree in the community) and the edge weights are represented by the normalized community overlap factor ($N_{p,q}$) as given in Eq. 8. Thus the resulting network is the network on which the eigenvector centrality algorithm is run to get the centrality values of the nodes.

The proposed influential community detection algorithm (starting from FRC detection to influence calculation) has been implemented in map-reduce fashion in order to make it scalable. The program comprises of 14 mapper-reduce pairs. The sequence of steps followed are presented in Algorithm 1.

Table 2. Observations for varying θ and ϵ

Serial no.	θ		ϵ		No. of communities	Convergence
	Quartile	Value	Quartile	Value		
1	Lower	0.7563	Lower	0.1151	2	Yes
2	Lower	0.7563	Middle	0.3647	3	No
3	Lower	0.7563	Upper	0.5503	7	Yes
4	Middle	1.0415	Lower	0.1151	2	Yes
5	Middle	1.0415	Middle	0.3647	3	No
6	Middle	1.0415	Upper	0.5503	5	Yes
7	Upper	1.1405	Lower	0.1151	2	Yes
8	Upper	1.1405	Middle	0.3647	3	No
9	Upper	1.1405	Upper	0.5503	2	Yes

7   Results and Observations

Identification of fuzzy-rough communities depends on two parameters namely, granular embeddedness threshold (ϵ) and granular degree (θ). The proposed algorithm has been executed on a small-scale network and three large scale networks. Since smaller networks are easier to visualize and analyze, a small scale network was used to optimize the value of ϵ and θ. The results obtained have been presented in Table 2.

The experiments have been performed on one small scale network and three large scale networks. The small-scale network used in this work is the Dolphin social network [20, 21]. Since the optimal values of ϵ and θ are unknown, three different combinations of θ and ϵ are chosen for running the experiments. The value of maximum granular embeddedness (ϵ_{max}) and the maximum possible value of granular degree (θ_{max}) might vary from one network to another. In order to generalize the optimal values of ϵ and θ, the values of θ and ϵ have been considered as the lower quartile, median and upper quartile from the range of values of θ and ϵ. The radius of the granules were set to three. Since real-world social networks show small-world property the average diameter of such networks is fixed to six [22, 23]. Searching for optimal values of ϵ and θ is important because if the values are not optimal two possible problems may be encountered:

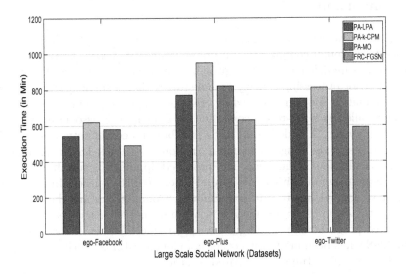

Fig. 2. Execution time (in Mins) for different algorithms

1. The network of community representatives obtained after the community detection is completed, may not have a dominant eigen value in its adjacency matrix form. Since the eigenvector centrality is calculated using power method it is not possible to obtain eigenvector for a matrix with more than one dominant eigen value [24].
2. The number of communities is either too small or too big.

Nine observations have been considered with varying values of θ and ϵ (lower, middle and upper quartile). The results are presented in Table 1.

From the Table 2, it can be observed that the number of communities obtained depends on the value of θ and ϵ. It can also be observed that the power method used for obtaining eigenvector centrality is converged only when value of θ and ϵ lie in the range of lower-quartile and upper-quartile respectively.

After obtaining the optimal values for θ and ϵ the algorithm was being executed for large scale networks like Facebook, Google circle and Twitter [25]. The proposed algorithm has been compared with few other community detection algorithms based on execution time. As the FRC-FGSN algorithm is implemented in distributed platform, for comparison we have considered the parallel version of Label Propagation (PA-LPA), k- Clique percolation Method (PA-k-CPM) and Modularity Optimization (PA-MO) algorithms. The execution time has been compared on large scale network only as for small scale network, the FRC-FGSN algorithm might take longer time than expectation due to communication latency in clustering setup. The execution time is observed to be least for FRC-FGSN as shown in Fig. 2.

8   Conclusion

In this work, we have presented an efficient algorithm (FRC-FGSN) to identify the fuzzy rough communities in granular social network. Real world social networks are modeled into fuzzy granular social network (FGSN), where the basic entity for processing is fuzzy granule rather than a single node. The identified communities are characterized by crisp lower and fuzzy upper memberships which are called as fuzzy-rough communities. Each node is associated with fuzzy membership value. A node is said to be member of a community, if its membership value lies in the range of boundary region $i.e.$, Upper-Lower. A node may belong to multiple communities. The proposed approach is suitable for exploring overlapping communities. We have also detected the outliers in the network which may not belongs to any communities. Communities are then quantified based on the eigen-centrality measures. We have implemented the model using distributed programming paradigm like map-reduce. The extensive comparison of FR-FGSN has been made with other parallel algorithms which conclude that, it has less execution time as compared to other.

In future some other distributed framework like spark can be adopted to measure the performance of the model. Other parameters like NMI, AUC, Accuracy may be considered in future to extend the experimental analysis.

References

1. Travers, J., Milgram, S.: The small world problem. Phychol. Today **1**, 61–67 (1967)
2. Stephen, A.T., Toubia, O.: Explaining the power-law degree distribution in a social commerce network. Soc. Netw. **31**(4), 262–270 (2009)
3. Fortunato, S.: Community detection in graphs. Phys. Rep. **486**(3), 75–174 (2010)
4. Albert, R., Jeong, H., Barabási, A.-L.: Internet: diameter of the world-wide web. Nature **401**(6749), 130–131 (1999)
5. Broder, A., et al.: Graph structure in the web. Comput. Netw. **33**(1), 309–320 (2000)

6. Kundu, S., Pal, S.K.: Fuzzy-rough community in social networks. Pattern Recogn. Lett. **67**, 145–152 (2015)
7. Kundu, S., Pal, S.K.: FGSN: fuzzy granular social networks-model and applications. Inf. Sci. **314**, 100–117 (2015)
8. Bonacich, P.: Some unique properties of eigenvector centrality. Soc. Netw. **29**(4), 555–564 (2007)
9. Landherr, A., Friedl, B., Heidemann, J.: A critical review of centrality measures in social networks. Bus. Inf. Syst. Eng. **2**(6), 371–385 (2010). https://doi.org/10.1007/s12599-010-0127-3
10. McAfee, A., Brynjolfsson, E., Davenport, T.H., et al.: Big data: the management revolution. Harvard Business Rev. **90**(10), 60–68 (2012)
11. Zaharia, M., et al.: Fast and interactive analytics over Hadoop data with Spark. USENIX Login **37**(4), 45–51 (2012)
12. Girvan, M., Newman, M.E.: Community structure in social and biological networks. Proc. Natl. Acad. Sci. **99**(12), 7821–7826 (2002)
13. Newman, M.E.: Fast algorithm for detecting community structure in networks. Phys. Rev. E **69**(6), 066133 (2004)
14. Raghavan, U.N., Albert, R., Kumara, S.: Near linear time algorithm to detect community structures in large-scale networks. Phys. Rev. E **76**(3), 036106 (2007)
15. Li, R.-H., Qin, L., Yu, J.X., Mao, R.: Influential community search in large networks. Proc. VLDB Endow. **8**(5), 509–520 (2015)
16. Kempe, D., Kleinberg, J., Tardos, É.: Maximizing the spread of influence through a social network. In: Proceedings of the Ninth ACM SIGKDD International Conference on Knowledge Discovery and Data Mining, pp. 137–146. ACM (2003)
17. Anagnostopoulos, A., Kumar, R., Mahdian, M.: Influence and correlation in social networks. In: Proceedings of the 14th ACM SIGKDD International Conference on Knowledge Discovery and Data Mining, pp. 7–15. ACM (2008)
18. Zadeh, L.A.: Fuzzy sets. In: Fuzzy Sets, Fuzzy Logic, and Fuzzy Systems: Selected Papers by Lotfi A Zadeh, pp. 394–432. World Scientific (1996)
19. Behera, R.K., Shukla, A., Mahapatra, S., Rath, S.K., Sahoo, B., Bhattacharya, S.: Map-reduce based link prediction for large scale social network. In: Proceedings of the 29th International Conference on Software Engineering and Knowledge Engineering, pp. 1–4. IEEE (2017)
20. Dolphins network dataset - KONECT, April 2017
21. Lusseau, D., Schneider, K., Boisseau, O.J., Haase, P., Slooten, E., Dawson, S.M.: The bottlenose dolphin community of Doubtful Sound features a large proportion of long-lasting associations. Behav. Ecol. Sociobiol. **54**, 396–405 (2003). https://doi.org/10.1007/s00265-003-0651-y
22. de Sola Pool, I., Kochen, M.: Contacts and influence. Soc. Netw. **1**(1), 5–51 (1978)
23. Zhang, L., Tu, W.: Six degrees of separation in online society. In: Proceedings of the WebSci 2009, Society On-Line, 18–20 March 2009, Athens, Greece, pp. 1–5 (2009)
24. Davidson, E.R.: The iterative calculation of a few of the lowest eigenvalues and corresponding eigenvectors of large real-symmetric matrices. J. Comput. Phys. **17**(1), 87–94 (1975)
25. Leskovec, J., Mcauley, J.J.: Learning to discover social circles in ego networks. In: Advances in Neural Information Processing Systems, pp. 539–547 (2012)

Human Factor on Software Quality: A Systematic Literature Review

Elcin Guveyi$^{(\boxtimes)}$ ⓘ, Mehmet S. Aktas ⓘ, and Oya Kalipsiz ⓘ

Department of Computer Engineering, Yıldız Technical University, Istanbul, Turkey
{eguveyi,aktas,kalipsiz}@yildiz.edu.tr

Abstract. Ensuring software quality is an important step towards a successful project. Since software development is a human-oriented process, it is possible to say that any factor affecting people will directly affect software quality and success. The aim of this study is to reveal which factors affect humans. For this purpose, we conducted a systematic literature review. We identified 80 related primary studies from the literature. We defined 7 research questions. For answering research questions, we extracted data from the primary studies. We researched human factors, methods for data collection and data analysis, publication types and years. Factors are grouped into 3 main groups: Personal factors, interpersonal factors, and organizational factors. The results show that personal factors are the most important category of human factors. It is seen that the most researched factors among personal factors are "experience" and "education".

Keywords: Human factor · Software quality · Systematic literature review

1 Introduction

The human effect plays a vital role in the software development process. At each step of the software development, human knowledge, intelligence, and experience affect product quality. Due to its importance, human factors have been the subject of software quality researches.

Software development process steps include analysis, design, development, testing, and maintenance. Every step is performed by humans. Good analysis and documentation bring a good implementation process. Good communication and harmony between these steps will improve the quality of the process. The best product will be produced at the planned time and with the estimated budget. Due to the human effect in the whole development process, software quality depends exactly on human behaviors. If we want to achieve quality software products, we should put the human effect in the center [1]. The main purpose of this review work is to show the importance of the human factors.

© Springer Nature Switzerland AG 2020
O. Gervasi et al. (Eds.): ICCSA 2020, LNCS 12252, pp. 918–930, 2020.
https://doi.org/10.1007/978-3-030-58811-3_65

In this work, we want to take a picture of literature that how many papers interested in "human impact on software quality". Since human is a social being, we cannot speak only intrinsic factors such as personality, mood, technical background, etc. There are also social and environmental factors such as relations with teammates and things about working place. While collecting primary studies, we encountered many different factors. So, we grouped them under three main categories: Personal Factors, Interpersonal Factors, and Organizational Factors.

Since the software development process includes teamwork, the relationship between teammates plays an important role. Firstly communication is crucial. Through the development process, healthy communication between people will increase product quality. We can say other factors under the interpersonal factors category such as collaboration, agreement, conflict, trust, share, etc.

Not only personal or social factors, but there are also environmental factors that affect humans. Because the developers spend most of the day in the office, working condition is the most researched topic on the studies. Factors like team size, team cultural diversity, gender diversity can affect employees. On the other hand, project properties have an impact on developers. We can say this project factors as project size, age, complexity, documentation, etc. Other most researched organizational factors are the approach of management, time pressure, and workload.

The literature seems to be quite lacking in the review studies on the effect of human factors. Some of the secondary studies about "human factor on software quality" are very old dated [2,3]. There is a master thesis about exact same subject but it's from 2010 [4]. So, we limited our work by receiving only the publications published in the last decade. We think we can get more up-to-date results in this way. Because the profile of the developer changes with the changing generation. The demands and expectations of young employees may be different. The hours they are productive during the day may vary [5]. The conditions of the office [6], gender distribution within the team [7] and cultural differences [8] may also affect the employees.

In the literature, some review papers focused only on personal [9] or environmental factors [10]. Another review studies focused on a factor and detailed it, for example, "motivation factor" [11,12]. We have kept our research area as large as possible. We tried to include all the factors affecting the developer in our study.

Our main motivation is to show which factors researched mostly. In this way, future researchers can conduct their work. With this roadmap study, they can focus on different factors other than these. Or they can research in a detailed way these factors.

The remainder of the paper is organized in this way. In Sect. 2, we describe our methodology while conducting this SLR. In Sect. 3, we answer the research questions and share the results. In Sect. 4, we explain the threats to validity. And we conclude the SLR in Sect. 5.

2   Methodology

Systematic literature review is defined as "a form of secondary study that uses a well-defined methodology to identify, analyse and interpret all available evidence related to a specific research question in a way that is unbiased and repeatable" [13]. In order to reveal the importance of the human factor in software quality, We conducted a systematic literature review. We applied the steps recommended by Kitchenham's guideline. First of all, we identified the right research questions. We then searched digital databases for primary studies. After getting of relevant studies, data extractions were conducted. All these processes will be detailed in the following sections.

2.1   Research Questions

According to [13], "Specifying the research questions is the most important part of any systematic review".

We planned the research questions to extract more information from primary studies about the human effect on software quality. Our research questions and the main motivation behind these questions have shown in Table 1.

Table 1. Research questions and main motivations.

ID	Research question	Main motivation
RQ1	What're the distribution of personal, interpersonal and organizational factors?	To identify which factor researched most
RQ2	Which software development step was researched?	To identify which software development step is more affected by the human factor
RQ3	Which data collection methods were used in the studies?	To identify how researchers collected the data
RQ4	Which methods were used for analyzing the data?	To identify how researchers analyzed the data
RQ5	What is the article type of primary studies?	To identify what are the distribution of journal articles and conference papers in primary studies
RQ6	What's the publication frequency of the papers?	To find out how many papers are published in every year
RQ7	Which factors studied most on software quality researches?	To provide an overview of the literature about factors research frequency

2.2   Search for Primary Studies

After we determined our research scope and research questions, we organized the search strings to receive the primary studies. We made this search at four well-known digital libraries: IEEE Xplore, ACM, SpringerLink, and ScienceDirect. The search was performed with the following search strings.

"software quality" AND ("human effect" OR "human effects" OR "human factor" OR "human factors" OR "human issue" OR "human issues")

We constrained the results by only getting papers published after 2009. All these search results are from 09.09.2019. After making a full-text search, we got the results shown in Table 2.

As the next step, we applied filters to these studies. The filters aim to get the most relevant papers about our research scope. On the other hand, a systematic filtering process will facilitate the choosing paper process and give an idea to the next researchers about how to move on to getting relevant papers.

Table 2. Search results in digital libraries

Digital Library	Number of papers
IEEE Xplore	87
ACM	621
SpringerLink	451
ScienceDirect	191
Total	**1350**

2.3 Inclusion and Exclusion Criteria

As a result of our searches on four databases, we obtained a total of 1350 articles. Of course, the vast majority of these articles were unrelated to our study. We have determined the inclusion and exclusion criteria to obtain related articles. The inclusion and exclusion criteria are outlined below:

Inclusion Criteria

– Study is written in English language.
– Study was published between 2009–2019.
– Study is about both software quality and human factor.

Exclusion Criteria

– Study is not written in English language.
– Study doesn't focus on software quality and human factor.
– Study is about human-computer interaction, user interface design and usability.
– Study is considering software productivity, but not software quality.
– Study is a secondary or tertiary study.
– Study is a short paper.

In line with inclusion and exclusion criteria, we determined the following filters.

Filter-1: In the first filter, we excluded video results, standards, conference program tables, indexes, appendices, articles except for English language, secondary studies (systematic literature reviews, mapping studies, etc.), tertiary studies.

Filter-2: In order to be sure that the papers include the search string words, we searched these words in the full text. Sometimes "references" section includes these words and search engines lists these papers as relevant results. But when we faced that kind of situation, or when we couldn't find these search words together in the paper (for example, just "software quality" is used and there is no other "human factor" or "human effect" word) we excluded this article.

Filter-3: Detailed reading was made in this filter. If the article is about another topic such as user experience, usability analysis, human-computer interaction, etc. we excluded these papers. We only got articles that focused on the factors affecting software quality.

By applying these filters to each database, we obtained Table 3.

Table 3. Filters applied to search results

Digital Library	Without filter	Filter-1	Filter-2	Filter-3
IEEE Xplore	87	72	72	25
ACM	621	495	92	29
SpringerLink	451	399	142	9
ScienceDirect	191	152	107	21
Total	**1350**			**84**

After filtering the papers we got a total of 84 primary studies. 4 of them were the same. We eliminate them, and finally got 80 papers [14].

2.4   Classification of the Articles

For the purpose of answering the research questions, we analyzed the articles. In this process, we specified the data extraction columns according to the research questions. These columns are listed in Table 4.

Definition of these column names are this way:

1. Article ID: We gave an identity number to all primary studies like A1, A2, etc.
2. Article Name: Bibliographic information of the articles.
3. Publication Year: Which year the article published.
4. Article Type: Defines that the article is a "conference paper", "journal article", "book chapter", etc.

Table 4. Data extraction columns

	Column name
1	Article ID
2	Article name
3	Publication year
4	Article type
5	Software development step
6	Data collection method
7	Data analysis method
8	Personal factors
9	Interpersonal factors
10	Organizational factors

5. Software Development Step: Defines that which software development step is researched: "analysis", "design", "implementation", "test" or "maintenance".
6. Data Collection Method: Defines which method that researchers used when they collect data from people. It can be a "survey", "interview" or "dataset".
7. Data Analysis Method: Defines which method, algorithm or theory that researchers used when they analyze the data.
8. Personal Factors: These are individual factors such as personal characteristics, technical background, experience, education, mood, etc. If the article contains this kind of factor, we put "+" to this column. And to see which factors are most researched, we noted them.
9. Interpersonal Factors: These factors are about the team and other peoples. For example communication, collaboration, conflicts, etc. If the article contains this kind of factor, we put "+" to this column. And to see which factors are most researched, we noted them.
10. Organizational Factors: These factors are about the working place and the project. For example office conditions, project age, time pressure, workload, etc. If the article contains this kind of factor, we put "+" to this column. And to see which factors are most researched, we noted them.

3 Results

After the data extraction process from the primary studies, we answered the research questions. The results of the study are shared and detailed in the following sections.

3.1   RQ1: What is the Distribution of Personal, Interpersonal, and Organizational Factors?

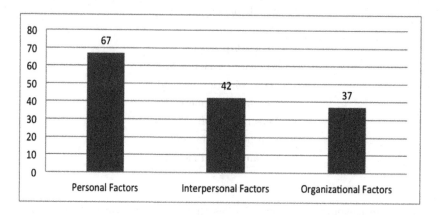

Fig. 1. Factors

The factors examined in the publications were grouped into three categories: personal, interpersonal, and organizational factors. As can be seen from the chart (see Fig. 1), the category which is thought to have the most effective and therefore included in the researches was "personal factors". From this point of view, we can say that the developer's characteristics affect the software product the most.

Another conclusion we draw from the graph is that interpersonal factors are investigated more than organizational factors. Generally speaking, the personal characteristics of the employees and their relations with their environment are more important than the conditions of the working environment. Office conditions and project features will, of course, not be ignored. However, in-team communication and the ability to work together are seen as more important than organizational factors.

3.2   RQ2: Which Software Development Step was Researched?

The studies we reviewed mostly followed developer activities or conducted surveys with developers (see Fig. 2). Therefore, we can say development as the most researched software process step.

Following this, we see that the test step is in second place. It is possible to say that testing processes have an important place in measuring software quality. The excess of faulty modules is an indication of a low-quality software product. In addition, it has been demonstrated that the conflict between test teams and software developers has a negative effect on quality [15].

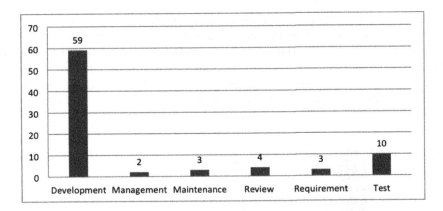

Fig. 2. Software development steps

3.3 RQ3: Which Data Collection Methods were Used in the Studies?

We found that the most frequently used data collection method at the researches was surveying (see Fig. 3). With online questionnaires and surveys, researchers were able to collect relevant data about employees. Another method of data collection was the use of a dataset that the researchers created or received. These datasets include collected projects, collected comments, collected logs, etc.

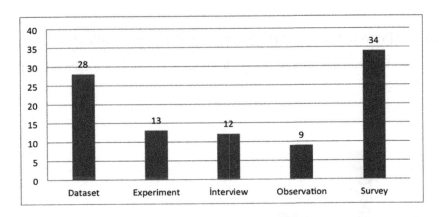

Fig. 3. Data collection methods

3.4 RQ4: Which Methods were Used for Analyzing the Data?

We have seen that different methods are used for data analysis. The chart (see Fig. 4) shows the four most commonly used methods. For correlation, Spearman's Rank Correlation was in the first place. Secondly, linear and logistic regression methods were used. Some of the researchers carried out the analysis using the appropriate tools to analyze the data. Some of them designed their own tools.

The methods used in the studies varied. Other methods can be listed as follows: Decision Tree, Naive Bayes, Chi-Square Test, Cluster Analysis, Principal Component Analysis, Structural Equation Modeling, Genetic Algorithm, Mann-Whitney U Test, Mean Score, Exploratory Factor Analysis.

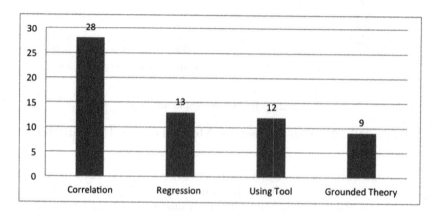

Fig. 4. Data analysis methods

3.5   RQ5: What is the Article Type of Primary Studies?

It is seen that the majority of the publications examined are conference papers. (see Fig. 5)

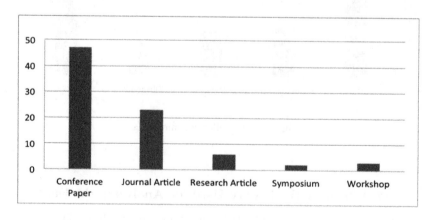

Fig. 5. Publication types

3.6   RQ6: What's the Publication Frequency of the Papers?

When we examine the distribution of publications by years (see Fig. 6), if we ignore the fluctuation in recent years, we can conclude that the human factor on software quality is an increasing field of research. However, when we look generally, the number of articles published yearly is quite low. Generally, articles in the literature evaluated the success of the software product according to the ratings of people. They did not take into account the quality of the software product. The number of studies conducted on software quality metrics is meager. This situation shows that new and more detailed studies are needed in this field.

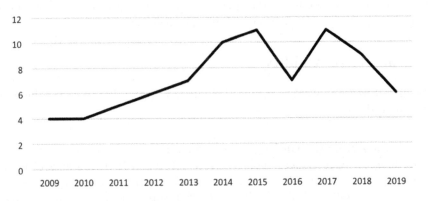

Fig. 6. Publications per year

3.7   RQ7: Which Factors are Studied Most on Software Quality Researches?

When we look at the most studied factors (see Fig. 7), we see that the characteristics and technical backgrounds of the employees are at the forefront.

Fig. 7. Most researched factors

While examining the personal characteristics, usually the Five-Factor Model was applied and the employees were evaluated through the five factors. Also known as the Big Five, these five personality factors are Agreeableness, Conscientiousness, Extraversion, Neuroticism, and Openness. In terms of the technical competence of people, experience, education, and knowledge have been evaluated.

For the interpersonal factors category, the most researched factors were communication and collaboration. Since the software is usually implemented by teams, communication and harmony between the people are very important.

The conditions of the working environment are of course also important. The number of people in the team and the size of the company were among the factors taken into account in the studies. Other prominent factors related to the company were as follows; the size of the project, distribution of roles in the team, time pressure, satisfaction with management, etc.

4   Threats to Validity

The main threats to validity in this SLR and our approaches to preventing them are shared down below.

Search for Primary Studies: For a systematic literature review, it's essential to get more relevant papers about the research topic. If the number of related articles we have reached is too small to provide an overview of the literature, our study's results will also be incorrect. For this reason, we aimed to reach as many primary studies as possible about our research topic. We applied the search to popular databases to get more studies. We cannot guarantee that we have collected all the studies in the literature, but we can say that we have reached as many studies as necessary to conduct a literature review.

Data Extraction: The most important process after the determination of the related articles is the accurate analysis of these papers. Conducting the entire analysis process by one person will be one of the factors threatening accuracy. For this reason, each article was assigned to at least two researchers for data extraction. We applied to cross-check in this process. The results obtained by one author have passed the approval of the other author.

5   Conclusion

In this systematic literature review, we aimed to give an overview of the literature about human factors on software quality. We made data extractions from the primary studies about this field. We determined which factors are studied in these papers. The factors were grouped into three main categories: "personal factors", "interpersonal factors", and "organizational factors".

Some of the personal factors that we collect from the papers were education, experience, technical background, motivation level, job satisfaction, happiness, gender, creativity, etc. In 67 of the 80 articles collected for the SLR study, we found that research was carried out on personal factors. The results of this SLR shows that personal factors are more important than interpersonal or organizational factors.

We have seen that surveys are frequently conducted to collect data (rate of 46%). For analyzing the data, researchers mostly used correlation (28%).

In future works, personal characteristics of people can be examined in a more detailed way. Except for education and experience, researchers can reach another important personal factor.

The results of this SLR study suggest that the human factor is very important for assuring software quality. For this reason, investing in people will affect the success and quality of the project positively. It is an obvious fact that successful projects will be carried out with better office conditions, less workload, and strongly communicated teams.

Acknowledgements. We would like to thank undergraduate students Halil İbrahim Uluoğlu and Yunus Emre Demir for their contribution to this SLR.

References

1. Fernández-Sanz, L., Misra, S.: Influence of human factors in software quality and productivity. In: Murgante, B., Gervasi, O., Iglesias, A., Taniar, D., Apduhan, B.O. (eds.) ICCSA 2011. LNCS, vol. 6786, pp. 257–269. Springer, Heidelberg (2011). https://doi.org/10.1007/978-3-642-21934-4_22

2. Laughery Jr., K.R., Laughery Sr., K.R.: Human factors in software engineering: a review of the literature. J. Syst.Softw. **5**(1), 3–14 (1985)

3. Nash, S.H., Redwine Jr., S.T.: People and organizations in software production: a review of the literature. ACM SIGCPR Comput. Pers. **11**(3), 10–21 (1988)

4. Pirzadeh, L.: Human factors in software development: a systematic literature review. Master's thesis (2010)

5. Meyer, A.N.: Fostering software developers' productivity at work through self-monitoring and goal-setting. In: ICSE (Companion Volume), vol. 2018, pp. 480–483 (2018)

6. Fagerholm, F., Ikonen, M., Kettunen, P., Münch, J., Roto, V., Abrahamsson, P.: How do software developers experience team performance in lean and agile environments? In: EASE, vol. 2014, pp. 7:1–7:10 (2014)

7. Catolino, G., Palomba, F., Tamburri, D.A., Serebrenik, A., Ferrucci, F.: Gender diversity and women in software teams: how do they affect community smells? In: ICSE-SEIS, vol. 2019, pp. 11–20 (2019)

8. Lee, D., Smith, A., Mortimer, M.: Cultural differences affecting quality and productivity in Western/Asian offshore software development. In: Proceedings of the 3rd International Conference on Human Computer Interaction, pp. 29–39 (2011)

9. Varona, D., Capretz, L.F., Piñero, Y., Raza, A.: Evolution of software engineers' personality profile. ACM SIGSOFT Softw. Eng. Notes **37**(1), 1–5 (2012)

10. Jia, J., Zhang, P., Capretz, L.F.: Environmental factors influencing individual decision-making behavior in software projects: a systematic literature review. In Proceedings of the 9th International Workshop on Cooperative and Human Aspects of Software Engineering, pp. 86–92 (2016)

11. Beecham, S., Baddoo, N., Hall, T., Robinson, H., Sharp, H.: Motivation in software engineering: a systematic literature review. Inf. Softw. Technol. **50**(9–10), 860–878 (2008)

12. França, A.C.C., Gouveia, T.B., Santos, P.C., Santana, C.A., da Silva, F.Q.: Motivation in software engineering: a systematic review update. In: 15th Annual Conference on Evaluation & Assessment in Software Engineering (EASE 2011), pp. 154–163. IET (2011)

13. Kitchenham, B., Charters, S.: Guidelines for performing systematic literature reviews in software engineering (2007)

14. Human Factor on Software Quality: SLR - Dataset. https://docs.google.com/spreadsheets/d/1GxDqVHlZNswT0kMmVpKsWby7XGu6kenaZuUBlwqBMfg/edit#gid=0

15. Gonçalves, W.F., de Almeida, C.B., de Arauújo, L.L., Ferraz, M.S., Xanduú, R.B., de Farias, I.: The influence of human factors on the software testing process: the impact of these factors on the software testing process. In: 2017 12th Iberian Conference on Information Systems and Technologies (CISTI), pp. 1–6. IEEE (2017)

Gamified e-Health Solution to Promote Postnatal Care in Morocco

Lamyae Sardi[1], Ali Idri[1,2(✉)], Taoufik Rachad[1], Leanne Redman[3], and Hassan Alami[4]

[1] Software Project Management Research Team ENSIAS, Mohammed V University, Rabat, Morocco
lamyasardi@gmail.com, rachad.taoufik@gmail.com, ali.idri@um5.ac.ma
[2] CSEHS-MSDA Mohamed VI Polytechnic University, Ben Guerir, Morocco
[3] Reproductive Endocrinology and Women's Health Lab, Pennington Biomedical Research Center, Baton Rouge, LA, USA
leanne.redman@prc.edu
[4] Faculty of Medicine, Mohammed V University, Rabat, Morocco
mhalami3@hotmail.com

Abstract. The postnatal period is a critical phase in both the lives of the mothers and the newborns. Due to all the inherent changes that occur during this period, quality care is crucial during this period to enhance the wellbeing of the mothers and the newborns. In Morocco, the neglection of postnatal care services are often associated to poor communication, financial difficulties and cultural barriers. Mobile technology constitutes therefore a promising approach to bridge this gap and promote postnatal care. In order to improve the effectiveness of mobile technology, gamification has become a powerful feature to boost motivation and induce fun and interactivity into the mobile solutions' tasks. Based on a previous review on mobile applications for postnatal care available in app repositories, a set of requirements have been identified to build a comprehensive mobile solution that cater the needs of both the mothers and the newborns. These requirements have, then, been enriched with real needs elicited at maternity Les orangers that belongs to the University Hospital Avicenne of Rabat. Along with the functional and non-functional requirements, gamification aspects have been also analyzed. After the analysis and design phases, a pilot version of the solution called 'Mamma&Baby' has been implemented using android framework. 'Mamma&Baby' is a mobile solution dedicated to assist new mothers during their postnatal period. As future work, it is expected to fully integrate the gamification elements into the solution and conduct an empirical evaluation of the overall quality and the potential of the solution with real puerperal women.

Keywords: Postnatal care · m-Health · Gamification · Quality evaluation

© Springer Nature Switzerland AG 2020
O. Gervasi et al. (Eds.): ICCSA 2020, LNCS 12252, pp. 931–946, 2020.
https://doi.org/10.1007/978-3-030-58811-3_66

1 Introduction

The postnatal period is a challenging phase in the lives of both mothers and newborns [1]. Commonly defined as the first weeks following childbirth, the postnatal period may last up to six months after delivery [2]; until the new mother regains her pre-pregnancy body shape, heals completely and builds a strong bond with her newborn baby.

Given the inherent physiological, psycho-emotional and social changes that occur during this period [3], an optimal care and a close attention to both mothers and newborn babies are needed to maintain and promote the health of the mother and her newborn baby and avert a substantial proportion of maternal and perinatal complications [4]. Postnatal care is therefore provided to meet the individual needs and preferences of the mothers and their newborn infants. It should be palliative and supportive for the mother to bolster her abilities to successfully adjust to motherhood [5]. According to international guidelines on reproductive health, postnatal care covers integrated maternal and newborn care practices that are provided in the health facility following childbirth, at home during the first crucial week, with subsequent visits to the facility during the remaining days and/or weeks of the postnatal period, when the mother is better able to leave her home. Postnatal care is also about empowering the mother to care for her baby and herself in order to promote their long-term physiological and emotional well-being [6]. Vaginal care, targeted postpartum hygiene and nutrition, newborn care and counselling on family planning and exclusive breastfeeding are the most preeminent pillars of postnatal care [7].

Albeit the critical importance of postnatal care in the lives of mothers and newborns, it consistently has the lowest coverage of interventions on the continuum of maternal and infant care. In this respect, postnatal care in Morocco is sub-optimal, hence substantially contributing to increasing maternal and infant mortality rates in the country. Poor communication, lack of awareness and information, financial difficulties are among the most prevalent factors hampering the utilization of postnatal care services [8]. A potential intervention that could reduce some of these modifiable factors is the incorporation of mobile technology.

In general, mHealth (mobile health) which refers to the continuous care delivered by mobile technology has been proven to have tremendous appeal in such it promises significant improvements in quality, convenience, reach and cost. With the outstanding technological advancements over the last decades, researchers have been more prompted to investigate ways of expanding and developing effective mHealth projects [9]. A significant attention is being drawn to leveraging mobile technology in the promotion of reproductive health care services including contraception and family planning, pregnancy monitoring and postnatal care [10–12]. As stated in a recent review most of postnatal care apps available in app repositories overlook addressing mothers needs during the postnatal period, specifically as regards to postpartum weight monitoring, mental wellbeing support and family planning [12].

Accordingly, the aim of the present study is to list the specifications of a comprehensive mHealth solution intended to advocate postnatal care. The completeness of this app consists of providing a functional content that combines newborn and maternal care along with the counselling sections on all aspects underpinning the postnatal period.

In an attempt to foster engagement with the app and induce pleasant use and experience, the present study also proposes a persuasive strategy that stands upon gamification and game-like principles. Commonly defined as the use of game elements in non-game contexts, gamification is a trending discipline that has been applied, to date, in several different fields and has yielded significant outcomes in terms of sustaining users' long-term engagement and motivation, promoting healthy behaviors and inducing positive emotional states [13].

2 Related Work

Although there is a plethora of apps available to promote postnatal care, the literature published in this area is still very scarce. The use of mobile technologies in promoting reproductive healthcare is not yet extensively leveraged by researchers given that a good number of studies published in the area only focused on developing systems based on Short Message Service (SMS) in order to enhance postnatal clinic attendance [14], increase health facility contact through antenatal care [15, 16] and disseminate text messages on important aspects of antenatal care at regular intervals [17]. Despite their perceived effectiveness, these developed systems are barely ubiquitous in that their accessibility is geographically limited. To alleviate this limitation, a few studies have designed and implemented mobile applications to improve postnatal care. For instance, Moment Health app has been developed for new and expectant mothers to self-screen for mental depression and anxieties associated to the prenatal and postnatal periods. The app also provides helpful guidance and practical strategies to cope with these mental disorders [18]. Another mobile application has been proposed to improve accessibility to nutritional information and tips during prenatal and postnatal period [19]. In a wider context, Shorey et al. have proposed an mHealth app for supporting parents during postnatal period called 'Home-but not Alone' [20]. Along with providing a continuity of care, it has been reported that this app has enhanced new parents' confidence and satisfaction with regards their parenting roles and has endorsed social support and empathy. Whereas, most of the available apps for postnatal care omit pertinent features in relation to maternal care or/and baby care, the novelty of the mobile solution presented in the present study lies, particularly, in the exhaustiveness of its functional content and its persuasive strategy based on gamification principles. To the best of our knowledge, this is the first mobile solution for postnatal care to include game elements.

3 Requirements Specification of the m-Health Solution for Postnatal Care

3.1 Purpose of the Solution

Mamma&Baby is the name given to the m-Health solution for postnatal care proposed in the present study. Being fully-fledged for women during the postnatal period, Mamma&Baby is a comprehensive user-centered app that is intended to accompany new mothers throughout their postnatal journey. The central objective of this app is to promote postnatal care through the provision of helpful tips for postpartum recovery and recommendations and advices on baby care. The postnatal period is often considered as an emotional roller coaster for new mothers who require attentiveness and social support. Therefore, Mamma&Baby app promises to alleviate the emotional burden that is correlated with the postnatal period by means of social integration and counselling on mental wellbeing.

3.2 Requirements Development Process

The development of requirements is a software engineering process that consists of four main activities:

1. *Requirements elicitation*: In order to build an m-Health solution that caters the needs of women in Morocco, a few visits to the Maternity Les Orangers that belongs to the University Hospital Avicenne of Rabat has been organized to closely observe the clinical intervention in terms of postnatal care. With the consent of the director of the maternity, several interviews have been conducted with the clinical staff (i.e. Doctors, interns and nurses) at the maternity to gather the maximum of information with regards postnatal care in Morocco.
2. *Requirements analysis*: The requirements identified in the first activity have been analyzed to ensure coherence and resolve conflicts between them. A scrupulous analytic review has been performed on existing apps for postnatal care to expand the set of requirements of the solution and assure its functional completeness [12].
3. *Requirements specification*: A Software Requirements Specification (SRS) covering functional and non-functional requirements for the m-Health solution for postnatal care has been elaborated according to the IEEE 29148 standard [21].
4. *Requirements validation:* The SRS developed has been finally presented to the clinical staff of the maternity for further validation.

3.3 The SRS

Initially, the following functional requirements have been specified:

- Baby management
  - The user shall be able to add multiple babies to her profile.
  - The user shall be able to select one of her babies to track her or his activities.

- Newborn's daily habits recording
  - The user shall be able to record the daily habits of her newborn including diaper changes, feeding and sleep patterns.
  - The user shall receive alerting messages if her newborn's feeding and sleep patterns are alarming or the number of diapers changes that her newborn needs significantly exceeds the average number.
- Growth measurements
  - The user shall record the anthropometric characteristics of her newborn including weight, height and head circumference.
  - The user shall be able to track her baby growth and compare it to standard child growth percentiles.
- Health checkups and medication
  - The user shall be able to schedule appointments for postnatal and pediatric checkups. Three postnatal checkups are considered by default at the 6th day, 6th week, 6th month after delivery.
  - Given that a user has scheduled an appointment, she shall receive a push notification to remind her of the upcoming medical visits (pediatric or postnatal visits).
  - The user shall be able to manage and record medications.
  - The user shall receive reminders of medication intake.
- Immunization
  - The user shall be able to track her newborn's vaccines.
  - The user shall be able to consult the immunization schedule as recommended by the ministry of health in Morocco.
  - The user shall schedule appointment for her newborn's vaccines and receive reminders accordingly.
- Postpartum recovery
  - The user shall be able to record and track her postpartum weight at any time.
  - The user shall be able to access information about postpartum recovery tips including nutrition, physical exercises and hygiene.
- Mental health
  - The user shall be able to learn more about the symptoms and signs of Post-partum Depression (PPD) and baby blues.
  - The user shall be able to acquire effective manners and strategies to cope with postpartum mental disorders.
  - The user shall be able to screen for postpartum depression by filling in a 10-item self-report measure based on the Edinburgh Postnatal Depression Scale (EDPS) [22]. Note that users can fill in this self-report only once a week.
- Community
  - The user shall be able to access the FAQ (Frequently Asked Questions) section to get answers about common doubts and concerns that new mothers have during their postnatal period.
  - The user shall be able to share her experiences and feelings with other new mothers through a forum.
  - The user shall be able to view and comment other users' posts.

- Guides
  - The user shall be able to get basic baby care tips including burping, bathing, soothing, swaddling, etc.
  - The user shall be able to access useful information on how to improve her breastfeeding experience.
  - The user shall be able to learn more about baby development milestones as regards the age of her baby.
  - The user shall be able to acquire information about signs and symptoms of potentially life-threatening postpartum conditions.
- Settings
  - The user shall be able to update her preferences with regards the unit of measurement.
  - The user shall be able to change language preferences.

Along with these functional requirements, a number of non-functional requirements have been identified to enhance the quality and design of the m-Health solution Mamma&Baby based on the international standard ISO/IEC 25010 [23] and mobile design guidelines [24]. The core aspects of quality that have been considered are as follows:

- **Functional suitability:** Mamma&Baby solution should cater users' needs through well integrated functions, useful and appropriate content.
- **Performance efficiency:** Mamma&Baby solution should take a short time to load and provide onscreen feedback to the user.
- **Availability:** Mamma&Baby solution should remain operational and accessible in a certain manner under possible circumstances (e.g. unavailable network, limited bandwidth).
- **Scalability:** Mamma&Baby solution should be able to deal with increasing use and handle more data as time progress.
- **Usability and user interaction:**
  - Mamma&Baby solution should support both landscape and portrait orientations.
  - The user should be able to understand the flow of the solution easily without further training or help.
  - Mamma&Baby solution should use intuitive and predictable navigation patterns.
  - Mamma&Baby solution should use common icons' system.
- **Visual quality:**
  - Mamma&Baby should use familiar and simple tone along with an intelligible writing style.
  - Mamma&Baby should display graphics, text and images without noticeable distortion.
  - Mamma&Baby should use a coherent color theme that recalls its purpose.
- **Security and privacy:**
  - Mamma&Baby should use a strong authentication mechanism.
  - All private data should be stored in the solution's internal storage.
  - Mamma&Baby must protect any stored sensitive personal data from unauthorized access.
  - Mamma&Baby should ensure encrypted communications.

- Mamma&Baby should include a privacy policy that is detailed, comprehensive and understandable.
- **Modifiability and maintainability:** Mamma&Baby should have a readable and extendible code to easily modify functions and implement new ones to avoid increasing maintenance cost.

With the aim to make the tedious and repetitive tasks included in the solution more fun, interactive and engaging, a gamification strategy is proposed to be implemented in the solution, and typically works in the following ways:

- **Point-based scoring:** Being one of the core gamification mechanics, allocating scores to users can motivate their willingness to continue to use the solution. Three point-based incentives are therefore proposed:
  - A user shall earn 15 points for filling in the self-report measure for postpartum depression screening.
  - A user shall earn 20 points for each medical appointment attended (gynecologic, pediatric or immunization visit).
  - A user shall earn 10 points for taking medication properly by marking the medication intake as complete.
  - A user shall earn 5 points for each measurement recorded; including baby growth parameters and mother's weight.
- **Badges:** These are simple virtual elements that symbolize rewards given to users for their achievements. Badges act as a target setting and as a recognition tool that motivate users to get actively involved in the solution and work hard towards gamification objectives. Four various achievements need to be completed to unlock badges and trophies as described below:
  - Once registered, the user shall receive a 'Welcome' badge.
  - A user shall be able to unlock the 'Best nursing Mamma' badge for breast-feeding her baby at least during his or her six first months.
  - A user shall be able to unlock the 'Super Mamma' badge when she attends five medical appointments.
  - A user shall be able to unlock the 'Fit Mamma' badge for losing at least 6 Kgs (13 lb) during the first six months of her postnatal period.
- **Progress bar:** It is perhaps one of the most straightforward gamification elements that displays operations' wholeness. It gives information about the progress users are making towards attaining a specific goal. In Mamma&Baby solution, the progress bar has been thought with regards baby growth measurements. In this respect, Mamma&Baby solution shall display the percentage users have completed as they enter values of their babies' vital parameters (height and weight) at a monthly basis during a twelve-month period.
- **Leaderboards:** The very presence of a leaderboard can elicit the desire to play. The simple goal of raising up the rankings serves as a powerful motivator to continue. Based on the amount of the points collected, users shall be able to see how they stack up against other users in the solution. The leaderboard is supposed to be displayed in the Community section where social interaction is endorsed.
- **Virtual goods:** Earned points can be exchanged for instant virtual rewards. Users shall be able to choose whether to redeem their points in the form of rewards and

subsequently reset their score to the remaining points or keep on accumulating points without spending them. Three virtual rewards are proposed in Mamma&Baby:

- A user shall be able to redeem '50 points' for a new display theme.
- A user shall be able to redeem '100 points' for an electronic personalized photo frame for a specific photo of her baby that she will uploads.
- A user shall be able to redeem '200 points' for a customized electronic photo album of ten uploaded photos.

4 Implementation

4.1 Tools and Technologies Used

From this initial system requirements specification, the structural and behavioral aspects of the system have been modeled using an open source UML (Unified Modeling Language) called StarUML[1]. The main purpose is to fill the gap between documents written in natural language and use cases by modeling requirements in a graphical and tabular way, which can significantly improve the requirements representation and enrich the relationship between them. In this vein, high-level requirements have been captured using Use cases and the domain model has been represented using a class diagram. The control flow drawn from an operation to another has been represented using activity diagrams. In conjunction with these UML diagrams, user interfaces have been sketched to explore the design space of the solution more fully and to openly investigate multiple design directions at low cost. In parallel, the SRS document has been transformed into logical structure, which contains detailed and complete set of specifications that can be implemented in a programming language. Afterwards, the design has been implemented into source code in Android studio being the official integration environment for Android app development. To build a powerful solution, Firebase; considered a Backend as a Service (BaaS) has been used to leverage its numerous features including real-time database, hosting, cloud storage and social authentication, among others.

4.2 User Interfaces

At the current stage of the development cycle, only the functional and non-functional requirements are fully implemented. The gamification aspects are now being analyzed in order to be incorporated in an updated version of the solution. Figure 1 depicts a few snapshots of user interfaces of Mamma&Baby. Once launched, the user will be primarily asked to complete the registration form to create a new account. When logged in, the user gets access to the home page where she can choose the section she is interested of. Six menu cards are available, assembling each of them two to four functionalities or features such as tracking baby's daily activities, setting appointments'

---

[1] http://staruml.io/.

reminders, learning tips on baby care, screening for postpartum depression and sharing experiences and concerns with other mothers, to cite but a few. It is possible to keep health records and tracking measurements of multiple babies, at any moment the user can switch between her tracked babies. Also, the user can change her preferences with regards language and measurement units from the drawer menu.

5 Experiment Design for Quality Assessment of the Solution

Following the development of Mamma&Baby solution and testing its different functionalities using specification-based testing, the clinical staff at the Maternity Les orangers have examined the different features and functionalities of the solution and have studied the overall content coherence in order to validate the solution from a clinical perspective. With the aim to assess the quality, effectiveness and usefulness of the solution, an experiment with real participants will be conducted at Maternity Les orangers under the close supervision of the same clinical staff already involved.

5.1 Participants and Study Procedures

Participants. A total of sixty-five puerperal women are expected to be enrolled in this experiment. These women have to fulfill the following inclusion criteria to guarantee their participation: IC1) Being aged between 20 and 45 years old, IC2) being resident in the region of Rabat, IC3) having an Android smartphone, IC4) having a moderate level of experience with mobile applications, IC5) willing to comply with the evaluation study procedures. A written informed consent form shall be administered to the prospective participants to be signed prior their effective enrollment in the evaluation. This informed consent will answer the common concerns and questions that cross participants' mind about the purpose of the evaluation, participation conditions, study procedures, confidentiality and withdrawal, before taking part of the study.

Evaluation Study Procedures. Before starting the experiment, all the participants enrolled will be initiated to the solution. The purpose and the main functionalities included in the solution will be explained in details and a quick video demonstration will be displayed to the participants to have a concrete idea on how to use the solution. Afterwards, the participants will be requested to have the Mamma&Baby solution running on their Android smartphone for up to six months of their postnatal period. They will have to complete all the tasks' instructions presented in Table 1 at a regular basis so that they will be able to provide a credible and well-founded feedback about the overall quality of the solution. After six months of use, the participants will be asked to complete two self-report questionnaires of quality assessment of the mobile solution.

5.2 Assessment Criteria

In order to assess the quality of the resulting gamified solution, two self-report questionnaires will be at disposal of the participants at the end of the experiment. The

Fig. 1. Screenshots of users' interfaces of the solution 'Mamma&Baby'

effectiveness and potential of the solution in promoting postnatal care and improving access to postnatal care services in Morocco will also be evaluated through a short questionnaire in which they will be asked to give their remarks and suggestions to improve the quality of the solution.

Product Quality. It refers to the degree to which a product or a service fits patterns of users or customers' expectations and preferences. The international standard IEC/ISO

Table 1. Tasks' participants

Tasks	Participants will be instructed to	Participants will be informed that
Task 1: Sign up/Create an account then log in	–Enter their personal information (Full name, phone number, weight, type of delivery, email, password) –Enter baby's details: Name, gender, birthday –Use their login credentials (email and password) to sign in	–The details entered should be accurate –Their personal details will be kept secured in our database
Task 2: Record regularly their baby's routine activities	–Have their smartphones at hand to record their baby's habits (feeding/sleep) with an accurate timing –Switch breasts multiple times when nursing and record the time spent on each breast until the breastfeeding session is over –Track daily diaper output –Get their baby's growth (height, weight and head circumference) measured at a monthly basis at each checkup or at any pharmacy,	–All the records made can be visualized on plots –Month-over-month measures can be compared with the OMS charts
Task 3: Set reminders for health checks appointments and medication intakes	–Enter information about their postnatal checkups' appointments or those of their baby's pediatric visits –Set a reminder for their appointments –Mark complete when the appointment is attended and add note if needed/preferred –Set a reminder to take their meds	–All the information related to the doctor visits or the medications should be correct
Task 4: Track the vaccine schedule and set reminders for upcoming shots	–Set reminders of upcoming vaccines in advance –Record/mark as complete the vaccines that babies received	–All the vaccines presented in the vaccine schedule are mandatory and should not be delayed or skipped
Task 5: Monitor postpartum weight	–Track their postpartum weight regularly	–All the postpartum weight measurements are graphically displayed
Task 6: Screen for postpartum depression	–Screen for PPD at least two times during the first 6 months after delivery	–Their answers to the quiz's questions should be honest

(*continued*)

Table 1. (*continued*)

Tasks	Participants will be instructed to	Participants will be informed that
	−Seek medical attention immediately is the quiz's result shows a possible presence of PPD symptoms	and correct to receive the most accurate feedback
Task 7: Become a member of new mothers' community	−Share their problems/concerns with other new mothers	−Their posts will be visible to all users
Task 8: Learn more about postnatal period	−Use our guides to acquire more information about numerous aspects of postnatal period such as: baby care, postpartum recovery, danger signs, postpartum mental health, etc. -Quickly get the answer to the most commonly asked questions by puerperal women	

25010 defines a model for software product quality that is composed of eight characteristics which are further subdivided into sub-characteristics that are related to static and dynamic properties of the software product [23]. Several studies have used this model to evaluate health solutions as for cardiology [25, 26], blood donation [27] and pregnancy monitoring [28]. Four characteristics pertaining to this model have been considered to develop the product quality questionnaire which are: Functional suitability, Operability, Reliability and Security. These characteristics have been found to significantly affect the quality of mHealth solutions [26–28]. The number of items per each characteristic depended on both the number of its sub-characteristics and the degree of its impact's relevance on the quality of the software product. However, despite having only three sub-characteristics, eleven items have been developed for functional suitability characteristic. In fact, functional suitability is one of the most important quality characteristics as it entails the ability of a software product to match the needs and requirements of its users [29].

On the other hand, operability has also included eleven items given its numerous sub-characteristics that are mainly focused on the degree to which the software product is attractive, easy to learn and appropriate to use [23]. Five additional items have been determined to cover reliability which bears on the capability of a software product to perform failure-free operation for a specified period of time. Security, for its part, has comprised three items primarily relying on data integrity, confidentiality and privacy. Considering the personal and sensitive information used and shared in healthcare solutions, several security and privacy concerns have arisen and have significantly disturbed the course of the software development cycle. This has obliged the developers to take into consideration a number of security requirements from the early stages of the software development [30]. Table 2 in Appendix summarizes the items of the product quality questionnaire. The possible answers to these items are either Yes/No or a 5-point Likert scale. The corresponding score to each of these answers are provided in Table 3 in Appendix. The resulting participants' scores will be obtained for each characteristic by summing all the scores obtained for their underpinning sub-characteristics. Further, they will be classified into five categories: i) very high if the score is between 4.5 and 5; ii) high if the score is between 3.5 and 4.5; iii) moderate if the score is between 2.5 and 3.5; iv) low if the score is between 1.5 and 2.5; v) very low if the score if between 1 and 1.5.

Quality-in-Use. The concept of quality in-use corresponds to the user's perception of the quality of the software product in its context of use. It can therefore be used to validate the degree to which the software product meets the users' needs [31]. According to the ISO/IEC 25010 standard, the quality in-use model is decomposed into the following five characteristics: Effectiveness, Efficiency, Satisfaction, Freedom from risk and Context coverage [23]. Given the gamification aspects that are expected to be implemented in the solution before the evaluation, an adapted model of the quality-in-use model presented in the ISO/IEC 25010 standard has been used to define the questions of the quality-in-use assessment questionnaire. The QU-GamSoft model has be constructed taking into consideration the specific elements in gamified software [32]. A total of thirteen items has been developed to cover three characteristics, namely: Effectiveness, efficiency and satisfaction as shown in Table 4 in Appendix.

These characteristics have been found to be significantly influenced in gamified software [32]. Effectiveness refers to the accuracy and completeness with which users achieve specified goals owing to the engagement caused by the gamification elements whereas efficiency designates the resources exploited as regards the completeness with which users achieve those goals [23]. Besides, satisfaction implies the extent to which user needs are satisfied and fulfilled when gamified software is used in specific context of use.

Unlike the efficiency and effectiveness characteristics, satisfaction is further divided into sub-characteristics including: enjoyment, usefulness and user trust [32]. The scoring system for this questionnaire is exactly similar to that of the product quality evaluation questionnaire. Accordingly, Table 5 in appendix displays the possible answers to this questionnaire's items along with their corresponding scores.

The Appendix can be found at the following link: https://www.um.es/giisw/ Mamma&Baby/Appendix.pdf.

Potential. The potential of the solution in promoting and improving postnatal care in Morocco will be assessed through the participants' evaluation of a few aspects of the solution as presented below:

- The solution provides valuable information on parenting and baby care.
- The solution offers useful advices and recommendations about postpartum recovery.
- The solution helps to track the vaccine schedule of your newborn.
- The solution leverages socialization in a way that it allows you to share your experiences with others.

Participants are invited to freely choose a value between 0 and 100% that better accommodate their perception with respect to these aspects. An additional open question is included in the questionnaire to give to the participants the opportunity to make critics, remarks and suggestions to enhance the overall quality of the solution.

5.3   Research Questions

The results of this empirical evaluation will be used to answer the following research questions:

RQ1. To What Extent the Solution Adheres to Quality Characteristics?
The aim of this question is to determine the degree of fulfillment of product quality characteristics (e.g. Functional suitability, Reliability and Security) by the solution. The overall average score for each product quality characteristic will be analyzed to answer this research question.

RQ2. To Which Degree does Gamification Elements Enhances the Quality-in-Use of the Solution?
This research question aims to investigate the importance of gamification aspects in improving user experience and user satisfaction with the solution. In order to answer this question, the overall score obtained in the quality-in-use assessment will be analyzed.

RQ3. Is there a Compliance Between the Solution's Product Quality, its Quality-in-Use and its Potential as Perceived and Reported by the Participants?
The goal of this research question is to compare between the perceived product quality and quality-in-use of the solution and its potential as reported by the participants. First, the correlation between the overall scores obtained in the product quality and quality-in-use assessments will be studied. Then, these overall scores will be contrasted, one by one, with the results of the solution's potential assessment. This will likely indicate whether the potential of the solution in improving postnatal care is tightly linked with its overall quality and vice versa.

6   Conclusions and Future Work

This paper presents the requirements specification of a gamified solution intended to promote postnatal care in Morocco. On the one hand, the elaboration of the SRS has been presented and the functional and non-functional requirements have been pointed out. The gamification aspects that are expected to be, soon, implemented into the solution have also been listed. On the other hand, the experiment design of quality evaluation of the solution with real participants has been thoroughly described. This evaluation will consist of regularly performing a set of tasks during a 6-months of use, followed by completing three distinct questionnaires on the solution's product quality, quality-in-use and potential. The results that will be obtained from these questionnaires will be scrutinized to determine the overall quality of the solution and the importance of gamification in yielding better outcomes. Further, these results will be used to guide the improvement process of the solution according to the participants' feedback.

For future work, it is, first, intended to complete the implementation of the solution by the integration of the gamification aspects. Second, it is planned to enforce this experiment design through conducting the evaluation with puerperal participants. Third, it is expected to answer the research questions, previously mentioned, based on the results obtained from the empirical evaluation study.

Acknowledgments. This work was conducted within the research project PEER, 7-246 supported by the US Agency for International Development. The authors would like to thank the NAS and USAID for their valued support.

References

1. World Health Organization: Postnatal Care for Mothers and Newborns Highlights from the World Health Organization 2013 Guidelines. https://bit.ly/31NSv4t
2. Romano, M., Cacciatore, A., Giordano, R., Rosa, B.La: Postpartum period: three distinct but continuous phases. J. Prenat. Med. **4**, 22–25 (2010)
3. Datta, S., Kodali, B.S., Segal, S.: Maternal physiological changes during pregnancy, labor, and the postpartum period. In: Obstetric Anesthesia Handbook. pp. 1–14 (2010)
4. World Health Organization: Postpartum Care of the Mother and Newborn: a practical guide. https://bit.ly/2ROdDCX
5. World Health Organization: A Handbook for Building Skills. Counselling for Maternal and Newborn Health Care. https://bit.ly/2xmvkjE
6. Dermott, K.: Clinical guidelines and evidence review for postnatal care: Routine postnatal care of recently delivered women and their babies (2006)
7. World Health Organization: A handbook for building skills Counselling for Maternal and Newborn Health (Updated). https://bit.ly/2NxqL0C
8. Elkhoudri, N., Baali, A., Amor, H.: Postnatal care: levels and determinants in Morocco. Iran. J. Public Health. **46**, 242–248 (2017)
9. Katusiime, J., Berlin, H., Linden, U.D., Linden, G.U.D.: Supporting maternal health education in developing countries using mobile phones- results of a pilot study. In: Proceedings of the First African Conference on Human Computer Interaction, pp. 48–57 (2016)
10. Bachiri, M., Idri, A., Fernández-alemán, J.L., Toval, A.: Mobile personal health records for pregnancy monitoring functionalities: analysis and potential. Comput. Methods Programs Biomed. **134**, 121–135 (2016)
11. Bachiri, M., Idri, A., Redman, Leanne M., Fernandez-Aleman, J.L., Toval, A.: A requirements catalog of mobile personal health records for prenatal care. In: Misra, S., et al. (eds.) ICCSA 2019. LNCS, vol. 11622, pp. 483–495. Springer, Cham (2019). https://doi.org/10.1007/978-3-030-24305-0_36
12. Sardi, L., Idri, A., Redman, L.M., Alami, H., Bezad, R., Fernández-alemán, J.L.: Mobile health applications for postnatal care : review and analysis of functionalities and technical features. Comput. Methods Programs Biomed. **184**, 105114 (2020)
13. Sardi, L., Idri, A., Fernández-alemán, J.L.: A systematic review of gamification in e-Health. J. Biomed. Inform. **71**, 31–48 (2017)
14. Adanikin, A.I., Olumnuyiwa, A.J., Adewale, A.: Role of reminder by text message in enhancing postnatal clinic attendance. Int. J. Gynecol. Obstet. **126**, 179 (2014)

15. Ngabo, F., et al.: Designing and implementing an innovative SMS-based alert system (RapidSMS-MCH) to monitor pregnancy and reduce maternal and child deaths in Rwanda. Pan Afr. Med. J. **13**, 1–15 (2012)

16. Parvin, M.S.: An effective m-health system for antenatal and postnatal care in rural areas of Bangladesh. J. Comput. Eng. **17**, 15–19 (2015)

17. Bangal, V.B., Borawake, S.K., Gavhane, S.P., Aher, K.H.: Use of mobile phone for improvement in maternal health: a randomized control trial. Int. J. Reprod. Contracept. Obstet. Gynecol. **6**, 5458–5463 (2017)

18. Moorhead, A., Bond, R., Mulvenna, M., O'Neil, S., Murphy, N.: A Self-management app for maternal mental health. In: British HCI Conference, pp. 1–5 (2018)

19. Mduma, N., Kalegele, K.: Enhancing management of nutrition information using mobile application: prenatal and postnatal requirements. In: IST-Africa, pp. 1–7 (2017)

20. Shorey, S., Yang, Y.Y., Dennis, C.: A mobile health app – based postnatal educational program (home-but not alone): descriptive qualitative study. J. Med. Internet Res. **20**, e119 (2018)

21. IEEE 29148 Standard. Systems and software engineering—Life cycle processes—Requirements engineering (2011)

22. Cox, J., Holden, J.: Perinatal mental health: a guide to the Edinburgh Postnatal Depression Scale (EPDS). Royal College of Psychiatrists (2003)

23. ISO/IEC-25010. Systems and software engineering—Systems and software Quality Requirements and Evaluation (SQuaRE)—System and software quality models (2011)

24. Android Developers: Reference Android Design Guidelines. https://bit.ly/1nKBw8N

25. Kadi, I., Idri, A., Ouhbi, S.: Quality evaluation of cardiac decision support systems using ISO 25010 standard. In: IEEE/ACS 13th International Conference of Computer Systems and Applications (AICCSA), pp. 1–8 (2016)

26. Ouhbi, S., Idri, A., Hakmi, R., Benjelloun, H., Fernández-alemán, J.L., Toval, A.: Requirements specification of an e-health solution to improve cardiovascular healthcare services in Morocco. In: The 11th International Conference on Intelligent Systems: Theories and Applications (SITA). pp. 16–21 (2016)

27. Idri, A., Sardi, L., Fernández-alemán, J.L.: Quality evaluation of gamified blood donation apps using ISO/IEC 25010 Standard. In: 12th International Conference on Health Informatics, pp. 607–614 (2018)

28. Idri, A., Bachiri, M., Fernández-alemán, J.L., Toval, A.: ISO/IEC 25010 based evaluation of free mobile personal health records for pregnancy monitoring. In: IEEE 41st Annual Computer Software and Applications Conference, pp. 262–267 (2017)

29. Rodríguez, M., Oviedo, J.R., Piattini, A.M.: Evaluation of software product functional suitability : a case study. Softw. Qual. Manag. **18**, 18 (2016)

30. Salinesi, C., Comyn-wattiau, I.: Reusable knowledge in security requirements engineering : a systematic mapping study. Requir. Eng. **21**(2), 251–283 (2015)

31. Bevan, N.: Quality in use: meeting user needs for quality. J. Syst. Softw. **49**, 89–96 (1999)

32. Vargas Enríquez, J.A.: Evaluating the quality in use of gamified software (2016)

Handling Faults in Service Oriented Computing: A Comprehensive Study

Roaa ElGhondakly, Sherin Moussa$^{(\boxtimes)}$ ⓘ, and Nagwa Badr

Information Systems Department, Faculty of Computer and Information
Sciences, Ain Shams University, Cairo, Egypt
{roaa.ahmed,sherinmoussa,nagwabadr}@cis.asu.edu.eg

Abstract. Recently, service-oriented computing paradigms have become a trending development direction, in which software systems are built using a set of loosely coupled services distributed over multiple locations through a service-oriented architecture. Such systems encounter different challenges, as integration, performance, reliability, availability, etc., which made all associated testing activities to be another major challenge to avoid their faults and system failures. Services are considered the substantial element in service-oriented computing. Thus, the quality of services and the service dependability in a web service composition have become essential to manage faults within these software systems. Many studies addressed web service faults from diverse perspectives. In this paper, a comprehensive study is conducted to investigate the different perspectives to manipulate web service faults, including fault tolerance, fault injection, fault prediction and fault localization. An extensive comparison is provided, highlighting the main research gaps, challenges and limitations of each perspective for web services. An analytical discussion is then followed to suggest future research directions that can be adopted to face such obstacles by improving fault handling capabilities for an efficient testing in service-oriented computing systems.

Keywords: Fault tolerance · Fault prediction · Fault injection · Quality of Service · Service testing · Service oriented computing

1 Introduction

Service-oriented systems are built through combining a set of distributed services that are previously developed for reuse. These loosely coupled services communicate with each other through a predefined protocol, forming a service composition to achieve a complex task [1, 2]. However, the performance and quality of the individual services might be higher than those of the resultant service composition, due to some integration issues, unavailability of services, dependability between services, etc., leading to faults occurrence. Four main mechanisms are investigated to achieve service dependability facing service compositions with respect to the quality, performance and reliability: fault avoidance, fault removal, fault prediction and fault tolerance. Fault avoidance methods minimize the occurrence of faults, whereas fault removal methods aim to remove faults as soon as possible. Fault prediction techniques predict the number of faults before

© Springer Nature Switzerland AG 2020
O. Gervasi et al. (Eds.): ICCSA 2020, LNCS 12252, pp. 947–959, 2020.
https://doi.org/10.1007/978-3-030-58811-3_67

occurrence, while fault tolerance detects faults and tries to solve them early from the system [3]. In this paper, a comprehensive study is conducted to investigate the studies handling web service faults with respect to different perspectives as shown in Fig. 1. A thorough analytical evaluation is discussed for the challenges and limitations encountered in each perspective in the state of art, revealing the main research gaps. In addition, a set of future directions are proposed for powerful testing in service-oriented computing (SOC) systems. The rest of the paper is organized as follows: Sect. 2 discusses the main research studies that tackle faults in service-oriented systems according to the given hierarchy. Section 3 analyzes the revealed challenges and limitations, whereas Sect. 4 proposes various future directions to consider maximizing testing benefits in service-orientation. Finally, Sect. 5 concludes the proposed study.

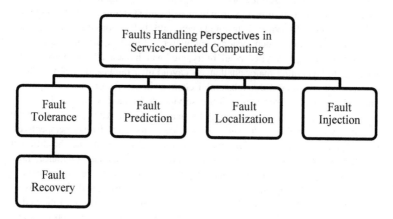

Fig. 1. The perspectives of faults handling in service-oriented computing (SOC)

2   Faults Manipulation in Service-Oriented Computing

Many studies have addressed diverse perspectives of faults handling in Service-oriented computing (SOC) systems, as fault tolerance, fault prediction, fault injection, etc. Following the hierarchy in Fig. 1, a comprehensive discussion is presented to investigate each perspective of faults handling in the following sub-sections.

2.1   Fault Tolerance

Fault tolerance allows a system to keep on operating while one or more of its components stop working or tend to fail [4]. Thus, fault tolerance should consist of a detection method and a recovery method. Most of the proposed approaches in this perspective required to combine other fault mechanisms in order to achieve fault tolerance, like fault localization, fault injection and fault recovery. Gupta et al. [5], considered fault tolerance from the web service composition point of view, taking into consideration some quality of service (QoS) attributes. A fault injection mechanism was used to inject two types of faults: network faults, by examining the unavailability of a service, and logical faults by observing incorrect values. Authors then tried to detect their existence and recover from them, without trying to find the already existed faults. In addition, only two types of faults were considered, ignoring any other types of faults.

In [6], the authors studied two existing fault tolerance mechanisms: Time redundancy and space redundancy, with their three strategies: Retry, Active replication and Passive replication. In Retry strategy, if a service fails, it would retry and run frequently to either work correctly or reach the limit of trials. Active and Passive replications depend on using replicas to overcome failures. In Active strategy, it invokes all services and the first returned suitable one is used, whereas in Passive strategy, the primary service is invoked first, then if it fails, a backup replication is used instead. They proposed integrated simulation algorithms combining all three strategies to control services and modify the ones that did not meet the desired requirements in the form of time, space, etc. However, although the simulation has given high reliability, they did not consider reliability after applying actual data. Fekih et al. [7] used a sensor-based method to detect and find faults' location, and then used two repair algorithms to correct faults before system crash; single service reconfiguration (SSR) and multiple service reconfiguration (MSR) with a metaheuristic search algorithm. However, they did not evaluate the efficiency of their results within comparison with other approaches. Authors in [8] used two ranking algorithms HITS based Service Component Ranking Algorithm (HSCR) and PageRank based Service Component Ranking Algorithm (PSCR) to rank services, where top services could be used later since their fault tolerance ability would be high. However, they encountered critical drawbacks, as they did not consider neither fault detection nor localization methods, whereas fault tolerance should include detection and recovery methods. In addition, localization methods help in finding the location of faulty service, which eases the recovery process. They only proposed the optimum services set to use instead of the faulty ones, in which only simple services were investigated neglecting QoS attributes.

A fault recovery approach was utilized in [9] through an error handling procedure, but it suffered from its weak response time that affected the overall performance. Chen et al. [10] proposed a 3-phase mechanism, in which these phases were invocation, synchronization and exception with the aid of petri nets to show the behavior of services. The invocation phase selected the services for composition, the synchronization phase obtained matching services for the selected ones, while the exception phase excluded the services that may cause faults as well as its connected ones. This mechanism was inefficient when services' resources increase, affecting the reliability of the proposed approach. Authors in [11] proposed a fault tolerance approach for mobile ad hoc networks based on a checkpointing technique, in which the faulty services were recovered by substituting them with the ones that satisfied QoS constraints using a fuzzy-rated system. However, their evaluation was based on simulation rather than real world problems. Besides, they encountered a single point of failure issue that would affect the reliability and availability of their approach.

Another rejuvenation fault tolerance scheme was introduced in [12], consisting of 3 sub phases: failure detection, age evaluation of components, and checkpointing method for rejuvenation. However, the results lacked accuracy as a fault detection metric, as well as maintaining availability. Miltiadis et al. in [13] proposed an approach for predicting the average execution time for faulty applications counting on a checkpoint mechanism. Although this approach improved the performance of faulty software, it did not propose a recovery method to overcome the existing faults. Authors in [14] investigated the impact of checkpointing interval selection on the cloud application performance, as well as finding the relation between the checkpointing interval and the failure probability. Yet, this study did not consider any fault recovery techniques. In [15], a fault injection method was used to inject faults in an application. It detected such faults using a logging mechanism in order to assess the performance of the applied fault tolerance mechanism, without discussing how faults were handled or recovered. Moreover, Jhawar and piuri in [16] analyzed the characteristics and reasons for failure of 2 fault types: crash and byzantine faults, as well as their corresponding fault tolerance mechanisms. The studies in [17] and [18] have considered fault tolerance approaches only, discarding other fault handling perspectives, in which one study addressed fault tolerance with load balancing algorithms, while the other addressed checkpointing approaches. In [19], Angarita et al. proposed a dynamic fault tolerance approach that could select the superior recovery strategy to correct faults based on analyzing some QoS parameters, the execution state and environment state. However, in practice, depending on the execution state and environment state criteria might not be possible [20]. Xu et al. in [21] discussed the impact of applying a fault recovery mechanism on time and cost, while addressing the problem of workflow scheduling in cloud computing via developing a heuristic-based algorithm. Nevertheless, they ignored that tasks might also fail, not only components.

Thus, most of the related studies applied fault detection and recovery to fulfill fault tolerance process, while ignored by few of them. Some have taken into consideration the QoS for its great impact on fault existence. Moreover, some studies applied their proposed approaches on simulated data rather than real data, which affected the truthfulness of their results.

2.2 Fault Prediction

Fault prediction is the process of predicting whether a software is faulty or not, as well as the number of faults that may appear in a software [22]. There exist only few studies that investigated fault prediction in the service-oriented computing paradigm. In [23], the authors proposed a framework to study the ability of source code metrics to predict faults in web services. They managed to predict whether a web service is faulty by applying 5 feature selection techniques to select such metrics. In addition, they considered 6 machine learning algorithms to predict faults: Naïve Bayes, Artificial Networks (ANN), Adaptive Boosting (AdaBoost), decision tree, Random Forests and Support Vector Machine (SVM). However, the main drawback was that they could not predict the number of faults. Ding et al. in [24] predicted the service composition reliability and located the faulty services using a spectrum-fault-localization technique, but the proposed method was not able to predict the number of faults as well. Authors in [25, 26] investigated some machine learning techniques for fault prediction, as classification algorithms and multi-layer perceptron, by developing a web service on Azure cloud platform to predict faulty services but neglected predicting the number of faults. Chatterjee et al. [27] proposed a prediction algorithm through integrating clustering and fuzzy algorithms to predict more than one fault at a time within one run, whereas in [28], a clustering method was proposed to detect faults using k-means++. A new set of metrics was introduced in [29] to make the fault detection process more efficient as well as to increase its performance, but they only validated their metrics on PHP based projects. However, the different approaches proposed in [27, 28] and [29] focused on predicting faulty components but neglected to predict the type and number of faults.

Consequently, most of the previous studies focused on predicting faults in service-oriented computing, ignoring the idea of predicting the number of faults, which would help in deciding how faulty the component is. In addition, it would allow controlling faults to increase services reliability and performance.

2.3   Fault Localization

Fault localization is the process of locating the faulty code or component [30, 31]. Despite of the existence of many software fault localization techniques, there were only few studies directed to fault localization in SOC paradigms [32]. Sun et al. in [33] proposed a fault localization approach for WS-BPEL programs, where switching and slicing methods were used. This study addressed fault localization for the interaction section of WS-BPEL programs only, neglecting the other sections. An automatic modeling mechanism was proposed in [34] using the "Policy View" of each service to identify fault location by building a belief network per service, but they ignored the types of located faults. Some studies have combined fault localization techniques to other fault handling perspectives, as with fault tolerance in [7] and with fault prediction in [24]. These combinations improved the reliability and availability of services, where locating their faults facilitated their correction timely and effectively.

Hence, there is still an eager need to investigate this perspective, with the aim of increasing web services reliability and performance. This includes considering different types of located faults, investigating different fault localization techniques, and defining the optimum techniques to apply in SOC systems. In addition, combining fault localization techniques with more fault handling perspectives is an encouraging trend that would elevate high performance and efficient fault handling.

2.4   Fault Injection

Fault injection is the process of injecting faults to the application to test its reliability and performance by trying to detect and remove such faults [35]. Qian et al. in [36] presented a fault injection process that counted on the place where faults can be injected and what type of faults can be injected. However, only sub-service stability coverage criterion was considered, in which more coverage criteria were highly required to evaluate the efficiency and reliability of the proposed approach. In [37], an approach was proposed using fault injection techniques to assist the failure diagnosis when the same failure takes place. In addition, it used fault localization to detect the root cause of the failure and to recover the system through fixing such faults. Some limitations were encountered, as the proposed approach could neither diagnose all kinds of failures, nor support multiple distributed systems paradigms. Another combined method was proposed in [38] to estimate the dependability of distributed systems. Contract-based and model-based cyber physical systems (CPS) were combined, applying a fault injection method to check the system dependability of the resulting model.

Thus, many studies have used fault injection methods for multiple reasons, as to evaluate and test a system [36, 38], to generate representative failure data [39], to check performance and reliability [36, 37], to assess dependability [40] and for security management [41, 42]. Furthermore, fault injection techniques were combined with other fault handling perspectives, as fault tolerance in [5] to increase the reliability and performance of the system under test. This indicates that there is still a growing interest on how and where to inject faults. A closer investigation is expected to study fault injection mechanisms with respect to SOC paradigms, considering its distributed nature and interoperability.

3   Challenges and Limitations of Faults Handling in SOC

Despite of having software faults as a comprehensive research field that has diverse contributions, handling faults in SOC is still insufficient. This is due to the different nature of web services rather than regular software systems, in which extra testing is highly demanded, and faults can occur easily for various reasons. In accordance with the related state of art, most of the previous studies considered fault tolerance as the main perspective for faults handling in service-oriented computing paradigms. Some combined it with other perspectives to boost the reliability of the system under test. A serious lack is witnessed in the research efforts proposed for the other fault handling perspectives. This raises many challenges and limitations as follows:

a) Fault tolerance methods-related Challenges
- Detecting many types of faults and their count is a persistent challenge, where the proposed studies did not cover multiple fault types, neglecting the number of faults. They only determined whether there exists a fault or not by injecting faults and trying to detect/localize them, ignoring the detection of actual faults rather than synthetic ones.
- Recovery strategies and fault prediction techniques require vital advancement with respect to the fault localization studies, in which only synthetic fault injection processes were considered, which lack to represent the diversity of faults that SOC systems can face. This would increase the performance and reliability of such systems.

b) Fault prediction methods-related Challenges
- The need for language-independent approaches, in which some studies proposed approaches for specific types of applications written in certain languages only, as WS-BPEL, PHP projects, etc.

- Semantic faults need to be considered, where most of the current studies detected faults that occur due to integration issues between components, unavailability of one of the composition services, etc., while ignoring faults that occur due to a semantic issue between services.

c) Fault injection and localization methods-related Challenges

- Handling faults in SOC systems should consider faults leading to task failure, not only faults leading to service failure. This would require new fault localization and injection approaches to address this different level of granularity.
- Investigating how and where to inject faults to improve the performance.

d) Generic Challenges

- Most of the current approaches showed high efficiency using simulated services, whereas in practice, these approaches could be inapplicable for real world applications.
- Addressing different evaluation measurements, metrics and coverage criteria to ensure the quality of the system under test.
- Consider other fault handling perspectives as fault prevention.
- The proposed approaches need to be more generic and applicable for different distributed systems.

Table 1 summarizes all deduced drawbacks and challenges at the main fault handling studies in the SOC paradigm, associated with the corresponding fault handling perspective considered, applied mechanisms, measured evaluation criteria, and the datasets used to examine the applied mechanisms.

Table 1. Deduced drawbacks and challenges in fault handling studies in SOC

Ref#	Fault handling perspective	Mechanism	Drawbacks	Challenges	Dataset	Evaluation
[5]	Fault tolerance and injection	Detect logic and network faults	Only two types of faults were considered	Detect the type and number of faults	Supply chain management system	Time complexity
[6]	Fault tolerance	Time and space redundancy with retry, active and passive replication	Reliability based on simulated data only	Consider actual faults	Composite web service of bank transaction	Reliability, round-trip time, failure rate
[7]	Fault tolerance	Single and multiple service reconfiguration	Considered only checkpointing techniques for faults detection	Fault detection techniques	QWS dataset [43]	Response time

(*continued*)

Table 1. (*continued*)

Ref#	Fault handling perspective	Mechanism	Drawbacks	Challenges	Dataset	Evaluation
[8]	Fault tolerance	HITS based and PageRank based service component ranking algorithms	Neglected QoS attributes, did not detect the faulty service	Consider more metrics	A real-world dataset	Failure rate
[9]	Fault tolerance	Selection of services, provided top-k compositions, fault recovery	Response time affected by similarity detection methods	Performance issues	OWLS-TC2 Semantic Web Services Ver 1.1	Response time, Efficiency, failure rate
[10]	Fault tolerance	Invocation, synchronization and exception with petri nets	Efficiency issues when service resources increase	Efficiency challenges	QWS dataset [43]	Run time, Reliability
[11]	Fault tolerance	Checkpointing technique then recovery via a fuzzy rated system	Considered checkpointing techniques only for fault detection	Fault detection techniques	Simulation of services	Service composition Efficiency, Failure rate, Recovery time
[12]	Fault tolerance	Rejuvenation fault tolerance scheme with detection, evaluation and checkpointing	Accuracy of fault detection	Performance measurements	A private cloud application	Accuracy and availability
[13]	Fault tolerance	Predict the average execution time of a program with presence of failure using checkpointing	Considered checkpointing only to improve the execution time and performance	Fault detection and recovery techniques	Multiple software applications with different loop sizes	Execution time
[14]	Fault tolerance	Investigate via simulation the impact of checkpointing interval selection on the performance of a SaaS cloud	Considered checkpointing to investigate the relation bet. the checkpointing interval and failure probability	Fault detection and recovery techniques	Simulated application	Performance metrics
[15]	Fault tolerance and injection	Inject fault and measure performance of fault tolerance	Did not state the used fault tolerance mechanism and how it recovered faults	Fault tolerance mechanisms	Some web services applications	Response time

(*continued*)

Table 1. (*continued*)

Ref#	Fault handling perspective	Mechanism	Drawbacks	Challenges	Dataset	Evaluation
[19]	Fault tolerance and recovery	Fault tolerance model to determine the best recovery strategy	Depended on metrics inapplicable for real world applications	Considering actual data	Generated 1000 CWSs	Efficiency and Effectiveness
[21]	Fault tolerance and recovery	Study the impact of fault recovery mechanism on time and cost	Did not discuss the optimum recovery strategy	Recovery strategy challenges	Real workflows	Cost and time
[23]	Fault prediction	Feature selection and machine learning algorithms	Stated whether a component is faulty or not	Detect type and number of faults	WSDL files from Multiple datasets	ROC, f-measure, Accuracy, Precision, RECALL
[24]	Fault prediction and localization	Spectrum-fault-localization technique	Did not state the type and number of faults	Detect the type and number of faults	An online shop example	Effectiveness and reliability
[26]	Fault prediction	Machine learning and classification algorithms	Did not state the type and number of faults	Detect the type and number of faults	Drupal, moodle datasets	Average fault prediction rate
[27]	Fault prediction	Integrate clustering and fuzzy algorithms	Focused on fault existence	Predict the type and number of existing faults	HTTP logs of certain web pages	Dynamic and dunn validity indices
[28]	Fault prediction	A clustering method for detecting faults using k-means ++	Detected faults only	Predict the type and number of existing faults	4 different datasets	Performance measurements and defect rate
[29]	Fault prediction	Applied a new set of metrics for efficient fault detection process	Detected faulty services only	Predict the type and number of faults, Tasks failure	Datasets from 3 open source web applications	Performance measurements
[34]	Fault localization	Automatic modeling mechanism using "Policy View" of each service	Consume more memory	Performance and quality limitations	Multiple topologies	Performance, System overhead and Viability
[36]	Fault injection	Analyzed multiple fault injection techniques	Needed to consider more coverage criteria	Coverage criteria limitation	Experiment subjects: ATM, NextDate	Performance, Response time

(*continued*)

Table 1. (*continued*)

Ref#	Fault handling perspective	Mechanism	Drawbacks	Challenges	Dataset	Evaluation
[37]	Fault injection and localization	Assisted failure diagnosis and applied fault localization and recovery	cannot diagnose all kinds of failures, cannot support multiple distributed systems	Generalization issue	OpenStack cloud platform	Variation, Accuracy

4 Suggested Future Directions in Faults Handling for SOC

New fault handling approaches in SOC systems should address the diversity of fault sources with respect to the interoperability and loose coupling of services, which generate emergent types of faults special to the nature of SOC systems. Future research should consider innovative approaches to anticipate the number of faults in a tested system, as well as discovering more fault types, as functionality faults, syntactic faults, control flow faults, semantic faults, service dependency in service compositions faults, etc. In addition, fault localization approaches should investigate hybrid methods by combining static, dynamic and execution slicing based methods and program spectrum-based methods, etc. [35].

Moreover, system recovery after finding faults is a very important process to consider. Therefore, new recovery strategies should be addressed that fit the distributed architecture, increased federation, expanded intrinsic interoperability and vendor diversification of the SOC paradigm. Besides, new fault handling perspectives, like fault prevention/avoidance techniques, should be tackled in order to improve the performance and quality of SOC systems. In addition, merging multi-fault perspectives together should be investigated to increase the dependability and reliability of the tested system. Consequently, fault handling in SOC is still an emerging field of research that expects more investigations to follow.

5 Conclusion

Even though software faults occur frequently, in case of service-oriented computing (SOC) systems, faults are more likely to exist due to the nature of web services, in which the availability of some services is not guaranteed. In this study, we thoroughly investigated the main fault handling approaches that have been presented with respect to the SOC paradigms from different perspectives, including fault tolerance, fault prediction, fault localization, fault recovery and fault injection. A detailed comparison is conducted to analyze the challenges and limitations of the current fault handling approaches directed to the SOC systems. Moreover, a set of suggested future directions are proposed for efficient fault handling capabilities in SOC systems, in which current research efforts are still insufficient.

References

1. Mikalsen, T., Wohlstadter, E., Desai, N., Rouvellou, I., Tai, S.: Transaction policies for service-oriented computing. Data Knowl. Eng. **51**(1), 59–79 (2004)
2. Rao, J., Su, X.: A survey of automated web service composition methods. In: Cardoso, J., Sheth, A. (eds.) SWSWPC 2004. LNCS, vol. 3387, pp. 43–54. Springer, Heidelberg (2005). https://doi.org/10.1007/978-3-540-30581-1_5
3. Griffiths, N., Chao, K.-M. (eds.): Agent-Based Service-Oriented Computing. AIKP. Springer, London (2010). https://doi.org/10.1007/978-1-84996-041-0
4. Agarwal, H., Sharma, A.: A comprehensive survey of fault tolerance techniques in cloud computing. In: 2015 International Conference on Computing and Network Communications (CoCoNet). IEEE (2015)
5. Gupta, R., Kamal, R., Suman, U.: A QoS-supported approach using fault detection and tolerance for achieving reliability in dynamic orchestration of web services. Int. J. Inf. Technol. **10**(1), 71–81 (2017). https://doi.org/10.1007/s41870-017-0066-z
6. Shu, Y., Wu, Z., Liu, H., Gao, Y.: A simulation-based reliability analysis approach of the fault-tolerant web services. In: 2016 7th International Conference on Intelligent Systems, Modelling and Simulation (ISMS), pp. 125–129. IEEE (2016)
7. Fekih, H., Mtibaa, S., Bouamama, S.: The dynamic reconfiguration approach for fault-tolerance web service composition based on multi-level VCSOP. Procedia Comput. Sci. **159**, 1527–1536 (2019)
8. Chen, L., Liu, L., Shang, J.: Fault tolerance for web service based on component importance in service networks. In: Proceedings of the Fifth International Conference on Network, Communication and Computing (2016)
9. Kargar, A., Emadi, S.: Fault tolerance in automatic semantic web service composition based on QoS-awareness using BTSC-DFS algorithm. In: 5th International Conference on Web Research (ICWR), pp. 50–54. IEEE (2019)
10. Chen, L., Fan, G., Liu, Y.: A formal method to model and analyse QoS-aware fault tolerant service composition. Int. J. Comput. Sci. Eng. **12**(2–3), 133–145 (2016)
11. Veeresh, P., Sam, R.P., Bin, C.S.: Reliable fault tolerance system for service composition in mobile Ad Hoc network. Int. J. Electr. Comput. Eng. **9**, 2523–2533 (2019)
12. Liu, J., Zhou, J., Buyya, R.: Software rejuvenation based fault tolerance scheme for cloud applications. In: 2015 IEEE 8th International Conference on Cloud Computing. IEEE (2015)
13. Siavvas, M., Gelenbe, E.: Optimum checkpoints for programs with loops. Simul. Model. Pract. Theory **97**, 101951 (2019). https://doi.org/10.1016/j.simpat.2019.101951. ISSN 1569-190X
14. Stavrinides, G.L., Karatza, H.D.: The impact of checkpointing interval selection on the scheduling performance of real-time fine-grained parallel applications in SaaS clouds under various failure probabilities. Concurrency Comput. Pract. Exp. **30**(12), e4288 (2018)
15. Farj, K., Smeda, A.: A methodology for evaluating fault tolerance in web service applications. In: Proceedings of the 15th International Conference on Applied Computer Science (ACS 2015), pp. 188–191 (2015)
16. Jhawar, R., Piuri, V.: Fault tolerance and resilience in cloud computing environments. In: Computer and Information Security Handbook, 1 January 2017, pp. 165–181. Morgan Kaufmann, Burlington (2017)
17. Kumar, S., Rana, D.S., Dimri, S.C.: Fault tolerance and load balancing algorithm in cloud computing: A survey. Int. J. Adv. Res. Comput. Commun. Eng. **4**(7), 92–96 (2015)
18. Vargas-Santiago, M., Hernández, S.E., Rosales, L.A., Kacem, H.H.: Survey on web services fault tolerance approaches based on checkpointing mechanisms. JSW **12**(7), 507–525 (2017)

19. Angarita, R., Rukoz, M., Cardinale, Y.: Modeling dynamic recovery strategy for composite web services execution. World Wide Web **19**(1), 89–109 (2015). https://doi.org/10.1007/s11280-015-0329-1

20. Bashari, M., Bagheri, E., Du, W.: Self-adaptation of service compositions through product line reconfiguration. J. Syst. Softw. **144**, 84–105 (2018)

21. Xu, H., Yang, B., Qi, W., Ahene, E.: A multi-objective optimization approach to workflow scheduling in clouds considering fault recovery. KSII Trans. Internet Inf. Syst. (2016)

22. Rathore, S.S., Kumar, S.: A study on software fault prediction techniques. Artif. Intell. Rev. **51**(2), 255–327 (2017). https://doi.org/10.1007/s10462-017-9563-5

23. Bhandari, G.P., Gupta, R., Upadhyay, S.K.: An approach for fault prediction in SOA-based systems using machine learning techniques. Data Technol. Appl. **53**(4), 397–421 (2019)

24. Ding, Z., Xu, T., Ye, T., Zhou, Y.: Online prediction and improvement of reliability for service oriented systems. IEEE Trans. Reliab. **65**(3), 1133–1148 (2016)

25. Malhotra, R.: A systematic review of machine learning techniques for software fault prediction. Appl. Soft Comput. **27**, 504–518 (2015)

26. Catal, C., Akbulut, A., Ekenoglu, E., Alemdaroglu, M.: Development of a software vulnerability prediction web service based on artificial neural networks. In: Kang, U., Lim, E.-P., Yu, J.X., Moon, Y.-S. (eds.) PAKDD 2017. LNCS (LNAI), vol. 10526, pp. 59–67. Springer, Cham (2017). https://doi.org/10.1007/978-3-319-67274-8_6

27. Chatterjee, S., Roy, A.: Novel algorithms for web software fault prediction. Qual. Reliab. Eng. Int. **31**(8), 1517–1535 (2015)

28. Öztürk, M.M., Cavusoglu, U., Zengin, A.: A novel defect prediction method for web pages using k-means++. Exp. Syst. Appl. **42**(19), 6496–6506 (2015)

29. Biçer, M.S., Diri, B.: Predicting defect prone modules in web applications. In: Dregvaite, G., Damasevicius, R. (eds.) ICIST 2015. CCIS, vol. 538, pp. 577–591. Springer, Cham (2015). https://doi.org/10.1007/978-3-319-24770-0_49

30. Wong, W.E., Gao, R., Li, Y., Abreu, R., Wotawa, F.: A survey on software fault localization. IEEE Trans. Softw. Eng. **42**(8), 707–740 (2016)

31. Zou, D., Liang, J., Xiong, Y., Ernst, M.D., Zhang, L.: An empirical study of fault localization families and their combinations. IEEE Trans. Softw. Eng. (2019)

32. Ghawate, S.B., Shinde, S.: Survey of software fault localization for web application. Int. J. Curr. Eng. Technol. **5**(3), 1525–1529 (2015)

33. Sun, C.A., Ran, Y., Zheng, C., Liu, H., Towey, D., Zhang, X.: Fault localisation for WS-BPEL programs based on predicate switching and program slicing. J. Syst. Softw. **135**, 191–204 (2018)

34. Tang, Y., Cheng, G., Xu, Z., Chen, F., Elmansor, K., Wu, Y.: Automatic belief network modeling via policy inference for SDN fault localization. J. Internet Serv. Appl. **7**(1), 1–13 (2016). https://doi.org/10.1186/s13174-016-0043-y

35. Wong, W.E., Debroy, V.: A survey of software fault localization. Department of Computer Science, University of Texas at Dallas (2009)

36. Qian, J., Wu, H., Chen, H., Li, C., Li, W.: Fault injection for performance testing of composite web services. Int. J. Performability Eng. **14**(6), 1314–1323 (2018)

37. Pham, C., et al.: Failure diagnosis for distributed systems using targeted fault injection. IEEE Trans. Parallel Distrib. Syst. **28**(2), 503–516 (2016)

38. Dal Lago, L., Ferrante, O., Passerone, R., Ferrari, A.: Dependability assessment of SOA-based CPS with contracts and model-based fault injection. IEEE Trans. Ind. Inf. **14**(1), 360–369 (2017)

39. Irrera, I., Vieira, M.: Towards assessing representativeness of fault injection-generated failure data for online failure prediction. In: 2015 IEEE International Conference on Dependable Systems and Networks Workshops. IEEE (2015)

40. Herscheid, L., Richter, D., Polze, A.: Experimental assessment of cloud software dependability using fault injection. In: Camarinha-Matos, L.M., Baldissera, T.A., Di Orio, G., Marques, F. (eds.) DoCEIS 2015. IAICT, vol. 450, pp. 121–128. Springer, Cham (2015). https://doi.org/10.1007/978-3-319-16766-4_13

41. Salas, M.I., De Geus, P.L., Martins, E.: Security testing methodology for evaluation of web services robustness-case: XML injection. In: 2015 IEEE World Congress on Services. IEEE (2015)

42. Bhor, R.V., Khanuja, H.K.: Analysis of web application security mechanism and attack detection using vulnerability injection technique. In: 2016 International Conference on Computing Communication Control and automation (ICCUBEA). IEEE (2016)

43. Yin, Y., Li, Y.: Towards dynamic reconfiguration for QoS consistent services based applications. In: Liu, C., Ludwig, H., Toumani, F., Yu, Q. (eds.) ICSOC 2012. LNCS, vol. 7636, pp. 771–778. Springer, Heidelberg (2012). https://doi.org/10.1007/978-3-642-34321-6_61

Requirements Re-usability in Global Software Development: A Systematic Mapping Study

Syeda Sumbul Hossain[1(✉)], Yeasir Arafat[1], Tanvir Amin[2], and Touhid Bhuiyan[1]

[1] Daffodil International University, Dhaka, Bangladesh
{syeda.swe,yeasir35-1501}@diu.edu.bd, t.bhuiyan@daffodilvarsity.edu.bd
[2] Infolytx, Dhaka, Bangladesh
tanviramin@ymail.com

Abstract. In global software development, requirements re-usability is a common practice which ultimately helps to maintain project quality and reduce both development time and cost. However, when a large-scale project is distributed, there are some critical factors needed to be maintained and managed for reusing requirements and it is considered a challenging job to interrelate the requirements between two identical projects. In this study, we have pointed out 48 challenges faced and 43 mitigation techniques used when implementing requirements re-usability in global software development projects among distributed teams. The challenges distributed teams frequently encounter can be divided into three considering issues as Communication, Coordination and Control of distributed teams in global software development. The results from this study can be used to plan development strategies while reusing requirements in distributed manners.

Keywords: Requirement re-usability · Agile · Distributed software development · Large-scale · Global Software Development (GSD) · Systematic mapping study

1 Introduction

Software engineering is a knowledge heightened work and this knowledge makes the software industry decline their cost in both helping co-located and distributed projects [2]. Close to these, practitioners in like manner get different sorts of methodology to constrain the cost of distributed projects. Regardless, distributed development as frequently as conceivable experience customary issues, for instance, communication, coordination, and control. Notwithstanding, software organization can be benefited by blending both of the advantages of agile and distributed software development, for instance, visit up close and personal interest, powerful correspondence, and client joint effort [57,58,63].

O. Gervasi et al. (Eds.): ICCSA 2020, LNCS 12252, pp. 960–974, 2020.
https://doi.org/10.1007/978-3-030-58811-3_68

In software development, the concept of re-usability helps the practitioners to reduce both cost and time. Requirement re-usability deals with efficient reuse of requirements and different software artifacts which help to minimize development cost and time [29]. Reliability of any product can also be increased by successfully applying the knowledge of previous projects. For reusing any requirements or software artifacts, some factors like cost of reuse, usefulness and quality of the reusable components need to be considered [18]. It is encouraged in [65] for agile development to use of reusable artifacts (e.g. design frameworks, patterns) where development costs will be reduced and the quality will be increased. Requirements reuse in a distributed system is used to increase system productivity, reliability, quality, to decrease system development sprint and to maintain consistency between two identical systems. In fact, development teams reuse requirements to reduce bug or error, and to maintain efficiency in a system. Hence, when it is a large-scale and distributed system, there are some critical factors are needed to be maintained and managed.

In a prior work [29], we have used survey study to pointed out requirement re-usability challenges and mitigation approaches in global software development. Using the semi-structured interview technique, 14 challenges and 10 mitigation approaches were splitted into three categories in respect of communication, coordination, and control. From that we are motivated to identify the challenges and mitigation techniques are stated in literature. We were driven by the following research question:

- *What are the requirements re-usability challenges and mitigation techniques in distributed large-scale agile projects reported in the up-to-the-minute?*

The remaining sections of this paper is structured as follows. Related works are presented at Sect. 2. In Sect. 3, the overall research methodology is described which is followed by results and analysis in Sect. 4. Discussion and conclusion are furnished in Sect. 5 and Sect. 6 respectively.

2   Related Work

Most of the studies have been claimed that requirement re-usability is a challenging job and practitioners face lots of challenges to reuse requirements in distributed and large-scale agile software development projects [11,14,28,61]. Different literature also stated that, software organizations face lots of problem if any changes occur in customer requirements or in technology. These changes result increase of project budget, slowing down the productivity, customers' dissatisfaction and lacking in professional behaviour among development team [5,24,51,60]. Successfully adaptations of reusable artifacts is not also fitted in agile development due to poor documentation and management of knowledge, experience, decisions and poor architecture [10,24]. In a study [1], it is shown a technique how to refactor software codes to reduce time and accelerate development.

A survey on requirement reuse conducted by Chernak, Y. [9], defined that, some participants of the survey were explaining some contradictory factors for instance maintenance cost of the project, resemblance of applications, existing requirements' quality and structure, and the level of abstraction at the time of reusing requirements. Those challenges arise at the time of distributed agile software development alongside with the customers' dissatisfaction while reusing requirements from any preceding similar projects [27]. Moreover, in different literature authors reported that, reuse of requirements is challenging due to many unknown requirements, external and internal forces, chances to miss important requirements, incomplete understanding, inconsistency or fault at the moment of person to person communication, sharing resources or pair programming, psychological impediments and knowledge reuse [6,51,70].

To improve product characteristics through requirement reuse, some well-known mitigation approaches adopted by the practitioners to overcome these challenges. For example, *Software Product Line Engineering (SPLE)* approach use to reduce time-to-market at reusing software components for a similar project, and that also reduce reuse overhead ratio or ratio of the reused asset integration effort to total development assets [9,47,48]. However, Wehrwein, B et al.[69] also sorted out some efficient re-usability approaches such as reusing design pattern, software architecture for component based, aspect oriented or service oriented software development, application framework, legacy system wrapping, Commercial off-the-shelf (COTS) integration, program libraries. These approaches help to increase productivity and effectiveness of development team, and reduce operational cost.

3   Research Methodology

3.1   Systematic Mapping Study

In this research, we have used systematic mapping study [37] as a research methodology to identify the current status of evidence reported in our research area and find out the literature ratio in related field. Systematic mapping studies reduce biasness of research, and also mitigate time and cost. To perform a systematic mapping study, we adopted following steps mentioned in [30,54]. Figure 1 represents the overall research methodology we have followed in this work.

Step 1: Define Research Questions (Research Scope). The research question is mentioned as one of the key factors of conducting systematic mapping study in [8]. This is essential to point out the related works and evidence according to research goal. For conducting this research, we stipulated our research question (RQ).

Step 2: Formulate and Execute Search Strings (All Studies). The search strings were drawn up according to intervention and scope area. Search string is used to identify primary studies from different digital sources or databases. For

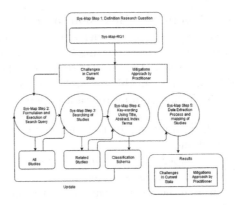

Fig. 1. Systematic mapping study

performing this step, first we have defined our search strategy to specify terms to be searched, searching process and resources where to search. Then we have formulate the search strings and execute those in different sources.

– Search Strategy
  • Searching terms were recognized by going through titles, abstracts and keywords of different studies.
  • Relevant papers were considered by forward and backward snowballing.
  • Lexicons are used to generate synonyms of keywords.
  • Boolean operators are used to formulate search strings.
– Search Strings
  • ("Requirements re-usability" OR "reusable requirements") AND ("Distributed" OR "dispersed") AND ("Agile" OR "scrum" OR "XP") AND ("Large-scale") AND ("Challenges" OR "Obstacles")
  • ("Requirements re-usability" OR "reusable requirements") AND ("Distributed" OR "dispersed") AND ("Agile" OR "scrum" OR "XP") AND ("Large-scale") AND ("Migitations" OR "Resolution")
– Scientific Databases
  We have chosen five different scientific data sources for executing the searching and set the time range between 1995 and 2020.
  • IEEE Xplore[1]
  • Association for Computing Machinery (ACM)[2]
  • Scopus[3]
  • Science Direct[4]
  • Springer[5]

---

[1] https://ieeexplore.ieee.org/Xplore/home.jsp.
[2] https://www.acm.org/.
[3] https://www.scopus.com/.
[4] https://www.sciencedirect.com/.
[5] https://www.springer.com/gp.

Step 3: Screen of Papers for Inclusion and Exclusion (Relevant Papers). Inclusion and exclusion criteria helps to include or exclude the studies according to relevant studies those relating with research area and question [52,54]. After applying inclusion and exclusion criterion at the end, we have finalized 52 papers out of 6832 papers in this research (See in Fig. 2). The following steps were followed to perform screening relevant papers.

– At first, we have picked only the papers which were written in English and only the peer-reviewed ones.
– For avoiding duplicate papers, we have used Mendeley[6]. It is one of mostly used online reference management systems.
– The researcher go through the abstracts and titles to identify relevant studies. In some cases, introduction and conclusion section are also considered for inclusion and exclusion process while abstracts and titles are not clear enough.
– We have excluded all the papers of which we have found no digital copies.

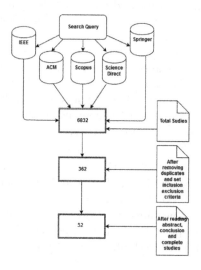

Fig. 2. Study results

Step 4: Develop Classification Scheme (Key-wording). Key-wording helps to achieve aim and objective in a targeted point [54]. We have used this step to get an overall high level idea of any relevant studies. Then we have categorized the relevant studies as per the nature and contribution.

---

[6] https://www.mendeley.com/.

Step 5: Extract Data and Map the Studies (Systematic Map). After development of classification scheme, all relevant studies are classified according to the classification scheme. Graph is used to generate report or visualized of mapping studies. After reading all the studies we identified challenges and mitigation approaches from different perspective and listed them. From listed findings, we removed the duplicate data and managed them by tables. Graphs and figures were used to distribute studies in different areas and sorted out publications year ratio.

3.2   Validity Threats

In this research, we have encountered different types of validity threats such as construct validity threat, internal validity threat, external validity threats and reliability as per the prior work [29]. We checked these threats throughout this research work. We have done systematic mapping study based on our research question and we formed search strings to find out the related studies from peer-reviewed database. Search strings were frequently reviewed and modified from the early phases of our research. Two researchers have done the searching query and inclusion-exclusion process in parallel, which minimized the risk of bias and lowered the internal validity threats. The presence of external validity threats is high as bias might be present in many literature. Two researchers work for finding all possible challenges and mitigation techniques, and then combined relevant and common ideas to achieve the final result. Our final result has been reviewed for several times. If any researchers search the queries according to our search string (within our searching time periods), will find the same data. This ensures the reliability of our research results.

4   Results and Analysis

In this section, we have reported the results of the systematic mapping study and also mentioned the analysis of studies in terms of the time distribution and categorizations based on our research theme.

4.1   Study Distribution

According to findings from the selected studies, we have observed, selected studies are distributed in the different sub-areas of requirement re-usability and most of the papers are published in requirements reuse and management area (See in Fig. 3).

In the below Fig. 4, we have represented the publications by year and we have seen that most of the papers published in between 2011 and 2020.

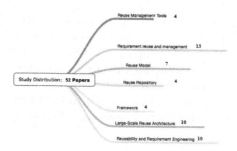

Fig. 3. Study distribution in different areas

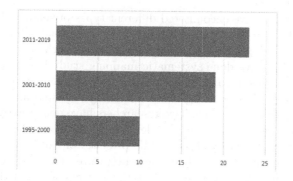

Fig. 4. Studies distribution over the publication years

4.2 Requirement Re-usability: Challenges

In Global Software Development (GSD), the development team confront some challenges like communication, coordination and control in managing the project as a consequence of distributed or dispersed nature of team structure. In this study, we have disjoint the findings of mapping studies into three grouping such as communication, coordination and control as per our prior work [29]. In Table 1 we have represent the challenges reported in the literature by categorize into three areas namely *Communication, Coordination,* and *Control.* As a whole, we have pointed out requirement re-usability challenges confronted by the practitioners in distributed large-scale agile projects. As we splitted the challenges into three sub-categories, we have observed that, distributed team struggling with control factor during requirement re-usability (See in Fig. 5, maximum challenges found in Control section).

4.3 Requirement Re-usability: Mitigations

We have also identified the mitigation techniques applied by practitioners that is found in literature in Table 2. Figure 6 depicts the number of mitigation techniques applied by the practitioners. Rather than the *communication* factor it

Table 1. Requirement re-usability challenges

Communication	Coordination	Control
Might miss important requirements [51]	Not sufficiently formalized [51]	Freezes the scope [51]
Incomplete understanding, Inconsistency or faulty between Team [5,51]	External and internal forces Often cause rapid changes Or growth of requirements [31,34,39,51]	Many unknowns Unclear vision of overall goal [6,51]
Communication gaps [6,16,17,34]	Tough job to pair programming and share resources [5] [62]	Trace-ability problem [3,27,34]
Low understanding the roles of others [6,9,12,17]	Dependency problem [3,4]	Organizational impediments [5,15]
Incompatible environments and conflicting assumptions [17]	Different identification [4]	Economic impediments[5]
Knowledge transfer [17]	Poor standard for reuse resources [4]	Administrative impediments[5]
Distributed access [12]	Trust issues [5]	Political impediments [5]
Reuse and corporate strategy [15]	Unstructured documentation [5,9]	Psychological impediments [5,17]
Distribution and collaboration [15]	Unclear requirements [6,9,17]	Continuous inflow of requirements [6]
Conflicts of interest [68]	User interface [12]	Low motivation to contribute at requested work [6]
	Incomplete requirements [9]	Overlapping requirements processes [6]
	Measurement and experimentation [15]	Keeping SRS updated [6]
	Common terminology [19]	Conflict between two system axioms [59]
	Volatile requirements [34]	Focus on process [15]
	Low architectural repository [1,36]	Lack of business analysis phase [27]
	Misunderstanding about reuse benefits [49]	Lack of traceability [27]
		Low coupling, high cohesion [32]
		Uncertain estimates [34]
		Architectural changes and code changes dependency [55]
		Informal model [44]
		Measurement quality of reusable requirement [50]
		Identify granularity [50]

seems that practitioners applying more mitigation techniques for both *coordination* and *control* factors during re-using requirement in a distributed large-scale agile project.

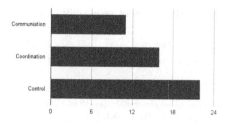

Fig. 5. Requirement re-usability challenges

Table 2. Mitigations techniques

Communication	Coordination	Control
Producer consumer model [51]	Test Driven Development [3,19,31,32,51]	Work flow control [17,51]
Cultural analysis [17]	Tailoring of transformation assets [3,12,13,31]	Platform Domain Analysis [3,5,12,13,20,27,32,33,59,64]
Face-to-face meeting [17]	Transformation composition [3,32]	Empirical knowledge analysis [4,7,17,67]
Local workshops [17]	Formal modeling approaches [7,15,19,25,32,39,44,51,59]	Theoretical knowledge analysis [3,4,17,41,47]
Distributed simulation approach [53]	Integrated knowledge utilization [4,5,12,55]	Schedule periodic check-ups[17]
	Semantic classification of experience element [12]	Use case driven approach [3,9,12,13]
	Packaging of analysis results [12,13,31,33,66]	Requirements interaction management [22,32,44,59,66]
	Shared repository for reusable requirements [10,12,13,17,32,36,68]	Multiple representations of experience elements [12,59]
	Reuse metrics [14,15,19,21,32,41,45,62]	Asset management units for project-related data [3,12]
	High-level reference model coordination [23,27]	Maintaining a project history [12,13]
	Evolutionary domain model [26]	Role Management [12]
	Pattern based software reuse [27,35]	Knowledge Based Tools [16,22,31,38,68]
	Architecture-centric software process [27,49]	Consistency Checker Tools [20,32]
	Requirement reasoning model [5,40]	Software Product Line Approach [4,15,44,46,64]
	Meta model to reengineered process [39,64,66,69]	Identifying commonalities and variations [39,64,66,68]
	Polymorphic reuse mechanism [42]	NFR or quality catalog [43]
	Incremental development approach [43]	Bottom-up Approach [64]
	Object oriented programming concept [56,60,64]	Prior in analysis phase [66]
	Variation points [68]	
	Linkage between product family [31]	

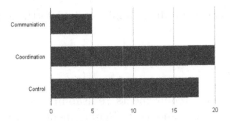

Fig. 6. Mitigations techniques

5   Discussion

Requirements re-usability is considered as an important technology [28], speeds up and aids in software development and maintenance processes. Other benefits of reusing requirements are increasing quality, reliability, efficiency, performance and productivity (faster, better, cheaper), minimizing developments and maintenance costs and time, reducing risk of project failures, reducing stress on technical people, and satisfying customers' needs [5,9,15,17,32,62] [14,44,60,64]. In a study, we have found that, one third errors of software occur from design and code, whereas, 40 to 60% of software errors occur from requirements errors [7].

Requirements reusing in agile software development, when it is distributed, needs supports like documentation, knowledge and risk management policies, experiences sharing, decisions, or architectural information [11,14,28]. In [13], re-using artifacts in software and product development domain is mentioned as a well-known concept. Project cost savings between 10 to 35%, in considered as well-planned reuse strategies in software development domain [14].

To build large and complex software as more reliable, less expensive and ready in internet time, reusing software artifacts can provide better way than traditional software engineering methods [15,39]. A literature through an experience mentioned that by reusing requirements defects reduced by 15%, and productivity increased by 57% [19]. Though requirements re-usability do not well fit in agile software development, however, modification and customization may be possible to adapt reusable artifacts successfully [60].

The motivation of the RQ was to find out the requirement re-usability challenges and mitigation techniques in distributed agile projects applied by the practitioners which are listed in the current-state-of-the-art. In response to RQ, through a systematic mapping study we have identified 48 challenges faced by the practitioners reported in different literature along with 43 mitigation techniques applied by the practitioners in large-scale distributed agile projects. We have divided literature findings into three categories which GSD teams frequently encounter. Identified challenges required to take into account during requirement re-usability in distributed large-scale agile projects which will help to reduce both time and cost. Test Driven Development (TDD), formal modeling, knowledge sharing and transfer, shared repository, Object Oriented Programming (OOP) concepts, linkage between product family and so forth help team to mitigate stated challenges.

6   Conclusions

In software development, requirements re-usability helps the practitioners in reducing development time and cost. Requirement re-usability is re-using of requirements and other artifacts which helps to minimize development cost, time and increase reliability by applying knowledge effectively from previously learned lesson. Sustainable software development can be achieved by applying the concept of reusing requirements. In this research, we have find out requirement re-usability challenges and mitigation techniques reported in different literature. In future, it would be interesting to map the current findings with industrial practice by applying either case studies or survey from large-scale agile distributed projects.

References

1. Adorf, C.S., Ramasubramani, V., Anderson, J.A., Glotzer, S.C.: How to professionally develop reusable scientific software-and when not to. Comput. Sci. Eng. **21**(2), 66–79 (2018)
2. Aurum, A., Jeffery, R., Wohlin, C., Handzic, M.: Managing Software Engineering Knowledge. Springer, Heidelberg (2013). https://doi.org/10.1007/978-3-662-05129-0
3. Basso, F.P., Pillat, R.M., Oliveira, T.C., Becker, L.B.: Supporting large scale model transformation reuse. In: ACM SIGPLAN Notices, vol. 49, pp. 169–178. ACM (2013)
4. Berzisa, S., Grabis, J.: Knowledge reuse in configuration of project management information systems: a change management case study. In: 2011 15th IEEE International Conference on Intelligent Engineering Systems (INES), pp. 51–56. IEEE (2011)
5. Biddle, R., Martin, A., Noble, J.: No name: just notes on software reuse. ACM SIGPLAN Not. **38**(12), 76–96 (2003)
6. Bjarnason, E., Wnuk, K., Regnell, B.: Requirements are slipping through the gapsóa case study on causes & effects of communication gaps in large-scale software development. In: 2011 19th IEEE International Requirements Engineering Conference (RE), pp. 37–46. IEEE (2011)
7. Brown, S., Felsing, M.: Reuse based requirements development & management (RBRDM) (2005)
8. Budgen, D., Turner, M., Brereton, P., Kitchenham, B.: Using mapping studies in software engineering. In: Proceedings of PPIG, vol. 8, pp. 195–204 (2008)
9. Chernak, Y.: Requirements reuse: the state of the practice. In: 2012 IEEE International Conference on Software Science, Technology and Engineering (SWSTE), pp. 46–53. IEEE (2012)
10. Daneva, M., Van Der Veen, E., Amrit, C., Ghaisas, S., Sikkel, K., Kumar, R., Ajmeri, N., Ramteerthkar, U., Wieringa, R.: Agile requirements prioritization in large-scale outsourced system projects: an empirical study. J. Syst. Softw. **86**(5), 1333–1353 (2013)

11. Decker, B., et al.: A framework for agile reuse in software engineering using wiki technology. Wissensmanagement **2005**, 411–414 (2005)
12. Feldmann, R.L., Geppert, B., Mahnke, W., Ritter, N., Rossler, F.: An ORDBMS-based reuse repository supporting the quality improvement paradigm-exemplified by the SDL-pattern approach. In: 34th International Conference on Technology of Object-Oriented Languages and Systems, TOOLS 34. Proceedings, pp. 125–136. IEEE (2000)
13. Feldmann, R.L., Geppert, B., Rossler, F.: An integrating approach for developing distributed software systems-combining formal methods, software reuse, and the experience base. In: Fifth IEEE International Conference on Engineering of Complex Computer Systems, ICECCS 1999, pp. 54–63. IEEE (1999)
14. Fortune, J., Valerdi, R.: Considerations for successful reuse in systems engineering. AIAA Space **2008** (2008)
15. Frakes, W.B., Kang, K.: Software reuse research: status and future. IEEE Trans. Software Eng. **31**(7), 529–536 (2005)
16. Carrillo de Gea, J.M., Nicolás, J., Fernández-Alemán, J.L., Toval, A.: Automated support for reuse-based requirements engineering in global software engineering. J. Softw. Evol. Process **29**(8), e1873 (2017)
17. de Gea, J.M.C., Nicolás, J., Alemán, J.L.F., Toval, A., Vizcaíno, A., Ebert, C.: Reusing requirements in global software engineering. In: Maalej, W., Thurimella, A. (eds.) Managing Requirements Knowledge, pp. 171–197. Springer, Heidelberg (2013). https://doi.org/10.1007/978-3-642-34419-0_8
18. Gill, N.S.: Reusability issues in component-based development. ACM SIGSOFT Softw. Eng. Not. **28**(4), 4 (2003)
19. Goldin, L., Matalon-Beck, M., Lapid-Maoz, J.: Reuse of requirements reduces time to market. In: 2010 IEEE International Conference on Software Science, Technology and Engineering (SWSTE), pp. 55–60. IEEE (2010)
20. Gomaa, H., Farrukh, G.: A software engineering environment for configuring distributed applications from reusable software architectures. In: Eighth IEEE International Workshop on Software Technology and Engineering Practice, Proceedings, [incorporating Computer Aided Software Engineering], pp. 312–325. IEEE (1997)
21. Gomaa, H., Farrukh, G.A.: An approach for generating executable distributed applications from reusable software architectures. In: Second IEEE International Conference on Engineering of Complex Computer Systems, Proceedings, pp. 442–449. IEEE (1996)
22. Gomaa, H., Farrukh, G.A.: Automated configuration of distributed applications from reusable software architectures. In: 12th IEEE International Conference Automated Software Engineering, Proceedings, pp. 193–200. IEEE (1997)
23. Gómez-Hérnandez, M.A., Asensio-Pérez, J.I., Gómez-Sánchez, E., Bote-Lorenzo, M.L., Dimitriadis, Y.A.: A high-level reference model for reusable object-level coordination support in groupware applications. In: 15th EUROMICRO International Conference on Parallel, Distributed and Network-Based Processing, PDP 2007, pp. 315–324. IEEE (2007)
24. Gunasekaran, A.: Agile manufacturing: enablers and an implementation framework. Int. J. Prod. Res. **36**(5), 1223–1247 (1998)
25. Hill, J.H., Schmidt, D.C., Edmondson, J.R., Gokhale, A.S.: Tools for continuously evaluating distributed system qualities. Software IEEE **27**(4), 65–71 (2010)
26. Hofmeister, C., Nord, R., Soni, D.: Global analysis: moving from software requirements specification to structural views of the software architecture. IEE Proc. Softw. **152**(4), 187–197 (2005)

27. Hong, W.: Architecture-centric software process for pattern based software reuse. In: WRI World Congress on Software Engineering, WCSE 2009, vol. 4, pp. 95–99. IEEE (2009)

28. Hoover, C.L., Khosla, P.K.: An analytical approach to change for the design of reusable real-time software. In: Second Workshop on Object-Oriented Real-Time Dependable Systems, 1996, Proceedings of WORDS 1996, pp. 144–151. IEEE (1996)

29. Hossain, S.S.: Challenges and mitigation strategies in reusing requirements in large-scale distributed agile software development: a survey result. In: Arai, K., Bhatia, R., Kapoor, S. (eds.) CompCom 2019. AISC, vol. 998, pp. 920–935. Springer, Cham (2019). https://doi.org/10.1007/978-3-030-22868-2_63

30. Hossain, S.S., Jubayer, S.A.M., Rahman, S., Bhuiyan, T., Rawshan, L., Islam, S.: Customer feedback prioritization technique: a case study on lean startup. In: Misra, S., Gervasi, O., Murgante, B., Stankova, E., Korkhov, V., Torre, C., Rocha, A.M.A.C., Taniar, D., Apduhan, B.O., Tarantino, E. (eds.) ICCSA 2019. LNCS, vol. 11623, pp. 70–81. Springer, Cham (2019). https://doi.org/10.1007/978-3-030-24308-1_6

31. Irshad, M.: Measuring cost avoidance through software reuse. Ph.D. thesis, Masterís thesis, Blekinge Institute of Technology, school of computing, Sweden, MSE-2010: 38 (2011)

32. Kakarontzas, G., Stamelos, I.: Component recycling for agile methods. In: 2010 Seventh International Conference on the Quality of Information and Communications Technology (QUATIC), pp. 397–402. IEEE (2010)

33. Kamalraj, R., Geetha, B., Singaravel, G.: Reducing efforts on software project management using software package reusability. In: IEEE International Advance Computing Conference, IACC 2009, pp. 1624–1627. IEEE (2009)

34. Karlsson, L., Dahlstedt, Å.G., Regnell, B., och Dag, J.N., Persson, A.: Requirements engineering challenges in market-driven software development-an interview study with practitioners. Inf. Softw. Technol. 49(6), 588–604 (2007)

35. Kavitha, C., Shidha, M., Jino, P.: Reusability and agile pattern mining. Int. J. Comput. Appl. 68(2) (2013)

36. Khan, M.Z., Khan, M.: Enhancing software reusability through value based software repository. Int. J. Softw. Eng. Its Appl. 8(11) (2014)

37. Kitchenham, B.: Procedures for performing systematic reviews. Keele, UK, Keele University 33(2004), 1–26 (2004)

38. Knauss, E., Liebel, G., Schneider, K., Horkoff, J., Kasauli, R.: Quality requirements in agile as a knowledge management problem: More than just-in-time. In: 2017 IEEE 25th International Requirements Engineering Conference Workshops (REW), pp. 427–430. IEEE (2017)

39. Kovacevic, J., et al.: Survey of the state-of the-art in requirements engineering for software product line and model-driven requirements engineering. Technical report, Technical Report D 1.1, Ample-project (2007)

40. Liang, P., Avgeriou, P., Clerc, V.: Requirements reasoning for distributed requirements analysis using semantic wiki. In: Fourth IEEE International Conference on Global Software Engineering, ICGSE 2009, pp. 388–393. IEEE (2009)

41. Liang, X.: Research on the distributive knowledge management system of logistic enterprise integrating context management. In: 2009 WRI World Congress on Computer Science and Information Engineering, vol. 5, pp. 204–210. IEEE (2009)

42. Liu, L., Zicari, R., Hursch, W., Lieberherr, K.J.: The role of polymorphic reuse mechanisms in schema evolution in an object-oriented database. IEEE Trans. Knowl. Data Eng. 9(1), 50–67 (1997)

43. López, C., Cysneiros, L.M., Astudillo, H.: NDR ontology: sharing and reusing NFR and design rationale knowledge. In: First International Workshop on Managing Requirements Knowledge, MARK 2008, pp. 1–10. IEEE (2008)
44. López, O., Laguna, M.A., Peñalvo, F.J.G.: Metamodeling for requirements reuse. In: WER, pp. 76–90 (2002)
45. Lucredio, D., de Almeida, E.S., Fortes, R.P.: An investigation on the impact of MDE on software reuse. In: 2012 Sixth Brazilian Symposium on Software Components Architectures and Reuse (SBCARS), pp. 101–110. IEEE (2012)
46. Mannion, M., Kaindl, H.: Product line requirements reuse based on variability management. In: 2012 19th Asia-Pacific Software Engineering Conference (APSEC), vol. 2, pp. 148–149. IEEE (2012)
47. Martinez, M.A., Toval, A.: COTSRE: a components selection method based on requirements engineering. In: Seventh International Conference on Composition-Based Software Systems, ICCBSS 2008, pp. 220–223. IEEE (2008)
48. Mili, A., Mili, R., Mittermeir, R.T.: A survey of software reuse libraries. Ann. Softw. Eng. 5, 349–414 (1998)
49. Mohagheghi, P.: The impact of software reuse and incremental development on the quality of large systems. Ph.D. thesis, Norwegian University of Science and Technology (2004)
50. Motahari-Nezhad, H.R., Li, J., Stephenson, B., Graupner, S., Singhal, S.: Solution reuse for service composition and integration. In: 2009 World Conference on Services-I, pp. 400–407. IEEE (2009)
51. Mugridge, R.: Managing agile project requirements with storytest-driven development. Software IEEE 25(1), 68–75 (2008)
52. Mujtaba, S., Petersen, K., Feldt, R., Mattsson, M.: Software product line variability: a systematic mapping study. Blekinge Institute of Technology, School of Engineering (2008)
53. Pan, K., Turner, S.J., Cai, W., Li, Z.: An efficient sort-based DDM matching algorithm for HLA applications with a large spatial environment. In: 21st International Workshop on Principles of Advanced and Distributed Simulation, PADS 2007, pp. 70–82. IEEE (2007)
54. Petersen, K., Feldt, R., Mujtaba, S., Mattsson, M.: Systematic mapping studies in software engineering. In: 12th International Conference on Evaluation and Assessment in Software Engineering, vol. 17. SN (2008)
55. Leite, J.C.S.P., Yu, Y., Liu, L., Yu, E.S.K., Mylopoulos, J.: Quality-based software reuse. In: Pastor, O., Falcão e Cunha, J. (eds.) CAiSE 2005. LNCS, vol. 3520, pp. 535–550. Springer, Heidelberg (2005). https://doi.org/10.1007/11431855_37
56. Przybyłek, A.: Systems evolution and software reuse in object-oriented programming and aspect-oriented programming. In: Bishop, J., Vallecillo, A. (eds.) TOOLS 2011. LNCS, vol. 6705, pp. 163–178. Springer, Heidelberg (2011). https://doi.org/10.1007/978-3-642-21952-8_13
57. Ramesh, B., Cao, L., Mohan, K., Xu, P.: Can distributed software development be agile? Commun. ACM 49(10), 41–46 (2006)
58. Sahay, S., Nicholson, B., Krishna, S.: Global IT Outsourcing: Software Development Across Borders. Cambridge University Press (2003)
59. Shehata, M., Eberlein, A.: Requirements interaction detection using semi-formal methods. In: 10th IEEE International Conference and Workshop on the Engineering of Computer-Based Systems, Proceedings, pp. 224–232. IEEE (2003)
60. Singh, S., Chana, I.: Enabling reusability in agile software development. arXiv preprint arXiv:1210.2506 (2012)

61. Souag, A., Mazo, R., Salinesi, C., Comyn-Wattiau, I.: Reusable knowledge in security requirements engineering: a systematic mapping study. Requirements Eng. **21**(2), 251–283 (2016)
62. Suri, P., Garg, N.: Software reuse metrics: measuring component independence and its applicability in software reuse. Int. J. Comput. Sci. Netw. Secur. **9**(5), 237–248 (2009)
63. Sutherland, J., Viktorov, A., Blount, J., Puntikov, N.: Distributed scrum: agile project management with outsourced development teams. In: 40th Annual Hawaii International Conference on System Sciences, HICSS 2007, p. 274a. IEEE (2007)
64. Thakur, S., Singh, H.: FDRD: feature driven reuse development process model. In: 2014 International Conference on Advanced Communication Control and Computing Technologies (ICACCCT), pp. 1593–1598. IEEE (2014)
65. Turk, D., France, R., Rumpe, B.: Assumptions underlying agile software development processes. arXiv preprint arXiv:1409.6610 (2014)
66. Villegas, O.L., Laguna, M.A.: Requirements reuse for software development. In: RE 01 Doctoral Workshop. In 5th-IEEE International Symposium on Requirements Engineering, Toronto, Canada, pp. 27–31. Citeseer (2001)
67. Wahid, S., Smith, J.L., Berry, B., Chewar, C.M., McCrickard, D.S.: Visualization of design knowledge component relationships to facilitate reuse. In: Proceedings of the 2004 IEEE International Conference on Information Reuse and Integration, IRI 2004, pp. 414–419. IEEE (2004)
68. Waldmann, B., Jones, P.: Feature-oriented requirements satisfy needs for reuse and systems view. In: 17th IEEE International Requirements Engineering Conference, RE 2009, pp. 329–334. IEEE (2009)
69. Wehrwein, B., Matos, G., Tanikella, R.: A requirements-driven and collaborative decision support approach for evaluating the viability of candidate implementation technologies. In: 12th International IEEE Enterprise Distributed Object Computing Conference, EDOC 2008, pp. 293–299. IEEE (2008)
70. Xiang, F., Ling, G., Jin, Y.: User-driven GIS software reuse solution based on SOA and web2. 0 concept. In: 2nd IEEE International Conference on Computer Science and Information Technology, ICCSIT 2009, pp. 5–9. IEEE (2009)

Inspecting JavaScript Vulnerability Mitigation Patches with Automated Fix Generation in Mind

Péter Hegedűs[✉]

MTA-SZTE Research Group on Artificial Intelligence, Szeged, Hungary
hpeter@inf.u-szeged.hu

Abstract. Software security has become a primary concern for both the industry and academia in recent years. As dependency on critical services provided by software systems grows globally, a potential security threat in such systems poses higher and higher risks (e.g. economical damage, a threat to human life, criminal activity).

Finding potential security vulnerabilities at the code level automatically is a very popular approach to aid security testing. However, most of the methods based on machine learning and statistical models stop at listing potentially vulnerable code parts and leave their validation and mitigation to the developers. Automatic program repair could fill this gap by automatically generating vulnerability mitigation code patches. Nonetheless, it is still immature, especially in targeting security-relevant fixes.

In this work, we try to establish a path towards automatic vulnerability fix generation techniques in the context of JavaScript programs. We inspect 361 actual vulnerability mitigation patches collected from vulnerability databases and GitHub. We found that vulnerability mitigation patches are not short on average and in many cases affect not just program code but test code as well. These results point towards that a general automatic repair approach targeting all the different types of vulnerabilities is not feasible. The analysis of the code properties and fix patterns for different vulnerability types might help in setting up a more realistic goal in the area of automatic JavaScript vulnerability repair.

Keywords: Security · Vulnerability · JavaScript · Prediction models · Automatic repair

The presented work was carried out within the SETIT Project (2018-1.2.1-NKP-2018-00004). Project no. 2018-1.2.1-NKP-2018-00004 has been implemented with the support provided from the National Research, Development and Innovation Fund of Hungary, financed under the 2018-1.2.1-NKP funding scheme and partially supported by grant TUDFO/47138-1/2019-ITM of the Ministry for Innovation and Technology, Hungary. Furthermore, Péter Hegedűs was supported by the Bolyai János Scholarship of the Hungarian Academy of Sciences and the ÚNKP-19-4-SZTE-20 New National Excellence Program of the Ministry for Innovation and Technology.

O. Gervasi et al. (Eds.): ICCSA 2020, LNCS 12252, pp. 975–988, 2020.
https://doi.org/10.1007/978-3-030-58811-3_69

1   Introduction

Software security is one of the most striking problems of today's software systems. With the advent of low-cost mobile/IoT devices connected to the Internet, the problem of insecure applications has risen sharply. Large impact security vulnerabilities are explored daily, for example, a serious flaw [18] has been discovered in 'Sudo', a powerful utility used in macOS this February. Security problems can cause not just financial damage [3] but can compromise vital infrastructure, or used to threaten entire countries.

Finding potential security vulnerabilities at the code level automatically is a very popular approach to aid security testing and to help explore potential security issues before they get into the release. However, most of the methods based on machine learning and statistical models stop at listing potentially vulnerable code parts and leave their validation and mitigation to the developers. Automatic program repair could fill this gap by automatically generating vulnerability mitigation code patches. Nonetheless, it is still immature, especially in targeting security-relevant fixes.

In this work, we inspect 361 actual vulnerability mitigation patches collected from vulnerability databases and GitHub to gain some knowledge about them that can help in establishing an automatic vulnerability repair mechanism. We formulated our particular research goals into the following three research questions that we address in this paper:

RQ1: What are the basic properties (the amount of added or removed files and lines) of the vulnerability mitigation code changes in JavaScript programs?
RQ2: How do vulnerability mitigation patches affect test code?
RQ3: How frequent are those small and concise code changes among real-world vulnerability patches that could be targeted by automated code fix generation?

We found that vulnerability mitigation patches are not short on average and in many cases affect not just program code but test code as well. The results point towards that a general automatic repair approach targeting all the different types of vulnerabilities is not feasible. Most of the security fixes containing many lines would be hard to generate automatically, however, some types of vulnerabilities are mitigated with a relatively small commit containing ten lines or less. These are the ones we would first target by an automatic repair tool. The analysis of the code properties and fix patterns for different vulnerability types might help in setting up a more realistic goal in the area of automatic JavaScript vulnerability repair.

The remaining of the paper is structured as follows. Section 2 collects the related works. In Sect. 3 we give details about the data we analyze. Section 4 contains the discussion of results we got and the answers to the research questions, while we conclude the paper in Sect. 5.

2   Related Work

Two lines of research works are very closely related to ours. First, the prediction of software vulnerabilities based on manual or automatic features extracted from the source code or related repositories, and second, automatic program repair with a special focus on security-related bugs.

Vulnerability prediction and data sets. In their preliminary study, Siavvas et al. [16] investigated if a relationship exists among software metrics and specific vulnerability types. They used 13 metrics and found that software metrics may not be sufficient indicators of specific vulnerability types, but using novel metrics could help.

In their work, Jimenez et al. [8] proposed an extensible framework (Vul-Data7) and dataset of real vulnerabilities, automatically collected from software archives. They presented the capabilities of their framework on 4 large systems, but one can extend the framework to meet specific needs.

Neuhas et al. [12] introduced a new approach (and the corresponding tool) called Vulture, which can predict vulnerable components in the source code, mainly relying on the dependencies between the files. They analyzed the Mozilla codebase to evaluate their approach using SVM for classification.

In their work, Shin et al. [14] created an empirical model to predict vulnerabilities from source code complexity metrics. Their model was built on the function level, but they consider only the complexity metrics calculated by Understand C++.[1] They concluded that vulnerable functions have distinctive characteristics separating them from "non-vulnerable but faulty" functions. They studied the JavaScript Engine from the Mozilla application framework. In another work Shin et al. [13] performed an empirical case study on two large code bases: Mozilla Firefox and Red Hat Enterprise Linux kernel, investigating if software metrics can be used in vulnerability prediction. They considered complexity, code churn, and developer activity metrics. The results showed that the metrics are discriminative and predictive of vulnerabilities.

Chowdhury et al. [5] created a framework that can predict vulnerabilities mainly relying on the CCC (complexity, coupling, and cohesion) metrics [4]. They also compared four statistical and machine learning techniques (namely C4.5 Decision Tree, Random Forests, Logistic Regression, and Naive Bayes classifier). The created model was accurate (with precision above 90%), but the recall was only 20% or lower which means an F-measure of 0.33 at most. The authors concluded that decision-tree-based techniques outperformed statistical models in their case.

Morrison et al. [11] built a model – replicating the vulnerability prediction model by Zimmermann et al. [20] – for both binaries and source code at the file level. The authors checked several learning algorithms including SVM, Naive Bayes, random forests, and logistic regression. On their dataset, Naive Bayes and random forests performed the best.

---

[1] https://scitools.com/.

Yu et al. introduced HARMLESS [19], a cost-aware active learner approach to predict vulnerabilities. They used a support vector machine-based prediction model with under-sampled training data, and a semi-supervised estimator to estimate the remaining vulnerabilities in a codebase. HARMLESS suggests which source code files are most likely to contain vulnerabilities. They also used Mozilla's codebase in their case study, with 3 different feature sets: metrics, text, and the combination of text mining and crash dump stack traces. The same set of source code metrics were used than that of Shin et al. [13].

Some works investigate the possible application of general fault prediction models for vulnerability prediction. Zimmermann et al. [20] argued in their work that vulnerabilities cannot be predicted as easily as defects. They used classical metrics widely used in defect prediction to see whether they can work as predictors of vulnerabilities at the binary level. They also planned to leverage specific metrics that are related to software security.

Shin et al. [15] investigated the usability of fault prediction models in the case of vulnerability prediction. They performed an empirical study on the code-base of Mozilla Firefox. The authors created 2 models: a traditional fault prediction model and a specialized, vulnerability prediction model. In their research, both models predicted vulnerabilities with high recall (90%) and low precision (9%) with F-measure around 0.16.

All the above works target file-level vulnerability prediction, while our focus is on identification and automatic repair of vulnerable JavaScript functions.

Automatic vulnerability repair. Automatic program repair research has matured a lot in the last couple of years. A lot of the challenges [9] have been solved but there are still a lot of open questions. Moreover, automatic program repair results targeting software vulnerabilities specifically are very sparse.

To assist developers to deal with multiple types of vulnerabilities, Ma et al. propose a new tool, called VuRLE [10], for automatic detection and repair of vulnerabilities. VuRLE (1) learns transformative edits and their contexts (i.e., code characterizing edit locations) from examples of vulnerable codes and their corresponding repaired codes; (2) clusters similar transformative edits; (3) extracts edit patterns and context patterns to create several repair templates for each cluster. VuRLE uses context patterns to detect vulnerabilities and customizes the corresponding edit patterns to repair them.

Smirnov and Chiueh introduce a program transformation system called DIRA [17] that can automatically transform an arbitrary application into a form that (1) can detect a control-hijacking attack when the control-sensitive data structure it tampers with is activated; (2) can identify the network packets that lead to the control-hijacking attack, and send these packets to a front-end content filter to prevent the same attack from compromising the application again, and (3) can repair itself by erasing all the side effects of the attack packets as if it never received them.

Gao et al. [7] present BovInspector, a tool framework for automatic static buffer overflow warnings inspection and validated bugs repair. Experimental results on real open source programs show that BovInspector can automatically inspect on average of 74.9% of total warnings, and false warnings account for about 25% to 100% (on average of 59.9%) of the total inspected warnings. In addition, the automatically generated patches fix all target vulnerabilities.

All of the above tools, however, focus primarily on general techniques and/or evaluate the approach on a limited number of particular security issues for general-purpose OO languages (Java and C++, respectively). We aim to explore the vulnerability fixes for JavaScript programs and to discover the possibilities of an automated vulnerability repair mechanism that could target many types of security issues.

3   Background

To inspect real-world JavaScript vulnerability mitigation patches, we had to collect them using data mining. We reused the processing tool-chain, data sources, and intermediate data files published in our previous work [6], where we built vulnerability prediction models based on the collected data using static source code metrics as predictors. We were able to collect 361 actual vulnerability fixing code changes from over 200 different JavaScript projects. The high-level process of collecting actual vulnerability patches is depicted in Fig. 1.

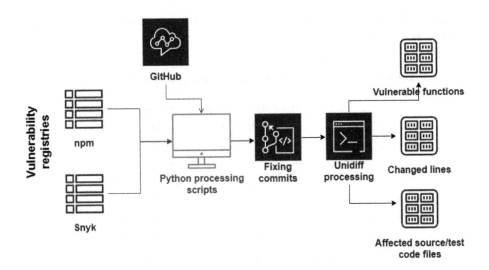

Fig. 1. Overall process of the data collection

We leveraged two publicly available vulnerability databases, nsp (the Node Security Platform, which is now part of npm) [1] and the Snyk Vulnerability Database [2]. Both of these projects aim to analyze programs for vulnerable third-party module usages. The main issue with these extracted raw vulnerability sources is that they contain unstructured data. The entries include a human-readable description of vulnerabilities with URLs of fixing commits, pull requests, or issues in GitHub or other repositories. However, these URLs are somewhat arbitrary, they can appear on multiple places within the entries and any of them might be missing entirely. To handle this, we wrote a set of Python scripts to process these vulnerability entries and create an internal augmented and structured representation of them.

Once we collected all the vulnerability fixing commits, we analyzed these unidiff format patches to extract added, removed, and modified files as well as added/removed program and test lines of code. We applied a simple heuristic to find test code, we searched for the term "test" in the path or name of the file or in the name of JavaScript function a code change affects. We also apply sophisticated mapping to be able to tell which functions are changed by the vulnerability fix. Therefore, we are not only able to tell how many lines of code is changed, but also how many and what particular functions are affected by the security fix. All the data we used for answering our research questions is available online.[2]

4   Results

4.1   RQ1: Basic Properties of Vulnerability Fixing Patches

Table 1 displays the descriptive statistics of the 361 real vulnerability mitigation patches we analyzed.

Table 1. Descriptive statistics of the vulnerability fixing patches

	Min	Max	Median	Average	Std.dev.
Added files	0	93	0	1.02	8.61
Modified files	0	132	2	3.88	12.72
Removed files	0	7	0	0.11	0.58
Added lines	0	7 521	10	138.53	771.55
Removed lines	0	3 205	4	74.17	315.70
All changed lines	0	9 179	15	212.69	978.27
Affected functions	0	466	2	10.48	40.01

At the file level, security fixes in JavaScript programs mostly modify existing files. The mitigation patches we analyzed contained almost 4 file modifications on average, but only around 1 file addition. File removal was very rare.

The number of line additions is twice as large as line removals. Note, that the unidiff file format marks line modifications as a line removal plus a line addition,

---

[2] https://doi.org/10.5281/zenodo.3767909.

thus some of the additions and removals together form line modifications. However, the average of the added lines by a patch is almost 140, while the removed line average is less than 75. Therefore, security fixes contain a lot of added lines together with some modifications and removals. It is also important to note that the average changed lines (any additions, removals, and modifications altogether) per vulnerability fixes are 212.69. So quite many lines are affected by fixes on average. However, as we can see, the standard deviation of these values is extra large as well, almost one thousand. Additionally, the median of the values is 15 only (half of the patches change 15 lines or less only). These suggest that far fewer lines are changed in most of the fix patches, but several very huge changes affect the average.

We also mapped the code change patches to actual JavaScript functions to see how many different functions are affected in the vulnerability fixes at the logical level. The same trend is true for the changed lines. On average, more than 10 functions are changed in the course of a vulnerability fix. However, the median of such values is only 2. Therefore, most of the patches affect a very small number of functions, with some patches containing an extremely large number of modified functions.

4.2   RQ2: Vulnerability Fixing Patches and Test Code

Table 2 contains the same descriptive statistics for the patches from the test code's perspective. The trends are similar, but the magnitude of values is one fourth that of the program code.

Table 2. Descriptive statistics of the vulnerability fixing patches

	Min	Max	Median	Average	Std.dev.
Added test files	0	4	0	0.15	0.55
Modified test files	0	14	0	0.68	1.40
Removed test files	0	1	0	0.01	0.12
Added test lines	0	1 027	0	32.81	108.35
Removed test lines	0	242	0	7.91	32.04
All changed test lines	0	1 269	0	40.72	135.60
Affected test functions	0	63	0	4.55	9.76

Figure 2 provides further details on the distribution of the changed program and test code lines. We can see the average number of changed code and test lines by the vulnerability fixing patches grouped by the CWE categories of the vulnerabilities. The vulnerability databases enumerated the associated CWE categorizations together with the vulnerability descriptions, therefore we could mine this information as well. It is noticeable that there are some vulnerability types where fixes do not introduce test code changes at all. However, where fixing patches do contain test code modifications, their magnitude is comparable to that of the program code's modifications on average.

4.3   RQ3: Possible Targets for Automated Fix Generation

In our previous work [6], we showed that it is possible to use machine learning models to predict JavaScript vulnerabilities effectively based on source code analysis results. In this work, we investigated how feasible it would be to generate also fixes for the detected vulnerabilities in an automated way, i.e. applying automated program repair techniques. Since the state-of-the-art of such techniques is still immature and efficient automatic patch generation works only for small code fragments, we inspected how many of the real-world vulnerability fixes are small and concise, thus being a good candidate for automatic repair.

According to Fig. 2, there are only 8 different CWE groups where the vulnerabilities belonging to them have fixes with 10 or less changed lines. Vulnerabilities of these types are definitely to best candidates for building automated repair techniques for fixing them. However, it is also evident, that there are much more short vulnerability fixes, so grouping them based on their CWE categories might not be the best strategy. Therefore, we plotted the number of vulnerabilities by CWE groups together with the number of fixes containing 10 or fewer lines of code changes. As can be seen in Fig. 3, a considerable proportion of each CWE group contains vulnerabilities with short fixing patches. Thus, automated patch generation could be extended to such fixes.

Going a bit deeper, we also examined a couple of vulnerability fixing patches with such short code-changes manually. Our goal was to evaluate the feasibility of automatic fix generation at the semantic level. It is not enough that a code we need to generate is short, but it should be such that its semantics is not overly complicated to apply automatic repair techniques for it.

Vulnerability fix in the Node.js WebSocket project.[3] A vulnerability of type CWE-410: Insufficient Resource Pool is fixed in one line (see Listing 41), changing the value of *maxPayload* from *null* to *100 * 1024 * 1024*. This is a simple, straightforward change and the occurrence of "null" is easy to detect. However, to come up with a proper payload value automatically would be a hard task for an automatic repair tool.

---

[3] npm:ws:20160624.

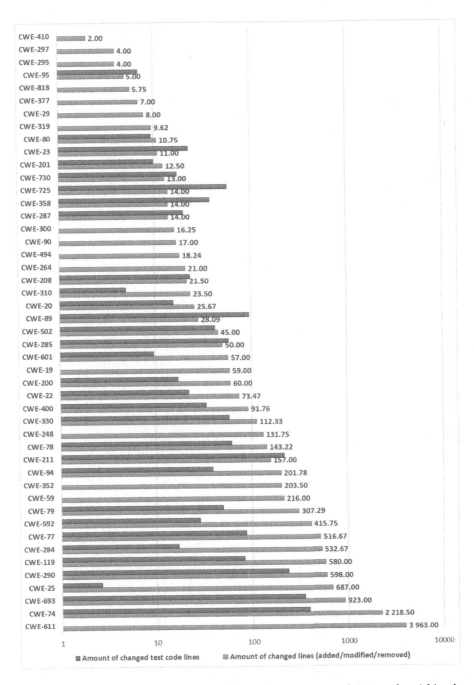

Fig. 2. The average number of changed lines in program and test code within the mitigation patches, grouped by CWE types

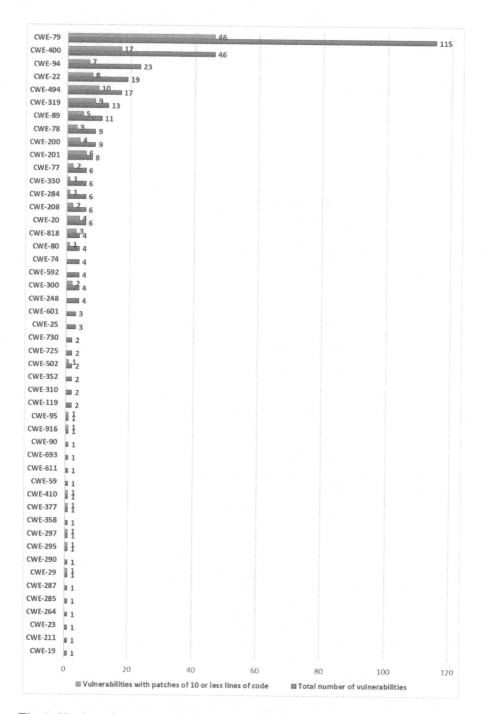

Fig. 3. Number of total vulnerabilities and mitigation patches with 10 lines or less, grouped by CWE categories

```
1   --- lib/WebSocketServer.js
2   +++ lib/WebSocketServer.js
3
4   @@ -37,7 +37,7 @@ function WebSocketServer(options, callback)
        {
5       disableHixie: false,
6       clientTracking: true,
7       perMessageDeflate: true,
8   -   maxPayload: null
9   +   maxPayload: 100 * 1024 * 1024
10    }).merge(options);
11
12    if (!options.isDefinedAndNonNull('port') && !options.
        isDefinedAndNonNull('server') && !options.value.
        noServer) {
```

Listing 41. Vulnerability fix in Node.js WebSocket

Vulnerability fix in the LinkedIn dust.js project.[4] A vulnerability of type CWE-95: Improper Neutralization of Directives in Dynamically Evaluated Code ('Eval Injection') is fixed by extending a simple conditional check with an additional condition (see Listing 42). These types of fixes are common in automatic repair for regular software bugs, thus they should be adapted to the vulnerability domain as well.

```
1   --- lib/dust.js
2   +++ lib/dust.js
3
4   @@ -851,7 +851,10 @@
5         SQUOT = /\'/g';
6
7     dust.escapeHtml = function(s) {
8   -   if (typeof s === 'string') {
9   +   if (typeof s === "string" || (s && typeof s.toString ===
        "function")) {
10  +       if (typeof s !== "string") {
11  +         s = s.toString();
12  +       }
13        if (!HCHARS.test(s)) {
14          return s;
15        }
```

Listing 42. Vulnerability fix in LinkedIn dust.js

Interestingly, this fix includes changes in the test code. The added condition is tested with a new test case as shown in Listing 43.

---

[4] npm:dustjs-linkedin:20160819.

```
1   --- test/jasmine-test/spec/coreTests.js
2   +++ test/jasmine-test/spec/coreTests.js
3
4   @@ -688,6 +688,13 @@ var coreTests = [
5               },
6       expected: "1",
7       message: "should test using a multilevel reference as a
                key in array access"
8   +           },
9   +           {
10  +       name: "Outputting an array calls toString and HTML-
                encodes",
11  +       source: "{array}",
12  +       context: { "array": ["You & I", " & Moe"] },
13  +       expected: "You &amp; I, &amp; Moe",
14  +       message: "should HTML-encode stringified arrays
                referenced directly"
15          }
16      ]
17  },
```

Listing 43. Added test case for the vulnerability fix in LinkedIn dust.js

Therefore, we should think of automatically generating new test cases upon automatic vulnerability fix generation. During future research, we have to put some effort into finding out which fixes are those that require such test case extensions.

Vulnerability fix in the Chrome driver project.[5] A vulnerability of type CWE-319: Cleartext Transmission of Sensitive Information is fixed by changing "http" to "https" (see Listing 44). The CWE-319 group of vulnerabilities appears to be a perfect candidate for generating fixes automatically. If we could find a method that identifies occurrences of "http" in contexts that are used as actual addresses, we could easily propose a fix automatically. In our future research, we will focus first on these vulnerability groups.

```
1   --- install.js
2   +++ install.js
3
4   @@ -15,7 +15,7 @@ var url = require('url')
5       var util = require('util')
6
7       var libPath = path.join(__dirname, 'lib', 'chromedriver')
8   -   var cdnUrl = process.env.npm_config_chromedriver_cdnurl ||
            process.env.CHROMEDRIVER_CDNURL || 'http://chromedriver.
            storage.googleapis.com'
9   +   var cdnUrl = process.env.npm_config_chromedriver_cdnurl ||
            process.env.CHROMEDRIVER_CDNURL || 'https://chromedriver.
            storage.googleapis.com'
10      // adapt http://chromedriver.storage.googleapis.com/
11      cdnUrl = cdnUrl.replace(/\/+$/, '')
12      var downloadUrl = cdnUrl + '/%s/chromedriver_%s.zip'
```

Listing 44. A vulnerability fix in Chrome driver

---

[5] npm:chromedriver:20161208.

5 Conclusions

In this paper, we inspected 361 real-world fixes of vulnerabilities explored in JavaScript programs. Our focus was on analyzing the various properties of such security fixing patches to aid further research on automatically generating such patches.

We found that security fixes in JavaScript programs mostly modify existing files and that the number of line additions and/or modifications overweight line removals. We also investigated if the test code is changed during vulnerability fixes. Although the overall amount of test code changed is significantly smaller than that of the program code, we observed that if a patch contains test code modifications, its magnitude is similar to the program code changes. That is, there are types of security issues that are fixed without test code adjustments, but for some security types, test code modifications are really important.

Finally, we examined the patches from the perspective of automatic repair techniques. In general, it would be hard to generate potential vulnerability fixes as the size of code changes and their types vary significantly. However, we showed that at least half of the fixes contain 15 or fewer code lines, which can be handled by automatic repair tools, but the semantic complexity of the changes is also important. We identified a couple of good candidates for starting with automatic security fix generation, like that of the vulnerabilities from the CWE-319 group.

A lot of further research is needed in this area, but we think our small scale empirical investigation contains some useful insights and guidance of further directions. We plan to develop automatic repair techniques for the above-mentioned vulnerability categories and evaluate their performance.

References

1. Node Security Platform - GitHub. https://github.com/nodesecurity/nsp. Accessed 16 Oct 2018
2. Vulnerability DB — Snyk. https://snyk.io/vuln. Accessed 16 Oct 2018
3. Anderson, R., et al.: Measuring the cost of cybercrime. In: Böhme, R. (ed.) The Economics of Information Security and Privacy, pp. 265–300. Springer, Heidelberg (2013). https://doi.org/10.1007/978-3-642-39498-0_12
4. Chidamber, S.R., Kemerer, C.F.: A metrics suite for object oriented design. IEEE Trans. Softw. Eng. 20(6), 476–493 (1994)
5. Chowdhury, I., Zulkernine, M.: Using complexity, coupling, and cohesion metrics as early indicators of vulnerabilities. J. Syst. Archit. 57(3), 294–313 (2011)
6. Ferenc, R., Hegedűs, P., Gyimesi, P., Antal, G., Bán, D., Gyimóthy, T.: Challenging machine learning algorithms in predicting vulnerable Javascript functions. In: Proceedings of the 7th International Workshop on Realizing Artificial Intelligence Synergies in Software Engineering, pp. 8–14. IEEE Press (2019)
7. Gao, F., Wang, L., Li, X.: BovInspector: automatic inspection and repair of buffer overflow vulnerabilities. In: Proceedings of the 31st IEEE/ACM International Conference on Automated Software Engineering, pp. 786–791 (2016)
8. Jimenez, M., Le Traon, Y., Papadakis, M.: Enabling the continous analysis of security vulnerabilities with VulData7. In: IEEE International Working Conference on Source Code Analysis and Manipulation, pp. 56–61 (2018)

9. Le Goues, C., Forrest, S., Weimer, W.: Current challenges in automatic software repair. Softw. Qual. J. **21**(3), 421–443 (2013)
10. Ma, S., Thung, F., Lo, D., Sun, C., Deng, R.H.: VuRLE: automatic vulnerability detection and repair by learning from examples. In: Foley, S.N., Gollmann, D., Snekkenes, E. (eds.) ESORICS 2017. LNCS, vol. 10493, pp. 229–246. Springer, Cham (2017). https://doi.org/10.1007/978-3-319-66399-9_13
11. Morrison, P., Herzig, K., Murphy, B., Williams, L.A.: Challenges with applying vulnerability prediction models. In: HotSoS (2015)
12. Neuhaus, S., Zimmermann, T., Holler, C., Zeller, A.: Predicting vulnerable software components. In: Proceedings of the ACM Conference on Computer and Communications Security, pp. 529–540, January 2007
13. Shin, Y., Meneely, A., Williams, L., Osborne, J.A.: Evaluating complexity, code churn, and developer activity metrics as indicators of software vulnerabilities. IEEE Trans. Softw. Eng. **37**(6), 772–787 (2011)
14. Shin, Y., Williams, L.: An empirical model to predict security vulnerabilities using code complexity metrics. In: Proceedings of the Second ACM-IEEE International Symposium on Empirical Software Engineering and Measurement, pp. 315–317. ACM (2008)
15. Shin, Y., Williams, L.A.: Can traditional fault prediction models be used for vulnerability prediction? Empirical Softw. Eng. **18**, 25–59 (2011)
16. Siavvas, M., Kehagias, D., Tzovaras, D.: A preliminary study on the relationship among software metrics and specific vulnerability types. In: 2017 International Conference on Computational Science and Computational Intelligence - Symposium on Software Engineering (CSCI-ISSE), December 2017
17. Smirnov, A., Chiueh, T.C.: DIRA: Automatic detection, identification and repair of control-hijacking attacks. In: NDSS (2005)
18. Sudo vulnerability in macOS (2020). https://www.techradar.com/news/linux-and-macos-pcs-hit-by-serious-sudo-vulnerability
19. Yu, Z., Theisen, C., Sohn, H., Williams, L., Menzies, T.: Cost-aware vulnerability prediction: the HARMLESS approach. CoRR abs/1803.06545 (2018)
20. Zimmermann, T., Nagappan, N., Williams, L.: Searching for a needle in a haystack: Predicting security vulnerabilities for windows vista. In: 2010 Third International Conference on Software Testing, Verification and Validation (ICST), pp. 421–428. IEEE (2010)

Software Process Improvement Assessment for Cloud Application Based on Fuzzy Analytical Hierarchy Process Method

Surjeet Dalal[1], Akshat Agrawal[2(✉)], Neeraj Dahiya[1], and Jatin Verma[3]

[1] SRM University Sonipat, Gurgaon, India
profsurjeetdalal@gmail.com,
neerajdahiya.cse@gmail.com
[2] Amity University Haryana, Gurugram, India
akshatag20@gmail.com
[3] G.B. Pant Engineering College, Delhi, India
vjatin83@gmail.com

Abstract. The miracles of ordinary programming development face exceptional difficulties which relate to Software process development. Main objective of this method is to make the prioritization-based intelligent plan for Software Process Improvement (SPI). Attainment elements utilizing the Fuzzy Analytical Hierarchy (AHP) Process technique. A special phase that was seen became additionally assessed through using a non-useful gathering with use of SPI. Inside subsequent stage, a multi-degree dynamic AHP tools became applied to fashion out and increase the perceptive depiction of the perceived segments and their requests. The repercussions of the Fuzzy AHP method are novel during this evaluation zone because it has been fairly utilized in cloud software improvement. This paper proposes the radical approach with use of Fuzzy AHP in the examination of Global Software Development (GSD) and SPI, which enables with expelling the untidiness and shortcoming inside the assessment of the procedure development phases related to cloud application headway.

Keywords: Fuzzy AHP · Software process improvement · Cloud computing

1 Introduction

These days, cloud computing is perceived as a predominant registering model in IT frameworks, empowering adaptable, universal, on-request and practical access to a wide pool of shared assets. It is commonly seen that huge and differing associations have embraced the cloud worldview for their data frameworks, getting a charge out of the accompanying two key highlights: low expenses by discharging them from the weight to contribute on equipment foundations and programming licenses, and diminished operational multifaceted nature, as associations can concentrate on the nature of their items and administrations as opposed to on the administration of complex IT frameworks [1]. A typical trait of every one of these applications is that they are information intensive, with the information being produced consistently and

© Springer Nature Switzerland AG 2020
O. Gervasi et al. (Eds.): ICCSA 2020, LNCS 12252, pp. 989–1001, 2020.
https://doi.org/10.1007/978-3-030-58811-3_70

originating from heterogeneous sources, for example, sensors or logical gadgets. Moreover, information generation rates can fluctuate altogether, and the applications may regularly need to process information in an opportune way empowering framework to take remedial/vital operational activities or respond at circumstances desperately (Fig. 1).

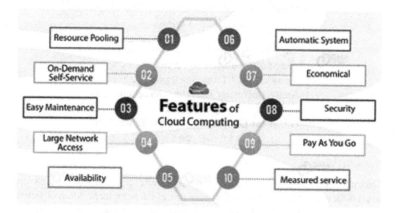

Fig. 1. Feature of Cloud computing environment [3]

Hence, such applications make frequently utilize computational assets. We will allude to this sort of utilizations as persistent, information stream applications (CDFA), including a wide scope of uses, for example, logical work processes, pipelines, gushing applications, or whatever other concentrated application where information conditions and simultaneousness play a significant angle [2].

Portability in the cloud can allude to two extraordinary yet interlinked angles:

Legacy programming's modernization planned for misusing current cloud-based advancements.

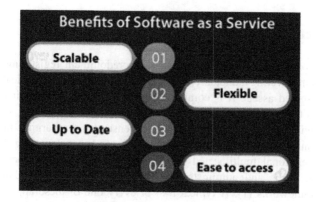

Fig. 2. Benefits of SaaS [1]

Portability of cloud-prepared applications among various cloud stages and suppliers (Fig. 2).

To continue with; we have recognized the purposes of contention which emerge while an application is ported starting with one cloud stages then onto the next. We have distinguished those parts of an application which should be tended to contrastingly in cloud stages. In this area we talk about the accompanying barely any potential clash focuses programming dialects and structures, stage explicit administrations and stage explicit design records [19].

Programming language or potentially systems - Each cloud stage has support for certain language, renditions and structures [4]. The programming dialects and systems that an application has been fabricated will be a significant concern while porting it to another stage. For instance, while Google App Engine (GAE) offers help for Python and Java, Amazon bolsters Java, .NET, PHP, Python and Ruby.

Platform explicit administrations – The time taken for application improvement can be radically decreased by utilizing API's. Rather than programming all of usefulness starting from the earliest stage, they can incorporate it into their application by official to the individual stage APIs [5].

1.1 SaaS App Development

Software-as-a-service (SaaS) applications have certainly become standard even among undertakings. In any case, building up an extraordinary SaaS application isn't trifling. It requires solid comprehension of multi-occupancy, configurability, security, apportioning to construct a genuine SaaS application that can be utilized to serve various sorts of customers.

The most widely recognized issue around the sending and ease of use of utilizations is the failure to test right off the bat in the development cycle intended to address those issues. In Fig. 3, we see that in the truth of undertakings, it is regularly restrictive to give engineers and analyzers situations proportionate to creation from the mix test stages. Surely, for arrangements on physical machines, this speaks to an expense of assets excessively high [7]. This implies the genuine operational design is not tried until the application comes to the pre-creation and creation conditions later in the cycle. This paper suggested approach based on Fuzzy Analytical Hierarchy Process which is applied for purpose of Software Process Improvement (SPI) assessment for Cloud application which emphasis on application deployment as well as migration of the application from one cloud to another.

2 Related Work

G. Fylaktopoulos et al. (2018) depicted the CIRANO stage, a separated Integrated Development Environment (IDE) for cloud-based applications. The proposed stage was attempted to help Model-Driven Development (MDD) and gathering facilitated exertion, empowering the fast improvement of forefront applications in the cloud. The paper introduced at the principal stage the front line in the field of cloud IDEs and delineates the structure, utilization, and nuances of the CIRANO stage. The essential

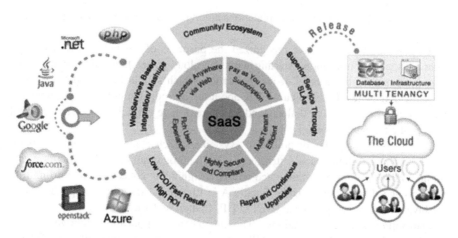

Fig. 3. Software-as-a-service (SaaS) applications [6]

featured of the proposed stage were presented in two relevant examinations concerning the headway of an application without any planning and porting of a current application. The paper discussed the revelations in relationship with existing instruments and proposed extensions of the phase as future work [8].

Polona Štefanič et al. (2019) expressed that time-fundamental applications, for instance, early notification systems or live event broadcasting, introduced explicit difficulties. They had hard cutoff focuses on Quality of Service necessities that must be kept up, paying little mind to orchestrating changes and moving apexes of weight. In this manner, such applications must modify deftly on-demand, in this way ought to be fit for reconfiguring themselves, nearby the fundamental cloud establishment, to satisfy their necessities. Programming building instruments and ways of thinking right presently did whatever it takes not to help such a perspective. In this paper, they portrayed a structure that had been planned to meet these objectives, as a significant part of the EU SWITCH adventure. SWITCH offers a versatile co-programming structure that gave a pondering layer and an establishment condition, which could help to both show and support the presence example of time-fundamental cloud neighborhood applications. They delineated the building, structure, and execution of the SWITCH parts and depicted how such instruments were applied to three time-fundamental authentic use cases [9].

Fahad Almudarra et al. (2015) discussed issues in making convenient cloud applications using deft programming progression strategies. Sha-Mo-Cloud, a crossbreed cloud framework was made using open cloud organizations for taking care of knowledge including pictures and chronicles got from customer's phones. Customers can move, get the chance to, manage, and share a singular substance-using web interface almost like a versatile application. Adaptable Cloud Computing has been an endless imaginative work zone. Various frameworks and middleware are developed starting late furnishing responses for utilizing appropriated figuring resources on resource-constrained mobile phones. A scarcely any number of works present sound structuring parts for becoming such programming. To spare customer security and modified data, some a part of the framework was made during a private cloud condition. This add like manner reports the structuring portions of the headway of ShaMoCloud. The item improvement bunch as lately made similar applications using the Team Software Process. The work presented here altogether examines the experiences of the ShaMoCloud progression bunch with four tantamount endeavors that did start late [10].

Philip Churchr et al. (2015) discussed issues in making convenient cloud applications using deft programming progression methods. Sha-Mo-Cloud, a crossbreed cloud framework was made using open cloud organizations for taking care of knowledge including pictures and chronicles got from customer's mobile phones. Customers could move, get the chance to, administer, and share a singular substance using web interface almost like an adaptable application. Adaptable Cloud Computing had been an endless imaginative work zone. Various frameworks and middleware had been developed starting late offering responses for utilizing disseminated registering resources on resource-constrained PDAs. A barely any number of works introduced sound structuring segments for becoming such programming. To spare customer security and altered data, some a part of the framework was made during a private cloud condition. This work moreover revealed the structuring portions of the headway of ShaMoCloud. The item advancement bunch as lately made near applications using the Team Software Process. The work presented here completely examines the experiences of the ShaMoCloud progression bunch with four equivalent endeavors that did start late [11].

Muhammad Shiraz et al. (2013) clarified that latest enhancements in PDA development had made PDAs as the future figuring and organization get to contraptions. Customers planned to run computational focused applications on Smart Mobile Devices (SMDs) correspondingly as stunning fixed PCs. In any case paying little mind to all the types of progress starting late, SMDs were still low potential figuring contraptions, which were constrained by CPU prospects, memory cutoff, and battery lifetime. Flexible Cloud Computing was the latest sensible response for diminishing this debilitating by expanding the organizations and resources of computational fogs to SMDs on demand premise. In MCC, application offloading was discovered as an item level response for developing application getting ready limits of SMDs. The current offloading figuring's offload computational concentrated applications to remote servers by using differing cloud models. A troublesome piece of such figuring's was the establishment of spread application planning stage at runtime which requires additional preparing resources on SMDs. This paper reviewed existing Disseminated Application Processing Frameworks (DAPFs) for SMDs in the MCC territory. The objective was to highlight gives what is progressively, hard to existing DAPFs in making, realizing, additionally, executing computational concentrated flexible applications inside MCC space [12]. It proposed topical logical arrangement of current DAPFs, reviews current offloading frameworks by using topical logical grouping, and researches the recommendations and essential pieces of ebb and flow offloading structures. Further, it analyzed shared qualities and deviations in such structures on the reason vital boundaries, for instance, offloading expansion, migration granularity, partitioning approach, and development plan. Finally, they put forth open examine issues in circled application planning for MCC that stay to be tended to.

Keiichi Shiohara et al. (2014) expressed that Web application progression was confronted with a growing system multifaceted nature, new specific necessities, dynamic changing of client terminal devices besides, security issues actuated by new parting strategies. During this novel condition, giving new procedures to suitably making Web applications in negligible exertion gets focal. This brought new specific troubles of developing new data showing and new methodology in the arrangement, database mapping, page progress control, endorsement, meeting the administrators, programming, and data and yield interface plan particular districts, as Web application improvement requires those strategies. At an equivalent time, because the significant progression of data and correspondence development (ICT) has been made, ICT propels were carrying exciting changes to our lives and business. Thus, there was a growing prerequisite for creating Web applications for business additionally, ordinary a day presence use. Developing past examination likewise, applications, this paper introduced that data models for creating Web applications might be built using spreadsheets considering a cloud application improvement stage, called FOCAPLAS. This spreadsheet-based making approach introduced their challenges on new frameworks of both the info showing and programming for Web application improvement [13, 14].

Fotis Gonidis et al. (2013) expressed that Cloud application stages picked up reputation and might change the way organization-based cloud applications were made including the utilization of stage basic organizations. A phase central assistance was considered as a bit of programming, which gave certain convenience and is when in doubt offered by methods for a web API, for instance, email, portion, confirmation organization. Regardless, the duplication and upgrade of stage major organizations and the available providers increased the test for the application originators to arrange them and deal with the heterogeneous providers' web APIs. Along these lines, another strategy of making applications should be grasped in which fashioner's impact distinctive stage basic organizations openly from the target application stages. To this end, this paper introduced an improvement framework whose goal was to engage the consistent coordination of the stage organizations and to allow the predictable use of the strong providers by relieving the heterogeneities among them [15].

Rear Benfenatk et al. (2014) described a nonexclusive methodology for self-loader improvement of cloud-based business applications. This could be used by non-IT experts, for example, colleagues, who set off a business application progression by simply communicating its necessities in the wording of business functionalities and constraints, QoS boundaries, likewise, her/his tendencies. From these functionalities and objectives, Linked USDL essentials reports are thus created. These records gave the reason to the cloud organization exposure and dispatch the customized improvement of cloud business applications. We present the essential enhancements in their model [16–18].

3 Problem Formulation

During the past decade, the software industry has been increasingly more worried about Software process improvement (SPI). Therefore, we have seen an expansion of models and activities all asserting to improve the probability of prevailing with SPI activities. SPI has its underlying foundations in quality administration and is intently identified with "second era" authoritative advancement draws near, explicitly to hierarchical learning. Understanding the "quality unrest" is, along these lines, a significant essential for comprehension SPI.

Software process improvement activities bolster the association in accomplishing its key business objectives more adequately, where the business objectives could be conveying programming quicker to the market, improving quality and decreasing or dispensing with squander [19, 20]. The goal is to work more astute and to fabricate programming better, quicker also, less expensive than contenders. Software process improvement makes business sense, and it gives an arrival on speculation. Software process improvement (SPI) is a drawn-out excursion, which is made agreeable by numerous methods.

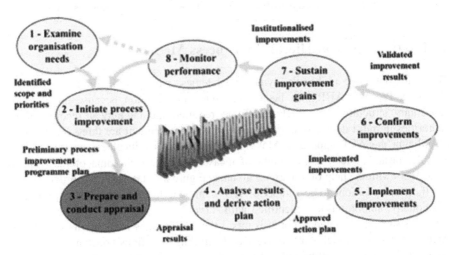

Fig. 4. Steps in process improvement [9]

The most predominant and favored arrangement is an information-driven technique with which programming advancement associations are testing. To see and feel of information and its administration, it has gotten fundamental to have normalized information the board apparatus (KMT) that involves determinations like-procurement, portrayal, sharing, and conveying. Albeit a few devices and strategies are accessible for overseeing information to take care of area issues, it is felt in the information society that no standard KM devices exist that would encourage SPI. In this bit of usage work, the creators plot the highlights that are considered noteworthy to execute a KMT that drives the excursion of SPI. Four procedure zones are picked, and four subsystems are distinguished in covering these procedure zones [20, 21]. A progression of studies directed among associations requiring the help of a KMT in making a definitive SPI activity is likewise talked about with intricate and noteworthy outcomes. Ramifications of this work request the participation of programming advancement organizations with the exploration network in finding a superior way to deal with their improvement program [22–24].

This section expands and coordinates models from earlier inquire about by playing out an observational examination of the key components for accomplishment in SPI. Cloud selection for a wide range of programming is expanding, and most associations no longer consider cloud framework as less secure than on-premises arrangements; rather, they consider it to be the main conceivable elective when versatility, cost, and time to esteem are significant variables. Late penetrates of security by government organizations have made cloud clients justifiably apprehensive, yet cloud suppliers are offering more options for the area of the cloud servers and improving security using private encryption keys that are held by the client as opposed to the supplier. It's additionally imperative to consider the relative hazard for the kind of data being put away in the cloud condition: With this approach, the models and examination put away in the open cloud may speak to some important licensed innovation, yet infrequently incorporate any actually recognizable data about the client association's clients [23].

4   Fuzzy Analytical Hierarchy Process Method

There are obtrusive multi-rule dynamic strategies, paying little brain to, Analytic Hierarchy Process (AHP) has been taken into consideration because the foremost elementary structure. The AHP technique required the theoretical records of the authorities in multi-degree dynamic issues. Arising subsequent are three center strides of utilizing the AHP approach. Making of the chain of criticalness structure of the irregular desire issue. Figure weight of measures at every diploma of the chain of criticalness with the help of a pairwise alliance. Figure the standardized burdens to pick out the final positions. The old-style AHP cannot influence a pioneer's peculiarity additionally, ambiguousness identified with surveying the necessities of various measures. As such, the woolen hypothesis mixes the AHP framework known as cushioned AHP that is used to pick capably right and fulfilling selections constantly and faulty issues. This approach will be utilized for each quantitative and exceptional data within the MCDM issues. Triangular warm numbers are applied all through this approach for slanting closer to reviews of the requirements and affect need the immensity of unequivocal models making use of the degree appraisal procedure [24, 25]. During this assessment, we have utilized the padded AHP proposed by Chang which affords incessantly correct and predictable results as disconnected to the standard AHP technique (Fig. 5).

The Fuzzy AHP approach has been applied to form the proclaimed fulfillment factors of SPI and its key classes.

A. Graphical levels of intensity version of the apparent sections and their classes.

In this examination, the graphical astounding structure turned into made established upon the gadget gave through Ramasubu and conversations with the review masters

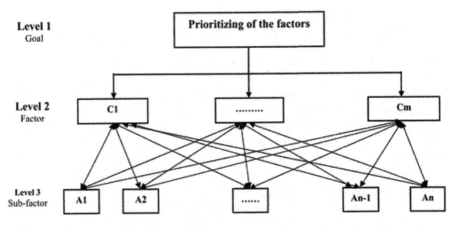

Fig. 5. Fuzzy AHP decision hierarchy [1]

(Fig. 4). The key goal of this assessment is gathered on the very fine degree of the chain of the noteworthiness of association (degree 1), while the delineations and their thriving sections at stage 2 and degree 3 autonomously.

B. examine development for inclining in the direction of the achievement factors the apparent achievement elements and their social affair turned into diagramed utilizing the survey examine method [26, 27]. The overview changed into made to amass statistics from the SPI masters to altogether chance underwrite the conspicuous achievement elements and their classes within the space of GSD. During this evaluation, the expertise became accrued from seventy-three directors together with prodigies, experience supervisors, programming engineers/engineers, programming sketchers, analyzers, instructive aces, and so on. The diagram human beings were welcomed making use of email and clean online life structures, which include ResearchGate, LinkedIn, and Facebook. The people have been the key masters that have been really pulled into the structure development experiences. The online information was amassed from latest timeline and for that reason the full-scale records collection takes one and half month. We have accrued a sum of seventy-five reactions given by means of the diagram people. The evaluation reactions have been explored by using the focal author of the paper and discovered six missing reactions. The missing reactions had been considering 75 reactions that had been considered at some point of this evaluation. We applied a 5-point Likert scale, and consequently the reactions have been referenced as: "very concur", "concur", "authentic", "veer off" and "mainly discredit this idea". It's great to believe the fair point inside the structure examination scale, considering the manner that the nonattendance of a neural choice could oblige the respondents to offer an unequal response (for example tremendous or however negative) [25–28].

C. Pilot trying out of the evaluate: - A pilot appraisal of the evaluation tool become driven by taking into consideration the substance and key factors of the audit. The examination turned into reviewed by using 5 experts identified with the SPI and GSD experiences, which includes the aspect organizing teachers from the metropolis. The going with facts turned into checked within the reactions of the pilot study. Responses were sketched bent test the consistency many of the respondents. Responses have been poor right down to understand any solicitation abandoned a vital open door by the respondents. The instrument was additionally amassed in subjects that could oppositely influence the reaction rate. The recommendation and comments gave through the pilot have a look at respondents may want to enhance the assessment response rate through and pretty [13]. During this assessment, the likelihood of the overview device changed into progressed via considering the proposals given by way of the pilot look at won-ders. The comments and proposals are abbreviated in going with focuses. Far and away most of the feedback had been identified with an instrument plan moreover, the experts proposed introducing the assessment factors during a stunning structure for clearness and insight. The ace's in addition quarreling over the obliged facts gave about the respondent association. It had been invigorated within the respectable series of the audit overview. Because the pilot looks at became fashioned and directed the have a look at approach, there has been no skipped question from the respondent. The tool has been adjusted and engaged problem to the appraisal given through the pilot observe people [29, 30].

5 Cloud Application Development Evaluation Using the Proposed Model

The proposed model is represented with a numerical case model. The point by point delineation is talked about beneath. A successful cloud-based Health application can help patients to improve their health. In any case, the determination of cloud-based Health applications is a moderately troublesome errand. The issue can be settled by applying AHP and Fuzzy TOPSIS procedures. The blend of AHP and Fuzzy TOPSIS has been discovered reasonable in various fields to take care of MCDM issues [30, 31]. The determinations of models and sub-rules for cloud-based Health applications are extremely pivotal. In the current examination, a double methodology was embraced to select the standards and sub-rules. In the primary stage, different measures were dis-tinguished by alluding to the writing in the important field. Consequently, suppositions from three specialists from the scholarly community and industry were taken on the distinguished components [32–34] (Fig. 6).

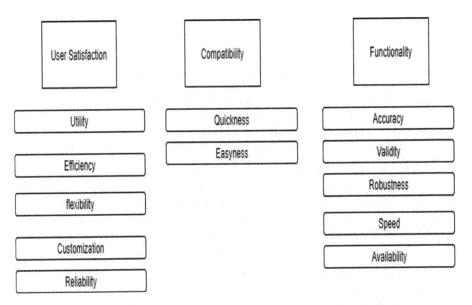

Fig. 6. Hierarchy of cloud based health application model [2]

6   Results Analysis and Conclusion

The health application has become fundamental as of late because of the digitization of society. This framework can oversee problems even more quickly if it very well may be amalgamated with the conventional human services framework. In this computerized world, a viable cloud Health application can assist individuals with dealing with their health and become progressively educated with respect to health.

Be that as it may, with the expanding number of health-related applications, it is hard to choose which applications are appropriate for the clients what is more, which are most certainly not. This examination has attempted to reveal insight into this course.

The point of this exploration is to frame a model dependent on AHP and fuzzy TOPSIS to look at and assess the exhibitions of various cloud-based health applications. For assessing exhibitions of various cloud-based health applications, nine rules and thirty-two sub-standards have been thought of. Diverse cloud-based health applications are looked at and organized dependent on the over thirty-two components. To catch the vulnerability relating to the human dynamic procedure, fuzzy ideas have been applied. Client fulfillment, usefulness, simple to learn and use, and data quality were significant factors for cloud-based health innovation determination. Solid Out has risen as the best cloud-based health application among all the options followed by Noom Weight Loss Coach. Strikingly, a huge variety of the positioning has been watched for weighted and unweighted techniques. The sub-rules assume a significant job in cloud-based health innovation choice. In any case, a leader can just utilize the fuzzy TOPSIS to rank the choices.

References

1. Khan, A.A., Basri, S., Dominic, P.D.D.: A propose framework for requirement change management in global software development. In: International Conference on Computer & Information Science, ICCIS, pp. 944–947 (2012)
2. Unterkal msteiner, M., Gorschek, T., Islam, M.M.K.A., Cheng, K.C., Permadi, R.B., Feldt, R.: Evaluation and measurement of software process improvement—a systematic literature review. IEEE Trans. Softw. Eng. **38**, 398–424 (2012)
3. Coleman, G., O'Connor, R.: Investigating software process in practice: a grounded theory perspective. J. Syst. Softw. **81**, 772–784 (2008)
4. Pettersson, F., Ivarsson, M., Gorschek, T., Öhman, P.: A practitioner's guide to lightweight software process assessment and improvement planning. J. Syst. Softw. **81**, 972–995 (2008)
5. Chen, L., Babar, M.A., Zhang, H.: Towards an evidence-based understanding of electronic data sources. In: Proceedings of the 14th International Conference on Evaluation and Assessment in Software Engineering, EASE, UK (2010)
6. Herbsleb, D.J., Moitra, D.: Global software development. IEEE Softw. **18**(2), 16–20 (2001)
7. Khan, A.A.: A framework for assisting software process improvement program in global software development: student research abstract. In: Proceedings of the 31st Annual ACM Symposium on Applied Computing. ACM (2016)
8. Kuhrmann, M., Konopka, C., Nellemann, P., Diebold, P., Münch, J.: Software process improvement: where is the evidence: initial findings from a systematic mapping study. In: Proceedings of the International Conference on Software and System Process (2015)
9. Paulk, M., Curtis, B., Chrissis, B.M., Weber, C.: Capability Maturity Model for Software, Version 1.1. CMU/SEI-93-TR-24 (1993)
10. SEI: Standard CMMI Appraisal Method for Process Improvement (SCAMPI)A, Version 1.3: Method Definition Document (CMU/SEI-2011-HB-001), Software Engineering Institute, Carnegie Mellon University, Pittsburgh, PA (2011)
11. SO: ISO 9000, Quality Management Systems-Fundamentals and Vocabulary International Organization for Standardization, Technical Report, ISO9000:2005 (2005)
12. Khan, A.A., Shameem, M., Kumar, R.R., et al.: Applied Soft Computing Journal 83 (2019) 10564823[13] ISO, ISO/IEC Information Technology- Process Assessment - Part 4: Guidance on Use for Process Improvement and Process Capability Determination, International Organization for Standardization, Technical ReportISO/IEC 15504-4:2004 (2004)
13. Gillies, A.: Software Quality: Theory and Management, International Thomson Computer Press (2011)
14. Abrahamsson, P.: Measuring the success of software process improvement: the dimensions. arXiv preprint arXiv:1309.4645 (2013)
15. Bano, M., Ikram, N.: Software process improvement: a systematic literature review. In: 15th International Multitopic Conference, INMIC, pp. 459–464 (2012)
16. Humphrey, W.S.: A Discipline for Software Engineering. Addison Wesley (1995)
17. Ayhan, M.B.: A fuzzy AHP approach for supplier selection problem: a case study in a Gear motor company. arXiv preprint arXiv:1311.2886 (2013)
18. Güngör, Z., Serhadlıoğlu, G., Kesen, S.E.: A fuzzy AHP approach to personnel selection problem. Appl. Soft Comput. **9**(2), 641–646 (2009)
19. Chamodrakas, I., Batis, D., Martakos, D.: Supplier selection in electronic marketplaces using satisficing and fuzzy AHP. Expert Syst. Appl. **37**(1), 490–498 (2010)
20. Ayhan, M.B.: Fuzzy tops is application for supplier selection problem. Int. J. Inf. Bus. Manag. **5**(2), 159–174 (2013)

21. Sulayman, M., Urquhart, C., Mendes, E., Seidel, S.: Software process improvement success factors for small and medium web companies: a qualitative study. Inf. Softw. Technol. **54**, 479–500 (2012)
22. Niazi, M., et al.: Challenges of project management in global software development: aclient-vendor analysis. Inf. Softw. Technol. **80**, 1–19 (2016)
23. Gillies, A.C.: Software Quality, 2nd edn. International Thomson Computer Press, London (1997)
24. Yamamura, G.: Software Process Satisfied Employees. IEEE Softw., 83–85 (1999)
25. Habib, Z.: The Critical success factors in implementation of software process improvement efforts: CSFs, motivators & obstacles, MSc. thesis, University of Gothenburg, Sweden (2009)
26. Paulk, M.: Capability Maturity Model for Software, Wiley Online Library (1993). S.E.I., Process Maturity Profile, Software Engineering Institute Carnegie Mellon University (2004)
27. Khan, A.A., Keung, J., Niazi, M., Hussain, S., Shameem, M.: GSEPIM: a road map for software process assessment and improvement in the domain of global software development. J. Softw. Evol. Process. **31**(1), e1988 (2019)
28. Niazi, M.: A framework for assisting the design of effective software process improvement implementation strategies, Ph.D. thesis, University of Technology Sydney (2004)
29. Babar, M.A., Niazi, M.: Implementing software process improvement initiatives: an analysis of Vietnamese practitioners' views. In: IEEE International Conference on Global Software Engineering, ICGSE 2008, pp. 67–76 (2008)
30. Khan, A.A., Basri, S., Dominic, P.D.D., Amin, F.E.: Communication risks and best practices in global software development during requirements change management: a systematic literature review protocol. Res. J. Appl. Sci. Eng. Technol. **6**, 3514–3519 (2013)
31. Dahiya, N.: A new variant of bat algorithm and clustering approach for optimization problems. In: Proceedings of First International Conference on Computational Intelligence and Communication Technologies (2017)
32. Behera, R.K., Shukla, S., Rath, S.K., Misra, S.: Software reliability assessment using machine learning technique. In: Gervasi, O., et al. (eds.) ICCSA 2018. LNCS, vol. 10964, pp. 403–411. Springer, Cham (2018). https://doi.org/10.1007/978-3-319-95174-4_32
33. Behera, R.K., Naik, D., Rath, S.K., Dharavath, R.: Genetic algorithm-based community detection in large-scale social networks. Neural Comput. Appl. **32**(13), 9649–9665 (2019). https://doi.org/10.1007/s00521-019-04487-0
34. Shukla, S., Behera, R.K., Misra, S., Rath, S.K.: Software Reliability Assessment Using Deep Learning Technique. In: Chakraverty, S., Goel, A., Misra, S. (eds.) Towards Extensible and Adaptable Methods in Computing, pp. 57–68. Springer, Singapore (2018). https://doi.org/10.1007/978-981-13-2348-5_5
35. Behera, R.K., Rath, S.K., Misra, S., Damaševičius, R., Maskeliūnas, R.: Large scale community detection using a small world model. Appl. Sci. **7**(11), 1173 (2017)

InDubio: A Combinator Library to Disambiguate Ambiguous Grammars

José Nuno Macedo[1,2]([✉]) (ID) and João Saraiva[1,2] (ID)

[1] University of Minho, Braga, Portugal
saraiva@di.uminho.pt
[2] HASLab/INESC TEC, Braga, Portugal
jose.n.macedo@inesctec.pt

Abstract. To infer an abstract model from source code is one of the main tasks of most software quality analysis methods. Such abstract model is called Abstract Syntax Tree and the inference task is called parsing. A parser is usually generated from a grammar specification of a (programming) language and it converts source code of that language into said abstract tree representation. Then, several techniques traverse this tree to assess the quality of the code (for example by computing source code metrics), or by building new data structures (e.g, flow graphs) to perform further analysis (such as, code cloning, dead code, etc). Parsing is a well established technique. In recent years, however, modern languages are inherently ambiguous which can only be fully handled by ambiguous grammars.

In this setting disambiguation rules, which are usually included as part of the grammar specification of the ambiguous language, need to be defined. This approach has a severe limitation: disambiguation rules are not first class citizens. Parser generators offer a small set of rules that can not be extended or changed. Thus, grammar writers are not able to manipulate nor define a new specific rule that the language he is considering requires.

In this paper we present a tool, name *InDubio*, that consists of an extensible combinator library of disambiguation filters together with a generalized parser generator for ambiguous grammars. *InDubio* defines a set of basic disambiguation rules as abstract syntax tree filters that can be combined into more powerful rules. Moreover, the filters are independent of the parser generator and parsing technology, and consequently, they can be easily extended and manipulated. This paper presents *InDubio* in detail and also presents our first experimental results.

Keywords: Parsing · Disambiguation filters · Combinators

1 Introduction

The evolution of programming languages in the 1960s was accompanied by the development of techniques for the syntactic analysis of programs. While techniques for processing text have evolved since then, the general approach has

© Springer Nature Switzerland AG 2020
O. Gervasi et al. (Eds.): ICCSA 2020, LNCS 12252, pp. 1002–1018, 2020.
https://doi.org/10.1007/978-3-030-58811-3_71

remained the same. To define and implement a new programming language, the general approach tends to be the use of context-free grammars to specify the programming language syntax. Then, a parser generator automatically generates programs known as *parsers*. Such parsers are able to syntactically recognize whether a text is a program in the specified programming language, described by a context-free grammar.

From such grammar, a parser generator produces a parser (implemented in a specific programming language) that given a text (i.e. a sequence of characters) accepts/rejects it. If the text is accepted a (abstract) syntax tree may be constructed. For unambiguous grammars, a single tree is built, meaning that there is only one possible way of accepting the text from such a grammar.

However, programmers often write ambiguous grammars [5]. Firstly, because they are easier to write/understand and evolve. Secondly, because modern languages provide a "cleaner" syntax, which make programs look nicer, but are easier to express by ambiguous grammars.

Listing 1.1. Grammar of arithmetic expressions

```
exp     : exp '+' exp
        | exp '-' exp
        | exp '*' exp
        | exp '/' exp
        | '(' exp ')'
        | number ;
```

The ambiguous grammar presented in Listing 1.1 follows closely the syntax nature of arithmetic expressions. For example, the text 1+2+3 can produce two different trees, prioritizing either the left sum or the right sum.

Regular parser generators do not support ambiguous grammars. Thus, ambiguity has to be dealt with by either refactoring the grammar to eliminate ambiguity (which can be complex, and results in a more complex and hard to understand grammar) or by providing disambiguation rules.

These disambiguation rules are pre-defined for most parser generators, and are directly imbued into the parser itself when it is generated, effectively modifying it. If the disambiguation rules are well-defined, there will be no ambiguity problems and the parser will be able to recognize text without any problem.

However, there are several problems with this approach: a) The only rules available are the pre-defined rules and they are not extensible: the parser generator itself would need to be updated in order to support new rules; b) Because disambiguation rules are part of the grammar, they are context-free too. Thus, it is impossible to define context-dependent rules like for example to express that '+' operator has a different priority/associative when inside a while loop; c) It is not modular and changing a disambiguation rule results in the generation of a new parser; d) Since the only rules available are the pre-defined rules, the developer is unable to observe the source code of these rules, instead opting to trust a black box that could potentially not behave as desired.

This paper presents an alternative to the classical approach, which does not suffer from these drawbacks: Disambiguation rules are modular combinators that are kept separate from the parser, being instead used as filters that are applied to the results of parsing an input. In this way, changes to the disambiguation rules do not affect the parser, allowing for an efficient development cycle around disambiguation rules. Because we express disambiguation rules as combinators, new rules can be easily defined by combining existing ones. Moreover, our approach allows the definition of context dependent disambiguation filters which behave differently according to the context they are applied to.

1.1 Motivation

In the early ages of programming languages, it was usual to purposely include certain symbols in a language's grammar so that the generated parser for said language was more efficient.

The most obvious example is found in the C programming language: the semicolon found at the end of each instruction is a statement terminator [15]. It is used to resolve some ambiguities that could be found in the grammar. However, modern programming languages tend to avoid the use of too many syntactic symbols. This not only allows developers to write fewer symbols and less code while programming, but also makes programs simpler and easier to understand. Although it helps program comprehension, it requires complex grammars and corresponding parsers to handle such programs.

This work focuses on generic parsing techniques that generate a parser for any context-free grammar. Due to the ambiguity, these parsers produce various results for the same program, and disambiguation rules are used to select the desired solution, but the existing tools that provide generic parsing techniques are still limited. These rules are to be implemented as combinators, which are simple code tools, that are easy to implement but very powerful when combined with other combinators.

2 State of the Art

There are various different parsing algorithms proposed to solve the parsing problem. The earliest solution to be used was to embed the grammar in the code, where there was no separation between the grammar and the rest of the code. This was a solution that made it very difficult to change the grammar once it was coded in, since it was mixed with the code.

2.1 BNF Notation

The BNF notation is a notation for specifying context-free grammar, generally used for specifying the exact grammar of programming languages. It was proposed by [4], to describe the language of what became known as ALGOL 59.

In the example in Listing 1.1, the BNF notation is used to describe the grammar of arithmetic expressions. This grammar is inherently recursive: an expression (Exp) can be defined as an expression (Exp), an arithmetic sign ('+')

and another expression (Exp). The entirety of a grammar is expressed in this way, which is simple to understand and powerful when compared to embedding the grammar in the code.

The BNF notation is extremely interesting as it laid the foundation to having the grammar separated from the code, such that it would be easy to change the grammar without having to change any of the remaining code.

However, this notation can be ambiguous. A concrete instance of text can be interpreted in different ways, all of them correct according to the specification. As an example, the text *1+2+3* can be considered. There are two possible ways to interpret this text according to the specification, which represent different order of operations, that is, whether the left sum or the right product is processed first.

2.2   Common Parsers

While it is common for programming languages to be expressed as grammars, for example using the BNF notation, there are various ways to generate a parser given such specification. Each alternative method has its own advantages and disadvantages. The first to be relevant were the most powerful in terms of compilation and execution time. As such, the grammars were changed to best fit the method: the developer had to both focus on writing the correct grammar and adapting it to fit the parser generator. The previous example uses left-recursion, which is impossible to parse [2] for some of these algorithms. Therefore, the previous example would have to be changed so as to not have left-recursion, before it could be used in some parser generators.

One of the most well-known parser generators, YACC, is a LALR parser generator [8]: this relies on a lightweight algorithm which was perfect for the time it was developed, that is, 1975, when it was much more necessary to restrict program runtime and memory size.

Another example of a popular parser generator is ANTLR [13], whose development started in 1989 as a LL(*) parser generator. The LL(*) algorithm allows for parsing decisions to be taken by looking at the following tokens in the input stream. ANTLR 4 uses the ALL(*)[14], which is $O(N^4)$ in theory but is shown to consistently perform linearly in practice.

While Yacc generates C code and ANTLR generates code for various programming languages, one of the most popular parser generators for Haskell is Happy [11], which enables the developer to supply a file with the specification of a grammar, and in turn generates a parser, that is, a module of code that can read text according to that grammar's specifications. Happy is part of the Haskell Platform, being one of the most famous Haskell parsing tools. Due to its rather big popularity and regular maintenance, it is a fairly well optimized tool.

2.3   Generalized Parsing

Several parsing techniques do not deal with ambiguity properly. The input is expected to be unambiguous, and when it is not, a certain interpretation of such ambiguity is chosen so as to continue parsing. This results in runtime-wise efficient but not so expressive parsers, as they ignore any ambiguity problems that could arise.

Ambiguity can be dealth with using GLR parsers, which are slower than their non-generalized counterparts, due to their additional flexibility in dealing with non-determinism: when faced with an input with several different possible outputs, a GLR parser [23] will produce all of the outputs instead of selecting one of them. If no non-determinism is present, a GLR parser will behave just like a LR parser [9], which is efficient. With the constant advances in technology, the limitations that made this technique undesirable are gone and there are parser generators that allow the use of the GLR algorithm, such as Happy.

However, GLR is not the only generalized algorithm. The GLL algorithm [21,22] is also generalized, but much less explored. This algorithm is worst-case cubic in both time and space and there are possible optimizations to it [1].

2.4   Scannerless Parsing

Generally speaking, parser applications are divided in two components: the lexer and the parser. The lexer takes the input and breaks it into a list of tokens [17], and then the parser takes those tokens and matches them with the production rules to produce the actual parsing result.

Scannerless parsing [16] consists of skipping the lexer entirely and treating each character from the input as a token, which is fed directly into the parser. Scannerless parsing removes the necessity of describing the tokens in the grammar specification, allowing the developer to write the grammar without worrying as much with conforming with the parser technology. Scannerless parsers are compositional, therefore allowing for two parsers to be merged without needing to change them.

2.5   Disambiguation Filters for Scannerless Generalized Parsing

In this work, the focus is on scannerless generalized parsers. For such, as they deal with ambiguous inputs, it is expected to get a list of outputs as a result, which represent all possible interpretations. However, not all possible interpretations are desired: depending on the situation, a developer might want to only get one or a small subset of parse trees, instead of all the possibilities.

The task of processing the list of the ambiguous parse trees produced by a parser and removing the undesired is called disambiguation. Typically, such filtering is done on the parser, that is, modifying part of the parser so that the undesired interpretations cannot be produced. Some new rules for disambiguation are needed when dealing with scannerless parsing. In this section, some filters for disambiguation are presented and described, according to the work of van den Brand et al. [5].

The **priority** filter specifies that certain productions have a higher priority than others, while the **associativity** filter specifies that an operator associates left or right.

The **reject** filter enables the creation of keywords in the grammar. In other words, it rejects some productions from deriving into certain sequences. This filter allows for a clean implementation of reserved keywords. For example, in the C programming language, it shouldn't be allowed for a variable to be named "while", as that is a reserved keyword used in defining loops.

The **follow** filter solves an ambiguity that arises in scannerless parsing. When the grammar dictates that a sequence of symbols can be parsed using one single production or a sequence of productions, for example, a sequence of digits which could be read as a single number or several numbers with no separators, the follow filter specifies that the longest match is to be performed.

When there are several correct interpretations of a given input but some are preferred over others, a **preference** filter is used. It specifies which parse results should be removed when there are several correct outputs but the developer wants to select only a part of them. This filter is the go-to filter to remove the dangling else problem, occurs when there are two *if* clauses and only one *else* clause, and thus it is not clear to which *if* clause the *else* clause associates to.

2.6 Haskell XML Toolbox and HaGLR

Syntax trees are generalized trees which can represent a program. Generalized trees are often called Rose Trees in the functional programming setting and are well studied in several contexts. One of them is XML, for which there are several generic tools that can be used. In this work, the filter variant of the Haskell XML Toolbox [20] is used as a base for building combinators for filtering syntax trees. The HaGLR tool [7] is a Haskell implementation of a GLR parser generator, which was implemented with pedagogic purposes. It produces as result a pure parse tree forest, which is a list of parse trees. This is not the case for all generalized parsers as some optimizations change the representation of the parse forests to save memory, which use a different, more compact approach, but are less intuitive to work around.

3 The InDubio Combinator Library

In this paper, a new approach for parser disambiguation is described. Instead of expressing the disambiguation rules in the parser itself, they are kept separate. The parser is generated once, and it produces a possibly ambiguous result. Afterwards, the disambiguation rules are applied to the forest of AST, removing some or all of the ambiguities, according to what the developer specified. There are several advantages and disadvantages in using this process instead of the classical approach. Since the parser that is used is unmodified, it is less efficient, as the classical approach removes parts of the parser reducing thus the number of results the parser has to output. However, while the parser itself is less efficient, the development cycle of the developer is more efficient, as there is no need to constantly produce a new parser after a change in a disambiguation rule. Only the disambiguation rules are to be changed, and this can be easily done if the implementation is user-friendly. Therefore, the disambiguation rules are implemented as filter combinators, where the developer starts with basic blocks that perform very simple filtering, combining them in easy-to-understand ways to produce complex filters that perform the desired disambiguation rules.

To be able to build complex filters to disambiguate the result of a parser, we use basic combinators defined in the Haskell XML Toolbox library. They enable the creation of filters, as well as manipulation and composition. Some new combinators were also created to better fit the needs of this work. They are available in the repository of this work, but as they are simple and intuitive, they are not described in this paper.

In the following sections, the types of filters described in Sect. 2.5 are implemented using these combinators. However, it is important to note that they apply to the parse trees produced by the parser, and if a different parser is used, it might be needed to change the filters accordingly.

To build a filter that defines disambiguation rules, it is first needed to take a look at a parse tree and devise an algorithm for checking if it is a valid parse tree. To do so, it is important to understand the structure of the parse trees produced by the parser.

In the remaining of this section, we will use the expression grammar *Filters* (available online at this work's repository) as running example.

Associativity Filter. Given a parser for the *Filters* grammar, and the simple input string "*1+2+3*", the output consists of two parse trees, as seen in Fig. 1. The left one shall be considered the correct interpretation and the right one the undesired interpretation for this example. As such, to write the filter, it is needed to locate what is the pattern that stands out in this example, and then describe a way to remove it using the combinators.

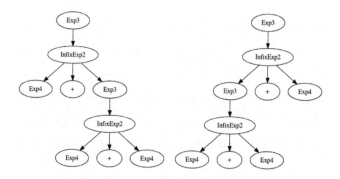

Fig. 1. Simplified parse trees for the string "1+2+3;"

The names of the nodes match with the names of the productions. As an example, the *Exp1* and *Exp2* nodes refer to the *Exp* production. *NTfromT2* refers to a terminal symbol, in this case, the + sign. *InfixExp2* refers to the

InfixExp production, which defines the additions. In this case, the difference between the two parse trees is in whether an *InfixExp2* node is to the left or to the right of their parent *InfixExp2* node. This represents the ambiguity, in which the addition can be left-associative or right-associative. Therefore, the ambiguity can be solved by implementing a filter that removes any tree where there is an *InfixExp2* node to the right (or left) of another *InfixExp2* node.

The implementation of this filter is rather trivial once the algorithm is defined. This filter will look at the root node, check if it is an *InfixExp2*, and, if it is, check if there is an *InfixExp2* node in the right child of said node. If there is not, then the tree is correct according to the filter.

```
associativity :: TFilter String
associativity = neg rightNodeCheck 'when' matches "InfixExp2"
  where rightNodeCheck = matches "InfixExp2" . head .
    ↪ getChildren . (!!2) . getChildren
```

Therefore, the filter is finished and can be read in a reasonably easy way. When the root matches the string *"InfixExp2"*, the rightmost child must not match the string *"InfixExp2"*. Of course, when the root does not match this string, the filter does nothing.

However, this filter does not work as expected on a real parse tree, because the filter only applies to the root. In reality, the ambiguity can exist deep into the tree, and so the *every* combinator is needed to apply the filter to all the tree, and discard the tree if any of the nodes fail to satisfy it.

Finally, we can generalize the resulting filter. This can be done by having the node's name passed as an argument, and not have it hard-coded in the definition.

```
left_assoc :: String -> TFilter String
left_assoc  p = neg (matches p . head . getChildren . (!!2) .
  ↪  getChildren) 'when' matches p

assocGeneric :: TFilter String
assocGeneric = every (left_assoc "InfixExp2")
```

Priority Filter. Given a parser for the *Filters* grammar, and the simple input string *"1+2*3"*, the output consists of two parse trees, as seen in Fig. 2.

These trees are rather similar to the ones displayed before, and the node naming conventions are the same. In this case, one of the parse trees represents the + symbol being processed first, while in the other tree is the * symbol that is processed first. To resolve this ambiguity, we use a simple algorithm: for any node in the tree, if it matches the * symbol, then the children nodes must not match the + symbol. If such nodes exist, they represent a situation where the product happens before the sum, which is not the desired behaviour.

```
priority :: TFilter String
priority = neg anyChildrenMatches 'when' matches "InfixExp2"
  where anyChildrenMatches = (matches "InfixExp1" $$). (
    ↪ concatMap getChildren) . getChildren
```

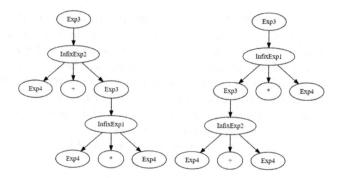

Fig. 2. Simplified parse trees for the string "1+2*3;".

As in previous filters, the *every* combinator is needed to apply the filter to all the nodes in the tree, so that it discards the tree if any of the nodes fail to satisfy it. Finally, it is possible to generalize this filter, so as to allow easier reuse.

```
before :: String -> String -> TFilter String
before x y = neg ((matches  x $$). (concatMap getChildren) .
    ↪ getChildren ) 'when' matches  y

priorityGeneric :: TFilter String
priorityGeneric = every (before "InfixExp1" "InfixExp2")
```

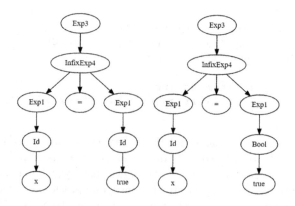

Fig. 3. Simplified parse trees for the string "x = true;".

Reject Filter. Given a parser for the *Filters* grammar, and the simple input string "*x = true*", the output consists of two parse trees, as seen in Fig. 3. The parser can interpret the string *true* as either a boolean value, that is, a "*Bool*" node, or an identifier, that is, an "*Id*" node. While both are technically correct, this ambiguity needs to be eliminated by not allowing the use of language keywords as language identifiers, thus the need for reject filters.

Since this parser is a scannerless parser, a string is actually a sequence of tokens, where each token is a character. To recover the string from the sequence of tokens, the *implodeSubTree* function is used. It is part of the tools available in the HaGLR parser, and it converts a sequence of tokens into a string. The resulting string is reversed, and thus the *reverse* function is used to fix the strings and enable adequate comparison between them.

According to the definition of this filter, when a node matches the *"Id"* production, then the string it derives into cannot match any of the desired keywords. The following implementation only considers the keywords *"true"* and *"false"* but it trivially generalizes to more language keywords.

```
reject :: TFilter String
reject = neg isOk 'when' matches "Id"
  where isOk = (matches (reverse "true") 'orElse' matches (
    ↪ reverse "false")).head.getChildren.implodeSubTree
```

As in previous disambiguation filter combinators, the *every* combinator is used to apply this filter to the whole tree. Of course, only the *"Id"* nodes can be affected by it, but they can be located anywhere on the tree, hence why this combinator is needed. One last step is to generalize this filter.

```
reject :: String -> String -> TFilter String
reject w p = neg (matches (reverse w) . head . getChildren .
  ↪ implodeSubTree) 'when' matches p

rejGeneric :: TFilter String
rejGeneric=every(reject "true" "Id" 'o' reject "false" "Id")
```

Follow Filter. Given a parser for the *Filters* grammar, and the simple input string *"int x [] = [12 3]"*, the output consists of two parse trees, as seen in Fig. 4. Since whitespace is not directly specified in the grammar, if there are not any other separators, the parser cannot distinguish whether the string *"12"* is one or two values. As such, the follow filters are used to solve this ambiguity.

In this situation, it is desired that the *"Values"* production has the longest match in each of its children, that is, tries to incorporate as many characters as possible into each children. In this situation, it is enough to specify that either the left child ends with a character that is not a number, or the right child starts with a value that is not a number. This forces the output to only contain this production when there are two values separated by a whitespace in the input, because if there are no whitespaces, the filter will reject the whole tree.

The implementation of this filter just specifies that, when the root node is a *"Values1"* node, then the first child's processed string must end with a desired character or the second child's processed string must start with one, so that between the two, there is at least one whitespace. It is important to note that the parser assembles whitespaces into various nodes automatically, and it is taken advantage of this fact to describe this filter.

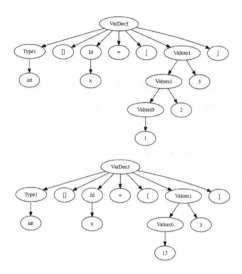

Fig. 4. Simplified parse trees for the string "int [] x = [12 3];".

```
follow :: TFilter String
follow = (p1 'orElse' p2) 'when' matches "Values1"
  where p1=isOf$not.isDigit.head.getLastTerm.(!!0).getChildren
      p2=isOf$not.isDigit.head.getFirstTerm.(!!1).getChildren
```

As before, the *every* combinator is used to apply this filter to the whole tree. Of course, only the *"Values1"* nodes can be affected by it, but they can be located anywhere on the tree, hence why this combinator is needed. One last step is to generalize this filter.

```
follow :: String -> String -> TFilter String
follow  t r = (p1 'orElse' p2) 'when' matches t
  where p1=isOf$flip notElem r.head.getLastTerm.(!!0).
      ↪ getChildren
      p2=isOf$flip notElem r.head.getFirstTerm.(!!1).getChildren

followGeneric :: TFilter String
followGeneric = every ( follow "Values1" "0123456789")
```

Preference Filter. Given a parser for the *Filters* grammar, and the simple input string *"if true then if false then 1 else 2"*, the output consists of two parse trees, as seen in Fig. 5. This is a rather famous ambiguity problem generally described as the *dangling else* problem. In this input string, there are two *if...then* clauses, and one *else* keyword, but the grammar allows the else to belong to either *if*. Therefore, the parser will generate two interpretations, in which the *else* keyword will associate with either of the *if...then* clauses.

In this situation, both interpretations are correct, but the developer may prefer one over the other. This is where the preference filter comes in.

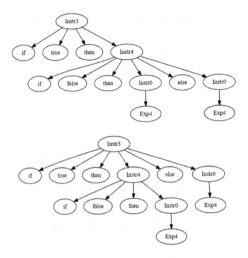

Fig. 5. Simplified parse trees for the string "if true then if false then 1 else 2;".

This filter, however, does not behave similarly to the other filters. It works by comparing different parse trees, and then choosing the best one, which is fundamentally different to the other filters which operate on a single tree. Therefore, the implementation of this filter is a simple function on filters, and the source code is available at the repository.

3.1 Context Dependent Filters

In our approach, disambiguation rules are embedded in the grammar description. As we presented in the previous sections, they can be used to implement already known disambiguation rules. However, they can also be used to implement new concepts and ideas that generally are not possible to implement in the disambiguation rules of most parser generators. This allows the developer to express any desired disambiguation rule - specific to the language the developer is defining - without the limitations of not being able to fine-tune the filters.

As an example, in this section, it will be presented a filter that associates any sum operations to the left, until an *if* clause is found, and inside the *if* blocks, the sum operations will associate to the right. While there is no immediate use for this filter in our running example language, it is a good example of different behaviour implemented into a filter.

```
ff :: TFilter String
ff = iff (matches "Instr3") rAssocAll leftUntil
  where rAssocAll = every (right_assoc "InfixExp2")
        leftUntil = isOf (all (satisfies ff) . getChildren) 'o
          ↪ ' left_assoc "InfixExp2"
```

The *iff* combinator is fed three arguments, where the first is just to check if the current node matches the *if* instruction. If so, the *rightAssocEverything* portion of the code is run, which just applies the *right_assoc* combinator shown before to all the subtrees from that point onwards. If the matching fails, as seen in the *leftAssocUntil* portion of the code, the *left_assoc* combinator is applied to the current node, and the whole filter is recursively applied to all the subtrees.

3.2   Embedded Filters

To allow an easier usage of these disambiguation filters, an easier way to use the well-known filters was developed. A new data type was developed, where each possible constructor represents a disambiguation rule, and a developer can specify the filters using this data type, coupled with a conversion function that transforms it into a filter that would be produced by using the equivalent combinators. The developer does not need to know the names of the productions to write the filters, and can use the symbols instead, which is generally more intuitive. However, the helper function that does this convertion is computationally intense, and so this approach is less efficient than the pure combinator approach. It is possible, however, to combine this approach with the combinator approach, allowing a developer to write the most trivial filters with this approach, and to write the most complex filters using combinators.

The following filter is an implementation of most of the filters previously described, combined into one filter, using this strategy. The priority filter is changed into a filter that defined priority between the modulus and equality operations, as these filters will be needed in the following section. This change is trivial using this strategy, as there is no need to know the production names, only the symbols that are relevant. The preference filter is not included as it cannot be described using this strategy.

```
filters :: TFilter String
filters = every $ gen_filters [LeftAssoc "+",
    "Values1" 'NotFollowedBy' "0123456789",
    Reject_List ["true", "false", "break"] "Id",
    ["=="] 'Before' ["%"]   ]
```

4   Disambiguation Filters in Practice

To test and validate our combinators[1], we have defined several grammars in HaGLR and expressed the disambiguation rules using our combinators: we consider the well known ambiguous expression grammar (a fragment of this grammar is shown in Sect. 1) and the Tiger grammar [3] (a real programming language defined with teaching purposes). For these two examples the grammars are pure CFGs: no alien notation for disambiguation rules is included. Moreover, the grammars are ambiguous since no care on expressing operator rules via nonterminals was considered.

---

[1] The work presented in this paper is available at our repository, at https://bitbucket.org/zenunomacedo/disambiguation-filters/.

Since the parsers produced by HaGLR for these two ambiguous grammars produce a forest of ASTs, we used our library to express the disambiguation rules for the two languages in order to select a single correct AST. Moreover, to validate that the selected tree is the correct one, we also express both languages via an equivalent non-ambiguous grammar. Those equivalent grammars were obtained by using grammar adaptation rules [10]. Thus, we compare the single AST produced by the non-ambiguous grammar, with the select AST produced by our filters from the AST forest produced by the HaGLR parser.

To automate this validation we used the QuickCheck [6] test case generator and property-based test framework: we define generators for random expressions, and used a set of pre-defined Tiger programs as input for our parsers. Then, we express a property to confirm that the resulting ASTs are equivalent: they produce semantically equivalent representations. For the expression grammars we developed an evaluator (that computes the result of the expression), and for the Tiger language we defined a translator to low-level code. Next, we show the QuickCheck property for the expression example.

```
prop_valid :: String -> Property
prop_valid x = forAll genExpr $ \e ->
  let rAmbig = disambiguation_small $ AP.glr_parser_aterm e
      rUnambig = UP.glr_parser_aterm e
  in singletonList rAmbig && singletonList rUnambig &&
  eval (head $ rAmbig) == eval (head $ rUnambig)
```

QuickCheck is then able to randomly generate inputs for the expression language and test this property for all of them: it states that both the ambiguous and non-ambiguous parsers produce a single result for the input, and that the semantic result of evaluating both expressions is equal. A similar property is defined for Tiger with the only difference of not randomly generating inputs, but instead selecting them from a pre-defined list. Thus, Quickcheck was used to confirm that both grammars produce equivalent semantic results.

4.1   Performance

As stated before, the HaGLR was developed with pedagogic purposes only. For example, it uses Haskell pre-defined lists to model parsing tables which is easy to understand but it is not the best data structure if we focus on performance. Thus, the resulting parsers are not optimized at all (unlike for example the parser produced by Happy [11]). Nevertheless, we performed some preliminary benchmarks to measure the cost of applying the disambiguation filters to the forest produced by the HaGLR parsers. For the two considered grammars we have the following results produced by Criterion [12] (a Haskell benchmark framework) (Table 1):

This table contains a single input for each grammar: an expression with 11 operators, and the Tiger program modelling the n-Queens problem (both available from our repository).

For the Expression grammar, applying the disambiguation filters reduces the parsing time by 17.6%, and for the Tiger grammar, applying the filters increases

Table 1. Comparison of the runtime without and with filters, in seconds, for the Expression and Tiger parsers.

	Expression	Tiger
No filters	5.811	2.119
With filters	4.789	2.829

the parsing time by 33.5%. We can conclude that using the filters improves the parsing performance when the grammar is highly ambiguous, because of Haskell's lazy evaluation, as the filters cut off the generation of unnecessary ASTs. However, for less ambiguous grammars such as Tiger's, the filters perform unnecessary verifications of non-ambiguous parts of the ASTs, which has a negative impact on performance.

5   Conclusions

In this paper, disambiguation rules are first-class citizens: new rules can be defined by combining existing ones and they can be also passed has input to parsers. As a result, grammar writers are not limited to a set of pre-defined and fixed rules offered by the parser generator, instead they can easily express new rules and experiment with them without having to re-generate a new parser.

We have developed InDubio: a combinator library of such disambiguation rules and we have defined rules to disambiguate both the well-known ambiguous expression language, and the Tiger language. We validate our library by combining our Haskell-based filter combinators with the HaGLR parser generator: The AST forest produced by the HaGLR parser is pruned into a single correct AST by our disambiguation filters. We presented our first preliminary benchmark results showing that although the generated parsers are non-optimized, for highly ambiguous grammars and due to the lazy evaluation of Haskell, by applying the filters, we actually produce faster parsers: lazy evaluation avoids the creation of unnecessary and redundant ASTs.

Because HaGLR was developed in a pedagogic setting, it does not use the most efficient data structures. Thus, we are optimizing HaGLR so that it uses a better parse-table representation, and we are also considering to use shared packed parse forests [24] and data structure free compilation [18], which both use sharing to reduce runtime and memory consumption. We are also integrating the disambiguation filters with BiYacc [25], a tool for generating both a parser and a reflective printer [26,27] for an unambiguous context-free grammar. The use of disambiguation filters can be helpful in extending this tool to also support ambiguous context-free grammars, therefore increasing its expressiveness and allowing for more test cases to be supported by this tool. Moreover, we also plan to combine our approach with Generic attribute grammars [19].

References

1. Afroozeh, A., Izmaylova, A.: Faster, practical GLL parsing. In: Franke, B. (ed.) CC 2015. LNCS, vol. 9031, pp. 89–108. Springer, Heidelberg (2015). https://doi.org/10.1007/978-3-662-46663-6_5
2. Aho, A.V., Lam, M.S., Sethi, R., Ullman, J.D.: Compilers: Principles, Techniques, and Tools, 2nd edn. Addison-Wesley, San Francisco (2006)
3. Appel, A.: Modern Compiler Implementation in ML. Cambridge University Press, Cambridge (1998)
4. Backus, J.W.: The syntax and semantics of the proposed international algebraic language of the Zurich ACM-GAMM conference. In: IFIP Congress, pp. 125–131 (1959)
5. van den Brand, M.G.J., Scheerder, J., Vinju, J.J., Visser, E.: Disambiguation filters for scannerless generalized LR parsers. In: Horspool, R.N. (ed.) CC 2002. LNCS, vol. 2304, pp. 143–158. Springer, Heidelberg (2002). https://doi.org/10.1007/3-540-45937-5_12
6. Claessen, K., Hughes, J.: Quickcheck: a lightweight tool for random testing of Haskell programs. ACM Sigplan Not. 46(4), 53–64 (2011)
7. Fernandes, J.P., Saraiva, J., Visser, J.: Generalised LR Parsing in Haskell (2004)
8. Johnson, S.C.: Yacc: yet another compiler-compiler (1979)
9. Johnstone, A., Scott, E., Economopoulos, G.: Generalised parsing: some costs, March 2004
10. Lämmel, R.: Grammar adaptation. In: Oliveira, J.N., Zave, P. (eds.) FME 2001. LNCS, vol. 2021, pp. 550–570. Springer, Heidelberg (2001). https://doi.org/10.1007/3-540-45251-6_32
11. Marlow, S., Gil, A.: Happy user guide (2001)
12. O'Sullivan, B.: Criterion: a Haskell microbenchmarking library (2009). http://www.serpentine.com/criterion/
13. Parr, T., Fisher, K.: Ll(*): the foundation of the ANTLR parser generator. In: Proceedings of the 32nd ACM SIGPLAN Conference on Programming Language Design and Implementation, PLDI 2011, pp. 425–436. ACM, New York (2011)
14. Parr, T., Harwell, S., Fisher, K.: Adaptive ll (*) parsing: the power of dynamic analysis. ACM SIGPLAN Not. 49(10), 579–598 (2014)
15. Perlis, A.J., Shaw, M., Sayward, F. (eds.): Software Metrics: An Analysis and Evaluation. MIT Press, Cambridge (1981)
16. Salomon, D.J., Cormack, G.V.: Scannerless NSLR(1) parsing of programming languages. In: Proceedings of the ACM SIGPLAN 1989 Conference on Programming Language Design and Implementation (PLDI 1989), pp. 170–178. ACM (1989)
17. Saraiva, J.: HaLeX: a Haskell library to model, manipulate and animate regular languages. In: Hanus, M., Krishnamurthi, S., Thompson, S. (eds.) Proceedings of the ACM Workshop on Functional and Declarative Programming in Education, pp. 133–140. University of Kiel Technical report 0210, September 2002
18. Saraiva, J., Swierstra, D.: Data Structure Free Compilation. In: Jähnichen, S. (ed.) CC 1999. LNCS, vol. 1575, pp. 1–16. Springer, Heidelberg (1999). https://doi.org/10.1007/978-3-540-49051-7_1
19. Saraiva, J., Swierstra, D.: Generic attribute grammars. In: Parigot, D., Mernik, M. (eds.) 2nd Workshop on Attribute Grammars and their Applications, WAGA 1999, pp. 185–204. INRIA Rocquencourt, March 1999
20. Schmidt, U., Schmidt, M., Kuseler, T.: HXT: a collection of tools for processing xml with Haskell (2016). https://github.com/UweSchmidt/hxt

21. Scott, E., Johnstone, A.: Gll parsing. Electron. Notes Theoret. Comput. Sci. **253**(7), 177–189 (2010)
22. Scott, E., Johnstone, A.: Gll parse-tree generation. Sci. Comput. Program. **78**(10), 1828–1844 (2013)
23. Tomita, M.: Efficient Parsing for Natural Language: A Fast Algorithm for Practical Systems. Kluwer Academic Publishers, Norwell (1985)
24. Tomita, M.: Efficient Parsing for Natural Language: A Fast Algorithm for Practical Systems, vol. 8. Springer Science & Business Media, New York (1985)
25. Zhu, Z., Ko, H., Martins, P., Saraiva, J., Hu, Z.: Biyacc: roll your parser and reflective printer into one. In: Proceedings of the 4th International Workshop on Bidirectional, L'Aquila, Italy, 24 July 2015, pp. 43–50 (2015)
26. Zhu, Z., Ko, H.-S., Zhang, Y., Martins, P., Saraiva, J., Hu, Z.: Unifying parsing and reflective printing for fully disambiguated grammars. New Gener. Comput. **38**(3), 423–476 (2020). https://doi.org/10.1007/s00354-019-00082-y
27. Zhu, Z., Zhang, Y., Ko, H.S., Martins, P., Saraiva, J.A., Hu, Z.: Parsing and reflective printing, bidirectionally. In: Proceedings of the 2016 ACM SIGPLAN International Conference on Software Language Engineering, SLE 2016, pp. 2–14. ACM (2016)

A Data-Mining Based Study of Security Vulnerability Types and Their Mitigation in Different Languages

Gábor Antal[1], Balázs Mosolygó[1], Norbert Vándor[1], and Péter Hegedűs[1,2(✉)]

[1] Department of Software Engineering, University of Szeged, Szeged, Hungary
hpeter@inf.u-szeged.hu
[2] MTA-SZTE Research Group on Artificial Intelligence, Szeged, Hungary

Abstract. The number of people accessing online services is increasing day by day, and with new users, comes a greater need for effective and responsive cyber-security. Our goal in this study was to find out if there are common patterns within the most widely used programming languages in terms of security issues and fixes. In this paper, we showcase some statistics based on the data we extracted for these languages. Analyzing the more popular ones, we found that the same security issues might appear differently in different languages, and as such the provided solutions may vary just as much.

We also found that projects with similar sizes can produce extremely different results, and have different common weaknesses, even if they provide a solution to the same task. These statistics may not be entirely indicative of the projects' standards when it comes to security, but they provide a good reference point of what one should expect. Given a larger sample size they could be made even more precise, and as such a better understanding of the security relevant activities within the projects written in given languages could be achieved.

Keywords: CVE · CWE · Data mining · Software security · Vulnerability analysis

1 Introduction

As more and more vital services are provided by software systems accessible on the Internet, security concerns are becoming a top priority. Mitigating the

The presented work was carried out within the SETIT Project (2018-1.2.1-NKP-2018-00004). Project no. 2018-1.2.1-NKP-2018-00004 has been implemented with the support provided from the National Research, Development and Innovation Fund of Hungary, financed under the 2018-1.2.1-NKP funding scheme and partially supported by grant TUDFO/47138-1/2019-ITM of the Ministry for Innovation and Technology, Hungary. Furthermore, Péter Hegedűs was supported by the Bolyai János Scholarship of the Hungarian Academy of Sciences and the ÚNKP-19-4-SZTE-20 New National Excellence Program of the Ministry for Innovation and Technology.

© Springer Nature Switzerland AG 2020
O. Gervasi et al. (Eds.): ICCSA 2020, LNCS 12252, pp. 1019–1034, 2020.
https://doi.org/10.1007/978-3-030-58811-3_72

risks posed by malicious third parties should be at the core of the development processes. However, eliminating all the security vulnerabilities is impossible, thus we have to be able to detect and understand the security issues in existing code bases. How and what types of security vulnerabilities appear in programs written in various languages, and how their developers react to them are questions still lacking answers with satisfying empirical evidence.

In this paper, we present the results of a small-scale, open-source study that aims to show the differences between some languages based on their activity when it comes to fixing security issues. We followed the basic ideas laid out by the work of Matt Bishop [3] with the design of our study approach.

We wanted to explore a set of patterns that could be later used as a point of reference. These are important not only when it comes to choosing the right language for a given task, but also to measure changes, improvements and deteriorations of the activity of the languages' communities. To be able to derive meaningful conclusions, we investigated C, C++, BitBake, Go, Java, JavaScript, Python, Ruby and Scheme programs. The choice to include so many languages had the advantage of not constraining our field of view to only certain kinds of projects.

For all the programs written in these different languages we extracted and analyzed the type of vulnerabilities found and fixed in the programs, the time it took for the fix to occur, the number of people working on a given project while an issue was active, and the required number of changes to the code and files to eliminate the issue. In short, the results show that while the severity of an issue may correlate with the time it takes to fix it, that is not the case in general. Averages show a similar pattern, which is likely because of the reintroduction of the same issues several times in larger projects.

CVEs (short for Common Vulnerabilities and Exposures) [10] are publicly disclosed cyber-security vulnerabilities and exposures that are stored and freely browsable online. These can be categorized into CWEs (short for Common Weakness Enumeration) [11]. We used these entries to gauge the speed at which developers fix major issues in different programming languages.

We extracted our proxy metrics for vulnerabilities based on the textual analysis of git logs and as such may not be indicative of the actual development process. Git is a free and open-source distributed version control system.[1] Commits are a way to keep previously written code organized and available. They usually have messages attached to them that explain what the contained changes are and what purpose do they serve. We have used these messages to collect data about CVEs from commit messages.

We used a PostgreSQL database to store the collected CVE and CWE entries extracted from commit logs. These were downloaded using an updated version of an open-source project called cve manager.[2] The commit messages were extracted using a mostly self-developed tool called git log parser.

---

[1] https://git-scm.com/.

[2] https://github.com/aatlasis/cve_manager.

We found that smaller and more user interface focused projects rarely document CVE fixes, however, larger-scale projects, especially those concerning back-end solutions and operating systems (package managers, etc.) are more inclined to state major bug fixes. We also found that in some projects, the developers prefer to only mention CVEs at larger milestones or releases, while in others, they were present in the exact commit they were fixed in. The paper also looks at CWEs more specifically, their prevalence in different languages. Some of these are language-specific, while others are more general.

2   Approach

Our main concern in this study was security, which led us to look for CVEs and CWEs in commit logs. This is a good way to identify major and confirmed vulnerabilities without the need for in-depth code analysis. We found that there are clear trends in some languages when it comes to handling various vulnerability types (CWEs). These can help others to apply a solution for an issue since these statistics can serve as guides that show what to watch out for.

The approach we took can be best explained through the tools we created to collect the necessary information. We will use the described tools as bullet points to illustrate the flow of the entire study and the inner workings of the miner. In the approach summary, we will explain things in more detail and also explain the design decisions we took during planning the approach.

2.1   CVE Manager

CVE Manager[3] is the backbone of most statistics and is essential to validating the found CVE entries. It is a lightweight solution that downloads the CVE data from the MITRE Corporation's[4] website. We store most of the collected data in a PostgreSQL[5] database. The tool is used to query for CVE entries found by the miner and some of their properties like their *id, impact score, severity*, and so on.

2.2   Git Log Parser

The other important tool used by the miner is our git log parser[6] solution. It simulates user commands using the Python subprocess module, which allows it to bypass some of the git's limitations. The script is prepared to mine local directories for data in the contained repository's commits. The parser first navigates to the path provided by the user through command line input, then issues the git log command that lists every commit and their meta-data.

---

[3] https://github.com/gaborantal/cve_manager.
[4] https://www.mitre.org/.
[5] https://www.postgresql.org/about/.
[6] https://github.com/gaborantal/git-log-parser.

It then saves this information into a list that will later be printed into a JSON file. This basic data is being extended with the line and file change information by comparing each commit to its predecessor with the git diff command.

The reports generated by the parser can be useful in a variety of situations, similar to ours, where an external utility needs the logs of a specific git repository. Some of its results are not used by the miner but are intended for later use, for example, the parser could check whether a commit is a merge or not, which is currently ignored in finding CVEs.

2.3   CVE Miner

The main tool of our project is the miner[7], which uses both the CVE Manager and the Git Log Parser to create a JSON file and a database entry for each CVE found and presumably, fixed in the actual repository. Figure 1 represents the inner working of the miner and its interaction with the other tools.

The miner requires some initial setup since the CVE data needs to be downloaded and inserted into a local PostgreSQL database. This is done in two steps. In the first step, the data is collected into a local NVD directory from which we read and upload it to the database in the second step.

There are multiple ways to start working with the CVE Miner. It can mine from both local and online sources. These options can be accessed using the command-line interface. When an online source is provided, a "repos" directory will be created if one does not already exist and the given repository will be automatically downloaded into it. Then the miner will continue as if a local directory had been provided. Multiple targets can be specified at once using a JSON file and the appropriate command-line argument.

The miner then processes the repositories by using Git Log Parser. After the JSON file is generated, the tool searches the messages attached to the commits for CVE entries. If a CVE is mentioned once, the miner assumes that the associated commit fixes the CVE. If it is mentioned multiple times, it is assumed that the first occurrence implies that the CVE is found in the code, and any subsequent mentions are the fixes for that vulnerability. During this process, other data is collected, including but not limited to the contributors, the number of changed files, and the number of commits between the finding and fixing of the CVE.

The next step is the calculation of statistics. The miner uses the previously acquired information to calculate the average time between the commit that found the CVE and the commit that fixed it. The other part of our statistics is correlation testing. The tool calculates the correlation between a CVE entry's severity and the time needed to fix it.

The last step is storing the data. By default, the miner creates a JSON file containing all the found CVEs and the calculated statistics. If chosen, the tool also uploads it to an Airtable[8] database.

---

[7] https://github.com/gaborantal/cve-miner.
[8] https://airtable.com/product.

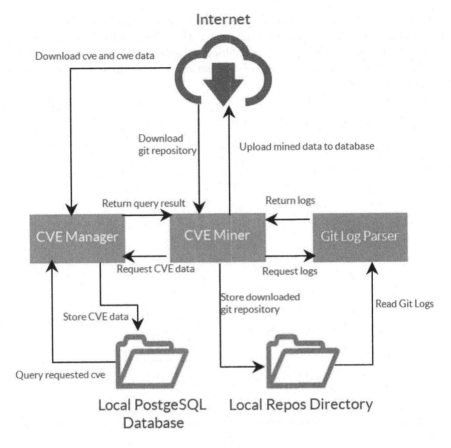

Fig. 1. A schematic representation of our miner

2.4 Approach Summary

Our main point of interest during this study was the collection of security-related data, thus a large emphasis has been put on it. We focused mainly on creating useful utilities for later research, and feel like we succeeded when it comes to most of the tools created.

We took the approach of looking only for mentions of the text "CVE" in commit logs as it is a fast solution providing sufficiently good approximation. The best way to improve current data is of course to collect a much larger amount of them.

3 Results

3.1 Time Based Statistics

Time Elapsed Between the Finding and Fixing Commit. This statistic can be interpreted in multiple ways. First, we will cover the intended purpose, showing how long it takes on average to fix a CVE entry. This is more accurate on projects at a smaller scale or lifespan since those have a lower chance of false fixing claims and reoccurring issues. Since we only check the textual references of CVE entries in commit logs not the actions taken, these properties of the projects are important.

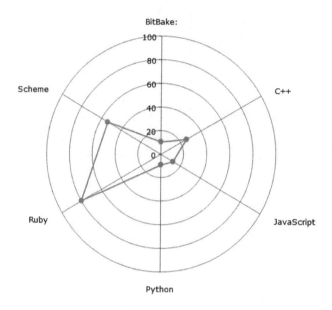

Fig. 2. The average time elapsed in days between finding and fixing a CVE

The second way the statistics can be interpreted is, as we mentioned previously, an indication of reoccurring vulnerabilities. Most of the time a CVE entry is mentioned in the context where it is claimed to be fixed, which is not surprising since you would not publicize an actual security issue in your system. Based on this, most CVEs should be mentioned only once. However, this is not the case with most large scale projects. We hypothesize that this happens because later changes may reintroduce a vulnerability previously fixed, which is likely because in larger systems it is a lot harder to foresee every possible outcome a change might have. Projects with longer code history usually have more reoccurring issues than others. When it comes to languages, a similar pattern can be observed (see Fig. 2). The differences are drastic since the scale and age of the analyzed projects vary. Most of the C++ and Scheme projects we looked at were larger projects, hence the reason for their dominance in the chart. Ruby is an outlier, there it is common for an issue to resurface years after the vulnerability has been fixed. The other reason vulnerabilities in some languages are more prevalent than in the others also has to do with the fact that larger systems usually do not allow developers to make changes directly to the working tree, merges that happen later can also increase this fixing time. This is not a huge issue since an error being fixed in a branch should not be considered fixed in the application until it has not been merged.

Time Elapsed Between the Publication and Fixing of a CVE. This statistic (see Fig. 3) is similar in nature to the previous one, however, it also takes into account the time each CVE spent in the code unnoticed after its publication. Most of the languages show similar attributes compared to the previous chart, however, when it comes to BitBake, a clear bump is visible, implying that it takes longer to come up with the first fix for an issue in BitBake programs.

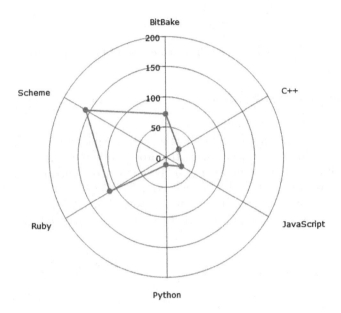

Fig. 3. The average time elapsed between the publication and fixing of a cve represented in days

Correlation Between Time and Severity. The chart in Fig 4 shows the correlation between the aforementioned statistics and the severity of the CVEs. The correlation between the fixing and the finding of a CVE can be attributed to the difficulty of the issue at hand, and the thoroughness of the testing.

The correlation between the publication date of CVEs and the time it took to fix them shows how prepared developers were when it came to fixing these vulnerabilities, since, for example, in the case of Python, the more severe problems were solved quicker than the others. This might imply that they put a larger emphasis on getting rid of more severe issues.

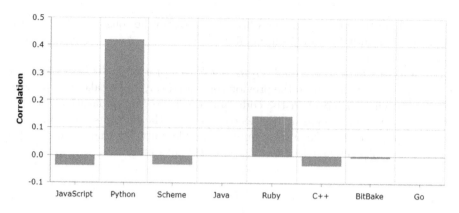

Fig. 4. The correlation between the base score(severity) and time taken fixing the cve

3.2   Activity Based Statistics

Active Contributors and Commit Count During the Fixing of a CVE. The results
in Figs. 5 and 6) showcase not only how quickly some issues might be fixed, but
the activity within the project during the process of fixing an issue. Both charts
show activities withing projects, Fig. 5 the number of contributors working on
the code between the first and last commit mentioning the same CVE. As we can
see several tens (e.g. JavaScript, Scheme) or even above 100 (Ruby) contributors
might work on a codebase in the period of fixing a security vulnerability.

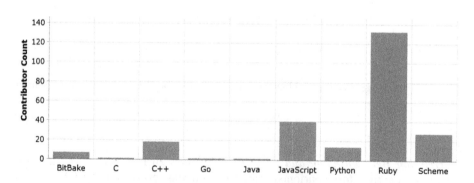

Fig. 5. The average number of contributors between the finding and fixing commit

The number of commits in the vulnerability fixing period is highest in Ruby
and Scheme (almost 1400). This implicates that a lot of code changes happen
while a security vulnerability is finally fixed.

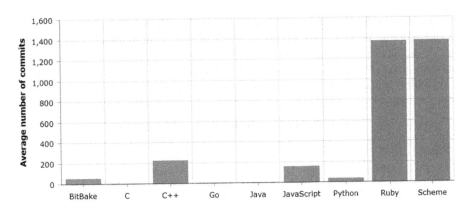

Fig. 6. The average number of commits between the finding and fixing of a CVE

3.3   Average File and Line Changes

The average changes to files and lines show how impactful an average CVE is in each language. These numbers are of course extremely varied not only per language but per project as well since some might use fewer, but longer files, to store the same code, while others might separate code a bit more. They also might only mention CVEs at larger milestones or merges, making some of the results disorderly high. Table 1 shows the average total lines and files changed per language upon fixing a CVE.

Table 1. Average total changes

Language	Average total lines changed	Average total files changed
BitBake	153.25	2.5
Go	123.23	5.69
JavaScript	288.46	4.53
Python	84.16	5.7
Ruby	58.77	4.19

3.4   Most Common CWEs by Language

The Usefulness of CWEs. CWEs are a grouping used for CVEs based on the weaknesses they cause. Knowing which CWE is most common in a language can be extremely useful when it comes to finding, fixing, and looking out for problems. This can reduce the time and energy needed to overcome certain vulnerabilities, and can raise the quality of code.

Our figures in Table 2 are of course not entirely indicative of each language as our scope is very limited, however, it might still give an idea of what to look for. As an example, the most common CWE in C++ is CWE-119[9] which has to do with incorrect memory management. An example of a more general CWE is CWE-20[10], a possible cause of this is an improper input validation in the code.

Table 2. Most common CWEs per languages

Language	CWE Group	Percentage
BitBake	CWE-119	21.40%
	CWE-20	11.74%
	CWE-125	18.87%
C	CWE-400	25.00%
	CWE-125	25.00%
	CWE-20	50.00%
C++	CWE-119	92.39%
	CWE-200	5.71%
Java	CWE-200	15.00%
	CWE-502	45.00%
	CWE-20	20.00%
JavaScript	CWE-119	6.45%
	NVD-CWE-Other	5.38%
	CWE-20	13.98%
	CWE-400	15.05%
	CWE-200	12.90%
	CWE-79	7.53%

Language	CWE Group	Percentage
Go	CWE-400	25.00%
Python	CWE-200	9.68%
	CWE-79	16.13%
	CWE-601	9.68%
	CWE-185	6.45%
	CWE-20	16.13%
	CWE-89	9.68%
Ruby	CWE-79	26.92%
	CWE-20	15.38%
	CWE-264	11.54%
	CWE-89	9.62%
	CWE-22	5.77%
	CWE-200	5.77%
Scheme	CWE-20	8.29%
	CWE-119	23.49%
	CWE-125	8.09%
	CWE-416	7.70%

For some of the languages with a more diverse set of CWEs, we created pie charts (see Fig. 7), to visually illustrate their distribution.

4   Related Work

There are plenty of previous works investigating different aspects of security vulnerabilities.

Li and Paxson [7] conducted a large-scale empirical study of security patches. They investigated more than 4,000 bug fixes that affected more than 3,000 vulnerabilities in 682 open-source software projects. They also used the National Vulnerability Database as a basis, but they used external sources (for example GitHub) to collect information about a security issue. We only rely on data that provided by NVD [20] or MITRE [10,11]. In their work, they investigated the life-cycle of both security and non-security patches, compared their impact on the code base, their characteristics. They found out that security patches have a lower footprint in code bases than non-security fixes; the third of all security issues were introduced more than 3 years before the fixing patch, and there were also cases when a security bugfix failed to fix the corresponding security issue.

---

[9] https://cwe.mitre.org/data/definitions/119.html.
[10] https://cwe.mitre.org/data/definitions/20.html.

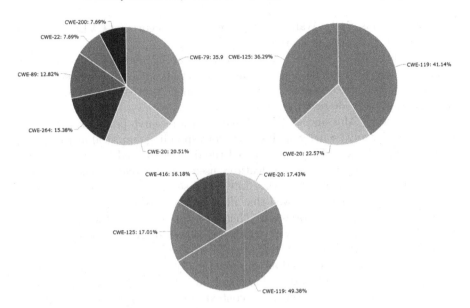

Fig. 7. A visual representation of some of the data found in Table 2 (top left Ruby, top right BitBake, bottom Scheme)

Frei et al. [5] presented a large-scale analysis of vulnerabilities, mostly concentrated on discovery, disclosure, exploit, and patch dates. The authors have found out that until 2006, the hackers reacted faster to vulnerability than the vendors.

Similar to the previous work, Shahzad et al. [16] presented a large-scale study about various aspects of software vulnerabilities during their life cycle. They created a large software vulnerability data set with more than 46,000 vulnerabilities. The authors also identified the most exploited forms of vulnerabilities (for example DoS, XSS). In our research, we also use categories, however, our categories are defined by CWE. They found that since 2008, the vendors have become more agile in patching security issues. They also validated the fact the vendors are getting faster than the hackers since than. Moreover, patching of vulnerabilities in closed-source software is faster than open-source software.

Kuhn et al. [6] analyzed the vulnerability trends between 2008 and 2016. They also analyzed the severity of the vulnerabilities as well as the categories. They found that number of design-related vulnerabilities is growing while there are several other groups (for example CWE-89 (SQL Injection)) that show a decreasing trend.

In their work, Wang et al. used Bayesian networks to categorize CVEs. They used the vulnerable product and CVSS[11] base metric scores as the observed variables. Although we do not use any machine learning methods in this study, our long term goal is to use various machine learning methods using the data

---

[11] Common Vulnerability Scoring System, as presented by Mell et al. [9].

presented in this study. Wang et al. proved that categorizing CVEs is possible and machine learning can do that.

Gkortzis et al. presented VulinOSS, a vulnerability data set containing the vulnerable open-source project versions, the details about the vulnerabilities, and numerous metrics related to their development process (e.g. whether they have tests, static code metrics).

In their work, Massacci et al. analyzed several research problems in the field of vulnerability and security analysis, the corresponding empirical methods, and vulnerable prediction. They summarized the databases used by several studies and identified the most common features used by researchers. They also conducted an experiment in which they integrated several data sources on Mozilla Firefox. The authors also showed that different data sources might lead to different results to a specific question. Therefore, the quality of the database is a key component. In our paper, we try our best to provide good quality and usable database for further researches.

Abunadi et al. [1] presented an empirical study aiming to clarify how useful cross-project vulnerability prediction could be. They conducted their research on a publicly available data set in the context of cross-project vulnerability prediction. In our research, we collected data from several programming languages. Hence we believe that our data set can be used in cross-project vulnerability prediction.

Xu et al. [25] presented a low-level (binary-level) patch analysis framework, that can identify security and non-security related patches by analyzing the binaries. Their framework can also detect patterns that help to find similar patches/vulnerabilities in the binaries. In contrast to their work, we use data mining and static process metrics. Therefore, our approach does not need any binaries, it does not require the project to be in an executable state which can be extremely useful when a project's older version could not be compiled.

Vásquez et al. [22] analyzed more than 600 Android-related vulnerabilities and the corresponding patches. Their approach uses NVD and Google Android security bulletins to identify security issues. Despite that we do not include Android security bulletins in this research, we plan to extend our scope in the future and include those vulnerabilities too as our framework is extensible.

Identifying whether a change contains security fix or not can be also challenging [18,19].

In our paper, we use the data of a vulnerability and we then we find the corresponding commits for a vulnerability.

Vaidya et al. [21] analyzed two language-based software ecosystems in the aspect of security. They investigated npm's and PyPI's ecosystem and some of the recent security attacks. They found out that automated detection of malicious packages is unfeasible, but using tools and metrics might help. In our work, we are providing some of the metrics and data that can help in detecting malicious commits.

In order to improve the quality of a software system, one has to evaluate the software's quality. This can be done in several ways, for example we can use data mining, textual analysis or we can estimate the software's quality and/or reliability. Some works uses machine learning [2,17] in order to capture the different characteristics of a software. That can also help to find vulnerable components.

Rahimi and Zargham proposed a method [15] to automatically predict vulnerability discovery in softwares. We believe that our data can be useful in learning models like the previously mentioned vulnerability discovery model.

Several works use bug reports to identify bugs and security issues in code bases [23,24].

In their work, Neuhaus et al. [13] use existing vulnerability database to mine vulnerability data and use the collected data to predict whether a given software component is likely to contain a vulnerability or not. Li et al. proposed [8] a vulnerability mining algorithm that also uses CVE, CWE data sets in order to mine the vulnerabilities. In contract to their work, we rely on only already fixed vulnerabilities that has a remark on the source code (and the corresponding version control system).

In their work, Gyimesi et al. [14] uses GitHub's issue management tools to find bugs and the corresponding code snippets. In contrast to their work, In contract to their work, we rely on only already fixed vulnerabilities that has a remark on the source code (and the corresponding version control system).

In our work, we did not try to reuse any of the existing bug databases as Munaiah et al. proved that there is only a weak correlation between number of bugs and number of vulnerabilites [4,12] in softwares.

5   Threats to Validity

The main weakness of our results is the limited scale at which we operated. We only had the resources to mine a few repositories for most languages. For this reason, some tables and graphs are missing some languages as one major project's practices had too large of an effect on the overall statistics.

One other major issue stems from the fact that we do not look at the code, but rely on the commit messages left by the developers. This can be troublesome when it comes to claiming that issues reappear since it could be the case that they were never fixed in the first place. The way we check for CVE fixes is also fairly limited, since we only look for the mention of a CVE in the commit message, but do not check the context in which it appears. We assume that the last commit at which a CVE is mentioned is the last time it occurred, and has therefore been fixed. This might not be the case, it is possible that later a fix happened, but the developer forgot to mention it.

We also do not account for merges, which can increase the number of lines needed for a fix. We believe that an issue is not fixed until it is merged into the master branch. However, if we count the lines in the commit that fixed the issue and the number of lines present in a merge that contains the commit getting rid of a vulnerability might not be indicative of the actual amount of work needed for a solution. In these cases, we currently just count the lines twice, but this has caused some statistics to be left out since they portrayed false information because of the practices the developers used when they merged larger pieces of code at once.

6 Conclusion

We presented a study that focuses on security issues. Our main goals were to determine if there were vulnerability types characteristic of languages. More specifically, what these issues are, how quickly they get fixed, and how efficiently does that fix happen.

We found that even at smaller sample sizes, specific weaknesses showed a clear trend in most of the tested languages. For example, in the case of C++ CWE-119 (memory handling problems) was the biggest group of issues faced by developers. This may not surprise those familiar with the language, but for a new developer, it can be a clear pointer as to what to watch out for.

The best example of how interesting these statistics truly are is Ruby. It is visible that for Ruby developers, the biggest issue is CWE-79, improper neutralization of inputs.[12] These issues take less effort to fix than others, requiring on average about 60 lines of code changes, and 4 file changes, however, the same issue might reappear later, as shown in Fig. 2. It is also visible that while in Ruby it takes the least amount of lines to fix an issue, more severe vulnerabilities take longer to get rid of, as seen in Fig. 4.

In conclusion, each language has its share of common weaknesses, which depend on a variety of factors, and being cautious of these is important.

References

1. Abunadi, I., Alenezi, M.: Towards cross project vulnerability prediction in open source web applications. In: Proceedings of the The International Conference on Engineering MIS 2015, ICEMIS 2015. Association for Computing Machinery, New York (2015). https://doi.org/10.1145/2832987.2833051
2. Behera, R.K., Shukla, S., Rath, S.K., Misra, S.: Software reliability assessment using machine learning technique. In: Gervasi, O., et al. (eds.) ICCSA 2018. LNCS, vol. 10964, pp. 403–411. Springer, Cham (2018). https://doi.org/10.1007/978-3-319-95174-4_32
3. Bishop, M.: Introduction to Computer Security, vol. 50. Addison-Wesley, Boston (2005)
4. Camilo, F., Meneely, A., Nagappan, M.: Do bugs foreshadow vulnerabilities? a study of the chromium project. In: 2015 IEEE/ACM 12th Working Conference on Mining Software Repositories, pp. 269–279 (2015)
5. Frei, S., May, M., Fiedler, U., Plattner, B.: Large-scale vulnerability analysis. In: Proceedings of the 2006 SIGCOMM Workshop on Large-Scale Attack Defense, pp. 131–138 (2006)
6. Kuhn, D., Raunak, M., Kacker, R.: An analysis of vulnerability trends, 2008–2016, pp. 587–588, July 2017. https://doi.org/10.1109/QRS-C.2017.106

---

[12] https://cwe.mitre.org/data/definitions/79.html.

7. Li, F., Paxson, V.: A large-scale empirical study of security patches. In: Proceedings of the 2017 ACM SIGSAC Conference on Computer and Communications Security, pp. 2201–2215 (2017)

8. Li, X., et al.: A mining approach to obtain the software vulnerability characteristics. In: 2017 Fifth International Conference on Advanced Cloud and Big Data (CBD), pp. 296–301 (2017)

9. Mell, P., Scarfone, K., Romanosky, S.: Common vulnerability scoring system. IEEE Secur. Privacy **4**(6), 85–89 (2006)

10. MITRE Corporation: CVE - Common Vulnerabilities and Exposures (2020). https://cve.mitre.org/. Accessed 29 Apr 2020

11. MITRE Corporation: CWE - Common Weakness Enumeration (2020). https://cwe.mitre.org/. Accessed 29 Apr 2020

12. Munaiah, N., Camilo, F., Wigham, W., Meneely, A., Nagappan, M.: Do bugs foreshadow vulnerabilities? an in-depth study of the chromium project. Empirical Softw. Eng. **22**, 1305–1347 (2016)

13. Neuhaus, S., Zimmermann, T., Holler, C., Zeller, A.: Predicting vulnerable software components. In: Proceedings of the 14th ACM Conference on Computer and Communications Security, CCS 2007, pp. 529–540. Association for Computing Machinery, New York (2007). https://doi.org/10.1145/1315245.1315311

14. Péter, G., et al.: BugsJS: a benchmark of JavaScript bugs. In: Proceedings of the 12th IEEE Conference on Software Testing, Validation and Verification (ICST), pp. 90–101. IEEE, April 2019. https://doi.org/10.1109/ICST.2019.00019

15. Rahimi, S., Zargham, M.: Vulnerability scrying method for software vulnerability discovery prediction without a vulnerability database. IEEE Trans. Reliab. **62**(2), 395–407 (2013)

16. Shahzad, M., Shafiq, M.Z., Liu, A.X.: A large scale exploratory analysis of software vulnerability life cycles. In: 2012 34th International Conference on Software Engineering (ICSE), pp. 771–781 (2012)

17. Shukla, S., Behera, R.K., Misra, S., Rath, S.K.: Software reliability assessment using deep learning technique. In: Chakraverty, S., Goel, A., Misra, S. (eds.) Towards Extensible and Adaptable Methods in Computing, pp. 57–68. Springer, Singapore (2018). https://doi.org/10.1007/978-981-13-2348-5_5

18. Sliwerski, J., Zimmermann, T., Zeller, A.: When do changes induce fixes? In: Proceedings of the 2005 International Workshop on Mining Software Repositories, MSR 2005. pp. 1–5. Association for Computing Machinery, New York (2005). https://doi.org/10.1145/1083142.1083147

19. Śliwerski, J., Zimmermann, T., Zeller, A.: When do changes induce fixes? In: Proceedings of the 2005 International Workshop on Mining Software Repositories, MSR 2005, pp. 1–5. Association for Computing Machinery, New York (2005). https://doi.org/10.1145/1083142.1083147

20. U.S. National Institute of Standards and Technology: National Vulnerability Database (2020). https://nvd.nist.gov/home. Accessed 29 Apr 2020

21. Vaidya, R.K., De Carli, L., Davidson, D., Rastogi, V.: Security issues in language-based software ecosystems. arXiv preprint arXiv:1903.02613 (2019)

22. Vásquez, M.L., Bavota, G., Escobar-Velasquez, C.: An empirical study on android-related vulnerabilities. In: Proceedings of the IEEE/ACM 14th International Conference on Mining Software Repositories (MSR), pp. 2–13 (2017)

23. Wijayasekara, D., Manic, M., Wright, J.L., McQueen, M.: Mining bug databases for unidentified software vulnerabilities. In: 2012 5th International Conference on Human System Interactions, pp. 89–96 (2012)

24. Wu, L.L., Xie, B., Kaiser, G.E., Passonneau, R.: Bugminer: Software reliability analysis via data mining of bug reports (2011)
25. Xu, Z., Chen, B., Chandramohan, M., Liu, Y., Song, F.: Spain: security patch analysis for binaries towards understanding the pain and pills. In: Proceedings of the IEEE/ACM 39th International Conference on Software Engineering (ICSE), pp. 462–472, May 2017. https://doi.org/10.1109/ICSE.2017.49

The SDK4ED Platform for Embedded Software Quality Improvement - Preliminary Overview

Miltiadis Siavvas[1](✉), Dimitrios Tsoukalas[1,3], Charalampos Marantos[2],
Angeliki-Agathi Tsintzira[3], Marija Jankovic[1], Dimitrios Soudris[2],
Alexander Chatzigeorgiou[3], and Dionysios Kehagias[1]

[1] Centre for Research and Technology Hellas, Thessaloniki, Greece
{siavvasm,tsoukj,jankovic,diok}@iti.gr
[2] National Technical University of Athens, Athens, Greece
{hmarantos,dsoudris}@microlab.ntua.gr
[3] Department of Applied Informatics, University of Macedonia, Thessaloniki, Greece
angeliki.agathi.tsintzira@gmail.com, achat@uom.gr

Abstract. Maintaining high level of quality with respect to important quality attributes is critical for the success of modern software applications. Hence, appropriate tooling is required to help developers and project managers monitor and optimize software quality throughout the overall Software Development Lifecycle (SDLC). Moreover, embedded software engineers and developers need support to manage complex interdependencies and inherent trade-offs between design and run-time qualities. To this end, in an attempt to address these issues, we are developing the SDK4ED Platform as part of the ongoing EU-funded SDK4ED project, a software quality system that enables the monitoring and optimization of software quality, with emphasis on embedded software. The purpose of this technical paper is to provide an overview of the SDK4ED Platform and present the main novel functionalities that have been implemented within the platform until today.

Keywords: Software quality · Verification and validation

1 Introduction

The SDK4ED[1] project aims to minimize cost, development time, and complexity of low-energy software development processes, by providing an innovative platform for automatic optimization and trade-off calculation among important design-time and run-time software quality attributes. In brief, the main goal that this project aims to achieve is the provision of a set of solutions (i.e., toolboxes) integrated into the form of an easy-to-use platform, which will enable the developers and project managers of software products monitor and optimize the

---

[1] https://sdk4ed.eu/.

© Springer Nature Switzerland AG 2020
O. Gervasi et al. (Eds.): ICCSA 2020, LNCS 12252, pp. 1035–1050, 2020.
https://doi.org/10.1007/978-3-030-58811-3_73

quality of their produced software, with emphasis on the quality attributes of Maintainability, Dependability, and Energy Consumption. Moreover, additional mechanisms for quality forecasting and trade-off analysis will support decision-making throughout the overall software development cycle.

In summary, the purpose of the present technical paper is to provide an overview of the SDK4ED Platform and present the main novel functionalities that have been implemented within the platform until today. More specifically, in [1], an overview of the overall SDK4ED concept was presented and the internal architecture of the envisaged platform was provided based on the collected functional and non-functional requirements, as well as technical specifications. In the present paper, we delve into the technical characteristics of the platform and we demonstrate how these requirements have been realized so far into an actual functional platform.

This paper is expected to provide an early overview of the novel features that the SDK4ED consortium is working on within the context of the project, and demonstrate how these features are being merged into a unified and operationalized platform. In addition, this paper can be used by practitioners and researchers as a guideline in order to perceive how the features specified in [1] can be implemented in practice, using cutting-edge technologies (e.g., Microservices, Docker Engine, ReactJS, etc.), and, in turn, help them extend or even build similar platforms from scratch.

It should be noted that although several tools and platforms (either commercial or open-source) have been proposed over the years for quantifying and improving software quality [2–4], none of them has managed to cover both runtime (e.g., Energy Consumption) and design-time (e.g., Maintainability) quality attributes in a unified manner. In addition, none of the existing platforms focuses on the trade-offs between conflicting quality criteria, nor on the provision of recommendations for code refactoring taking into account the inter-relationships between different quality attributes. The SDK4ED project attempts to fill this gap by providing a platform that enables the evaluation of software with respect to both runtime and design-time quality attributes, and the improvement of its quality through refactoring recommendations that are produced based on the trade-offs among these quality criteria.

The main motivation of this paper is to raise the awareness of the software quality community about our ongoing work within the context of the SDK4ED project and especially regarding the novel features that we are integrating into a unified software engineering platform. We believe that a platform capable of monitoring important software quality attributes and evaluating the trade-offs between them is of paramount importance for both researchers and practitioners working on the embedded systems industry. In addition to this, we aim at showcasing how cutting-edge technologies are used for the implementation of the overall software evaluation platform, with the purpose to provide ideas to potential engineers for following a similar approach for the development of similar platforms.

The rest of the paper is structured as follows. Section 2 provides the overview of the SDK4ED Platform, along with important details regarding its technical implementation. In Sect. 3 a detailed description of the individual features (i.e., toolboxes) of the SDK4ED Platform is provided. In Sect. 4 the real-world applications that are used as pilot cases for the evaluation of the SDK4ED Platform are described. Finally, Sect. 5 concludes the paper and presents the next steps of the SDK4ED Project.

2 The SDK4ED Platform Overview

2.1 Overall Architecture

The high-level architecture of the SDK4ED Platform is illustrated in Fig. 1. As can be seen by Fig. 1 the overall platform consists of five core modules (i.e., toolboxes), namely Technical Debt Management, Energy Optimization, Dependability Optimization, Forecaster, and Decision Support. The first three modules provide features for monitoring and optimizing the quality attributes of Maintainability, Energy Consumption, and Dependability respectively. The latter two provide additional features (i.e., quality forecasts and trade-off analysis), which can further support decision-making during software development. At the moment, the SDK4ED Platform is able to analyze software applications written in Java, C, and C++ programming languages, covering a wide range of embedded software applications. To better understand the overall goal of the SDK4ED Platform, its core modules are briefly described in the rest of this section. A more detailed description is provided in Sect. 3.

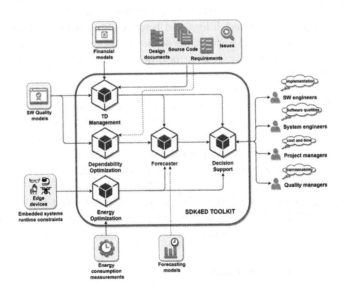

Fig. 1. The high-level overview of the SDK4ED platform.

Technical Debt Management. The Technical Debt (TD) management module is responsible for monitoring and optimizing the *Maintainability* of software products through the notion of Technical Debt [5]. More specifically, its main goal is to provide efficient support for TD quantification, prioritization, and handling in Embedded Software systems. TD is actually a measure of software Maintainability, similar to software metrics [6–9]. As discussed in Sect. 3.1, this is achieved through the provision of both state-of-the-art and novel mechanisms for TD Principal and TD Interest estimation, as well as extraction of refactoring opportunities.

Energy Optimization. The Energy Optimization module is responsible for measuring and minimizing the *Energy Consumption* of a given software application. In particular, as detailed in Sect. 3.2, this module provides mechanisms for estimating the energy consumption of a software application, identifying energy-hungry parts, and providing recommendations for potential energy optimizations.

Dependability Optimization. The Dependability Optimization module is responsible for assessing and optimizing the *Dependability* of software products. In particular, this module provides solutions for evaluating and optimizing two important facets of the Dependability [10] of the analyzed software, namely Security [11,12] and Reliability [13,14]. As discussed in Sect. 3.3, both security- and reliability-related services are provided by this module.

Forecaster. The Forecaster module is responsible for predicting the future evolution of the three quality attributes of interest, namely Maintainability (in fact, Technical Debt), Dependability, and Energy Consumption. This is achieved through the provision of advanced time series and machine-learning models (see Sect. 3.4). As depicted in Fig. 1, this module depends highly on the outputs of the three aforementioned modules.

Decision Support. The main purpose of the Decision Support module is to facilitate decision-making during the development and maintenance of embedded software applications. More specifically, as discussed in Sect. 3.5, the main responsibility of this module is to inform developers and project managers about the impact that refactorings for improving a specific quality attribute (e.g., Maintainability) will have on the other two attributes of interest (i.e., Dependability and Energy Consumption). Hence, this module receives input from all the other modules of the SDK4ED Platform and performs a trade-off analysis in order to determine these impacts and provide useful recommendations.

2.2   Technical Specifications

The SDK4ED Platform is actually a software quality monitoring system. As opposed to the majority of the existing software quality monitoring systems that are built as offline applications, we opted for a cloud-based web application.

The reasoning that led us to this option is (i) the increased visibility that a cloud-based platform offers, (ii) the high accessibility that is provided through the Internet, and (iii) the ease of use, since the tedious part of manually installing and configuring the tool is avoided. In addition to this, the platform can be used by end-users working on highly different operating systems, thus offering a cross-platform experience that would be extremely difficult to achieve in the case of an offline application.

For the development of the cloud-based SDK4ED Platform, we decided to use the Microservice Architecture (MOA) pattern [15], instead of the traditional Service-oriented Architecture (SOA) pattern. Both patterns are based on the concept of implementing the main functionalities of the application as individual services. The main difference between the two patterns is that while SOA requires all the services to be centrally implemented in the form of a monolithic application, in MOA, similar functionalities are grouped into components (i.e., microservices) with their own lifecycles, which can then be distributed over a network. These services can then collaborate together in order to form the broader application. Some of the main advantages of MOA over SOA (which helped us reach our final decision) are listed below [15]:

- Microservices can be deployed independently
- Microservices can be implemented using different technologies
- Microservices can be developed quickly, deployed and maintained by a small, independent team
- Microservices offer modular maintenance

Based on the MOA pattern, each one of the core modules of the SDK4ED Platform (see Fig. 1) has been implemented as an individual Microservice and the main functionalities of each module as individual web services. For the actual implementation of the Microservices, the Docker Engine[2] was used. Docker is an Enterprise Container Platform that allows applications to be packaged as individual containers along with their required parts (e.g., tools, configuration, dependencies, etc.) and communicate with each other through dedicated channels. In fact, the Microservices of the SDK4ED Platform are implemented as individual Docker Images, which are then deployed as independent Docker Containers.

Docker encompasses a set of key features that played an important role in our final selection. First of all, each Microservice (i.e., Docker Image) can be developed independently of one another, adopting different tools, frameworks, configurations, etc., without posing any restrictions to the other Microservices. Hence, Docker provides flexibility in the sense that it allows the individual applications to be implemented using highly different languages and technologies, encouraging in that way agile software development. In addition, the implemented Docker Images can be deployed and executed as Docker Containers either on the same machine or distributed over different locations. The execution of one Docker Container does not affect the execution of the others, increasing, in that

---

[2] https://www.docker.com/.

way, the reliability of the overall platform. Finally, the installation of the final integrated toolbox becomes an easy process, as it is reduced to the deployment of the individual Docker Containers that correspond to the Microservices of the platform, which can be performed automatically based on a description provided as a compose file.

Apart from the individual Docker Containers (i.e., Microservices) that form the back-end of the SDK4ED Platform, a front-end is also available in the form of a dashboard that facilitates its adoption in practice. The Home Page of the SDK4ED Dashboard is depicted in Fig. 2. The Home Page, built using the React[3] framework, provides a general overview of the analyzed projects by concentrating information retrieved from the individual web services.

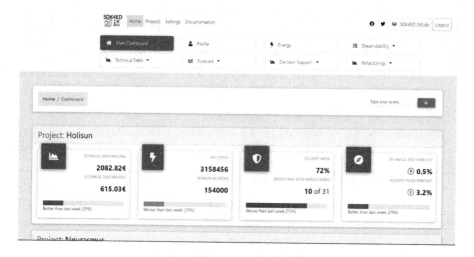

Fig. 2. The Home page of the SDK4ED Dashboard.

3 SDK4ED Toolboxes

3.1 Technical Debt Toolbox

The Technical Debt Management Toolbox is responsible for assessing the code quality (i.e., Maintainability) of a given software product, providing also suggestions on how to improve it (i.e., refactoring opportunities). It also provides novel mechanisms for assessing the TD that is introduced by new code added to the software product. More specifically, it comprises three main functionalities (i.e., components), which have been implemented in the form of individual web services. These services are described below:

---

[3] https://reactjs.org/.

- **Technical Debt Analysis:** This web service is responsible for analyzing and evaluating the TD aspects of a software application through its entire evolution. These TD aspects include TD Principal and Interest [16], as well as TD Interest Probability [17] and the Breaking Point [18] of the application. While the SonarQube[4] platform is used as the basis for the calculation of these TD-related aspects, Technical Debt Management Toolbox has been extended by introducing new tools developed in the context of the SDK4ED project to support the quantification of additional TD indicators (e.g., long methods, effort to resolve an inefficiency, etc.), as well as to provide appropriate rule configuration for the cases of C/C++, tailored to the needs of an embedded system developer.
- **Technical Debt New Code:** This web service is responsible for analyzing the commit history and providing a quality gate for the new code. In this way, if the new commit adds more TD in the existed code then the quality gate fails and an alert is sent to the user.
- **Refactorings:** This web service is responsible for analyzing the source code and suggesting potential refactoring opportunities based on Long Method code smell [19], as well as suggesting an optimal code design based on coupling and cohesion between the files.

The TD Management toolbox has been implemented as an individual Microservice, which encapsulates the three aforementioned web services. From a technical perspective, it has been deployed as an independent Docker Container, which actually constitutes the back-end of the TD Management toolbox. Dedicated front-end pages have been implemented as part of the broader SDK4ED Dashboard, in order to facilitate the invocation of the aforementioned services and the effective presentation of their results. In Fig. 3, the main front-end panel of the TD Management toolbox is presented.

As can be seen by Fig. 3, the user is able to select a specific project from the dedicated drop-down list, and then, the historical TD analysis is presented. More specifically, important TD-related measures are illustrated, including TD Principal, TD Interest, and TD Interest probability. Additional low-level information is also provided in the panel (e.g., code smells, bugs, etc.). Similar panels have been developed for the other two services. However, for reasons of brevity, screenshots are not provided in the present paper.

3.2 Energy Optimization Toolbox

The main purpose of the Energy Optimization toolbox is to provide support for measuring the energy consumption of a given software application, and for minimizing the energy consumption through the recommendation of energy optimizations that can be applied to the source code of the application. Hence, this toolbox provides two main functionalities, which have been implemented in the form of individual web services and are described below:

---

[4] https://www.sonarqube.org/.

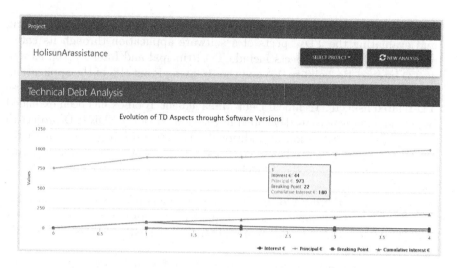

Fig. 3. The main front-end page of the Technical Debt toolbox.

– **Consumption Analysis**: The purpose of this service is the identification of the critical parts of the application source code in terms of CPU cycle. The identification of critical parts (i.e., hotspots) is based on the dynamic analysis of the application by integrating popular profiling tools, such as Valgrind[5] and Linux Perf[6]. The outcome of the analysis is a list containing the identified hotspots of the application source code (usually loops) and the values of a set of energy consumption indicators for each hotspot. The indicators are: (i) CPU-related (e.g., CPU cycles), (ii) memory-related (e.g., number of memory accesses) (iii) multithreaded-related (e.g., Lock contention), and (iv) accelerator-specific (e.g., memory/control/integer operations) indicators.

– **Estimation & Optimization.** This service is responsible for identifying possible optimizations at the level of the source code and then, for recommending these optimizations to application developers for improving the energy efficiency of the analyzed application. The identification of possible optimizations is indicated by the values of the energy consumption indicators for each one of the identified hotspots (as produced by the previous service). The service recommends the most suitable energy optimization for each one of the identified hotspots. These optimizations include: (i) data-flow optimizations (e.g., cache blocking), (ii) optimizations for concurrent data accesses (e.g., alternative lock mechanisms), and (iii) offloading recommendations (e.g., suggestion to offload the hotspot on GPU accelerators).

The aforementioned web services are part of the Energy Optimization toolbox Microservice, which, similarly to the other toolboxes, is deployed as an individual Docker Container. A dedicated front-end has been implemented as part of

---

[5] http://www.valgrind.org/.

[6] https://perf.wiki.kernel.org/index.php/Main_Page.

the SDK4ED Dashboard, with the purpose of facilitating the invocation of the services and presenting the results in an easy-to-understand manner. In Fig. 4 a screenshot of the Energy Optimization toolbox front-end page is illustrated. As can be seen by this figure, the user is informed about the hotspots that were identified in the analyzed project, along with their calculated energy indicators. For each hotspot, a specific energy optimization is provided in a separate table.

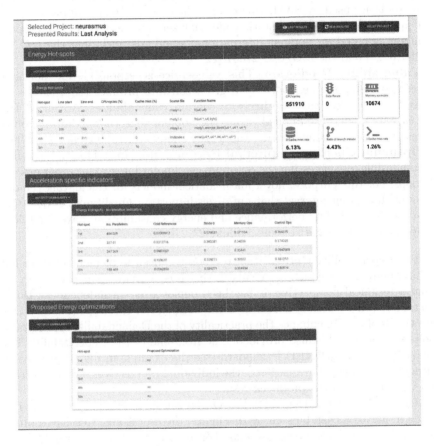

Fig. 4. The front-end page of the Energy Optimization toolbox.

3.3   Dependability Optimization Toolbox

As already mentioned, the purpose of the Dependability Optimization toolbox is to provide tools (i.e., services) for monitoring and optimizing the Dependability (i.e., Security and Reliability) of software applications. Hence, this toolbox offers three main features implemented in the form of individual web services. These services are listed below:

- **Quantitative Security Assessment:** This web service is responsible for evaluating the internal security level of a given software application. More specifically, it applies static analysis to a selected software application and aggregates the results in order to compute a high-level security indicator using a novel Security Assessment Model (SAM) [20], which has been developed within the course of the SDK4ED Project. For the case of software applications written in Java, the PMD[7] and CKJM Extended[8] static analysis tools are used by SAM, whereas for the case of C/C++ applications the CppCheck[9] and CCCC[10] static code analyzers are employed. The proposed model is based on popular international standards, including the ISO/IEC 25010 [21] and the ISO/IEC 27001 [22].
- **Vulnerability Prediction:** This web service is responsible for identifying security hotspots, i.e., parts of a given software product (e.g., classes and source code files) that are likely to contain vulnerabilities. Advanced Deep Learning models are applied (using the popular tensorflow[11] library) on the results of text mining in order to identify these vulnerability hotspots [11].
- **Optimum Checkpoint Interval Recommendation:** This web service is responsible for suggesting the optimum checkpoint interval for programs with loops. For this purpose, novel mathematical models for calculating the optimum checkpoint interval that optimizes important Quality-of-Service (QoS) attributes, including performance and energy consumption, have been developed and used as part of this module [23, 24].

The Dependability Optimization toolbox has been implemented as an individual Microservice, which encapsulates the three aforementioned web services. From a technical perspective, it has been deployed as an independent Docker Container, which actually constitutes the back-end of the Dependability Optimization toolbox. To enhance the practicality of the Dependability Optimization toolbox, a front-end is also provided. The front-end of the Dependability Toolbox is part of the SDK4ED Dashboard (see the example in Fig. 5), whereas its purpose is to allow: (i) invocation of the individual web services, and (ii) retrieval and visualization of the produced results.

An example of the Dependability Optimization toolbox front-end is illustrated in Fig. 5. As can be seen by this figure, the user is able to select a project from a dedicated drop-down list and then decide whether they would like to perform a New Analysis or display the results of the previous analysis that has been performed for the selected project. Several useful information is displayed to the user regarding the selected project. For instance, in the example presented in Fig. 5, the user is informed about the overall Security Index of the selected application, whereas more detailed information about the dependability of the project is also provided through dedicated charts.

---

[7] https://pmd.github.io/.

[8] http://gromit.iiar.pwr.wroc.pl/p_inf/ckjm/.

[9] http://cppcheck.sourceforge.net/.

[10] http://cccc.sourceforge.net/.

[11] https://www.tensorflow.org/.

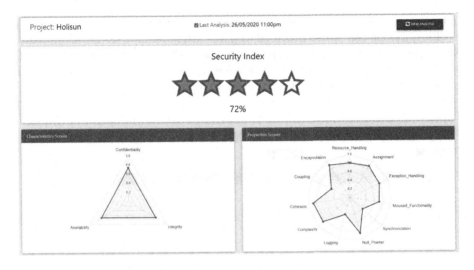

Fig. 5. The front-end page of the Dependability Optimization toolbox.

3.4 Forecasting Toolbox

The purpose of the Forecasting Toolbox is to provide predictive forecasts regarding the evolution of the three core quality attributes targeted by the SDK4ED platform, namely TD, Energy, and Dependability. Towards building a solid basis for the Forecasting Toolbox realization, the suitability of various dedicated time series was investigated [25], whereas advanced ML models have been introduced as part of the business logic of the toolbox, following the overall concept described in [26]. Hence, this toolbox offers three main features implemented in the form of individual web services. These services are briefly described below:

- **TD Forecaster:** This web service is responsible for generating TD forecasts for a given software application. A TD forecast represents the predicted evolution of the total remediation effort (measured in minutes) to fix all code issues (e.g. code smells, bugs, code duplication, etc.) of a software application, up to a future point specified by the user.
- **Energy Forecaster:** This web service is responsible for generating Energy forecasts for a given software application. An Energy forecast represents the predicted evolution of the total energy consumption (measured in Joules) of a software application, up to a future point specified by the user.
- **Dependability Forecaster:** This web service is responsible for generating Security forecasts for a given software application. A Security forecast represents the predicted evolution of the Security Index (see Sect. 3.3) of a software application, up to a future point specified by the user.

Similarly to the other Toolboxes of the SDK4ED platform, the Forecasting Toolbox has also been implemented as an individual Microservice, which encapsulates the three aforementioned web services and has been deployed as an independent Docker Container. In addition to the back-end of the Forecasting Toolbox, a front-end is also provided as part of the overall SDK4ED Dashboard. More specifically, there are three panels on the navigation menu of the SDK4ED Dashboard that are dedicated to TD, Energy, and Security forecasting. As an example, the main screen of the TD Forecasting panel is depicted in Fig. 6.

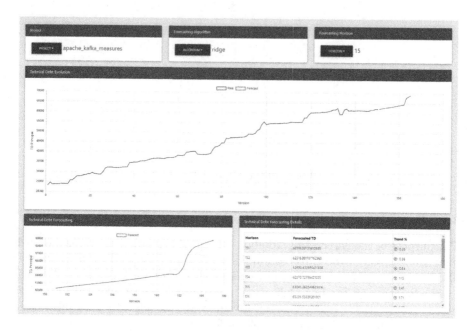

Fig. 6. The front-end page of the Forecasting toolbox.

The main screen of the TD Forecasting panel comprises a dropdown button, two interactive plots, and one table. The dropdown button allows the user to select the forecasting horizon for which they would like to see predictions. Once the forecasting horizon is selected, the back-end server invokes the proper forecasting algorithm (depending on the selected horizon) and returns the predictions back to the dashboard. The first plot shows the entire evolution followed by the forecasted evolution of the application, whereas the second plot focuses solely on the forecast, giving a more fine-grained view. In addition to the plots, a complementary table comprising the detailed results of the forecasts is presented at the bottom-right part of the screen. This table presents the forecasted TD values for the upcoming weeks, as well as the difference between the current TD value and the forecasted TD values per week, which may serve as an indicator of whether the TD Principal will increase or decrease, and to what extent. This additional information is expected to help the developers take even more informed decisions regarding the prioritization of their TD repayment activities.

3.5   Decision Support Toolbox

The main purpose of the decision support module is to facilitate the decision-making process during the development and maintenance of embedded software applications. More specifically, the main objective of this toolbox is to aggregate the refactoring suggestions provided by the individual toolboxes for improving a single quality attribute and then perform a trade-off analysis in order to determine how the refactorings for improving a specific quality attribute (e.g., Maintainability) may affect the other two quality attributes of interest (i.e., Dependability and Energy Consumption). This is expected to allow the developers and project managers make more informed decisions regarding which sub-group of refactorings to apply to the source code of their software application.

The Decision Support system is an ongoing research task, which is expected to be delivered as part of the final version of the SDK4ED Platform. Numerous theoretical and empirical analyses have been conducted within the course of the SDK4ED Project regarding the inter-relationships between the quality attributes of Maintainability, Dependability, and Energy Consumption [27–29]. The results of these studies identified various observable impacts that refactorings may have and led us to develop an approach (along with its tooling) that will perform this trade-off analysis. Concepts from the field of fuzzy multi-criteria decision making were also adopted (e.g., [30]). In addition to this, more advanced concepts for facilitating decision-making from interdisciplinary fields will be also studied (e.g., [31–33]).

4   Applications of the SDK4ED Platform

As already mentioned in Sect. 1, the SDK4ED Platform targets mainly the embedded software community, in which Energy Consumption and Dependability are aspects of major concern. However, it should be noted that the SDK4ED Platform is not limited only to embedded software and can be leveraged for improving the quality of any kind of software in general. Within the context of the SDK4ED project, real-world software applications were utilized as the basis for showcasing the capabilities of the produced platform, as well as for evaluating its correctness. These applications come from the airborne, automotive, and healthcare domains, and are provided by three industries, namely Airbus, Holisun, and Neurasmus respectively.

Regarding the airborne use case, embedded software running on Unmanned Aerial Vehicles (UAV) provided by Airbus Defence is used as a testbed. These software applications are written in C/C++ programming language and are responsible for critical tasks of UAVs missions, including algorithms for real-time obstacle avoidance, algorithms for improving autonomy capacity, and algorithms for route planning and navigation. Airbus is interested in optimizing the software running on UAVs with respect to their energy consumption, as improved energy efficiency will lead to longer flight duration, maintaining at the same time high-levels of Dependability and Maintainability.

As far as the automotive use case is concerned, specific focus is given on augmented reality software applications that are running on smart glasses, with the purpose to facilitate the remote assistance of technicians operating in the industrial field with engineers in support centers. Solutions provided by Holisun are used as testbeds. These software applications are actually Java (i.e., Android) applications, with high demands in computational power, data transmission volumes, and latency. Holisun, through the adoption of the SDK4ED Platform, is willing to improve the real-time performance and energy efficiency of their application, while maintaining their Dependability and Maintainability.

Finally, as far as the healthcare use case is concerned, embedded software running on implantable devices is used as a testbed. These applications, which are developed by Neurasmus, are written in C programming language and they are characterized by high demands with respect to energy efficiency and dependability. Hence, through the SDK4ED Platform, Neurasmus will attempt to improve the energy consumption and the dependability of their applications, while maintaining the code sufficiently maintainable.

5   Conclusion

In this paper, we presented the current state of the SDK4ED Platform (developed as part of the ongoing EU-funded SDK4ED Project), the purpose of which is to enable the monitoring and optimization of important quality attributes (i.e., Maintainability, Energy Consumption, and Dependability) of software applications, with emphasis on embedded software. More specifically, the overview of the SDK4ED Platform was initially provided, followed by a more detailed description of its core modules. Emphasis was given on their technical characteristics, as well as on the main research achievements that have been achieved so far. Building upon [1], in which the overall concept, requirements, and architecture of the SDK4ED Platform were presented, this paper demonstrated our progress towards the actual realization of these specifications into an actual operationalized platform.

In the remaining period until the end of the project, emphasis will be given on the finalization of the Decision Support module of the SDK4ED Platform, which is the only module currently in progress. More specifically, a novel trade-off analysis mechanism will be developed, which will be based on the outputs of the other four modules of the platform and multi-criteria decision-making techniques that encompass fuzzy logic. Subsequently, the effort will be directed towards the implementation of the final version of the SDK4ED Platform, and its release as an open-source software application.

Acknowledgements. This work is partially funded by the European Union's Horizon 2020 Research and Innovation Programme through SDK4ED project under Grant Agreement No. 780572.

References

1. Jankovic, M., Kehagias, D., Siavvas, M., Tsoukalas, D., Chatzigeorgiou, A.: The SDK4ED approach to software quality optimization and interplay calculation. In: 15th China-Europe International Symposium on Software Engineering Education (2019)
2. Heitlager, I., Kuipers, T., Visser, J.: A practical model for measuring maintainability. In: 6th International Conference on the Quality of Information and Communications Technology (2007)
3. Wagner, S., et al.: Operationalised product quality models and assessment: the quamoco approach. Inf. Softw. Technol. **62**, 101–123 (2015)
4. Siavvas, M.G., Chatzidimitriou, K.C., Symeonidis, A.L.: Qatch-an adaptive framework for software product quality assessment. Expert Syst. Appl. **86**, 350–366 (2017)
5. Cunningham, W.: The wycash portfolio management system. ACM SIGPLAN OOPS Messenger **4**(2), 29–30 (1993)
6. Misra, S., Akman, I., Colomo-Palacios, R.: Framework for evaluation and validation of software complexity measures. IET Softw. **6**(4), 323–334 (2012)
7. Misra, S., Adewumi, A., Fernandez-Sanz, L., Damasevicius, R.: A suite of object oriented cognitive complexity metrics. IEEE Access **6**, 8782–8796 (2018)
8. Kumar, L., Misra, S., Rath, S.K.: An empirical analysis of the effectiveness of software metrics and fault prediction model for identifying faulty classes. Comput. Stand. Interfaces **53**, 1–32 (2017)
9. Baski, D., Misra, S.: Metrics suite for maintainability of extensible markup language web services. IET Softw. **5**(3), 320–341 (2011)
10. Sommerville, I.: Software Engineering. Addison-Wesley, Boston (1995)
11. Siavvas, M., Gelenbe, E., Kehagias, D., Tzovaras, D.: Static analysis-based approaches for secure software development. In: Gelenbe, E., et al. (eds.) EuroCYBERSEC 2018. CCIS, vol. 821, pp. 142–157. Springer, Cham (2018). https://doi.org/10.1007/978-3-319-95189-8_13
12. Gelenbe, E., et al.: NEMESYS: enhanced network security for seamless service provisioning in the smart mobile ecosystem. In: Gelenbe, E., Lent, R. (eds.) Information Sciences and Systems 2013. LNEE, vol. 264, pp. 369–378. Springer, Cham (2013)
13. Behera, R.K., Shukla, S., Rath, S.K., Misra, S.: Software reliability assessment using machine learning technique. In: Gervasi, O., et al. (eds.) ICCSA 2018. LNCS, vol. 10964, pp. 403–411. Springer, Cham (2018). https://doi.org/10.1007/978-3-319-95174-4_32
14. Shukla, S., Behera, R.K., Misra, S., Rath, S.K.: Software Reliability Assessment Using Deep Learning Technique. Towards Extensible and Adaptable Methods in Computing (2018)
15. Wolff, E.: Microservices: Flexible Software Architecture. Addison-Wesley, Boston (2016)
16. Ampatzoglou, A., Michailidis, A., Sarikyriakidis, C., Ampatzoglou, A., Chatzigeorgiou, A., Avgeriou, P.: A Framework for Managing Interest in Technical Debt: An Industrial Validation (2018)
17. Charalampidou, S., Ampatzoglou, A., Chatzigeorgiou, A., Avgeriou, P.: Assessing code smell interest probability: a case study. In: XP2017 Workshops (2017)
18. Chatzigeorgiou, A., Ampatzoglou, A., Ampatzoglou, A., Amanatidis, T.: Estimating the breaking point for technical debt. In: IEEE 7th International Workshop on Managing Technical Debt (2015)

19. Charalampidou, S., Arvanitou, E.M., Ampatzoglou, A., Avgeriou, P., Chatzigeorgiou, A., Stamelos, I.: Structural Quality Metrics as Indicators of the Long Method Bad Smell. In: 44th Conference on Software Enginering and Advanced Applications (2018)
20. Siavvas, M.: Static analysis for facilitating secure and reliable software. Ph.D. thesis, Imperial College London (2019)
21. ISO/IEC: ISO/IEC 25010 - Systems and software engineering - Systems and software Quality Requirements and Evaluation (SQuaRE) - System and software quality models. ISO/IEC (2011)
22. ISO/IEC: ISO/IEC 27001:2013(en) Information technology - Security techniques - Information security management systems - Requirements. ISO/IEC (2013)
23. Siavvas, M., Gelenbe, E.: Optimum checkpoints for programs with loops. Simul. Modell. Practice Theory **97**, 101951 (2019)
24. Siavvas, M., Gelenbe, E.: Optimum interval for application-level checkpoints. In: 6th International Conference on Cyber Security and Cloud Computing (2019)
25. Tsoukalas, D., Jankovic, M., Siavvas, M., Kehagias, D., Chatzigeorgiou, A., Tzovaras, D.: On the Applicability of Time Series Models for Technical Debt Forecasting. In: 15th China-Europe International Symposium on Software Engineering Education (2019)
26. Tsoukalas, D., Siavvas, M., Jankovic, M., Kehagias, D., Chatzigeorgiou, A., Tzovaras, D.: Methods and tools for td estimation and forecasting: a state-of-the-art survey. In: 2018 International Conference on Intelligent Systems (IS) (2018)
27. Papadopoulos, L., Marantos, C., Digkas, G., Ampatzoglou, A., Chatzigeorgiou, A., Soudris, D.: Interrelations between software quality metrics, performance and energy consumption in embedded applications. In: Proceedings of the 21st International Workshop on Software and Compilers for Embedded Systems (2018)
28. Siavvas, M., et al.: An empirical evaluation of the relationship between Technical Debt and Software Security. In: 9th International Conference on Information Society and Technology (2019)
29. Siavvas, M., Marantos, C., Papadopoulos, L., Kehagias, D., Soudris, D., Tzovaras, D.: On the relationship between software security and energy consumption. In: 15th China-Europe International Symposium on Software Engineering Education (2019)
30. Guo, S., Zhao, H.: Fuzzy best-worst multi-criteria decision-making method and its applications. Knowl. Based Syst. **121**, 23–31 (2017)
31. Behera, R.K., Rath, S.K., Misra, S., Damaševičius, R., Maskeliūnas, R.: Large scale community detection using a small world model. Appl. Sci. **7**(11), 1173 (2017)
32. Vafeiadis, T., et al.: Data analysis and visualization framework in the manufacturing decision support system of COMPOSITION project. Procedia Manuf. **28**, 57–62 (2019)
33. Behera, R.K., Naik, D., Rath, S.K., Dharavath, R.: Genetic algorithm-based community detection in large-scale social networks. Neural Comput. Appl. **32**(13), 9649–9665 (2019). https://doi.org/10.1007/s00521-019-04487-0

Author Index

Printed in the United States
By Bookmasters